Turpin & Tomkins' British Government and the Constitution

A lot has happened to the UK Constitution in the last seven years. We've witnessed the UK's exit from the EU, further devolution to Scotland and Wales, a number of prominent cases by the Supreme Court, two early parliamentary general elections, major governmental defeats and two Prime Ministerial resignations. Alison Young has built on the text of Colin Turpin and Adam Tomkins' earlier edition, keeping their unique historical and contextual approach, whilst bringing the material up to date with more contemporary examples, including references to Brexit, the recent prorogation and Brexit case law, and the Covid-19 pandemic. The book continues to include substantial extracts from parliamentary and other political sources as well as from legislation and case law. It also provides a full yet accessible account of the British constitution at the culmination of a series of dramatic events, on the threshold of possible further constitutional reform.

Alison Young is the Sir David Williams Professor of Public Law at the University of Cambridge. She has taught constitutional law and administrative law for over 20 years at both Oxford and Cambridge. She regularly appears on the media commenting on constitutional developments, including BBC and Sky News, The Briefing Room and Law in Action, and also appears before parliamentary committees on issues of public law. She co-edits the UKCLA blog and is a trustee of the Constitution Society. Her other publications include *Democratic Dialogue and the UK Constitution* (2017).

Law in Context

Editors: Kenneth Armstrong (University of Cambridge), Maksymilian Del Mar (Queen Mary, University of London) and Sally Sheldon (University of Kent)

Since 1970, the Law in Context series has been at the forefront of a movement to broaden the study of law. The series is a vehicle for the publication of innovative monographs and texts that treat law and legal phenomena critically in their cultural, social, political, technological, environmental and economic contexts. A contextual approach involves treating legal subjects broadly, using materials from other humanities and social sciences, and from any other discipline that helps to explain the operation in practice of the particular legal field or legal phenomena under investigation. It is intended that this orientation is at once more stimulating and more revealing than the bare exposition of legal rules. The series includes original research monographs, coursebooks and textbooks that foreground contextual approaches and methods. The series includes and welcomes books on the study of law in all its contexts, including domestic legal systems, European and international law, transnational and global legal processes, and comparative law.

Books in the Series

Harlow & Rawlings: *Law and Administration*
Harris: *An Introduction to Law*
Harris, Campbell & Halson: *Remedies in Contract and Tort*
Harvey: *Seeking Asylum in the UK: Problems and Prospects*
Hervey & McHale: *Health Law and the European Union*
Holder & Lee: *Environmental Protection, Law and Policy*
Kostakopoulou: *The Future Governance of Citizenship*
Lewis: *Choice and the Legal Order: Rising above Politics*
Likosky: *Law, Infrastructure and Human Rights*
Likosky: *Transnational Legal Processes*
Maughan & Webb: *Lawyering Skills and the Legal Process*
McGlynn: *Families and the European Union: Law, Politics and Pluralism*
Moffat: *Trusts Law: Text and Materials*
Monti: *EC Competition Law*
Morgan & Yeung: *An Introduction to Law and Regulation: Text and Materials*
Norrie: *Crime, Reason and History*
O'Dair: *Legal Ethics*
Oliver: *Common Values and the Public–Private Divide*
Oliver & Drewry: *The Law and Parliament*
Picciotto: *International Business Taxation*
Reed: *Internet Law: Text and Materials*
Richardson: *Law, Process and Custody*
Roberts & Palmer: *Dispute Processes: ADR and the Primary Forms of Decision-Making*
Rowbottom: *Democracy Distorted: Wealth, Influence and Democratic Politics*
Scott & Black: *Cranston's Consumers and the Law*
Seneviratne: *Ombudsmen: Public Services and Administrative Justice Stapleton: Product Liability*
Stewart: *Gender, Law and Justice in a Global Market*
Tamanaha: *Law as a Means to an End: Threat to the Rule of Law*
Turpin & Tomkins: *British Government and the Constitution: Text and Materials*
Twining: *General Jurisprudence: Understanding Law from a Global Perspective*
Twining: *Globalisation and Legal Theory*
Twining: *Human Rights, Southern Voices: Francis Deng, Abdullahi An-Na'im, Yash Ghai and Upendra Baxi*
Twining: *Rethinking Evidence*
Twining & Miers: *How to Do Things with Rules*
Ward: *A Critical Introduction to European Law*
Ward: *Law, Text, Terror*
Ward: *Shakespeare and Legal Imagination*
Wells & Quick: *Lacey, Wells and Quick: Reconstructing Criminal Law*
Young: *Turpin & Tomkins' British Government and the Constitution*
Zander: *Cases and Materials on the English Legal System*
Zander: *The Law-Making Process*

Turpin & Tomkins' British Government and the Constitution

Text and Materials

Eighth edition

ALISON L. YOUNG

Sir David Williams Professor of Public Law

University of Cambridge

CAMBRIDGE
UNIVERSITY PRESS

CAMBRIDGE
UNIVERSITY PRESS

University Printing House, Cambridge CB2 8BS, United Kingdom

One Liberty Plaza, 20th Floor, New York, NY 10006, USA

477 Williamstown Road, Port Melbourne, VIC 3207, Australia

314–321, 3rd Floor, Plot 3, Splendor Forum, Jasola District Centre,
New Delhi – 110025, India

79 Anson Road, #06–04/06, Singapore 079906

Cambridge University Press is part of the University of Cambridge.

It furthers the University's mission by disseminating knowledge in the pursuit of
education, learning, and research at the highest international levels of excellence.

www.cambridge.org
Information on this title: www.cambridge.org/9781108707381
DOI: 10.1017/9781108752268

First published by Weidenfeld & Nicholson 1985
Second edition published by Northwestern University Press 1991
Third edition published by Butterworths 1995
Fourth edition published by Butterworths 1999
Fifth edition published by Butterworths 2002
Sixth edition published by Cambridge University Press 2007
Seventh edition published by Cambridge University Press 2012
Eighth edition published by Cambridge University Press 2021

Printed in the United Kingdom by TJ Books Limited, Padstow Cornwall

A catalogue record for this publication is available from the British Library.

ISBN 978-1-108-70738-1 Paperback

In memory of Colin Turpin, 1928–2019

Government without a Constitution is power without a right.

Thomas Paine, *Rights of Man* (1792)

Contents

Preface

This book is concerned with the organisation, powers and accountability of government in the British constitution. It has always been written from a lawyer's perspective, modified by an awareness that the British constitution is far from being exclusively the handiwork of lawyers. Judges and other practitioners of the discipline of law have made a notable contribution to it, but so have political actors, controversialists of many hues, party organisations, peers, rebels in and out of parliament and the legions of special interests. Yet lawyers sometimes pretend that the constitution is theirs, teaching and writing about it in myopic isolation.

In updating this book, I have endeavoured to continue this tradition. In spite of the fact that the UK constitution seems to have been continually in the news, studying the UK constitution can often seem strange and abstract to students. This book endeavours to make the UK constitution relevant, placing it in its historical context while also using contemporary examples to demonstrate how far the UK constitution has an impact on the day-to-day lives of those living in the UK. It is impossible to understand the UK constitution without a grasp of the law, found in statutes and case law. It is equally impossible to understand the British constitution without an evaluation of constitutional principles and ideas or of how the constitution operates in practice. As such, any study of the constitution would be incomplete without an account of the practices that take place outside as well as within the law. Those studying constitutional law have much to learn from political scientists, historians and political theorists, as well as public administrators and politicians. While they all may have different perspectives, they are all studying or practising in areas governed by the British constitution.

This new edition continues the book's longstanding tradition of presenting the essential features of British Government that offer a wide range of views from a wide range of sources. It continues to include references to official and unofficial publications, the writings of political scientists and parliamentarians and commentators on the constitution, in addition to law reports, legislation and legal works. The constitution is made of a variety of sources and can only be fully understood when all are taken into account, including the interrelationship between different sources of constitutional law and different governmental institutions.

Given the recent turbulent constitutional times – particularly surrounding Brexit – any student of the constitution may be forgiven for thinking that the predominant characteristic of the UK constitution is one of change. This is only added to when we examine the continuing evolution of devolution since 1998. The flexible, evolving nature of the UK constitution can be regarded as a strength that allows it to adapt pragmatically as society develops. We need to ensure that the constitution can adapt when required, particularly when the assumptions supporting the justification for these constitutional rules and practices change. But it can also be a weakness if change strays too far from, or even begins to undermine, longstanding principles of the UK constitution. Moreover, piecemeal change, resolving one practical issue without recognising its potential impact on other issues, and overly rapid change without proper deliberation may result in unintended future consequences. It is also important to ensure all have a role in shaping the UK constitution – the electorate and not just the elites.

This edition – the first to have been updated by Alison Young – adopts the same basic structure as the previous edition. The book is divided into four parts. Part I (Chapters 1–5) deals with the fundamental ideas that govern the constitution (democracy, sovereignty, the rule of law and so forth) and with the multiplicity of sources, both domestic and European, that now contribute to it. It has been substantially rewritten, in particular, to take account of the UK's ever-evolving relationship with Europe in the light of Brexit and the rapid evolution of devolution, particularly to Wales, as well as discussion of possible future developments. Part II (Chapters 6–7) is concerned with central government, with its institutions, personnel and powers. Part III (Chapters 8–10) focuses on the various ways in which British Government is subject to forms of accountability. In this Part, we consider, in turn, the relative roles of the people, of parliament and of the courts of law in this regard. When we come to the courts (in Chapter 10), both the law of judicial review and the principles of liability are discussed. Part IV (Chapter 11) considers the extent to which, and the means by which, the British constitution seeks to secure a degree of personal liberty. This is an element of the constitution that has been sorely tested in recent years in the face of a series of apparent threats to national and international security and the response to the Covid-19 pandemic. We consider in some detail the ways in which British constitutional law has responded to this challenge. I would like to thank Duncan, Imogen (and Bagheera) for their support and patience, as well as all of the students she has ever taught at both Oxford and Cambridge, whose enthusiasm and constant questioning keep the subject alive.

I would like to acknowledge the pleasure it has again been to work with our publishers at Cambridge University Press.

I have endeavoured to state the legal and constitutional position as of 31 May 2020.

Acknowledgements

Every attempt has been made to secure permission to reproduce copyright material in this title and grateful acknowledgement is made to the authors and publishers of all reproduced material. In particular, the publishers would like to acknowledge the following for granting permission to reproduce material from the sources set out below:

Robert Blackburn and Andrew Kennon (eds.), *Griffith & Ryle on Parliament: Functions, Practice and Procedures* (2nd edition 2003), pp. 409–11. Reprinted with permission by Sweet & Maxwell.

Vernon Bogdanor, *The Monarchy and the Constitution* (1997), pp. 61–3. Reprinted with permission by Oxford University Press.

Rodney Brazier, *The Constitution in the New Politics* (1978) PL 117, pp. 117–20. Reprinted with permission by Sweet & Maxwell.

Rodney Brazier, *Constitutional Practice* (1988), p. 296. Reprinted with permission by Oxford University Press.

Ronald Butt, *The Power of Parliament* (2nd edition 1969), pp. 317–18. Reprinted with permission by Margaret Butt.

Nick Cohen, 'Without Prejudice: Return of the H Block', *Observer*, 18 November 2001. © Guardian News and Media Ltd 2001. Reprinted with permission.

Bernard Crick, *The Reform of Parliament* (revised 2nd edition 1970), pp. 79–81. Reprinted with permission by Weidenfeld & Nicolson, a division of the Orion Publishing Group.

SE Finer, 'The Individual Responsibility of Ministers' (1956) 34 *Pub Adm* 377 at 393–4. Reprinted with permission by Blackwell Publishing.

JAG Griffith, 'The Place of Parliament in the Legislative Process' (1951) 14 *MLR* 279 at 287–8. Reprinted with permission by Blackwell Publishing.

Harris *v.* Minister of the Interior 1952 (2) SA 428 (Appellate Division of the Supreme Court of South Africa). Reprinted with permission by Juta & Company, Cape Town.

HLA Hart, *The Concept of Law* (2nd edition 1994), pp. 149–50. Reprinted with permission by Oxford University Press.

Kavanagh and Butler, *General Election Figures of 2005* (2005). Reprinted with permission by Palgrave Macmillan.

Robert Leach in Maurice Mullard, *Policymaking in Britain*, pp. 34–5. © Taylor & Francis 2005. Reproduced by permission of Taylor & Francis Books UK.

Lord Lester and Lydia Clapinska, 'Human Rights and the British Constitution', in Jowell and Oliver (eds.), *The Changing Constitution* (5th edition 2004), pp.67–9. Reprinted with permission by Oxford University Press.

Martin Loughlin, 'The Underside of the Law: Judicial Review and the Prison Disciplinary System' (1993) 46 CLP 23, 25–6. Reprinted with permission by Martin Loughlin and Oxford University Press.

Martin Loughlin, *Sword and Scales* (2000), pp. 141–5. Reprinted with permission by Hart Publishing.

MacCormick *v.* Lord Advocate 1953 SC 396 (Court of Session) Scottish Council of Law Reporting. Reproduced from Session Cases® by permission of the Scottish Council of Law Reporting, all rights reserved.

Ralph Miliband, *The State in Capitalist Society* (1969), pp. 49–54. Reprinted with permission by Merlin Press.

Philip Norton, *The House of Commons and the Constitution: The Challenges of the 1970s* (1981) 34 *Parliamentary Affairs* 253, 254–5, 266–7. Reprinted with permission by Oxford University Press.

Frederick Schauer, *Free Speech* (1982). Reprinted with permission by Cambridge University Press.

HWR Wade, *The Basis of Legal Sovereignty* (1995) CLJ 172, pp. 187–9. Reprinted with permission by John Bell, editor of the *Cambridge Law Journal*.

Patrick Weller, 'Cabinet Government: An Elusive Ideal?' (2003) 81 Pub Adm 701, 703–4, 716. Reprinted with permission by Blackwell Publishing.

All public sector information has been licensed under the Open Government Licence v1.0.

Table of Cases

Table of Statutes

Table of European Treaties

Abbreviations

ACAS	Advisory, Conciliation and Arbitration Service
AFSJ	area of freedom, security and justice
AMS	additional member system
AV	alternative vote
BJ Pol S	*British Journal of Political Science*
CFSP	common foreign and security policy
CLJ	*Cambridge Law Journal*
CLP	*Current Legal Problems*
Cm	Command Paper (1986–present)
Cmd	Command Paper (1919–56)
CML Rev	*Common Market Law Review*
Cmnd	Command Paper (1956–86)
COREPER	Committee of Permanent Representatives
Crim LR	*Criminal Law Review*
DUP	Democratic Unionist Party
EC	European Community
ECB	European Central Bank
ECHR	European Convention on Human Rights
ECtHR	European Court of Human Rights
ECJ	European Court of Justice
EEC	European Economic Community
EHRLR	*European Human Rights Law Review*
EL Rev	*European Law Review*
EP	European Parliament
EU	European Union
FPTP	first-past-the-post
GCHQ	Government Communications Headquarters
HC	House of Commons Paper
HC Deb	House of Commons Debates
HL	House of Lords Paper
HL Deb	House of Lords Debates
HRA	Human Rights Act 1998
ICLQ	*International and Comparative Law Quarterly*

IPPR	Institute for Public Policy Research
JCHR	Joint Committee on Human Rights
JHA	justice and home affairs
JLS	*Journal of Law and Society*
JMC	Joint Ministerial Committee
JR	*Judicial Review*
LQR	*Law Quarterly Review*
LS	Legal Studies
MEP	Member of the European Parliament
MLR	*Modern Law Review*
MP	Member of Parliament
MSP	Member of the Scottish Parliament
NDPB	non-departmental public body
NEDC	National Economic Development Council
NILQ	*Northern Ireland Legal Quarterly*
NLJ	*New Law Journal*
OJLS	*Oxford Journal of Legal Studies*
Parl Aff	Parliamentary Affairs
PL	*Public Law*
Pol Q	*Political Quarterly*
PPB	party political broadcast
PR	proportional representation
Pub Adm	Public Administration
QMV	qualified majority voting
Quango	quasi-autonomous non-governmental organisation
SDLP	Social Democratic and Labour Party
SIAC	Special Immigration Appeals Commission
SNP	Scottish National Party
Stat LR	*Statute Law Review*
STV	single transferable vote
TEU	Treaty on European Union
TFEU	Treaty on the Functioning of the European Union
UNSCR	United Nations Security Council Resolution
UUP	Ulster Unionist Party

Part I

Constitution, State and Beyond

1

The British Constitutional Order

Contents

Introduction

On 23 June 2016, a referendum was held in the UK to determine whether the country should continue as a member of the European Union. The referendum generated a high turnout of 71.8 per cent of those entitled to vote – more than 30 million people. Of that number, 51.9 per cent voted to leave the EU, with 48.1per cent voting to remain. The UK officially left the EU on 31 January 2020 and is currently in the 'implementation period' governed by the Withdrawal Agreement until 31 December 2020, unless an agreed extension is reached. This decision will give rise to the most important constitutional change in the UK since it joined the European Union over forty years ago. The subject of Brexit divided the UK with support for leave and remain cutting across party lines. It also cut across the four nations of the United Kingdom. While in England and Wales a majority voted to leave the European Union, in Scotland and Northern Ireland there were majority votes in favour of remain.

The Brexit referendum and subsequent events challenge the fundamental nature of the UK constitution. As will be discussed in more detail later, the UK is traditionally understood as having an uncodified constitution, founded on the sovereignty of Parliament. However, the continuing use of referendums to determine key constitutional issues – such as the UK's membership of the EU – questions this foundation. Is the UK constitution based on the sovereignty of Parliament or on that of the people? More importantly, what should Parliament do when the majority view in Parliament is contradicted by the voice of the people as expressed through a referendum?

The UK is a union but is not a federal state. However, there has been a growing use of devolution to grant more powers to Scotland, Wales and Northern Ireland, culminating in the Scotland Act 2016 and the Wales Act 2017. Brexit places the union under pressure. Although the 2014 Scottish independence referendum voted in favour of Scotland remaining part of the UK, there has since been a rise in calls for a second Scottish independence referendum post-Brexit, it being perceived that Scots may prefer to leave the UK and remain part of the EU than to remain part of the UK and leave the EU. The largest impact will fall on Northern Ireland. Concerns as to the resurrection of the 'troubles' between Northern Ireland and Ireland led to the creation of the 'Northern Ireland backstop' in the Withdrawal Agreement – the Agreement negotiated between the UK and the EU concerning the terms of the UK's withdrawal from the EU. This backstop proved to be one of the most controversial elements of the Withdrawal Agreement, with a majority of MPs voting against it on three occasions. As things stand, there will be no hard border between Northern Ireland and Ireland. Nevertheless, neither the UK as a whole nor Northern Ireland will be part of the EU customs union and Northern Ireland, unlike the UK, is required to mirror some EU measures regarding goods. In addition, goods moving from the UK to Northern Ireland that are likely to then travel from Northern Ireland to Ireland will be subject to checks. Meanwhile, political tensions in Northern Ireland meant that Northern Ireland was effectively without a government during most of the Brexit negotiations, with Westminster enacting legislation to empower civil servants to take governmental decisions rather than either moving to direct rule or calling for a general election in Northern Ireland. The new government was finally formed in January 2020. Post-Brexit, common frameworks for trade that are established through EU rules may be eroded as powers from the EU are returned to the UK, with those in devolved areas returning to Scotland, Wales and Northern Ireland. This may require further mechanisms to ensure more coordinated law-making across the UK, with Westminster working more closely with the devolved legislatures and governments.

The UK is often described as having more of a political than a legal constitution. This is not to deny the growing use of legislation, codes and the common law to regulate constitutional matters. However, Brexit has seen a greater use of the courts to resolve constitutional issues. From 5 to 8 December 2016, Gina Miller and others appeared before the Supreme Court, arguing that the UK's notification of withdrawal from the EU could not be made by ministers alone and required legislation from Parliament to empower ministers to notify the EU. *R (Miller)* v. *Secretary of State for Exiting the European Union*, [2017] UKSC 5, [2018] AC 61 was the first case in the Supreme Court to be heard en banc, with a panel consisting of all of the then eleven Justices of the Supreme Court. It prompted global as well as national media coverage, with live media streaming of the case with commentary, news reports and live twitter feeds and blogs. Protestors on both sides gathered outside the court. While some media coverage was neutral, there was also strident criticism in some newspapers – most famously, the three members of the judiciary who decided the case in the High Court were labelled 'Enemies of the People' by the *Daily Mail*, it being perceived that their conclusion that the prerogative could not be used was a deliberate strategy by the applicants to delay Brexit with the judiciary being complicit in bringing this to fruition. Regardless of one's views on Brexit, it cannot be denied that, although deciding a clear legal issue based on legal precedent, the decision of the Supreme Court would determine an issue of constitutional law that could have dramatic political consequences for a divisive issue. UK constitutional law, and its Supreme Court, were thrust into the global spotlight.

Neither was this the final case related to Brexit to require a sitting of eleven Justices of the Supreme Court. On 28 August 2019, a prorogation order was issued proroguing (i.e. suspending) Parliament from no earlier than 9 September 2019, and no later than 12 September 2019, until 14 October 2019. This would have had the effect of suspending Parliament for five out of the eight weeks in the run-up to what was, at the time, the date of the UK's exit from the EU on 31 October 2019. In *R (Miller)* v. *Prime Minister; Cherry* v. *Advocate General for Scotland* [2019] UKSC 41, [2020] AC 373, the Supreme Court, again sitting en banc with eleven justices, held that the prorogation was unlawful. The principles of parliamentary sovereignty and parliamentary accountability placed limits on the prorogative power of pro-rogation that could not be transgressed, unless there were reasonable justifica-tion. In this instance, the length of the prorogation of Parliament, at such a crucial time, transgressed those limits. The Government had failed to provide any justification for the prorogation, let alone a reasonable one. The Court therefore quashed the prorogative order in council that had prorogued Parliament – in essence, as far as the law is concerned, Parliament had never been prorogued and MPs could return to the House of Commons.

Neither has the impact of Brexit been seen only in the courts. The process of legislating to ensure the UK's exit from the EU, and the implementation of the Withdrawal Agreement, gave rise to a series of dramatic events in the Westminster Parliament: snap general elections; votes of no confidence; the use of indicative votes; modifications of the rules governing Parliament to facilitate debate and to enact legislation initiated by opposition and backbench MPs; the creative use of standing orders to initiate and enact private members' bills; the use of legislation to add an extra polling day to call an early parlia-mentary general election following the failure to obtain the two-thirds majority required to hold an early parliamentary general election; a series of ministerial resignations; and the resignation of Theresa May as Prime Minister. It has led some to regard Brexit as a 'constitutional moment', which may lead to the adoption of a written constitution (on this, see Bogdanor, *Beyond Brexit: Towards a British Constitution* (2019)). While this chapter will focus on the nature of the British constitution, the impact of Brexit will run through the rest of this book. However, it is important also not to overestimate its importance. There are many rules in the UK constitution and not all of them are touched by Brexit. It is hard to deny, however, its impact and potential repercussions – placing questions as to the nature of the UK constitution and whether it should be reformed centre stage. This chapter will first explain the nature of the British constitution, before analysing constitutional change and constitutional reform.

1.1 Nature of the British Constitution

Almost every country in the world has a written constitution that is a declaration of the country's supreme law. All other laws and all the institutions of such a state are subordinate to the written constitution, which is intended to be an enduring statement of fundamental principles. The absence of this kind of supreme instrument in the governmental system of the United Kingdom is unusual, leaving many observers to wonder where our constitution is to be found and, indeed, whether we have a constitution at all.

What, then, do we mean when we speak of the British constitution? Plainly, there exists a body of rules that govern the political system, the exercise of public authority and the relations between citizen and state. The fact that the main rules of these kinds are not set out in a single, formal document does make for some difficulty in describing our constitution, although even in a country with a written constitution we soon discover that not all the arrangements for its government are to be found there: many elements of the constitution will have to be looked for elsewhere than in the primary document labelled 'the constitution'. (The formal constitution may even be misleading, for, as we are warned by a Frenchman, Léon Duguit, 'the facts are stronger than constitutions' and by an American, Roscoe Pound, that the 'law in books' is not necessarily the same as the 'law in action'.) But at all events a written constitution is a place from where a start can be made. Lacking this, how do we set about describing the British constitution?

We might begin in a specific way by taking note of particular *rules and practices* that are observed in the working of the political system – for example, the rule that the Civil Service is politically objective and impartial (Constitutional Reform and Governance Act 2010, section 7(4)) – or the practice by which ministers answer questions in the House of Commons. Rules and practices such as these, relating to the government of the country, are of great number and variety: if it were possible to make a complete statement of them, this could no doubt be presented as a formal description of the British constitution. (It would include much that elsewhere would be put into a written constitution and much more that would be left out.) We should then have the material for a definition of the British constitution, which might run something like this:

> a body of rules, conventions and practices that describe, regulate or qualify the organisation, powers and operation of government and the relations between persons and public authorities.

But such a definition, even if formally adequate, would fail to reveal some important features of the constitution.

Shifting our point of view slightly, we might think next of the *institutions and offices* that constitute the machinery of British Government. An institutional description of the constitution would include Parliament, the government and the courts, the monarchy and the Civil Service, devolved legislatures and administrations in Scotland, Wales and Northern Ireland and offices such as those of the Parliamentary Ombudsman, the Comptroller and Auditor General and the Director of Public Prosecutions. Of course, these institutions and offices are themselves to be explained by reference to rules and practices that constitute them or define their powers and activity. But we do not think of them simply as bundles of rules. Rather, they have what might be described as their own reality and momentum – often loaded with history and tradition – in what is sometimes called 'the living constitution'.

Reflecting further on the constitution, there would come to mind certain *ideas*, *doctrines* or *organising principles* that have influenced or inspired the rules and practices of the constitution or that express essential features of our institutions of government or of relations between them. There can be no true understanding of the British constitution without an appreciation of the role within it of such commanding principles as those of democracy, parliamentary sovereignty, the rule of law, the separation of powers and ministerial responsibility (on each of which, see Chapter 2).

We also have to think of the ways these various institutions and ideas are now required to operate in the context of globalisation and of the rise to prominence of international and supranational organisations such as the Council of Europe, with its influential European Convention on Human Rights (ECHR), and the European Union (EU), with its vast and continually growing body of EU law (on both of which, see Chapter 5), some of which continue to have an effect in the UK even post-Brexit.

Until now we have spoken rather loosely of 'rules and practices' of the constitution and we now need to be more definite. The *legal* rules that make up part of the constitution are either statutory rules or rules of common law. Many of the more important practices of the constitution also have the character of rules and, like legal rules, may give rise to obligations and entitlements. These non-legal rules are called *conventions*. (The nature of conventions and their relation to law is one of the fundamental problems of the constitution and is more fully explored in Chapter 3.)

As already indicated, the attempt might be made to enumerate all the rules relating to the system of government in a comprehensive statement of the contents of the British constitution (although it would not remain up to date for long). One problem that would arise in doing this would be that of deciding whether rules were sufficiently connected with the machinery of government to count as part of the constitution. Should the statement include the rules and practices relating to the control of immigration, the organisation of the armed forces or the administration of social security? This sort of question would have to be answered rather arbitrarily, for there are no natural boundaries of the system of government or of the constitution. As Finer, Bogdanor and Rudden have commented (*Comparing Constitutions* (1995), p. 40), the British constitution is 'indeterminate, indistinct and unentrenched'. Moreover, much of it would remain so even were it to be codified.

Unsurprisingly, no official comprehensive list or statement of the kind under consideration has been attempted. In 2006, Vernon Bogdanor and Stefan Vogenauer conducted a series of seminars at the University of Oxford, in which students were asked to produce an account of the current principles of the UK constitution (see Bogdanor, Vogenauer and Khaitan, 'Should Britain have a Written Constitution?' (2007) 78 *Political Quarterly* 499). The UK is said to have an 'ancient' constitution, but given the plethora of statutes on constitutional law dating from only the last forty years, this would seem to be not exactly the case.

A comprehensive list of constitutional rules would not tell us what is distinctive in the British constitution or what is of especial value. For the constitution is not mere machinery for the exercise of public power, but establishes an *order* by which public power is itself to be constrained. Some constitutional rules express social or political values that are thought important to preserve or that help to maintain a balance between different institutions of government or safeguard minorities or protect individual rights. These rules, we may say, have 'something fundamental' about them and are distinguishable from much that is circumstantial, temporary, simply convenient or merely mechanical in the constitution.

This distinction, however, is not straightforward. There is often disagreement about what is vital in the constitution and what is inessential. It is easy to fall into a very conservative way of regarding the constitution and to categorise what is old and traditional in our rules and practices as necessarily to be cherished and preserved, although no longer conformable to a changed society, a transformed public consciousness and new conceptions of justice and morality. There is a contrary tendency to view the whole constitution in an instrumental way, holding all its rules to be equally malleable or dispensable in the interest of immediate political ends or administrative convenience.

Profound changes in society and politics in the past century created stresses in Britain's historical constitution, particularly, more recently, through the Brexit process. However, a lack of consensus, together with official inertia or contentment with the status quo, for a long time inhibited thoroughgoing constitutional reform. The response to revealed defects was to adjust or tinker with the constitutional mechanism, sometimes without due deliberation or debate, rather than to redesign the system. These piecemeal tinkerings often had unintended consequences. Towards the close of the twentieth century, questions were increasingly raised about the suitability of the constitution to the political realities of the post-industrial, multiracial, multi-party, relatively non-deferential and egalitarian (if still unequal) society that Britain had become. We find Samuel Beer observing that 'the new stress on participant attitudes and behaviour collides with values anciently embedded in the political system' (*Britain Against Itself* (1982), p. 112). Constitutional rules that had seemed deeply rooted were coming under critical scrutiny – for example, the electoral system, rules for maintaining governmental secrecy and the law and conventions regulating the working of Parliament. Government was seen to be over-centralised and insufficiently controlled.

In response to such criticisms and dissatisfactions, the Blair Government, taking office in 1997, launched an ambitious – but not comprehensive – project of constitutional reform, which we consider in the final section of this chapter. In their own way, the Brown Government (2007–10) and the Coalition Government (2010–15) both continued to place questions of constitutional reform prominently on their political and legislative agendas. More recently, it is events that have placed the British constitution under pressure that have led for further calls for a codified constitution. Constitutional change is occurring through the way in which rules and practices are being modified in response to the difficulties surrounding the Brexit process. It remains to be seen whether these changes will have any long-term effect.

The still uncompleted reform project and the complications of Brexit have given a renewed impetus to constitutional debate. It is timely for us to ask what in the British constitution has outlived its usefulness, what needs reform and what expresses fundamental values that it is important to maintain and strengthen?

1.1.1 Fundamentals, Fluidity and Safeguards

It may be expected that Parliament, the government and the courts should have a particular concern for rules that reflect fundamental values, upholding them against prejudice or transient passions and departing from them only on the strength of open and principled argument.

Unfortunately, this expectation is sometimes disappointed. The abrogation by Parliament of long-established rules that may be deemed fundamental is not always supported by either full investigation or convincing justification. This criticism has been made, for instance, of the abolition by the Criminal Justice Act 1988 of the defendant's right of peremptory challenge of jurors and also of the abolition by the Criminal Justice and Public Order Act 1994 of an accused person's 'right to silence', which had 'stood out as one of the proudest boasts of Britain's commitment to civil liberties' (Robertson, *Freedom, the Individual and the Law* (7th edn. 1993), p. 32). Similar challenges arise from the increasing use of referendums, the modification of the office of the Lord Chancellor and the unintended consequences of the Fixed-Term Parliaments Act 2011 applied in circumstances other than the Coalition Government against the backdrop of Brexit.

By the Anti-terrorism, Crime and Security Act 2001, Parliament authorised the indefinite detention without trial of non-British nationals who were suspected of being international terrorists. To forestall challenges to the adoption of this power, the Government derogated from Article 5(1) of the ECHR (the right to liberty and security of person). Derogation is allowed by the Convention (Article 15) if strictly necessary in the event of a 'public emergency threatening the life of the nation'. In *A* v. *Secretary of State for the Home Department* [2004] UKHL 56, [2005] 2 AC 68, it was held by the House of Lords that the Government's derogation on this ground went beyond what was strictly necessary and was, therefore, unlawful. It was further held that section 23 of the Act, the provision for detention, was incompatible with Article 5(1) of the Convention. The case resulted in Parliament re-legislating, replacing the scheme of indefinite detention without trial with a system of 'control orders', themselves deeply controversial from a human rights point of view (see the Prevention of Terrorism Act 2005), which were, in turn, replaced by TPIMs (Terrorism, Prevention and Investigative Measures Act 2011. These matters are more fully considered in Chapter 11).

Judicial decisions, too, may undo what had been previously considered fundamental. Here follows an example of judicial subversion of a fundamental rule – although happily it was only a temporary aberration and after a time the rule was restored.

The writ of habeas corpus (meaning 'thou shalt have the body brought into court'), for securing a judicial inquiry into the legality of a person's detention, has its origin in early common law and a series of Habeas Corpus Acts. The efficacy of the writ of habeas corpus will often depend in practice on the onus of proof and the courts established the rule that the custodian must prove, to the satisfaction of the court, the circumstances alleged to justify the detention. This rule, in assuring effective protection of the right of the individual to personal freedom, certainly has the appearance of 'something fundamental': it was expressed as follows by Lord Atkin in *Eshugbayi Eleko* v. *Government of Nigeria* [1931] AC 662, 670:

> In accordance with British jurisprudence no member of the executive can interfere with the liberty or property of a British subject except on the condition that he can support the legality of his action before a court of justice.

However, in a number of cases arising under the Immigration Act 1971, the courts reversed the rule as to onus of proof in habeas corpus proceedings, holding that the onus was on the applicant to establish that his or her detention was unlawful. It was further held that this onus could be discharged only by showing that the immigration authority – the immigration officer or the Secretary of State – had *no reasonable grounds* for reaching the conclusions on which the detention was based. (See *R* v. *Secretary of State for the Home Department, ex p Choudhary* [1978] 1 WLR 1177 and *Zamir* v. *Secretary of State for the Home Department* [1980] AC 930.) The effect of these rulings was, as Templeman LJ observed in *R* v. *Secretary of State for the Home Department, ex p Akhtar* [1981] QB 46, 52, to deny 'the effective recourse of an individual to the courts which administer justice in this country'. Must we not say of this judicial deviation, in which the courts overturned the rule of the Habeas Corpus Acts and robbed the individual of an effective remedy for unlawful detention, that it violated fundamental constitutional principle? In *Khawaja* v. *Secretary of State for the Home Department* [1984] AC 74, the House of Lords restored the true principle, holding that the burden of proof rested on the custodian and that the issue was not whether there were reasonable grounds for the decision to detain, but whether the detention could be justified in law.

To whom are we to look for the defence of what is fundamental in the constitution – for the preservation of 'constitutionalism'?

First, the courts have a cardinal role to play in upholding fundamental principle, although, as we have just seen, they have themselves the capability to reinterpret or displace constitutional rules, which itself calls for vigilance: *quis custodiet ipsos custodes*? (who will guard the guardians?). We rely on the courts to maintain fundamental legal rules against excessive zeal or malpractice of administrators and others who exercise public power, but their role as constitutional guardians is necessarily limited. They are restricted, as regards legislation, by the doctrine of parliamentary sovereignty (see Chapter 2); and they work within a tradition (itself resting on a fundamental idea of the constitution) of judicial restraint, for they are, after all, unelected, largely unaccountable and not especially qualified to resolve issues of political judgment and policy. In recent years, the courts have, however, found a new boldness in developing the principles of judicial review, focusing on the role of the court as the guardian of the constitution, particularly of the rule of law. This, in turn, has led to criticism of the judiciary, expressed most recently in a powerful critique of the judicial role by Lord Sumption in his Reith lectures (available at www.bbc.co.uk/programmes/m00057m8; see also Sumption, *Trials of the State: Law and the Decline of Politics* (2020); Rozenburg *Enemies of the People: How Judges Shape Society* (2020)). The balance between a proper judicial restraint and a legitimate judicial activism remains a critical feature of the constitution. (See, further, Chapters 10 and 11.)

Second, we depend on the political actors themselves to observe the 'rules of the game': ministers, civil servants and parliamentarians operate in a framework of generally well-understood procedures that are designed to make the governmental machine work not merely efficiently but with respect for fundamentals. A veteran parliamentarian showed an awareness of this in remarking: 'We have no constitution in this country: we have only procedure – hence its importance' (Mr St John-Stevas, HC Deb vol. 991, col 721, 30 October 1980). Procedures, it is true, may not hold up in a time of crisis. Admitting this, Gough nevertheless asked whether, in 'a time of crisis or of embittered emotions', we should be 'any safer with laws, even with fundamental laws and a written constitution' (*Fundamental Law in English Constitutional History* (1955), p. 212). The observance of procedures is checked in certain respects by parliamentary select committees – such as the Public Accounts Committee, the Select Committee on Standards and the Commons Select Committee on Privileges, in the Commons and the Privileges and Conduct Committee and the Constitution Committee in the House of Lords – and by the Comptroller and Auditor General of the National Audit Office, the Committee on Standards in Public Life, the Parliamentary Ombudsman and the Commissioner for Public Appointments. (See, further, Chapter 9.)

Third, and in the last resort, we depend on the force of public opinion, pronounced in the general verdicts of elections, in the growing use of referendums and expressed in more specific ways through the media, political parties, public protest and private interest groups and organisations of many kinds. A valuable role is performed by those organisations such as Liberty, which exist for the purpose of defending individuals' rights. (See, further, Chapter 8.)

Part of the problem, perhaps, is a lack of certainty about what is truly fundamental to our constitutional order. We may wish to claim that trial by jury, the right to silence or habeas corpus are fundamental values inherent in the constitutional order, but on what basis can such a claim actually be grounded, beyond one's own desire? How can an argument be made, either legally or politically, that this value or that right is so fundamental to our sense of constitutionalism, whatever that may mean, that it should remain untouched by legislative amendment or judicial re-interpretation? As we have already mentioned, and as we shall see further later, the British constitution has been subject to considerable and significant reform in recent years. Much of the reform is both welcome and overdue. But the current climate of reform poses in stark form the question of whether there is anything that ought to lie beyond the reformers' reach. Is anything sacred or is the entirety of the British constitution 'up for grabs'? (For an intriguing analysis, see Murkens, 'The Quest for Constitutionalism in UK Public Law Discourse' (2009) 29 *OJLS* 427.)

Sir John Baker, reflecting on these questions in an absorbing analysis, warns that the government 'constantly tinkering with constitutional arrangements as a routine exercise of power and without regard to the consequences', *even if many of the changes are themselves desirable*, may lead to 'the dismal reflection that we no longer have a constitution, in the sense of a set of conventions which set the bounds of executive power and keep the government within those bounds' (Sir John Baker, 'Our Unwritten Constitution' (2010) 167 *Proc Brit Acad* 91, 117). If the government no longer exercises constitutional self-restraint, then to whom must we turn for safeguards? Sir John's answer is a traditional one in the British context: this is Parliament's role, he argues, and, in particular, it is the role of select committees ('one of the most fruitful reforms of the last thirty years') and of the House of Lords (which has 'become the principal defender of constitutional liberties, and arguably the more significant legislative chamber, albeit at the cost of endangering its own existence'). A written constitution might help, he argues (p. 108), although it would not necessarily do so:

> In practice the true function of a written constitution is not so much to improve the clarity of the rules as to empower the highest court to strike down legislation according to its own interpretation of the words. The question is therefore whether the time has come to transfer more power to the judges, on the footing that the political constitution has broken down beyond repair. This is far from straightforward, since we cannot assume that the traditional juristic standards of the judiciary will be maintained once they have a political role.

The ongoing tensions (or, if you prefer, the balance) between the parliamentary aspects of our constitution and its judicial aspects is one of the central themes of contemporary constitutional debate in Britain, and we shall touch on it throughout this book.

1.2 The Constitution, the State and the Nation

Definitions of the constitution often focus on the concept of the state and its organs. For example, Hood Phillips and Jackson's *Constitutional and Administrative Law* (8th edn. 2001, p. 5), defines a constitution as:

> the system of laws, customs and conventions which define the composition and powers of organs of the state, and regulate the relations of the various state organs to one another and to the private citizen.

Regarded from the perspective of international law the UK is undoubtedly a state, but our constitutional system has been constructed largely without the use of the concept of the state. In Britain, there is no legal entity called 'the state' in which powers are vested or to which allegiance or other duties are owed. The non-admission of the idea of the state helps to explain the tardy and partial development in Britain of a system of public law. As Kenneth Dyson remarks (*The State Tradition in Western Europe* (1980), p. 117), there was 'no conception of the state to which principles and rules could be attributed' and ordinary private law occupied much of the field in which relations between public officers and private citizens were conducted. For issues savouring more of policy than of property, the courts were inclined to assign to Parliament the function of controlling governmental action (a classic example is *R* v. *Halliday, ex p Zadig* [1917] AC 260). It has been said, too, that the absence of a concept of the state has frustrated 'the development of a rational-legal theory of the constitution' and has excluded from our constitutional culture 'the notion of an authority higher than the government of the day' (Madgwick and Woodhouse, *The Law and Politics of the Constitution of the United Kingdom* (1995), p. 75; see, further, Mitchell, 'The Causes and Effects of the Absence of a System of Public Law in the United Kingdom' [1965] *PL* 95 and Laborde, 'The Concept of the State in British and French Political Thought' (2000) 48 *Pol Stud* 540).

The idea of the state is familiar enough in English political thought, and even lawyers have to deal with such expressions as 'offences against the state', 'act of state' and the 'interests of the state'. By way of contrast, as Sedley LJ remarked in *A* v. *Head Teacher and Governors of Lord Grey School* [2004] EWCA Civ 382, [2004] 4 All ER 628, [3], 'the law of England and Wales does not know the state as a legal entity'. Accordingly, there is no single legal definition of the state for all purposes and the courts have had to decide, in various contexts, whether a particular public body is an organ of the state. In *D* v. *National Society for the Prevention of Cruelty to Children* [1978] AC 171, it was argued that the NSPCC, a voluntary charity incorporated by royal charter and authorised by statute to bring care proceedings for the protection of children, was not part of 'the state' and accordingly could not rely on 'public interest immunity' (a prerogative immunity of the Crown) as justifying its refusal to disclose the identity of its informants. Lord Simon of Glaisdale disposed of this argument in the following words (pp. 235–6):

'[T]he state' cannot on any sensible political theory be restricted to the Crown and the departments of central government (which are, indeed, part of the Crown in constitutional law). The state is the whole organisation of the body politic for supreme civil rule and government – the whole political organisation which is the basis of civil government. As such it certainly extends to local – and, as I think, also statutory – bodies in so far as they are exercising autonomous rule.

(See further on Crown prerogatives, Chapters 6 and 7.)

The phrase 'the interests of the state' occurs in the Official Secrets Act 1911 and was considered in the following case.

Chandler v. *Director of Public Prosecutions* [1964] AC 763 (HL)

The appellants had attempted to enter and immobilise an airfield, which was a 'prohibited place' within the meaning of the Official Secrets Act 1911, as a demonstration of opposition to nuclear weapons. They were charged with conspiracy to commit a breach of section 1 of the Act, which makes it an offence to enter any prohibited place 'for any purpose prejudicial to the safety or interests of the State'. It was argued for the appellants that what they had intended to do was not *in fact* prejudicial to the safety or interests of the state, and further that it was their *purpose* to benefit and not to harm the state. Counsel argued also that the word 'State' in the Act meant the inhabitants of the country and not the organs of government.

> **Lord Reid:** ... Next comes the question of what is meant by the safety or interests of the State. 'State' is not an easy word. It does not mean the Government or the Executive. 'L'Etat c'est moi' was a shrewd remark, but can hardly have been intended as a definition even in the France of the time. And I do not think that it means, as counsel argued, the individuals who inhabit these islands. The statute cannot be referring to the interests of all those individuals because they may differ and the interests of the majority are not necessarily the same as the interests of the State. Again we have seen only too clearly in some other countries what can happen if you personify and almost deify the State. Perhaps the country or the realm are as good synonyms as one can find and I would be prepared to accept the organised community as coming as near to a definition as one can get.

Lord Hodson also took the state to mean 'the organised community' (p. 801).

> **Lord Devlin:** ... What is meant by 'the State'? Is it the same thing as what I have just called 'the country'? Mr Foster, for the appellants, submits that it means the inhabitants of a particular geographical area. I doubt if it ever has as wide a meaning as that. I agree that in an appropriate context the safety and interests of the State might mean simply the public or national safety and interests. But the more precise use of the word 'State', the use to be expected in a legal context, and the one which I am quite satisfied ... was intended in this statute, is to denote the organs of government of a national community. In the United Kingdom, in relation at any rate to the armed forces and to the defence of the realm, that organ is the Crown.

In the view of all their Lordships, the interests of the state were in this matter identical with those of the Crown or at all events were determined by the Crown – in effect, by the government of the day. Lord Pearce, for example, said (p. 813):

> In such a context the interests of the State must in my judgment mean the interests of the State according to the policies laid down for it by its recognised organs of government and authority.

Consequently, it could not be argued that the military dispositions decided on by the *government* were not in the interests of the *state*. The arguments for the appellants having failed in this and other respects, their convictions were confirmed. (See, further, Thompson [1963] *PL* 201.)

In *R* v. *Ponting* [1985] Crim LR 318, McCowan J, in directing the jury on the meaning of 'the interest of the State' in section 2(1) (since repealed) of the Official Secrets Act 1911, followed Lord Pearce in saying that the expression meant the policies of the state laid down for it by the recognised organs of government and authority. This ruling neutralised Ponting's argument, in defending a charge of disclosure of official information in breach of section 2(1), that he had acted in the interest of the state as an institution distinct from the government of the day. (The jury nevertheless acquitted Ponting in a verdict welcomed by many observers, including Lord Denning: see HL Deb vol. 461, col 563, 20 March 1985. On the *Ponting* case, see, further, MacCormick, *Questioning Sovereignty* (1999), ch. 3.)

If the interests of the state and of the government are in law to be considered the same, the possibility remains that those interests may differ from what is in the real interest of the community as a whole. This was perceived by Lord Radcliffe, when he said, in *Glasgow Corpn* v. *Central Land Board* 1956 SC (HL) 1, 18–19, that 'The interests of government ... do not exhaust the public interest.' That the interests of the government may have to yield to the wider public interest is clearly shown by the *Spycatcher* case, *Attorney General* v. *Guardian Newspapers Ltd (No 2)* [1990] 1 AC 109, where the desire of Mrs Thatcher's Government to ban the publication of the memoirs of a former Security Service (MI5) officer, Peter Wright, was weighed against the broader public interests of freedom of expression and open government. These latter interests were (eventually) held to prevail over the declared interest of the government of the day (see, further, Chapter 11). It might make for a better understanding of constitutional relationships if we had a coherent concept of the state, clearly distinguished from those who exercise power within it.

Who speaks for (or represents) the national interest and, indeed, whether there even exists in our constitutional law a conception of the national interest that is any higher (or any deeper) than the political interest of the government of the day are matters that continue to cause trouble. The 'national interest' is as confused and as under-developed a notion in British constitutional law as is the state. As we saw earlier in this chapter, among the questions for the House of Lords in *A* v. *Secretary of State for the Home Department* [2004] UKHL 56, [2005] 2 AC 68 was whether (as the Government claimed) there was a 'public emergency threatening the life of the nation'. Their Lordships ruled 8–1 that there was, a verdict subsequently endorsed (17–0) by the Grand Chamber of the European Court of Human Rights (ECtHR) (in *A* v. *United Kingdom* (2009) 49 EHRR 29). The sole dissentient on this point was Lord Hoffmann (at [91]–[96]), who took the words 'threatening the life of the nation' to require something more than 'threatening the lives of some of those who live in the nation':

> What is meant by 'threatening the life of the nation'? The 'nation' is a social organism, living in its territory (in this case, the United Kingdom) under its own form of government and subject to a system of laws which expresses its own political and moral values. When one speaks of a threat to the 'life' of the nation, the word life is being used in a metaphorical sense. The life of the nation is not coterminous with the lives of its people. The nation, its institutions and values, endure through generations. In many important respects, England is the same nation as it was at the time of the first Elizabeth or the Glorious Revolution. The Armada threatened to destroy the life of the nation, not by loss of life in battle, but by subjecting English institutions to the rule of Spain and the Inquisition. The same was true of the threat posed to the United Kingdom by Nazi Germany in the Second World War. This country, more than any other in the world, has an unbroken history of living for centuries under institutions and in accordance with values which show a recognisable continuity . . .
>
> The Home Secretary has adduced evidence . . . to show the existence of a threat of serious terrorist outrages . . .
>
> But the question is whether such a threat is a threat to the life of the nation. The [government's] submissions . . . treated a threat of serious physical damage and loss of life as necessarily involving a threat to the life of the nation. But in my opinion this shows a misunderstanding of what is meant by 'threatening the life of the nation'. Of course the government has a duty to protect the lives and property of its citizens. But that is a duty which it owes all the time and which it must discharge without destroying our constitutional freedoms. There may be some nations too fragile or fissiparous to withstand a serious act of violence. But that is not the case in the United Kingdom . . .
>
> This is a nation which has been tested in adversity, which has survived physical destruction and catastrophic loss of life. I do not underestimate the ability of fanatical groups of terrorists to kill and destroy, but they do not threaten the life of the nation. Whether we would survive Hitler hung in the balance, but there is no doubt that we shall survive Al Qaida. The Spanish people have not said that what happened in Madrid, hideous crime as it was, threatened the life of their nation. Their legendary pride would not allow it. Terrorist violence, serious as it is, does not threaten our institutions of government or our existence as a civil community.

None of the other judges hearing the appeal took this approach. Lord Bingham ruled that the court should defer to the government on the point, stating that 'great weight should be given' to the Home Secretary and his colleagues on the question 'because they were called on to exercise a preeminently political judgment' (at [29]). Lord Hope agreed, ruling that 'the questions whether there is an emergency and whether it threatens the life of the nation are preeminently for the executive and Parliament. The judgment that has to be formed on these issues lies outside the expertise of the courts' (at [116]). Similar views were expressed by the other Law Lords hearing the appeal (see, e.g., Baroness Hale at [226]). The Grand Chamber of the ECtHR agreed with these views, stating that 'while it is striking that the United Kingdom was the only Convention State to have lodged a derogation in response to the danger from Al Qaida ... the Court accepts that it was for each government, as the guardian of their own people's safety, to make their own assessment on the basis of the facts known to them. Weight must, therefore, attach to judgment of the United Kingdom's executive and Parliament on this question' (at [180]).

While this does not suggest that there can be no circumstances in which a court may overturn the judgment of the government that there is a 'public emergency threatening the life of the nation', it is clear that the government will have to have done something outrageous – taken leave of its senses, perhaps – before a court will intervene (see, further, Chapters 10 and 11).

Other recent cases in which the courts have struggled with concepts of the national interest or with the question of who, constitutionally, speaks for the national interest include *Secretary of State for the Home Department* v. *Rehman* [2001] UKHL 47, [2003] 1 AC 153, in which the House of Lords unanimously ruled that it was lawful for the Secretary of State to deport an individual from the UK on the basis that he was a threat to *national* security even where he was a threat not directly to the security of the UK but to the security of a foreign country, thus appearing to merge 'national security' and 'international security' together. In *R (Corner House Research)* v. *Director of the Serious Fraud Office* [2008] UKHL 60, [2009] 1 AC 756 the director of the Serious Fraud Office discontinued a criminal investigation into British Aerospace (BAe) which concerned a lucrative arms deal that BAe had secured with Saudi Arabia. He had been prevailed on to do so by ministers and diplomats on the basis that the investigation, if taken further, would threaten future Saudi provision of intelligence to the UK. This, it was feared, would be so contrary to British national security that it would jeopardise 'British lives on British streets'. The Divisional Court held that it was a monstrous breach of the rule of law for an independent prosecutor to have yielded to such political and diplomatic threats (see [2008] EWHC 714 (Admin), [2008] 4 All ER 927). The House of Lords swiftly overruled the lower court, unanimously holding that the director of the Serious Fraud Office had not acted unlawfully. The case throws into sharp relief ongoing tensions as to what is in the national interest, and who decides this (we return to the *Corner House* case in Chapter 2).

Yet a further complication arises when it is remembered that not all those in the UK would equate 'the national interest' with 'the British national interest'. The Scottish National Party, for example, is strongly of the view that the national interest north of the border means the Scottish national interest. Some parties in Wales and Northern Ireland take similar views. The tension between the wishes of England, Scotland, Wales and Northern Ireland came to the fore in the light of the Brexit referendum. Those voting in England and Wales voted in favour of the UK leaving the European Union. Those voting in Scotland and Northern Ireland voted in favour of remaining in the EU. There were growing tensions over the lack of involvement of the devolved govern-ments in the negotiation process. Although a joint ministerial council was formed to facilitate co-operation, the devolved governments felt that their wishes were insufficiently regarded. This appeared to be borne out as papers from the Welsh and Scottish legislatures on the future relationship between the UK and the EU demonstrated a preference for a softer form of Brexit than that preferred by the Westminster Government.

These latent tensions came to the fore during the enactment of the European Union (Withdrawal) Act 2018. The legislation altered the distribution of competences between Westminster and the devolved legislatures. As such, the Sewel convention would apply – the legislation would not normally be enacted without the consent of the devolved legislatures. The UK's member-ship of the EU meant that law-making powers were transferred to the EU. On the UK's exit from the EU, these powers would be transferred back to the UK. Some of these powers – for example, fisheries and agriculture – had been devolved. As such, the powers would be repatriated from the EU to the devolved legislatures. However, the Westminster Government was concerned that this could lead to the undermining of the single market in the UK, with the devolved legislatures enacting measures regulating goods that were different from those in England. Consequently, the European Union (Withdrawal) Bill 2017–19 originally included a provision that all areas of power would return to the Westminster Government, for at least the first two years post-Brexit. These powers would then be returned to the devolved legislatures once common frameworks had been established.

Both the Welsh and the Scottish legislatures were unhappy with these arrangements, as well as other aspects of the EU (Withdrawal) Bill – e.g. the decision not to include the EU's Charter of Fundamental Rights and Freedoms in domestic law post-exit day. It became clear that neither would grant its consent to the Bill. Moreover, Scotland and Wales enacted their own versions of the European Union (Withdrawal) Act 2018 – the Law Derived from the European Union (Wales) Act 2018 and the UK Withdrawal from the European Union (Legal Continuity)(Scotland) Bill 2018 (Scottish Continuity Bill). The European Union (Withdrawal) Bill 2017–19 was subsequently modified. Powers from the EU in the areas that had been devolved would vest in the devolved legislatures. However, ministers in Westminster were able to enact delegated legislation to transfer these powers to Westminster for a fixed period of time (see European Union (Withdrawal) Act 2018, section 12). Section 12 does require Westminster to seek the consent of the devolved legislatures to these orders. However, even if consent is refused the ministerial order to transfer power to Westminster may still be made. This modification was sufficient for the Welsh Government, which gave its consent to the Bill. Although the Law Derived from the European Union (Wales) Act 2018 came into force before the European Union (Withdrawal) Act 2018, the Welsh government subsequently repealed the Act by a ministerial order, being empowered to do so by section 22 of the

2018 Act. The same was not true for Scotland, which continued to refuse to grant its consent. Nevertheless, the European Union (Withdrawal) Act 2018 came into force without Scotland's consent.

In addition, the AG of the UK and the Advocate General of Scotland used the provisions of section 33 of the Scotland Act 1998 for the first time, challenging the validity of the bill, before it received royal assent, before the Supreme Court (in *re UK Withdrawal from the European Union (Legal Continuity) Scotland Bill* [2018]UKSC 64, [2019] AC 1022). In a long and complex judgment, the Supreme Court concluded that the Scottish Continuity Bill as a whole was not outwith the competences of the Scottish Parliament. However, this was not the case for clause 17 of the bill. This clause stated that Westminster ministers were not able to enact measures that modify the powers of the Scottish Parliament without the consent of the Scottish Parliament. This provision was 'inconsistent with the continued recognition of . . . unqualified Sovereignty' of the Westminster Parliament and 'therefore tantamount to an amendment of section 28(7) of the Scotland Act'. In addition, by the time the case was heard before the Supreme Court, the European Union (Withdrawal) Act 2018 had received royal assent. The European Union (Withdrawal) Act 2018 added itself to the list of legislation that the Scottish Parliament was unable to amend. As such, those provisions of the Scottish Legal Continuity Bill that contradicted the European Union (Withdrawal) Act 2018 would be unlawful when the Scottish Legal Continuity Bill came into force, even though they were not beyond the scope of the Scottish Parliament when they were enacted (see Rawlings, 'Brexit and the Territorial Constitution: Devolution, Reregulation and Inter-governmental Relations' Report of the Constitution Society 2017; McCorkindale and McHarg 'Continuity and Confusion: Legislating for Brexit in Scotland and Wales' (available on the UK Constitutional Law Blog https://ukconstitutionallaw.org/).

In addition, the European Union (Withdrawal Agreement) Act 2020 was enacted without the consent of any of the three devolved legislatures. Tensions continue to rise between Scotland and Westminster over Brexit. It remains to be seen whether the calls of the Scottish first minister and the Scottish Parliament for a further referendum on Scottish independence in the light of Brexit will come to fruition, particularly as discussions were suspended during the Covid-19 pandemic. However, it would be no understatement to say that these developments have placed considerable strain on the Union. These tensions will only be exacerbated, particularly given the division over issues of the border between Ireland and Northern Ireland post-exit day. (See Chapter 4 for further discussion.)

1.3 Constitutional Law Beyond the State

In recent years, a number of commentators have argued that the traditional focus in constitutional studies (both legal and political) on the state is no longer appropriate or that, at the least, such a focus needs now to be supplemented with additional perspectives. Gavin Anderson, for example, urges that we need to do no less than to 'reconfigure our understandings of constitutional law and constitutional rights according to . . . [a new] paradigm that enables us to understand better, and respond to, the challenges facing constitutionalism in an age of globalization' (*Constitutional Rights after Globalization* (2005), p. 3).

The state, it is claimed, is coming under pressure both internally and externally. On the one hand, the devolutionary forces of regionalism and localism are investing sites of constitutional authority within the state with increasing power. In the UK, for example, we can no longer understand the fullness of our constitutional arrangements if we confine our attention to matters in London, Westminster and Whitehall. The Scottish Parliament at Holyrood and the National Assembly for Wales at Cardiff Bay are essential institutions not only if you are studying British constitutional law in Scotland or Wales but so, too, if you are studying it in England. On the other hand, the forces of globalisation (in the economic, political, social, cultural and legal spheres) and the rise to constitutional prominence of both international and supranational organisations such as the World Trade Organization (WTO), the United Nations (UN), the Council of Europe and the EU (among a number of others) also require us to shift our gaze beyond national borders. To this end, recent years have seen a voluminous literature with such suggestive titles as *The End of Sovereignty?* (Camilleri and Falk (1992)), *Losing Control? Sovereignty in an Age of Globalization* (Sassen (1996)) and *The Retreat of the State* (Strange (1996)), while a number of EU lawyers have written articles that talk of such things as 'post-national constitutionalism' and the need to find 'constitutional substitutes' (see, e.g., Shaw (1999) 6 *JEPP* 579; Chalmers (2000) 27 *JLS* 178).

Two different sets of claim are made in this literature. The first, more moderate, claim is that even if the state continues to be the primary site of constitutional authority, the way in which it operates is now *conditioned* by both sub-state and super-state forces. The second, bolder, claim is that, in some senses at least, the state is no longer the primary site of constitutional authority and has been replaced in that regard by a combination of sub-state and super-state forces. The following extract surveys the issues.

Martin Loughlin, *Sword and Scales* (2000), pp. 141–5

The nation-state is a relatively modern phenomenon. Its emergence has been traced to the period after the Treaty of Westphalia of 1648, an era in which the western world was divided into more clearly delineated jurisdictions and the modern map of Europe began to take shape. But the idea of the nation-state which emerged in modern European history is not one in which a close congruence between ethnicity and the structure of government has been forged. Given the circumstances in which states have been formed, such congruency is almost never realized. Rather, nation-states are best viewed as 'imagined communities' [Benedict Anderson] or 'groups which *will* themselves to persist' [Ernest Gellner]. They exist despite differences of race and language, and largely because they are united by 'common sympathies' [JS Mill] or a history of common suffering . . . This is what might be called a civic conception of the nation-state. The French, for instance, constitute a nation-state, whether their ancestors were Gauls, Bretons, Normans, Franks, Romans or whatever. Similarly, the English, Irish, Scots and Welsh – notwithstanding their ethnic differences – have been forged into the nation-state of the United Kingdom. In this civic conception, the nation-state can be seen as a device through which class, ethnic and religious tensions within a defined territorial unit can be managed.

These nation-states present themselves as independent units in the international arena. From . . . the mid-eighteenth century, it has generally been accepted that the fundamental principle of international law is that of the formal equality of states, a principle which in turn yields those of independence and territorial integrity. These principles of the independence, equality and territorial integrity of sovereign states form the basis for the conduct of international relations . . .

[C]ertain structural changes are occurring in the international arena which appear to challenge the traditional role of the nation-state in political and economic affairs. These structural changes involve the twin processes of integration and fragmentation. Although these processes seem to be pulling in opposite directions, both present threats to the position of the nation-state as the predominant actor in . . . political affairs.

The process of integration is the result of the global impact of economic and technological change. The world which we inhabit is now genuinely global. It has been noted, for example, that today even illiterate labourers working in the deepest recesses of tropical rain forests understand that their livelihoods are not determined by forces operating at the level of their localities or even within the territorial borders of their states, but by the vagaries of world markets and the habits, tastes and capacities of consumers in distant countries. But this observation now applies not only to the cocoa labourers of Ghana but also to workers in the semi-conductor plants of Scotland and north-east England. With the emergence of global markets we see the growth in scale and power of transnational corporations and also the establishment of a variety of international organizations trying to respond to the regulatory issues which are presented. This process of world-wide economic integration necessitates a reconfiguration of the international political arena.

The process of fragmentation is, to some extent, a by-product of economic and political integration. With the growth of world markets, for example, the trend has been towards the regionalization of economies, and some of these regional entities (e.g., Singapore/Indonesia or Vancouver/Seattle) have become linked primarily to the global economy rather than to their host nation-states. In response to these economic trends, which have contributed to the resurgence of issues of ethnic identity, more extensive powers of government have been given to regional bodies within the nation-state. This has occurred throughout Europe, notably in the autonomous regions of Spain and the *Länder* of Germany and as the recent establishment of a Welsh Assembly and a Scottish Parliament indicates, this process has also affected governmental arrangements within the United Kingdom . . . Fragmentation undermines the traditional structures of the nation-state and has prompted the reconfiguration of the national political system. Such contemporary trends of integration and fragmentation are commonly viewed as responses to one powerful phenomenon – globalization.

Since the end of the Second World War, there has been a spectacular growth in transnational investment, production and trade. In turn, this has led to the establishment of global financial markets as the major US, European and Japanese banks have become locked into an international circuit regulating the flow of capital. The major transnational corporations which have emerged now account for a large proportion of the world's production and these corporations, able to disperse their centres of production, are no longer bounded by the territories of any particular State.

Many of these changes have been driven by technological development. A revolution has occurred in transportation and communications systems and, in conjunction with the microchip revolution and the digitalization of information, this has had a profound impact on economic activity. Production is now much less tied to specific localities; enterprises increasingly possess the capacity to shift capital and labour at low cost and high speed. Money is now able to circulate around the world through invisible networks, in vast quantities and at high velocity. These developments – universalized communication, supersonic transportation, hi-tech weaponry and the like – have presented a series of serious challenges to the nation-state. The success of the modern State over the last two hundred years has been based mainly on its ability to promote economic well-being, to maintain physical security and to foster a distinctive cultural identity of its citizens. Yet it is precisely these claims which are now being undermined by [the forces of globalisation].

Having surveyed the issues, Loughlin's verdict is that, powerful as the simultaneously integrationist and fragmentary forces of globalisation may be, the state will survive them, and will survive them intact (pp. 145–6):

Globalization has created a world of greater interdependence. Nevertheless, although the phenomenon seems to undermine the power of the nation-state, it is unlikely to lead to its demise. Indeed, there seems little doubt but that the modern State will remain the primary form of political organization for the foreseeable future . . .

The State is still the principal agency for managing the economy and promoting the welfare of its citizens. The critical point for our purposes is that, as a result of structural changes, the State must acknowledge that, to be effective, it must be prepared to work with other powerful agencies. To be successful, the State must be able to harness the immense power now located in private corporations and it must also work in tandem with a range of supra-national governmental bodies. The State, in short, is obliged to share power.

Loughlin's analysis is supported by Helen Thompson, who comes to a similar conclusion ('The Modern State and its Adversaries' (2006) 41 *Gov and Opp* 23, 26, emphasis in the original):

[F]or the modern state to be heading towards crisis, or significant long-term change, at least one of three things would have to be true: first, consent to particular and *reasonably long-established* sites of authoritative rule is breaking down either through large-scale resistance to the rule of law, or through the rejection of the rules of rule of such a state by a significant section of the political community constituted by it, and those who command the state's power cannot contain such developments; secondly, *previously capable* states are unable to command coercive power against those over whom they rule and against their external enemies; thirdly, the laws and demands of international institutions and organizations have enforceable claims against *historically sovereign* states.

In a compelling overview, Thompson argues that while each of these three phenomena has occurred at least somewhere in the world in recent times, there is no overall pattern that may be attributable to overarching forces of globalisation. She argues, for example, that the 'most crucial coercive powers that states enjoy are to tax and to command military forces' and that the evidence 'does not suggest that states are actually taxing less than they did ... Neither can it be plausibly claimed that the coercive power of well-established states to tax is diminishing ... [and] Even more clearly, the ability of previously capable states to mobilize armed force has been unimpaired by the end of the Cold War' (pp. 30–3). While she concedes that not all states today 'enjoy the same degree of external sovereignty as they did at the end of the 1970s' (p. 34):

such intervention in the internal affairs of nominally sovereign states does not represent a move beyond Westphalia. In the spirit of Westphalia, powerful states have long tried to curtail the activities of other states as states.

According to Thompson, and contrary to popular myth, the Peace of Westphalia (1648) 'did not result in external state sovereignty against all other states'. Rather, it 'legitimized the sovereignty of powerful modern states and the right of those states to impose limits on the statehood of defeated and aspiring states. It defined an external world in which sovereignty depended on power and in which distinctions were made between strong and weak states (pp. 25–6). Seen in this light, the policies of contemporary institutions such as the World Bank and the IMF, where tough conditions are imposed on states in the developing world, conditions that increasingly speak to constitutional values such as 'good governance', 'accountability' and 'transparency', are not so much a break from the Westphalia model as its continuation by new means: 'An international economy in which indebted states find that richer states succeed in controlling their economic decision-making and the parameters of their internal politics is repeating past history' (p. 36). Thompson's conclusions are as follows (pp. 39–40):

> Whilst the internal authority of some poorer states has certainly buckled under the pressure of economic liberalization, it is the external sovereignty of many poor and small states that has diminished most significantly, leaving them unable to resist the demands of other states and international institutions without inviting their own destruction. This is not because of anything that can sensibly be called 'globalization'. Neither does it mean that the modern state is heading towards a general crisis. Rather it suggests that the number of modern states that can lay claim to effective external sovereignty is diminishing towards the numbers seen in the more distant past. We are returning to some aspects of an older political world in which empire – the rule of a state over territory where it does not, at least at the moment of subjugation, recognize the subjects as its own – was central to the language and practice of politics. The modern state and empire have long been historical bedfellows.

In a lengthy and thoughtful analysis, Neil Walker examines a variety of critiques of modern constitutionalism, including those associated with globalisation and post-nationalism. He suggests (as does Gavin Anderson, *Constitutional Rights after Globalization* (2005)) that what is needed to account for constitutionalism in today's world is a developed sense of 'constitutional pluralism' ('The Idea of Constitutional Pluralism' (2002) 65 *MLR* 317). Walker says, first, that any successful notion of constitutionalism must (p. 334):

> continue to take the state seriously as a significant host to constitutional discourse. Even those who would most urgently contend that constitutionalism has to encompass post-national trends or that constitutionalism is an increasing irrelevance or obstacle to understanding or steering forms of social and political organisation, would hardly deny the state its place in the constitutional scheme.

He goes on to suggest, however, that:

> almost equally uncontroversially, a revised conception of constitutionalism should of course then also be open to the discovery of meaningful constitutional discourse and processes in non-state sites . . . Even for those who are most sceptical or pessimistic about the viability of constitutionalism beyond the state, their position is based either upon an incapacity to imagine the form in which such post-state constitutionalism might be effectively articulated and institutionalised or upon an unwillingness to concede that the time is yet ripe for such an enterprise, rather than upon a refusal *in principle* to contemplate that a constitutional steering mechanism, or its functional equivalent, might be appropriate for significant circuits of transnational power.

Be this as it may, in this book, we focus in most of our chapters on British constitutional law and practice, albeit that we aim to explain and demonstrate how the British constitution accommodates – sometimes relatively smoothly, but sometimes not – sites of constitutional authority both within the UK (see especially Chapter 4) and beyond its borders (see especially Chapter 5). In this, perhaps it may be said that we are siding with John Dunn's judgment (in *The Cunning of Unreason* (2000), p. 66) that, in the UK at least, 'Only massive selective inattention could stop anyone recognizing that states today remain (as they have been for some time) the principal institutional site of political experience.'

1.4 Constitutional Reform and Constitutional Change

In recent years the United Kingdom has been 'going through a period of profound constitutional change' (Oliver, *Constitutional Reform in the United Kingdom* (2003), p. v). The changes are regarded by some commentators to amount to no less than a 'new British constitution' (Bogdanor, *The New British Constitution* (2009), p. x). We would not go so far. Indeed, as we shall show later in this section, there is a very great deal of the 'old' constitution that remains. This said, however, there should be no doubting the significance of the reforms that have occurred in recent years and, indeed, that remain ongoing. In the pages that follow, we first set out what the main reforms have been, before offering some commentary on how they might best be understood. These reforms need to be put in the context of the pressure under which Brexit has placed the UK constitution, causing some to regard this as a constitutional crisis.

1.4.1 An Outline

1.4.1.1 The Blair Governments (1997–2007)

The 'New Labour' Government that took office in Britain in 1997 did so on a series of manifesto commitments to reform aspects of the constitution. In particular, it undertook as follows: to modernise the composition of the House of Lords and the procedures of the House of Commons; to enact freedom of information legislation designed to lead to more open government; to devolve power to Scotland and Wales; to reform local government; to establish a directly elected 'strategic authority' and mayor for London; to strengthen regional government in England; to enact human rights enforceable in UK courts; and to continue to work on a bipartisan basis for sustained peace and reform in Northern Ireland (Labour Party manifesto, *Because Britain Deserves Better* (1997), pp. 32–5).

The 1997–2001 Parliament passed legislation or introduced other measures in fulfilment of each of the Labour Party's manifesto pledges on constitutional reform. Thus, the Human Rights Act 1998 (HRA) incorporated most of the substantive provisions of the ECHR (1950) into domestic law; the Scotland Act 1998 and the Government of Wales Act 1998 devolved power to Scotland and

Wales; the 'Good Friday' or 'Belfast' Agreement led to the enactment of the Northern Ireland Act 1998, under which power was devolved to Northern Ireland; the House of Lords Act 1999 removed most of the hereditary peers from the House of Lords; a Freedom of Information Act was passed in 2000; the Greater London Authority Act 1999 created a mayor and a Greater London Authority for the nation's capital; the Local Government Act 2000 sought to give a new lease of life to local democracy; and the Regional Development Agencies Act 1998 made provision, albeit modest, for the development of aspects of economic policy on a regional basis. Meanwhile, a newly established Modernisation Committee of the House of Commons considered an array of ways in which Commons procedure could be modernised.

A number of these policies had been relatively newly adopted by the Labour Party, whose traditional hostility to a Bill of Rights, for example, had been founded on a fear that a conservative judiciary would use its provisions to defeat progressive or socialist legislation (see Griffith, *The Politics of the Judiciary* (5th edn. 1997) and Ewing and Gearty, *Freedom under Thatcher* (1990), ch. 8). Others were more firmly established. Most of these policies had long been advocated by pressure groups campaigning for constitutional reform (Charter 88, for example, or Liberty or the Campaign for Freedom of Information) and several of them had been subjected to detailed analysis by think tanks such as the Institute for Public Policy Research and the Constitution Unit. The latter, in particular, published a series of detailed reports on how to make devolution work, which, along with the groundbreaking work of the Scottish Constitutional Convention (on which, see Chapter 4), greatly contributed to the way in which the new Labour Government was able to 'hit the ground running' and to embark on its most ambitious constitutional reforms early in its first term.

After 2001, the pace of change – especially of legislative change – slowed somewhat, although 2005 saw the enactment of the (slightly misleadingly named) Constitutional Reform Act, which substantially reformed the powers and responsibilities of the Lord Chancellor and the judicial appointments process for England, Wales and Northern Ireland, and provided for the creation of a new Supreme Court to replace the appellate committee of the House of Lords and the judicial committee of the Privy Council. (The UK Supreme Court commenced its work in 2009.) Also important in this period was the Legislative and Regulatory Reform Act 2006, which concerns the relationship between the government's and Parliament's law-making powers.

An important difference between the reforms before and after the 2001 election concerned the process by which they were introduced. A notable feature of the 1997–2001 reforms, especially so given the magnitude of the reforms legislated for, was the smoothness of their implementation. Projects such as devolution or the incorporation of fundamental rights are considerable endeavours. Yet each was legislated for and implemented with efficiency and apparent ease of effort – at least in part explained by the years of careful thought and planning that had been devoted to these issues by think tanks and pressure groups while the Labour Party was in opposition. The measure that became the Constitutional Reform Act 2005, by contrast, was born of blunder. In June 2003 the prime minister announced a cabinet reshuffle, one element of which was that the Lord Chancellor and his department would cease to exist, to be replaced by a Secretary of State of (and Department for) Constitutional Affairs. Only afterwards did it apparently occur to the prime minister and the Cabinet Office that the position of Lord Chancellor was a statutory one and that it could therefore be abolished only by an act of Parliament (the prime minister can effect 'machinery of government' changes through announcing them himself but may not amend or repeal legislation; ordinarily only an act of Parliament may amend or repeal legislation). As the cabinet secretary later told the House of Lords Constitution Committee, 'it was a complete mess-up' (see House of Lords Constitution Committee, *The Cabinet Office and the Centre of Government*, 4th report of 2009–10, HL 30, para 193). A fresh Lord Chancellor had therefore to be appointed (Lord Falconer); he steered the required legislation through Parliament, the result being the Constitutional Reform Act 2005. The Constitution Committee was damning in its criticism of this sorry episode, which, it said (at [208]–[210]):

> involved wholly inadequate consultation both within Government (the Lord Chancellor [Lord Irvine of Lairg] was not consulted before decisions were taken) and outside Government (in particular, the failure to consult the senior judiciary). There was no justification for the failure to consult on these important reforms . . . [T]he scale of the constitutional changes involved, and the content of the necessary legislation, were not properly appreciated. This problem could not have arisen but for the fact that the Lord Chancellor and the senior judiciary were not consulted. Consultation on important constitutional reform is essential to good government.

(For further criticism of the process of constitutional reform under Labour, see Baker, 'Our Unwritten Constitution' (2010) 167 *Proc Brit Acad* 91; Flinders, *Delegated Governance and the British State* (2008).)

The measures outlined above are the main reforms of the constitution during the years of the Blair Governments, but they are far from the only measures to have affected aspects of our constitutional law. The period 1997–2007 witnessed significant legislative change in several other areas that touch on constitutional law and practice. The funding and conduct of political parties was (partially) reformed by the Political Parties, Elections and Referendums Act 2000; human rights and civil liberties were substantially affected by such legislation as the Crime and Disorder Act 1998, the Regulation of Investigatory Powers Act 2000, the Extradition Act 2003, the Asylum and Immigration (Treatment of Claimants) Act 2004 and the Serious Organised Crime and Police Act 2005, among several others; and the period saw a raft of counterterrorism legislation, including the Terrorism Act 2000, the Anti-terrorism, Crime and Security Act 2001, the Prevention of Terrorism Act 2005 and the Terrorism Act 2006; see also in this regard the Civil Contingencies Act 2004.

(This legislation and the various matters it concerns are considered throughout this book: the HRA is considered in Chapters 2, 10 and 11; the devolution legislation is considered in Chapter 4, as is reform of local government; reforms to Parliament are considered in Chapter 9; the Constitutional Reform Act is considered in Chapter 2; and aspects of the counterterrorism legislation are considered in Chapter 11.)

1.4.1.2 The Brown Government (2007–10)

The story of constitutional reform during Gordon Brown's time as Prime Minister is an astonishing one and makes for a sobering case study of the gulf in British government between rhetoric and reality or, from a different point of view, of how little government can be expected to deliver, no matter how grand its aspirations. It started in the opening week of Mr Brown's premiership, no less, as the most ambitious and exciting programme of reform ever seen in the modern era; it ended with a relative mouse of a measure, the Constitutional Reform and Governance Act 2010, in which only a fraction of the programme set out in the summer of 2007 was realised.

The main events in the story are as follows: (a) the publication of a Green Paper (a government consultation document) in July 2007, within a week of Mr Brown's becoming Prime Minister, *The Governance of Britain* (Cm 7170); (b) the simultaneous publication in March 2008 of a White Paper (a government policy document), *The Governance of Britain: Constitutional Renewal* (Cm 7342) and of a Draft Constitutional Renewal Bill (the Draft Bill was thoroughly scrutinised by a parliamentary Joint Committee on the Draft Constitutional Renewal Bill: see that Committee's *1st report of 2007–08*, HL 166, HC 551, July 2008); (c) the introduction more than a year later of the Government's Constitutional Reform and Governance Bill; (d) the enactment in the mad rush immediately before the general election of 2010 of some, but far from all, of the provisions contained in the bill, in the form of the Constitutional Reform and Governance Act 2010. Each of these events will be discussed in turn.

The *Governance of Britain* Green Paper was cast in broad and grand terms, and sought to limit the powers of the executive, to make the executive more accountable, to reinvigorate British democracy and to review the relationship between the individual and the state. It aimed to provide for a better constitutional balance, making the executive more accountable to Parliament, aiming to place the executive's powers on a statutory footing leading to greater parliamentary oversight and control over the executive. It also suggested that the House of Lords should become 'substantially or wholly' elected (para 137), the House of Commons should be 'revitalised' (para 139) and new forms of 'direct democracy' should be encouraged. A new Bill of Rights and Duties was proposed. All of this, it was thought, would have the potential to lead at least to a new 'concordat between the executive and Parliament' or, perhaps, even to a written constitution (para 212). (See further Le Sueur, 'Gordon Brown's New Constitutional Settlement' [2008] *PL* 21.)

The Draft Constitutional Renewal Bill and the accompanying White Paper of eight months later brought forward only a few of these proposals. The very large gulf between the promise of the Green Paper and the provisions of the Draft Bill was obvious to everyone. Whatever the merits of the individual reforms provided for by the Draft Bill, its contents could hardly be described as 'constitutional renewal'!

The Constitutional Reform and Governance Bill was long delayed, not being published until July 2009 (fifteen months after the Draft Bill and twelve months after the Joint Committee's report on the Draft Bill). No reason for this delay was given. The bill included provisions on the Civil Service, on the ratification of treaties, on demonstrations in the vicinity of Parliament and on judicial appointments. Added to the bill were provisions concerning member-ship of the House of Lords. These were tidying-up measures, falling a long way short of the stated ideal of the 'substantially or wholly' elected House referred to in the *Governance of Britain* Green Paper. It was proposed that the ninety-two remaining hereditary peers should no longer be replaced, one by one, such that the number of remaining hereditaries would instead dwindle over time rather than being kept at ninety-two. Further clauses provided for the expul-sion, suspension or resignation of members from the House of Lords.

As the bill progressed through its legislative stages in the House of Commons, a considerable number of provisions were added to it by way of government amendments. Fresh clauses were added on the conduct of refer-endums; clauses were also added that would have established a nationwide referendum to be held on whether the electoral system for the House of Commons should be changed from first-past-the-post to the alternative vote system ('AV' – see further on this below); clauses were introduced that substantially amended the Parliamentary Standards Act 2009; new provisions were added concerning the tax status of MPs and members of the House of Lords; and an amendment to the Freedom of Information Act 2000 was also introduced at a late stage in the bill's passage through the Commons.

The bill as amended was eventually passed by the Commons and was sent to the House of Lords in March 2010. Parliament was dissolved early the follow-ing month, as a general election had been called for 6 May 2010. Thus, what had started out in the summer of 2007 as such a grand 'renewal' of Britain's constitution had been reduced to an omnibus bill of constitutional miscellany, much delayed, much amended and, now, much rushed. The House of Lords had time to hold a second reading debate on the bill (that is, a debate on its general principles) but detailed consideration of its many and various provi-sions proved impossible, owing to time having run out. In the event, the bill went into what is called the 'wash-up', the curious and frenetic few days in the dying days of a Parliament in which the political parties engage in crude horse-trading, deciding behind closed doors which provisions from which bills before Parliament will be allowed to pass into law. The House of Lords Constitution Committee was far from alone in expressing its dismay, sadness and, indeed, anger that such were the depths to which Labour's once-cherished plans for constitutional reform had fallen. 'This is no way to undertake the task of constitutional reform', it flatly stated, in a damning verdict that was echoed on all sides of the House (see House of Lords Constitution Committee, *Constitutional Reform and Governance Bill*, 11th report of 2009–10, HL 98, para 47; HL Deb vol. 718, cols 958–1056, 24 March 2010).

The enactment that came out of the wash-up contains only about half of the provisions that had found their way into the bill by the time it had arrived in the Lords: thus, the principal provisions of the Constitutional Reform and Governance Act 2010 place the Civil Service on a statutory footing; provide for Parliament to approve (or, as the case may be, not to approve) treaties ratified by ministers; make substantial amendments to the Parliamentary Standards Act 2009; and impose new requirements on the tax status of MPs and members of the House of Lords.

One of the main themes of the *Governance of Britain* Green Paper was that the non-statutory (or prerogative) powers of the government should be placed either on a legislative footing or, at least, made subject to greater parliamentary oversight. The Constitutional Reform and Governance Act achieves this for two such powers: the constitutional position of civil servants is now governed by statute (rather than, as formerly, under the prerogative) and powers to ratify treaties are now, as a matter of statute, subject to parliamentary scrutiny (the ratification of treaties is a prerogative power). But the vast bulk of the government's prerogative powers remain unaffected, in spite of the promises of the 2007 Green Paper.

1.4.1.3 The Coalition Government (2010–15)

Both parties in the Coalition Government that took office following the 2010 general election went into that election committed to a series of constitutional reforms. While full-scale constitutional reform is a policy most often associated with the Liberal Democrats, David Cameron's Conservative Party had, by 2010, also pledged itself to a variety of reforms. Among the Liberal Democrats' priorities were: a proportionate system of voting to replace the first-past-the-post system used for elections to the House of Commons; the introduction of fixed-term parliaments; an elected House of Lords; a written constitution; and a Freedom Bill designed to roll back the incursions into civil liberties witnessed under previous governments. Conservative policies included the following: to reduce by 10 per cent the size of the House of Commons; to establish a system of 'English votes for English laws', meaning that only MPs representing constituencies in England would be permitted to vote on measures affecting only England; the repeal of the Human Rights Act and its replacement with a British Bill of Rights; a Referendum Bill, requiring a referendum to be held before the UK could ratify any future EU treaty; and a Sovereignty Bill, re-affirming the supremacy of Parliament.

The Coalition Government's *Programme for Government*, published in May 2010, set out a series of policies that sought to combine aspects of these ideas. The *Programme for Government* had six themes: parliamentary reform; electoral reform; reforms related to Europe; greater decentralisation; greater transparency; commitments to freedom of information and civil liberties. As with other proposals of constitutional reform, practical and political problems – exacerbated by maintaining a Coalition Government – meant that many of the provisions were watered down or failed to come to fruition. Nevertheless, as will be seen, although the reforms that were made appeared moderate or cosmetic, they nevertheless had important unintended consequences down the line.

In terms of parliamentary reform, the most important change was the enactment of the Fixed-Term Parliaments Act 2011. This act fixes parliamentary terms to five years. It also provides for two ways of holding a general election before the end of the five-year term. First, two-thirds of the whole House of Commons can vote in favour of a motion to hold an early general election. Second, a successful vote of no confidence in the government will lead to a two-week period in which an alternative government can be formed. If a vote of confidence in the alternative government is successful, then no general election is held. If this is not the case, then a general election will take place. Although intended to remove the ability of the prime minister to call a general election at a favourable time, thus placing more control in Parliament over the executive, as will be seen below the act has not removed politics from the timing of general elections. Moreover, given the events of 2019, its utility has been questioned. Other measures of parliamentary reform were less successful. The commitment to implement the recommendations of the Wright Committee, introducing, inter alia, a Commons Business Committee, only gave rise to the introduction of a Backbench Business Committee. A more successful change was the election of the chairs of select committees by the House of Commons, which has seen select committees play a more active role in holding the government to account. However, the plan to replace the House of Lords with a wholly elected chamber failed due to a lack of support from the Conservative Party. A similar issue of lack of support arose with regard to proposals for electoral reform. Although the relevant legislation was enacted to hold a referendum on electoral reform, the proposals for an alternative voting mechanism were rejected.

Other changes included the establishment of e-petitions, where a government response is required when a petition obtains 10,000 signatures, with 100,000 signatures triggering a debate and the introduction of a power of recall. The Recall of MPs Act 2015 provides a means through which to recall

MPs convicted of certain criminal offences, or who have been suspended from the House for a period of ten working (or fourteen during a recess) days or more, or those convicted of giving false or misleading information relating to parliamentary allowances. A petition may be initiated and, if signed by 10 per cent of those registered to vote in that constituency, the MP is recalled and a by-election is held. However, the proposal to hold more public reading stages for bills failed to fully materialise.

Although the proposed 'Sovereignty Bill' did not materialise, the European Union Act 2011 did initiate a series of complex referendum locks as regards certain transfers of power from the UK to the EU, as well as including a clause, section 18, reaffirming that UK legislation provided for the effect of EU law in national law. Following a transfer of power from Westminster to Holyrood, a referendum on Scottish independence was held in 2014. Although the referendum outcome was not in favour of independence, the close outcome, as well as political concerns that there could be a vote in favour of independence, led to the transfer of more powers to Scotland – referred to as devo-max. Similarly, the Wales Act 2014 devolved more powers to Wales, including fiscal powers for the first time. Further devolution proved less successful, with a mixed reaction to the provision of referendums for local mayors and elections of police and crime commissioners. The West Lothian question also remained unresolved. There was also little movement on civil liberties. The Commission on a British Bill of Rights failed to reach a consensus, although small changes were made regarding the protection of civil liberties.

This patchwork of achievements was perhaps to be expected, given the general difficulties of achieving constitutional reform. What may appear as attractive constitutional reform while in opposition may lose its shine once in government. The reforms were also hampered by competing ideologies of the Conservatives and the Liberal Democrats and the difficulties faced by the Liberal Democrats when moving from opposition to a position of power. It is perhaps no surprise that the most successful policies either made minor changes or did not require legislation. Neither is it a surprise that those changes that did require legislation were either needed to maintain the Coalition Government (e.g. the Fixed-Term Parliaments Act 2011), or stemmed from apparent necessary political concessions from the government (e.g. devolution). This did not deter the parties in the 2015 general election from including programmes for constitutional reform in their manifestos, the consequences of one such proposal triggering what is likely to lead to dramatic and as yet unpredictable changes to the UK constitution.

1.4.1.4 Constitutional Change Post-2015: Brexit and Beyond

Earlier editions have evaluated past changes, concluding that for all of the programmes of constitutional reform, the main features of the UK constitution had remained essentially the same. In the excitement of the early years of the Blair Government's reforms, it was easy, perhaps, to get carried away. In the introduction to their edited collection of essays, *Constitutional Reform* (1999), Robert Blackburn and Raymond Plant stated, for example, that 'taken as a whole, the parameters and range of subjects affected [by the Government's plans in the field of constitutional reform] cover virtually the entire terrain of our constitutional structure' (p. 1). This was never the case. The 'Westminster model' is still intact. Britain remains a constitutional monarchy and parliamentary democracy with a bicameral legislature; the prime minister and the cabinet continue to be constitutionally accountable for their policies and decisions to Parliament; and the judiciary continues to be independent, even if its constitutional powers have grown since 1972 (and again since 1997).

There are significant aspects of the British constitution that remain largely untouched by the pre-2015 reforms. These include the monarchy, most of the Crown's prerogative powers, the structure of government and the relationship between ministers and civil servants (see Chapters 6 and 7); rule- and law-making by the government – delegated legislation and suchlike (see Chapter 7); the UK's relationship with the EU, and the impact of EU law on the constitution (see Chapter 5); and the relationship between the House of Commons and the House of Lords, which has not been altered substantially since 1911. The great constitutional statutes of the past continue since 1997 as they did before to shape the constitutional order of today: Magna Carta, the Bill of Rights 1689, the Act of Settlement 1701 and so on. As we shall see throughout this book, were we to confine our attention to events and laws that occurred or have been passed only since 1997, it would result in our having an extremely odd – and untenable – view of the constitution. It is essential that students and scholars of the constitution grasp the venerable and the continuing, as well as the new and the changing, elements of our constitutional order. To privilege either over the other would be a serious error.

Vernon Bogdanor, then Professor of Government at Oxford, claimed that the changes witnessed since 1997 cannot 'be understood in evolutionary terms' and that 'they represent nothing less than a revolution in our constitutional affairs, a radical discontinuity from what has happened before' (Bogdanor, *The New British Constitution* (2009), p. 276). In *The British Constitution* (2007), Professor King agrees with Vernon Bogdanor, that the 'old' constitution has been replaced by a new one. But this is about the limit of their agreement. Whereas Bogdanor sees a logic to the new constitution (a logic of the dispersal of power), in King's analysis what we now have is merely 'a mess' (The *British Constitution*, p. 345): 'some of the changes were intended, some were unintended, some were intended but had unintended consequences, and some were undoubtedly intended, but not as part of any scheme of constitutional change', he says (p. 349).

King's words are almost prophetic when we analyse the process of constitutional change post-2015. The 2015 general election produced a surprise – the expected second hung Parliament instead produced a Conservative Government, albeit with a relatively small majority. The Conservative Party manifesto had focused less on plans of constitutional reform. Moreover, most of the changes related to the completion of earlier promised programmes of reform. In terms of political reform, the manifesto reiterated the promise to make boundary changes and reduce the number of MPs in the House of Commons from 650 to 600. There was no commitment to replace the House of Lords with an elected chamber. Other commitments were to continue with the process of devolution, implementing the Smith Commission, devolving greater fiscal and welfare powers to Scotland, as well as implementing the Silk Commission and the St David's Day agreement, moving Wales to a system of reserved powers. Mention was also made of the introduction of 'English Votes for English Laws' to resolve the West Lothian issue.

If our narrative stopped there, then we may have concluded that the Conservative Government of 2015 to 2017 had made good on most of its plans. We might also have been tempted to join Bogdanor in seeing a logical progression of constitutional reform. English Votes for English Laws was introduced to the Commons through a new standing order in Parliament. If the Speaker certifies a bill as pertaining to English or English and Welsh matters only, then the committee stage of the bill is considered only by MPs from English or English and Welsh constituencies. Moreover, a legislative grand committee, composed of MPs representing English or English and Welsh constituencies, must vote in favour of the bill before its third reading before the full House. The Scotland Act 2016 and the Wales Act 2017 succeeded in granting greater powers to Scotland and Wales, as well as recognising the permanent nature of the Scottish Parliament and the Welsh Assembly – now Senedd – their removal requiring a referendum of the Scottish or Welsh electorate respectively, although there has been no modification of boundaries or of the number of MPs in the House of Commons.

However, the above account does not include two of the key commitments of the Conservative Party manifesto – the promise to hold an 'in-out' referendum on the UK's continued membership of the European Union and to 'scrap' the Human Rights Act and replace it with a British Bill of Rights. Of the two proposed changes, it is the last one that was designed to produce constitutional change. The referendum promise is probably best understood as a means of responding to the political challenge posed by the rise of the UK Independence Party and of resolving tensions that were arising from divergent views regarding European Union membership within the Conservative Party. It was not conceived as a means of instituting constitutional change. If understood as a political tactic to bolster the chances of the Conservative Party of winning the election, then the tactic succeeded. However, if it was designed to maintain the status quo and to silence division on Europe, it can only be regarded as a spectacular failure, the vote in favour of the UK's exit from the EU instigating a fundamental constitutional change. Moreover, far from removing the divisions in the

Conservative Party over Europe, these divisions have continued to persist, dividing not just one but several political parties, with these divisions being felt across the whole country.

The most obvious constitutional change from the referendum is the UK's exit from the EU, which took place on 31 January 2020. In short, the European Union (Withdrawal) Act 2018 aims to preserve most of the regulations stemming from the EU, incorporating these into domestic law as retained EU law. However, retained EU law does not include the EU's Charter of Fundamental Rights and Freedoms. In addition, human rights protected through general principles will only be able to be used as interpretative principles post-exit day. The supremacy of EU law will also only continue as regards legislation enacted prior to exit day. The European Union (Withdrawal Agreement) Act 2020 incorporates the Withdrawal Agreement into UK law. It preserves the effect of the European Communities Act 1972 – which was repealed on exit day – for those aspects of EU law that the UK is still required to adhere to according to the Withdrawal Agreement. This will remain in place until the end of the transition period – 31 December 2020. After that, the provisions of the European Union (Withdrawal) Act 2018 will apply as concerns retained EU law. These changes will be discussed in more detail in Chapter 5, since our focus here is the inadvertent consequences of earlier measures of constitutional reform and the further inadvertent changes as a consequence of the Brexit process. These changes led some to conclude that the Brexit process pushed the UK into a constitutional crisis.

1.4.1.5 Inadvertent Consequences: The Fixed-Term Parliaments Act 2011

The Fixed-Term Parliaments Act 2011 fixed parliamentary terms to five years and replaced the prerogative power of the dissolution of Parliament with a statutory provision governing an early general election, set out in section 2 below.

2 Early Parliamentary General Elections

(1) An early parliamentary general election is to take place if—
    (a) the House of Commons passes a motion in the form set out in subsection (2), and
    (b) if the motion is passed on a division, the number of members who vote in favour of the motion is a number equal to or greater than two thirds of the number of seats in the House (including vacant seats).
(2) The form of motion for the purposes of subsection (1)(a) is—
    "That there shall be an early parliamentary general election."
(3) An early parliamentary general election is also to take place if—
    (a) the House of Commons passes a motion in the form set out in subsection (4), and

> (b) the period of 14 days after the day on which that motion is passed ends without the House passing a motion in the form set out in subsection (5).
>
> (4) The form of motion for the purposes of subsection (3)(a) is—
>
>   "That this House has no confidence in Her Majesty's Government."
>
> (5) The form of motion for the purposes of subsection (3)(b) is—
>
>   "That this House has confidence in Her Majesty's Government."
>
> (6) Subsection (7) applies for the purposes of the Timetable in rule 1 in Schedule 1 to the Representation of the People Act 1983.
>
> (7) If a parliamentary general election is to take place as provided for by subsection (1) or (3), the polling day for the election is to be the day appointed by Her Majesty by proclamation on the recommendation of the Prime Minister (and, accordingly, the appointed day replaces the day which would otherwise have been the polling day for the next election determined under section 1).

While the term of office of the Coalition Government was fixed at five years, this was not the case for the 2015 Conservative Government, with Theresa May using section 2(1)(a) on 18 April 2017 in support of a snap general election to take place on 8 June 2017. The requirement of a vote of two-thirds of the members of the House of Commons may have seemed such a high hurdle that it would tip the balance of power away from the government to Parliament. However, the fact that Theresa May's motion succeeded – by 522 votes to 13 – suggests otherwise. The use of a motion for a snap general election can be likened to a game of political chicken. To vote against a general election suggests both a lack of a commitment to democracy and a lack of confidence in your political party's chances in the next general election. However, the outcome of the 2017 general election may suggest that prime ministers are far from infallible when it comes to choosing an election date to suit their political cause. The 2015 Conservative majority Government was replaced with a minority Conservative Government, shored up by a 'confidence and supply' agreement from the DUP.

While, in theory, the balance of power rests with Parliament, in practice it appeared to be difficult to see when a prime minister would be unable to obtain the majority needed for a general election at the time of his or her choosing, suggesting that the transfer of power from the government to Parliament was only illusory. Nevertheless, these circumstances arose in 2019. Boris Johnson tabled three early general election motions – 4 September, 9 September and 28 September. On all three occasions, the government was able to obtain a majority of votes in favour of an early parliamentary general election, but was not able to obtain the two-thirds required due to the abstention of the opposition. In order to escape this impasse, the government tabled the Early Parliamentary General Election

Bill 2019, which became the Early Parliamentary General Election Act 2019 which provided as follows:

1 Early Parliamentary General Election

(1) An early parliamentary general election is to take place on 12 December 2019 in consequence of the passing of this Act.

(2) That day is to be treated as a polling day appointed under section 2(7) of the Fixed-Term Parliaments Act 2011.

This effectively bypassed the two-thirds requirement. Although section 3(2) of the Fixed-Term Parliaments Act 2011 states that Parliament may not be dissolved other than through its provisions, these exceptions include in order to hold a poll on a date as set out in section 2(7) of the act. The Early Parliamentary General Election Act added an extra polling date. While this did not require two-thirds of the Commons, it did require legislation that meant that it also needed a majority vote in the House of Lords and the assent of the monarch in addition to a majority vote in the House of Commons. In addition, the 2019 Act empowered Parliament to define the polling date. This is not the case for an early parliamentary general election under the Fixed-Term Parliaments Act 2011, where the polling date is determined by the monarch, on the recommendation of the prime minister (section 2(7)).

The 2011 Act has also challenged one of the most fundamental conventions of the UK constitution – that the UK Government only remains in power to the extent that it holds the confidence of the House of Commons. Prior to the act, the government, by convention, would resign if it lost a vote of no confidence. Votes of no confidence were often called were the government to lose a vote in the House on a major policy issue. As such, it was rare, if not impossible, for the government to claim to retain the confidence of the House after losing a vote on a key element of governmental policy. The events of 15 and 16 January 2019 blatantly demonstrate that, post the 2011 Act, this may no longer be the case.

On 15 January 2019, the House of Commons was asked to vote on the Withdrawal Agreement, under the so-called meaningful vote provisions found in section 13 of the European Union (Withdrawal) Act 2018. Section 13 requires that the Withdrawal Agreement (the Agreement between the UK and the EU setting out the conditions of the UK's withdrawal from the European Union) can only be ratified if, inter alia, its contents are approved by a motion of the House of Commons. The House of Commons voted overwhelming against the Withdrawal Agreement by 432 votes to 202, suffering the heaviest parliamentary defeat of any prime minister in the democratic era. It may have been thought that such a dramatic defeat on the key aspect of the government's policy could be seen as an indication that the government no longer enjoyed the confidence of the House of Commons. However, given the provisions of the 2011 Act, Theresa May was not in a position where she could offer the resignation of her government, leading to a general election. Rather, a general election could only be called either if Theresa May proposed a motion for an early general election or following a vote of no confidence. Jeremy Corbyn MP, then Leader of the Opposition, duly tabled a motion of no confidence in the government, which was debated on 16 January. However, Theresa May's government survived the vote of no confidence, the motion being defeated by 325 votes to 306.

The experience of the Fixed-Term Parliaments Act is a stark illustration of the dangers of piecemeal constitutional change. Fixing parliamentary terms and involving the Commons in the process of the calling of an early general election provided an effective means of maintaining a stable Coalition Government. However, it has not resulted in a general rebalancing of power from the executive to the legislature and some argue that its operation in 2019 undermined the fundamental convention that a government only stays in power to the extent that it enjoys the confidence of the House of Commons. It is perhaps for this reason that the Conservative Party manifesto for 2019, and the following Queen's Speech in December 2019, included a commitment to repeal the Fixed-Term Parliaments Act 2011. However, it should be recalled that 2019 was an unusual set of circumstances.

1.4.1.6 Continuing Constitutional Consequences of Brexit and Constitutional Change

The last edition of this book evaluated two emerging trends of constitutional change – a revival of the powers of Parliament and a perceived moved towards juristocracy. Both of these trends can be said to have continued post-2015, although the Brexit referendum has also undermined the legitimacy and the powers of Parliament.

The last ten years has witnessed a growing use of referendums. Referendums bear an uneasy relationship with the traditional understanding of the UK constitution. As will be discussed in Chapter 2, if there were a key to understanding the nature of the UK constitution, it was the principle of parliamentary sovereignty. According to this principle, Parliament is the most powerful institution in the UK constitution. Each successive Parliament may enact laws on any subject matter it desires – including, as we have seen, instigating constitutional change – by using the standard law-making procedure of obtaining the agreement of the House of Commons, the House of Lords and the consent of the monarch.

Referendums, however, challenge this assumption. They prioritise direct as opposed to representative democracy. The people have spoken. The people have also spoken through electing MPs to the House of Commons. What should the House of Commons do when the voice of the people on a particular issue as expressed in a referendum provides an outcome different from the one hoped for by Parliament? This tension was exacerbated by the provisions of the European Union Referendum Act 2015. Unlike other legislation providing for referendums, the 2015 Act did not impose any legally binding obligation on ministers in response to the outcome of the referendum. Rather, the referendum was only 'politically advisory'. Yet, this advice was clearly particularly strong. It led to the resignation of David Cameron as Prime Minister, with Theresa May being chosen by the Conservative Party as their leader – and hence Prime Minister – in his stead. It became a matter of governmental policy to implement the outcome of the referendum. Moreover, the House of Commons voted twice to adopt the outcome of the referendum (on opposition day motions on 12 October 2016 and 7 December 2016).

The strength of the Brexit vote, and the ensuing undermining of the House of Commons, is clearly illustrated by the swift enactment of the European Union (Notification of Withdrawal) Act 2017. Following the conclusion in *Miller I* (above) that the UK Government could not use its prerogative powers to leave the European Union, legislation was required. This placed Parliament in the position where it could have placed limits on this power or conditions on its exercise. This would not have been available to Parliament had the executive been able to trigger the Brexit process merely by exercising its prerogative powers. However, there is little evidence of the House of Commons using this power. The European Union (Notification of Withdrawal) Bill 2017/19 was introduced in the House of Commons a mere two days after the *Miller I* decision. A mere thirteen days later, the bill was agreed to at a third reading in the House of Commons by 494 votes to 122, with no amendments. The House of Lords did approve two amendments: seeking to protect the rights of EU citizens living in the UK and to provide for parliamentary approval over the agreement forged between the UK and the EU. Neither of these amendments was ultimately successful.

Further evidence of the erosion of Parliament can be found in the provisions of the European Union (Withdrawal) Act 2018. This time the transfer of power is from Parliament to the executive. The act needed to ensure that modifications were made to domestic law to ensure that it could be applied correctly following the UK's exit from the EU. Given the volume of necessary changes, this was achieved through a grant of power to the executive to enact delegated legislation, including Henry VIII clauses empowering ministers to 'make any provision that could be made by an Act of Parliament' (see section 8 (5) and 9 (2)). Moreover, these powers can be exercised whenever a minister considers it appropriate. These provisions were soundly criticised by the House of Lords' Constitution Committee (*European Union (Withdrawal) Bill, 9th Report of 2017–19*, HL Paper 69), p. 4):

> The Bill also represents a challenge for the relationship between Parliament and the Executive. While we acknowledge that the Government needs some broad delegated powers—including Henry VIII powers to amend primary legislation—to deliver legal continuity post-exit, these powers need to be restricted and subject to appropriate scrutiny. However, here too the Bill falls short. The Bill grants ministers overly-broad powers to do whatever they think is 'appropriate' to correct 'deficiencies' in retained EU law. This gives ministers far greater latitude than is constitutionally acceptable. The Bill also includes an unacceptably wide urgent procedure, allowing the Government to make regulations lasting up to a month without any scrutiny by Parliament. In addition, the Bill provides for a power to implement the withdrawal agreement that is no longer required in light of Government commitments to bring forward a further withdrawal and implementation bill.

(See also 'European Union (Withdrawal) Bill: Interim Report' House of Lords, Select Committee on the Constitution, 3rd Report of Session 2017–19, HL Paper 19.)

However, it would be wrong to conclude that these changes, added to the unintended consequences of the Fixed-Term Parliaments Act 2011 (discussed earlier) have led to the emaciation of Parliament. The snap general election of 2017, coupled with the provisions of section 13 of the European Union (Withdrawal) Act 2018, have led to an increase in the powers of the Commons in particular. Theresa May effectively called for a general election in 2017 in order to increase her parliamentary majority, thus enabling her to implement Brexit with little parliamentary resistance. However, the election gave rise to a hung Parliament. It was therefore easier for Parliament to exert its control over the government. Section 13 of the European Union (Withdrawal) Act 2018 provides for the so-called 'meaningful vote' over the Withdrawal Agreement. First, it provides that the Withdrawal Agreement cannot be ratified unless there is a motion in the House of Commons voting in favour of the agreement, a motion in the House of Lords to take note of the motion in the House of Commons and legislation to implement the provisions of the Withdrawal Agreement. Moreover, the section provides for a series of motions in neutral terms should the House of Commons vote against the Withdrawal Agreement, or should there be no Withdrawal Agreement, or no prospect of it being agreed to, by a series of deadlines.

This provision transfers powers from the executive to the legislature. The normal constitutional arrangement is that it is for the executive to negotiate international agreements. The role of the legislature is found in the provisions of the Constitutional Reform and Government Act 2010, which requires, normally, that the legislature approves international agreements in order for them to be ratified. The neutral motions could also provide the Commons with an opportunity to guide the executive as to how to proceed in the light of the rejection of a Withdrawal Agreement, or no Withdrawal Agreement being reached in time. The legislature used both of these provisions. The House of Commons rejected the Withdrawal Agreement twice during the 2017–19 parliamentary session, on 15 January and 12 March 2019. Moreover, the Commons twice held indicative votes, on 27 March and 1 April 2019, using the neutral motions to vote on a range of possible options to guide the government. However the indicative votes provided no clear preference.

Both of these examples illustrate a strengthening of the power of the legislature over the executive. The means through which these powers were obtained also illustrate a growing power of Parliament. The origins of section 13 can be tracked to the European Union (Notification of Withdrawal) Act 2017. We noted above that this was enacted quickly and without amendment. However, one of the reasons that its provisions were enacted without amendment was because the government provided a political assurance that 'the Government will bring forward a motion on the final agreement, to be approved by both Houses of Parliament before it is concluded. [The Government] expect and intend that this will happen before the European Parliament debates and votes on the final agreement' (HC Deb, vol. 621, col 264, 7 February 2017). The original provisions of section 13 were amended by the House of Lords to include motions that were not neutral. A neutral motion is unamendable. Other motions could have been amended by the Commons. On its return to the House of Commons, the Commons voted to reject the amendments of the House of Lords. However, prior to the debates on the first meaningful vote, the government proposed a business motion setting out the timing of the debates. This motion was successfully amended by Dominic Grieve MP, such that the Commons would be able to propose amendments to neutral votes. This amendment paved the way for the later indicative votes. This display of the strengthening of the powers of Parliament culminated in the enactment of the European Union (Withdrawal) Act 2019 and the European Union (Withdrawal) (No 2) Act 2019. The House of Commons successfully pushed through a business motion to suspend Standing Order No. 14 – the standing order that prioritises the business of the government in the House. Instead, debate would be held on the European Union (Withdrawal) Act 2019, legislation that had originated from opposition and backbench MPs (the bill was mostly initiated by Yvette Cooper, a Labour MP). The legislation was designed to prevent a no-deal exit from the EU on 12 April and demonstrates a dramatic show of strength of the Commons. On 3 September 2019, the Speaker interpreted Standing Order No. 24 – which allows for a motion on an urgent matter – to include a vote to suspend Standing Order No. 14, timetabling instead the enactment of what became the European Union (Withdrawal) (No 2) Act 2019 – known as the Benn/Burt Bill. This act required the prime minister to seek an extension from the then deadline of 31 October 2019, should the House of Commons fail to vote in favour of the Withdrawal Agreement, or fail to vote in favour of exiting the EU with no deal, by 19 October 2019. These votes having failed, the prime minister was required to seek an extension, despite making it clear that this was not governmental policy.

These events took place in unprecedented times, when a series of events undermined the assumptions that normally underpin the UK's parliamentary system of government: a minority as opposed to a strong government; a key policy issue which divides across party lines; a strict deadline set by EU law whose extension is not under the sole control of the UK and an issue that, regardless of how it is resolved, will have a dramatic impact on the UK constitution. It may also be dependent on the personalities of those involved and the judgment of the then Speaker, John Bercow. Moreover, previous attempts of Yvette Cooper to initiate and enact legislation had been less successful; the European Union (Withdrawal) Act 2019 was her fifth attempt. However, they now set a precedent. These events demonstrate that it is possible for backbench and opposition MPs to amend business orders and to use urgent motions to suspend Standing Order No.14, and initiate and successfully enact legislation. Governments would be wise to realise that a route once found to be successful may be tried again. Perhaps this demonstrates the real power of the legislature – a possible show of strength may require the government to pre-emptively decide to act before it is forced to do so by the legislature. (See Russell and Gover, *Legislation at Westminster: Parliamentary Actors and Influence in the Making of the Law* (2017); Craig, 'Brexit and the UK Constitution' in Jowell and O'Cinneide, *The Changing Constitution* (9th edn. 2019). It is perhaps no surprise that, after obtaining a large majority in the December 2019 general election, the government was able to push the European Union (Withdrawal Agreement) Act 2020 through the Commons in three days, with the Act repealing section 13 of the European Union (Withdrawal) Act 2018.

The second trend noted in the last edition of this book was the growing power of the judiciary – the move towards juristocracy. It is frequently claimed that a key idea underpinning a number of the post-1997 reforms has been significantly and substantially to enhance the constitutional power and authority of the judiciary, to such an extent that it is now to the courts (rather than to Parliament) that we should look to take the lead responsibility in seeking to hold government to account. As Robert Hazell has claimed, 'the judges would not admit it, but they have emerged immensely stronger' ('The Continuing Dynamism of Constitutional Reform' (2007) 60 *Parl Aff* 3, 17). Regardless of whether we should express the position in terms as bold as these, what is clear – to opponents and supporters of enhanced judicial power alike – is that the constitutional power and authority of the courts has increased markedly in recent years (and not only since 1997). While reforms such as the HRA may not by themselves have *caused* the growth in judicial power, they have certainly made a significant *contribution* to it. Indeed, Vernon Bogdanor goes so far as to claim that the HRA is 'the cornerstone of the new constitution' (*The New

British Constitution (2009), p. xiii). (These matters are considered further throughout this book: see, in particular, Chapters 2, 10 and 11.)

The UK is far from alone in having recently witnessed constitutional changes the effect of which is to enhance the power of the courts. In a compelling analysis, Ran Hirschl has documented similar moves in a variety of common law jurisdictions: namely, Canada, Israel, New Zealand and South Africa (see *Towards Juristocracy: The Origins and Consequences of the New Constitutionalism* (2004)). In the UK, while the influence of comparable common law jurisdictions has played its role, the greater pressures and influences have come from Europe – that is, both from the European Court of Human Rights and from the law of the EU, as shaped and developed by the Court of Justice of the European Communities (see, further, Chapter 5). (For an informed exchange of views on the 'juridification' of the British constitution, see Bevir, 'The Westminster Model, Governance and Judicial Reform' (2008) 61 *Parl Aff* 559; Masterman, 'Labour's "Juridification" of the Constitution' (2009) 62 *Parl Aff* 476; Bevir's response to Masterman at (2009) 62 *Parl Aff* 493; Masterman's further response at (2009) 62 *Parl Aff* 499.)

Events surrounding Brexit further illustrate this trend. Two cases have played a key role in determining constitutional issues surrounding Brexit: *R (Miller)* v. *Secretary of State for Exiting the European Union* [2017] UKSC 5, [2018] AC 61 and *Wightman* v. *Secretary of State for Exiting the European Union* [2018] CSIH 62, [2019] 1 CMLR 795 (before the Scottish Court of Session) and C-621/18, [2018] 3 WLR 1965 before the Court of Justice of the European Union. *Miller* (discussed already) concluded that the government could not use the prerogative power to notify the EU of the UK's intention to withdraw from the European Union treaties. *Wightman* concerned an application for an Article 267 reference from the Scottish courts, to ask whether, as a matter of EU law, it was possible for the UK to unilaterally revoke Article 50. The CJEU concluded that the UK did have the power unilaterally to revoke Article 50. A statement expressing the UK's intention to revoke Article 50 would have to be clear and unequivocal and comply with the UK's constitutional requirements in order to successfully revoke the Article 50 notification.

In determining these key issues, these cases influenced the Brexit process. Without *Miller*, there would have been no need for the European Union (Notification of Withdrawal) Act 2017. The political commitment given to the House of Commons to help smooth the passage of that legislation through Parliament may not have been made, which may have then meant that the meaningful vote provisions were not included in the European Union (Withdrawal) Act 2018. *Wightman* provided MPs with information relevant to their decisions to accept or reject the Withdrawal Agreement and when proposing alternatives to the government through the indicative vote process. Moreover, both demonstrate a growing recognition of the ability to use the courts as a supplement to the political process. *Miller* marks the first case where a crowdfunded applicant (the people's challenge, later Pigney who intervened on the case) brought a case to the Supreme Court. *Wightman* was an application from, among others, members of both the Scottish Parliament and the Westminster Parliament. They also demonstrate how constitutionally important cases may be brought to the courts even though there is no challenge to a particular decision of a public body. In *Miller*, the government had not used the prerogative power to trigger Article 50, but had stated that it intended to do so. In *Wightman*, the government had stated that there was no governmental policy to revoke Article 50, nevertheless it was important for the question to be answered given that it would be useful information for MPs in Westminster when voting on motions concerning the Withdrawal Agreement.

The most important constitutional case illustrating this move towards the growing role of the courts in the determination of constitutional issues is the second *Miller* decision, *R (Miller)* v. *Prime Minister; Cherry* v. *Advocate General for Scotland* [2019] UKSC 41, [2020] AC 373. As discussed earlier, the issue arose from the prime minister's decision to prorogue Parliament. The Supreme Court unanimously agreed that the prorogation of Parliament in September 2019 was unlawful. The Supreme Court used the constitutional principles of parliamentary sovereignty and parliamentary accountability to place limits on the scope or extent of the prerogative power of prorogation. The long length of the prorogation of Parliament, at a time of great constitutional importance, transgressed parliamentary sovereignty and parliamentary accountability. The government could have prorogued for this length of time had it provided a reasonable justification for doing so. Such a justification was, in the event, lacking.

However, it is also important to recognise that these cases do not illustrate a transfer of power to the courts. In *Miller I*, the court was determining the scope of a prerogative power. If its decision altered the balance of power between institutions of the constitution, it modified that between Parliament and the government. The same can be said of *Wightman*, in that the information provided helped the legislature to exercise its powers. It also, arguably, empowered the UK Parliament by confirming its sovereign power to determine both whether to leave and whether to remain in the EU. In *Miller II; Cherry*, the court was also upholding the powers of Parliament, restricting the scope of a prerogative power when this seriously undermined parliamentary sovereignty, or the principle that the executive should be held to account by the legislature. Nevertheless, these cases have been criticised due to their political consequences and the way in which the court is becoming involved in key constitutional issues that would have previously been resolved through political mechanisms alone. It also remains to be seen whether the powers of the judiciary will be reversed. Following the Queen's Speech in December 2019, the government committed to establishing a Commission to Investigate the Constitution, Democracy and Rights – although to date no commission has been established. (See Sir Stephen Laws, 'Judicial Intervention in

Parliamentary Proceedings' Policy Exchange Paper available at https://policy
exchange.org.uk/wp-content/uploads/2018/11/Judicial-Intervention-in-
Parliamentary-Proceedings.pdf; Ekins and Gee '*Miller*, Constitutional Realism
and the Politics of Brexit' in Elliott, Williams and Young (eds.) *The UK
Constitution after Miller: Brexit and Beyond* (2018).)

1.4.1.7 A Written Constitution?

Most of the rules of our constitution do, of course, exist in written form *somewhere*. Lord Scarman has said that 'today our constitution is not "unwritten" but
hidden and difficult to find' (*Why Britain Needs a Written Constitution* (1992),
p. 4). Besides the great number of statutes that may be labelled as 'constitutional',
the written sources of our constitution include law reports as the repository of
many common law or judge-made rules affecting constitutional powers and
relationships. In addition, as we shall see, some constitutional conventions have
been put on written record in the interests of clarity and for the avoidance of
doubt. There are also many informal but authoritative codes, memoranda, notices
and other documents produced within government that direct the behaviour of
ministers or officials and can be seen as belonging to the written part of our
constitution, even though they do not have the status of law. Some of these
documents are of great importance to the way in which government operates
and some of the rules and procedures that they contain might be included in
a written constitution, were we to have one. As it is, documents of these kinds are
easily overlooked in any attempt to enumerate the sources or written elements of
the constitution. Among the more important of them are the *Civil Service Code*
(rules of conduct for civil servants); the *Ministerial Code*; the so-called
'Osmotherly Rules'; *Departmental Evidence and Response to Select Committees*;
and *Government Accounting* (Treasury guidance on the financial procedures and
responsibilities of government departments).

   In the 1970s, a written constitution, as a remedy for the perceived ills of the
body politic, was urged by, among others, Hood Phillips ('Need for a Written
Constitution', in Stankiewicz (ed.), *British Government in an Era of Reform*
(1976)) and Lord Hailsham (*Elective Dictatorship* (1976), pp. 12–14).
Arguments for a written constitution were renewed in the 1990s and significant contributions to the debate were made by the publication of three draft
constitutions for the UK: the 'MacDonald Constitution', drawn up by John
MacDonald QC and published in a Liberal Democrat paper (*We, The People*
(1990)); Tony Benn's Commonwealth of Britain Bill, presented to the House of
Commons in May 1991; and *The Constitution of the United Kingdom*, published by the Institute for Public Policy Research in 1991. (These essays in
constitution-making are analysed by Oliver, 'Written Constitutions: Principles
and Problems' (1992) 45 *Parl Aff* 135; see also Cornford, 'On Writing
a Constitution' (1991) 44 *Parl Aff* 558; Brazier, 'Enacting a Constitution'
(1992) 13 *Stat LR* 104.)

The MPs' expenses scandal of 2009, combined with disquiet on a number of fronts about the process by which constitutional reform had been undertaken since 2001, and augmented in some quarters by concern as to the negative impact on civil liberties of a number of government policies, led, in 2008–10, to fresh calls to consider enacting a written constitution. We saw earlier the powerfully expressed views of Sir John Baker in this regard (p. X), but perhaps the most sustained plea that an earnest and urgent debate be commenced as to a new written constitution came from Richard Gordon QC, a leading public law barrister at the English bar. In his *Repairing British Politics: A Blueprint for Constitutional Change* (2010), Gordon set out an argument as to why a written constitution might be required at this point in Britain's history and followed this with a draft constitutional text which, he claimed, was based on the 'central principle' of seeking to 'reflect as strongly as possible a representative democracy' (p. 29). Gordon's constitution would create a 'sovereign, democratic, secular state with power conferred by the people'; the constitution would be the supreme law, thereby replacing the doctrine of parliamentary sovereignty with a doctrine of constitutional supremacy; the Upper House of Parliament (renamed the Senate) would be 70 per cent elected and 30 per cent appointed; the monarchy would remain but its powers would be defined and limited by the constitution; and the Supreme Court's powers would grow yet further, as it would have the power to strike down laws that it held to be in violation of the constitution. Richard Gordon's constitution was very much a lawyer's constitution, giving extensive powers to courts and seeking to use law to curtail political institutions. It was also a curiously Anglo-centric constitution, saying precious little about the position of Scotland, Wales or Northern Ireland. (See also Barber, 'Against a Written Constitution' [2008] *PL* 11; Bogdanor and Vogenauer, 'Enacting a British Constitution: Some Problems' [2008] *PL* 38; Beatson, 'Reforming an Unwritten Constitution' (2010) 126 *LQR* 48.)

The arguments for a written constitution deserve serious consideration. There is a case for giving to our most highly valued constitutional principles the special status and authority that would result from their embodiment in a constitution that was intended to endure. A more complete separation of powers might be instituted in the written constitution, reducing the power of the executive to control and direct the workings of Parliament. The relations between the countries and regions of the UK could be put on a firmer and clearer basis, possibly on a federal plan. The status of local government could be confirmed and protected, preventing the sort of erosion of its independence that occurred under the Thatcher Governments (see Chapter 4). The fluidity and uncertainty of some of our most important conventions might be corrected by putting them into writing. The constitution would rest on the authority not of Parliament but of the people: a referendum could be held to approve it and be required for its amendment.

If these arguments are weighty, there is much to be said on the other side. The security that can be given to leading principles and fundamental rights by an entrenched written constitution should not be exaggerated. Certainly the constitution could be made difficult to amend – if not, much of the point of having a written constitution would be lost – but this might work as a brake on the necessary adaptation of the constitution to social change. Sir Stephen Sedley aptly remarks (in Lord Nolan and Sir Stephen Sedley, *The Making and Remaking of the British Constitution*, The *Radcliffe Lectures* (1997), p. 88) that a written constitution:

> has to be negotiated with and by an infinite range of interests and viewpoints, among whom there will be the winners and losers dictated by the balance of power at the moment of enactment. Simply to put in writing our arrangements for the distribution and exercise of state power at a point of history where no comprehensive new consensus has emerged is to risk consolidating state power wherever it happens at that moment to reside.

Compare the following comments by Andrew Gamble (in Holliday, Gamble and Parry (eds.), *Fundamentals in British Politics* (1999), p. 26):

> For its proponents the great virtue of the British state as a liberal state lies precisely in its undefined character, because it is this which gives it its flexibility and pragmatism, its ability to respond to new interests and demands and, by making timely concessions and accommodations, to preserve its essential institutional core intact ... The danger of any kind of codified constitution from this perspective is that it locks in a particular set of arrangements which may be the best available at that time, but may later be judged inappropriate and then may be very difficult to change.

Ours has traditionally been a political constitution, in which change is directed and conflicts are largely resolved through the political process (see Griffith, 'The Political Constitution' (1979) 42 *MLR* 1). When a written constitution is in place, arguments about its effect are conducted in legal terms, as an exercise in interpretation, and are displaced from the political forum into the courts. As Ian Holliday remarks (in Parry and Moran (eds.), *Democracy and Democratization* (1994), p. 253), 'juridification of politics is one of the major problems created by a written constitution': much power and much trust are given to judges. The role that they may assume is exemplified by the history of the US Supreme Court. Rights guaranteed by the United States Constitution were in the years 1880–30 used by Supreme Court justices, imbued with ideas of *laissez-faire* capitalism, as weapons against progressive social welfare legislation. (See, e.g., *Lochner* v. *New York* 198 US 45 (1905), in which the US Supreme Court held that a statute limiting employment in bakeries to sixty hours a week and ten hours a day was invalid as an arbitrary interference with the freedom to contract guaranteed by the Fourteenth Amendment to the Constitution.) Again, the New Deal programme, undertaken by President

Roosevelt to counter the results of economic depression, was substantially nullified by Supreme Court decisions in the years 1934 to 1936. In its active phases, the Supreme Court has been the source of far-reaching judicial legislation, whether of a conservative or a liberal tendency, and has had a substantial influence on social and political affairs in the USA.

This is the kind of role that our courts might be given by a written constitution. As we have seen, it may be that we are already taking that course, with the enhanced constitutional adjudication entrusted to our courts by the HRA and the devolution legislation. Perhaps it is becoming true here, as in the USA, that the constitution 'is whatever the judges say it is' (Sedley, 'The Sound of Silence: Constitutional Law without a Constitution' (1994) 110 *LQR* 270, 277). Perhaps we are moving from a political constitution to a law-based or perhaps even a judge-based constitution. In the chapters that follow, we will come back to this question many times.

(On constitutional reform, see, further, Oliver, *Constitutional Reform in the United Kingdom* (2003); Johnson, *Reshaping the British Constitution* (2004); King, *The British Constitution* (2007); Bogdanor, *The New British Constitution* (2009); Gordon, *Repairing British Politics: A Blueprint for Constitutional Change* (2010); Hazell, *The Conservative-Liberal Democrat Agenda for Constitutional and Political Reform* (2010); McLean, *What's Wrong with the British Constitution?* (2010); Norton (ed.) *A Century of Constitutional Reform* (2011); King, 'The Democratic Case for a Written Constitution' in Jowell and O'Cinneide *The Changing Constitution* (9th edn. 2019).)

2

The Ideas of the Constitution

Contents

The previous chapter explained that the UK's constitution is in some senses unique due to its uncodified nature, its provisions evolving over time. Nevertheless, calls are often made that the actions of the government are 'unconstitutional'. This has been particularly true throughout the Brexit process. Would it have been 'unconstitutional' for the government to have decided not to implement the outcome of the referendum or to have delayed the UK's notification of its intention to leave the EU in order for Parliament to more fully debate the precise nature of the UK's future relationship with the EU post-Brexit? Is it unconstitutional for the UK as a whole to leave the EU given that only England and Wales voted in favour of leaving the EU, whereas Northern Ireland and Scotland did not? Is it unconstitutional for Parliament to play a role in directing the government through its negotiations with the EU? Was it unconstitutional for the prime minister to prorogue Parliament in September 2019? Was it unconstitutional for backbench and opposition MPs to 'take control' of the Commons, pushing through private members' bills that directed the prime minister to act in a manner directly contrary to the government's policy? Would it be unconstitutional for a prime minister to refuse to resign after losing a vote of no confidence that was not enacted under the terms of the Fixed-Term Parliaments Act 2011 or to seek the prorogation of Parliament during the fourteen-day period allowed for the formation of an alternative government after losing a vote of no confidence in the terms proscribed by the Fixed-Term Parliaments Act 2011?

When asking and answering these questions, we can look at statutes, common law, conventions and parliamentary rules – for example the standing orders governing parliamentary business. We could also be using 'unconstitutional' merely as a term of disapproval, motivated more by political concerns, in the hope that using 'unconstitutional' adds strength to our argument. This chapter explains how 'unconstitutional' also refers to values and ideas about good constitutionalism. When we use 'unconstitutional' in this sense, we mean that an action breaches democracy, parliamentary sovereignty, the rule of law or the separation of powers – it undermines the ideas on which the UK constitution is based.

2.1 Democracy and the Constitution

Democracy is not to be taken for granted. Neither is its contemporary acceptance as the only form of government able to claim legitimacy to rule. As John Dunn asks in his account of the history of democracy, *Setting the People Free: The Story of Democracy* (2005), pp. 13, 15:

> Why does democracy loom so large today? Why should it hold such sway over the political speech of the modern world? What does its recent prominence really mean? When Britain and America set out to bury Baghdad in its own rubble, why was it in the name of democracy of all words in which they claimed to do so? Is its novel dominance in fact illusory: a sustained exercise in fraud or an index of utter confusion? Or does it mark a huge moral and political advance, which only needs to cover the whole world, and be made a little more real, for history to come to a reassuring end?

> Why should it be the case that, for the first time in the history of our still conspicuously multi-lingual species, there is for the present a single world-wide name of the legitimate basis of political authority?

Democracy came late to the British constitution. Much of our constitutional architecture was constructed at a time when to accuse someone of harbouring democratic sympathies was a grave political insult. This is not to say that democracy came late to Britain in comparison with other countries. But it is to say that several key elements of the British constitution predate the emergence of democracy as an accepted form of government. Anthony King puts the point well (*The British Constitution* (2009), p. 249):

> The United Kingdom was a monarchy before it became a constitutional monarchy. It was a constitutional monarchy before it became a system of government built around ministers of the Crown. It was a system of government built around ministers of the Crown before it became a parliamentary system. And it was a parliamentary system before it became a parliamentary democracy. Democracy . . . was a novel feature grafted on to a pre-existing constitutional structure.

Nonetheless, democracy deserves to be treated as the first of our constitutional themes since the working assumption of all the principal actors on the constitutional stage, even those who (such as the monarch and the House of Lords) are not themselves democratically elected, is that Britain is, and ought to consider itself as, a modern democracy. Even if the assumption is sometimes misplaced or overstated, it is impossible to understand the way the contemporary British constitution works without taking on board this basic working assumption. Equally, however, like all assumptions, it is rebuttable. On no account could today's British constitutional order accurately be described as entirely or unambiguously democratic. (Valuable introductions to the idea of democracy abound. Among the better ones, see Dahl, *On Democracy* (2015); Crick, *Democracy: A Very Short Introduction* (2002); Held, *Models of Democracy* (3rd edn. 2006).)

2.1.1 Representative Democracy

Democracy may be said to consist of two main elements: representation and participation. As to the first, since the achievement of universal suffrage with the enactment of the Representation of the People Acts 1918 and 1928 it can be claimed that the British constitution has embodied the principle of representative democracy, at least as far as elections to the House of Commons are concerned. As it is from the House of the Commons that the government of the day is drawn, it may be said that British Government is democratic, the fact that no one actually elects it as such notwithstanding. The members of Parliament who become ministers in the government are elected as members of Parliament, but not as ministers. Ministers are appointed by the prime minister; they are not elected to ministerial office. The prime minister is appointed by the monarch, who is also not elected, but who now appoints as prime minister the person most likely to be able to command majority support in the House of Commons. There had been advocates of the democratic principle before the early twentieth century, but democracy was 'still a pejorative term on both sides of the House in 1831–2' (Wright, *Democracy and Reform 1815–1885* (1970), p. 38) and the idea of government by the whole people, as it would be understood today, was not accepted by political leaders at any time in the nineteenth century. Nonetheless, the first Reform Act of 1832 began a process by which the claims of representative democracy were progressively accommodated with the existing institutions of government. There was no sudden triumph of democracy. Even after the third Reform Act of 1884, only about 60 per cent of the adult male population, or about 28 per cent of the total adult population, had the vote. The Representation of the People Act 1918 introduced universal adult male suffrage (on condition of six months' residence in a constituency) and gave the right to vote to women aged over thirty. The Act of 1928 lowered the voting age for women to twenty-one, which was the same as for men and the principle of 'one man or woman, one vote' was finally achieved when the Representation of the People Act 1948 abolished the business and university franchises that had qualified certain persons to cast more than one vote.

Democracy as established in the UK is a form of 'liberal democracy'. With us it occurs as a system of representative and responsible government in which voters elect the members of a representative institution, the House of Commons, and the government is largely chosen from and, in turn, accountable through the Commons to the electorate itself.

Jack Lively, *Democracy* (1975), pp. 43–4

What then are the conditions necessary for the existence of responsible government? What is needed to ensure that some popular control can be exerted over political leadership, some governmental accountability can be enforced? Two main conditions can be suggested, that governments should be removable by electoral decisions and that some alternative can be substituted by electoral decision. The alternative, it should be stressed, must be more than an alternative governing group. It must comprehend alternatives in policy, since it is only if an electoral decision can alter the actions of government that popular control can be said to be established. The power of replacing Tweedledum by Tweedledee (the 'Ins' by the 'Outs', as Bentham had it) would be an insufficient basis for such control. To borrow the economic analogy, competition is meaningless, or at any rate cannot create consumer sovereignty, unless there is some product differentiation.

In detail there might be a great deal of discussion about the institutional arrangements necessary to responsible government, but in general some are obvious. There must be free elections, in which neither the incumbent government nor any other group can determine the electoral result by means other than indications of how they will act if returned to power. Fraud, intimidation and bribery are thus incompatible with responsible government …. Another part of the institutional frame necessary to responsible government is freedom of association. Unless groups wishing to compete for leadership have the freedom to organize and formulate alternative programmes, the presentation of alternatives would be impossible. Lastly, freedom of speech is necessary since silent alternatives can never be effective alternatives. In considering such arrangements, we cannot stick at simple legal considerations; we must move from questions of 'freedom from' to questions of 'ability to'. The absence of any legal bar to association will not, for example, create the ability to associate if there are heavy costs involved which only some groups can bear. Nor will the legal guarantee of freedom of speech be of much use if access to the mass media is severely restricted.

This could be summed up by saying that responsible government depends largely upon the existence of, and free competition between, political parties.

The degree of influence or control over government that is exercisable by the electorate depends on a variety of factors, among them the electoral system adopted, party organisation and the particular concept of representation ('delegation' or 'authorisation') that the constitution embodies. These matters are considered in Chapter 8.

A simple, majoritarian version of democracy would claim for the elected representatives of the people an unqualified power to act upon whatever view they might take of the public interest. In this version, no individual or minority rights or interests could legitimately be opposed to decisions supported by a majority in the elected assembly. 'We are the masters now' would be a conclusive response to opposition or protest and the credentials of democracy might be invoked to exclude or victimise those who dissented, were unpopular or belonged to vulnerable minorities such as single parents, homeless young people, asylum-seekers and the impoverished underclass of the long-term unemployed.

This would surely be a narrow understanding of democracy that would empty it of much of its virtue. A democracy that admitted no restraints on the will of the majority would be liable quickly to lose legitimacy and moral justification and would endure only as long as it commanded enough force to contain dissent and dissatisfaction. A more inclusive and more viable version of democracy accepts limitations on majority rule in a toleration of minority values, opposition and dissent, in a willingness to share information and to consult, and in respect for fundamental individual rights and freedoms. Cass Sunstein (*Designing Democracy* (2001)) speaks in this connection of the 'internal morality of democracy', which includes a commitment to the equality of citizens, the protection of fundamental rights and processes of decision-making based on openness, consultation, receptivity to argument and the giving of reasons. Exclusive reliance on voting power in a majoritarian system disregards values such as those that are integral to a mature and fully realised democracy. They need not (and perhaps cannot entirely) be given formal expression in a written constitution, but they are standards by which the claim that our unwritten constitution is in accord with democratic principle must be judged. One question, of course, is who should do the judging: should democratic institutions be self-regulating in terms of these values, should it be the people who decide or should it be some other body, such as the courts of law? (See, further, Prosser, 'Understanding the British constitution' (1996) 44 *Political Studies* 473.)

In *Chassagnou* v. *France* (2000) 29 EHRR 615, the ECtHR stated (at [112]) that:

> pluralism, tolerance and broadmindedness are hallmarks of a 'democratic society'. Although individual interests must on occasion be subordinated to those of a group, democracy does not simply mean that the views of a majority must always prevail: a balance must be achieved which ensures the fair and proper treatment of minorities and avoids any abuse of a dominant position.

We may also note the view of Sir John Laws that the 'moral force' of democracy 'depends in large measure upon the extent to which it vindicates individual liberty' and that 'the rule of reasonableness' in the exercise of public power 'is a requirement of democracy itself': *The Golden Metwand and the Crooked Cord* (eds. Forsyth and Hare (1998), pp. 194–6). Even within the idea of democracy, then, we can see a clear tension between the extent to which a constitution should give expression to the will of the majority and the extent to which it should impose limitations on the will of the majority, in the interests of openness, opposition, dissent and individual rights.

2.1.2 Participatory Democracy

The kind of liberal, representative and largely indirect democracy that is reflected in our present constitutional arrangements is neither flawless nor immutable. As such, we should be careful to consider the claims of other models of democracy.

C.B. Macpherson, *The Life and Times of Liberal Democracy* (1977), pp. 6–8

Would it not be simpler to set up a single model of present liberal democracy, by listing the observable characteristics of the practice and theory common to those twentieth-century states which everyone would agree to call liberal democracies, that is, the systems in operation in most of the English-speaking world and most of Western Europe? Such a model could easily be set up. The main stipulations are fairly obvious. Governments and legislatures are chosen directly or indirectly by periodic elections with universal equal franchise, the voters' choice being normally a choice between political parties. There is a sufficient degree of civil liberties (freedom of speech, publication, and association, and freedom from arbitrary arrest and imprisonment) to make the right to choose effective. There is formal equality before the law. There is some protection for minorities. And there is general acceptance of a principle of maximum individual freedom consistent with equal freedom for others.

It is all too easy, in using a single model, to block off future paths; all too easy to fall into thinking that liberal democracy, now that we have attained it, by whatever stages, is fixed in its present mould. Indeed, the use of a single contemporary model almost commits one to this position. For a single model of current liberal democracy, if it is to be realistic as an explanatory model, must stipulate certain present mechanisms, such as the competitive party system and wholly indirect (i.e. representative) government. But to do this is to foreclose options that may be made possible by changed social and economic relations. There may be strong differences of opinion about whether some conceivable future forms of democracy can properly be called *liberal* democracy, but this is something that needs to be argued, not put out of court by definition. One of the things that needs to be considered is whether liberal democracy in a large nation-state is capable of moving to a mixture of indirect and direct democracy: that is, is capable of moving in the direction of a fuller participation, which may require mechanisms other than the standard party system.

The democratic ideal is imperfectly realised in existing political institutions: the processes of government are remote from the mass of the people, who participate only indirectly and to a limited extent in public decision-making. Democratic representation, it has been said, 'has served not only as a necessary instrument of accountability, but also as a means of keeping the people at arm's length from the political process' (Beetham, in Held (ed.), *Prospects for Democracy* (1993), p. 60). Indeed, as Bernard Manin has demonstrated, representative government was designed by its founders to be an alternative to, and not a species of, democratic government. One of the remarkable transformations in political thought since the eighteenth century is the now commonplace acceptance of representative government as a plausible variant of democracy. (See Manin, *The Principles of Representative Government* (1997).) As Macpherson indicates, the theory of representative democracy may be opposed to or supplemented by one of participatory democracy, which would accord a more active political role to the people. Could new institutional arrangements be devised that would provide for greater participation by the people in the working of the constitution? Active citizenship and participation might be furthered by policies of decentralisation (devolution of power to localities), subsidiarity (decision-taking at the lowest practicable level) and improved processes of consultation, as well as by the democratisation of political parties and of the management of social institutions (schools, hospitals) and the workplace. The UK has seen recent developments in this direction, through greater devolution to Scotland and Wales and the possibility of greater powers to other areas through the use of elected mayors. There has also been the development of e-petitions. In addition, some would argue for an extended recourse to direct democracy, in the form of referendums. The UK has seen a greater use of referendums, most notably the recent referendum on Scottish Independence in 2014 and the Brexit referendum in 2016.

(See, further, Pateman, *Participation and Democratic Theory* (1970); Held and Pollitt (eds.), *New Forms of Democracy* (1986); Budge, *The New Challenge of Direct Democracy* (1996); Pinkney, 'The Sleeping Night-Watchman and Some Alternatives' (1997) 32 *Government and Opposition* 340; Saward, 'Reconstructing democracy: current thinking and new directions' (2001) 36 *Government and Opposition* 559; Flinders, 'Majoritarian Democracy in Britain' (2005) 28 *W Eur Pol* 62.)

Concerns as to the extent to which representative democracy creates political elites, who are removed from the real people, has given rise to an increase in populist movements in the UK and across Europe. Populism is not easy to define. It can refer to a movement or to a political philosophy. Moreover, it is thin-centred – in that populism can be right-wing, left-wing or even have no particular political tendency. At its core lies a mistrust of representative institutions, of experts and political elites, combined with a call for politics to reflect the wishes of 'the real people'; the 'real people' being defined in terms of their nationality, social class or general non-membership of the political elite. In addition, populist movements homogenise the will of the people – the will of a majority on a particular issue or the will of a particular group is defined as 'the' will of the people. Populist movements and populist leaders also appeal to emotion as opposed to rationality, undermining democratic deliberation and expertise.

Populism can also be fuelled by the use of referendums. While it may be contestable to argue that the UK is now governed by populist leaders, it is hard to refute the impact of the Brexit referendum in pushing the UK towards populism. In particular, the outcome of the referendum has been equated with the will of the people, despite the fact that the referendum outcome in favour of exiting the EU did not represent the votes of all citizens in the UK of voting age – it was a majority of votes from those who chose to vote. In addition, the referendum outcome has been referred to as supporting either a hard or a no-deal Brexit, even though the referendum itself did not provide a specific vote in favour of a particular form of exit and those voting in favour of leaving the EU may have had differing intentions as to the UK's future relationship with the EU. In addition, campaigns for the referendum on both sides relied on emotion as well as rational arguments, including appeals to the need for the people to decide as opposed to the out-of-touch political elites.

It is the homogenisation of the will of the people and the lack of engagement with compromise solutions or political deliberation that are particularly dangerous, leading to populism's potential – some would argue inevitable – collapse into authoritarianism (see Müller *What is Populism?* (2017)). This is not to argue against referendums per se. Neither is it to question the outcome of the Brexit referendum. Referendums may also enhance democracy through enhancing participation in public deliberation. (See Tierney, 'The Scottish Independence Referendum: A Model of Good Practice in Direct Democracy' in McHarg, Mulle, Page and Walker (eds.) *The Scottish Independence Referendum: Constitutional and Political Implications* (2016).) Neither is it the case that systems with constitutional protections of democracy, civil liberties and human rights are less prone to populism. However, there is a need to ensure that deliberative democracy is also protected, enabling discussion and deliberation to better facilitate compromises between competing political positions and ideals. (See, further, Young, 'Populism and the UK constitution' (2018) 71 *CLP* 17; Allan, 'Democracy, Liberalism and Brexit' (2017) 39 *Cardozo Law Review* 879; Koch, 'Democracy as Punishment: Brexit and Austerity Politics' in Koch (ed.), *Personalising the State: An Anthropology of Law, Politics and Welfare in Austerity Britain* (2018).)

Macpherson reminds us in *The Real World of Democracy* ((1972), p. 4) that a liberal democracy, like any other organisation of government, is a system of power – a system 'by which power is exerted by the state over individuals and groups within it' and, further, that:

> a democratic government, like any other, exists to uphold and enforce a certain kind of society, a certain set of relations between individuals, a certain set of rights and claims that people have on each other both directly, and indirectly through their rights to property. These relations themselves are relations of power – they give different people, in different capacities, power over others.

Representative democracy is a great achievement, no doubt, but it does not necessarily prevent an over-centralisation of state power, the dominance of a political elite or the emergence of unaccountable private corporations wielding considerable economic power. Democracy is 'unfinished business' (Clarke, *Deep Citizenship* (1996), p. 23) and the search must go on for means of extending the democratisation of our country and institutions. Paul Hirst has argued that this may be achieved by building on voluntary associations and communities as the reinvigorated, democratically managed units of a pluralist state: *Representative Democracy and its Limits* (1990); *Associative Democracy* (1994); *From Statism to Pluralism* (1997); 'Renewing Democracy through Associations' (2002) 73 *Pol Q* 409. James Tully would go further, calling for a revised constitutionalism founded on cultural diversity and extending 'self-rule' to the variety of cultures of which society is composed: *Strange Multiplicity: Constitutionalism in an Age of Diversity* (1995).

The observance of democratic principles in practice in the UK is critically examined by Weir and Beetham, *Political Power and Democratic Control in Britain* (1999) and Beetham *et al.*, *Democracy under Blair* (2003). For a different perspective, see Graham, *The Case Against the Democratic State* (2002).

Questions about the nature and vitality of British democracy are raised by new developments and arguments concerning the electoral system, referendums, the role of pressure groups and the organisation of political parties (see in more detail in Chapter 8).

2.1.3 Democracy and Accountability

Accountability is a liability or obligation attached to those invested with public powers or duties. Its primary ingredient is an obligation to explain and justify decisions made or action taken. Normanton says of it ('Public Accountability and Audit: A Reconnaissance', in Smith and Hague (eds.), *The Dilemma of Accountability in Modern Government* (1971), p. 312):

> Accountability is a device as old as civilised government itself; it is indispensable to regimes of every kind. It provides the post-mortem of action, the test of obedience and judgement, the moment of truth; it can validate the power of command, or it can create favourable conditions for individual responsibility and initiative.

Accountability is retrospective: it is an obligation to answer *after the event* for acts or decisions. But an awareness that an account will have to be given may have a bracing effect on the quality of decision-making.

We can find in accountability a link with democracy, in that those elected by the people to govern are given power not for their own ends but for the public good, and a link with the rule of law, which demands that those to whom power is granted should not exceed the limits of their authority. Accountability for the use of power is supportive of both democracy and the rule of law, and we may claim it as a leading principle of our constitution even if it is only imperfectly realised in practice.

The ultimate accountability in a democracy is to the electorate, but more precisely targeted systems of accountability are needed between elections or for application to those (such as civil servants) over whom the electorate has no power of sanction. None who wields the power or discharges the functions of the state should be exempt from the requirements of accountability. We therefore expect that ministers, their battalions of officials, the chief executives of central government agencies, local government councillors and officers, health authorities, the police, immigration officers and other public bodies and officers will be subject to mechanisms of accountability.

Accountability in a democratic state under the rule of law in principle implies a duty to account to an independent agency outside the organisation whose actions are in question. The outside agency may be the legislature, a court, a tribunal or some other independent body or officer. In actuality, we find that for some activities the only form of direct accountability provided is internal (or 'managerial') by which account has to be rendered to superior officers in the organisation or its head: the personal accountability of civil servants in the UK is, in general, of this kind. Managerial accountability has a part to play in a structure of accountable government, but we will normally expect that the organisation itself or its head should be accountable in the fuller, 'public' sense to an outside body.

Accountability may be legal, directed towards ensuring that action taken is in accordance with law, or it may relate to any (or several) other desirable features of executive action such as rationality, economy, efficiency and fairness. (What a particular authority is to be accountable *for* depends on its range of functions, degree of autonomy, etc.)

When acts of the administration may affect individual rights or interests, accountability also requires that appropriate reparation should be made to the victim of illegal action or maladministration. (This may be called 'amendatory' or 'remedial' accountability.) Here accountability overlaps with the redress of grievances. *Legal* accountability for decisions of public authorities depends on the availability of a right of appeal to a court or tribunal or on access to judicial review (see Chapter 10). The principal mechanism of *political* accountability in the UK is found in the doctrine of ministerial responsibility to Parliament. At the end of the nineteenth century, the legal and political responsibility of ministers was, as Vile says (*Constitutionalism and the Separation of Powers* (1967), p. 231), 'the crux of the English system of government'. The legal responsibility of ministers to the courts was complemented by their political responsibility to Parliament. Ministerial responsibility in the political sense was the result of the development of conventions by which the sovereign had become bound to act on the advice of ministers, and ministers had become answerable to Parliament for the advice given. The principle of ministerial responsibility, as an element in the theory of the British constitution, was derived from the reality of constitutional practice. 'The accountability of ministers to Parliament, and through Parliament to the nation, is the theoretical basis of our modern English Constitution', wrote Sidney Low in 1904 (The *Governance of England*, p. 133).

According to this theory, the power of government was 'placed under the check of a strict responsibility and control' (Earl Grey, *Parliamentary Government* (new edn. 1864), p. 5). But it was only for a few decades in the middle of the nineteenth century, when a Parliament not yet infiltrated by disciplined parties showed its ability to bring down governments, that so strong a statement of the theory might have been justified by the facts. Since then the government has established an ascendancy over Parliament, and the traditional parliamentary techniques of control and accountability, focused on ministers, have struggled to check the use of power in the corridors of the departmental bureaucracies and in the outworks of government occupied by quasi-autonomous organisations.

This modern development has led some to dismiss the theory of ministerial responsibility as mere fiction: it is now 'little more than a formal principle used by ministers to deter parliamentary interference in their affairs' says Vile (p. 341). But it can still be maintained that '[t]he British constitution is built, however precariously, on the political accountability of ministers to Parliament' (Flinders, *The Politics of Accountability in the Modern State* (2001), p. xvi). No other theory of government has taken its place; it still explains much of what happens in government and Parliament, and it is through the mechanisms of ministerial responsibility that Parliament persists in its effort to 'watch and control' the government. The extent to which it is able to do so in practice is considered in detail in Chapter 9.

There are many actions of public authorities for which ministers have no or only limited responsibility to Parliament, and there is therefore a need for supplementary mechanisms of accountability. Several such mechanisms are in place. For instance, central government expenditure is overseen by the National Audit Office, headed by the Comptroller and Auditor General, and by the House of Commons Public Accounts Committee. Public inquiries have become a frequent occurrence in Britain, examining in detail a variety of problems and scandals in governmental and public life. As the House of Commons Public Administration Committee put it (*Government by Inquiry*, HC 51 of 2004–05, para 2), 'the public inquiry has become a pivotal part of public life in Britain, and a major instrument of accountability'. As regards accountability for actions affecting individual citizens, there is a great variety of arrangements, in some cases providing an avenue for redress of grievances. An example is the ombudsman system for resolving complaints of maladministration against government departments or local authorities. The investigation of complaints against the police is supervised by the Independent Police Complaints Commission established by the Police Reform Act 2002, replacing a previous complaints-handling system that had not enjoyed public confidence.

Traditional mechanisms of accountability have been put under strain by the fragmentation that has taken place in central government through a proliferation of autonomous decision-making bodies (executive agencies and non-departmental public bodies (NDPBs)) and the development of collaborative arrangements and networks in the policy-making process. These have included the involvement of private sector bodies (e.g., through advisory groups, contracting out and public–private partnerships) in the development and implementation of policy. (See, further, Bovens, *The Quest for Responsibility: Accountability and Citizenship in Complex Organisations*

(1998); M Flinders, *The Politics of Accountability in the Modern State* (2001); Philp, 'Delimiting Democratic Accountability' (2009) 57 *Pol Studies* 28.)

'Information', says Jackson, 'is the essential lubricant of any system of accountability and control' (*The Political Economy of Bureaucracy* (1982), p. 246). Sir Richard Scott is of the same mind (*Scott Report* (1996), vol. I, para D4.58): 'Without the provision of full information it is not possible for Parliament, or for that matter the public, to hold the executive fully to account.' It is when information is withheld, or Parliament and the public are misled, that accountability most signally fails. The question of accountability is therefore closely interwoven with that of 'open government', considered below (pp. 664–667).

Opacity, and blurred accountability, may result from the complexity of decision-making processes in the modern state. Rhodes ('The Hollowing Out of the State' (1994) 65 *Pol Q* 138, 147) remarks that:

> sheer institutional complexity obscures who is accountable to whom for what. Policy networks, or professional-bureaucratic functional alliances, are a characteristic feature of policy-making in Britain. Such networks restrict who contributes to policy-making and policy implementation ... They are also a form of private government; much of their work is invisible to the parliamentary and public eye. With the growth of trans-national networks linking UK networks to the EC, the policy process becomes more complex and the lines of accountability ever more difficult to identify.

It may be assumed that Brexit would reduce this complexity, by removing an extra layer of regulation. Many of the areas previously regulated by the EU would return to the UK. However, Brexit could add further layers of complication as measures previously regulated by the EU that fall within the sphere of devolved powers will return to Scotland, Wales and Northern Ireland, although this return may be delayed by governmental ministerial order. This may lead to further layers of complication and the need to build more intergovernmental cooperation to develop common frameworks. In addition, the secondary legislation designed to deal with deficiencies following the UK's withdrawal from the EU has demonstrated a tendency to remove regulation, hollowing out the state even further (see Sinclair and Tomlinson, 'Deleting the Administrative State?' UK Const. L. Blog (7 February 2019) available at https:// ukconstitutionallaw.org).

2.2 Parliamentary Sovereignty

For Dicey, the greatest British constitutional lawyer of the nineteenth century, whose magisterial *The Law of the Constitution* was first published in 1885, it was 'the very keystone of *the law of the constitution* 'that Parliament is the sovereign or supreme legislative authority in the state.

Dicey, *The Law of the Constitution* (1885), pp. 39–40

The principle of Parliamentary sovereignty means neither more nor less than this, namely, that Parliament . . . has, under the English constitution, the right to make or unmake any law whatever; and, further, that no person or body is recognised by the law of England as having a right to override or set aside the legislation of Parliament.

The legislative supremacy of Parliament, increasingly asserted in the sixteenth and seventeenth centuries, was assured by Parliament's victory in the Civil Wars of the 1640s and by the so-called 'Glorious' Revolution of 1688–9, which, among other things, established the primacy of statute over prerogative. Academic lawyers, drawing on works of political science, subsequently embraced it as orthodox doctrine, and the courts propounded it as law. It was at once historical reality, constitutional theory and a fundamental principle of the common law. In accordance with this principle the courts have held that statutes enacted by Parliament must be enforced and must be given priority over rules of common law, over international law binding on the UK, over the enactments of subordinate legislative authorities and over earlier enactments of Parliament itself. The sovereignty of Parliament, although it pre-dates the emergence of democracy in the UK, is closely connected with democracy. This was recognised by Lord Hoffmann when he observed that: 'The principle of the sovereignty of Parliament, as it has been developed by the courts over the past 350 years, is founded upon the unique authority Parliament derives from its representative character' (*R (Bancoult)* v. *Secretary of State for Foreign and Commonwealth Affairs (No 2)* [2008] UKHL 61, [2009] 1 AC 453, at [35]).

'Parliamentary sovereignty' was, as we have seen, Dicey's phrase, and it has become widely accepted. But while convenient shorthand, it is not the most accurate label that could have been chosen. What the doctrine establishes, as the quotation from Dicey's *Law of the Constitution* reveals, is the legal supremacy of *statute*, which is not quite the same thing as the sovereignty of *Parliament*. It means that there is no source of law higher than – i.e., more authoritative than – an act of Parliament. Parliament may by statute make or unmake any law, including a law that is violative of international law or that alters a fundamental principle of the common law. And the courts are obliged to uphold and enforce it.

For the avoidance of doubt, it should be added that it is only Acts of the Westminster Parliament that enjoy this legal status. Acts of the Scottish Parliament are not legally supreme, neither are the measures adopted by the other devolved institutions in Wales and Northern Ireland. Courts may strike down Acts of the Scottish Parliament if they violate the terms of the Scotland Act 1998 or if they are incompatible with Convention rights or with EU law. In Dicey's terms, the Scottish Parliament has the power to make or unmake only those laws that it is authorised by the Scotland Act 1998 to make or unmake; and, further, courts are recognised as having a right to override or set aside the legislation of the Scottish Parliament in the circumstances as laid down in the Scotland Act. While we are on the subject of Scotland, the references to 'the English constitution' and to 'the law of England' in Dicey's quotation should not go unnoticed. The doctrine of the sovereignty of Parliament has not always been accepted by Scots lawyers as warmly as it has been received in England. There is a body of opinion in Scots law that the Westminster Parliament is not free to legislate in contravention of the terms on which the Union of Scotland and England was settled in 1707. That union, so the argument goes, abolished the old Scottish and English Parliaments and replaced them with a new British Parliament in Westminster, the new Parliament being subject to the terms of its creation as laid out in the Acts (or Treaties) of Union. This argument was accepted, albeit obiter, by the Lord President of the Court of Session (Lord Cooper) in the famous case of *MacCormick* v. *Lord Advocate* 1953 SC 396, but it is by no means clear that Lord Cooper stated the Scots law position accurately. We consider these matters in more detail in Chapter 4.

The sovereignty of (the Westminster) Parliament is a doctrine whose cardinal importance to the British constitution would be difficult to exaggerate. As the 'keystone' of the constitution (as Dicey expressed it), what is meant is that the doctrine is no less than 'the central principle' of the system 'on which all the rest depends' (to quote from the definition offered in the *Oxford English Dictionary*). However, while it is elemental, in a comparative sense it is also quite unusual. Most constitutional orders do not confer supremacy on statute. Most constitutional orders confer supremacy on the constitutional text itself, a text that normally binds not only judges and governments but also Parliaments. The British constitution is unusual in not stating that acts of Parliament are subject to constitutional limitations. This unusualness has caused a good number of commentators and, in recent times, also some judges to suggest that, the fundamental role that the doctrine has played in the past notwithstanding, the time has come for it to be at least reconsidered, if not discarded altogether. We will explore some of these arguments in the pages that follow.

In this part of the chapter, we consider, first, the Diceyan orthodoxy and, in particular, the way in which it was accepted in the leading twentieth-century case law. Then we move on to examine the impact on the sovereignty of Parliament of the break-up of the British Empire. When Dicey wrote, the Westminster Parliament made laws not only for Britain but also for a large number of colonies and dominions across the globe. How may the territorial extent of parliamentary sovereignty be reduced? If Parliament may make or unmake any law whatsoever, could it make a law granting independence to a colony and subsequently repeal that law, withdrawing the grant of independence and reasserting British rule over the territory? In the third section, we consider the question of whether a Parliament is able to bind its successor

Parliaments. Is every Parliament equally sovereign or may Parliament today limit the way in which the Parliament of tomorrow may make laws? In the final section of this part, we consider three contemporary challenges to the doctrine of parliamentary sovereignty: the challenge that came from the UK's membership of the EU; the challenge that comes from the inclusion since 1998 within our legal system of fundamental rights; and the challenge that may be beginning to come from the common law itself.

2.2.1 Diceyan Orthodoxy

Both the positive and the negative aspects of Dicey's formulation of the sovereignty of Parliament are illustrated by the following cases.

Cheney v. *Conn* [1968] 1 All ER 779 (Ungoed-Thomas J)

A taxpayer appealed against an assessment to income tax made under the Finance Act 1964. One of the grounds of the appeal was that, since the money would be used in part for the construction of nuclear weapons, and since (it was argued) such use was contrary to international law, the illegal purpose to which the statute was being applied invalidated the assessment. This argument failed; in dealing with it, Ungoed-Thomas J said:

> What the statute itself enacts cannot be unlawful, because what the statute says and provides is itself the law, and the highest form of law that is known to this country. It is the law which prevails over every other form of law, and it is not for the court to say that a parliamentary enactment, the highest law in this country, is illegal.

That statute prevails over treaties binding on the UK was reaffirmed by the House of Lords in *R* v. *Lyons* [2002] UKHL 44, [2003] 1 AC 976, Lord Hoffmann saying:

> The sovereign legislator in the United Kingdom is Parliament. If Parliament has plainly laid down the law, it is the duty of the courts to apply it, whether that would involve the Crown in breach of an international treaty or not.

By the same token, the courts acknowledge a duty to *interpret* statutes, if possible, as being in conformity with international law and treaty obligations, and we shall see that this interpretative power may be very far-reaching (below, pp. 86–87).

The supremacy of statute has also been sustained in a negative way by a consistent judicial disclaimer of any power of interference with acts of Parliament. In *Manuel* v. *Attorney General* [1983] Ch. 77, 86, Sir Robert Megarry V-C said:

> I am bound to say that from first to last I have heard nothing in this case to make me doubt the simple rule that the duty of the court is to obey and apply every Act of Parliament, and that the court cannot hold any such Act to be ultra vires. Of course there may be questions about what the Act means, and of course there is power to hold statutory instruments and other subordinate legislation ultra vires. But once an instrument is recognised as being an Act of Parliament, no English court can refuse to obey it or question its validity.

Plainly the instrument before the court must be recognised as being an act of Parliament. In *R* v. *Secretary of State for the Environment, ex p Hammersmith and Fulham London Borough Council* [1991] 1 AC 521, 562, Lord Donaldson MR, after allowing for the impact of EU law on parliamentary sovereignty, said:

> Parliament has a limitless right to alter or add to the law by means of primary legislation, enacted by the full constitutional process of debate and decision in both Houses on first and second readings of the Bill, committee and report stages and third readings, followed by Royal Assent. The result is a statute and in relation to statutes the only duty of the judiciary is to interpret and apply them.

Resolutions of one or of both houses of Parliament do not have the force of law. Accordingly, in *Bowles* v. *Bank of England* [1913] 1 Ch. 57, Parker J held that a resolution of the House of Commons was not enough to empower the Crown to levy income tax: only an act of Parliament could authorise such taxation.

But if an act is expressed to have been enacted by Crown, Lords and Commons, the courts will not inquire whether it was properly passed or represents the will of Parliament. This was affirmed in a famous dictum of Lord Campbell in *Edinburgh and Dalkeith Railway Co* v. *Wauchope* (1842) 8 Cl & Fin 710. In this case, it had been argued in the court below that a private act of Parliament was inoperative because notice to those affected by it had not been given as required by parliamentary standing orders. (Private acts commonly affect private rights and are subject to a special parliamentary procedure.) Although this argument was abandoned in the House of Lords, Lord Campbell expressed a clear view on the point:

> [A]ll that a Court of Justice can do is to look to the Parliamentary roll: if from that it should appear that a bill has passed both Houses and received the Royal Assent, no Court of Justice can inquire into the mode in which it was introduced into Parliament, nor into what was done previous to its introduction, or what passed in Parliament during its progress in its various stages through both Houses.

Some years later in *Lee* v. *Bude and Torrington Junction Rly Co* (1871) LR 6 CP 576, there was again a challenge to the validity of a private act, this time on the ground that the promoters of the act had fraudulently misled Parliament as to the facts and the promoters' true purposes. In rejecting this argument, Willes J said:

> Are we to act as regents over what is done by parliament with the consent of the Queen, lords, and commons? I deny that any such authority exists. If an Act of Parliament has been obtained improperly, it is for the legislature to correct it by repealing it: but, so long as it exists as law, the Courts are bound to obey it. The proceedings here are judicial, not autocratic, which they would be if we could make laws instead of administering them.

Despite these unequivocal rulings the question of the validity of a private act was once more argued in the courts in an important case in the 1970s.

British Railways Board v. *Pickin* [1974] AC 765 (HL)

In Acts of Parliament by which the old railway companies acquired land for laying railway lines it was provided that, if the lines should be discontinued, the land taken was to revert to the adjoining landowners. In 1968 the British Railways Board promoted a private bill that would extinguish the rights of reverter; it was passed as the British Railways Act 1968. Pickin, who had acquired land adjoining a railway line that had been discontinued, brought an action in which he asserted that the relevant provision (section 18) of the Act of 1968 was invalid and ineffective to deprive him of his rights in the track. The act, he maintained, had been improperly passed through Parliament as an unopposed private bill, in that notice had not been given to affected landowners as required by standing orders, and Parliament had been misled by false statements in the preamble to the bill that notices and plans of the land had been published.

On the application of the Railways Board, these contentions were ordered to be struck out of the pleadings as an abuse of the process of the court, but they were restored by the Court of Appeal as raising a triable issue. The board's appeal against this decision was allowed by a unanimous House of Lords.

> **Lord Reid:** . . . The idea that a court is entitled to disregard a provision in an Act of Parliament on any ground must seem strange and startling to anyone with any knowledge of the history and law of our constitution, but a detailed argument has been submitted to your Lordships and I must deal with it.
>
> I must make it plain that there has been no attempt to question the general supremacy of Parliament. In earlier times many learned lawyers seem to have believed that an Act of Parliament could be disregarded in so far as it was contrary to the law of God or the law of nature or natural justice, but since the supremacy of Parliament was finally demonstrated by the Revolution of 1688 any such idea has become obsolete.

> The respondent's contention is that there is a difference between a public and a private Act. There are of course great differences between the methods and procedures followed in dealing with public and private Bills, and there may be some differences in the methods of construing their provisions. But the respondent argues for a much more fundamental difference. There is little in modern authority that he can rely on. The mainstay of his argument is a decision of this House, *Mackenzie v Stewart* in 1754.

The Court of Appeal had been persuaded that in *Mackenzie* v. *Stewart*, the House of Lords had refused to give effect to a private act obtained by fraud. Lord Reid reexamined this old and ill-reported case, and concluded that it had been decided by putting a particular construction on the act in question and not by holding it invalid. Lord Reid continued:

> The function of the court is to construe and apply the enactments of Parliament. The court has no concern with the manner in which Parliament or its officers carrying out its Standing Orders perform these functions. Any attempt to prove that they were misled by fraud or otherwise would necessarily involve an inquiry into the manner in which they had performed their functions in dealing with the Bill which became the British Railways Act 1968 . . .
>
> For a century or more both Parliament and the courts have been careful not to act so as to cause conflict between them. Any such investigations as the respondent seeks could easily lead to such a conflict, and I would only support it if compelled to do so by clear authority. But it appears to me that the whole trend of authority for over a century is clearly against permitting any such investigation.
>
> The respondent is entitled to argue that section 18 should be construed in a way favourable to him and for that reason I have refrained from pronouncing on that matter. But he is not entitled to go behind the Act to show that section 18 should not be enforced. Nor is he entitled to examine proceedings in Parliament in order to show that the appellants by fraudulently misleading Parliament caused him loss. I am therefore clearly of opinion that this appeal should be allowed.

The House of Lords expressly approved what had been said by Lord Campbell in *Wauchope* and by Willes J in *Lee* (as quoted above). Lord Simon of Glaisdale relied in particular on the privilege of Parliament declared in Article 9 of the Bill of Rights 1689 as disallowing any questioning of parliamentary proceedings. (See below, p. 173.) He also drew attention to a practical consideration:

> [I]f there is evidence that Parliament may have been misled into an enactment, Parliament might well - indeed, would be likely to - wish to conduct its own inquiry. It would be unthinkable that two inquiries - one parliamentary and the other forensic - should proceed concurrently, conceivably arriving at different conclusions; and a parliamentary examination

> of parliamentary procedures and of the actions and understandings of officers of Parliament would seem to be clearly more satisfactory than one conducted in a court of law – quite apart from considerations of Parliamentary privilege.

Lord Morris was mindful of Parliament's character as the supreme judicial body in the land – a medieval conception not yet quite extinct:

> It would be impracticable and undesirable for the High Court of Justice to embark upon an inquiry concerning the effect or the effectiveness of the internal procedures in the High Court of Parliament or an inquiry whether in any particular case those procedures were effectively followed.

Jackson v. *Attorney General* [2005] UKHL 56, [2006] 1 AC 262

The normal procedure for the enactment of statute is that a bill must be 'read' and passed three times by each house – Commons and Lords – and will then receive the royal assent (see in more detail Chapter 7). Thus, acts of Parliament are formally made by the Crown, the Lords and the Commons acting together. Since the Parliament Act 1911, however, the Commons and the Crown have enjoyed a limited power to legislate without the consent of the House of Lords. If the Commons passes a bill that is then repeatedly rejected by the Lords, after a certain period, the bill may nonetheless proceed to receive the royal assent (and thereby become an Act) in spite of any opposition of the House of Lords. The effect of the Parliament Act 1911 was, for most bills, to replace the Lords' veto over legislation with a power to delay the legislation. The one exception written into the statute is that a bill to extend the life of a Parliament (i.e., to postpone a general election) continues to require the assent of both houses. These arrangements were amended by the Parliament Act 1949, which reduced the length by which the House of Lords may delay a bill from two years to one year (much shorter periods of delay apply to 'money bills', but that need not concern us here). The 1949 Act was itself passed under the Parliament Act procedure. Since 1949, only four acts have been passed using this proced-ure: the War Crimes Act 1991, the European Parliamentary Elections Act 1999, the Sexual Offences (Amendment) Act 2000 and the Hunting Act 2004. (See, further, Chapter 9.)

In *Jackson* v. *Attorney General* a challenge was launched to the constitu-tional validity of the Hunting Act 2004 and the Parliament Act 1949. *Jackson* is a very important case in the developing law of the sovereignty of Parliament, and we shall consider it in detail later in this chapter. For now, what concerns us is solely the point raised in *Wauchope, Lee* and *Pickin*: namely, do the courts have the jurisdiction to examine whether a purported statute is properly a statute? The Attorney General did not seek to argue that the challenge to the 1949 and 2004 acts was non-justiciable. The government knew that the hunting legislation was controversial and considered that a clear verdict from the courts as to its validity was preferable to there being any continuing doubt about the matter. Accordingly, he conceded that the courts did have jurisdiction. The courts accepted, albeit in some instances with qualification, that he was right to do so.

> **Lord Bingham:** . . . Like the Court of Appeal . . . I feel some sense of strangeness at the exercise which the courts have (with the acquiescence of the Attorney General) been invited to undertake in these proceedings. The authority of *Pickin v British Railways* Board [1974] AC 765 is unquestioned, and it was there very clearly decided that 'the courts in this country have no power to declare enacted law to be invalid' (per Lord Simon of Glaisdale at p 798). I am, however, persuaded that the present proceedings are legitimate, for two reasons. First, in *Pickin*, unlike the present case, it was sought to investigate the internal workings and procedures of Parliament to demonstrate that it had been misled and so had proceeded on a false basis. This was held to be illegitimate . . . [his Lordship cited the quotation from Lord Campbell in *Wauchope* and continued]. Here, the courts look to the parliamentary roll and sees bills (the 1949 Act, and then the 2004 Act) which have not passed both Houses. The issue concerns no question of parliamentary procedure such as would, and could only, be the subject of parliamentary inquiry, but a question whether, in Lord Simon's language, these Acts are 'enacted law'. My second reason is more practical. The appellants have raised a question of law which cannot, as such, be resolved by Parliament. But it would not be satisfactory, or consistent with the rule of law, if it could not be resolved at all. So it seems to me necessary that the courts should resolve it, and that to do so involves no breach of constitutional propriety.

> **Lord Nicholls:** . . . These proceedings are highly unusual. At first sight a challenge in court to the validity of a statute seems to offend the fundamental constitutional principle that courts will not look behind an Act of Parliament and investigate the process by which it was enacted. Those are matters for Parliament, not the courts. It is for each House to judge the lawfulness of its own proceedings. The authorities establishing this principle can be found gathered in *Pickin v British Railways Board* [1974] AC 765 . . . In the present case the claimants do not dispute this constitutional principle . . . Their challenge to the lawfulness of the 1949 Act is founded on a different and prior ground: the proper interpretation of section 2(1) of the 1911 Act. On this issue the court's jurisdiction cannot be doubted. This question of statutory interpretation is properly cognisable by a court of law even though it relates to the legislative process. Statutes create law. The proper interpretation of a statute is a matter for the courts, not Parliament, This principle is as fundamental in this country's constitution as the principle that Parliament has exclusive cognisance (jurisdiction) over its own affairs.

The House of Lords unanimously upheld the validity of both the Parliament Act 1949 and the Hunting Act 2004. Along the way, several of their Lordships commented on various aspects of the sovereignty of Parliament. We shall examine a number of these comments later in this chapter (pp. 83–84).

2.2.2 Territorial Extent of Sovereignty: Post-Colonial Independence

Britain is still an imperial power. To this day, it continues to possess a number of 'overseas territories', as they are now called. Matters of imperial law continue to come before the British courts. *R (Bancoult) v. Secretary of State for Foreign and Commonwealth Affairs* [2001] QB 1067, *R (Bancoult) v. Secretary of State for Foreign and Commonwealth Affairs (No 2)* [2008] UKHL 61, [2009] 1 AC 453 and *R v. Secretary of State for Foreign and Commonwealth Affairs, ex p Quark Fishing* [2005] UKHL 57, [2006] 1 AC 529 are three recent examples, the first two cases concerning an appalling (and still ongoing) episode in the government of the British Indian Ocean Territory (also known as the Chagos Islands) and the last case concerning South Georgia and the South Sandwich Islands. However, that said, it is of course the case that the vast majority of the nations formerly included within the British Empire have now obtained their independence (from the British Parliament, if not always from the Crown – many countries in the Commonwealth continue to recognise Queen Elizabeth as head of state). Post-colonial independence poses a number of legally difficult questions for the doctrine of parliamentary sovereignty. The granting of independence to a former colony requires legislative power to be transferred from Westminster to the newly independent state. How may this be achieved? We saw above that, as Dicey explained, Parliament 'may make or unmake any law whatever'. Suppose that Parliament passes a statute granting independence to a former colony or dominion. What would be the legal effect of a later Parliament repealing that legislation and reasserting its right to make laws for the territory?

First, it may be argued (with equivocal support from Dicey, *The Law of the Constitution* (1885), p. 69 note) that Parliament can surrender its sovereign authority over particular territory to some other body of persons. The Statute of Westminster 1931 may be thought to have accomplished this. The statute removed existing limitations of the competence of dominion Parliaments and reinforced this conferment of legislative power with a provision, in section 4, intended to give a legal underpinning to the convention (itself reaffirmed in the preamble to the statute) that the UK Parliament should not legislate for a dominion without its consent. Section 4 provides:

> No Act of Parliament of the United Kingdom passed after the commencement of this Act shall extend, or be deemed to extend, to a Dominion as part of the law of that Dominion unless it is expressly declared in that Act that that Dominion has requested, and consented to, the enactment thereof.

(The 'dominions' to which the act applied in 1931 were Canada, Australia, New Zealand, South Africa, the Irish Free State and Newfoundland, all of which at that time were autonomous members of the British Commonwealth, owing a common allegiance to the Crown.)

In more recent times, acts have been passed to transfer sovereign authority to former colonies and dependencies that have gained independence. In most of these independence acts, the renunciation of legislative competence was not qualified by a 'request and consent' provision such as that in section 4 of the Statute of Westminster. For example, section 1(2) of the Zimbabwe Act 1979) provided:

> On and after Independence Day Her Majesty's Government in the United Kingdom shall have no responsibility for the government of Zimbabwe; and no Act of the Parliament of the United Kingdom passed on or after that day shall extend, or be deemed to extend, to Zimbabwe as part of its law[.]

In a heaven of orthodoxy inhabited by lawyers, it is held that the transfers of sovereignty effected by the Statute of Westminster and the independence Acts are in strict law only conditional, in that Parliament can at any time repeal or disregard these enactments and resume its entire legislative authority over the countries concerned. This was, indeed, the view expressed in an obiter dictum of Lord Sankey, with reference to the application of section 4 of the Statute of Westminster to the Dominion of Canada, in *British Coal Corpn* v. *R* [1935] AC 500, 520:

> It is doubtless true that the power of the Imperial Parliament to pass on its own initiative any legislation that it thought fit extending to Canada remains in theory unimpaired: indeed, the Imperial Parliament could, as a matter of abstract law, repeal or disregard s 4 of the Statute.

But he went on to say:

> But that is theory and has no relation to realities.

The position taken by Lord Sankey as a matter of 'abstract law' was countered by the assertion of a South African judge (Stratford ACJ in *Ndlwana* v. *Hofmeyr* 1937 AD 229, 237) that: 'Freedom once conferred cannot be revoked.' This was echoed by Lord Denning in *Blackburn* v. *Attorney General* [1971] 1 WLR 1037, 1040:

> We have all been brought up to believe that, in legal theory, one Parliament cannot bind another and that no Act is irreversible. But legal theory does not always march alongside political reality. Take the Statute of Westminster 1931, which takes away the power of

Parliament to legislate for the Dominions. Can any one imagine that Parliament could or would reverse that Statute? Take the Acts which have granted independence to the Dominions and territories overseas. Can anyone imagine that Parliament could or would reverse those laws and take away their independence? Most clearly not. Freedom once given cannot be taken away. Legal theory must give way to practical politics.

These constitutional issues arose in the following case.

Manuel v. Attorney General [1983] Ch. 77, 95 (Sir Robert Megarry V-C)

The Canada Act 1982, making provision for a new constitution of Canada, had been passed by the UK Parliament on a request submitted by the Senate and the House of Commons of Canada with the agreement of nine of the ten provincial governments. The claimants were Canadian Indian Chiefs whose complaint was that the new constitution took away the special protection that had been accorded to the rights of the Indian peoples of Canada under the prior constitutional arrangements. They sought a number of declarations claiming that: (1) the UK Parliament had no power to amend the constitution of Canada so as to prejudice the Indian nations of Canada without their consent; and (2) the Canada Act 1982 was ultra vires and void. The defendant, the Attorney General, moved that the statement of claim be struck out as disclosing no reasonable cause of action.

Sir Robert Megarry: . . . On the face of it, a contention that an Act of Parliament is ultra vires is bold in the extreme. It is contrary to one of the fundamentals of the British Constitution . . . As was said by Lord Morris of Borth-y-Gest [in *British Railways Board* v. *Pickin*, above] it is not for the courts to proceed 'as though the Act or some part of it had never been passed'; there may be argument on the interpretation of the Act, but 'there must be none as to whether it should be on the Statute Book at all' . . .

Mr Macdonald [counsel for the claimants] was, of course, concerned to restrict the ambit of the decision in *Pickin v British Railways Board*. He accepted that it was a binding decision for domestic legislation, but he said that it did not apply in relation to the Statute of Westminster 1931 or to the other countries of the Commonwealth . . . [This point] is founded upon the theory that Parliament may surrender its sovereign power over some territory or area of land to another person or body . . . After such a surrender, any legislation which Parliament purports to enact for that territory is not merely ineffective there, but is totally void, in this country as elsewhere, since Parliament has surrendered the power to legislate; and the English courts have jurisdiction to declare such legislation ultra vires and void.

Before I discuss this proposition, and its application to Canada, I should mention one curious result of this theory which emerged only at a late stage. In response to a question, Mr Macdonald accepted that as the theory applied only to territories over which Parliament had surrendered its sovereignty, it did not affect territories over which Parliament had never exercised sovereignty. Thus if one adapts an example given by Jennings [The *Law and the*

Constitution (5th edn. 1959) at pp. 170, 171], an English statute making it an offence to smoke in the streets of Paris or Vienna would be valid, though enforceable only against those who come within the jurisdiction, whereas an English statute making it an offence to smoke in the streets of Bombay or Sydney would be ultra vires and void, and an English court could make a declaration to this effect. At this stage I need say no more than that I find such a distinction surprising.

The claimants had argued that the Statute of Westminster had transferred sovereignty to Canada, subject only to section 7 of the statute by which the UK Parliament retained power to enact amendments to the Canadian constitution (contained in the British North America Acts). This power could be exercised (in what was argued to be the true meaning of section 4, set out above) only on condition that the actual request and consent of the dominion had been forthcoming, and such consent must be expressed by all the provincial legislatures and by the Indian nations of Canada as well as by the federal Parliament. No such general consent of the dominion had been given, and without it the UK Parliament could not legislate for Canada on any subject.

Sir Robert Megarry: . . . In the present case I have before me a copy of the Canada Act 1982 purporting to be published by Her Majesty's Stationery Office. After reciting the request and consent of Canada and the submission of an address to Her Majesty by the Senate and House of Commons of Canada, there are the words of enactment:

> 'Be it therefore enacted by the Queen's Most Excellent Majesty, by and with the advice and consent of the Lords Spiritual and Temporal, and Commons, in this present Parliament assembled, and by the authority of the same, as follows:'
>
> There has been no suggestion that the copy before me is not a true copy of the Act itself, or that it was not passed by the House of Commons and the House of Lords, or did not receive the Royal Assent . . . The Canada Act 1982 is an Act of Parliament, and sitting as a judge in an English court I owe full and dutiful obedience to that Act.

I do not think that, as a matter of law, it makes any difference if the Act in question purports to apply outside the United Kingdom. I speak not merely of statutes such as the Continental Shelf Act 1964 but also of statutes purporting to apply to other countries. If that other country is a colony, the English courts will apply the Act even if the colony is in a state of revolt against the Crown and direct enforcement of the decision may be impossible: see *Madzimbamuto v Lardner-Burke* [1969] 1 AC 645 . . . Similarly if the other country is a foreign state which has never been British, I do not think that any English court would or could declare the Act ultra vires and void. No doubt the Act would normally be ignored by the foreign state and would not be enforced by it, but that would not invalidate the Act in this country. Those who infringed it could not claim that it was void if proceedings within the jurisdiction were taken against them. Legal validity is one thing, enforceability is another. Thus a marriage in Nevada may constitute statutory bigamy punishable in England (*Trial of Earl Russell* [1901] AC 446), just as acts in Germany may be punishable here as statutory

> treason: *Joyce v Director of Public Prosecutions* [1946] AC 347. Parliament in fact legislates only for British subjects in this way; but if it also legislated for others, I do not see how the English courts could hold the statute void, however impossible it was to enforce it, and no matter how strong the diplomatic protests.
>
> I do not think that countries which were once colonies but have since been granted independence are in any different position. Plainly once statute has granted independence to a country, the repeal of the statute will not make the country dependent once more; what is done is done, and is not undone by revoking the authority to do it . . . But if Parliament then passes an Act applying to such a country, I cannot see why that Act should not be in the same position as an Act applying to what has always been a foreign country, namely, an Act which the English courts will recognise and apply but one which the other country will in all probability ignore.

Sir Robert Megarry accordingly held that the claimants' statement of claim disclosed no reasonable cause of action. He concluded:

> Perhaps I may add this. I have grave doubts about the theory of the transfer of sovereignty as affecting the competence of Parliament. In my view, it is a fundamental of the English constitution that Parliament is supreme. As a matter of law the courts of England recognise Parliament as being omnipotent in all save the power to destroy its own omnipotence. Under the authority of Parliament the courts of a territory may be released from their legal duty to obey Parliament, but that does not trench on the acceptance by the English courts of all that Parliament does. Nor must validity in law be confused with practical enforceability.

The claimants appealed. The Court of Appeal was content to assume in favour of the claimants (while expressly refraining from deciding) the correctness of the proposition 'that Parliament can effectively tie the hands of its successors, if it passes a statute which provides that any future legislation on a specified subject shall be enacted only with certain specified consents'. But was this what Parliament had done in enacting section 4 of the Statute of Westminster? The judgment of the court (delivered by Slade LJ) proceeded on the basis that precise compliance with section 4 was necessary if the Canada Act 1982 was to be valid and effective. The attack on the validity of the act failed. The Court of Appeal construed section 4 of the Statute of Westminster as requiring no more than a declaration in an act that the dominion had requested and consented to it. The court thereby avoided having to decide the constitutional issues, whether Parliament can effectively renounce its sovereign legislative power in respect of a particular territory, and whether it can make the consent of some other body necessary for the validity of its acts. Contrariwise, the judgment of Sir Robert Megarry at first instance had left no room for doubt as to the answers to these questions. (For further analysis, see Hadfield [1983] *PL* 351; and Marshall, *Constitutional Conventions* (1984), ch. XII.) Parliament has since expressly renounced, without qualification, its surviving legislative competences in respect of Canada (in the Canada Act 1982, section 2) and Australia (Australia Act 1986, section 1).

2.2.3 Continuing Sovereignty and the 'New View'

Let us now put to one side the unlikely prospect of legislation by the UK Parliament purporting to alter the law of a state such as Zimbabwe or Canada to which it has ostensibly made an unqualified transfer of legislative sovereignty.

The wider question remains, which has important practical implications, as to whether Parliament can bind itself (including succeeding Parliaments) either as to the content of future legislation or as to the manner and form in which future legislation must be passed. As we shall see, consideration of this question takes us into the treacherous waters of what the legal basis of the doctrine of parliamentary sovereignty is. The sovereignty of the UK Parliament has traditionally been held to be of that transcendent kind that cannot be limited even by Parliament itself.

Godden v. *Hales* (1686) 11 St Tr 1165 (KB)

Herbert CJ: . . . [I]f an act of parliament had a clause in it that it should never be repealed, yet without question, the same power that made it, may repeal it.

Professor H.L.A. Hart holds that the rule of parliamentary sovereignty is part of what he calls the 'rule of recognition' of our legal system. This is the fundamental or ultimate rule of the system that states the criteria for identifying valid rules of law: unlike all the other rules, the rule of recognition is binding simply because it is accepted by the community, in particular by its judges and officials. The rule of recognition sustaining our constitutional system is said to include the proposition that Parliament cannot bind itself.

H.L.A. Hart, *The Concept of Law* (2nd edn. 1994), pp. 149–50

Under the influence of the Austinian doctrine that law is essentially the product of a legally untrammeled will, older constitutional theorists wrote as if it was a logical necessity that there should be a legislature which was sovereign, in the sense that it is free, at every moment of its existence as a continuing body, not only from legal limitations imposed *ab extra*, but also from its own prior legislation. That Parliament is sovereign in this sense may now be regarded as established, and the principle that no earlier Parliament can preclude its 'successors' from repealing its legislation constitutes part of the ultimate rule of recognition used by the courts in identifying valid rules of law. It is, however, important to see that no necessity of logic, still less of nature, dictates that there should be such a Parliament; it is only one arrangement among others, equally conceivable, which has come to be accepted with us as the criterion of legal validity. Among these others is another principle which might equally well, perhaps better, deserve the name of 'sovereignty'. This is the principle that Parliament should *not* be incapable of limiting irrevocably the legislative competence of its successors but, on the contrary, should have this wider self-limiting power. Parliament would then at least once in its history be capable of exercising an even larger sphere of legislative competence than the accepted established doctrine allows to it. The requirement that at every moment of its existence Parliament should be free from legal limitations including even those imposed by itself is, after all, only one interpretation of the ambiguous idea of legal omnipotence. It in effect makes a choice between a *continuing* omnipotence in all matters not affecting the legislative competence of successive parliaments, and an unrestricted *self-embracing* omnipotence the exercise of which can only be enjoyed once. These two conceptions of omnipotence have their parallel in two conceptions of an omnipotent God: on the one hand, a God who at every moment of his existence enjoys the same powers and so is incapable of cutting down those powers, and, on the other, a God whose powers include the power to destroy for the future his omnipotence. Which form of omnipotence – continuing or self-embracing – our Parliament enjoys is an empirical question concerning the form of rule which is accepted as the ultimate criterion in identifying the law. Though it is a question about a rule lying at the base of a legal system, it is still a question of fact to which at any given moment of time, on some points at least, there may be a quite determinate answer. Thus it is clear that the presently accepted rule is one of continuing sovereignty, so that Parliament cannot protect its statutes from repeal.

The rule of recognition, which affirms the continuing sovereignty of Parliament, may change over time; political developments may eventually – or even suddenly – cause the courts to give obedience to a modified or new rule of recognition. But while it stands it has, as Hart says, a 'unique authoritative status'. The rule of parliamentary sovereignty is not alterable by Parliament acting alone.

H.W.R. Wade, 'The Basis of Legal Sovereignty' [1955] *CLJ* 172, 187–9

But to deny that Parliament can alter this particular rule [that the courts will enforce statutes] is not so daring as it may seem at first sight; for the sacrosanctity of the rule is an inexorable corollary of Parliament's continuing sovereignty. If the one proposition is asserted, the other must be conceded. Nevertheless some further justification is called for, since there must be something peculiar about a rule of common law which can stand against a statute.

The peculiarity lies in this, that the rule enjoining judicial obedience to statutes is one of the fundamental rules upon which the legal system depends. That there are such rules, and that they are in a very special class, is explained with great clarity by Salmond [*Jurisprudence* (10th edn. 1947), p. 155]:

'All rules of law have historical sources. As a matter of fact and history they have their origin somewhere, though we may not know what it is. But not all of them have legal sources. Were this so, it would be necessary for the law to proceed *ad infinitum* in tracing the descent of its principles. It is requisite that the law should postulate one or more first causes, whose operation is ultimate and whose authority is underived . . . The rule that a man may not ride a bicycle on the footpath may have its source in the by-laws of a municipal council; the rule that these by-laws have the force of law has its source in an Act of Parliament. But whence comes the rule that Acts of Parliament have the force of law? This is legally ultimate; its source is historical only, not legal . . . It is the law because it is the law, and for no other reason that it is possible for the law itself to take notice of. *No statute can confer this power upon Parliament, for this would be to assume and act on the very power that is to be conferred.'*

Once this truth is grasped, the dilemma is solved. For if no statute can establish the rule that the courts obey Acts of Parliament, similarly no statute can alter or abolish that rule. The rule is above and beyond the reach of statute, as Salmond so well explains, because it is itself the source of the authority of statute. This puts it into a class by itself among rules of common law, and the apparent paradox that it is unalterable by Parliament turns out to be a truism. The rule of judicial obedience is in one sense a rule of common law, but in another sense – which applies to no other rule of common law – it is the ultimate *political fact* upon which the whole system of legislation hangs. Legislation owes its authority to the rule: the rule does not owe its authority to legislation. To say that Parliament can change the rule, merely because it can change any other rule, is to put the cart before the horse.

For the relationship between the courts of law and Parliament is first and foremost a political reality. Historical illustrations of this are plentiful. When Charles I was executed in 1649 the courts continued to enforce the Acts of the Long Parliament, the Rump, Barebones' Parliament, and the other Commonwealth legislatures. For a revolution took place, and the courts (without any authority from the *previous* sovereign legislature) spontaneously transferred their allegiance from the King in Parliament to the kingless Parliaments. In other words, the courts altered their definition of 'an Act of Parliament' and recognised that the seat of sovereignty had shifted. This was a political fact from which legal consequences flowed. But in 1660 there was a counter-revolution: Charles II was restored, and it was suddenly discovered that all Acts passed by the Commonwealth Parliaments were void for want of the royal assent. The courts, again without any prior authority, shifted their allegiance back to the King in Parliament, and all the Commonwealth legislation was expunged from the statute book. The 'glorious revolution' of 1688 was, in its *legal* aspect if in no other, much like the revolution of 1649, for the courts, recognising political realities but without any legal justification, transferred their obedience from James II to William and Mary. Had the Jacobite rebellions of 1715 and 1745 succeeded, the courts might once again have held all intervening legislation – including the Bill of Rights and Act of Settlement – void for lack of the assent of the proper monarch. The fact that William and Mary's Parliament had passed Acts confirming their title to the Crown and its own legislative authority would obviously not have availed in the least.

What Salmond calls the 'ultimate legal principle' is therefore a rule which is unique in being unchangeable by Parliament – it is changed by revolution, not by legislation; it lies in the keeping of the courts, and no Act of Parliament can take it from them. This is only another way of saying that it is always for the courts, in the last resort, to say what is a valid Act of Parliament; and that the decision of this question is not determined by any rule of law which can be laid down or altered by any authority outside the courts. It is simply a political fact.

The 'revolution' which, in the view of Sir William Wade, is required for any change in the ultimate legal principle of parliamentary sovereignty, may be a gradual event rather than a sudden political convulsion.

Sir William Wade, *Constitutional Fundamentals* (rev edn. 1989), p. 37

I have never suggested that no shift in judicial loyalty is possible. One has only to look at the shifts which took place in seventeenth-century England, in eighteenth-century America and in the twentieth-century dissolution of the British Empire, latterly in particular in Zimbabwe. These shifts are revolutions, breaks in continuity and in the legal pedigree of legislative power. Even without such discontinuity there might be a shift of judicial loyalty if we take into account the dimension of time. Suppose that Parliament were to enact a Bill of Rights entrenched by a clause saying that it was to be amended or repealed only by Acts certified to be passed by two-thirds majorities in both Houses. Suppose also that Parliament scrupulously observed this rule for 50 or 100 years, so that no conflicting legislation came before the courts. Meanwhile new generations of judges might come to accept that there had been a new constitutional settlement based on common consent and long usage, and that the old doctrine of sovereignty was ancient history, to be classed with the story of the Witenagemot, Bonham's case, the Rump, Barebones' Parliament and the Jacobite pretenders. The judges would then be adjusting their doctrine to the facts of constitutional life, as they have done throughout history.

If a bill of rights with entrenched provisions such as Sir William Wade supposes (and unlike the HRA which, not being entrenched, is reconcilable with the orthodox doctrine of parliamentary sovereignty) were to be introduced with general political and popular support, it might perhaps, in a much shorter time than 50 or 100 years, establish itself in the British political culture and be recognised by the judges as having worked a change in the ground rules of the constitution.

It is argued by some constitutional theorists (whose position derives an arguably gratuitous advantage from being sometimes described as the 'new view' of parliamentary sovereignty) that the orthodox doctrine of sovereignty does not prevent Parliament from binding itself as to the 'manner and form' (as opposed to the content) of future legislation. (See, e.g., Heuston, *Essays in Constitutional Law* (2nd edn. 1964), ch. 1.) According to this view, Parliament could effectively provide that an act might be repealed or amended only by a specified majority in both houses, or only with the approval of the electorate in a referendum, or only by the use of a prescribed verbal formula in the amending act. The 'new view' that such self-imposed procedural limitations would be binding on Parliament relies largely on Commonwealth cases, of which the following is an example.

Harris v. Minister of the Interior 1952 (2) SA 428 (Appellate Division of the Supreme Court of South Africa)

The South Africa Act 1909, an act of the UK Parliament, joined together four colonies as the Union of South Africa and created the Parliament of the Union. This was initially a non-sovereign legislature, which, by reason of the Colonial Laws Validity Act 1865, had no general power to legislate inconsistently with UK statutes extending to South Africa. But section 152 of the South Africa Act empowered the Union Parliament to 'repeal or alter any of the provisions of this Act'.

Those who framed the South Africa Act were concerned to protect and entrench existing voting rights, in particular the rights of the 'Cape Coloured' voters of the former Cape Colony. Accordingly, section 35(1) of the act provided that no act of the Union Parliament should disqualify any person in the Cape Province as a voter by reason of his race or colour, unless the bill:

> be passed by both Houses of Parliament sitting together, and at the third reading be agreed to by not less than two-thirds of the total number of members of both Houses.

Section 35 was itself entrenched in a proviso to section 152, by which any repeal or alteration of section 35, or indeed of section 152, could be effected only by the same method of a bill passed by a two-thirds' majority in a joint sitting of both houses.

In 1948 a National Government came into power and initiated an intensified policy of white supremacy under the name of apartheid. By that date, South Africa had, as a result of constitutional convention and the Statute of Westminster 1931, shed its colonial status and was acknowledged to be an independent and sovereign state within the Commonwealth. In 1951, the Union Parliament passed by a simple majority, the two houses sitting separately, a Separate Representation of Voters Act (Act 46 of 1951), which deprived Cape Coloured voters of their existing voting rights by providing for their registration on a separate voters' roll. Some of the disqualified voters brought proceedings to challenge the validity of the act.

The argument of counsel for the government was that the Union Parliament, having acquired full legislative sovereignty as a result of the Statute of Westminster, was free to disregard the limitations contained in sections 35 and 152 of the South Africa Act 1909.

A unanimous Appellate Division held that the Separate Representation of Voters Act was null and void.

> **Centlivres CJ:** ... It is common cause that Act 46 of 1951 was passed by the House of Assembly and the Senate sitting separately and assented to by the Governor-General and that it was not passed in conformity with the provisions of sec. 35(1) and sec. 152 of the South Africa Act ...

> If Act 46 of 1951 had been passed before the Statute of Westminster, it is clear ... that that Act would not have been a valid Act, as it was not passed in accordance with the procedure prescribed by secs 35(1) and 152 ...
>
> The effect of sub-sec (1) of sec 2 [of the Statute of Westminster] is that the Colonial Laws Validity Act no longer applies to any law made ... by the Union Parliament. Consequently the Union Parliament can now make a law repugnant to a British Act of Parliament in so far as that Act extends to the Union ... [I]t is clear that when [the Statute of Westminster] refers to a law made by a Dominion, such law means in relation to South Africa a law made by the Union Parliament functioning either bicamerally or unicamerally in accordance with the requirements of the South Africa Act.
>
> [The judge referred to the argument of counsel for the Government that the effect of the Statute of Westminster was that the Union was a sovereign state and that all fetters binding the Union Parliament had fallen away, and continued:]
>
> A State can be unquestionably sovereign although it has no legislature which is completely sovereign. As Bryce points out in his *Studies in History and Jurisprudence* legal sovereignty may be divided between two authorities. In the case of the Union, legal sovereignty is or may be divided between Parliament as ordinarily constituted and Parliament as constituted under ... the proviso to sec 152. Such a division of legislative powers is no derogation from the sovereignty of the Union and the mere fact that that division was enacted in a British Statute (viz, the South Africa Act) which is still in force in the Union cannot affect the question in issue.
>
> The South Africa Act, the terms and conditions of which were, as its preamble shows, agreed to by the respective Parliaments of the four original Colonies, created the Parliament of the Union. It is that Act and not the Statute of Westminster which prescribes the manner in which the constituent elements of Parliament must function for the purpose of passing legislation. While the Statute of Westminster confers further powers on the Parliament of the Union, it in no way prescribes how that Parliament must function in exercising those powers.
>
> [T]he Statute of Westminster has left the entrenched clauses of the South Africa Act intact, and, that being so, it follows that ... courts of law have the power to declare Act 46 of 1951 invalid on the ground that it was not passed in conformity with the provisions of secs 35 and 152 of the South Africa Act ... To hold otherwise would mean that courts of law would be powerless to protect the rights of individuals which were specially protected in the constitution of this country.

(The judicial vindication in this great case of the rule of law and the rights of individuals was countered by further measures taken by the National Government, which succeeded eventually in removing the Cape Coloured voters from the common roll. The whole course of the constitutional battle is considered by Marshall, *Parliamentary Sovereignty and the Commonwealth* (1957), ch II and by Forsyth, *In Danger for their Talents* (1985), pp. 61–74.)

The *Harris* case is a demonstration of the principle that a Parliament may be sovereign and yet be subject to requirements of manner and form for the legally effective expression of its will. But this does not justify our concluding that the UK Parliament can impose legally binding requirements of manner and form on itself. The Union Parliament owed its existence to the South Africa Act, which therefore had a special status as the constituent instrument of that Parliament. Only when functioning in accordance with the procedural requirements of the constituent act could it be said that the Union Parliament functioned at all. Other Commonwealth cases that are invoked in support of the 'new view' of parliamentary sovereignty, such as *Attorney General for New South Wales* v. *Trethowan* [1932] AC 526 and *Bribery Comr* v. *Ranasinghe* [1965] AC 172, also depend on the special authority of the instrument containing the limiting provisions. In the constitution of the UK, by way of contrast, as the Privy Council observed in *Ranasinghe*, 'there is no governing instrument which prescribes the law-making powers and the forms which are essential to those powers'.

As regards requirements of manner and form imposed by the UK Parliament on itself, the following case gives no encouragement to exponents of the 'new view'.

Ellen Street Estates Ltd v. *Minister of Health* [1934] 1 KB 590 (CA)

The Acquisition of Land (Assessment of Compensation) Act 1919 laid down the principles on which compensation was to be assessed for the compulsory acquisition of land for public purposes. Section 7(1) said that the provisions of any act authorising compulsory acquisition 'shall . . . have effect subject to this Act, and so far as inconsistent with this Act those provisions shall cease to have or shall not have effect'. On one view section 7(1) is correctly construed as applying only to past enactments, but it was argued in this case that it applied also to later acts and that, as a consequence, inconsistent provisions in the Housing Act 1925 were of no effect. It was not disputed that a later act could amend the 1919 Act, but it was contended that only express provision in the later act would achieve this: in effect, Parliament had in 1919 bound its successors as to the *form* of any amendment of the provisions of its enactment of that year. The Court of Appeal held, however, that even if section 7(1) of the Act of 1919 was intended to apply to later acts, it could not control future Parliaments, and the Housing Act 1925 therefore overrode those provisions of the 1919 Act with which it was inconsistent.

> **Scrutton LJ:** . . . Such a contention involves this proposition, that no subsequent Parliament by enacting a provision inconsistent with the Act of 1919 can give any effect to the words it uses . . . That is absolutely contrary to the constitutional position that Parliament can alter an Act previously passed, and it can do so by repealing in terms the previous Act . . . and it can do it also in another way – namely, by enacting a provision which is clearly inconsistent with the previous Act.
>
> **Maugham LJ:** . . . The Legislature cannot, according to our constitution, bind itself as to the form of subsequent legislation, and it is impossible for Parliament to enact that in

a subsequent statute dealing with the same subject-matter there can be no implied repeal. If in a subsequent Act Parliament chooses to make it plain that the earlier statute is being to some extent repealed, effect must be given to that intention just because it is the will of the legislature.

The same conclusion on this point had been reached earlier by the Divisional Court in *Vauxhall Estates Ltd* v. *Liverpool Corpn* [1932] 1 KB 733. These cases are not necessarily conclusive of the matter: in each of them the 'manner and form' question arose in a specific and narrow context and in neither case was the nature of parliamentary sovereignty examined in depth. The 'new view' continues to find support, for instance, in a thoughtful analysis by Craig, 'Sovereignty of the United Kingdom Parliament after *Factortame*' '(1991) 11 *Yearbook of European Law* 221. An unqualified acceptance of the new view would, however, bestow a dangerous power on any government looking for a way to shore up partisan legislation against being overturned by a future Parliament of a different political composition.

Several members of the House of Lords commented on the 'manner and form' argument in their opinions in *Jackson* v. *Attorney General* [2005] UKHL 56, [2006] 1 AC 262 (for the background to which, see above). All such comments were obiter and none resolves the matter definitively. Even after *Jackson*, there can be no certainty as to whether the manner and form argument is, or is not, part of the law governing the Westminster Parliament. The clearest support in *Jackson* for the manner and form argument comes from Lord Steyn [81]; the clearest criticism of the manner and form argument comes from Lord Hope [113] (but see also Baroness Hale of Richmond [161–163], who says that the question 'is for another day').

Lord Steyn: . . . The word Parliament involves both static and dynamic concepts. The static concept refers to the constituent elements which make up Parliament: the House of Commons, the House of Lords, and the Monarch. The dynamic concept involves the constituent elements functioning together as a law making body. The inquiry is: has Parliament spoken? The law and custom of Parliament regulates what the constituent elements must do to legislate: all three must signify consent to the measure. But, apart from the traditional method of law making, Parliament acting as ordinarily constituted may functionally redistribute legislative power in different ways. For example, Parliament could for specific purposes provide for a two-thirds majority in the House of Commons and the House of Lords. Such redefinition could not be disregarded. Owen Dixon neatly summarised this idea in 1935: '. . . The very power of constitutional alteration cannot be exercised except in the form and manner which the law for the time being prescribes. Unless the legislature observes that manner and form, its attempt to alter its constitution is void. It may amend or abrogate for the future the law which prescribes that form or that manner. But, in doing so, it must comply with its very requirements.' See 'The Law and the Constitution' (1935) 51 LQR

590, 601. This formulation can be traced to the majority judgment in *Attorney General for New South Wales v Trethowan* (1931) 44 CLR 394.

Lord Hope: . . . it is a fundamental aspect of the rule of sovereignty that no Parliament can bind its successors. There are no means whereby, even with the assistance of the most skilful draftsman, it can entrench an Act of Parliament. It is impossible for Parliament to enact something which a subsequent statute dealing with the same subject matter cannot repeal.

It may be that no single theory of parliamentary sovereignty is unequivocally established in our constitution, doing service for every occasion. Allan, 'Parliamentary Sovereignty: Lord Denning's Dexterous Revolution' (1983) 3 *OJLS* 22, argues that the 'fundamental' rule about parliamentary sovereignty is, in fact, indeterminate: it does not specify whether sovereignty is 'continuing' or 'self-embracing'. It is therefore for the judges to decide on the effectiveness of any self-imposed limitation of manner and form as and when the question arises, and they may respond in the future to a perceived 'readiness of the political climate for change' in upholding such a limitation in a particular context.

(See, further, Goldsworthy, *Parliamentary Sovereignty: Contemporary Debates* (2010), chs. 5–7.)

2.2.4 Sovereignty Re-appraised: Three Contemporary Challenges

2.2.4.1 Membership of the EU

When the UK joined the European Community (now the EU) in 1972 it was already an established principle of the EU legal order that laws issuing from it, within the area of the EU's competence, should have supreme authority in all the member states. To this end, the ECJ insisted that the member states had, in transferring powers to the EU, necessarily limited their own sovereign authority (see Case 26/62 *Van Gend en Loos* [1963] ECR 1 and Case 6/64 *Costa v. ENEL* [1964] ECR 585). Accordingly, the European Communities Act 1972 (the legal instrument governing the status of EU law in the UK) provides that UK legislation – including acts of Parliament – is to have effect *subject to* authoritative provisions of EU law. The significance of this provision was illustrated in the *Factortame* litigation, the leading case in the UK on the relationship between the sovereignty of Parliament and the claims of EU law to legal supremacy. This was confirmed in *Benkharbouche* v. *Embassy of the Republic of Sudan* [2017] UKSC 62, [2017] 3 WLR 957 where the Supreme Court disapplied primary legislation that was incompatible with provisions of the EU Charter of Fundamental Rights and Freedoms. *Factortame* and *Benkharbouche* are considered in detail in Chapter 5. The broad issues concerning the implications for our constitutional law and politics of the UK's membership of the EU and the impact of Brexit are also addressed in that chapter.

The effect of the European Communities Act 1972 may seem equivalent to a transfer of (a portion of) Parliament's sovereignty to the EU, but since the act is, like any other enactment, in principle repealable by Parliament, the restriction of sovereignty effected by it is not irreversible: we may say that sovereignty has been lent rather than given away. While previous editions suggested that, as Lord Sankey said about the Statute of Westminster and its application to Canada, 'that is theory and has no relation to realities', Brexit illustrates that it is possible for the UK to leave the EU. However, the full impact of this decision in practice remains to be seen. As will be discussed below (in Chapter 5), the European Union (Withdrawal) Act 2018 preserves the sovereignty of retained EU law, but only as this applies to legislation enacted prior to 31 December 2020 – the completion day of the implementation period. The Withdrawal Agreement preserves the sovereignty of the provisions of EU law contained in the agreement until the end of the implementation period. This is achieved through the provisions of the European Union (Withdrawal Agreement) Act 2020, which preserves the effect of the European Communities Act 1972, in spite of its having been repealed on exit day by section 1 of the European Union (Withdrawal) Act 2018.

What is clear is that EU law had, and until the end of the implementation period continues to have, effect in the UK *only* because Parliament has said so. It had been suggested by counsel in *Thoburn* v. *Sunderland City Council* [2003] QB 151 that this was not the case and that EU law had some force in the UK independently of the European Communities Act 1972, but the judge (Laws LJ) was emphatic in rejecting this claim (at [58]–[59]). Section 18 of the European Union Act 2011 underscored the point: 'Directly applicable or directly effective EU law (that is, the rights, powers, liabilities, obligations, restrictions, remedies and procedures referred to in section 2(1) of the European Communities Act 1972) falls to be recognised and available in law in the United Kingdom only by virtue of that Act or where it is required to be recognised and available in law by virtue of any other Act.' (The European Union Bill 2010–11 is considered further below, in Chapter 5.) Although this act has now been repealed by the European Union (Withdrawal) Act 2018, its sentiment is nevertheless repeated in section 38 of the European Union (Withdrawal Agreement) Act 2020, which states that 'it is recognised that the Parliament of the United Kingdom is sovereign', the provisions of the 2020 Act that preserves the effect of the European Communities Act 1972 notwithstanding. After the completion day of the implementation period, sections 5(1) and 5(2) of the European Union (Withdrawal) Act 2018 preserve the principle of the supremacy of EU law.

It is a matter of (hotly contested) interpretation whether the UK's membership of the EU constituted a revolutionary alteration to the rule of recognition or a mere evolution of legal principle. For the former view, see Sir William Wade, 'Sovereignty – Revolution or Evolution?' (1996) 112 *LQR* 568; for the latter, see Allan, 'Parliamentary Sovereignty: Law, Politics and Revolution' (1997) 113 *LQR* 443; and for fuller consideration of all of this, see Chapter 5.

2.2.4.2 European Human Rights Law

The European Convention on Human Rights (ECHR) was developed under the auspices of the Council of Europe. This is a quite different body from the EU and the two need to be distinguished from one another. The ECHR is enforced by the European Court of Human Rights (ECtHR) in Strasbourg; the law of the EU is enforced by the European Court of Justice (ECJ) in Luxembourg. Judgments of the ECtHR may have an impact on parliamentary sovereignty where they hold that particular statutory provisions are contrary to the terms of the ECHR. An ongoing example concerns the franchise and the general exclusion from it of convicted prisoners. The Grand Chamber of the ECtHR held by a majority of 12:5 that this rule was unlawful: *Hirst* v. *United Kingdom (No 2)* (2006) 42 EHRR 41 (this ruling was in contrast to that of the domestic court, the Divisional Court having ruled that the matter was one that should be left for Parliament to determine). The incumbent government did nothing to effect a change in the law, not least because it knew that any change would be deeply unpopular in Parliament, the press and beyond. The Coalition Government was no more eager than its predecessor to amend the law so as to enable convicted prisoners to vote, but it feared that further inaction would result in a large number of compensation claims being brought. In February 2011, the House of Commons debated the matter (with a view to exploring the issue: not with a view to changing the law). On a free (unwhipped) vote, after a high-quality, thorough and (generally) well-informed debate, MPs voted overwhelmingly in favour of maintaining the general ban on prisoners' voting and, moreover, in favour of the view that the matter should be decided by Parliament and not by a court of law: see HC Deb vol. 523, cols 493–586, 10 February 2011. In spite of this general unwillingness to change the law, the Coalition Government published a draft bill. The joint Committee of the House of Commons and the House of Lords on the Eligibility (Prisoners) Draft Bill recommended that prisoners serving prison sentences of twelve months or fewer should be given the right to vote. The government did not formally respond to these proposals. In December 2015, the government indicated that it would produce a substantive report in response to the report of the Joint Committee. However, this report was not forthcoming. In 2017, the government published further proposals that would have allowed prisoners on temporary licence to vote. These proposals were accepted by the Council of Europe and have now been implemented, The Scottish Elections (Franchise and Representation) Act 2020 enables prisoners serving terms of twelve months or under to vote in local elections. The Welsh Senedd is currently considering whether to grant the right to vote in local elections to prisoners serving terms of four years or under.

As a matter of *international* law, the UK has been bound by the terms of the ECHR since its inception in the 1950s. This means that litigants could complain to the ECtHR if they felt their rights were being violated by the UK. But it was not until the HRA came into force in 2000 that litigants could make such arguments in the *domestic* courts. The relationship between fundamental rights, domestic judicial review and parliamentary sovereignty was summarised in the following way in an important ruling by Lord Hoffmann.

R v. *Secretary of State for the Home Department, ex p Simms* [2000] 2 AC 115 (HL)

Lord Hoffmann: . . . Parliamentary sovereignty means that Parliament can, if it chooses, legislate contrary to fundamental principles of human rights . . . But the principle of legality means that Parliament must squarely confront what it is doing and accept the political cost. Fundamental rights cannot be overridden by general or ambiguous words. This is because there is too great a risk that the full implications of their unqualified meaning may have passed unnoticed in the democratic process. In the absence of express language or necessary implication to the contrary, the courts therefore presume that even the most general words were intended to be subject to the basic rights of the individual. In this way the courts of the United Kingdom, though acknowledging the sovereignty of Parliament, apply principles of constitutionality little different from those which exist in countries where the power of the legislature is expressly limited by a constitutional document.

However, while the ruling in *Simms* is undoubtedly important as a statement of principle, it is not always as rigorously enforced as a bare reading of Lord Hoffmann's words may lead one to imagine. The rule in *Simms* has been held to be of a lesser value where Parliament has 'squarely confronted what it is doing' – where the rights implications of legislation have not 'passed unnoticed' but have been addressed in it: see, for example, *McE* v. *Prison Service of Northern Ireland* [2009] UKHL 15, [2009] 1 AC 908. Other cases in which the rule in *Simms* was apparently overlooked or set aside include *R (Bancoult)* v. *Secretary of State for Foreign and Commonwealth Affairs (No 2)* [2008] UKHL 61, [2009] 1 AC 453 (see pp. 199–200 below) and *R (Gillan)* v. *Metropolitan Police Commissioner* [2006] UKHL 12, [2006] 2 AC 307 (see p. 951 below). (See, further, on *Simms*, Sales (2009) 125 *LQR* 598.)

The following convention rights are incorporated into domestic law under the Human Rights Act: the right to life, freedom from torture, freedom from slavery, the right to liberty, the right to a fair trial, the right to privacy, freedom of thought, conscience and religion, freedom of expression, freedom of assembly and association, the right to marry, freedom from discrimination, the right to property and the right to education, as well as others (see, in more detail, Chapter 11). Sections 3 and 4 of the HRA govern the relationship between these convention rights and acts of Parliament. Section 3(1) provides that: 'So far as it is possible to do so, primary legislation and subordinate legislation must be read and given effect in a way which is compatible with the Convention rights.' Section 4 provides that, if a court is satisfied that a provision of primary legislation is incompatible with a convention right, the court 'may make a declaration of that incompatibility'. Such a declaration 'does not affect the validity, continuing operation or enforcement of the provision in respect of which it is given' (section 4(6)(a)). Thus, courts in the UK do not have the power, even after the HRA, to strike down acts of Parliament that they deem to be incompatible with convention rights. All they may do is 'declare' the incompatibility. It is then a matter for Parliament to decide whether it wishes to continue with the legislation, to amend it or to replace it.

The difference between the consequences of an incompatibility of legislation with convention right or with provisions of EU law is clearly illustrated by *Benkharbouche* (above). Ms Benkharbouche argued that her employment contract with the Sudan Embassy breached the Working Time Directive – an EU law measure – as well as other aspects of UK law. However, she faced a problem bringing her case as the State Immunity Act 1978 was interpreted so as to prevent her bringing her claim to court. The Supreme Court concluded that this breached Ms Benkharbouche's right of access to the courts, found in Article 6 ECHR and Article 47 of the EU Charter of Fundamental Rights and Freedoms. Where the difference arose was as to the remedy: 'a conflict between EU law and English domestic law must be resolved in favour of the former, and the latter must be disapplied; whereas the remedy in the case of inconsistency with article 6 of the Human Rights Convention is a declaration of incompatibility' (Lord Sumption at [78]).

We will consider these matters in greater detail in Chapter 11. For now, what is important are the implications of these provisions for the sovereignty of Parliament. The key issue is: when should the courts use section 4 and when should they use section 3? Suppose that the courts are faced with a statutory provision that they consider to be incompatible with a convention right. Depending on the wording of the provision and on the nature of the incompatibility, it may be that the court has a choice. Either it could use its power under section 3 to interpret the provision so as to make it compatible with convention rights or it could declare the provision to be incompatible. The more the courts use section 4, the more the matter will remain one for Parliament. Conversely, by using section 3 to stretch or perhaps even to change the meaning of legislation, the more it will be the case that Parliament legislates subject to the interpretation imposed by the courts. In other words, an overuse of section 3 will lead to the HRA becoming a greater restriction on the sovereignty of Parliament. There is already a considerable body of case law (and attendant academic commentary) on this issue. Early tensions within the Appellate Committee of the House of Lords were revealed in *R v. A* [2002] 1 AC 45, where Lord Steyn considered that the only limit on the use of section 3 was where the provision in question expressly contradicted a convention right. Other members of the House of Lords hearing the appeal were not prepared to go so far, and Lord Steyn's position was criticised by Lord Nicholls in *Re S* [2002] 2 AC 291. In *R (Anderson)* v. *Secretary of State for the Home Department* [2003] 1 AC 837, Lord Steyn seems to have relented somewhat, as he stated that 'section 3(1) is not available where the suggested interpretation is contrary to express statutory words or is by implication necessarily contradicted by the statute'. In *Bellinger* v. *Bellinger* [2003] 2 AC 467, the House of Lords declined to interpret a provision of the Matrimonial Causes Act 1973 to include single-sex marriages when one of the parties had undergone a gender reassignment. Lord Nicholls stated that:

> the recognition of gender reassignment for the purposes of marriage is part of a wider problem which should be considered as a whole and not dealt with in piecemeal fashion. There should be a clear, coherent policy. The decision regarding recognition of gender reassignment for the purpose of marriage cannot sensibly be made in isolation from a decision on the like problem in other areas where a distinction is drawn between people on the basis of gender. These areas include education, child care, occupational qualifications, criminal law.

For these reasons, the issue should be one for Parliament, not for the courts, and the House of Lords granted a declaration of incompatibility under section 4. If *Re S*, *Anderson* and *Bellinger* seemed to indicate that the more robust approach proposed by Lord Steyn in *R* v. *A* was not to be preferred, the following case has once again cast doubt on the matter and has reopened the question of how far section 3 of the HRA may be used by the courts to force a rethinking of traditional understandings of the sovereignty of Parliament. (See, further, Bennion [2000] *PL* 77; Marshall [2003] *PL* 236; Kavanagh (2004) 24 *OJLS* 259 and [2004] *PL* 537.)

Ghaidan v. *Godin-Mendoza* [2004] UKHL 30, [2004] 2 AC 557

This case concerned a claim of discrimination, contrary to Articles 8 and 14 of the ECHR, in the application of the Rent Act. The background was as follows: on the death of a protected tenant of a dwelling house, his or her surviving spouse, if then living in the house, becomes a statutory tenant by succession. Marriage is not essential for this purpose. A person who was living with the original tenant 'as his or her wife or husband' is treated as the spouse of the original tenant (Rent Act 1977, Schedule 1, para 2(2), as amended by the Housing Act 1988). In *Fitzpatrick* v. *Sterling Housing Association* [2001] 1 AC 27 the House of Lords decided that this provision did not include people in a same-sex relationship. The question in *Ghaidan* v. *Godin-Mendoza* was whether this reading of the provision survived the coming into force of the HRA. The House of Lords ruled that it did not. The majority reinterpreted the provision under section 3 of the HRA. Lord Millett, by way of contrast, ruled that a declaration of incompatibility under section 4 should have been granted. It is instructive to compare the two approaches. Lord Nicholls was one of the judges in the majority.

Lord Nicholls: . . . One tenable interpretation of the word 'possible' would be that section 3 is confined to requiring courts to resolve ambiguities . . . This interpretation of section 3 would give the section a comparatively narrow scope. This is not the view which has prevailed . . . [T]he interpretative obligation decreed by section 3 is of an unusual and far-reaching character. Section 3 may require a court to depart from the unambiguous meaning the legislation would otherwise bear. In the ordinary course the interpretation of legislation involves seeking the intention reasonably to be attributed to Parliament in using the language in question. Section 3 may require the court to depart from this legislative intention, that is, depart from the intention of the Parliament which enacted the legislation. The question of difficulty is how far, and in what circumstances, section 3 requires a court to depart from the intention of the enacting Parliament. The answer to this question depends upon the intention reasonably to be attributed to Parliament in enacting section 3 . . .

[T]he intention of Parliament in enacting section 3 was that, to an extent bounded only by what is 'possible', a court can modify the meaning, and hence the effect, of primary and secondary legislation. Parliament, however, cannot have intended that in the discharge of this extended interpretative function the courts should adopt a meaning inconsistent with a fundamental feature of the legislation. That would be to cross the constitutional boundary section 3 seeks to demarcate and preserve. Parliament has retained the right to enact legislation in terms which are not Convention-compliant. The meaning imported by application of section 3 must be compatible with the underlying thrust of the legislation being construed. Words implied must . . . 'go with the grain of the legislation'. Nor can Parliament have intended that section 3 should require courts to make decisions for which they are not equipped. There may be several ways of making a provision Convention-compliant, and the choice may involve issues calling for legislative deliberation.

[His Lordship referred to *Bellinger* v. *Bellinger*, cited earlier, and continued:] No difficulty arises in the present case. Paragraph 2 of Schedule 1 to the Rent Act 1977 is unambiguous. But the social policy underlying the . . . extension of security and tenure under paragraph 2 to the survivor of couples living together as husband and wife is equally applicable to the survivor of homosexual couples living together in a close and stable relationship. In this circumstance I see no reason to doubt the application of section 3 to paragraph 2 has the effect that paragraph 2 should be read and given effect to as though the survivor of such a homosexual couple were the surviving spouse of the original tenant.

Lord Millett: . . . I agree with all my noble and learned friends . . . that [the] discriminatory treatment of homosexual couples is incompatible with their Convention rights and cannot be justified by any legitimate aim . . .

The question [of whether section 3 or section 4 should be used] is of great constitutional importance, for it goes to the relationship between the legislature and the judiciary, and hence ultimately to the supremacy of Parliament. Sections 3 and 4 of the Human Rights Act were carefully crafted to preserve the existing constitutional doctrine, and any application of the ambit of section 3 beyond its proper scope subverts it. This is not to say that the doctrine of parliamentary supremacy is sacrosanct, but only that any change in a fundamental constitutional principle should be the consequence of deliberate legislative action and not judicial activism, however well meaning.

[His Lordship proceeded to outline two sorts of case in which use of section 3 would be inappropriate.] In some cases (*Re S* and *Anderson* [cited above] are examples) it would have been necessary to repeal the statutory scheme and substitute another. This is obviously impossible without legislation, and cannot be achieved by resort to section 3. In other cases (*Bellinger* is an example) questions of social policy have arisen which ought properly to be left to Parliament and not decided by the judges.

[S]ection 3 requires the court to read legislation in a way which is compatible with the Convention only 'so far as it is possible to do so'. It must, therefore, be possible, *by a process of interpretation alone*, to read the offending statute in a way which is compatible with the Convention. This does not mean that it is necessary to identify an ambiguity or absurdity in the statute . . . before giving it an abnormal meaning in order to bring it into conformity . . . [The court] can read in and read down; it can supply missing words, so long as they are consistent with the fundamental features of the legislative scheme; it can do considerable violence to the language and stretch it almost (but not quite) to breaking point. The court must 'strive to find a *possible* interpretation compatible with Convention rights' (citing Lord Steyn in *R v A*). But it is not entitled to give it an impossible one, however much it would wish to do so. In my view section 3 does not entitle the court to supply missing words which are inconsistent with a fundamental feature of the legislative scheme; nor to repeal, delete, or contradict the language of the offending statute.

(See, further, Kavanagh, *Constitutional Review under the UK Human Rights Act* (2009).)

Further controversy about the relationship between sections 3 and 4 of the HRA arose in cases and parliamentary reports concerned with control orders. Control orders were coercive measures that the Secretary of State was empowered to impose on individuals under the Prevention of Terrorism Act 2005. They were replaced by TPIMs – terrorism prevention and investigation measures, in 2012 (see, further, Chapter 11). In two cases decided on the same day, the House of Lords ruled that the regime of control orders under the 2005 Act was lawful (as long as it was 'read down' with reference to section 3 of the HRA: see above), albeit that certain restrictions contained in particular control orders were excessive and therefore disproportionate (and unlawful): *Secretary of State for the Home Department* v. *JJ* [2007] UKHL 45, [2008] 1 AC 385 and *Secretary of State for the Home Department* v. *MB* [2007] UKHL 46, [2008] 1 AC 440. Parliament's Joint Committee on Human Rights (JCHR) later argued that their Lordships should have declared aspects of the regime to be incompatible with convention rights, thereby forcing Parliament to revisit the 2005 Act (the JCHR published a long series of reports that were deeply critical of control orders).

In *Secretary of State for the Home Department* v. *MB*, a majority of the House of Lords ruled that the question of whether legal proceedings in cases where a control order is challenged are fair is one that should be determined on a case-by-case basis in the light of section 3 of the HRA (that is to say, in the light of the rule that the relevant statutory framework must if possible be read and given effect in a way that makes it compatible with convention rights). The JCHR argued that their Lordships should instead have employed section 4 (JCHR, *Counter-Terrorism Bill*, 9th report of 2007–08, HL 50, HC 199, paras 46–7). This was for the following, constitutionally significant, reasons:

> we are surprised at the Lords' interpretation of the scope of their power under s 3 of the Human Rights Act to read words into a statute to avoid an incompatibility with a Convention right. In 2005, in the Prevention of Terrorism Act, Parliament grappled with how to strike the right balance between the right to a fair hearing and keeping sensitive information secret. It decided (against our advice) to strike that balance by placing a duty on courts in control order proceedings to receive and act on material even the gist of which is not disclosed to the controlled person. It used mandatory language to make that clear. To weaken Parliament's clear mandatory language by 'reading in' the words 'except where to do so would be incompatible with the right of the controlled person to a fair trial' does, as Lord Bingham observed, 'very clearly fly in the face of Parliament's intention' [*MB* at [44]]. The scheme of the Human Rights Act deliberately gives Parliament a central role in deciding how best to protect the rights protected in the ECHR . . . In our view it would have been more consistent with the scheme of the Human Rights Act for the House of Lords to have given a declaration of incompatibility, requiring Parliament to think again about the balance it struck in the control order legislation . . .

As we shall see in Chapter 11, the judgments in *JJ* and *MB* proved unsatisfactory (and even unworkable) in a number of respects, and both had to be revisited in subsequent litigation: see *Secretary of State for the Home Department* v. *AF* [2009] UKHL 28, [2010] 2 AC 269 and *Secretary of State for the Home Department* v. *AP* [2010] UKSC 24, [2010] 3 WLR 51. In *Secretary of State for the Home Department* v. *AF*, the House of Lords concluded, following the Grand Chamber decision of the European Court of Human Rights in *A* v. *United Kingdom*, that Article 6 ECHR would be breached if a party were denied knowledge of the essence of the case made against him. The House of Lords confirmed that legislation could be read down to achieve this objective, in a similar manner to *MB*: effectively creating an exception to what appeared to be a general prohibition. Both parties before the court agreed to using section 3 in this manner rather than issuing a declaration of incompatibility. This raises issues for the separation of powers as well as parliamentary sovereignty. Should the government be able to suggest convention-compatible interpretations of legislation to avoid the use of a section 4 declaration of incompatibility where Parliament would have potentially played a greater role in modifying legislation, or even deciding that no modification was required?

2.2.4.3 Challenge of Common Law Radicalism

The undoubted importance of the European Communities Act 1972 and the HRA notwithstanding, it may be that the most potent challenge to the continuing status of parliamentary sovereignty as the 'keystone' of the British constitution comes not from any legislation that Parliament has passed but from the common law. The past fifteen years or so have seen a remarkable renaissance in what might be called common law radicalism. There have been common law radicals in previous centuries. Sir Edward Coke (1552–1634), the most famous and the most innovative common lawyer of the early seventeenth century, Chief Justice under James I turned parliamentarian and leading author of the Petition of Right (1628), was one such who more than left his mark on constitutional law. Common law radicals believe that the entire constitution, including the doctrine of the sovereignty of Parliament, is based on the common law. The recent renaissance of common law radicalism has seen several judges and academic commentators arguing, for example, that the common law includes a 'higher-order law' to which even legislation is subject (Sir John Laws, 'Law and Democracy' [1995] *PL* 72).

So far has the argument developed that some discern an 'emerging constitutional paradigm, no longer of Dicey's supreme parliament to whose will the rule of law must finally bend, but of a bi-polar sovereignty of the Crown in Parliament and the Crown in its courts' (Sir Stephen Sedley [1995] *PL* 386, 389). In a series of remarkable dicta in the 1980s a New Zealand judge, Cooke J (who later became Lord Cooke of Thorndon), questioned whether the New Zealand Parliament (acknowledged as possessing a legal sovereignty comparable to that of the UK Parliament) could lawfully override certain fundamental common law rights. For instance, in *Taylor* v. *New Zealand Poultry Board* [1984] 1 NZLR 394, 398 he said: 'I do not think that literal compulsion [to answer questions from an official], by torture for instance, would be within the lawful powers of Parliament. Some common law rights presumably lie so deep that even Parliament could not override them.' Along similar lines, albeit extra-judicially, Lord Woolf has said (in '*Droit Public* – English Style' [1995] *PL* 57, 69) that if Parliament 'did the unthinkable' in depriving the High Court of its role in reviewing the legality of executive action:

> then I would say that the courts would also be required to act in a manner which would be without precedent. Some judges might choose to do so by saying that it was an unrebuttable presumption that Parliament could never intend such a result. I myself would consider there

> were advantages in making it clear that ultimately there are even limits on the supremacy of Parliament which it is the courts' inalienable responsibility to identify and uphold. They are limits of the most modest dimensions which I believe any democrat would accept. They are no more than are necessary to enable the rule of law to be preserved.

The current case law illustrates two main challenges to parliamentary sovereignty from the common law. The first is similar to the challenge posed by section 3 of the Human Rights Act 1998, where courts read legislation in a manner that appears to contradict the will of Parliament. The second stems from Lord Woolf's statement, where the courts suggest that there are limits to Parliament's law-making powers; there are legislative provisions that the courts would either fail to recognise, or would not enforce. *Robinson* v. *Secretary of State for Northern Ireland, Evans* v. *Attorney General* and *R (UNISON)* v. *Lord Chancellor* provide a stark illustration of how far courts may appear to 'bend' statutory wording to achieve an interpretation that preserves constitutional stability, or fundamental common law rights. *Jackson* v. *AG*, and its development of the 'exceptional circumstances' dicta, illustrates how far courts may go in refusing to recognise legislation. This is illustrated most starkly with regard to recent interpretations of ouster clauses – i.e. clauses in which the legislature appears to remove judicial review of the courts over decisions of inferior courts and tribunals.

As Laws LJ stated in *International Transport Roth* v. *Secretary of State for the Home Department* [2002] EWCA Civ 158, [2003] QB 728, [71]: 'In its present state of evolution, the British system may be said to stand at an intermediate stage between parliamentary supremacy and constitutional supremacy.' (See further on these ideas, Knight, 'Bi-polar Sovereignty Restated' [2009] *CLJ* 361 and 'Striking Down Legislation Under Bi-polar Sovereignty' [2011] *PL* 90; Lakin, 'Debunking the Idea of Parliamentary Sovereignty: The Controlling Factor of Legality in the British Constitution' (2008) 28 *OJLS* 709.)

The common law radicalism of which these statements are illustrative examples has not gone unchallenged: for criticism, see Griffith, 'The Brave New World of Sir John Laws' (2000) 63 *MLR* 159; Poole, 'Back to the Future? Unearthing the Theory of Common Law Constitutionalism' (2003) 23 *OJLS* 435; and Goldsworthy, *Parliamentary Sovereignty: Contemporary Debates* (2010), especially chs 2–4.

Robinson v. *Secretary of State for Northern Ireland* [2002] UKHL 32, [2002] NI 390
Robinson concerned a challenge to the legality of the election in November 2001 of David Trimble and Mark Durkan as First Minister (FM) and Deputy First Minister (DFM), respectively, of Northern Ireland. Section 16(1) of the Northern Ireland Act 1998 provides that: 'Each Assembly shall, within a period of six weeks beginning with its first meeting, elect from among its members the First Minister and the Deputy First

Minister.' Section 16(3) provided that: 'Two candidates standing jointly shall not be elected to the two offices without the support of a majority of the members voting in the election, a majority of the designated Nationalists voting and a majority of the designated Unionists voting' (this provision has subsequently been amended such that the candidates for FM and DFM are now merely nominated by their parties). Section 16 left open the question of what was to happen if the six-week period expired with no FM and DFM being elected. The nearest the act came to answering this question was in section 32(3), which provided that: 'If the period mentioned in section 16 ends without a First Minister and a Deputy First Minister having been elected, the Secretary of State *shall* propose a date for the poll for the election of the next Assembly' (emphasis added).

Since devolution to Northern Ireland under the 1998 Act commenced, it has been suspended and restored on numerous occasions. When it was restored on 23 September 2001, the offices of FM and DFM were vacant. The six-week period provided for by section 16(1) would therefore expire on 4 November 2001. On 2 November, the Assembly held an election to fill the offices but the candidates (Messrs Trimble and Durkan) did not receive the measure of cross-community support then required under section 16(3). After a number of previously non-designated members of the Assembly redesignated themselves as Unionists for the purpose of electing a FM and DFM, a further election was held on 6 November 2001, at which the candidates did obtain the support they needed.

Robinson, a leading member of the Democratic Unionist Party (DUP) and a member of the assembly, challenged the legality of this election. He argued that the assembly had no power to elect a FM and DFM after the expiry of the six-week period and that fresh elections to the assembly should have been called, in accordance with section 32(3). The assembly, according to this argument, is a creature of statute and has only such powers as are conferred on it by the 1998 Act. The Court of Appeal of Northern Ireland held, by a 2:1 majority, that the election was lawful. On appeal, the House of Lords agreed, albeit by a 3:2 majority. The contrast between the approaches of the judges in the majority and those in the minority is striking. Consider, for example, the following extracts from the opinions of Lords Bingham and Hoffmann (in the majority) and Lord Hutton (in the minority).

Lord Bingham: . . . The 1998 Act . . . was passed to implement the Belfast Agreement, which was itself reached, after much travail, in an attempt to end decades of bloodshed and centuries of antagonism. The solution was seen to lie in participation by the Unionist and Nationalist communities in shared political institutions . . . If these shared institutions were to deliver the benefits which their progenitors intended, they had to have time to operate and take root.

The 1998 Act does not set out all the constitutional provisions applicable to Northern Ireland, but it is in effect a constitution. So to categorise the Act is not to relieve the courts of their duty to interpret the constitutional provisions in issue. But the provisions should, consistently with the language used, be interpreted generously and purposively, bearing in mind the values which the constitutional provisions are intended to embody. [Counsel for Robinson] submitted that the resolution of political problems by resort to the vote of the people in a free election lies at the heart of any democracy and that this democratic principle is one embodied in this constitution. He is of course correct . . . But elections held with undue frequency are not necessarily productive. While elections may produce solutions they can also deepen divisions. Nor is the democratic ideal the only constitutional ideal which this constitution should be understood to embody. It is in general desirable that the government should be carried on, that there be no governmental vacuum.

Lord Hoffmann: . . . [Counsel for Robinson] politely but firmly reminded your Lordships that your function was to construe and apply the language of Parliament and not merely to choose what might appear on political grounds to be the most convenient solution. It is not for this House, in its judicial capacity, to say that new elections in Northern Ireland would be politically inexpedient . . . I unreservedly accept those principles. A judicial decision must rest on 'reasons that in their generality and their neutrality transcend any immediate result that is involved' [citing Wechsler, 'Towards Neutral Principles of Constitutional Law' (1959) 73 *Harvard LR* 1]. But I think that the construction which I favour satisfies those requirements. The long title of the [1998] Act is 'to make new provision for the government of Northern Ireland for the purpose of implementing the agreement reached at multi-party talks on Northern Ireland . . .'. According to established principles of interpretation, the Act must be construed against the background of the political situation in Northern Ireland and the principles laid down by the Belfast Agreement for a new start. These facts and documents form part of the admissible background for the construction of the Act just as much as the Revolution, the Convention and the Federalist Papers are the background to construing the Constitution of the United States.

Lord Hutton (dissenting): . . . My Lords, despite the attractiveness of the . . . argument based on the purpose of the Belfast Agreement, I have come to the conclusion that the appeal should succeed. The Northern Ireland Assembly is a body created by a Westminster statute and it has no powers other than those given to it by statute . . . In my opinion the wording of section 32(3) . . . makes it clear that Parliament intended that if there was not a successful election with in the six weeks' period, the Secretary of State would fix an early date for the poll . . . [T]he objective of the Belfast Agreement cannot operate to alter the meaning of the [statutory] words.

Had there been a further election to the assembly, it was likely that the DUP would have replaced Mr Trimble's UUP (the Ulster Unionists) as the largest unionist party. Likewise, it was felt that Sinn Fein would stand a good chance of replacing Mr Durkan's SDLP as the largest nationalist party. Coalition government was difficult enough with the UUP and SDLP as the largest parties. With the DUP and Sinn Fein as the largest parties, it was considered at the time to be all but unthinkable.

This is the political background to the dispute in *Robinson*. The question of constitutional law that the case raises is the extent to which the courts should take political background such as this into consideration when interpreting what Lord Bingham described as a constitutional statute. The majority of the House of Lords interpreted the legislation purposively, the purpose being to maintain devolved government in Northern Ireland. Why should this purpose have been privileged over other purposes embodied in the 1998 Act and in the Belfast Agreement that preceded it? Why, in particular, should it have been privileged over the value of electoral democracy? Is the fact that elections may sometimes 'deepen divisions', as Lord Bingham expressed it, a proper and relevant consideration for the court? Even if the purposive approach was appropriate in principle, what of Lord Hutton's objection that no matter how noble, no purpose should be permitted to displace the clear meaning of the statutory language in sections 16 and 32 of the Act? *Robinson* suggests that, when it comes to the interpretation of what the courts deem to be 'constitutional statutes' (whatever that may mean in our unwritten constitution), different rules may apply from those that govern the interpretation of ordinary (i.e., non-constitutional) legislation. Later case law has called this into question. Purposive interpretations that take constitutional background into account are not adopted for all constitutional statutes, or even for all of the provisions of the same constitutional statute. Rather, context determines the interpretation adopted by the court. (See, further, Morison and Lynch, 'Litigating the Agreement: Towards a New Judicial Constitutionalism for the UK from Northern Ireland?', in Morison, McEvoy and Anthony (eds.), *Judges, Transition and Human Rights* (2007), ch. 7. (For another case in which the notion of 'constitutional statutes' has been considered, albeit in a different context, see the decision of the Divisional Court in *Thoburn* v. *Sunderland City Council* [2003] QB 151, considered below, pp. 193–194.)

We mentioned the principle of legality earlier when assessing the extent to which European Human rights challenges parliamentary sovereignty. This principle has also been used to provide statutory interpretations that appear to contradict the will of Parliament.

Evans v. *Attorney General* [2015] UKSC 21, [2015] AC 1787

Evans concerned the so-called 'black spider memos' written by Prince Charles to a range of government departments. The *Guardian* newspaper had made a freedom of information request to obtain the memos, arguing that their disclosure was in the public interest. This request was initially refused by the information commissioner and the First Tier Tribunal, but an appeal to the Upper Tribunal was successful. However, despite its successful appeal, the *Guardian* newspaper was unsuccessful in its bid to obtain the memos. Section 53 of the Freedom of Information Act 2000 empowered an 'accountable person' to veto the decision to disclose information on 'reasonable grounds'. The Attorney General, who was the 'accountable person' for the purposes of

this information, issued a certificate vetoing the decision to disclose information. Evans, the journalist who had made the initial freedom of information
request, challenged this decision. A majority of the Supreme Court interpreted
the provisions of section 53 such that they did not empower the Attorney
General to issue a certificate vetoing the requirement to release information
merely because he disagreed with the certificate. The different approaches of
the judiciary illustrate divergent views as to the extent to which courts can
interpret legislation to uphold requirements of the rule of law before they cross
a line and undermine parliamentary sovereignty.

> **Lord Neuberger:** [52]. First, subject to being overruled by a higher court or (given
> Parliamentary supremacy) a statute, it is a basic principle that a decision of a court is
> binding between the parties, and cannot be ignored or set aside by anyone, including
> (indeed it may fairly be said, least of all) the executive. Secondly, it is also fundamental to
> the rule of law that decisions and actions of the executive are, subject to necessary well
> established exceptions (such as declarations of war), and jealously scrutinised statutory
> exceptions, reviewable by the court at the suit of an interested citizen. Section 53, as
> interpreted by the Attorney General's argument in this case, flouts the first principle and
> stands the second principle on its head. It involves saying that a final decision of a court can be
> set aside by a member of the executive (normally the minister in charge of the very
> department against whom the decision has been given) because he does not agree with it . . .

Lord Neuberger then referred to the principle of legality that 'unless there is the
clearest provision to the contrary, Parliament must be presumed not to legislate contrary to the rule of law' before concluding:

> [58]. Accordingly, if section 53 is to have the remarkable effect argued for by Mr Eadie QC for
> the Attorney General, it must be 'crystal clear' from the wording of the FOIA 2000, and
> cannot be justified merely by 'general or ambiguous words'. In my view, section 53 falls very
> far short of being 'crystal clear' in saying that a member of the executive can override the
> decision of a court because he disagrees with it . . .
>   [71]. If section 53 does not entitle an accountable person to issue a certificate simply on
> the ground that he disagrees with the determination of a court to uphold, or issue, a decision
> notice, then, given that it is agreed that section 53 can be invoked once a court has reached
> such a determination, the question arises: on what grounds can it be issued in such
> circumstances? The specific examples mentioned by the Court of Appeal in answer to this
> question may be found in para 38 of Lord Dyson MRs judgment, and they are 'a material
> change of circumstances since the tribunal decision, or that the decision of the tribunal was
> demonstrably flawed in fact or in law'.

Lord Mance and Lord Wilson disagreed with Lord Neuberger's interpretation,
believing that Parliament had intended the provisions of section 53 to apply in

a wider range of circumstances than those set out by Lord Neuberger. However, they disagreed both as to the meaning that should be ascribed to section 53 and as to the approach to the interpretation of legislation more generally. While Lord Mance agreed that the Attorney General could not issue a certificate merely because he disagreed, he focused on how judicial review meant that the courts would check whether the Attorney General had issued a certificate that was within the proper bounds of his power.

Lord Mance [129]. On any view, the Attorney General must under the express language of section 53(2) be able to assert that he has reasonable grounds for considering that disclosure was not due under the provisions of the FOIA. That is, I consider, a higher hurdle than mere rationality would be. Under section 53(6) he must also express his reasons for this opinion, unless, under section 53(7) this would involve disclosure of exempt information. On judicial review, the reasonable grounds on which the Attorney General relies must be capable of scrutiny . . .

[130]. . . . It would, in my view, require the clearest possible justification, which I might accept only be possible to show in the sort of unusual situation in which Lord Neuberger PSC contemplates that a certificate may validly be given. This is particularly so, when the Upper Tribunal heard evidence, called and cross-examined in public, as well as submissions on both sides. In contrast, the Attorney General, with all due respect to his public role, did not. He consulted in private, took into account the views of the Cabinet, former ministers and the Information Commissioner and formed his own view without inter partes representations. But disagreement about the relative weight to be attributed to competing interests found by the tribunal is a different matter, and I would agree with Lord Wilson JSC that the weighing of such interests is a matter which the statute contemplates and which a certificate could properly address, by properly explained and solid reasons.

Lord Wilson, who dissented, was scathing in his assessment of the judgment of the Court of Appeal, which had also determined that the certificate issued by the Attorney General was unlawful, as well as of the interpretation of section 53 found in the judgment of Lord Neuberger.

Lord Wilson [168]. I would have allowed the appeal. How tempting it must have been for the Court of Appeal (indeed how tempting it has proved even for the majority in this court) to seek to maintain the supremacy of the astonishingly detailed, and inevitably unappealed, decision of the Upper Tribunal in favour of disclosure of the Prince's correspondence! But the Court of Appeal ought (as, with respect, ought this court) to have resisted the temptation. For, in reaching its decision, the Court of Appeal did not in my view interpret section 53 FOIA. It re-wrote it. It invoked precious constitutional principles but among the most precious is that of parliamentary sovereignty, emblematic of our democracy . . .

After considering the conclusion of Lord Neuberger, and the Court of Appeal, that 'reasonable grounds' for issuing a certificate could only occur when the decision of Information Commissioner had made an error of law, or where there was a material change of circumstances, Lord Wilson dismissed this approach as

[177]. . . . far-fetched and thus serving only to illuminate the deficiency of the Court of Appeal's analysis of section 53. Its effect is that, for all practical purposes, no certificate can be given under section 53 by way of override of a decision notice upheld or substituted by the Upper Tribunal or, probably, by the First-tier Tribunal. In other words, namely in those of Ms Rose, it will 'almost never' be reasonable for an accountable person to disagree with the decision of a court in favour of disclosure. The trouble is that, as is agreed, Parliament made clear, by subsection (4)(b), that such a certificate could be given in such circumstances.

R (UNISON) v. Lord Chancellor [2017] UKSC 51, [2017] 3 WLR 409

UNISON concerned the setting of fees for employment tribunals and employment appeal tribunals by the Lord Chancellor. Section 42(1) of the Tribunals, Courts and Enforcement Act 2007 provided that the Lord Chancellor may by order set the fees to be payable in tribunals, including employment tribunals. The Lord Chancellor used this power to set fees that *UNISON*, a trade union, believed were too high. There was the opportunity to have fees remitted. However, the guidelines on the remission of fees required those obtaining a remission to be earning less than the current minimal wage. *UNISON* argued that this effectively meant that many did not have a means of access to the courts. The Supreme Court agreed. It read down the broad statutory provisions such that they did not empower the Lord Chancellor to act in a manner that would undermine the rule of law. By setting tribunal fees at a rate that made it practically impossible for many to come to court, the Lord Chancellor had acted beyond the scope of his powers. Lord Reed gave the judgement of the court.

[65]. In determining the extent of the power conferred on the Lord Chancellor by section 42(1) of the 2007 Act, the court must consider not only the text of that provision, but also the constitutional principles which underlie the text, and the principles of statutory interpretation which give effect to those principles. In that regard, there are two principles which are of particular importance in this case. One is the constitutional right of access to justice: that is to say, access to the courts (and tribunals: *R v Secretary of State for the Home Department, ex p Saleem* [2001] 1 WLR 443). The other is the rule that "specific statutory rights are not to be cut down by subordinate legislation passed under the vires of a different Act" (*R v Secretary of State for Social Security, ex p Joint Council for the Welfare of Immigrants* [1997] 1 WLR 275, 290 per Simon Brown LJ) . . .

[86]. The 2007 Act does not state the purposes for which the power conferred by section 42(1) to prescribe fees may be exercised. There is however no dispute that the purposes which underlay the making of the Fees Order are legitimate. Fees paid by litigants can, in principle, reasonably be considered to be a justifiable way of making resources available for the justice system and so securing access to justice. Measures that deter the bringing of frivolous and vexatious cases can also increase the efficiency of the justice system and overall access to justice.

[87]. The Lord Chancellor cannot, however, lawfully impose whatever fees he chooses in order to achieve those purposes. It follows from the authorities cited that the Fees Order will be ultra vires if there is a real risk that persons will effectively be prevented from having access to justice. That will be so because section 42 of the 2007 Act contains no words authorising the prevention of access to the relevant tribunals. That is indeed accepted by the Lord Chancellor.

[88]. But a situation in which some persons are effectively prevented from having access to justice is not the only situation in which the Fees Order might be regarded as ultra vires. As appears from such cases as *Leech* and *Daly,* even where primary legislation authorises the imposition of an intrusion on the right of access to justice, it is presumed to be subject to an implied limitation. As it was put by Lord Bingham in *Daly,* the degree of intrusion must not be greater than is justified by the objectives which the measure is intended to serve.

In one sense, *UNISON* appears to be a standard application of the principle of legality. A broad power was read down in a manner that upheld the rule of law by preserving access to courts and tribunals. Moreover, the court did not completely remove the power of the Lord Chancellor, who was still able to set court fees provided that these did not render access to tribunals impossible, or place too great a restriction on access to tribunals. Contrariwise, it illustrates how court decisions indirectly impinge on policy choices. While measures of austerity may be made to other services, the courts will ensure that access to justice is preserved. Some criticise the judgment for effectively making a policy choice. However, such policy choices are, in some sense, inevitable. A determination of the bounds of discretionary powers will inevitably restrict some policy choices and it would be open to the legislature to specifically empower the Lord Chancellor to set tribunal fees in a manner that imposed a disproportionate restriction on access to justice. A stronger challenge to parliamentary sovereignty is found in cases that suggest that, in exceptional circumstances, the courts may refuse to enforce or recognise legislation.

Jackson v. *Attorney General* [2005] UKHL 56, [2006] 1 AC 262
The second case to reveal something of the challenge that is posed for parliamentary sovereignty by common law radicalism is *Jackson*, the facts of which were set out above (pp. 69–70). The comments made in *Jackson* about the sovereignty of Parliament were obiter and, moreover, they were uttered in the context of litigation concerning statutes passed without the consent of

the House of Lords. It may be, for that reason, that they prove to be of little precedential value. That said, however, their Lordships' opinions do not expressly state that their comments about parliamentary sovereignty should apply only in the context of legislation passed under the Parliament Act procedure (see Plaxton (2006) 69 *MLR* 249, 259). Moreover, as will be seen, these dicta have been repeated in later cases and have been added to by a further distinct dictum in relation to ouster clauses.

In *Jackson*, as in *Robinson*, one of the matters considered was the category of 'constitutional statutes'. The Court of Appeal in *Jackson* ruled that, while neither the Parliament Act 1949 nor the Hunting Act 2004 was invalid, the Parliament Act procedure would not be available to pass *any* bill into law. A bill, for example, to abolish the House of Lords would be a change so fundamental to the constitution that it could be enacted only in the usual way (i.e., with the assent of the Commons, Lords and Crown) and could not be lawfully enacted under the Parliament Act procedure (see [2005] EWCA Civ 126, [2005] QB 579). This view was comprehensively rejected by the panel of nine Law Lords who heard the appeal in the House of Lords. Lord Carswell did say that: 'Despite the general lack of enthusiasm for the proposition espoused by the Court of Appeal, . . . I incline very tentatively to the view that its instinct may be right [and] . . . I wish to reserve my opinion on it', but his judicial colleagues in the House of Lords distanced themselves from the Court of Appeal's view, not least because when it was passed in 1911 both houses knew well that the Parliament Act was more than likely to be used to enact measures of considerable constitutional importance: that is, the Government of Ireland Act 1914 and the Welsh Church Act 1914.

Among the most interesting obiter comments in *Jackson* are the following from Lords Bingham, Steyn and Hope.

Lord Bingham of Cornhill: . . . The bedrock of the British constitution is, and in 1911 was, the supremacy of the Crown in Parliament . . . Then, as now, the Crown in Parliament was unconstrained by any entrenched or codified constitution. It could make or unmake any law it wished. Statutes, formally enacted as Acts of Parliament, properly interpreted, enjoyed the highest legal authority.

Lord Steyn: . . . We do not in the United Kingdom have an uncontrolled constitution . . . In the European context the second *Factortame* decision made that clear: [1991] 1 AC 603. The settlement contained in the Scotland Act 1998 also points to a divided sovereignty. Moreover, the European Convention on Human Rights as incorporated into our law by the Human Rights Act 1998 created a new legal order . . . The classic account given by Dicey of the doctrine of the supremacy of Parliament, pure and absolute as it was, can now be seen to be out of place in the modern United Kingdom. Nevertheless, the supremacy of Parliament is still the general principle of our constitution. The judges created this principle. If that is so, it is not unthinkable that circumstances could arise where the courts may have to qualify a principle established on a different hypothesis of constitutionalism. In exceptional circumstances involving an attempt to abolish judicial review or the ordinary role of the courts, the Appellate Committee of the House of Lords or a new Supreme Court may have to consider whether this is a constitutional fundamental which even a sovereign Parliament acting at the behest of a complaisant House of Commons cannot abolish. It is not necessary to explore the ramifications of this question in this opinion. No such issues arise on the present appeal.

Lord Hope of Craighead: ... Our constitution is dominated by the sovereignty of Parliament. But parliamentary sovereignty is no longer, if it ever was, absolute ... Step by step, gradually but surely, the English principle of the absolute sovereignty of Parliament which Dicey derived from Coke and Blackstone is being qualified ... The rule of law enforced by the courts is the ultimate controlling factor on which our constitution is based ...

Each of the two main parties has made use of the 1949 Act's timetable, and in subsequent legislation passed by both Houses each of these Acts has been dealt with in a way that has acknowledged its validity ... The political reality is that of a general acceptance by all the main parties and by both Houses of the amended timetable which the 1949 Act introduced. I do not think that it is open to a court of law to ignore that reality ...

Trust will be eroded if the [Parliament Act] procedure is used to enact measures which are, as Lord Steyn puts it, exorbitant or are not proportionate. Nevertheless, the final exercise of judgment on these matters must be left to the House of Commons as the elected chamber.

Several comments may be made about these various statements. First, as the contrast of approaches between Lord Bingham, on the one hand, and Lords Steyn and Hope, on the other, shows, their Lordships were not unanimous in terms of their thoughts about sovereignty. For Lord Bingham, outwith contexts in which the EU was relevant (and it was not relevant here) there was no difference between the doctrine of sovereignty as it stood in 1911 and the doctrine of sovereignty now. For Lords Steyn and Hope, by contrast, even if the sovereignty of Parliament persists as a 'general' doctrine, it does so in a way that is heavily qualified both by statute and by the common law. For Lord Steyn, moreover, Dicey's account, while apparently accepted by Lord Bingham, is 'out of place in the modern United Kingdom'.

Second, is there not something curious about the construction of Lord Steyn's argument? At the beginning of the passage from his opinion he cites three respects in which, in his view, the sovereignty of Parliament is now limited. These are: the UK's membership of the EU, the devolution 'settlement' of 1998 and the incorporation by the HRA of fundamental rights into domestic law. Each of these, it is to be observed, came about as a result of legislation. Yet from this starting point his Lordship goes on to state that the sovereignty of Parliament is a 'construct of the common law', 'created' by judges and alterable by them. Even if this is correct (on which more below) does the conclusion follow from the evidence his Lordship cites? The changes he outlines were made through legislation by Parliament, not through common law adjudication by judges.

Third, two of Lord Steyn's descriptions are worth noting. First, he describes the devolution legislation of 1998 as pointing to 'a divided sovereignty'. It is not at all clear what this means. The Scottish Parliament, created by the Scotland Act 1998, which his Lordship cites, is anything but a sovereign legislature, as the Scotland Act makes abundantly plain. Moreover, the existence of the Scottish Parliament has done nothing to limit the legal power of the Westminster Parliament to legislate for Scotland, even on ostensibly devolved matters (see the Scotland Act 1998, section 28(7)). The political reality may be, for the time being, that the Westminster Parliament will not legislate for Scotland on devolved matters without the consent of the Scottish Parliament, but this behaviour results from a political agreement that is not legally enforceable and has nothing to do with the legal principles that Lord Steyn is concerned with in this passage. Moreover, the European Union (Withdrawal) Act 2018 was enacted in spite of Scotland's refusing to agree to its provisions under a legislative consent motion. The European Union (Withdrawal Agreement) Act 2020 became law despite all three devolved legislatures refusing to grant legislative consent motions, although it is arguable that no legislative consent motion was required under the terms of the Sewel Convention. Second, he describes the HRA as having created a 'new legal order'. This is obvious mimicry of the ECJ, which in 1963 famously described the EU as having created a 'new legal order of international law', a new legal order that dealt with matters of national sovereignty, for example, differently from the way in which they were understood in ordinary international law. Again, however, is his Lordship's terminology not somewhat tendentious? Lord Steyn may wish that the HRA had created a new legal order of judicial supremacy, but is the reality not that it was expressly intended to do no such thing? As we saw above, the act seeks to *balance* convention rights with parliamentary sovereignty and to ensure that the sovereignty of Parliament is *preserved* in the scheme of the act (see Ewing, 'The Human Rights Act and Parliamentary Democracy' (1999) 62 *MLR* 79). It should be noted that Lord Steyn's dicta in *Jackson* were subsequently described as 'unargued and unsound', 'historically false' and 'jurisprudentially absurd' (Ekins, 'Acts of Parliament and the Parliament Acts' (2007) 123 *LQR* 91, 103) and, moreover, that Lord Bingham seemed to ally himself with these criticisms. In *The Rule of Law* (2010, p. 167), Lord Bingham wrote of Lord Steyn's comments that: 'No authority was cited to support them, and no detailed reasons were given.'

Third, there is some difficulty in reconciling all of the statements that Lord Hope makes. He starts with the (some would say) sweeping proposition that the rule of law is the 'ultimate controlling factor on which our constitution is based'. This sounds very much like the common law radicalism of Lord Steyn and others, as outlined above. But Lord Hope goes on to make two further comments, which seem significantly to dent the extent to which he can really believe what he says about the rule of law. First, he offers as a reason for the court holding that the Parliament Act 1949 is valid that each of the two main parties have made use of the act, that both houses have treated legislation made under the act as valid, that the political reality is of a 'general acceptance' of the act's procedures and, moreover, that 'it is not open to a court of law to ignore that reality'. Second, and similarly, he states that the 'final exercise of judgment' as to when the Parliament Act procedures may be used should be left to the House of Commons 'as the elected chamber', not to a court of law. Now, if the constitution really were based on the rule of law as its 'ultimate controlling factor', neither of these would be the case. Neither the 'political reality' nor the judgment of the House of Commons would stand in the way of the court stating that the rule of law had been violated. The rule of law would trump both. As it is, Lord Hope holds that the rule of law has to be conditioned by – has to give way, even? – to political reality and to the Commons' democratic superiority. Given this, how can the rule of law be the ultimate controlling factor on which the constitution is based?

Finally, and related to the previous point, what is perhaps most important about Lord Hope's opinion is the reliance he places on political fact. This brings us back to what Sir William Wade wrote about the sovereignty of Parliament half a century before *Jackson* was decided (see above, pp. 79–80). What is the source of the authority for the proposition that acts of Parliament enjoy legal supremacy in the British constitution? Lord Steyn and the common law radicals would say that it is a rule of the common law, which, like any other rule of the common law, was created and may be altered by the courts. Wade and Lord Hope, however, take the view that its source lies in political fact – or, more precisely, in judicial recognition of political fact. As Wade argued, it was the political fact of Parliament's seventeenth-century victories over the Crown that the courts took into account when articulating the orthodoxy of parliamentary sovereignty. Similarly, the political facts of the UK's membership of the EU and of its incorporation into domestic law of convention rights may be recognised by the courts as conditioning the constitutional environment in which the doctrine of sovereignty now operates. This, it is submitted, is the better view. Just as the sovereignty of Parliament is a doctrine that Parliament, acting alone, would struggle to change, so too is it a legal doctrine that the courts, acting alone, should not imagine they could change. As Lord Hope correctly states in *Jackson*, the doctrine of the sovereignty of Parliament results from 'a delicate balance between the various institutions ... maintained to a large degree by the mutual respect which each institution has for the other'. Lord Hope cited with approval what Lord Reid had stated in *Pickin*: namely, that 'for a century or more both Parliament and the courts have been careful to act so as not to cause conflict between them.' As Lord Hope added, 'this is as much a prescription for the future as it was for the past'. And it is a reminder as much to the common law radicals as it is to Parliament that the doctrine of the sovereignty of Parliament is not to be abused.

Lord Bingham, in *The Rule of Law* (2010), stated (at p. 167) that: '[I]t has been convincingly shown that the principle of parliamentary sovereignty has been recognised as fundamental in this country not because the judges invented it but because it has for centuries been accepted as such by judges and others officially concerned in the operation of our constitutional system. The judges did not by themselves establish the principle and they cannot, by themselves, change it.'

Nevertheless, the dicta concerning both the ability of the courts to refuse to recognise or enforce legislation in exceptional circumstances have been repeated in later cases. In *AXA General Insurance* v. *Lord Advocate* [2011] UKSC 46, [2012] 1 AC 868, Lord Hope repeated his assertion that 'the rule of law enforced by the courts is the ultimate controlling factor on which our constitution is based' (at para [51]). He went on to assert that:

> It is not entirely unthinkable that a government which has that power may seek to use it to abolish judicial review or to diminish the rule of the courts in protecting the interests of the individual . . . The rule of law requires that the judges must retain the power to insist that legislation of that extreme kind is not law which the courts will recognise.

Neither is it the case that dicta of the court are restricted to examples of the removal of judicial review or the role of the courts. In *Moohan* v. *Lord Advocate* [2014] UKSC 67, [2015] AC 901, Lord Hodge asserted (at para [67]) that he did:

> not exclude the possibility that in the very unlikely event that a parliamentary majority abusively sought to entrench its power by a curtailment of the franchise or similar device, the common law, informed by principles of democracy and the rule of law and international norms, would be able to declare such legislation unlawful.

Not only does Lord Hodge expand the possible exceptional circumstances – to include the removal of the right to vote – but also he appears to suggest that the courts could go beyond merely not recognising legislation. Could they also declare legislation unlawful, in a manner similar to section 4 declarations of incompatibility?

A further potential restriction on parliamentary sovereignty can be found in the courts' treatment of ouster clauses. The courts have been particularly protective of ensuring their ability to review decisions of inferior courts and tribunals, regarding this as an aspect of the rule of law. In 2003–4, the government proposed to remove judicial review over almost all asylum decisions in its Asylum and Immigration (Treatment of Claimants etc.) Bill. This was greeted with uproar. Lord Woolf CJ stated in a widely publicised lecture that the provision 'was fundamentally in conflict with the rule of law' and that 'if this clause were to become law, it would be so inconsistent with the spirit of mutual respect between the different arms of government that it could be the catalyst for a campaign for a written constitution', a written constitution, his Lordship implied, that would not include the doctrine of parliamentary sovereignty among its provisions (see Lord Woolf, 'The Rule of Law and a Change in the Constitution' [2004] *CLJ* 317, 328–9). Two former Lord Chancellors, including Lord Irvine of Lairg (who had, until 2003, been a member of the government that was now proposing the measure) made it clear that they would denounce it in the House of Lords. In the event, the government dropped the clause before the measure could be debated in the Lords. The Act as passed does not include it, although it does contain a range of measures designed to make it more difficult to gain the assistance of the courts in seeking asylum in the UK (for a valuable and thorough commentary, see Rawlings, 'Review, Revenge and Retreat' (2005) 68 MLR 378).

In spite of this show of force, ouster clauses continue to be included in legislation. The most recent Supreme Court decision on these clauses contained a dictum that suggested a further limitation on parliamentary sovereignty.

R (Privacy International) v. *Investigatory Powers Tribunal* [2019] UKSC 22, [2019] 2 WLR 1219

The Investigatory Powers Tribunal investigates complaints raised against the use of the security services of their powers to hack computers and tap phones. The legislation establishing the powers of the tribunal included an ouster clause, ousting determinations of the tribunal from review of the court, including determinations as to whether the tribunal had jurisdiction to act. Lord Carnwath, with whom Lord Kerr and Lady Hale agreed, stated in dictum (at para [144]) that there was a

> strong case for holding that, consistently with the rule of law, binding effect cannot be given to a clause which purports wholly to exclude the supervisory jurisdiction of the High Court to review a decision of an inferior court or tribunal, whether for excess or abuse of jurisdiction, or error of law.

Lord Lloyd-Jones agreed with the conclusion of Lord Carnwath, Lord Kerr and Lady Hale that the specific ouster clause did not remove the jurisdiction of the court to control decisions of the IPT as concerns legal errors made by the IPT when determining its own jurisdiction – the ouster clause only removing the judicial review over jurisdictional errors of fact. However, he did so for different reasons and did not express a view on when it would be possible for legislatures more generally to oust judicial review. Lord Sumption, Lord Kerr and Lord Wilson all dissented. However, Lord Wilson also appeared to express sympathy with Lord Carnwath's dictum, provided this was limited to the possibility of Parliament removing judicial review for jurisdictional error of decisions of inferior courts and tribunals with limited jurisdiction (at [236]).

This purports to place a further restriction on parliamentary sovereignty. Lord Carnwath separates this restriction from the 'exceptional circumstances' dicta found in *Jackson, AXA General Insurance* and *Moohan*. The dictum was not applied in *Privacy International*, with the majority of the Supreme Court reading down the broad ouster clause so as not to apply to the specific decision of the Investigatory Powers Tribunal at issue in the case. (This case is discussed further in Chapter 10.)

2.2.5 Conclusions

For the time being, and the various challenges to it outlined in the previous section notwithstanding, parliamentary sovereignty remains formally intact as a matter of law. That said, however, the practical realism of the doctrine may be questioned. In the first place, as Professor Lauterpacht observes, 'the reality of that sovereignty [of the Crown in Parliament] ends where Britain's international obligations begin' ((1997) 73 *International Affairs* 137, 149). Again, who can doubt that Parliament has in reality relinquished its power to legislate for Canada and other independent Commonwealth states, Sir Robert Megarry's ruling in the *Manuel* case (above) that sovereignty over such territories continues notwithstanding?

Another kind of constraint on the exercise of sovereignty arises from the phenomenon of 'globalisation' – the growth of a global economy dominated by transnational corporations and characterised by a free movement of capital, advanced technology and communications, regulation by international agreements and agencies, and a diminished exposure to national controls. These developments place limits on national economic policy-making and to this extent reduce the scope for the effective exercise of parliamentary sovereignty. (See Himsworth, 'In a State no Longer: The End of Constitutionalism?' [1996] *PL* 639; see, further, Chapter 1.)

Further, Parliament is limited in its legislative activity by its (or rather by the government's) awareness of what is politically unfeasible or likely to provoke an adverse public reaction. This restraint has been most marked following the outcome of the Brexit referendum. A more 'constitutional' form of constraint consists in Parliament's recognition of *conventions* as to the use of its legislative power. These may be quite specific, for instance, that Parliament should not legislate for the domestic affairs of the Channel Islands or the Isle of Man without their consent (the islands having their own legislative authorities). Similar conventions have emerged as to Parliament's respect for the autonomy of the elected institutions in Scotland, Wales and Northern Ireland to which legislative powers have been transferred under the devolution settlements of 1998. Broader and less precise conventions constrain Parliament from enacting oppressive laws, such as violate fundamental rights or unjustly discriminate between citizens. (The significance of conventions for sovereignty theory is explored by Elliott, 'Parliamentary Sovereignty and the New Constitutional Order' (2002) 22 *LS* 340.)

Even if parliamentary sovereignty must be qualified in these ways, it continues to embody a considerable and wide-ranging power – within its acknowledged sphere of application it is still a power not misdescribed as supreme. It provides a party elected into office by the people with the fullest legal capacity to put its policies into effect, and in this respect serves the claims of democracy. Governments have been able to call on the sovereign power of Parliament in attacking the great issues of poverty and inequality and in establishing a welfare state, just as, in more recent years, thoroughgoing policies concerning trade unions, local government, devolution and the privatisation of public sector undertakings were put into effect by means of the same sovereign authority. (See Ewing, 'Human Rights, Social Democracy and Constitutional Reform', in Gearty and Tomkins (eds.), *Understanding Human Rights* (1996), ch. 3.)

However serviceable for realising the goals of elected governments, must a legally unlimited power be regarded as something alien to the idea of constitutionalism, creating a constant danger of arbitrary rule? It is 'Parliament's sovereign power', said Lord Scarman, 'more often than not exercised at the will of an executive sustained by an impregnable majority, that has brought about the modern imbalance in the legal system' (*English Law – The New Dimension* (1974), p. 74). Or is constitutional balance preserved by constraints on Parliament such as those we have noted above as well as by countervailing features of the democratic system: elections, opposition parties in Parliament and organised groups in civil society?

Jeffrey Goldsworthy, *The Sovereignty of Parliament: History and Philosophy* (1999)
What is at stake is the location of ultimate decision-making authority – the right to the 'final word' – in a legal system. If the judges were to repudiate the doctrine of parliamentary sovereignty, by refusing to allow Parliament to infringe unwritten rights, they would be claiming that ultimate authority for themselves. In settling disagreements about what fundamental rights people have, and whether particular legislation is consistent with them, the judges' word rather than Parliament's would be final. Since virtually all significant moral and political controversies in contemporary Western societies involve disagreements about rights, this would amount to a massive transfer of political power from parliaments to judges. Moreover, it would be a transfer of power initiated by the judges, to protect rights chosen by them, rather than one brought about democratically by parliamentary enactment or popular referendum.

2.3 The Rule of Law

The idea of the rule of law is rooted in the history of European political thought and constitutionalism, although with us it was first given a clear definition in

Dicey's *The Law of the Constitution* in 1885. Indeed, Dicey's argument in this book was that the *law* of the constitution contained two fundamental doctrines: the sovereignty of Parliament and the rule of law. (Dicey recognised, of course, that there was considerably more to the constitution than law alone, but he focused, in this book, on its legal elements.) The sovereignty of Parliament concerns the relationship of Parliament to the law; the rule of law concerns that of the government to the law.

Edward McWhinney rightly sees the English version of the concept as a 'historically received notion' and says that it is, in essence, 'a distillation of English common law legal history from the great constitutional battles of the seventeenth century onwards' (*Constitution-making: Principles, Process, Practice* (1981), p. 10; see, further, Jaffe and Henderson, 'Judicial Review and the Rule of Law: Historical Origins' (1956) 72 *LQR* 345). The rule of law is both a legal rule and a political ideal or principle of governance comprising values that should be reflected in the legal system and respected by those concerned in the making, development, interpretation and enforcement of the law. Through the courts' acknowledgment of the demands of the rule of law, it has acquired the status of an 'overarching principle of constitutional law' (Lord Steyn, 'Democracy Through Law' [2002] *EHRLR* 723, 727).

The ideal of the rule of law has been formulated in many ways, both broad and narrow, and there is much disagreement as to the values or principles that it embraces. The argument has often focused on Dicey's classic exposition of the rule of law, and in particular on the first two meanings he gives to this expression.

Dicey, *The Law of the Constitution* (1885), pp. 202–3

[The rule of law] means, in the first place, the absolute supremacy or predominance of regular law as opposed to the influence of arbitrary power, and excludes the existence of arbitrariness, of prerogative, or even of wide discretionary authority on the part of the government. Englishmen are ruled by the law, and by the law alone; a man may with us be punished for a breach of law, but he can be punished for nothing else.

It means, again, equality before the law, or the equal subjection of all classes to the ordinary law of the land administered by the ordinary law courts; the 'rule of law' in this sense excludes the idea of any exemption of officials or others from the duty of obedience to the law which governs other citizens or from the jurisdiction of the ordinary tribunals.

The rule of law is formally recognised in statute, section 1 of the Constitutional Reform Act 2005 somewhat cryptically providing that: 'This Act does not adversely affect . . . the existing constitutional principle of the rule of law' (see further on the Constitutional Reform Act below, pp. 160–163). It was the enactment of this provision, perhaps, that inspired Lord Bingham to consider the meaning of the rule of law, first in a public lecture delivered in

Cambridge (and published at [2007] *CLJ* 67) and subsequently in his book, *The Rule of Law* (2010). In *Privacy International* (discussed earlier) Lord Carnwath (at para [121]) refers to both Lord Bingham's account of the rule of law and the 2005 Act, asserting that 'Parliament having recognised this "existing constitutional principle", and providing no definition, there is nothing controversial in the proposition that it is for the courts, and ultimately the Supreme Court (created by the same Act), to determine its content and limits'. Lord Bingham divided the rule of law into eight sub-rules, as follows (page references are to the *CLJ* article):

The law must be accessible and, so far as possible, intelligible, clear and predictable. [Among other matters, Lord Bingham noted that this sub-rule precludes 'excessive innovation and adventurism by the judges' (71).]

Questions of legal right and liability should ordinarily be resolved by application of the law and not the exercise of discretion.

The laws of the land should apply equally to all, save to the extent that objective differences justify differentiation.

The law must afford adequate protection of fundamental human rights. [On this sub-rule, Lord Bingham noted that 'a state which savagely repressed or persecuted sections of its people could not . . . be regarded as observing the rule of law' but that, in his view, the rule of law does not address the 'full range of freedoms protected by bills of rights'. He conceded that there is 'an element of vagueness about the content of this sub-rule, since the outer edges of fundamental human rights are not clear-cut' (76–7).]

Means must be provided for resolving, without prohibitive cost or inordinate delay, bona fide civil disputes which the parties themselves are unable to resolve. ['The rule of law', he added, 'plainly requires that legal redress should be an affordable commodity' (78).]

Ministers and public officials at all levels must exercise the powers conferred on them reasonably, in good faith, for the purpose for which the powers were conferred and without exceeding the limits of such powers.

Adjudicative procedures provided by the state should be fair.

The existing principle of the rule of law requires compliance by the state with its obligations in international law.

In the pages that follow, we shall explore the extent to which these 'sub-rules' are reflected in our law.

In the following section, we consider, first, what is probably the most basic sense of the rule of law: namely, the notion that government must act in accordance with, and not beyond, its legal powers. As we shall see, even this aspect of the rule of law has not escaped controversy in the British context. In the second section, we then consider the claim of the rule of law that government should not be treated differently in law from the ways in which ordinary persons are treated. We shall see, again, that, in the UK (as, in fact, in most other countries), the government is able to benefit from a number of legal immunities and privileges, which distinguish its legal position from that of others, albeit that important House of Lords' case law has in recent years attempted to limit the range of these immunities. In the third section, we consider something of the problem that executive and administrative discretion poses for the rule of law. In the final sections, we outline a number of wider conceptions of the rule of law, conceptions that British constitutional law has not yet embraced, at least, not in full.

2.3.1 Government Under Law

The minimum element in the rule of law is that the government is subject to the law and may exercise its power only in accordance with law. A government that claimed to be above the law and to be subject to no legal restraint in issuing commands to give effect to its view of the public (or its own) interest would undoubtedly be a government that did not acknowledge the rule of law. In England, it was established long ago in the following case that the use of public power must be justified by law and not by the claims of state necessity.

Entick v. *Carrington* (1765) 19 St Tr 1029 (Court of Common Pleas)

The King's messengers, armed with a warrant of the Secretary of State to arrest the plaintiff (claimant), John Entick, alleged to be the author of seditious writings, and to seize his books and papers, broke into and entered his house and took away his papers. Entick sued the officers for trespass to his house and goods, and the defendants sought to justify the legality of the warrant. Unable to find specific authority in law, they argued that such warrants had been issued frequently in the past and executed without challenge, and that the power of seizure was essential to government.

> **Lord Camden CJ:** . . . This power, so claimed by the Secretary of State, is not supported by one single citation from any law book extant . . .
>
> If it is law, it will be found in our books. If it is not to be found there, it is not law.
>
> By the laws of England, every invasion of private property, be it ever so minute, is a trespass. No man can set his foot upon my ground without my licence, but he is liable to an action, though the damage be nothing . . . if he admits the fact, he is bound to shew by way of justification, that some positive law has empowered or excused him. The justification is submitted to the judges, who are to look into the books; and [see] if such a justification can be maintained by the text of the statute law, or by the principles of common law. If no such excuse can be found or produced, the silence of the books is an authority against the defendant, and the plaintiff must have judgment . . .
>
> I come now to the practice since the Revolution, which has been strongly urged, with this emphatical addition, that a usage tolerated from the era of liberty, and continued downwards to this time through the best ages of the constitution, must necessarily have a legal commencement . . .

With respect to the practice itself, if it goes no higher, every lawyer will tell you, it is much too modern to be evidence of the common law . . .

This is the first instance I have met with, where the ancient immemorable law of the land, in a public matter, was attempted to be proved by the practice of a private office.

The names and rights of public magistrates, their power and forms of proceeding as they are settled by law, have been long since written, and are to be found in books and records

[W]hoever conceived a notion, that any part of the public law could be buried in the obscure practice of a particular person?

To search, seize, and carry away all the papers of the subject upon the first warrant: that such a right should have existed from the time whereof the memory of man runneth not to the contrary, and never yet have found a place in any book of law; is incredible . . .

But still it is insisted, that there has been a general submission, and no action brought to try the right.

I answer, there has been a submission of guilt and poverty to power and the terror of punishment. But it would be strange doctrine to assert that all the people of this land are bound to acknowledge that to be universal law, which a few criminal booksellers have been afraid to dispute . . .

It is then said, that it is necessary for the ends of government to lodge such a power with a state officer; and that it is better to prevent the publication before than to punish the offender afterwards . . . [W]ith respect to the argument of state necessity, or a distinction that has been aimed at between state offences and others, the common law does not understand that kind of reasoning, nor do our books take notice of any such distinctions.

It was held that the warrant was illegal and void, and Entick was awarded damages.

The principle affirmed in this great case, that a public officer must show express legal authority for any interference with the person or property of the citizen, is still the law. But nowadays there are many statutes that authorise such interferences and some do so in very general terms. One statute of this sort, the Taxes Management Act 1970, was said by Lord Scarman in *IRC* v. *Rossminster Ltd* [1980] AC 952, 1022, to make 'a breath-taking inroad upon the individual's right of privacy and right of property'. The act authorises officers of the Board of Inland Revenue, acting under a search warrant, to enter premises by day or night, if necessary by force, and seize 'any things whatsoever' reasonably believed to be evidence of an offence involving serious fraud in connection with tax. The search warrant is issued by a judge who must be satisfied that there is reasonable ground for suspecting that an offence of fraud in relation to tax has been committed. The warrant in the *Rossminster* case simply followed the wording of the statute without specifying what particular offence was suspected and the Court of Appeal ([1980] AC 967) held the warrant invalid for this reason. Lord Denning cited *Entick* v. *Carrington* among other cases and said (974):

> When the officers of the Inland Revenue come armed with a warrant to search a man's home or his office, it seems to me that he is entitled to say: 'Of what offence do you suspect me? You are claiming to enter my house and to seize my papers.' And when they look at the papers and seize them, he should be able to say: 'Why are you seizing these papers? Of what offence do you suspect me? What have these to do with your case?' Unless he knows the particular offence charged, he cannot take steps to secure himself or his property. So it seems to me, as a matter of construction of the statute and therefore of the warrant – in pursuance of our traditional role to protect the liberty of the individual – it is our duty to say that the warrant must particularise the specific offence which is charged as being fraud on the revenue.

The House of Lords, however, reversed the Court of Appeal's ruling and held that there was nothing in the statute to require the particular offence to be stated in the warrant. Since the provisions of the statute had been complied with, there was no violation of the principle of *Entick* v. *Carrington* . (See, too, Duffy and Hunt, 'Goodbye *Entick v Carrington*: The Security Service Act 1996' (1997) 2 *EHRLR* 11.)

The requirement of the rule of law that express legal authority must be shown for interferences with individual rights was doubtless formally satisfied in this case. But is it diluted in substance, when the legal power is conferred in very wide terms that do not have to be particularised before the power is used against an individual?

Although the courts do in many cases uphold the rights of the citizen against executive action that is not justified by law, a contrary tendency in our legal system allows certain kinds of interference with private interests to be committed by a public authority without express legal justification. This is because there are in the common law relatively few positively constituted civil rights: the 'rights' of the citizen have often been no more than the residue of liberty that is beyond the limits of lawfully exercised public power. (This remains the position at common law even after the HRA: see, further, Chapter 11.) If the citizen's interest is not supported by a legally acknowledged right, a public authority may be able to act to the detriment of that interest without having to show specific legal authority for its action.

Malone v. *Metropolitan Police Commissioner* [1979] Ch. 344 (Chancery Division)

The plaintiff (claimant) had been charged with handling stolen property; in the course of the trial, counsel for the Crown admitted that the plaintiff's telephone line had been 'tapped' in order to hear and record his conversations, for the purpose of criminal investigation. The tapping had been done on the authority of a warrant issued by the Home Secretary in accordance with usual practice.

The plaintiff brought proceedings against the Metropolitan Police commissioner for declarations that the tapping was unlawful, inter alia, on the ground that it was authorised neither by statute nor by common law.

Sir Robert Megarry V-C: ... England, it may be said, is not a country where everything is forbidden except what is expressly permitted: it is a country where everything is permitted except what is expressly forbidden.

... if the tapping of telephones by the Post Office at the request of the police can be carried out without any breach of the law, it does not require any statutory or common law power to justify it: it can lawfully be done simply because there is nothing to make it unlawful. The question, of course, is whether tapping can be carried out without infringing the law.

[T]here is admittedly no statute which in terms authorises the tapping of telephones, with or without a warrant. Nevertheless, any conclusion that the tapping of telephones is therefore illegal would plainly be superficial in the extreme. The reason why a search of premises which is not authorised by law is illegal is that it involves the tort of trespass to those premises: and any trespass, whether to land or goods or the person, that is made without legal authority is prima facie illegal. Telephone tapping by the Post Office, on the other hand, involves no act of trespass. The subscriber speaks into his telephone, and the process of tapping appears to be carried out by Post Office officials making recordings, with Post Office apparatus on Post Office premises, of the electrical impulses on Post Office wires provided by Post Office electricity. There is no question of there being any trespass on the plaintiff's premises for the purpose of attaching anything either to the premises themselves or to anything on them: all that is done is done within the Post Office's own domain. As Lord Camden CJ said in *Entick v Carrington*, 'the eye cannot by the laws of England be guilty of a trespass'; and, I would add, nor can the ear.

Sir Robert Megarry was also of the opinion that where tapping was carried out under warrant, its lawfulness had been recognised by the Post Office Act 1969. Arguments for the plaintiff based on alleged infringements of rights of privacy and confidentiality and breaches of the ECHR were also unsuccessful.

Malone subsequently took his case to the ECtHR, which ruled that there had been a violation of Article 8 of the Convention (the right to respect for private life and correspondence). Since the law of England failed to provide a clear delimitation of the power of interception, 'the minimum degree of legal protection to which citizens are entitled under the rule of law in a democratic society is lacking' (*Malone* v. *United Kingdom* (1984) 7 EHRR 14). Following this ruling, the government brought forward legislation to provide a 'comprehensive framework' for the interception of communications (Interception of Communications Act 1985; see now the Regulation of Investigatory Powers Act 2000). The rights conferred by Article 8 of the Convention have since been given domestic legal effect by the HRA.

According to the principle affirmed by Sir Robert Megarry in the *Malone* case, the act of a public authority will be upheld if it was 'in accordance with law' in the sense that it did not infringe any law. In this respect, the administration is treated like a private individual, who is free to do whatever the law does not prohibit. Is it not, however, a rather dubious constitutional principle that places government, with the great resources at its command and its responsibility for the public interest, on the same footing as the private citizen? As Tony Prosser remarks ((1996) 44 *Political Studies* 473, 476), if government is able:

> to avail itself of the same legal rights and privileges as the private citizen . . . this leaves no room for constraints on power based explicitly on responsibilities to the broader public interest or for rights owed by the state through its status as an institution transcending the chaos of particular interests.

The licence allowed to the state by the *Malone* principle was countered by Laws J in *R* v. *Somerset County Council, ex p Fewings* [1995] 1 All ER 513, 524, in saying:

> For private persons, the rule is that you may do anything you choose which the law not does prohibit . . . But for public bodies the rule is opposite, and so of another character altogether. It is that any action to be taken must be justified by positive law . . . The rule is necessary in order to protect the people from arbitrary interference by those set in power over them.

Surely the view of Laws J (as he then was) is to be preferred over that of Sir Robert Megarry in the *Malone* case? Yet, this does not appear to be the current position in English law. The real issue is how public bodies are able to obtain lawful authority for their actions. On the traditional Diceyan reading, there are only two sources of power – statute and the prerogative. However, as confirmed by the Supreme Court in *R (on the application of New London College)* v. *Secretary of State for the Home Department* [2013] UKSC 51, [2013] 1 WLR 2358: '[T]he Crown possesses some general administrative powers . . . which are not exercises of the royal prerogative and do not require statutory authority' (Lord Sumption, at para [28], with whom Lords Hope, Clarke and Reed agreed). Lord Carnwath disagreed, expressing the opinion that all powers of the Crown are either statutory or prerogative. These powers now include adopting policies or guidelines, as well as placing wiretaps. (See, further, Harris (1992) 108 *LQR* 626 and (2010) 126 *LQR* 373; Cohn (2005) 25 *OJLS* 97; Perry (2015) 131 *LQR* 672 .)

In at least the limited sense that executive action must not contravene the law, the rule of law is a part of British law. This is not to say that the principle is always scrupulously observed by public authorities, and the rule of law is most at risk of violation in times of crisis or danger to the community. A notorious instance of disregard of the rule of law was the officially authorised but unlawful physical ill-treatment applied to detainees in Northern Ireland in 1971. (See the Compton and Parker Reports, Cmnd 4823/1971 and Cmnd 4901/1972; Brownlie (1972) 35 *MLR* 501; *Ireland* v. *United Kingdom* (1978) 2 EHRR 25 (ECtHR).) The conflict in Northern Ireland was again to raise concern for the rule of law when allegations of the gravest nature were made that a 'shoot to kill' policy had been applied by the security forces in the 1970s and 1980s. An inquiry by Mr John Stalker, Deputy Chief Constable of Greater Manchester, into the circumstances in which seven persons were shot by members of the Royal Ulster Constabulary met with obstruction and Mr Stalker was suspended from duty before his inquiry was completed. The facts of these and other shooting incidents, and of Mr Stalker's suspension, remain in a fog of obscurity. (See, further, Jennings (ed.), *Justice Under Fire* (1988), ch. 5; Ewing and Gearty, *Freedom Under Thatcher* (1990), pp. 230–5; *McKerr v. United Kingdom* (2002) 34 EHRR 553.)

Subsequently, the murders of the Belfast solicitor Patrick Finucane and of a number of other people by loyalist paramilitary organisations led to allegations that members of the security forces had colluded in the murders. These allegations were investigated by Sir John Stevens, the Metropolitan Police Commissioner, who concluded that there had been collusion in the murders of Finucane and one other victim (*Stevens Enquiry, Overview and Recommendations*, 2003). An additional investigation was carried out, at the request of the British and Irish Governments, by Justice Peter Cory, a retired member of the Canadian Supreme Court, who found 'strong evidence that collusive acts were committed' by the Army, the Special Branch of the Royal Ulster Constabulary and the Security Service, and urged that a public inquiry should be held (*Cory Collusion Inquiry Report: Patrick Finucane*, HC 470 of 2003–04). The government responded by announcing that a public inquiry would be held under the Inquiries Act 2005. But this procedure was objected to (as being insufficiently independent) by a number of parties and, to date, no inquiry has been established. In 2007, the police ombudsman for Northern Ireland found that members of the Royal Ulster Constabulary had colluded in murders committed by loyalist paramilitary informers (see www.policeombudsman.org). In 2019, the Supreme Court declared that the failure to hold a public inquiry was a breach of Article 2 ECHR. In addition, the statement of the intention to hold a public inquiry created a legitimate expectation that an inquiry would be held, but the court concluded that there were good reasons for the government to not be held to this legitimate expectation (*In the Matter of an Application by Geraldine Finucane for Judicial Review* [2019] UKSC 7, [2019] NI 292).

The police, in their zeal to secure convictions, have sometimes resorted to fabrication of evidence and other malpractices, contributing to a series of grave miscarriages of justice in cases such as the 'Guildford Four', the 'Birmingham Six', the 'Bridgewater Three' and the 'Tottenham Three'. (See, respectively, the May Report, *The Guildford and Woolwich Bombings*, HC 449 of 1993–4; *R v. McIlkenny* [1992] 2 All ER 417, *The Times*, 31 July 1997, p. 4; Griffith, *The Politics of the Judiciary* (5th edn. 1997), p. 211.)

In interrogating servicemen in Cyprus in 1984, the service police were found to have acted in good faith but to have committed illegalities in their concern to protect the national interest. Mr David Calcutt QC said in his Report (Cmnd 9781/1986):

> In our society, it is for Parliament and not for investigators, however genuinely and well motivated, to decide if and when, and in what circumstances, the interests of an individual should be subordinated to the interests of society as a whole.

Again, political demonstrations, industrial action and other forms of militant activism have on occasion provoked reactions from authority going beyond what is proper or legal. (See, e.g., McCabe and Wallington, *The Police, Public Order and Civil Liberties: Legacies of the Miners' Strike* (1988).) (On policing and public protest, see, further, Chapter 11.)

The rule of law is undermined if the state exercises its powers in such a way as to make it impossible, or even very difficult, for persons affected to challenge the legality of the state's action. In *R (Karas)* v. *Secretary of State for the Home Department* [2006] EWHC 747 (Admin), immigration officers detained a husband and his pregnant wife at 8.30pm with a view to their being deported at 7.45am the following day. Prior to this time, the husband and wife had no idea that they were to be deported at all. They had been regularly reporting, as required, to the immigration authorities, who had not previously mentioned it to them. Munby J held that the Home Office's action was 'deliberately planned with a view to ... the spiriting away of the claimants from the jurisdiction before there was likely to be time for them to obtain and act upon legal advice or apply to the court'. Damages were awarded to the husband and wife. Munby J added that the case revealed 'at best an unacceptable disregard by the Home Office of the rule of law, at worst an unacceptable disdain by the Home Office for the rule of law, which is as depressing as it ought to be concerning.'

In *R (Al-Sweady)* v. *Secretary of State for Defence* [2009] EWHC 2387 (Admin), [2010] HRLR 2 the Divisional Court expressed strongly worded criticisms of the deliberate failure of the Ministry of Defence to comply with its duties regarding the disclosure of documents.

The rule of law is also undermined when the state commits or connives at breaches of the law. In 1984, the Home Office issued guidelines that purported to authorise the police to install listening devices in homes and other private premises in specified circumstances in the investigation of serious crimes. There was no legal basis for such authorisation and the installation of the devices by the police with Home Office approval involved unlawful acts of civil trespass and damage to property. (See *R* v. *Khan* [1997] AC 558.) Legal authority to enter property and plant listening devices (or seize documents) was eventually provided by Part 3 of the Police Act 1997. Authorisations to interfere with property may be given by a senior police officer but are subject to supervision by a judicial commissioner. (See also the Intelligence Services Act 1994, sections 5–7; and Part 2 of the Regulation of Investigatory Powers Act 2000.)

Serious allegations of state connivance in the most grotesque violations of law were made by a number of British residents who had been imprisoned by the USA at Guantanamo Bay. The residents claimed that they had been tortured and subjected to inhuman, degrading and cruel treatment either by the USA or by third parties while in US captivity, or both. They further claimed that the British Government and the British Security and Secret Intelligence Services (MI5 and MI6) knew of their ill-treatment and facilitated it by cooperating with the US authorities in their interrogations. Among the men's allegations were that they were subjected to the most appalling treatment over a prolonged period of time, in some cases for more than two-and-a-half years. We are not talking only about such practices as sleep deprivation, starvation and water-boarding here, shameful and illegal though those practices are; we are talking about the use of razor blades and the infliction of serious bodily injury, as well as devastating psychological oppression.

The episode has sorely tested the British commitment to the rule of law. One of the Guantanamo detainees, Binyam Mohamed, sought discovery of information passed by the Americans to the British Government which, he claimed, he required in order to defend himself in legal actions that the US authorities were preparing to bring against him. This information would show that he had been tortured and mistreated such that any confession evidence on which the USA may wish to rely would be unsafe and inadmissible. The British Government sought strenuously to resist having to disclose this information. The Secretary of State (who at the material time was David Miliband) argued that the information in question was American information, passed in confidence to the UK, and that, given its origin, only the US authorities could disclose it. For Binyam Mohamed ('BM'), it was countered that any public interest in maintaining confidentiality was outweighed first by BM's interests in securing justice as a victim of torture and, second, by the legitimate public interest in knowing the extent to which British authorities were complicit in the torture and ill-treatment of its residents.

The case resulted in an extraordinary series of court judgments – six from the Divisional Court and two from the Court of Appeal – as the courts contested with the government the extent to which the details of this story could be made public. The government not only resisted having to disclose the information BM sought but also objected to the public release of sections of the courts' judgments in which aspects of the information were summarised or commented on. The government argued that these passages should be kept secret. During the (protracted) course of the litigation before the Divisional Court it was clear that the court became increasingly frustrated with and, indeed, disbelieving of the government's arguments. After BM's lawyers obtained from a US court the information that BM had sought from the

British authorities, the Divisional Court eventually ruled that all of the passages from its judgments that the government wanted kept secret should be published. The government appealed to the Court of Appeal, which agreed with the lower court. But the majority of the Court of Appeal so ruled only on a technicality – BM may have 'won', but the case can hardly be seen as a ringing endorsement of open justice or of the public vindication of the rule of law. On the morning of the final Court of Appeal judgment, Mr Miliband was proudly explaining to the House of Commons how the court had endorsed his position – that the British courts should not order the disclosure of information emanating from a foreign intelligence service: HC Deb vol. 505, col 913, 10 February 2010. It seemed that, for the government, upholding this principle – which had never previously been claimed to be a legal principle – was more important than uncovering the truth about torture.

(The key judgments of the Divisional Court in this case are the following: *R (Binyam Mohamed)* v. *Secretary of State for Foreign and Commonwealth Affairs (No 1)* [2008] EWHC 2048 (Admin), [2009] 1 WLR 2579; *R (Binyam Mohamed)* v. *Secretary of State for Foreign and Commonwealth Affairs (No 4)* [2009] EWHC 152 (Admin), [2009] 1 WLR 2653; and *R (Binyam Mohamed)* v. *Secretary of State for Foreign and Commonwealth Affairs (No 5)* [2009] EWHC 2549 (Admin), [2009] 1 WLR 2653. The judgments of the Court of Appeal are as follows: *R (Binyam Mohamed)* v. *Secretary of State for Foreign and Commonwealth Affairs* [2010] EWCA Civ 65, [2010] 3 WLR 554; and *R (Binyam Mohamed)* v. *Secretary of State for Foreign and Commonwealth Affairs* [2010] EWCA Civ 158, [2010] 3 WLR 554. For a full analysis of the saga, see Tomkins, 'National Security and the Due Process of Law' (2011) 64 *CLP 215*; and see, further, pp. 373–5.)

The allegation underpinning this litigation is that the British Government and, specifically, MI5 and MI6 and their parent departments, the Home Office and the Foreign Office, were complicit in torture. There is no allegation that MI5 or MI6 themselves engaged in torture directly. But complicity in torture is itself illegal in international law: it is expressly prohibited by Article 4 of the UN Convention against Torture (which the UK ratified in 1988).

That said, however, allegations have been made that British armed forces committed acts of torture in Iraq. The Baha Mousa Inquiry reported in 2011. It investigated the death of Baha Mousa, an Iraqi civilian, arrested and detained in Basra by the British armed forces, who later died in custody. An extensive report, extending to three volumes, concluded that there was sufficient evidence that the armed forces carried out low-level assaults against the detainees, and that some, if not all, had had toilet water flushed over them. The report also concluded that there was evidence that other detainees had been hooded, forced to adopt stress positions, and beaten (see www.gov.uk/government/publications/the-baha-mousa-public-inquiry-report). Others have been made in various cases, including (as regards Afghanistan) *R (Evans)* v. *Secretary of State for Defence* [2010]

EWHC 1445 (Admin) and (as regards Iraq) *R (Ali Zaki Mousa)* v. *Secretary of State for Defence* [2010] EWHC 3304 (Admin). See, further, JCHR, *Allegations of UK Complicity in Torture*, 23rd Report of 2008–09, HL 152, HC 230; and Human Rights Watch, *Cruel Britannia: British Complicity in the Torture and Ill-Treatment of Terror Suspects in Pakistan* (2009).

In July 2010, Prime Minister David Cameron announced a public inquiry into allegations of British complicity in torture. In 2018, two reports of the Intelligence and Security Committee (*Detainee Mistreatment and Rendition: 2001–2010* HC1113 and *Detainee Mistreatment and Rendition: Current Issues* HC1114) concluded that, although there was no evidence of the direct involvement of UK personnel in mistreatment, there were thirteen recorded incidents 'where it appears that UK personnel witnessed at first hand a detainee being mistreated by others – such that it must have caused alarm and should have led to action' as well as '25 incidents recorded where UK personnel were told by detainees that they had been mistreated by others' (HC 1113, p. 3). The committee also investigated the UK's involvement in rendition – that is, transporting individuals to detention centres outside the usual controls of national and international law (e.g. Guantanamo Bay). The committee summarised its conclusions as follows (at pp. 3–4):

> The one aspect of UK policy which was clear was that the UK does not conduct rendition operations itself. However, in three individual cases SIS or MI5 made, or offered to make, a financial contribution to others to conduct a rendition operation. Given that the operations were to countries such as LEEDS and DORNOCH (code words were used in the report to protect classified information), these can be described as 'extraordinary renditions' due to the real risk of torture or cruel, inhuman or degrading treatment of the detainees. The Agencies' financing of these operations was completely unacceptable. In our view this amounts to simple outsourcing of action they knew they were not allowed to undertake themselves.
>
> The Agencies also suggested, planned or agreed to rendition operations proposed by others in 28 cases. We have seen a further 22 cases where SIS or MI5 provided intelligence to enable a rendition operation to take place; and 23 cases where they failed to take action to prevent a rendition – this latter category includes instances where there were opportunities to intervene and prevent the rendition of a British national or resident, but the UK Government conspicuously failed to act.
>
> There is, however, no evidence in the primary material that any US rendition flight transited the UK with a detainee on board, although two detainees are now known to have transited through the British Overseas Territory of Diego Garcia. The Committee has seen nothing to indicate that detainees have ever been held on Diego Garcia. We note, however, that the policy on recording flights was woefully inadequate, and the records available are patchy and cannot be relied on.

Recently, the Supreme Court considered whether it was possible for individuals to bring an action for compensation against the UK government as a result of its involvement in rendition processes, as well as mistreatment and torture. *Belhaj* v. *Straw* [2017] UKSC 3, [2017] AC 964, concerned Abdel Hakim Belhaj and his wife, Fatima Boudchar, who were detained in Libya after being rendered there from China. Both were tortured during their detention. Mr Belhaj alleged that his detention and rendition were instigated by the UK. The government wished to strike out the claim, arguing that as the torture was carried out by agents of a foreign state, they could rely on the defence of a foreign act of state. In a complex judgment, where it can be hard to discern the precise ratio of the case, it was nevertheless clear that the doctrine of foreign act of state would not apply to exclude the court from examining serious breaches of international human rights law such as the allegations of torture. However, in *Rahmatullah* v. *Ministry of Defence* [2017] UKSC 1, [2017] 3 All ER 179, the Supreme Court concluded that the UK could rely on the doctrine of act of state to exclude the tort action – this doctrine applying to actions of the UK carried out against non-UK nationals on non-UK territory. Mr Rahmatullah was captured by British forces in Iraq, and then transferred to US custody where he was detained without charge. He alleged that he had been tortured during his detention. On 10 May 2018, the then Prime Minister, Theresa May, wrote a letter of apology to Mr Belhaj and his wife. The letter set out that they would receive £500,000 in compensation.

In *R* v. *Loosely* [2001] UKHL 53, [2001] 1 WLR 2060 the House of Lords reconsidered the law of entrapment. A prosecution founded on entrapment is an abuse of the court's process. The House of Lords ruled that police conduct that brings about state-created crime is unacceptable and improper, and to prosecute in such circumstances is an affront to the public conscience. (See, further, Ho, 'State Entrapment' (2011) 31 *LS* 71.) Lord Nicholls commenced his opinion with the following remarks:

> Every court has an inherent power and duty to prevent abuse of its process. This is a fundamental principle of the rule of law. By recourse to this principle courts ensure that executive agents of the state do not misuse the coercive, law enforcement functions of the courts and thereby oppress citizens of the state. Entrapment, with which these two appeals are concerned, is an instance where such misuse may occur. It is simply not acceptable that the state through its agents should lure its citizens into committing acts forbidden by the law and then seek to prosecute them for doing so. That would be entrapment. That would be a misuse of state power, and an abuse of the process of the courts. The unattractive consequences, frightening and sinister in extreme cases, which state conduct of this nature could have are obvious. The role of the courts is to stand between the state and its citizens and make sure this does not happen.
>
> These propositions, I apprehend, are not controversial. The difficulty lies in identifying conduct which is caught by such imprecise words as lure or incite or entice or instigate. If

police officers acted only as detectives and passive observers, there would be little problem in identifying the boundary between permissible and impermissible police conduct. But that would not be a satisfactory place for the boundary line. Detection and prosecution of consensual crimes committed in private would be extremely difficult. Trafficking in drugs is one instance. With such crimes there is usually no victim to report the matter to the police. And sometimes victims or witnesses are unwilling to give evidence.

Moreover, and importantly, in some instances a degree of active involvement by the police in the commission of a crime is generally regarded as acceptable.

In the following case, the rule of law was strongly vindicated and was held to prevail over the public interest in the prosecution and punishment of crime.

R v. Horseferry Road Magistrates' Court, ex p Bennett [1994] 1 AC 42 (HL)

Bennett, a New Zealand citizen, was wanted for criminal offences allegedly committed by him in the UK. He was discovered to be in South Africa but proceedings for his extradition to this country were not instituted. He was, however, arrested by South African police and placed, handcuffed to the seat, on a flight to Heathrow, where he was arrested by English police officers and subsequently committed by a magistrate for trial in the Crown Court.

Bennett applied for judicial review of his committal. He contended that he had been unlawfully removed from South Africa, at the request of and in collusion with the English police, on the pretext that he was being deported to New Zealand via Heathrow.

The question that was tried as a preliminary issue was whether, on the assumption that the facts asserted by Bennett were true, he could lawfully be put on trial in England for the offences he was alleged to have committed in this country. The Divisional Court held that the courts' concern was only that a defendant should have a fair trial: there was no legal authority for the proposition that a court could prevent a prosecution because of the methods by which the police had secured the defendant's presence within the jurisdiction.

This decision was reversed by the House of Lords (Lord Oliver dissenting).

Lord Griffiths: ... Your Lordships have been urged by the respondents to uphold the decision of the Divisional Court and the nub of their submission is that the role of the judge is confined to the forensic process. The judge, it is said, is concerned to see that the accused has a fair trial and that the process of the court is not manipulated to his disadvantage so that the trial itself is unfair: but the wider issues of the rule of law and the behaviour of those charged with its enforcement, be they police or prosecuting authority, are not the concern of the judiciary unless they impinge directly on the trial process.

Lord Griffiths considered the cases in which the courts had exercised a jurisdiction to prevent abuse of process and continued:

> Your Lordships are now invited to extend the concept of abuse of process a stage further. In the present case there is no suggestion that the appellant cannot have a fair trial, nor could it be suggested that it would have been unfair to try him if he had been returned to this country through extradition procedures. If the court is to have the power to interfere with the prosecution in the present circumstances it must be because the judiciary accept a responsibility for the maintenance of the rule of law that embraces a willingness to oversee executive action and to refuse to countenance behaviour that threatens either basic human rights or the rule of law.
>
> My Lords, I have no doubt that the judiciary should accept this responsibility in the field of criminal law. The great growth of administrative law during the latter half of this century has occurred because of the recognition by the judiciary and Parliament alike that it is the function of the High Court to ensure that executive action is exercised responsibly and as Parliament intended. So also should it be in the field of criminal law and if it comes to the attention of the court that there has been a serious abuse of power it should, in my view, express its disapproval by refusing to act upon it . . .
>
> In my view your Lordships should now declare that where process of law is available to return an accused to this country through extradition procedures our courts will refuse to try him if he has been forcibly brought within our jurisdiction in disregard of those procedures by a process to which our own police, prosecuting or other executive authorities have been a knowing party.
>
> **Lord Bridge of Harwich:** . . . There is, I think, no principle more basic to any proper system of law than the maintenance of the rule of law itself. When it is shown that the law enforcement agency responsible for bringing a prosecution has only been enabled to do so by participating in violations of international law and of the laws of another state in order to secure the presence of the accused within the territorial jurisdiction of the court, I think that respect for the rule of law demands that the court take cognisance of that circumstance. To hold that the court may turn a blind eye to executive lawlessness beyond the frontiers of its own jurisdiction is, to my mind, an insular and unacceptable view. Having then taken cognisance of the lawlessness it would again appear to me to be a wholly inadequate response for the court to hold that the only remedy lies in civil proceedings at the suit of the defendant or in disciplinary or criminal proceedings against the individual officers of the law enforcement agency who were concerned in the illegal action taken. Since the prosecution could never have been brought if the defendant had not been illegally abducted, the whole proceeding is tainted.

The matter was remitted to the Divisional Court to determine whether Bennett's factual allegations were well-founded. In *R* v. *Horseferry Road Magistrates' Court, ex p Bennett (No 4)* [1995] 1 Cr App R 147, the Divisional Court was not satisfied that Bennett had been properly available for arrest at Heathrow and quashed the order committing him for trial. (See also *R* v. *Grant* [2005] EWCA Crim 1089, [52]–[58].)

The government and other public authorities cannot always be relied on to respect the law and observe its constraints. A state can therefore claim to uphold the rule of law only if it provides effective means for the prevention and redress of illegal action by those who wield public powers. Accordingly, it is a further requirement of the rule of law that there should be independent courts or other agencies that will check and control the actions of public authorities to ensure their compliance with the law. Lord Irvine of Lairg LC emphasised this in *Boddington* v. *British Transport Police* [1999] 2 AC 143, 161, saying that:

> It is well recognised to be important for the maintenance of the rule of law and the preservation of liberty that individuals affected by legal measures promulgated by executive public bodies should have a fair opportunity to challenge these measures and to vindicate their rights in court proceedings.

(See, to similar effect, Lord Hope in *Secretary of State for the Home Department* v. *AF* [2009] UKHL 28, [2010] 2 AC 269, at [84].)

Interference with legal process may be said to be an infringement of the rule of law. Perverting the course of justice is a criminal offence. In 2006, the director of the Serious Fraud Office (SFO) was prevailed on to discontinue a criminal investigation into a deal between British Aerospace and Saudi Arabia. The Divisional Court held that the political and diplomatic pressure that had been placed on the director of the SFO to secure this result was an affront to the rule of law that 'invites at least dismay, if not outrage' (*R (Corner House Research)* v. *Director of the Serious Fraud Office* [2008] EWHC 714 (Admin), [2008] 4 All ER 927, at [34]). The court ruled that the director's decision to discontinue the investigation was unlawful. On appeal, the House of Lords saw matters differently. Their Lordships ruled that continuing with the investigation would have entailed a risk to national security (Saudi Arabia having apparently threatened to withdraw intelligence cooperation with the UK were the investigation not abandoned) and the director of the SFO was entitled to take such considerations into account when deciding whether it was in the public interest to press ahead with a prosecution: *R (Corner House Research)* v. *Director of the Serious Fraud Office* [2008] UKHL 60, [2009] 1 AC 756. (See, further on this case, Chapter 10.)

It is a requirement of the rule of law that the government should comply with judgments of the courts given against it. Indeed, it was this concern that led Lord Neuberger to reach his conclusion in *Evans* (discussed above) that the executive was not able to set aside the judgment of a tribunal. In particular, it would not be consistent with the rule of law for a government to resort to retrospective legislation in order to nullify those judgments that it preferred not to obey. Nevertheless, there are examples where the UK government appears to have done precisely that. In *Burmah Oil Co Ltd* v. *Lord Advocate* [1965] AC 75, the Burmah Oil Company claimed compensation for the wartime destruction of its installations in Burma, which had been ordered by the British military authorities to prevent their falling into the hands of advancing Japanese forces. The destruction had been a lawful exercise of the war prerogative of the Crown, but the House of Lords held that the use of the prerogative in these circumstances imported an obligation to pay compensation. In a dissenting speech, Lord Radcliffe observed that in no previous case had a court of law awarded compensation for a taking or destruction of property under the war prerogative, and that there was no clear body of legal opinion that would justify the declaration, for the first time, of a legal right to compensation.

The company's victory in this case raised the spectre of a governmental liability (to other claimants also) in a considerable amount, greatly exceeding the sum it had made available for a partial compensation of war losses, out of which many claims had already been settled. The government, arguing that it was necessary to maintain the integrity of its scheme of compensation, then brought about the enactment of the War Damage Act 1965, which provided:

> (1) No person shall be entitled at common law to receive from the Crown compensation in respect of damage to, or destruction of, property caused (whether before or after the passing of this Act, within or outside the United Kingdom) by acts lawfully done by, or on the authority of, the Crown during, or in contemplation of the outbreak of, a war in which the Sovereign was, or is, engaged.
> (2) Where any proceedings to recover at common law compensation in respect of such damage or destruction have been instituted before the passing of this Act, the court shall, on the application of any party, forthwith set aside or dismiss the proceedings, subject only to the determination of any question arising as to costs or expenses.

After the introduction of the bill, which became the War Damage Act 1965, JUSTICE published the following statement:

> At a recent meeting of the Executive Committee of JUSTICE the members present, who included lawyers who are members of all the main political parties, considered the War Damage Bill in the context of the principles of the Rule of Law which JUSTICE is pledged to uphold.
>
> It was the unanimous view of the meeting that the passage of this Bill into law would constitute a serious infringement of the Rule of Law by which is understood the supremacy of the Courts. The refusal to meet a legitimate claim for compensation affirmed by the highest Court in the land, namely the House of Lords, is in the view of JUSTICE an action

inconsistent with the Rule of Law and a dangerous precedent for the future. It is entirely wrong that when a litigant has won his case, legislation should be produced revising decisions retrospectively so that the successful plaintiff is deprived of his victory.

The fact that a threat of legislative action was made during an early stage of the proceedings, and long after the right of legal action had arisen, so far from justifying the enactment of this Bill, makes it clear, in the opinion of JUSTICE, that both Conservative and Labour Governments have failed to recognise the over-riding need to respect the decisions of the judiciary.

The issues raised by the *Burmah Oil* case and the government's response to it were perhaps more complex than this statement would suggest, but if the executive were to make a practice of retrospectively overturning adverse judicial rulings, there would be no equality before the law and no public confidence in the legal process. Since the War Damage Act 1965 there have been other instances, also of questionable propriety, of legislation retrospectively nullifying judicial decisions. (See Zellick [1985] *PL* 283, 290; see, further, *McE* v. *Prison Service of Northern Ireland* [2009] UKHL 15, [2009] 1 AC 908.)

Two more controversial examples occurred more recently. In *Ahmed* v. *Her Majesty's Treasury* [2010] UKSC 2, [2010] 2 AC 534, the Supreme Court struck down the Terrorism (United Nations Measures) Order 2006 and the Al-Qaida and Taliban (United Nations Measures) Order 2006. Both introduced asset freezing mechanisms in order to implement UN Security Council measures brought in in response to 9/11. Both were deemed to harm human rights, yet the legislation empowering these orders – the United Nations Act 1946 – did not expressly empower the government to enact measures that contravened human rights. Moreover, the 1946 legislation empowered the government to enact orders that were necessary to implement UN obligations. The United Nations order included provisions that went beyond what was necessary to implement UN obligations. In response, the government introduced the Terrorist Asset-Freezing (Temporary Provisions) Act 2010, which provided retrospective validity for these measures, albeit on a temporary basis. This act was repealed by the Terrorist Asset-Freezing etc. Act 2010, which provided an alternative statutory basis for these measures. At first sight, this looks like an egregious breach of the rule of law, similar to that which occurred in *Burmah Oil*. However, the decision of the court to strike down these measures placed the UK in breach of its obligations in international law, in addition to potentially endangering national security. It also provided an opportunity for more detailed democratic scrutiny of these measures, to balance human rights and national security. Alas, this opportunity was not fully utilised, the Terrorist Asset-Freezing etc. Act 2010 being enacted in just four days. A better solution may have been to have adopted the same remedy as the European Court of Justice, which struck down the EU's implementation of the UN order in C-402/05P *Kadi and Albarakaat* v. *Council and Commission of the European Union*, but delayed the implementation of the judgment by three months in order to provide the EU with the time to enact replacement measures to uphold its UN obligations.

It is not possible for UK courts to strike down legislation because it is retrospective. To do so would breach parliamentary sovereignty. However, there is one example in which a court was able to declare legislation incompatible with Convention rights, in part, because of its retrospectivity. However, the breach of Article 6 ECHR – the right to a fair trial – occurred because the legislation was enacted retrospectively to remedy a declaration of incompatibility made under the Human Rights Act 1998 against earlier legislation, this being made after the Court of Appeal had issued a declaration of incompatibility and while the case was on appeal to the Supreme Court (see *Reilly and Hewstone* v. *Secretary of State for Work and Pensions* [2016] EWCA Civ 413, [2017] QB 657). The Court of Appeal made it clear that enacting retrospective legislation, alone, would not breach convention rights. The problem occurred due to the timing, the legislation interfering with judicial proceedings that were before the court at that time.

2.3.2 Equality Before the Law

'The most basic tenet of any constitutional society is the shared belief that, by virtue of being citizens of a state, all persons are equal in the eyes of the law' (Franklin and Baun (eds.), *Political Culture and Constitutionalism* (1995), p. 5). For Dicey, as we have seen (above, p. 97), the rule of law included 'equality before the law' – the equal subjection of all, including officials, to the ordinary law administered by the ordinary courts. Here, Dicey directed his fire at the French system of administrative law (*droit administratif*) applied by separate administrative courts, declaring that it rested 'on ideas foreign to the fundamental assumptions of our English common law, and especially to what we have termed the rule of law' (*The Law of the Constitution* (1885), p. 329). Dicey later qualified this insular and faulty judgment: the French system was not then well-understood in England but is now recognised as being fully compatible with justice and the rule of law.

Dicey was, however, on surer ground in saying that officials (and those in government) should enjoy no special exemption from obedience to the law. He was convinced that this principle was respected in England – with us, he said (p. 193):

> every official, from the Prime Minister down to a constable or a collector of taxes, is under the same responsibility for every act done without legal justification as any other citizen.

Admittedly, Dicey was not here telling the whole truth for, while an official who committed a tort (or for that matter a crime) would be liable like anyone else, in Dicey's day, the Crown was immune from tortious liability and so could not be made vicariously liable for the torts of its servants. Yet Dicey was surely right to insist on a principle that officials, ministers and other public authorities should not be exempted from the rules and processes of the law and, in particular, should submit to the jurisdiction and comply with the decisions of the courts. Now today, it is true that immunities of the executive from legal process have, in general, been removed – for instance, the Crown was made liable in tort by the Crown Proceedings Act 1947 – but governments may still resort to expedients for limiting their answerability to the courts, as by inducing Parliament to invest them with wide discretionary powers or to exclude some kinds of decision from judicial control through the employment of 'ouster' clauses.

Judgments given by the courts against executive officers or bodies are generally fully respected and obeyed, but until recently there was believed to be a significant surviving immunity of ministers of the Crown from the process of law. An injunction – a judicial order requiring something to be done or not done (a mandatory or prohibitory injunction) – was not only acknowledged to be unavailable against the Crown itself but also, it was believed, could not be granted against a minister acting in his or her official capacity. The exclusion of injunctive relief in such cases was considered to be the effect, in civil proceedings, of section 21 of the Crown Proceedings Act 1947; furthermore, the view was taken in *R v. Secretary of State for Transport, ex p Factortame Ltd* [1990] 2 AC 85 that a like exclusion applied in (public law) proceedings for judicial review. Some other remedy, such as a declaration, might be available instead of a final injunction, but if urgent provisional relief were needed, there was no effective alternative to an interim (temporary) injunction.

Since ministers were thought to be immune, in their official capacities, from the coercive jurisdiction of the courts, it appeared also that there was no jurisdiction to make a finding of contempt against a minister who disregarded a court's order. Yet if an argument in these terms were to be upheld, said Lord Templeman in *M v. Home Office* (below), it would 'establish the proposition that the executive obey the law as a matter of grace and not as a matter of necessity, a proposition which would reverse the result of the Civil War'.

M v. Home Office [1994] 1 AC 377 (HL)

M, a citizen of Zaire (now Democratic Republic of Congo), arrived in the UK and claimed political asylum. His application was considered by the Asylum Division of the Home Office and rejected in the name of the Home Secretary, whereon directions were given for his removal from the UK. An initial application by M for permission to apply for judicial review was unsuccessful, but a fresh application to a judge in chambers was made on his behalf as he was about to be put on a flight to Zaire via Paris. The judge (Garland J) adjourned the application for fuller consideration on the following day, stating that M should not be removed in the meantime. Garland J understood and formally recorded that counsel for the Home Office had given an express undertaking to this effect, but counsel had not intended to give such an undertaking and no efforts were then made to procure M's return from Paris after the aircraft's arrival there. Informed of the departure of M's flight from Paris to Zaire, Garland J made a mandatory order requiring the Home Secretary to arrange for M's return to the jurisdiction. When this order was received and considered by the Home Secretary, Kenneth Baker, he decided – on legal advice that the judge had exceeded his powers – that M should not be brought back to this country.

Proceedings for contempt of court were brought against the Home Office and Home Secretary Baker. Simon Brown J held that he had no power to make a finding of contempt against either the Home Office or Baker. The Court of Appeal disagreed, holding that Baker had been guilty of contempt of court, although not finding it necessary that he should be punished otherwise than in being ordered to pay the costs. Baker appealed to the House of Lords.

The essential question in the case was whether the courts have jurisdiction to make coercive orders against ministers of the Crown. Lord Woolf delivered the principal speech, with which the other Law Lords concurred.

Lord Woolf first considered the prohibition in section 21(2) of the Crown Proceedings Act 1947 on granting, in any civil proceedings, an injunction against an officer of the Crown if the effect of the injunction would be 'to give any relief against the Crown which could not have been obtained in proceedings against the Crown'.

> **Lord Woolf:** ... [Section 21(2)] is restricted in its application to situations where the effect of the grant of an injunction or an order against an officer of the Crown will be to give any relief against the Crown which could not have been obtained in proceedings against the Crown prior to the Act. Applying those words literally, their effect is reasonably obvious. Where, prior to 1947, an injunction could be obtained against an officer of the Crown, because he had personally committed or authorised a tort, an injunction could still be granted on precisely the same basis as previously since ... to grant an injunction could not affect the Crown because of the assumption that the Crown could do no wrong. The proceedings would, however, have to be brought against the tortfeasor personally in the same manner as they would have been brought prior to the Act of 1947. If, on the other hand, the officer was being sued in a representative capacity [as an authorised representative for defending civil proceedings against the Crown in terms of section 17 of the 1947 Act] no injunction could be granted because in such a situation the effect would be to give relief against the Crown. The position would be the same in those situations where proceedings would previously have been brought by petition of right or for a declaration but could now be brought against the authorised department.
>
> There appears to be no reason in principle why, if a statute places a duty on a specified minister or other official which creates a cause of action, an action cannot be brought for breach of statutory duty claiming damages or for an injunction, in the limited circumstances

where injunctive relief would be appropriate, against the specified minister personally by any person entitled to the benefit of the cause of action. If, on the other hand, the duty is placed on the Crown in general, then section 21(2) would appear to prevent injunctive relief being granted, but as Professor Sir William Wade QC has pointed out ('Injunctive Relief against the Crown and Ministers' (1991) 107 *LQR* 4, 4–5) there are likely to be few situations when there will be statutory duties which place a duty on the Crown in general instead of on a named minister. In broad terms therefore the effect of the Act can be summarised by saying that it is only in those situations where prior to the Act no injunctive relief could be obtained that section 21 prevents an injunction being granted. In other words it restricts the effect of the procedural reforms that it implemented so that they did not extend the power of the courts to grant injunctions. This is the least that can be expected from legislation intended to make it easier for proceedings to be brought against the Crown.

As regards proceedings for judicial review, Lord Woolf disagreed with the view taken by Lord Bridge in *R* v. *Secretary of State for Transport, ex p Factortame Ltd* [1990] 2 AC 85 (above) that injunctions could not be granted against a minister of the Crown in such proceedings.

Turning to the injunction granted by Garland J in the present case, Lord Woolf concluded that the judge had jurisdiction to make the order and that it was appropriately made. The advice which Home Secretary Baker had been given that the order was made without jurisdiction notwithstanding, it was an order of the High Court that was to have been treated as a valid order and one to be obeyed until set aside.

Lord Woolf then considered the jurisdiction to make a finding of contempt:

The Court of Appeal were of the opinion that a finding of contempt could not be made against the Crown, a government department or a minister of the Crown in his official capacity. Although it is to be expected that it will be rare indeed that the circumstances will exist in which such a finding would be justified, I do not believe there is any impediment to a court making such a finding, when it is appropriate to do so, not against the Crown directly, but against a government department or a minister of the Crown in his official capacity. Lord Donaldson of Lymington MR considered that a problem was created in making a finding of contempt because the Crown lacked a legal personality. However, at least for some purposes, the Crown has a legal personality. It can be appropriately described as a corporation sole or a corporation aggregate: per Lord Diplock and Lord Simon of Glaisdale respectively in *Town Investments Ltd v Department of the Environment* [1978] AC 359. The Crown can hold property and enter into contracts. On the other hand, even after the Act of 1947, it cannot conduct litigation except in the name of an authorised government department or, in the case of judicial review, in the name of a minister. In any event it is not in relation to the Crown that I differ from the Master of the Rolls, but as to a government department or a minister.

Nolan LJ ... considered that the fact that proceedings for contempt are 'essentially personal and punitive' meant that it was not open to a court, as a matter of law, to make a finding of contempt against the Home Office or the Home Secretary. While contempt proceedings usually have these characteristics and contempt proceedings against a government department or a minister in an official capacity would not be either personal or punitive (it would clearly not be appropriate to fine or sequestrate the assets of the Crown or a government department or an officer of the Crown acting in his official capacity), this does not mean that a finding of contempt against a government department or minister would be pointless. The very fact of making such a finding would vindicate the requirements of justice. In addition an order for costs could be made to underline the significance of a contempt. A purpose of the courts' powers to make findings of contempt is to ensure that the orders of the court are obeyed. This jurisdiction is required to be coextensive with the courts' jurisdiction to make the orders which need the protection which the jurisdiction to make findings of contempt provides. In civil proceedings the court can now make orders (other than injunctions or for specific performance) against authorised government departments or the Attorney-General. On applications for judicial review orders can be made against ministers ... [I]f such orders are made and not obeyed, the body against whom the orders were made can be found guilty of contempt ...

In cases not involving a government department or a minister the ability to punish for contempt may be necessary. However, as is reflected in the restrictions on execution against the Crown, the Crown's relationship with the courts does not depend on coercion and in the exceptional situation when a government department's conduct justifies this, a finding of contempt should suffice. In that exceptional situation, the ability of the court to make a finding of contempt is of great importance. It would demonstrate that a government department has interfered with the administration of justice. It will then be for Parliament to determine what should be the consequences of that finding. In accord with tradition the finding should not be made against the 'Crown' by name but in the name of the authorised department (or the Attorney-General) or the minister so as to accord with the body against whom the order was made. If the order was made in civil proceedings against an authorised department, the department will be held to be in contempt. On judicial review the order will be against the minister and so normally should be any finding of contempt in respect of the order.

However, the finding under appeal is one made against Mr Baker personally in respect of an injunction addressed to him in his official capacity as the Secretary of State for the Home Department. It was appropriate to direct the injunction to the Secretary of State in his official capacity since, as previously indicated, remedies on an application for judicial review which involve the Crown are made against the appropriate officer in his official capacity. This does not mean that it cannot be appropriate to make a finding of contempt against a minister personally rather than against him in his official capacity provided that the contempt relates to his own default. Normally it will be more appropriate to make the order against the office which a minister holds where the order which has been breached has been made against that office since members of the department concerned will almost certainly be involved and investigation as to the part played by individuals is likely to be at least extremely difficult, if not impossible, unless privilege is waived (as commendably happened in this case). In addition the object of the exercise is not so much to punish an individual as to vindicate the rule of law by a finding of contempt. This can be achieved equally by a declaratory finding of the court as to the contempt against the minister as representing the department. By making the finding against the minister in his official capacity the court will be indicating that it is the department for which the minister is responsible which has been guilty of contempt. The minister himself may or may not have been personally guilty of contempt. The position so far as he is personally concerned would be the equivalent of that which needs to exist for the court to give relief against the minister in proceedings for judicial review. There would need to be default by the department for which the minister is responsible.

While [Mr Baker] was Home Secretary the order was one binding upon him personally and one for the compliance with which he as the head of the department was personally responsible. He was, therefore, under a strict liability to comply with the order. However, on the facts of this case I have little doubt that if the Court of Appeal had appreciated that they could make a finding against Mr Baker in his official capacity this is what the court would have done. The conduct complained of in this case which justified the bringing of contempt proceedings was not that of Mr Baker alone and he was acting on advice. His error was understandable and I accept that there is an element of unfairness in the finding against him personally.

Baker's appeal was dismissed, save that 'the Home Secretary' was substituted as the person against whom the finding of contempt was made.

Sir William Wade remarked of this decision that it had 'put the rule of law back on the rails' (*The Times*, 17 August 1993). The case has received extensive comment. On *M v. Home Office* in the Court of Appeal, see Wade (1992) 142 *NLJ* 1275, 1315 and (1992) 108 *LQR* 173; Marshall [1992] *PL* 7; and, in the House of Lords, Allan [1994] *CLJ* 1; Gould [1993] *PL* 568; Harlow (1994) 57 *MLR* 620. For a more sceptical view of the achievements of *M v. Home Office*, see Tomkins, *Public Law* (2003), pp. 51–4.

The position in Scotland was historically different and was confused by an unfortunate mix of some unhelpful English precedents being applied in Scotland and some remarkably poor drafting in the Crown Proceedings Act 1947. However, Scots law has now been (more or less) brought into line with the English law position as set out in *M v. Home Office*: see *Davidson v. Scottish Ministers* [2005] UKHL 74, 2006 SLT 110. See, further, Tomkins, 'The Crown in Scots law', in McHarg and Mullen (eds.), *Public Law in Scotland* (2006).

It should be noted that the Law Lords in *M v. Home Office* did not question the continuing immunity of *the Crown itself* from judicial process. Sir Stephen Sedley has remarked that the supposition of the immunity of the Crown as executive 'groans under an unnecessary burden of history and myth' (Forsyth and Hare (eds.), *The Golden Metwand and the Crooked Cord* (1998), p. 262) but, even after *M* v. *Home Office*, it remains the law, as Sedley LJ himself ruled in *Chagos Islanders* v. *Attorney General* [2004] EWCA Civ 997.

2.3.3 Discretion and the Rule of Law

Statutes often entrust ministers and other public authorities with discretionary power, allowing them – within whatever limits may be fixed – to choose whether or in what way to exercise the power. Can such discretion in executive decision-making be reconciled with the principle that all uses of executive power should be governed by law? Dicey was apprehensive of the danger implicit in discretion, saying that the rule of law excluded 'wide discretionary authority on the part of the government'. In this, Gavin Drewry remarks that Dicey 'gave currency to a cripplingly restricted view of public law which failed to accommodate the looming reality of a twentieth century interventionist state' ((1995) 73 *Pub Adm* 41, 46). Today we have a better understanding of the necessity and value of discretionary power in many branches of public administration, in order that varying circumstances as well as the needs of justice in individual cases can properly inform the making of decisions.

> ### *Kenneth Culp Davis, Discretionary Justice* (1971), pp. 17, 42
>
> Rules without discretion cannot fully take into account the need for tailoring results to unique facts and circumstances of particular cases. The justification for discretion is often the need for individualized justice. This is so in the judicial process as well as in the administrative process.
>
> Every governmental and legal system in world history has involved both rules and discretion. No government has ever been a government of laws and not of men in the sense of eliminating all discretionary power. Every government has always been *a government of laws and of men* . . .
>
> Elimination of all discretionary power is both impossible and undesirable. The sensible goal is development of a proper balance between rule and discretion. Some circumstances call for rules, some for discretion, some for mixtures of one proportion, and some for mixtures of another proportion . . . [T]he special need is to eliminate *unnecessary* discretionary power, and to discover more successful ways to confine, to structure, and to check necessary discretionary power.

Davis was of the opinion that the degree of discretion allowed to administrative authorities was often too great and that injustice was more likely to result from discretion than from the application of rules. But rules are not always the most apt means of achieving goals of efficiency and justice, and it has been argued that the British tradition favours discretion as opposed to 'the rigidities of legal formalism': 'Administration is viewed as in the first place a discretionary activity, the benefits of which are likely to be reduced if it has to be conducted within a framework of detailed legal regulation' (Nevil Johnson, Memorandum to the Treasury and Civil Service Committee, *5th Report of 1993–94*, HC 27-III, Appendix 10). In particular, a discretion that is 'structured' in a framework of published policies and fair procedures may be a more just and effective method of dealing with claims on public resources than the application of a mass of detailed and complex rules. The system of social security provision for those in need makes use of both rules and discretion, government policy showing a preference sometimes for rules and sometimes for discretion or arriving at a blend of the two techniques.

The administrative process cannot, in any event, be understood as involving a simple choice between rules and discretion. They can work in combination, and procedures of decision-making should be constructed that are appropriate to the objectives sought and have regard for values such as fairness, efficiency, openness and accountability. (See, further, Galligan, *Discretionary Powers* (1986), ch. 2; Hawkins (ed.), *The Uses of Discretion* (1992); Baldwin, *Rules and Government* (1995), ch. 3.)

If discretionary power is conferred in wide and unqualified terms, there is a risk – we must concede to Dicey – that its exercise may be infected by uncertainty, inconsistency or even perversity. We may see it as a function of the rule of law to ensure that well-founded claims, individual interests and, indeed, civil liberties are not at the mercy of uncontrolled discretion, and generally to prevent discretionary power from degenerating into arbitrariness by insisting on effective limits, standards and controls. How, in practice, are such limits to be established?

A statute that confers discretionary power will often specify criteria and limits to be observed by the decision-maker. Consider, for example, a statute such as the Animals (Scientific Procedures) Act 1986, which gives the Secretary of State a discretionary power to grant licences allowing the use of animals for experimental purposes. Section 5 provides that, before granting a licence, the Secretary of State must be satisfied as to a specified range of matters (e.g., that the purpose of the research cannot be achieved satisfactorily by any other reasonably practicable method) and must 'weigh the likely adverse effects on the animals concerned against the benefit likely to accrue' from the experiments.

Where the terms of a statute do not disclose limits on the exercise of a power conferred by it, such limits may be imported by common law principles of fairness and legality. We have already seen this in the *UNISON* case, discussed earlier with regard to upholding the rule of law and access to the courts. This is well-illustrated by the following case.

R v. Secretary of State for the Home Department, ex p Pierson [1998] AC 539 (HL)
In terms of section 35 of the Criminal Justice Act 1991, the Home Secretary had a discretionary power to release on licence a prisoner serving a mandatory life sentence for murder. (This power has since been removed by the Criminal Justice Act 2003: see below, p. 930.) Successive Home Secretaries had adopted

and applied a policy of fixing a penal element of the sentence (the 'tariff'), which is intended as a period that would satisfy the requirements of retribution and deterrence, to be followed by any further period of detention considered by the Home Secretary to be necessary for the protection of the public. In a policy statement issued in 1993 the then Home Secretary announced that the tariff set at the beginning of a mandatory life sentence would be reviewed before the prisoner was released and might exceptionally be increased if it was not then believed to be adequate.

In the case of the appellant, Pierson, a mandatory life prisoner, a previous Home Secretary had, in 1988, at the beginning of the sentence, fixed the tariff at twenty years on the basis that the appellant had committed double premeditated murder. This decision was subsequently communicated to the appellant who was invited (in accordance with *R* v. *Secretary of State for the Home Department, ex p Doody* [1994] 1 AC 531) to make representations about it. In responding, the appellant objected that the two murders had been part of a single incident and that they were alleged not to have been premeditated. The Home Secretary accepted that it had been wrong to proceed on the basis of premeditation and acknowledged that the murders were part of a single incident, but decided nevertheless that twenty years was appropriate to meet the requirements of retribution and deterrence. This decision was challenged in proceedings for judicial review.

The House of Lords held that the decision to confirm a tariff period originally fixed on the basis of aggravating circumstances erroneously taken into account amounted in substance to an increase in the tariff. A majority of three Law Lords held that the decision was unlawful and must be quashed, but differed in their reasons. Lords Steyn and Hope, of the majority, held that the power conferred on the Home Secretary must be exercised in accordance with minimum standards of fairness and did not allow him to increase the penal tariff once it had been fixed and communicated to a prisoner. In the present context the speech of Lord Steyn is of interest for its reliance on the rule of law or 'principle of legality'.

Lord Steyn held it to be a general principle of English law 'that a lawful sentence pronounced by a judge may not retrospectively be increased' and that 'a convicted criminal is entitled to know where he stands so far as his punishment is concerned'. His Lordship continued as follows.

Lord Steyn: . . . The question must now be considered whether the Home Secretary, in making a decision on punishment, is free from the normal constraint applicable to a sentencing power. It is at this stage of the examination of the problem that it becomes necessary to consider where in the structure of public law it fits in. Parliament has not expressly authorised the Home Secretary to increase tariffs retrospectively. If Parliament had done so that would have been the end of the matter. Instead Parliament has by section 35(2) of the Act of 1991 entrusted the power to take decisions about the release of mandatory life sentence prisoners to the Home Secretary. The statutory power is wide enough to authorise the fixing of a tariff. But it does not follow that it is wide enough to permit a power retrospectively to increase the level of punishment.

The wording of section 35(2) of the Act of 1991 is wide and general. It provides that 'the Secretary of State may . . . release on licence a life prisoner who is not a discretionary life prisoner'. There is no ambiguity in the statutory language. The presumption that in the event of ambiguity legislation is presumed not to invade common law rights is inapplicable. A broader principle applies. Parliament does not legislate in a vacuum. Parliament legislates for a European liberal democracy founded on the principles and traditions of the common law. And the courts may approach legislation on this initial assumption. But this assumption only has prima facie force. It can be displaced by a clear and specific provision to the contrary . . .

[A] general power to increase tariffs duly fixed is in disharmony with the deep rooted principle of not retrospectively increasing lawfully pronounced sentences. In the absence of contrary indications it must be presumed that Parliament entrusted the wide power to make decisions on the release of mandatory life sentence prisoners on the supposition that the Home Secretary would not act contrary to such a fundamental principle of our law. There are no contrary indications. Certainly, there is not a shred of evidence that Parliament would have been prepared to vest a general power in the Home Secretary to increase retrospectively tariffs duly fixed. The evidence is to the contrary. When Parliament enacted section 35(2) of the Act of 1991 – the foundation of the Home Secretary's present power – Parliament knew that since 1983 successive Home Secretaries had adopted a policy of fixing in each case a tariff period, following which risk is considered. Parliament also knew that it was the practice that a tariff, once fixed, would not be increased. That was clear from the assurance in the 1983 policy statement [by the Home Secretary, Mr Leon Brittan] that 'except where a prisoner has committed an offence for which he has received a further custodial sentence, the formal review date will not be put back'. What Parliament did not know in 1991 was that in 1993 a new Home Secretary would assert a general power to increase the punishment of prisoners convicted of murder whenever he considered it right to do so. It would be wrong to assume that Parliament would have been prepared to give to the Home Secretary such an unprecedented power, alien to the principles of our law . . .

The correct analysis of this case is in terms of the rule of law . . .

Unless there is the clearest provision to the contrary, Parliament must be presumed not to legislate contrary to the rule of law. And the rule of law enforces minimum standards of fairness, both substantive and procedural. I therefore approach the problem in the present case on this basis.

It is true that the principle of legality only has prima facie force. But in enacting section 35(2) of the Act of 1991, with its very wide power to release prisoners, Parliament left untouched the fundamental principle that a sentence lawfully passed should not retrospectively be increased. Parliament must therefore be presumed to have enacted legislation wide enough to enable the Home Secretary to make decisions on punishment on the basis that he would observe the normal constraint governing that function. Instead the Home Secretary has asserted a general power to increase tariffs duly fixed. Parliament did not confer such a power on the Home Secretary.

It follows that the Home Secretary did not have the power to increase a tariff lawfully fixed ...

It was agreed before your Lordships' House that the Home Secretary's decision letter of 6 May 1994 did communicate a decision to Mr Pierson to increase the tariff in his case. That decision was in my judgment unlawful and ought to be quashed.

An authority vested with discretionary power may itself adopt policies or rules for the exercise of its discretion. Indeed, a discretionary power may be of a kind, and of such width, that it 'calls out for the development of policy as to the way it will in general be exercised' (Lord Woolf MR in *R* v. *Secretary of State for the Home Department, ex p Venables* [1998] AC 407, 432). Adoption of a policy can be helpful in preventing inconsistency or arbitrariness in the use of discretion (see *R* v. *Secretary of State for the Home Department, ex p Yousaf* [2000] 3 All ER 649, at [44]). Any policy adopted must, of course, be compatible with the purposes of the statute conferring the power. In addition, the authority must not apply its self-imposed rules in an inflexible way so as to *fetter* the discretion it is required to exercise and must remain willing to listen to those with something new to say.

In *Gillan* v. *United Kingdom* (2010) 50 EHRR 45 the ECtHR ruled that the police powers to stop and search contained in sections 44–7 of the Terrorism Act 2000 were so widely framed that they failed 'to offer the individual adequate protection against arbitrary interference' (at [79]). Unlike the stop and search powers conferred by section 1 of the Police and Criminal Evidence Act 1984, for example, those in the Terrorism Act did not require the police to have reasonable suspicion of wrongdoing before a stop and search could be made. While the powers in sections 44–7 of the Terrorism Act were attended by a range of safeguards, it had been shown to the satisfaction of the ECtHR that the safeguards had not worked in practice. For example, although the act required there to be an authorisation before the powers could be exercised, and although the scheme of the Act was that such an authorisation should be granted for a specific location and for a limited amount of time, a rolling authorisation had, in fact, been in place for the whole of Greater London since the Act had come into force. For these reasons, the ECtHR held that the safeguards ostensibly contained in the Act did not 'constitute a real curb on the wide powers afforded to the executive' (at [79]). The court ruled that the powers breached Article 8 of the ECHR (the right to respect for private life), the interference with privacy not being 'in accordance with the law' by virtue of the arbitrary manner in which the stop and search powers could be exercised. The Protection of Freedoms Bill 2011 will, if enacted in the form in which it was introduced, repeal sections 44–7 of the Terrorism Act and will replace these powers with new, more narrowly constrained, stop and search powers.

The judgment of the ECtHR stands in marked contrast to that of the House of Lords, in which the lawfulness of the powers had been upheld: see *R (Gillan)* v. *Metropolitan Police Commissioner* [2006] UKHL 12, [2006] 2 AC 307.

(See also on the rule of law and the requirement of certainty *R (Purdy)* v. *Director of Public Prosecutions* [2009] UKHL 45, [2010] 1 AC 345.)

2.3.4 The Rule of Law: Wider Conceptions?

The rule of law in its minimal sense of government according to law may seem to be a relatively unexacting principle, which is satisfied by any state that has taken the trouble to invest its officers with legal authority to do what is required of them. The rule of law in this limited sense is not inconsistent with despotic government if the despot is scrupulous about using the forms of law. Despotic governments, however, are not generally distinguished by a punctilious observance of the law, even law of their own making and, indeed, even democratic governments do not always show a fastidious regard for legal requirements. Broader conceptions of the rule of law demand more than a mere formal compliance by public authorities with the rules of the legal system. In this light, several commentators have argued that the doctrine should be seen as including a number of other values. (We saw an important example of this from Lord Bingham, above, pp. 111–112.)

In its wider sense, the rule of law has been said to require, for example, that laws should be general, prospective, open, clear and stable. (See, especially, Joseph Raz, 'The Rule of Law and its Virtue' (1977) 93 *LQR* 195, who sees these and other principles of the rule of law as resting on the 'basic idea that the law should be capable of providing effective guidance' and on respect for the dignity and autonomy of the individual.)

The *generality* of a legal order would distinguish it from a regime in which specific commands were issued without regard to reasoned principle – or in which, in the words of Lon Fuller, governmental power expressed itself in 'unpredictable and patternless interventions in human affairs' (*The Morality of Law* (2nd edn. 1969), pp. 157–8). It is impossible to conceive of a legal *system* of which this was the characteristic feature, but a government might show a tendency to act in this way in particular branches of administration.

The law should be *prospective* and should not, as Willes J observed in *Phillips* v. *Eyre* (1870) LR 6 QB 1, 23, 'change the character of past transactions carried on upon the faith of the then existing law'. In *Lauri* v. *Renad* [1892] 3 Ch. 402, 421, Lindley LJ held it to be a 'fundamental rule of English law that no statute shall be construed so as to have a retrospective operation unless its language is such as plainly to require such a construction'. Retrospective legislation is sometimes justified, as Willes J conceded in *Phillips* v. *Eyre* (above), to avoid 'practical public inconvenience and wrong', and an element of retrospectivity is an unavoidable feature of some fiscal legislation in particular. (See, further, Dickinson, 'Retrospective Legislation and the British Constitution' 1974 *SLT*

25; Feldman (1992) 108 *LQR* 212; *L'Office Cherifien des Phosphates* v. *Yamashita-Shinnihon Steamship Co Ltd* [1994] 1 AC 486.) Retrospective *penal* legislation is especially offensive to the rule of law and is besides contrary to Article 7 of the ECHR. Our courts will interpret penal statutes as not having retrospective effect unless they are compelled by unequivocal statutory provision to hold otherwise: see *Waddington* v. *Miah* [1974] 1 WLR 683. In *Welch* v. *United Kingdom* (1995) 20 EHRR 247, it was held by the ECtHR that the UK had breached Article 7 by reason of the retrospective operation of confiscation orders made under the Drug Trafficking Offences Act 1986.

Laws should be *open*, that is to say, made known by sufficient publication. As Lord Diplock remarked in *Fothergill* v. *Monarch Airlines* [1981] AC 251, 279, elementary justice 'demands that the rules by which the citizen is to be bound should be ascertainable by him (or, more realistically, by a competent lawyer advising him) by reference to identifiable sources that are publicly accessible'. In *Salih* v. *Secretary of State for the Home Department* [2003] EWHC 2273 (Admin), Stanley Burnton J declared it to be 'a fundamental requisite of the rule of law that the law should be made known'. In this case, the Home Secretary had discretion under statute to provide 'hard cases support' (facilities for accommodation) for failed asylum-seekers. He adopted a set of criteria for the provision of hard cases support, but decided that he would neither publicise his scheme nor inform failed asylum-seekers of the possibility of applying for support. Stanley Burnton J held that it was 'inconsistent with the constitutional imperative that statute law be made known for the government to withhold information about its policy relating to the exercise of a power conferred by statute'. The judge concluded that the Home Secretary's decision not to inform failed asylum-seekers of his policy on hard cases was unlawful. See also *R (Anufrijeva)* v. *Secretary of State for the Home Department* [2003] UKHL 36, [2004] 1 AC 604, in which Lord Steyn declared that a constitutional state under the rule of law 'must accord to individuals the right to know of a decision before their rights can be adversely affected'. See, to like effect, *Walumba Lumba* v. *Secretary of State for the Home Department* [2011] UKSC 12, esp. at [34].

If laws are to be an effective and reliable guide to conduct, it is evident that they should be *clear*. Expressed as a requirement of *certainty*, this was said by Lord Nicholls in *R* v. *Secretary of State for the Environment, ex p Spath Holme Ltd* [2001] 2 AC 349, 397, to be 'one of the fundamental elements of the rule of law'. Our laws do not always measure up to this. The Law Commission observed in 1994 that 'laws which so many people have to use, often at great personal expense, remain unsimple, unmodern, inaccessible and unreformed': *Twenty-eighth Annual Report* (Law Com No 223, 1994), para 1.21. More recently, the Supreme Court was outspoken in its criticism of the unnecessary complexity of aspects of our criminal justice law. In *R (Noone)* v. *Governor of HMP Drake Hall* [2010] UKSC 30, [2010] 1 WLR 1743, Lord Judge CJ stated (at [87]) that 'it is outrageous that so much intellectual effort, as well as public time and resources, have had to be expended in order to discover a route through the legislative morass to what should be ... the simplest and most certain of questions – the prisoner's release date.' The ECtHR declared in *Sunday Times* v. *United Kingdom* (1979) 2 EHRR 245, 271, that 'a norm cannot be regarded as a "law" unless it is formulated with sufficient precision to enable the citizen to regulate his conduct' (see also *Gillan* v. *United Kingdom*, above).

Laws should be *stable* because frequent changes in them make it difficult to know the law or to plan for the future. (See Raz, 'The Rule of Law and its Virtue' (1977) 93 *LQR* 195, 199.)

The rule of law as we have so far considered it may appear to be neutral with regard to the distribution of power in society and might not be an obstacle to a legal order designed to maintain social and economic inequality and to serve the interests of a governing elite. (Cf. Thompson, *Whigs and Hunters* (1975), pp. 258–69.) Unger (*Law in Modern Society* (1977)) observes that the rule of law has failed to solve the problem of power: it is, he says (p. 239):

> the liberal state's most emphatic response to the problems of power and freedom. But ... whatever its efficacy in preventing immediate government oppression of the individual, the strategy of legalism fails to deal with these issues in the basic relationships of work and everyday life.

The rule of law has sometimes been invoked in defence of private interests against the actions of 'interventionist' government directed to social reform and public welfare. Friedmann (The *State and the Rule of Law in a Mixed Economy* (1971), p. 95) responds as follows:

> The proposition that the rule of law in modern democracy is incompatible with any kind of economic planning by the state or ... that the planned state 'commands people which road to take', whereas the rule of law only provides 'signposts', [von Hayek, *The Road to Serfdom* (1944), p. 54] is of course incompatible with the reality of any contemporary democracy. It would be a useless exercise for us to attempt to define the rule of law in a way that bears no relation to the minimum functions of social welfare, urban planning, regulatory controls, entrepreneurship and other essential functions of the state in a mixed economy.

The achievement of great social ends, such as the removal of economic, racial and sexual injustice, and the provision of welfare services, is impossible without state activity and the assumption of the necessary powers. It would be a distorted conception of the rule of law that denied the validity of these ends or frustrated their accomplishment. If in recent times a new orthodoxy of the non-interventionist state, of deregulation and privatisation, has been in the ascendancy, it cannot claim the specific endorsement of the rule of law.

Among those who have argued for an enlarged conception of the rule of law, going beyond an exclusive insistence on requirements of legality and procedural fairness, the International Commission of Jurists has taken the most radical position. In a congress held in Delhi in 1959, it declared:

> that the Rule of Law is a dynamic concept for the expansion and fulfilment of which jurists are primarily responsible and which should be employed not only to safeguard and advance the civil and political rights of the individual in a free society, but also to establish social, economic, educational and cultural conditions under which his legitimate aspirations and dignity may be realized.

The impulse to redefinitions of this kind comes from an awareness that a neutral conception of the rule of law seems to distance lawyers and the ideals of law from the most compelling issues of our time – of poverty, social deprivation and the denial of political rights and elementary justice by authoritarian governments. The lawyers at Delhi were conscious that law is, too often, mainly of service to limited and powerful interests in unequal societies.

Others still insist on a stricter definition of the rule of law, saying with Raz ((1977) 93 *LQR* 195, 195–6): 'If the rule of law is the rule of the good law then to explain its nature is to propound a complete social philosophy. But if so the term lacks any useful function. We have no need to be converted to the rule of law just in order to discover that to believe in it is to believe that good should triumph.' Can the wider objectives declared in Delhi be accommodated within a workable concept of the rule of law? (See, further, Craig, 'Formal and Substantive Conceptions of the Rule of Law' [1997] *PL* 467.)

2.3.5 The Rule of Law and Parliamentary Sovereignty

For Dicey, as we have seen, the fundamental principles of the British constitution were parliamentary sovereignty and the rule of law. But Dicey, it has been objected (Lane, *Constitutions and Political Theory* (1996), p. 44), 'did not fully understand that his model is contradictory', for:

> If Parliament has sovereignty, then how could it be bound by the rule of law . . . ? If the rule of law is the foundation of the State, then how can Parliament claim a power not bound by any legal restrictions?

Dicey was not wholly oblivious of the contradiction but believed that the rule of law was not at risk from a Parliament that was subject, in his view, to both internal and external limits to the exercise of its sovereignty. Parliament was restrained internally, he thought, by its representative character, which identified it with the interests and wishes of the electorate, and externally by the force of a public opinion that would oppose serious resistance to 'reactionary legislation'.

Today there is less confidence in the effectiveness of such constraints to reconcile parliamentary sovereignty with the rule of law. Can the dilemma be resolved only by admitting legal limits to parliamentary sovereignty or has the rule of law to be qualified by democratic principle? (See, for example, the arguments in 2003–4 concerning the proposed ouster clause in the Asylum and Immigration (Treatment of Claimants) Bill, considered above, p. 106–107.) See, further, Allan, *Constitutional Justice* (2001), ch. 7; *The Sovereignty of Law: Freedom, Constitution and Common Law* (2013), ch. 1; and contrast Goldsworthy, *Parliamentary Sovereignty: Contemporary Debates* (2010), ch. 3.

(See generally, on the rule of law, Allan, *Law, Liberty, and Justice* (1993), ch. 2; Dyzenhaus (ed.), *Recrafting the Rule of Law: The Limits of Legal Order* (1999); Craig, 'Constitutional Foundations, the Rule of Law and Supremacy' [2003] *PL* 92; Ekins, 'Judicial Supremacy and the Rule of Law' (2003) 119 *LQR* 127; Lord Bingham, *The Rule of Law* (2010).)

2.4 Separation of Powers

A doctrine of the separation of powers was formulated by English writers and controversialists of the mid-seventeenth century who argued for the separation of the legislative and executive (then including judicial) functions of government, seeing in this a means to restrain the abuse of governmental power. The theory of the separation of powers was subsequently developed by John Locke in his *Second Treatise of Civil Government* (1690) and, more systematically, in France, by Montesquieu in *The Spirit of the Laws* (1748). Montesquieu, in the context of his description of an idealised English constitution, distinguished the legislative, executive and judicial functions of government, which he maintained should be exercised by different persons, and insisted on the independence of the judiciary. (Montesquieu also held that the judiciary should not be identified with any one estate or class of persons in the state.) 'All would be lost', he wrote (*The Spirit of the Laws*, Book XI, ch. 6), 'if the same man or the same ruling body, whether of nobles or of the people, were to exercise these three powers, that of law-making, that of executing the public resolutions, and that of judging crimes and civil causes.' He also held that the legislature and the executive should have powers to enable each to check or limit the other.

Montesquieu's work ensured the lasting influence of the theory of the separation of powers. In England, however, this theory was opposed in the eighteenth century by the doctrine of the mixed or balanced constitution, in which monarchical, aristocratic and democratic elements were *joined* and held in equilibrium, rather than strictly separated. Accordingly, the theory of the separation of powers was not to prevail as an explanation of English constitutional arrangements; neither did it provide a focus for constitutional reform. It was in America (and in France) that the theory was to be embraced by political leaders and makers of constitutions, the US Constitution of 1789, for example, being based on a conception of the separation of powers qualified by a machinery of checks and balances (see, further, Claus, 'Montesquieu's Mistakes and the True Meaning of Separation' (2005) 25 *OJLS* 419).

The system of parliamentary government that evolved in the UK in the nineteenth century under the impetus of the Reform Act of 1832 was evidently not based on a theory of the separation of powers. The modern constitution is perhaps even less conformable to that theory as traditionally understood, for nowadays 'rules are made by civil servants and by judges as well as by legislatures; rules are applied by the courts as well as by "the executive"; and judgements are made by civil servants and ministers as well as by judges' (Vile, *Constitutionalism and the Separation of Powers* (1967), p. 317). While we may concede that the British constitution has not been *based on* the separation of powers, this does not mean that the separation of powers has been of no relevance to it. One consequence of the constitutional reforms that have been enacted since 1998 is that the separation of powers has grown in importance. Indeed, Vernon Bogdanor in *The New British Constitution* (2010, p. 285) goes so far as to suggest that:

> The old constitution was based upon the sovereignty of Parliament. The new constitution is based on the idea of a constitutional state based upon a separation of powers.

(On Bogdanor's argument, see above, pp. 43–44.)

It is not the case, however, that the separation of powers carried no weight before 1998. Consider, for example, the reliance placed on it by the Donoughmore Committee, which inquired into delegated legislation and administrative adjudication in the 1930s.

Report of the Committee on Ministers' Powers (Donoughmore Committee), Cmd 4060/1932, pp. 4, 5

In the British Constitution there is no such thing as the absolute separation of legislative, executive, and judicial powers; in practice it is inevitable that they should overlap. In such constitutions as those of France and the United States of America, attempts to keep them rigidly apart have been made, but have proved unsuccessful. The distinction is none the less real, and for our purposes important. One of the main problems of a modern democratic state is how to preserve the distinction, whilst avoiding too rigid an insistence on it, in the wide borderland where it is convenient to entrust minor legislative and judicial functions to executive authorities.

It is customary today for parliament to delegate minor legislative powers to subordinate authorities and bodies. Ministers of the Crown are the chief repositories of such powers; but they are conferred also, in differing degrees, upon Local Authorities, statutory corporations and companies, Universities, and representative bodies of solicitors, doctors and other professions. Some people hold the view that this practice of delegating legislative powers is unwise, and might be dispensed with altogether. A similar view is held with regard to the delegation to Ministers by statutory authority of judicial and quasi-judicial functions. It has even been suggested that the practice of passing such legislation is wholly bad, and should be forthwith abandoned. We do not think that this is the considered view of most of those who have investigated the problem, but many of them would like the practice curtailed as much as possible.

The Donoughmore Committee was appointed in a political atmosphere that was generally hostile to the delegation by Parliament of legislative and judicial functions to ministers and other public authorities. It had been asserted that the practice of delegation, in its denial of the separation of powers, presented a threat to parliamentary sovereignty and the rule of law. The committee, however, declined to give its imprimatur to a strict separation of powers, seeing the doctrine as no more than a 'rule of political wisdom' that 'must give way where sound reasons of public policy so require' (p. 95). Moreover, it rejected the view that the delegation of law-making and judicial powers had led to a 'new despotism' of officials.

While the necessity for the delegation of legislative powers to the executive is not nowadays contested, the nature and extent of such delegations may raise questions about compliance with the separation of powers. For instance, a House of Lords committee expressed concern about the delegation of powers contained in the Access to Justice Bill and questioned whether 'control by the state of the means of access to justice may erode the separation of powers and put individuals at a disadvantage when seeking to defend themselves against claims brought by the very government which also has the power to prescribe how effectively they may be represented' (Constitution Committee, *1st report of 2001–02*, HL 11: Memorandum by the Delegated Powers and Deregulation Committee, p. 8). (See Ganz, 'Delegated Legislation: A Necessary Evil or a Constitutional Outrage?', in Leyland and Woods (eds.), *Administrative Law Facing the Future* (1997), ch. 3; and Page, *Governing by Numbers* (2001); see, further, Chapter 7.)

Issues also arise as to the appropriate level of parliamentary scrutiny over delegated powers. The Sanctions and Anti-Money Laundering Act 2018, for example, empowers ministers to make regulations imposing sanctions for the purposes of compliance with UN obligations, to comply with other international law obligations, or for a range of purposes set out in the legislation – for instance, to prevent terrorism, or to 'promote respect for democracy, the rule of law and good governance' (section 1(2)(i)). Moreover, the minister is empowered to make such regulations 'where that minister considers it appropriate' (section 1(1)). The Select Constitution Committee of the House of Lords criticised this broad delegation of power, focusing in particular on the minister only needing to consider it 'appropriate' to enact regulations to make sanctions, the breadth of purposes for which these regulations could be made, in addition to considering it 'constitutionally inappropriate for ministers to have the power, by regulations, to create new forms of sanctions' ('Sanctions and Anti-Money Laundering Bill', 8th Report of Session 2017–2019 HL Paper 39). The committee also concluded that it was constitutionally unacceptable for ministers to be given the power to create new criminal offences that could impose penalties of up to ten years' imprisonment. Similar criticisms were also made by the Delegated Powers and Regulatory Reform Committee of the House of Lords (7th *Report* of Session 2017–19). Following these criticisms, the bill was amended and the act now includes a requirement that, when exercising a power to make regulations that are not required by international law, the minister has to consider 'good reasons' for adopting the sanctions measure and whether the adoption of these sanctions is a 'reasonable course of action' (section 2(2)). These must be set out in a report laid before Parliament. This provides a means for Parliament to check the minister's reasons for making such sanctions, in addition to facilitating later judicial checks on the powers of the minister. These measures are also subject to the affirmative resolution procedure (see section 55 of the Act). Concerns have also been raised about the breadth of delegated powers in order to achieve Brexit, found both in the European Union (Withdrawal) Act 2018 and the European Union (Withdrawal Agreement) Act 2020, discussed further in Chapter 5.

Powers of delegated legislation and executive law-making are particularly controversial when they extend to an ability of ministers and civil servants to amend primary legislation. Such powers are known as Henry VIII clauses. It may be thought that only Parliament ought to be able to amend or repeal its (primary) legislation – statutes. Henry VIII clauses extend that power, in certain circumstances, to the executive. Such clauses are included, for example, in the European Communities Act 1972 and in the Human Rights Act, as well as the European Union (Withdrawal) Act 2018 and the European Union (Withdrawal Agreement) Act 2020. (See Barber and Young, 'The Rise of Prospective Henry VIII Clauses and their Implications for Sovereignty' [2003] *PL* 112.)

Extensive Henry VIII clauses were included in the Deregulation and Contracting Out Act 1994 and the Regulatory Reform Act 2001. The government proposed to take these further in its Legislative and Regulatory Reform Bill of 2006. As the government drafted it, this measure would have permitted ministers to make orders amending, repealing or replacing almost *any* legislation, primary or secondary, for almost *any* purpose. The only exceptions would have been that such orders could not have: imposed or increased taxation; created or increased criminal penalties; or authorised forcible entry, search or seizure. These powers were so sweeping that the bill was frequently dubbed the 'Abolition of Parliament Bill'. The bill was introduced in order to streamline the procedure available under the Regulatory Reform Act 2001, under which only twenty-seven regulatory reform orders had been made. The 2006 Bill met with very considerable hostility, with both the Hansard Society and several parliamentary committees calling for significant amendments (the bill was scrutinised – indeed, condemned – in reports of the House of Commons Regulatory Reform Committee (HC 878 of 2005–06), the House of Commons Procedure Committee (HC 894 of 2005–06), the House of Commons Public Administration Committee (HC 1033 of 2005–06) and the House of Lords Constitution Committee (HL 194 of 2005–06)). As a result, the government was forced to make a series of substantial amendments which, on the one hand, reduced the scope of ministerial powers to make and unmake the law and, on the other hand, increased the degree of parliamentary scrutiny of ministerial orders made under the act. Even after these amendments, however, the bill was still thought by the House of Lords Constitution Committee to contain 'over-broad and vaguely drawn' ministerial powers to which 'further safeguards' should have been attached (HL 194 of 2005–06, para 5). For a thorough analysis of this important episode, see Davis [2007] *PL* 677.

Depressingly, the government does not seem to have learned the lessons of 2006. In October 2010, the Coalition Government introduced into Parliament the Public Bodies Bill. The measure is designed to reduce the number of public bodies (or 'quangos') in the UK. Unfortunately, it seeks to achieve this aim through the use of astonishingly broad Henry VIII powers that would enable ministers to abolish, merge or modify a very large number of public bodies, as listed in the various schedules to the bill. Moreover, as introduced, the Henry VIII powers in the Public Bodies Bill were not accompanied by the sorts of constraints and safeguards that Parliament had insisted be included in the Legislative and Regulatory Reform Act 2006. The Public Bodies Bill, like its 2006 predecessor, was swiftly and robustly condemned in a series of parliamentary reports, led by the House of Lords Constitution Committee (see its *6th Report of 2010–11*, HL 51; see also House of Lords Delegated Powers and Regulatory Reform Committee, *5th Report of 2010–11*, HL 57; and House of Commons Public Administration Committee, *5th Report of 2010–11*, HC 537). The bill is liable to be substantially amended in Parliament.

The misuse of Henry VIII clauses generally, and those contained in the Public Bodies Bill specifically, has also attracted the strong criticism of the Lord Chief Justice, Lord Judge (see, e.g., his evidence to the House of Lords Constitution Committee, 15 December 2010, published as that Committee's *9th Report of 2010–11*, HL 89 and also Judge *The Safest Shield: Lectures, Speeches and Essays* (2015)). Nevertheless, Henry VIII clauses continue to be used, most recently and controversially in the European Union (Withdrawal) Act 2018 and the European Union (Withdrawal Agreement) Act 2020. While both the House of Lords Delegated Powers and Regulatory Reform Committee and the Committee on the Constitution criticised the broad Henry VIII powers in the bill, little was done to restrict these powers. Although both committees recognised that Henry VIII powers may be required in order to facilitate necessary legislative changes to facilitate Brexit, the House of Lords Constitution Committee nevertheless concluded that the Henry VIII power was still too broad and that there was insufficient parliamentary scrutiny over these powers (see 'European Union (Withdrawal) Bill' 9th report of session 2017–19, HL Paper 69, discussed further in Chapter 5).

(For more information on ministerial law- and rule-making powers, see Chapter 7.)

Most of this part of this chapter is concerned with the separation of the judicial roles in the constitution from those of government and Parliament. While the separation (or, perhaps, the lack of it) between government and Parliament is briefly considered towards the end of the section, this topic is considered in more detail in Chapter 9. Here we ask, first, whether the separation of powers in the British constitutional order is more a political ideal than a judicially enforceable rule of law, before considering in detail the judicial role and the matter of judicial independence. The changing role of the Lord Chancellor and the difficult issue of judicial appointments are discussed, before we close our consideration of the judiciary with an outline of the separation of the courts from Parliament.

2.4.1 A Political Ideal or a Legal Principle?

A doctrine of the separation of powers can be put into service for different purposes. It may be used in support of a principle that functions should be allocated to the most appropriate body in the state, whether an elected assembly, a court, a tribunal, a body of elected or appointed officials, or something else. This is a matter of allotting functions and powers in such a way that they can be operated with the greatest possible effectiveness. By the same token, the separation of powers is also invoked in support of arrangements for preventing the abuse of power, whereby public powers are so distributed among different institutions that each has a necessary freedom of action and also some capacity for checking other power-holding bodies – a system of checks and balances. As Vile (*Constitutionalism and the Separation of Powers* (1967), p. 10) aptly says:

> We are not prepared to accept that government can become, on the grounds of 'efficiency', or for any other reason, a single undifferentiated monolithic structure, nor can we assume that government can be allowed to become simply an accidental agglomeration of purely pragmatic relationships.

And he goes on to say (p. 15): 'The diffusion of authority among different centres of decision-making is the antithesis of totalitarianism or absolutism.'

The doctrine of the separation of powers in each of these uses (which are complementary) has traditionally been supposed to require a threefold classification of functions and corresponding institutions: legislative, executive and judicial. But in the diverse and complex activity of a modern state like the UK, the processes of law-making, administration and adjudication are neither clearly demarcated nor assigned exclusively to separate institutions. Values once associated with a doctrine of the formal separation of legislative, executive and judicial powers may now depend on the pluralist arrangements of the modern state, in which the powerful departments of central government operate in a world of countervailing powers exercised by Parliament, courts, the devolved administrations, local government and other public bodies, political parties and the empire of pressure groups. We cannot, however, be confident that this pluralist diversity will necessarily give balance to the constitution and prevent undue and dangerous concentrations of power. Questions must be constantly asked as to whether powers are appropriately allocated and what checking mechanisms should be set up, both between and within different branches of the state apparatus.

The question of the proper location of power arises in a wide variety of contexts. Is it right, for instance, that a member of the executive should have any role in determining how long a convicted offender should remain in custody? Formerly, if a young offender were convicted of murder and sentenced to be detained during Her Majesty's pleasure, the practice was for the Home Secretary to fix a period of detention (the 'penal element' or 'tariff') sufficient to meet the requirements of retribution and deterrence, which must be served before the release of the offender could be considered by the Parole Board. In *R v. Secretary of State for the Home Department, ex p Venables* [1998] AC 407, 526, Lord Steyn said: 'In fixing a tariff the Home Secretary is carrying out, contrary to the constitutional principle of separation of powers, a classic judicial function.' The House of Lords did not conclude that the infringement of the separation of powers made the ministerial fixing of a tariff unlawful (although it was held on other grounds that the Home Secretary had acted unlawfully). But in subsequent proceedings in this case, in the ECtHR it was ruled by that court (*V and T v. United Kingdom* (1999) 30 EHRR 121) that the fixing of the tariff amounted to a sentencing exercise, that the Home Secretary as a member of the executive was not an 'independent and impartial tribunal' and accordingly that there had been a breach of Article 6(1) of the ECHR (the right to a fair trial). As a result of this decision it was provided by section 60 of the Criminal Justice and Courts Services Act 2000 that in respect of young offenders convicted of murder and detained at Her Majesty's pleasure, the tariff should be set by the trial judge in open court.

A different regime, resting on section 29 of the Crime (Sentences) Act 1997, continued to apply to an adult prisoner serving a mandatory life sentence for murder. In this case, the Home Secretary remained responsible for setting the penal tariff and for the eventual decision on release. Here, it was contended that the Home Secretary was not fixing the sentence but was deciding whether a person sentenced by a court to life imprisonment should be prematurely released. Somewhat surprisingly, this argument found favour with the ECtHR in *Wynne* v. *United Kingdom* (1994) 19 EHRR 333.

The Home Secretary's power to decide on the release of mandatory life sentence prisoners was again considered by the ECtHR in *Stafford* v. *United Kingdom* (2002) 35 EHRR 32. The Home Secretary had rejected a recommendation of the Parole Board that Stafford, who was serving a life sentence for murder, should be released on licence, on the ground that he might, if released, commit non-violent imprisonable offences. (He had served a sentence for cheque fraud.) A challenge to this decision in the English courts having failed (see *R* v. *Secretary of State for the Home Department, ex p Stafford* [1999] 2 AC 38), Stafford took his complaint to the ECtHR. The ECtHR reassessed its decision in the *Wynne* case (above) and concluded that Stafford's continued detention by decision of the executive, on the ground relied on, was not in accordance with the spirit of the European Convention 'with its emphasis on the rule of law and protection from arbitrariness' and was not compatible with Article 5(1) of the convention (the right to liberty and security of person). Moreover, the fact that Stafford's continued detention was dependent on the discretion of the Home Secretary constituted a violation of Article 5(4) (the right of a detained person to have the lawfulness of his detention decided by a court). In the course of its judgment, the court noted that 'the continuing role of the Secretary of State in fixing the tariff and in deciding on a prisoner's release following its expiry, has become increasingly difficult to reconcile with the notion of separation of powers between the executive and the judiciary'.

The government took a different view regarding the fixing of the tariff and the Home Secretary continued to carry out this function, albeit after taking advice in each instance from the trial judge and the Lord Chief Justice. The procedure was challenged in the following case.

R (Anderson) v. *Secretary of State for the Home Department* [2002] UKHL 46, [2003] 1 AC 837

The appellant, Anderson, had been sentenced by a court to mandatory life imprisonment for murder. The trial judge and the Lord Chief Justice recommended a tariff of fifteen years to be served by him in order to satisfy the requirements of retribution and deterrence. The Home Secretary rejected this advice and fixed the tariff at twenty years. Shortly before the lapse of the judicially recommended minimum term, Anderson brought proceedings to challenge the Home Secretary's decision to set the twenty-year tariff. This decision, it was contended for Anderson, was contrary to Article 6(1) of the ECHR, given effect in the UK by the HRA. So far as material in this case, Article 6(1) provides:

> In the determination of his civil rights and obligations or of any criminal charge against him, everyone is entitled to a fair and public hearing within a reasonable time by an independent and impartial tribunal established by law.

It was argued for Anderson that setting the tariff was a sentencing exercise and as such was part of the determination of a criminal charge in terms of Article 6(1): it must accordingly be carried out by an independent and impartial tribunal and not by a member of the executive. For the Home Secretary, however, the argument was renewed that had been accepted by the ECtHR in *Wynne* (above) but rejected on reconsideration in *Stafford* (above) – that fixing the tariff was not the imposition of a sentence but the administration of a sentence of life imprisonment already passed by the trial court. On this central point, the lords (sitting as a panel of seven) unhesitatingly accepted the reasoning of *Stafford* v. *United Kingdom*: setting the tariff was a sentencing exercise.

> **Lord Bingham:** . . . What happens in practice is that, having taken advice from the trial judge, the Lord Chief Justice and departmental officials, the Home Secretary assesses the term of imprisonment which the convicted murderer should serve as punishment for his crime or crimes. That decision defines the period to be served before release on licence is considered. This is a classical sentencing function. It is what, in the case of other crimes, judges and magistrates do every day.

The Lords approved the following passage from the judgment in *Stafford*:

> The Court considers that it may now be regarded as established in domestic law that there is no distinction between mandatory life prisoners, discretionary life prisoners and juvenile murderers as regards the nature of tariff-fixing. It is a sentencing exercise. The mandatory life sentence does not impose imprisonment for life as a punishment. The tariff, which reflects the individual circumstances of the offence and the offender, represents the element of punishment.

It followed from the Lords' conclusion on this central point that the existing procedure did not comply with Article 6(1), for it was plain, and was not in dispute, that the imposition of a sentence was part of the criminal trial and that the Home Secretary was not independent of the executive.

In arriving at this result, the lords emphasised that it was in accordance with the fundamental principle of the separation of powers between the executive and the judiciary, a principle essential to both the rule of law and democracy:

> **Lord Steyn:** . . . In a series of decisions . . . the House of Lords has described the Home Secretary's role in determining the tariff period to be served by a convicted murderer as punishment akin to a sentencing exercise. In our system of law the sentencing of persons convicted of crimes is classically regarded as a judicial rather than executive task. Our constitution has, however, never embraced a rigid doctrine of separation of powers. The

> relationship between the legislature and the executive is close. On the other hand, the separation of powers between the judiciary and the legislative and executive branches of government is a strong principle of our system of government ... It is reinforced by constitutional principles of judicial independence, access to justice, and the rule of law.

In response to the judgment in this case, provision was made in the Criminal Justice Act 2003 for the tariff or minimum term to be served by mandatory life prisoners to be fixed by the sentencing judge. When the minimum term has been served, the Parole Board decides on the prisoner's suitability for release.

Article 6(1) of the Convention and its interpretation by the courts have given a powerful reinforcement to the domestic principle of the separation of judicial and executive powers. As Lord Steyn expressed it in *Anderson*, 'Article 6(1) requires effective separation between the courts and the executive, and further requires that what can in shorthand be called judicial functions may only be discharged by the courts.' (See also *R (Hammond)* v. *Secretary of State for the Home Department* [2005] UKHL 69, [2006] 1 AC 603, especially the opinion of Lord Hoffmann.)

It may be that one effect of the incorporation by the HRA of the ECHR into domestic law is to encourage British courts to enforce the separation of powers as a legal principle more than they were prepared to do in earlier times. As we have seen, before the HRA, the separation of powers was a political ideal that could be variously used to describe or to criticise aspects of the British constitution, but it was not generally regarded as being a judicially enforceable rule. The sentencing context is one area where the courts have begun to talk of the separation of powers in more juridical terms, but it is not the only one.

Matthews v. *Ministry of Defence* [2003] UKHL 4, [2003] 1 AC 1163

Matthews concerned an unsuccessful challenge to the legality of a statutory bar that prevented servicemen from suing the Crown in tort for personal injury suffered in the course of military duty (see the Crown Proceedings Act 1947, section 10, now repealed by the Crown Proceedings (Armed Forces) Act 1987). Matthews argued that the bar constituted a breach of Article 6(1) (the right to a fair trial before an independent and impartial tribunal). The House of Lords disagreed. In the course of his speech, Lord Hoffmann made the following statements about the separation of powers:

> **Lord Hoffmann:** ... In the great case of *Golder v United Kingdom* (1975) 1 EHRR 524 the Strasbourg court decided that the right to an independent and impartial tribunal for the determination of one's civil rights did not mean only that if you could get yourself before a court, it had to be independent and impartial. It meant that if you claimed on arguable grounds to have a civil right, you had a right to have that question determined by a court. A right to the independence and impartiality of the judicial branch of government would not

> be worth much if the executive branch could stop you from getting to the court in the first place. The executive would in effect be deciding the case against you. That would contravene the rule of law and the principle of the separation of powers.
>
> These principles require not only that you should be able to get to the court room door. The rule of law and separation of powers would be equally at risk if the executive government was entitled, as a matter of arbitrary discretion, to instruct the court to dismiss your action. There are different ways in which one could draft a law to give the executive such a power. It might say that the cause of action was not complete without the government's consent. That would look like a rule of substantive law. Or it could provide that the government could issue a certificate saying that the action was not to proceed. That looks like a procedural bar. But provided one holds onto the underlying principle, which is to maintain the rule of law and the separation of powers, it should not matter how the law is framed. What matters is whether the effect is to give the executive a power to make decisions about people's rights which under the rule of law should be made by the judicial branch of government.

Lord Hoffmann's remarks have since been cited with approval by Lord Nicholls in a case concerning the enforceability of consumer credit agreements (*Wilson* v. *Secretary of State for Trade and Industry* [2003] UKHL 40, [2004] 1 AC 816) and by Lord Hope in a case concerning child maintenance and the Child Support Agency (*R (Kehoe)* v. *Secretary of State for Work and Pensions* [2005] UKHL 48, [2006] 1 AC 42). However, in spite of the variety of factual contexts in which the separation of powers is mentioned in recent House of Lords case law, the work being done by the principle is the same in all these cases. All are concerned with demarcating *judicial* power (none is concerned, for example, with the relationship of legislative to executive power, although, on that issue, see *R* v. *Secretary of State for the Home Department, ex p Fire Brigades Union* [1995] 2 AC 513, *R (Miller)* v. *Secretary of State for Existing the European Union* [2017] UKSC 5 and *R (Miller)* v. *Prime Minister; Cherry v Advocate General for Scotland* [2019] UKSC 41 discussed below). Their Lordships are concerned, on the one hand, that judicial functions (such as sentencing) are undertaken by judicial bodies (and not by the Home Secretary) but, on the other hand, that the requirements of Article 6(1) are not so strictly interpreted that they mean that all determinations of social security or of economic benefits need necessarily to be taken to the courts. To the extent that Article 6(1) has encouraged the courts to consider the separation of powers as a juridical principle, it has done so only in this context of properly demarcating judicial power. It has not transformed the separation of powers into a general principle of constitutional law beyond this context. (On the proper demarcation of judicial power, see, further, *R (Alconbury)* v. *Secretary of State for the Environment* [2003] 2 AC 295 and *Begum* v. *Tower Hamlets London Borough Council* [2003] 2 AC 430, *Ali* v. *Birmingham City Council*

[2010] UKSC 8, [2010] AC 39 and *Poshteh* v. *Kensington Royal London Borough Council* [2017] UKSC 36, [2017] AC 64 considered in Chapter 10.)

2.4.2 The Courts in the Constitution: Judicial Review and Judicial Law-Making

As *Anderson* and *Matthews* suggest, the idea of the separation of powers has particular relevance to the role and authority of the courts in the constitution. There are claims and conflicts that are most appropriately resolved by a process of adjudication, in which decisions are reached after hearing arguments and by reference to legal rules and principles. Some of these questions are best adjudicated by courts staffed by judges who are experts in the law and independent of Parliament and the executive. In deciding whether a particular matter is suitable for judicial determination, account must be taken of the nature of the process of adjudication and of the expertise and resources available to the courts. Some questions are 'non-justiciable' because they cannot be satisfactorily decided by the process of legal argument and rule application, or because they raise issues of policy or the public interest of which it is impossible for the courts to inform themselves adequately within the limits of existing judicial procedures and rules of evidence. These questions should be referred to other agencies that are better equipped to decide them.

The courts will themselves decline to inquire into matters that they identify as non-justiciable: for example, one of the grounds of decision in *Chandler* v. *DPP* [1964] AC 763 (above, pp. 14–16) was that the question whether it was in the interests of the state for the armed forces to be provided with nuclear weapons was a political question that was not appropriate for judicial determination. Again, in *Council of Civil Service Unions* v. *Minister for the Civil Service* [1985] AC 374, the House of Lords indicated that the exercise by ministers of certain kinds of prerogative power is not controllable by the courts because (said Lord Roskill) 'their nature and subject matter are such as not to be amenable to the judicial process'. The courts, Lord Roskill continued, 'are not the place wherein to determine whether a treaty should be concluded or the armed forces disposed in a particular manner or Parliament dissolved on one date rather than another'. It is important, however, that courts should not acquiesce in the abuse of executive power by taking refuge in the notion of non-justiciability. In *Abbasi* v. *Secretary of State for Foreign and Commonwealth Affairs* [2002] EWCA Civ 1598 the Court of Appeal re-affirmed that the courts could not enter the 'forbidden area' of the government's decisions in the conduct of foreign policy. Even so, the court envisaged that judicial review would be possible if the government, in failing to take action to protect British citizens from violations by a foreign government of their fundamental rights, could be shown to have acted irrationally or contrary to legitimate expectations created by its own assurances or policy statements. (The law of judicial review is considered more fully in Chapter 10.)

It is nowadays generally accepted that judges 'do and must make law in the gaps left by Parliament' (per Steyn LJ in *R* v. *Brown* [1994] 1 WLR 1599, 1604) and that the development of the common law is part of the constitutional role of the courts. As Lord Wilberforce said in *British Railways Board* v. *Herrington* [1972] AC 877, 921, 'the common law is a developing entity as the judges develop it, and so long as we follow the well tried method of moving forward in accordance with principle as fresh facts emerge and changes in society occur, we are surely doing what Parliament intends we should do'. Certain kinds of subject matter are considered to be especially suited to judicial creativity, and a claim of this sort was made by Lord Scarman in *Furniss* v. *Dawson* [1984] AC 474, 514, for the judicial development of the principle that 'every man is entitled if he can to order his affairs so as to diminish the burden of tax':

> The limits within which this principle is to operate remain to be probed and determined judicially. Difficult though the task may be for judges, it is one which is beyond the power of the blunt instrument of legislation. Whatever a statute may provide, it has to be interpreted and applied by the courts: and ultimately it will prove to be in this area of judge-made law that our elusive journey's end will be found.

Are there limits beyond which the courts should not go in creating new rules? Lord Reid sounded a note of caution in *Pettitt* v. *Pettitt* [1970] AC 777, 794–5:

> Whatever views may have prevailed in the last century, I think that it is now widely recognised that it is proper for the courts in appropriate cases to develop or adapt existing rules of the common law to meet new conditions. I say in appropriate cases because I think we ought to recognise a difference between cases where we are dealing with 'lawyer's law' and cases where we are dealing with matters which directly affect the lives and interests of large sections of the community and which raise issues which are the subject of public controversy and on which laymen are as well able to decide as are lawyers. On such matters it is not for the courts to proceed on their view of public policy for that would be to encroach on the province of Parliament.

In *Woolwich Equitable Building Society* v. *IRC* [1993] AC 70 a majority of the House of Lords formulated a new rule that the citizen who makes a payment of money to a public authority in response to an unlawful (ultra vires) demand of tax is entitled to restitution of the sum paid. Lord Goff, one of the majority, took note of an objection to the recognition of such a right of recovery:

> This is that for your Lordships' House to recognise such a principle would overstep the boundary which we traditionally set for ourselves, separating the legitimate development of the law by the judges from legislation. It was strongly urged by Mr Glick, in his powerful

> argument for the revenue, that we would indeed be trespassing beyond that boundary if we were to accept the argument of Woolwich. I feel bound however to say that, although I am well aware of the existence of the boundary, I am never quite sure where to find it. Its position seems to vary from case to case. Indeed, if it were to be as firmly and clearly drawn as some of our mentors would wish, I cannot help feeling that a number of leading cases in your Lordships' House would never have been decided the way they were. For example, the minority view would have prevailed in *Donoghue v Stevenson* [1932] AC 562; our modern law of judicial review would have never developed from its old, ineffectual, origins; and *Mareva* injunctions would never have seen the light of day. Much seems to depend upon the circumstances of the particular case.

The majority were convinced by the arguments of justice in favour of judicial recognition of the principle of recovery of tax paid pursuant to an unlawful demand. If limits to the application of the principle were required for reasons of policy or good administration, it would be for Parliament to introduce them. Lord Keith, dissenting, was of the opinion that to accept the argument of the building society would 'amount to a very far-reaching exercise of judicial legislation'. He added:

> It seems to me that formulation of the precise grounds upon which overpayments of tax ought to be recoverable and of any exceptions to the right of recovery, may involve nice considerations of policy which are properly the province of Parliament and are not suitable for consideration by the courts.

In *Kleinwort Benson Ltd* v. *Lincoln City Council* [1999] 2 AC 349 the House of Lords, taking (in Lord Goff's words) 'a more robust view of judicial development of the law', abrogated 'in the public interest' the longstanding rule that money paid under a mistake of law was not recoverable. The courts have not refrained from making innovative decisions in areas of social controversy, as in *Airedale NHS Trust* v. *Bland* [1993] AC 789 (where the withholding of treatment from a patient in a persistent vegetative state was held to be lawful) and *R v. R (Rape: Marital Exemption)* [1992] 1 AC 599.

Can the limits of judicial creativity be expressed in terms of a distinction between *principle* and *policy*? While the legislature makes decisions on grounds of policy, according to its view of what is required for the good of the country, judicial decisions, it has been suggested, should be grounded not in policy but in principle, according with 'a coherent conception of justice and fairness' (Dworkin, *Law's Empire* (1986), ch. 7). In *McLoughlin* v. *O'Brian* [1983] 1 AC 410 Lord Scarman endorsed such a limitation of the judicial function, but Lord Edmund-Davies in the same case emphatically rejected it, and in practice policy considerations are frequently adduced by judges in deciding cases. No doubt the courts must proceed with special caution as the safe waymarks of legal principle are left behind for the contested ground of social policy, but if judges are to continue to develop and modernise branches of law in which Parliament chooses not to intervene, it does not seem realistic to demand that they should eschew all consideration of policy.

It might be thought that judicial law-making should stop short of the creation of new criminal offences, resulting in the punishment of acts that were not unlawful at the time of their commission. Yet in *Shaw* v. *DPP* [1962] AC 220 the House of Lords made a ruling that amounted to the creation of a wide new offence of conspiracy to corrupt public morals, a decision at odds with many understandings of the separation of powers and also with the 'principle of legality' (*nullum crimen sine lege*), which is an aspect of the rule of law. (See, further, Smith, 'Judicial Law-Making in the Criminal Law' (1984) 100 *LQR* 46 and compare *R* v. *R* [1992] 1 AC 599, in which the House of Lords discarded the 'marital exception' in rape, approving the observation of Lord Lane CJ in the Court of Appeal that 'This is not the creation of a new offence, it is the removal of a common law fiction which has become anachronistic and offensive.')

The principle of the separation of powers presupposes that the authority conferred on judges to decide disputes and develop legal principles is given on the condition that no political preference will influence their judgments. Sir John Donaldson MR affirmed the principle of judicial neutrality in *British Airways Board* v. *Laker Airways Ltd* [1984] QB 142, 193, in saying:

> It is a matter of considerable constitutional importance that the courts should be wholly independent of the executive, and they are. Thus, whilst the judges, as private citizens, will be aware of the 'policy' of the government of the day, in the sense of its political purpose, aspirations and programme, these are not matters which are in any way relevant to the courts' decisions and are wholly ignored.

Our judiciary can be acquitted of conscious political bias. Contrariwise, it has been said that judges, by virtue of their background, training and associations, are generally deeply conservative and have attitudes that lead them to look with favour on property owners, employers and the established social order. (See Griffith, *The Politics of the Judiciary* (5th edn. 1997) and compare Dworkin, 'Political Judges and the Rule of Law' (1978) 64 *Proc Brit Acad* 259.)

2.4.3 Judicial Independence and the Position of the Lord Chancellor

The British version of the separation of powers was for a long time able to accommodate the ancient office of Lord Chancellor even though it would have presented an affront to purer forms of the doctrine. The Lord Chancellor was a senior judge and the head of the judiciary in England and Wales while also being a member of the government, with a seat in the cabinet, and presiding in the upper house of the legislature. It was remarked by a Law Lord, Lord Steyn, in an address to the Administrative Law Bar Association in 1996, that the ambivalent role of the Lord Chancellor was 'no longer sustainable on either constitutional or pragmatic grounds'. He noted that the Lord Chancellor was 'a spokesman for the government in furtherance of its party political agenda' and that, even in respect of matters affecting the administration of justice, he was 'subject to collective Cabinet responsibility'. (See also Lord Steyn, 'The Case for a Supreme Court' (2002) 118 *LQR* 382.) Lord Irvine of Lairg, as Lord Chancellor, himself underlined the political nature of his office (HL Deb vol. 622, col 814, 21 February 2001):

> It is not the case that Lord Chancellors are not party political. They are appointed by the Prime Minister; they take the party Whip; they speak and vote for the Government in Parliament; they sit in Cabinet; and they campaign for their party.

Paradoxically, the multiple role of the Lord Chancellor was defended as supporting the separation of powers, even if incompatible with a 'purist' version of the doctrine. Lord Irvine said that the office 'stands at a critical cusp in the separation of powers', so that 'the judiciary has a representative in the Cabinet and the Cabinet in the judiciary', and further that the protection of the judiciary from executive interference is 'a high order duty' of any Lord Chancellor: 'The office is a buffer between the judiciary and the Executive which protects judicial independence.' (HL Deb vol. 597, col 734, 17 February 1999. Compare Lord Steyn's article cited above.)

That the Lord Chancellor might – and from time to time did – sit as a judge on the Appellate Committee of the House of Lords gave rise to particular concern, although it was said that his doing so fostered 'the necessary close relationship with the senior judiciary' (Parliamentary Secretary, Lord Chancellor's Department, HL Deb vol. 344, col 1364, 22 February 2000). If there was complacency about the Lord Chancellor's judicial role, it was disturbed by the decision of the ECtHR in *McGonnell* v. *United Kingdom* (2000) 30 EHRR 289.

McGonnell owned land in Guernsey that was not zoned for residential use under the island's development plan. His appeal against a refusal of permission for residential use of the land was dismissed by the Royal Court of Guernsey, composed of the bailiff of Guernsey and lay members, the bailiff being the sole judge of the law. The bailiff also presided (and could exercise a casting vote) in the States of Deliberation (the legislative assembly), which had adopted the development plan. The ECtHR held that the bailiff's participation in the adoption of the plan gave objective grounds for doubt to be cast on his judicial impartiality, and accordingly that the hearing by the Royal Court constituted a breach of Article 6(1) of the ECHR (the right to a fair trial by an independent and impartial tribunal).

The court accepted the submission of the UK Government that the convention does not require states 'to comply with any theoretical concepts as such' – so that adherence to some particular understanding of the separation of powers is not demanded – and said that the question is always 'whether, in a given case, the requirements of the Convention are met'.

Compatibility with Article 6(1) would be in doubt if the Lord Chancellor were to sit in a case in which governmental interests were at stake or legislation in which the Lord Chancellor had participated came into question. After the *McGonnell* decision, Lord Irvine of Lairg said (HL Deb vol. 610, col 33WA, 23 February 2000):

> The Lord Chancellor would never sit in any case concerning legislation in the passage of which he had been directly involved nor in any case where the interests of the executive were directly engaged.

Indeed, it was by then 'unthinkable that he could now sit in any of the major cases which come before the Law Lords every year, such as cases involving constitutional law, public law, devolution, human rights, important points of statutory construction, and so forth' (Lord Steyn, 'The Case for a Supreme Court' (2002) 118 *LQR* 382, 387).

Some took the view that all that was necessary to ensure constitutional fitness was for the Lord Chancellor to relinquish his role as a judge. But other features of the office were also problematic. It was doubted whether, as a senior minister with extensive executive responsibilities, owing loyalty to his colleagues in government and bound by collective ministerial responsibility, the Lord Chancellor could as head of the judiciary effectively defend the independence of the judges, protecting them from political interference. His responsibility for the appointment of judges, too, had come under increasingly critical scrutiny (see below).

As a result, the government decided on radical reform: the office of Lord Chancellor would be abolished and those of his functions that were to be retained would be redistributed. These changes, it was claimed, would 'put the relationship between the executive, the judiciary and the legislature on a modern footing, and clarify the independence of the judiciary' (*Constitutional Reform: Reforming the Office of the Lord Chancellor*, Department of Constitutional Affairs (2003)). A new Secretary of State for constitutional affairs would have responsibility for safeguarding judicial independence. The Lord Chief Justice would become the head of the judiciary of England and Wales. A Constitutional Reform Bill to implement the government's proposals was introduced in the House of Lords in 2004: see now the Constitutional Reform Act 2005. In the event, the office of Lord Chancellor was retained by the act, albeit that the office is now shorn of its judicial role. (For extensive analysis of the passage of the legislation, including commentary on its impact on the separation of powers, see Windlesham [2005] *PL* 806 and [2006] *PL* 35.)

Senior judges were initially disturbed by the proposal to abolish the office of Lord Chancellor, fearing that the protection of judicial independence would be weakened, but, in the second reading debate on the Constitutional Reform Bill in the House of Lords, the Lord Chief Justice, Lord Woolf, said that, following an agreement (known as the 'concordat') reached between himself and the Secretary of State for constitutional affairs in January 2004 and reflected in the terms of the bill, the constitutional independence of the judiciary was satisfactorily assured (HL Deb vol. 658, col 1004, 8 March 2004; see also Lord Woolf [2004] *CLJ* 317, 324). It is of fundamental importance that the judicial authorities of the state should be independent, so that their decisions are reached in accordance with law and not in submission to the wishes of government or on other extraneous considerations. Invited to give a definition of judicial independence, a former Lord Chancellor, Lord Mackay of Clashfern, responded (HL Deb vol. 576, col 106 WA, 16 December 1996):

> Judicial independence requires that judges can discharge their judicial duties in accordance with the judicial oath and the laws of the land, without interference, improper influence or pressure from any other individual or organisation.

It is plainly necessary that judges should be secure in their tenure of office, and with us this has been assured, for the senior judiciary, since the Act of Settlement of 1701. Section 11(3) of the Senior Courts Act 1981 now provides:

> A person appointed to an office to which this section applies [ie the office of a judge of the Court of Appeal or the High Court of Justice] shall hold that office during good behaviour, subject to a power of removal by Her Majesty on an address presented to Her by both Houses of Parliament.

The Constitutional Reform Act 2005 makes equivalent provision for judges of the Supreme Court (section 33) and for judges of the High Court and Court of Appeal in Northern Ireland (section 133). A judge of the Court of Session in Scotland may be removed from office by the Crown on a recommendation by the first minister of Scotland, supported by a resolution of the Scottish Parliament following a report by an independent tribunal that the judge is unfit for office (Scotland Act 1998, section 95).

The Act of Settlement and its modern successors are generally understood as meaning that a judge may be removed by the Crown either for misbehaviour or for another cause following an address from both houses, but it is thought unlikely in practice that a judge would be removed for misbehaviour except in pursuance of an address from Parliament. Rodney Brazier comments (*Constitutional Practice* (3rd edn. 1999), p. 296):

> The reluctance of any government to remove any senior judge other than by the long-winded address procedure; the refusal of successive governments to initiate that procedure, even when a judge has been convicted of an offence as serious as drunken driving; the government's ability to control Commons' business and thereby to prevent discussion of any early-day motion critical of the judiciary; and the government's power to vote down any Opposition motion debated in Opposition time, taken together all mean that the tenure of office of the senior judiciary is extremely secure.

The only instance since 1701 of removal of a judge under the Act of Settlement procedure was that in 1830 of Sir Jonah Barrington, a judge of the High Court of Admiralty in Ireland, who had been found guilty of embezzlement. Motions for the removal of a judge have been tabled by backbenchers from time to time – for instance, a motion supported by over 100 MPs called for the removal of the Chief Justice, Lord Lane, in 1991, after the revelation of a miscarriage of justice in the case of the 'Birmingham Six' (see *R* v. *McIlkenny* [1992] 2 All ER 417). But such motions are intended rather as an expression of criticism of judicial conduct than to bring about the judge's dismissal, and they are not debated.

There is little likelihood of the Act of Settlement procedure being invoked because a judge's decisions are unwelcome to the executive. However, vigilance is called for in case of covert pressures being brought to bear on judges, for instance, pressure to resign, or changes in the administrative arrangements for the courts that may have an adverse impact on the conduct of cases and the independent functioning of the whole judicial process. (See Woodhouse, *In Pursuit of Good Administration* (1997), pp. 117–20; Malleson, 'Judicial Training and Performance Appraisal: The Problem of Judicial Independence' (1997) 60 *MLR* 655.) The Constitutional Reform Act 2005 should help to counter threats of these kinds. As we saw above, the office of Lord Chancellor is retained, but he is replaced as head of the judiciary in England and Wales by the Lord Chief Justice, who is also the president of the courts of England and Wales. The Lord Chief Justice has an enhanced capacity to influence decisions relating to the administration of the court system, including decisions on resources for the administration of justice.

The 2004 concordat declared that judicial independence should be expressly guaranteed. Accordingly, section 3(1) of the Constitutional Reform Act places a general obligation on the Lord Chancellor, other ministers of the Crown and 'all with responsibility for matters relating to the judiciary or otherwise to the administration of justice' to 'uphold the continued independence of the judiciary'.

This is supplemented by particular duties imposed 'for the purpose of upholding that independence'. These are set out in section 3(5) and (6) as follows:

> (5) The Lord Chancellor and other Ministers of the Crown must not seek to influence particular judicial decisions through any special access to the judiciary.
> (6) The Lord Chancellor must have regard to
>
>   (a) the need to defend that independence;
>   (b) the need for the judiciary to have the support necessary to enable them to exercise their functions;
>   (c) the need for the public interest in regard to matters relating to the judiciary or otherwise to the administration of justice to be properly represented in decisions affecting those matters.

The duty placed on ministers and others by section 3(1) is of a declaratory rather than specifically enforceable nature, although it may be hoped that it will be taken seriously and contribute to sustaining a culture of judicial independence. The obligation of the Lord Chancellor to have regard to 'the need to defend that independence' (section 3(6)) seems to add little to his duty to 'uphold the continued independence of the judiciary', but it emphasises that he has a special responsibility in this matter, over and above that resting on other ministers.

In terms of the oath that must be taken by the Lord Chancellor, he swears to 'defend the independence of the judiciary and discharge my duty to ensure the provision of resources for the efficient and effective support of the courts for which I am responsible' (section 17). If matters of concern should not be satisfactorily resolved, the Chief Justice of any part of the UK may invoke the power conferred by section 5(1) to:

> lay before Parliament written representations on matters that appear to him to be matters of importance relating to the judiciary, or otherwise to the administration of justice, in that part of the United Kingdom.

(With regard to the independence of the judiciary in Northern Ireland, see sections 4, 10 and 11 of the Act.)

The tenure of members of the lower judiciary is not secured by the Act of Settlement procedure. Circuit judges and recorders, for instance, may be dismissed by the Lord Chancellor on the ground of misbehaviour or incapacity, but only with the agreement of the Lord Chief Justice and in accordance with procedures prescribed by regulations made under the Constitutional Reform Act 2005 (section 115). The question arose, in respect of part-time or temporary judicial office, whether the officeholder was an 'independent' tribunal in the meaning of Article 6(1) of the ECHR (the right to a fair trial by an independent and impartial tribunal). In *Starrs v. Ruxton* 2000 SLT 42 the High Court of Justiciary in Scotland held that trial before a temporary sheriff, who held office at pleasure, could be removed from office at any time and the renewal of whose appointment was within the unfettered discretion of the executive, did not constitute a fair hearing before an independent tribunal as required by Article 6(1). (See O'Neill (2000) 63 *MLR* 429.) As a consequence of the ruling in *Starrs*, no further use was made of temporary sheriffs and the Bail, Judicial Appointments etc. (Scotland) Act 2000 provided for the appointment of part-time sheriffs who would have security of tenure. New arrangements were also made to strengthen the security of tenure of part-time judicial officers in England and Wales (e.g., deputy High Court Judges, deputy circuit judges and recorders).

Security of tenure is essential to judicial independence, but it has been rightly said that this 'cannot justify judicial immunity from proper investigation of allegations of misconduct' (Pannick, *The Times*, 24 February 1998). Complaints about judicial conduct were formerly made to the Lord Chancellor who, as head of the judiciary, could, after investigation, 'guide, counsel, advise or rebuke' or, rarely, exercise his powers of dismissal in respect of the lower judiciary. (A circuit judge was dismissed in 1983 for the offence of smuggling whisky.) The matter is now regulated by sections 108–21 of the Constitutional Reform Act 2005. It is there provided (section 115) that the Lord Chief Justice may, with the agreement of the Lord Chancellor, make regulations for the procedure to be followed in investigating allegations of judicial misconduct. The Lord Chief Justice is authorised to give formal advice, a formal warning or reprimand to judicial officeholders – or in certain circumstances to suspend them from office – with the agreement of the Lord Chancellor (section 108(2)–(7)).

In the following speech, the Lord Chief Justice offered a series of reflections on judicial independence:

Lord Judge CJ, *Keynote Speech to the Commonwealth Magistrates' and Judges' Association Conference, September 2010*

Our independence is an essential ingredient in our abilities as judges to fulfil our responsibilities. Sitting in our courts we must, adapting the works of Edmund Burke, be sure that we can offer the litigant seeking justice, the calm neutrality of the impartial judge . . .

[J]udicial independence has two manifestations. First there is the independence of the judiciary as an institution, which is a concept well understood by right thinking men and woman within our communities. What is much more difficult to understand and to convey is that the concept of judicial independence means the independence of every individual judge from one another . . .

Of course, just as our independence has both an institutional and an individual aspect, so too we have a collective as well as an individual responsibility for the efficient and economic administration of justice ... the principle of judicial independence is not and cannot be an excuse, let alone a justification, for judicial inefficiency or idleness.

Next, I do not believe that the principle of judicial independence necessarily and inevitably leads to judicial isolationism. Whatever may have been the views of an earlier generation, and their views are well known and well documented, we cannot be divorced from the realities of the world we live in, and in particular the new methods of communication with their inevitable impact on public thinking and public perception, nor can we assume that our adherence to the principles of judicial independence will be understood if they are never explained. There are times when the judiciary should be accessible beyond and over and above the pronouncements that individual judges make in court. I am not suggesting that every judge should automatically make himself or herself available for interview with any media representative. And we must beware the judge who is seeking headlines for himself or herself. But there is room for avoiding isolationism ...

If we are not clear about what the principle means it can sound like special pleading ... We must understand that judicial independence is a prize enjoyed by our communities. It is their privilege ... [T]he community as a whole, and each individual citizen in it, is entitled to have its disputes, particularly when it is in dispute with the government of the day, or any of the large institutions which play a dominating part in our lives, decided by an impartial judge, independent of all of them. It is after all our responsibility to see that the rule of law applies to every single litigant equally and without distinction or discrimination or prejudice, favourable or unfavourable to one side or the other. So when we are discussing judicial independence we are doing no more but no less than cherishing a crucial ingredient of any community that truly embraces the rule of law.

It is essential that the appointment of judges should not be affected by political partiality. The Lord Chancellor formerly had a decisive role in the appointment of judges by Queen Elizabeth, in making recommendations either directly to her or to the prime minister as her adviser on appointments to the most senior judicial offices. The Lord Chancellor, besides being a high judicial officer, was a member of the government. There were no formal safeguards against politically motivated appointments; as with so much in our constitution, the avoidance of malpractice depended on those concerned observing the conventions and acting with respect for constitutional principles. Before the Second World War, appointments to the judiciary were sometimes made as a reward for political services, but such impropriety has not, since then, blemished the system.

The selection of those to be recommended for appointment by Queen Elizabeth was made by the Lord Chancellor after informal and confidential consultations with the senior judiciary and senior members of the profession. Lord Scarman once described the process of appointment as 'all too haphazard' and an 'oldboy network' which had resulted in some 'terrible mistakes'

(*The Times*, 8 October 1987, p. 7). A president of the Law Society warned of the risk that the system might discriminate 'in favour of those who fit the present mould of the existing judiciary' ((1990) 140 *NLJ* 1594). In response to such misgivings, JUSTICE (the British Section of the International Commission of Jurists) proposed the establishment of a judicial commission, including lawyers and judges but with a majority of lay members, which would make recommendations on judicial appointments to the Lord Chancellor (The *Judiciary in England and Wales*, a report by JUSTICE (1992), ch. 6). Successive Lord Chancellors declined to adopt proposals of this kind, but in 1997 Lord Irvine of Lairg decided on more limited reforms of the system of appointment. He announced that appointments to the High Court would no longer be by invitation only and that applications would be solicited from all eligible members of the professions. An annual report would be presented to Parliament on the operation of the judicial appointments system. Following an independent scrutiny of appointment procedures carried out by Sir Leonard Peach at the request of the Lord Chancellor, a Commission for Judicial Appointments was established, not to advise on appointments but to provide an independent oversight of the system.

The Constitutional Reform Act 2005 placed the system of judicial appointments on a modern footing. The role of the Lord Chancellor remains important, in advising the monarch on appointments to high judicial offices and in himself appointing many judicial officeholders, for instance, assistant recorders, deputy district judges, justices of the peace, and chairmen and members of a great number of tribunals. His role is, however, complemented by sections 63–107 of the Act, which established a new Judicial Appointments Commission of fifteen members: a lay person as chairman; five judicial members; two members from the legal professions; five lay members; a tribunal chairman, tribunal member or arbitrator; and a justice of the peace. Commissioners are appointed by the monarch on the recommendation of the Lord Chancellor who acts in accordance with procedures, set out in Schedule 12 to the Act, which are designed, through the involvement of the Judges' Council or an independent panel, to exclude partisan considerations from appointments.

The Judicial Appointments Commission has a critical role in the appointment of the Lord Chief Justice, other heads of division, Lords Justices of Appeal, High Court judges and other judicial officeholders. When an appointment is to be made, the commission (in the case of a High Court judge or listed officeholder) or a selection panel appointed by it (in the case of the Lord Chief Justice, head of division or Lord Justice of Appeal) decides on the selection process to be applied and proceeds to apply it. Its selection of one person is presented in a report to the Lord Chancellor. (What follows is described here in summary form: for the full details, see sections 67–96 of the Constitutional Reform Act.)

On receiving the report (stage 1), the Lord Chancellor has three options: (a) to accept the selection; (b) to reject it; (c) to require the commission or panel to reconsider the selection. Following a *rejection* or *requirement to reconsider*, the commission or panel must again make a selection. The Lord Chancellor has then (stage 2) the same three options – to accept, reject or require reconsideration – but he may reject the selection only if it was made following a reconsideration at stage 1, and may require reconsideration of the selection only if it was made following a rejection at stage 1. Following a further selection after rejection or reconsideration at stage 2, the Lord Chancellor must, at stage 3, accept the selection. If the Lord Chancellor rejects or requires reconsideration of a selection at stage 1 or 2, the commission or panel in proceeding to a further selection may not select the person rejected, but following a reconsideration may select the person reconsidered. Selection by the commission or a selection panel 'must be solely on merit'; subject to this the commission must in performing its functions 'have regard to the need to encourage diversity in the range of persons available for selection for appointments' (sections 63–4 of the Act). (See, further, Malleson (2006) 33 *JLS* 126.) (On appointments to the UK Supreme Court, see below.)

(See, further, www.judicialappointments.gov.uk. For Scotland, see the Judiciary and Courts (Scotland) Act 2008 and www.judicialappointmentsscotland.gov.uk; and for Northern Ireland, see the Justice (Northern Ireland) Act 2002 and www.nijac.org.)

The independence of the judiciary may be put in contention when judges become involved in issues of acute political controversy. It is at such times that the greatest circumspection is called for from all those concerned in the judicial process, as well as particular restraint from politicians and members of the government. There were lapses in these respects during the miners' strike of 1984–85 (see Oliver, 'The Independence of the Judiciary' (1986) 39 *CLP* 237 and 'Politicians and the Courts' (1988) 41 *Parl Aff* 13) and a singular lack of governmental restraint in the 1990s is chronicled by Loveland, 'The War Against the Judges' (1997) 68 *Pol Q* 162. This 'war' was not succeeded by a permanent peace and Lord Irvine, as Lord Chancellor, made it known that he had many times had to argue in government 'in ways that ensure that the independence of the judiciary is upheld' (Committee on the Lord Chancellor's Department, *Evidence*, HC 611-I of 2002–03, Q 29). Lord Irvine added that:

> In all governments some ministers have spoken out against decisions that they do not like and I have to say that I disapprove of that. I think that it undermines the rule of law and . . . that when you get court decisions you favour, you do not clap and when you get a court decision which is against you, you do not boo.

Lord Irvine's disquiet had been provoked by some ill-judged responses by ministers to judicial decisions that displeased them, for instance, a decision by Collins J in 2003 that the Home Secretary had acted unfairly in denying support to destitute asylum-seekers. (The Home Secretary's appeal against this decision was dismissed by the Court of Appeal: *R (Q)* v. *Secretary of State for the Home Department* [2003] EWCA Civ 364, [2004] QB 36. On this episode, see Bradley [2003] *PL* 397; and see generally Stevens, 'A Loss of Innocence?: Judicial Independence and the Separation of Powers' (1999) 19 *OJLS* 365.)

Now that the Lord Chancellor is no longer a judge, it has been felt in some quarters that the judiciary may be less effectively protected from outspoken ministerial criticism of their decisions. When John Reid, as Home Secretary, condemned what he considered to be too lenient a sentence in 2006, the incumbent Lord Chancellor (Lord Falconer) was slow to come publicly to the judges' defence. The House of Lords Constitution Committee was highly critical of this, arguing that 'there was a systemic failure' and that Lord Falconer had not fulfilled his duties satisfactorily (*6th Report of 2006–07*, para 49; see, further, Bradley [2008] *PL* 470).

While, in the past, Home Secretaries in both Conservative and Labour governments have on occasion been intemperate in their criticisms of individual judges, there had been no recurrence of this since 2006 and in 2010 the Lord Chief Justice told the House of Lords Constitution Committee that he enjoyed an 'extremely equable' relationship with the Lord Chancellor, that he had 'no particular concerns at the moment' about judicial independence and that he welcomed the fact that the ministerial habit of criticising judges 'has gone', adding that he 'did not think it would return'. This, he said, was because 'everybody understands [the] conventions and why they are important'. (See House of Lords Constitution Committee, *9th Report of 2010–11*, HL 89, evidence of Lord Judge CJ.) By way of contrast, consider the prime minister's reaction to the decision of the Supreme Court in *R (F and Thompson)* v. *Secretary of State for the Home Department* [2010] UKSC 17, [2010] 2 WLR 992, in which it was ruled that notification requirements imposed on a person placed indefinitely on a sex offenders' register without provision for review were incompatible with the right to respect for private life (under Article 8 of the ECHR). Prime Minister David Cameron stated in the House of Commons that it was 'completely offensive' to have a ruling by a court that 'flies in the face of common sense' and he described himself as 'appalled' by the decision (HC Deb vol. 523, col 955, 16 February 2011). Consider also the outspoken attack on the Supreme Court's alleged lack of knowledge of Scots Law by Kenny MacAskill, Justice Secretary in the Scottish Government, in May 2011 (see, e.g., *Daily Telegraph*, 2 June 2011).

Similar criticisms arose over the lack of action of the Lord Chancellor following attacks on the judiciary by the media surrounding the first *Miller* decision – most notably the headline in the *Daily Mail* 'Enemies of the people: 'Fury over "out of touch" judges who have "declared war on democracy" by defying 17.4 m Brexit voters and who could trigger constitutional crisis' in reaction to the decision of the High Court. The Lord Chancellor – then Liz Truss – did not respond immediately, and her later response was then criticised for merely making a statement confirming the independence of the judiciary and the high respect in which the UK judiciary was held due to its independence and impartiality. This has led some to argue that the Lord Chancellor is no longer in a position to adequately protect the judiciary from criticism in the media, particularly given the move to the appointment of those to the office who do not have a legal background.

A different sort of circumstance to have provoked disquiet in recent years about the independence of the judiciary from the executive is the government's use of judges to chair politically sensitive public inquiries. Several such inquiries have been chaired by judges, although not all are. Examples include the Scott Inquiry into the 'arms to Iraq' affair in the 1990s, the Phillips Inquiry into BSE ('mad cow disease'), the Hutton Inquiry into the death of Dr David Kelly and the Saville Inquiry into 'Bloody Sunday' (on which see, respectively, Tomkins, *The Constitution after Scott: Government Unwrapped* (1998), www.bseinquiry.gov.uk, www.the-hutton-inquiry.org.uk and www.bloody-sunday-inquiry.org). The Butler Inquiry into the state and use of secret intelligence on Iraqi weapons of mass destruction is an example of such an inquiry being chaired by someone other than a judge, Lord Butler being a former cabinet secretary. The House of Commons Public Administration Select Committee investigated the use of judges to chair such inquiries and recommended as follows (*Government by Inquiry*, HC 51 of 2004–05, paras 57–8):

> We recognise the value of using senior judges to chair some inquiries. Their training and experience give them important transferable skills, and they provide reassurance that an inquiry will be independent and fair. Their use is most appropriate in fact-finding inquiries which are at a distance from government. Inquiries into issues at the centre of government are, however, politically contentious, as well as requiring an understanding of how government works. Criticism of their reports in such cases may undermine the impact of the inquiry and the judiciary as an institution, as well as being detrimental to the reputation of the individual judges. With developments in public law, Human Rights Act considerations about impartiality and the … establishment of a Supreme Court, which involves the institutional separation of the judges from the House of Lords, care needs to be exercised in the future use of judges for such work, particularly those from the highest court, and especially in relation to politically sensitive cases. We … recommend that decisions about the appointment of judges to undertake inquiries should be taken co-equally by the government and the Lord Chief Justice or senior law lord.

The government rejected the committee's recommendation, but section 10 of the Inquiries Act 2005 now provides that if a minister proposes to appoint a judge to be a member of an inquiry, he must first *consult* the Lord Chief

Justice or the president of the Supreme Court. Whether this provision will be sufficient to allay concerns about judicial independence and the chairing of sensitive public inquiries remains to be seen. (For further consideration, see Beatson, 'Should Judges Conduct Public Inquiries?' (2005) 121 *LQR* 221.)

2.4.4 The Courts and Parliament

When we turn to the separation of judiciary and legislature – the courts and Parliament – we are at once struck by the presence, until very recently, of judges in the Upper House of Parliament. Until 2009, the Law Lords (Lords of Appeal in Ordinary), appointed under the Appellate Jurisdiction Act 1876, sat as the final court of appeal for England, Wales, Northern Ireland and (in civil cases) Scotland. Besides sitting as judges in the Appellate Committee of the House of Lords, the Law Lords might also – and frequently did – take part in debates and in the legislative functions of the Upper House.

The decision of the ECtHR in *McGonnell* v. *United Kingdom* (2000) 30 EHRR 289 (above) also had implications for the dual role of the Law Lords as both judges and legislators. In 2000, the Law Lords adopted a statement of principles for their guidance in participating in the business of the house so that they should not be disqualified from adjudicating on issues that might come before them in their judicial capacity. The statement embodied two broad principles (HL Deb vol. 614, col 419, 22 June 2000):

> As full members of the House of Lords the Lords of Appeal in Ordinary have a right to participate in the business of the House. However, mindful of their judicial role they consider themselves bound by two general principles when deciding whether to participate in a particular matter, or to vote: first, the Lords of Appeal in Ordinary do not think it appropriate to engage in matters where there is a strong element of party political controversy; and secondly the Lords of Appeal in Ordinary bear in mind that they might render themselves ineligible to sit judicially if they were to express an opinion on a matter which might later be relevant to an appeal to the House.

This act of self-denial was thought by some to provide a sufficient assurance of the independence and impartiality of the Law Lords in adjudicating any case that came before them. But while it restricted their ability to make a useful contribution to the work of the Upper House, it did not eliminate all possibility of confusion – at least in public perception – of the legislative and judicial roles of the Law Lords. The government concluded that the continuance of the Law Lords in their existing roles could not be reconciled with Article 6 of the ECHR, which demands of judges that they should be manifestly independent and impartial – that they should be so in fact and that they should present an objective appearance of being so. In the government's view, it was in any event desirable in principle that the final court of appeal should be clearly separated from Parliament, saying that it was not 'appropriate in a twenty-first century democracy for the highest appellate court to be part of the legislature' (*Judicial Appointments and a Supreme Court*, Cm 6150/2004, para 11).

The Constitutional Reform Act 2005 accordingly provided for the Lords of Appeal in Ordinary to be removed from the Upper House of Parliament and for the creation of a new Supreme Court as a final court of appeal for the UK. This reform came into effect in 2009, when in October of that year the Supreme Court opened for business. The Supreme Court assumed the jurisdiction of the former Appellate Committee of the House of Lords, along with the devolution jurisdiction (see Chapter 4) of the Judicial Committee of the Privy Council. The existing lords of appeal in ordinary became the first justices of the Supreme Court. Succeeding Supreme Court judges are formally appointed by the monarch on the recommendation of the prime minister, after a process of selection in which an independent selection commission, convened by the Lord Chancellor, has the decisive role. The selection procedures are similar to those established by the Constitutional Reform Act for other judicial appointments as described above. Whether these procedures remain effective and/or free from controversy in the long term remains to be seen (for developments, see this book's companion website).

(See, further, Carnwath, 'Do We Need a Supreme Court?' (2004) 75 *Pol Q* 249; Hale, 'A Supreme Court for the United Kingdom?' (2004) 24 *LS* 36; Woodhouse, 'The Constitutional and Political Implications of a United Kingdom Supreme Court' (2004) 24 *LS* 134; Pannick, 'Replacing the Law Lords by a Supreme Court' [2009] *PL* 723.)

If it could be said without qualification that 'Parliament makes the laws, the courts enforce them', there would be a complete separation of functions between the legislature and the judiciary. In reality, however, the common law has been made by the courts, which continue to have a law-making role in the modern constitution, as we have seen. It is, however, a subordinate role, not to be extended so as to usurp the primary legislative power of Parliament. In *Duport Steels Ltd* v. *Sirs*, the separation of powers was invoked as defining the relation of the courts to Parliament. In this case, the House of Lords reversed the decision of the Court of Appeal in which an unwarrantably restrictive interpretation had been placed on section 13(1) of the Trade Union and Labour Relations Act 1974 (as amended in 1976), which conferred immunity from liability in tort for an act done by a person 'in contemplation or furtherance of a trade dispute'.

Duport Steels Ltd v. *Sirs* [1980] 1 WLR 142 (HL)

Lord Diplock: . . . My Lords, at a time when more and more cases involve the application of legislation which gives effect to policies that are the subject of bitter public and parliamentary controversy, it cannot be too strongly emphasised that the British constitution, though largely unwritten, is firmly based upon the separation of powers; Parliament makes the laws, the judiciary interpret them. When Parliament legislates to remedy what the majority of its members at the time perceive to be a defect or a lacuna in the existing law (whether it be the written law enacted by existing statutes or the unwritten common law as it has been expounded by the judges in decided cases), the role of the judiciary is confined to ascertaining from the words that Parliament has approved as expressing its intention what that intention was, and to giving effect to it. Where the meaning of the statutory words is plain and unambiguous it is not for the judges to invent fancied ambiguities as an excuse for failing to give effect to its plain meaning because they themselves consider that the consequences of doing so would be inexpedient, or even unjust or immoral. In controversial matters such as are involved in industrial relations there is room for differences of opinion as to what is expedient, what is just and what is morally justifiable. Under our constitution it is Parliament's opinion on these matters that is paramount.

A statute passed to remedy what is perceived by Parliament to be a defect in the existing law may in actual operation turn out to have injurious consequences that Parliament did not anticipate at the time the statute was passed; if it had, it would have made some provision in the Act in order to prevent them. It is at least possible that Parliament when the Acts of 1974 and 1976 were passed did not anticipate that so widespread and crippling use as has in fact occurred would be made of sympathetic withdrawals of labour and of secondary blacking and picketing in support of sectional interests able to exercise 'industrial muscle'. But if this be the case it is for Parliament, not for the judiciary, to decide whether any changes should be made to the law as stated in the Acts, and, if so, what are the precise limits that ought to be imposed upon the immunity from liability for torts committed in the course of taking industrial action. These are matters on which there is a wide legislative choice the exercise of which is likely to be influenced by the political complexion of the government and the state of public opinion at the time amending legislation is under consideration.

It endangers continued public confidence in the political impartiality of the judiciary, which is essential to the continuance of the rule of law, if judges, under the guise of interpretation, provide their own preferred amendments to statutes which experience of their operation has shown to have had consequences that members of the court before whom the matter comes consider to be injurious to the public interest.

Lord Scarman: . . . My basic criticism of all three judgments in the Court of Appeal is that in their desire to do justice the court failed to do justice according to law. When one is considering law in the hands of the judges, law means the body of rules and guidelines within which society requires its judges to administer justice. Legal systems differ in the width of the discretionary power granted to judges: but in developed societies limits are invariably set, beyond which the judges may not go. Justice in such societies is not left to the unguided, even if experienced, sage sitting under the spreading oak tree.

In our society the judges have in some aspects of their work a discretionary power to do justice so wide that they may be regarded as law-makers. The common law and equity, both of them in essence systems of private law, are fields where, subject to the increasing intrusion of statute law, society has been content to allow the judges to formulate and develop the law. The judges, even in this, their very own field of creative endeavour, have accepted, in the interests of certainty, the self-denying ordinance of 'stare decisis', the doctrine of binding precedent: and no doubt this judicially imposed limitation on judicial law-making has helped to maintain confidence in the certainty and evenhandedness of the law.

But in the field of statute law the judge must be obedient to the will of Parliament as expressed in its enactments. In this field Parliament makes, and un-makes, the law: the judge's duty is to interpret and to apply the law, not to change it to meet the judge's idea of what justice requires. Interpretation does, of course, imply in the interpreter a power of choice where differing constructions are possible. But our law requires the judge to choose the construction which in his judgment best meets the legislative purpose of the enactment. If the result be unjust but inevitable, the judge may say so and invite Parliament to re-consider its provision. But he must not deny the statute. Unpalatable statute law may not be disregarded or rejected, merely because it is unpalatable. Only if a just result can be achieved without violating the legislative purpose of the statute may the judge select the construction which best suits his idea of what justice requires . . .

Within these limits, which cannot be said in a free society possessing elective legislative institutions to be narrow or constrained, judges, as the remarkable judicial career of Lord Denning himself shows, have a genuine creative role. Great judges are in their different ways judicial activists. But the constitution's separation of powers, or more accurately functions, must be observed if judicial independence is not to be put at risk. For, if people and Parliament come to think that the judicial power is to be confined by nothing other than the judge's sense of what is right (or, as Selden put it, by the length of the Chancellor's foot), confidence in the judicial system will be replaced by fear of it becoming uncertain and arbitrary in its application. Society will then be ready for Parliament to cut the power of the judges. Their power to do justice will become more restricted by law than it need be, or is today.

(See the comments on this case by Allan, *Law, Liberty, and Justice* (1993), pp. 62–4 and by Tomkins [1999] *PL* 525, 530–1.) It is right that judges should have regard, in resolving the uncertainties and ambiguities of statutory language, to the broad objective of the statute and also to fundamental rights and principles that the courts should seek to uphold. What Lord Diplock was warning against was a substitution by the judge of his own view of the public interest or of justice or fundamental principle for the clear expression of Parliament's will. Reforming legislation has sometimes failed in its purpose when it has encoun-tered discordant ideas or principles embedded in the judicial tradition. (See, for instance, the discussion of section 17(1) and (2) of the Trade Union and Labour Relations Act 1974 by Lord Wedderburn, 'The Injunction and the Sovereignty of Parliament' (1989) 23 *The Law Teacher* 4.)

It was aptly said by Lord Diplock in *Black-Clawson International Ltd* v. *Papierwerke Waldhof-Aschaffenburg AG* [1975] AC 591, 638, that 'Parliament, under our constitution, is sovereign only in respect of what it expresses by the words used in the legislation it has passed.' As we saw when considering the sovereignty of Parliament above, the courts have the function of interpreting parliamentary legislation, and although that judicial task is expressed as one of ascertaining the will or intention of Parliament, the process of interpretation is far from being mechanical and allows for a significant injection of judicial policy into the application of statutes. 'Parliament is accustomed', says Sir Stephen Sedley, 'to accepting from the judges that it meant things which may never have crossed its collective mind' (Richardson and Genn (eds.), *Administrative Law and Government Action* (1994), p. 36). Lord Bridge observed in *X Ltd* v. *Morgan-Grampian Ltd* [1991] 1 AC 1, 48, that:

> In our society the rule of law rests upon twin foundations: the sovereignty of the Queen in Parliament in making the law and the sovereignty of the Queen's courts in interpreting and applying the law.

The courts may not question what takes place in Parliament, as was declared long ago in Article 9 of the Bill of Rights 1689:

> That the freedom of speech and debates or proceedings in Parliament ought not to be impeached or questioned in any court or place out of Parliament.

Article 9 was said by Lord Browne-Wilkinson in *Pepper* v. *Hart* [1993] AC 593, 638, to be a provision 'of the highest constitutional importance' in ensuring the freedom of members of Parliament to discuss freely whatever matter they choose without incurring any civil or criminal penalty.

R (Wheeler) v. *Office of the Prime Minister* [2008] EWHC 1409 (Admin)

In *Wheeler*, the claimant contended that a referendum was required to have been held before the UK could lawfully ratify the Lisbon Treaty (reforming the EU: see Chapter 5). Ratification of the treaty had been approved by act of Parliament (the European Union (Amendment) Act 2008).

> **Richards LJ:** . . . In our reasoning to date we have taken account of the fact that any decision on a referendum lies in Parliament. But the position of Parliament gives rise to further, more specific difficulties for the claimant's case.
>
>   In his submissions on behalf of the Speaker [of the House of Commons], Mr Lewis QC drew attention to two distinct constitutional principles relating to the position of Parliament. They are conveniently summarised by Stanley Burnton J (as he then was) in *Office of Government Commerce v Information Commissioner* [2008] EWHC 774 (Admin) . . .:
>
>   'These authorities demonstrate that the law of Parliamentary privilege is essentially based on two principles. The first is the need to avoid any risk of interference with free speech in Parliament. The second is the principle of the separation of powers, which in our Constitution is restricted to the judicial function of government, and requires the executive

and the legislature to abstain from interference with the judicial function, and conversely requires the judiciary not to interfere with or to criticise the proceedings of the legislature. These basic principles lead to the requirement of mutual respect by the Courts for the proceedings and decisions of the legislature and by the legislature (and the executive) for the proceedings and decisions of the Courts.'

The first of those principles is particularly relevant to the use to which certain Parliamentary material may be put, and is considered later. The second goes to the core of the claimant's case. In *R v Parliamentary Commissioner for Standards, ex p Al Fayed* [1998] 1 WLR 669, 670, Lord Woolf MR said it was clearly established that 'the courts exercise a self-denying ordinance in relation to interfering with the proceedings of Parliament'. In *R v Her Majesty's Treasury, ex p Smedley* [1985] QB 657, 666C–E, Sir John Donaldson MR said that 'it behoves the courts to be ever sensitive to the paramount need to refrain from trespassing upon the province of Parliament or, so far as this can be avoided, even appearing to do so'; and against that background he went on to say, in relation to the particular Order in Council under challenge in those proceedings, that 'it would clearly be a breach of the constitutional conventions for this court, or any court, to express a view, let alone take any action, concerning the decision to lay this draft Order in Council before Parliament or concerning the wisdom or otherwise of Parliament approving the draft'. The court in that case was willing to consider whether such an Order, if approved by Parliament, would be *ultra vires* the enabling statute, but made very clear the care that needed to be exercised in relation to the limits of the court's role.

In the light of that principle, the claimant has already cut back his claim heavily . . . The case as reformulated still depends, however, on satisfying the court that the defendants are in breach of legitimate expectation by failing to introduce a Bill into Parliament to provide for a referendum (or, as might have been the case while the European Union (Amendment) Bill was still before Parliament, by failing to move an amendment providing for a referendum). That reformulation creates an unsatisfactory disconnection between the expectation originally asserted and the relief now claimed, as well as producing the odd result that the defendants are said to be under a duty to introduce into Parliament a Bill which they can then work to defeat by their own votes and by all other means available to them. More importantly, it also fails to meet the problem created for the claimant's case by the principle to which we have referred.

In our judgment, it is clear that the introduction of a Bill into Parliament forms part of the proceedings within Parliament. It is governed by the Standing Orders of the House of Commons (see, in particular, Standing Order 57(1)). It is done by a Member of Parliament in his capacity as such, not in any capacity he may have as a Secretary of State or other member of the government. *Prebble* ([1995] 1 AC 321) supports the view that the introduction of legislation into Parliament forms part the legislative process protected by Parliamentary privilege. To order the defendants to introduce a Bill into Parliament would therefore be to order them to do an act within Parliament in their capacity as Members of Parliament and would plainly be to trespass impermissibly on the province of Parliament. Nor can the point be met by the grant of a declaration, as sought by the claimant, instead of a mandatory order. A declaration tailored to give effect to the claimant's case would necessarily involve some indication by the court that the defendants were under a public law duty to introduce a Bill into Parliament to provide for a referendum. The practical effect of a declaration would be the same as a mandatory order even if, in accordance with longstanding convention, it relied on the executive to respect and give effect to the decision of the court without the need for compulsion.

There was also a certain amount of argument addressed to the question of laying before Parliament an order under section 101(4) of the Political Parties, Elections and Referendums Act 2000. In our view, however, that is not the proper focus of attention. It is clear from the statements made by the Prime Minister and the Foreign Secretary in 2004 that the promised referendum on the Constitutional Treaty was to take place after the Parliamentary process had been completed: it was not envisaged that there would be a referendum before the relevant Bill had become a statute. Moreover an order under section 101(4) cannot be made unless there is before Parliament a Bill containing provision for a referendum. The question therefore comes back to the introduction of a Bill into Parliament to provide for a referendum, and we are not concerned with the laying of an order before Parliament under powers conferred by an existing statute, where different considerations might apply.

The fact that the claim would involve an interference by the court with the proceedings of Parliament is a further decisive reason why the claim must fail.

While it is important to ensure that courts abstain from improper interference in proceedings in Parliament, it is also necessary to ensure that this abstention does not prevent MPs being held to account for their actions.

R v. *Chaytor and others* [2010] UKSC 52, [2011] 1 AC 684

Chaytor and others had been committed for trial for false accounting in respect of their alleged dishonest claims for expenses and allowances made while they had been serving MPs. Chaytor argued that the continuance of the criminal prosecution would breach parliamentary privilege, both because it was for Parliament, exclusively, to investigate this conduct and because expenses claims were part of the proceedings in Parliament and, therefore, could not be questioned by the courts. The Supreme Court dismissed both arguments. Parliament did not assert an exclusive jurisdiction to investigate criminal conduct and there were examples of the House of Commons coordinating with the police over criminal investigations. Moreover, the submission of expense claims and the claiming of allowances was not a proceeding in Parliament. Lord Phillips stated that:

[47] . . . the principal matter to which article 9 is directed is freedom of speech and debate in the Houses of Parliament and in parliamentary committees. This is where the core or essential business of Parliament takes place. In considering whether actions outside the Houses and committees fall within parliamentary proceedings because of their connection to them, it is necessary to consider the nature of that connection and whether, if such actions

do not enjoy privilege, this is likely to impact adversely on the core or essential business of Parliament.

[48]. If this approach is adopted, the submission of claim forms for allowances and expenses does not qualify for the protection of privilege. Scrutiny of claims by the courts will have no adverse impact on the core or essential business of Parliament, it will not inhibit debate or freedom of speech. Indeed it will not inhibit any of the varied activities in which Members of Parliament indulge that bear in one way or another on their parliamentary duties. The only thing that it will inhibit is the making of dishonest claims.

While the courts must abstain from improper interference in proceedings in Parliament, it is also a constitutional principle that Parliament should not interfere in or prejudice the judicial process. This is expressed in the *sub judice* rule, which is part of the law and custom of Parliament. The *sub judice* rule, which applies to motions, debates and questions in each house, disallows consideration of cases in which proceedings are active in UK courts. Observance of the rule is ensured by the Speaker in the House of Commons and by the Leader of the House of Lords, each of whom has discretion to waive the rule. The *sub judice* rule is in any event subject to the right of the two houses to legislate on any matter (or to discuss delegated legislation) and is relaxed where a case concerns a ministerial decision or issues of national importance such as the economy, public order or essential services. (See the Appendix to the House of Commons Standing Orders and HL Deb vol. 612, cols 1725–6, 11 May 2000 and House of Commons Procedure Committee, *The Sub Judice Rule of the House of Commons*, HC 125 of 2004–05.)

Judges are shielded from criticism in Parliament by a rule that charges against a judge can be made only on a substantive motion on which a vote will be taken. The Speaker of the House of Commons ruled on 4 December 1973 (HC Deb vol. 865, col 1092):

Reflections on [a] judge's character or motives cannot be made except on a motion. No charge of a personal nature can be raised except on a motion. Any suggestion that a judge should be dismissed can be made only on a motion.

A qualifying ruling was given by the Speaker on 19 July 1977 (HC Deb vol. 935, col 1381):

Yet the rule is not so restrictive as some Hon. Members may think. It is not necessary to have a substantive motion before the House to allow Members to argue that a judge has made a mistake, that he was wrong, and the reasons for those contentions can be given within certain limits, provided that moderate language is used.

2.4.5 Parliament and the Executive

As long ago as 1867 Walter Bagehot highlighted 'the close union, the nearly complete fusion, of the executive and legislative powers' (*The English Constitution* (1963 edn.), p. 65). The executive is headed (under the monarch as formal and ceremonial head of state) by ministers who sit in Parliament and are normally able to exercise significant control of proceedings in the elected house. The Leader of the House in both the Commons and the Lords is a minister and government whips arrange the business of each house, although the government's powers to control the Lords are far weaker than is the case in the Commons. Parliamentary government depends on party, and it has been remarked that Parliament 'has little distinct life or identity of its own, separate from government and party' (Weir and Beetham, *Political Power and Democratic Control in Britain* (1999), p. 372).

In spite of the popularity of this view, however, it stands in need of substantial revision, first as a result of the recent researches of Philip Cowley, who has chronicled in detail how the Labour backbench MPs of the 1997 and 2001 Parliaments have been more rebellious than any since the mid-nineteenth century, rebelling against the government line on a broad range of issues, from counterterrorism and foreign policy (particularly over the Iraq war) to education reform and from university fees to reform of the NHS. (See Cowley, *The Rebels: How Blair Mislaid his Majority* (2005).) Second, the extent to which backbench members, as opposed to government whips, may set the Commons' agenda has grown through a series of recent reforms to parliamentary procedure. There is also evidence of the extent to which perceptions of backbench rebellion or opposition may lead the government to amend bills (see Russell and Gover *Legislation at Westminster* (2017)). As discussed in the previous chapter, the relative power of the executive over the legislature has been significantly challenged through the Brexit process, particularly in the face of a minority Conservative Government led first by Theresa May and then Boris Johnson as Prime Minister during 2019. These are considered in detail in Chapter 9.

Despite these advances, the domination of the House of Commons by party and government continues to be seen as a formidable obstacle to Parliament's performance of its traditional – and democratically essential – function of scrutinising and checking the operations of the executive. So far as there is a separation of powers between Parliament and government, it is not one in which equal powers are counter-balanced. Nonetheless, it would be wrong to see Parliament as a cowed and supine body, the mere instrument of the government's will. A spirit of independence still stirs in the House of Commons and may ignite rebellion or foster subversive alliances among backbenchers. Members of non-conformist outlook, of whom there are not a few, preserve a sense of Parliament's separateness and autonomy, and look for reforms in practice and procedure that would strengthen Parliament's authority in its relations with the executive. However, the rules governing parliamentary business – in particular Standing Order No. 14 which prioritises governmental business – can make it difficult for the Commons to exert control. (These matters are further considered in Chapter 9.)

On occasion, it may fall to the courts to ensure that the government is respectful of legal limits in its relations with Parliament. This can be seen in the following cases.

Secretary of State for the Home Department, ex p Fire Brigades Union [1995] 2 AC 513 (HL)

Parliament had made provision in the Criminal Justice Act 1988 for a scheme for the compensation of victims of crime. The Act provided further that the statutory scheme should come into force on a day to be appointed by the Secretary of State in a commencement order. The Secretary of State then decided that he would not make a commencement order to implement the scheme and instead used prerogative power to introduce a different, less generous scheme. The House of Lords held by a majority that in so doing the minister had frustrated the will of Parliament and had acted unlawfully. While it was for the minister to decide when it might be appropriate to bring the statutory scheme into force, this was a matter that he was required to keep under continuing review: instead, he had 'written off' the statutory scheme, had 'struck out down a different route and thereby disabled himself from properly discharging his statutory duty in the way Parliament intended' (Lord Nicholls). 'It is for Parliament, not the executive', said Lord Browne-Wilkinson, 'to repeal legislation.' We may see the judgment of the majority as upholding the separation of powers in preventing an attempt by the executive to legislate (under prerogative) in defiance of the intention of Parliament.

By the same token, it was a dissenting law lord in this case, Lord Mustill, who expressly invoked the separation of powers in warning that *the courts* must not overstep the boundaries that were set between them, the executive and Parliament: '[I]t is the task of Parliament and the executive in tandem, not of the courts, to govern the country.' Similarly, Lord Keith, also dissenting, considered the majority ruling to be 'an unwarrantable intrusion by the court into the political field and a usurpation of the function of Parliament'. (For comment, see Barendt [1995] *PL* 357; Tomkins, *Public Law* (2003), ch. 1.)

R (Miller) v. *Secretary of State for Exiting the European Union* [2017] UKSC 5

Gina Miller and others challenged the decision of the government to use its prerogative powers to notify the EU of the UK's intention to withdraw from the EU treaties. The majority of the Supreme Court concluded that the prerogative power of foreign relations could not be used to withdraw from the EU treaties. One of the arguments used to justify this conclusion was because to use the prerogative in this manner would frustrate legislation; 'ministers cannot frustrate the purpose of a statute or a statutory provision, for example by emptying it of content or preventing its effectual operation'. Although the minority concluded that the government could use the prerogative, they did not directly disagree with the frustration principle. They did, however, conclude that the European Communities Act 1972 would not be rendered devoid of purpose by the UK's notification of its intention to withdraw from the EU treaties. More controversial is Lord Neuberger's statement, at para [81], concerning the ability of ministers to use prerogative powers to make sweeping changes to the constitution:

> It would be inconsistent with long-standing and fundamental principle for such a far-reaching change to the UK constitutional arrangements to be brought about by ministerial decision or ministerial action alone.

This statement is consistent with both the constitutional principle of parliamentary sovereignty and the separation of powers. It could also be justified as a parallel to the principle of legality. If broad legislative powers are to be read down so as to prevent the executive from enacting measures which undermine the rule of law or other fundamental common law rights, then the same could be said to be true of broad prerogative powers. However, it is hard to see any specific case providing direct support for this principle. Moreover, it may be difficult to apply in practice – how 'far-reaching' must a change to UK constitutional arrangements be such that it cannot be made by ministerial decision alone? It is not clear how far this statement is an alternative justification for the conclusion reached by the majority, or whether it is dictum as not strictly necessary to decide the case. However, it could provide a strong means for the courts to protect the division between the legislature and the executive, particularly as the UK continues to work its way through the Brexit process or when the UK continues to have a minority government, or a government with only a small working majority. (For contrasting views on this principle, see Elliott, 'The Supreme Court's Judgment in *Miller*: In Search of Constitutional Principle' (2017) 76 *CLJ* 257; Young, '*R (Miller)* v. *Secretary of State for Exiting the European Union*: Thriller or Vanilla?' (2017) 42 *ELRev* 280.)

The use of constitutional principles to control the relationship between the executive and the legislature was recently exemplified most powerfully in the second *Miller* case.

R (Miller) v. *Prime Minister; Cherry* v. *Advocate General for Scotland* [2019] UKSC 41

On 28 August 2019, an order in council stated that the Westminster Parliament would be prorogued from the 9 or 12 September until 14 October 2019. The issue arose as to whether this use of the prerogative power was lawful. Gina Miller and Joanna Cherry, a Westminster MP, commenced proceedings in England and Scotland respectively. At first instance, the English High Court, in the *Miller* case, and the Inner House of the Court of Session in the *Cherry* case, concluded that the issue was non-justiciable. The prorogation of Parliament was a political as opposed to a legal matter and not one suited to determination by the court. However, on appeal, the Outer House of the Court of Session in the *Cherry* case concluded both that the issue was justiciable, and that there prorogation was unlawful. Both cases were then heard by an eleven-bench Supreme Court.

The Supreme Court unanimously concluded that the use of the prerogative was unlawful. In reaching this conclusion, the court used two background constitutional principles – parliamentary sovereignty and parliamentary accountability – to place limits on the scope of the prerogative power of prorogation. Before setting out these principles, the court clarified that 'although the courts cannot decide political questions, the fact that a legal dispute concerns the conduct of politicians, or arises from a matter of political controversy, has never been sufficient reason for the courts to refuse to consider it'. As the Divisional Court observed in para 47 of its judgment, almost all important decisions made by the executive have a political hue to them. Nevertheless, the courts have exercised a supervisory jurisdiction over the decisions of the executive for centuries. 'Many if not most of the constitutional cases in our legal history have been concerned with politics in that sense' ([32]). The Supreme Court delineated and applied these constitutional principles as follows:

[41]. Two fundamental principles of our constitutional law are relevant to the present case. The first is the principle of Parliamentary sovereignty: that laws enacted by the Crown in Parliament are the supreme form of law in our legal system, with which everyone, including the Government, must comply. However, the effect which the courts have given to Parliamentary sovereignty is not confined to recognising the status of the legislation enacted by the Crown in Parliament as our highest form of law. Time and again, in a series of cases since the 17th century, the courts have protected Parliamentary sovereignty from threats posed to it by the use of prerogative powers, and in doing so have demonstrated that prerogative powers are limited by the principle of Parliamentary sovereignty. To give only a few examples, in the Case of Proclamations the court protected Parliamentary sovereignty directly, by holding that prerogative powers could not be used to alter the law of the land. Three centuries later, in the case of *Attorney General v De Keyser's Royal Hotel Ltd* [1920] AC 508, the court prevented the Government of the day from seeking by indirect means to bypass Parliament, in circumventing a statute through the use of the prerogative. More recently, in the *Fire Brigades Union* case, the court again prevented the Government from rendering a statute nugatory through recourse to the prerogative, and was not deflected by the fact that the Government had failed to bring the statute into effect. As Lord Browne-Wilkinson observed in that case at p 552, 'the constitutional history of this country is the history of the prerogative powers of the Crown being made subject to the overriding powers of the democratically elected legislature as the sovereign body'.

[42]. The sovereignty of Parliament would, however, be undermined as the foundational principle of our constitution if the executive could, through the use of the prerogative,

prevent Parliament from exercising its legislative authority for as long as it pleased. That, however, would be the position if there was no legal limit upon the power to prorogue Parliament (subject to a few exceptional circumstances in which, under statute, Parliament can meet while it stands prorogued). An unlimited power of prorogation would therefore be incompatible with the legal principle of Parliamentary sovereignty.

. . .

[44]. It must therefore follow, as a concomitant of Parliamentary sovereignty, that the power to prorogue cannot be unlimited. Statutory requirements as to sittings of Parliament have indeed been enacted from time to time, for example by the Statute of 1362 (36 Edward III c 10), the Triennial Acts of 1640 and 1664, the Bill of Rights 1688, the Scottish Claim of Right 1689, the Meeting of Parliament Act 1694, and most recently the Northern Ireland (Executive Formation etc) Act 2019, section 3. Their existence confirms the necessity of a legal limit on the power to prorogue, but they do not address the situation with which the present appeals are concerned.

[45]. On the other hand, Parliament does not remain permanently in session, and it is undoubtedly lawful to prorogue Parliament notwithstanding the fact that, so long as it stands prorogued, Parliament cannot enact laws. In modern practice, Parliament is normally prorogued for only a short time. There can be no question of such a prorogation being incompatible with Parliamentary sovereignty: its effect on Parliament's ability to exercise its legislative powers is relatively minor and uncontroversial. How, then, is the limit upon the power to prorogue to be defined, so as to make it compatible with the principle of Parliamentary sovereignty?

[46]. The same question arises in relation to a second constitutional principle, that of Parliamentary accountability, described by Lord Carnwath in his judgment in the first Miller case as no less fundamental to our constitution than Parliamentary sovereignty *(R (Miller) v Secretary of State for Exiting the European Union* [2017] UKSC 5; [2018] AC 61, para 249). As Lord Bingham of Cornhill said in the case of *Bobb v Manning* [2006] UKPC 22, para 13, 'the conduct of government by a Prime Minister and Cabinet collectively responsible and accountable to Parliament lies at the heart of Westminster democracy'. Ministers are accountable to Parliament through such mechanisms as their duty to answer Parliamentary questions and to appear before Parliamentary committees, and through Parliamentary scrutiny of the delegated legislation which ministers make. By these means, the policies of the executive are subjected to consideration by the representatives of the electorate, the executive is required to report, explain and defend its actions, and citizens are protected from the arbitrary exercise of executive power.

[47]. The principle of Parliamentary accountability has been invoked time and again throughout the development of our constitutional and administrative law, as a justification for judicial restraint as part of a constitutional separation of powers (see, for example, *R v Secretary of State for the Environment, Ex p Nottinghamshire County Council* [1986] AC 240, 250), and as an explanation for non-justiciability (*Mohammed (Serdar) v Ministry of Defence* [2017] UKSC 1; [2017] AC 649, para 57). It was also an animating principle of some of the statutes mentioned in para 44, as appears from their references to the redress of grievances.

As we have mentioned, its importance as a fundamental constitutional principle has also been recognised by the courts.

[48]. That principle is not placed in jeopardy if Parliament stands prorogued for the short period which is customary, and as we have explained, Parliament does not in any event expect to be in permanent session. But the longer that Parliament stands prorogued, the greater the risk that responsible government may be replaced by unaccountable government: the antithesis of the democratic model. So the same question arises as in relation to Parliamentary sovereignty: what is the legal limit upon the power to prorogue which makes it compatible with the ability of Parliament to carry out its constitutional functions?

[49]. In answering that question, it is of some assistance to consider how the courts have dealt with situations where the exercise of a power conferred by statute, rather than one arising under the prerogative, was liable to affect the operation of a constitutional principle. The approach which they have adopted has concentrated on the effect of the exercise of the power upon the operation of the relevant constitutional principle. Unless the terms of the statute indicate a contrary intention, the courts have set a limit to the lawful exercise of the power by holding that the extent to which the measure impedes or frustrates the operation of the relevant principle must have a reasonable justification. That approach can be seen, for example, in *R (UNISON) v Lord Chancellor* [2017] UKSC 51; [2017] 3 WLR 409, paras 80-82 and 88-89, where earlier authorities were discussed. A prerogative power is, of course, different from a statutory power: since it is not derived from statute, its limitations cannot be derived from a process of statutory interpretation. However, a prerogative power is only effective to the extent that it is recognised by the common law: as was said in the *Case of Proclamations*, 'the King hath no prerogative, but that which the law of the land allows him'. A prerogative power is therefore limited by statute and the common law, including, in the present context, the constitutional principles with which it would otherwise conflict.

[50]. For the purposes of the present case, therefore, the relevant limit upon the power to prorogue can be expressed in this way: that a decision to prorogue Parliament (or to advise the monarch to prorogue Parliament) will be unlawful if the prorogation has the effect of frustrating or preventing, without reasonable justification, the ability of Parliament to carry out its constitutional functions as a legislature and as the body responsible for the supervision of the executive. In such a situation, the court will intervene if the effect is sufficiently serious to justify such an exceptional course.

The Supreme Court concluded both that the exceptionally long period of prorogation, at a time when one would expect Parliament to play a role in determining such a constitutionally, politically and socially significant issue as Brexit, justified the interference of the court. Such a prorogation had restricted both parliamentary sovereignty and parliamentary accountability. In addition, the government had failed to provide a justification for this interference. Consequently, the decision was struck down as ultra vires. The outcome of the decision was that Parliament had never been prorogued and MPs could return to Parliament. In reaching this conclusion, the Supreme Court provided its most constitutionally significant judgment to date demonstrating how the court will intervene in extreme circumstances to prevent the powers of the legislature from abuse from the executive. (The judgment has split opinion in the academic community – Craig, 'The Supreme Court, Prorogation and Constitutional Principle' [2020] *PL* 248; Loughlin, 'A Note on Craig on *Miller; Cherry*' [2020] *PL* 278; Craig, 'Response to Loughlin's Note on *Miller; Cherry*' [2020] *PL* 282; Thiel, 'Unconstitutional Prorogation of Parliament' [2020] *PL* 529; Young, '*R (Miller) v Prime Minister; Cherry v Advocate General for Scotland*: Re-inventing the Constitution, or Re-imagining Constitutional Scholarship? (forthcoming).)

(See generally, on the separation of powers, Allan, *Law, Liberty, and Justice* (1993), ch. 3; Barendt, 'Separation of Powers and Constitutional Government' [1995] *PL* 599; Bellamy, 'The Political Form of the Constitution: The Separation of Powers, Rights and Representative Democracy' (1996) 44 *Political Studies* 436; Munro, *Studies in Constitutional Law* (2nd edn. 1999), ch. 9; Barber, 'Prelude to the Separation of Powers' [2001] *CLJ* 59; Bradley, 'Relations Between Executive, Judiciary and Parliament: An Evolving Saga?' [2008] *PL* 470; Carolan, *The New Separation of Powers: A Theory for the Modern State* (2009); Masterman and Wheatle, 'Unpacking the Separation of Powers: Judicial Independence, Sovereignty and Conceptual Flexibility in the UK Constitution' [2017] *PL* 469; Young, 'The Relationship between Parliament, the Executive and the Judiciary', in Jowell and O'Cinneide, *The Changing Constitution* (9th edition) (2019).)

3

Constitutional Sources

Contents

In previous chapters, we have touched on the way in which Brexit has challenged traditional understandings of the UK constitution. We have also mentioned both *Miller* decisions in the Supreme Court. In *R (Miller) v. Secretary of State for Exiting the European Union* [2017] UKSC 5, Lord Neuberger, who delivered the judgment of the majority of the court, set out his characterisation of the constitutional background of the UK as follows (at para [40]):

> Unlike most countries, the United Kingdom does not have a constitution in the sense of a single coherent code of fundamental law which prevails over all other sources of law. Our constitutional arrangements have developed over time, in a pragmatic as much as a principled way, through a combination of statutes, events, conventions, academic writings and judicial decisions.

In *R (Miller) v. Prime Minister; Cherry v Advocate General for Scotland* the unanimous judgment of the UK Supreme Court, given by Lady Hale and Lord Reed – the then President and Deputy President of the UK Supreme Court – described the UK constitution as follows:

[39]. Although the United Kingdom does not have a single document entitled 'The Constitution' it nevertheless possesses a Constitution, established over the course of our history by common law, statutes, conventions and practice. Since it has not been codified, it has developed pragmatically, and remains sufficiently flexible to be capable of further development. Nevertheless, it includes numerous principles of law, which are enforceable by the courts in the same way as other legal principles. In giving them effect, the courts have the responsibility of upholding the values and principles of our constitution and making them effective. It is their particular responsibility to determine the legal limits of the powers conferred on each branch of government, and to decide whether any exercise of power has transgressed those limits. The courts cannot shirk that responsibility merely on the ground that the question raised is political in tone or context.

[40]. The legal principles of the constitution are not confined to statutory rules, but include constitutional principles developed by the common law. We have already given two examples of such principles, namely that the law of the land cannot be altered except by or in accordance with an Act of Parliament, and that the Government cannot search private premises without lawful authority. Many more examples could be given. Such principles are not confined to the protection of individual rights, but include principles concerning the conduct of public bodies and the relationships between them. For example, they include the principle that justice must be administered in public (*Scott v Scott* [1913] AC 417), and the principle of the separation of powers between the executive, Parliament and the courts (*Ex p Fire Brigades Union*, pp 567–568). In their application to the exercise of governmental powers, constitutional principles do not apply only to powers conferred by statute, but also extend to prerogative powers. For example, they include the principle that the executive cannot exercise prerogative powers so as to deprive people of their property without the payment of compensation (*Burmah Oil Co Ltd v Lord Advocate* [1965] AC 75).

This chapter will focus on statutes, the common law and conventions, all of which played a role in both *Miller* decisions. Both concerned prerogative powers. In *Miller*, the case concerned whether the government enjoyed a prerogative power that it could use to inform the EU of the UK's intention to withdraw from the EU treaties. If not, then legislation would be needed to empower the government to act. A second question was then raised as to whether, if legislation were needed, the Scottish, Welsh and Northern Irish legislatures should be consulted. In *Miller; Cherry*, the Supreme Court determined whether the specific exercise of a prorogative power to prorogue Parliament was unlawful as beyond the scope of the prerogative power, established by constitutional principles developed by the common law.

Prerogative powers stem, historically, from the powers of the Crown. They are governed by the common law. When examining the scope of prerogative powers in *Miller*, the majority judgment of the Supreme Court referred to case law, including the *Case of Proclamations*. The court also referred to the Bill of Rights 1688, the Claim of Rights 1689 in Scotland and the Acts of Union of 1706 and

1707. Both the common law and statute law imposed restrictions on prerogative powers:

> [44]. In the early 17th century *Case of Proclamations* (1610) 12 Co Rep 74, Sir Edward Coke CJ said that 'the King by his proclamation or other ways cannot change any part of the common law, or statute law, or the customs of the realm'. Although this statement may have been controversial at the time, it had become firmly established by the end of that century. In England and Wales, the Bill of Rights 1688 confirmed that 'the pretended power of suspending of laws or the execution of laws by regall authority without consent of Parlyament is illegall' and that 'the pretended power of dispensing with laws or the execution of laws by regall authoritie as it hath beene assumed and exercised of late is illegall'. In Scotland, the Claim of Right 1689 was to the same effect, providing that 'all Proclamationes asserting one absolute power to Cass [i.e. to quash] annull and Disable lawes . . . are Contrair to Law'. And article 18 of the Acts of Union of 1706 and 1707 provided that (with certain irrelevant exceptions) 'all. . .laws' in Scotland should 'remain in the same force as before . . .but alterable by the Parliament of Great Britain'.

In *Miller; Cherry*, the Supreme Court clearly recognised that '[t]he legal principles of the constitution are not confined to statutory rules, but include constitutional principles developed by the common law.' It was these common law principles that were used to determine the scope of the prerogative power of prorogation.

Statutes and common law are examples of legal sources of the UK constitution. Both provided legally enforceable limits on the scope of prerogative powers that could be applied by the courts. Whether the use of prerogative powers to notify the EU of the UK's intention to withdraw from the EU treaties would modify either statute or common law – thus being outwith the scope of the prerogative power of foreign relations, which included entering in to and withdrawing from treaties – depended on the courts' interpretation of other legislative provisions, including most notably the European Communities Act 1972. Common law principles of parliamentary sovereignty and parliamentary accountability were also used in *Miller; Cherry* to determine the scope of a prerogative power, the courts having the ability to recognise and enforce the common law.

Conventions, however, are currently not legally enforceable rules. According the majority of the Supreme Court in *Miller*, 'Judges . . . are neither the parents nor the guardians of political conventions; they are merely observers' (at para [146]). In other words, conventions are not created by the courts. Neither are courts charged with overseeing their application, or enforcing breaches of convention. It remains to be seen whether this means that all courts can do is observe conventions. As will be discussed below, earlier case law suggests that courts may do more than merely observe, although no case law to date suggests that courts can enforce a breach of convention in and of itself. In the *Miller* case, this meant that, if the Sewel Convention applies to legislation and consent is not obtained from the devolved legislatures, there is no legal argument that can be used to enforce the convention. Consequently, the European Union (Withdrawal) Act 2018 is valid legislation, in spite of the fact that Westminster sought the consent of the devolved legislatures, but the Scottish Parliament voted against granting consent. Similarly, the European Union (Withdrawal Agreement) Act 2020 is valid in spite of its being enacted without the consent of all three devolved legislatures, although it is arguable that consent was not required as the legislation did not fall within the scope of the Sewel Convention, being legislation that altered the devolution settlement but which did not legislate in a devolved area of power.

During the course of the chapter, we shall consider further the distinctive features of constitutional laws and conventions, and also the relationship between these two kinds of rules. In doing so, we are also thinking about issues relevant to the separation of powers, the rule of law and parliamentary sovereignty. How far should Parliament and the courts determine the content of, and enforce, different sources, and different rules, of the UK constitution?

3.1 Legal Rules

Dicey (*The Law of the Constitution* (1885), p. 203) held it to be one aspect of the rule of law in England that:

> the principles of private law have with us been by the action of the courts and Parliament so extended as to determine the position of the Crown and of its servants; thus the constitution is the result of the ordinary law of the land.

Dicey's statement needs qualification. It fails to take account of the *extraordinary* powers deriving from the royal prerogative, or of the 'law and custom of Parliament', which has developed separately from the 'ordinary' law. But the statement is more seriously misleading in that a large part of modern constitutional law consists of enactments conferring powers on public authorities, principles developed by the courts in interpreting and giving effect to those enactments, and remedies of exclusive application to public bodies: a corpus of public law, in short, that cannot be explained as a mere extension of private law rules to the administration.

It remains true that the legal rules of the constitution have, in general, evolved by the same processes, and from the same sources, as the law governing the relations between private individuals. Thus, we find constitutional rules mingled with the rest of the law, in statutes and subordinate legislation, in the common law and decisions of judges.

3.1.1 Statute

Although our constitution is frequently described as 'unwritten', almost all of it is written down *somewhere*. What we do not have is a 'codified' constitution or any sort of overarching, superior constitutional text. A considerable part of the British constitution consists of written Acts of Parliament that regulate the system of government or the exercise of public power. These include statutes that have established fundamental features of the constitution, for example, by defining or redefining the terms of the union between England, Scotland and Northern Ireland (Acts of Union with Scotland 1707 and with Ireland 1800 and the devolution statutes of 1998 and thereafter), defining the relations between the two Houses of Parliament (Parliament Acts 1911 and 1949), effecting changes in the law of the UK following accession to the EU (European Communities Act 1972, as amended, and the European Union Act 2011), and the UK's exit from the EU, (European Union (Withdrawal) Act 2018 and European Union (Withdrawal Agreement) Act 2020), giving domestic legal effect to the rights protected by the ECHR (Human Rights Act 1998), creating the Supreme Court (Constitutional Reform Act 2005), fixing the terms of Parliament and governing early general elections (Fixed-Term Parliaments Act 2011), and placing the Civil Service on a statutory footing (Constitutional Reform and Governance Act 2010). Elements of the constitution are also to be found in statutes directed against public disorder (Public Order Acts 1936 and 1986, Criminal Justice and Public Order Act 1994), conferring powers on the police and on the security and secret intelligence agencies (Police and Criminal Evidence Act 1984, Police Acts 1996 and 1997, Police Reform Act 2002, Policing and Crime Act 2017, Security Service Act 1989, Intelligence Services Act 1994, Regulation of Investigatory Powers Act 2000, Investigatory Powers Act 2016), remedying maladministration in government (Parliamentary Commissioner Act 1967), providing for civil proceedings by and against the Crown (Crown Proceedings Act 1947), regulating the franchise and the conduct of elections (Representation of the People Acts, Political Parties, Elections and Referendums Act 2000) and others far too numerous to mention.

Among these statutes are certain great constitutional Acts and instruments that were enacted in confirmation of the results of political upheaval or revolution, or as emphatic statements of what were conceived as fundamental rights or privileges. The antiquity of these Acts, the great historical events with which they are associated, or the lasting worth of the principles contained in them – or a combination of these features – have invested them with a kind of sanctity (in the minds of lawyers and to some extent in public sentiment) that is not unlike that elsewhere attaching to written constitutions. They include Magna Carta 1215, the Habeas Corpus Act 1679, the Bill of Rights 1689, the Act of Settlement 1701, the Act of Union with Scotland 1707 and the Statute of Westminster 1931. The Human Rights Act 1998 and the various Acts governing the devolution of power to Scotland, Wales and Northern Ireland may in time take their place among them.

The following extracts are taken from the Bill of Rights 1689:

> [The] Lords Spirituall and Temporall and Commons pursuant to their respective Letters and Elections being now assembled in a full and free Representative of this Nation . . . Does in the first place (as their Ancestors in like Case have usually done) for the Vindicating and Asserting their ancient Rights and Liberties, Declare
>
> That the pretended Power of Suspending of Laws or the Execution of Laws by Regal Authority without Consent of Parliament is illegal.
>
> That the pretended Power of Dispensing with Laws or the Execution of Laws by Regal Authority as it hath been assumed and exercised of late is illegal.
>
> That levying Money for or to the Use of the Crown by pretence of Prerogative without Grant of Parliament . . . is illegal.
>
> That the raising or keeping a standing Army within the Kingdome in time of Peace unless it be with Consent of Parliament is against Law.
>
> That the Subjects which are Protestants may have Arms for their Defence suitable to their Conditions and as allowed by Law.
>
> That Election of Members of Parliament ought to be free.
>
> That the Freedom of Speech and Debates or Proceedings in Parliament ought not to be impeached or questioned in any Court or Place out of Parliament.
>
> That excessive Bail ought not to be required nor excessive Fines imposed nor cruel and unusual Punishments inflicted.
>
> And that for Redress of all Grievances and for the amending strengthening and preserving of the Laws Parliaments ought to be held frequently.

The provisions of the Bill of Rights are not inviolate, and some have been altered by subsequent legislation; for example, it hardly needs saying that Protestant subjects no longer enjoy a special privilege in the keeping of arms. Some other provisions have lost their importance. There remains, however, a core of provisions that the courts will still uphold against the Crown or government (but not against specific and clear contrary provision by Parliament).

Attorney General v. *Wilts United Dairies Ltd* (1921) 37 TLR 884 (CA)

It was the statutory duty of the food controller to regulate the supply and consumption of food, and he had power under the Defence of the Realm Acts and Regulations to make orders for this purpose. He made orders that fixed maximum prices for milk and provided for the licensing of wholesale dealers. The maximum price fixed for the more productive counties of Cornwall, Devon, Dorset and Somerset was 2d a gallon less than for other areas, but dealers who took milk from these counties for sale elsewhere were required to pay 2d a gallon to the food controller. Licences were granted to the defendants to purchase milk in the four counties on the express condition that they should pay the 2d a gallon, but they afterwards refused to pay and proceedings were brought to recover the amount claimed to be due.

   The Court of Appeal held that the statutory provisions relied on by the food controller did not give him power to levy a financial charge and, accordingly, that the imposition of the charge was illegal.

> **Scrutton LJ:** ... [T]he Bill of Rights ... forbids 'levying money for the use of the Crown without grant of Parliament', and the requirement of this twopence appears to me clearly to come within these words. It is true that the fear in 1689 was that the King by his prerogative would claim money; but excessive claims by the Executive Government without grant of Parliament are, at the present time, quite as dangerous, and require as careful consideration and restriction from the Courts of Justice.

The judgment of the Court of Appeal was affirmed by the House of Lords: (1922) 38 TLR 781. (The same article of the Bill of Rights was one of the grounds of the decision of the Court of Appeal in *Congreve* v. *Home Office* [1976] QB 629.)

   In *Williams* v. *Home Office (No 2)* [1981] 1 All ER 1211, it was argued that the plaintiff's (claimant's) detention in a special control unit, while serving a sentence in Wakefield Prison, violated the prohibition in the Bill of Rights of the infliction of cruel and unusual punishments. Since the regime in the control unit was authorised only by delegated legislation (the Prison Rules) and not by the Prison Act 1952, it would be illegal if contrary to the Bill of Rights. It was held, however, on the evidence that the regime was neither cruel nor unusual and therefore that there had been no breach of the Bill of Rights. Challenges in cases of this sort are now more likely to be founded on the HRA, giving effect to Article 3 of the ECHR in its prohibition of 'inhuman or degrading treatment or punishment'. (See, e.g., *Davidson* v. *Scottish Ministers* 2006 SLT 110.)

R v. *Chaytor and Others* [2010] EWCA Crim 1910, [2010] 2 Cr App R 34

Article 9 of the Bill of Rights (parliamentary proceedings not to be questioned outside Parliament) has frequently arisen for consideration in modern times: see, for example, *Pepper* v. *Hart* [1993] AC 593, 623–4, 638–40; *Prebble* v. *Television New Zealand Ltd* [1995] 1 AC 321; *Hamilton* v. *Al Fayed* [2001] 1 AC 395; and *R (HS2 Alliance)* v. *Secretary of State for Transport* [2014] UKSC 3, [2014] 1 WLR 324. In *Chaytor*, three MPs and one member of the House of Lords faced prosecution for false accounting (contrary to the Theft Act 1968, section 17) with regard to their parliamentary expenses (on the expenses scandal, see above, p. 47). In a preliminary action, they contended that the law of parliamentary privilege as articulated in Article 9 conferred on them an immunity from such prosecution. The Court of Appeal had no difficulty in ruling that it did not: *R* v. *Chaytor and Others* [2010] EWCA Crim 1910. The court's judgment, delivered by the Lord Chief Justice, set the law in its historical and constitutional contexts (at [5] and [14]).

> **Lord Judge CJ:** ... Properly understood, the privileges of Parliament are the privileges of the nation, and the bedrock of our constitutional democracy. Members of the House of Commons are elected to represent the community on the basis of universal suffrage. Subject to limited processes of delay and amendment in the House of Lords, the members of the House of Commons are responsible for the enactment of the legislation by which the country is governed. Among the privileges enjoyed by members of Parliament is the privilege of freedom of speech. Because it is now so long established, it is easy to underestimate its pivotal role in our democracy. Privilege is a concept which has, in recent times, developed unfortunate connotations, but freedom of speech is described as a privilege because that is how it was described during the struggles of the seventeenth century to establish the principle that members of Parliament should be entitled as a matter of incontrovertible right to speak their minds with total freedom. Subject only to self imposed parliamentary ordinance, this is nothing more and nothing less than an absolute, uncircumscribed, and indeed cherished, entitlement ...
>
> This provision [i.e. Article 9 of the Bill of Rights] has remained in force for over 300 years. Its importance cannot be overestimated. It has never been questioned. It is not questioned in these proceedings. No one has suggested that parliamentary privilege should be diminished. These appeals are concerned with its ambit, and whether it extends to criminal proceedings against members of Parliament for fraudulent claims for parliamentary expenses. We simply record that on a first reading, and save always in relation to freedom of speech, it is difficult to read into Article 9 that members of Parliament are immune from prosecution for criminal conduct on the grounds of privilege just because the crime in question was committed in Parliament.

The Supreme Court subsequently upheld this ruling, dismissing Chaytor's appeal: see [2010] UKSC 52, [2010] 3 WLR 1707 (see Chapter 2). In *R (HS2)* v. *Secretary of State for Transport* (discussed below), Lord Neuberger and Lord Mance referred to Article 9 (at para [203] as 'one of the pillars of constitutional settlement which established the rule of law in England in the seventeenth century' and reiterated the description of Lord Browne-Wilkinson in the House of Lords in *Pepper* v. *Hart* [1993] 1 All ER 42, that Article 9 was 'a provision of the highest constitutional importance' that 'should not be narrowly construed'.

Certain provisions of Magna Carta, too, continue to be relied on in judicial proceedings. In *R* v. *Secretary of State for the Home Department, ex p Phansopkar* [1976] QB 606, for example, the Court of Appeal held that a person seeking a certificate of entitlement to enter the UK as a patrial (one having the 'right of abode' under provisions of the Immigration Act 1971 then in force) had the right to prompt and fair consideration of her application for the certificate, and could not be required first to return to her country of origin, there to suffer the same delays as affected those requiring leave to enter the UK. The court cited Magna Carta: 'To none will we sell: to no one will we delay or deny right or justice.' (See also *Re S-C (Mental Patient: Habeas Corpus)* [1996] QB 599, 603 and *Belhaj* v. *Straw* [2017] UKSC 3, [2017] 2 WLR 456, which cited article 29, that 'no free-man shall be taken or imprisoned . . . except by the legal judgment of his peers' as a fundamental right limit on the doctrine of act of state – see Chapter 2.)

Magna Carta was invoked by the applicant for judicial review in *R (Bancoult)* v. *Secretary of State for Foreign and Commonwealth Affairs* [2001] QB 1067, where it was argued that the exiling in the 1960s of the Chagossians from the Chagos Islands, a British overseas territory now known as the British Indian Ocean Territory, in order to make way for an American airforce base, was contrary to chapter 29 of Magna Carta, which provides that 'no freeman shall be taken or imprisoned, or be disseised of his freehold, or liberties, or free customs, or be outlawed, or exiled, or any other wise destroyed . . . but by . . . the law of the land.' The argument was unsuccessful, but in the course of his judgment Laws LJ emphasised the 'enduring significance' of Magna Carta, saying that it was 'in truth the first general declaration . . ., in the long run of our constitutional jurisprudence, of the principle of the rule of law'. The court held on other grounds that the exile of the Chagossians had been unlawful (see Tomkins, 'Magna Carta, Crown and colonies' [2001] *PL* 571). The government subsequently reconfirmed their exile by a fresh order in council (see below). The Divisional Court and the Court of Appeal thought this, too, to be unlawful but the House of Lords, by the narrowest of margins, overruled the lower courts and the Chagossians remain exiled: see *R (Bancoult)* v. *Secretary of State for Foreign and Commonwealth Affairs (No 2)* [2008] UKHL 61, [2009] 1 AC 453.

3.1.1.1 Constitutional Statutes

When discussing the relationship between EU and UK law, Laws LJ developed the concept of constitutional statutes, which appeared to have two attributes: (i) they could not be impliedly repealed and (ii), their provisions were interpreted differently from 'ordinary' legislation (see *Robinson* v. *Secretary of State for Northern Ireland* [2002] UKHL 32, considered in Chapter 2). While there is now case law from the Supreme Court supporting the existence of constitutional statutes, and even of a developing hierarchy between these statutory provisions, it would no longer appear to be the case that constitutional statutes are interpreted differently. Rather, 'constitutional status' may be one feature, among many, influencing principles of statutory interpretation. As such, this section will focus more specifically on whether constitutional legislation has a special status, making it harder to repeal than ordinary legislation.

Thoburn v. *Sunderland City Council* [2002] EWHC 195, [2003] QB 151

The Weights and Measures Act 1985 authorised the use of both metric and imperial measures for the purposes of trade without preference of one over the other. Subsequently regulations were made, under power conferred by section 2(2) of the European Communities Act 1972, which prohibited such use and gave priority to the metric system. It was argued that the regulations were inconsistent with the 1985 Act and that this later act must be taken as having impliedly amended section 2(2) of the European Communities Act 1972, restricting the power it conferred in respect of matters regulated by the 1985 Act (the argument of 'implied repeal').

The court reached the conclusion that there was no inconsistency between the Weights and Measures Act 1985 and section 2(2) of the European Communities Act 1972, so that the argument of implied repeal fell away. Laws LJ nevertheless considered the question of principle, whether the European Communities Act 1972 could be *impliedly* repealed or amended by inconsistent provision in a later act.

Laws LJ: . . . We should recognise a hierarchy of Acts of Parliament: as it were 'ordinary' statutes and 'constitutional' statutes. The two categories must be distinguished on a principled basis. In my opinion a constitutional statute is one which (a) conditions the legal relationship between citizen and State in some general, overarching manner, or (b) enlarges or diminishes the scope of what we would now regard as fundamental constitutional rights. (a) and (b) are of necessity closely related: it is difficult to think of an instance of (a) that is not also an instance of (b). The special status of constitutional statutes follows the special status of constitutional rights. Examples are Magna Carta 1297, the Bill of Rights 1689, the Union with Scotland Act 1706, the Reform Acts which distributed and enlarged the franchise (Representation of the People Acts 1832, 1867 and 1884), the Human Rights Act 1998, the Scotland Act 1998 and the Government of Wales Act 1998. The [European Communities Act 1972] clearly belongs in this family. It incorporated the whole corpus of substantive Community rights and obligations, and gave overriding domestic effect to the judicial and administrative machinery of Community law. It may be there has never been a statute having such profound effects on so many dimensions of our daily lives. The 1972 Act is, by force of the common law, a constitutional statute.

Ordinary statutes may be impliedly repealed. Constitutional statutes may not. For the repeal of a constitutional Act or the abrogation of a fundamental right to be effected by statute, the court would apply this test: is it shown that the legislature's *actual* – not imputed, constructive or presumed – intention was to effect the repeal or abrogation? I think the test could only be met by express words in the later statute, or by words so specific that the inference of an actual determination to effect the result contended for was irresistible. The ordinary rule of implied repeal does not satisfy this test. Accordingly, it has no application to constitutional statutes . . . A constitutional statute can only be repealed, or amended in a way which significantly affects its provisions touching fundamental rights or

> otherwise the relation between citizen and state, by unambiguous words on the face of the later statute.

Laws LJ's invention in this case of a class of 'constitutional statutes' was both novel and significant. It may be argued that it was not so innovatory as it might appear, for the courts had already recognised the existence of constitutional *rights*, which will not be overridden by an act of Parliament unless Parliament's intention to do so is expressed in terms that are compellingly clear (see the rule in *R* v. *Secretary of State for the Home Department, ex p Simms* [2000] 2 AC 115). Although, Laws LJ's views were regarded as exceptional at the time, the existence of constitutional statutes, and their immunity from implied repealed, has now been approved by the Supreme Court. In *H* v. *Lord Advocate* [2012] UKSC 24, [2013] 1 AC 413. Lord Hope (at para [30]) referred to the

> fundamental constitutional nature of the settlement that was achieved by the Scotland Act. This in itself must be held to render it incapable of being altered otherwise than by an express enactment. Its provisions cannot be regarded as vulnerable to alteration by implication from some other enactment in which an intention to alter the Scotland Act is not set forth expressly on the face of the statute.

The existence of constitutional statutes was further confirmed by the Supreme Court in 2014, where the Supreme Court also suggested a potential hierarchy between constitutional provisions.

R (HS2) v. *Secretary of State for Transport* [2014] UKSC 3, [2014] 1 WLR 324

This case concerned the plans to build HS2, a high-speed rail link from London to the West Midlands and, eventually, further north. In order to obtain consent for the scheme, two hybrid bills were placed before Parliament. However, questions arose as to whether this procedure would satisfy requirements under EU law. It was argued that the plans for HS2 fell under the provisions of the Strategic Environmental Assessment Directive, which required 'effective public participation' in the planning decision for HS2. The government argued that the requirement for 'effective public participation' did not apply given that Article 1(4) of the Directive provided an exemption for projects 'adopted by a specific act of national legislation' as the objectives of the Directive, including effective public participation 'are achieved through the legislative process'. However, HS2 relied on interpretations of this Directive that had suggested that the exemption only applied if it could be demonstrated that the legislative process would enable effective public participation. It was argued that this would not be the case, particularly for legislation adopted under the hybrid bill procedure, due to the operation of government whips and the principle of ministerial responsibility. In short, it was argued that the government had proposed the plan, was backing the plan, and the structures of Parliament meant that there would be little the legislature could do to ensure that the environmental impact of HS2 was fully debated, particularly given the large amount of complex data concerned.

The Supreme Court rejected this argument. In particular, it concluded that EU law would not require the provisions of a directive to be interpreted in a manner that would undermine fundamental constitutional principles. The protection of debate in Parliament was a constitutional principle common to the legislatures of the member states and, as such, the UK courts would not be required to examine the quality of legislative debate. Rather, the fact that a legislative procedure was used would be sufficient to satisfy the provisions of the Directive, particularly in the light of the wording of Article 1(4) of the Directive. Lord Neuberger, who gave the leading judgment of the court also considered, in dicta, the possible resolution of a contradiction between Article 9 of the Bill of Rights, which would prevent an assessment of whether parliamentary procedures satisfied a test of effective public participation, and directly effective provisions of EU law which obtain their force from the European Communities Act 1972.

> [207]. The United Kingdom has no written constitution, but we have a number of constitutional instruments. They include Magna Carta, the Petition of Right 1628, the Bill of Rights and (in Scotland) the Claim of Rights Act 1689, the Act of Settlement 1701 and the Act of Union 1707. The European Communities Act 1972, the Human Rights Act 1998 and the Constitutional Reform Act 2005 may now be added to this list. The common law itself also recognises certain principles as fundamental to the rule of law. It is, putting the point at its lowest, certainly arguable (and it is for United Kingdom law and courts to determine) that there may be fundamental principles, whether contained in other constitutional instruments or recognised at common law, of which Parliament when it enacted the European Communities Act 1972 did not either contemplate or authorise the abrogation.
>
> [208]. We are not expressing any view on whether or how far art 9 of the Bill of Rights would count among these, but the point is too important to pass without mention. We would wish to hear full argument upon it before expressing any concluded view. It is not a point upon which the parties before us proposed to make any submissions until it was raised by the court. We were then told that the attention of the Parliamentary authorities (and we deliberately use a vague expression) had been drawn to this appeal, and they elected not to be represented. If and when the point does fall to be considered, the Parliamentary authorities may wish to reconsider whether they should be represented, and, particularly if they still regard that course as inappropriate, it may well be the sort of point on which the Attorney General should appear or be represented. Important insights into potential issues in this area are to be found in their penetrating discussion by Laws LJ in the Divisional Court in *Thoburn v Sunderland City Council* [2002] EWHC 195 (Admin), [2003] QB 151, [2002] 4 All ER 156 (*The Metric Martyrs* case), especially paras 58–70, although the focus there was the possibility of conflict between an earlier 'constitutional' and later 'ordinary' statute, rather

than, as here, between two constitutional instruments, which raises yet further considerations.

R (Miller) v. *Secretary of State for Existing the European Union* (discussed above) also confirmed the constitutional status of the European Communities Act 1972.

As well as ensuring that provisions in constitutional legislation are not impliedly repealed, other principles of statutory interpretation used to resolve potential conflicts between statutory provisions may not apply to constitutional legislation if their application would result in ordinary legislation overriding the provisions of constitutional legislation. An example can be found in *R (Governors of Brynmawr Foundation School* v. *The Welsh Ministers* [2011] EWHC 519 (Admin). Welsh ministers exercised their powers under the Government of Wales Act 2006 to enter into an arrangement with Blaenau Gwent County Borough Council to consult about proposals to close sixth form provision at Brynmawr Foundation School. The Government of Wales Act 2006, classified in the case as a constitutional statute, provided Welsh ministers with broad powers to regulate education in Wales. However, the School Standards and Framework Act 1998 provided more specific powers to regulate education. These provisions did not provide ministers with the ability to reorganise sixth form provision in Welsh schools. It was argued that, as the Government of Wales Act 2006 provided for a general power, and the 2000 Act for a more specific power, the standard principle of statutory interpretation should apply – that general provisions are not able to overturn specific provisions. The High Court concluded that this interpretation failed to take account of the constitutional nature of the Government of Wales Act 2006, whose provisions 'should not, absent clear words, be avoided or circumvented by resort to a specific provision in a non-constitutional statute' (at para [77]).

Despite the special deference with which the Bill of Rights, Magna Carta and other great constitutional statutes are cited by the courts, none of them are immune from repeal by Parliament and many of their provisions have, in fact, been so repealed. Most notably, the European Communities Act 1972 was repealed by section 1 of the European Union (Withdrawal) Act 2018 on exit day – 31 January 2020. In this respect, their legal status may seem to be no greater than that of the National Lottery etc. Act 1993.

In a comment on the *Thoburn* case ((2002) 118 *LQR* 493), Geoffrey Marshall sees difficulty in the thesis of 'two-tier' legislation:

The proffered definitions are undeniably vague and it is hard to see any clear dividing line between ordinary statutes and statutes that deal with rights of a kind that we would now regard as fundamental. Are rights to education, medical services or pensions basic or fundamental, or are they mere run-of-the-mill entitlements? And where statutes condition the legal relationship between citizen and State, when is the manner in which they do it general or overarching? Are Police Acts or Taxation Acts or trade union legislation general or overarching enough to qualify?

What, in any event, is the rationale for supposing that some Acts of Parliament, whatever their subject matter, embody the intentions of the legislature in a more forceful way or in a more protected form than others, in the absence of any explicit Parliamentary expression of intention to create first and second class statutes? Is it really consistent with the sovereignty of Parliament that such a difference in status should be imposed on different segments of its handiwork? In the absence of a consistent and workable definition it seems likely that whatever statutes are judicially determined to be unamenable, for whatever reason, to implied repeal will turn out to be constitutional. This seems to inject an unwelcome element of uncertainty into our public law.

This uncertainty was exacerbated by the recognition in *HS2* of a potential hierarchy between constitutional provisions, including the possible suggestion that Article 9 of the Bill of Rights 1689 was more important than the European Communities Act 1972, such that the latter statute could not abrogate the former. There are competing arguments not only as to whether specific statutes are constitutional or otherwise, but also has to how we should determine whether a statute is 'constitutional'. David Feldman proposed an alternative definition to that proposed by Sir John Laws LJ in *Thoburn*, classing as constitutional legislation that 'establishes state institutions and confers functions, responsibilities and powers on them' seeing the 'key function of a constitution' as 'to constitute the state and its institutions and confer functions, powers and duties on them' (Feldman, 'The Nature and Significance of "Constitutional" Legislation' (2013) 129 *LQR* 343, 353–4). Paul Craig classifies legislation as constitution due to its 'normative importance' in addition to its regulation of constitutional matters. (Craig, 'Constitutionalising Constitutional Law:*HS2*' [2014] *PL* 373). Farrah Ahmed and Adam Perry build on concerns of 'normative importance' by providing a more complex, multilayered definition: (Ahmed and Perry 'Constitutional Statutes' (2017) 37 *OJLS* 461 at p. 470).

A constitutional statute is a statute at least a part of which (1) creates or regulates a state institution and (2) is among the most important elements of our government arrangements, in terms of (a) the influence it has on what state institutions can and may do, given our other governing norms, and (b) the influence it has on what state institutions can and may do through the difference it makes to our other norms. Simplifying a bit, a constitutional statute is a statute that is about state institutions and which substantially influences, directly or indirectly, what those institutions can and may do.

Concerns about the precise definition of constitutional legislation have also meant that there are no special procedural requirements – for instance, a super majority – for constitutional legislation to be enacted differently from ordinary legislation. The situation is different in the Scottish Parliament and the Welsh Senedd, both of which are empowered to enact legislation determining the franchise, voting system, the number of constituencies and the number of members of the legislature to be elected to those constituencies for the Scottish Parliament and the Welsh Senedd respectively, but can only do so with a two-thirds majority of the legislature (Scotland Act 1998, s 31; Government of Wales Act 2006, s 111A). The nearest equivalent as regards the Westminster Parliament is the requirement under the Fixed-Term Parliaments Act 2011 that a motion for an early parliamentary general election requires two-thirds of the votes of the entire House of Commons if it is to succeed. However, as demonstrated by the enactment of the Early Parliamentary General Elections Act 2019, this can be circumvented by enacting legislation that sets an additional date for an early parliamentary general election.

The Constitution Committee of the House of Lords concluded that special procedures – for example, the use of super majorities – should not be required for constitutional legislation. Nevertheless, it did recommend that significant constitutional legislation should be subject to pre-legislative scrutiny, following the publication of a draft bill beforehand, to help facilitate public participation in constitutional change. It also recommended that the best way to ensure constitutional legislation was enacted properly was to strengthen the scrutiny roles of the committees of both Houses of Parliament over the legislation as a whole. This would indirectly provide better scrutiny for constitutional legislation, for example, the committee recommended that the written statements to be produced by ministers when proposing a government bill, should include a statement as to the impact of the proposed legislation on existing constitutional arrangements (*The Process of Constitutional Change, 5th Report of 2010–2012*, HL paper 177).

One difference is apparent. For ordinary public bills, the committee stage in the House of Commons, when their clauses are discussed in detail, is normally taken 'upstairs' in a public bill committee, rather than in a committee of the whole House. The Procedure Committee recommended in 1945 (*1st Report of 1945–46*, HC 9–1, para 6) that the committee stage of bills of 'first-class constitutional importance' should be taken on the floor of the House so that every member should have the opportunity of discussing their detailed provisions. This principle was approved by the House of Commons (HC Deb vol. 415, col 2402, 15 November 1945) and has since generally been followed (e.g., in the proceedings on the Human Rights Bill in 1998, on the House of Lords Bill in 1999 and on the Constitutional Reform and Governance Bill in 2010), although there is sometimes disagreement as to whether a bill is 'constitutional' or of the first class of importance. The matter is usually settled through 'the usual channels' of consultation between government and opposition, but cannot always be resolved in this way. For instance, a motion to commit the Intelligence Services Bill 1994 to a committee of the whole House, on the ground that it involved 'clear constitutional issues', was resisted and not carried. (Note also the controversy as to the 'constitutional' character of the British Nationality Bill 1980: HC Deb vol. 995, cols 649 et seq, 4 December 1980; vol. 996, col 1138, 12 January 1981.) There was initial disagreement between government and opposition about the legislative programmes for the Scotland Bill and the Government of Wales Bill in the 1997–8 session of Parliament, but after discussion between the usual channels each bill had its committee stage on the floor of the house. The entire committee stage of the Constitutional Reform Bill (2004–5) was taken on the floor of the House rather than, as the government initially proposed, parts of it being taken in committee (see HC Deb vol. 430, cols 589–90, 31 January 2005). (The committee stage of constitutional bills can be split, matters of principle being considered on the floor and more technical provisions in standing committee.) For a thorough analysis, see Hazell, 'Time for a New Convention: Parliamentary Scrutiny of Constitutional Bills 1997–2005' [2006] *PL* 247.

3.1.2 Subordinate Legislation

Subordinate legislation, in the sense of legislation by the executive, is normally made under the authority of Acts of Parliament (*delegated legislation*), but orders in council on a strictly limited range of subjects can be made (by the monarch in council) under prerogative power – a type of primary, not delegated, legislation. Of this class are the Civil Service orders in council, which until recently provided the legal base for the regulation of the Civil Service. These orders in council were revoked by and replaced with primary legislation under the Constitutional Reform and Governance Act 2010.

Delegated legislation is normally concerned with matters of detail but is sometimes of wider significance, and some orders in council and regulations made under statutory authority have a place among the sources of constitutional law. Subordinate legislation of this kind may reallocate functions of central government or regulate the exercise of powers by local or other public authorities. For instance, orders in council made under the Ministers of the Crown Act 1975 can be used to dissolve government departments, establish new ministerial offices or transfer functions between ministers. (See, further, Daintith and Page, *The Executive in the Constitution* (1999), pp. 32–3, 36–7.)

Subordinate legislation affecting matters of constitutional concern has been the subject of two decisions of the UK's highest court. *R (Bancoult)* v. *Secretary of State for Foreign and Commonwealth Affairs (No 2)* [2008] UKHL 61, [2009] 1 AC 453 concerned the validity of section 9 of the British Indian Ocean Territory (Constitution) Order 2004, an order in council made under the prerogative. Among other matters, section 9 provided that 'no person is entitled to enter or be present in the Territory except as authorised'. Section

9 therefore sought to continue on a fresh legal basis the exile of the Chagossians from the British Indian Ocean Territory (otherwise known as the Chagos Islands), which had been ruled unlawful in earlier litigation (*R (Bancoult) v. Secretary of State for Foreign and Commonwealth Affairs* [2001] QB 1067: see above). As we saw earlier, the Divisional Court and the Court of Appeal ruled that section 9 was unlawful; the House of Lords was divided on the matter, the majority (Lords Hoffmann, Rodger and Carswell) ruling that section 9 was lawful, with Lords Bingham and Mance dissenting. The Chagossians' argument was that the Crown's power to legislate by order in council (that is, with no parliamentary input) was limited and could not extend to legislating for the abolition of a right of abode in a British overseas territory. While the lower courts and the dissenting Law Lords accepted this argument, the majority of the House of Lords ruled that there was no such limitation. The exile of the Chagossians from their homeland has been aptly described by a former British high commissioner to Mauritius as 'one of the worst violations of human rights perpetrated by the UK in the twentieth century' (David Snoxell, *The Times*, 26 May 2007). Lord Rodger agreed that it had been 'in many respects disgraceful' (*Bancoult (No 2)* at [75]). It is, with respect, enormously disappointing that the House of Lords should have chosen to interpret colonial law in such a manner as to allow for this grotesque violation of the Chagossians' fundamental rights to continue. (For commentary on various aspects of the decision in *Bancoult (No 2)*, see Cohn [2009] *PL* 260; Elliott and Perreau-Saussine [2009] *PL* 697; Poole (2010) 60 *UTLJ* 81; for fuller accounts of the Chagossian story, see Sand, *United States and Britain in Diego Garcia* (2009); Vine, *Island of Shame* (2009).)

Ahmed and others v. *HM Treasury* [2010] UKSC 2, [2010] 2 WLR 378 concerned the lawfulness of two orders in council that had been made under the United Nations Act 1946. The orders, known as the Terrorism Order (TO) and the Al-Qaida Order (AQO), had been made in order to comply with requirements as to the freezing of terrorist assets laid down in a series of resolutions of the UN Security Council (see especially UNSC Resolution 1267 and UNSC Resolution 1373). The TO and the AQO conferred on the Treasury broad powers to freeze all financial and economic resources of persons reasonably suspected to be involved in terrorism. The consequences of the exercise of these powers were described by the Supreme Court as 'so drastic and so oppressive' that the persons affected were to be considered 'effectively prisoners of the state' (Lord Hope at [4] and [6]). Section 1 of the United Nations Act 1946 confers on ministers the power to make such orders in council as appear 'necessary or expedient' for the purpose of implementing in the UK the requirements of international law as laid down by the UN. The Treasury relied on this power in making the TO and the AQO. The Supreme Court, sitting in a panel of seven, ruled that the general words of the 1946 Act did not confer on ministers the power to make orders in council that overrode individuals' fundamental rights. The court applied the rule in *Simms* (above, p. 87) that general legislative provisions need to be read subject to fundamental rights. (The AQO was subsequently replaced with a new order in council based not on the United Nations Act but on the European Communities Act 1972: see the Al Qaida and Taliban (Asset Freezing) Regulations 2010 (SI 1197/2010); the TO has now been replaced by the Terrorist Asset-Freezing etc. Act 2010 (for criticisms of this measure, see House of Lords Constitution Committee, *2nd Report of 2010–11*, HL 25; and JCHR, *3rd Report of 2010–11*, HL 41, HC 535).

Subordinate legislation made by ministers under the devolution statutes may relate to constitutional matters, for instance, in transferring functions to the Scottish Ministers (Scotland Act 1998, section 30(2)). Section 30 was used to transfer power to the Scottish Parliament to hold an independence referendum in Scotland, the terms being set out in the Edinburgh Agreement. Subordinate legislation had been widely used to enlarge the legislative competence of the National Assembly for Wales. Under section 95 of the Government of Wales Act 2006, a 'legislative competence order' (LCO) may be made to this effect where the UK Parliament, the National Assembly and the Secretary of State for Wales are in agreement. Several such LCOs have been made, each one amending Schedule 5 to the Government of Wales Act 2006 (this is the schedule to the Act which lists the competences of the National Assembly). This resulted in Schedule 5 becoming so difficult to navigate that it had been described as 'unwieldy and incomprehensible' (House of Commons Welsh Affairs Committee, *12th report of 2008–09*, HC 678, para 41). These difficulties were partially resolved following the enactment of the Wales Act 2017. (See, further, Chapter 4.)

R (Munir) v. Secretary of State for the Home Department [2012] UKSC 32, [2012] 1 WLR 2192 and R (Alvi) on Secretary of State for the Home Department [2012] UKSC 33, [2012] 1 WLR 2208

As both Bancoult and Ahmed illustrate, restrictions on individual liberty may have their source in subordinate legislation. Further examples of this come from the immigration rules. Section 3(2) of the Immigration Act 1971 provides that: 'The Secretary of State shall from time to time . . . lay before Parliament statements of the rules, or of any changes to the rules, laid down by him as to the practice to be followed in the administration of this Act for regulating the entry into and stay in the United Kingdom of persons required by this Act to have leave to enter.' In 2008, a points-based system was introduced to govern immigration. The Secretary of State also issues policy guidance as to how these rules are to be implemented by immigration officials, as well as regulating how the points-based system is to be determined. This has given rise to issues as to the distinction between guidelines – which do not need to be laid before Parliament – and modifications to the immigration rules, which do.

In *Secretary of State for the Home Department* v. *Pankina* [2010] EWCA Civ 719, [2010] 3 WLR 1526, the various applicants before the court were graduates of UK institutions who wished to remain and work in the UK. The

Secretary of State issued policy guidance relating to the new rule, which stated that the applicant must have 'at least £800 of personal savings which must have been held for at least three months prior to the date of application'. The three-month requirement was contained in the Secretary of State's policy guidance but not in the immigration rules themselves. The Court of Appeal held that, for this reason, the three-month criterion formed no part of the rules applicable to the cases before it. Following *Pankina*, a series of cases sought to draw the distinction between guidelines and rules.

Alvi had applied for leave to remain in the UK as a physiotherapy assistant. However, the codes of practice governing the classification of skilled workers did not include physiotherapy assistants on the list of jobs of level 3, as required for Mr Alvi to remain in the UK. In *Munir*, an issue arose as to a concession. A lengthy residence would not normally provide a justification for permission to remain in the UK. However, a concession was made that enforcement action would not normally be taken with regard to children born in the UK who had resided in the UK for seven years or more, or who had come to the UK at an early age and had resided continuously in the UK for seven years or more. The Secretary of State then withdrew this concession. In both cases, the question arose as to whether these were rules that should have been laid before Parliament. The Supreme Court concluded in *Alvi* that the measure determining the types of job that met the required level for a skilled worker was a rule that should have been laid before Parliament. This was not the case for the withdrawal of a concession.

Lord Dyson SJC: [82] ... As I said in *Munir's* case, the whole point of s 3(2) is to give Parliament a degree of control over the practice to be followed by the Secretary of State in the administration of the 1971 Act for regulating immigration control. If she were free not to lay down rules as to her practice, the plain purpose of s 3(2) would be frustrated. Parliament has required of the Secretary of State that she lay *all* rules as to her practice, although the content of the rules is a matter for her. As Lord Windlesham said in the passage that I quoted in para [25] of my judgment in *Munir's* case, migrants are entitled to know under what rules they are expected to act and it would be impossible for the immigration service to operate otherwise than on the basis of published rules.

[83]. Nevertheless, s 3(2) raises a difficult question of interpretation. What is a rule 'as to the practice to be followed in the administration' of the 1971 Act? Parliament drew a distinction between rules within the meaning of s 3(2) and 'instructions (not inconsistent with the immigration rules)' given to immigration officers by the Secretary of State within the meaning of para 1(3) of Pt 1 of Sch 2 to the 1971 Act. Rules cannot, therefore, encompass the instructions and guidance issued to caseworkers and other staff to assist them with processing applications, although in a sense these documents describe some of the practice followed in the administration of the 1971 Act. But the statute itself recognises that instructions to immigration officers as to how they are to apply the rules are different from the rules themselves. The recognition that the 1971 Act distinguishes

between rules and instructions to immigration officers does not, however, shed light on where the statute draws the line between them

. . .

[94]. In my view, the solution which best achieves these objects is that a rule is any requirement which a migrant must satisfy as a condition of being given leave to enter or leave to remain, as well as any provision 'as to the period for which leave is to be given and the conditions to be attached in different circumstances' (there can be no doubt about the latter since it is expressly provided for in s 3(2)). I would exclude from the definition any procedural requirements which do not have to be satisfied as a condition of the grant of leave to enter or remain. But it seems to me that any requirement which, if not satisfied by the migrant, will lead to an application for leave to enter or remain being refused is a rule within the meaning of s 3(2). That is what Parliament was interested in when it enacted s 3(2). It wanted to have a say in the rules which set out the basis on which these applications were to be determined.

[95]. It may be said that Parliament would not have been interested in scrutinising details such as increases in the appropriate salaries stated in SOC 3221 or changes in the requirements of the resident labour test or even changes in what constitutes a job at or below NVQ/SVQ level 3. I do not think that we can be confident as to what Parliament would have said if it had foreseen the possibility that immigration control would become as complicated as it has become. We know that Parliament wanted to control the making of immigration rules. The most important rules are those by which applications for leave to enter and remain are determined. I see no reason to think that Parliament would not have been interested in having the opportunity to scrutinise the critical aspects of those rules, in particular the provisions which set out the criteria which determine the outcome of applications.

[96]. It seems to me that this approach best reflects what Parliament must be taken to have intended when it enacted s 3(2). There is no evidence that it would be unduly burdensome, let alone administratively unworkable for the Secretary of State. It causes her no administrative difficulty to make the most detailed rules and lay them before Parliament. I acknowledge the burdens that would be imposed on the Scrutiny Committee to which Lord Hope refers at para [65], above. It is, however, a striking fact that the Immigration Rules are already hugely cumbersome. The complexity of the machinery for immigration control has (rightly) been the subject of frequent criticism and is in urgent need of attention. But that is not relevant to the present issue.

[97]. If the boundary is drawn where I have suggested, that should introduce a degree of certainty which ought to reduce the scope for legal challenges. The key requirement is that the Immigration Rules should include all those provisions which set out criteria which are or may be determinative of an application for leave to enter or remain.

These cases illustrate the extent to which important issues are governed by secondary legislation, and the need to ensure effective parliamentary scrutiny over delegated legislation. The immigration rules are extensive. They also illustrate the extent to which changes in policy direction can occur through the use of delegated legislation, most notably through the recent adoption of a 'culture of hostility' giving rise to the Windrush scandal.

(For detailed accounts and case studies of the making of delegated legislation, see Le Sueur, Sunkin and Murkens, *Public Law: Text, Cases, and Materials* (1997), chs 10 and 11; Page, *Governing by Numbers: Delegated Legislation and Everyday Policy-Making* (2001). The making and scrutiny of delegated legislation is considered further in Chapters 7 and 9.)

3.1.3 Common Law

A substantial part of the law of the constitution is common law. '[W]hile other areas of substantive law have become land-masses of statute', remarks Sir Stephen Sedley, 'our constitutional law remains a common law ocean dotted with islands of statutory provision' ('The Sound of Silence' (1994) 110 *LQR* 270, 273). Even if, some years on, this seems a somewhat exaggerated view, there should be no doubting the common law's continuing importance as a source of constitutional law. The doctrine of the rule of law, considered in the previous chapter, owes its authority to the common law. It is in the common law that we find a number of important powers of government, notably the 'prerogative' powers. These are the inherent legal powers of the Crown. Some continue to be exercised by the monarch, but most have now transferred to government ministers. Among the former are the power to appoint the prime minister, the power to dismiss the government, the power to prorogue, but not dissolve, Parliament (i.e., bring a parliamentary session to an end, but not to dissolve Parliament and call a new general election, this now being governed by the Fixed-Term Parliaments Act 2011), and the power to grant (or, exceptionally, to refuse to grant) the royal assent to legislation. All of these are legal powers for which there is no statutory authority: their source lies in the Crown prerogative, recognised by force of the common law. Among the prerogative powers of ministers are the powers to sign and withdraw from treaties, to conduct diplomacy, to deploy the armed forces (both within the UK and abroad), to employ and organise the Civil Service, to issue and revoke passports, and to grant pardons. Ministerial appointment (and removal), appointment to the peerage and the conferring of honours also fall within the prerogative. (The prerogative powers of the monarch are considered in Chapter 6, while those exercisable by government ministers are considered in Chapter 7.)

In addition, judges have created a broad variety of common law principles in matters that they see as touching the safety of the state, public order, the prevention of crime or the moral welfare of society. Accordingly, and controversially, the police enjoy common law powers of arrest, in addition to their statutory powers (see, for example, *Duncan v. Jones* [1936] 1 KB 218), and common law powers of entry, in addition to their statutory powers (see *Thomas v. Sawkins* [1935] 2 KB 249). (For critical commentary, see Ewing and Gearty, *The Struggle for Civil Liberties* (2000), pp. 261–74, 289–95.) Indeed, the courts have allowed the police to exercise very considerable 'preventive' powers: further examples include *Piddington* v. *Bates* [1961] 1 WLR 162, *Moss* v. *McLachlan* [1985] IRLR 76 and *R (Hicks)* v. *Metropolitan Police Commissioner* [2017] UKSC 9, [2017] AC 256. In other cases, however, common law powers have been confined so as to protect the citizen from the arbitrary use of police power, for instance, in *Lindley* v. *Rutter* [1981] QB 128 (disallowing automatic search of persons in custody); *Brazil* v. *Chief Constable of Surrey* [1983] 1 WLR 1155 (requiring reasons to be given before a search of the person is conducted: see now the Police and Criminal Evidence Act 1984, section 54); *Redmond-Bate* v. *DPP* [2000] HRLR 249 (disapproving police action directed against persons whose conduct is lawful and unprovocative, but which is the occasion for the use of violence by others); and *R (Laporte)* v. *Chief Constable of Gloucestershire Police* [2006] UKHL 55, [2007] 2 AC 105 (ensuring that actions short of arrest taken to prevent a breach of a peace can only be taken if the breach of the peace is sufficiently imminent to justify arrest).

Statutes are interpreted by the courts against a background of common law principles, and some of these are regarded as having so fundamental a character that only very clear statutory language is accepted by the courts as effective to displace them.

Pyx Granite Co Ltd v. *Ministry of Housing and Local Government* [1960] AC 260 (HL)

By statute, a person wishing to develop his land had normally to obtain the permission of the local planning authority or of the minister. The relevant legislation also provided that the minister's decision on the question whether permission was needed in a particular case should be final. The appellant company had applied for planning permission, and the minister, having ruled that permission was required, refused permission for part of the land and granted it for another part only on certain conditions. The company brought proceedings in which it claimed that the proposed developments did not require planning permission and that, as a consequence, the minister's decisions were invalid. It was argued against the company that the courts had no jurisdiction to entertain the action because the Act had provided the only procedure for having the question of the need for permission determined.

Viscount Simonds: . . . The question is whether the statutory remedy is the only remedy and the right of the subject to have recourse to the courts of law is excluded . . . It is a principle not by any means to be whittled down that the subject's recourse to Her Majesty's courts for the determination of his rights is not to be excluded except by clear words. That is, as McNair J called it in *Francis v Yiewsley and West Drayton Urban District Council*, a 'fundamental rule' from which I would not for my part sanction any departure . . . There is nothing in the Act to suggest that, while a new remedy, perhaps cheap and expeditious, is given, the old and, as we like to call it, the inalienable remedy of Her Majesty's subjects to seek redress in her courts is taken away.

Their Lordships held that the jurisdiction of the courts was not excluded and that the company did not require planning permission for the proposed development. (See also *Raymond* v. *Honey* [1983] 1 AC 1, 12–13, 14–15; *R* v. *Secretary of State for the Home Department, ex p Leech (No 2)* [1994] QB 198; *Boddington v British Transport Police* [1999] 2 AC 143, 161; *R* v. *Secretary of State for the Home Department, ex p Simms* [2000] 2 AC 115; *Evans* v. *Attorney General* [2015] UKSC 21, [2015] AC 1787; *R (UNISON)* v. *Lord Chancellor* [2017] UKSC 51.)

The common law supplies the bulk of the legal principles by which the exercise of public powers may be qualified. While these common law principles have in recent years been supplemented with statutory principles (such as the principle of proportionality derived from the Human Rights Act), it remains the case that most of the standards against which the courts may judge the exercise of governmental powers originate in the common law of judicial review. This is true both of the substantive tests of legality and rationality (sometimes known as 'ultra vires') and also of the procedural grounds of review, also known as 'natural justice' (see, in more detail, Chapter 10). The law of natural justice provides a good example of the contribution that the common law has made to our constitutional order.

Natural justice requires of decision-makers that they should act without bias (*nemo judex in causa sua*: no one should be judge in his own cause), allow those affected by the decision to be heard (*audi alteram partem*: hear the other side of the question) and reach their conclusion honestly and fairly. (These may, indeed, be seen as requirements of the rule of law.)

It offends against natural justice if a decision-maker is biased or has some financial or personal interest in the matter to be decided. Also a decision may be of such a kind (e.g., a decision of a court or tribunal) that justice must be *seen* to be done, so that a 'real possibility' of bias – from the viewpoint of a 'fair-minded and informed observer' – will invalidate the decision, even if no actual bias is shown. (See *R* v. *Bow Street Metropolitan Stipendiary Magistrate, ex p Pinochet Ugarte (No 2)* [2000] 1 AC 119; *Porter* v. *Magill* [2001] UKHL 67, [2002] 2 AC 357; *Lawal* v. *Northern Spirit Ltd* [2003] UKHL 35, [2004] 1 All ER 187. Bias or the appearance of bias may also constitute an infringement of Article 6(1) of the ECHR.)

The obligation to give a hearing was declared long ago in the case of *Dr Bentley* (1723) 1 Stra 557, who had been deprived of his degrees by the University of Cambridge without notice. Fortescue J said in this case (567):

[T]he objection for want of notice can never be got over. The laws of God and man both give the party an opportunity to make his defence, if he has any. I remember to have heard it observed by a very learned man upon such an occasion, that even God himself did not pass sentence upon Adam, before he was called upon to make his defence. Adam (says God) where art thou? Hast thou not eaten of the tree, whereof I commanded thee that thou shouldst not eat? And the same question was put to Eve also.

The growth in modern times of governmental powers affecting the individual has extended the reach of natural justice – often expressed in its newer applications as a 'duty to act fairly' – and the courts continually work out its content and application in a great variety of circumstances. Lord Morris of Borth-y-Gest said in *Wiseman* v. *Borneman* [1971] AC 297, 309:

> Natural justice, it has been said, is only 'fair play in action'. Nor do we wait for directions from Parliament. The common law has abundant riches: there may we find what Byles J called 'the justice of the common law' (*Cooper v Wandsworth Board of Works* (1863) 14 CBNS 180, 194).

Lord Reid said in the same case (308) that where a procedure for decision-making was laid down by statute, the courts might supplement it with further safeguards if that was necessary to ensure the observance of natural justice, provided that 'to require additional steps would not frustrate the apparent purpose of the legislation'. It is presumed that Parliament, in conferring a power of decision-making, however wide, 'implicitly requires the decision to be made in accordance with the rules of natural justice' (*R* v. *Secretary of State for the Home Department, ex p Pierson* [1998] AC 539, 574, per Lord Browne-Wilkinson). In *Leech* v. *Deputy Governor of Parkhurst Prison* [1988] AC 533 the House of Lords overruled earlier authority in holding that the courts could intervene to ensure the observance of natural justice by a prison governor exercising disciplinary authority over prisoners. This disciplinary function, said Lord Oliver (578), 'is a public function which affects the liberty and, to a degree, the status of the persons affected by it. As such it must ... be subject to the general common law principle which imposes a duty of procedural fairness when a public authority makes a decision not of a legislative nature affecting the rights, privileges and interests of individuals'.

Subject to any further development of common law radicalism (discussed in the previous chapter), common law principles, however fundamental they may seem, have always to yield to unequivocal statutory provision. In addition, it may be clear that a statute is intended to implement a policy that runs counter to older ideas enshrined in common law. An example is the opposition between private rights of property, traditionally defended by the common law, and modern public welfare legislation (see, e.g., *Belfast Corpn* v. *OD Cars Ltd* [1960] AC 490, 523–4, per Lord Radcliffe).

By inventing new common law doctrines, the courts may bring about changes in the constitutional system, but they must be slow to do so 'by entering, or re-entering, a field regulated by legislation' (Lord Nicholls in *Re McKerr* [2004] UKHL 12, [2004] 1 WLR 807, [32]). Constitutional reform is primarily the responsibility of Parliament. This is not to say, however, that common law rules of constitutional law cannot be changed by the courts: they clearly may be and, indeed, sometimes are. *M* v. *Home Office* [1994] 1 AC 377, considered in the previous chapter, is a good example, as is the case study to which we now turn.

3.1.3.1 Developing Constitutional Common Law: A Case Study

The common law is (subject to Parliament) under the control of the judges, who may by their decisions modify and reinterpret constitutional powers and relationships, and redefine the rights of citizens. In the following case, the court extended a common law principle and added to the government's armoury for the protection of cabinet secrecy.

3.1.3.1.1 *Attorney General v. Jonathan Cape Ltd* [1976] QB 752 (Lord Widgery CJ)

Richard Crossman, a minister in the 1964–70 Labour Government, kept a diary of cabinet proceedings that he meant to publish in full, with the object of challenging the traditional secrecy of British government and giving a detailed public account of the workings of the cabinet. Crossman died before the diaries could be published, but after his death, the *Sunday Times* began to publish extracts from them, and Crossman's literary executors proposed to publish the diaries in full as a book. In accordance with the usual practice as to ministerial memoirs, the *Sunday Times* and the executors first submitted the diaries to the secretary to the cabinet for his comments. Ordinarily, if the cabinet secretary asked for the deletion of particular items that he thought infringed the confidentiality of cabinet proceedings, or would be damaging to national security, the publishers would comply. In this instance, however, the *Sunday Times*, faithful to Crossman's intentions, began to publish the extracts, although the cabinet secretary had refused to give them clearance.

The Attorney General brought proceedings for injunctions to prevent the further publication of the diaries. In no previous case had an injunction been granted or sought in similar circumstances, but the Attorney General argued that the courts had power to protect the confidentiality of cabinet proceedings in the public interest. Counsel for the defendants contended, by way of contrast, that if publication of cabinet proceedings was contrary to the public interest, that was a matter to be remedied by legislation.

Lord Widgery CJ: . . . It has always been assumed by lawyers and, I suspect, by politicians, and the Civil Service, that Cabinet proceedings and Cabinet papers are secret, and cannot be publicly disclosed until they have passed into history. It is quite clear that no court will compel the production of Cabinet papers in the course of discovery in an action [but see now *Air Canada v Secretary of State for Trade (No 2)* [1983] 2 AC 394, 432], and the Attorney-General contends that not only will the court refuse to compel the production of such matters, but it will go further and positively forbid the disclosure of such papers and proceedings if publication will be contrary to the public interest.

The basis of this contention is the confidential character of these papers and proceedings, derived from the convention of joint Cabinet responsibility whereby any policy decision reached by the Cabinet has to be supported thereafter by all members of the Cabinet whether they approve of it or not, unless they feel compelled to resign. It is contended that Cabinet decisions and papers are confidential for a period to the extent at least that they must not be referred to outside the Cabinet in such a way as to disclose the attitude of individual Ministers in the argument which preceded the decision. Thus, there may be no objection to a Minister disclosing (or leaking, as it was called) the fact that a Cabinet meeting has taken place, or, indeed, the decision taken, so long as the individual views of Ministers are not identified.

There is no doubt that Mr Crossman's manuscripts contain frequent references to individual opinions of Cabinet Ministers, and this is not surprising because it was his avowed object to obtain a relaxation of the convention regarding memoirs of ex-Ministers ... There have, as far as I know, been no previous attempts in any court to define the extent to which Cabinet proceedings should be treated as secret or confidential, and it is not surprising that different views on this subject are contained in the evidence before me. The Attorney-General does not attempt a final definition but his contention is that such proceedings are confidential and their publication is capable of control by the courts at least as far as they include (a) disclosure of Cabinet documents or proceedings in such a way as to reveal the individual views or attitudes of Ministers; (b) disclosure of confidential advice from civil servants, whether contained in Cabinet papers or not; (c) disclosure of confidential discussions affecting the appointment or transfer of such senior civil servants.

The Attorney-General contends that all Cabinet papers and discussions are prima facie confidential, and that the court should restrain any disclosure thereof if the public interest in concealment outweighs the public interest in a right to free publication ...

I do not understand ... the Attorney-General to be contending, that it is only necessary for him to evoke the public interest to obtain an order of the court. On the contrary, it must be for the court in every case to be satisfied that the public interest is involved, and ... after balancing all the factors which tell for or against publication, to decide whether suppression is necessary.

The defendants' main contention is that whatever the limits of the convention of joint Cabinet responsibility may be, there is no obligation enforceable at law to prevent the publication of Cabinet papers and proceedings, except in extreme cases where national security is involved. In other words, the defendants submit that the confidential character of Cabinet papers and discussions is based on a true convention ... namely, an obligation founded in conscience only. Accordingly, the defendants contend that publication of these Diaries is not capable of control by any order of this court.

If the Attorney-General were restricted in his argument to the general proposition that Cabinet papers and discussions are all under the seal of secrecy at all times, he would be in difficulty. It is true that he has called evidence from eminent former holders of office to the effect that the public interest requires a continuing secrecy, and he cites a powerful passage from the late Viscount Hailsham to this effect ...

The defendants, however, in the present action, have also called distinguished former Cabinet Ministers who do not support this view of Lord Hailsham, and it seems to me that the degree of protection afforded to Cabinet papers and discussion cannot be determined by a single rule of thumb. Some secrets require a high standard of protection for a short time. Others require protection until a new political generation has taken over. In the present action against the literary executors, the Attorney-General asks for a perpetual injunction to restrain further publication of the Diaries in whole or in part. I am far from convinced that he has made out a case that the public interest requires such a Draconian remedy when due regard is had to other public interests, such as the freedom of speech . . . .

I have already indicated some of the difficulties which faced the Attorney-General when he relied simply on the public interest as a ground for his actions. That such ground is enough in extreme cases is shown by the universal agreement that publication affecting national security can be restrained in this way. It may be that in the short run (for example, over a period of weeks or months) the public interest is equally compelling to maintain joint Cabinet responsibility and the protection of advice given by civil servants, but I would not accept without close investigation that such matters must, as a matter of course, retain protection after a period of years.

However, the Attorney-General has a powerful reinforcement for his argument in the developing equitable doctrine that a man shall not profit from the wrongful publication of information received by him in confidence. This doctrine, said to have its origin in *Prince Albert v Strange* (1849) 1 H & TW 1, has been frequently recognised as a ground for restraining the unfair use of commercial secrets transmitted in confidence. . . . It is not until the decision in *Duchess of Argyll v Duke of Argyll* [1967] Ch 302, that the same principle was applied to domestic secrets such as those passing between husband and wife during the marriage. It was there held by Ungoed-Thomas J, that the plaintiff wife could obtain an order to restrain the defendant husband from communicating such secrets, and the principle is well expressed in the headnote in these terms, at p 304:

'A contract or obligation of confidence need not be expressed but could be implied, and a breach of contract or trust or faith could arise independently of any right of property or contract . . . and that the court, in the exercise of its equitable jurisdiction, would restrain a breach of confidence independently of any right at law.'

This extension of the doctrine of confidence beyond commercial secrets has never been directly challenged, and was noted without criticism by Lord Denning MR in *Fraser v Evans* [1969] 1 QB 349, 361. I am sure that I ought to regard myself, sitting here, as bound by the decision of Ungoed-Thomas J.

Even so, these defendants argue that an extension of the principle of the *Argyll* case to the present dispute involves another large and unjustified leap forward, because in the present case the Attorney-General is seeking to apply the principle to public secrets made confidential in the interests of good government. I cannot see why the courts should be powerless to restrain the publication of public secrets, while enjoying the *Argyll* powers in regard to domestic secrets. Indeed, as already pointed out, the court must have power to deal with publication which threatens national security, and the difference between such a case and the present case is one of degree rather than kind. I conclude, therefore, that

> when a Cabinet Minister receives information in confidence the improper publication of such information can be restrained by the court, and his obligation is not merely to observe a gentleman's agreement to refrain from publication.

Lord Widgery went on to deal with the argument for the *Sunday Times* that the evidence did not establish the existence or scope of a convention of collective or joint ministerial responsibility:

> I find overwhelming evidence that the doctrine of joint responsibility is generally understood and practised and equally strong evidence that it is on occasion ignored. The general effect of the evidence is that the doctrine is an established feature of the English form of government, and it follows that some matters leading up to a Cabinet decision may be regarded as confidential. Furthermore, I am persuaded that the nature of the confidence is that spoken for by the Attorney-General, namely, that since the confidence is imposed to enable the efficient conduct of the Queen's business, the confidence is owed to the Queen and cannot be released by the members of Cabinet themselves. I have been told that a resigning Minister who wishes to make a personal statement in the House, and to disclose matters which are confidential under the doctrine obtains the consent of the Queen for this purpose. Such consent is obtained through the Prime Minister. I have not been told what happened when the Cabinet disclosed divided opinions during the European Economic Community referendum. But even if there was here a breach of confidence (which I doubt) this is no ground for denying the existence of the general rule. I cannot accept the suggestion that a Minister owes no duty of confidence in respect of his own views expressed in Cabinet. It would only need one or two Ministers to describe their own views to enable experienced observers to identify the views of the others . . .
>
> The Cabinet is at the very centre of national affairs, and must be in possession at all times of information which is secret or confidential. Secrets relating to national security may require to be preserved indefinitely. Secrets relating to new taxation proposals may be of the highest importance until Budget day, but public knowledge thereafter. To leak a Cabinet decision a day or so before it is officially announced is an accepted exercise in public relations, but to identify the Ministers who voted one way or another is objectionable because it undermines the doctrine of joint responsibility.
>
> It is evident that there cannot be a single rule governing the publication of such a variety of matters. In these actions we are concerned with the publication of diaries at a time when 11 years have expired since the first recorded events. The Attorney-General must show (a) that such publication would be a breach of confidence; (b) that the public interest requires that the publication be restrained, and (c) that there are no other facets of the public interest contradictory of and more compelling than that relied upon. Moreover, the court, when asked to restrain such a publication, must closely examine the extent to which relief is necessary to ensure that restrictions are not imposed beyond the strict requirement of public need.

Applying those principles to the present case, what do we find? In my judgment, the Attorney-General has made out his claim that the expression of individual opinions by Cabinet Ministers in the course of Cabinet discussion are matters of confidence, the publication of which can be restrained by the court when this is clearly necessary in the public interest.

The maintenance of the doctrine of joint responsibility within the Cabinet is in the public interest, and the application of that doctrine might be prejudiced by premature disclosure of the views of individual Ministers.

There must, however, be a limit in time after which the confidential character of the information, and the duty of the court to restrain publication, will lapse. Since the conclusion of the hearing in this case I have had the opportunity to read the whole of volume one of the Diaries, and my considered view is that I cannot believe that the publication at this interval of anything in volume one would inhibit free discussion in the Cabinet of today, even though the individuals involved are the same, and the national problems have a distressing similarity with those of a decade ago. It is unnecessary to elaborate the evils which might flow if at the close of a Cabinet meeting a Minister proceeded to give the press an analysis of the voting, but we are dealing in this case with a disclosure of information nearly 10 years later.

It may, of course, be intensely difficult in a particular case, to say at what point the material loses its confidential character, on the ground that publication will no longer undermine the doctrine of joint Cabinet responsibility. It is this difficulty which prompts some to argue that Cabinet discussions should retain their confidential character for a longer and arbitrary period such as 30 years, or even for all time, but this seems to me to be excessively restrictive. The courts should intervene only in the clearest of cases where the continuing confidentiality of the material can be demonstrated. In less clear cases – and this, in my view, is certainly one – reliance must be placed on the good sense and good taste of the Minister or ex-Minister concerned.

In the present case there is nothing in Mr Crossman's work to suggest that he did not support the doctrine of joint Cabinet responsibility. The question for the court is whether it is shown that publication now might damage the doctrine notwithstanding that much of the action is up to 10 years old and three general elections have been held meanwhile. So far as the Attorney-General relies in his argument on the disclosure of individual ministerial opinions, he has not satisfied me that publication would in any way inhibit free and open discussion in Cabinet hereafter.

It remains to deal with the Attorney-General's two further arguments, namely, (a) that the Diaries disclose advice given by senior civil servants who cannot be expected to advise frankly if their advice is not treated as confidential; (b) the Diaries disclose observations made by Ministers on the capacity of individual senior civil servants and their suitability for specific appointments. I can see no grounds in law which entitle the court to restrain publication of these matters. A Minister is, no doubt, responsible for his department and accountable for its errors even though the individual fault is to be found in his subordinates. In these circumstances, to disclose the fault of the subordinate may amount to cowardice or bad taste, but I can find no ground for saying that either the Crown or the individual civil servant has an enforceable right to have the advice which he gives treated as confidential for all time.

For these reasons I do not think that the court should interfere with the publication of volume one of the Diaries, and I propose, therefore, to refuse the injunction sought but to grant liberty to apply in regard to material other than volume one if it is alleged that different considerations may there have to be applied. *Injunction refused.*

The report of the case concludes with an afterword by the Chief Justice:

Lord Widgery CJ said that the statement in his judgment that the courts would not restrict publication of confidential communications between civil servants and Ministers was restricted to the present proceedings and did not amount to a general ruling that the courts had no power to do so in any circumstances.

The Attorney General may be said to have been victorious in this case in gaining judicial acceptance of the *principle* that a legal obligation of confidentiality attaches to cabinet proceedings, even though the court decided that the Crossman diaries no longer, after the lapse of ten years, retained their confidential character, and so fell outside the protection of the law. The court fashioned from the 'developing equitable doctrine' of confidentiality, which had in previous cases found its application in commercial and domestic relations, a new rule for maintaining the secrecy of cabinet proceedings.

It is important, however, to note Lord Widgery's insistence that publication of confidential cabinet papers or discussions should be restrained only if the public interest was shown to require such restraint and if there were 'no other facets of the public interest contradictory of and more compelling than that relied upon'.

The new common law rule established in *Attorney General* v. *Jonathan Cape Ltd* was not considered by the government to give sufficient protection to the confidentiality of government business. More stringent rules of non-disclosure, recommended by a Committee of Privy Counsellors (the Radcliffe Committee, Cmnd 6386/1976), were adopted by the government in 1976 as rules of practice to which ministers would be required to agree. The Radcliffe rules do not supplant the common law but impose on ministers obligations, of a non-legal kind, which are more precise and of wider scope than the legal obligation of confidentiality established in the *Crossman Diaries* case. The rules stipulate that, in general, ministers are not to disclose confidential discussions for a period of fifteen years. The *Ministerial Code* (2019) provides in para 8.10 that 'former Ministers intending to publish their memoirs are required to submit the draft manuscript in good time before publication to the Cabinet Secretary and to conform to the principles set out in the Radcliffe Report of 1976.'

It has been said that, although depending on voluntary observance, the system 'works reasonably well' (HC Deb vol. 194, col 17, 1 July 1991. Cf. R Brazier, *Ministers of the Crown* (1997), pp. 314–15.) The protection of government information through the doctrine of confidentiality, as endorsed in *Jonathan Cape*, was at the core of the *Spycatcher* litigation in 1986–8 (see Chapter 11).

3.2 Conventions

The working of our system of government is conditioned by a mass of usages or practices that must be taken into account if the system is to be understood. Some of these usages affect the behaviour of the principal organs of the state or their mutual relations, while others operate at lower levels of the conduct of official business and may not be dignified as having a constitutional character. Among these usages are some that have the status of 'conventions of the constitution'. For Dicey, conventions were principally those customary rules that determined the way in which the discretionary (or prerogative) powers of the executive should be used (*The Law of the Constitution* (1885), pp. 428–9). The modern conception is somewhat broader than this, and Lord Wilson of Dinton has a helpful description of constitutional conventions as 'the main political principles which regulate relations between the different parts of our constitution and the exercise of power but which do not have legal force' ('The Robustness of Conventions in a Time of Modernisation and Change' [2004] *PL* 407, 408–9). For Jaconelli, conventions are social rules of a constitutional character that govern the relations between political parties or the institutions of government, regulating the manner in which government is to be conducted ('The Nature of Constitutional Convention' (1999) 19 *LS* 24).

Usages do not have the character and force of constitutional conventions unless they are generally acknowledged – by those involved in the constitutional relationships in which the usages have their setting – as having an obligatory character. (Some conventions, it has been noted, 'do not in fact impose obligations or duties but confer rights or entitlements': Marshall, *Constitutional Conventions* (1984), p. 7; but these too will have been raised above the level of mere usage or practice by a general acknowledgment, not of their obligatory character, but of their legitimising authority.) Conventions, that is to say, are *rules* and are part of the constitutional order, interwoven with but distinguishable from rules of law. On this view, breach of a constitutional convention is every bit as unconstitutional as breach of a constitutional law. The difference lies in the nature of the enforcement and of the sanction. Laws, of course, are enforced in courts. Conventions are not: they are non-legal but nonetheless binding rules of constitutional behaviour. Their enforcement is political rather than legal and is the responsibility of political bodies such as the House of Commons. The conventions of ministerial responsibility are a good example. It is a convention that ministers are collectively and individually responsible to Parliament. If a minister knowingly misleads Parliament, for instance, he or she will be expected to resign from office. If no resignation is forthcoming, the minister will be acting unconstitutionally, but he or she will not be acting illegally. No court of law could compel a resignation in these circumstances: it would be a matter for Parliament. (The operation of ministerial responsibility is considered further in Chapter 9.)

That said, the consequences of a breach of convention are various and are not always easily predictable. On the one hand, a breach may simply confirm a general view that the convention is inconvenient and should be changed or abandoned. On the other, the breach may provoke accusations of unconstitutional behaviour and lead to serious political controversy. On occasion, the response to a breach has been the passage of legislation to give a legal reinforcement to the convention or replace it with legally binding rules. This was what happened after the House of Lords exceeded conventional limits on its powers in rejecting, in 1909, a finance bill (Lloyd George's 'People's Budget') passed by the Commons. The Parliament Act 1911 removed the Lords' veto over money bills.

Geoffrey Marshall has suggested that it is no less than the 'major purpose' of conventions 'to give effect to the principles of governmental accountability that constitute the structure of responsible government' (*Constitutional Conventions* (1984), p. 18). The relations between the Crown and Parliament are fundamental to this structure, and are regulated as much by convention as they are by law. For example, while the Triennial Act 1694 requires only that 'a Parliament shall be holden once in three years at the least', by convention, Parliament is summoned to meet every year. (This convention is fortified by the need to obtain the consent of Parliament to annual Acts providing for the raising of revenue and the expenditure of public money.) Governmental accountability to Parliament depends not only on the conventions of ministerial responsibility referred to above, but also on a host of ancillary conventions which help to safeguard the rights of Parliament, its select committees, opposition parties and individual MPs. For instance, one of these conventions has to do with the 'estimates', a principal mechanism for parliamentary control of governmental expenditure. It is an established convention that significant changes in the form of the estimates presented to Parliament by government departments are not to be made without the prior approval of both the Public Accounts Committee and the Treasury Committee of the House of Commons. (See Treasury and Civil Service Committee, *4th Report of 1994–95*, HC 212, para 4.) The rules of parliamentary procedure are supplemented by conventions. (We shall encounter some of these conventions in Chapter 9.)

Other conventions serve a variety of purposes connected with many different aspects of government. Such is the conventional rule that governs access by ministers to the papers of a previous administration of a different political party. The terms of the convention were set out by the prime minister in a written answer to a parliamentary question on 24 January 1980 (HC Deb vol. 977, cols 305–7 W) declaring it to be:

> an established rule that after a General Election a new Administration does not have access to the papers of a previous Administration of a different political complexion. This rule applies especially to Cabinet papers.

In general, documents are withheld from the new administration if they reveal the personal views of the previous ministers on matters of policy or administration, or advice submitted to them on matters which they had under consideration. (For further details, see para 11.23 of the *Cabinet Manual*.)

Another area regulated by convention is that of government communications. Governments spend substantial sums of money on publicity and advertising. Publicity campaigns have accompanied successive privatisations and such projects as the New Deal jobs programme. In addition, governments mount campaigns on social questions such as road safety and avoidance of AIDS, and publish information about recent legislation and new policy initiatives. There is an evident necessity to ensure that public money should not be spent for party political purposes under the guise of government publicity, and for many years there have been conventions within government as to what is and is not allowable. When the Widdicombe Committee was inquiring into publicity campaigns in local government in 1984–5, it asked to be provided with information about the practice in central government (*Interim Report of the Committee of Inquiry into the Conduct of Local Authority Business* (1985), paras 116–19). As a result, the conventions were formally recorded in writing by the Cabinet Office, and they afterwards became known as the 'Widdicombe Conventions'. They provide a fuller statement of the principle, affirmed in both the *Ministerial Code* (2019) and the *Civil Service Code*, that public resources must not be used for party political purposes. Guidelines based on the Widdicombe Conventions were drawn up by a government working group in 1997. These guidelines, as revised from time to time, are followed by civil servants working as communicators. The 'Government Communication Service Propriety Guidance' (https://gcs.civilservice.gov.uk/wp-content/uploads/2015/09/Government-Communication-Propriety-Guidance.pdf) issued by the Cabinet Office defines how civil servants can properly and effectively present the policies and programmes of the government of the day and sets out the basic conventions:

> The following basic criteria have been applied to government communications by successive administrations. The communication:
>
> - should be relevant to government responsibilities;
> - should be objective and explanatory, not biased or polemical;
> - should not be – or liable to be – misrepresented as being party political;
> - should be conducted in an economic and appropriate way, and should be able to justify the costs as expenditure of public funds.

> Publicly funded government communications cannot be used primarily or solely to meet party political objectives. However, it is recognised that the governing party may derive incidental benefit from activities carried out by the Government.
>
> The Ministerial Code requires ministers to uphold the impartiality of the Civil Service. They must not ask civil servants to act in any way that conflicts with the Civil Service Code. Ministers must ensure that public resources are not used to support publicity for party political purposes.

Governments have a tendency to blur the distinction between (legitimate) publicity for government policies and party-political propaganda. The Treasury and Civil Service Committee of the House of Commons suggested in 1988 that there was a case for giving statutory authority to the Widdicombe Conventions, but the government disagreed, saying that ministers were collectively committed to the conventions and were accountable to Parliament for their observance in particular cases. (See the Committee's *7th Report of 1987–88*, HC 506, para 17 and its *1st Special Report of 1988–89*, HC 180, para 2. See, further, Munro [1990] *PL* 1; Oborne in Sutherland (ed.), *The Rape of the Constitution?* (2000), pp. 318–24.)

As is clear from the above examples, conventions may be written or unwritten. Whether they are written or unwritten makes no difference to their force as conventions, although it may make a difference to their clarity. As Jaconelli states, when conventions are written down 'the formula *records*, rather than *creates*, the convention' ('Do Constitutional Conventions Bind?' [2005] *CLJ* 149, 169). Unlike enacted laws, the conventions would be conventions even if they were not written down. Some conventions are even codified. Among these are the conventions of ministerial responsibility, which are included in the *Ministerial Code* (a document formerly known as *Questions of Procedure for Ministers*), which is issued on appointment to all ministers by the Prime Minister (for the full text, see https://assets.publishing.service.gov.uk/government/uploads/system/uploads/attachment_data/file/826920/August-2019-MINISTERIAL-CODE-FINAL-FORMATTED-2.pdf).

Ministerial Code (2010, updated August 2019), Section 1

1.1 Ministers of the Crown are expected to maintain high standards of behaviour and to behave in a way that upholds the highest standards of propriety.
1.2 Ministers should be professional in all their dealings and treat all those with whom they come into contact with consideration and respect. Working relationships, including with civil servants, ministerial and parliamentary colleagues and parliamentary staff should be proper and appropriate. Harassing, bullying or other inappropriate or discriminating

behaviour wherever it takes place is not consistent with the Ministerial Code and will not be tolerated.

1.3 *The Ministerial Code* should be read alongside the background of the overarching duty on Ministers to comply with the law and to protect the integrity of public life. They are expected to observe the *Seven Principles of Public Life* set out at Annex A and the following principles of Ministerial conduct:

a. The principle of collective responsibility applies to all Government Ministers;

b. Ministers have a duty to Parliament to account, and be held to account, for the policies, decisions and actions of their departments and agencies;

c. It is of paramount importance that Ministers give accurate and truthful information to Parliament, correcting any inadvertent error at the earliest opportunity. Ministers who knowingly mislead Parliament will be expected to offer their resignation to the Prime Minister;

d. Ministers should be as open as possible with Parliament and the public, refusing to provide information only when disclosure would not be in the public interest, which should be decided in accordance with the relevant statutes and the *Freedom of Information Act 2000*;

e. Ministers should similarly require civil servants who give evidence before Parliamentary Committees on their behalf and under their direction to be as helpful as possible in providing accurate, truthful and full information in accordance with the duties and responsibilities of civil servants as set out in the *Civil Service Code*;

f. Ministers must ensure that no conflict arises, or appears to arise, between their public duties and their private interests;

g. Ministers should not accept any gift or hospitality which might, or might reasonably appear to, compromise their judgement or place them under an improper obligation;

h. Ministers in the House of Commons must keep separate their roles as Minister and constituency Member;

i. Ministers must not use government resources for Party political purposes;

j. Ministers must uphold the political impartiality of the civil service and not ask civil servants to act in any way which would conflict with the *Civil Service Code* as set out in the *Constitutional Reform and Governance Act 2010*.

1.4 It is not the role of the Cabinet Secretary or other officials to enforce the Code. If there is an allegation about a breach of the Code, and the Prime Minister, having consulted the Cabinet Secretary, feels that it warrants further investigation, he may ask the Cabinet Office to investigate the facts of the case or refer the matter to the independent adviser on Ministers' interests.

1.5 The Code provides guidance to Ministers on how they should act and arrange their affairs in order to uphold these standards. It lists the principles which may apply in particular situations. It applies to all members of the Government and covers Parliamentary Private Secretaries . . .

1.6 Ministers are personally responsible for deciding how to act and conduct themselves in the light of the Code and for justifying their actions and conduct to Parliament and the public. However, Ministers only remain in office for so long as they retain the confidence of the

> Prime Minister. He is the ultimate judge of the standards of behaviour expected of a Minister and the appropriate consequences of a breach of those standards.
>
> 1.7 Ministers must also comply at all times with the requirements which Parliament itself has laid down in relation to the accountability and responsibility of Ministers . . . Ministers must also comply with the Codes of Conduct for their respective Houses and also any requirements placed on them by the Independent Parliamentary Standards Authority.

There are two notable differences between this version of the code and the original 2010 version. First, the addition of section 1.2. designed to protect parliamentary colleagues and staff from bullying and harassment. Second, the removal from ministers of acting in line with the Coalition Agreement – which was only relevant to the 2010–15 Coalition Government – and of the obligation of ministers to act in line with the law, including international law and treaty obligations. These obligations were removed by then Prime Minister, David Cameron, in 2015. This change gave rise to concerns that ministers may no longer have drawn to their attention the need to comply with international law requirements, even though it did not modify their legal obligations.

There is also a further significant change between the most recent 2019 version of the *Ministerial Code* and the 2018 version regarding section 1.4. In the 2018 version, enacted when Theresa May was Prime Minister, an allegation of a breach of the code 'will' be referred to the independent adviser on ministers' interests if 'the Prime Minister, having consulted the Cabinet Secretary, feels that it warrants further investigation'. However, the 2019 version, enacted when Boris Johnson was Prime Minister, adds in an extra layer of discretion – the prime minister may refer, as opposed to will refer a breach if he feels this warrants further investigation. Moreover, the prime minister does not consult with the cabinet secretary before reaching this conclusion, and may refer the matter to the Cabinet Office instead of the independent adviser on ministers' interests. This is a dilution of independence and accountability, suggesting a potential lowering of the seriousness of breaches of the *Ministerial Code*, which may in turn result in fewer resignations for breaches of the code in future.

The *Cabinet Manual*

The *Cabinet Manual* codifies a wide range of rules, practices and constitutional conventions, although it is not always clear whether the *Manual* is an account of a convention, rule or practice. It was drafted by Sir Gus O'Donnell, with the approval of the then prime minister, the first version of the *Manual* being produced in October 2011 (available at https://assets.publishing.service.gov.uk/government/uploads/system/uploads/attachment_data/file/60641/cabinet-manual.pdf). It deals with the following subject matter: the sovereign; elections and government formation; the structure of central government;

collective cabinet decision-making; ministers and Parliament; ministers and the law; ministers and the Civil Service; relations between central government and the devolved institutions; relations between central government the EU and other international organisations; government finance and expenditure; and official information.

Before its publication, draft chapters were produced, including most notably the draft chapter on the process of government formation which helped to facilitate the formation of the Coalition Government following the hung Parliament of 2010. In particular, it clarified (for example) that Gordon Brown was acting perfectly properly (and constitutionally) in not resigning as Prime Minister immediately after it was apparent that his party had lost its overall majority of seats in the House of Commons. Some newspapers hostile to Mr Brown accused him of 'squatting' in Downing Street. They were wholly wrong to do so and it was useful to have the draft chapter of the *Manual* to hand to point this out. (See, further, House of Commons Political and Constitutional Reform Committee, *Lessons from the Process of Government Formation after the 2010 General Election, 4th Report of 2010–11*, HC 528.)

The aims and objectives of the *Cabinet Manual*, its authorship and ownership, as well as its constitutional status and the drafting of some of its content, attracted criticism, although the broad project was welcomed by commentators such as the Constitution Unit and the Institute for Government. Several parliamentary committees took evidence and published reports on the draft *Manual* (including the House of Commons Political and Constitutional Reform Committee and the House of Lords Constitution Committee). Further developments with regard to the *Cabinet Manual* will be posted as appropriate on this book's companion website.

The Political and Constitutional Reform Committee carried out a report on the *Cabinet Manual* in 2015 (*Revisiting the Cabinet Manual, Fifth Report of 2014–15*, HC233). The report was broadly in favour of the *Manual* and it did not recommend that its provisions should be put on a statutory footing. However, the committee was concerned about the lack of general public awareness of the *Cabinet Manual*, particularly as this now set out the 'rules of the game'. The committee stated that 'in the run up to the 2015 general election, the public is entitled to clear, objective and unambiguous information about the process whereby administrations are formed' and recommended that the 'Cabinet Office plan for an enhanced programme of public engagement with the contents of the Manual after the 2015 election'. Alas, this process has not taken place at a time where there is, perhaps, even greater need for knowledge of its provisions. Since 2015, there have been two changes of prime minister that have occurred through changes in the leadership of the particular political party in power as opposed to through a general election (Theresa May in 2016 and Boris Johnson in 2019). Whereas concerns originally arose as to the formation of a coalition government, which are covered by the *Cabinet Manual*, there are now issues surrounding the conduct of a minority government, and the behaviour of an incumbent prime minister during the fourteen days after a vote of no confidence, as well as the residual powers of the monarch to prorogue Parliament on the advice of the prime minister. The committee also recommended regular revision of the *Manual*, being revised at least every Parliament and 'especially on the arrival of a new administration'.

The committee also made more specific recommendations for the revision of the *Cabinet Manual*

> • It is vital that there should be a clear and shared understanding of the conventions governing the position of an incumbent Prime Minister who may not be able to command the confidence of the House of Commons after a general election: the principle that there must always be a government, and the Sovereign must always have a principal constitutional adviser in the form of a Prime Minister, is unambiguous and ought to be made clear;
> • In the new era of fixed-term Parliaments, it is in the interests of good government for pre-election contacts between the opposition parties and the Civil Service to be authorised to begin 12 months out from a general election as a matter of course, and
> • Any revision to the Manual must reflect the present scope of uncertainty over the use of the convention regarding consultation of the House of Commons before UK armed forces are committed to military action overseas.

These revisions have also not been made. This has been of particular concern as to the convention regarding consultation of the House of Commons before the commitment of the armed forces to military action overseas (discussed below).

Perhaps one of the most currently relevant provisions of the *Cabinet Manual* concerns votes of no confidence, now regulated by the Fixed-Term Parliaments Act 2011:

> 2.19 Under the Fixed-Term Parliaments Act 2011, if a government is defeated on a motion that 'this House has no confidence in Her Majesty's Government', there is then a 14-day period during which an alternative government can be formed from the House of Commons as presently constituted, or the incumbent government can seek to regain the confidence of the House. If no government can secure the confidence of the House of Commons during that period, through the approval of a motion that 'this House has confidence in Her Majesty's Government', a general election will take place. Other decisions of the House of Commons which have previously been regarded as expressing 'no confidence' in the government no longer enable or require the Prime Minister to hold a general election. The Prime Minister is expected to resign where It Is clear that he or she does not have the confidence of the House of Commons and that an alternative government does have the confidence.

2.20 Where a range of different administrations could be formed, discussions may take place between political parties on who should form the next government. In these circumstances the processes and considerations described in paragraphs 2.12–2.17 would apply.

. . .

2.12 Where an election does not result in an overall majority for a single party, the incumbent government remains in office unless and until the Prime Minister tenders his or her resignation and the Government's resignation to the Sovereign. An incumbent government is entitled to wait until the new Parliament has met to see if it can command the confidence of the House of Commons, but is expected to resign if it becomes clear that it is unlikely to be able to command that confidence and there is a clear alternative.

2.13 Where a range of different administrations could potentially be formed, political parties may wish to hold discussions to establish who is best able to command the confidence of the House of Commons and should form the next government. The Sovereign would not expect to become involved in any negotiations, although there are responsibilities on those involved in the process to keep the Palace informed. This could be done by political parties or the Cabinet Secretary. The Principal Private Secretary to the Prime Minister may also have a role, for example, in communicating with the Palace.

2.14 If the leaders of the political parties involved in any negotiations seek the support of the Civil Service, this support may only be organised by the Cabinet Secretary with the authorisation of the Prime Minister. If the Prime Minister authorises any support it would be focused and provided on an equal basis to all the parties involved, including the party that was currently in government. The Civil Service would continue to advise the incumbent government in the usual way.

2.15 Following the election in May 2010, the Prime Minister authorised the Civil Service to provide such support to negotiations between political parties.

2.16 As long as there is significant doubt following an election over the Government's ability to command the confidence of the House of Commons, certain restrictions on government activity apply; see paragraphs 2.27–2.34.

2.17 The nature of the government formed will be dependent on discussions between political parties and any resulting agreement. Where there is no overall majority, there are essentially three broad types of government that could be formed:

- single-party, minority government, where the party may (although not necessarily) be supported by a series of ad hoc agreements based on common interests;
- formal inter-party agreement, for example the Liberal–Labour pact from 1977 to 1978; or
- formal coalition government, which generally consists of ministers from more than one political party, and typically commands a majority in the House of Commons.

The restrictions on government activity are designed to prevent an incumbent government from 'initiating any new action of a continuing or long-term character', including such activity as 'taking or announcing major policy decisions'.

The *Cabinet Manual* has provided greater clarity over the content of some constitutional conventions. This clarity has helped to enhance accountability. For example, it enhances accountability over ministers who breach individual or collective ministerial responsibility. However, as will be discussed below, the *Cabinet Manual* does not provide a definitive account of conventions. Their content can change with practice. Without continual renewal and change, this can lead to confusion and can continue to provide an opportunity for the government to evade accountability for its actions.

3.2.1 How Do Conventions Arise?

Whether a convention exists is sometimes a matter of uncertainty. Sir Ivor Jennings, in his *The Law and the Constitution* (5th edn. 1959, p. 136), suggested the following approach:

> We have to ask ourselves three questions: first, what are the precedents; secondly, did the actors in the precedents believe that they were bound by a rule; and thirdly, is there a reason for the rule? A single precedent with a good reason may be enough to establish the rule. A whole string of precedents without such a reason will be of no avail, unless it is perfectly certain that the persons concerned regarded them[selves] as bound by it.

This approach, while in many respects commendable, is not authoritative, although it was accepted and applied in *Evans* v. *Information Commissioner* [2012] UKHT 313 (AAC) (see below). Furthermore, even if Jennings' approach is applied, it may not always give a clear result (e.g., there may be a difference of opinion as to whether the precedents are compelling or whether there is a good reason for the rule). There are many conventions that are generally acknowledged to exist, but they are not always precisely formulated and the limits of their application may be unclear. On the one hand, this imprecision makes for a flexibility which allows a congruous development of the constitution in response to experience and changes in society. On the other hand, as Peter Madgwick and Diana Woodhouse have noted (*The Law and Politics of the Constitution of the United Kingdom* (1995), p. 35):

> The imprecision, flexibility and absence of sanctions work to the advantage of those in positions of power, for it becomes difficult to determine, and thus appeal to, the constitutional position and constitutional limitations.

Conventions, as Geoffrey Marshall says, 'are unlike legal rules because they are not the product of a legislative or of a judicial process' (*Constitutional Conventions* (1984), p. 216). Many conventions are the result of a gradual hardening of usage over a period of years or generations. Jaconelli suggests that 'their essence is found to subsist in a stream of concordant actions and expectations deriving from such actions' ('Do Constitutional Conventions Bind?' [2005] *CLJ* 149, 170). Both elements are important: for a constitutional convention to have been established, it is not enough that a repeated course of behaviour has occurred. It is necessary, in addition, that such behaviour must be *expected* to continue to recur. This is true, for example, of what is perhaps the cardinal convention of our constitutional monarchy: that the monarch must act on the advice of his/her ministers. Queen Victoria might not have assented to this obligation (see Le May, *The Victorian Constitution* (1979), p. 74), but in 1910 the prime minister reminded King George V of what had become an incontrovertible convention. King George had proposed to meet the leader of the unionist opposition in the House of Lords, Lord Lansdowne, to discover his views on the progress of the Liberal Government's Parliament Bill, in the light of the Liberal victory in the general election of December 1910.

Mr Asquith's Minute to King George V, December 1910

The part to be played by the Crown, in such a situation as now exists, has happily been settled by the accumulated traditions and the unbroken practice of more than 70 years. It is to act upon the advice of the Ministers who for the time being possess the confidence of the House of Commons, whether that advice does or does not conform to the private and personal judgment of the Sovereign. Ministers will always pay the utmost deference, and give the most serious consideration, to any criticism or objection that the Monarch may offer to their policy; but the ultimate decision rests with them; for they, and not the Crown, are responsible to Parliament. It is only by a scrupulous adherence to this well-established Constitutional doctrine that the Crown can be kept out of the arena of party politics.

It follows that it is not the function of a Constitutional Sovereign to act as arbiter or mediator between rival parties and policies; still less to take advice from the leaders on both sides, with the view to forming a conclusion of his own. George III in the early years of his reign tried to rule after this fashion, with the worst results, and with the accession of Mr Pitt to power he practically abandoned the attempt. The growth and development of our representative system, and the clear establishment at the core and centre of our Constitution of the doctrine of Ministerial responsibility, have since placed the position of the Sovereign beyond the region of doubt or controversy.

(The prime minister withdrew his objection to the interview with Lord Lansdowne on King George's assurance that his purpose was to obtain information and not advice; further correspondence between King George V and Prime Minister Asquith concerning the constitutional position of the monarch and dating from 1913 is usefully reproduced in McLean, *What's Wrong with the British Constitution?* (2010), pp. 273–83.)

In a valuable analysis, Aileen McHarg tells us that 'conventions are typically thought of as the embodiment of constitutional custom or tradition; the product of a slow process of evolution' ('Reforming the United Kingdom constitution: Law, Convention, Soft Law' (2008) 71 *MLR* 853, 857). Yet, as she points out, from time to time an attempt is made to *declare* a constitutional convention – even, occasionally, to declare a *new* constitutional convention. McHarg takes as her principal example Gordon Brown's Green Paper, *The Governance of Britain* (Cm 7170, 2007), which was discussed in Chapter 1 (see pp. 30–31). As we saw, this document proposed (among other matters) to develop a new convention whereby the government would be required to obtain parliamentary consent before deploying Her Majesty's armed forces in conflict. It is not unknown for conventions to be declared in this manner (a further example is the Salisbury Convention, considered in the next section) but, as McHarg argues (p. 859), it is the 'subsequent practice, rather than the initial statement, which ... determine[s] both the status and the scope' of the constitutional norm.

It may be difficult to say with certainty that a usage or practice has come to be accepted as a binding convention. We can often only infer that a supposed convention is considered to be binding from the consistency of the behaviour over a period of those affected by it: the shorter the period, the more doubtful the inference. Between 1964 and 1983, no new hereditary peerages were created, and it seemed that a new convention in this sense was on the way to becoming established. But in 1983 hereditary peerages were again conferred, on the recommendation of Prime Minister Thatcher, and it was not objected that there had been a breach of convention. Conventions are always emerging, crystallising and dissolving, and it is sometimes questionable whether a convention has been broken or has simply changed.

3.2.2 Doubtful Conventions

3.2.2.1 Going to War

The royal prerogative includes the power, by convention exercisable by the government, to declare war or engage the armed forces of the Crown in military expeditions or armed conflict. As a matter of law, a decision to exercise the prerogative in these ways does not require the authority of Parliament (although the expenses of such engagements must be met from the funds voted by Parliament for expenditure by the Ministry of Defence and other departments).

It was not the practice of governments to seek parliamentary approval for decisions on the use of armed force, although a recent report of the Public Administration and Constitutional Affairs Committee on the House of Commons found evidence of a convention in place since the Second World War of consulting the Commons in order to ensure that the deployment of the military had the approval of the Commons (*The Role of Parliament in the UK*

Tony Blair
invasion of
Iraq

Constitution: Authorising the Use of Military Force, 20th Report of 2017–19, HC 1891). In 2003, the government thought it right, or expedient, to obtain the support of the House of Commons *before* embarking on military intervention in Iraq. The House was asked to vote on the prime minister's substantive motion requesting approval for the use of all necessary means, including military force, 'to ensure the disarmament of Iraq's weapons of mass destruction' (HC Deb vol. 401, col 760, 18 March 2003). The motion was carried.

It has been said that this event established a *convention* that parliamentary approval must be obtained before the use of military force is undertaken by the government (or, at all events, in case of action taken in an emergency, at the earliest opportunity thereafter). The Foreign Secretary, Mr Jack Straw, seemed to give support to this view in saying, at the conclusion of the Iraq debate, that it was 'constitutionally proper in a modern democracy' that the government should seek the 'explicit support' of the House of Commons for military action (col 900). Lord Wilson of Dinton has suggested that the precedent of March 2003 'will almost certainly have to be followed in similar circumstances in the future' ([2004] *PL* 407, 414). This was also recognised by a resolution of the House of Commons on 15 May 2007, as well as resolving that 'the time has come for Parliament's role to be made more explicit in approving, or otherwise, decisions of the Government relating to the major, or substantial, deployment of British forces overseas into actual, or potential, armed conflict; ... and calls upon the Government, after consultation, to come forward with more detailed proposals for Parliament to consider' (see HC Deb vol. 460, col 582). This convention is also included in the *Cabinet Manual*:

> 5.38 In 2011 the Government acknowledged that a convention had developed in Parliament that before troops were committed the House of Commons should have an opportunity to debate the matter and said that it proposed to observe that convention except when there was an emergency and such action would not be appropriate.

This most recent formulation of the convention makes it clear that exceptions exist, particularly where there is a need to respond quickly. In these circumstances, the convention is that the government is expected to come to Parliament to explain this exceptional action so that the House of Commons can hold the government to account for its actions. However, a recent committee report concluded that there was uncertainty surrounding these exceptions. Evidence provided to the committee by the government suggested four exceptions: 'where it could compromise the effectiveness of UK operations and the safety of British service men and women; to protect the UK's sources of secret intelligence; so as not to undermine the effectiveness or security of operational partners; and where the legal basis for action has previously been agreed by Parliament' (*The Role of Parliament in the UK Constitution:*

Authorising the Use of Military Force, 20th Report of 2017–19, HC 1891, at pp. 23–4). The committee also recommended the modification of the *Cabinet Manual* to take account of these exceptions and reinforce the importance of obtaining Common's approval of military action, even when exceptions meant that this approval should be obtained after as opposed to before the deployment of troops.

3.2.2.2 The Salisbury–Addison Convention on the House of Lords

The result of the 1945 general election was that a Labour Government was formed with Clement Attlee as Prime Minister. The Labour Party enjoyed a large majority in the House of Commons but the Conservative Party had an even larger majority in the House of Lords. The Leader of the House of Lords (Viscount Addison, a government minister) entered into an agreement with the Leader of the Opposition in that House (Viscount Cranborne, later the fifth Marquess of Salisbury) that government bills bringing forward proposals that had been put before the electorate would not be opposed in the House of Lords. This agreement became known as the Salisbury Convention. It came to be understood as meaning in practice that the House of Lords will 'not seek to vote down a manifesto Bill at second or third reading' (Lord Hesketh, Government Chief Whip, HL Deb vol. 545, col 1809, 19 May 1993). A 'manifesto bill' is a bill in which the government brings forward a proposal contained in its manifesto for the preceding general election.

Whether the rule is properly understood as being a constitutional convention or not may be open to doubt on two fronts. First, it should be noted that the rule originated as an agreement between two political parties. The Addison-Cranborne agreement did not involve all parties in the House of Lords; certainly it was not an agreement between the House of Lords and the House of Commons. Inquiring into the *Conventions of the United Kingdom Parliament* in 2006, a specially appointed joint committee of both houses accepted that, its origins notwithstanding, the rule had by 1999 evolved into a constitutional convention: it bound the House as a whole and not only the political parties that had made the agreement in 1945 (Joint Committee on Conventions, *1st Report of 2005–06*, HL 265, HC 1212, para 97). Nevertheless, evidence provided to the Constitution Committee of the House of Lords from Lord Newby, the then Leader of the Liberal Democrats in the House of Lords, the Liberal Party recognises this 'convention' as an agreement between two political parties and, as such, not binding on either Liberal or unaligned peers (*The Salisbury–Addison Convention, 5th Report 2017–19*, HL Paper 28).

Second, the question was raised whether the reforms to the membership of the House of Lords made by the House of Lords Act 1999 effectively killed the Salisbury–Addison Convention. Rodney Brazier, professor of constitutional law at Manchester, told the 2006 joint committee that this was a 'well-known view' (ibid, para 93), although he conceded that it did not appear to be accepted by the government. In *The New British*

Constitution (2009, p. 16) Vernon Bogdanor identifies the Salisbury–Addison Convention as having become 'highly problematic'. It was born, he says, of the particular political circumstances of 1945. After the Act of 1999, it ceased to be the case that any one political party enjoyed a majority in the House of Lords. These new political circumstances placed the ongoing relevance of the convention in serious doubt. The joint committee seemed to be of the view that the Salisbury–Addison Convention continued to be valid. It defined it in the following terms (para 99):

> In the House of Lords:
>
> - A manifesto Bill is accorded a Second Reading;
> - A manifesto Bill is not subject to 'wrecking amendments' which change the Government's manifesto intention as proposed in the Bill; and
> - A manifesto Bill is passed and sent (or returned) to the House of Commons, so that they have the opportunity, in reasonable time, to consider the Bill or any amendments the Lords may wish to propose.

Issues also arose as to whether the convention should apply during the 2010–15 Coalition Government and the 2017 minority government. In its report, *Constitutional Implications of Coalition Government, 5th Report of 2013–14* HL Paper 130, the House of Lords Select Committee on the Constitution concluded (at paras 98–100);

> that the Salisbury-Addison convention – whereby bills foreshadowed in a government's manifesto are given a second reading in the Lords, are not subject to wrecking amendments and are passed in reasonable time – does not, strictly speaking, apply to measures in a coalition agreement. This is because a coalition agreement cannot be said to have a mandate from the electorate in the way that a manifesto can.
>
> However, if all parties in a coalition made the same or a substantially similar commitment in their manifestos, then they should be entitled to the benefit of the Salisbury-Addison convention in respect of that commitment.
>
> We recognise that a practice has evolved that the House of Lords does not normally block government bills, whether they are in a manifesto or not. There is no reason why this practice should not apply when there is a coalition government.

Evidence submitted to the Constitution Committee in 2017 demonstrated divergence as to whether the convention applied to a minority government supported by a confidence and supply agreement. Baroness Evans of Bowes Park, the then Leader of the House of Lords, stated that the government believed that the convention continued to apply to manifesto promises of minority governments, but not to those manifesto promises of the party providing confidence and supply to the government. Baroness Smith of Basildon, the then Shadow Leader of the House of Lords, stated that it was far from clear that the convention applied to minority governments. However, she also stated that the convention recognises the primacy of the elected House over the unelected House of Lords and that the House of Lords would only reject a bill at second reading in extremis, drawing on the presumption that the House of Lords does not normally reject a bill that has been accepted by the House of Commons. Lord Newby, then leader of the Liberal Democrats in the House of Lords focused on the extent to which the bill represented the views of the Commons rather than its connection to the manifesto of a minority government, while wanting to ensure that the Lords were able to provide proper scrutiny over the bill. Lord Hope of Craighead, then Convener of the Crossbench Peers in the House of Lords, did not think that the convention applied to a minority government with a confidence and supply agreement, but that nevertheless the presumption would still apply that the House of Lords would not reject bills that had been accepted at second reading at the Commons, given that this presumption was based on a government enjoying the confidence of the House of Commons.

3.2.2.3 Law Officers' Advice

It is from time to time declared to be a settled convention that the advice of the law officers to the government or to individual ministers is not to be made public. For instance, the Attorney General informed the House of Commons on 29 July 1997 (HC Deb vol. 299, col 122 W) that:

> It is the established convention that the advice of the Law Officers is not disclosed, nor whether they have advised on a given question.

In the *Ministerial Code* (2019), the rule is expressed as follows (para 2.13):

> The fact that the Law Officers have advised or have not advised and the content of their advice must not be disclosed outside Government without their authority.

In *The Attorney General, Politics and the Public Interest* (1984, p, 225), John Edwards instanced a number of occasions when advice given by the law officers to the government had been disclosed to the House of Commons. The rule against disclosure was, he said, a flexible one, and he continued:

> Talk of an absolute prohibition against such disclosure is totally unsupportable. Expressed in realistic terms, the rule enables considerations of political advantage or embarrassment to

> the government to govern the decision whether to reveal what advice the Law Officers have given a ministerial colleague or the government as a whole.

Before taking military action against Iraq in 2003, the government received advice from the Attorney General as to the legality of the proposed action. The terms of the Attorney General's (Lord Goldsmith's) advice were not made public, but in a parliamentary answer on 17 March 2003 he gave a brief summary of the basis for his opinion that military action would be lawful under Security Council resolutions (HL Deb vol. 646, cols 2–3WA). The government rebuffed attempts to obtain full disclosure of Lord Goldsmith's legal advice, reiterating that there was 'a long-standing convention' against disclosure and 'a strong public interest in maintaining the confidentiality of Law Officers' advice' (HL Deb vol. 659, col 105WA, 25 March 2004. The Attorney General's legal advice was eventually published on 28 April 2005 after it had been extensively 'leaked' to the media without authority). On whom might this 'convention' be said to be binding? It has not been unreservedly endorsed by Parliament and it seems to bind the government, or the law officers, only if they choose that it should.

This ability for the convention to bind when the government wishes that it should caused issues with regard to the legal advice surrounding Brexit. MPs were of the opinion that this legal advice, particularly concerning the status of the Northern Ireland backstop, was crucial to the exercise of their vote on the Withdrawal Agreement. Nevertheless, the government did not wish to disclose this legal advice. The Commons found a means through which to seek disclosure of this legal advice. On 13 November 2018, an opposition day was used to table a humble address, a motion from the House of Commons addressed directly to the monarch. This humble address sought the release of 'any legal advice in full, including that provided by the attorney general, on the proposed withdrawal agreement on the terms of the UK's departure from the European Union including the Northern Ireland backstop and framework for a future relationship between the UK and the European Union' (Hansard HC vol. 649, col 189). The motion having been agreed to (Conservative MPs being instructed to abstain from voting), the Speaker confirmed that the government needed to respond to the motion. On 4 December 2018, the Commons voted in favour of a contempt motion, finding ministers in contempt for failing to produce the 'final and full legal advice provided by the Attorney General to the Cabinet concerning the EU Withdrawal Agreement and the framework for the future relationship, and orders its immediate publication' (Hansard HC vol. 650, col 732). While this may provide a means for the Commons to hold the government to account and ensure it is properly informed, it may well be that the success of this motion was due to the peculiarities of Brexit, the legal requirement of the Commons to vote on the Withdrawal Agreement in order for it to be ratified (European Union Withdrawal Act 2018, section 13) and the existence of a minority government. Nevertheless, it sets a precedent that may be used in the future for the Commons to obtain legal advice, particularly when this is needed to hold the government to account.

3.2.3 Conventions and Laws

To illustrate the close nexus in practice between law and convention, consider the following examples. We know it as a rule of law that the monarch may give or refuse assent to a bill passed by both Houses of Parliament; it is a constitutional convention that she should always (or in all but very exceptional circumstances: see de Smith and Brazier, *Constitutional and Administrative Law* (8th edn. 1998, pp. 127–8) give her assent (see, further, Chapter 6). Likewise, as a matter of law the monarch may appoint anyone she wishes to be prime minister (indeed, if she wished, she would be legally entitled to appoint no one to the office: there is no legal requirement that there always be a prime minister). It is a convention, however, that where one party has a majority of seats in the House of Commons, the monarch should appoint as prime minister the leader of that party. It is the law that a writ for a parliamentary by-election must be issued by the Clerk of the Crown in Chancery on receipt of a warrant from the Speaker of the House of Commons (Representation of the People Act 1983, Schedule 1, rr 1, 3); it is a convention, resulting from agreement in an all-party speaker's conference in 1973, that when a vacancy occurs in the House, the chief whip of the party to which the former member belonged shall, normally within three months, move that the Speaker issue the warrant for a writ (see *Conference on Electoral Law*, Cmnd 5500/1973; HC Deb vol. 41, cols 164–8, 19 April 1983). Convention prescribes that there should be a prime minister who is a member of the House of Commons; the law directs that he or she should receive a salary (Ministerial and other Salaries Act 1975).

On occasion, a constitutional convention may be placed on a legal footing: a recent example comes from the Constitutional Reform and Governance Act 2010. Sections 20–5 of this act concern Parliament's role with regard to approving (or, as the case may be, not approving) treaties that have been signed by government ministers. Before this act, the matter had been governed by constitutional convention – it had been known as the Ponsonby Rule.

Dicey formulated the distinction between the law of the constitution and constitutional conventions as follows.

> ### Dicey, *The Law of the Constitution* (1885), pp. 23–4
>
> [T]he rules which make up constitutional law, as the term is used in England, include two sets of principles or maxims of a totally distinct character.
>
> The one set of rules are in the strictest sense 'laws', since they are rules which (whether written or unwritten, whether enacted by statute or derived from the mass of custom,

tradition, or judge-made maxims known as the common law) are enforced by the courts; these rules constitute 'constitutional law' in the proper sense of that term, and may for the sake of distinction be called collectively 'the law of the constitution'.

The other set of rules consist of conventions, understandings, habits or practices which, though they may regulate the conduct of the several members of the sovereign power, of the Ministry or of other officials, are not in reality laws at all since they are not enforced by the courts. This portion of constitutional law may, for the sake of distinction, be termed the 'conventions of the constitution', or constitutional morality.

To put the same thing in a somewhat different shape, 'constitutional law', as the expression is used in England, both by the public and by authoritative writers, consists of two elements. The one element, here called the 'law of the constitution', is a body of undoubted law; the other element, here called the 'conventions of the constitution', consists of maxims or practices which, though they regulate the ordinary conduct of the Crown, of Ministers, and of other persons under the constitution, are not in strictness laws at all.

The distinction made by Dicey in this passage has been rejected by some who have denied that there is any difference in principle between laws and conventions. Sir Ivor Jennings, in particular, argued that enforceability by the courts was not a valid basis for a distinction between laws and conventions and that both rested essentially on the acquiescence of those to whom they applied (*The Law and the Constitution* (5th edn. 1959, pp. 103–36). But Dicey's analysis can be defended on the ground that laws are given effect or 'enforced' by courts or tribunals in a sense which cannot be applied to the treatment of conventions by these bodies. Moreover, law is not usually defined in terms that can include conventions, and those who are involved in or observe the political process are aware of a difference between laws and conventions, and are rarely uncertain as to the category to which a particular rule belongs. A civil servant who, without authority, gives information to a newspaper about the issue of warrants for 'telephone tapping' is in no doubt that he or she is breaking the law (Official Secrets Act 1989, section 4(3)(a)); a cabinet secretary knows that it is convention and not law that prevents him from disclosing to a new administration the papers of the previous government of a different party. By the same token, Allan has argued that constitutional conventions provide 'a primary source of legal principle': *Law, Liberty, and Justice* (1993), ch. 10. A similar argument is developed by Mark Elliott in an inquiry into 'Parliamentary Sovereignty and the New Constitutional Order' ((2002) 22 *LS* 340). Conventions properly understood, he says, rest on or give effect to constitutional principles and these may 'influence the evolution of constitutional law'. In this way, conventions may acquire 'legal weight' and 'help to shape the constitution's legal contours'. (For a rebuttal of this view, see Jaconelli, 'Do Constitutional Conventions Bind?' [2005] *CLJ* 149.)

This is not to say that a convention, as such, can be directly enforced by a court.

Madzimbamuto v. *Lardner-Burke* [1969] 1 AC 645 (PC)

After the unlawful declaration of independence by the government of the Crown colony of Southern Rhodesia in 1965, the UK Parliament passed the Southern Rhodesia Act 1965 to deal with the circumstances arising from this unconstitutional action. In the *Madzimbamuto* case, the question arose whether Parliament could properly legislate for Southern Rhodesia, the colony having already progressed, before the declaration of independence, to a substantial degree of self-government. The UK Government had indeed formally acknowledged in 1961 that:

> it has become an established convention for Parliament at Westminster not to legislate for Southern Rhodesia on matters within the competence of the Legislative Assembly of Southern Rhodesia except with the agreement of the Southern Rhodesia Government.

Lord Reid (delivering the majority judgment) referred to the convention set out in the UK Government's statement of 1961 and continued:

> That was a very important convention but it had no legal effect in limiting the legal power of Parliament.
> It is often said that it would be unconstitutional for the United Kingdom Parliament to do certain things, meaning that the moral, political and other reasons against doing them are so strong that most people would regard it as highly improper if Parliament did these things. But that does not mean that it is beyond the power of Parliament to do such things. If Parliament chose to do any of them the courts could not hold the Act of Parliament invalid. It may be that it would have been thought, before 1965, that it would be unconstitutional to disregard this convention. But it may also be that the unilateral Declaration of Independence released the United Kingdom from any obligation to observe the convention. Their Lordships in declaring the law are not concerned with these matters. They are only concerned with the legal powers of Parliament.

[handwritten margin note: unconstitutional ≠ unlawful]

In the following case, there was an unpromising attempt to persuade a court to make a declaration as to the existence of a constitutional convention.

R (Southall) v. *Secretary of State for Foreign and Commonwealth Affairs* [2003] EWCA Civ 1002

The applicant in this case had sought permission to bring proceedings for judicial review. His principal contention was that for the government to ratify the proposed treaty establishing a constitution for the EU, and for Parliament to enact its provisions as law, without the approval of the electorate, would be contrary to constitutional convention. He wished the reviewing court to grant a declaration to this effect.

A judge having refused permission for the applicant to proceed to judicial review, he applied to the Court of Appeal for permission to appeal against that refusal.

> **Schiemann LJ** (giving the judgment of the court): ... [Counsel for the applicant] submitted that there was a convention that no Act of Parliament would be passed which altered our constitution in a fundamental way without it first having received the approval of the electorate either through a general election or a referendum.

The court was presented with evidence about the holding of referendums in the past but was not persuaded that it was arguable that a convention such as was asserted by the applicant in fact existed – although, arguably, recent events may alter this conclusion. In any event, said the court, 'we know of no occasion when in this country declarations similar to those sought have been made by the courts'. Permission to appeal was accordingly refused. (On the circumstances in which a referendum should be held, see now House of Lords Constitution Committee, *Referendums in the United Kingdom*, 12th Report of 2009–10, HL 99, para 94; see, further, Chapter 8.)

Although conventions are not *enforced* by courts – even in the form of a declaratory judgment – nevertheless, the existence and content of a convention may form part of a judge's reasoning in coming to a decision. For example, in *Attorney General* v. *Jonathan Cape Ltd* (above, p. 208) the court held that an injunction can in a proper case be granted to protect the confidentiality of cabinet proceedings on the ground that confidentiality is necessary for the maintenance of the convention of joint (or collective) cabinet responsibility, a convention which the court considered to be in the public interest. Here the court's evaluation of the convention of collective ministerial responsibility as an essential feature of our governmental system was a crucial element in its argument and conclusions. Ian Loveland remarks that it is arguable that in this case the court in effect 'enforced a convention by cloaking it with a common law label' (*Constitutional Law, Administrative Law and Human Rights* (5th edn. 2009, p. 279). It is, indeed, contended by Allan (above) that the distinction between recognition and enforcement of conventions dissolves in the process of adjudication and that it is wrong 'to attribute to convention an intrinsic inferiority' to rules of law – even enacted law. Jaconelli, in contrast, insists on a 'clear conceptual divide' between law and convention, while acknowledging that in some respects 'the two phenomena may intertwine' (see above). (See, generally, Barber, 'Laws and Constitutional Conventions' (2009) 125 *LQR* 294.)

Evans v. *Information Commissioner (Correspondence with Prince Charles in 2004 and 2005)* [2012] UKUT 313 (AAC)
Evans, a *Guardian* journalist, sought disclosure of the 'advocacy' correspondence between Prince Charles and various government ministers under the

Freedom of Information Act. This would require the correspondence to be disclosed when this was in the public interest. In determining this issue, the Upper Tribunal recognised that it was being invited to determine the scope of a constitutional convention. In particular, the constitutional convention that the heir to the throne is 'entitled and bound by constitutional convention to be educated in and about the business of government' (at [64]). The existence and content of this convention was, in turn, based on other conventions, referred to by Professor Brazier in evidence given to the tribunal as the 'cardinal convention', that the monarch acts on advice, and the 'tripartite convention' that the monarch has a right to be consulted by and to encourage and warn her government. In order to ensure that these conventions operate, it is in the public interest for the communications between the monarch and the government to remain confidential, particularly to ensure the neutrality of the monarch. However, the question arose as to whether the convention that the heir to the throne should be educated in the business of government meant that confidentiality should also extend to communication between the heir to the throne and the government. After consulting two expert witnesses – Professors Brazier and Tomkins – and applying the three-stage Jennings test, the Upper Tribunal concluded that the education convention did not extend to letters between Prince Charles and government ministers where he was advocating for particular causes. The tribunal also obtained evidence from government departments, including its evidence in a series of annexes to its judgment. In reaching this conclusion, the tribunal stated the following regarding the role of conventions and their relationship to law.

[66]. What are constitutional conventions? The first thing to stress is that they are not law. They are not enforced by courts. For example, there is a convention that an incumbent Prime Minister must resign if, after a general election, another party has won a majority in the House of Commons. But no-one can seek to enforce this in the courts – there is no law which says that such a Prime Minister must resign. Because it is a constitutional convention, however, a Prime Minister who broke it could be said to have acted unconstitutionally . . .

[67]. The second thing to stress is that the major constitutional conventions are core elements in the United Kingdom's parliamentary democracy. Two of them in particular need to be borne firmly in mind. They were labelled – for the purposes of this case only – by Professor Brazier as the 'cardinal convention' and the 'tripartite convention'. We say more about them below. As to the constitutional convention that the heir to the throne is entitled and bound to be instructed in and about the business of government, we shall call it the 'education convention'. Professor Brazier labelled it – again as regards this case only – as the 'apprenticeship convention'. For reasons which we explain below, we think that such a label involves an element of controversy.

[68]. The third thing to stress follows in part from the first. The parties invite us to decide the extent of the constitutional convention. It is only rarely that a court or tribunal has to decide a question of that kind, and it is a task which we undertake with circumspection. We

> are not deciding an issue of law. Questions about constitutional conventions have been the subject of much academic and political debate. So it is important to understand precisely what we were invited to do.

After considering the competing tests for establishing the existence of a constitutional convention, the tribunal went on to state:

> [75]. Accordingly for the purposes of the present case, the answer to the question we posed above is that a particular constitutional obligation will be a constitutional convention if the Jennings test is met. As regards the scope of the education convention, we must apply the three elements of that test. First, we must consider whether there is at least one precedent underpinning such a scope. Second, we must consider whether both parties to it considered themselves to be bound to treat Prince Charles's education in the business of government, with its special constitutional status and associated special degree of confidentiality, as extending not merely – as Mr Evans accepts – to government informing Prince Charles about what it is doing and responding to queries from him. Third, we must consider whether there is a reason, in the sense used by Jennings and described above, for the convention to have that scope.

All three elements of the Jennings test pointed against the expansion of the education convention to include elements of apprenticeship, such that the public interest would require that the content of Prince Charles' communications to ministers advocating for particular causes should remain confidential.

R (Miller) v. Secretary of State for Exiting the European Union [2017] UKSC 5

In addition to determining the scope of prerogative powers, *Miller* required the Supreme Court to examine the Sewel Convention. This convention requires that Westminster will not normally legislate on matters that have been devolved or, understood more broadly, that modify the distribution of powers between Westminster and the devolved legislatures, without first obtaining the consent of the devolved legislatures. The majority of the Supreme Court stated the following about the relationship between law and convention.

> [141]. Before addressing the more recent legislative recognition of the convention, it is necessary to consider the role of the courts in relation to constitutional conventions. It is well established that the courts of law cannot enforce a political convention. In *Re Resolution to Amend the Constitution* [1981] 1 SCR 753, the Supreme Court of Canada addressed the nature of political conventions. In the majority judgment the Chief Justice (Laskin) and Dickson, Beetz, Estey, McIntyre, Chouinard and Lamer JJ stated at pp 774 to 775:
>   'The very nature of a convention, as political in inception and as depending on a consistent course of political recognition by those for whose benefit and to whose

detriment (if any) the convention developed over a considerable period of time is inconsistent with its legal enforcement.'

[142]. In a dissenting judgment on one of the questions before the court, the Chief Justice and Estey and MacIntyre JJ developed their consideration of conventions at p 853:

'[A] fundamental difference between the legal, that is the statutory and common law rules of the constitution, and the conventional rules is that, while a breach of the legal rules, whether of statutory or common law nature, has a legal consequence in that it will be restrained by the courts, no such sanction exists for breach or non-observance of the conventional rules. The observance of constitutional conventions depends upon the acceptance of the obligation of conformance by the actors deemed to be bound thereby. When this consideration is insufficient to compel observance no court may enforce the convention by legal action. The sanction for non-observance of a convention is political in that disregard of a convention may lead to political defeat, to loss of office, or to other political consequences, but will not engage the attention of the courts which are limited to matters of law alone. Courts, however, may recognise the existence of conventions.'

[143]. Martland, Ritchie, Dickson, Beetz, Chouinard and Lamer JJ made the same point at pp 882 to 883:

'It is because the sanctions of convention rest with institutions of government other than courts . . . or with public opinion and ultimately, the electorate, that it is generally said that they are political.'

[144]. Attempts to enforce political conventions in the courts have failed. Thus in *Madzimbamuto v Lardner-Burke* [1969] 1 AC 645, the Judicial Committee of the Privy Council had to consider a submission that legal effect should be given to the convention which applied at that time that the UK Parliament would not legislate without the consent of the government of Southern Rhodesia on matters within the competence of the Legislative Assembly. In its judgment delivered by Lord Reid the Board stated at p 723 that:

'That is a very important convention but it had no legal effect in limiting the legal power of Parliament. It is often said that it would be unconstitutional for the UK Parliament to do certain things, meaning that the moral, political and other reasons against doing them are so strong that most people would regard it as highly improper if Parliament did these things. But that does not mean that it is beyond the power of Parliament to do such things. If Parliament chose to do any of them the courts could not hold the Act of Parliament invalid.'

More recently, the political nature of the Sewel Convention was recognised by Lord Reed in a decision of the Inner House of the Court of Session, *Imperial Tobacco v Lord Advocate* 2012 SC 297, para 71.

[145]. While the UK government and the devolved executives have agreed the mechanisms for implementing the convention in the Memorandum of Understanding, the convention operates as a political restriction on the activity of the UK Parliament. Article 9 of the Bill of Rights, which provides that 'Proceedings in Parliament ought not to be impeached or questioned in any Court or Place out of Parliament', provides a further reason why the courts cannot adjudicate on the operation of this convention.

[146]. Judges therefore are neither the parents nor the guardians of political conventions; they are merely observers. As such, they can recognise the operation of a political

convention in the context of deciding a legal question (as in the Crossman diaries case – *Attorney General v Jonathan Cape Ltd* [1976] 1 QB 752), but they cannot give legal rulings on its operation or scope, because those matters are determined within the political world. As Professor Colin Munro has stated, 'the validity of conventions cannot be the subject of proceedings in a court of law' – (1975) 91 LQR 218, 228.

It is hard to reconcile the statement that the courts are 'merely observers' with the way in which the Upper Tribunal approached the assessment of the existence of the education convention, and its scope, in *Evans* v. *Information Commissioner*. While the Upper Tribunal was clear that it was not enforcing the convention, nevertheless its detailed evaluation of the convention, applying the Jennings test, determined whether the release of the advocacy correspondence was in the public interest. Legislation may have required the court to determine whether the release of information was in the public interest; but it was the court's evaluation of the convention that essentially concluded that the advocacy correspondence had to be released. This may seem to lend weight to Allan's argument that there is little, if any difference, between convention and law. However, the difference lies in the legal authority from legislation for the court to determine, on the facts, whether it is in the public interest to release information. The convention provides this factual evidence. While the Upper Tribunal was using evidence to determine the content of a convention, it was not thereby endorsing the convention as a sound principle of constitutional governance that could be enforced by the courts. The tribunal also did not look to legal principle, but to factual evidence of observation by government officials and the views of academics as to the constitutional importance of particular conventions. While it may be hard to regard this as mere observation, nevertheless it is clear that the courts are not the parents or guardians of convention. They do not determine their content in the same way as they determine the content of the common law. Neither do they enforce conventions through providing legal consequences for the mere breach of a constitutional convention.

There has also been criticism of the more recent *Miller; Cherry* case, which some would argue effectively enforced a constitutional convention. It will be recalled that in *R (Miller)* v. *Prime Minister; Cherry* v. *Advocate General for Scotland*, the Supreme Court used the constitutional principle of accountability to place limits on the scope of the prerogative power of prorogation. However, although there was evidence of prior case law that could be regarded as upholding or relying on the principle of parliamentary accountability (the Supreme Court referred to *R (Miller)* v. *Secretary of State for Exiting the European Union* [2017] UKSC 5, [2018] AC 61; *Bobby* v. *Manning* [2006] UKPC 22; *R* v. *Secretary of State for the Environment, ex parte Nottinghamshire County Council* [1986] AC 240; and *Mohammed (Serdar)* v. *Ministry of Defence* [2017] UKSC 1, [2017] AC 649), there was no prior case law referring to

parliament sovereign
↓
parliamentary accountability reigns supreme

parliamentary accountability specifically as a fundamental principle of the common law. Moreover, it was felt that parliamentary accountability was best understood either as a convention or as a principle enforced through specific conventions. Did this mean that the Supreme Court was effectively enforcing a constitutional convention? A better reading of the case is that the constitutional principle of parliamentary accountability can be used both to underpin the development of specific constitutional conventions and of the common law. In *Miller; Cherry*, the principle was used to develop the common law by setting the limits on the prerogative power of prorogation. This, again, adds credence to Allan's argument that conventions may crystallise into law as both are based on constitutional principles. However, it is important to recognise an important further step when developing the common law – a step of which the Supreme Court in *Miller; Cherry* was all too aware – that of ensuring that the common law takes account of issues of whether a particular principle is best enforced by political means through convention, or through legal means by the courts.

3.2.4 Patriation of the Canadian Constitution: A Case Study

To close this chapter, we offer a detailed case study of convention in action. The case study concerns the patriation of the Canadian constitution in the early 1980s. It shows the importance of convention, it illustrates the close working relationship of convention to constitutional law and it demonstrates the ways in which courts may make, in this instance quite extensive, use of convention. In this respect, this case study may be contrasted with *Attorney General* v. *Jonathan Cape Ltd*, the *Crossman Diaries* case, considered above.

The basic constitutional structure of Canada was established by the British North America Act 1867, an act of the UK Parliament incorporating the terms on which the Canadian Provinces were united in the Federation of Canada. Any necessary amending legislation was to be enacted by the UK Parliament.

Although Canada was a fully independent state, at the latest after the Statute of Westminster 1931, the Canadian Parliament remained incompetent to amend the British North America Acts. There was in 1931 no agreement in Canada as to the terms on which the power of constitutional amendment might be transferred to Canadian institutions, and the Statute of Westminster left this power with the UK Parliament. While section 2 of the Statute allowed full efficacy in general to the legislation of the Canadian Parliament (and the parliaments of the other independent dominions), section 7(1) provided:

> Nothing in this Act shall be deemed to apply to the repeal, amendment or alteration of the British North America Acts, 1867 to 1930.

And section 7(3) provided:

> The powers conferred by this Act upon the Parliament of Canada or upon the legislatures of the Provinces shall be restricted to the enactment of laws in relation to matters within the competence of the Parliament of Canada or of any of the legislatures of the Provinces respectively.

The British North America (No 2) Act 1949, which transferred a power of constitutional amendment to the Parliament of Canada, excepted amendments affecting the distribution of powers between the provincial and federal governments.

Even before 1931, a convention had become established which governed legislation by the UK Parliament for the self-governing dominions. This convention was formally reaffirmed in the preamble to the Statute of Westminster in the following words:

> It is in accord with the established constitutional position that no law hereafter made by the Parliament of the United Kingdom shall extend to any of the said Dominions as part of the law of that Dominion otherwise than at the request and with the consent of that Dominion.

(A *legal* reinforcement of this convention was provided by section 4 of the Statute, considered in the previous chapter.)

On a number of occasions, both before and after 1931, the British North America Act 1867 was amended by the UK Parliament, in each case on the request of the Canadian Parliament. When the requested legislation would directly affect federal–provincial relations, the request was made and acted on only after the Federal Government had obtained the agreement of the governments of the affected provinces.

In 1980 the Canadian Government decided that the time had come to 'patriate' the Canadian constitution, i.e., to terminate the power of the UK Parliament to legislate for Canada and provide for all future constitutional amendments to be effected in Canada in accordance with a prescribed procedure. It was proposed at the same time to incorporate in the patriated constitution a Charter of Rights and Freedoms, which would prevail over inconsistent federal or provincial laws. Only the UK Parliament could pass the necessary legislation to bring about the desired patriation of the constitution. The legislation would clearly affect the distribution of powers in the Canadian Federation, and the Federal Government tried to obtain the agreement of the provincial governments to the proposal. However, only two provinces (Ontario and New Brunswick) agreed, while the remaining eight provinces were opposed to patriation on the Federal Government's terms. Nevertheless, the Federal Government decided to proceed on the basis of this limited agreement. A proposed resolution was submitted to the Canadian Parliament in the form of an address to Queen Elizabeth, requesting her to cause a bill to be introduced in the UK Parliament that would incorporate a Constitution Act for Canada, including a Charter of Rights and Freedoms and a procedure for constitutional amendment in Canada.

In response to these developments the Foreign Affairs Committee of the (British) House of Commons undertook an inquiry into the role of the UK Parliament in the expected event that a request for patriation should be supported only by the Federal Government and Parliament and two provincial governments. Would the UK Parliament be bound to accede to such a request? The answer would depend on the applicable conventions rather than on law. The following memorandum was submitted to the Foreign Affairs Committee.

First Report from the Foreign Affairs Committee (Kershaw Report), vol. II, HC 42-II of 1980–81: Memorandum by Professor HWR Wade (p. 102)

(1) The Government of Canada claims that the United Kingdom Parliament is obliged to enact, without questions asked, any amendment of the British North America Acts which is submitted by the Government of Canada and backed by the usual resolutions of the two Houses of Parliament in Ottawa, even though the amendment affects the rights of the Provinces.

(2) The Government of the UK may be tempted to accept this claim since it would enable the Parliament of the UK to play a purely formal and automatic part and to avoid embroiling itself in a Canadian constitutional controversy which ought to be decided in Canada alone and in which no one in the UK wishes to intervene.

(3) Are the Government and Parliament of the UK entitled to take this line of least resistance? The answer depends upon constitutional convention rather than upon law. In law there is no doubt that the Canadian courts recognise that in matters affecting the Provinces the British North America Acts can be amended only by the UK Parliament in accordance with the Statute of Westminster 1931, section 7. They may be expected to recognise also (a) that no law sets any limit upon this amending power of the UK Parliament; and (b) that no law sets any limit upon the freedom of the Canadian Government to submit amendments affecting the constitutional powers and position of the Provinces – though if they should decide otherwise this will be an internal Canadian matter. The important question for the UK Government and Parliament is whether it is required by constitutional convention that any amendment legislation should be enacted without question at Westminster, even though it affects and is opposed by some or all of the Provinces.

(4) In British constitutional theory and practice there is a clear-cut distinction between law and convention. Law derives from common law and statute and is enforceable by the courts. Convention derives from constitutional principle and practice and is not enforceable by courts. Law remains in force until changed by statute. Convention may change with changing times. Law, at least if statutory, is ascertainable in precise form. Convention is often imprecise and may be nowhere formulated in categorical terms.

(5) The correct attitude for the UK Government and Parliament to adopt must be found by looking at (a) constitutional principle and (b) past practice.

A. Constitutional Principle

(6) The essential elements of a federal constitution are that powers are divided between the central and provincial governments and that neither has legal power to encroach upon the domain of the other, except through the proper process of constitutional amendment. The system of local government in the UK, for example, contains no element of federalism because the powers of local authorities are wholly at the mercy of Parliament . . .

(7) If it were correct that the UK Parliament is obliged to enact any amendment of the British North America Acts proposed by the Canadian Government, this would obviously contradict the federal principle. It would then lie wholly within the power of the Canadian Government, de facto, to obtain amendments derogating from the powers of the Provinces and against the will of the Provinces. The Canadian constitution would cease to be federal in the true sense, since the Provinces would be at the mercy of the central government. By agreeing to act merely as an automaton at the direction of the Canadian Government, the UK Parliament would be subverting the whole foundation of the Constitution of Canada. It would put into the hands of the Canadian government powers which are not possessed by the central government of the United States, Australia, India and other federal countries, and which cannot be possessed by the central government without destroying the federal basis of the constitution. It would be idle then to say that the UK was refraining from taking sides in a Canadian controversy. In fact the UK would be taking sides with the Canadian government in undermining the constitutional rights and powers of the Provinces, contrary to the whole system of the British North America Acts and the fundamentals of Canadian constitutional law . . .

(8) Section 7 of the Statute of Westminster 1931 was inserted at the instance of the Provinces expressly for the purpose of preserving the federal principle. Had that not been done, the Canadian Parliament would have obtained full legal power to amend the British North America Acts under section 2 . . .

(9) The provisions of the Statute of Westminster make it quite clear that it cannot have been supposed in 1931 that convention required the UK Parliament to enact without question any British North America Bill put forward by the Canadian Government and Parliament. If there had been any such convention, section 7 would have been useless to the Provinces, and the security which it was intended to give them would have been nugatory, since the Canadian Government could at any time have called upon the UK Parliament to enact an amendment taking away constitutional powers of the Provinces. It is inconceivable that the Provinces would have been satisfied with this situation. Yet they were satisfied with section 7, thus clearly disproving the existence of any convention of the kind now claimed.

They must have felt fully assured that they enjoyed not only strictly legal but also genuinely constitutional protection for their rights.

(10) Constitutional principle, therefore, is entirely opposed to any alleged convention that the UK Parliament is obliged to enact amendments of the Constitution of Canada which reduce the rights of the Provinces without the consent of the Provinces concerned and without inquiring whether that consent has been given.

B. Past Practice

(11) It would be unprofitable to itemise all the amendments of the British North America Acts effected by the UK Parliament since 1867. The majority of them had no effect on the legislative powers of the Provinces and the fact that provincial consent was not obtained is immaterial.

(12) The only amendments affecting the legislative powers of the Provinces were those of 1940, 1951, 1960 and 1964. In each one of these cases all the Provinces were consulted and their agreement was obtained. The amendment of 1940 was delayed for some years until the agreement of Quebec could be obtained. By accepting this delay of the amendment (which gave the Canadian Parliament power to legislate for unemployment insurance) the Canadian Government (in the words of the federal Prime Minister) –

'avoided the raising of a very critical constitutional question, namely, whether or not in the amending of the British North America Act it is absolutely necessary to secure the consent of all the Provinces, or whether the consent of a certain number of Provinces would of itself be sufficient.' (Canadian Commons Debates, 1940 (25 June), pp 1117–18.)

It is clear from this remark that the Canadian Government accepted that in the case of such amendments, convention made it 'absolutely necessary' that the consent of at least some Provinces was obtained. In principle it would seem right that the consent of all Provinces suffering any diminution of their legislative powers should be obtained, and this is corroborated by the fact that unanimous consent was obtained for the amendments of 1951, 1960 and 1964.

(13) In addition, there is the very significant case of non-amendment represented by the Statute of Westminster 1931. This would have gravely affected Provincial legislative independence, as already pointed out, had not section 7 been inserted at the instance of the Provinces. In this case not only the Canadian Government but also the UK Government and Parliament felt bound to take account of the Provinces' objections.

(14) It hardly seems necessary to argue that convention requires the prior agreement of Provinces whose powers will be affected by the amendment, since the Canadian Government expressly admitted as much in the White Paper of 1965 entitled 'The Amendment of the Constitution of Canada'. It said:

'The *fourth general principle* is that the Canadian Parliament will not request an amendment directly affecting federal-provincial relationships without prior consult-ation and agreement with the provinces. This principle did not emerge as early as others but since 1907, and particularly since 1930, has gained increasing recognition and acceptance. The nature and the degree of provincial participation in the amending process, however, have not lent themselves to easy definition.'

> This statement, it is important to observe, was agreed by all the Provinces before the White Paper was published . . . It therefore represents a 'convention' in the literal sense, being an agreed statement of the federal-provincial relationship. It is thus as authoritative a source of constitutional convention as can be imagined.
>
> (15) It is therefore acknowledged by all concerned that as the conventions of the Canadian constitution have developed they have hardened in favour of the protection of the rights of the Provinces . . .
>
> (16) The 'fourth general principle' quoted above is framed in terms of convention binding the Canadian Parliament rather than the UK Parliament. But it by no means follows that it will not concern the UK Parliament. The whole object of section 7 of the Statute of Westminster was to make the UK Parliament the guardian of the rights of the Provinces and as already shown, constitutional principles make it essential that the UK Parliament should not act as a mere automaton at the Canadian Government's instance. It is inexorably necessary, therefore, that the UK Parliament should be assured that the Canadian conventions for the protection of the Provinces have been duly observed. If the UK Parliament failed to satisfy itself of this, it would be acting as an automaton and failing in its function of constitutional guardian. Where the requested amendment will affect the Provinces, therefore, the UK Parliament must make sure that the Provinces concerned have consented. As the precedents since 1930 make clear, the consent of the Provinces to amendments affecting them has in fact always been sought and obtained by the Canadian Government, so that the UK Parliament has not had to make any inquiry. But it would be entirely wrong to conclude from that that the UK Parliament will never look behind the Canadian Government's request . . .
>
> (17) The inescapable conclusion is that section 7 of the Statute of Westminster 1931 has left the UK Parliament with not only legal but also political responsibility for upholding the federal constitution of Canada and acting as guardian of the rights of the Provinces. Anachronistic and unwelcome as this responsibility may be, it was deliberately preserved in 1931 and nothing has since happened to alter it. The UK Parliament therefore has the duty, when requested to amend the British North America Acts, to ask itself two questions: first, does the amendment adversely affect Provincial legislative powers; and secondly, if so, have the Provinces affected signified their consent?

In its report to the House of Commons, the Foreign Affairs Committee concluded that the UK Parliament was not constitutionally bound – in particular, was not bound by convention – to act automatically on a request from the Canadian Parliament for the repatriation of the Canadian constitution. The committee advised that it was 'in accord with the established constitutional position for the UK Government and Parliament to take account of the federal character of Canada's constitutional system, when considering how to respond' to such a request (para 14.4). By way of contrast, the committee was not persuaded that the UK Parliament could properly act on a request for patriation only if it was supported by *all* the provinces. In the committee's view, the request must have a sufficient degree of provincial support for Parliament to be satisfied that it represented 'the wishes of the Canadian people as a federally structured community' (para 114). The committee proposed a criterion for determining whether the required degree of support existed (para 114).

Meanwhile some of the dissenting provinces had instituted proceedings in the Canadian courts to obtain a ruling on the constitutionality of the action being taken by the Federal Government to secure patriation. Appeals from the rulings of three provincial Courts of Appeal were heard by the Supreme Court of Canada, which gave its judgment before the resolution of the Canadian Parliament had been submitted to Queen Elizabeth.

Reference re Amendment of the Constitution of Canada (1981) 125 DLR (3d) 1 (Supreme Court of Canada)

The Supreme Court decided by a majority of seven to two that there was no *legal* impediment to the submission by the Canadian Parliament, without the agreement of the provinces, of a request for the constitutional amendments necessary to effect patriation, and no legal restraint on the power of the UK Parliament to act on such a request. But the court had also been asked to decide the following question:

> Is it a constitutional convention that the House of Commons and Senate of Canada will not request Her Majesty the Queen to lay before the Parliament of the United Kingdom of Great Britain and Northern Ireland a measure to amend the Constitution of Canada affecting federal-provincial relationships or the powers, rights or privileges granted or secured by the Constitution of Canada to the provinces, their legislatures or governments without first obtaining the agreement of the provinces?

The Supreme Court decided by a majority of 6:3 that this question should be answered in the affirmative, and further that 'at least a substantial measure of provincial consent' was required for compliance with the convention. Since the necessary measure of provincial agreement was wanting, it would be 'unconstitutional in the conventional sense' for the proposed request for constitutional amendment to be submitted to Her Majesty the Queen. Passages quoted below are from the majority opinion of Martland, Ritchie, Dickson, Beetz, Chouinard and Lamer JJ.

In giving general consideration to the nature of conventions the court said:

> The conventional rules of the Constitution present one striking peculiarity. In contradistinction to the laws of the Constitution, they are not enforced by the Courts. One reason for this situation is that, unlike common law rules, conventions are not judge-made

rules. They are not based on judicial precedents but on precedents established by the institutions of government themselves. Nor are they in the nature of statutory commands which it is the function and duty of the Courts to obey and enforce. Furthermore, to enforce them would mean to administer some formal sanction when they are breached. But the legal system from which they are distinct does not contemplate formal sanctions for their breach.

Perhaps the main reason why conventional rules cannot be enforced by the Courts is that they are generally in conflict with the legal rules which they postulate and the Courts are bound to enforce the legal rules. The conflict is not of a type which would entail the commission of any illegality. It results from the fact that legal rules create wide powers, discretions and rights which conventions prescribe should be exercised only in a certain limited manner, if at all.

The following example was given to illustrate this point:

As a matter of law, the Queen, or the Governor General or the Lieutenant-Governor could refuse assent to every bill passed by both Houses of Parliament or by a Legislative Assembly [of a Province] as the case may be. But by convention they cannot of their own motion refuse to assent to any such bill on any ground, for instance because they disapprove of the policy of the bill. We have here a conflict between a legal rule which creates a complete discretion and a conventional rule which completely neutralizes it. But conventions, like laws, are sometimes violated. And if this particular convention were violated and assent were improperly withheld, the courts would be bound to enforce the law, not the convention. They would refuse to recognize the validity of a vetoed bill.

It had been argued that a question about the existence of a convention was a political one and did not raise a justiciable issue appropriate for a court to decide. This argument was dismissed on the ground, inter alia, that the statutes empowering the provincial governments to put questions for resolution by the courts did so in terms wide enough to entitle them to obtain an answer to a question of this kind. Although the question was 'not confined to an issue of pure legality', it had to do with 'a fundamental issue of constitutionality and legitimacy'. The court had not been asked to enforce a convention but rather 'to recognise it if it exists'. This the courts in England and the Commonwealth had done many times:

In so recognizing conventional rules, the Courts have described them, sometimes commented upon them and given them such precision as is derived from the written form of a judgment. They did not shrink from doing so on account of the political aspects of conventions, nor because of their supposed vagueness, uncertainty or flexibility.

> In our view, we should not, in a constitutional reference, decline to accomplish a type of exercise that Courts have been doing of their own motion for years.

Did the convention exist? In addressing this question the court adopted Sir Ivor Jennings' view of the requirements for establishing a convention (*The Law and the Constitution*, p. 161). The court proceeded to examine in turn the precedents, the beliefs of the 'actors' or participants in government and the reason for the alleged rule. The court found five precedents where constitutional amendments had changed provincial legislative powers and so had directly affected federal–provincial relationships:

> Every one of these five amendments was agreed upon by each Province whose legislative authority was affected.
>
> In negative terms, no amendment changing provincial legislative powers has been made since Confederation when agreement of a Province whose legislative powers would have been changed was withheld ...
>
> The accumulation of these precedents, positive and negative, concurrent and without exception, does not of itself suffice in establishing the existence of the convention; but it unmistakably points in its direction. Indeed, if the precedents stood alone, it might be argued that unanimity is required.

Turning to the question whether the convention had been acknowledged by the 'actors in the precedents', the court cited the official statement of Federal Government policy, endorsed by all the provinces and published in the White Paper of 1965. (This statement, affirming the general principle of prior consultation and agreement with the provinces on amendments affecting federal–provincial relationships, is quoted in Wade's Memorandum, above, para 15.) Government ministers, the court found, had expressed themselves in similar terms on a number of occasions, and successive discussions between the federal and provincial governments on the subject of constitutional amendment had proceeded on the assumption that a substantial degree of provincial consent was required. It was clear to the court that not all the actors concerned had accepted a principle of *unanimous* provincial consent. The court concluded as follows:

> It would not be appropriate for the Court to devise in the abstract a specific formula which would indicate in positive terms what measure of provincial agreement is required for the convention to be complied with. Conventions by their nature develop in the political field and it will be for the political actors, not this Court, to determine the degree of provincial consent required.
>
> It is sufficient for the Court to decide that at least a substantial measure of provincial consent is required and to decide further whether the situation before the Court meets with

> this requirement. The situation is one where Ontario and New Brunswick agree with the proposed amendments whereas the eight other Provinces oppose it. By no conceivable standard could this situation be thought to pass muster. It clearly does not disclose a sufficient measure of provincial agreement.

Finally, the court considered the reason for the rule, finding this in the federal principle embodied in the constitution of Canada as a federal union.

As a result, the conclusion of the Supreme Court was that while the law did not require provincial consent to the proposed resolution of the federal Houses of Parliament, the evolution of convention had made a substantial measure of provincial consent constitutionally necessary. Convention had become settled in this sense without affecting the legal position for, as the court held, it is impossible for a convention to crystallise into law.

The court's judgment did not indicate what would be a 'substantial measure of provincial consent', but its decision that the support of only two provinces did not meet this condition caused the Federal Government to seek wider agreement on a revised set of proposals for patriation. As a result, nine provinces (all except Quebec) agreed to support the revised scheme. In pursuance of this agreement, an 'Address to the Queen' was approved by both Houses of the Canadian Parliament in December 1981, requesting the passage of legislation which would enact a new constitution for Canada, incorporating a Charter of Rights, and transfer the power of constitutional amendment to Canadian institutions. The Canada Bill 1982, the long title of which was 'A Bill to give effect to a request by the Senate and House of Commons of Canada', was accordingly laid before the UK Parliament. The Lord Privy Seal, Mr Humphrey Atkins, moved the second reading of the bill in the House of Commons.

House of Commons, 17 February 1982 (HC Deb vol. 18, cols 295, 297)

Mr Atkins: It is, of course, a matter for regret that the present proposals do not have the unanimous support of the Canadian provinces. But ... the Supreme Court of Canada considered that the consent of all the provinces was not required, either by law or by constitutional convention, to the making of a request to us. No one would deny that nine out of 10 provinces constitutes the substantial measure of provincial consent to which the Supreme Court referred.

After referring to the preamble to the Statute of Westminster 1931, Mr Atkins continued:

> It would, of course, be inconsistent with this 'request and consent' convention for Parliament to make amendments which have not been requested and consented to by Canada in the

first place ... In the light of this, I have to state the clear view of the Government that any amendment to the Canada Bill which may be put forward should not be passed by the House.

The Canada Bill was duly passed by both Houses without amendment.

Richard Kay ((1982) 4 *Supreme Court Law Review* 23, 33) remarks that the Canadian Supreme Court's part in the process that resulted in agreement between the Federal Government and nine of the ten provincial governments was crucial, and that perhaps it was only the court's intervention that could have broken the political logjam. He adds: 'But the Court intervened as another political actor, not as a court of law.' Is this a right understanding of the court's involvement?

4

Devolution and the Structure of the UK

Contents

In 2018, the United Kingdom marked the twentieth anniversary of devolution. The period since 1998 has seen a rapid evolution in the transfer of powers to the devolved legislatures, particularly to Wales and to Scotland. However, while devolution is strongly politically entrenched in Scotland, Wales and Northern Ireland, the same is not true in England. There is little understanding of the United Kingdom as a devolved nation from the English perspective, given the lack of devolution in England. There is no specific English Parliament. However, there have been a series of 'devolution deals', which transfer greater powers to combined authorities in England with elected mayors. Each of these deals is specific, negotiated between the Westminster Government and the particular combined authority.

Devolution furthers democracy through enabling decisions to be taken more closely to those directly affected by those decisions. It is also particularly pertinent when a distinct community has a different viewpoint or political persuasion from the rest of the country. It also enables each component part of the United Kingdom to reach different conclusions on specific issues. This was illustrated starkly by the diverse outcomes in the Brexit referendum. It has also been illustrated clearly by the response to the Covid-19 pandemic. As health is a devolved matter, Scotland, Wales, Northern Ireland and England all enacted different regulations in response to the pandemic. While, for the most part, these regulations were similar, there were nevertheless differences between them, particularly as regards the frequency with which individuals were allowed to exercise within the first stage of lockdown, in addition to the approach taken to the closure of national parks. These differences have caused confusion in a situation where the prime minister makes announcements in his role as prime minister of the United Kingdom, when these measures may be different across the United Kingdom.

It can be difficult to understand the complex interactions between each of the devolved legislatures and governments and Westminster. The key is to recognise that devolution is asymmetrical. This is reflected in the different histories of Scotland, Wales and Northern Ireland, in addition to the diverse pace of devolution, the range of powers devolved and the distinct political aims of the devolved governments. While the current Scottish Government, for example, wishes to pursue an independent Scotland and, at the time of writing, is in the process of requesting a second independence referendum (albeit that this is currently on hold during the Covid-19 pandemic), the current government in Wales would sooner pursue a move towards a more federal structure, granting a greater role to Wales. Northern Ireland's complex history makes it harder still to determine its long-term future, particularly in the light of Brexit. To date, there is little support for further devolution to England, or to specific English regions.

It is also important to understand that devolution is a constantly evolving story. This means that there is no clear constitutional design to devolution. The powers have evolved through a series of negotiations, without adhering to models of multi-layered government – for example the principle of subsidiarity, which prioritises the taking of decisions closest to those most directly affected by that decision, is not incorporated into devolution legislation, neither does it appear to have influenced those powers that have been devolved and those that are reserved to the United Kingdom. The question remains as to where this series of ad hoc, evolving, asymmetrical devolutions of power will lead, particularly given the tension that has been placed on the union of the United Kingdom through the Brexit process. This chapter will explore this issue through describing the history of devolution, as well as explaining the relationship between devolution and Brexit and the organisation of local government in the United Kingdom.

4.1 The United Kingdom as a Union State

The United Kingdom is a union of England, Scotland, Wales and Northern Ireland in a single state. The Channel Islands and the Isle of Man, which are internally self-governing dependencies of the Crown, are not part of the UK (on the Crown dependencies and their constitutional relationship with the UK, see House of Commons Justice Committee, *8th Report of 2009–10*, HC 56 and the Government's Response, Cm 8837, March 2014).

It used to be generally thought that the UK has a *unitary* constitution, like those of France, Italy, Japan, the Netherlands, Sweden and New Zealand, and unlike the *federal* constitutions of Germany ('the Federal Republic of Germany'), Switzerland, the USA, Australia, Brazil, Canada, India, Nigeria and the Russian Federation. However, it may be that the better view is that the UK has a *union* constitution that is neither straightforwardly unitary nor systematically federal in character (see Walker, 'Beyond the Unitary Conception of the United Kingdom Constitution?' [2000] *PL* 384; this is a strong theme, too, of Iain McLean's book, *What's Wrong with the British Constitution?* (2010)). This perhaps is particularly true since the advent of the current devolution arrangements in 1998. That said, however, it should not be thought that all such differences as exist in the government and public law of England, Scotland, Wales and Northern Ireland were created by devolution. A number of differences between English and Welsh law, on the one hand, and Scots law, on the other hand, are several centuries old. Others, while more recent in origin, nonetheless have nothing to do with devolution. Examples include differences in the law pertaining to the Crown, in judicial review proceedings and in the law of remedies (see, generally, McHarg and Mullen (eds.), *Public Law in Scotland* (2006), especially chapters by McHarg, Tierney and Tomkins).

In this chapter, we outline, first, some general issues concerning federalism and devolution. We then examine the various schemes of devolution as now exist in Scotland, Wales and Northern Ireland. In the final section of the chapter, we outline the UK's scheme of local government.

4.1.1 Federalism

K.C. Wheare, *Modern Constitutions* (2nd edn. 1966), p. 19

In a federal Constitution the powers of government are divided between a government for the whole country and governments for parts of the country in such a way that each government is legally independent within its own sphere. The government for the whole country has its own area of powers and it exercises them without any control from the governments of the constituent parts of the country, and these latter in their turn exercise their powers without being controlled by the central government. In particular the legislature of the whole country has limited powers, and the legislatures of the states or provinces have limited powers. Neither is subordinate to the other; both are coordinate. In a unitary Constitution, on the other hand, the legislature of the whole country is the supreme

> law-making body in the country. It may permit other legislatures to exist and to exercise
> their powers, but it has the right, in law, to overrule them; they are subordinate to it.

From this it appears that the essential features of a federal constitution are that the central and regional governments have limited powers and that, within those limits, each government is independent of the other.

Other definitions of federalism have been proposed. Preston King, in *Federalism and Federation* (1982), pp. 140–1, sees the distinguishing feature of a federation as the entrenched role of the regional units in national decision-making:

> a federation may conveniently be defined as a constitutional system which instances
> a division between central and regional governments and where special or entrenched
> representation is accorded to the regions in the decision-making procedures of the central
> government.

The regions in a federation will sometimes have been independent countries that agreed to join together in a federal union, but an existing unitary state may transform itself into a federation, as Belgium has done, by redistributing sovereign powers between central and regional governments. However created, a federal system seems to embody a *contractual* idea in that the central and the regional governments hold their powers on a condition of respect for the independence of the other. The terms of the 'contract' under which power is distributed are expressed in a written constitution and are unalterable by either the central or the regional legislatures acting unilaterally. To that extent, the constitution is supreme.

The formal analysis of federal and unitary constitutions assumes a regularity that is not always to be found in the shifting and diverse patterns of modern governmental systems. Wheare observed that a federal constitution might include elements that diverged from *the federal principle* as formally defined; indeed, if it had 'considerable unitary modifications', it would be better classified as 'quasi-federal' (Wheare, *Federal Government* (4th edn. 1963), p. 19). Moreover, when we consider the actual practice of governments it appears that a country 'may have a federal constitution, but, in reality, it may work that constitution in such a way that its government is not federal', or again that 'a country with a non-federal constitution may work it in such a way that it provides an example of federal government' (p. 20).

History and our own time show us such a variety of systems for the distribution of power between central and regional governments, and so many exceptions, qualifications, understandings and compromises in the working of constitutions, that there is often disagreement about whether a system of government is federal or unitary. The Constitution of the United

States is generally regarded as the paradigm of federal constitutions, yet even there the limits on the powers of the federal and state governments are blurred by innumerable arrangements for shared or cooperative governmental activity, and the central government, with its vast financial resources, has gained an ascendancy that transcends its formal powers. A centralising tendency is, indeed, a feature of most modern federal systems (see, e.g., Nagel, *The Implosion of American Federalism* (2001), although in Canada, exceptionally, a contrary tendency may be apparent). No constitution, remarks Finer, 'is an entirely realistic description of what actually happens' (*Five Constitutions* (1979), p. 16), and in federal constitutions, the formal distribution of powers is commonly qualified by networks of consultation, bargaining and joint planning. This means that the classification of a governmental system as federal or unitary (if we can agree on it) does not tell us much about how the system actually works. Equally, it is open to doubt whether either a federal or a unitary system, in the abstract, has the advantage in assuring good, efficient or strong government. Rufus Davis disposes in the following passage of judgments like that of Dicey, who concluded (in *The Law of the Constitution* (1885), pp. 171–2) that 'federal government means weak government' and that a federation 'will always be at a disadvantage in a contest with unitarian states of equal resources'.

S. Rufus Davis, *The Federal Principle* (1978), pp. 211–12

The truth of the matter is – and experience has been the teacher – that some 'federal' systems fail, some do not; some are able to resist aggression, some are not; some inhibit economic growth, some do not; some frustrate *some* kinds of economic planning, some frustrate *other* kinds; some develop a great diversity of public services, some do not; some promote a great measure of civil liberty, some do not; some are highly adaptive, some are not; some are highly efficient in servicing the needs of a modern state, some are not; some gratify values that others do not. Indeed, over a long or short span of time, some are always something (socially, economically, politically, administratively, constitutionally) which other federal systems are not. But whatever their condition at any one time (eg, adaptive/maladaptive, conservative/progressive, efficient/inefficient, etc), it is rarely clear that it *is* so because of their federalness, or the particular character of their federal institutions, or the special way they practice federalism, or in spite of their federalness. And further: when at some moment federal systems resemble or differ from each other in some respect or other (eg, efficiency or inefficiency in the delivery of public services, tepidity or zealotry in the pursuit of civil liberties), the reasons, though sometimes traceable to similarities or differences in their constitutional structure, flow more often than not from the things they share in common as societies or the things that distinguish them as societies.

In a word, we are dealing with things that are only partly the same. And if there is . . . a common 'logic' running through all federal systems, it lacks the force to transcend their different political cultures and impose a common political direction. This is the massive fact we have come to learn. To expect to give a common explanation for, say, the failure of the

Weimar Federal Republic and the Central African Federation in any other than trivial generalizations, or to expect that political performance will necessarily differ because states are federal or unitary, is to exaggerate the limited potentialities of contemporary federal theory and mistake the limited value of the distinction between federal and unitary systems.

If there are regionally based ethnic communities in a country, federalism can give them protection against oppression by majoritarian central government. It is also claimed that in the dismantling of a single, all-embracing sovereign power in the state, federal systems foster a more vigorous democratic polity, providing 'an encouragement to diversity, greater responsiveness of government, and an opportunity for broader citizen participation in public affairs' (Saunders in Hesse and Wright (eds.), *Federalizing Europe?* (1996), p. 47; see, too, Stephen Breyer's interesting account of the working of American federalism, 'Does Federalism Make a Difference?' [1999] *PL* 651, esp. 661–2).

The UK, at all events, is clearly recognisable as a state in which a supreme central authority is firmly established on the principle of parliamentary sovereignty. When a Government and Parliament of Northern Ireland were constituted by the Government of Ireland Act 1920, these institutions were subordinate to the UK Parliament. In practice, the UK Parliament refrained from exercising its power to legislate on matters 'transferred' to the Parliament of Northern Ireland, and it may therefore have been correct to describe the *system of government* in Northern Ireland – at all events until the period of crisis which began in 1968 – as 'quasi-federal' (Bogdanor, *Devolution* (1979), pp. 50–1). The overriding sovereignty of the Parliament at Westminster was, however, demonstrated when the Government of Northern Ireland was suspended and its Parliament prorogued by the Northern Ireland (Temporary Provisions) Act 1972. Institutions of *local* government in the UK owe their existence and powers to Parliament and can at any time be re-organised, abridged in their powers or extinguished by Parliament.

There has never been serious official consideration of a restructuring of the UK on a federal plan. The Kilbrandon Commission, in a rather sketchy (and, perhaps, now somewhat dated) survey of federalism (Cmnd 5460/1973, paras 501–23), concluded that 'in the modern world federal countries are hampered by an inflexible system of government'. The commission rejected federalism as inappropriate for the UK on a number of grounds. Among these were: the role which in the commission's view would be assumed, in a federal system, by the courts; and the dominant position of England, which could not be satisfactorily accommodated in a fully federal UK. The latter consideration remains striking: 84 per cent of the UK's population resides in England (as of 2010, England had 56.3 million inhabitants and the UK had 66.8 million).

Report of the Royal *Commission on the Constitution*, vol. 1, Cmnd 5460/1973

527. We have noted that a federal system of government would require a written constitution, a special procedure for changing it and a constitutional court to interpret it. None of these features has been present in our constitutional arrangements before, and we doubt very much whether they would now find general acceptance ...

529. In a federal system ... there is more than one legislature and the powers of each are strictly defined. There may be provision for federal law to override provincial law where the two conflict, but this rule is designed for those fields in which the federal and provincial governments have joint responsibility. It cannot be used by the federal government to encroach upon legislative territory specifically assigned under the constitution to the provinces. Disputes about governmental powers which cannot otherwise be resolved go to a constitutional court. The effect is therefore to place elected bodies in a position subordinate to the judiciary. Inevitably there are some constitutional questions which have to be decided more as a matter of individual judgement than in accordance with the rules laid down in the constitution ... The work of the judges therefore tends to become political, and their known political views are taken into account when they are appointed. This situation, probably unavoidable in a federal system, is foreign to our own tradition of unitary government based upon the complete sovereignty of Parliament and upon the complete dissociation of the judiciary from matters of political policy ...

The Dominant Position of England

531. As far as we are aware no advocate of federalism in the United Kingdom has succeeded in producing a federal scheme satisfactorily tailored to fit the circumstances of England. A federation consisting of four units – England, Scotland, Wales and Northern Ireland – would be so unbalanced as to be unworkable. It would be dominated by the overwhelming political importance and wealth of England. The English Parliament would rival the United Kingdom federal Parliament; and in the federal Parliament itself the representation of England could hardly be scaled down in such a way as to enable it to be out-voted by Scotland, Wales and Northern Ireland, together representing less than one-fifth of the population. A United Kingdom federation of the four countries, with a federal Parliament and provincial Parliaments in the four national capitals, is therefore not a realistic proposition.

532. The imbalance would be corrected if England were to be divided into a number of units, each having the status of a federal province. It is clear, however, that this artificial division into provinces with independent sovereign powers would be unacceptable to the people of England. Advocates of federalism have attempted to get round the difficulty by an arrangement in which the regions of England would not have the full status of federal provinces; they would have elected assemblies with fewer powers than the legislatures of Scotland, Wales and Northern Ireland, and a separate body would be established to deal with all-England affairs. But no matter how this body were to be constituted and its powers

> shared with the regional assemblies, the fact would remain that England by its weight of numbers and wealth would continue to dominate the federation.

The nub of the case for federalism is that it allows for autonomy and diversity in a system of shared power, while keeping sufficient authority at the centre to uphold common standards (e.g., of respect for human rights) and to maintain the unity, security and prosperity of the state. Are the arguments of the Kilbrandon Commission conclusive against the case for a United Kingdom federation? (See, further, Olowofoyeku, 'Decentralising the UK: The Federal Argument' (1999) 3 *Edinburgh L Rev* 57.)

The federal principle has not been without influence in British history. If dismissed by Dicey as incompatible with fundamentals of the British constitution, it has been embraced by other writers of his time and ours and on occasion by politicians, and it provided the framework for a number of constitutions established for former British colonies. (See Kendle, *Federal Britain: A History* (1997); Crozier, 'Federalism and Anti-federalism in the United Kingdom'; Bosco, 'The British Federalist Tradition', in Knipping (ed.), *Federal Conceptions in EU Member States* (1994).) The political impetus for the introduction of a federal system of government does not, however, at present exist in the UK. The devolutionary projects of 1998 for Scotland, Wales and Northern Ireland were not designed to refashion the UK as a federal state. Tierney argues that federalism may be flexible enough to provide a future model for the UK (Tierney, 'The Territorial Constitution and the Brexit Process' (2019) 72 *Current Legal* Problems 59).

4.1.2 Devolution

A system of devolved government applied in Northern Ireland from 1921 to 1972, replaced in the last year by direct rule from Whitehall. (See below, pp.301–316.)

The 1974–9 Labour Government launched a scheme for the devolution of powers to Scotland and Wales. Responding to an upsurge of Scottish and Welsh nationalism in the 1960s (rather than acting on a cool appraisal of constitutional deficiencies and the need for reform), the Wilson Government initiated the appointment in 1969 of a Royal Commission on the Constitution. The Kilbrandon Report (so named from Lord Kilbrandon, who had become Chairman of the Commission in 1972) was published in 1973 (Cmnd 5460). The report adopted a broad meaning of the term 'devolution' so as to include both the 'deconcentration' of functions within the governmental hierarchy, which it termed 'administrative devolution', and the more advanced devolution, which involves a *transfer* of central government powers to regional bodies, although 'without the relinquishment of sovereignty'. Devolution of the more advanced kind might extend to the transfer of powers to determine policies and enact legislation to put them into effect – *legislative devolution*; alternatively, major policies and primary legislation might be kept at the centre, while powers of subordinate policy-making and administration were transferred to the regions – *executive devolution*. The question for the commission was whether the case had been made for going beyond the existing system of administrative devolution in favour of either legislative or executive devolution to any of the countries or regions of the UK.

All the commissioners were persuaded that central government had become overloaded and remote, and that there had been a weakening of public confidence in the democratic process. As a remedy for these infirmities of the body politic, twelve commissioners – all but one – prescribed the introduction of schemes of legislative or executive devolution, but there was disagreement about the application of the schemes. Eight commissioners proposed a scheme of legislative devolution for Scotland, six wished to see it extended to Wales, two favoured executive devolution for Scotland, Wales and eight English regions, three wanted an elected assembly for Wales with advisory functions only and nine recommended non-elected regional advisory councils for England. In a memorandum of dissent (Cmnd 5460-I), two commissioners proposed a more thoroughgoing scheme of executive devolution for Scotland, Wales and five English regions.

The Labour Government responded to these discordant voices by deciding in 1974 to establish elected assemblies in Scotland and Wales, the former with legislative and the latter with executive powers (*Democracy and Devolution: Proposals for Scotland and Wales*, Cmnd 5732). The difference of treatment was justified by the government as resting on the need for distinctive legislation in Scotland, with its separate legal system, and the lack of public demand in Wales for a legislative assembly. The government ruled out the creation of an English assembly or regional assemblies in England with legislative powers, but canvassed the possibility of executive devolution to new regional authorities (*Devolution: The English Dimension* (1976)). A year later, it announced that it had found no 'broad consensus of popular support' for devolution in England, and the matter was dropped.

A Scotland and Wales Bill introduced in the House of Commons in 1976 provided for directly elected assemblies in Scotland and Wales: the Scottish Assembly would have legislative powers, while the Welsh Assembly would have executive powers only, to be exercised within a framework of Westminster legislation. The bill was strongly contested, made little progress and was withdrawn. A fresh start was made after the government had concluded a bargain with the Liberal Party (the 'Lib-Lab' pact of 1977–8) and separate devolution bills for Scotland and Wales were passed by Parliament in 1978. It was a condition of each bill that its provisions should not take effect unless approved by 40 per cent of the electorate in, respectively, Scotland and Wales. After royal assent, both acts were submitted to referendums as so required and, since the 40 per cent threshold was achieved in neither country, the acts were repealed, as provided, by orders in council.

Devolution remained on the political agenda in spite of the loss of the Scotland and Wales Acts. In Scotland, in particular, where 52 per cent of those voting in the referendum (albeit only 33 per cent of the electorate) had been in favour of putting the Scotland Act 1978 into effect, there was continuing and substantial support for the revival of the devolution project. Such support grew through the 1980s and early 1990s, as Scotland saw itself as governed by a government it did not vote for and one, moreover, that showed little regard for the economic priorities of the Scots. The government's apparent non-reaction to the collapse of shipbuilding on the Clyde and to the economic hardships that resulted for Glasgow, and its imposition of the hated poll tax (or community charge) one year earlier in Scotland than in England and Wales were merely the headlines in a prolonged story of Scotland's disaffection with the British Government. In the 1950s, half of Scotland's MPs were Conservatives. After the 1987 and 1992 general elections, however, fewer than a dozen of Scotland's (then) seventy-two MPs were Conservatives and, in the 1997 election, the Conservatives were wiped out altogether, as not a single Tory MP was returned from a Scottish constituency. In the 1980s and 1990s, Scotland was governed by the Conservatives because the majority of English MPs were Conservative and in spite of the fact that, within Scotland, there were clear and overwhelming majorities in favour of what, in British terms, were then the opposition parties. (See, further, Marr, *The Battle for Scotland* (1992), chs 5 and 6.)

Scotland did not simply take all of this lying down. A remarkable and broadly constituted Scottish Constitutional Convention convened in 1989, composed of Scottish Labour and Liberal Democrat MPs together with representatives of local authorities, churches, trade unions and other bodies. (The Conservative Party and the Scottish National Party declined to take part, the latter on the ground that the convention resolved to focus on devolutionary solutions that envisaged Scotland remaining in the UK; the SNP desired to see an independent Scottish state, outside the UK but remaining within the EU.) The first act of the convention was to adopt a Claim of Right for Scotland which declared as follows:

> We, gathered as the Scottish Constitutional Convention, do hereby acknowledge the sovereign right of the Scottish people to determine the form of Government best suited to their needs, and do hereby declare and pledge that in all our actions and deliberations their interests shall be paramount.
>
> We further declare and pledge that our actions and deliberations shall be directed to the following ends: to agree a scheme for an Assembly or Parliament for Scotland; to mobilise Scottish opinion and ensure the approval of the Scottish people for that scheme; and to assert the right of the Scottish people to secure the implementation of that scheme.

As Neil MacCormick has suggested ('Sovereignty or Subsidiarity? Some Comments on Scottish Devolution', in Tomkins (ed.), *Devolution and the British Constitution* (1998), p. 5), this is a 'bold, categorical, and even revolutionary' statement of intent. But it was meant as no mere piece of grandstanding rhetoric, as the work of the convention went on to demonstrate. After a lengthy period of discussion and consultation, the convention agreed in 1995 on a scheme of devolution, published in its report (and, again, note the boldness of the claim) *Scotland's Parliament: Scotland's Right*.

What Scotland would have done about the matter had the Conservatives enjoyed a fifth successive general election victory in 1997 we will never know. In the event, of course, Tony Blair's Labour Party won with a landslide majority and a manifesto commitment to create a Scottish Parliament 'firmly based on the agreement reached in the Scottish Constitutional Convention' (*Because Britain Deserves Better* (1997), p. 33). True to its word, the Labour Government's proposals for Scottish devolution, contained in the White Paper, *Scotland's Parliament* (Cm 3658/1997), were indeed broadly based on the scheme outlined in *Scotland's Parliament: Scotland's Right*.

Significantly, there was no equivalent preparation of a devolutionary scheme for Wales. Neither was there political pressure of a similar intensity for a restructuring of the system of government of Wales. But the Labour Party had committed itself before the 1997 general election to devolution of powers to Wales as well as to Scotland, and the new government's project for Welsh devolution was set out in its White Paper, *A Voice for Wales* (Cm 3718/1997).

The proposals in the White Papers were submitted to referendums in the two countries in September 1997 in accordance with the Referendums (Scotland and Wales) Act 1997 (which did not stipulate a threshold such as the one that had shackled the earlier devolution project). In Scotland, in a turnout of 60.4 per cent, 74.3 per cent of those voting agreed that there should be a Scottish Parliament and 63.5 per cent also agreed that the Parliament should have tax-varying powers. The Welsh electorate voted only on the question whether there should or should not be a Welsh Assembly. In a turnout of 50 per cent, 50.3 per cent of those voting agreed that there should be a Welsh Assembly, while 49.7 per cent disagreed – a narrow margin of affirmative votes but a significant shift from the 1979 Welsh referendum result, when a mere 20 per cent of those voting (in a turnout of 59 per cent) had been in favour of devolution.

The Scotland Bill and the Government of Wales Bill which were introduced in the House of Commons at the end of 1997 were based on the white papers. Each bill received the royal assent in the following year. In that year, too, the Northern Ireland Act 1998 was enacted, devolving powers to an elected assembly in Northern Ireland. One commentator has suggested that these acts brought about 'the most radical constitutional reform this country has seen since the Great Reform Act of 1832' (Bogdanor, in University of Cambridge Centre for Public Law, *Constitutional Reform in the United Kingdom* (1998), p. 9).

As we shall see in more detail below, the progress of devolution has been markedly different in the three countries since 1998. Devolution in Northern Ireland has been suspended and reinstated on several occasions, as the various parties have cooperated and fallen out with one another over aspects of security policy and other matters. Devolution in Wales was subjected to a major review in 2002–4 (see www.richardcommission.gov.uk), leading to fresh legislation in 2006 that significantly reformed the 1998 settlement: see the Government of Wales Act 2006, replacing the Government of Wales Act 1998. In 2010, the members of the Welsh Assembly voted in favour of holding a referendum on the transfer of more legislative powers to Wales, the vote in favour broadened its law-making capacity. This was followed in 2014 by the transfer of fiscal powers (Wales Act 2014) and a move to a reserved powers model following the Wales Act 2017. In 2020 the Welsh Assembly changed its name to the Senedd Cymru (Welsh Parliament) and assembly members are now referred to as members of Senedd (MS). Scotland saw an independence referendum in 2014, where the majority voted in favour of remaining in the UK, in addition to a transfer of additional powers to Scotland – the Scotland Act 2012, which saw a large transfer of fiscal powers, and the Scotland Act 2016, which devolved further tax and welfare powers. Given growing tension over Brexit, there are continuing calls in Scotland for a further independence referendum, although the Scottish Government placed talks with the UK Government to request a transfer of powers to hold a second referendum on hold in 2020 due to the impact of the Covid-19 pandemic. Importantly, both the Scotland Act 2016 and the Wales Act 2017 recognise both the permanence of the Scottish Parliament and the Welsh Senedd, and that it was for the people of Scotland and Wales respectively to remove devolution.

The essential features of the devolution settlement are now to be found in the Scotland Act 1998, the Government of Wales Act 2006 and the Northern Ireland Act 1998, as amended. These are complemented by a variety of more or less formal arrangements, principally a series of agreements between the UK Government and the devolved administrations which set out the principles on which they conduct their mutual relations.

The main agreement is the *Memorandum of Understanding and Supplementary Agreements* (as revised in 2012; available at https://assets.publishing.service.gov .uk/government/uploads/system/uploads/attachment_data/file/316157/ MoU_between_the_UK_and_the_Devolved_Administrations.pdf), which provides for the establishment of a joint ministerial committee as a consultative forum for ministers from the four administrations (the UK, Scotland, Wales and Northern Ireland). The joint ministerial committee considers matters of common interest or overlapping responsibilities and seeks to resolve intergovernmental disputes. In addition there are three multilateral 'overarching' agreements or concordats, which deal respectively with arrangements for cooperation on EU business, international relations and financial assistance to industry. Individual departments of the UK Government have also concluded bilateral concordats with the devolved administrations. Although concordats are not intended to be legally binding, they may turn out to be justiciable in proceedings for judicial review: for instance, a concordat might give rise to a legitimate expectation that its terms would be properly adhered to. (On legitimate expectations, see below, pp. 850–855.) (See, further, Rawlings, 'Concordats of the Constitution' (2000) 116 *LQR* 257; House of Lords Constitution Committee, *Devolution: Inter-Institutional Relations in the United Kingdom*, 2nd Report of 2002–03, HL 28.)

Devolution in Britain, as it has been experienced since 1998, 'is variable, an untidy, asymmetrical constitutional architecture' (O'Neill, 'Great Britain: From Dicey to Devolution' (2000) 53 *Parl Aff* 69, 78). Similarly, Robert Hazell, in *The State and the Nations* (2000, p. 269), remarks: 'Asymmetry runs through every clause and schedule of the devolution legislation, from the fundamentals of powers and functions down to the niceties of nomenclature.' He goes on to stress that these variations are not accidental:

> They are deliberate differences chosen to emphasise the difference in style and substance between the three devolved assemblies, and in particular between each of the devolved assemblies and their parent body at Westminster.

The different constitutional structures were devised so as to match the particular historical and political circumstances of each country. This is not to say that the match is in every respect apposite, and it is evident that we cannot think of the settlement as being in each case fixed and permanent. This is, indeed, acknowledged in provisions of the devolution statutes, which allow for future extensions of the areas of competence of the devolved institutions.

The former Secretary of State for Wales, Mr Ron Davies, in insisting that devolution was 'a process, not an event', highlighted a feature not only of the settlement for Wales but of the whole devolution project.

Although it is clear that devolution has not resulted in a federal constitution of the UK, it has been remarked that 'in political terms, these new settlements are significantly closer to the federalist end of the continuum than their predecessors in the Northern Ireland Act 1920 and the abortive Scotland Act 1978' (Walker, 'Beyond the Unitary Conception of the United Kingdom Constitution?' [2000] *PL* 384, 396). This author goes on to say (at p. 397) that:

> the British state has come closer than ever before to conceding that its retention of legislative omnicompetence in the context of a devolution process is a matter of legal form rather than political substance; in other words, while ritual deference continues to be paid to the legal theory of the unitary state, the developing culture of negotiation and balanced settlement reflects a rather different political understanding.

The terms of the devolution settlements for Scotland, Wales and Northern Ireland are considered in the next section.

4.2 Scotland, Wales, Northern Ireland and England

The UK is a multinational state in which the inhabitants of Scotland, Wales and Northern Ireland identify themselves not only as 'British' but also – indeed, often exclusively – as Scots, Welsh, Ulstermen or Irish. In law, there is, however, a single British citizenship for all those sufficiently connected by birth or descent with the UK (British Nationality Act 1981).

The structure of the UK as we now know it dates from 1922, when southern Ireland withdrew from the Union as the Irish Free State.

Legislation of the UK Parliament has usually extended to all parts of the Kingdom, but some public acts have not extended to Northern Ireland or have applied only to Scotland, Wales or Northern Ireland (rarely only to England). The former Parliament of Northern Ireland (1921–72) enacted many laws for the province that are still in force. The devolution arrangements of 1998, while not restricting the legal competence of Parliament to legislate for the whole of the UK, do affect the exercise of its power in respect of devolved matters: the government undertook that it would 'proceed in accordance with the convention that the UK Parliament would not normally legislate with regard to devolved matters except with the agreement of the devolved legislature' (*Memorandum of Understanding*, 2012, para 14). Devolution has increased the diversity of the law in force in different parts of the Kingdom.

There is freedom of movement throughout the UK for those settled there.

4.2.1 Scotland

4.2.1.1 Scotland in the Union

Scotland covers about one-third of the area of the UK and has a population of 5.4 million or about 8.4 per cent of the total UK population.

Scotland and England, under the same Crown from 1603 but with separate institutions of government, were joined in the United Kingdom of Great Britain in 1707 by the Treaty and Acts of Union. Articles of union, agreed in 1706 by commissioners acting on behalf of the Parliament of each country, were adopted by Acts of Union passed by the English Parliament in 1706 and the Scottish Parliament in 1707. In terms of these instruments, the two Parliaments were superseded by a Parliament of Great Britain – 'a new Parliament for a new State' (Scottish Law Commission, Memorandum No 32 (1975), p. 16).

In entering the union, the Scots were concerned to ensure, as far as they could, that certain of their cherished rights and institutions should not be at risk from a Parliament in which English members would be in a majority. The union legislation accordingly declared, as a 'fundamental and essential condition' of the union, that the Presbyterian religion and Church of Scotland should 'remain and continue unalterable' in Scotland, and affirmed that the Scottish superior courts (the Court of Session and the Court of Justiciary) should remain 'in all time coming' with their authority and privileges. While the Parliament of Great Britain was authorised to alter the laws of Scotland, it was stipulated that no alteration should be made in private law 'except for evident utility of the subjects within Scotland'. From a modern point of view, the Acts of Union are defective in that they include no safeguards against violation of their 'fundamental' provisions, neither do they include any special machinery for amending these as changed conditions might require. At least one of the fundamental provisions, obliging professors of Scottish universities to make a formal submission to Presbyterianism, was repealed by the Universities (Scotland) Acts 1853 and 1932; the issue was not a contentious one and the Scots may be said to have acquiesced in the repeal.

It would seem to follow from the doctrine of parliamentary sovereignty that an act of Parliament is valid even if it violates fundamental provisions of the union legislation. Against this it is argued that the Acts of Union are constituent Acts that, in creating the Parliament of the UK, imposed limitations on its powers that remain effective. English constitutional lawyers have not, in general, accepted this argument. The argument has been heard in the Scottish courts and although it has not prevailed there, neither has it been summarily dismissed.

MacCormick v. *Lord Advocate* 1953 SC 396 (Court of Session)

The Chairman and Secretary of the Scottish Covenant Association petitioned the Court of Session for a declaratory order that a proclamation describing the Queen as 'Elizabeth the Second of the United Kingdom of Great Britain' was illegal. They argued that the adoption of the numeral 'II', since it implied that Elizabeth I had been Queen of Great Britain, was contrary to Article I of the Treaty and Acts of Union that had brought about the union of the two kingdoms in 1707. For the Crown, the Lord Advocate denied that the proclamation conflicted with Article I, and maintained further that the use of the numeral 'II' was authorised by the Royal Titles Act 1953. The petitioners contended that the act could not validly permit the violation of a fundamental provision of the treaty.

The Lord Ordinary (Lord Guthrie) dismissed the petition on the grounds: (1) that the Royal Titles Act had authorised the adoption of the numeral, and an act of Parliament could not be challenged as being in breach of the treaty or on any other ground; (2) that in any event the treaty did not expressly or impliedly prohibit the use of the numeral; and (3) that the petitioners had no sufficient interest to bring the proceedings.

The petitioners' appeal to the First Division of the Inner House was dismissed, the court agreeing with Lord Guthrie that there was nothing in Article I of the Treaty against the use of the numeral, and that the petitioners had no title to sue. The court was of the opinion that the Royal Titles Act had no relevance in the case:

it was enacted only after the proclamation of the Queen as Elizabeth II and was not concerned in any way with the numeral adopted. The Lord President nevertheless expressed his opinion on the questions of the validity of an Act of Parliament that conflicted with the treaty, and the jurisdiction of the courts if such an issue were to arise.

Lord President (Cooper): . . . The principle of the unlimited sovereignty of Parliament is a distinctively English principle which has no counterpart in Scottish constitutional law. It derives its origin from Coke and Blackstone, and was widely popularised during the nineteenth century by Bagehot and Dicey, the latter having stated the doctrine in its classic form in his *Law of the Constitution*. Considering that the Union legislation extinguished the Parliaments of Scotland and England and replaced them by a new Parliament, I have difficulty in seeing why it should have been supposed that the new Parliament of Great Britain must inherit all the peculiar characteristics of the English Parliament but none of the Scottish Parliament, as if all that happened in 1707 was that Scottish representatives were admitted to the Parliament of England. That is not what was done. Further, the Treaty and the associated legislation, by which the Parliament of Great Britain was brought into being as the successor of the separate Parliaments of Scotland and England, contain some clauses which expressly reserve to the Parliament of Great Britain powers of subsequent modification, and other clauses which either contain no such power or emphatically exclude subsequent alteration by declarations that the provision shall be fundamental and unalterable in all time coming, or declarations of a like effect. I have never been able to understand how it is possible to reconcile with elementary canons of construction the adoption by the English constitutional theorists of the same attitude to these markedly different types of provisions.

The Lord Advocate conceded this point by admitting that the Parliament of Great Britain 'could not' repeal or alter such 'fundamental and essential' conditions. He was doubtless influenced in making this concession by the modified views expressed by Dicey in his later work entitled *Thoughts on the Scottish Union*, from which I take this passage (pp 252-253): – 'The statesmen of 1707, though giving full sovereign power to the Parliament of Great Britain, clearly believed in the possibility of creating an absolutely sovereign Legislature which should yet be bound by unalterable laws'. After instancing the provisions as to Presbyterian Church government in Scotland with their emphatic prohibition against alteration, the author proceeds: – 'It represents the conviction of the Parliament which passed the Act of Union that the Act for the security of the Church of Scotland ought to be morally or constitutionally unchangeable, even by the British Parliament . . . A sovereign Parliament, in short, though it cannot be logically bound to abstain from changing any given law, may, by the fact that an Act when it was passed had been declared to be unchangeable, receive a warning that it cannot be changed without grave danger to the Constitution of the country.' I have not found in the Union legislation any provision that the Parliament of Great Britain should be 'absolutely sovereign' in the sense that that Parliament should be free to alter the Treaty at will . . .

> But the petitioners have still a grave difficulty to overcome on this branch of their argument. Accepting it that there are provisions in the Treaty of Union and associated legislation which are 'fundamental law', and assuming for the moment that something is alleged to have been done – it matters not whether with legislative authority or not – in breach of that fundamental law, the question remains whether such a question is determinable as a justiciable issue in the Courts of either Scotland or England, in the same fashion as an issue of constitutional *vires* would be cognisable by the Supreme Courts of the United States, or of South Africa or Australia. I reserve my opinion with regard to the provisions relating expressly to this Court and to the laws 'which concern private right' which are administered here. This is not such a question, but a matter of 'public right' (articles 18 and 19). To put the matter in another way, it is of little avail to ask whether the Parliament of Great Britain 'can' do this thing or that, without going on to inquire who can stop them if they do ... This at least is plain, that there is neither precedent nor authority of any kind for the view that the domestic Courts of either Scotland or England have jurisdiction to determine whether a governmental act of the type here in controversy is or is not conform to the provisions of a Treaty, least of all when that Treaty is one under which both Scotland and England ceased to be independent states and merged their identity in an incorporating union. From the standpoint both of constitutional law and of international law the position appears to me to be unique, and I am constrained to hold that the action as laid is incompetent in respect that it has not been shown that the Court of Session has authority to entertain the issue sought to be raised.

Lord Carmont expressed agreement with the views of the Lord President, and Lord Russell in a concurring judgment was in general agreement with those views.

It has been said of Lord Cooper's conclusion that the courts have no jurisdiction to rule on the validity of an act of Parliament contradicting the Treaty of Union, that 'what he gave with the right hand he took away with the left' (Himsworth and O'Neill, *Scotland's Constitution: Law and Practice* (2nd edn. 2009), p. 112). (See, further, MacCormick, 'Does the United Kingdom Have a Constitution? Reflections on *MacCormick v Lord Advocate*' (1978) 29 *NILQ* 1; Tomkins, 'The Constitutional Law in *MacCormick v Lord Advocate*' [2004] *Juridical Rev* 213.)

Similar statements can be found in *Gibson* v. *Lord Advocate* 1975 SLT 134 (Court of Session), where the applicant argued that the equal access to fishing rights for all EU nationals, incorporated into UK law through the provisions of the European Communities Act 1972, was unlawful as it contravened Article XVIII of the Act of Union 1707, which prohibited the alteration of private rights 'except for the evident utility of the subjects within Scotland'. The claim did not succeed. Nevertheless, the case is important as a further reiteration, in dicta, of the scope in Scots law of the sovereignty of Parliament.

Lord Keith: . . . In addition to the argument on relevancy there were addressed to me interesting arguments upon the question of jurisdiction and the competency of the action. These arguments raised constitutional issues of great potential importance, in particular whether the Court of Session has power to declare an Act of the United Kingdom Parliament to be void, whether an alleged discrepancy between an Act of that Parliament and the Treaty or Act of Union is a justiciable issue in this court, and whether, with particular reference to article XVIII of the Act of Union, this court has power to decide whether an alteration of private law bearing to be effected by an Act of the United Kingdom Parliament is 'for the evident utility' of the subjects in Scotland. Having regard to my decision on relevancy, these are not live issues in the present case. The position was similar in *MacCormick v Lord Advocate* [above], a case concerned with the validity of the proclamation as Queen of Her present Majesty under a title which incorporated the numeral 'second'. The First Division held that no question properly arose concerning the validity of the Royal Titles Act 1953, but delivered certain obiter dicta upon the constitutional position as regards the Treaty and Act of Union . . . Like Lord President Cooper, I prefer to reserve my opinion on what the question would be if the United Kingdom Parliament passed an Act purporting to abolish the Court of Session or the Church of Scotland or to substitute English law for the whole body of Scots private law. I am, however, of opinion that the question whether a particular Act of the United Kingdom Parliament altering a particular aspect of Scots private law is or is not 'for the evident utility' of the subjects within Scotland is not a justiciable issue in this court. The making of decisions upon what must essentially be a political matter is no part of the function of the court, and it is highly undesirable that it should be. The function of the court is to adjudicate upon the particular rights and obligations of individual persons, natural or corporate, in relation to other persons or, in certain instances, to the state. A general inquiry into the utility of certain legislative measures as regards the population generally is quite outside its competence.

(See the note by Thomson (1976) 92 *LQR* 36, who draws attention to an earlier case, *Laughland* v. *Wansborough Paper Co Ltd* 1921 1 SLT 341, in which Lord Ashmore thought it right to consider the utility of a statutory rule that had been challenged as contrary to Article XVIII, finding it to be of general benefit to Scotland. Compare, too, the opinions expressed in *Stewart* v. *Henry* 1989 SLT (Sh Ct) 34 and *Fraser* v. *MacCorquodale* 1992 SLT 229, the decision of the Court of Session in *Pringle, Petitioner* 1991 SLT 330, discussed by Edwards (1992) 12 *Legal Studies* 34, and *Murray* v. *Rogers* 1992 SLT 221.)

MacCormick and *Gibson* contain interesting dicta but give no definite ruling on the question as to whether Parliament's powers are limited by the Treaty and Acts of Union. It is evident, however, that anyone seeking to challenge an Act on this ground will have the difficult task of persuading a court to assume jurisdiction to decide the question. If a court should agree to entertain the matter, arguments for the fundamental status of the Treaty of Union, while likely to carry substantial weight in a Scottish court, might be countered by arguments that the new Parliament created in 1707 succeeded to the sovereignty of its English predecessor and was unlimited in *law* by the terms of the Treaty of Union, or alternatively that any initial limitations on the power of the UK Parliament have been overcome by the full maturing of the doctrine of parliamentary sovereignty since 1707.

It is nevertheless the fact that the essential conditions of the Treaty of Union have, in substance, been respected. Scottish lawyers, politicians and others still hold them to be significant. Custom, Scottish national sentiment and political calculation are factors that have qualified the exercise of Parliament's powers with regard to the Treaty of Union.

(See, further, Smith, 'The Union of 1707 as Fundamental Law' [1957] *PL* 99; Upton, 'Marriage Vows of the Elephant: The Constitution of 1707' (1989) 105 *LQR* 79; Walker and Himsworth, 'The Poll Tax and Fundamental Law' [1991] *Juridical Rev* 45; MacCormick, *Questioning Sovereignty* (1999), ch. 4; Munro, *Studies in Constitutional Law* (2nd edn. 1999), ch. 5; Wicks, 'A New Constitution for a New State? The 1707 Union of England and Scotland' (2001) 117 *LQR* 109; Ford, 'The Legal Provisions in the Acts of Union' [2007] *CLJ* 106.)

4.2.1.2 Government of Scotland Before Devolution

After the union of 1707, the Scottish administration was absorbed into an administration of Great Britain centred in London. The Lord Advocate held an office of ancient origin in Scotland and, as well as being a law officer of the Crown, had far-reaching executive responsibilities. Public boards with governmental functions were established in Scotland in the nineteenth century. A new system of administration was instituted in 1885 when a secretary for Scotland was appointed as ministerial head of a Scottish Office in Whitehall. The Scottish Secretaryship was replaced in 1926 by the more senior office of Secretary of State, and in 1939 the Scottish Office was moved to Edinburgh (with a branch in London).

Except in the war years, the Secretary of State for Scotland always had a seat in the cabinet, which was necessary if he was to be able to press the case for Scotland on equal terms. In 1998, the responsibilities of the Secretary of State, heading a team of five subordinate ministers, covered a wide range of Scottish affairs corresponding to functions that were spread over no fewer than seven Whitehall departments. The Scottish Office and its agencies employed some 10,000 civil servants.

There were special arrangements for the conduct of Scottish business in Parliament. In the House of Commons, a Scottish Grand Committee, comprising all MPs representing Scottish constituencies, resembled a sub-Parliament for Scotland within the House, debating bills relating exclusively to Scotland and questioning Scottish Office ministers. There were also Scottish standing committees to examine the detail of Scottish bills and a Select Committee on Scottish Affairs to review the work of the Scottish Office.

These arrangements provided much work for Scottish MPs and involved them closely and constantly in Scottish business at Westminster. This business was, however, firmly set in a UK context in which collective ministerial responsibility and centralised policy-making were the rule.

4.2.1.3 Devolution under the Scotland Act 1998

The devolution settlement for Scotland rests on the provisions of the Scotland Act 1998, described in the Supreme Court as being 'on any view a monumental piece of constitutional legislation' (*Martin* v. *HM Advocate* [2010] UKSC 10, 2010 SC (UKSC) 40, at [44] (Lord Walker)). The act put the union of Scotland with the rest of the UK on a new basis, devolving primary legislative powers and administrative responsibilities to newly created institutions in Scotland. Section 37 provides: 'The Union with Scotland Act 1706 and the Union with England Act 1707 have effect subject to this Act.' The Act's provisions do not, however, seem to violate any of the fundamentals of the Treaty and Acts of Union.

The Scotland Act established a unicameral, law-making Scottish Parliament and a Scottish Administration, consisting of ministers, certain non-ministerial officeholders and their Civil Service staff. The term 'Scottish Administration' was never widely used. Until 2007 the term 'Scottish Executive' was commonly in use. Since that time the preferred term has been 'Scottish Government'.

Scottish devolution has, in broad terms, been accepted by all the major UK political parties, albeit that there remains more disquiet among Conservatives than there is in Labour or Liberal Democrat ranks about certain aspects of devolution. The Scottish National Party (SNP) continues to advocate a version of independence for Scotland and is less accepting of devolution as a 'settlement' than is the case for the main UK parties. But even the SNP has worked within the devolution arrangements: the party did not use its term of office following the 2007 Scottish parliamentary election to seek to undermine or overturn devolution, although it succeeded in holding a Scottish independence referendum in 2014 and has twice since instigated votes in the Scottish Parliament in favour of a second independence referendum. That the SNP took power after 2007 provided Britain's unionist parties with the opportunity to review the success and the future operation of Scottish devolution. In 2008–9, the Conservative, Labour and Liberal Democrat Parties worked together on the Calman Commission to develop cross-party agreement as to the ways in which Scottish devolution could be enhanced (the SNP did not participate in the Calman Commission). Calman's recommendations were contained in a report, *Serving Scotland Better: Scotland and the United Kingdom in the 21st Century*, published in June 2009. The most important recommendations concerned the ways in which the fiscal autonomy of the Scottish Parliament could be increased, thereby decreasing its dependence on the Treasury in London. Its further recommendations represented a tidying-up exercise rather than a root-and-branch reform of the arrangements set down in the Scotland Act 1998 (see below). The Scotland Act 2012 broadly implemented the Calman Commission, transferring to Scotland the power to raise its own taxes, which came into force fully in 2016. This empowered the Scottish Parliament to raise or lower income tax by up to 10p in the pound, as well as devolving stamp duty and landfill tax to Scotland. It also led to the renaming of the Scottish Executive as the Scottish Government.

Following the election of a majority SNP government in 2011, the Scottish Government sought to hold a referendum on independence in fulfilment of its manifesto commitment. The Scottish Parliament published a consultation paper *Your Scotland, Your Referendum* and a draft Referendum Bill, which asserted the power of the Scottish Parliament to hold a referendum. This was challenged by the UK Government. Rather than referring this to the courts, the Scottish and Westminster governments settled this potential dispute through the Edinburgh Agreement, which framed the referendum process. The UK Government made an order in council, under section 30 of the Scotland Act 1998, devolving the competence to the Scottish Parliament to hold an independence referendum before the end of 2014. The Scottish Parliament had the power to set the date for the referendum, the franchise, and to determine the detailed procedural process rules. The question for the referendum was agreed to by both governments, using the process set out in the Political Parties, Elections and Referendums Act 2000: 'Should Scotland be an independent country? Yes/No.' The referendum attracted a high turnout – 84.59 per cent of the electorate – with 55 per cent voting 'no' and 45 per cent voting 'yes' to independence.

The Smith Commission was convened following the referendum outcome and it recommended the transfer of more powers to the Scottish Parliament, including the power to regulate elections and the franchise in Scotland, greater fiscal powers and greater regulation of social welfare provisions. In addition, it recommended the reformation of intergovernmental arrangements, including a concordat concerning Scottish Government representation of the UK in the EU. It also recommended that the Scottish Parliament and Scottish Government should be recognised as permanent institutions, and that the 'Sewel Convention will be put on a statutory footing'. The recommendations of the Smith Commission were implemented through the Scotland Act 2016. However, in spite of the increase in powers, there were concerns both at the speed of the Smith Commission, the extent to which the increase powers were hedged with legal restrictions, and of the implementation of its outcome without a broader discussion of devolution in the UK as a whole (see House of Lords, Select Committee on the Constitution, *The Union and Devolution 10th Report of 2015–16*, HL Paper 149). As will be discussed in more detail below, the Scottish Parliament has called for a second independence referendum in the light of the outcome of the Brexit referendum and the negotiations surrounding the UK's exit from the European Union.

The main characteristics and powers of the Scottish Parliament may be summarised as follows:

(1) The Scottish Parliament and Government are recognised as a 'permanent part of the United Kingdom's constitutional arrangements', it being declared also that 'the Scottish Parliament and the Scottish Government are not to be abolished except on the basis of a decision of the people of Scotland voting in a referendum' (section 63A, Scotland Act 1998). This does not provide a legally binding constitutional guarantee. Rather it is a statement of the commitment of the UK Government to the devolution settlement.

(2) The Parliament has at present 129 members (MSPs). Scottish Parliament constituency boundaries were initially linked with those for the House of Commons. This link was removed by the Scottish Parliament (Constituencies) Act 2004, which preserved the number of 129 constituencies. The proposed modification of the constituencies of the Westminster Parliament, therefore, will not lead to the automatic modification of constituencies of the Scottish Parliament.

(3) The Parliament is elected by the additional member (or 'mixed member') system, which is designed to achieve a degree of proportionality between votes cast and seats won through a combination of the plurality or 'first-past-the-post' (FPTP) system with a regional list system. At present, seventy-three MSPs are elected in single-member constituencies by FPTP and seven additional members are elected in each of eight regions of Scotland by the list system, the parties presenting closed lists of their chosen candidates for each region. An elector may vote for a constituency candidate and has a second, regional vote to be cast for a party (or for an independent candidate standing in the region). The additional member system has a tendency to bring about coalition or minority government. After each of the first two elections (in 1999 and 2003), a coalition of Labour and the Liberal Democrats took office in Scotland; after the 2007 election, a minority SNP administration took office; but the SNP's overwhelming victory in 2011 resulted in its winning a majority of seats in the Scottish Parliament. This was maintained in the 2016 election, with the SNP winning fifty-nine of the constituency seats and four regional seats (sixty-three of 129 seats) and 46.5 per cent of the vote.

(4) The Parliament is normally elected for a fixed term of four years, but, exceptionally, it may be dissolved before the term has run. This will happen if the Parliament resolves, by a two-thirds majority of its members, that it should be dissolved, or if the Parliament is deadlocked in the choice of a first minister. The elections to the Scottish Parliament may not take place on the same day as a parliamentary general election to the Westminster Parliament or a European parliamentary general election (see section 2A Scotland Act 1998, although this is likely to be repealed

following the UK's exit from the European Union). The Scottish Elections (Dates) Act 2016 set the date for the next poll for the Scottish Parliament to take place on 6 May 2021 as opposed to 6 May 2020.

(5) The Parliament is a legislature of limited powers, its powers limited both by the Scotland Act 1998 and the common law (for relevant case law, see below). It is competent to legislate for Scotland on devolved matters, its laws being known as Acts of the Scottish Parliament (ASPs). Unlike Westminster, the Scottish Parliament has no competence to legislate in a way that is incompatible with convention rights or, until the end of the implementation period completion day, with EU law (Scotland Act 1998, section 29).

(6) The scheme adopted in the Scotland Act is to specify the powers *retained* at Westminster, not those devolved. Accordingly, the Act specifies in detail (in Schedule 5) the 'reserved matters', which are outside the competence of the Scottish Parliament, those matters that are not reserved being generally devolved.

The reserved matters include: the constitutional framework (the Crown, the Union of Scotland and England, the UK Parliament, the continued existence of the High Court of Justiciary and the Court of Session); international relations and the European Union (until the end of the implementation period completion day); the regulation of international trade; the Civil Service; defence and the armed forces; fiscal, economic and monetary policy; immigration and nationality; national security and official secrets; competition policy; consumer protection; ownership and exploitation of coal, oil and gas; nuclear energy; social security (subject to exceptions); employment and industrial relations; broadcasting; and equal opportunities.

Within the reserved categories many exceptions are made. For instance, the reservation of fiscal, economic and monetary policy is subject to the exception of local taxation to fund local authority expenditure, which is devolved, and devolved taxation following the inclusion in the Scotland Act 2012 to empower the Scottish Parliament to modify income tax. This was accompanied by a decrease in the 'block grant' transferred from the Treasury to the Scottish ministers. The block grant is calculated by reference to the 'Barnett formula', which pre-dates devolution. While there are many who consider that the Barnett formula may have outlived its usefulness, securing agreement on its replacement is unlikely to be straightforward, especially in a time of austerity. The Calman Commission recommended that 'until such times as a proper assessment of relative spending need across the UK is carried out, the Barnett formula should continue to be used as the basis for calculating the proportionality of the block grant' (recommendation 3.4). (For criticisms of the Barnett formula, see House of Lords Select Committee on the Barnett Formula, *1st Report of 2008–09*, HL 139; House of Commons Justice Committee, *Devolution: A Decade On*, 5th Report of 2008–09, HC

529, paras 231–52.) The 2016 Scotland Act also created a range of exceptions as regards the reserved category of social security, empowering Scotland to enact measures, inter alia, for disability benefits, carer's benefits, the provision of financial assistance for maternity expenses, funeral expenses, cold weather payments and to those receiving housing benefits.

The list of reserved matters in Schedule 5 is lengthy but leaves a wide range of matters to fall within the competence of the Scottish Parliament. The devolved matters include Scots private law (including judicial review) and criminal law; the prosecution service, police and prisons; the judiciary and the court system; agriculture, forestry and fisheries; economic development, tourism, roads and transport; planning and environmental protection; education and training; health; local government, social work and housing; and sport and the arts. Some matters within these fields are reserved in Schedule 5: for instance, abortion, surrogacy, medicines and regulation of the health professions are reserved, although, in general, health is a devolved matter.

(7) Since the judiciary and the court system are devolved matters, the Scottish Parliament has power to alter the structure and jurisdiction of the courts in Scotland. By the same token, the continued existence of the High Court of Justiciary as a criminal court of first instance and of appeal, and of the Court of Session as a civil court of first instance and of appeal, as well as the determination of judicial salaries, are reserved matters. The Scotland Act includes provisions for the appointment and removal of judges that are designed to safeguard the independence of the judiciary (section 95).

(8) Changes to the list of reserved matters – as by transfer of additional powers to the Scottish Parliament – may be made by order in council under section 30 of the 1998 Act. This can be done only if the Westminster and Scottish Parliaments agree on the change, for the order in council has to be approved in draft by both Houses at Westminster and by the Scottish Parliament. If the change is effected by primary legislation, an agreed convention requires that the prior approval of the Scottish Parliament should be obtained.

(9) Section 29 of the 1998 Act places certain restrictions on the competence of the Scottish Parliament to enact valid legislation. In particular, an Act of the Scottish Parliament may not relate to reserved matters and may not include provisions that are incompatible with convention rights or with EU law (until the end of the implementation period completion day).

(10) In general, the Scottish Parliament may repeal or amend acts of the Westminster Parliament in relation to devolved matters. However, this is subject to Schedule 4, which lists legislation that may not be modified by the Scottish Parliament – for example, the Scotland Act 1998 itself, the Human Rights Act 1998 and the European Union (Withdrawal) Act 2018.

(11) The Parliament decides on its own procedures and working practices, which are incorporated in standing orders and may be amended as necessary. The standing orders provide for the establishment of committees of the Parliament, some of which are mandatory (e.g., on procedures of the Parliament, European and external relations, finance and equal opportunities), while 'subject' committees scrutinise departments of the Scottish Government and legislative proposals, and may themselves initiate legislation ('committee bills'). (See, in detail, McFadden and Lazarowicz, *The Scottish Parliament: An Introduction* (4th edn. 2010), ch. 4.)

(12) A bill becomes an Act of the Scottish Parliament 'when it has been passed by the Parliament and has received Royal Assent' (Scotland Act 1998, section 28(2)). The Scotland Act provides (in section 36) for a framework of legislative procedure, comprising three stages that loosely correspond to the second reading, committee stage and third reading of bills in the House of Commons. However, despite this basic similarity, there are numerous important differences between legislative procedure in Westminster and in the Scottish Parliament. The most significant – and most obvious – is that the Scottish Parliament is unicameral: there is no second, revising chamber. But important too is the way in which the relationship between committee work and plenary debates is structured, with a higher profile given to the former in the Scottish Parliament, not only in terms of scrutinising government bills but also in terms of legislative initiative. There is no Westminster equivalent of the system employed in the Scottish Parliament of 'committee bills', for example. (See, further, McFadden and Lazarowicz, above, ch. 5.) A further difference is the requirement of a two-thirds majority to enact measures relating to a protected subject matter (Scotland Act 1998, section 31A).

Since the Scottish Parliament is a legislature of limited competence, provision is made in the Scotland Act for resolving questions of vires that may arise in the passage of a bill or after its enactment. The Scotland Act 1998 includes provisions intended to reduce the likelihood of an ultra vires bill being passed by the Parliament. A person in charge of a bill is required to state, on or before the introduction of the bill, that in his or her view its provisions would be within the legislative competence of the Parliament (section 31(1)). In addition, the presiding officer of the Parliament – a politically impartial officer similar to the Speaker of the House of Commons – has to decide and state on or before the introduction of the bill whether or not in his or her view the bill's provisions would be within the Parliament's competence (section 31(2)). The presiding officer also has to state, after the last time the bill is amended and before it is passed or rejected, whether in his or her view the provisions of the bill relate to a protected subject matter – these include provisions that would modify the franchise, voting system, number of constituencies or number of members to be returned for each constituency of the Scottish Parliament, which require a two-thirds majority. It is for the Parliament to decide on the appropriate course of action – such as a corrective amendment – if the presiding officer should conclude that provisions of the bill would be ultra vires.

If it should nevertheless happen that the Parliament passes a bill which it is thought may be (wholly or in part) ultra vires, the Advocate General for Scotland, the Lord Advocate or the Attorney General may within a period of four weeks refer the question of vires to the Supreme Court (Scotland Act 1998, section 33). If the Supreme Court decides that the bill or any of its provisions would not be within the Parliament's legislative competence, the Parliament has an opportunity of reconsidering the bill with a view to its amendment or rejection (section 36(4)). The presiding officer may not submit a bill in its unamended form for the royal assent if the Supreme Court has ruled that it or any of its provisions is ultra vires (section 32(3)(a)). To date, only one case has been brought, concerning the UK Withdrawal from the European Union (Legal Continuity) (Scotland) Bill 2018. Section 29(1) of the 1998 Act provides:

> An Act of the Scottish Parliament is not law so far as any provision of the Act is outside the legislative competence of the Parliament.

Questions of competence, which include the requirement of compatibility with convention rights and EU law, are termed 'devolution issues'. After a bill has received the royal assent and become an Act of the Scottish Parliament, a devolution issue – as to whether the Act's provisions are within the competence of the Parliament – may arise in the course of legal proceedings, whether in the Scottish courts or elsewhere in the UK.

4.2.1.3.1 Judicial Review of Acts of the Scottish Parliament

The legality of Acts of the Scottish Parliament may be judicially reviewed, both in terms of the competences set out in section 29 of the Scotland Act 1998 and as regards some common law standards of review. Relatively few legal challenges have yet been made to Acts of the Scottish Parliament on the ground that the legislation has trespassed onto territory that is reserved to Westminster: most legal challenges to Acts of the Scottish Parliament have been based on convention rights grounds (there was a series of early cases concerned with the compatibility of aspects of Scots criminal law with convention rights – for instance, *Macklin* v. *HM Advocate* [2015] UKSC 77, [2017] 1 All ER 32), or a potential breach of EU law (see, for example, *Scotch Whisky Association* v. *The Lord Advocate* [2017] UKSC 76), or even both (see, for example, *Christian Institute* v. *Lord Advocate* [2016] UKSC 51).

Cases that have concerned the distinction between reserved and devolved powers amply illustrate just how difficult it may be to clearly separate reserved from devolved matters. In *Martin* v. *HM Advocate* [2010] UKSC 10, 2010 SC (UKSC) 40, for example, the Supreme Court split 3:2, with one of the Scottish justices of the Supreme Court in the majority and the other dissenting. The case concerned section 45 of the Criminal Proceedings etc. (Reform) (Scotland) Act 2007. This provision was designed to increase the range of statutory offences that could be tried summarily. Among these offences were road traffic offences. At the material time, road traffic law was reserved, while criminal procedure was devolved. Thus, section 45 was a rule of criminal procedure that related, among other matters, to road traffic offences (such offences being reserved). As such, was section 45 within or outside the legislative competence of the Scottish Parliament? The question needed to be answered with very close reference to the detailed provisions of the Scotland Act, the key provision of which, in the view of the Supreme Court, was para 2(3) of Schedule 4. This provides that, in general, an Act of the Scottish Parliament may not modify the law on reserved matters but that this prohibition 'applies in relation to a rule of Scots private law or Scots criminal law ... only to the extent that the rule in question is special to a reserved matter'. The majority of the Supreme Court ruled that section 45 was not 'special to a reserved matter'; the minority ruled that it was.

Two main constitutional issues have arisen: are Acts of the Scottish Parliament subject to judicial review under the common law in the same way as other statutory bodies and should the Scotland Act 1998, as a constitutional statute, be interpreted in a more purposive manner (see *Robinson* v. *Secretary of State for Northern Ireland* [2002] UKHL 32)? Our discussion will focus on the two most constitutionally important decisions: *AXA* v. *General Insurance* and the first reference using the section 33 of the Scotland Act, *Reference re the UK Withdrawal from the European Union (Legal Continuity)(Scotland) Bill (Legal Continuity Bill)*. The former answers the first question, setting out the extent to which Acts of the Scottish Parliament are subject to common law review. The second issue was answered in *Imperial Tobacco* [2012] UKSC 61, where the Supreme Court concluded that it was not the case that the Scotland Act 1998 should be interpreted generally in a more purposive manner as a constitutional statute, but rather that the interpretation of the act was context-specific. The *Legal Continuity Bill* reference provides the most recent account of the approach adopted by the UK Supreme Court to the determination of devolution issues.

AXA General Insurance v. *Lord Advocate* [2011] UKSC 46, [2012] 1 AC 868

The Damages (Asbestos-Related Conditions) (Scotland) Act 2009, an act of the Scottish Parliament, provided that pleural plaques and certain other asbestos-related conditions were actionable (in Scotland) for the purposes of damages in the law of personal injury. In 2007, the House of Lords had ruled in a series of English appeals that pleural plaques did not constitute recoverable damage for the purposes of the law of negligence (see *Rothwell* v. *Chemical and Insulating*

Co Ltd [2007] UKHL 39, [2008] 1 AC 281). AXA and other insurance companies sought to challenge the 2009 Act on both common law and convention rights grounds. *Whaley* v. *Watson* [2000] SC 340 had suggested that Acts of the Scottish Parliament could be subject to judicial review on the same grounds as any other body created by statute. This approach was rejected by the Supreme Court. The ordinary grounds of judicial review did not apply as the Scottish Parliament, although created by legislation, is a democratically elected body. Nevertheless, Acts of the Scottish Parliament can be challenged when they violate fundamental principles of the rule of law. The leading judgments were given by Lords Hope and Reed – who were then the two Scottish judges in the Supreme Court. While Lord Hope reached his conclusion by reasoning from first principles, looking at the extent to which democratically elected bodies should be subject to judicial review, Lord Reed focused on an interpretation of the scope of powers granted to the Scottish Parliament under the Scotland Act 1998, applying the principle of legality.

> **Lord Hope** [43]. The issue can be broken down into its component parts in this way. First, there is the question whether measures passed by the devolved legislatures are amenable to judicial review, other than in the respects expressly provided for by the devolution statutes, at all. If not, that will be the end of the argument. But if they are open to judicial review on common law grounds at all, there is the question as to what these grounds are. At the one extreme are the grounds that the appellants' second plea in law encapsulates: that the legislation is unreasonable, irrational or arbitrary. At the other is the proposition that judicial intervention is admissible only in the exceptional circumstances that Lord Steyn had in mind in *R (Jackson) v Attorney General* [2005] UKHL 56, [2006] 1 AC 262, para 102; see also my own speech at paras 104–107 and Baroness Hale of Richmond's observations at para 159. To answer these questions in their proper context it is necessary to set out the background in a little more detail. Although I am conscious of the implications of what the court decides in this case for the other devolved legislatures, I shall concentrate on the position of the Scottish Parliament. As was common ground before us, I consider that, while there are some differences of detail between the Scotland Act 1998 and the corresponding legislation for Wales and Northern Ireland, these differences do not matter for present purposes. The essential nature of the legislatures that the legislation has created in each case is the same.
>
> . . .
>
> [46] . . . The Scottish Parliament takes its place under our constitutional arrangements as a self-standing democratically elected legislature. Its democratic mandate to make laws for the people of Scotland is beyond question. Acts that the Scottish Parliament enacts which are within its legislative competence enjoy, in that respect, the highest legal authority. The United Kingdom Parliament has vested in the Scottish Parliament the authority to make laws that are within its devolved competence. It is nevertheless a body to which decision making powers have been delegated. And it does not enjoy the sovereignty of the Crown in Parliament that, as Lord Bingham said in Jackson, para 9, is the bedrock of the British

constitution. Sovereignty remains with the United Kingdom Parliament. The Scottish Parliament's power to legislate is not unconstrained. It cannot make or unmake any law it wishes. Section 29(1) declares that an Act of the Scottish Parliament is not law so far as any provision of the Act is outside the legislative competence of the Parliament. Then there is the role which has been conferred upon this court by the statute, if called upon to do so, to judge whether or not Acts of the Parliament are within its legislative competence: see section 33(1) and paragraphs 32 and 33 of Schedule 6, as amended by section 40 and paragraphs 96 and 106 of Schedule 9 to the Constitutional Reform Act 2005. The question whether an Act of the Scottish Parliament is within the competence of the Scottish Parliament is also a devolution issue within the meaning of paragraph 1(a) of Schedule 6 to the Scotland Act in respect of which proceedings such as this may be brought in the Scottish courts.

[47]. Against this background, as there is no provision in the Scotland Act which excludes this possibility, I think that it must follow that in principle Acts of the Scottish Parliament are amenable to the supervisory jurisdiction of the Court of Session at common law. The much more important question is what the grounds are, if any, on which they may be subjected to review.

[48]. There is very little guidance as to how this question should be answered in the authorities. I do not think that we get much help from cases such as *R v Secretary of the State for the Environment, Ex P Nottinghamshire County Council* [1986] AC 240, *R v Secretary of State for the Environment, Ex p Hammersmith and Fulham London Borough Council* [1991] 1 AC 521 and *Edinburgh District Council v Secretary of State for Scotland* 1985 SC 261. They were concerned with the exercise of delegated powers by ministers and, as the judges of the First Division said, 2011 SLT 439, para 83, none of them is directly in point in this case. All I would take from them is that, even in these cases, a high threshold has been set. I also think that the situation that was considered in *R (Asif Javed) v Secretary of State for the Home Department* [2001] EWCA Civ 789, [2002] QB 129 which was concerned with a draft order which was laid by the Secretary of State and approved by both Houses of Parliament is so different from that which arises here that it can safely be left on one side. The fact is that, as a challenge to primary legislation at common law was simply impossible while the only legislature was the sovereign Parliament of the United Kingdom at Westminster, we are in this case in uncharted territory. The issue has to be addressed as one of principle.

[49]. The dominant characteristic of the Scottish Parliament is its firm rooting in the traditions of a universal democracy. It draws its strength from the electorate. While the judges, who are not elected, are best placed to protect the rights of the individual, including those who are ignored or despised by the majority, the elected members of a legislature of this kind are best placed to judge what is in the country's best interests as a whole. A sovereign Parliament is, according to the traditional view, immune from judicial scrutiny because it is protected by the principle of sovereignty. But it shares with the devolved legislatures, which are not sovereign, the advantages that flow from the depth and width of the experience of its elected members and the mandate that has been given to them by the electorate. This suggests that the judges should intervene, if at all, only in the most exceptional circumstances. As Lord Bingham of Cornhill said in *R (Countryside Alliance)*

v Attorney General [2007] UKHL 52, [2008] AC 719, para 45, the democratic process is liable
to be subverted if, on a question of political or moral judgment, opponents of an Act achieve
through the courts what they could not achieve through Parliament.

Lord Reed: [135]. The appellants maintain in their pleadings that, in passing the 2009
Act, the Scottish Parliament acted in a manner which was unreasonable, irrational and
arbitrary, and that the Act should therefore be quashed by the court. The Lord Ordinary
accepted that Acts of the Scottish Parliament were subject to judicial review on the
ground of irrationality, but considered that the scope for review could be no wider, and
might be narrower, than that permitted in respect of United Kingdom subordinate
instruments carrying direct Parliamentary approval, as explained by Lord Bridge of
Harwich in *R v Secretary of State for the Environment, Ex p Hammersmith and Fulham
London Borough Council* [1991] 1 AC 521 at p 597: that is to say, an Act of the Scottish
Parliament was not open to challenge on the ground of irrationality short of the extremes
of bad faith, improper motive or manifest absurdity. He added that even if he had taken
a contrary view, he would not in any event have closed the door on the possibility that
the courts might require to intervene in defence of the rule of law and the fundamental
rights and liberties of the subject. The judges of the First Division considered that review
for irrationality was not apt in the context of the 2009 Act because the aspects of the Act
whose rationality was challenged were essentially political questions which a court would
not enter upon. The court appears therefore to have considered that whether an Act of
the Scottish Parliament could be judicially reviewed on the ground of irrationality would
depend upon an assessment of the justiciability of the issue raised in the particular case.
They added that the court might well hold itself entitled to intervene in the event of
a deliberate misuse of power, or if the Scottish Parliament were to take a measure of the
kind contemplated by Lord Steyn in *R (Jackson) v Attorney General* [2005] UKHL 56,
[2006] 1 AC 262, para 102.

. . .

[140]. It cannot however be assumed that the grounds upon which the lawfulness of an
Act of the Scottish Parliament may be reviewed include all, or any, of the grounds upon
which the Court of Session may exercise its supervisory jurisdiction in other contexts. In *West
v Secretary of State for Scotland*, Lord President Hope referred at p 397 to: 'the distinction
which must be made between the question of competency as to whether a decision is open
to review by the Court of Session in the exercise of its supervisory jurisdiction, and the
substantive grounds on which it may do so. The extent of the supervisory jurisdiction is
capable of a relatively precise definition, in which the essential principles can be expressed.
But the substantive grounds on which that jurisdiction may be exercised will of course vary
from case to case. And they may be adapted to conform to the standards of decision-taking
as they are evolved from time to time by the common law.' As that dictum makes clear, the
grounds of review must be related to the nature of the power whose exercise is under
review.

. . .

[151]. As I have said, the court determines the powers of the Scottish Parliament by
applying the principles of statutory interpretation, taking into account the nature and

purpose of the statute under consideration. One familiar principle of statutory interpretation is the principle of legality explained by Lord Hoffmann in *R v Secretary of State for the Home Department, Ex p Simms* [2000] 2 AC 115 at p 131, in the dictum to which Lord Steyn referred in the case of *Anufrijeva*: 'Fundamental rights cannot be overridden by general or ambiguous words. This is because there is too great a risk that the full implications of their unqualified meaning may have passed unnoticed in the democratic process. In the absence of express language or necessary implication to the contrary, the courts therefore presume that even the most general words were intended to be subject to the basic rights of the individual. In this way the courts of the United Kingdom, though acknowledging the sovereignty of Parliament, apply principles of constitutionality little different from those which exist in countries where the power of the legislature is expressly limited by a constitutional document.'

[152]. The principle of legality means not only that Parliament cannot itself override fundamental rights or the rule of law by general or ambiguous words, but also that it cannot confer on another body, by general or ambiguous words, the power to do so . . .

[153]. The nature and purpose of the Scotland Act appear to me to be consistent with the application of that principle. As Lord Rodger of Earlsferry said in *R v HM Advocate* [2002] UKPC D 3, 2003 SC (PC) 21, para 16, the Scotland Act is a major constitutional measure which altered the government of the United Kingdom; and his Lordship observed that it would seem surprising if it failed to provide effective public law remedies, since that would mark it out from other constitutional documents. In *Robinson v Secretary of State for Northern Ireland* [2002] UKHL 32, [2002] NI 390, para 11, Lord Bingham of Cornhill said of the Northern Ireland Act 1998 that its provisions should be interpreted 'bearing in mind the values which the constitutional provisions are intended to embody'. That is equally true of the Scotland Act. Parliament did not legislate in a vacuum: it legislated for a liberal democracy founded on particular constitutional principles and traditions. That being so, Parliament cannot be taken to have intended to establish a body which was free to abrogate fundamental rights or to violate the rule of law.

The *UK Withdrawal from the European Union (Legal Continuity)(Scotland) Bill Reference* [2018] UKSC 64, [2019] AC 1022 (*The Scottish Continuity Bill*)

This case marks the first and, to date, only reference to the UK Supreme Court by the UK Government of the compatibility of an Act of the Scottish Parliament prior to its enactment. It raised important constitutional issues in the context of Brexit (discussed more fully below). In addition, issues arose both as to the interpretation of the Scotland Act 1998 and as to the time as to when the legality of an Act of the Scottish Parliament should be assessed – when it is enacted or when it would come into force? This issue arose as, in the interim between the enactment of the legislation and the hearing of the Supreme Court, the UK Parliament enacted the European Union (Withdrawal) Act 2018, which included a provision adding this legislation to the list of those in Schedule 4 of the Scotland Act 1998 that may not be modified or amended by the Scottish Parliament.

First, the Supreme Court concluded that the validity of legislation has to be determined when the court decides on the legality of this legislation and not when it is enacted. This is of particular constitutional importance as it means that not only can the UK Government challenge the validity of Acts of the Scottish Parliament, but also it is then possible for the UK Government to persuade the UK Parliament to enact legislation to specifically limit the powers of the Scottish Parliament, potentially undermining or restricting the Act of the Scottish Parliament that is subject to a legal challenge. If this power is abused, it has the potential to undermine the devolution settlement.

Second, the Supreme Court concluded that the common law limit on the law-making power of the Scottish Parliament was not applicable to a reference brought under section 33(1) of the Scotland Act 1998. This procedure was limited to determinations as to whether the Scottish Parliament had acted beyond the scope of its powers as set out in section 29 of the Scotland Act 1998.

Third, the decision clarified what was meant by a modification of UK legislation for the purposes of the application of Schedule 4 of the Scotland Act 1998. Modification did not arise if the Scottish Parliament merely enacted legislation in the same field of law as a UK statute listed in Schedule 4. However, modification need not be express. An implied amendment, disapplication or repeal, in whole or in part, would suffice. This issue arose in particular as regards section 17 of the bill. This clause required Westminster ministers to obtain the consent of Scottish ministers when exercising delegated powers in a devolved area, specifically relating to legislation granted powers to UK ministers to modify retained EU law.

[51]. As appears from the authorities cited by the Lord Advocate, one enactment does not modify another merely because it makes additional provision in the same field of law. If it did, the important distinction between the protection of enactments from modification under Schedule 4 to the Scotland Act, and the inability of the Scottish Parliament to legislate in relation to reserved matters under Schedule 5, would become obscured. When the UK Parliament decides to reserve an entire area of the law to itself, it does so by listing the relevant subject matter in Schedule 5. When it has not taken that step, but has protected a particular enactment from modification by including it in Schedule 4, it is not to be treated as if it had listed the subject matter of the enactment in Schedule 5. Where the only relevant restriction on the legislative power of the Scottish Parliament is the protection of an enactment from modification under Schedule 4, the Parliament has the power to enact legislation relating to the same subject matter as the protected enactment, provided it does not modify it. Without attempting an exhaustive definition, a protected enactment will be modified by a later enactment, even in the absence of express amendment or repeal, if it is implicitly amended, disapplied or repealed in whole or in part. That will be the position if the later enactment alters a rule laid down in the protected enactment, or is otherwise in conflict

with its unqualified continuation in force as before, so that the protected enactment has to be understood as having been in substance amended, superseded, disapplied or repealed by the later one.

[52]. Applying that approach, we are unable to accept the Lord Advocate's submission that section 28(7) of the Scotland Act would not be modified by section 17 of the Bill. As the Lord Advocate acknowledges, the power of the UK Parliament to make laws for Scotland includes the power to make laws authorising the making of subordinate legislation by Ministers and other persons. An enactment of the Scottish Parliament which prevented such subordinate legislation from having legal effect, unless the Scottish Ministers gave their consent, would render the effect of laws made by the UK Parliament conditional on the consent of the Scottish Ministers. It would therefore limit the power of the UK Parliament to make laws for Scotland, since Parliament cannot meaningfully be said to 'make laws' if the laws which it makes are of no effect. The imposition of such a condition on the UK Parliament's law-making power would be inconsistent with the continued recognition, by section 28(7) of the Scotland Act, of its unqualified legislative power. Thus, in order for section 17 of the Bill and section 28(7) of the Scotland Act to operate concurrently, the former would have to be treated as impliedly amending the latter, so that it read:

'(7) Subject to section 17 of the UK Withdrawal from the European Union (Legal Continuity) (Scotland) Act 2018, this section does not affect the power of the Parliament of the United Kingdom to make laws for Scotland.'

[53]. That conclusion is not altered by the other arguments advanced by the Lord Advocate. In relation to the first argument (para 47 above), a provision which made the effect of laws made by the UK Parliament for Scotland conditional on the consent of the Scottish Ministers, unless it disapplied or repealed the provision in question, would for that very reason be inconsistent with the continued recognition of its unqualified sovereignty, and therefore tantamount to an amendment of section 28(7) of the Scotland Act. In relation to the second argument (para 48 above), the question before the court is whether, if the Bill were to receive Royal Assent, section 17 would be law. If not, there would be no question of its having to be disapplied or repealed by the UK Parliament: it would be of no legal effect whatsoever ('not law', in terms of section 29(1) of the Scotland Act). It is therefore no answer to an argument that section 17 of the Bill would be outside legislative competence, to say that it could be disapplied or repealed. In relation to the third argument (para 49 above), this submission resembles the Lord Advocate's first argument, and for similar reasons we are unable to accept it. A provision which imposes a condition on the legal effect of laws made by the UK Parliament, in so far as they apply to Scotland, is in conflict with the continuation of its sovereign power to make laws for Scotland, and is therefore equivalent to the amendment of section 28(7) of the Scotland Act. The suggested analogy reinforces the point. If a provision of a Bill passed by the Scottish Parliament were to prevent legislation enacted by the UK Parliament from coming into force without the Scottish Ministers' consent, that provision would undoubtedly limit the UK Parliament's power to make laws for Scotland.

[54]. For these reasons, we conclude that section 17 of the Bill would modify section 28(7) of the Scotland Act, contrary to section 29(2)(c) and paragraph 4(1) of Schedule 4. Having reached that conclusion, it is unnecessary for us to consider whether section 17 of the Bill would also breach the restriction in paragraph 4(1) of Schedule 4 by modifying section 63(1).

Fourth, the decision clarified the approach of the Supreme Court when determining whether Acts of the Scottish Parliament 'relate to' a reserved matter, and are thereby outwith the competence of the Scottish Parliament. The UK Government had argued that the Scottish Continuity Bill as a whole related to a reserved matter as it regulated how EU law would be retained in Scotland post-Brexit, and thereby was 'related to' 'relations with the European Union', which are reserved to the Westminster Parliament. In making this argument, the UK Government adopted a purposive approach to the Scottish Continuity Bill, regarding its purpose as dealing with relations with the EU in a manner specific to Scotland, whereas this issue was reserved to the UK. The Supreme Court rejected this argument. In doing so, it reaffirmed the approach in *Martin* v. *Most* and *Imperial Tobacco Ltd* v. *Lord Advocate* that in order to 'relate to' a reserved matter, the provisions of the proposed Act of the Scottish Parliament must have 'more than a loose or consequential connection' to the reserved matter. While it was important to examine the purpose and not just the specific provisions of the Scottish bill, the Supreme Court should not take account of the political motivations of the Scottish Parliament when enacting the legislation in question before the court. Applying this approach to the Scottish Continuity Bill, the Supreme Court concluded (at [31]) that it was:

not within the carve-out from the reserved matter for the observation or implementation of obligations under EU law. It has nothing to do with the observation or implementation of those obligations. If the Scottish Bill becomes law, its provisions will not affect the law of Scotland until after withdrawal, i.e. at a time when the UK has no EU law obligations . . . The Scottish Bill is concerned with the purely domestic rules of law which at that point will replace EU law. The fact that those domestic rules may be substantially the same as the rules which previously applied as a matter of EU law does not make them obligations under EU law. Their juridical source is purely domestic.

Neither did the bill relate to the reserved matter of the UK's relations with the EU.

[33]. In our judgment, the Scottish Bill does not 'relate to' relations with the EU. It will take effect at a time when there will be no legal relations with the EU unless a further treaty is made with the EU. The Bill does not purport to deal with any legal rule affecting the power of Ministers of the Crown to negotiate such a treaty or otherwise to conduct the UK's relations

with the EU. It does not purport to affect the way in which current negotiations between the UK and the EU are conducted. It simply regulates the legal consequences in Scotland of the cessation of EU law as a source of domestic law relating to devolved matters, which will result from the withdrawal from the EU already authorised by the UK Parliament. This is something that the Scottish Parliament is competent to do, provided (i) that it does it consistently with the powers reserved in the Scotland Act to the UK Parliament, and with legislation and rules of law protected under Schedule 4, and (ii) that its legislation does not relate to other reserved matters. Parts of the argument of the UK Law Officers appear to suggest a wider objection that separate Scottish legislation about the consequences of withdrawal is legally untidy, politically inconvenient or redundant in the light of the corresponding UK legislation. But we are not concerned with supposed objections of this kind, which go to the wisdom of the legislation and not to its competence.

[34]. Different considerations may arise if and when further legislation is required to implement any agreement which Ministers of the Crown may negotiate with the EU governing the terms of withdrawal or the subsequent relations of the UK with the EU. But that is a matter which will have to be addressed when that legislation comes to be proposed.

[35]. The UK Law Officers' case on these points is not assisted by reference to the constitutional framework underlying the devolution settlement or the principles of legal certainty and legality. The constitutional framework underlying the devolution settlement is neither more nor less than what is contained in the Scotland Act construed on principles which are now well settled. And there is nothing legally uncertain or otherwise contrary to the rule of law about the enactment of legislation governing the domestic legal consequences of withdrawal at both the UK and the Scottish level, provided that they do not conflict, a question which is addressed below.

The final paragraph is particularly important. It makes it clear that the UK Government cannot object to the Scottish Parliament's enacting legislation that diverges from that of the Westminster Parliament, even when this concerns an issue of constitutional importance. All that matters is whether the legislation is within the competence of the Scottish Parliament as set out in the provisions of the Scotland Act 1998. This rebutted the claim by the Westminster Government that the Scottish Continuity Bill was beyond the scope of the powers of the Scottish Parliament as it was contrary to the constitutional framework that underpins devolution.

4.2.1.3.2 The Scottish Government

The Scotland Act 1998 provides for a Scottish Government consisting of ministers, other officeholders and their staff. All these are servants of the Crown. Non-ministerial officeholders and members of staff belong to the unified home Civil Service of the UK.

The Crown is one and indivisible but may have distinct capacities, and the Scotland Act distinguishes between 'the Crown in right of Her Majesty's

Government in the United Kingdom' and 'the Crown in right of the Scottish Administration'. By section 99, the Crown in either of these capacities may enter into legal relations with, and take legal proceedings against, the Crown in its other capacity. Accordingly, contracts and other legal arrangements may be made between the Scottish and the UK Governments, and may be enforced in legal proceedings.

Within the Scottish Government executive power is exercised in devolved matters, in a 'cabinet-style' government. What follows is a summary of its main attributes and powers (see, in more detail, Himsworth, 'The Domesticated Executive of Scotland', in Craig and Tomkins (eds.), *The Executive and Public Law* (2006), ch. 6):

(1) The Scottish Government is composed of a first minister, ministers appointed by the first minister, including a deputy first minister, and the Scottish law officers (the Lord Advocate and the Solicitor General for Scotland). They are known collectively as the Scottish ministers. They may be assisted by junior ministers. These latter, together with all members of the government except the law officers, must be members of the Parliament. Consistent with the Westminster model of cabinet government, Scottish ministers are individually responsible for their portfolios (the matters allocated to them by the first minister), take part in decision-making and are collectively responsible for the decisions taken. The first minister is nominated by the Parliament and appointed by the monarch; ministers and junior ministers are appointed by the first minister with the agreement of the Parliament and the approval of the monarch. The law officers are appointed by the monarch on the recommendation of the first minister, acting with the agreement of the Parliament. In 2020 there were eleven cabinet secretaries or senior ministers (including the first minister), together with sixteen junior ministers.

(2) The Scottish Government is accountable to the Scottish Parliament. Its members may be required by the Parliament or its committees to appear before them and give evidence. If the Parliament resolves that the government no longer enjoys its confidence, the government must resign.

(3) Functions (powers and duties, including powers of subordinate legislation) that formerly belonged to the Secretary of State for Scotland, or to other UK ministers in regard to Scotland, have been transferred generally – so far as they fall within the devolved field – to Scottish ministers (section 53). Additional functions may be transferred by order in council ('executive devolution orders') from ministers of the Crown to Scottish ministers under section 63. The first executive devolution order (SI 1999/1750) transferred over 400 functions to the Scottish ministers and further transfers have been made by subsequent orders. Legislation of the Scottish Parliament itself may entrust new functions to

Scottish ministers in devolved matters and may empower them to make subordinate legislation.

(4) The Scottish Government is bound to implement EU obligations in the devolved field and may not act incompatibly with EU law (section 57(2)) until the end of the implementation period completion day.

(5) Subordinate legislation and other acts of the Scottish Government must be compatible with convention rights (Scotland Act 1998, section 57(2)).

(6) There continues to be a Secretary of State for Scotland with a seat in the cabinet, although the transfer of almost all the functions of the Scotland Office to Scottish ministers greatly reduces the range of his or her responsibilities. Under the Scotland Act, the Secretary of State (it can be *any* Secretary of State) has certain powers of intervention to safeguard UK interests. Under section 35, the Secretary of State may make an order prohibiting the presiding officer of the Parliament from submitting a bill for royal assent if he or she has reasonable grounds to believe that its provisions would be incompatible with international obligations or the interests of defence or national security, or would adversely affect the operation of the law in reserved matters. Section 58 gives the Secretary of State the power to revoke subordinate legislation of the Scottish Government on similar grounds and to give directions to the Scottish Government to ensure compliance with international obligations. (Note also the further powers conferred on UK ministers by section 107.) A new law officer, the Advocate General for Scotland, was created by section 87 of the Scotland Act. The Advocate General for Scotland is responsible for advising the UK government on matters of Scots law. (The far older offices of Lord Advocate and Solicitor General became the law officers of the Scottish Government.)

4.2.2 Wales

Wales is about one-twelfth the size of the UK and has a population of just over 3 million, or about 5 per cent of the total UK population. Wales came under the rule of the English Crown in the thirteenth century. There was no treaty of union, then or later, between the two countries, and the Act of Union of 1536 was a unilateral act of the English Parliament, extending the English administrative system to Wales and providing for Welsh representation in Parliament.

In the early years of the twentieth century, a number of departments with Welsh responsibilities were created (e.g., the Welsh Board of Health and the Welsh Department of the Board of Education) and from 1951 a senior departmental minister (at first the Home Secretary) was given a general responsibility for Wales with the title of Minister for Welsh affairs. A secretaryship of state for Wales was created by the Wilson Government in 1964, and since then there has been a Secretary of State for Wales, with a seat in the Cabinet, in charge of the Welsh Office (since 1999, the Wales Office).

The responsibilities of the Secretary of State for Wales were substantially increased in the years after 1964. They did not become quite so wide-ranging as those of the Secretary of State for Scotland, for, as we have seen, the Scottish Office had a longer history of 'separateness' and administered Scotland's own judicial and legal systems. To a great extent government policies were executed in Wales by local authorities and by some twenty-four (in 1998) executive NDPBs overseen by the Welsh Office (e.g., the Welsh Development Agency and the Welsh Language Board).

It was remarked by the House of Commons Welsh Affairs Committee that the framework of policy was generally 'set by English government departments and copied by the Welsh Office with greater or lesser variations to suit Welsh circumstances' (*1st Report of 1992–93*, HC 259, para 3). The secretary of state and the Welsh Office were also, no doubt, sometimes able to bring Welsh interests into account when government policies were being formulated. Contrariwise, the Welsh secretary was bound by collective responsibility and by the policies of the governing party, whether or not these were to the advantage of Wales or coincided with the wishes of a majority of Welsh voters (see Bogdanor, *Devolution in the United Kingdom* (1999), pp. 160–1).

At present, Wales returns forty MPs to the House of Commons. Wales is over-represented in the house on the basis of the size of its electorate, which would strictly entitle it to no more than thirty-three seats. To begin with, no change was made in Welsh representation in consequence of devolution, but under the Parliamentary Voting System and Constituencies Act 2011 the number of Welsh seats is scheduled to be reduced to thirty. This change has yet to be implemented – although constituency boundary changes formed part of the manifesto of the current Conservative Government.

Parliamentary legislation relating exclusively to Wales was uncommon before devolution: examples are the Welsh Language Act 1993 and the Local Government (Wales) Act 1994. Arrangements were put in place in the House of Commons for debating Welsh affairs and for scrutinising the administration of Wales. A Welsh grand committee, consisting of all MPs for Wales and up to five other members, considered bills and other matters relating exclusively to Wales and could question Welsh Office ministers. In addition, a Select Committee on Welsh Affairs examined 'the expenditure, administration and policy of the Welsh Office and associated public bodies'. Both committees have continued to function since devolution.

4.2.2.1 First Phase: Devolution under the Government of Wales Act 1998 – Executive Devolution

In the 1980s and 1990s, Wales, like Scotland, was governed by a Conservative administration that only a minority of voters in Wales supported. Unlike Scotland, however, Wales experienced no equivalent of the Scottish

Constitutional Convention. There was no Welsh equivalent to the Scottish Claim of Right (see above, p. 259) and, by the time of Labour's election victory in 1997, there was no fresh blueprint for Welsh devolution to supersede the discredited model of the 1970s. Nonetheless, the new Labour Government, conscious of what it described as Wales' distinctive 'language and cultural traditions', was committed to 'meet the demand for decentralisation of power to ... Wales, once established in [a] referendum' (Labour Party manifesto, *Because Britain Deserves Better* (1997), p. 33). As we saw above (p. 260), the referendum produced a positive result (albeit by only the tightest of margins) and the result was the Government of Wales Act 1998. Commenting on the differences between Scotland and Wales, Sir David Williams observed as follows (in University of Cambridge Centre of Public Law, *Constitutional Reform in the United Kingdom* (1998), p. 44):

> There has never been an independent Welsh Parliament on an established basis and hence no overall executive government. Welsh law – at least in this millennium ... has been English law; and, despite the Courts of Great Sessions (finally abolished in 1830) there has been no separate system of courts for Wales. The 'trappings' of legislative devolution are not, as they are to some extent in Scotland, in place, and the process of administrative decentralisation has been more recent and less extensive. For many Scots legislative devolution might appear, especially in the light of three decades of deliberations, to be a small step in constitutional terms; for many Welsh it might appear to be a giant leap.

The original arrangement for Wales, unlike that for Scotland, was to be a scheme of *executive* devolution: no powers of primary law-making or of taxation were devolved. The essential purpose of the Government of Wales Act 1998 was to place the existing Welsh administration and its NDPBs (quangos) under the control of an elected Welsh Assembly, which would have the power to make delegated or secondary legislation, but not primary legislation.

To this end, the Act established an Assembly for Wales, known as the National Assembly for Wales or *Cynulliad Cenedlaethol Cymru*. The assembly was a body corporate that exercised its functions 'on behalf of the Crown' (section 1). Like the Scottish Parliament, it is a unicameral assembly. It comprises sixty members (known as AMs), forty elected in single member constituencies under the first-past-the-post system and twenty by the party list system. The functions of the Welsh Office that were devolved to Wales were transferred to the assembly by the Government of Wales Act 1998 itself, by subsequent acts of Parliament and by orders in council made under section 22 of the 1998 Act. These functions fell within the eighteen fields listed in Schedule 2 to the Act as follows: agriculture, forestry, fisheries and food; ancient monuments and historic buildings; culture (including museums, galleries and libraries); economic development; education and training; the environment; health; highways; housing; industry; local government;

planning; social services; sport; tourism; transport; water and flood defence; and the Welsh language.

A considerable devolution of functions and powers (deriving from some 300 statutes) took place, but there remained many functions exercisable in relation to Wales by ministers of the Crown that were not transferred. (These include such matters as are reserved under the Scotland Act, as well as others.)

Unlike the provision made for Scotland, the Government of Wales Act did not establish a separate executive body for the government of Wales: functions to be devolved, with corresponding powers and duties, were conferred on the assembly itself as a corporate body. In practice, however, a form of cabinet government emerged, most of the assembly's executive powers being delegated to the assembly first secretary and assembly secretaries, who, from 2002 onwards, came to be known as Welsh ministers and collectively, together with civil servants, as the Welsh Assembly Government.

The Welsh Office (Wales Office) continues to exist as a department of central government, headed by the Secretary of State for Wales. The Secretary of State for Wales is the key government figure liaising with the devolved administration in Wales and represents Wales' interests in the cabinet and in Parliament. (See, further, Welsh Affairs Select Committee, *Wales and Whitehall, 11th Report of 2009–10*, HC 246.)

4.2.2.2 Dissatisfaction with the 1998 Scheme for Wales

Unlike in Scotland, it was never clear that the Government of Wales Act 1998 solved the problem it was designed to address. Perhaps this is because (again, unlike in Scotland) it was not clear what the problem was in the first place. It was as if Wales were being dragged along in Scotland's wake, offered something of devolution but never as much as was offered to (or demanded by) the Scots. This was nothing new: as Sir David Williams put it ('Devolution: The Welsh Perspective', in Tomkins (ed.), *Devolution and the British Constitution* (1998), pp. 21–2): 'In the 1970s the dominance of Scotland in the devolution debates largely obscured the Welsh dimension, and the process has been repeated in the later 1990s.' Further, he continued, 'there is little or no constitutional framework or context in which the proposals for executive devolution can properly be assessed.' What led Welsh devolution in the late 1990s, it seems, was not an echo of the consistent and coherent demand for home rule that had been heard so resoundingly in Scotland, but an inchoate and far from unanimous sense within the Labour Party that, in the light of developments in Scotland, *something* ought also to be offered to Wales. Exactly what that 'something' should amount to, it seems, was determined as much by reference to internal squabbles within the Labour Party as to any constitutional road map. As Rawlings has written, 'the original scheme suffered from a lack of constitutional vision, [being the] product of a closed and elite form of constitution-making grounded in internal party compromise' ('Hastening Slowly: The

Next Phase of Welsh Devolution' [2006] *PL* 824, 826; see, further, Rawlings, *Delineating Wales* (2003), pp. 1–52).

In an effort to add constitutional clarity and direction to the uncertain start of Welsh devolution, the Welsh Assembly Government commissioned a report in 2002 on 'the powers and the electoral arrangements of the National Assembly for Wales'. A commission of ten members, chaired by the Labour peer Lord Richard, reported in March 2004 (see www.richardcommission.gov.uk).

The report of the Richard Commission offered two ways forward, one of which could be accommodated within the framework of the Government of Wales Act 1998 and the other of which would require new Westminster legislation. The former possibility was outlined in chapter 13 of the report:

> [A] possibility would be for the powers of the Assembly to develop within the existing Government of Wales Act framework, but with much broader legislative powers. The objective would be to enable the Government in the Assembly to deliver its programme, but through specific powers delegated to it by Parliament.
>
> There are no formal legal or constitutional rules that define what should be the subject of primary rather than secondary legislation … [T]he current settlement depends on what Parliament decides, on a measure by measure basis, shall be provided through primary legislation and what through secondary legislation. Accordingly, the Assembly's powers could be strengthened within the current settlement by including in future primary legislation new framework provisions designed to allow the Assembly to, for example, make through secondary legislation any changes it wishes within the field covered by the Act …
>
> There are precedents for a more permissive approach to the Assembly's powers: the Education Act 2002; and the NHS Reform and Healthcare Professions Act 2002 and the Health (Wales) Act 2003, which confer on the Assembly powers to amend certain primary legislation. Although the powers granted under these Acts do not give the Assembly the freedom to do anything it chooses within the scope of the Act, the two Health Acts in particular do confer some broad powers on the Assembly to shape NHS delivery in Wales.

The second solution recommended by the Richard Commission was to confer by fresh legislation new powers on the assembly to make primary legislation. In the event, the UK Government opted for a combination of the two schemes, albeit that the ability of the assembly to make primary legislation would come in a series of steps, and not immediately: see its White Paper, *Better Governance for Wales* (Cm 6582/2005) and the legislation it spawned: the Government of Wales Act 2006, to which we can now turn.

4.2.2.3 Second Phase: Devolution under the Government of Wales Act 2006 – The Move Towards Legislative Devolution

The Government of Wales Act 2006, when enacted, had three main aims: to effect a formal separation of powers between the executive and the legislative branches of the assembly; to reform electoral arrangements; and to enhance the legislative powers of the assembly.

To take each of these in turn, under the act, the Welsh Assembly Government is established for the first time as an entity separate from, but accountable to, the national assembly (sections 45–8). Welsh ministers act on behalf of the Crown rather than as delegates of the assembly, but will have to resign from office if they lose the confidence of the assembly. A new office of counsel general is created, the postholder being responsible for providing legal advice to the assembly government on matters relating to their devolved functions (section 49). Most of the statutory functions that under the 1998 Act were exercised in the name of the assembly have under the 2006 Act formally become the responsibility of the Welsh ministers (sections 56–8).

The main change in the electoral arrangements is the new rule that individuals are no longer able to be candidates in constituency elections and at the same time be eligible for election as regional members from party lists (section 7). In the 2003 assembly elections, seventeen of the twenty AMs elected from the regional party lists were candidates who had stood in, but had lost, constituency elections. These included the candidates who had come second, third and even fourth in the Clwyd West constituency. In the government's view, this was both confusing for electors and unfair, making winners out of losers, but in the view of other parties the change was nothing more than a crude attempt on the part of the government to rig future elections in favour of the Labour Party, as it would be the Liberal Democrats and Plaid Cymru that would be most adversely affected by the new rule. Consequently, the proposed change was a matter of considerable controversy as the Government of Wales Bill made its progress through Parliament. Indeed, there was some doubt whether the bill would be passed at all, such was the hostility to this provision in the House of Lords. In the event, however, the government got its way.

The enhancement of the assembly's legislative powers was complex and was divided into three stages. The first (as recommended by the Richard Commission, above) saw the conferral of wider powers on the assembly to make subordinate legislation. This change, as explained above, did not require fresh legislation and had already commenced under the framework of the Government of Wales Act 1998. The second and third stages were provided for in the Government of Wales Act 2006. The second stage consisted of an order in council mechanism whereby Parliament could confer enhanced legislative powers on the assembly in relation to specified subject matters which fall within devolved fields. Such orders in council – known as legislative competence orders (LCOs) – enabled the assembly to pass its own legislation within the scope of the powers delegated by Parliament. Such legislation was known as 'assembly measures' (sections 93–102).

It is important to note that, under these provisions, the 2006 Act did not itself confer additional powers on the assembly. Rather, it provided a mechanism whereby such powers could be conferred on a case-by-case basis as appropriate, with parliamentary consent. The 'devolved fields' with regard to which LCOs could have been made included: agriculture, fisheries, forestry and rural development; ancient monuments and historic buildings; culture; economic development; education and training; the environment; fire and rescue services and fire safety; food; health and health services; highways and transport; housing; local government; public administration; social welfare; sport and recreation; tourism; town and country planning; water and flood defence; and the Welsh language. The Act provided for the assembly and both Houses of Parliament to approve draft LCOs before they come into force.

In addition to the LCO process, an ordinary Act of Parliament could amend Schedule 5 to the Government of Wales Act 2006 by adding to (or, indeed, by reducing) the law-making powers of the assembly. The combination of legislative amendment and LCOs resulted in a heavily revised Schedule 5, which set out the legislative competences of the Welsh Assembly, that was so lengthy and complex it became difficult to navigate.

The third stage in the enhancement of the assembly's legislative powers was to confer primary legislative powers on the assembly to pass 'assembly acts' within devolved fields (sections 103–16). However, under the terms of the 2006 Act, these powers could not come into force unless they were approved in a further Welsh referendum (section 103). Such a referendum was held on 3 March 2011, resulting in a 'Yes' vote, replacing the power to enact assembly measures with the power to enact Acts of the Welsh Assembly.

4.2.2.4 Third Phase of Devolution: Power of the Assembly to Make Legislative Acts

The referendum outcome transferred legislative powers to the Welsh Assembly. However, devolution in Wales remained a system of conferred powers. These were found in section 108 of the Act, which empowers the Welsh Assembly to enact any measures that could have been made by an Act of Parliament, provided that this was in the sphere of legislative competences set out in Part 1 of Schedule 7 to the Act. This empowered the Welsh Assembly to enact measures that 'relate to one or more' of a list of areas of power, which included: agriculture, fisheries, forestry and rural development; ancient monuments and historical buildings; culture; economic development; education and training; the environment; fire and rescue; food; health and health services, highways and transport; housing; local government; public administration; social welfare; sport and recreation; tourism; town and country planning; water and flood defence; and the Welsh language. Section 108(7) states that the determination of whether legislation 'relates to' a subject matter set out in the Schedule 'is to be determined by reference to the purpose of the provision, having regard (among other things) to its effect in all the circumstances'. In addition, legislative acts of the Welsh Assembly could not be incompatible with EU law, or with convention rights (section 108(6)). All these broad areas of competence were subject to a series of exceptions, making it difficult to determine the precise scope of legislative competences conferred on the Welsh Assembly.

Difficulties arose as to the interpretation of the competences of the Welsh Assembly. This gave rise to a series of referrals using the procedure under section 112 of the Government of Wales Act 2006, which permits bills to be scrutinised to ensure they are within the competence of the Welsh Assembly prior to their enactment; focusing on whether the purpose and effect of the proposed bill was within the scope of conferred powers.

Re Agriculture Sector (Wales) Bill [2014] UKSC 43, [2014] 4 All ER 789

The Welsh legislature enacted measures to reinstate a regulatory framework for agricultural wages after the UK enacted legislation to abolish the Agricultural Wages Board. The question arose as to whether this amounted to the regulation of agricultural matters, which was within the competences conferred on the Welsh Assembly, or the regulation of an employment matter that had not been conferred. The Supreme Court concluded that the purpose of the bill was to support and protect the agricultural industry in Wales through regulating agricultural wages. Although the bill had an effect on wages, this did not mean that the bill was beyond the legislative competences of the Welsh Assembly. In reaching this conclusion, the Supreme Court set out the following principles of interpretation, drawn from the case law on Welsh and Scottish cases (at [6]):

i) The question whether a provision is outside the competence of the Assembly must be determined according to the particular rules that section 108 of, and Schedule 7 to, the GWA [Government of Wales Act] 2006, have laid down: see the *Local Government Byelaws (Wales) Bill 2012* case at para 79.

ii) The description of the GWA 2006 as an Act of great constitutional significance cannot be taken, in itself, to be a guide to its interpretation. The statute must be interpreted in the same way as any other statute: *Local Government Byelaws (Wales) Bill 2012*, para 80.

iii) When enacting the GWA 2006 Parliament had to define, necessarily in fairly general and abstract terms, permitted or prohibited areas of legislative activity. The aim was to achieve a constitutional settlement. It is proper to have regard to that purpose if help is needed as to what the words mean: see the *Local Government Byelaws (Wales) Bill 2012* case at para 80.

The Supreme Court defined 'agriculture' broadly – it could include regulation of the agricultural sector, including the regulation of wages which 'will have a direct effect on the agricultural industry in Wales' ([53]). Difficulties arose as the regulation of wages falls within the sphere of employment or industrial relations. However, the Government of Wales Act 2006 was 'silent' on whether 'employment' or 'industrial relations' fell within the competences of the Welsh

Assembly. They were neither specifically conferred on the Welsh Assembly in Schedule 7, nor listed as specific exceptions. There were some aspects of employment that were listed as exceptions to other areas of conferred powers – for example, the regulation of occupational pensions was specifically exempted from the conferred power of the regulation of economic development. Did this mean that the regulation of employment writ large was beyond the competences of the Welsh Assembly?

[60]. The model of devolution to Wales in the third phase of devolution . . . was to give the Assembly legislative competence only in relation to subjects expressly listed. Whether a provision relates to a listed subject is, as we have explained, to be determined under section 108 by considering the purpose and effect of the provision.

[61]. In the present case, for the reasons we have given, the Bill might in principle be regarded not only as relating to a subject listed as devolved, but also as relating to subjects which are not mentioned at all in the legislation. Employment and industrial relations are neither listed as devolved subjects, nor specified as exceptions.

[62]. It is therefore necessary to consider as the fourth issue the position where a Bill which relates to a listed subject might also be regarded as relating to other subjects of legislative activity which, although not specified as exceptions, are not listed as devolved. Is the consequence that such a Bill is not within the legislative competence of the Assembly?

[63]. It appears unlikely that this issue will frequently arise in relation to Welsh devolution. That is because Schedule 7, although briefer than the schedule of reserved matters in the Scotland Act 1998, contains a considerable number of exceptions which are applicable irrespective of the heading under which the exception is specified. The issue only arises in this reference because there is no exception of employment or industrial relations specified in the GWA 2006.

[64]. The Attorney General contended that the court should in a case such as this determine the 'real' purpose and objective effect of the Bill. He submitted that in reality the purpose and objective effect of the Bill did not relate to agriculture but to employment and industrial relations. It should therefore be so characterised. This was the way that the UK Ministry, the Department of the Environment Food and Rural Affairs, had characterised the issue when consulting on the future of the Agricultural Wages Board in October 2012. 'The Government is committed to providing an environment for all sectors of the economy in which private enterprise and businesses can flourish. To do so, the Government wishes to remove unnecessary red tape and administrative burden. A key coalition commitment is a cross-Government review of employment-related law which is taking forward a number of measures aimed at reducing burdens on business by simplifying employment legislation to give employers the flexibility to run their business effectively and have the confidence to take on staff and grow. The proposed abolition of the agricultural minimum wage and the Agricultural Wages Board is part of that overall wider review.'

[65]. We cannot accept that this is the approach which the language of the GWA 2006 requires or permits. We acknowledge that, in principle, there may be more than one way in which the purpose and effect of a Bill may be capable of being characterised. The present is

a case in point. A Bill which establishes a scheme for the regulation of agricultural wages can in principle reasonably be classified either as relating to agriculture or as relating to employment and industrial relations. Which classification is the more apt depends on the purpose for which the classification is being carried out, and on the classificatory scheme which has to be employed.

[66]. As we explained in para 6, the question whether a provision is outside the competence of the Assembly must be determined according to the particular rules that section 108 of, and Schedule 7 to, the GWA 2006, have laid down. The rules must be interpreted according to the ordinary meaning of the words used. In that way, a coherent, stable and workable outcome can be achieved.

[67]. As we have explained, the scheme of the conferred powers model adopted for Welsh devolution, as embodied in the GWA 2006, is to limit the legislative powers of the Assembly in relation to subjects listed in Schedule 7 by reference to the express exceptions and limitations contained in the Act, rather than via some dividing up of the subjects in Schedule 7 along lines not prescribed in the legislation. Under section 108(4) and (7), the Assembly has legislative competence if the Bill relates to one of the subjects listed in Part 1 of Schedule 7, provided it is not within one of the exceptions. In most cases, an exception will resolve the issue. Where however there is no exception, as in the present case, the legislative competence is to be determined in the manner set out in section 108. Provided that the Bill fairly and realistically satisfies the test set out in section 108(4) and (7) and is not within an exception, it does not matter whether in principle it might also be capable of being classified as relating to a subject which has not been devolved. The legislation does not require that a provision should only be capable of being characterised as relating to a devolved subject.

[68]. The Attorney General's submission would in effect compel us to re-write section 108 to make it operate in such a way as to add to the exceptions specified in Schedule 7. Instead of the specific exception which Parliament created in respect of occupational pension schemes, the court would create a much wider exception in respect of the remuneration of employees, or perhaps employment generally. Not only is that impermissible in principle, but it would in practice restrict the powers of the Assembly to legislate on subjects which were intended to be devolved to it: as the present case demonstrates, a Bill which undoubtedly relates to a devolved subject may also be capable of being classified as relating to a subject which is not devolved. Such an interpretation of section 108 would therefore give rise to an uncertain scheme that was neither stable nor workable. In contrast, the application of the clear test in section 108 provides for a scheme that is coherent, stable and workable.

The importance of this judgment stems both from the narrow reading of the specific exceptions and the recognition that, provided that a bill falls within the sphere of competences conferred on the Welsh Assembly, it does not matter if it could also fall within a sphere of competence on which the Government of Wales Act 2006 is silent. This provided a broad interpretation of the powers of the Welsh Assembly.

However, there are also examples of the powers being construed more narrowly. *In re Recovery of Medical Costs for Asbestos Diseases (Wales) Bill* [2015] UKSC 3, [2015] AC 1016, the counsel general requested a reference to the Supreme Court. Although he was confident that the legislation was within the powers of the Welsh Assembly, he wished to make a referral to prevent any future uncertainty on this issue. The bill, inter alia, imposed liability on those who had been legally required to make compensation payments to victims of asbestos-related diseases to pay the charges for the NHS services provided to those victims. Was this within the competence of the Welsh Assembly, as part of its competences of 'organising and funding the NHS,' or beyond its competences, given that, at the time, the Welsh Assembly had no general fiscal or revenue raising powers? The decision in *Re Agricultural Sector (Wales) Bill* might appear to suggest that the legislation *was* within the competence of the Welsh Assembly. It 'related to' the funding of the NHS by providing a means of funding the NHS. The minority in the Supreme Court agreed with this assessment. The 'organising and funding of the NHS' included a broad power to raise money for the NHS which extended to a policy of making the tortfeasor pay for the costs imposed on the NHS.

However, the majority concluded that the bill was beyond the powers of the Welsh legislature, concluding that the bill did not 'relate to' 'the organisation and funding of the national health service' because there was only an indirect connection between funding of the NHS and the bill:

> [26]. The provision of health services and the organisation and funding of the Welsh Health Service clearly cannot permit the Welsh Assembly to raise monies generally, by relying on the fact that any monies raised from any source increase the funds available for all its spending, including spending on the Health Service. The question is whether the position is different if the monies raised can be said to be specifically intended or hypothecated to provide funds for use in the Health Service. But, if that were sufficient, it would be difficult to see any real limit to the persons on whom or basis on which such charges might be imposed, provided only that the charges were levied on that express basis. The reality is also that, unless the charges are for research, treatment or other services which would not otherwise be undertaken or provided by the National Health Service, even a hypothecated charge is in substance no different from a general charge boosting the Welsh Government's resources.
>
> [27]. In these circumstances, any raising of charges permissible under para 9 would have, in my opinion, to be more directly connected with the service provided and its funding. The mere purpose and effect of raising money which can or will be used to cover part of the costs of the Welsh NHS could not constitute a sufficiently close connection. In the case of prescription or other charges to users of the Welsh NHS service, a direct connection with the service and its funding exists, in that users are directly involved with and benefitting by the service. In the case of charges under section 2, the argument would have to be that a sufficient connection can be found in the actual or alleged wrongdoing that led to a compensator making a compensation payment to or in respect of a sufferer from an

asbestos-related disease. But that is at best an indirect, loose or consequential connection. The expression 'organisation and funding of national health service' could not, in my opinion, have been conceived with a view to covering what would amount in reality to rewriting the law of tort and breach of statutory duty by imposing on third persons (the compensators), having no other direct connection in law with the NHS, liability towards the Welsh Ministers to meet costs of NHS services provided to sufferers from asbestos-related diseases towards whom such third persons decide to make a compensation payment for liability which may or may not exist or have been established or admitted.

All of the Supreme Court concluded that the bill was beyond the competence of the Welsh Assembly as it breached Article 1 of the First Protocol of the ECHR.

Understandably, there were concerns as to the uncertainty surrounding the scope of devolved powers to Wales. These issues were exacerbated due to the asymmetries between devolution in Wales and Scotland.

4.2.2.5 Fourth Phase of Devolution: Greater Fiscal Powers and the Move to a Reserved Powers Model – Wales Act 2014 and Wales Act 2017

Following the outcome of the referendum, the Silk Commission was established in 2011. Its remit was to examine, in part 1, fiscal devolution and accountability, and, in part 2, the constitutional settlement, with the reports being produced in 2012 and 2013 respectively. The Silk Commission took place shortly after the Calman Commission, investigating devolution in Scotland, and the Holtham Commission, which was established to review the funding of Welsh devolution. The Holtham Commission, which published its final report in 2010, concluded that there should be some devolution of tax powers to Wales, but that, in practice, this was unlikely to be achieved before 2015. The commission was chaired by Paul Silk and consisted of four members nominated by each of the political parties in the then National Assembly for Wales and two independent members. The Silk Commission did not consider the Holtham Commission's proposals in the first part of its report, which was considered in intergovernmental discussion between Westminster and Wales.

In its first report, the Silk Commission was concerned that the then block grant system for Wales meant that, whilst the Welsh Government and Welsh Assembly were responsible to the Welsh electorate for how money was spent, it was not responsible in the same manner for how money was raised. The commission recommended a combination of a block grant and the devolution of some tax powers; including stamp duty, landfill tax, aggregates levies, long-haul air passenger tax rates and business rates. It also recommended a partial devolution of income tax. The majority of the recommended changes were implemented in the Wales Act 2014. In addition to providing for devolved taxation powers (Part 2 of the Act) and the provision to hold a referendum on whether to empower the Welsh Assembly to modify income tax by up to 10 pence in the pound, the Act also enables ordinary general elections in Wales to take place every five years as opposed to every four years, and removed the restriction on individuals standing as both a constituency and a regional candidate, provided that this was for the same party in the same constituency. This was seen as a means of providing a better ability for smaller parties to gain representation in the Welsh Assembly.

The second part of the Silk Commission made sixty-one recommendations. Its main recommendations included: a move from a conferred powers to a reserved powers model; improvements in intergovernmental relations, including recommending a statutory code on intergovernmental relations and a Welsh intergovernmental committee (composed of representatives from Wales and from Westminster) to oversee devolution in Wales; further devolution of transport powers, powers over natural resources, policing and the youth justice system, and greater control to the Welsh Assembly over its own proceedings and an increase in membership from sixty to, potentially, eighty members. The Secretary of State for Wales established a series of cross-party negotiations – the St David's Day Process. At the conclusion of this process, an agreed document was produced *Powers for a Purpose: Towards a Lasting Devolution Settlement for Wales* (2015, Cm 9020), which reported that there was a consensus for most, but not all, of the recommendations of Part II of the Silk Commission. The government then published a draft Wales bill.

Although there was general agreement surrounding a move to a reserved powers model, there were concerns both as to the content of the draft bill and the process through which the reserved powers had been determined. The Welsh affairs committee, for example, was critical of the lack of constructive consultation between the Welsh Office and the Welsh Government during the St David's Day process, focusing on how the government looked more to seeking a consensus rather than ensuring there was sufficient deliberation surrounding the scope of reserved powers (*Pre-Legislative Scrutiny of the Draft Wales Bill. First Report of 2015–16* HC 449, paras 26–7):

> There is a range of ways in which Government departments could have gathered views on where the devolution boundary should lie. One end of the spectrum would include an approach similar to that adopted for the Government's work on the balance of competences between the UK and the EU, whereby Government departments would consult widely and look in depth at each subject area. The results of the write-around suggest that the Whitehall departments replied with a list that maps out the existing legislative competence. We note the Secretary of State's comments that there has been pushback from the Wales Office with regard to the list of reservations, and we would welcome examples of where this has happened, and how Westminster departments responded.

It is in the interests of everyone that this settlement is long lasting and we are concerned that the approach to drawing up the reservations could undermine this. We conclude that a more hands-on approach from the Wales Office would have been preferable, whereby each department was asked to consult widely and was then challenged as to what they were and were not proposing should go on the list of reservations.

The Welsh Affairs Committee was also concerned that the draft Wales bill had responded to the Supreme Court's decision in the *Re Agricultural Sector (Wales) Bill* on silent powers by including the majority of these powers in the list of reserved powers; essentially repatriating a power within the powers of the Welsh Assembly under the conferred powers model and placing it back in the hands of Westminster. (See also Wales Governance Centre and the Constitution Unit, 'Challenge and Opportunity: The Draft Wales Bill 2015' (available at www.cardiff.ac.uk/data/assets/pdf_file/0011/1288694/Challenge-and-Opportunity-The-Draft-Wales-Bill-2015.pdf) and Welsh Assembly, Constitutional and Legislative Affairs Committee, 'Report on the UK Government's Draft Wales Bill' (available at https://senedd.wales/laid%20documents/cr-ld10468/cr-ld10468-e.pdf).) Concerns were also raised that Wales would only be able to legislate to modify the law on reserved matters, or to modify private law or criminal law 'if necessary' to implement policy. Given that these areas fell within 'silent powers' this was, again, seen to transfer power back to the UK, as well as creating a test that would be difficult to apply in practice. Concerns also arose as to whether the legislation enacted by the Welsh Assembly created a new body of law and, as such, whether this required Wales to be recognised as a separate legal jurisdiction. The Government of Wales was also critical of the draft bill, publishing its own alternative draft bill, the Government and Laws in Wales Bill 2016.

Given the criticisms of the original draft bill, this bill was put on pause. A different bill was later laid before Parliament – the Wales Bill 2016–17, which improved on the earlier draft bill. However, the new bill did not assuage all concerns, in particular, concerns still remain as to the extent to which silent powers have become reserved powers. Moreover, complexities persist given the exceptions listed to some of the powers reserved to Westminster, and the continuance of some of the necessity clauses.

The main characteristics of the powers of the Welsh Assembly – now the Senedd – can be summarised as follows:

(1) As with the Scottish Parliament and Government, the Senedd and the Welsh Government are recognised as a 'permanent part of the United Kingdom's constitutional arrangements', its being declared also that 'the Assembly and the Welsh Government are not to be abolished except on the basis of a decision of the people of Wales voting in a referendum'

(section A1 Government of Wales Act 2006). As with the provision in the Scotland Act 1998, this is intended to be merely declaratory.

(2) The Senedd has at present sixty members (MSs), elected by the additional member (or 'mixed member') system. Forty MSs are constituency MSs and twenty are regional MSs. After the most recent 2016 election, the government (thirty-one) is formed of twenty-nine Labour, one Liberal Democrat and one independent member. The opposition (twenty-nine) is composed of Conservative, Plaid Cymru, Brexit Party, UKIP, the Welsh National Party and independent MSs. Since the enactment of the Wales Act 2014, it is possible for an individual to be a candidate both for a constituency and a regional seat, provided that these are in the same area. The Senedd conducts debates in both English and Welsh.

(3) The Parliament is normally elected for a fixed term of five years, but exceptionally may be dissolved before the term has run. This will happen if the Senedd resolves, by a two-thirds majority of its members, that it should be dissolved, or if the Senedd is deadlocked in the choice of a first minister.

(4) The Parliament is a legislature of limited powers, its powers limited both by the Government of Wales Act 2006 (as amended) and the common law (see above). It is competent to legislate for England and Wales on devolved matters. However, an Act of the Senedd may not apply 'otherwise than in relation to Wales' or confer, impose, modify or remove 'functions exercisable otherwise than in relation to Wales' unless this is ancillary to the Act and 'has no greater effect otherwise than in relation to Wales, or in relation to functions exercisable otherwise than in relation to Wales, than is necessary to give effect to the purpose of that provision' (section 108A 2(b) and 108A (3)). Like the Scottish Parliament, the Senedd has no competence to legislate in a manner that is incompatible with convention rights or, until the end of the implementation period completion day, with EU law (Government of Wales Act 2006, section 108A(2)(e)).

(5) The Wales Act 2017 moved the Senedd to a system of reserved powers. The Government of Wales Act 2006 now specifies the powers *retained* at Westminster, not those devolved. Acts of the Senedd must not relate to a reserved matter. Schedule 7A provides the list of reserved matters. The UK Government may transfer more powers to Wales by an order in council (section 109).

The reserved matters include: the constitutional framework (the Crown, the union of the nations of Wales and England and the UK Parliament); international relations and the European Union (until the end of the implementation period completion day); the regulation of international trade; the Civil Service; defence and the armed forces; fiscal, economic and monetary policy; elections; immigration and nationality; national security and official secrets; crime, public order and policing; competition policy; intellectual property; import and export control; consumer protection;

ownership and exploitation of coal, oil and gas; nuclear energy; transport; social security (subject to exceptions); employment and industrial relations; broadcasting; registration of land and equal opportunities.

As with the provisions of the Scotland Act 1998, many exceptions are made to the reserved categories. For instance, the reservation of fiscal, economic and monetary policy is subject to the exception of local taxation to fund local authority expenditure, which is devolved, and devolved taxation.

(6) The Senedd may not modify reserved matters, set out in Schedule 7B of the Government of Wales Act 2006. This includes modifications of private law or criminal law and of the Government of Wales Act 2006 itself, or other legislation listed in Schedule 7B (e.g., the Human Rights Act 1998, the Civil Contingencies Act 2004 and the European Union (Withdrawal) Act 2018, subject to specific exceptions).

(7) Unlike Scotland, the judiciary and the court system are not devolved matters, other than the regulation of devolved tribunals. The legal system of Wales has long been enmeshed with that of England. However, with the growth of Acts of the Senedd providing for distinct legal provisions in Wales, there have been calls for a distinct approach to justice in Wales. Section A2 of the Government of Wales Act 2006 recognises Welsh law, including the ability of the Senedd to 'make law forming part of the law of England and Wales'. The Commission on Justice in Wales recommended legislative devolution of justice to Wales, in order to bring Wales in line with Scotland and Northern Ireland, as well as recommending that Wales should be placed in a similar position to Scotland and Northern Ireland as regards appointments to the Supreme Court (*Justice in Wales for the People of Wales*, October 2019).

(8) The Senedd may regulate elections to the Senedd, although this requires a super majority of two-thirds of the MSs (section 111A). The Senedd and Elections (Wales) Act 2020 extended the franchise to the Senedd to 16 and 17 year olds.

(9) A bill becomes an Act of the Senedd when it has been enacted by the Senedd and received royal assent (Government of Wales Act 2006, section 107(2)). Acts are enacted in both Welsh and English, which have equal status (Legislation (Wales) Act 2019).

(See, further, Rawlings, *Delineating Wales* (2003); Jones and Williams, 'Wales as a Jurisdiction' [2004] *PL* 78; Rawlings, 'Hastening Slowly: The Next Phase of Welsh Devolution' [2005] *PL* 824; Trench, 'Wales and the Westminster Model' (2010) 63 *Parl Aff* 117; Moon and Thomas, 'Welsh Devolution and the Problem of Legislative Competence' (2017) 12 British Politics 335; Rawlings 'The Strange Reconstitution of Wales [2018] *PL* 62; Rawlings, 'The Welsh Way/Y Ffordd Gymreig', in Jowell and O'Cinneide *The Changing Constitution* (9th edn. 2019).)

4.2.3 Northern Ireland

Northern Ireland, a land of 5,000 square miles, has a population of 1.8 million or 2.9 per cent of the total UK population. Ruled, if not entirely controlled, by the English Crown since the twelfth century, all Ireland was united with Great Britain by the Acts of Union of the British and Irish Parliaments in 1800. (The Act of the Irish Parliament was passed in unedifying circumstances but was doubtless formally valid.) The Acts of Union ended the life of the Irish Parliament and transferred its authority to a Parliament of the UK, which was to include Irish members. The two countries were to be united into one kingdom 'for ever after' and the union of the Churches of England and Ireland was declared to be established forever as 'an essential and fundamental part' of the union.

As with the earlier Acts of Union between England and Scotland (above), it can be argued that the Acts of Union of 1800 were constituent Acts of a new (UK) Parliament that set legal limits to the powers of that Parliament. But in this instance, the argument has not fared well. The Irish Church Act 1869 disestablished the Church of Ireland, dissolving its union with the Church of England, the explicit provision of the Acts of Union notwithstanding. A challenge to the validity of the Act (although not expressly for its non-conformity with the Acts of Union) was unsuccessful: *Ex p Canon Selwyn* (1872) 36 JP 54. The Acts of Union were abrogated in a fundamental respect in 1921–2 when the Irish Free State was separated from the UK as a free dominion within the Commonwealth. (See the Irish Free State (Agreement) Act 1922, the Irish Free State Constitution Act 1922 and the Irish Free State (Consequential Provisions) Act 1922.) It became a republic with the name Éire or, in the English language, Ireland, in 1937 and withdrew from the Commonwealth in 1949.

The six counties of the northeast remained within the UK, with their own Parliament and government in Belfast established by the Government of Ireland Act 1920. The Ireland Act 1949 included, in statutory form, a political assurance to the unionist (mainly Protestant) community of Northern Ireland which was reaffirmed in subsequent legislation and now appears in the following terms in section 1(1) of the Northern Ireland Act 1998:

> It is hereby declared that Northern Ireland in its entirety remains part of the United Kingdom and shall not cease to be so without the consent of a majority of the people of Northern Ireland voting in a poll held for the purposes of this section in accordance with Schedule 1.

Sub-section (2) makes provision for action to be taken if the vote in such a poll is in favour of Northern Ireland becoming part of a united Ireland:

But if the wish expressed by a majority in such a poll is that Northern Ireland should cease to be part of the United Kingdom and form part of a united Ireland, the Secretary of State shall lay before Parliament such proposals to give effect to that wish as may be agreed between Her Majesty's Government in the United Kingdom and the Government of Ireland.

4.2.3.1 Devolved Government 1921–72

The constitution of Northern Ireland established by the Government of Ireland Act 1920 endured until 1972. The Act provided for a system of devolved government, with a bicameral Parliament of Northern Ireland and an executive headed by a governor as the representative of the Crown.

The Parliament of Northern Ireland consisted of a Senate and a House of Commons. Elections to the House of Commons were by proportional representation (the single transferable vote system) until 1929, and from then by the plurality ('first-past-the-post') system used in UK parliamentary elections. The UK Parliament retained its entire sovereignty in matters affecting Northern Ireland, but there was an extensive transfer of legislative power to the Parliament at Stormont in Belfast, the Act specifying the subjects to be *retained* at Westminster rather than those to be *transferred*. The convention was soon established that the UK Parliament should not legislate for Northern Ireland in the 'transferred' area unless requested to do so by the Northern Ireland Government. Representation of Northern Ireland in the UK Parliament continued, but with a reduced number of seats while the system of devolved government remained in place (thirteen until 1948, thereafter twelve).

Report of the Royal Commission on the Constitution (Kilbrandon Report), vol. 1, Cmnd 5460/1973

172. [T]he constitution was placed under … stresses stemming from the division of the population into two sharply distinct communities, a majority, predominantly Protestant and in favour of the maintenance of the union with Great Britain, and a minority, predominantly Roman Catholic and opposed to the union. For the whole period of the existence of the Northern Ireland Parliament, politics in the province were dominated by this single issue. Parliamentary elections were concerned almost exclusively with it, and only those political parties whose positions in relation to it were clearly defined were able to attract substantial support …

1251. [T]he Act applied to Northern Ireland the system of Parliamentary democracy in use at Westminster, which depends for its smooth working on an alternation between Government and Opposition. The rule that the 'winner takes all' – that the Government is formed exclusively from the party that has a majority, be it large or small, in the legislature, and that the Opposition is totally excluded – is far easier to accept when electoral victory passes from party to party. Balance and equity are achieved by alternation. But in Northern Ireland the winner was always the Unionist Party. There was nothing contrived or improper

> about this; whatever may have been true, from time to time and from place to place, about local government elections, there is no room for doubt that at every general election for the Northern Ireland House of Commons a clear majority of the electors deliberately intended the Unionist Party to form the government. The permanent majority was a permanent and cohesive majority in the electorate. But such a result, so often repeated, and apparently so likely to continue, inevitably produced great dissatisfaction in the minority and raised the question of the suitability of that particular form of government in the special circumstances of Northern Ireland.

In spite of these flaws, the Kilbrandon Commission was in agreement with other commentators who judged the devolved or 'home rule' government of Northern Ireland to have been broadly successful in providing laws and administration suitable to the particular needs of the province. It had been an instrument of progress at all events 'in the large areas of government which were unaffected, or at least were not dominated, by the community problem' (para 1264). But a different aspect of the period of home rule was emphasised in the 1984 *Report of the New Ireland Forum* (composed of representatives of democratic nationalist parties of north and south). The identity of the nationalist community in the North, it said (para 3.9), had been effectively disregarded:

> The symbols and procedures of the institutions to which nationalists are required to give allegiance have been a constant reminder of the denial of their identity . . . [T]hey have had virtually no involvement in decision-making at the political level. For over 50 years they lived under a system of exclusively unionist power and privilege and suffered systematic discrimination. They were deprived of the means of social and economic development, experienced high levels of emigration and have always been subject to high rates of unemployment.

Civil liberties were not well protected during this period. The Civil Authorities (Special Powers) Act (Northern Ireland) enacted by the Stormont Parliament in 1922 established a wide-ranging system of controls, including powers of arrest, search, internment and the banning of organisations, which, in general, did not prove to be amenable to successful challenge in the courts. (See, e.g., *McEldowney* v. *Forde* [1971] AC 632, of which it has been said that it finally convinced the minority community of 'the futility of pursuing the civil rights campaign through the courts': Boyle et al., *Law and State: the Case of Northern Ireland* (1975), p. 15.)

For the whole period 1921–72, the Unionist Party had an absolute majority in the Northern Ireland House of Commons. (No such long-lasting single-party hegemony has been known at Westminster since the Reform Act of 1832.) The dominance of the Unionist Party extended to local government, where unionist majorities were sometimes assured by gerrymandering and the manipulation of housing allocations. Inflexible single-party rule contributed to the resentments of a disadvantaged Catholic community in the poorest part of the UK, and these resentments were at last to explode in the so-called 'troubles' – the political violence and terrorism – of 1968 and the following years.

Between 1968 and 1972 some important constitutional reforms were instituted by the Northern Ireland Government, under a degree of pressure from Whitehall. Electoral law was reformed and local government was reorganised. A Northern Ireland Parliamentary Commissioner for Administration and a Commissioner for Complaints were appointed to investigate complaints of maladministration by public authorities. A Community Relations Commission was set up to promote action to improve community relations and a Housing Executive took over responsibility for public housing in the province. Despite these reforms, the nationalist community was 'still discriminated against in social, economic, cultural and political terms' (*Report of the New Ireland Forum* (1984), para 3.17) and the province experienced continuing violence and disorder, the despatch of troops and the reintroduction of internment. The deepening crisis elicited increasing involvement by the UK Government in the affairs of Northern Ireland, and finally in March 1972 direct rule from Whitehall was imposed on the province. By the Northern Ireland (Temporary Provisions) Act 1972 the Parliament of Northern Ireland was prorogued and provision was made for legislation by order in council on the subjects within its competence. The powers of the Northern Ireland Government were transferred to a Secretary of State for Northern Ireland.

4.2.3.2 Direct Rule

The first period of direct rule ran from 1972 to 1974. A considerable amount of time was given at Westminster to legislation for Northern Ireland (Acts and orders in council). A Northern Ireland (Border Poll) Act 1972 provided for a referendum in the province on the question of whether Northern Ireland should remain part of the UK or be joined with the Republic of Ireland. In the 'border poll' of March 1973, only 58.7 per cent of the electorate cast a vote (nationalist political leaders had urged their supporters not to vote): 591,820 voted to remain part of the UK and 6,463 to join with the Republic of Ireland.

A new system of devolution, based on the principle of power-sharing between the two communities, was instituted by the Northern Ireland Constitution Act 1973 and the Northern Ireland Assembly Act 1973. There was to be an assembly, with legislative powers, elected by proportional representation, and an executive constituted from parties representative of both communities. The assembly was duly elected and the Secretary of State appointed an executive, composed of members of the Official Unionist Party, the Social Democratic and Labour Party (SDLP) and the Alliance

Party. The leaders of these parties joined with ministers of the UK and Irish Governments in a conference at Sunningdale in December 1973, and agreement was reached on the formation of a Council of Ireland, which would be an instrument for cooperation between the province and the republic.

This first attempt to achieve an intercommunal constitutional settlement in Northern Ireland collapsed when a general strike of loyalist workers organised by the Ulster Workers' Council brought down the executive in May 1974 after only five months. The assembly was dissolved and direct rule from Whitehall was resumed under arrangements made by the Northern Ireland Act 1974. Direct rule was to have been for an 'interim period' of one year, but was extended annually by orders made under the Act in the conviction that a return to single-party government in Northern Ireland would offer no prospect of a solution to the problems of the province.

Renewed attempts were made to devise a scheme of devolved government that would have broad support in the two communities. A Northern Ireland Assembly was reconstituted by the Northern Ireland Act 1982 with scrutinising, deliberative and consultative functions and a requirement to bring forward proposals for a broadly acceptable scheme of devolution. Within a few years, the endeavour broke down in dissension and the assembly was dissolved by order in council in 1986. Direct rule continued until 1998.

Under the system of direct rule, the government of Northern Ireland was the responsibility of a Secretary of State, assisted later by four subordinate ministers. Policy on law and order, constitutional development, etc. was directed by the Northern Ireland Office in Whitehall; departments in Belfast (staffed by the Northern Ireland Civil Service, which is a distinct service under the Crown) administered agriculture, economic development, education, the environment, and health and social services.

Acts of Parliament might be enacted for or extend to Northern Ireland, but the Northern Ireland Act 1974 conferred a wide power to legislate specifically for Northern Ireland by order in council, subject to affirmative resolutions of both Houses of Parliament, and this was the method usually adopted. However, various other enactments allowed the 'negative resolution' procedure – with less scope for parliamentary control (see below, p. 573) – to be used for orders in council relating to Northern Ireland.

The representation of Northern Ireland in the UK Parliament was increased by the House of Commons (Redistribution of Seats) Act 1979, which provided that the number of constituencies for Northern Ireland should be seventeen, unless the Boundary Commission for Northern Ireland should find it necessary to vary this number to sixteen or eighteen for the time being. There are at present eighteen Northern Ireland seats in the House of Commons.

A Northern Ireland Grand Committee was established in the House of Commons, consisting of all MPs for Northern Ireland constituencies and up to twenty-five other members. Its business has included the holding of short debates, hearing ministerial statements, putting questions to ministers for oral answer and considering bills, proposed orders in council and statutory instruments relating to Northern Ireland. A select committee on Northern Ireland Affairs was constituted to examine the expenditure, administration and policy of the Northern Ireland Office and the Northern Ireland departments in Belfast. Both committees continue to have a role, under new standing orders, in the devolution settlement (see below).

Direct rule was unavoidable while agreement could not be reached on a system of devolved government with broad support in the two communities, but it lacked legitimacy in Northern Ireland, was wanting in democratic credentials and did not assure the effective accountability of government.

4.2.3.3 Renewed Search for a Settlement

In the 1980s and 1990s, the UK Government sought the active cooperation of the Government of the Republic of Ireland in the quest for a political settlement.

On 15 November 1985, at an intergovernmental meeting held at Hillsborough Castle near Belfast, a formal and binding agreement was signed by the prime minister of the UK and the taoiseach of the Republic of Ireland (Cmnd 9657). The Anglo-Irish Agreement provided for improved cooperation between the north and south of Ireland in cross-border security and other matters, and set up an intergovernmental conference that would meet regularly and be concerned with Northern Ireland affairs and with relations between the two parts of the island of Ireland.

The agreement was unwelcome to unionists in Northern Ireland and members of the Ulster Unionist Council sought leave to apply for judicial review to challenge its implementation, principally on the ground that the proposed intergovernmental conference 'would amount to the establishment in the United Kingdom of a new standing body for the purpose of influencing the conduct of the government without the authority of the Queen in Parliament, and would be contrary to law'. In *Ex p Molyneaux* [1986] 1 WLR 331 the court refused leave to apply, holding that the establishment of the intergovernmental conference, which would have no legislative or executive power, did not contravene 'any statute, any rule of common law or any constitutional convention'.

Among changes that were influenced by the discussions in the intergovernmental conference may be instanced the enactment of the Fair Employment (Northern Ireland) Act 1989, strengthening the existing legislation to eliminate religious discrimination and promote equality in employment, as well as the repeal of the Flags and Emblems (Display) Act (Northern Ireland) 1954, the establishment of an Independent Commission for Police Complaints and the introduction of a Code of Conduct for the Royal Ulster Constabulary (as it then was).

In the 1990s, discussions continued with the main parties in Northern Ireland on new political institutions for the province and between the UK and Irish Governments on 'fundamental aspects of relationships within the island of Ireland' and new structures for cooperation between the two governments. In spite of the IRA's repudiation in 1996 of the first 'ceasefire' maintained by the nationalist and loyalist armed movements since 1994, a continuing effort was made to proceed with negotiations between all democratically mandated political parties in Northern Ireland. The Northern Ireland (Entry to Negotiations, etc.) Act 1996 made provision for negotiations to take place between elected delegates of Northern Ireland political parties that had expressed their commitment to democracy and non-violence (the 'Mitchell principles'). Representatives of the British and Irish Governments would also take part. The all-party negotiations, which began in June 1996, were intended to lead to 'a comprehensive political settlement in relation to Northern Ireland'. Initially, they showed little promise of doing so, but an impetus to progress was given by a renewed ceasefire by the IRA on 20 July 1997 in response to a more flexible approach taken by the British Government to the Northern Ireland question after the 1997 general election. Agreement – styled 'the Multi-Party Agreement' and since known as the Belfast Agreement (or Good Friday Agreement) – was reached by the participants in the talks on 10 April 1998 (Cm 3883/1998). It set out the agreed arrangements for the devolution of legislative and executive powers to an elected Northern Ireland Assembly. At the same time, a new agreement was concluded between the British and Irish Governments, replacing the Anglo-Irish Agreement of 1985. It entered into force on 2 December 1999.

Writing in 2001, Brendan O'Leary said of the British-Irish Agreement (or Treaty) and the Multi-Party (Belfast) Agreement that they represented 'the most comprehensive, ambitious, and successful attempt at constitutional conflict regulation of the last three decades' (in Reynolds (ed.), *The Architecture of Democracy* (2002), p. 294).

Agreement between the Government of the United Kingdom of Great Britain and Northern Ireland and the Government of Ireland, Cm 4705/2000, Article 1

The two Governments:

(i) recognise the legitimacy of whatever choice is freely exercised by a majority of the people of Northern Ireland with regard to its status, whether they prefer to continue to support the Union with Great Britain or a sovereign united Ireland;

(ii) recognise that it is for the people of the island of Ireland alone, by agreement between the two parts respectively and without external impediment, to exercise their right of self-determination on the basis of consent, freely and concurrently given, North and South, to bring about a united Ireland, if that is their wish, accepting that this right must be achieved and exercised with and subject to the agreement and consent of a majority of the people of Northern Ireland;

(iii) acknowledge that while a substantial section of the people in Northern Ireland share the legitimate wish of a majority of the people of the island of Ireland for a united Ireland, the present wish of a majority of the people of Northern Ireland, freely exercised and legitimate, is to maintain the Union and accordingly, that Northern Ireland's status as part of the United Kingdom reflects and relies upon that wish; and that it would be wrong to make any change in the status of Northern Ireland save with the consent of a majority of its people;

(iv) affirm that, if in the future, the people of the island of Ireland exercise their right of self-determination on the basis set out in sections (i) and (ii) above to bring about a united Ireland, it will be a binding obligation on both Governments to introduce and support in their respective Parliaments legislation to give effect to that wish;

(v) affirm that whatever choice is freely exercised by a majority of the people of Northern Ireland, the power of the sovereign government with jurisdiction there shall be exercised with rigorous impartiality on behalf of all the people in the diversity of their identities and traditions and shall be founded on the principles of full respect for, and equality of, civil, political, social and cultural rights, of freedom from discrimination for all citizens, and of parity of esteem and of just and equal treatment for the identity, ethos and aspirations of both communities;

(vi) recognise the birthright of all the people of Northern Ireland to identify themselves and be accepted as Irish or British, or both, as they may so choose, and accordingly confirm that their right to hold both British and Irish citizenship is accepted by both Governments and would not be affected by any future change in the status of Northern Ireland.

In Article 2, the two governments undertook to support and implement the provisions of the Belfast Agreement.

A referendum was held in Northern Ireland on 22 May 1998 in accordance with the Northern Ireland Negotiations (Referendum) Order 1998 (SI 1998/1126) (made under power conferred by section 4 of the Northern Ireland (Entry to Negotiations, etc.) Act 1996). Of the 81 per cent of electors who voted on the question whether they supported the Belfast Agreement, 71 per cent expressed their support. In a simultaneous referendum held in the Republic of Ireland, 94 per cent of those voting approved the changes to the Irish Constitution that were required by the agreement, acknowledging the existing status of Northern Ireland.

Following the approval of the Belfast Agreement in the referendum, a new Northern Ireland Assembly was elected by proportional representation (single transferable vote) on 25 June 1998, in accordance with the Northern Ireland (Elections) Act 1998. It was initially to be a 'shadow' assembly, which would settle its standing orders and working practices and elect a first minister and deputy first minister. Provision for the devolution of legislative and executive powers to the assembly was made subsequently by the Northern Ireland Act 1998. Devolved government was to be brought into operation once it appeared to the Secretary of State that 'sufficient progress has been made in implementing the Belfast Agreement' (Northern Ireland Act 1998, section 3). In November 1999 the Secretary of State determined that there had been sufficient progress and an order in council made under section 3 brought devolution into effect on 2 December 1999. The devolved institutions assumed their functions, but a continuing political failure to achieve full implementation of the Belfast Agreement, marked by dissension in regard to the decommissioning of arms, demilitarisation and policing arrangements, as well as outbreaks of paramilitary activity, resulted in repeated suspensions of devolved government, the last of which, in October 2002, continued for four-and-a-half years, until May 2007. During this period, direct rule was resumed, with legislation by order in council in matters that would have been within the competence of the Northern Ireland Assembly.

Yet, discussions continued on the issues that divided the parties. A momentous event occurred in July 2005 when the IRA announced an end to its armed campaign and, in September 2005, the Independent Commission on Decommissioning (the de Chastelain Commission) reported – and confirmed in a further report in January 2006 – that the IRA had put all its arms beyond use.

In October 2006, intensive talks were held in St Andrews, Scotland, between the British and Irish Governments and the various Northern Ireland parties. In the St Andrews Agreement of 13 October 2006, the two governments reaffirmed their full commitment to the 'fundamental principles' of the Belfast (or Good Friday) Agreement:

consent for constitutional change, commitment to exclusively peaceful and democratic means, stable inclusive partnership government, a balanced institutional accommodation of the key relationships with Northern Ireland, between North and South and within these islands, and for equality and human rights at the heart of the new dispensation in Northern Ireland.

The St Andrews Agreement made a number of revisions to the Belfast Agreement but it did so on the basis of the foundations that had been laid in 1998. Such changes agreed at St Andrews as required legislation were implemented under the Northern Ireland (St Andrews Agreement) Act 2006, which made amendments to the Northern Ireland Act 1998.

The two governments made it clear that a failure to implement the St Andrews Agreement would result in the dissolution of the assembly. In this event, Northern Ireland would have been governed not on a scheme of devolution but on the basis of fresh British–Irish partnership arrangements – a revised form of direct rule that would have substantially involved Dublin in aspects of the government of Northern Ireland. As it turned out, however, devolution was restored in May 2007 and (to date) there have been no further suspensions of devolution since that time. A further significant step was taken when, under the Northern Ireland Act 2009, policing and justice functions were finally devolved.

Overall, the record since 2007 is mixed. Rick Wilford reports that, while there remain 'undoubted and unresolved tensions' among the main parties in Northern Ireland, 'the vastly changed context means that they have not as yet fallen prey to the same intensity of in-fighting that hobbled' earlier attempts at devolution under the 1998 Act ('Northern Ireland: The Politics of Constraint' (2010) 63 *Parl Aff* 134, 152). However, progress in terms of developing policy and law-making has been slow. Wilford writes of there being 'a dearth of policy initiatives and something of a legislative famine for much of the period since 2007' (p. 147).

4.2.3.4 Devolution Under the Northern Ireland Act 1998

The purpose of the Northern Ireland Act 1998 was to give legal effect to the substantive provisions of the Belfast Agreement in their entirety, establishing a polity in which power would be shared and opposed viewpoints accommodated.

Strand One of the Agreement, setting out the terms of the proposed devolutionary settlement, was closely adhered to in the Act. The system of devolution adopted for Northern Ireland drew on the previous scheme of devolved government under the Northern Ireland Constitution Act 1973 and on the model of the Scotland Act 1998.

The Northern Ireland Assembly has ninety members, elected for a five-year term by the single transferable vote system, each of the eighteen Northern Ireland parliamentary (Westminster) constituencies returning five members. The assembly has powers of primary legislation in respect of all *transferred* matters, that is, all matters that are not 'excepted' or 'reserved' in terms of the Act (Schedules 2 and 3 respectively). Transferred matters include the wide range of social and economic matters that were within the responsibility of the six Northern Ireland departments immediately prior to devolution. These matters include agriculture and rural development, arts and culture, economic development, education, the environment, health, social services, training and employment. (The Northern Ireland departments were to continue in existence, subject to the power of the assembly to transfer functions between them or to create or dissolve departments.)

The *excepted* matters listed in Schedule 2 are not within the competence of the assembly and cannot be transferred to it (other than by Act of Parliament amending the Northern Ireland Act). They include international relations and relations with the EU, defence and the armed forces, national security, the appointment and removal of judges, taxation, elections and the main provisions of the Northern Ireland Act itself. The act includes some

further specific limitations of the assembly's competence. Certain enactments are 'entrenched' by section 7 of the Act so that they may not be
modified by an act of the assembly (or by subordinate legislation made by
a Northern Ireland minister): these include the European Union
(Withdrawal) Act 2018 and the Human Rights Act 1998. An Act of the
assembly is outside competence if it is incompatible with a convention right
under the HRA or with EU law, or if it discriminates against persons on the
ground of religious belief or political opinion: section 6(2). The Northern
Ireland Assembly also has a limited power to modify EU retained law within
the sphere of its devolved competence, save that it cannot modify retained
EU law as set out in an order of council enacted under the European Union
(Withdrawal) Act 2018.

The *reserved* matters listed in Schedule 3 are not within the competence of
the assembly but are capable of being transferred. They include criminal justice
and policing, public order, firearms and explosives, financial services and
markets, import and export controls, intellectual property, telecommunica-
tions and broadcasting, and consumer safety. The transfer of reserved matters
to assembly competence may be effected by order in council, provided that the
assembly has passed, with cross-community support (see below), a resolution
requesting the transfer and a draft of the order has been approved by each
House of Parliament. (Removal of a transferred matter to the reserved list may
be effected in the same way.) The possibility of transfer from the reserved list
introduces an element of flexibility into the devolution settlement. Additional
flexibility ensues from provisions of the Act that enable the assembly to
legislate on a reserved matter with the consent of the Secretary of State given
in any particular instance, subject to parliamentary controls. (See sections 8,
10, 14 and 15.)

The Belfast Agreement provided for safeguards 'to ensure that all sections of
the community can participate and work together successfully' in the assembly. The Act accordingly provides that certain important decisions of the
assembly may be taken only with 'cross-community support'. The mechanism
for achieving this requires that assembly members must identify themselves
and be designated as 'nationalist' or 'unionist' (or 'other'). 'Cross-community
support' is defined as follows (section 4(5)):

(a) the support of a majority of the members voting, a majority of the
    designated nationalists voting and a majority of the designated unionists
    voting [parallel consent]; or
(b) the support of 60 per cent of the members voting, 40 per cent of the
    designated nationalists voting and 40 per cent of the designated unionists
    voting [weighted majority].

Questions of vires arising in relation to assembly legislation are dealt with in
the Act (sections 9–12 and Schedule 10) in a manner similar to the corresponding provision made in the Scotland Act 1998 (above).

Executive authority in transferred matters is exercised on behalf of the assembly by a first minister and deputy first minister and up to ten Northern Ireland ministers. The number and functions of ministerial posts are determined by the first minister and deputy first minister acting jointly, subject to approval by the assembly on a cross-community basis.

The first minister and deputy first minister are elected jointly by the assembly, in effect so as to represent, respectively, the largest unionist and the largest nationalist party. The remaining ministerial posts are allocated in proportion to party strengths in the assembly (in accordance with a formula known as the 'd'Hondt system' set out in section 18). Statutory committees of the assembly are appointed 'to advise and assist each Northern Ireland Minister in the formulation of policy' (section 29). They scrutinise the work of ministers and their departments and can initiate legislation. The person who chairs a statutory committee must not be of the same party as the minister.

A coordinating Executive Committee of the Assembly consists of all Northern Ireland ministers presided over jointly by the first minister and deputy first minister. It agrees on a policy programme and budget for each year, subject to approval by the assembly on a cross-community basis.

The first minister, deputy first minister and Northern Ireland ministers (and also any junior ministers appointed in accordance with section 19) must affirm the pledge of office (set out in Schedule 4). This includes a 'commitment to non-violence and exclusively peaceful and democratic means' as well as undertakings 'to serve all the people of Northern Ireland equally, and ... to promote equality and prevent discrimination', 'to support, and act in accordance with, all decisions of the Executive Committee and Assembly' and 'to comply with the Ministerial Code of Conduct' set out in Schedule 4. The failure of a minister to observe any term of the pledge of office may result in exclusion from office by resolution of the assembly passed with cross-community support (section 30).

The devolution of legislative competence to the Northern Ireland Assembly does not, it goes without saying (but is said in section 5(6) of the Act), 'affect the power of the Parliament of the United Kingdom to make laws for Northern Ireland'. Parliament may indeed have occasion to make such laws in relation to excepted or reserved matters (and has done so in the Northern Ireland (Miscellaneous Provisions) Act 2006, providing for the devolution of police and justice), but will undoubtedly be at pains to respect fully the terms of the original devolutionary settlement or subsequent revisions of it that may be agreed on. In respect of some reserved matters, the order in council procedure may be used instead of parliamentary enactment. This is permitted by section 85.

The Northern Ireland Constitution Act 1973 established a Standing Advisory Commission on Human Rights to advise the Secretary of State on the 'adequacy and effectiveness' of the law in preventing, and providing redress for, religious or political discrimination. In practice, with the approval of successive secretaries of state, the commission assumed responsibility to advise on the whole range of human rights issues in Northern Ireland. It produced valuable reports and was forthright in its criticism of some government policies and legislation for Northern Ireland, but had only a limited influence on the decisions taken. The parties to the Belfast Agreement affirmed their commitment to 'the civil rights and the religious liberties of everyone in the community' and to a number of specific rights of special concern in the Northern Ireland context, among them 'the right to equal opportunity in all social and economic activity, regardless of class, creed, disability, gender or ethnicity'. These goals were translated into law by the Human Rights Act, which extends to Northern Ireland, and by the Northern Ireland Act 1998.

The Northern Ireland Act established a new Northern Ireland Human Rights Commission, with a membership reflecting the community balance, which is to 'keep under review the adequacy and effectiveness in Northern Ireland of law and practice relating to the protection of human rights' (section 69(1)). The commission has a responsibility to advise the assembly whether bills are compatible with human rights and to advise the Secretary of State and the Executive Committee of the Assembly on measures that ought to be taken to protect human rights. It also has the power to assist individuals in proceedings relating to the protection of human rights and may itself bring proceedings in such cases.

The commission was also given the task of advising the Secretary of State on the scope for defining a bill of rights for Northern Ireland, supplementing the 'convention rights' included in the HRA and reflecting, as provided in the Belfast Agreement, 'the particular circumstances of Northern Ireland' and 'principles of mutual respect for the identity and ethos of both communities and parity of esteem'. It published draft proposals for consultation and engaged in discussions with political parties, human rights lawyers and other representatives of civil society on the terms of a bill of rights. Previous editions of this book reported that the provisions proved contentious, and that further progress had stalled. Unfortunately, this remains the case. (See Harvey and Schwartz, 'Designing a Bill of Rights for Northern Ireland' (2009) 60 *NILQ* 181.)

(See, further, McCrudden, 'Northern Ireland and the British Constitution Since the Belfast Agreement', in Jowell and Oliver (eds.), *The Changing Constitution* (6th edn. 2007), ch. 10; Anthony and Morison, 'The Story of Lawmaking for Post-1998 Northern Ireland', in Hazell and Rawlings (eds.), *Devolution, Law-Making and the Constitution* (2005), ch. 5; Wilford, 'Northern Ireland: The Politics of Constraint' (2010) 63 *Parl Aff* 134.)

4.2.3.5 2017–19: Political Impasse and the Lack of a Northern Ireland Government

In spite of a relatively successful period of devolved government from 2007 to 2017, difficulties arose after the 2016 election to the Northern Irish Assembly.

Support had been obtained for Arlene Foster, DUP, as the First Minister with Martin McGuiness, Sinn Féin, as the Deputy First Minister. However, difficulties arose over the appointment of the minister of justice. The Alliance Party refused to make a nomination following concerns that the DUP had made too great a use of petitions of concern, which would then require decisions on a particular issue to be taken with cross-community support. Political scandal then arose over the Renewable Heat Incentive Scheme – the subject of a public inquiry that should deliver its report in 2020. It transpired that, unlike the schemes in England and Wales, the Northern Ireland scheme had not included cost controls in its implementation. As such, individuals were able to make a profit on the scheme by needlessly burning wood pellets. It was reported that this had cost the public purse close to £500 million. Nevertheless, Arlene Foster, who had been responsible for the scheme during her time as the Minister for Enterprise, Trade and Investment, did not comply with calls for her resignation. Following the resignation of Deputy First Minister McGuiness, for reasons of ill health and the DUP's refusal to support a bursary scheme designed to promote the learning of Irish, First Minister Arlene Foster was required to resign.

It proved impossible for a consensus to be reached over the appointment of a new first minister and deputy first minister. Given the reluctance to govern through direct rule from the UK, government was effectively carried out by civil servants who were performing the role of their ministerial equivalents. The Northern Ireland Act 1998 required that these positions should be filled within fourteen days. The failure to do so led to the calling of an election by the Secretary of State for Northern Ireland. The election to the Northern Ireland Assembly in March 2017 was the first with the smaller number of seats – a reduction from 108 to ninety seats. A series of talks were held to reach an agreement on a new first minister and a new deputy first minister. All of these talks failed to produce agreement. This led to the UK Government enacting measures to extend the period for negotiation to find a new leader. Of particular note was the Northern Ireland (Executive Formation and Exercise of Functions) Act 2018, section 1(1) of which states that 'For the purposes of filling the Ministerial offices on the first occasion following the election of the Northern Ireland Assembly at the poll on 2 March 2017, the Northern Ireland Act 1998 has effect as if in section 16A(3) for the words before paragraph (a) there were substituted "Within the period beginning with the first meeting of the Assembly and ending with 26 March 2019".' This retrospectively replaced a fourteen-day period in which to agree a new first minister and deputy first minister with a two-year period. This, in turn, was extended to 25 August 2019 by delegated legislation (Northern Ireland (Extension of Period for Executive Formation) Regulations 2019, and again to 21 October 2019 by the Northern Ireland (Executive Formation etc.) Act 2019. This Act included a further power to extend the period for forming an executive to 13 January 2020. Eventually, a few days before this final deadline, agreement was reached and a new first minister and deputy first minister were appointed, with the terms agreed between the two main parties being published in a document *New Decade, New Approach* (available at https://assets.publishing.service.gov.uk/govern ment/uploads/system/uploads/attachment_data/file/856998/2020–01-08_a_new_decade__a_new_approach.pdf).

This meant that Northern Ireland was without a government for almost three years. Moreover, this occurred during a crucial time, as Brexit and the controversial Northern Ireland backstop were being negotiated. During this time, Northern Ireland was effectively governed by civil servants. This position was challenged in *Re Buick's Application* [2018] NICA 26 which concerned the approval of planning application for a major incinerator and waste treatment centre in County Antrim by a civil servant. The first instance court concluded that the decision was unlawful as the decision could only be taken by a minister and not by a civil servant. The Northern Ireland Court of Appeal agreed, but the majority reached this conclusion for a different reason. Due to the cross-cutting nature of the decision it could only be taken by the Northern Ireland executive as a whole and not by a single minister. As such, it could not be taken by a civil servant acting on behalf of a minister. In addition to extending the period for the formation of a Northern Ireland Executive, the Northern Ireland (Executive Formation and Exercise of Functions) Act 2018 also empowered civil servants to perform ministerial functions.

4.2.4 England

It may seem odd to include England, given that the English Parliament and the Westminster Parliament are effectively the same and there has been no devolution per se to England – save for aspects of local devolution in 'devolution deals' to combined authorities discussed below. This means that the Westminster Parliament is composed of members representing Scotland, Wales and Northern Ireland, in addition to those from England. While this is required to enact legislation for the United Kingdom, should the situation be different when the Westminster Parliament enacts legislation that only takes effect in England? This is known as the 'West Lothian question'. In the 1976–8 devolution debates, Labour MP for West Lothian, Mr Tam Dalyell, had repeatedly protested that, since the representation of Scotland in the UK Parliament was to be maintained, Scottish MPs might have a decisive voice in legislation on a matter concerned only with England and Wales, whereas English and Welsh MPs would have forfeited their right to take part in legislation devolved to Scotland. An amendment designed to deal with the West Lothian question was made to the 1978 Scotland Bill, although it had been resisted by the government as a 'constitutional imbecility'. It provided that if the second reading of an 'English' bill was approved only with the support of MPs for Scottish constituencies, there would have to be a second vote after an interval of fourteen days. (It was contemplated that the Scottish

MPs would be induced to abstain in the second vote.) However, the Scotland Act 1998 provided no provision for dealing with the West Lothian question. Concern continued to be expressed that 'West Lothian' introduces an imbalance into the constitutional system; Mr Tam Dalyell (as MP for Linlithgow) concluded that 'some legislative entity is going to have to emerge in England to fill the vacuum left by Scottish home rule' (HC Deb vol. 311, col 741, 6 May 1998).

In the 2010 general election, the Conservative Party included a pledge in its manifesto to provide for 'English Votes for English Laws'. The 2010 Coalition Government then established the McKay Commission on the Consequences of Devolution for the House of Commons. The commission recommended that the House of Commons should adopt a constitutional convention that legislation that only affects England or England and Wales should not be adopted without the majority consent of MPs from England or England and Wales. The commission proposed modifying the standing orders to facilitate this change, alongside other recommendations concerning the House of Lords, the consideration of delegated legislation, and the need for a devolution committee to consider the cross-border effects of legislation. However, these measures were not implemented by the Coalition Government. A commitment to introducing 'English Votes for English Laws' was included in the 2015 manifesto of the Conservative Party. The Conservative Government then introduced a proposal for a new standing order. Following criticisms of the speed with which this was introduced, its original imposition was delayed, allowing select committees to take evidence and produce reports evaluating the new proposals.

The new provisions can be found in Standing Order No 83 J. They require that legislation in a devolved area that only affects England, or only affects England and Wales, is agreed to by a majority of English only, or English and Welsh only MPs, in addition to a majority of the House of Commons. First, it requires the Speaker to determine whether a government bill, or certain clauses in that bill, applies exclusively to England or to England or Wales and is within devolved legislative competence. If so, the Speaker is required to certify the bill. Any bill certified in this way proceeds through the provisions for English Votes for English Laws (EVEL). After the second reading of the bill, it is either sent to a public bill committee, whose composition consists only of English or English and Welsh MPs and reflects the party share of English or English and Welsh only MPs, or to the Legislative Grand Committee (England) – i.e. all of the English or English and Welsh MPs in the House of Commons. The bill is then considered on report by the whole house. If no changes are made, then the bill is passed to the Legislative Grand Committee (England) for consent. If consent is obtained, the bill then goes to the whole House of Commons for consent. If the bill is amended at committee stage, the Speaker is required to consider any amendments to determine if any new certification of the bill is required. Similar provisions apply to amendments from the House of Lords. Any vote held on an amendment from the House of Lords that is certified as concerning a devolution matter and as only affecting the law in England, or in England and Wales only, requires a double majority – i.e. a majority of all of those voting, and a majority of English only or English and Welsh only MPs.

Although this provides a partial solution to the democratic deficit created by the West Lothian question, nevertheless there are problems with the new EVEL standing orders. First, there are concerns that the requirement for the Speaker to certify a bill may politicise the role of the Speaker. Evidence of the application of this principle, however, would suggest that this is not the case. Second, there are problems as to the potential under-inclusiveness of EVEL. It only applies to votes in the House of Commons and not to those in the House of Lords. Also, problems arise as to potential cross-over issues – although legislation may only have spending implications in England or in England and Wales, they will have an impact on the Barnett formula, which is used to calculate the block grant from Westminster to Scotland, Wales and Northern Ireland. Although fiscal devolution has reduced the impact of such a crossover, the concern nevertheless remains. The procedures are also very technical. Prior to the modification of the standing orders, concerns were raised as to the creation of two classes of MP which gives rise to possible intractable technical and political difficulties. (See Hazell (ed.), *The English Question* (2006), pp. 225–6; Bogdanor, 'The West Lothian Question' (2010) 63 *Parl Aff* 156.) However, research into the first year of application of the EVEL procedures suggested that the need for a double majority meant that these difficulties had not arisen. (Kenny and Gover, *Finding the Good in EVEL: An Evaluation of 'English votes for English Laws' in the House of Commons*, available at www .ucl.ac.uk/constitution-unit/sites/constitution-unit/files/EVEL_Report_ A4_FINAL.pdf.)

(See, further, Hadfield, 'Devolution, Westminster and the English Question' [2005] *PL* 286; Hazell (ed.), *The English Question* (2006); House of Commons Justice Committee, *Devolution: A Decade On*, 5th Report of 2008–09, HC 529, paras 153–230; Kenny and Lodge, *The English Question: The View from Westminster* (2009), House of Commons Procedure Committee *English Votes for English Laws Standing Orders: Report of the Committee's Technical Evaluation. Third Report of 2016–17* HC 189.)

4.3 Parliamentary Sovereignty and the Devolution Settlement

In the White Paper *Scotland's Parliament* (Cm 3658/1997), para 4.2, it was insisted that the UK Parliament 'is and will remain sovereign in all matters' and that it 'will be choosing to exercise that sovereignty by devolving legislative responsibilities to a Scottish Parliament without in any way diminishing its own powers'. This understanding is replicated in the devolution legislation. The Scotland Act 1998, the Government of Wales Act 2006 and the Northern Ireland Act 1998 all now include clauses that make it clear that the devolution of legislative powers to these legislatures 'does not affect the power of the Parliament of the United Kingdom to make laws for' Scotland, Wales and Northern Ireland (Scotland Act 1998, section 28(7); Government of Wales Act 2006, section 107(5); and Northern Ireland Act 1998, section 5(6)).

In the course of proceedings on the Scotland Bill in the House of Commons, Mr Tam Dalyell MP remarked of this sub-section that it 'may conceivably be true in an arcane legal sense, but in the political reality of 1998 it is palpably misleading and about as true as it would be to say that the Queen can veto any legislation' (HC Deb vol. 305, col 366, 28 January 1998). A similar view was taken by Vernon Bogdanor in concluding that after devolution the supremacy of Parliament 'will become merely a nebulous right to supervise the Scottish Parliament, together with the right under pathological circumstances, to abolish it' ('Devolution: The Constitutional Aspects', in University of Cambridge Centre for Public Law, *Constitutional Reform in the United Kingdom* (1998), p. 12). This view may appear to be reinforced following the enactment of the Scotland Act 2016 and the Wales Act 2017. Both the Scotland Act 1998 and the Government of Wales Act 2006 now contain a new provision recognising the permanence of the devolution settlement. See, for example, section 63A of the Scotland Act 1998:

63A Permanence of the Scottish Parliament and Scottish Government

(1) The Scottish Parliament and the Scottish Government are a permanent part of the United Kingdom's constitutional arrangements.

(2) The purpose of this section is, with due regard to the other provisions of this Act, to signify the commitment of the Parliament and Government of the United Kingdom to the Scottish Parliament and the Scottish Government.

(3) In view of that commitment it is declared that the Scottish Parliament and the Scottish Government are not to be abolished except on the basis of a decision of the people of Scotland voting in a referendum.

A similarly worded provision is found in Section A1 of the Government of Wales Act 2006, referring to the Welsh Parliament and Government and the people of Wales. Section 1 of the Northern Ireland Act 1998 contains a provision with a similar purpose, a product of the particular history of Northern Ireland and which implements the Belfast Agreement signed by the UK and Irish Governments:

Status of Northern Ireland

(1) It is hereby declared that Northern Ireland in its entirety remains part of the United Kingdom and shall not cease to be so without the consent of a majority of the people of

> Northern Ireland voting in a poll held for the purposes of this section in accordance with Schedule 1.
>
> (2) But if the wish expressed by a majority in such a poll is that Northern Ireland should cease to be part of the United Kingdom and form part of a united Ireland, the Secretary of State shall lay before Parliament such proposals to give effect to that wish as may be agreed between Her Majesty's Government in the United Kingdom and the Government of Ireland.

All three recognise the permanence of the institutions of devolution, in addition to recognising the importance of the will of the people governed by these institutions. The provisions in the Scotland Act 1998 and the Government of Wales Act 2006 are intended as expressions of political commitment, such that they are not legally binding and do not place a legal restriction on the powers of the Westminster legislature. The provisions are similarly of a declaratory nature, however they also place a legally binding obligation on the UK Government to enter into negotiations with the Government of Ireland to implement the will of the people of Northern Ireland should they vote in favour of unification with Ireland.

While these provisions do not place a legal restriction on the Westminster Parliament, and so do not challenge the legal sovereignty of the Westminster Parliament, nevertheless, the declarations of permanence might reinforce earlier accounts that a time might come when the courts will be persuaded to hold that devolution were irreversible, in accordance with a judicially revised account of parliamentary sovereignty. (See Loughlin, *Sword and Scales* (2000), p. 154; Little, 'Scotland and Parliamentary Sovereignty' (2004) 24 *LS* 540.) These legislative provisions also provide a further indirect challenge to parliamentary sovereignty. They suggest that, as regards devolution, sovereignty rests with the people and not with Parliament.

However, it would appear that the UK courts have not yet reached a point where they would be willing to recognise that devolution cannot be legally reversed. This can be seen both in the treatment of issues of sovereignty in the recent reference regarding Scotland's Legal Continuity Bill, and treatment of the Sewel Convention by courts.

The UK Withdrawal from the European Union (Legal Continuity) (Scotland) Bill [2018] UKSC 64, 2019] AC 1022 (The Scottish Continuity Bill)

The Attorney General argued that section 17 of the bill was beyond the competence of the Scottish Parliament as it would modify section 28(7) of the Scotland Act 1998 – a provision contained in Schedule 4 of the Scotland Act meaning that it could not be modified by the Scottish Parliament. Clause 17 of the bill would have required any delegated legislation made by a Westminster minister, which modified retained EU law in an area devolved to Scotland, to obtain the consent of Scottish ministers to that delegated legislation. It was argued that this would modify section 28(7), which sets out that the legislative power granted to Scotland 'does not affect the power of the Parliament of the United Kingdom to make laws for Scotland'. By requiring consent in this manner, clause 17 arguably affected the power of the Westminster Parliament to enact law for Scotland, as any law devolving power to a UK minister to modify retained EU law in an area devolved to Scotland would require the consent of a Scottish minister. It thereby placed a condition on how the Westminster Parliament could exercise its power to enact legislation for Scotland. The Lord Advocate rejected this argument. Instead, he argued that the provision did not modify the powers of the Westminster Parliament to enact legislation for Scotland as, inter alia, if the Westminster Parliament were to enact legislation that did not include a provision requiring the consent of Scottish ministers, this would impliedly repeal the requirements of clause 17 requiring consent. The Supreme Court rejected these arguments as follows:

[51]. As appears from the authorities cited by the Lord Advocate, one enactment does not modify another merely because it makes additional provision in the same field of law. If it did, the important distinction between the protection of enactments from modification under Schedule 4 to the Scotland Act, and the inability of the Scottish Parliament to legislate in relation to reserved matters under Schedule 5, would become obscured. When the UK Parliament decides to reserve an entire area of the law to itself, it does so by listing the relevant subject-matter in Schedule 5. When it has not taken that step, but has protected a particular enactment from modification by including it in Schedule 4, it is not to be treated as if it had listed the subject-matter of the enactment in Schedule 5. Where the only relevant restriction on the legislative power of the Scottish Parliament is the protection of an enactment from modification under Schedule 4, the Parliament has the power to enact legislation relating to the same subject-matter as the protected enactment, provided it does not modify it. Without attempting an exhaustive definition, a protected enactment will be modified by a later enactment, even in the absence of express amendment or repeal, if it is implicitly amended, disapplied or repealed in whole or in part. That will be the position if the later enactment alters a rule laid down in the protected enactment, or is otherwise in conflict with its unqualified continuation in force as before, so that the protected enactment has to be understood as having been in substance amended, superseded, disapplied or repealed by the later one.

[52]. Applying that approach, we are unable to accept the Lord Advocate's submission that section 28(7) of the Scotland Act would not be modified by section 17 of the Bill. As the Lord Advocate acknowledges, the power of the UK Parliament to make laws for Scotland includes the power to make laws authorising the making of subordinate legislation by Ministers and other persons. An enactment of the Scottish Parliament which prevented such subordinate legislation from having legal effect, unless the Scottish Ministers gave their consent, would render the effect of laws made by the UK Parliament conditional on the consent of the Scottish Ministers. It would therefore limit the power of the UK Parliament to

make laws for Scotland, since Parliament cannot meaningfully be said to 'make laws' if the laws which it makes are of no effect. The imposition of such a condition on the UK Parliament's law-making power would be inconsistent with the continued recognition, by section 28(7) of the Scotland Act, of its unqualified legislative power. Thus, in order for section 17 of the Bill and section 28(7) of the Scotland Act to operate concurrently, the former would have to be treated as impliedly amending the latter, so that it read: '(7) Subject to section 17 of the UK Withdrawal from the European Union (Legal Continuity) (Scotland) Act 2018, this section does not affect the power of the Parliament of the United Kingdom to make laws for Scotland.'

[53]. That conclusion is not altered by the other arguments advanced by the Lord Advocate. In relation to the first argument (para 47 above), a provision which made the effect of laws made by the UK Parliament for Scotland conditional on the consent of the Scottish Ministers, unless it disapplied or repealed the provision in question, would for that very reason be inconsistent with the continued recognition of its unqualified sovereignty, and therefore tantamount to an amendment of section 28(7) of the Scotland Act. In relation to the second argument (para 48 above), the question before the court is whether, if the Bill were to receive Royal Assent, section 17 would be law. If not, there would be no question of its having to be disapplied or repealed by the UK Parliament: it would be of no legal effect whatsoever ('not law', in terms of section 29(1) of the Scotland Act). It is therefore no answer to an argument that section 17 of the Bill would be outside legislative competence, to say that it could be disapplied or repealed. In relation to the third argument (para 49 above), this submission resembles the Lord Advocate's first argument, and for similar reasons we are unable to accept it. A provision which imposes a condition on the legal effect of laws made by the UK Parliament, in so far as they apply to Scotland, is in conflict with the continuation of its sovereign power to make laws for Scotland, and is therefore equivalent to the amendment of section 28(7) of the Scotland Act. The suggested analogy reinforces the point. If a provision of a Bill passed by the Scottish Parliament were to prevent legislation enacted by the UK Parliament from coming into force without the Scottish Ministers' consent, that provision would undoubtedly limit the UK Parliament's power to make laws for Scotland.

[54]. For these reasons, we conclude that section 17 of the Bill would modify section 28(7) of the Scotland Act, contrary to section 29(2)(c) and paragraph 4(1) of Page 22 Schedule 4. Having reached that conclusion, it is unnecessary for us to consider whether section 17 of the Bill would also breach the restriction in paragraph 4(1) of Schedule 4 by modifying section 63(1).

It was further argued that section 17 of the bill was beyond the competence of the Scottish Parliament as it 'related to' a reserved matter, 'the Parliament of the United Kingdom'. The Supreme Court concluded that this reservation should be interpreted as referring to attributes of the UK Parliament that are relevant to the nature of the UK constitution. This would include a provision which undermined the sovereignty of Parliament. Merely enacting an Act of the Scottish Parliament that contradicted UK legislation would not 'relate' to the reserved matter of the UK Parliament. The Scottish Parliament can enact legislation for Scotland that contradicts a UK Act of Parliament, provided that this does not modify legislation listed in Schedule 4 to the Act. The Supreme Court then considered whether section 17 challenged the sovereignty of the Westminster Parliament and concluded:

> [63]. Nor are we persuaded that section 17 impinges upon the sovereignty of Parliament. Section 17 does not purport to alter the fundamental constitutional principle that the Crown in Parliament is the ultimate source of legal authority; nor would it have that effect. Parliament would remain sovereign even if section 17 became law. It could amend, disapply or repeal section 17 whenever it chose, acting in accordance with its ordinary procedures.
>
> [64]. The preferable analysis is that although section 17, if it became law, would not affect Parliamentary sovereignty, it would nevertheless impose a condition on the effect of certain laws made by Parliament for Scotland, unless and until Parliament exercised its sovereignty so as to disapply or repeal it. It would therefore 'affect the power of the Parliament of the United Kingdom to make laws for Scotland', and so modify section 28(7) of the Scotland Act.

This appears, at first sight, to give rise to a contradiction. How can section 17 both impose a condition on the exercise of the enactment of legislation by the Westminster Parliament and also not restrict the sovereignty of the Westminster Parliament? Surely section 17 does not 'modify' section 28(7) of the Scotland Act 1998 if the Westminster Parliament can just enact legislation that contradicts section 17, thereby disapplying or repealing the condition imposed by section 17? One possible means of resolving this conundrum is to see these statements of the Supreme Court as supporting a 'manner and form' account of parliamentary sovereignty. While the UK Parliament can overturn the conditions imposed by section 17 of the Scottish Legal Continuity Bill, it can only do so through express or specific wording, particularly given that the Scotland Act 1998 is an example of a constitutional statute. If this is correct, then it may provide further support for the possible entrenchment of devolution. However, a better interpretation is to realise that the perceived sovereignty conundrum is really an issue of the timing at which the potential modification of section 28(7) of the Scotland Act 1998 takes place and when the court assesses whether legislation enacted by the Scottish Parliament 'relates to' the sovereignty of Parliament. As paragraph 64 of the judgment makes clear, section 17 does impose a condition that exists until the moment that the Westminster Parliament acts to alter this condition. At the time of its enactment, therefore, section 17 does purport to modify section 28(7), even though it does not limit the sovereignty of the Westminster Parliament. Sovereignty is not altered as Westminster still remains the ultimate source of legal authority in the UK. It would appear, therefore, that the UK courts are not yet at the stage where they would regard the devolution legislation of being incapable of being repealed.

This interpretation is reinforced when we analyse the status of the Sewel Convention in UK law. Although Westminster may continue to legislate for Scotland, Wales and Northern Ireland, when the Scotland Act 1998 was enacted it was envisaged that the Westminster Parliament should legislate on devolved matters only with the agreement of the Scottish Parliament. This understanding was confirmed by a minister, Lord Sewel, when the Scotland Bill was before the House of Lords, in saying (HL Deb vol. 592, col 791, 21 July 1998):

> we would expect a convention to be established that Westminster would not normally legislate with regard to devolved matters in Scotland without the consent of the Scottish Parliament.

After discussion and agreement between the UK and the Scottish Governments, a 'Sewel Motion' (also known as a legislative consent motion) was introduced in the Scottish Parliament for approval of the legislation to be enacted at Westminster. This also includes legislation enacted for Wales and Northern Ireland. The convention is contained in a memorandum of understanding between the UK and the devolved governments which states:

> The UK Government will proceed in accordance with the convention that the UK Parliament would not normally legislate with regard to devolved matters except with the agreement of the devolved legislature. The devolved administrations will be responsible for seeking such agreement as may be required for this purpose on an approach from the UK Government.

Over time, legislative consent motions were also sought not only when the UK Parliament legislated for the UK in an area of devolved competence, but also when the UK enacted measures that altered the devolved competences. The original content of the Sewel Convention is now also recognised in legislation. The Wales Act 2017, for example, inserted the following provision into the Government of Wales Act 2006, immediately after the recognition that the Westminster Parliament still has the power to legislate for Wales, in section 107(6):

> But it is recognised that the Parliament of the United Kingdom will not normally legislate with regard to devolved matters without the consent of the Assembly.

A similarly worded provision is now found in section 28(8) of the Scotland Act 1998, inserted by the Scotland Act 2016. However, rather than the Sewel Convention being regarded as a limit on the powers of Westminster, it has rather been regarded as a means of empowering Westminster to legislate for Scotland, Wales and Northern Ireland, subject to obtaining the consent of the relevant devolved legislature. As Barry Winetrobe has argued ('A Partnership of the Parliaments?', in Hazell and Rawlings (eds.), *Devolution, Law Making and the Constitution* (2005), pp. 41–2):

> What began life as a 'negative' safeguard and assurance against any unilateral exercise of Westminster legislative supremacy over devolved matters has become in practice a positive mechanism authorising the exercise, albeit with consent, by Westminster of just such legislative authority. Far from being the exception, as was originally suggested, it has become a regular, virtually institutionalised feature of the Scottish devolved law making scene.

This concern is all the more worrying given that, in spite of its being recognised in legislation, the Sewel Convention remains a convention. The courts will not legally enforce any perceived breach of this convention. In *R (Miller)* v. *Secretary of State for Exiting the European Union* [2017] UKSC 5, [2018] AC 61 (discussed in Chapter 3), the Supreme Court confirmed that, as a convention, the Sewel Convention could not be enforced by the courts. The Supreme Court also considered the effect of the legislative recognition of the convention by the Scotland Act 2016, concluding, at para [149], that:

> In the Scotland Act 2016, the recognition of the Sewel Convention occurs alongside the provision in section 1 of that Act. That section, by inserting section 63A into the Scotland Act 1998, makes the Scottish Parliament and the Scottish government a permanent part of the United Kingdom's constitutional arrangements, signifies the commitment of the UK Parliament and government to those devolved institutions, and declares that those institutions are not to be abolished except on the basis of a decision of the people of Scotland voting in a referendum. This context supports our view that the purpose of the legislative recognition of the convention was to entrench it as a convention.

This interpretation further confirms the preservation of the sovereignty of the Westminster Parliament, recognising the power of the Westminster Parliament both to enact legislation for the UK in a devolved area of power and to modify the devolution settlement. While the Sewel Convention, broadly understood, may require consent of the devolved legislatures, if such consent is not obtained, the legislation enacted by Westminster is nevertheless legally binding. As will be seen in the following section, this has given rise to tension between Westminster and the devolved legislatures.

(See, further, Bradley, 'Constitutional Reform, the Sovereignty of Parliament and Devolution', in University of Cambridge Centre for Public Law, *Constitutional Reform in the United Kingdom* (1998); McFadden and Lazarowicz, *The Scottish Parliament* (4th edn. 2010); Page, in Hazell and Rawlings (eds.), *Devolution, Law Making and the Constitution* (2005), ch. 1; Mitchell, in Trench (ed.), *The Dynamics of Devolution* (2005), ch. 2; Mitchell, *Devolution in the UK* (2011); Deacon,

Devolution in the United Kingdom (2nd edn. 2012); Schütze and Tierney (eds.), *The United Kingdom and the Federal Idea* (2017).)

4.4 Devolution and Brexit: An Uncertain Future?

The Brexit referendum brought inherent tensions in the devolution process to the fore. These tensions were evident from the enactment of the Referendum Act 2015 authorising the referendum and have persisted through the negotiation process, particularly concerning the repatriation of powers from the EU following implementation period completion day. The Brexit process also illustrates the asymmetrical nature of devolution in the UK, and the way in which, while devolution is deeply embedded in Scotland, Wales and Northern Ireland, the view from Westminster may often appear different. Brexit has placed the union of the United Kingdom under severe pressure – perhaps pushing this to breaking point. This is particularly true in Scotland. Those voting against independence in the 2014 referendum may have been persuaded by the fact that, by remaining as part of the United Kingdom, Scotland would remain in the European Union. Brexit, however, reversed this fact. Both of the calls for a second independence referendum in Scotland have focused on this change. While the 2014 independence referendum may have been seen as a once in a generation opportunity, the change in direction over EU membership has been seen in Scotland as a sufficiently important change to justify a further independence referendum. While there are not the same calls for independence in Wales, there is a desire to see a stronger role for Wales in the United Kingdom. In Northern Ireland, there is still the possibility of a border poll, particularly given the contentious issue of the Northern Ireland Protocol designed to enable Northern Ireland to be a part of the same customs regulations as the UK, while preventing the need for a hard border between Ireland and Northern Ireland. Nevertheless, in spite of these tensions, Brexit may also provide an opportunity to improve intergovernmental and interlegislative relations in the United Kingdom, through its creation of shared powers and the need to develop common frameworks across the United Kingdom.

The European Union Referendum Act 2015 provided an opportunity for the United Kingdom as a whole to decide whether to remain in or to leave the European Union. During the progress of the bill, Alex Salmond proposed an amendment to the bill, requiring not just a vote in favour of leaving from the UK as a whole, but also from a majority of the component parts of the United Kingdom (HC Deb 16 June 2015, vol. 597, col 190; similar arguments were made by Ms Ahmed-Sheikh: HC Deb 16 June 2015, vol. 597, cols 260–1). However, this amendment was rejected. While this fits the understanding that the relationship of the UK with the EU is reserved to the United Kingdom, this nevertheless reflects a lack of recognition of the importance of the range of voices across the United Kingdom. The outcome of the referendum also reflected this divergence. While England and Wales voted to leave the European Union, Scotland and Northern Ireland voted to remain.

The lack of a requirement of consent for all four components of the United Kingdom also illustrates a clear distinction between a devolved and a federal nation. A federal constitution often ensures that the component states or nations in that federation have a potential veto power over constitutional change. This lack of a veto was reinforced by the approach of the UK Supreme Court to the Sewel Convention in *R (Miller)* v. *Secretary of State for Exiting the European Union* (discussed above). The Supreme Court both confirmed that courts cannot legally enforce conventions, and that the recognition of the Sewel convention in legislation (at that time in the Scotland Act 2016, the Wales Act 2017 having not yet been enacted) did not convert the Sewel Convention into a legally enforceable provision. Rather, it recognised the convention as a convention, effectively entrenching it as a convention. This made it clear that any veto the devolved nations had over constitutional change, and the implementation of that change, would be political and not legal. In other words, if there were not effective political mechanisms to uphold the Sewel Convention, any objection from the devolved nations could, legally, be ignored.

The divergence expressed in the Brexit referendum was reflected in, and to a certain extent exacerbated by, the different policy documents produced by the Scottish Government, and the Welsh Government and Plaid Cymru and the eventual negotiation stance taken by the UK Government. In *Scotland's Place in Europe*, the Scottish Government argued in favour of a soft form of Brexit: remaining in the single market and the customs union and enabling Scotland to mirror EU regulations post-Brexit. In *Securing Wales' Future: Transition from the European Union to a New Relationship*, the Welsh Government and Plaid Cymru also argued against a hard Brexit advocating: the retention of full and unfettered access to the single market for goods, services and capital; enabling EU citizens to remain in Wales with reciprocal arrangements for Welsh citizens residing in EU countries; and the retention of high social standards, consumer protection and environmental protections. Both advocated for a role for Scotland and Wales in the negotiation process. However, there was divergence as to their desired future relationship with the Westminster Government. The Scottish Government's desired outcome was for an independent Scotland in the European Union, in addition to an assurance of the repatriation of powers in devolved areas from the EU to Scotland. The Welsh Government and Plaid Cymru advocated for more shared powers between Westminster and the devolved nations, focusing on the development of more federal structures and a stronger role for Wales in the United Kingdom.

The United Kingdom's White paper *The Future Relationship between the United Kingdom and the European Union* (Cm 9593, July 2018), advocated a hard form of Brexit, including leaving both the single market and the customs union. This was replicated in both of the withdrawal agreements negotiated between the UK and the EU. Although the Westminster Government established a specific Joint Ministerial Committee on European Negotiations, there were criticisms of this process. The committee met only sporadically, at the initiation of the Westminster Government, and there was very little, if any, transparency of the negotiation process. This led to concerns that the process provided an ineffectual means of deliberation. This process, and the divergent outcomes, furthered tensions between Westminster, Scotland and Wales. These tensions were exacerbated by the first iteration of the European Union (Withdrawal) Act 2018, particularly concerning the repatriation of powers from the EU to the UK.

Following the UK's exit from the European Union, powers that had been transferred to the EU would return to the UK. Some of those powers would be within the sphere of devolved powers – for example, agriculture and fishing. The question arose as to whether these should return to the devolved legislatures, or whether they should be transferred to the UK. Prior to Brexit, the devolved legislatures had the power to implement EU law within the area of devolved powers. However, all three devolved legislatures were unable to enact legislation or act contrary to EU law. This ensured that there was a system of commonality, established through EU law, with smaller divergence surrounding how the devolved legislatures and Westminster implemented EU obligations found in EU directives. While the devolved legislatures wished to see powers in devolved areas to be repatriated from the EU to the devolved legislatures, Westminster was concerned that this could lead to too much divergence, undermining the existing common frameworks established by EU law and, potentially, threatening to damage the common market in goods and services across the UK.

When it was introduced to the House of Commons, the European Union (Withdrawal) Bill 2017–19 stated, in clause 11, that the devolved legislatures would not have the power to modify retained EU law, either through primary or delegated legislation, for the first two years following the UK's exit from the EU. During this period, the UK, through delegated legislation enacted by orders in council, could transfer power back to the devolved legislatures to modify retained EU law. This was perceived as a power grab by the devolved legislatures. It led both Scotland and Wales to enact their own legislation to ensure the retention of EU law in Scotland and Wales – the Scottish legislation was challenged by the Attorney General before the Supreme Court (see above, at p. 320). The pressure from both the Welsh Assembly and the Scottish Parliament led to amendments to the bill. These amendments are found in section 12 of the European Union (Withdrawal) Act 2018. This empowers the delegated legislatures to modify retained EU law within the sphere of its devolved powers. However, ministers of the UK Government, by delegated legislation, can limit the scope of these powers for two years, enabling the UK to enact common frameworks where required. Any order to retain power at Westminster in this manner is subject to obtaining 'consent' from the devolved legislatures. However, consent is described as follows (section 30A(4) into the Scotland Act 1998; section 109A(5) Government of Wales Act 2006 and section 6A(4) Northern Ireland Act 1998):

(a) a decision to agree a motion consenting to the laying of the draft,
(b) a decision not to agree a motion consenting to the laying of the draft, or
(c) a decision to agree a motion refusing to consent to the laying of the draft;

> and a consent decision is made when the Parliament first makes a decision falling within any of paragraphs (a) to (c) (whether or not it subsequently makes another such decision).

In other words, consent does not require the devolved legislatures to agree to delegated legislation transferring aspects of retained EU law in devolved areas to Westminster in order to empower Westminster to establish common frameworks. The Scottish Parliament was unhappy with these modifications, and refused to approve the Legislative Consent Motion on the European Union (Withdrawal) Act 2018. The Welsh Assembly also initially refused consent and enacted its own legislation to ensure the continuity of EU law in Wales – the Law Derived from the European Union (Wales) Act 2018. However, following modification to the European Union (Withdrawal) Act 2018, Wales consented to the 2018 Act. The Welsh Government entered into negotiations with the UK Government, obtaining an agreement as to the use of section 12. Following this agreement, the Welsh Government used its powers under the Law Derived from the European Union (Wales) Act 2018 (found in section 22) to revoke the legislation.

The tension between the devolved legislatures and Westminster did not stop there. All three of the devolved legislatures were asked to approve a legislative consent motion for the European Union (Withdrawal Agreement) Act 2020, which implements the Withdrawal Agreement between the UK and the European Union into domestic law. All three legislatures refused to give their consent. Nevertheless, the European Union (Withdrawal Agreement) Act 2020 was enacted without consent. On the one hand, this could be perceived as a further breach of the Sewel Convention which, as discussed above, has been applied not only when Westminster enacts legislation on a devolved matter but also, as in the case of the 2020 Act, when Westminster enacts legislation that modifies the devolution settlement. However, this could also be perceived not as an extension of the Sewel Convention, but as an additional practice, given that this was not within the original expression of the Sewel Convention in the memoranda of understanding between Westminster and the devolved legislatures. Neither is it found in the legislative recognition of the Sewel Convention in the new provisions of the Scotland Act 1998 and the Government of Wales Act 2006.

Most of our discussion to date has concerned the tensions between Westminster and Scotland and Wales. This was because, as discussed above, there was neither a government nor a legislature in Northern Ireland during the Brexit negotiation process, Stormont was recomposed in January 2020, enabling the scrutiny of the European Union (Withdrawal Agreement) Act 2020. The future relations between the UK and the devolved legislatures would appear to be the most precarious as regards Northern Ireland. This is because a hard Brexit, without the UK's membership of the common market, requires a border between Northern Ireland and Ireland as goods and services move from one to the other. However, given the longstanding tensions between the two communities in Northern Ireland, a hard border is – to say the least – undesirable. The solution to this situation is the Northern Ireland Protocol. Although Northern Ireland will be part of the same customs union as the UK, it will also, for a fixed period after the end of the implementation period completion day, ensure that its laws comply with EU laws on goods. There will also be customs checks on goods travelling from the UK to Northern Ireland when it is likely that the goods will then move from Northern Ireland to Ireland. The extension of the protocol beyond this fixed period is taken by a simple majority – there is no need for cross-community support. It remains to be seen whether this will provide a workable solution for Northern Ireland. If not, there remains the possibility that Northern Ireland could hold a border poll, which as we saw above, would place a legal obligation on the UK Government to initiate discussions with Ireland should the people of Northern Ireland vote to join Ireland. Brexit provides a reason for why some in Northern Ireland may wish to do so – in order to continue as a member of the European Union.

Brexit also provides greater opportunity for the devolved government and legislatures and Westminster to work together. Schedule 2 of the European Union (Withdrawal) Act 2018 empowers the devolved governments, either acting alone or acting jointly with a minister of the Crown, to enact delegated legislation to remedy deficiencies in retained EU law. The same ability to act jointly is found in Schedule 1 of the European Union (Withdrawal Agreement) Act 2020. This could provide an opportunity to build better mechanisms for facilitating the different devolved governments and Westminster ministers to work together. It remains to be seen whether this will help repair relations between the component parts of the United Kingdom, or further exacerbate existing tensions.

(See, further, Tierney, 'The Territorial Constitution and the Brexit Process' (2019) 72 Current Legal Problems 59; European Union Committee *Brexit: Devolution 4th Report 2017–19* HL Paper 9; McHarg and Mitchell, 'Brexit and Scotland' (2017) 19 *British Journal of Politics and International Relations* 512; V Bogdanor *Beyond Brexit: Towards a British Constitution* (2019), ch. 6.)

4.5 Local Government

Every modern state, unless of minute size, needs a system of local administration. Even if all important decisions were taken at the centre, there would need to be local agencies to implement them, issuing commands and services to local populations, and some subsidiary decision-making would have to be delegated to these agencies. Of course, there are many possible kinds of arrangement for local administration. In the UK, part of this task is performed by local branches of central government, such as the outposts of HM Revenue and Customs and of the Department of Work and Pensions, as well as by a host of unelected local public-spending bodies (local 'quangos'); however, the most wide-ranging responsibilities fall to elected local government.

It would be generally agreed that local government in the UK has the following main objectives:

- to reduce the load on the centre – central government in the modern state would be greatly overloaded if the burden of administration were not shared with local institutions;
- to provide opportunities for democratic choice and popular participation in the government of local areas – in this way government can be made more accountable to local communities, and ordinary citizens can take a fuller part in the democratic process and in public life;
- to achieve more responsive and rational decision-making through institutions that are well informed about local conditions and aware of local needs and demands – specific policies can be developed to match local circumstances, and national policies can be adapted to the needs of different areas and communities.

The Redcliffe-Maud Commission, in its report on the structure of local government in England, gave some attention to the purposes of local government.

Report of the Royal Commission on Local Government in England (Redcliffe-Maud Report) vol. 1, Cmnd 4040/1969

28. Our terms of reference . . . require us to bear in mind the need to sustain a viable system of local democracy: that is, a system under which government by the people is a reality. This we take to be of importance at least equal to the importance of securing efficiency in the provision of services. Local government is not to be seen merely as a provider of services. If that were all, it would be right to consider whether some of the services could not be more efficiently provided by other means. The importance of local government lies in the fact that it is the means by which people can provide services for themselves; can take an active and constructive part in the business of government; and can decide for themselves, within the limits of what national policies and local resources allow, what kind of services they want and what kind of environment they prefer. More than this, through their local

representatives people throughout the country can, and in practice do, build up the policies which national government adopts – by focusing attention on local problems, by their various ideas of what government should seek to do, by local initiatives and local reactions. Many of the powers and responsibilities which local authorities now possess, many of the methods now in general use, owe their existence to pioneering by individual local authorities. Local government ... being, by its nature, in closer touch than Parliament or Ministers can be with local conditions, local needs, local opinions, is an essential part of the fabric of democratic government. Central government tends, by its nature, to be bureaucratic. It is only by the combination of local representative institutions with the central institutions of Parliament, Ministers and Departments, that a genuine national democracy can be sustained.

29. We recognise that some services are best provided by the national government: where the provision is or ought to be standardised throughout the country, or where the decisions involved can be taken only at the national level, or where a service requires an exceptional degree of technical expertise and allows little scope for local choice. Even here, however, there is a role for local government in assessing the impact of national policies on places and on people, and in bringing pressure to bear on the national government for changes in policy or in administration, or for particular decisions. And wherever local choice, local opinion and intimate knowledge of the effects of government action or inaction are important, a service is best provided by local government, however much it may have to be influenced by national decisions about the level of service to be provided and the order of priorities to be observed.

30. We conclude then that the purpose of local government is to provide a democratic means both of focussing national attention on local problems affecting the safety, health and well-being of the people, and of discharging, in relation to these things, all the responsibilities of government which can be discharged at a level below that of the national government. But in discharging these responsibilities local government must, of course, act in agreement with the national government when national interests are involved.

The Widdicombe Committee, in its report on *The Conduct of Local Authority Business* (Cmnd 9797/1986), saw the value of local government as stemming from its attributes of *participation* (by the local community), *responsiveness* (to local needs) and also *pluralism*, or 'the spreading of power within the state' (paras 3.13–13.17).

In a balanced assessment of the claimed benefits of local government, Anne Phillips concludes that its strongest justification is to be found in its role in 'enhancing and developing democracy', in particular through providing 'the most accessible avenue for political participation'. She argues for the development of procedures for the 'deepening' of local democracy, so that 'the locality can play a crucial role in extending discussion and deliberation and debate' ('Why Does Local Democracy Matter?', in Pratchett and Wilson (eds.), *Local Democracy and Local Government* (1996)).

4.5.1 Structure of Local Government

Until well into the nineteenth century the local government of England and Wales was a Byzantine structure of borough corporations, parishes, justices of the peace and ad hoc authorities of various kinds – 'a chaos of institutions, areas and rates' (Richards, *The Reformed Local Government System* (4th edn. 1980), p. 15). The Local Government Acts of 1888 and 1894 created a more rational system, which was to endure in its essentials until the reorganisation effected by the Local Government Act 1972.

The structure of local government established by the acts of 1888 and 1894 was based on democratically elected local authorities. County councils were the upper-tier authorities in the counties; below them were rural district councils and, for the smaller towns, urban district councils or non-county borough councils. Within the rural districts, some minor functions were retained by parishes. Larger towns were separately administered as 'county boroughs' by all-purpose authorities independent of the counties. London was given its own county government – the London County Council (LCC) – in 1888, and the London Government Act 1899 created twenty-eight metropolitan borough councils within the area of the LCC. (The City of London kept its own ancient institutions.)

The system created by these enactments assumed a separation between town and country which was to become ever more unreal. Suburban development, population growth and mobility, and the increasing scale of local government activity (including such new services as education, environmental planning, health, housing and social welfare) demanded a radical reorganisation of the structure and working of local government. The groundwork for reform was done by a series of royal commissions on *Local Government in Greater London* (Herbert Report, Cmnd 1164/1960), on *Local Government in England* (Redcliffe-Maud Report, Cmnd 4040/1969) and on *Local Government in Scotland* (Wheatley Report, Cmnd 4150/1969).

The Herbert Commission's proposals were implemented by the London Government Act 1963. The LCC was replaced by the Greater London Council (GLC), with jurisdiction extending over a much larger built-up area and responsibilities in such matters as strategic planning, transport, main roads, fire protection, etc. The bulk of local services, including education, health, housing, local planning and social welfare, were to be discharged by thirty-two London borough councils. The Redcliffe-Maud Commission's proposals for the rest of England were criticised on their merits and generated political contention. In the event, the Local Government Act 1972 departed in some important respects from the Redcliffe-Maud scheme, in particular in adopting a two-tier structure of local government instead of the Redcliffe-Maud proposal of all-purpose unitary authorities. In Scotland, there was, from 1975, a two-tier system of nine regional councils (responsible for education, social work, strategic planning and transport) and fifty-six district councils (responsible for local planning and housing).

If these reforms were directed towards increasing the efficiency of local government, the scheme as implemented, and the reduction in the number of local authorities, may have furthered a movement towards greater centralisation of powers. Martin Loughlin, for instance, has suggested that 'the reforms which were enacted were not part of a programme of creating functionally effective units through which the trend towards centralisation could be reversed ... but part of the centralisation process itself' (*Local Government in the Modern State* (1986), p. 9). The process of centralisation continued after the return of a Conservative Government in 1979. The new government was resolved to abolish the GLC and the metropolitan councils as 'a wasteful and unnecessary tier of government' (Conservative Party manifesto, 1983). (They also had the demerit of being strongholds of opposition to the government's policies.) Their dissolution was accomplished by the Local Government Act 1985.

The reformed local government system of 1972–3 was not universally acclaimed. It had endured for less than twenty years when the government embarked on a further reorganisation of local government in England, Scotland and Wales. In announcing the review to be undertaken for England, the Secretary of State for the Environment remarked that 'local government cannot be a fully independent power in the land. It traditionally derives its power from Parliament, and it must complement and not compete with central Government in its activities' (HC Deb vol. 188, col 401, 21 March 1991). In a consultation paper (*Local Government Review: The Structure of Local Government in England* (1991)), the government found the two-tier system of county and district councils to be unsatisfactory in several respects. Although it was not proposed to establish a uniform pattern of authorities throughout England, it was contemplated that single-tier government would be the norm. Similar consultation produced a like result in Scotland.

The Local Government Act 1992 established a Local Government Commission for England with the task of reviewing local government areas as directed by the Secretary of State and recommending appropriate boundaries, electoral changes and administrative structures for each such area. The Act empowered the Secretary of State to give effect to the commission's recommendations, in his discretion, by laying orders before Parliament.

The commission completed its review at the beginning of 1995; its recommendations fell far short of the government's preference for an England of predominantly single-tier local government. The Secretary of State's insistence on a radical reconsideration by the commission provoked the resignation of its chairman. The review was resumed under his successor. In the event, forty-six new unitary local authorities were established in England (and a further nine in 2009), but the two-tier structure of county and district councils remains in place in most of the non-metropolitan counties. This 'hybrid' structure of local government lacks a logical foundation and it has been doubted whether it will prove a durable solution. That said, the claimed merits of a general adoption of unitary local government – more effective management, planning and service delivery – are much debated.

Local authorities in English towns and cities were given the option by the Local Government Act 2000 of having a directly elected mayor and/or of adopting an 'executive structure' in place of the 'committee structure' that had been traditional for local authorities. These options were streamlined by the Local Government and Public Involvement in Health Act 2007. By the end of 2009, twelve local authorities in England and Wales had elected mayors. The Localism Act 2011 facilitated further restructuring. Referendums in the twelve largest English cities took place to create directly elected mayors in Birmingham, Leeds, Sheffield, Bradford, Manchester, Liverpool, Bristol, Wakefield, Coventry, Leicester, Nottingham and Newcastle-upon-Tyne. Of those, only Leicester, Liverpool and Bristol voted in favour of establishing an elected mayor. The 2011 Act also empowers local authorities to abolish local mayors, following a referendum. A referendum can take place either from a decision of the council to hold a referendum, or following a local petition.

Following the Scottish independence referendum, the government announced the possibility of 'devolution deals' to devolve more power to local areas, also through a system with an elected major, but in combined as opposed to local authorities. At the time of writing, devolution deals had been made in Greater Manchester, the Sheffield City Region, West Yorkshire, Cornwall, North of Tyne, Tees Valley, West Midlands, Liverpool City Region, Cambridgeshire/Peterborough and West of England. These deals are negotiated between the government and the specific combined authority. There are now powers under the Cities and Local Government Devolution Act 2016 to enact orders in council to transfer statutory functions (although, controversially, this appeared to grant retrospective validity for earlier transfers).

In 1998 the Labour Government published new proposals for the government of London 'to fill the democratic deficit created by the abolition of the GLC in 1986, to provide strong strategic leadership and restore accountability' (A Mayor and Assembly for London, Cm 3897/1998). The government's proposals were approved in a referendum held in Greater London on 7 May 1998 and were implemented by the Greater London Authority Act 1999, establishing a Greater London Authority (GLA), a new type of city government in the UK, consisting of a mayor of London and a London Assembly, each elected for a term of four years. If there are three or more candidates, the mayor is elected by the supplementary vote system in which each voter may express a first and second preference. A candidate who wins more than half the first-preference votes is elected as mayor; otherwise, all but the two candidates with the most votes are eliminated and the second-preference votes of the eliminated candidates are allocated between the two who remain in the contest: the candidate who then has more votes is elected. (If there are only two candidates, the election is by the 'first-past-the-post' system.) The twenty-five London Assembly members are elected by the additional member system, each voter having a constituency vote and a London vote. Fourteen 'constituency members' are elected by 'first-past-the-post' in single-member constituencies and eleven 'London members' by the party list system (or as independents) on a London-wide vote. Following the enactment of the Police and Social Responsibility Act 2011, the mayor is also the Police and Crime Commissioner for London.

The GLA has responsibility, and a general power, to promote economic development and wealth creation, social development and the improvement of the environment in Greater London. Following the enactment of the Localism Act 2011, the mayor also has powers of land acquisition and social housing, maintaining economic development strategy and the power to establish mayoral development corporations for specified areas. The mayor also oversees the London Environment Strategy. The London Assembly can reject mayoral strategies on a two-thirds majority vote. In 2017, the London Finance Commission, convened by the London Mayor Sadiq Khan, produced a report recommending the devolution of taxes to London – including stamp duty, air passenger duty, vehicle excise duty, and a share of income tax and VAT revenue. The GLA has already imposed transport-related levies – e.g. the congestion charge and an emissions levy.

The structure of local government in Scotland and Wales was reorganised in 1994 by legislation instituting single-tier local government in the two countries. The Local Government (Scotland) Act 1994 established thirty-two all-purpose authorities for Scotland – fewer elected councils and larger areas than before. Responsibility for local government in Scotland (including questions of structure) was devolved to the Scottish Parliament by the Scotland Act 1998. The Local Governance (Scotland) Act 2004 introduced the single transferable vote system for local government elections with effect from 2007. (See, further, Himsworth, 'Local Government in Scotland', in McHarg and Mullen (eds.), *Public Law in Scotland* (2006), ch. 8, and see further below.)

The Local Government (Wales) Act 1994 replaced the existing eight county councils and thirty-seven district councils in Wales with twenty-two unitary authorities. The devolution settlement for Wales initially left responsibility for the structure and boundaries of local government with the Secretary of State but these have now been devolved. The Local Government and Elections (Wales) Bill 2019 will extend the franchise in local elections to sixteen and seventeen year olds and foreign citizens legally resident in Wales (similar to the Senedd Cymru) as well as proposing a new legislative framework for the regulation of local government in Wales.

Local government in Northern Ireland was reformed by the Local Government (Northern Ireland) Act 1972. The Act established a lower tier of twenty-six district councils with limited functions, while many local government services were to be discharged for the whole province by the Parliament and Government of Northern Ireland as the upper tier. A 'review of public administration' was completed in 2005. It was decided to reduce the number of local authorities from twenty-six first to seven and subsequently to eleven, covering larger areas and with substantially increased responsibilities and powers: see now the Local Government (Boundaries) (Northern Ireland) Act 2008. These reforms were completed in 2015.

4.5.2 Functions and Powers

Martin Loughlin has identified 'multi-functionality' as one of the basic characteristics 'of critical importance in shaping the institution of local government' (see above). In *Legality and Locality: The Role of Law in Central-Local Government Relations* (1996, pp. 80–1), he instances the transfer of functions, in the late nineteenth and early twentieth centuries, from single-purpose local boards (e.g., for education and for poor relief) to local authorities as exemplifying the idea 'that the local inhabitants might look to a single institution for the basic services which government should provide at the level of the locality'. During this period, local authorities steadily acquired additional functions, such that their total spending came to be roughly a quarter of all public expenditure. Loughlin observes, however, that since the 1930s 'local authorities have been stripped of various responsibilities, including trunk roads in 1936, electricity in 1947, gas in 1948, water and sewerage in 1974, public assistance between 1934 and 1948, hospitals in 1946 and the remaining local health services in 1974' (*Local Government in the Modern State* (1986), p. 6).

The removal of functions from local government was intensified after 1979 under the auspices of a Conservative Government committed to a fundamental transformation of local authorities, to become, in the words of a Secretary of State for the Environment, 'enablers and regulators rather than providers of services' (*Municipal Review*, April 1989, p. 9; see also *Competing for Quality*, Cm 1730/1991, p. 22). In the 1980s and 1990s, a tide of legislation curtailed local government responsibilities in respect of education, housing, police services and public transport. While, on the one hand, local authorities acquired some new functions, notably in assuming community care responsibilities (National Health Service and Community Care Act 1990), on the other, there was a dispersal of local functions, resulting in 'an institutionally differentiated structure of local governance' (Loughlin, *Legality and Locality* (1996), p. 108).

The loss of functions by local government was a matter of concern to the House of Lords Select Committee on Relations between Central and Local Government. It noted the view of the local authority associations that local authorities had become mere agents of central policy 'at the expense of an independent role in their own communities'.

Report of the Select Committee on Relations between Central and Local Government, vol. I, HL 97 of 1995–96, paras 6.2–6.3

For a long time, and under different governments, power in this country has been moving away from local authorities, either to central government or to appointed or elected bodies, often not involving local authorities, some of which operate at a local level, and which are mostly single-purpose bodies. We do not believe this movement to be necessarily due to any over-arching central philosophy aimed at attacking local government itself. Central government has on occasions wished to promote national standards, to correct perceived mismanagement or overspending by local authorities, or to deal with those which have over-stepped their place. It has found that the easiest way to achieve these aims is to take powers away from local government.

There have been many such changes which, while individually explicable, have, taken together, resulted in a significant if incremental shift in the balance of power to the centre.

The fragmentation of local responsibilities had resulted in the loss of an overall view of the needs of the local area and a blurring of accountability (see paras 4.46 and 6.9 of the *Report*). The committee concluded that if nothing were done to strengthen the position of local government, there was a risk of 'a continued attrition of powers and responsibilities' from local authorities 'until nothing meaningful is left' (para 6.30).

Local authorities nevertheless retain a wide range of functions relating to such matters as consumer protection, culture and entertainment, education, environmental health, fire, highways and public transport, housing, licensing, personal social services, planning and development control.

Local authorities owe their existence to statute and their powers are conferred on them (and can, therefore, be taken away) by Parliament. All local government expenditure requires statutory authorisation.

Many statutes give powers to local authorities to enable them to carry out their functions. The statutory powers of local authorities were marginally extended by section 111 of the Local Government Act 1972, which provides that a local authority 'shall have power to do any thing . . . which is calculated to facilitate, or is conducive or incidental to, the discharge of any of their functions'. As to the limits (some would say the emasculation) of this power, see the controversial decision of the House of Lords in *Hazell* v. *Hammersmith and Fulham London Borough Council* [1992] 2 AC 1, critiqued in Loughlin, *Legality and Locality* (1996), ch. 6.

Local authorities had been constrained in taking action for the benefit of their communities by the ultra vires principle: they have been able to act only within the limits of the powers conferred on them. In a series of cases, the courts have construed this restriction strictly: *Hazell* (above) and *Bromley London Borough Council* v. *Greater London Council* (below) are notorious examples. Section 2 of the Local Government Act 2000 empowered local authorities to do anything they considered likely to promote or improve the economic, social or environmental wellbeing of their local community. While welcome as an attempt to confer greater freedom on local authorities, even after the 2000 Act it was reported that 'in the great majority of cases councils will continue to act under specific, detailed and limited statutory powers' (Leigh, 'The New Local Government', in Jowell and Oliver (eds.), *The Changing Constitution* (6th edn. 2007), p. 300). The Localism Act 2011 now provides a general power of competence to local authorities in England: a local authority now 'has power to do anything that individuals generally may do' (section 1(1)), subject to statutory limitations.

In some cases, the courts have held local authorities to be constrained, in decisions involving the expenditure of money, by a duty – commonly if dubiously characterised as a 'fiduciary' duty – owed to local taxpayers (formerly 'ratepayers'). For instance, in *Prescott* v. *Birmingham Corpn* [1955] Ch. 210, the Court of Appeal decided, on this principle, that the corporation's scheme of free travel facilities for old people in the city was ultra vires and illegal. Although the corporation was authorised by statute, in operating its passenger transport service, to charge such fares as it thought fit, it was held that it owed a duty to its ratepayers to run the undertaking 'on business lines' and was not permitted to confer rights of free travel 'on any class or classes of the local inhabitants appearing to them to be deserving of such benefits by reason of their advanced age and limited means'. (The effect of this restrictive decision was removed, in respect of local public transport service undertakings, by the Public Service Vehicles (Travel Concessions) Act 1955; see now the Transport Act 1985, sections 93–105.)

The principle of a fiduciary duty to ratepayers was again invoked in *Bromley London Borough Council* v. *Greater London Council* [1983] 1 AC 768. The GLC, in implementing an election manifesto promise of its Labour majority to cut London transport fares by 25 per cent, paid a subsidy to the London Transport Executive (LTE), which then ran London's buses and tubes, to enable it to make the reduction. To raise money for the subsidy, the GLC issued a supplementary rate precept to the London boroughs, to be met from additional rates, and this decision was challenged by Bromley Council. The House of Lords ruled that the GLC, in exercising in this way its discretionary power under the Transport (London) Act 1969 to make grants to the LTE, had acted ultra vires and unlawfully. Their Lordships held that the Act required the GLC to strike a fair balance between users of London transport and the ratepayers from whose resources any subsidy would be supplied. The GLC, in the view of the house, had failed properly to strike this balance in introducing low fares without due regard to ratepayers' interests or the requirement of the Act that the LTE should, so far as practicable, break even in its operations. In reaching this conclusion, their Lordships interpreted the Act as requiring that London transport should be run on business principles, not for objects of social policy, and placed a strong emphasis on the GLC's fiduciary duty to ratepayers, interpreting provisions of the Act As being implicitly qualified by this duty.

The reasoning of the five Law Lords in the *Bromley* case differed markedly in detail in interpreting a statute that was by no means explicit as to the extent of the GLC's power to pay revenue subsidies to the LTE. (See, further, Dignan, 'Policy-Making, Local Authorities and the Courts: The "GLC Fares" Case' (1983) 99 *LQR* 605; Griffith, 'Judicial Decision-making in Public Law' [1985] *PL* 564, 575–82.)

The decisions of local authorities may be challenged in proceedings for judicial review on the usual grounds (see Chapter 10; and see also Sunkin et al., 'Mapping the Use of Judicial Review to Challenge Local Authorities in England and Wales' [2007] *PL* 545). Complaints of maladministration or failures in the provision of services by local authorities may be taken to a local government and social care ombudsman under the Local Government Act 1974 as amended. (See also the Public Services Ombudsman (Wales) Act 2019, the Scottish Public Services Ombudsman Act 2002 and the Local Government (Northern Ireland) Act 2014.)

4.5.3 Central-Local Government Relations

Part of the constitutional importance of local government is that power in the state is dispersed: the autonomy of local authorities, answerable to their own electorates, is a counterweight to the authority of Whitehall. Contrariwise, central government, ever since it assumed a responsibility for economic progress and social welfare, has laid claim to the support of local government for national policies and has intervened to maintain uniform standards in local services.

Since we have no written constitution that fixes the boundary between central and local government, it can be shifted by the actions of successive governments so that, as George Jones and John Stewart say (*The Case for Local Government* (1983), pp. 110–11): 'Apparently minor and administrative changes can accumulate into a fundamental constitutional change, unnoticed until too late.' The Widdicombe Committee showed an awareness of this danger in warning that 'care is needed before taking decisions which, singly or cumulatively, might alter local government's status in the political system. This need is increased rather than diminished by the lack of a written consti-tution' (*The Conduct of Local Authority Business*, Cmnd 9797/1986, para 3.51). Both Labour and Conservative Governments have extended central control over local authorities, and this trend accelerated after 1979 with an avalanche of legislation affecting the resources, functions and powers of local authorities and, in its cumulative effect, significantly reducing local autonomy.

A flourishing local democracy requires that elected authorities should have substantial freedom to raise and spend money in the interests of their local communities, but in the 1980s and 1990s, central government took firm control of local government finance. At present, local authorities have three main ways of raising funds: government grants, council tax and business rates. About one-third of the money received by local authorities comes from the government grant. Large cuts in government grants have placed severe financial constraints on local authorities that do not have the power to borrow money. The Localism Act 2011 also limits the extent to which local authorities may raise council tax – any increase above an annual 2 per cent increase requires a referendum. The current government is carrying out a spending review and a fair funding review.

Statutes provide central government with a range of administrative controls of local government action. Some acts of local authorities are subject to ministerial *approval*. Local authorities may be required by statute to 'have regard' to *guidance* issued by ministers. Other statutes empower ministers to give *directions* to local authorities. There are also various statutory 'default powers' by which a minister may, for instance, issue directions to a local authority which has failed to perform its duty, or may transfer its responsibilities to another authority, or assume them himself or herself. See, in this connection, *Secretary of State for Education and Science* v. *Tameside Metropolitan Borough Council* [1977] AC 1014. (For a comprehensive survey of the issues, see House of Commons Communities and Local Government Committee, *The Balance of Power: Central and Local Government*, 6th Report of 2008–09, HC 33; see also the government response, published as Cm 7801/ 2010.)

(See, generally, Loughlin, *Legality and Locality: The Role of Law in Central-Local Government Relations* (1996); Leigh, *Law, Politics, and Local Democracy* (2000); Carmichael and Midwinter (eds.), *Regulating Local Authorities: Emerging Patterns of Central Control* (2003); Stoker and Wilson (eds.), *British Local Government into the 21st Century* (2004); Loughlin, 'The Demise of Local Government', in Bogdanor (ed.), *The British Constitution in the Twentieth Century* (2003); Bailey and Elliott, 'Taking Local Government Seriously: Democracy, Autonomy and the Constitution' [2009] *CLJ* 436.)

5

The European Dimensions

Contents

The previous edition of this book noted that 'no successful account of the British constitution can now be confined to institutions, events or laws which are exclusively British. Over the past half-century, as the constitutional importance of the Commonwealth has declined, so has the significance of "Europe" grown and grown again.' While this is hard to deny, it is impossible to ignore the impact of Brexit and the UK's exit from the European Union on 31 January 2020. Neither can we ignore the constitutional and legal modifications caused by this event.

This chapter will focus on the two most important European institutions and the UK's relationship with these institutions. It will look first at the Council of Europe and its European Convention on Human Rights (ECHR); and, second, at the European Union (EU). The UK is still a member of the ECHR, which focuses on protecting human rights in the UK. This chapter will set out the nature of the ECHR and its relationship with UK law. We will then provide an outline of the UK's membership of the EU, before analysing the impact of Brexit on the UK constitution, focusing in this chapter on the ever-changing relationship between the UK and the EU and between UK and EU law.

5.1 The European Convention on Human Rights

The ECHR is an international treaty made under the auspices of the Council of Europe, which is based in Strasbourg in eastern France (a list of the principal rights protected under the Convention was given above, p. 87). The UK was the first country to ratify the ECHR, in March 1951. The Convention came into force in 1953 and the European Court of Human Rights handed down its first judgment in 1961. From these slow post-war beginnings has grown an extra-ordinary and genuinely pan-European human rights regime. The Council of Europe now has forty-seven member states, all of whom are parties to, and are hence bound by, the convention. This membership stretches from Iceland to Turkey, from Finland to Malta, and from Portugal to Russia. Ukraine, Azerbaijan, Armenia and Georgia are all members, as are all twenty-six member states of the EU.

Under present arrangements any individual claiming to be a victim of a violation of the convention may lodge an application directly with the ECtHR in Strasbourg. When first established, cases were first referred to the commission, which determined their admissibility, before their referral to the Strasbourg Court. However, the continuing rise in cases lodged before the commission led to the enactment of Protocol 11 to the Convention, which came into force in 1998, abolishing the commission and turning the court into a full-time body. There is one judge on the court for each state party to the convention – judges are elected to the court by the Parliamentary Assembly of the Council of Europe from lists of three candidates submitted by the governments of the state parties for a non-renewable term of nine years. A Grand Chamber (composed of seventeen judges) hears cases that raise a serious question of interpretation of the convention or where there is a risk of departing from existing case law.

In spite of these changes, the backlog before the ECHR continued to rise – reaching a peak of more than 160,000 in 2011. In reaction to the ever-growing number of cases, the Council of Europe organised a series of conferences on the future of the European Court of Human Rights: the Interlaken Conference in 2010; the Izmir Conference in 2011; the Brighton Conference in 2012; the Brussels Conference in 2015 and the Copenhagen Conference in 2018. Two recurring themes run through these discussions: the need to tackle the docket problem, particularly as concerns repeat applications for the same or similar issues, and the need to respond to concerns from some states that the convention interferes too greatly in issues more suited to resolution by national democracies. Protocol 14 was developed to tackle the first issue. This moved to the system of a single judge, as well as changing the criteria for admissibility to the 'significantly disadvantaged' criterion, enabling judges to refuse applications where the applicant would not be significantly disadvantaged. Protocol 15 – which is not yet in force – aims to tackle this problem further by reducing the time limit for applications from six to four months. There is some evidence that these measures have had an impact. However, as of 1 January 2020, there were still 59,800 applications pending before the court. While this is an impressive reduction, it would suggest that there is still some way to go.

Protocol 15 was designed to implement the Brighton declaration. It adds a new recital at the end of the preamble to the convention, which contains a reference to the principle of subsidiarity and the doctrine of the margin of appreciation:

> Affirming that the High Contracting Parties, in accordance with the principle of subsidiarity, have the primary responsibility to secure the rights and freedoms defined in this Convention and the Protocols thereto, and that in doing so they enjoy a margin of appreciation, subject to the supervisory jurisdiction of the European Court of Human Rights established by this Convention.

Although this protocol has been signed by all forty-seven signatory states, at the time of writing, the protocol was not yet in force as two states – Italy and Bosnia and Herzegovina – had not yet ratified it. Further measures to facilitate effective dialogue between the national courts and the European Court of Human Rights can be found in Protocol 16, which provides national courts with a discretionary power to request an advisory opinion from the European Court of Human Rights. Although this has been signed and ratified by some signatory states, at the time of writing this protocol had not been signed by the United Kingdom.

Of the 59,800 cases pending before the court as of the end of 2019, 25.2 per cent were from Russia, 15.5 per cent from Turkey, 14.8 per cent from Ukraine and 13.2 per cent from Romania. In 2019, the court decided 40,667 cases, with 38,480 being struck out or declared inadmissible and 2,187 being decided by judgment of the court – as some of these were joined applications, the number of specific judgments was 884 in total. Very few cases progress to a judgment. In 2019, 84 per cent of the cases disposed of were found to be inadmissible, 10 per cent were struck out (including those struck out due to a friendly settlement or a unilateral declaration) and only 5 per cent proceeded to judgment. It continues to be the case that the overwhelming majority of applications received by the court are inadmissible and that, among those applications which are admissible, the vast majority of the court's caseload is routine. The court also continues to be swamped with very large numbers of repetitive applications from a relatively small number of states in which there are systemic human rights failures that are taking an excessively long time to put right. The length of court proceedings and the non-enforcement of judicial decisions appear to be among the biggest problems. The largest number of violations are found in cases concerning the right to a fair trial, the right to property, the right to liberty, the right to an effective remedy and freedom from inhuman or degrading treatment.

It is remarkable, perhaps, that in the meantime and in spite of its sometimes very high-profile critics (see, e.g., Lord Hoffmann, 'The Universality of Human Rights' (2009) 125 *LQR* 416), the court continues to be able to make genuinely important contributions to both the development and the application of international human rights law. To take two recent examples from the UK alone, in 2019 the court concluded that Schedule 7 of the Terrorism Act 2000 was incompatible with Article 8 ECHR. Schedule 7 empowered officers to stop, question and detain individuals at ports and airports if those individuals appeared to be, or have been, concerned in the commission, preparation or instigation of acts of terrorism. These powers do not require the officer in question to form a reasonable suspicion that the individual in question is involved in terrorist activity (see *Beghal* v. *United Kingdom* [2019] ECHR 4755/16). In 2018, the court concluded that the bulk surveillance activities of GCHQ breached Article 8 ECHR, given that there were insufficient safeguards concerning the collection and use of this data (*Big Brother Watch* v. *United Kingdom* [2018] ECHR 58170/13).

5.1.1 The ECtHR and its Impact on British Constitutional Law

What impact have the judgments of the ECtHR had on British constitutional law? This matter is addressed in the following extract. (By way of explanation, states parties to the convention were not required to accept the jurisdiction of the court (as opposed to that of the now defunct commission) until 1998: before that date this was optional among states that had ratified the convention. The UK accepted the jurisdiction of the court with effect from January 1966.)

Colm O'Cinneide, 'Human Rights and the UK Constitution', in Jowell and O'Cinneide *The Changing Constitution* (9th edn. 2019), pp. 64–5 and 66

The political momentum in favour of reform was also influenced by the development of international and European human rights law since 1945. Beginning with the ECHR in 1951, the UK ratified a variety of UN and Council of Europe treaty instruments designed to set out universally applicable human rights standards. In the Cold War era, compliance with these standards came to be seen as a key marker of respect for basic democratic principles. As a consequence, the civil and political rights set out in the ECHR and the interpretation given to these rights by the European Court of Human Rights in Strasbourg became an important reference point for all European legal systems. From the early 1970s on, judgments of the Strasbourg Court began to expose the existence of human rights 'blind spots' in UK law.

This contributed to growing disenchantment with the Diceyan constitutional orthodoxy, and encouraged a new focus on expanding the protection afforded by domestic UK law to human rights. So too did the development of various modes of constitutional rights review in many European jurisdictions after 1945, and the impact of the civil rights jurisprudence of the US Supreme Court during the 'Warren Court' period of the 1950s and the 1960s. The development of EU law also had an effect, as the provisions of rights-protective European legislation such as the Equal Treatment and Pregnant Workers Directives were applied by national courts and the ECJ to read down or suspend conflicting UK laws . . .

By 1997, when the Labour Party returned to power after eighteen years of being in opposition, the political climate was thus ripe for reform – which cleared the way for Parliament to enact the HRA in 1998 . . . this incorporated most of the ECHR rights into UK law and empowered the courts to overturn acts by public authorities which violated these rights, while preserving parliamentary sovereignty: courts were given the power to issue declarations of incompatibility to the effect that legislation was in their view incompatible with ECHR rights, but such declarations are not legally binding. The HRA thus preserved the existing ground rules of the UK constitutional system, while giving courts new powers to protect individual rights.

Significantly, the new devolution legislation introduced at the same time also required the devolved legislatures in Northern Ireland, Scotland and Wales to comply with Convention rights. The devolved legislatures were also to have the authority to take measures to give further effect to the UK's international human rights obligations when acting within the scope of their powers, including but not confined to those that arise under the ECHR. In addition, the 1998 Belfast Agreement, which brought the Northern Ireland conflict to an end, provided that compliance with the ECHR was an essential 'safeguard' of the peace process. It also affirmed that ECHR rights should be incorporated into, and made enforceable by, Northern Irish law. The Agreement also made provision for the establishment of a Human Rights Commission – which would play a leading role in considering whether a new Bill of Rights should be introduced containing supplemental rights to those contained in the ECHR 'to reflect the particular circumstances of Northern Ireland'.

ECHR compliance – and respect for human rights more generally – was thus built into the devolved system of governance from the beginning. This reflected the wide political support that existed in 1998 for ECHR incorporation, and more generally for the embrace of human rights law represented by enactment of the HRA.

This illustrates the influence of both the European Convention of Human Rights, and the EU, in the development of the protection of human rights in the UK. It marks the move away from a system of negative liberties, towards not only a system of positive rights, but also a developing human rights culture. Respect for human rights was built in to the devolution settlements and also played an important role in the peace process in Northern Ireland.

Conor Gearty, in a compelling analysis, has suggested that the core of the ECHR's influence can be reduced to three main areas: the first is due process, or the procedural safeguards afforded to individuals in criminal, civil or administrative law; the second is the protection of minority groups, most notably prisoners or those detained under mental health legislation, in respect of which there has been a considerable volume of Strasbourg case law emanating from the UK; and the third is what Gearty calls the protection of 'traditional civil liberties' such as privacy, freedom of expression and freedom of assembly (Gearty, 'The United Kingdom', in Gearty (ed.), *European Civil Liberties and the ECHR: A Comparative Study* (1997)).

An example of a case in Gearty's first category is *Brogan* v. *United Kingdom* (1988) 11 EHRR 117, in which the Court held that a provision of the (now repealed) Prevention of Terrorism Act 1984 allowing detention without charge for up to seven days violated Article 5(3) of the Convention, which provides that those arrested or detained should be brought 'promptly before a judge'. Unfortunately, the British Government's response to this judgment was to derogate from the convention, arguing that the troubles of Northern Ireland rendered the requirements of Article 5(3) inapplicable. Equally unfortunately, the ECtHR later upheld the legality of the derogation (see *Brannigan and McBride* v. *United Kingdom* (1993) 17 EHRR 539; on derogations from the convention, see Article 15 of the Convention and see further Chapter 11). The government withdrew the derogation in February 2001 after the Terrorism Act 2000 repealed the earlier legislation and made provision for extensions of detention to be authorised by a judicial officer.

Perhaps the best-known example of a case in Gearty's second category is *Golder* v. *United Kingdom* (1975) 1 EHRR 524. While Golder was an inmate in a British jail, he wished to sue a prison officer for libel, but the authorities refused him permission to consult a solicitor. After his release, Golder took the case to Strasbourg, where the court ruled that the authorities' action had infringed both Golder's right under Article 8(1) of the Convention to respect for his correspondence (part of the right to privacy) and his right under Article 6(1) to access to the courts (part of the right to a fair trial). The government's response was to amend the prison rules so as to allow a prisoner 'to correspond with a solicitor for the purpose of obtaining legal advice concerning any cause of action in relation to which the prisoner may become a party to civil proceedings or for the purpose of instructing the solicitor to issue such proceedings'. (In more recent times, prisoners' rights have received rather more robust protection from the domestic courts than was normal at the time *Golder* was decided. A number of the more important cases decided in light of the Human Rights Act have concerned prisoners' rights and may be seen to continue the work started in *Golder*: see, e.g., *R* v. *Secretary of State for the Home Department, ex p Simms* [2000] 2 AC 115 (above, p. 87) and *R (Daly)* v. *Secretary of State for the Home Department* [2001] 2 AC 532 (see Chapter 10).

Finally, a good example of a case in Gearty's last category is *Sunday Times* v. *United Kingdom* (1979) 2 EHRR 245. The *Sunday Times* wished to publish an article alleging that Distillers, a pharmaceutical company, had taken insufficient care before putting the drug thalidomide on the market. Thalidomide was a sedative that had been prescribed to numerous pregnant women, many of whom then gave birth to babies with severe deformities. At the material time almost 400 negligence actions had been brought against Distillers. The Attorney General brought proceedings seeking an injunction preventing the

Sunday Times from running its story. The House of Lords granted the injunction, holding that it would be in contempt of court for a newspaper to publish an article where there was a possibility that publication would prejudice legal proceedings (see *Attorney General* v. *Times Newspapers* [1974] AC 273). The *Sunday Times* took the matter to Strasbourg, where the ECtHR ruled that the test applied by the House of Lords failed to give sufficient weight to the newspaper's freedom of expression. The government's reaction was to place much of the law of contempt of court (which had previously been largely common law) on a statutory footing, the new Contempt of Court Act 1981 changing the test so that publication could be prevented in the future only where there was a substantial risk of serious prejudice to legal proceedings (section 2(2)). (Other important cases in this category include *Malone* v. *United Kingdom* (1984) 7 EHRR 14, concerned with telephone tapping and considered in Chapter 2, and the *Spycatcher* cases, concerned with the restrictions sought by the Thatcher Government on the publication of the memoirs of a former security service (MI5) officer: see *Observer and Guardian* v. *United Kingdom* (1991) 14 EHRR 153 and *Sunday Times* v. *United Kingdom* (No 2) (1991) 14 EHRR 229.

These examples illustrate something of the range of responses that the British Government has taken to judgments of the ECtHR where the court has found a violation of the convention. In the first, the government derogated and the offensive provision of the Prevention of Terrorism Act continued in force; in the second, the defect was cured by a change in the prison rules (delegated legislation made under the authority of the Prison Act); and, in the third, a new act of Parliament was passed. The Contempt of Court Act 1981 is far from the only statute to have been directly influenced by a judgment of the ECtHR. Other examples include the Interception of Communications Act 1985 (which followed the ruling in *Malone*; see now the Regulation of Investigatory Powers Act 2000), the Mental Health Act 1983, the Education (No 2) Act 1986, the Criminal Justice Act 1991 and the Special Immigration Appeals Commission Act 1997, as well as numerous others.

It should be noted that not all the cases outlined here concerned *legislative* violations of the convention. It was the *common law* judgment of the House of Lords that was found wanting in the *Sunday Times* case, as it was the common law of breach of confidence that was found to be violative of the right to freedom of expression in the *Spycatcher* cases. For all their embracement of human rights since the 1998 Act, British judges have not always been the keenest practitioners of European human rights standards, as these cases illustrate. When it is the common law that is found wanting in Strasbourg, the response may be to enact legislation to replace the common law (as with the Contempt of Court Act 1981) or it may be to issue a practice direction or some similar instruction so that the common law may change course.

While the UK has a generally good record in this regard, it does not always respond as quickly or as fully as it might in implementing measures required to comply with adverse rulings of the ECtHR. In *Hirst* v. *United Kingdom* (2006) 42 EHRR 41, in a judgment delivered in October 2005, the court ruled that the general ban on prisoners voting in UK elections was contrary to Article 3 of Protocol 1 (the right to free and fair elections). Yet, despite issuing two consultation exercises, nothing had been done by the 2010 general election to comply with the court's ruling in *Hirst*. This was in spite of a second decision of the European Court of Human Rights in *Greens and MT* v. *UK* (2010) 53 EHRR 710, which resulted in the European Court of Human Rights setting a six-month deadline for the UK to introduce legislation to remedy the violation of convention rights (this was then extended to take account of the Grand Chamber decision in *Scoppola* v. *Italy (No 3)* (2012) 56 EHRR 663). The Coalition Government indicated that it would amend the law and published a draft bill. This provided for three options: to continue the outright ban; to impose a ban for prisoners sentenced to terms of four years or more and a ban for prisoners sentenced to more than six months. A joint committee established to scrutinise the draft legislation recommended that those prisoners serving sentences of twelve months or under should be entitled to vote. However, neither the recommendations of the draft bill, nor of the joint committee, were taken forward by the Coalition Government of 2010 to 2015. In the meantime, further cases confirmed that the UK law was in breach of the convention (*Firth* v. *UK* [2014] EHRR 874 and *McHugh* v. *UK* [2015] Application No 5198/07 – however, in neither case was compensation awarded as, although an outright ban on prisoner voting was not permitted, it was not clear which prisoners should be allowed to vote) and a declaration of incompatibility in Scotland (*Smith* v. *Scott* [2007] SC 345) and a confirmation by the UK Supreme Court that the blanket ban on prisoner voting breached convention rights, although there was no further declaration of incompatibility issued in that case (*R (Chester)* v. *Secretary of State for Justice; R (McGeoch* v. *The Lord President of the Council (Scotland)* [2013] UKSC 63, [2014] AC 271).

In 2015, the general election returned a Conservative Government with David Cameron as Prime Minister. That same year also saw the Council of Europe's Committee of Ministers publish a decision calling on the UK to amend its legislation in line with convention rights. This was followed by an interim resolution in December 2015, where the Committee of Ministers '[e]xpressed profound concern that the blanket ban on the right of convicted prisoners remained in place'. The following year, the UK gave a commitment to the Committee of Ministers that it would bring forward proposals to address the convention breach. In 2017, David Liddington, then Minister of Justice, announced a change to the guidelines, such that prisoners released on a temporary licence could vote, alongside those released on licence with an electronic tag who already had the right to vote. The Council of Europe accepted these changes even though, in effect, it was thought to have only changed the law for about 100 prisoners. In 2020, Scotland enacted legislation allowing prisoners serving sentences of twelve months or under to vote in local Scottish elections

(Scottish Elections (Franchise and Representation Act 2020, section 5(3)). At the time of writing, the Welsh Senedd was also considering whether to extend the franchise in local elections to include prisoners serving terms of under four years.

5.1.2 Domestic Influence of the ECHR

So much for the impact of decisions of the ECtHR on our constitutional affairs. What remains to be considered is the influence of the convention within the case law of the domestic courts. This is a matter that has, of course, been completely transformed by the Human Rights Act. Here we will briefly consider the position within domestic law *before* the HRA, before moving to consider aspects of the present position. Fuller treatment of the impact of the HRA is contained elsewhere in this book, and what follows should be read alongside our more detailed consideration of the HRA's impact on parliamentary sovereignty (Chapter 2); of its impact on the law of judicial review (Chapter 10); and of its impact on the protection in the UK of human rights and civil liberties (Chapter 11).

5.1.2.1 Before the HRA

The mere conclusion of a treaty by the Crown cannot itself effect any alteration in the domestic law of the UK. Since the convention came into force on 3 September 1953 its provisions have been binding on the UK in international law, but prior to the entry into force of the HRA, they did not have direct internal legal effect and were not enforceable by the courts of this country: *R v. Secretary of State for the Home Department, ex p Brind* [1991] 1 AC 696.

However, even though the domestic courts could not enforce the terms of the convention, this does not mean to say that the convention had no indirect effect on domestic courts before the HRA. Indeed, in the period before the HRA the English courts were neither oblivious of the existence of the convention nor unreceptive to the principles it embodies. (Scots courts, by contrast, were considerably more resistant to the influence of the convention: in *Kaur v. Lord Advocate* 1980 SC 319 it was ruled that Scots courts should not have regard to the convention even in cases of statutory ambiguity. This line was overturned only in 1997: see *T, Petitioner* 1997 SLT 724.) English courts applied the 'prima facie presumption that Parliament does not intend to act in breach of international law, including therein specific treaty obligations': *Salomon v. Customs and Excise Comrs* [1967] 2 QB 116, 143 (Diplock LJ). Accordingly, if a statutory provision were ambiguous or unclear, the courts would interpret it in the sense that was more consonant with the provisions of the convention (see, e.g., *Waddington v. Miah* [1974] 1 WLR 683). As Lord Bridge remarked in *R v. Secretary of State for the Home Department, ex p Brind*, above, at 747–8, 'it is already well settled that, in construing any provision in domestic legislation which is ambiguous in the sense that it is capable of a meaning which either conforms to or conflicts with the Convention, the courts will presume that Parliament intended to legislate in conformity with the Convention, not in conflict with it.'

The courts also showed an increasing willingness to take account of the European Convention in developing the common law, sometimes taking the view that provisions of the convention marched with or were an articulation of principles underlying the common law (see, e.g., *Rantzen* v. *Mirror Group Newspapers* [1994] QB 670, 691). The convention was seen as having a particular relevance when questions of legal or public policy had to be determined: see, for instance, *R* v. *Chief Metropolitan Stipendiary Magistrate, ex p Choudhury* [1991] 1 QB 429. In *Derbyshire County Council* v. *Times Newspapers* [1992] QB 770, the Court of Appeal ruled that when developing a previously unclear rule of common law, the courts *must* have regard to relevant provisions of the convention. The House of Lords, while agreeing with the Court of Appeal in the result, did not expressly endorse this reasoning (see [1993] AC 534). Further remarks about the relationship between domestic law and the convention were uttered in the various *Spycatcher* cases: *Attorney General* v. *Guardian Newspapers* [1987] 1 WLR 1248 and *Attorney General* v. *Guardian Newspapers Ltd (No 2)* [1990] 1 AC 109.

A limit was reached with the *Brind* case, however, in which the House of Lords unanimously ruled that breach of the convention did not, of itself, constitute a ground of judicial review. That is to say, until the HRA, it could not be argued in a domestic court that government ministers or other public authorities had acted unlawfully solely because they had acted in a way that was in breach of a convention right: see *R* v. *Secretary of State for the Home Department, ex p Brind* [1991] 1 AC 696. Under domestic law as it stood before the HRA, judicial review was available only where it could be shown that government ministers or other public authorities had acted illegally, irrationally or procedurally unfairly. (The law of judicial review is discussed in more detail in Chapter 10.)

5.1.2.2 The HRA: Its General Scheme

The scheme of the HRA is to incorporate most of the substantive provisions of the European Convention into domestic law, with the effect that these become directly enforceable by British courts. It should be noted that not quite all of the substantive provisions of the convention are incorporated: in particular, Article 13 of the Convention, the right to an effective remedy, is not incorporated (for the consequences of this, see Chapter 10). The provisions of the convention are incorporated in two main ways. The first regards Parliament and the second government and other public authorities. As we saw in Chapter 2, sections 3 and 4 of the HRA govern the relationship between convention rights and acts of Parliament. Section 3(1) provides that: 'So far as it is possible to do so, primary legislation and subordinate legislation must be read and given effect in a way which is compatible with the Convention rights.' Section 4 provides that, if a court is satisfied that a provision of primary legislation is incompatible with a convention right, the court 'may make a declaration of that incompatibility'. Such a declaration 'does not affect the validity, continuing operation or enforcement of the provision in respect of which it is given' (section 4(6)(a)). Thus, as we saw in Chapter 2, courts in the UK do not have the power, even after the HRA, to strike down Acts of Parliament that they deem to be incompatible with convention rights. All they may do is 'declare' the incompatibility. It is then a matter for Parliament to decide whether it wishes to continue with the legislation, to amend it or to replace it.

Section 6 of the HRA governs the relationship between convention rights and the government and other public authorities. It provides that: 'It is unlawful for a public authority to act in a way which is incompatible with a Convention right.' This provision effectively overturns the ruling in *Brind* (above) and makes breach of a convention right a ground of judicial review in domestic law.

It should be noted that it is only the *text* of certain convention *articles* that is incorporated under the HRA. The case law of the ECtHR is not incorporated, although, as we saw above, section 2 of the HRA provides that domestic courts must take it into account in appropriate cases. This means that the techniques of interpretation employed by the European Court need not be followed by our domestic courts (see further on this matter Chapter 10).

Two further provisions of the HRA should be noted at this stage: section 10, which empowers ministers to make orders amending legislation where that legislation has been found to be violative of a convention right; and section 19, which provides that:

> A Minister of the Crown in charge of a Bill in either House of Parliament must, before Second Reading of the Bill
>
> (a) make a statement to the effect that in his view the provisions of the Bill are compatible with the Convention rights ('a statement of compatibility'); or
> (b) make a statement to the effect that although he is unable to make a statement of compatibility the government nevertheless wishes the House to proceed with the Bill.

Section 10 raises concerns about ministerial powers to legislate (considered in connection with the separation of powers in Chapter 2); section 19 reminds us that when we think about the impact of the HRA we must think not only of its impact on the case law of the courts but also of its impact on legislation and on parliamentary affairs generally (see below). Two points are worth making about section 19: the first is that it applies only to primary legislation. It does not apply to delegated legislation (although explanatory memoranda accompanying affirmative instruments do, as a matter of practice, include statements of ministerial views as to compatibility with convention rights). The second is that ministers do not have to give reasons as to why they consider that a bill is or is not compatible with convention rights. As a matter of practice, the explanatory notes that accompany bills do now include such reasons, but this is not a requirement of the HRA.

5.1.2.3 A Human Rights Culture in the UK?

While the section 19 statements are undoubtedly important, the more pressing reminder within Parliament of the importance of compliance with European human rights standards has come from the impressive, energetic and persistent work of Parliament's Joint Committee on Human Rights (JCHR). The committee was established with effect from January 2001. Among other tasks, it examines the compatibility with human rights of all bills introduced into Parliament. The committee's first legal adviser, David Feldman, has written that, as a result of the section 19 statements and, even more, as a result of the work of the committee, 'human rights are gaining in influence, particularly at the drafting stage of legislation' (Feldman, 'The Impact of Human Rights on the UK Legislative Process' (2004) 25 *Statute LR* 91). Feldman cites a number of bills that were amended as a result of concerns expressed by, and pressure exerted by, the committee. Among those he lists are the Anti-Terrorism, Crime and Security Act 2001, the Criminal Justice and Police Act 2001, the Enterprise Act 2002 and the Extradition Act 2003.

In the 2005–10 Parliament, the JCHR continued to play an active and highly visible role. It published reports on a large number of bills and enjoyed considerable success in bringing to the attention of both Houses of Parliament the human rights implications of the legislation they were considering. It took a particular interest in counterterrorism legislation, publishing no fewer than seventeen reports on this subject during the lifetime of the 2005–10 Parliament: a reflection, perhaps, of how central that topic had become both to British politics and to human rights law. While it undoubtedly succeeded in raising the profile of the human rights implications of the UK's counterterrorism legislation, the JCHR enjoyed only a partial success in terms of persuading Parliament that bills required amendment in order to make them compatible with human rights law. Perhaps its biggest success on this front came when the House of Lords defeated the government's proposal to extend pre-charge detention in terrorism cases to forty-two days (see HL Deb vol. 704, cols 491–544, 13 October 2008). The government's defeat in the House of Lords was so comprehensive that it immediately dropped its proposal and did not attempt to reintroduce it in the House of Commons. By the same token, the JCHR was as unsuccessful as were the human rights campaign groups in persuading the government that the regime of control orders needed amendment in order to comply with human rights law (For an overview, see Hiebert, 'Parliament and the HRA: Can the JCHR Help Facilitate a Culture of Rights?' (2006) 4 *ICON* 1; and JCHR, *Counter-Terrorism Policy and Human Rights, 16th Report of 2009–10*, HL 86, HC 111.)

The JCHR has continued to focus its analysis on terrorism legislation, with further reports on terrorist asset-freezing legislation, the regulation of TPIMs to replace control orders and legislation designed to tackled terrorism and extremism in the UK. The committee also investigated the impact of Brexit on human rights, as well as an influential report into human rights abuses surrounding the Windrush generation, confirming that two individuals had been wrongfully detained due to systemic failures in the Home Office (*Windrush Generation Detention: Sixth Report of 2017–19*, HC 1034, HL Paper 160). There is no equivalent of the JCHR in the devolved legislatures, although each has committees that focus on human rights and equality issues.

The Equality and Human Rights Commission (EHRC) is a statutory body established under the Equality Act 2006, whose remit is to promote and monitor human rights and to protect, enforce and promote equality. The law of equality and non-discrimination was codified and extended by the Equality Act 2010, an enactment of considerable constitutional importance. The EHRC seeks: (a) to enforce the law by bringing and participating in litigation; (b) to influence the development of the law and government policy; and (c) to promote best practice. Also important in this arena is the work of a variety of charities and campaign groups, such as the British Institute of Human Rights, Liberty and JUSTICE. Extensive information about these organisations is available from their websites.

As we stated earlier, full consideration of the impact of the HRA on case law in the UK is contained elsewhere in this book. As is made plain in each of these sections of the book, through the HRA, the ECHR exerts a growing and powerful influence over British constitutional law. Such influence is not always welcomed, not least by the government. Although the commission on a British bill of rights, established under the Coalition Government, did not recommend the replacement of the Human Rights Act with a British bill of rights, there have been repeated calls by the Conservative Party to repeal the Human Rights Act 1998. The Queen's Speech of 2019 included a promise to establish a commission on the constitution, democracy and rights, part of whose remit would be to investigate whether the balance between human rights and effective government needs to be redressed. However, although these arguments continue, Brexit and the response to the Covid-19 pandemic appear to have pushed human rights reforms off the immediate agenda.

5.2 Brexit and the European Union

For the remainder of this chapter, we shall consider the impact on the British constitution of the UK's membership of and exit from the EU, and the current uncertainty surrounding the UK's future relationship with the EU following implementation period completion day on 31 December 2020. The UK voted to leave the EU in a referendum that took place on 23 June 2016. The impact of Brexit on various aspects of the UK constitution has been discussed throughout this book. The purpose of this section is, first, to provide an overview of the nature of the UK's membership of the EU and the problems this was seen to pose for the UK constitution, before, second, providing an account of the legal journey through the Brexit process.

5.2.1 The EU

The UK became a member state of what is now the European Union (EU) on 1 January 1973. The EU, then the European Economic Community (EEC) was established in 1957 by six founding member states: France, West Germany, Italy, Belgium, the Netherlands and Luxembourg. Its creation was a key part of the international attempts made in the aftermath of the Second World War to rebuild Europe, and to do so in a manner that sought to prevent the recurrence of war. The EU was awarded the Nobel Peace Prize in 2012. One of the most impressive achievements of the EU was the creation of the single market (originally the common market). The EEC was renamed the European Community (EC) in the early 1990s; since the coming into force of the Lisbon Treaty (in 2010 – see below) the only correct name for the organisation is the EU. While we use the labels 'EU' and 'EU law' in the text of this book, several of our extracts date from times when 'European Community' and 'community law' were the correct terms. We have not altered the terminology used in the extracts. The EU now has twenty-seven member states: Austria, Belgium, Bulgaria, Croatia, Cyprus, Czech Republic, Denmark, Estonia, Finland, France, Germany, Greece, Hungary, Ireland, Italy, Latvia, Lithuania, Luxembourg, Malta, Netherlands, Poland, Portugal, Romania, Slovakia, Slovenia, Spain and Sweden. The UK left the EU on 31 January 2020. Its current relationship with the EU is governed by the Withdrawal Agreement, which will remain in force until 31 December 2020, unless extended.

The provisions of EU law are now found in the Lisbon Treaty, which is 'shorthand' for the Treaty on European Union (TEU) and the Treaty on the Functioning of the European Union (TFEU). The Lisbon Treaty provides the foundation not only for the single market, but also for greater economic and political Union between the member states of the European Union, including, for some, monetary union and a shared currency, the euro.

The TEU is much shorter than the TFEU. The TEU sets out the general values on which the EU is based (Articles 2–3) and outlines the core principles of EU law (Articles 4–6). It contains a series of provisions on democracy (Articles 9–12) and explains in outline the functions of each of the main EU institutions (the European Parliament, the European Council, the European Commission, the ECJ, etc.; we consider each of these institutions below). Most of the remainder of the TEU is concerned with the Common Foreign and Security Policy (CFSP) (Articles 21–46). There are then some closing provisions, including Article 48, which sets out new and important provisions governing how the treaties may be amended further in the future. Significantly, this includes Article 50 TEU, which for the first time, made it clear that a member state had the power to decide to leave the EU and set out the legal mechanism whereby a member state may do so.

The TFEU opens with a series of provisions concerning the EU's competences (that is to say, with provisions concerning the EU's powers). They seek to set out what EU law had already established: thus, while new as treaty provisions, they do not significantly alter EU law. The TFEU lists the areas in which the EU has exclusive competence. These are few. It then lists the areas in which the EU has shared competence (i.e., law- and policy-making powers that the EU's institutions share with member state governments). The vast majority of the EU's competences fall into this category. There is no list in the TFEU of the competences that remain exclusive to the member states, but Article 4 of the TEU describes the following as 'essential state functions': ensuring the territorial integrity of the state, maintaining law and order, and safeguarding national security; and Article 6 of the TFEU lists a series of policy areas in which the powers of the EU are limited to supporting, coordinating or supplementing the actions of the member states (these include health, culture and education, as well as others).

Part Two of the TFEU contains constitutionally important provisions on non-discrimination and citizenship. Article 18 of the TFEU sets out what is one of the most important and powerful rules of EU law: that 'any discrimination on grounds of nationality shall be prohibited' within the scope of application of EU law. Part Three of the TFEU, forming the bulk of the Treaty (Articles 26–197), contains detailed provisions governing the EU's policy areas. It commences with the internal market and the free movement of goods before turning to agriculture; the free movement of persons, services and capital; the area of freedom, security and justice; transport; competition, state aids and taxation; economic and monetary policy; employment; social policy; as well as numerous others, of which the environment has been perhaps the most notable. The TFEU also contains provisions on the EU's external actions (such as with regard to world trade policy and development aid) and on its budget. Part Six of the TFEU contains in Articles 223–309 detailed and, for our purposes, very important provisions governing the composition and powers of the EU's institutions and other bodies, the law-making procedures of the EU and the jurisdiction of the European Court of Justice.

In addition to the 358 Articles of the TFEU, a series of protocols and declarations are appended to it. The protocols enjoy the same legal force as the articles, but the declarations do not. From a constitutional point of view, a number of the protocols are of prime importance, including Protocol No 1, which outlines the roles to be played in EU law by national parliaments; Protocol No 2, which concerns the application of the core principles of subsidiarity and proportionality (discussed below); and Protocol No 30, which concerned the application in the UK (when a member state) and Poland of the EU's Charter of Fundamental Rights (discussed below).

One final and, from a student's point of view, undoubtedly awkward feature of Lisbon is that it renumbered the articles of the treaties. Moreover, this is not the first time this has happened: Amsterdam (1997) also renumbered the articles of both the TEU and the EC Treaty. Thus, an existing provision of either treaty that pre-dates Amsterdam will now have had three different numbers! So, for example, the provision on equal pay was Article 119 of the Treaty of Rome, which became Article 141 EC and is now Article 157 of the TFEU, and the provision governing preliminary references to the Court of Justice was Article 177 of the Treaty of Rome, which became Article 234 EC and is now Article 267 of the TFEU. This is nightmarish, not least because when reading a case from an earlier period, that case will, of course, use the numbers that applied at that time. Many of the leading cases on what is now Article 267 of the TFEU were decided long before Lisbon, so tracing the numeric history of that article becomes important. There is no getting around this. For simplicity's sake, in this book, we use the current, post-Lisbon numbering, but we give pre-Lisbon numbers alongside where we think it may be helpful.

Legally, at the heart of economic union lie the four 'fundamental freedoms' of EU law: the free movement of goods, the free movement of persons, the free movement of services and the free movement of capital. To this day, these principles continue to form the core of the EU's internal market. Alongside these provisions, the other major features of economic union concern competition law and the common agricultural policy. All of these matters have been central to the European project since the EEC's foundation in the 1950s, and they continue to be so. In addition, the Treaty of Rome contained a number of provisions concerned with social policy. Among the most important of these is the provision that: 'Each Member State shall ensure that the principle of equal pay for male and female workers for equal work or work of equal value is applied' (now Article 157 of the TFEU). Since the 1950s, a range of matters have been added to the legislative and policy-making competence of the EU. For example, provisions concerning environmental law were added by the Single European Act; provisions concerning CFSP and certain matters of freedom, security and justice were added at Maastricht; and provisions on employment policy and on visas, asylum and immigration were added at Amsterdam.

Article 1 of the TEU sets out what may be regarded as the overarching goal of the EU: to create 'an ever closer union among the peoples of Europe'. Article 2 of the TEU is in the following rather grand terms:

The Union is founded on the values of respect for human dignity, freedom, democracy, equality, the rule of law and respect for human rights, including the rights of persons belonging to minorities. These values are common to the Member States in a society in which pluralism, non-discrimination, tolerance, justice, solidarity and equality between women and men prevail.

The human rights language of this provision is notable. At its very opening, then, Lisbon seeks to reorient the EU beyond its economic origins, as an international organisation focused on the *overall* wellbeing of its member states and citizens: economic, social, cultural and political.

Articles 4 and 5 of the TEU set out some of the core constitutional principles of EU law as follows:

Article 4

1. In accordance with Article 5, competences not conferred upon the Union in the Treaties remain with the Member States.
2. The Union shall respect the equality of Member States before the Treaties as well as their national identities, inherent in their fundamental structures, political and constitutional, inclusive of regional and local self-government. It shall respect their essential State functions, including ensuring the territorial integrity of the State, maintaining law and order and safeguarding national security. In particular, national security remains the sole responsibility of each Member State.
3. Pursuant to the principle of sincere cooperation, the Union and the Member States shall, in full mutual respect, assist each other in carrying out tasks which flow from the Treaties.

The Member States shall take any appropriate measure, general or particular, to ensure fulfilment of the obligations arising out of the Treaties or resulting from the acts of the institutions of the Union.

The Member States shall facilitate the achievement of the Union's tasks and refrain from any measure which could jeopardise the attainment of the Union's objectives.

Article 5

1. The limits of Union competences are governed by the principle of conferral. The use of Union competences is governed by the principles of subsidiarity and proportionality.
2. Under the principle of conferral, the Union shall act only within the limits of the competences conferred upon it by the Member States in the Treaties to attain the objectives set out therein. Competences not conferred upon the Union in the Treaties remain with the Member States.
3. Under the principle of subsidiarity, in areas which do not fall within its exclusive competence, the Union shall act only if and in so far as the objectives of the proposed action cannot be sufficiently achieved by the Member States, either at central level or at regional and local level, but can rather, by reason of the scale or effects of the proposed action, be better achieved at Union level . . .

> 4. Under the principle of proportionality, the content and form of Union action shall not exceed what is necessary to achieve the objectives of the Treaties . . .

Five major principles of EU constitutional law are enshrined in these provisions. The *first* is the principle of conferred powers, also known as the principle of limited competences. The EU has only those powers that are conferred on it by the treaties. This has been a rule of European law since the founding of the EEC in 1957. As the treaties are made by the national governments of the member states, this means that the EU has only those powers that are conferred on it by national governments. To this critically important point of constitutional principle, however, needs to be added a rider. Article 352 of the TFEU (formerly Article 308 EC) provides that, if action by the EU should prove necessary in order to attain one of the objectives of the treaties, and if the treaties have not provided the EU with the necessary powers to undertake that action, measures may be taken to confer on the EU the power to take the necessary action, but only if all member state governments agree. There are limitations as to the circumstances in which Article 352 may be used (it cannot apply, for example, to a matter of CFSP) but it has nonetheless been extensively relied on by the EU's law-makers and it represents a hotly contested matter of EU constitutional law.

The *second* point of constitutional principle contained in Articles 4–5 of the TEU is the identification of essential state functions that the EU must respect. This is a new provision, written into the treaties at Lisbon.

If the first two points of constitutional principle are designed to protect the member states from improper expansion of the EU's powers, the *third* is designed to protect the EU by imposing an important constitutional obligation on the member states. This is the provision in the final two sentences of Article 4 of the TEU (before Lisbon, the equivalent provision was Article 10 EC). This 'fidelity clause' or duty of loyal cooperation was relied on by the Court of Justice in a series of groundbreaking cases in which the court developed means of giving European law real force in the face of what it perceived to be member state resistance. (Among the most important examples are Case 14/83 *Von Colson and Kamann* v. *Land Nordrhein-Westfalen* [1984] ECR 1891 and Joined Cases C-6 and 9/90 *Francovich and Bonifaci* v. *Italy* [1991] ECR I-5357, both of which are discussed further below.)

The *fourth* point of constitutional importance in Articles 4–5 of the TEU is the principle of *subsidiarity*, defined in Article 5(3). As is the case with all the constitutional principles enshrined in Articles 4–5, subsidiarity is judicially enforceable. But whereas the court has developed a considerable jurisprudence with regard to competence, fidelity and proportionality, it has struggled to give juridical teeth to the principle of subsidiarity. Indeed, to date, the court has yet to invalidate a single piece of EU legislation on the basis of its violation of the principle of subsidiarity. While subsidiarity is, in principle, justiciable, it is as much a political principle as it is a legal requirement. Protocols No 1 and No 2 of the TFEU seek to find ways of allowing the principle of subsidiarity to be policed politically. These protocols grant to national parliaments within member states a power formally to voice their concerns if they are of the 'reasoned opinion' that a legislative proposal fails to comply with the principle of subsidiarity. Such reasoned opinions must be taken into account by the EU's law-makers, but they do not necessarily have to be followed (reasons have to be given if the views of the national parliaments are to be overridden). Thus, national parliaments have no veto, no matter how strongly they believe a legislative proposal to be in violation of the principle of subsidiarity.

The *fifth* constitutional principle articulated by Articles 4–5 of the TEU is the principle of *proportionality*, which is as core to EU law as it is to European human rights law (see further below). For a case illustrative of the use made by the Court of Justice of the principle of proportionality, see Case C-491/01 *R v. Secretary of State for Health, ex p British American Tobacco* [2002] ECR I-11453 concerning the EU's controversial directive on the sale and marketing of certain tobacco products.

The constitutional principles enshrined in Articles 4–5 of the TEU are far from an exhaustive list. Fundamental rights are separately provided for in Article 6 of the TEU (we consider this matter later in this chapter: see pp. 371– 380). But as notable as their contents are the omissions from Articles 4, 5 and 6. There is no reference to the supremacy of EU law, to the law of direct or indirect effect, or to the principles of member state liability. Yet all of these are core to EU constitutional and administrative law.

5.2.2 The Backdrop to Brexit: Principles of EU Law

The clear message of the referendum campaign to leave the EU focused on the UK's need to 'take back control'. The growth of the EU, and key principles of EU law, were regarded as undermining the UK's sovereign law-making power. Not only was this seen as a limitation of the UK's powers, it was also seen as a transfer of power from a democratic decision-making body to a less democratically accountable body – or at least one which was less accountable to the British people. To understand these arguments, we need to understand four key principles of EU law – supremacy, direct and indirect effect, state liability and fundamental rights – and the impact of these principles on the UK constitution.

5.2.2.1 Supremacy

Supremacy concerns the relationship between EU law and national law. Suppose that a provision of EU law provides that x should be the law, whereas a provision of, say, British, German or Polish law provides that y should be the law. In the event that x and y are mutually incompatible, which should prevail? Surprisingly, perhaps, the treaties themselves are silent on this question. The

Court of Justice first declared what it considered the right answer to be in 1964, in one of its most significant constitutional decisions to date.

Case 6/64 *Costa* v. *ENEL* [1964] ECR 585 (ECJ)

European Court of Justice: ... By contrast with ordinary international treaties, the EEC Treaty has created its own legal system which, on the entry into force of the Treaty, became an integral part of the legal systems of the Member States and which their courts are bound to apply.

By creating a Community of unlimited duration, having its own institutions, its own personality, its own legal capacity and capacity of representation on the international plane and, more particularly, real powers stemming from a limitation of sovereignty or a transfer of powers from the States to the Community, the Member States have limited their sovereign rights, albeit within limited fields, and have thus created a body of law which binds both their nationals and themselves.

The integration into the laws of each Member State of provisions which derive from the Community, and more generally the terms and the spirit of the Treaty, make it impossible for the States, as a corollary, to accord precedence to a unilateral and subsequent measure over a legal system accepted by them on a basis of reciprocity. Such a measure cannot therefore be inconsistent with that legal system. The executive force of Community law cannot vary from one State to another in deference to subsequent domestic laws, without jeopardizing the attainment of the objectives of the Treaty ...

[T]he law stemming from the Treaty, an independent source of law, could not, because of its special and original nature, be overridden by domestic legal provisions, however framed, without being deprived of its character as Community law and without the legal basis of the Community itself being called into question. The transfer by the States from their domestic legal system to the Community legal system of the rights and obligations arising under the Treaty carries with it a permanent limitation of their sovereign rights, against which a subsequent unilateral act incompatible with the concept of the Community cannot prevail.

The doctrine of supremacy has been many times reaffirmed by the Court of Justice, with no mitigation of its rigour. National legal provisions of whatever order (even if part of the constitution of a member state) must yield precedence to EU law and, to the extent of any conflict with it, must be treated as inapplicable (see Case 11/70 *Internationale Handelsgesellschaft* [1970] ECR 1125). This is so even if the national law is of more recent date than the European rule with which it conflicts. The *Simmenthal* case was another landmark in the evolution of this doctrine.

Case 106/77 Amministrazione delle Finanze dello Stato v. *Simmenthal SpA*
[1978] ECR 629 (ECJ)
The Simmenthal company had been charged a fee for a public health inspection of beef that it had imported into Italy from France. The company

reclaimed the fee in an Italian magistrate's court on the ground that its imposition was contrary to provisions of EU law on the free movement of goods. This contention was upheld by the ECJ on a reference made to it by the Italian court. The Italian authorities then raised a new argument: the Italian law providing for the fee had been enacted *after* the relevant EU provisions, and although under Italian law an enactment could be held invalid if it conflicted with prior treaty obligations, only the Italian Constitutional Court had jurisdiction to give such a ruling; in the meantime, other courts must give effect to the enactment. The Italian magistrate then made a second reference to the European Court for a ruling on this question. In the course of its judgment, the Court of Justice restated the principle of the supremacy of EU law (as it now is: then community law) as follows (emphasis added).

European Court of Justice: ... [R]ules of Community law must be fully and uniformly applied in all the Member States from the date of their entry into force and for so long as they continue in force.

These provisions are therefore a direct source of rights and duties for all those affected thereby, whether Member States or individuals, who are parties to legal relationships under Community law.

This consequence also concerns any national court whose task it is as an organ of a Member State to protect, in a case within its jurisdiction, the rights conferred upon individuals by Community law.

Furthermore, in accordance with the principle of the precedence of Community law, the relationship between provisions of the Treaty and directly applicable measures of the institutions on the one hand and the national law of the Member States on the other is such that those provisions and measures *not only by their entry into force render automatically inapplicable any conflicting provision of current national law but* – in so far as they are an integral part of, and take precedence in, the legal order applicable in the territory of each of the Member States – *also preclude the valid adoption of new national legislative measures to the extent to which they would be incompatible with Community provisions.*

Indeed any recognition that national legislative measures which encroach upon the field within which the Community exercises its legislative power or which are otherwise incompatible with the provisions of Community law had any legal effect would amount to a corresponding denial of the effectiveness of obligations undertaken unconditionally and irrevocably by Member States pursuant to the Treaty and would thus imperil the very foundations of the Community ...

It follows from the foregoing that every national court must, in a case within its jurisdiction, apply Community law in its entirety and protect rights which the latter confers on individuals and must accordingly set aside any provision of national law which may conflict with it, *whether prior or subsequent to the Community rule.*

Accordingly any provision of a national legal system and any legislative, administrative or judicial practice which might impair the effectiveness of Community law by withholding from the national court having jurisdiction to apply such law the power to do everything necessary at the moment of its application to set aside national legislative provisions which might prevent Community rules from having full force and effect are incompatible with those requirements which are the very essence of Community law.

... [A] national court which is called upon, within the limits of its jurisdiction, to apply provisions of Community law is under a duty to give full effect to those provisions, if necessary refusing of its own motion to apply any conflicting provision of national legislation, even if adopted subsequently, and it is not necessary for the court to request or await the prior setting aside of such provision by legislative or other constitutional means.

The challenge posed by the principle of supremacy, as articulated by the Court of Justice in *Costa* and *Simmenthal*, is clear. In the UK context, the challenge is how the principle may be reconciled with the British constitutional doctrine of the sovereignty of Parliament. This doctrine, discussed in Chapter 2, provides, of course, that the UK Parliament may make or unmake any law whatever, and that no court may override or set aside an Act of Parliament. The Court of Justice, however, ruled in *Simmenthal* that it would be *invalid* for member states to adopt measures that are incompatible with EU law.

5.2.2.2 Direct and Indirect Effect

While it may be the clash between the principle of supremacy and the sovereignty of Parliament that has caught most of the headlines, it is in the doctrine of direct effect that the true radicalism of EU law lies. If a provision of EU law has direct effect, this means it may be invoked and relied on by a litigant in proceedings before a national court and that the national court must give due effect to it. Thus, making EU law directly effective is a means by which it may be enforced by national courts. Like supremacy, direct effect is not expressly provided for in the treaties, but is the creation of the case law of the Court of Justice. Here it is *Van Gend en Loos*, arguably the most important case in the Court's history, that is central.

Case 26/62 Van Gend en Loos v. Nederlandse Administratie der Belastingen [1963] ECR 1

The question for the Court of Justice was whether as a matter of EU law an importer (Van Gend en Loos) could plead before a Dutch court that certain provisions of European law had been infringed and, more specifically, whether the importer could as a matter of EU law claim the protection of rights conferred on them by European law, rights that the national court was under a duty to protect. The relevant provision of EU law was Article 12 EEC (now Article 30 of the TFEU), which provides that 'customs duties on imports and exports and charges having equivalent effect shall be prohibited between the Member States'.

European Court of Justice: . . . To ascertain whether the provisions of an international treaty extend so far in their effects it is necessary to consider the spirit, the general scheme and the wording of those provisions.

The objective of the EEC Treaty, which is to establish a common market, the functioning of which is of direct concern to interested parties in the Community, implies that this Treaty is more than an agreement which merely creates mutual obligations between the contracting states. This view is confirmed by the preamble to the Treaty which refers not only to governments but to peoples. It is also confirmed more specifically by the establishment of institutions endowed with sovereign rights, the exercise of which affects Member States and also their citizens. Furthermore, it must be noted that the nationals of the states brought together in the Community are called upon to cooperate in the functioning of this Community through the intermediary of the European Parliament and the Economic and Social Committee.

In addition the task assigned to the Court of Justice under [Article 267 of the TFEU, the preliminary reference procedure], the object of which is to secure uniform interpretation of the Treaty by national courts and tribunals, confirms that the states have acknowledged that Community law has an authority which can be invoked by their nationals before those courts and tribunals. The conclusion to be drawn from this is that the Community constitutes a new legal order of international law for the benefit of which the states have limited their sovereign rights, albeit within limited fields, and the subjects of which comprise not only Member States but also their nationals. Independently of the legislation of Member States, Community law therefore not only imposes obligations on individuals but is also intended to confer upon them rights which become part of their legal heritage. These rights arise not only where they are expressly granted by the Treaty, but also by reason of obligations which the Treaty imposes in a clearly defined way upon individuals as well as upon the Member States and upon the institutions of the Community.

With regard to the general scheme of the Treaty as it relates to customs duties and charges having equivalent effect it must be emphasized that [the Treaty], which bases the Community upon a customs union, includes as an essential provision the prohibition of these customs duties and charges. This provision is found at the beginning of the part of the Treaty which defines the 'foundations of the Community'. It is applied and explained by [Article 30 of the TFEU].

The wording of [Article 30] contains a clear and unconditional prohibition which is not a positive but a negative obligation. This obligation, moreover, is not qualified by any reservation on the part of states which would make its implementation conditional upon a positive legislative measure enacted under national law. The very nature of this prohibition makes it ideally adapted to produce direct effects in the legal relationship between Member States and their subjects.

The implementation of [Article 30] does not require any legislative intervention on the part of the states. The fact that under this Article it is the Member States who are made the subject of the negative obligation does not imply that their nationals cannot benefit from this obligation . . .

It follows from the foregoing considerations that, according to the spirit, the general scheme and the wording of the Treaty, [Article 30] must be interpreted as producing direct effects and creating individual rights which national courts must protect.

In the view of the Court of Justice, then, EU law is not simply a supranational body of law but is to enter the legal orders of the member states and be enforced by the national courts as well as by the Court of Justice itself. The English Court of Appeal judge Lord Denning was quick to see the radicalism of this as he gave typically vivid expression of the impact of direct effect in the course of his judgment in *Bulmer* v. *Bollinger* [1974] Ch. 401, 418–19, a case decided soon after the UK's accession to the EU:

> [W]hen we come to matters with a European element, the Treaty is like an incoming tide. It flows into the estuaries and up the rivers. It cannot be held back. Parliament has decreed that the Treaty is henceforward to be part of our law. It is equal in force to any statute. . . . Any rights or obligations created by the Treaty are to be given legal effect in England [sic] without more ado. Any remedies or procedures provided by the Treaty are to be made available here without being open to question. In future, in transactions which cross the frontiers, we must no longer speak or think of English law as something on its own. We must speak and think of Community law, of Community rights and obligations, and we must give effect to them.

It should be noted that, according to *Van Gend en Loos*, not all provisions of European law are directly effective. On the contrary, only those provisions that are clear, unconditional and negative may have direct effect. However, these conditions have been substantially liberalised in subsequent case law. The requirement that the provision be negative was dropped in Case 2/74 *Reyners* v. *Belgium* [1974] ECR 631 and the requirement that the provision must be unconditional and not in need of national implementing legislation was dropped in Case 43/75 *Defrenne* v. *Sabena* [1976] ECR 455. Most controversial has been the (partial) extension of the doctrine of direct effect to directives. In Case 41/74 *Van Duyn* v. *Home Office* [1974] ECR 1337 the Court of Justice ruled as follows:

> It would be incompatible with the binding effect attributed to a directive by Article [288 of the TFEU] to exclude, in principle, the possibility that the obligation which it imposes may be invoked by those concerned. In particular, where the Community authorities have, by directive, imposed on Member States the obligation to pursue a particular course of conduct, the useful effect of such an act would be weakened if individuals were prevented from relying on it before their national courts and if the latter were prevented from taking it into consideration as an element of Community law. Article [267 of the TFEU], which empowers national courts to refer to the Court questions concerning the validity and interpretation of all acts of the Community institutions, without distinction, implies furthermore that these acts may be invoked by individuals in the national courts. It is necessary to examine, in every case, whether the nature, general scheme and wording of the provisions in question are capable of having direct effects on the relations between Member States and individuals.

The importance of this extension becomes apparent when we contrast different forms of EU law, as set out in Article 288 TFEU:

> To exercise the Union's competences, the institutions shall adopt regulations, directives, decisions, recommendations and opinions.
>
> A regulation shall have general application. It shall be binding in its entirety and directly applicable in all Member States.
>
> A directive shall be binding, as to the result to be achieved, upon each Member State to which it is addressed, but shall leave to the national authorities the choice of form and methods.
>
> A decision shall be binding in its entirety. A decision which specifies those to whom it is addressed shall be binding only on them.
>
> Recommendations and opinions shall have no binding force.

A regulation, being 'directly applicable', has automatic effect as law in all the member states without any intervention by the national authorities of those member states. As such, it is the most powerful form of law available to the EU, apart from treaty provisions themselves. Regulations avoid the possibility that the law might be distorted or delayed in being re-enacted by agencies of the member states, and are especially apt when what is wanted is a prompt, precise and uniform application of rules throughout the union. The EU has the power to adopt regulations only where the treaty expressly so provides. If the EU has the power in a certain field to adopt only directives, it may not adopt regulations instead.

Directives are binding 'as to the result to be achieved': the member states are obliged to implement them but use their own legislative or administrative techniques in doing so. Unlike regulations, then, directives can come into force only when implemented (or 'transposed' into national law) by the member states. In other words, they are not 'directly applicable'. In the British context, such transposition will not always require primary legislation: sometimes secondary legislation (such as an order in council) will be sufficient. This will depend on the subject matter. Directives are an appropriate legislative instrument when a precisely uniform implementation is not necessary or would be difficult to realise because of differing legal, administrative or economic structures in the member states. They are particularly suitable for achieving a 'harmonisation' or 'approximation' of national laws, when that is required, for example, for the operation of the internal market (see Article 115 of the TFEU). A directive usually leaves to the member states a margin of discretion in carrying out its objectives. Directives normally set time limits for their implementation. Direct effect provides an effective means of ensuring that member states do not diverge too greatly from one another so as to harm the need for uniform application of EU law, and ensure that EU citizens can rely on directives that should have been implemented by their member state.

Contrariwise, it potentially removes member state discretion as to how to implement a directive.

The reasoning employed to extend direct effect to directives is neither particularly full nor convincing, and the judgment in *Van Duyn* was greeted with such hostility that the Court of Justice had to rethink its justification for extending direct effect to directives. This it did in Case 148/78 *Ratti* [1979] ECR 1629, where the court constructed an 'estoppel' argument as the basis for allowing directives, in certain circumstances, to have direct effect. The argument runs as follows: directives impose a duty on member states to adopt the appropriate implementing measures by a certain date; it would be wrong for member states to be able to rely on and gain advantage through their failure to carry out this obligation; they are thus 'estopped' or prevented from denying the direct effect of directives once the time limit for their implementation into national law has expired.

This reasoning has had an important consequence: namely, that directives may have direct effect and may be relied on by litigants in proceedings in national courts *where those proceedings are brought against a public authority of a member state*, but not otherwise. It is the *member state* that is estopped from gaining an advantage by failing to implement a directive, not any other body. Thus, an important difference has emerged between the direct effect of directives and the direct effect of treaty provisions and regulations. Whereas the latter may be directly effective, the identity of the party against whom legal proceedings are brought in the national court notwithstanding, directives may be relied on only where the party proceeded against is a public authority. This is called 'vertical' direct effect. Treaty provisions and regulations may be both vertically and horizontally directly effective, but directives may be only vertically directly effective. Thus, in Case 152/84 *Marshall* v. *Southampton and SW Hampshire Area Health Authority* [1986] ECR 723 Marshall sought to rely on and enforce a provision of the Equal Treatment Directive (76/207/EEC) against her employer. She was successful on the basis that her employer (the health authority) was a public authority. But had her employer been a private sector employer, she would have been unsuccessful. This distinction has been repeatedly and roundly criticised, but it remains the law (see Case C-91/92 *Faccini Dori* v. *Recreb* [1994] ECR I-3325).

Ever since *Marshall*, the Court of Justice has tried to find a number of other ways of giving greater effect to directives in the legal orders of the member states, without overruling its decisions that directives are incapable of having full (horizontal) direct effect. Several of these alternative means have had profound constitutional consequences. Here we shall consider three: the extension of the notion of the state, the doctrine of indirect effect and the development of state liability. If directives can have direct effect against the state, or against public authorities, it clearly becomes critical to know what is and what is not a public authority. The Court of Justice showed that, for the purposes of EU law, 'public authority' could have a very broad meaning. In

Case C-188/89 *Foster* v. *British Gas* [1990] ECR I-3313, for example, the court ruled that the pre-privatised British Gas could be regarded as a public authority. Rather than attempting to construct a pan-European definition, the court ruled that this was a matter best left for national courts to determine; although there are four indications that a body is a public body: (i) that it is performing a public service; (ii) that the performance of this service was transferred to the body by the state; (iii) that the state oversees the performance of this service and (iv) that the body in question has powers over and above those of ordinary individuals.

More important, perhaps, is the doctrine of indirect effect, otherwise known as the 'duty of consistent interpretation'. This doctrine amounts to a duty, imposed by the Court of Justice on national courts, in certain circumstances to interpret national law in a particular way. In Case 14/83 *Von Colson and Kamann* v. *Land Nordrhein-Westfalen* [1984] ECR 1891 the Court of Justice ruled that:

> in applying national law and in particular the provisions of national law specifically introduced in order to implement [a] directive, national courts are required to interpret their national law in the light of the wording and purpose of the directive.

Von Colson concerned the interpretation of a piece of German law that had been passed in order to give effect to a directive. To start with, it appeared that the duty of consistent interpretation applied only in the context of interpreting national law whose purpose was the implementation of a directive, but in Case C-106/89 *Marleasing* v. *La Comercial Internacionale de Alimentacion* [1990] ECR I-4135 the Court of Justice broadened the reach of the duty, ruling that (emphasis added):

> in applying national law, *whether the provisions in question were adopted before or after the directive*, the national court called upon to interpret it is required to do so, as far as possible, in the light of the wording and purpose of the directive in order to achieve the result pursued by the latter.

5.2.2.3 State Liability

The third and arguably most radical way in which the Court of Justice has sought to give greater effect to directives is through the doctrine of state liability. According to this doctrine member states will in certain circumstances be liable in damages to individuals who suffer loss as a result of the member state's failure properly to implement a directive into national law. The leading authority on state liability in the context of directives remains the *Francovich* case.

Joined Cases C-6 and 9/90 *Francovich and Bonifaci v Italy* [1991] ECR I-5357 (ECJ)

European Court of Justice: . . . It should be borne in mind at the outset that the EEC Treaty has created its own legal system, which is integrated into the legal systems of the Member States and which their courts are bound to apply. The subjects of that legal system are not only the Member States but also their nationals. Just as it imposes burdens on individuals, Community law is also intended to give rise to rights which become part of their legal patrimony. Those rights arise not only where they are expressly granted by the Treaty but also by virtue of obligations which the Treaty imposes in a clearly defined manner both on individuals and on the Member States and the Community institutions [citing *Van Gend en Loos* and *Costa* v. *ENEL*].

Furthermore, it has been consistently held that the national courts whose task it is to apply the provisions of Community law in areas within their jurisdiction must ensure that those rules take full effect and must protect the rights which they confer on individuals [citing *Simmenthal*].

The full effectiveness of Community rules would be impaired and the protection of the rights which they grant would be weakened if individuals were unable to obtain redress when their rights are infringed by a breach of Community law for which a Member State can be held responsible.

The possibility of obtaining redress from the Member State is particularly indispensable where, as in this case, the full effectiveness of Community rules is subject to prior action on the part of the State and where, consequently, in the absence of such action, individuals cannot enforce before the national courts the rights conferred upon them by Community law.

It follows that the principle whereby a State must be liable for loss and damage caused to individuals as a result of breaches of Community law for which the State can be held responsible is inherent in the system of the Treaty.

A further basis for the obligation of Member States to make good such loss and damage is to be found in Article [4(3) of the TEU], under which the Member States are required to take all appropriate measures, whether general or particular, to ensure fulfilment of their obligations under Community law. Among these is the obligation to nullify the unlawful consequences of a breach of Community law . . .

It follows from all the foregoing that it is a principle of Community law that the Member States are obliged to make good loss and damage caused to individuals by breaches of Community law for which they can be held responsible.

Although State liability is thus required by Community law, the conditions under which that liability gives rise to a right to reparation depend on the nature of the breach of Community law giving rise to the loss and damage.

Where, as in this case, a Member State fails to fulfil its obligation under the third paragraph of Article [288 of the TFEU] to take all the measures necessary to achieve the result prescribed by a directive, the full effectiveness of that rule of Community law requires that there should be a right to reparation provided that three conditions are fulfilled.

The first of those conditions is that the result prescribed by the directive should entail the grant of rights to individuals. The second condition is that it should be possible to identify the content of those rights on the basis of the provisions of the directive. Finally, the third condition is the existence of a causal link between the breach of the State's obligation and the loss and damage suffered by the injured parties.

Those conditions are sufficient to give rise to a right on the part of individuals to obtain reparation, a right founded directly on Community law.

Subject to that reservation, it is on the basis of the rules of national law on liability that the State must make reparation for the consequences of the loss and damage caused. In the absence of Community legislation, it is for the internal legal order of each Member State to designate the competent courts and lay down the detailed procedural rules for legal proceedings intended fully to safeguard the rights which individuals derive from Community law . . .

Further, the substantive and procedural conditions for reparation of loss and damage laid down by the national law of the Member States must not be less favourable than those relating to similar domestic claims and must not be so framed as to make it virtually impossible or excessively difficult to obtain reparation.

Since the *Francovich* decision the principle of state liability has been broadened. Originally a means of giving greater domestic legal effects to directives, in Joined Cases C-46/93 and C-48/93 *Brasserie du Pêcheur* v. *Germany* and *R* v. *Secretary of State for Transport, ex p Factortame Ltd (No 3)* [1996] ECR I-1029, the Court of Justice ruled that member states could be held liable in damages for a variety of breaches of EU law, including, significantly for our purposes, breaches attributable to national legislation:

the Court held in *Francovich* that the principle of State liability for loss and damage caused to individuals as a result of breaches of Community law for which it can be held responsible is inherent in the system of the Treaty.

It follows that that principle holds good for any case in which a Member State breaches Community law, whatever be the organ of the State whose act or omission was responsible for the breach . . .

The fact that, according to national rules, the breach complained of is attributable to the legislature cannot affect the requirements inherent in the protection of the rights of individuals who rely on Community law and, in this instance, the right to obtain redress in the national courts for damage caused by that breach.

Member states would be liable where the following three conditions were met:

In such circumstances, Community law confers a right to reparation where three conditions are met: the rule of law infringed must be intended to confer rights on individuals; the breach must be sufficiently serious; and there must be a direct causal link between the breach of the obligation resting on the State and the damage sustained by the injured parties.

State liability, while it is a doctrine of EU law, is principally for the national courts of the member states to enforce. The Court of Justice had the following to say about the sorts of factors that national courts could take into account:

> The factors which the competent court may take into consideration include the clarity and precision of the rule breached, the measure of discretion left by that rule to the national or Community authorities, whether the infringement and the damage caused was intentional or involuntary, whether any error of law was excusable or inexcusable, the fact that the position taken by a community institution may have contributed towards the omission, and the adoption or retention of national measures or practices contrary to Community law.
>
> On any view, a breach of Community law will clearly be sufficiently serious if it has persisted despite a judgment finding the infringement in question to be established, or a preliminary ruling or settled case-law of the Court on the matter from which it is clear that the conduct in question constituted an infringement.

The doctrine of state liability was further extended in Case C-224/01 *Köbler* v. *Austria* [2003] ECR I-10239, where the Court of Justice controversially ruled that decisions of national courts that fail to give sufficient weight to matters of EU law could, in principle, incur state liability (for comment, see Scott and Barber (2004) 120 *LQR* 403). The ruling in *Köbler* was reconfirmed by the ECJ in Case C-173/03 *Traghetti del Mediterraneo* v. *Italy* [2006] ECR I-5177.

5.2.2.4 Fundamental Rights

The Court of Justice first considered aspects of fundamental rights in case law dating back to the early 1970s (in Case 11/70 *Internationale Handelsgesellschaft* [1970] ECR 1125, for example). However, human rights were originally less central to EU law than the four fundamental freedoms of the internal market (free movement of goods, workers, services and capital). Gradually, however, human rights have grown in prominence in EU law. This was particularly so for those rights enshrined in the ECHR. As matters stand the ECHR is not formally part of EU law, and the EU still has not acceded to the ECHR, in spite of an obligation in the EU treaties for the EU to seek accession. Nevertheless, the Court of Justice has on numerous occasions referred to it in its case law and has stated that it enjoys a special status in EU law (see, e.g., Case 36/75 *Rutili* [1975] ECR 1219 and Case C-299/95 *Kremzow* [1997] ECR I-2629).

During 2000, a specially appointed convention drafted a charter of fundamental rights for the EU. This was 'proclaimed' by the European Council at Nice, but the Treaty of Nice did not incorporate this charter into the treaties and its legal status was left in flux. During the opening years of the twenty-first century Advocates General began to cite the charter with increasing frequency in their opinions, and the court itself did likewise for the first time in 2006, albeit that it was always careful to rely on the charter as an additional source and not as an exclusive source of rights (see, e.g., Case C-540/03 *European*

Parliament v. *Council* [2006] ECR I-5769). Lisbon changed all this and brought fundamental rights into the core of EU law for the first time. The central provision is Article 6 of the TEU, which reads as follows:

1. The Union recognises the rights, freedoms and principles set out in the Charter of Fundamental Rights of the European Union of 7 December 2000, as adopted at Strasbourg, on 12 December 2007, which shall have the same legal value as the Treaties.

   The provisions of the Charter shall not extend in any way the competences of the Union as defined in the Treaties.

   The rights, freedoms and principles in the Charter shall be interpreted in accordance with the general provisions in Title VII of the Charter governing its interpretation and application and with due regard to the explanations referred to in the Charter, that set out the sources of those provisions.

2. The Union shall accede to the European Convention for the Protection of Human Rights and Fundamental Freedoms. Such accession shall not affect the Union's competences as defined in the Treaties.

3. Fundamental rights, as guaranteed by the European Convention for the Protection of Human Rights and Fundamental Freedoms and as they result from the constitutional traditions common to the Member States, shall constitute general principles of the Union's law.

It is immediately apparent that Article 6 of the TEU brings the charter into full legal force, giving it the same status in EU law as the treaties themselves.

The charter, while it is partly based on the ECHR, goes significantly beyond it. All the substantive rights protected in the ECHR are also protected in the charter. Thus, both instruments include the right to life; freedom from torture; prohibition of slavery; the right to liberty; the right to a fair trial; the right to privacy; freedom of thought, conscience and religion; freedom of expression; freedom of assembly; the right to education; and the right to property, as well as others. The charter provides that '[i]n so far as this Charter contains rights which correspond to rights guaranteed by the [ECHR], the meaning and scope of those rights shall be the same as those laid down by' the ECHR (Article 52(3)).

Also included in the charter are numerous other rights that are not found in the ECHR. The following are examples: rights of the child (Article 24); rights of the elderly (Article 25); solidarity rights (Articles 27–38), including the right of collective bargaining and action (Article 28), the right to fair and just working conditions (Article 31), rights to social security and social assistance (Article 34), rights to health care (Article 35) and rights to environmental protection (Article 37); and citizens' rights (Articles 39–46), including the right to good administration (Article 41).

Of great importance is Article 51 of the charter (which appears in Title VII of the charter, referred to in Article 6(1) of the TEU). Article 51 provides as follows:

1. The provisions of this Charter are addressed to the institutions, bodies, offices and agencies of the Union with due regard for the principle of subsidiarity and to the Member States only when they are implementing Union law. They shall therefore respect the rights, observe the principles and promote the application thereof in accordance with their respective powers and respecting the limits of the powers of the Union as conferred on it in the Treaties.
2. The Charter does not extend the field of application of Union law beyond the powers of the Union or establish any new power or task for the Union, or modify powers and tasks as defined in the Treaties.

The charter therefore binds the EU's institutions and bodies: now that Lisbon has brought the charter into force, it is illegal as a matter of EU law for an institution or body of the EU to act in a manner that fails to respect a right enshrined in the charter. The charter also binds the member states, *but only when they are within the scope of EU law* (C-617/10 *Åklagaren v Hans Åkerberg Fransson*). This occurs, in particular, when member states implement EU law, or enact measures in an area that is regulated by EU law.

The UK (joined by Poland) negotiated the inclusion of a protocol to the Lisbon Treaty: Protocol No 30 on the Application of the Charter of Fundamental Rights to Poland and to the UK. This protocol provides as follows:

Article 1

1. The Charter does not extend the ability of the Court of Justice of the European Union, or any court or tribunal of Poland or of the United Kingdom, to find that the laws, regulations or administrative provisions, practices or action of Poland or of the United Kingdom are inconsistent with the fundamental rights, freedoms and principles that it reaffirms.
2. In particular, and for the avoidance of doubt, nothing in Title IV of the Charter [that is, the solidarity rights contained in Articles 27–38] creates justiciable rights applicable to Poland or the United Kingdom except in so far as Poland or the United Kingdom has provided for such rights in its national law.

Article 2

To the extent that a provision of the Charter refers to national law and practices, it shall only apply to Poland or the United Kingdom to the extent that the rights or principles that it contains are recognised in the law or practices of Poland or of the United Kingdom.

This protocol is not an opt-out from the charter, but it seeks to emphasise that, at least in respect of Poland (and the UK when it was an EU member state), the charter is not to be interpreted as extending the reach of EU law or as creating new rights. The Court of Justice of the European Union has interpreted the charter in tandem with human rights protected as general principles of EU law. However, it has expanded the meaning of 'implementing EU law' to include any situation where the member state is acting within the scope of EU law. Also, as we saw above, the UK courts have used charter provisions to disapply UK legislation, achieving a better remedy than was available under the Human Rights Act 1998 where the courts can only issue a declaration of incompatibility (see *Benkharbouche* v. *Embassy of the Republic of Sudan* [2017] UKSC 62, [2019] AC 777).

The charter has significantly raised the profile of rights in the EU legal order. Moreover, it has done so by describing them as 'fundamental'. Even if the charter of itself does not alter the *content* of EU law (by adding to its rights), it has added to the *weight* to be accorded in EU law to such rights as are contained in the charter. In addition, it has become clear in later cases that some provisions of the charter, in the same manner as some fundamental rights found in general principles of EU law, are capable of having horizontal and not just vertical direct effect – that is, they can impose obligations on individuals as well as on public bodies (C-569/16 and C-570/16 *Bauer et al.* [2019] 1 CMLR 1271).

There is one final point to make about the charter. It describes itself as the charter of fundamental *rights*. But not everything in the charter is a 'right'. The preamble to the charter proclaims that the EU 'recognises the rights, freedoms and principles set out' in the charter. Article 52(1) and 52(5) of the charter help to decode this (emphasis added):

Article 52

1. Any limitation on the exercise of the *rights and freedoms* recognised by this Charter must be provided for by law and respect the essence of those rights and freedoms. Subject to the principle of proportionality, limitations may be made only if they are necessary and genuinely meet objectives of general interest recognised by the Union or the need to protect the rights and freedoms of others.

   ...

5. The provisions of this Charter which contain *principles* may be implemented by legislative and executive acts taken by institutions, bodies, offices and agencies of the Union, and by acts of the Member States when they are implementing Union law, in the exercise of their respective powers. *They shall be judicially cognisable only in the interpretation of such acts and in the ruling on their legality.*

Thus, a distinction is drawn between rights and freedoms, on the one hand, and principles, on the other hand. Rights and freedoms are to be protected as they generally are under the ECHR: that is, the rights and freedoms are not absolute, but may be limited where this is: (a) provided for by law; (b) proportionate; and (c) necessary in the interests of a particular objective. Under the charter, rights and freedoms are free-standing in the sense that they are judicially enforceable whether or not they are implemented by legislation. Principles, by contrast, are not independently justiciable. Where they are implemented through legislation, the courts are to interpret that legislation in the light of the principles enshrined in the charter. But without such legislation, the charter's principles are not justiciable.

Despite this rather sizeable difference of effect between rights and principles, there is no means set out in the charter that clearly demarcates which of its articles describe rights or freedoms and which of its articles concern principles. In some instances, of course, it is obvious. Thus, the right to life, freedom of expression and the right to a fair trial are straightforwardly rights or freedoms, which are enforceable without further enactment in accordance with Article 52(1) (as they are under the ECHR). Equally, some provisions, even when described as 'rights', are clearly principles. The 'rights of the elderly' protected under Article 25 are an example – this can readily be inferred from the language which the article uses: '[T]he Union recognises and respects the rights of the elderly to lead a life of dignity and independence and to participate in social and cultural life.' The language of 'recognise and respect' is the language of principle, not of judicially enforceable obligation. In other instances, however, it is not so clear, and it will be for the courts to determine whether we are in the territory of rights or principles. Article 20 is an example. This simply declaims that 'everyone is equal before the law'. Is that a right in EU law or a principle? Or what about Article 1, which provides that 'human dignity is inviolable. It must be respected and protected' – is that a right or a principle? And by what criteria are we to make this distinction?

One answer to the riddle would be to say that civil and political rights (of the kind found in the ECHR) are rights or freedoms, whereas economic, social or cultural rights are principles. But this approach is difficult to reconcile with the language of the charter. Several of the provisions in Title IV (solidarity) are crafted in the language of rights, not principles. Among these are Article 29 ('everyone has the right of access to a free placement service'), Article 30 ('every worker has the right to protection against unjustified dismissal'), Article 31(2) ('every worker has the right to limitation of maximum working hours') and Article 32(1) ('the employment of children is prohibited'), among others. Further, the charter is not structured in a way which clearly delineates the old distinction between civil and political rights, on the one hand, and economic, social and cultural rights, on the other. The 'right to engage in work', for example, (Article 15) appears in Title II ('freedoms') alongside such classic civil and political rights as freedom of expression. And with some rights, such as that in Article 13 (providing that 'the arts and scientific research shall be free of constraint'), it is not at all obvious whether the right is best classified as civil, political, economic, social or cultural.

Among the most striking cases which the Court of Justice has thus far decided in the area of fundamental rights is *Kadi*. Kadi's assets were frozen under United Nations Security Council Resolution (UNSCR) 1267. Among other matters, UNSCR 1267 requires all states to 'freeze funds and other financial resources . . . as designated' by a sanctions committee, established under UNSCR 1267 with the task of designating funds derived or generated from, and property owned or controlled by, the Taliban, Osama bin Laden or Al-Qaida. Under Regulation 881/2002 the Council of Ministers decided that designations under UNSCR 1267 would be implemented within the EU at EU level rather than separately by the twenty-seven member states. Article 2 of Regulation 881/2002 provides that 'all funds and economic resources belonging to, or owned or held by, a natural or legal person . . . designated by the Sanctions Committee and listed in [the Annex to the Regulation] shall be frozen'. Kadi was designated by the sanctions committee, he was added to the list in the annex and his assets in the EU were accordingly frozen under Article 2 of Regulation 881/2002. The case gave rise to three decisions of the CJEU. These decisions are important both in terms of the extent to which the EU is prepared to protect human rights – in this case, rights to a fair hearing, property rights and the right to an effective remedy– against the need to protect national security and the extent to which the EU was prepared to protect rights even when this meant, potentially, applying rights over and above a UN security council resolution.

In C-402 and C-415/05P *Kadi & Al Barakaat International Foundation* v. *Commission (Kadi I)* [2008] ECR I-6352, the European General Court (formerly the Court of First Instance) was reluctant to review the regulation enacted to implement the UN Security resolution according to EU human rights standards, as the EU was in essence bound by the UN Charter as a matter of EU law. As such, to examine the legality of the regulation would contradict the primacy of the UN Charter. Nevertheless, the General Court was prepared to examine the validity of the regulation according to international law principles of *jus cogens* – the higher rules of international law that bind all international bodies. However, the General Court concluded that these principles, which included fundamental rights, had not been breached by the EU's regulation.

Kadi appealed to the Court of Justice, which overturned the decision of the General Court. First, the Court of Justice concluded that the General Court had erred in law. The regulation was not immune from judicial review. The court stated that 'respect for human rights is a condition of the lawfulness of Community acts . . . and that measures incompatible with respect for human rights are not acceptable in the Community' (at [284]) and ruled that it followed that 'the obligations imposed by an international agreement cannot have the effect of prejudicing the constitutional principles of the EC Treaty, which include the principle that all Community acts must respect fundamental rights' (at [285]).

Second, the Court of Justice concluded that the regulation had breached the rights of defence, given that Kadi had not been informed why he had been placed on the list of those whose assets were to be frozen. He had also received no right to be heard. Consequently, Kadi's right to effective judicial review over a decision that severely restricted his property rights had been breached. This lack of an effective defence also meant that the regulation was an unjustifiable restriction of the right to property.

However, Kadi's assets remained frozen even after the judgment. The court gave the council and the commission three months in which to comply with the requirements of the judgment: that is, three months in which to offer Kadi some form of hearing compatible with EU law. The commission forwarded to Kadi the narrative summaries of the reasons provided by the UN sanctions committee as to why his assets should be frozen and Kadi commented on them. The commission considered Kadi's comments and concluded that 'the listing of Mr Kadi is justified for reasons of his association with the Al Qaida network'. It therefore decided that Kadi's assets should remain frozen (see Commission Regulation 1190/2008). Kadi successfully challenged this regulation before the European General Court (*T-85/09 Kadi* v. *Commission* [2010] ECR II 5177).

However, the commission, council and the UK lodged an appeal, giving rise to the *Kadi II* decision (C-584, C-593 and C 595/10P *Commission* v. *Kadi*). The Court of Justice upheld this appeal, confirming both the need to ensure that all acts of the EU complied with human rights and ensuring a detailed scrutiny of these rights.

97. As stated by the General Court in paragraphs 125, 126 and 171 of the judgment under appeal, the Court held, in paragraph 326 of the Kadi judgment, that the Courts of the European Union must, in accordance with the powers conferred on them by the Treaties, ensure the review, in principle the full review, of the lawfulness of all Union acts in the light of the fundamental rights forming an integral part of the European Union legal order, including review of such measures as are designed to give effect to resolutions adopted by the Security Council under Chapter VII of the Charter of the United Nations (see also, to that effect, *Hassan and Ayadi v Council and Commission*, paragraph 71, and *Bank Melli Iran v Council*, paragraph 105). That obligation is expressly laid down by the second paragraph of Article 275 TFEU.

98. Those fundamental rights include, inter alia, respect for the rights of the defence and the right to effective judicial protection.

99. The first of those rights, which is affirmed in Article 41(2) of the Charter of Fundamental Rights of the European Union ('the Charter') (see, to that effect, Case C-27/09 P *France v People's Mojahedin Organization of Iran* [2011] ECR I-13427, paragraph 66), includes the right to be heard and the right to have access to the file, subject to legitimate interests in maintaining confidentiality.

100. The second of those fundamental rights, which is affirmed in Article 47 of the Charter, requires that the person concerned must be able to ascertain the reasons upon which the decision taken in relation to him is based, either by reading the decision itself or by requesting and obtaining disclosure of those reasons, without prejudice to the power of the court having jurisdiction to require the authority concerned to disclose that information, so as to make it possible for him to defend his rights in the best possible conditions and to decide, with full knowledge of the relevant facts, whether there is any point in his applying to the court having jurisdiction, and in order to put the latter fully in a position to review the lawfulness of the decision in question (see judgment of 4 June 2013 in Case C-300/11 *ZZ*, paragraph 53 and case-law cited).

In order to satisfy the requirements of Article 47 of the charter (the right to effective judicial protection), the court has to ensure both that the commission complied with procedural safeguards and also that the decision 'is taken on a sufficiently solid factual basis ... with the consequence that judicial review cannot be restricted to an assessment of the cogency in the abstract of the reasons relied on, but must concern whether those reasons, or, at the very least, one of those reasons, deemed sufficient in itself to support that decision, is substantiated' (para 119). The court then added:

120. To that end, it is for the Courts of the European Union, in order to carry out that examination, to request the competent European Union authority, when necessary, to produce information or evidence, confidential or not, relevant to such an examination (see, by analogy, *ZZ*, paragraph 59).

121. That is because it is the task of the competent European Union authority to establish, in the event of challenge, that the reasons relied on against the person concerned are well founded, and not the task of that person to adduce evidence of the negative, that those reasons are not well founded.

122. For that purpose, there is no requirement that that authority produce before the Courts of the European Union all the information and evidence underlying the reasons alleged in the summary provided by the Sanctions Committee. It is however necessary that the information or evidence produced should support the reasons relied on against the person concerned.

123. If the competent European Union authority finds itself unable to comply with the request by the Courts of the European Union, it is then the duty of those Courts to base their decision solely on the material which has been disclosed to them, namely, in this case, the indications contained in the narrative summary of reasons provided by the Sanctions Committee, the observations and exculpatory evidence that may have been produced by the person concerned and the response of the competent European Union authority to those observations. If that material is insufficient to allow a finding that a reason is well founded, the Courts of the European Union shall disregard that reason as a possible basis for the contested decision to list or maintain a listing.

124. If, on the other hand, the competent European Union authority provides relevant information or evidence, the Courts of the European Union must then determine whether the facts alleged are made out in the light of that information or evidence and assess the probative value of that information or evidence in the circumstances of the particular case and in the light of any observations submitted in relation to them by, among others, the person concerned.

125. Admittedly, overriding considerations to do with the security of the European Union or of its Member States or with the conduct of their international relations may preclude the disclosure of some information or some evidence to the person concerned. In such circumstances, it is none the less the task of the Courts of the European Union, before whom the secrecy or confidentiality of that information or evidence is no valid objection, to apply, in the course of the judicial review to be carried out, techniques which accommodate, on the one hand, legitimate security considerations about the nature and sources of information taken into account in the adoption of the act concerned and, on the other, the need sufficiently to guarantee to an individual respect for his procedural rights, such as the right to be heard and the requirement for an adversarial process (see, to that effect, the *Kadi* judgment, paragraphs 342 and 344; see also, by analogy, *ZZ*, paragraphs 54, 57 and 59).

126. To that end, it is for the Courts of the European Union, when carrying out an examination of all the matters of fact or law produced by the competent European Union authority, to determine whether the reasons relied on by that authority as grounds to preclude that disclosure are well founded (see, by analogy, *ZZ*, paragraphs 61 and 62).

127. If the Courts of the European Union conclude that those reasons do not preclude disclosure, at the very least partial disclosure, of the information or evidence concerned, it shall give the competent European Union authority the opportunity to make such disclosure to the person concerned. If that authority does not permit the disclosure of that information or evidence, in whole or in part, the Courts of the European Union shall then undertake an examination of the lawfulness of the contested measure solely on the basis of the material which has been disclosed (see, by analogy, *ZZ*, paragraph 63).

128. On the other hand, if it turns out that the reasons relied on by the competent European Union authority do indeed preclude the disclosure to the person concerned of information or evidence produced before the Courts of the European Union, it is necessary to strike an appropriate balance between the requirements attached to the right to effective judicial protection, in particular respect for the principle of an adversarial process, and those flowing from the security of the European Union or its Member States or the conduct of their international relations (see, by analogy, *ZZ*, paragraph 64).

The court concluded that none of the evidence provided was sufficient to justify the imposition of these sanctions on Kadi. This judgment demonstrates the potential strength of judicial review. The Court of Justice did not see these as political questions outside the scope of judicial review. While recognising the need for some information to be kept sensitive, the court nevertheless required the rule of law to be upheld, ensuring that the court review factual evidence in full to ensure that it supported the restriction on property rights.

5.2.3 The Backdrop to Brexit: EU Law in the UK

5.2.3.1 Impact of EU Membership on Government and Parliament

When ministers of the Crown exercised the royal prerogative in concluding the Treaty of Accession of the UK to the European Communities in 1972, this act produced no effects in the law of the UK. British courts act on a dualist theory of the relation between international law and municipal (national) law in holding that treaties can bring about changes in the law of the UK only through the intervention of Parliament (see *Attorney General for Canada* v. *Attorney General for Ontario* [1937] AC 326, 347). It was therefore necessary for Parliament to enact a statute that would make the changes in the law required by the UK's membership of the European Communities. Not only would existing European law have to be incorporated as a whole but provision would also have to be made for future European legislation to take effect in the UK in accordance with the treaties.

Both these commitments were implemented by the European Communities Act 1972 – an enactment effecting a radical transformation of the legal system of the UK. Indeed, Laws LJ suggested in *Thoburn* v. *Sunderland City Council* [2003] QB 151 that: 'It may be there has never been a statute having such profound effects on so many dimensions of our daily lives.' The European Communities Bill introduced in Parliament in 1972 was given a second reading in the House of Commons by a majority of eight votes after Prime Minister Edward Heath had announced that the vote would be regarded as one of confidence in the government. Although strongly contested, the bill was passed by both houses without a single amendment. So Parliament exercised its sovereignty and the European Communities Act 1972 came into force on 1 January 1973. Over time, the European Communities Act was amended to add new treaties to the list of those the 1972 Act incorporated into UK law. Also, the UK enacted the European Union Act 2011. This legislation added in specific requirements as regards the ratification of certain EU treaties – specifically any provision to amend or replace the treaties, in addition to measures deemed to transfer further competences from the UK to the EU. The ratification of these provisions required a statement to be made to Parliament, the approval of the treaty by an act of Parliament, and a vote in a referendum in favour of adopting the new treaty. The 2011 Act also added in a so-called sovereignty clause in section 18:

> Directly applicable or directly effective EU law (that is, the rights, powers, liabilities, obligations, restrictions, remedies and procedures referred to in section 2(1) of the European Communities Act 1972) falls to be recognised and available in law in the United Kingdom only by virtue of that Act or where it is required to be recognised and available in law by virtue of any other Act.

The clause was designed to assert that, to the extent that EU law is recognised in the UK, this is through the provisions of an act of parliament, challenging assertions in *Thoburn* that the common law had accommodated the primacy of EU law into UK law.

5.2.3.2 European Communities Act 1972

The provisions of the European Communities Act 1972 to be discussed below are set out here for reference:

> 2. (1) All such rights, powers, liabilities, obligations and restrictions from time to time created or arising by or under the Treaties, and all such remedies and procedures from time to time provided for by or under the Treaties, as in accordance with the Treaties are without further enactment to be given legal effect or used in the United Kingdom shall be recognised and available in law, and be enforced, allowed and followed accordingly; and the expression 'enforceable Community right' and similar expressions shall be read as referring to one to which this subsection applies.
>
> (2) Subject to Schedule 2 to this Act, at any time after its passing Her Majesty may by Order in Council, and any designated Minister or department may by regulations, make provision –
>
> (a) for the purpose of implementing any Community obligation of the United Kingdom, or enabling any such obligation to be implemented, or of enabling any rights enjoyed or to be enjoyed by the United Kingdom under or by virtue of the Treaties to be exercised; or
>
> (b) for the purpose of dealing with matters arising out of or related to any such obligation or rights or the coming into force, or the operation from time to time, of subsection (1) above;
>
> and in the exercise of any statutory power or duty, including any power to give directions or to legislate by means of orders, rules, regulations or other subordinate instrument, the person entrusted with the power or duty may have regard to the objects of the Communities and to any such obligation or rights as aforesaid. In this subsection 'designated Minister or department' means such Minister of the Crown or government department as may from time to time be designated by Order in Council in relation to any matter or for any purpose, but subject to such restrictions or conditions (if any) as may be specified by the Order in Council . . .

(4) The provision that may be made under subsection (2) above includes, subject to Schedule 2 to this Act, any such provision (of any such extent) as might be made by Act of Parliament, and any enactment passed or to be passed, other than one contained in this Part of this Act, shall be construed and have effect subject to the foregoing provisions of this section; but, except as may be provided by any Act passed after this Act, Schedule 2 shall have effect in connection with the powers conferred by this and the following sections of this Act to make Orders in Council and regulations.

3. (1) For the purposes of all legal proceedings any question as to the meaning or effect of any of the Treaties, or as to the validity, meaning or effect of any Community instrument, shall be treated as a question of law (and, if not referred to the European Court, be for determination as such in accordance with the principles laid down by and any relevant decision of the European Court or any court attached thereto).

Schedule 1 to the European Union (Amendment) Act 2008 changed the terminology employed in these provisions so that it accords with the current (post-Lisbon) terminology of EU law. So, for example, 'enforceable Community right' in section 2(1) became 'enforceable EU right', 'any Community obligation' in section 2(2)(a) became 'any EU obligation' and so on.

We have seen that the European Communities Act had to provide for the application in the UK of European law – both extant law and that which would issue in the future. Some specific alterations of UK law were immediately necessary and these were made by sections 4–12 of the act; for example, section 9(1) modified the doctrine of ultra vires in company law to conform to a directive of 1968. For the rest, existing European law to be given effect in the UK was incorporated *en bloc* by section 2(1) of the act.

The rights and remedies, etc. to which section 2(1) refers are those that are required by EU law to be given legal effect 'without further enactment' – that is, are to be directly enforceable in the courts of the member states. The subsection means that all directly applicable and directly effective EU law is to be recognised and enforced in the UK; by this provision the act adopted at a stroke almost the entire existing corpus of EU regulations together with the directly effective provisions of directives, decisions and the treaties. As a result, some 1,500 instruments of European law came into force in the UK on 1 January 1973.

It will be noticed that the law made applicable by section 2(1) keeps its separate identity as European law: it is not made a part of English (or Scots) law but is to be enforced together with that law in the courts of the UK. British courts regularly acted on section 2(1) of the European Communities Act in giving effect to European law. Once it is established – it may be by reference to the case law of the Court of Justice, in accordance with section 3(1) – that the provision of EU law in question is of the kind that produces direct effects, it is enforced accordingly. What, however, was to be done about *future* EU legislation that was to be given direct effect in the UK? A government White Paper of 1967 had drawn attention to the 'constitutional innovation' that would be necessary for 'the acceptance in advance as part of the law of the UK of provisions to be made in the future by instruments issued by the Community institutions – a situation for which there is no precedent in this country' (*Legal and Constitutional Implications of United Kingdom Membership of the European Communities*, Cmnd 3301, para 22). The situation was even more unprecedented in that future EU legislation was not only to be accepted in advance but was to be given that supremacy over domestic law, which is a keystone of the EU's legal order.

The way was not taken of attempting to make an express transfer of legislative power from Parliament to the EU's institutions. Rather, the subtle mechanism of section 2(1) was made to serve a dual purpose. For the sub-section gave effect in the UK to what it terms enforceable rights as 'from time to time' arising under the treaties, and so covered prospective European law as well as the law in existence when the Act came into force.

Neither was it thought right (or politic?) to make an express declaration in the Act of the primacy or supremacy of EU law over the laws of the UK. The words designed to achieve this are to be found oddly sandwiched in the middle of section 2(4) and read as follows:

> any enactment passed or to be passed . . . shall be construed and have effect subject to the foregoing provisions of this section.

The enormous effect of this provision is not immediately apparent on its face, but among 'the foregoing provisions' are those in sub-section (1) giving the force of law in the UK to the 'enforceable rights' there defined. It is therefore intended that any enactment (including any Act of Parliament) is to be construed and have effect *subject to* EU law having force in the UK.

The same principle is impressed on the judges by some bracketed words in section 3(1): it is there provided that any question of the validity, meaning or effect of EU law is to be decided by our courts 'in accordance with the principles laid down by and any relevant decision of the European Court'. That Court of Justice has, as we have seen, consistently upheld the precedence of EU law over national law.

The provisions we have considered were apt to ensure that EU law, of whatever date, that had legal force in the UK overrode any inconsistent provisions in UK legislation enacted before 1 January 1973, when the European Communities Act came into force. This follows from the simple rule that the later act (the European Communities Act) must prevail over any earlier enactment.

A more difficult problem arises if an Act of Parliament passed *after* 1 January 1973 should conflict with a provision of EU law (of whatever date). Here, the simple rule mentioned above would give precedence to the Act of Parliament as the latest expression of Parliament's will, but the doctrine of supremacy in EU law and the apparent intention of section 2(4) of the European Communities Act required the provision of EU law to prevail. This conflict raised the question of the continuing sovereignty of Parliament. We shall see in the following section how the British courts responded to it.

EU legislation (directives in particular) will often call for implementing action by the national authorities. In the UK, this was sometimes done, especially in important matters, by Act of Parliament: an example is the Data Protection Act 1998, passed to implement the Data Protection Directive (95/46/EC). More often, subordinate legislation was the chosen method of implementation: section 2(2) of the European Communities Act authorised the making of orders in council or departmental regulations for this purpose. The power given was a wide one, for it was amplified by section 2(4) to include 'any such provision (of any such extent) as might be made by Act of Parliament', subject only to certain limitations in Schedule 2 to the Act. (These related to taxation, retrospective legislation, sub-delegated legislation and the creation of new criminal offences.) It follows that orders in council or regulations made under section 2(2) could repeal or amend Acts of Parliament. This was done, for instance, when the Equal Pay (Amendment) Regulations 1983 (SI 1983/1794), made by the Secretary of State for Employment under the authority of section 2(2), amended the Equal Pay Act 1970 so as to bring it into line with European law.

5.2.3.3 Impact of EU Membership on Questions of Public Law

Naturally, the UK's membership of the EU had a profound effect on the areas of substantive law over which the EU had competence. Thus, British trade law, competition law, environmental protection law, labour law and discrimination law, to name just a few such areas, have been transformed by virtue of our membership of the EU. But the UK's membership of the EU also had a considerable impact on various matters of British constitutional law. In the remainder of this chapter, the EU's impact on four areas of constitutional law will be examined. We start with the most famous: the challenge EU membership posed for the doctrine of the sovereignty of Parliament. We then consider the EU's impact on statutory interpretation (particularly in light of the doctrine of indirect effect or the duty of consistent interpretation) and, more briefly, the impact on judicial review and on the law of remedies.

5.2.3.3.1 Supremacy and Sovereignty

It did not take long for English judges to acknowledge the supremacy of European law. EU law was soon applied by British courts so as to override contrary provisions in laws made before the European Communities Act came into force on 1 January 1973. This early acceptance was understandable as this aspect of the supremacy of EU law was consistent with the normal operation of UK statutes and is uncontroversial.

When a statute enacted after 1 January 1973 was in question, the courts first strove to interpret the statute in such a way as to reconcile it with any relevant EU law in force in the UK. Such an approach was demanded by section 2(4) of the European Communities Act, by which enactments must be 'construed and have effect' subject to the application in the UK of directly effective European law. The novel and creative use of modes of interpretation, enabled courts to resolve many apparent inconsistencies between post-1972 UK statutes and instruments of EU law. In taking that course, courts could claim to give due recognition both to the intentions of Parliament and to the obligation to accord priority to EU law. If such an interpretation of the statute proved impossible, however, the court had nevertheless to find a way of assuring to EU law its full force and effect.

In the following case, *Macarthys Ltd* v. *Smith* [1979] 3 All ER 325 (CA), the question arose of the relation between the Equal Pay Act 1970 (as re-enacted with amendments by the Sex Discrimination Act 1975 *after* the European Communities Act had come into force) and EU law.

Macarthys Ltd had employed Mr McCullough as stockroom manager. Some time after he left, Mrs Smith was employed in the same position, with similar duties, but at lower pay. A tribunal held that she was entitled to be paid at the same rate as Mr McCullough, and the Employment Appeal Tribunal, with Phillips J presiding, affirmed that decision. Macarthys Ltd appealed.

Lord Denning MR: . . .The employers say that this case is not within the Equal Pay Act 1970. In order to be covered by that Act, the employers say that the woman and the man must be employed by the same employer on like work *at the same time*: whereas here Mrs Smith was employed on like work *in succession* to Mr McCullough and not at the same time as he.

To solve this problem I propose to turn first to the principle of equal pay contained in the EEC Treaty, for that takes priority even over our own statute.

The EEC Treaty
Article 119 of the EEC Treaty [as it then was: see now Article 157 of the TFEU] says:

'Each Member State shall . . . ensure and subsequently maintain the application of the principle that men and women should receive equal pay for equal work.'

That principle is part of our English law. It is directly applicable in England. So much so that, even if we had not passed any legislation on the point, our courts would have been bound to give effect to art 119. If a woman had complained to an industrial tribunal or to the High Court and proved that she was not receiving equal pay with a man for equal work, both the industrial tribunal and the court would have been bound to give her redress . . .

In point of fact, however, the United Kingdom has passed legislation with the intention of giving effect to the principle of equal pay. It has done it by the Sex Discrimination Act 1975 and in particular by s 8 of that Act amending s 1 of the Equal Pay Act 1970. No doubt the Parliament of the United Kingdom thinks that it has fulfilled its obligations under the Treaty. But the European Commission take a different view. They think that our statutes do not go far enough.

What then is the position? Suppose that England passes legislation which contravenes the principle contained in the Treaty, or which is inconsistent with it, or fails properly to implement it. There is no doubt that the European Commission can report the United Kingdom to the European Court of Justice; and that court can require the United Kingdom to take the necessary measures to implement art 119 ...

It is unnecessary, however, for these courts to wait until all that procedure has been gone through. Under s 2(1) and (4) of the European Communities Act 1972 the principles laid down in the Treaty are 'without further enactment' to be given legal effect in the United Kingdom; and have priority over 'any enactment passed or to be passed' by our Parliament. So we are entitled and I think bound to look at art 119 of the EEC Treaty because it is directly applicable here; and also any directive which is directly applicable here: see *Van Duyn v Home Office*. We should, I think, look to see what those provisions require about equal pay for men and women. Then we should look at our own legislation on the point, giving it, of course, full faith and credit, assuming that it does fully comply with the obligations under the Treaty. In construing our statute, we are entitled to look to the Treaty as an aid to its construction; but not only as an aid but as an overriding force. If on close investigation it should appear that our legislation is deficient or is inconsistent with Community law by some oversight of our draftsmen then it is our bounden duty to give priority to Community law. Such is the result of s 2(1) and (4) of the European Communities Act 1972.

I pause here, however, to make one observation on a constitutional point. Thus far I have assumed that our Parliament, whenever it passes legislation, intends to fulfil its obligations under the Treaty. If the time should come when our Parliament deliberately passes an Act with the intention of repudiating the Treaty or any provision in it or intentionally of acting inconsistently with it *and says so in express terms* [emphasis added] then I should have thought that it would be the duty of our courts to follow the statute of our Parliament. I do not however envisage any such situation ... Unless there is such an intentional and express repudiation of the Treaty, it is our duty to give priority to the Treaty. In the present case I assume that the United Kingdom intended to fulfil its obligations under art 119. Has it done so?

Article 119

Article 119 is framed in European fashion. It enunciates a broad general principle and leaves the judges to work out the details. In contrast the Equal Pay Act is framed in English fashion. It states no general principle but lays down detailed specific rules for the courts to apply (which, so some hold, the courts must interpret according to the actual language used) without resort to considerations of policy or principle.

Now consider art 119 in the context of our present problem. Take the simple case envisaged by Phillips J. A man who is a skilled technician working single-handed for a firm receives £1.50 an hour for his work. He leaves the employment. On the very next day he is replaced by a woman who is equally capable and who does exactly the same work as the man but, because she is a woman, she is only paid £1.25 an hour. That would be a clear case of discrimination on the ground of sex. It would, I think, be an infringement of the principle in art 119 which says 'that men and women should receive equal pay for equal work'. All the more so when you take into account the explanatory sentence in art 119 itself which says:

> 'Equal pay without discrimination based on sex means . . . that pay for work at time rates shall be the same for the same job.'

If you go further and consider the Council directive of 10th February 1975, it becomes plain beyond question:

> 'The principle of equal pay for men and women outlined in Article 119 of the Treaty, hereinafter called "principle of equal pay", means, for the same work or for work to which equal value is attributed, the elimination of all discrimination on ground of sex with regard to all aspects and conditions of remuneration.'

. . . In my opinion therefore art 119 is reasonably clear on the point; it applies not only to cases where the woman is employed on like work *at the same time* with a man in the same employment, but also when she is employed on like work in succession to a man, that is, in such close succession that it is just and reasonable to make a comparison between them. So much for art 119.

The Equal Pay Act 1970

Now I turn to our Act to see if that principle has been carried forward into our legislation. The relevant part of this Act was passed not in 1970 but in 1975 by s 8 of the Sex Discrimination Act 1975.

Section 1(2)(a)(i) of the Equal Pay Act 1970 introduces an 'equality clause' so as to put a woman on an equality with a man 'where the woman is employed on like work with a man in the same employment'. The question is whether the words *'at the same time'* are to be read into that subsection so that it is confined to cases where the woman and the man are employed *at the same time* in the same employment.

After considering this and related provisions, Lord Denning concluded that section 1(2)(a)(i) of the Equal Pay Act should *not* be read as if it included the words 'at the same time', but should be interpreted so as to apply to cases where a woman was employed on like work *in succession* to a man. He continued:

> So I would hold, in agreement with Phillips J, that both under the Treaty and under the statutes a woman should receive equal pay for equal work, not only when she is employed *at the same* time as the man, but also when she is employed at the same job *in succession* to him, that is, in such close succession that it is just and reasonable to make a comparison between them.

If I Am Wrong

Now my colleagues [Lawton and Cumming-Bruce LJJ] take a different view. They are of opinion that s 1(2)(a)(i) of the Equal Pay Act should be given its natural and ordinary meaning, and that is, they think, that it is confined to cases where the woman is employed *at the same time* as a man.

> So on our statute, taken alone, they would allow the appeal and reject Mrs Smith's claim. My colleagues realise, however, that in this interpretation there may be a conflict between our statute and the EEC Treaty. As I understand their judgments, they would hold that if art 119 was clearly in favour of Mrs Smith it should be given priority over our own statute and Mrs Smith should succeed. But they feel that art 119 is not clear, and, being not clear, it is necessary to refer it to the European Court at Luxembourg for determination under art 177 of the Treaty [now Article 267 TFEU].
>
> **Conclusion**
> For myself I would be in favour of dismissing the appeal, because I agree with the decision of the Employment Appeal Tribunal. I have no doubt about the true interpretation of art 119.
>   But, as my colleagues think that art 119 is not clear on the point, I agree that reference should be made to the European Court at Luxembourg to resolve the uncertainty in that article.
>   Pending the decision of the European court, all further proceedings in the case will be stayed.

The case duly came before the Court of Justice for a preliminary ruling under (what is now) Article 267 of the TFEU. The European Court ruled that the principle of equal pay enshrined in Article 119 of the treaty was not confined to situations in which men and women were employed contemporaneously by the same employer: see Case 129/79 *Macarthys Ltd* v. *Smith* [1980] ECR 1275. In the light of this answer, the employers conceded defeat when the case returned to the Court of Appeal: *Macarthys Ltd* v. *Smith* [1981] QB 180. Lord Denning took the opportunity of saying (at 200):

> The majority of this court felt that article 119 was uncertain. So this court referred the problem to the European Court at Luxembourg. We have now been provided with the decision of that court. It is important now to declare – and it must be made plain – that the provisions of article 119 of the EEC Treaty take priority over anything in our English statute on equal pay which is inconsistent with article 119. That priority is given by our own law. It is given by the European Communities Act 1972 itself. Community law is now part of our law: and, whenever there is any inconsistency, Community law has priority. It is not supplanting English law. It is part of our law which overrides any other part which is inconsistent with it.

Macarthys Ltd v. *Smith* was not a case in which a provision of a domestic statute was deprived of its effect by an overriding obligation of EU law: rather the EU law extended to employees a right to equal pay in circumstances that fell outside the scope of the UK statute. Nevertheless, as the Court of Appeal recognised, there was an inconsistency between the UK statute and EU law, and the court held unequivocally that the EU law had 'priority'. TRS Allan, drawing attention to Lord Denning's proposition that Parliament could override provisions of the treaty if it stated 'in express terms' its intention to do so, comments as follows ('Parliamentary Sovereignty: Lord Denning's Dexterous Revolution' (1983) 3 *OJLS* 22, 25):

The attempt to entrench section 2(1) of the European Communities Act by means of section 2(4) has to some extent succeeded: the effect of the decision seems to be to impose a requirement of form (express wording) on future legislation designed to override [EU] law. In short, Parliament in 1972 accomplished the impossible and (to a degree) bound its successors.

5.2.3.3.2 The *Factortame* Saga

As Allan's comment suggests, questions of sovereignty pervaded the judgment in *Macarthys Ltd* v. *Smith* even if that case did not confront them squarely. That confrontation came a decade later, with the *Factortame* series of cases, to which we now turn.

The background is as follows. The Council of Ministers had fixed national quotas of allowable catches of fish by the fishing fleets of the member states. The UK Parliament enacted the Merchant Shipping Act 1988, Part II of which specified requirements for the registration of fishing vessels as British (whose catches would then count as part of the British quota). The act stipulated that only British-owned vessels managed and controlled from within the UK could be registered as British fishing vessels. In substance, a vessel would be 'British-owned' only if the owners (or shareholders of corporate owners) were British citizens and were resident and domiciled in the UK. Regulations made by the Secretary of State under the Act brought this scheme into operation and as a result ninety-five fishing vessels, previously registered as British under an Act of 1894 but managed and controlled from Spain or owned by Spanish nationals or companies, would not qualify for registration under the 1988 Act. The owners of these vessels sought judicial review, claiming a declaration that the 1988 legislation should not apply to them, on the ground that it denied their rights under directly enforceable provisions of EU law.

The Divisional Court decided to obtain a preliminary ruling from the ECJ under (what is now) Article 267 of the TFEU on the questions of EU law arising in the case. Since there would be a delay of two years before the ruling of the Court of Justice was given, and the owners of the fishing vessels would suffer severe hardship if obliged to refrain from fishing during that time, the Divisional Court granted them interim relief, ordering that Part II of the 1988 Act and the regulations should be 'disapplied' and that the Secretary of State should be constrained from enforcing the legislation pending final judgment in the case.

In *R* v. *Secretary of State for Transport, ex p Factortame Ltd* the Court of Appeal ([1989] 2 CMLR 353) and then the House of Lords ([1990] 2 AC 85) held that the Divisional Court had had no power, as a matter of *English* law, to make an interim order in such terms. This was for two reasons. In the words of Lord Bridge, the first was that:

> An order granting the applicants the interim relief which they seek will only serve their purpose if it declares that which Parliament has enacted to be the law . . . not to be the law until some uncertain future date . . . [T]he effect of [such] interim relief would be to [confer] upon [the applicants] rights directly contrary to Parliament's sovereign will.

The second reason was more technical. It was that, as the law then stood, there was simply no such thing in English law as an interim injunction against the Crown, and this was precisely the remedy which the Divisional Court had granted (the respondent in the case, the Secretary of State for Transport, being an officer of the Crown). There was, at the time, no such thing as an interim injunction against the Crown because section 21(2) of the Crown Proceedings Act 1947 provides that: 'The court shall not in any civil proceedings grant any injunction or make any order against an officer of the Crown.' (The interpretation of this provision was subsequently changed in *M* v. *Home Office* [1994] 1 AC 377 to exclude judicial review proceedings from its scope, judicial review proceedings being public law proceedings rather than civil proceedings. See above, pp. 129–133.)

Having decided that there was no such remedy in English law, the House of Lords then went on to consider whether an appropriate interim remedy might be available to the applicants *as a matter of European law*. After all, it was their rights in *EU law* that the applicants argued had been violated. Might EU law not be expected to say something about how those rights could be judicially protected? Their Lordships decided that EU law on the matter was unsettled and accordingly sent a second reference to the Court of Justice.

In the meantime, another actor had entered the stage. The European Commission brought an action in the Court of Justice for a declaration under (what is now) Article 258 of the TFEU that in imposing the nationality requirements in Part II of the Merchant Shipping Act 1988, the UK had failed in its obligations under the treaty. In Case 246/89 R *Commission* v. *United Kingdom* [1989] ECR 3125 the Court of Justice made an interim order that, pending the delivery of its judgment in the action for a declaration, the UK was to suspend the application of the nationality requirements as regards the nationals of other member states. The UK Government complied with this ruling: see the Merchant Shipping Act 1988 (Amendment) Order 1989 (SI 1989/2006). In the debate in the House of Commons on a motion to approve the order, MPs expressed their concern about the implications for parliamentary sovereignty, one of them seeing the order as 'an historic surrender of some constitutional importance' (Mr Jonathan Aitken). The Solicitor General said in reply: 'This case involves no erosion of sovereignty over and above that which we accepted in 1972–73.'

When the question of interim relief referred to it by the House of Lords came before the Court of Justice, the ECJ held that a national court was obliged to set aside provisions of domestic law that might prevent, even temporarily, rights in EU law from having full force and effect (see Case C-213/89 *R* v. *Secretary of State for Transport, ex p Factortame Ltd* [1990] ECR I-2433). Accordingly:

> a national court which, in a case before it concerning Community law, considers that the sole obstacle which precludes it from granting interim relief is a rule of national law must set aside that rule.

The House of Lords, when the case returned to it, obliged now to disregard obstacles to interim relief under English law, granted an injunction against the Secretary of State, requiring him to suspend the application of the requirements of British residence and domicile in the Merchant Shipping Act to nationals of other Member States: *R* v. *Secretary of State for Transport, ex p Factortame Ltd (No 2)* [1991] 1 AC 603. (The nationality requirements had already been suspended by order in council: see above.) In this profoundly important decision, the House of Lords acknowledged that its obligation to comply with a principle of EU law as affirmed by the ECJ required it to deny effect to the terms of an Act of Parliament. In the event, the Merchant Shipping Act 1988 yielded to the superior force of an earlier statute, the European Communities Act 1972. As Craig sees it (in Sunkin and Payne (eds.), *The Nature of the Crown* (1999), p. 332) the House of Lords was seeking by its ruling in *Factortame (No 2)* 'to bring constitutional doctrine up to date with political reality'. In the course of his opinion in *Factortame (No 2)*, Lord Bridge made the following observations.

> **Lord Bridge:** My Lords, when this appeal first came before the House last year ... your Lordships held that, as a matter of English law, the courts had no jurisdiction to grant interim relief in terms which would involve either overturning an English statute in advance of any decision by the European Court of Justice that the statute infringed Community law or granting an injunction against the Crown. It then became necessary to seek a preliminary ruling from the European Court of Justice as to whether Community law itself invested us with such jurisdiction ...
>
> [We later] received the judgment of the European Court of Justice (Case C 213/89), replying to the questions we had posed and affirming that we had jurisdiction, in the circumstances postulated, to grant interim relief for the protection of directly enforceable rights under Community law and that no limitation on our jurisdiction imposed by any rule of national law could stand as the sole obstacle to preclude the grant of such relief. In the light of this judgment we ... unanimously decided that relief should be granted ...
>
> Some public comments on the decision of the European Court of Justice, affirming the jurisdiction of the courts of Member States to override national legislation if necessary to enable interim relief to be granted in protection of rights under Community law, have suggested that this was a novel and dangerous invasion by a Community institution of the

sovereignty of the United Kingdom Parliament. But such comments are based on a misconception. If the supremacy within the European Community of Community law over the national law of Member States was not always inherent in the E.E.C. Treaty it was certainly well established in the jurisprudence of the European Court of Justice long before the United Kingdom joined the Community. Thus, whatever limitation of its sovereignty Parliament accepted when it enacted the European Communities Act 1972 was entirely voluntary. Under the terms of the Act of 1972 it has always been clear that it was the duty of a United Kingdom court, when delivering final judgment, to override any rule of national law found to be in conflict with any directly enforceable rule of Community law. Similarly, when decisions of the European Court of Justice have exposed areas of United Kingdom statute law which failed to implement Council Directives, Parliament has always loyally accepted the obligation to make appropriate and prompt amendments. Thus there is nothing in any way novel in according supremacy to rules of Community law in those areas to which they apply and to insist that, in the protection of rights under Community law, national courts must not be inhibited by rules of national law from granting interim relief in appropriate cases is no more than a logical recognition of that supremacy.

We shall come back to consider Lord Bridge's comments in detail in a moment. First, let us finish the saga. In the next chapter of the *Factortame* annals, the Court of Justice gave its ruling on the original reference from the Divisional Court, holding that nationality, residence and domicile requirements such as were stipulated by the Merchant Shipping Act 1988 were contrary to EU law (in particular, what is now Article 49 of the TFEU on freedom of establishment): Case C-221/89 *R* v. *Secretary of State for Transport, ex p Factortame (No 3)* [1992] QB 680. The Divisional Court thereon granted a declaration to that effect, and the government duly took the necessary steps to bring domestic law into conformity with the judgment: see section 3 of the Merchant Shipping (Registration, etc.) Act 1993 and the Merchant Shipping (Registration of Ships) Regulations 1993 (SI 1993/3138). The sequel to the ECJ's ruling that the UK legislation was in breach of EU law was a claim for damages against the UK Government brought by the Spanish trawler owners who had, during the course of the *Factortame* litigation, been deprived of their right to fish in British waters. It was held by the House of Lords, after yet another reference to the Court of Justice, that the claimants were entitled to damages: see *R* v. *Secretary of State for Transport, ex p Factortame Ltd (No 5)* [2000] 1 AC 524.

It was clear after *Factortame (No 2)* that British courts would no longer necessarily be inhibited from suspending the application of a statute when such action was required to give effective interim protection to rights under EU law. Moreover, the *Factortame* litigation indicated that a ruling by the Court of Justice that provisions in a UK statute were incompatible with EU law would, where possible, be acted on by British courts in granting declaratory relief to a party adversely affected by the application of those provisions. This was reinforced by the decision of the House of Lords in *R* v. *Secretary of State for Employment, ex p Equal Opportunities Commission* [1995] 1 AC 1. In this case the Equal Opportunities Commission (EOC) objected to provisions of the Employment Protection (Consolidation) Act 1978 on the ground that they were contrary to EU law. No decision had been taken by the Secretary of State such as might have been open to review, but the EOC mounted a challenge, in proceedings for judicial review, directed to the statutory provisions themselves. The House of Lords granted declarations that the provisions in question were incompatible with (what is now) Article 157 of the TFEU and with the Equal Pay and Equal Treatment Directives. In response to this ruling, the act was amended by delegated legislation so as to remove the incompatibility (see, on this case, Harlow and Szyszczak (1995) 32 *CML Rev* 641). Furthermore, the Supreme Court disapplied section 1 of the State Immunity Act 1978 in *Benkharbouche* v. *Embassy of the Republic of Sudan* [2017] UKSC 62, [2019] AC 777 as this contradicted Article 47 of the EU Charter, the right to an effective remedy.

What are we to make of the *Factortame* story and, in particular, of the decision of the House of Lords in *Factortame (No 2)*? Academic opinion remains sharply divided on how the decision should be interpreted and, especially, on what it meant – and potentially may still mean – for the sovereignty of Parliament. There are perhaps two main camps, which may be dubbed the 'revolution view' and the 'evolution view'. In the former (perhaps we should say, leading the former) is the late Sir William Wade who, with his customary clarity and robustness, argued as follows ('Sovereignty: Revolution or Evolution?' (1996) 112 *LQR* 568):

> When in the second *Factortame* case the House of Lords granted an injunction to forbid a minister from obeying an Act of Parliament, and the novel term 'disapplied' had to be invented to describe the fate of the Act, it was natural to suppose that something drastic had happened to the traditional doctrine of Parliamentary sovereignty. The established rule about conflicting Acts of Parliament, namely that the later Act must prevail, was evidently violated, since the later Act in this case was the Merchant Shipping Act 1988, yet it was disapplied under the European Communities Act 1972. The Act of 1972 had provided for the subordination of English law to European Community law by section 2(4), enacting that European Community law was to prevail over Acts of Parliament 'passed or to be passed'. When that Act was nevertheless held to prevail it seemed to be fair comment to characterise this, at least in a technical sense, as a constitutional revolution. The Parliament of 1972 had succeeded in binding the Parliament of 1988 and restricting its sovereignty, something that was supposed to be constitutionally impossible. It is obvious that sovereignty belongs to the Parliament of the day and that, if it could be fettered by earlier legislation, the Parliament of the day would cease to be sovereign.

For Wade, a constitutional revolution had occurred because the House of Lords had recognised that the result of the European Communities Act 1972 was that future Parliaments were, unless and until they expressly repealed it, bound by its terms. Parliament remained sovereign in the sense that it retained the power expressly to repeal the 1972 Act – which, as we will see, occurred as part of the Brexit process. But, for as long as the UK continued to be a member of the EU on the terms set out in the 1972 Act, the UK Parliament remained tied to the terms of that statute.

An alternative, more evolutionary, set of views has been suggested by a variety of other commentators, including Sir John Laws and Professor TRS Allan. Sir John Laws has argued as follows ('Law and Democracy' [1995] *PL* 72, 89):

> The effect is that section 2(4) of the European Communities Act falls to be treated as establishing a rule of construction for later statutes, so that any such statute has to be read (whatever its words) as compatible with rights accorded by European Law. Sir William Wade regards this development as 'revolutionary', because in his view it represents an exception to the rule that Parliament cannot bind its successors. But I do not think that is right. It is elementary that Parliament possesses the power to repeal the European Communities Act in whole or in part (I leave aside the political realities); and the most that can be said, in my view, is that the House of Lords' acknowledgement of the force of European law means that the rule of construction implanted by section 2(4) cannot be abrogated by an implied repeal. Express words would be required. That, however, is hardly revolutionary: there are a number of areas where a particular statutory construction is only likely to be accepted by the courts if it is vouchsafed by express provision [as where a statute is said to exact taxes, impose criminal liability or to have retroactive effect]. Although *Factortame* and *EOC* undoubtedly demonstrate what may be described as a devolution of legislative power to Europe, it is not true devolution of sovereignty. In legal (though certainly not political) terms, the organs of European legislation may in truth be described, for so long as the Act of 1972 remains on the statute book, as Parliament's delegates; the law of Europe is not a higher-order law, because the limits which for the time being it sets to the power of Parliament are at the grace of Parliament itself.

Allan's challenge to Wade is slightly different. He attacks the jurisprudential basis of Wade's account of sovereignty (outlined in Chapter 2, above, pp. 79-80). For Wade, the sovereignty of Parliament is ultimately a judicially recognised 'political fact'. And when the judges recognise that the political facts have changed, the meaning of sovereignty changes accordingly. So, for Wade, what the House of Lords recognised in *Factortame (No 2)* was that the political fact of sovereignty had changed – Parliament since 1972 legislates not in the splendid isolation of a supreme being but in a geopolitical environment in which the UK is a loyal and (largely) obedient member of the EU. Allan disputes this analysis on the basis that sovereignty should be seen not as judicial recognition of political fact, but as a rule of the common law based on reason just like any other rule of the common law. For him, what occurred in *Factortame (No 2)*, 'far from any dramatic, let alone unauthorised, change', was that 'the House of Lords merely determined what the existing constitutional order required in novel circumstances' ('Parliamentary Sovereignty: Law, Politics, and Revolution' (1997) 113 *LQR* 443, 445). As he recognises and, indeed, welcomes, the consequences of Allan's analysis are potentially great (pp. 448–9): 'If it is possible to recognise limits on the power of Parliament to enact legislation which conflicts with [EU] law, even if only to the extent of requiring express wording, it is equally possible to countenance other limits on parliamentary sovereignty which reflect the demands of constitutional principle. Since the requirement of judicial obedience to statutes constitutes a principle of common law ... its nature and scope are matters of reason, governed by our understanding of the constitution as a whole.' Here we are back to the common law radicalism that we saw posing such a potent challenge to the sovereignty of Parliament in Chapter 2 (see above, pp. 93–108).

(For a full and balanced analysis of the issues, see Craig, 'Sovereignty of the United Kingdom Parliament after *Factortame*' (1991) 11 *YEL* 221; for further commentary, see Wade (1991) 107 *LQR* 1; Oliver (1991) 54 *MLR* 442; Gravells [1991] *PL* 180.)

These matters were revisited and taken further in *Thoburn* v. *Sunderland City Council* [2003] QB 151. This was a first instance decision only, albeit that it was a decision made by a leading public law judge, Sir John Laws (Laws LJ). The case arose out of the prosecution of a number of traders (known popularly as the 'metric martyrs') for continuing to trade in imperial measures (pounds and ounces) after EU laws had been brought into effect in Britain that required trade to be conducted in metric measures only (i.e., in grams and kilograms). The traders argued that the Weights and Measures Act 1985, which, until it was amended by orders in council in 1994 to bring it into line with European requirements, had allowed trading in either imperial or metric measures, had impliedly repealed the government's statutory power (in section 2(2) of the European Communities Act 1972) to make the 1994 orders in council. The argument was unsuccessful, principally on the ground that there was no inconsistency between the 1972 and 1985 Acts (and, without such inconsistency, there could be no question of implied repeal). What is of more interest, however, is Laws LJ's reasoning, albeit that (rather like their Lordships' comments on sovereignty in *Jackson* v. *Attorney General* in Chapter 2), it is almost all obiter.

Laws LJ: ... Being sovereign, [the UK Parliament] cannot abandon its sovereignty. Accordingly there are no circumstances in which the jurisprudence of the Court of Justice can elevate Community law to a status within the corpus of English domestic law to which it could not aspire by any route of English law itself. This is, of course, the traditional doctrine of sovereignty. If it is to be modified, it certainly cannot be done by the incorporation of external texts. The conditions of Parliament's legislative supremacy in the United Kingdom necessarily remain in the United Kingdom's hands. But the traditional doctrine has in my judgment been modified. It has been done by the common law, wholly consistently with constitutional principle.

The common law has in recent years allowed, or rather created, exceptions to the doctrine of implied repeal: a doctrine which was always the common law's own creature. There are now classes or types of legislative provision which cannot be repealed by mere implication. These instances are given, and can only be given, by our own courts, to which the scope and nature of parliamentary sovereignty are ultimately confided. The courts may say – have said – that there are certain circumstances in which the legislature may only enact what it desires to enact if it does so by express, or at any rate specific, provision. The courts have in effect so held in the field of European law itself . . .

It seems to me that there is no doubt but that in *Factortame* the House of Lords effectively accepted that section 2(4) [of the European Communities Act 1972] could not be impliedly repealed, albeit the point was not argued . . .

In the present state of its maturity the common law has come to recognise that there exist rights which should properly be classified as constitutional or fundamental [citing *R v Secretary of State for the Home Department, ex p Simms* [2000] 2 AC 115 and *R v Secretary of State for the Home Department, ex p Pierson* [1998] AC 539, among other authorities: see chapter 2]. And from this a further insight follows. We should recognise a hierarchy of Acts of Parliament: as it were 'ordinary' statutes and 'constitutional' statutes . . . The European Communities Act 1972 [along with Magna Carta, the Bill of Rights 1689, the Act of Union, the Reform Acts, the Human Rights Act and the devolution legislation] is, by force of the common law, a constitutional statute.

Ordinary statutes may be impliedly repealed. Constitutional statutes may not.

Laws LJ's distinction between ordinary and constitutional statutes was novel. However, this has now been accepted in future case law (see *Robinson v. Secretary of State for Northern Ireland* [2002] UKHL 32; *H v. Lord Advocate* [2012] UKSC 34, [2013] 1 AC 413; *R (HS2 Action Alliance Ltd) v. Secretary of State for Transport* [2014] UKSC 3; [2014] 1 WLR 324); and *R (Governors of Brynmawr Foundation School) v. The Welsh Ministers* [2011] EWHC 519, considered in Chapter 2). But it will be seen that, in this judgment, his Lordship develops aspects of both his own and of TRS Allan's 'evolutionary' accounts of what happened in 1972 and of what the constitutional implications are of the House of Lords' decisions in *Factortame*.

It seems that, on any of Wade's, Laws' or Allan's views, we must recognise the assertion of a judicial power to redefine the extent and limits of parliamentary sovereignty. In the context of EU law, that power was furnished to the courts by Parliament itself in the European Communities Act 1972, as confirmed in section 18 of the European Union Act 2011. Parliament retained its ultimate sovereignty as long as it had the power to terminate the application of

EU law in the UK (and its overriding force) by repealing or further amending the European Communities Act 1972. As we will see, this is precisely what occurred following the Brexit referendum, with the European Union (Withdrawal) Act 2018 specifically and expressly repealing the European Communities Act 1972 on the UK's exit from the European Union on 31 January 2020.

A more difficult issue would have arisen during the UK's membership of the EU had Parliament deliberately legislated in contradiction of a rule of EU law, perhaps even with the *expressly stated* purpose of negating the effect of the rule in the UK. (Cf Lord Denning MR in *Macarthys Ltd* v. *Smith*, above.) A bill to this effect was introduced in Parliament in 2005 (the Food Supplements (European Communities Act 1972 Disapplication) Bill, sponsored by a group of well-known 'Eurosceptic' MPs). The bill had no chance of being enacted. Its provisions, however, make interesting reading. Its long title stated that the bill was 'to provide that a specified Community instrument relating to food supplements shall not have effect in the United Kingdom notwithstanding the provisions of the European Communities Act 1972'. To this end, clause 1 of the bill provided that 'Notwithstanding the provisions of the European Communities Act 1972 (a) Directive 2002/46/EC . . . on the approximation of the laws of the Member States relating to food supplements, and (b) any judgment of the European Court of Justice relating to the [Directive], shall not have effect in the United Kingdom.'

If an Act had been passed in terms such as these, the courts could not have refused to apply it without asserting a power which our constitution has not hitherto accorded to them and to which no English court has yet laid claim. Yet, should the issue have arisen, the response of the British courts could not have been predicted with certainty. One thing was certain, however: the commission would have had the power to bring infringement proceedings before the Court of Justice against the UK (under Article 258 of the TFEU) and, if the UK had ignored the court's judgment, the country would have been heavily fined under the penalty payment procedure of Article 260 of the TFEU. What would have happened if the UK – a net contributor to the EU's budget – had refused to pay such a penalty payment, insisting on its national sovereignty, is a question that will now remain unanswered, at least as regards the actions of the UK. However, this issue may arise in regard to a recent decision of the German Federal Constitutional Court. The court concluded that a decision of the European Court of Justice, which had judged that the European Central Banks Public Sector Purchase Programme was lawful, was ultra vires and wrong given that the European Court of Justice had failed to carry out a proportionality analysis of these measures. As such, the German Federal Constitutional Court refused to follow the decision of the European Court of Justice. It then carried out its own review of the Public Sector Purchasing Programme, concluding that it was disproportionate. At the time of writing, the saga was still unfolding as to whether the commission would commence further action against Germany, or as to the consequences of this action. (The judgment

can be found, in English, at: www.bundesverfassungsgericht.de/SharedDocs/
Entscheidungen/EN/2020/05/rs20200505_2bvr085915en.html.)

5.2.3.3.3 Statutory Interpretation

We saw above (p. 368) that in *Von Colson* and again in *Marleasing* the ECJ
introduced and developed a duty on the courts of member states to interpret
national law consistently with EU law. As we saw, to start with this duty was
expressed in the specific context of the interpretation of national law that was
itself designed to implement provisions of EU law into the relevant national
legal system. Only in *Marleasing*, it will be recalled, was this duty extended
more generally. A series of three House of Lords cases, all decided after *Von
Colson* but before *Marleasing*, illustrate the impact of this obligation on British
practices of statutory interpretation.

These cases do not, strictly speaking, concern sovereignty, although matters of statutory interpretation may sometimes have an indirect impact on
sovereignty (as we saw, for example, with regard to section 3 of the HRA,
above, pp. 86–93). There is a difference – in theory if not always in practice –
between judicial interpretation of Parliament's legislation and judicial invali-
dation of legislation. In any case, not all of these three cases concern the
interpretation of statute – of primary legislation. One of them concerns the
interpretation of secondary legislation, where no question of parliamentary
sovereignty arises.

The first case is *Duke* v. *GEC Reliance* [1988] AC 618. This case concerned
the interpretation of certain provisions of primary legislation (the Sex
Discrimination Act 1975) that had *not* been passed for the purpose of giving
domestic effect to EU law. One purpose of that legislation was to preserve
different retirement ages for men and women. In 1986 the ECJ ruled (in
Marshall, above, p. 367) that such discrimination was, as a matter of EU law,
unlawful as being in breach of the Equal Treatment Directive (Directive 76/
207/EEC). In *Duke*, the House of Lords was invited to follow that approach and
to construe and give effect to the 1975 Act accordingly. This their Lordships
refused to do, holding that *Von Colson* was 'no authority for the proposition
that a court of a Member State must distort the meaning of a domestic statute
so as to conform to Community law which is not directly applicable' (Lord
Templeman). (Directives, of course, are not directly applicable: Article 288 of
the TFEU.) Neither could section 2(4) of the European Communities Act 1972
be relied on to achieve this purpose: Lord Templeman stated that section 2(4)
'does not in my opinion enable or constrain a British court to distort the
meaning of a British statute in order to enforce against an individual
a Community directive which has no direct effect between individuals' (a
reference to the fact that, as we saw above, directives may have vertical but
not horizontal direct effect; in *Duke*, the dispute was between two private
parties.)

The second case is *Pickstone* v. *Freemans* [1989] AC 66, which saw the House of Lords adopt an altogether different approach to interpretation. The case did not overrule *Duke* v. *GEC Reliance*, but it clearly distinguished it. The Equal Pay Act 1970, as amended, provided for equality of benefits for a female employee if her work was (in terms of the demands made on her) of equal value to that of a man in the same employment. The amendment so providing was made to the Equal Pay Act 1970 by the Equal Pay (Amendment) Regulations 1983 (SI 1983/ 1794) in order to give effect to Article 119 EC (as it then was – see now Article 157 of the TFEU) as elaborated by the Equal Pay Directive (Directive 75/117/EC).

Mrs Pickstone was employed by Freemans as a 'warehouse operative' and was paid less than a man in the same employment who was employed as a 'checker warehouse operative'. She contended that her work was of equal value with that of the man and that she was therefore entitled to equal pay. The employers replied that one of the warehouse operatives was a man, doing the same work as Mrs Pickstone and receiving the same pay. They argued that the amended Equal Pay Act excluded a woman's entitlement to equal pay on the basis of work of equal value to that of a man if she was paid as much as another man who was employed on like work with her.

A literal construction of the relevant section of the Equal Pay Act supported the argument of the employers but would thus allow a new form of discrimination against women which would be inconsistent with EU law: the Equal Pay (Amendment) Regulations 1983 would have failed, through defective drafting, in their purpose of bringing the act into accord with the treaty and the Equal Pay Directive. To avoid this result the House of Lords departed from the 'well-established' rule of construction that the intention of Parliament 'has . . . to be ascertained from the words which it has used and those words are to be construed according to their plain and ordinary meaning' (Lord Oliver). It was necessary to adopt instead a 'purposive' construction.

Lord Oliver: . . . [A] construction which permits the section to operate as a proper fulfilment of the United Kingdom's obligation under the Treaty involves not so much doing violence to the language of the section as filling a gap by an implication which arises, not from the words used, but from the manifest purpose of the Act and the mischief it was intended to remedy. The question is whether that can be justified by the necessity – indeed the obligation – to apply a purposive construction which will implement the United Kingdom's obligations under the Treaty . . .

The fact that a statute is passed to give effect to an international treaty does not, of itself, enable the treaty to be referred to in order to construe the words used other than in their plain and unambiguous sense . . . I think, however, that it has also to be recognised that a statute which is passed in order to give effect to the United Kingdom's obligations under the EEC Treaty falls into a special category and it does so because, unlike other treaty obligations, those obligations have, in effect, been incorporated into English law by the European Communities Act 1972 . . .

> In the instant case, the strict and literal construction of the section does indeed involve the conclusion that the Regulations, although purporting to give full effect to the United Kingdom's obligations under article 119, were in fact in breach of those obligations. The question . . . is whether they are reasonably capable of bearing a meaning which does in fact comply with the obligations imposed by the Treaty . . .
>
> I am satisfied that the words of [the section], whilst on the face of them unequivocal, are reasonably capable of bearing a meaning which will not put the United Kingdom in breach of its Treaty obligations. This conclusion is justified, in my judgment, by the manifest purpose of the legislation, by its history, and by the compulsive provision of section 2(4) of the [European Communities Act 1972].

Lord Templeman, in agreeing with Lord Oliver, expressly relied on *Von Colson*. He stated that, in that case, the Court of Justice 'advised that in dealing with national legislation designed to give effect to a directive, "it is for the national court to interpret and apply the legislation adopted for the implementation of the directive in conformity with the requirements of Community law, in so far as it is given discretion to do so under national law"'. Lord Templeman then went on to state that:

> In *Duke v GEC Reliance* this House declined to distort the construction of an Act of Parliament which was not drafted to give effect to a directive and which was not capable of complying with the directive as subsequently construed by the European Court of Justice. In the present case I can see no difficulty in construing the regulations of 1983 in a way which gives effect to the declared intention of the Government of the United Kingdom responsible for drafting the regulations and is consistent with the objects of the EEC Treaty, the provisions of the Equal Pay Directive and the rulings of the European Court of Justice.

Thus, their Lordships were in agreement that the words of the Act inserted by the Equal Pay (Amendment) Regulations 1983 must be modified – by implication of additional words – to the extent necessary to ensure compliance with EU law, thus giving effect to the intention of the government in introducing the regulations and of Parliament in approving them.

Such a purposive approach to statutory interpretation was again taken by the House of Lords in *Litster* v. *Forth Dry Dock and Engineering* [1990] 1 AC 546, where their Lordships recognised, indeed emphasised, that what they were doing was a requirement of EU law rather than something they were doing purely voluntarily. As Lord Keith put it, 'it is the duty of the court to give [the relevant legislation, here the Transfer of Undertakings (Protection of Employment) Regulations 1981 (SI 1981/1794)] a construction which accords with the decisions of the European Court upon the corresponding provisions of the directive to which the [national legislation] was intended by Parliament to give effect. The precedent established by *Pickstone v Freemans* indicates that this is to be done by implying the words necessary to achieve that result.'

As was noted earlier, all these decisions were handed down before *Marleasing*. While *Marleasing* extended the scope of the duty of consistent interpretation (so that it applies not only in the context of interpreting national legislation that has been passed in order to give EU law domestic effect), even after *Marleasing*, the duty is not an absolute one. It applies only where an interpretation consistent with EU law is 'possible'. *Marleasing* does not require a court to give a meaning to UK legislation that it is incapable of bearing: as the House of Lords ruled in *Webb* v. *EMO Air Cargo* [1993] 1 WLR 49, the statute 'must be open to an interpretation consistent with the directive whether or not it is also open to an interpretation inconsistent with it' and a conformable interpretation is to be adopted only 'if that can be done without distorting the meaning of the domestic legislation' (Lord Keith).

In *Webb* v. *EMO Air Cargo*, the appellant, Mrs Webb, had been engaged by the company to take the place of another employee who had been given maternity leave. Soon after starting work, Mrs Webb reported that she had herself become pregnant and she was dismissed. She claimed that her dismissal was contrary to the Sex Discrimination Act 1975. The House of Lords concluded that if the Act were considered in isolation, the appellant must fail: she would not have suffered discrimination according to its terms. The question then arose whether Mrs Webb's dismissal was contrary to the Equal Treatment Directive (Directive 76/207/EEC, which could not have direct effect in the circumstances of the case and had been adopted after the 1975 Act). The House of Lords made a reference to the Court of Justice for its ruling on the correct interpretation of the directive to enable the house to decide whether it was possible to construe the 1975 Act so as to accord with that interpretation. In Case C-32/93 *Webb* v. *EMO Air Cargo* [1994] ECR I-3567, the Court of Justice ruled that Directive 76/207 precluded the dismissal of an employee in the position of Mrs Webb. When the matter returned to it in *Webb* v. *EMO Air Cargo (No 2)* [1995] 1 WLR 1454, the House of Lords did find it possible, without doing violence to the language of the act, to interpret it so as to conform to the directive.

5.2.3.3.4 Judicial Review

The third and fourth consequences for British public law of the UK's membership of the EU can be relatively quickly dealt with. EU law has had an important impact on judicial review. As we shall see in detail in Chapter 10, judicial review is the legal procedure by which the actions and decisions of government and other public authorities may be challenged in court. Applicants may seek (or, in Scotland, petition for) judicial review where they consider that a public authority has acted or is proposing to act illegally, irrationally or procedurally unfairly (*Council of Civil Service Unions* v. *Minister for the Civil Service* [1985] AC 374). Each of these grounds of review – illegality, irrationality and procedural unfairness – has detailed and developed meanings in domestic law, as we shall see in Chapter 10. EU law has made two substantive changes to the way in which the grounds of judicial review are applied.

First, it has supplemented the notion of irrationality with a doctrine of proportionality. It may be that, in this respect, it is the law of the ECHR rather than EU law that will have the greater impact on domestic proceedings, proportionality being a principle of considerable importance in European human rights law (on which see *R (Daly)* v. *Secretary of State for the Home Department* [2001] 2 AC 532, considered in Chapter 10). However, prior to Brexit, there were cases in which proportionality as a general principle of EU law featured, a notable example being *R* v. *Chief Constable of Sussex, ex p International Trader's Ferry* [1999] 2 AC 418. This case concerned the legality of the decision of the chief constable of Sussex police force, taken principally for resource reasons, to limit the number of days on which his force was able to police ports from which live animals were being exported to France. Without a significant police presence, animal rights protesters would force the ports to close. The House of Lords ruled that the chief constable's decision was neither irrational in domestic law nor disproportionate in EU law, the point of EU law arising because the ferry operators considered that their inability to continue with the exports infringed their right to freedom of movement of goods under Article 34 of the TFEU. However, it is important to note that even the EU's standard of proportionality can apply more or less stringently. This was recently illustrated in *R (on the application of Plan B Earth Ltd)* v. *The Secretary of State for Transport* [2020] EWCA Civ 214, concerning judicial review of the planned third runway at Heathrow Airport. It was argued, inter alia, that the plan was contrary to the EU's Habitats Directive (Directive 92/43/EEC). When applying this directive, the Court of Justice recognises that, due to the fact that this requires complex scientific and technical assessments, in an area which grants a broad discretion, the proportionality standard applied is one of 'manifest error'. The Court of Appeal agreed that the equivalence of this standard in English law was that of *Wednesbury* unreasonableness, as opposed to proportionality. This was contested by the applicants, who argued that the standard applied should be one of proportionality given that the issue in question concerned fundamental rights of environmental protection, which are protected in the EU Charter. At the time of writing, an appeal against this decision had been lodged before the Supreme Court.

Second, EU law has significantly influenced the protection that the courts will give under domestic law to 'legitimate expectations'. If you legitimately expect that the government will treat you in a certain way (because, for example, the government has told you that it will treat you in a certain way and you have relied on that assurance), English law would traditionally have protected your expectation by affording you a right to be heard before your expectation could be frustrated (see, e.g., *R* v. *Secretary of State for the Home*

Department, ex p Hargreaves [1997] 1 WLR 906). This amounts to a procedural protection of legitimate expectations: what you get is a right to be heard; what you do not get is the right necessarily to have your expectation fulfilled. Under EU law, however, legitimate expectations may be protected substantively: what you may get is not merely a right to be heard but the right to have your expectation satisfied. Accordingly, albeit only in limited cases, English law too has started (not only in the context of EU law) to afford substantive protection to legitimate expectations (see, e.g., *R* v. *Minister for Agriculture, Fisheries and Food, ex p Hamble* [1995] 2 All ER 714 and *R* v. *North and East Devon Area Health Authority, ex p Coughlan* [2001] QB 213). (See, further, pp. 851–855.)

5.2.3.3.5 Remedies

The final area to be considered is the law of remedies. We saw above that the Court of Justice has developed a doctrine of state liability according to which, in certain circumstances, member states will be liable in damages for 'sufficiently serious' breaches of EU law. Under domestic public law, damages were only rarely available. Whereas damages are a central remedy in domestic private law, they have not been so in public law. In public law, the principal remedies are injunctions, by which public officers may be ordered to act or to refrain from acting in certain ways, and declarations, by which, as its name implies, the court may declare what the legal position is. It was thought that, under the combined influence of the EU doctrine of state liability and European human rights law (see the HRA, section 8), that was beginning to change, as damages became more important in public law (see, e.g., Amos, 'Extending the Liability of the State in Damages' (2001) 21 *LS* 1). It remains to be seen whether this development will continue post-Brexit. Questions of liability and public law are considered further in Chapter 10.

5.2.4 The Backdrop to Brexit: Discontent and Democratic Deficit

The previous sections have explained how the UK's membership of the EU had an impact on the UK constitution, particularly as concerns the supremacy of directly effective provisions of EU law. This effectively restricted the law-making power of the UK Parliament. If the UK Parliament were to enact legislation that was incompatible with directly effective provisions of EU law, then the UK courts were able to disapply that legislation, even when it was enacted after 1972. If the UK Parliament wished to legislate contrary to directly effective EU law, it might have been possible for it to do so if it were to enact legislation that took effect 'notwithstanding' the provisions of directly effective EU law, or to enact legislation to specifically or expressly repeal the European Communities Act 1972. However, it was not even clear that this would have succeeded, unless the UK were also to leave the European Union. If the UK had tried to act in this manner, prior to leaving the EU, it would have always been possible for the commission to bring legal proceedings against the UK for breaching EU law, leading to the possibility of the imposition of substantial fines.

There had always been concerns as to the way in which the UK's membership of the EU would limit the law-making power of the UK Parliament. These concerns were hinted at in the previous edition of this book – where note was taken of undertakings of the Coalition Government in its *Programme for Government* (2010) following the 2010 general election:

[a] We will ensure that the British Government is a positive participant in the European Union ...

[b] We will ensure that there is no further transfer of sovereignty or powers [from the UK to the EU] over the course of the next Parliament. We will examine the balance of the EU's existing competences ...

[c] We will amend the 1972 European Communities Act so that any proposed future treaty that transferred areas of power, or competences, would be subject to a referendum on that treaty – a 'referendum lock'. We will amend the 1972 European Communities Act so that the use of any passerelle would require primary legislation.

[d] We will examine the case for a United Kingdom Sovereignty Bill to make it clear that ultimate sovereignty remains with Parliament.

Although the Coalition Government did not propose a UK Sovereignty Bill, nevertheless, as discussed above, the European Union Act 2011 was enacted, which provided for referendum locks on further transfers of power to the European Union, in addition to adding in a sovereignty clause – in section 18 of the Act – reinforcing that any transfer of power to the EU from the UK came from the Westminster Parliament and that sovereignty remains with the Westminster Parliament.

There were two main concerns: first that the EU's powers were expanding and had strayed into areas that went beyond the intentions of the member states and second, that the European Union suffered from a democratic deficit. The former questioned the extent to which the UK Parliament remained sovereign. The second questioned the legitimacy of allowing EU laws to override UK legislation if the EU laws were not enacted in a democratically legitimate manner. It is not the place of a text and materials book to evaluate these political arguments. However, it is the place of this book to provide an outline of the facts underpinning these claims. As we saw earlier, both the principle of the supremacy of EU law and of direct effect were established through the case law of the European Union. We also saw that the Court of Justice had played a key role in the development of the protection of human rights in the European Union. Are these examples of the court going beyond the scope of the treaties, enhancing the competences of the European Union? Similar accusations have been laid at the door of the court, both in terms of its lack of control over the legislative competences of the EU and its control over the principle of subsidiarity, which is designed to ensure that, within the area of competences shared between the member states and the European Union, action is only taken by the EU when the aim of that action can only be achieved through the EU, or by reason of its scale and effect can best be achieved by the EU (Article 5 TEU). However, although we can point to examples of legislation that the Court of Justice has struck down as beyond the competences of the EU, these are few and far between. Also, the CJEU has never struck down legislation on the grounds of a breach of the principle of subsidiarity.

In terms of the claims of a democratic deficit, we need to look more clearly at the law-making processes of the European Union. Space precludes a detailed account of all of the possible law-making procedures in the EU. The most commonly used law-making procedure, post-Lisbon, is the ordinary legislative procedure that is set out in Article 294 TFEU as follows:

1. Where reference is made in the Treaties to the ordinary legislative procedure for the adoption of an act, the following procedure shall apply.
2. The Commission shall submit a proposal to the European Parliament and the Council.

First reading

3. The European Parliament shall adopt its position at first reading and communicate it to the Council.
4. If the Council approves the European Parliament's position, the act concerned shall be adopted in the wording which corresponds to the position of the European Parliament.
5. If the Council does not approve the European Parliament's position, it shall adopt its position at first reading and communicate it to the European Parliament.
6. The Council shall inform the European Parliament fully of the reasons which led it to adopt its position at first reading. The Commission shall inform the European Parliament fully of its position.

Second reading

7. If, within three months of such communication, the European Parliament:
    (a) approves the Council's position at first reading or has not taken a decision, the act concerned shall be deemed to have been adopted in the wording which corresponds to the position of the Council;
    (b) rejects, by a majority of its component members, the Council's position at first reading, the proposed act shall be deemed not to have been adopted;
    (c) proposes, by a majority of its component members, amendments to the Council's position at first reading, the text thus amended shall be forwarded to the Council and to the Commission, which shall deliver an opinion on those amendments.
8. If, within three months of receiving the European Parliament's amendments, the Council, acting by a qualified majority:

(a) approves all those amendments, the act in question shall be deemed to have been adopted;

(b) does not approve all the amendments, the President of the Council, in agreement with the President of the European Parliament, shall within six weeks convene a meeting of the Conciliation Committee.

9. The Council shall act unanimously on the amendments on which the Commission has delivered a negative opinion.

Conciliation

10. The Conciliation Committee, which shall be composed of the members of the Council or their representatives and an equal number of members representing the European Parliament, shall have the task of reaching agreement on a joint text, by a qualified majority of the members of the Council or their representatives and by a majority of the members representing the European Parliament within six weeks of its being convened, on the basis of the positions of the European Parliament and the Council at second reading.

11. The Commission shall take part in the Conciliation Committee's proceedings and shall take all necessary initiatives with a view to reconciling the positions of the European Parliament and the Council.

12. If, within six weeks of its being convened, the Conciliation Committee does not approve the joint text, the proposed act shall be deemed not to have been adopted.

Third reading

13. If, within that period, the Conciliation Committee approves a joint text, the European Parliament, acting by a majority of the votes cast, and the Council, acting by a qualified majority, shall each have a period of six weeks from that approval in which to adopt the act in question in accordance with the joint text. If they fail to do so, the proposed act shall be deemed not to have been adopted.

14. The periods of three months and six weeks referred to in this Article shall be extended by a maximum of one month and two weeks respectively at the initiative of the European Parliament or the Council . . .

The law-making process provides the European Parliament with a veto power. This applies not only to most legislation, but also to the budget, where the Parliament has the power to veto the EU's annual budget. However, it is rare for the European Parliament to veto legislation outright. Nevertheless, the European Parliament can be more successful in ensuring the success of its amendments to legislation than backbench and opposition MPs in the Westminster Parliament.

The European Parliament is the only directly democratically composed institution in the European Union. It is elected every five years. Following the exit of the UK from the European Union, the European Parliament is currently composed of 705 members (MEPs) elected from the twenty-seven member states. The last election took place in May 2019. At the time of that election, the UK was a member state of the European Union, and so duly elected its quota of MEPs. The UK's seats were redistributed on 1 February 2020, following the UK's exit from the EU. This led to the reduction in numbers of the European Parliament from 751 to 705. Each member state decides the electoral system used to elect the MEPs. Although there are no 'European' political parties, there are political groups across the different political parties in the European Union. There are currently seven political groups – the two largest groups are the centre-right and centre-left groups: the European People's Party (Christian Democrats) and the Progressive Alliance of Socialists and Democrats, who have 187 and 146 members, respectively. Even though the Parliament is directly elected, there is often little turnout for elections to the European Parliament, and very little engagement in most countries with the issues before the European Parliament. It is in this regard that it is felt that, despite the growth in the role of the European Parliament, the European Union still suffers from a democratic deficit.

However, as the ordinary legislative procedure makes clear, legislation is not enacted by the European Parliament alone. A key role is also played by the council and the commission. The council has to agree to all legislation, enjoying a veto power in the same way as the European Parliament. The commission initiates all legislation. There are also circumstances in which the council and the commission can enact legislation on their own, or without a role for the European Parliament beyond its consultation or consent. This is particularly true of Article 352 TFEU, paragraph one of which states that:

> If action by the Union should prove necessary, within the framework of the policies defined in the Treaties, to attain one of the objectives set out in the Treaties, and the Treaties have not provided the necessary powers, the Council, acting unanimously on a proposal from the Commission and after obtaining the consent of the European Parliament, shall adopt the appropriate measures. Where the measures in question are adopted by the Council in accordance with a special legislative procedure, it shall also act unanimously on a proposal from the Commission and after obtaining the consent of the European Parliament.

As discussed above, the EU has limited competences. It can only act within the sphere of powers conferred on it by the Lisbon Treaty. However, Article 352 provides a means whereby the EU can act to achieve its objectives, even if there is no specific provision of the Lisbon Treaties empowering the EU to act:

Article 352 (1)

If action by the Union should prove necessary, within the framework of the policies defined in the Treaties, to attain one of the objectives set out in the Treaties, and the Treaties have not provided the necessary powers, the Council, acting unanimously on a proposal from the Commission and after obtaining the consent of the European Parliament, shall adopt the appropriate measures. Where the measures in question are adopted by the Council in accordance with a special legislative procedure, it shall also act unanimously on a proposal from the Commission and after obtaining the consent of the European Parliament.

If we are to evaluate the democratic credentials of the European Union, we also need to examine the composition of the commission and the council.

The commission is a large body, whose composition is split into three categories: the college of commissioners, the directorates-general and the cabinets. The college of commissioners is composed of a representative from each member state, currently under the presidency of Ursula von der Leyen. The president of the commission is nominated by the European Council and elected by the European Parliament. The president then nominates the commissioners, whose appointment is also subject to a vote of approval from the European Parliament for the commission as a whole. Commissioners are appointed for a renewable five-year term, to run concurrently with that of the European Parliament. Each commissioner is allocated a portfolio by the president of the commission; thus, there is a commissioner for competition, a commissioner for agriculture, a commissioner for the environment and so on (for the current list in full, see the commission's website http://ec.europa.eu/index_en.htm). Article 17 of the TEU provides that the commissioners shall act 'in the general interest of the Union' and that they must be 'completely independent' in the performance of their duties. In particular, they 'shall neither seek nor take instructions from any Government'. Additionally, the commission as a college is 'responsible' to the European Parliament (Article 17(8) of the TEU), the Parliament having the power to 'censure' the commission. If a motion of censure is passed by a two-thirds majority of the European Parliament, the college of commissioners is required to resign as a body, albeit that it will remain in office until a new commission is appointed (Article 234 of the TFEU). The directorates-general, in which most of the commission's staff work, are akin to government departments. The cabinets are the political offices of each commissioner. These are small, comprising no more than eight individuals each (except the president's cabinet, which has eleven members).

The council is composed of ministers from the member states. The European Council is composed of the heads of government of the member states. Article 15 of the TEU sets out the tasks of the European Council:

1. The European Council shall provide the Union with the necessary impetus for its development and shall define the general political directions and priorities thereof. It shall not exercise legislative functions.

2. The European Council shall consist of the Heads of State or Government of the Member States, together with its President and the President of the Commission. The High Representative of the Union for Foreign Affairs and Security Policy shall take part in its work.
3. The European Council shall meet twice every six months, convened by its President . . .
4. Except where the Treaties provide otherwise, decisions of the European Council shall be taken by consensus.

The president of the European Council is elected for a term of two and a half years, which is renewable once. The current president, elected on 1 December 2019, is Charles Michel. The Council of Ministers consists of representatives of the governments of the member states at ministerial level. Its membership varies according to the subject under consideration – ministers responsible for agriculture, for example, meeting as the 'Agriculture and Fisheries Council' when issues of the common agricultural policy are to be discussed.

Almost all substantive decisions in council are made through either one of two means: unanimously or by 'qualified majority voting' (QMV) (for some procedural matters a simple majority is all that is required). Clearly, when unanimity is required, the power of each member state government is increased, as each has a veto. Where legislation may be adopted by QMV, by way of contrast, it may be passed even against the wishes of a number of member state governments. Lisbon made QMV the 'default' position for decision-making in council and transferred a number of areas from unanimity to QMV. The rules of QMV have been complex and hotly contested; they remain politically sensitive. Lisbon reformed the rules of QMV, simplifying them such that as from November 2014, 'a qualified majority shall be defined as at least 55% of the members of the Council, comprising at least fifteen of them and representing Member States comprising at least 65% of the population of the Union' (Article 16(4) of the TEU). The aim of this formulation is to achieve some sort of balance between preserving each national voice, on the one hand, while reflecting the vastly different population sizes of the member states, on the other.

The council is assisted by a committee of permanent representatives (COREPER), which consists of representatives of the member states who have ambassadorial rank and head the staffs of officials constituting the permanent representation of each member state to the EU. This committee has responsibility for preparing the work of the council and for carrying out the tasks assigned to it by the council It sets up its own specialised working groups of national officials, examines proposals that have been submitted to the council and tries to reach an accommodation of national viewpoints. COREPER and its working groups take no decisions themselves but exercise an important influence in settling and defining the issues for council decision. These official bodies operate beyond the reach of democratic control and accountability. Uncontroversial proposals agreed by COREPER are generally adopted without debate by the council. Decisions of the council on more contentious matters are the product of intergovernmental bargaining and compromise. Ministers may often be compelled to make concessions on one issue in return for support on another. Since Lisbon, the TEU has provided that: 'The Council shall meet in public when it deliberates and votes on a draft legislative act. To this end, each Council meeting shall be divided into two parts, dealing respectively with deliberations on Union legislative and non-legislative activities' (Article 16(8) of the TEU).

When assessing the democratic credentials of the EU, it is also important to take account of the extent to which political mechanisms in addition to legal mechanisms help to ensure the EU acts within its sphere of competences – particularly as regards controls over subsidiarity – as well as the role of national parliaments when scrutinising EU legislation. The Lisbon Treaty included a revised protocol on the principles of subsidiarity and proportionality. First, the protocol provides a means for national parliaments to be made aware of draft legislation, requiring the commission to forward draft legislative acts to the national parliaments at the same time as they are sent to the council and the European Parliament. The European Parliament also forwards its draft legislative acts and its amendments to draft legislative acts to national parliaments. All draft legislation is also required to include a statement as to how the measure complies with the principles of subsidiarity and proportionality. In addition, the protocol creates what are colloquially referred to as the 'yellow card' and the 'orange card' mechanisms. National parliaments may, within eight weeks of received a draft legislative proposal, raise concerns as to subsidiarity. The yellow card refers to the situation that arises if one-third of the national parliaments raise concerns as to subsidiarity, which triggers a requirement on the commission to decide whether to maintain, change or withdraw its legislative proposal, giving reasons for this conclusion. If a majority of the national parliaments raise concerns, this then triggers the orange card mechanism. As with the yellow card mechanism, the commission may decide to maintain, modify or withdraw its legislative proposal and must give reasons. This justification must be provided to the European Parliament and the council. If 55 per cent of council members, or a simple majority of the European Parliament find that the principle of subsidiarity has been breached, then the proposal is dropped and will not be considered further. At the time of writing, the yellow card procedure had been used three times (on the first occasion, the commission withdrew its proposal, on the other two, it provided reasons and maintained its proposal). The orange card procedure has not yet been triggered. The commission also submits an annual report on the application of the principles of subsidiarity and proportionality.

In the UK, the House of Lords European Union Select Committee 'considers EU documents and other matters related to the EU'. It aims to hold the government to account for its actions at the EU level. Since the UK's exit from the EU, the committee has also scrutinised the conduct of the UK's negotiations with the EU, in addition to its implementation of the Withdrawal Agreement. The Lords Committee is currently composed of nineteen members appointed by the House of Lords. In turn, the committee appoints members to five sub-committees on the EU: environment, goods, international agreements, justice and services. The international agreements committee scrutinises all international agreements laid before Parliament under the terms of the Constitutional Reform and Governance Act 2010. The committee also conducts inquiries and produces reports. Its work is highly praised – not just in the UK but, at least prior to Brexit, across the EU. Its work will be discussed in more detail in the following section.

Ultimately, however, these issues are not dependent on facts alone. They are heavily influenced by values. It is hard to deny that the EU has moved on beyond its initial foundations and that this has included greater political union, with some perceiving this as a move, eventually, towards a federal Europe. It is also hard to deny the impact of EU law in the UK. Whether this is seen as a means of countries working together to achieve objectives that could not be achieved alone, or whether we agree with, in particular, the protections of workers' rights, environmental rights, consumer protection, and the agricultural and trade policies of the EU as a move in the right direction, is a policy choice. The advantages – or otherwise – of EU membership did come at the cost of sharing law-making power with the EU. The question continually arose as to whether this was a price worth paying.

5.3 Brexit and Beyond

The build-up to Brexit was not just concerned with issues of law and policy. It was also a matter of politics. In its 2015 manifesto, the Conservative Party promised that it would hold an in/out referendum on Brexit by the end of 2017. This promise was motivated by two factors. First, there was evidence of division within the Conservative Party on European issues. Second, there was concern as to the rise of the popularity of the UK Independence Party (UKIP). In the 2014 elections to the European Parliament, for example, UKIP obtained twenty-four seats with 27 per cent of the popular vote. This meant that it was the most successful political party in those elections. A referendum was perceived as providing a means of settling this issue. There were also good constitutional reasons for resolving issues as to the UK's membership of the EU through a referendum. We discussed earlier that the UK became a member of the EU on 1 January 1973, when the European Communities Act 1972 came into force. However, this is not the full story. In 1975, the then Labour Government held a referendum on the UK's continued membership of the

EU. In that referendum, the UK voted to continue to remain in the EU. We can also track a consistent pattern of using referendums to determine issues of constitutional importance – for example, the use of referendums for devolution and on the issue of whether the Westminster Parliament should adopt an alternative voting system. The UK's continued membership of the EU did not divide on party lines, meaning that a general election might not fully reflect opinion on continued membership of the EU. Surely if a referendum were needed to confirm remaining in the EU, a further referendum would be required to leave the EU, even if this requirement were only one of politics or constitutional ideology and not a matter of law.

The referendum was regulated by the European Union Referendum Act 2015. The act provided for the holding of a referendum to be held no later than 31 December 2017, excluding 5 May 2016 and 4 May 2017. It also established the question that would be placed on the ballot paper: 'Should the United Kingdom remain a member of the European Union or leave the European Union?'; and the possible responses: 'Remain a Member of the European Union' and 'Leave the European Union' (European Union Referendum Act 2015, section 1). Everyone entitled to vote in elections for the Westminster Parliament was entitled to vote in the Brexit referendum, including peers who may not vote for the Westminster Parliament, but who were entitled to vote either in local elections or elections for the European Parliament. This included Commonwealth citizens and Irish citizens, and UK citizens living in Gibraltar, but did not include EU citizens exercising their right to reside in the UK. In addition, as discussed in Chapter 4, the outcome of the referendum was determined on a simple majority of votes cast. There was no need for a majority of the component parts of the UK. The convention of ministerial collective responsibility did not apply to the referendum campaign. This meant that cabinet and governmental ministers were free to campaign according to their conscience and did not need to comply with the line of the government.

The Brexit referendum took place on 23 June 2016. The referendum generated a large turnout: 72.2 per cent of the electorate. Of those, 17,412,742 (51.9 per cent) voted to leave the EU and 16,141,241 (48.1 per cent) voted to remain in the EU. The referendum outcome led to the resignation of David Cameron, then Prime Minister, who had been responsible for initiating the referendum and who had campaigned in favour of the UK remaining in the EU. Following a leadership campaign in the Conservative Party, Theresa May became the next Prime Minister of the UK, taking on the mantle of implementing the outcome of the referendum and securing the UK's exit from the European Union. As will be discussed below, this was no simple task. While the referendum provided an answer to the simple question of whether the UK should remain within or leave the EU, it did not provide a clear answer as to the type of relationship the electorate wished to have with the EU in the future. In addition, the UK's exit from the EU raised questions as to the relative powers of the executive and the legislature. Article 50 of the TEU provided for the regulation of a member state's exit from the European Union as follows:

1. Any Member State may decide to withdraw from the Union in accordance with its own constitutional requirements.
2. A Member State which decides to withdraw shall notify the European Council of its intention. In the light of the guidelines provided by the European Council, the Union shall negotiate and conclude an agreement with that State, setting out the arrangements for its withdrawal, taking account of the framework for its future relationship with the Union. That agreement shall be negotiated in accordance with Article 218(3) of the Treaty on the Functioning of the European Union. It shall be concluded on behalf of the Union by the Council, acting by a qualified majority, after obtaining the consent of the European Parliament.
3. The Treaties shall cease to apply to the State in question from the date of entry into force of the withdrawal agreement or, failing that, two years after the notification referred to in paragraph 2, unless the European Council, in agreement with the Member State concerned, unanimously decides to extend this period.
4. For the purposes of paragraphs 2 and 3, the member of the European Council or of the Council representing the withdrawing Member State shall not participate in the discussions of the European Council or Council or in decisions concerning it.
   A qualified majority shall be defined in accordance with Article 238(3)(b) of the Treaty on the Functioning of the European Union.
5. If a State which has withdrawn from the Union asks to rejoin, its request shall be subject to the procedure referred to in Article 49.

This required, first, that the UK notify the European Council of the UK's decision to leave the European Union. Prime Minister May announced that the government would use the prerogative power to notify the European Council (for a discussion of prerogative powers, see pp. 575–577). As such, the timing of notification, and the content of that notification, was a decision for the government. Parliament would not have a say. However, the intention of the prime minister to use the prerogative was subject to challenge. In *R (Miller)* v. *Secretary of State for Exiting the European Union* [2016] EWHC 2768 (Admin), [2017] 2 WLR 583, the high court – which, unusually and as a mark of the importance of the case – was composed of Lord Thomas, the Chief Justice, Sir Terence Etherton, the Master of the Rolls, and Sales LJ (then a member of the Court of Appeal), concluded that the prerogative power of international relations, which included entering and exiting treaties, did not include the specific power to notify the European Council of the UK's intention to exit the European Union. The judges reaching this conclusion were subject to strong criticism in the press, most notoriously in the headline of the *Daily Mail* of 4 November 2016, which referred to the three judges who decided the case as 'Enemies of the People'. The government appealed the decision, which was leapfrogged to the Supreme Court and which, for the first time in its history, sat in its maximum sitting as eleven justices of the Supreme Court.

R (Miller) v. *Secretary of State for Exiting the European Union* [2017] UKSC 5,
[2018] AC 61

The UK Supreme Court was asked to determine two issues. First, did the
government enjoy a prerogative power that could be used to notify the
European Council of the UK's intention to exit the EU treaties. Second, if
legislation was required, did the devolved legislatures need to consent to this
legislation? In a historic judgment, the Supreme Court concluded, by
a majority of eight to three, that the prerogative did not include a specific
power to withdraw from the EU treaties. This judgment has important implications for legal controls over prerogative powers, and for the extent to which
the courts can recognise, but not enforce, constitutional conventions. The
focus in this chapter will be on the impact of the *Miller* decision on our
understanding of the nature of EU law and the purpose of the European
Communities Act 1972. The justices of the Supreme Court diverged on these
issues.

The Supreme Court set out the limits on prerogative powers. Prerogative
powers do not include an ability to modify domestic law, or to frustrate
legislation. It will be recalled from the above discussion that international
treaties do not form part of UK law unless and until they are incorporated
into UK law through the enactment of legislation. As regards the UK's
membership of the EU, this occurred through the provisions of the
European Communities Act 1972, set out above. In particular, disagreement
arose as to the interpretation of section 2(1) of the Act which provides that:

> All such rights, powers, liabilities, obligations and restrictions from time to time created or
> arising by or under the Treaties, and all such remedies and procedures from time to time
> provided for by or under the Treaties, as in accordance with the Treaties are without further
> enactment to be given effect or used in the United Kingdom shall be recognised and
> available in law, and be enforced, allowed and followed accordingly.

The majority's interpretation of the 1972 Act led them to conclude both that
the UK's withdrawal from the EU would modify domestic law and frustrate the
European Communities Act 1972. The minority disagreed. In order to understand this disagreement, it helps first to set out Lord Reed's dissenting judgment, before providing an account of the majority judgment delivered by Lord
Neuberger.

> **Lord Reed:** [184]. Considering section 2(1) in greater detail, it is a long and densely-packed
> provision, whose syntax is complex, and whose meaning is not immediately clear. It requires
> to be read with care. Its essential structure can be expressed in this way: All such [members
> of a specified category] as [satisfy a specified condition] shall be [dealt with in accordance
> with a specified requirement]. Rules in that form can be used in many contexts: for example,

all such prisoners as are charged with conduct contrary to good order and discipline shall be brought before the Governor; all such incoming passengers as are displaying symptoms of ebola shall be placed in quarantine.

[185]. Two features of such rules should be noted. First, the rule is conditional in nature: the application of the requirement which it imposes depends on there being members of the specified category that satisfy the relevant condition. In the examples just given, for example, the relevant conditions are being charged with conduct contrary to good order and discipline; and displaying symptoms of ebola. Secondly, although a rule in that form contemplates the possibility that the condition may be satisfied, the form of the rule does not convey any intention that the condition will be satisfied. In the examples just given, for example, the rule does not convey an intention that there will be prisoners who are charged, or passengers who display symptoms of ebola. The intention of the rule-maker, so far as it can be derived from the rule, would not therefore be thwarted or frustrated if, either immediately, or at some point in the future, there were no members of the relevant category which satisfied the relevant condition.

[186]. In section 2(1), the relevant category is:

'rights, powers, liabilities, obligations and restrictions from time to time created or arising by or under the Treaties, and . . . remedies and procedures from time to time provided for by or under the Treaties.'

The words 'from time to time', which appear twice, mean that section 2(1) is concerned not only with the Treaties, and the Regulations and other legal instruments made under them, as they stood at the time of accession, but also with the Treaties and instruments made under them as they may change over time in the future. This recognises the fact that the 'rights, powers, liabilities, obligations and restrictions . . . created or arising by or under the Treaties', and the 'remedies and procedures . . . provided for by or under the Treaties', alter from time to time, as a result of changes to the Treaties or to the laws made under the procedures laid down in the Treaties.

[187]. This is relevant in the present context, since it demonstrates that Parliament has recognised that rights given effect under the 1972 Act may be added to, altered or revoked without the necessity of a further Act of Parliament (something which is also apparent from section 1(3)). In response to this point, the majority of the court draw a distinction, described as 'a vital difference', between changes in domestic law resulting from variations in the content of EU law arising from new EU legislation, and changes resulting from withdrawal by the UK from the European Union. There is no basis in the language of the 1972 Act for drawing any such distinction. Under the arrangements established by the Act, alterations in the UK's obligations under the Treaties are automatically reflected in alterations in domestic law. That is equally the position whether the alterations in the UK's obligations under the Treaties result from the Treaties' ceasing to apply to the UK, in accordance with article 50EU, or from changes to the Treaties or to legislation made under the Treaties. The Act simply creates a scheme under which the effect given to EU law in domestic law reflects the UK's international obligations under the Treaties, whatever they may be. There is nothing in the Act to suggest that Parliament's intention to ensure an exact match depends on the reason why they might not match.

[188]. The requirement imposed by section 2(1) is: *'shall be recognised and available in law, and be enforced, allowed and followed accordingly.'* This phrase gives effect in domestic law to all such rights, powers and so forth as satisfy the relevant condition.

[189]. The condition which must be satisfied, in order for that requirement to apply, is set out in the following phrase: 'All such ... as *in accordance with the Treaties are without further enactment to be given legal effect or used in the United Kingdom.'* This phrase is of particular importance to the resolution of the *Miller* appeal. It follows from this phrase that rights, powers and so forth created or arising by or under the Treaties are not automatically given effect in domestic law. Legal effect is given only to such rights, powers and so forth arising by or under the Treaties as 'in accordance with the Treaties' are without further enactment to be given legal effect 'in the United Kingdom'. In this respect, once more, the 1972 Act creates a scheme under which the effect given to EU law in domestic law exactly matches the UK's international obligations, whatever they may be.

[190]. The words 'without further enactment' reflect the EU law concept of direct effect, established by *Van Gend en Loos* and *Costa v ENEL* as explained above (and, in so far as it may be regarded as distinct, the concept of direct applicability, established by article 189 of the Treaty of Rome and now stated in article 288FEU of the FEU Treaty: see section 18 of the European Union Act 2011). Accordingly, where 'in accordance with the Treaties', rights, powers and so forth are to be directly applicable or directly effective in the law of the UK, section 2(1) achieves that effect. But there is no obligation 'in accordance with the Treaties' to give effect in the UK to EU rights, powers and so forth merely because they are directly effective under EU law: such an obligation arises only if and for so long as the Treaties apply to the UK. The extent to which the effect given by section 2(1) to rights, powers and so forth arising under EU law is dependent on the Treaties cannot therefore be confined to the question whether the rights, powers and so forth are, under the Treaties, directly effective: it also depends, more fundamentally, on whether the Treaties impose any obligations on the UK to give effect to EU law.

[191]. Whether rights, powers and so forth are to be given legal effect in the UK, in accordance with the Treaties, therefore depends on whether the Treaties apply to the UK. As the majority of the court state, at para 77:

'Parliament cannot have intended that section 2 should continue to import the variable content of EU law into domestic law, or that the other consequences of the 1972 Act described in paras 62–64 above should continue to apply, after the United Kingdom had ceased to be bound by the EU Treaties.'

If the Treaties do not apply to the UK, then there are no rights, powers and so forth which, in accordance with the Treaties, are to be given legal effect in the UK.

Lord Reed concludes both that withdrawing from the EU treaties would not modify domestic law and that it would not frustrate the European Communities Act 1972. EU law is international law. It is not part of domestic law until it has been incorporated into UK law by travelling through the pipeline provided by the 1972 Act. Leaving the EU treaties would not modify domestic law. It would just prevent provisions of EU law being incorporated into the UK. While this would modify the law, including potentially removing rights, the law modified is not domestic. It is international law that, following the UK's exit from the EU, would no longer be incorporated into UK law as EU law would no longer require its incorporation. In a similar manner, the provisions of the 1972 Act are not frustrated as, when we read section 2(1), we realise that it is conditional. The 1972 Act incorporates the provisions of EU law that arise from time to time. If the UK withdraws from the EU treaties, then there are no rights or obligations of EU law that need to be incorporated into UK law through the Act. The Act is not frustrated as its provisions are conditional. Its purpose is to incorporate into domestic law whatever EU law requires – even if that is essentially nothing following the UK's exit from the EU.

Lord Reed's approach can be contrasted with that of the majority, whose judgment was delivered by Lord Neuberger.

[60]. Many statutes give effect to treaties by prescribing the content of domestic law in the areas covered by them. The 1972 Act does this, but it does considerably more as well. It authorises a dynamic process by which, without further primary legislation (and, in some cases, even without any domestic legislation), EU law not only becomes a source of UK law, but actually takes precedence over all domestic sources of UK law, including statutes. This may sound rather dry or technical to many people, but in constitutional terms the effect of the 1972 Act was unprecedented. Indeed, it is fair to say that the legal consequences of the United Kingdom's accession to the EEC were not fully appreciated by many lawyers until the Factortame litigation in the 1990s – see the House of Lords decisions in *R v Secretary of State for Transport, Ex p Factortame Ltd* (No 2) [1991] 1 AC 603 and (*No 5*) [2000] 1 AC 524. Of course, consistently with the principle of Parliamentary sovereignty, this unprecedented state of affairs will only last so long as Parliament wishes: the 1972 Act can be repealed like any other statute. For that reason, we would not accept that the so-called fundamental rule of recognition (i e the fundamental rule by reference to which all other rules are validated) underlying UK laws has been varied by the 1972 Act or would be varied by its repeal.

[61]. In one sense, of course, it can be said that the 1972 Act is the source of EU law, in that, without that Act, EU law would have no domestic status. But in a more fundamental sense and, we consider, a more realistic sense, where EU law applies in the United Kingdom, it is the EU institutions which are the relevant source of that law. The legislative institutions of the EU can create or abrogate rules of law which will then apply domestically, without the specific sanction of any UK institution. It is true that the UK Government and UK-elected members of the European Parliament participate in the EU legislative processes and can influence their outcome, but that does not diminish the point. Further, in the many areas of EU competence which are subject to majority decision, the approval of the United Kingdom is not required for its legislation to take effect domestically. It is also true that EU law enjoys its automatic and overriding effect only by virtue of the 1972 Act, and thus only while it remains in force. That point simply reflects the fact that Parliament was and remains sovereign: so, no new source of law could come into existence without Parliamentary sanction – and without

being susceptible to being abrogated by Parliament. However, that in no way undermines our view that it is unrealistic to deny that, so long as that Act remains in force, the EU Treaties, EU legislation and the interpretations placed on these instruments by the Court of Justice are direct sources of UK law.

[62]. The 1972 Act did two things which are relevant to these appeals. First, it provided that rights, duties and rules derived from EU law should apply in the United Kingdom as part of its domestic law. Secondly, it provided for a new constitutional process for making law in the United Kingdom. These things are closely related, but they are legally and conceptually distinct. The content of the rights, duties and rules introduced into our domestic law as a result of the 1972 Act is exclusively a question of EU law. However, the constitutional processes by which the law of the United Kingdom is made is exclusively a question of domestic law.

[63]. Under the terms of the 1972 Act, EU law may take effect as part of the law of the United Kingdom in one of three ways. First, the EU Treaties themselves are directly applicable by virtue of section 2(1). Some of the provisions of those Treaties create rights (and duties) which are directly applicable in the sense that they are enforceable in UK courts. Secondly, where the effect of the EU Treaties is that EU legislation is directly applicable in domestic law, section 2(1) provides that it is to have direct effect in the United Kingdom without the need for further domestic legislation. This applies to EU Regulations (which are directly applicable by virtue of article 288FEU of the FEU Treaty). Thirdly, section 2(2) authorises the implementation of EU law by delegated legislation. This applies mainly to EU Directives, which are not, in general, directly applicable but are required (again by article 288) to be transposed into national law. While this is an international law obligation, failure of the United Kingdom to comply with it is justiciable in domestic courts, and some Directives may be enforced by individuals directly against national governments in domestic courts. Further, any serious breach by the UK Parliament, government or judiciary of any rule of EU law intended to confer individual rights will entitle any individual sustaining damage as a direct result to compensation from the UK Government: *Brasserie du Pêcheur SA v Federal Republic of Germany* (Joined Cases C-46/93 and C-48/93) [1996] QB 404 (provided that, where the breach consists in a court decision, the breach is not only serious but also manifest: *Köbler v Republik Österreich* (Case C-224/01) [2004] QB 848).

[64]. Thus, EU law in EU Treaties and EU legislation will pass into UK law through the medium of section 2(1) or the implementation provisions of section 2(2) of the 1972 Act, so long as the United Kingdom is party to the EU Treaties. Similarly, so long as the United Kingdom is party to the EU Treaties, UK courts are obliged (i) to interpret EU Treaties, Regulations and Directives in accordance with decisions of the Court of Justice, (ii) to refer unclear points of EU law to the Court of Justice, and (iii) to interpret all domestic legislation, if at all possible, so as to comply with EU law: see *Marleasing SA v La Comercial Internacional de Alimentación SA* (Case C-106/89) [1990] ECR I-4135. And, so long as the United Kingdom is party to the EU Treaties, UK citizens are able to recover damages from the UK Government in cases where a decision of one of the organs of the state based on a serious error of EU law has caused them loss.

[65]. In our view, then, although the 1972 Act gives effect to EU law, it is not itself the originating source of that law. It is, as was said on behalf of the Secretary of State echoing the illuminating analysis of Professor Finnis, the 'conduit pipe' by which EU law is introduced into UK domestic law. So long as the 1972 Act remains in force, its effect is to constitute EU law an independent and overriding source of domestic law.

. . .

[76]. We accept the proposition that the ambit of the rights and remedies etc which are incorporated into domestic law through section 2 of the 1972 Act varies with the United Kingdom's obligations from time to time under the EU Treaties. This proposition is reflected in the language of subsections (1) and (2) of section 2, which are quoted in paras 18 and 19 above. However, this proposition is also limited in nature. Thus, the provisions of new EU Treaties are not automatically brought into domestic law through section 2: only once they have been statutorily added to 'the Treaties' and 'the EU Treaties' in section 1(2) can section 2 give effect to new EU Treaties. And section 2 can only apply to those rights and remedies which are capable of being 'given legal effect or used' or 'enjoyed' in the United Kingdom.

[77]. We also accept that Parliament cannot have intended that section 2 should continue to import the variable content of EU law into domestic law, or that the other consequences of the 1972 Act described in paras 62–64 above should continue to apply, after the United Kingdom had ceased to be bound by the EU Treaties. However, while acknowledging the force of Lord Reed JSC's powerful judgment, we do not accept that it follows from this that the 1972 Act either contemplates or accommodates the abrogation of EU law upon the United Kingdom's withdrawal from the EU Treaties by prerogative act without prior Parliamentary authorisation. On the contrary: we consider that, by the 1972 Act, Parliament endorsed and gave effect to the United Kingdom's membership of what is now the European Union under the EU Treaties in a way which is inconsistent with the future exercise by ministers of any prerogative power to withdraw from such Treaties.

[78]. In short, the fact that EU law will no longer be part of UK domestic law if the United Kingdom withdraws from the EU Treaties does not mean that Parliament contemplated or intended that ministers could cause the United Kingdom to withdraw from the EU Treaties without prior Parliamentary approval. There is a vital difference between changes in domestic law resulting from variations in the content of EU law arising from new EU legislation, and changes in domestic law resulting from withdrawal by the United Kingdom from the European Union. The former involves changes in EU law, which are then brought into domestic law through section 2 of the 1972 Act. The latter involves a unilateral action by the relevant constitutional bodies which effects a fundamental change in the constitutional arrangements of the United Kingdom.

. . .

[80]. One of the most fundamental functions of the constitution of any state is to identify the sources of its law. And, as explained in paras 61 to 66 above, the 1972 Act effectively constitutes EU law as an entirely new, independent and overriding source of domestic law, and the Court of Justice as a source of binding judicial decisions about its meaning. This proposition is indeed inherent in the Secretary of State's metaphor of the 1972 Act as

a conduit pipe by which EU law is brought into the domestic UK law. Upon the United Kingdom's withdrawal from the European Union, EU law will cease to be a source of domestic law for the future (even if the Great Repeal Bill provides that some legal rules derived from it should remain in force or continue to apply to accrued rights and liabilities), decisions of the Court of Justice will (again depending on the precise terms of the Great Repeal Bill) be of no more than persuasive authority, and there will be no further references to that court from UK courts. Even those legal rules derived from EU law and transposed into UK law by domestic legislation will have a different status. They will no longer be paramount, but will be open to domestic repeal or amendment in ways that may be inconsistent with EU law.

[81]. Accordingly, the main difficulty with the Secretary of State's argument is that it does not answer the objection based on the constitutional implications of withdrawal from the EU. As we have said, withdrawal is fundamentally different from variations in the content of EU law arising from further EU Treaties or legislation. A complete withdrawal represents a change which is different not just in degree but in kind from the abrogation of particular rights, duties or rules derived from EU law. It will constitute as significant a constitutional change as that which occurred when EU law was first incorporated in domestic law by the 1972 Act. And, if Notice is given, this change will occur irrespective of whether Parliament repeals the 1972 Act. It would be inconsistent with long-standing and fundamental principle for such a far-reaching change to the UK constitutional arrangements to be brought about by ministerial decision or ministerial action alone. All the more so when the source in question was brought into existence by Parliament through primary legislation, which gave that source an overriding supremacy in the hierarchy of domestic law sources.

There are three main differences between the two judgments. First, the majority judgment delivered by Lord Neuberger does not merely regard the European Communities Act 1972 as providing a means for EU law to travel through the 'conduit pipe' and then be incorporated into UK law. It also recognises EU law as a valid source of domestic law. The provisions of EU law, once enacted by the EU institutions under the requirements of EU law, are recognised as domestic law. These provisions then travel through the conduit pipe provided by the act into the UK. Consequently, different consequences from those stated by Lord Reed would arise if the UK withdraws from the EU. This automatically removes EU law as a source of domestic law and the EU provisions – which are recognised as a source of domestic law – are removed as the UK withdraws from the EU treaties. Second, the purpose of the European Communities Act 1972 is not merely to incorporate EU law into the UK, but also to facilitate the UK's membership of the EU. While the purpose of the 1972 Act is not frustrated by modifying the content of the rights, principles and liabilities, etc., that are incorporated into UK law as the content of EU treaties change, it is frustrated if the UK cuts off all of this source of law by withdrawing from the EU treaties. Third, the majority adds that to withdraw from the EU treaties by an act of the executive alone would breach a longstanding constitutional principle.

The outcome of the first *Miller* decision was that the government could not use the prerogative to notify the European Council on the UK's intention to withdraw from the EU treaties. Instead, legislation would be required. Shortly after the decision was delivered by the UK Supreme Court, the UK Government introduced the European Union (Notification of Withdrawal) Bill 2017. The requirement of legislation provided Parliament with the opportunity to place conditions on the delegation of power to the government. Amendments in the House of Lords were originally successful, both as regards providing a role for Parliament in the negotiation of the Withdrawal Agreement and to require the government to produce a report on the impact of Brexit on the rights of EU citizens residing in the UK. However, neither of these amendments was accepted by the House of Commons and they were then withdrawn by the House of Lords. In the end, the legislation placed no conditions on the government. The entire act is reproduced below:

The European Union (Notification of Withdrawal) Act 2017
Section 1: Power to notify withdrawal from the EU

(1) The Prime Minister may notify, under Article 50(2) of the Treaty on European Union, the United Kingdom's intention to withdraw from the EU.
(2) This section has effect despite any provision made by or under the European Communities Act 1972 or any other enactment.

Section 2: Short title

This Act may be cited as the European Union (Notification of Withdrawal) Act 2017.

On 29 March 2017, Prime Minister Theresa May notified the European Council of the UK's intention to withdraw from the EU treaties. This started the negotiation period of two years – subject to an agreed extension by both parties – as established in Article 50 TFEU.

(For further discussion of the *Miller* decision, see Barber, Hickman and King, 'Reflections on Miller' (2016–2017) 8 *UK Supreme Court Yearbook*' Craig, '*Miller*, Structural Constitutional Review and the Limits of Prerogative Power' (2017) *Public Law* 48; Ekins, 'Constitutional Practice and Principle in the Article 50 Litigation' (2017) 133 *LQR* 347; Elliott, 'The Supreme Court's Judgment in *Miller*: In Search of Constitutional Principle' [2017] *CLJ* 257; Endicott, 'Lord Reed's Dissent in Gina Miller's Case and the Principles of our Constitution'(2016–2017) 8 *UK Supreme Court Yearbook*; essays in Elliott, Williams and Young, *The UK Constitution After Miller: Brexit and Beyond* (Hart 2019).

After notifying the European Council, the UK Government then had to undertake three further tasks: to negotiate the content of the Withdrawal Agreement between the UK and the EU, to negotiate the future relationship between the UK and the EU, and to provide a legislative solution to the UK's withdrawal from the EU, recognising the need to ensure certainty and continuity of law as well as the future flexibility for the UK to be able to legislate contrary to EU law should it wish to do so. The first two tasks required both the UK to establish its own position in addition to negotiating with the European Union. Problems arising from this process, particularly as regards the relationship between Westminster and the devolved legislatures, were discussed above in Chapter 4. The UK's position became clearer following the publication of a White Paper by the Government in July 2018: *The Future Relationship between the United Kingdom and the European Union* (Cm 9593). The prime minister's Foreword to the White Paper set out its aims:

> In the referendum on 23 June 2016 – the largest ever democratic exercise in the United Kingdom – the British people voted to leave the European Union.
>
> And that is what we will do – leaving the Single Market and the Customs Union, ending free movement and the jurisdiction of the European Court of Justice in this country, leaving the Common Agricultural Policy and the Common Fisheries Policy, and ending the days of sending vast sums of money to the EU every year. We will take back control of our money, laws, and borders, and begin a new exciting chapter in our nation's history.

This made it clear that the UK aimed to achieve a hard as opposed to a soft Brexit, i.e., that it wished to leave both the single market and the customs union.

5.3.1 The European Union (Withdrawal) Act 2018

In tandem with carrying out negotiations with the European Union, the UK Government introduced the European Union (Withdrawal) Bill 2017–19, which became the European Union (Withdrawal) Act 2018. Although the focus in this chapter is an explanation and evaluation of how well the Act achieved its aim of ensuring the continuity of law post-Brexit, any evaluation also has to take account of the further constitutional consequences of the Act. Also, these provisions have to be read with care. The 2018 Act was amended by the European Union (Withdrawal Agreement) Act 2020. In particular, the provisions referring to 'exit date' were amended to refer to 'implementation period completion date'. However, in order to understand the Brexit process, we will refer here to the provisions of the 2018 Act as originally enacted, before explaining when examining the European Union (Withdrawal Agreement) Act 2020 why this change was later needed.

First, the bill received a lot of parliamentary scrutiny. It received its first reading in the House of Commons on 13 July 2017 and its first reading in the

House of Lords on 17 January 2018. After the third reading of the bill in the House of Lords on 16 May 2018, the bill returned to the Commons on 12 and 13 June, back to the Lords on 18 June, and then to the Commons and the Lords again on 20 June, before receiving royal assent on the 26 June 2018. Reports on the bill, and the operation of the act, were produced by the House of Lords Constitution Committee (*The 'Great Repeal Bill' and Delegated Powers, 9th Report of 2016–17* HL Paper 123, *The European Union (Withdrawal) Bill: Interim Report 3rd Report of 2017–19* HL Paper 19, *The European Union (Withdrawal) Bill 9th Report of 2017–19* HL Paper 69), the Delegated Powers and Regulatory Reform Committee of the House of Lords (*European Union (Withdrawal) Bill 3rd Report 2017–19* HL Paper 22), the House of Commons Procedure Committee (*Scrutiny of Delegated Legislation under the European Union (Withdrawal) Bill: Interim Report 1st Report of 2017–19* HC 386, *Scrutiny of Delegated Legislation under the European Union (Withdrawal) Bill 6th Report of 2017–19* HC 1395 and *Motions under section 13(1) of the European Union (Withdrawal) Act 2018 8th Report of 2017–19* HC 1664); the House of Commons Exiting the EU Committee (*European Union (Withdrawal) Bill, First Report of 2017–19* HC 373, *Response to the Vote on the Withdrawal Agreement and Political Declaration: Assessing the Options, 12th Report 2017–19* HC 1908 and *Response to the 12 March 2019 vote on the Withdrawal Agreement and Political Declaration: Next Steps for Parliament 13th Report of 2017–19* HC 2703) and the House of Commons Public Administration and Constitutional Affairs Committee (*Devolution and Exiting the EU and Clause 11 of the European Union (Withdrawal) Bill: Issues for Consideration, First Report of 2017–19* HC 484, *Devolution and Exiting the EU: Reconciling Differences and Building Strong Relationships 8th Report of 2017–19* HC 1485), in addition to reports from the Welsh Senedd and the Scottish Parliament. The bill was also significantly amended, particularly through the government's accepting amendments, or proposing similar amendments, to those voted on by the House of Lords. This is particularly important concerning the volte face regarding the extent to which powers reallocated from the EU to the UK in devolved areas of power would remain in the competence of the devolved legislatures (now section 12 of the Act – discussed in Chapter 4) and the provisions on the so-called meaningful vote (now section 13 of the Act) over the Withdrawal Agreement.

Second, section 13 of the Act modified the traditional understanding of the separation of powers as regards international relations. The executive has a general prerogative power to enter into foreign relations. Parliament normally has a very limited role, if any, during treaty negotiations. Although Parliament does play a role in the ratification of treaties, under the provisions of Part 2 of the Constitutional Reform and Governance Act 2010, this role is limited to a potential indefinite delay of the ratification of the international treaty, with no requirement for a debate to be held on the treaty once laid before Parliament. Section 13 modified this in three ways. First, it provided the

House of Commons with an effective veto over the Withdrawal Agreement. This is found in section 13(1) of the Act, produced below:

European Union (Withdrawal) Act 2018, section 13

(1) The Withdrawal Agreement may be ratified only if –

    (a) a Minister of the Crown has laid before each House of Parliament –

        (i) a statement that political agreement has been reached,

        (ii) a copy of the negotiated withdrawal agreement, and

        (iii) a copy of the framework for the future relationship,

    (b) the negotiated withdrawal agreement and the framework for the future relationship have been approved by a resolution of the House of Commons on a motion moved by a Minister of the Crown,

    (c) a motion for the House of Lords to take note of the negotiated withdrawal agreement and the framework for the future relationship has been tabled in the House of Lords by a Minister of the Crown and –

        (i) the House of Lords has debated the motion, or

        (ii) the House of Lords has not concluded a debate on the motion before the end of the period of five Lords sitting days beginning with the first Lords sitting day after the day on which the House of Commons passes the resolution mentioned in paragraph (b), and

    (d) an Act of Parliament has been passed which contains provision for the implementation of the withdrawal agreement.

Second, section 13(2) of the Act not only required a minister to ensure that a debate on the motion of ratification of the treaty took place, but also it ensured that this would take place in a timely manner, before the European Parliament provided its consent to the Withdrawal Agreement as required by Article 50 TFEU. Third, section 13 provided for a series of motions should the government fail to obtain a Withdrawal Agreement by 21 January, or if the government before then made a statement that no agreement in principle could be reached by 21 January, or if the motion to approve the Withdrawal Agreement was defeated. These motions provided an opportunity for the House of Commons to direct the government as to the possible course of action in future negotiations.

While the first and second features of the Act demonstrate greater powers for the legislature through greater democratic oversight and in terms of the legislative scrutiny of the Act, the provisions of the Act were also strongly criticised for providing broad sweeping powers to the executive. While it was recognised that these were needed to ensure that necessary changes could be made in time to ensure the continuity of the law post-Brexit, concern was expressed as to the number of Henry VIII clauses (i.e. clauses that empowered the executive to overturn or modify primary legislation), in addition to the powers that were granted to ministers to exercise when the minister considered it 'appropriate'. Although the Act does provide that some of these delegated powers can only be exercised through the affirmative as opposed to the negative resolution procedure, and a sifting committee was established to make recommendations as to when delegated legislation that could be enacted through the negative resolution procedure should nevertheless be enacted through the affirmative resolution procedure, concerns still arose due to the lack of time to ensure that all these measures were scrutinised effectively to ensure that they only provided for technical changes necessary to remedy deficiencies, as opposed to taking policy choices that had received too little scrutiny from the legislature.

Having set out these three general features of the European Union (Withdrawal) Act 2018, we now need to assess how the Act facilitated the implementation of Brexit. The Act needed to ensure that provisions of EU law that had been part of UK law were able to continue to be a part of UK law post-Brexit in order to ensure the continuity of law. The Act also needed to ensure that measures would be put in place that would be able to accommodate any possible outcome – for instance, the UK leaving the EU without a deal and with a range of possible deals set out in the Withdrawal Agreement. Finally, the act needed to ensure that there would be the sufficient flexibility moving forward for the UK to decide those elements of EU law it wished to keep and those it wished to modify or remove. In doing so, the legislation had to take account of the different types of EU law discussed above: treaty provisions, regulations and directives, in addition to decisions and opinions of the EU institutions. Moreover, it had to recognise that there are three types of EU rights – as set out in the *Miller* decision: rights that the UK can replicate (e.g., provisions of EU law regulating employment law in the UK); rights that the UK could not replicate as they are reciprocal rights, which rely on the implementation by all member states of the EU (e.g., the right of UK citizens to move and reside in other EU countries) and 'membership' rights enjoyed by virtue of being a member of the EU (e.g., the right to vote for a member of the European Parliament). The first set of rights can continue easily post-Brexit, however, the second set of rights are, in practice, protected by other member states, although the UK would have to ensure that rights of EU citizens residing in the UK were protected. Moreover, the content of the second and third set of rights would depend on the content of the Withdrawal Agreement.

The 2018 Act first implemented Brexit through expressly repealing the European Communities Act 1972, in section 1 of the Act. It then incorporated the provisions of EU law by effectively taking a snapshot of the provisions of EU law in place on exit day (but note that this was later modified to the EU law in place at the end of the implementation period completion day) following the enactment of the European Union (Withdrawal Agreement) Act 2020). This was then incorporated into UK law by creating a new type of domestic law – retained EU law. This was achieved through section 2, for delegated legislation enacted to incorporate EU law into UK law; through section 3 for 'direct EU legislation' – for example, regulations, directives and tertiary legislation; and through section 4 for 'rights, powers, liabilities, obligations, restrictions, remedies and procedures' of EU law that were incorporated into UK law through section 2(1) of the European Communities Act 1972.

However, not all provisions of EU law were incorporated in this manner. The noticeable exception is EU law relating to human rights (discussed above at pp. 371–380.) Section 5(4) stated that: 'The Charter of Fundamental Rights is not part of domestic law on or after exit day' (now implementation period completion day). Moreover, although fundamental rights that form part of the general principles of EU law are retained, they will no longer have the same force in UK law after the end of the implementation period. These fundamental rights cannot be used to form a right of action in domestic law. Moreover, they cannot be used to disapply or quash any legal provision, or to quash conduct that would otherwise be lawful (Schedule 1, paragraph 3). In addition, *Francovich* can no longer be used post-exit day, preventing individuals from bringing an action against the state for damages because of a sufficiently serious breach of retained EU law (Schedule 1, paragraph 4).

In addition, the Act provides a broad power to enact delegated legislation to deal with deficiencies that arise in retained EU law. These deficiencies can arise as retained EU law may refer to EU institutions in their provisions, or may empower EU institutions to act, or rely on reciprocal actions from member states. This power is found in section 8 of the Act:

8 Dealing with Deficiencies Arising from Withdrawal

(1) A Minister of the Crown may by regulations make such provision as the Minister considers appropriate to prevent, remedy or mitigate –
   (a) any failure of retained EU law to operate effectively, or
   (b) any other deficiency in retained EU law,
      arising from the withdrawal of the United Kingdom from the EU.

Further provisions of this section provide examples of possible deficiencies, as well as providing a means for ministers to add to the list of deficiencies through delegated legislation. There are also limits on these regulations, for example, they may not impose or increase taxation or fees, make retrospective provisions, create criminal offences or establish a public authority. Section 8 includes Henry VIII clauses, enabling delegated legislation to modify or amend primary legislation. However, the powers under section 8 cannot be used to 'amend, repeal or revoke' the Human Rights Act 1998, the Scotland Act 1998, the Government of Wales Act 2006 and the Northern Ireland Act 1998. It was estimated that around 1,000 pieces of delegated legislation would be needed. Hundreds of statutory instruments have been enacted, some of which were enacted under the power to make delegated legislation found in primary legislation other than the European Union (Withdrawal) Act 2018.

In order to ensure that the UK was able to modify retained EU law post-exit day (now implementation period completion day), section 5 provided for the partial preservation of the supremacy of EU law.

> (1) The principle of the supremacy of EU law does not apply to any enactment or rule of law passed or made on or after exit day.
> (2) Accordingly, the principle of the supremacy of EU law continues to apply on or after exit day so far as relevant to the interpretation, disapplication or quashing of any enactment or rule of law passed or made before exit day.
> (3) Subsection (1) does not prevent the principle of the supremacy of EU law from applying to a modification made on or after exit day of any enactment or rule of law passed or made before exit day if the application of the principle is consistent with the intention of the modification.

In other words, if there is a conflict between retained EU law and legislation enacted prior to exit day (now implementation period completion day), the courts are to apply retained EU law that can disapply or quash the earlier legislation. However, this is not the case as regards legislation enacted after this date, unless this is applied to legislation modified after exit day (implementation period completion day) and the modification was intended to continue to preserve the supremacy of EU law. This allows for retained EU law to continue to operate in the same manner, while preserving the ability of the UK Parliament to enact legislation that contradicts retained EU law. To this extent, the UK will 'regain sovereignty', in that it will be able to legislate contrary to retained EU law.

While the 2018 Act does achieve its objectives, and was subject to detailed criticisms, concerns remain as to the constitutional cost of achieving these objectives, particularly as regards the broad delegation of powers to the executive and the practical difficulty of ensuring there is sufficient parliamentary scrutiny over delegated legislation to make sure that it is not used to take policy decisions that are unchecked by the legislature. It is also important to note the political consequences that ensued from the requirements of section 13. The Withdrawal Agreement was defeated three times in the House of Commons. In addition, legislation initiated by a combination of backbench and opposition MPs was used to require the UK Government to – twice – seek an extension to the Article 50 negotiation process (the European Union (Withdrawal) Act 2019 and the European Union (Withdrawal) (No 2) Act 2019).

The inability to negotiate a Withdrawal Agreement that the Commons was able to approve led to the resignation of Theresa May as the leader of the Conservative Party and, hence, as Prime Minister. Difficulties arose in particular surrounding the Northern Ireland Protocol attached to the Withdrawal Agreement. Following her resignation, Boris Johnson was elected leader of the Conservative Party and hence Prime Minister. However, the political path to Brexit was not necessarily made any easier with the appointment of a new prime minister. Concerns still persisted as to the content of the Northern Ireland Protocol and other aspects of the Withdrawal Agreement. Boris Johnson was determined to leave the EU on the then agreed exit date of 31 October 2019. However, this was not to prove to be the case. In the run-up to the prorogation of the Commons – later quashed as unlawful by the Supreme Court in *R (Miller)* v. *Prime Minister; Cherry and Advocate General for (Scotland)* [2019] UKSC 41, [2020] AC 373) – the European Union (Withdrawal Agreement) (No 2) 2019 was enacted, which required the prime minister to seek an extension to the negotiation period until 31 January 2020, should the House of Commons either fail to vote in favour of the current or a newly negotiated Withdrawal Agreement, or to vote in favour of leaving the EU with no deal, by 19 October 2019. This gave rise to a historic sitting of the House of Commons on a Saturday. Having failed to obtain a majority in favour of the newly negotiated Withdrawal Agreement, the prime minister notified the European Council of the UK's request for an extension of the Article 50 negotiation period. He did so through sending a copy of the appendix to the European Union (Withdrawal Agreement) (No 2) Act 2019, in addition to a letter explaining why the law required him to send this appendix requesting an extension, and a third letter signed by the prime minister making it clear that this request was not the government's policy, which was to leave the EU on 31 October 2019, even if this was without a deal, as the UK had been unable to approve the Withdrawal Agreement.

The troubled political waters over Brexit did not stop there. The European Council and the UK Government had agreed the terms of a second Withdrawal Agreement, and a new Political Declaration on the Future Relationship between the UK and the EU, on 17 October. On 21 October, the UK Government published the European Union (Withdrawal Agreement) Bill 2019, designed to implement the new Withdrawal Agreement. The government then proposed a programme motion for this bill, which would have provided for the bill to pass through the House of Commons in only three sitting days. This motion was defeated in the House of Commons by 322 votes to 308. This effectively stopped the progress of the bill, making it extremely difficult, if not impossible, for the Withdrawal Agreement to be ratified according to the provisions of section 13 of the European Union (Withdrawal) Act 2018. This prompted Boris Johnson to table a motion for the holding of an early parliamentary general election on 28 October 2019 (he had previously tabled motions for an early parliamentary general election on 4 September and 9 September). Although 299 voted in favour and only 70 voted against an early parliamentary general election, this did not reach the threshold of two-thirds of the entire House of Commons as required by the Fixed-Term Parliaments Act 2011. The government was then successful in enacting the Early Parliamentary General Elections Act 2019, which provided for a general election to be held on 12 December 2019. After obtaining a large majority in that election, the newly elected Conservative Government was able to introduce a new European Union (Withdrawal Agreement) Bill to Parliament. This became the European Union (Withdrawal Agreement) Act 2020.

5.3.2 The European Union (Withdrawal Agreement) Act 2020

As with the 2018 Act, the main purpose of this chapter is to evaluate the extent to which the 2020 Act achieved its purpose of incorporating the provisions of the Withdrawal Agreement into UK law. However, as with the 2018 Act, it is helpful to first take note of the way in which the 2020 Act was enacted and also some of the differences between the bill as first proposed and the second bill, which became the 2020 Act.

When discussing the European Union (Withdrawal) Act 2018, we noted the extent to which the bill had been subject to detailed political scrutiny on the floor of the House of Commons and the House of Lords, in Westminster parliamentary committees, and in debates and committee reports of the devolved legislatures. The same is not true of the European Union (Withdrawal Agreement) Act 2020, which was speedily enacted through Parliament to ensure that its provisions were in place for 31 January 2020. After receiving its first and second reading on 19 and 20 December 2019, the bill was allocated two days of discussion at the committee stage, taking place in a committee of the whole house, on 7 and 8 January 2020, receiving its third reading in the House of Commons and the first reading in the House of Lords on 9 January. The bill had three days of debate at committee stage, and two days at the report stage, before, after a ping pong between the Commons and the Lords, the bill received royal assent on 23 January 2020. Moreover, the House of Commons had only recently been composed following the election in December 2019. This meant that there had not been time for the new committees to be composed in the House of Commons, meaning, in turn, that it was not possible for any commons committees to produce reports on the bill. Nevertheless, both the Constitution Committee and the Delegated Powers and Regulatory Reform Committee of the House of Lords were able to produce reports on the bill, having to do so to a very quick timeframe. This is a stark contrast to the amount of time spent on the European Union (Withdrawal) Act 2018 and almost mirrors the programme motion that the Commons voted against as regards the first European Union (Withdrawal Agreement) Bill placed before Parliament in October 2019.

It is also important to note some of the differences between the earlier and the later version of the European Union (Withdrawal Agreement) Bills and between the European Union (Withdrawal) Act 2018 and the European Union (Withdrawal Agreement) Act 2020. While the 2018 Act provided examples of greater powers for the Commons vis-à-vis the government, there is a reversal of this modification of the separation of powers in the 2020 Act. The 2020 Act repealed section 13 of the European Union (Withdrawal) Act 2018, in addition to removing the Withdrawal Agreement from the provisions of the Constitutional Reform and Governance Act 2010 (sections 31 and 32). The first version of the bill included a provision empowering a minister to agree to an extension of the period by which the deal on the future relationship between the UK and the EU needed to be agreed, provided that the minister laid a statement before Parliament and the House of Commons voted in favour of a motion to agree to an extension, alongside a vote in the House of Lords to take note of the vote in the Commons. However, the second bill, which became the 2020 Act, states that a minister may not agree to an extension of the negotiation period (section 33). Moreover, the first version of the bill included a requirement that a minister must make a statement before the House of Commons, thirty days before the end of exit day, setting out the statement of future objectives. The Commons then had a power to enact a resolution on this statement, with the Crown being required to seek to achieve these objectives, in addition to producing reports. There are no such requirements in the 2020 Act, placing all of the powers of negotiation in the hands of the government.

As with the European Union (Withdrawal) Act 2018, the European Union (Withdrawal Agreement) Act 2020 also transfers a large amount of delegated powers to the executive, including Henry VIII clauses. According to the report of the House of Lords Delegated Powers and Regulatory Reform Committee, the Act uses the statement 'an appropriate authority may by regulations make such provision as the authority considers appropriate' nine times in an Act with only forty-two sections. In addition, the expression 'a minister of the Crown may by regulations' occurs fifteen times (*European Union (Withdrawal Agreement) Bill, First*

Report of 2019–20 HL Paper 3). Sections 8(3), 11(4) and 21(4) are all Henry VIII clauses, with the broadest Henry VIII clause being found in section 41, which states that: 'A Minister of the Crown may by regulations make such provision as the Minister considers appropriate in consequence of this Act', including a power of 'modifying any provision made by or under an enactment' where an 'enactment' is defined as not including 'primary legislation passed or made after IP completion date'.

The implementation of the Withdrawal Agreement required, in particular, for the UK to ensure that the aspects of EU law in Part 4 of the Withdrawal Agreement would continue to have direct effect and supremacy from exit day until the end of the implementation period. In addition, it required the UK to guarantee residency rights for those EU citizens who had exercised their right to move to and reside in the UK before the end of the implementation period, and to implement the EU Settlement Scheme for those moving to the UK from the EU and EEA from 30 June 2021. We will focus on the extent to which the 2020 Act achieves the broader aims of implementing the Withdrawal Agreement, in particular looking at ensuring that EU law continued to have effect during the transition period.

It will be recalled that section 1 of the European Union (Withdrawal) Act 2018 repealed the European Communities Act 1972 on exit day. As this was the mechanism through which EU law was incorporated into domestic law, the European Union (Withdrawal Agreement) Act 2020 had to find an alternative means of ensuring that those elements of EU law retained through the Withdrawal Agreement continued to have effect during the transition period. This is achieved by sections 1 and 2 of the 2020 Act, which inserts two new sections, sections 1A and 1B into the European Union (Withdrawal) Act 2018, the relevant provisions of which are as follows:

1A Saving for ECA for Implementation Period

(1) Subsections (2) to (4) have effect despite the repeal of the European Communities Act 1972 on exit day by section 1.
(2) The European Communities Act 1972, as it has effect in domestic law or the law of a relevant territory immediately before exit day, continues to have effect in domestic law or the law of the relevant territory on and after exit day so far as provided by subsections (3) to (5).

...

1B Saving for EU-Derived Domestic Legislation for Implementation Period

(1) Subsections (2) to (5) have effect despite the repeal of the European Communities Act 1972 on exit day by section 1.

(2) EU-derived domestic legislation, as it has effect in domestic law immediately before exit day, continues to have effect in domestic law on and after exit day, subject as follows.

(3) Any enactment which continues to have effect by virtue of subsection (2) is to be read, on and after exit day and so far as the context permits or requires, as if –

   (a) any reference to an expression which is to be read in accordance with Schedule 1 to the Interpretation Act 1978 and is an expression defined by section 1 of, or Part 2 of Schedule 1 to, the European Communities Act 1972 were a reference to that expression as defined by that section or that Part of that Schedule as it continues to have effect by virtue of section 1A(2) to (4) of this Act,

   (b) any reference (however expressed and subject to paragraph (a) above) to –

      (i) EU law,

      (ii) any particular EU Treaty or any part of it,

      (iii) any EU instrument, or other document of an EU entity or of the EU, or any part of any such instrument or document,

      (iv) any part of EU law not falling within sub-paragraph (ii) or (iii),

      (v) any tax, duty, levy or interests of the EU, or

      (vi) any arrangement involving, or otherwise relating to, the EU of a kind not falling within sub-paragraph (i), (ii), (iii), (iv) or (v), were a reference to any such thing so far as it is applicable to and in the United Kingdom by virtue of Part 4 of the withdrawal agreement,

   (c) any reference (however expressed and subject to paragraph (a) above) to the European Communities Act 1972 were or (as the case may be) included a reference to the Act of 1972 as it continues to have effect by virtue of section 1A(2) to (4) of this Act,

   (d) any reference (however expressed) to the area of the EU or of the EEA included the United Kingdom,

   (e) any reference (however expressed) to a citizen of the EU or a national of the EEA included a United Kingdom national (within the meaning given by Article 2(d) of the withdrawal agreement), and

   (f) such other modifications were made as –

      (i) are provided for by regulations under section 8A or Part 1A of Schedule 2, or

      (ii) so far as not so provided, are necessary for any purpose of Part 4 of the withdrawal agreement and are capable of being ascertained from any such purpose or otherwise from that Part of that agreement.

(4) Any EU-derived domestic legislation which is an enactment passed or made on or after exit day and before IP completion day is, unless the contrary intention appears, to be read in accordance with subsection (3) (and anything done or omitted to be done in connection with any such enactment is to be understood, and has effect, accordingly).

(5) Subsections (2) to (4) are subject to any regulations made under section 8A or 23 or Part 1A of Schedule 2 or otherwise under this Act or under the European Union (Withdrawal Agreement) Act 2020.

(6) Subsections (1) to (5) are repealed on IP completion day.

These provisions mean that, although the European Communities Act 1972 has been repealed, its effect is preserved as regards the provisions of Part 4 of the Withdrawal Agreement Act and all of EU law that had been incorporated into UK law by exit day – that is, 31 January 2020. Part 4 of the Withdrawal Agreement is best understood as preserving those provisions of EU law that we can replicate in the UK, and the reciprocal rights. However, all of what we referred to as membership rights of the EU are no longer part of UK law. In terms of the UK, this means that UK ministers no longer attend council or European Council meetings. Also, the members of the CJEU and the commission, and the MEPs who represented the UK are now no longer members of these EU institutions. In addition, UK citizens no longer have a right to vote for an MEP. Also, any EU law created during the implementation period is incorporated into UK law. During the implementation period – that is, until (unless extended) the 31 December 2020 – these provisions of EU law continue to have direct effect and supremacy, in other words, they can be used to disapply legislation. However, on 31 December 2020, (implementation period completion day) all of EU law in force on that date is incorporated into UK law as retained EU law, as per the provisions of the European Union (Withdrawal) Act 2018 discussed above.

The European Union (Withdrawal Agreement) Act 2020 also provides ministers with the power to make regulations to implement the Withdrawal Agreement, including the provisions relating to citizenship of EU and EEA citizens after IP completion day (sections 3 to 6). From a constitutional law perspective, three further provisions are of interest. First, section 29 of the Act, which inserts section 13A into the European Union (Withdrawal) Act 2018. This establishes a process whereby the European Scrutiny Select Committee of the House of Commons scrutinises measures enacted by the EU during the implementation period. If the committee is of the opinion that this measure 'raises a matter of vital interest to the United Kingdom', it may word a motion in response to this measure and a minister must ensure that this motion is debated in the House of Commons within fourteen sitting days. Similar provisions are also provided as regards the House of Lords in respect to the EU Select Committee of the House of Lords.

Second, the European Union (Withdrawal Agreement) Act 2020 potentially modifies the extent to which UK courts are bound to follow decisions of the CJEU when interpreting provisions of retained EU law. During the implementation period, the UK continues to be bound by the provisions of the EU Treaty requiring mutual cooperation, requiring UK courts to follow decisions of the CJEU. Under section 6 of the European Union (Withdrawal) Act 2018, UK courts continued to be bound by decisions of the CJEU enacted prior to exit day, apart from the UK Supreme Court, which was free to depart from these decisions in the same manner as it would depart from its own precedents. Courts are not bound by decisions of the CJEU enacted after exit day, and may not make references to the CJEU under Article 267 TFEU. However, courts could have regard to decisions of the CJEU enacted after exit day so far as it is relevant to a matter before the court. The 2020 Act changes 'exit day' to 'implementation period completion day'. In addition, section 26 of the European Union (Withdrawal Agreement) Act 2020 inserts section 5A into the European Union (Withdrawal) Act 2018. This provision empowers a minister of the Crown to determine the extent to which any court is bound by decisions of the CJEU, and the test that the court or tribunal should apply when deciding whether to be bound by the decisions of the CJEU, as well as the conditions that the Supreme Court should apply when determining whether it is to be bound by decisions of the CJEU. This provision is problematic in two ways. First, it breaches the separation of powers, empowering the executive to determine when and how courts are bound by decisions of another court. Further breaches of this principle arise from the manner in which this power can be exercised. The minister has to consult the president of the Supreme Court, the Lord Chief Justice, the Lord President of the Court of Session, the Lord Chief Justice of Northern Ireland and the senior president of tribunals before enacting these regulations. This potentially places these senior law officials in a very difficult position – should they be allowed to sit in cases applying these regulations if they have been consulted on their content, or would this undermine their impartiality or independence? Second, it can potentially create problems for the rule of law. The old provisions created a form of legal certainty as only the UK Supreme Court could decide to depart from decisions of the CJEU enacted prior to implementation period completion day. Now it is possible that any court may have this power. This could create uncertainty as different courts disagree about whether they should or should not adhere to decisions of the CJEU, creating divergent views on the same provision of retained EU law. It may also give rise to more litigation.

Third, section 38 takes us back to the key issue that has run through this chapter and Brexit more generally – did the UK's membership of the EU limit the sovereignty of the Westminster Parliament and, if so, does the UK regain that sovereignty on exit day or on implementation period completion day? Section 38 appears to provide an answer to this question:

38 Parliamentary Sovereignty

(1) It is recognised that the Parliament of the United Kingdom is sovereign.
(2) In particular, its sovereignty subsists notwithstanding –
    (a) directly applicable or directly effective EU law continuing to be recognised and available in domestic law by virtue of section 1A or 1B of the European Union (Withdrawal) Act 2018 (savings of existing law for the implementation period),

     (b) section 7A of that Act (other directly applicable or directly effective aspects of the withdrawal agreement),

     (c) section 7B of that Act (deemed direct applicability or direct effect in relation to the EEA EFTA separation agreement and the Swiss citizens' rights agreement), and

     (d) section 7C of that Act (interpretation of law relating to the withdrawal agreement (other than the implementation period), the EEA EFTA separation agreement and the Swiss citizens' rights agreement).

(3) Accordingly, nothing in this Act derogates from the sovereignty of the Parliament of the United Kingdom.

However, it is hard to know what difference, if any, this provision makes. In the same manner of section 18 of the European Union Act 2010 – now repealed – it asserts that, to the extent that EU law disapplies UK legislation, this is achieved through legislation enacted by the UK Parliament – the provisions of the European Communities Act 1972 preserved by the European Union (Withdrawal Agreement) Act 2020. Section 38(1) makes a more general assertion, recognising the sovereignty of the UK Parliament. However, as we saw with regard to the recognition of the Sewel Convention in *Miller*, merely recognising the sovereignty of Parliament does not make this a legal principle, or mean that the source of the sovereignty of Parliament is UK legislation, or the common law, or a political fact.

It is impossible to underestimate the impact of Brexit on the UK constitution. These implications are discussed throughout this book, whereas this chapter has focused on its impact on the European dimension of the UK constitution. At the time of writing, the UK is within the implementation period. This comes to an end on 31 December 2020. As discussed above, 'A Minister of the Crown may not agree in the Joint Committee to an extension of the implementation period' (section 33). However, this provision does not say that a minister may not ask for an extension. In addition, as we saw with the Early Parliamentary General Elections Act 2019, there is nothing to prevent the UK from enacting legislation to repeal this section. It may even be possible for a minister to use section 41 of the 2020 Act to overturn section 33, should this be required to ensure the purposes of the 2020 Act interpreted as ensuring the UK is able to negotiate a successful treaty as to the future relationship between the UK and the EU. What this chapter has shown is that it can be hard to predict the future when it comes to Brexit, and that the legal and constitutional changes required to accommodate Brexit are complex and may well continue to have repercussions in UK law for a long time post-implementation period completion day.

(See, further, Craig, 'Constitutional Principle, the Rule of Law and Political Reality: The European Union (Withdrawal) Act 2018' (2019) 82 MLR 319; Elliott and Tierney, 'Political Pragmatism and Constitutional Principle: The

European Union (Withdrawal) Act 2018 [2019] *PL* 37; Gordon, 'Brexit: A Challenge for the UK Constitution, of the UK Constitution', (2016) 12 *European Constitutional Law Review* 409; McHarg, 'Navigating without Maps: Constitutional Silence and the Management of the Brexit Crisis' (2018) 16 *ICON* 952; Douglas-Scott, 'Brexit, Article 50 and the Contested British Constitution' (2016) 79 *MLR* 1019.)

Part II
Government

6

Crown and Government

Contents

In 2020, the world was changed due to the Covid-19 pandemic. While it may seem odd to mention this at the beginning of a chapter on the government, the need to respond rapidly to the pandemic provides a clear importance of the role of government in any constitution. The government was needed to provide a quick and coordinated response to the pandemic, to coordinate medical advice, to develop a phased plan in response to the virus (to contain, delay and research into the virus – *Coronavirus: Action Plan – What You Can Expect Across the UK* (3 March 2020)), as well as determine a plan for the recovery from the pandemic: *Our Plan to Rebuild: The UK Government's Covid-19 Recovery Strategy* (CP 239, May 2020). As health is a devolved matter, the response to the Covid-19 pandemic has required actions from the Scottish, Welsh and Northern Irish governments, in addition to the UK Government, which enacts regulations for England, as well as overseeing the UK as a whole.

Government is not only needed to respond to emergencies. The everyday business of the country requires government. The government will be the focus of this chapter and the next. For the most part, we consider British Government, although reference is made from time to time to government in the devolved administrations. This chapter mainly concerns the 'architecture' – the institutions, personnel and structure – of British Government. In it, we consider the constitutional positions of the Crown, the monarchy, the prime minister, cabinet and other ministers, and civil servants. In the next chapter, we move on to examine the various powers of British Government, paying particular attention to the government's rule- and law-making powers.

6.1 The Crown

We saw in Chapter 1 that constitutional thought and doctrine in the United Kingdom have largely dispensed with the concept of the state. Instead of the state we have the Crown, which serves as a central, organising principle of government. The Crown may denote the monarch in the constitutional role, but more broadly it 'personifies the executive government of the country' (Diplock LJ in *BBC* v. *Johns* [1965] Ch. 32, 79): it is associated with the idea of executive authority rather than with that of the common interest. The major public powers are vested in the Crown or, more commonly, in ministers who, in strict theory, are servants of the Crown.

Town Investments Ltd v. *Department of the Environment* [1978] AC 359 (HL)
The Secretary of State for the Environment, a minister of the Crown, had acquired a leasehold interest in certain premises for use as office accommodation by civil servants employed not in his own but in other government departments. The question arose whether the premises were 'occupied' by their tenant under a 'business tenancy' and were therefore subject to a rent freeze imposed on such tenancies by statutory instrument. If the minister were the tenant, could he be said to be in occupation of the premises? The House of Lords held that it was the Crown, not the minister, that became the tenant of the premises, and further that the Crown was in occupation for the purposes of a business (the activity or business of government) carried on by it. The premises were therefore occupied under a 'business tenancy'.

Lord Diplock: ... [I]t is not private law but public law that governs the relationships between Her Majesty acting in her political capacity, the government departments among which the work of Her Majesty's government is distributed, the ministers of the Crown in charge of the various departments and civil servants of all grades who are employed in those departments. These relationships have in the course of centuries been transformed with the continuous evolution of the constitution of this country from that of personal rule by a feudal landowning monarch to the constitutional monarchy of today; but the vocabulary used by lawyers in the field of public law has not kept pace with this evolution and remains more apt to the constitutional realities of the Tudor or even the Norman monarchy than to the constitutional realities of the 20th century. To use as a metaphor the symbol of royalty, 'the Crown', was no doubt a convenient way of denoting and distinguishing the monarch when doing acts of government in his political capacity from the monarch when doing private acts in his personal capacity, at a period when legislative and executive powers were exercised by him in accordance with his own will. But to continue nowadays to speak of 'the Crown' as doing legislative or executive acts of government, which, in reality as distinct from legal fiction, are decided on and done by human beings other than the Queen herself, involves risk of confusion. We very sensibly speak today of legislation being made by Act of Parliament – though the preamble to every statute still maintains the fiction that the maker was Her Majesty and that the participation of the members of the two Houses of Parliament had been restricted to advice and acquiescence. Where, as in the instant case, we are concerned with the legal nature of the exercise of executive powers of government, I believe that some of the more Athanasian-like features of the debate in your Lordships' House could have been eliminated if instead of speaking of 'the Crown' we were to speak of 'the government' – a term appropriate to embrace both collectively and individually all of the ministers of the Crown and parliamentary secretaries [junior ministers] under whose direction the administrative work of government is carried on by the civil servants employed in the various government departments. It is through them that the executive powers of Her Majesty's government in the United Kingdom are exercised, sometimes in the more important administrative matters in Her Majesty's name, but most often under their own official designation. Executive acts of government that are done by any of them are acts done by 'the Crown' in the fictional sense in which that expression is now used in English public law.

The executive acts of government with which the instant case is concerned are the acceptance of grants from lessors who are private subjects of the Queen of leasehold interests in premises for use as government offices and the occupation of the premises by civil servants employed in the work of various government departments. The leases were executed under his official designation by the minister of the Crown in charge of the government department to which, for administrative and accounting purposes, there is entrusted the responsibility for acquiring and managing accommodation for civil servants employed in other government departments as well as that of which the minister himself is the official head. In my opinion, the tenant was the government acting through its appropriate member or, expressed in the term of art in public law, the tenant was the Crown.

Lord Diplock's analysis is open to criticism in so far as it holds that executive acts done by ministers are necessarily to be considered as acts done by the Crown. (See Sir William Wade, in Sunkin and Payne (eds.), *The Nature of the Crown* (1999), pp. 23–6 and compare the analysis by Martin Loughlin in chapter 3 of the same work.) Ministers are commonly themselves invested by statute with powers or duties and are then legally answerable for any excess or improper exercise of such powers or failure of duty and cannot shelter behind immunities of the Crown. This principle was authoritatively confirmed in *M* v. *Home Office* [1994] 1 AC 377 (above, p 113).

Its continuing formal centrality notwithstanding, the constitutional concept of the Crown has suffered a substantial decay. The original or inherent powers of the Crown embraced in the royal prerogative, although still significant (see below), have been greatly reduced in extent by the intervention of statute. Individual ministers (or 'the Secretary of State': see below, pp. 468–515), rather than the Crown itself, are normally the recipients of statutory powers. From the viewpoint of political science, if not of law, the concept of the Crown distorts reality in representing the different elements of the executive as a unified whole, concealing their interrelationships – for example, the conflicts and accommodations that take place between the prime minister and other ministers, the Treasury and the spending departments, ministers and civil servants, departments and their associated public bodies, irregular or special advisers and established civil servants, and so on. As Rodney Barker observed (in Borthwick and Spence (eds.), *British Politics in Perspective* (1984), p. 5):

> Constitutional theory is concerned to determine coherent principles, and as such the notion of the crown has a limited use since it cannot be employed over a wide range of constitutional behaviour without losing precisely that coherence, and referring to powers which are separate, conflicting or independent of one another.

Lord Simon of Glaisdale's characterisation of the Crown, in *Town Investments* (p. 440), as a corporation aggregate – a corporation composed of many persons – headed by the Queen seems to capture the complex and fragmented nature of central executive power in the UK, but Lord Diplock's designation of the Crown, in the same case, as a corporation sole is generally followed. As a corporation, the Crown has an inherent legal capacity, for instance, to enter into contracts, although this assessment has been criticised, particularly as regards the existence of a third source of power of the Crown that is not granted to the Crown either in legislation or through the prerogative.

R (New London College) v. *Secretary of State for the Home Department* [2013] UKSC 51, [2013] 1 WLR 2358

The case concerned a statement of change to the immigration rules. The immigration rules enabled students to come to the UK to study under a tier-4 student visa. Education establishments could register themselves as sponsoring students, enabling these students to obtain their visas. The Secretary of State established new guidelines regulating this sponsorship system, modifying the criteria that education establishments had to satisfy in order to qualify for a sponsorship licence. New London College did not satisfy the new criteria, meaning that its sponsorship licence was revoked. The college challenged the decision, arguing that the change to the sponsorship criteria were provisions that determined immigration and, therefore, had to be laid before Parliament according to section 3(2) of the Immigration Act 1971. The guidelines had not been laid before Parliament. The government argued that the guidelines were valid as the provisions were not rules that regulated immigration. The college argued, in the alternative, that the government did not possess a power to enact these guidelines outside the provisions of the immigration rules. The Supreme Court concluded both that the provisions were not immigration rules, and so did not need to be laid before Parliament, but that the government nevertheless had the power to enact these guidelines. This power was an ancillary power to the statutory powers granted to the minister to regulate immigration issues.

In reaching this conclusion, Lord Sumption revisited the argument as to the existence of residual powers of the Crown, due to the classification of the Crown as a corporation sole:

> [28] . . . It has long been recognised that the Crown possesses some general administrative powers to carry on the ordinary business of government which are not exercises of the royal prerogative and do not require statutory authority: see Harris, 'The "Third Source" of Authority for Government Action Revisited' (2007) 123 *LQR* 225. The extent of these powers and their exact juridical basis are controversial. In *R v Secretary of State for Health, Ex p C* [2000] 1 FLR 627 and *R (Shrewsbury and Atcham Borough Council) v Secretary of State for Communities and Local Government* [2008] 3 All ER 548, the Court of Appeal held that the basis of the power was the Crown's status as a common law corporation sole, with all the capacities and powers of a natural person subject only to such particular limitations as were imposed by law. Although in *R (Hooper) v Secretary of State for Work and Pensions* [2005] 1 WLR 1681, para 47 Lord Hoffmann thought that there was 'a good deal of force' in this analysis, it is open to question whether the analogy with a natural person is really apt in the case of public or governmental action, as opposed to purely managerial acts of a kind that any natural person could do, such as making contracts, acquiring or disposing of property, hiring and firing staff and the like. But the question does not need to be resolved on these appeals because the statutory power of the Secretary of State to administer the system of immigration control must necessarily extend to a range of ancillary and incidental administrative powers not expressly spelt out in the Act, including the vetting of sponsors.

Lord Carnwath agreed that the power of the minister to regulate the licensing scheme for educational sponsors was an adjunct to his statutory powers, but disagreed with Lord Sumption as to the precise identification of the statutory provisions in question. He regarded this as an adjunct to the power to provide for entry to the UK to study, rather than as an adjunct to the general power to regulate immigration.

All ministers are in law 'servants of the Crown' (or of the monarch); civil servants work under the direction of ministers but are themselves also servants of the Crown, not of the departmental minister. (See *Bainbridge*

v. *Postmaster-General* [1906] 1 KB 178.) In *Robertson* v. *Minister of Pensions* [1949] 1 KB 227, the appellant was assured by an official of the War Office that a disability from which he suffered had been accepted as attributable to military service, thus entitling him to certain disablement benefits. Later, the minister of pensions decided that the appellant's disability was not attributable to war service. The court (Denning J) held that the assurance given by the War Office was legally binding, and since the War Office was the agent of the Crown, it was binding on the Crown and therefore bound the minister of pensions, who was also only a servant or agent of the Crown. This decision seems to rest on a principle of the 'indivisibility of the Crown', which acts as a restraint on the pursuit of contradictory policies and inconsistent decision-making by different government departments. The limits of the principle are not altogether clear and in *R (Bapio Action Limited)* v. *Secretary of State for the Home Department* [2008] UKHL 27, [2008] 1 AC 1003, Lord Scott, in a dissenting opinion, was dismissive of the principle of a unitary or indivisible Crown as 'an archaic constitutional theory that has become legal fiction'. Legal fictions may, however, give shorthand expression to useful principles! (See on this case Elliott [2008] *CLJ* 453.)

In the larger realm of the Commonwealth, by way of contrast, the Crown had been perceived as divisible and the monarch's government is a separate legal entity in each of the territories still owing allegiance to the Crown: see *R* v. *Secretary of State for Foreign and Commonwealth Affairs, ex p Indian Association of Alberta* [1982] QB 892; and *R (Quark Fishing Ltd)* v. *Secretary of State for Foreign and Commonwealth Affairs* [2005] UKHL 57; [2006] 1 AC 529. (Cf. the critical analysis of *Quark Fishing Ltd* and discussion of the meaning of 'the Crown' by Twomey [2008] *PL* 742.) The majority view in *Quark Fishing* was also criticised by Professor John Finnis, ('Common Law Constraints: Whose Common Good Counts?' University of Oxford Faculty of Law Research Series, Working Paper 10/2008). This led Lord Hoffmann, in *R (Bancoult)* v. *Foreign Secretary (No 2)* ([2009] 1 AC 453), to express a preference for the dissenting view in *Quark Fishing*. In *R (Barclay)* v. *Secretary of State for Justice (No 1)*, [2014] UKSC 54 [at para [52]], Lady Hale cited with approval a passage from Halsbury's Laws of England, itself approved in *Bancoult (No 2)*:

> The United Kingdom and its dependent territories within Her Majesty's dominions form one realm having one undivided Crown. This general principle is not inconsistent with the further principle that on the grant of a representative legislature, and perhaps even as from the setting up of courts, a legislative council and other such structures of government, Her Majesty's government in a colony is to be regarded as distinct from Her Majesty's government in the United Kingdom. To the extent that a dependency has responsible government, the Crown's representative in the dependency acts on the advice of local ministers responsible to the local legislature, but in respect of any British overseas territory

> or other dependency of the United Kingdom, acts of Her Majesty herself are performed only on the advice of the United Kingdom government.

What is important is the advice on which the Crown is acting when it adopts a measure, as well as determining the consequence of establishing why the court needs to determine whether a measure was enacted by the Crown on behalf of the UK or a dependent territory. In *Bancoult (2)*, the Crown was acting on the advice of ministers in the UK when enacting an order in council establishing the British and Indian Overseas Territory (BIOT). This is hardly surprising as there were no local BIOT ministers to consult at the time the order in council was enacted, the constitution of BIOT effectively being established by the order in council. In *Barclay*, the applicants sought judicial review of an order in council granting royal assent to the Reform (Sark) (Amendment)(No 2) Law 2010, it being claimed that this law was incompatible with convention rights. It was argued that the Crown was acting on behalf of Guernsey, suggesting that the UK courts would not have jurisdiction to hear a challenge to an order in council in order to determine its compatibility with Convention rights. However, Lady Hale concluded that the order in council affected the UK's international law obligations, the UK having continued responsibility for the actions of Guernsey in international law. As such, the order in council concerned the UK as well as Guernsey and, therefore, could be challenged in the UK courts. Nevertheless, Lady Hale also concluded that there were good reasons for the UK courts not to hear this claim.

(See, further, Allen 'The Office of the Crown' [2018] *CLJ* 298; Twomey *The Veiled Sceptre: Reserve Powers of Heads of State in Westminster Systems* (2018).)

6.1.1 Privileges and Immunities of the Crown

In a vivid aphorism, Walter Bagehot remarked of the England of Queen Victoria that: 'A Republic has insinuated itself beneath the folds of a Monarchy' (*The English Constitution* (Fontana edn. 1963), p. 94). Modern governments, having assumed the attributes of the Crown, are invested with most of those common law powers, privileges and immunities that formerly constituted the 'royal' prerogative, but of which relatively few are now exercised or enjoyed by the monarch in person. Some of these are necessary governmental powers that, if they did not belong to the government as part of the prerogative, would have to be provided by statute: indeed, statute might be a better ground for the definition and regulation of such powers. (On the powers of government, see Chapter 7.) The prerogative also includes, however, certain privileges and immunities that, as the legacy of a former royal pre-eminence, may lack justification in a modern democratic state.

The Crown may be able to avoid liability under a statute that is not expressed as being applicable to it, by virtue of a principle commonly, although misleadingly, described as 'Crown immunity'. In effect, the principle functions as a rule of construction or a presumption (one that is rebuttable) that the Crown is not bound by statute. It is preserved by section 40(2)(f) of the Crown Proceedings Act 1947, which provides that nothing in the Act shall 'affect any rules of evidence or any presumption relating to the extent to which the Crown is bound by any Act of Parliament'.

Madras Electric Supply Corpn Ltd v. *Boarland* [1955] AC 667 (HL)

In this case, the liability of the appellant company to income tax was in issue, the company having transferred its business to the Crown in the course of the year of assessment. It was not disputed that the Crown itself was immune from the taxing provisions of the relevant statute, but some of their Lordships found it necessary, in dealing with the contentions of the parties, to consider the basis of the Crown's immunity.

> **Lord Macdermott:** . . . Whatever ideas may once have prevailed on the subject, it is, in my opinion, today impossible to uphold the view that the Crown can find in the prerogative an immunity from tax if the statute in question, according to its true construction, includes the Crown amongst those made liable to the tax it imposes. The appropriate rule, as I understand it, is that in an Act of Parliament general words shall not bind the Crown to its prejudice unless by express provision or necessary implication.
>
> **Lord Reid:** . . . I do not think that it has ever been suggested, at least since 1688, that, if an Act in its terms and on its true construction applies to the Crown, its operation can be prevented by the royal prerogative. It is true that there does not appear to be in the authorities any statement which precisely negatives this argument, but that is not surprising. As the point has never been raised it has not been necessary to formulate the answer to it.
>
> Chitty states the rule as follows: 'But Acts of Parliament which would divest or abridge the King of his prerogatives, his interests or his remedies, in the slightest degree, do not in general extend to, or bind the King, unless there be express words to that effect.' (*Prerogatives of the Crown*, [1820], p. 383.) I draw attention to the words 'extend to, or bind the King'. It is not a matter of the King preventing the operation of an Act which extends to the Crown, but of the scope of provisions which prejudice the Crown being so limited that they never extend to the Crown.

Dicta of Lord Keith of Avonholm in this case found the basis of the rule in a prerogative power of the Crown to override statutory words that were capable of applying to it, but this is no longer a tenable view of the matter.

In *Province of Bombay* v. *Municipal Corpn of the City of Bombay* [1947] AC 58 (PC), a stringent test was applied in deciding whether a statute was effective to bind the Crown. The Privy Council held that the Crown would be bound only if made subject to the Act by express words or *necessary implication*, and placed a strict interpretation on the latter alternative. The City of Bombay Municipal Act 1888 gave power to the Bombay Municipality to carry water mains 'into, through or under any land whatsoever within the city'. The municipality wished to lay a water main in certain Crown land within the city, but its right to do so was contested by the Crown. The High Court of Bombay was satisfied that the Act could not operate with reasonable efficiency unless it applied to Crown land, and accordingly held that it must be taken to bind the Crown by necessary implication. This decision was reversed by the Privy Council. The judgment of the board was delivered by Lord du Parcq, who defined 'necessary implication' as applying when 'it is manifest from the very terms of the statute, that it was the intention of the legislation that the Crown should be so bound'. The argument that legislation was 'for the public good' was insufficient to demonstrate that legislation applied to the Crown by necessary implication.

It was argued in *Lord Advocate* v. *Dumbarton District Council* [1990] 2 AC 580 that the rule of construction that the Crown is not bound by statute, unless named expressly or by necessary implication, applied only if the statute was one that would, if binding on the Crown, prejudice or restrict its property, rights or interests. This argument was accepted by the First Division of the Court of Session (1988 SLT 546) but was controversially rejected by the House of Lords, which declined to place any gloss on 'the simple rule that the Crown is not bound by any statutory provision unless there can somehow be gathered from the terms of the relevant Act an intention to that effect' (per Lord Keith). (See, further, Tomkins, 'The Crown in Scots Law', in McHarg and Mullen (eds.), *Public Law in Scotland* (2006) and compare the more flexible formulation of the rule by the High Court of Australia in *Bropho* v. *State of Western Australia* (1990) 171 CLR 1: see also Kneebone [1991] *PL* 361; Berry (1993) 14 *Stat LR* 204.)

The assumption that legislation does not bind the Crown, unless through express words or necessary implication, was recently discussed in the Supreme Court. Lady Hale, who delivered the judgment of the court, accepted that the interpretative presumption was outdated and that there were good reasons for changing the presumption, such that legislation should bind the Crown, unless there were express words that it should not bind the Crown. Nevertheless, the Supreme Court concluded that it was not for courts to change this presumption.

R (Black) v. *Secretary of State for Justice* [2017] UKSC 81, [2016] 1 WLR 3623

Black was a prisoner serving an indeterminate sentence. He was also a non-smoker with myriad health problems that were exacerbated by tobacco smoke. He complained that the prison in which he was incarcerated was not properly enforcing the smoking ban in common areas of prisons. The provisions relating to the smoking ban in public places were found in Chapter 1 of

Part 1 of the Health Act 2006. Black asked that the Smoke-Free Compliance Line be placed on the prison phone system. He also issued a pre-action protocol letter as a prelude to bringing an action for judicial review. However, although it looked initially as if Black would be successful in his bid for the installation of the compliance line, the Secretary of State responded to the pre-action protocol letter by stating that provisions of the Health Act did not bind the Crown. Therefore, there was no requirement on prisons to enforce the smoking ban found in the provisions of the Health Act 2006. If there were no smoking ban, there was no need for a compliance line to ensure that organisations adhered to the smoking ban. Black subsequently challenged the decision of the Secretary of State, arguing that the statutory presumption should be reversed in this specific case, such that the government was bound by the smoking ban found in the Health Act.

Lady Hale accepted that the classic position was that 'a statutory provision does not bind the Crown save by express words or "necessary implication"' (at [22]). Nevertheless, the barrister for Black argued that the Supreme Court should either revisit or modify the rule, or apply the rule in such a way that the Crown, including the prison service, should be bound by the smoking ban. Lady Hale was unwilling to revisit the rule:

[33]. Mr Havers points out that the rule has been subject to criticism from distinguished commentators, ranging from Glanville Williams, who called it 'a gap made in the "rule of law"' (in *Crown Proceedings,* London, Stevens, 1948, at p. 49); and *Bennion on Statutory Interpretation*, which describes insistence on necessary implication as 'typical of the unrealistic attitude displayed by some judges in resisting implied meaning in statutes' (London, LexisNexis, 6th edn., Oliver Jones (ed.), 2013, at p. 181), to Paul Craig, who describes the present law as unsatisfactory, unclear and the product of a misinterpretation of earlier authority (in *Administrative Law*, London, Sweet & Maxwell, 8th edn. (2016), at para 29.003). In his view, careful thought is not always given to whether the Crown should be bound, which may be overlooked or receive scant attention when legislation is drafted.

[34]. Two solutions have been canvassed. One, favoured by Glanville Williams and Paul Craig, is to reverse the presumption, so that the Crown is bound unless expressly excluded from some or all of the Act's provisions. This would have the merit of clarity and certainty. It would force the Crown to think carefully about whether and to what extent it should be bound and to justify any exemption. The other, favoured by Bennion, is that there should be a single test: what did Parliament intend? In other words, there would be no presumption either way and no requirement that any implication be 'necessary'. This would be to apply the general rule of statutory interpretation to the question, but it would not produce the clarity and certainty of the alternative suggestion.

[35]. It is easy to see the merits of the solution put forward by Glanville Williams and Paul Craig. However, the problem for this Court in adopting either of the solutions proposed is that the presumption, as stated in the *Bombay, Madras* and above all the *Dumbarton* cases,

is so well established in modern times that many, many states will have been drafted and passed on the basis that the Crown is not bound except by express words or necessary implication. Decisions of this Court, or indeed any court, generally operate retrospectively to alter the previous understanding of the law. It may be possible for the Court to declare that a new understanding of the law will operate only prospectively: the possibility was canvassed at length in *In re Spectrum Plus Ltd* [2005] UKHL 41; [2005] 2 AC 680. But such a course would be wholly exceptional and the case for doing so has certainly not been made before us. I would therefore decline to abolish the rule or reverse the presumption, although I would urge Parliament, perhaps with the assistance of the Law Commission, to give careful consideration to the merits of doing so.

Lady Hale was also unwilling to modify the test. Neither did she feel the need for further clarification than the following provisions (at [36]).

(1) The Crown is not bound by a statutory provision except by express words or necessary implication.

(2) This is not an immunity from liability, strictly so-called, but a rule of statutory interpretation.

(3) The goal of all statutory interpretation is to discover the intention of the legislation.

(4) That intention is to be gathered from the words used by Parliament, considered in the light of their context and their purpose. In this context, it is clear that Lord Hobhouse's dictum in *R (Morgan Grenfell & Co Ltd) v Special Commissioner of Income Tax* [2002] UKHL 21; [2003] 1 AC 563, at para 45, that 'A *necessary* implication is one which necessarily follows from the express provisions of the statute construed in their context' must be modified to include the purpose, as well as the context, of the legislation.

(5) In considering the intention of the legislation, it is not enough that it is intended for the public good or that it would be even more beneficial for the public if the Crown were bound.

(6) However, it is not necessary that the purpose of the legislation would be 'wholly frustrated' if the Crown were not bound. In the *Bombay case*, it is clear that the Board was only using this as one example of where the Crown would be bound by necessary implication. In this case, it is accepted that the *Liverpool Coroner's case* was rightly decided. The purpose of the Coroners Act would not have been 'wholly frustrated' had it not bound the Crown. But one very important purpose of the Act would have been frustrated: that was to render the inquest process compliant with the United Kingdom's obligations under the European Convention on Human Rights, so that deaths for which the state might bear some responsibility could be properly investigated.

(7) In considering whether the purpose of the Act can be achieved without the Crown being bound, it is permissible to consider the extent to which the Crown is likely voluntarily to take action to achieve it. Inaction cannot be assumed. It may be that the Act's purpose can as well be achieved by the Crown exercising its powers properly and in the public interest. But if it cannot, that is a factor to be taken into account in determining the intention of the legislation.

Although accepting that there were good reasons for applying the legislation to the Crown, particularly when considering the objectives of the Health Act which would apply equally to Crown employees as to other employees, nevertheless Lady Hale concluded that the legislation did not apply to the Crown. Other provisions of the Health Act 2006 had specifically stated that they were to apply to the Crown. As such, Lady Hale concluded that, had Parliament wanted the provisions in the Health Act regarding the smoking ban to apply to the Crown, then Parliament would have also specifically included express words to ensure that the provisions applied to the Crown. Lady Hale also believed that it would be possible for the Crown to voluntarily comply with the smoking ban, even if not required to do so by legislation; although Lady Hale did admit that she reached this conclusion 'not without considerable reluctance' (at [50]).

It is easy to understand Lady Hale's reluctance. The Crown's (qualified) immunity from statute has enabled Crown bodies to escape the operation of social welfare and other legislation enacted in the public interest, including the provisions in the Health Act 2006 designed to protect the health of workers and others. Indeed, some statutes make express provision for the Crown's immunity, in whole or in part; for example, section 13 of the Rent Act 1977 provides that tenants of the Crown shall not, in general, qualify as protected tenants under the Act, and section 191 of the Employment Rights Act 1996 excludes persons in Crown employment from the Act's provisions on redundancy payments. However, the rule of law concerns are understandable – considerable practical difficulties and uncertainty would arise were courts to reverse this statutory presumption. It may be best for this modification to be achieved by statute, particularly to ensure greater certainty and clarity. However, in the current political climate, it is unlikely that time will be found to enact this legislative change. Moreover, in a climate where there are ministerial suggestions that ministers need not abide by legislative provisions, it may be time for the court to revisit whether prospective overruling is required, providing Parliament with an opportunity to specifically modify legislation where there are grounds for maintaining that specific legislative provisions should not bind the Crown.

Alternative arrangements have sometimes been made to ensure conformity by Crown bodies with general standards and requirements imposed by statute. For instance, Crown servants, while ineligible for redundancy payments under the Employment Rights Act (above), may qualify for equivalent benefits under a Civil Service Compensation Scheme established, and from time to time revised, in consultation with the Civil Service unions. Again, while the Crown formerly enjoyed immunity from statutory planning controls and accordingly was not required to obtain planning permission for the development of Crown land, a non-statutory administrative procedure, involving consultation with the local planning authority, provided equivalent safeguards. The Crown's immunity was removed by the Planning and Compulsory Purchase Act 2004, subject to a number of exceptions and qualifications, for instance in relation to enforcement action and compulsory acquisition of land.

The Planning Act 2008, amending the planning regime (e.g., introducing a new consent system for nationally significant infrastructure projects) is, in essentials, binding on the Crown (section 226).

Part I of the Health and Safety at Work etc. Act 1974, which deals with the health, safety and welfare of employees and the protection of public health and safety, is declared to be binding on the Crown, but with important exceptions relating to enforcement procedures (section 48). In 1978, the Health and Safety Commission initiated a non-statutory procedure of Crown enforcement notices, issued in lieu of the statutory improvement and prohibition notices served on private sector employers. A failure by a Crown body to act on an enforcement notice may result in a 'Crown censure' – a formal recording by the Health and Safety Executive that the body concerned has failed to comply with health and safety law. The Labour Government undertook to introduce legislation that would remove Crown immunity from statutory health and safety enforcement. (See *Third Special Report, Work and Pensions Committee*, HC 837 of 2007–08, para 12.) This was in accordance with government policy to remove or restrict Crown immunity from statutory duties 'as legislative opportunities arise' (HL Deb vol. 606, col 98WA, 4 November 1999). For instance, section 60 of the National Health Service and Community Care Act 1990 removed Crown immunities (e.g., respecting food hygiene, health and safety and fire prevention legislation) from NHS bodies.

Section 159 of the Environmental Protection Act 1990 exemplifies an approach to Crown immunity that is characteristic of recent statutes:

159 Application to Crown

(1) Subject to the provisions of this section, the provisions of this Act and of regulations and orders made under it shall bind the Crown.

(2) No contravention by the Crown of any provision of this Act or of any regulations or order made under it shall make the Crown criminally liable; but the High Court or, in Scotland, the Court of Session may, on the application of any public or local authority charged with enforcing that provision, declare unlawful any act or omission of the Crown which constitutes such a contravention.

(3) Notwithstanding anything in subsection (2) above, the provisions of this Act and of regulations and orders made under it shall apply to persons in the public service of the Crown as they apply to other persons.

(4) If the Secretary of State certifies that it appears to him, as respects any Crown premises and any powers of entry exercisable in relation to them specified in the certificate that it is requisite or expedient that, in the interests of national security, the powers should not be exercisable in relation to the premises, those powers shall not be exercisable in relation to those premises; and in this subsection 'Crown premises' means premises held or used by or on behalf of the Crown.

(5) Nothing in this section shall be taken as in any way affecting Her Majesty in her private capacity . . .

The government confirmed that any declaration of non-compliance in terms of section 159(2) 'would be followed by immediate corrective action' (*The Citizen's Charter*, Cm 1599/1991, p. 46).

The Equality Act 2010 harmonises and strengthens discrimination law, protecting from discrimination on grounds of personal characteristics such as age, disability, race, religion and sex. In general, its provisions apply to Crown acts as they apply to acts done by private persons, while duties are imposed on ministers, government departments and other specified public bodies regarding the advancement of equality of opportunity, the reduction of socioeconomic inequalities and the fostering of good relations.

The Crown benefited in the past from a far-reaching privilege relating to the production of evidence in court, to which the name 'Crown privilege' was aptly applied. This doctrine, rooted in the royal prerogative, enabled a minister of the Crown to disallow the production of any document in a court of law by invoking the public interest. The courts were obliged, although with increasing reluctance, to submit to the minister's decision. The coup de grâce to this absolute ministerial discretion was administered in *Conway* v. *Rimmer* [1968] AC 910, in which the House of Lords upheld the power of the courts to review and, in an appropriate case, to set aside the objection of the executive to disclosure. In *Rogers* v. *Home Secretary* [1973] AC 388, 'Crown privilege' was reinterpreted as a rule of 'public interest immunity', which gives a qualified protection to documents bearing on important state interests: it is for the court to balance any such interest against the public interest in the due administration of justice. In coming to its decision, the court must ensure that a party's right to a fair trial (Article 6 of the ECHR) is not infringed by the exclusion of evidence. (See as to this *R* v. *H* [2004] UKHL 3, [2004] 2 AC 134.) The government's use (in some instances abuse) of public interest immunity has on occasion caused deep legal and political controversy, as when ministers sought in the early 1990s to rely on the doctrine to withhold material evidence from the criminal trials of directors of companies that had been engaged in covert trading (including, it was alleged, arms trading) with Saddam Hussein's Iraq. The defendants argued that such trade as their companies had undertaken was done with the full knowledge, indeed with the positive encouragement, of the UK's Secret Intelligence Service (MI6). It was this controversy that led to the establishment of the Scott Inquiry (see Tomkins, *The Constitution after Scott* (1998), ch. 5).

Questions of fundamental importance were raised by claims of public interest immunity (PII) in the following case.

R (Binyam Mohamed) v. *Secretary of State for Foreign and Commonwealth Affairs* [2010] EWCA Civ 65

Attempts were made in the *Binyam Mohamed* litigation to prevent, by reliance on PII, the disclosure to the lawyers of Binyam Mohamed (BM) of documents that were essential for his defence to serious charges of terrorism brought against him in the United States. The documents contained information provided on a confidential basis by the intelligence services of the US to the security service (MI5) and the Secret Intelligence Service (MI6) in the United Kingdom. The information was of a kind that would provide support for allegations that BM had been tortured while in the hands of US authorities, so that confessions made by him could not be relied on. In proceedings brought on behalf of BM in the Divisional Court, it was claimed that the documents should be made available to his lawyers.

In the first of a series of judgments, the Divisional Court ruled that the documents should be disclosed, subject to any claim to be made by the foreign secretary that they should be withheld on PII grounds. The judgment itself included a summary of the information, derived from the US intelligence services, about the treatment and interrogation of BM while held by the American authorities or on their behalf. This summary was provisionally 'redacted' or excluded from the published version of the judgment, pending a further hearing.

In response to this judgment, the foreign secretary claimed PII on the ground that disclosure of the documents to BM's lawyers would be damaging to national security in that it would seriously harm the intelligence-sharing relationship between the UK and the USA. Before any ruling had been made on this claim, the US Government itself provided the documents in issue to BM's lawyers.

The question remained for decision whether the summary of BM's treatment that had been redacted from the first judgment should be restored to the open version of the judgment. Its restoration was sought by BM himself, whose US lawyers now had the documents they had sought for his defence, but who was still prevented from seeing the full reasons for the Divisional Court's decision, as principles of open justice and the equal treatment of parties to litigation would ordinarily require. Restoration of the redacted passages was also sought by representatives from the media, urging that, in the public interest the serious allegations of mistreatment or torture should be exposed. In contrast, the PII certificates from the foreign secretary asserted that the redacted part of the judgment should remain closed to avert what he claimed was a real risk that its publication would cause the US Government to restrict the future provision of intelligence, thus inflicting serious harm to national security. The case had taken on a new aspect: the demands of national security were no longer to be considered in the context of BM's right to a fair trial, but must be balanced against 'the public interest in open justice, the rule of law and democratic accountability', due account being taken also of 'the right to receive and impart information' under Article 10 of the ECHR: *R (Binyam Mohamed)* v. *Secretary of State for Foreign and Commonwealth Affairs* [2009] EWHC 152 (Admin), at [18], [48]. The final conclusion of the Divisional Court, after receiving new evidence as to the position likely to be taken by the US Government, was that the redacted passages should be published. The foreign secretary appealed against this decision.

The Court of Appeal was required, in the words of Lord Judge CJ, 'to address fundamental questions about the relationship between the executive and the judiciary in the context of national security in an age of terrorism and the interests of open justice in a democratic society': [2010] EWCA Civ 65 at [3]. The court emphasised that, even though national security was engaged in the case, the question whether to give effect to the minister's PII certificate and uphold the exclusion of the redacted material was 'a matter for judicial, not executive, determination' [132]. Nevertheless, 'very substantial weight' was to be accorded to the foreign secretary's view and 'cogent reasons' would be required for a court to differ from his assessment of the risk to national security: only if his opinion were irrational or without a sufficient evidential basis should the court override it.

Approaching the question in this way, the court decided that the redacted passages should be published. Considerations that supported and those that weighed against the position taken by the foreign secretary were held to be finely balanced, but a new factor had emerged – given particular emphasis in the judgments of Lord Neuberger MR and Sir Anthony May – which was decisive. This was a finding in an open judgment of a US district court (*Farhi Saeed Bin Mohamed* v. *Barak Obama*) that BM's account of the brutal torture that he had undergone, as set out in the district court's judgment, was true. The details of his treatment contained in the redacted passages had, as a result, entered the public domain. This being so, there was no need for the court to conduct a balancing exercise. The foreign secretary's contention that the publication by an English court of matter already published by a court in the United States might cause the American authorities to restrict the future transmission of intelligence to the United Kingdom security services was without an evidential basis and indeed was irrational. Had the US court not made these findings, however, the majority of the Court of Appeal would have ruled against BM, and would have allowed the foreign secretary's appeal.

The PII claims in the *Binyam Mohamed* litigation, and the judicial responses to them, prompted the issue by the Treasury solicitor in January 2010 of *Guidance on Discharging the Duty of Candour and Disclosure in Judicial Review Proceedings*. Government departments and agencies were reminded that, when facing claims for judicial review, their 'objective must not be to win the litigation at all costs but to assist the court in reaching the correct result and thereby to improve standards in public administration'. Public authorities, in responding to applications for judicial review, are subject to 'a very high duty of candour' and must 'set out fully and fairly all matters that are relevant to the decision that is under challenge'. PII applies only 'where disclosure of material would cause serious harm or real damage to the public interest'.

(See further on the *Binyam Mohamed* litigation above, pp. 119–120. On PII, see also *R (Al-Sweady)* v. *Secretary of State for Defence* [2009] EWHC 2387

(Admin), [2010] HRLR 2. On judicial review and irrationality, see, further, Chapter 10; on human rights and national security, see, further, Chapter 11.)

The Crown still enjoys certain privileges and immunities in legal proceedings to which it is a party – in particular, the remedies of injunction and specific performance are not available in civil proceedings against the Crown: section 21 of the Crown Proceedings Act 1947. A declaration can be granted in lieu of these remedies and, as Lord Bridge observed in *Factortame Ltd v. Secretary of State for Transport* [1990] 2 AC 85, 150: 'A declaration of right made in proceedings against the Crown is invariably respected.' Judicial interpretation of section 21 has caused particular problems in Scots law, on which, see *Davidson v. Scottish Ministers* 2002 SC 205 (Court of Session) and 2006 SLT 110 (House of Lords); and *Beggs v. Scottish Ministers* 2005 SC 342 (Court of Session) and [2007] UKHL 3, [2007] 1 WLR 455, [31–4], [51] (see Tomkins, in McHarg and Mullen (eds.), *Public Law in Scotland* (2006)).

Some public bodies are set up to perform managerial or administrative functions on behalf of the Crown and so may benefit from privileges or immunities of the Crown – in particular, they may share in Crown immunity from statutory liability. A statute constituting a new public body will often say expressly whether or not it is to be regarded as acting on behalf of the Crown. For instance, section 55(2) of the Local Democracy, Economic Development and Construction Act 2009 provides that the Local Government Boundary Commission for England established by the Act 'is not to be regarded as a servant or agent of the Crown or as enjoying any status, immunity or privilege of the Crown', whereas section 34(1) of the Water Act 2003 provides that the functions of the Water Services Regulation Authority established by the act are performed 'on behalf of the Crown'. If the statute is not explicit on this point, the question has to be resolved on a consideration of the functions of the public body and the degree of its independence: see *Tamlin v. Hannaford* [1950] 1 KB 18. Even if a public body acts as the agent of the Crown, it is not necessarily to be identified with the Crown for all purposes. In *British Medical Association v. Greater Glasgow Health Board* [1989] AC 1211, the House of Lords held that the health board, although set up to perform functions on behalf of the Crown, was not within the protection of section 21 of the Crown Proceedings Act 1947 (see above).

Crown bodies are, at common law, immune from criminal liability, but exceptions may be made by statute. The Corporate Manslaughter and Corporate Homicide Act 2007, which created new offences of corporate manslaughter and (in Scotland) corporate homicide, is binding on the Crown. A corporate body that is a servant or agent of the Crown is not immune from prosecution under the Act by reason of its Crown status (section 11(1)), while Schedule 1 to the Act specifies a number of government departments and other public bodies that, although not corporations, may be guilty of an offence under the Act.

Other than as provided by statute, the Crown enjoys no special immunity from civil liability at common law. As Lord Walker said in *Deutsche Morgan Grenfell* v. *Inland Revenue Commissioners* [2006] UKHL 49, [2007] 1 AC 558 (at [133]), 'under the rule of law, the Crown (that is the executive government in its various manifestations) is in general subject to the same common law obligations as ordinary citizens'. A former immunity of the Crown from liability in tort for injury or death caused to members of the armed forces, as provided in section 10 of the Crown Proceedings Act 1947, was abolished by the Crown Proceedings (Armed Forces) Act 1987, but not retrospectively. In *Matthews* v. *Ministry of Defence* [2003] UKHL 4, [2003] 1 AC 1163, the House of Lords held that the surviving immunity under section 10 was not incompatible with convention rights (Article 6(1) of the Convention, given effect by the HRA).

(See, generally, Tomkins, 'Crown Privileges', in Sunkin and Payne (eds.), *The Nature of the Crown* (1999).)

6.2 Monarchy and the Prerogative

In a constitutional monarchy like ours, the sovereign is the head of state and symbolically represents the nation, but he or she is not the head of government. As Vernon Bogdanor succinctly observes (*The Monarchy and the Constitution*, below, at p. 65), in a constitutional monarchy we find 'a set of conventions which limit the discretion of the sovereign so that his or her public acts are in reality those of ministers'.

Vernon Bogdanor, *The Monarchy and the Constitution* (1997), pp. 61–2, 63

The functions of a head of state, where that office is separated from that of the head of government, are generally of three main kinds. First, there are constitutional functions, primarily of a formal and residual kind, such as appointing a prime minister and dissolving the legislature. Secondly, the head of state carries out a wide variety of public engagements and ceremonial duties. Thirdly, and perhaps most important, there is the symbolic or representative function, by means of which the head of state represents and symbolizes not just the state but the nation. It is this role of interpreting the nation to itself that is the crucial one; the ceremonial activities – once dismissed by President de Gaulle as opening exhibitions of chrysanthemums – are means through which the head of state can be seen as fulfilling his or her representative functions. That is why the long withdrawal from public duties of Queen Victoria after the death of the Prince Consort in 1861 proved so damaging to the monarchy. To be an effective symbol, a head of state and particularly a sovereign has to be seen. There is a theatrical element to effective representation, and, unless this is recognized, a head of state will lack the authority which comes from public support. Then, in the long run, he or she will find it impossible, lacking that authority, to perform his or her constitutional functions effectively.

In his book *The English Constitution*, first published in 1867, Walter Bagehot drew a famous distinction between the 'efficient' and the 'dignified' elements of the constitution. The 'efficient' elements were those with the power to make and carry out policy, such as the cabinet. The 'dignified' elements, by contrast, such as the monarchy, enjoyed little effective power. This did not mean, however, that they were unimportant or superfluous. On the contrary, they were of fundamental significance in symbolizing and reinforcing national unity. They helped to reconcile the ruled to the rulers. It was the 'dignified' elements in the constitution which created the aura of authority that helped to render government legitimate.

It is easier for a head of state to fulfil this 'dignified' function if the 'efficient' functions are located elsewhere, for any exercise of the efficient functions is almost bound to be controversial. Thus, when he or she exercises the 'efficient' functions, the head of state will cease to be able to represent all of the people; he or she will be representing only the particular cross-section who agree with his or her activities. That is a fundamental problem with countries where the positions of head of state and head of government are combined.

Bogdanor remarks that a head of state in a republic, even if not the same person as the head of government, is likely to be a figure with a political history:

[T]he fact that the head of state has a political history must always make it more difficult to fulfil the symbolic and representative role successfully. In a monarchy, by contrast, the head of state has no political history. Provided that the sovereign carries out the constitutional functions in an impartial way, he or she is in a better position to represent the nation as a whole and to be a representative whom everybody can accept.

A republican riposte might be that a hereditary monarch, albeit without a political history, embodies a regal history and patrician associations which may also be a disability in representing the nation as a whole. (See Tom Nairn, *The Enchanted Glass: Britain and its Monarchy* (rev edn. 1994).)

In the modern constitution, the sovereign still possesses certain residual rights and powers. As a source of influence on government he or she has, as Bagehot remarked (*The English Constitution* (Fontana edn. 1963, p. 111)), 'three rights – the right to be consulted, the right to encourage, the right to warn'. Occasions for the exercise of these rights still exist, for instance, in the prime minister's weekly audience with the sovereign, but to what extent they are asserted it is difficult to know, especially as regards the living monarch. Peter Hennessy is persuaded of 'the continuing political influence of the monarchy as practised by George VI and Elizabeth II' (*The Hidden Wiring* (1995), p. 49 and see pp. 63–70). Likewise, one of the present queen's biographers, Ben Pimlott, chronicles her personal involvement in the selection of the prime minister in 1957 and 1963, judging her action in the latter year, 'in effect to collude with' outgoing Prime Minister Harold Macmillan's scheme for 'blocking' the frontrunner RA Butler from replacing him, as 'the biggest political misjudgement of her reign' (Ben Pimlott, *The Queen: Elizabeth II and the Monarchy* (2nd edn. 2002), p. 335). That said, however, there can be little doubt that royal influence on government has declined since the reign of Queen Victoria. (See Hardie, *The Political Influence of the British Monarchy 1868–1952* (1970); Lord Simon, 'The Influence and Power of the Monarch in the United Kingdom' (1982) 63 *The Parliamentarian* 61; Brazier, *Constitutional Texts* (1990), pp. 127–8, 417–35; Bogdanor, *The Monarchy and the Constitution* (1997), pp. 69–74.)

It has been conjectured that Prince Charles as king may prove to be less restrained than the present monarch in urging his personal views on matters of public policy. (See Blackburn, *King and Country* (2006), pp. 13–22.) A High Court judge, Vos J, was moved in *CPC Group* v. *Qatari Diar Real Estate* [2010] EWHC 1535 (Ch.), at [124], to describe the prince's intervention in a planning dispute (concerning the Chelsea Barracks site in London) as 'unexpected and unwelcome'. The prince's involvement in communications with ministers also came to light following the disclose of the 'Black Spider' memos (see *Evans* v. *Information Commissioner (Correspondence with Prince Charles in 2004 and 2005)* [2012] UKUT 313 (AAC) and *R (Evans)* v. *Attorney General* [2015] UKSC 21, [2015] AC 1787). As heir to the throne, Prince Charles has intervened in numerous matters of public policy: does this not undermine the political neutrality of the monarchy?

We have already seen that most of the surviving powers, privileges and immunities that were once aspects of the *royal* prerogative have been appropriated by the government. Even when it is the sovereign who acts, this is normally because of an obligation by convention to do so in accordance with the advice of Crown ministers. There are, however, grounds for the view that there remain a few prerogative powers – aptly named 'reserve powers' by Geoffrey Marshall [2002] *PL* 4 – that may still fall to be exercised by the sovereign in his/her own judgment in exceptional circumstances.

6.2.1 Appointment of the Prime Minister

Legally, the monarch has the power to appoint whomsoever he or she wishes to be the prime minister. Indeed, there exists the legal power to appoint no one at all to the office, for there is no *legal* requirement that there should at all times be a prime minister. While this remains the formal legal position, in reality the monarch's prerogative is governed by the fundamental constitutional convention, grounded in political necessity, that he or she must appoint as prime minister the person who can form a government that will have the confidence of the House of Commons. Normally, this convention clearly indicates the party leader who, having majority support in the house, has an indisputable claim to be appointed.

Formerly, if a prime minister died or personally resigned (other ministers remaining in office), the sovereign might have had to use his or her own judgment in making an appointment, but now the main parties all have procedures for electing a successor in such an event. The recent resignations of David Cameron and Theresa May were both announced in advance. Both resigned as leader of the party, allowing for internal mechanisms of the Conservative Party to provide a new leader. Each then resigned as prime minister so as to allow the new leader of the party – in this instance, Theresa May, followed by Boris Johnson, who then became Prime Minister. A similar pattern occurred when Harold Wilson announced his resignation as Prime Minister in March 1976 (see Wilson, *The Governance of Britain* (1976), pp. 21–2) and when Mrs Thatcher in 1990, having decided to withdraw after the first round of the Conservative leadership election, waited to resign as PM until John Major had been elected as leader. In such cases, there is no room for the exercise of discretion by the sovereign.

In the event of a sudden death or resignation of the prime minister, the governing party would doubtless expedite its election procedures. If there were still to be substantial delay before a successor could be chosen, the cabinet could be expected to bring forward a minister who would assume temporary leadership of the government, the sovereign being invited to confirm his or her authority to act. Otherwise, the monarch might call on the deputy prime minister or, if there was none, the minister ranking highest in precedence to take this responsibility. (See, further, Brazier, *Constitutional Practice* (3rd edn. 1999), ch. 2.)

If, in a general election, the main opposition party wins an overall majority of seats, as did the Labour Party in May 1997, the government will resign and the sovereign will call on the leader of the opposition to form a new government. But, if no party gains an overall majority, it may not be immediately clear whether the existing prime minister, or the leader of the opposition, or some other party leader, will have sufficient support in the House of Commons to govern effectively. This indeed was the position after the general election of February 1974, which gave rise to considerable uncertainty (see Brazier, 'The Constitution in the New Politics' [1978] PL 117).

A general election that fails to give an overall majority to one party may produce a result allowing of either a single-party minority government or a government formed from any of various combinations of parties under one or other of a number of party leaders. In these circumstances, the established conventions and precedents do not give an unequivocal indication of the way in which the prerogative of appointment should be exercised. The hitherto unusual phenomenon of a 'hung' Parliament, with no party enjoying an overall majority, occurred again in the general election of 6 May 2010. Opinion polls had indicated the possibility of such a result, giving rise to much speculation about the process of selection of a prime minister and the formation of a government in that event. As we saw in Chapter 3, this situation is now governed by the *Cabinet Manual* (see above, pp. 221–222).

What should the role of the sovereign in the choice of a prime minister in such circumstances be? The 'golden rule', as Robert Hazell expressed it, 'is not to draw the monarch into controversy or political negotiations' (*Making Minority Government Work* (2009), p. 68). Witnesses who gave evidence to the justice committee in its inquiry into constitutional processes following a general election 'were unanimous that, in circumstances of a House with no overall majority, it was for the politicians to conduct negotiations to clarify who was most likely to be able to command the House's confidence and the Sovereign would not, and should not be expected to, take a role in that process' (Justice Committee, *5th Report of 2009–10*, HC 396, para 19).

In the hung Parliament resulting from the May 2010 general election, no party had come close to winning the 326 seats needed for an overall majority in a House of Commons of 650 seats. The Conservatives, led by David Cameron, had the largest number of seats (307) and could have chosen to form a minority government sustained by a formal 'confidence and supply agreement' with other parties or with a view to making deals with other parties on specific issues as they arose. The minority government option was not, however, pursued by the Conservative leadership, which instead opened discussions with the Liberal Democrats, led by Nick Clegg, on the formation of a coalition government. An attempt by Gordon Brown, still in office as Prime Minister, to negotiate a Labour/Liberal Democrat coalition was unsuccessful, whereupon Mr Brown arranged to meet Queen Elizabeth in Buckingham Palace. The Queen had been kept fully informed of developments through her private secretary, and Mr Brown, having declared his inability to form an administration having the confidence of the House of Commons, tendered his resignation as Prime Minister. The Queen then invited Mr Cameron to form a government. (See, further, Blackburn, 'The 2010 General Election Outcome and Formation of the Coalition Government' [2011] *PL* 30; House of Commons Political and Constitutional Reform Committee, *Lessons from the Process of Government Formation after the 2010 General Election*, 4th Report of 2010–11, HC 528.)

Following the 2017 snap general election, although the Conservative Party received the most number of seats (317), it did not obtain an overall majority. Theresa May remained as Prime Minister, obtaining a confidence and supply agreement with the DUP, although the agreement was only finalised after Parliament had reconvened and the Queen's Speech had taken place.

Some contend that there may still be a role for the sovereign in the choice of a prime minister, albeit one of last resort, in the unlikely event that political leaders should fail to reach any conclusion on the formation of a government in the context of a hung Parliament. (See, e.g., Brazier [2005] *PL* 45; Bogdanor, *The Times*, 29 April 2010, p. 71.) This view is contested by Blackburn, *King and Country* (2006), pp. 86–90 and *The Times*, 28 November 2009 (Letters), asserting that the sovereign should not 'become embroiled in exercising any discretion over who should be prime minister'. Any uncertainty of this kind would be resolved by the adoption of the proposal of the Institute for Public Policy Research, in its draft *Constitution of the United Kingdom* (1991), that the head of state should 'appoint as the Prime Minister the person elected to that office by the House of Commons'. A similar solution was urged by the Fabian Society in its report on *The Future of the Monarchy* (2003), p. 56. In devolved Scotland and Wales, the first minister is chosen, respectively, by the Scottish Parliament and the Welsh Assembly, to be formally appointed by the sovereign: sections 45 and 46 of the Scotland Act 1998; and sections 46 and 47 of the Government of Wales Act 2006.

6.2.2 Dismissal of Ministers

The monarch has a prerogative power to dismiss ministers singly or collectively but, again, the legal power is overlaid by convention. In practice, the fate of individual ministers is in the hands of the prime minister. Although constrained by political factors, he or she has, by convention, the power to require the resignation of any minister. (In the last resort, the prime minister could advise the sovereign to exercise the power of dismissal.)

In *Adegbenro* v. *Akintola* [1963] AC 614, the Privy Council had to decide a question about the power vested by the Constitution of Western Nigeria in the governor of the region to dismiss the regional premier if he had lost the confidence of the elected house. Arguments addressed to the court had sought to draw analogies from the monarch's prerogative of dismissal in the United Kingdom. Lord Radcliffe said (at 631):

> British constitutional history does not offer any but a general negative guide as to the circumstances in which a Sovereign can dismiss a Prime Minister. Since the principles which are accepted today began to take shape with the passing of the Reform Bill of 1832 no British Sovereign has in fact dismissed or removed a Prime Minister, even allowing for the ambiguous exchanges which took place between William IV and Lord Melbourne in 1834. Discussion of constitutional doctrine bearing upon a Prime Minister's loss of support in the House of Commons concentrates therefore upon a Prime Minister's duty to ask for liberty to resign or for a dissolution, rather than upon the Sovereign's right of removal, an exercise of which is not treated as being within the scope of practical politics.

Having regard to the facts that governments are sustained in office by a democratically elected House of Commons, and that no prime minister has been dismissed by the sovereign since 1783, when George III dismissed the Fox-North coalition government (or perhaps since 1834, when the circumstances of Melbourne's departure were equivocal), it must now be unconstitutional for the sovereign to dismiss the prime minister and his or her colleagues in all but the most exceptional circumstances. George V contemplated dismissing the Asquith Government in 1914 with a view to a general election being called by a new prime minister, in order to forestall the passage of a Home Rule Bill and avert an apparent threat of civil war in Ulster. In the event, the crisis was resolved without royal recourse to this extreme remedy. The power of dismissal is said still to survive for use should a government act to destroy the democratic or parliamentary bases of the constitution. But unless the sovereign's judgment of the necessity to dismiss ministers on these grounds should be generally supported by public opinion, the monarchy itself would be placed in jeopardy.

What consequences might follow if a government, defeated on a vote of confidence in the House of Commons, refused to resign or request a dissolution of Parliament? Would this be an occasion for the exercise of the prerogative of dismissal? For Geoffrey Marshall, this is a plain case: 'Ministers who clearly ignored a loss of confidence by the House of Commons and defied the conventional rule might properly be dismissed' (Marshall, *Constitutional Conventions: The Rules and Forms of Political Accountability* (1986), p. 27). The provisions of the Fixed-Term Parliaments Act 2011 now render this issue moot: it replaces the prerogative of dissolution with statutory provisions fixing parliamentary terms to five years, with two possible means of calling an early general election. A vote of no confidence does not now require the resignation of the prime minister or the dissolution of the house. Following the vote of no confidence according to the specific wording of the motion set out in the Fixed-Term Parliaments Act 2011, a period of fourteen days takes place in which it is possible for the house to pass a motion of confidence in the government, be that the incumbent government or a differently composed government. Should a government lose a vote of confidence, the *Cabinet Manual* specifies that the government remains in office during that fourteen-day period. However, its provisions lead to a further issue – what if the incumbent prime minister failed to resign even in the face of a vote of confidence in a differently composed government? This would appear to be a similar case in which it would be appropriate for the monarch to exercise the prerogative power of dismissal. It would be clear that the incumbent prime minister no longer had the confidence of the house. The incumbent prime minister would also be frustrating the purpose of the Fixed-Term Parliaments Act 2011 designed to facilitate the dissolution of Parliament and to regulate the holding of general elections.

When, in 1975, the Governor-General of Australia, Sir John Kerr, acting in the name of Queen Elizabeth, but on his own initiative, dismissed the Prime Minister of Australia, Mr Whitlam, and all the ministers of the Labour Government with the object of resolving a political and constitutional impasse, his action provoked much controversy and reactions of an intense and bitter kind. The crisis had resulted from the refusal of the Upper House of the Australian Parliament, where the opposition had a majority, to pass appropriation bills providing necessary supply (authorisation of expenditure) for the government. This unprecedented action of the Senate was designed to bring down the government, which attempted to extricate itself from a critical situation by devising unorthodox expedients for raising money. In this crisis, the Governor-General Kerr acted by dismissing Mr Whitlam and his government and appointing as Prime Minister then leader of the opposition, Mr Fraser, who had first assured the Governor-General that the appropriation bills would be passed and that he would as Prime Minister advise a dissolution of both Houses of Parliament in order that the deadlock might be resolved by the verdict of the people. The subsequent election was convincingly won by the opposition Liberal and Country parties, and a coalition government was formed under Mr Fraser.

Sir John Kerr's drastic action has been defended in that it brought about the immediate passage of the obstructed supply bills and placed the resolution of the conflict in the hands of the electorate. But he was also criticised for acting precipitately when a political solution was still possible.

These events took place in a political and constitutional context different from that in which the sovereign has to operate in the UK and they do not provide us with a directly applicable precedent (even if any clear principle can be deduced from them). They do demonstrate, however, that dismissal of a government may still be an available measure of last resort, but also that it is likely to generate vehement public controversy.

(See, further, Howard and Saunders, in Evans (ed.), *Labor and the Constitution 1972–1975* (1997); Sir John Kerr, *Matters for Judgment* (1978), especially chs 16–22; Low, 'Wearing the Crown: New Reflections on the Dismissal 1975' (1984) 19 *Politics* 18; Low (ed.), *Constitutional Heads and Political Crises* (1988), ch. 6.)

6.2.3 Dissolution of Parliament

The maximum duration of Parliament was fixed at five years by the Septennial Act 1715 as amended by section 7 of the Parliament Act 1911, but Parliament could be dissolved before its expiry by the exercise of the royal prerogative, in practice, on a request from the prime minister. Until the First World War, the decision to request the sovereign to dissolve Parliament was taken by the cabinet collectively, but the power to request a dissolution was appropriated by the prime minister early in the twentieth century, it seems through a misunderstanding of the precedents: see Lord Blake, *The Office of Prime Minister* (1975), p. 59 and Marshall, *Constitutional Conventions: The Rules and Forms of Political Accountability*, pp. 48–53. Marshall argued that the justification for this arrogation of the power was weak, but it nevertheless became established as a constitutional convention that the responsibility for invoking the prerogative power rested with the prime minister alone.

The unfairness was manifest of entrusting decisions on dissolution and consequently the timing of a general election to the prime minister of the day, who could be depended on to use the power for political advantage. Misuse of the power was scarcely mitigated by the practice, usually followed by prime ministers, of consulting senior colleagues before asking for a dissolution. There was also an uncertain safeguard in the possibility, in ill-defined circumstances, of refusal by the sovereign to grant a requested dissolution, notably if, as Vernon Bogdanor observed (*The Monarchy and the Constitution* (1995), p. 162), 'the grant of a dissolution would be an affront to, rather than an expression of, democratic rights.'

In the closing years of the twentieth century, there were those who urged the radical solution that the House of Commons should be elected for a fixed term, so that the power of dissolution should not ordinarily be available during the five-year (or a shorter) term. The arguments for a fixed-term Parliament attracted increasing support in more recent years: see, for instance, Hazell and Willan, *Fixed Term Parliaments* (2006); the debate on David Howarth MP's Fixed-Term Parliaments Bill at HC Deb vol. 475, cols 1703 et seq (16 May 2008); and Blackburn [2009] *PL* 766 at 784–9. The Coalition Agreement of May 2010 included an undertaking to bring forward legislation providing for fixed-term Parliaments of five years. The Fixed-Term Parliaments Act 2011 fixes the term of Parliament to five years. It provides two opportunities for an early general election: following a motion for an early general election or following a vote of no confidence. An early general election can be called if the House of Commons passes a motion 'that there shall be an early general election'. A number of MPs equal to or greater than two-thirds of the number of seats in the house must vote in favour of the motion if it is to pass (section 2(1) and (2)). On 19 April 2017, Theresa May placed a motion before the House of Commons calling for an early general election. The motion was passed by 522 votes to 13. As a result, a general election took place on 8 June 2017. Boris Johnson proposed three motions for an early general election; on 4 September, 9 September and 28 October 2019. Although he won all three motions, he failed to obtain the majority required to trigger an early general election on all three occasions. Having failed to obtain the requisite number of votes, the government introduced a bill, which became the Early Parliamentary General Elections Act 2019. Section 1 of the Act provided that an early parliamentary general election would take place on 12 December 2019. This date was deemed to be a polling day for the purposes of the Fixed-Term Parliaments Act 2011. This would appear to be an easy means of forcing an early parliamentary general election – only a simple and not a two-thirds majority is needed in the House of Commons to vote in favour of legislation. However, this may not always be as easy to achieve as it appeared to be in 2019. First, legislation also requires the consent of the House of Lords. Second, enacting legislation in this manner means that Parliament as a whole – and not, in effect, solely the prime minister – determines the date of a general election. As with most things in 2019, the backdrop of Brexit means it can be difficult to determine long-term changes in behaviour as a result of what happened in this extraordinary time for Parliament and the UK constitution.

The Fixed-Term Parliaments Act also triggers an early general election if the House of Commons votes in favour of a motion 'that this House has no confidence in Her Majesty's Government'. If this motion is passed, then a general election is called if, following a period of fourteen days from the vote of no confidence, the House of Commons does not pass a motion 'that this House has confidence in Her Majesty's Government' (sections 2(3) to (7)). (See the report of the Public Administration and Constitutional Affairs Committee: *The Role of Parliament in the UK Constitution: Interim Report The Status and Effect of Confidence Motions and the Fixed Term Parliaments Act, 2011, 14th Report 2017–2019, HC 1813.*)

The Act 'does not affect Her Majesty's power to prorogue Parliament' (section 6(1). Prorogation brings a parliamentary session to an end and suspends proceedings. It normally only occurs for a limited period, a few days at the end of each parliamentary session, to enable time to prepare the Queen's Speech, which sets out the legislative agenda for the next parliamentary session. This power was used, controversially, by the Prime Minister, Boris Johnson, to prorogue Parliament from 10 September to 14 October 2019. The advice given to Her Majesty was challenged in both the Scottish and the English courts. In *Cherry* v. *Advocate General for Scotland* [2019] SCOH 70, the Outer House of the Court of Session concluded that the prerogative power of prorogation was non-justiciable, as a matter of politics. The divisional court in England reached the same conclusion in *R (Miller)* v. *Prime Minister* [2019] EWHC 2381 (QB). The Inner House of the Court of Session in Scotland then concluded that the prerogative power of prorogation was justiciable, and that its exercise by the prime minister was unlawful as an abuse of power. He had used the prerogative for an improper purpose. The case was then heard by the Supreme Court, sitting as a panel of eleven, where the Supreme Court concluded that the advice given to the monarch was unlawful and that, therefore, the prorogation was a nullity. In essence, Parliament had never been prorogued.

The Supreme Court focused on determining the limits placed on the prerogative power of prorogation by the common law. In particular, it concluded that the constitutional principles of parliamentary sovereignty and of parliamentary accountability placed limits on the prerogative of prorogation. These limits had been transgressed by the proposed prorogation, meaning that the advice of the prime minister was unlawful.

R (Miller) v. *Prime Minister; Cherry* v. *Advocate General for Scotland* [2019] UKSC 41 [2020] AC 373

[50]. For the purposes of the present case, therefore, the relevant limit upon the power to prorogue can be expressed in this way: that a decision to prorogue Parliament (or to advise the monarch to prorogue Parliament) will be unlawful if the prorogation has the effect of frustrating or preventing, without reasonable justification, the ability of Parliament to carry

out its constitutional functions as a legislature and as the body responsible for the supervision of the executive. In such a situation, the court will intervene if the effect is sufficiently serious to justify such an exceptional course.

[51]. That standard is one that can be applied in practice. The extent to which prorogation frustrates or prevents Parliament's ability to perform its legislative functions and its supervision of the executive is a question of fact which presents no greater difficulty than many other questions of fact which are routinely decided by the courts. The court then has to decide whether the Prime Minister's explanation for advising that Parliament should be prorogued is a reasonable justification for a prorogation having those effects. The Prime Minister's wish to end one session of Parliament and to begin another will normally be enough in itself to justify the short period of prorogation which has been normal in modern practice. It could only be in unusual circumstances that any further justification might be necessary. Even in such a case, when considering the justification put forward, the court would have to bear in mind that the decision whether to advise the monarch to prorogue Parliament falls within the area of responsibility of the Prime Minister, and that it may in some circumstances involve a range of considerations, including matters of political judgment. The court would therefore have to consider any justification that might be advanced with sensitivity to the responsibilities and experience of the Prime Minister, and with a corresponding degree of caution. Nevertheless, it is the court's responsibility to determine whether the Prime Minster has remained within the legal limits of the power. If not, the final question will be whether the consequences are sufficiently serious to call for the court's intervention.

. . .

[61]. It is impossible for us to conclude, on the evidence which has been put before us, that there was any reason – let alone a good reason – to advise Her Majesty to prorogue Parliament for five weeks, from 9th or 12th September until 14th October. We cannot speculate, in the absence of further evidence, upon what such reasons might have been. It follows that the decision was unlawful.

The decision has been criticised as an example of the court imposing legal limits on a political power, thereby transgressing the separation of powers between the court and the executive. Nevertheless, it is important to recognise that the Supreme Court stressed that this was a control over the scope of a prerogative power and not over the manner in which it was exercised. The Supreme Court did not determine the proper or improper purposes of pro-rogation, or determine the precise length of prorogation. Neither did it ques-tion the motives of the prime minister when he gave advice to the monarch to prorogue Parliament. The court, instead, focused on using constitutional principles to determine the scope of the prerogative power. Moreover, the Supreme Court stressed the unique set of circumstances before the court, given the constitutional importance of Brexit and legislation (e.g. the European Union (Withdrawal) Act 2018; the European Union (Withdrawal) Act 2019 and the European Union (Withdrawal) (No 2) Act 2019), which provided for

Parliament, particularly the House of Commons, to have a say in how the UK was to exit the European Union. The court also stressed that it would exercise sensitivity when assessing both whether the restriction placed on parliamentary sovereignty and parliamentary accountability by a particular prorogation was sufficiently serious to warrant the exceptional course of action of the courts controlling this prorogation and also when evaluating whether the reasoning of the prime minister provided a reasonable justification for such an unusual prorogation.

The case may well be seen as one decided on its own specific and unique facts. Nevertheless, it also demonstrates a growing role of the Supreme Court in protecting the common law constitution and in controlling prerogative powers.

6.2.4 Royal Assent to Legislation

The monarch is part of Parliament and his or her assent to a bill passed by both houses is necessary for the bill to become an Act. There has been no refusal of the royal assent since Queen Anne refused to assent to a Scotch Militia Bill in 1707 and it must now be regarded as an established constitutional convention that the monarch must give assent, irrespective of any views held on the bill's merits, at all events unless otherwise advised by the prime minister and provided that he or she is satisfied that parliamentary procedures were properly observed in the bill's passage. Robert Blackburn concludes succinctly that: 'The royal act of Assent is in the nature of a certificate that the Bill has passed through all its established parliamentary procedures' (*King and Country* (2006), p. 94). (See, further, Marshall, *Constitutional Conventions* (1986), pp. 21–3; Bogdanor, *The Monarchy and the Constitution* (1995), pp. 129–32; Twomey, 'The Refusal or Deferral of Royal Assent' [2006] *PL* 580.)

Tensions arose surrounding the prerogative power of royal assent following the enactment of the European Union (Withdrawal) Act 2019. This Act was a private members bill, led, inter alia, by Oliver Letwin and Yvette Cooper, requiring the then Prime Minister, Theresa May, to seek an extension to the negotiation period governing the UK's exit from the European Union in order to prevent the UK leaving the EU with no deal. It was argued that it may be possible for ministers to advise the monarch not to give assent to the Act. Two views emerged: first, that the monarch should always give royal assent to legislation, even when advised by ministers not to do so and, second, that the monarch could refuse to give royal assent to legislation when advised by ministers not to do so, with different criteria advocated regarding the circumstances in which it would be constitutionally acceptable for ministers to advise the monarch not to grant royal assent. In the end, no advice to refuse assent was forthcoming from ministers. As such, the question remains unresolved (see Twomey, *The Veiled Sceptre: Reserve Powers of Heads of State in Westminster Systems* (2018), pp. 616–790 for a full evaluation of this prerogative power). (See also various blog posts on this issue on the UKCLA website: https://ukconstitutionallaw.org/tag/royal-assent/and from Mark Elliott (https://publiclawforeveryone.com/2019/01/21/can-the-government-veto-legisla tion-by-advising-the-queen-to-withhold-royal-assent/) and Thomas Poole (www .lrb.co.uk/blog/2019/april/the-executive-power-project).)

A sceptical view of the 'personal prerogatives' of the sovereign is taken by Robert Blackburn, who argues that the sovereign exercises his or her legal powers exclusively in accordance with established conventions and procedures, leaving no room for personal discretion (Blackburn, above, ch. 3). For a more expansive interpretation of the continuing constitutional authority of the monarch, see Tomkins, *Public Law* (2003), pp. 62–72. Nevil Johnson concludes a survey of the monarch's residual powers in saying that: '[T]here is no prerogative power that can in the normal conditions of political life be exercised independently by the monarch' (*Reshaping the British Constitution* (2004), p. 60). This is surely right, although it should always be remembered that politics does not invariably keep to its 'normal conditions'. In abnormal or emergency conditions, it is clear that the monarch retains an array of extraordinary *legal* powers. Whether the exercise of such powers would ever again be considered *constitutional* is impossible to say unless and until it happens. Such is the nature of conventions. What we can say, perhaps, is that, as is suggested by the examples of Scotland and Wales and more recently by the Fixed-Term Parliaments Bill, statutory provisions could relatively easily be crafted that would do away with any lingering doubts. Why have they not been? In whose interests is it that the present circumstances continue to persist?

(See, generally, Sunkin and Payne (eds.), *The Nature of the Crown* (1999); Johnson, *Reshaping the British Constitution* (2004), ch. 4; Blackburn, *King and Country: Monarchy and the Future King Charles III* (2006); McLean, *What's Wrong with the British Constitution?* (2010), ch. 12; Twomey *The Veiled Sceptre: Reserve Powers of Heads of State in Westminster Systems* (2018).)

6.3 Central Government

6.3.1 Ministers

The executive powers of government are, in general, exercised by or on behalf of ministers of the Crown, who in the theory of the constitution are themselves servants of the Crown. It has been argued (by Rodney Brazier, *Ministers of the Crown* (1997), pp. 23–31) that the term 'ministers of the Crown' is properly restricted to those senior ministers who have sole charge of a government department, and in whom the legal powers of government are vested. Usage is not consistent, however, and 'ministers of the Crown' sometimes refers to all ministers of whatever rank (e.g., in the Ministers of the Crown Act 1975). The choice of the people (MPs or peers) to be appointed as ministers by the monarch is a matter within the exclusive judgment of the prime minister, but, in practice, is subject to the constraints of politics and party. Such constraints were particularly compelling in the formation of the Coalition Government in 2010 when the Conservative Prime Minister, David Cameron, appointed five Liberal Democrat MPs (including their leader, Nick Clegg) to be members of the cabinet and a further ten and one peer as junior ministers (ministers of state or parliamentary secretaries). Prime Minister Cameron agreed that any new ministerial appointments in the Coalition Government would be made only after consultation with the deputy prime minister. As ministers hold office 'at the pleasure of the Crown', they may lawfully be dismissed by the Crown, but in this, the monarch must act in accordance with convention, as we have already seen.

Town Investments Ltd v. *Department of the Environment* [1978] AC 359 (HL)

Lord Simon: . . . Once central government was firmly established in England, power – what in modern political science would be known as executive, judicial and legislative power – was concentrated in the King. No line was drawn at first between the private and the public business of the King. But, as the latter grew, administrative convenience called for some devolution. Offices were hived off from the King's household. There was the Chancery presided over by the Chancellor. Then there was the Privy Seal Office under a Keeper of the Privy Seal, and the Exchequer with a Treasurer and a Chancellor of its own. And so on. All these officials holding offices of ancient origin had their action 'confined within rigid limits, expressed by the commissions by which they were appointed and the procedure which their acts must follow'. The motive force behind their departments –

'was the King's command. They all existed to give effect to his will. The officials who presided over them were appointed and dismissible by him. Each was charged with the fulfilment of the royal pleasure within his own appropriate sphere.'

However, for centuries thereafter the King's secretary remained within the royal household. Unlike the officials holding offices of ancient origin, the King's secretary was therefore 'free to enter every new branch of royal administration as it developed'. So it was that with the increase in the powers of the Crown in the 16th century the Secretary rose to the first rank among the King's servants. But under the Restoration the Secretaries (for their office was now duplicated) too became heads of departments of state, charged like the holders of the ancient offices with executing the royal will. (For the foregoing historical development, see D.L. Keir, *The Constitutional History of Modern Britain* 1485–1937 . . ., whence also came the quotations.)

With the development of modern government fresh departments were formed to be headed by ministers or by Secretaries of State. Just as all were originally appointed to carry out departmentally the royal will, so today all ministers are appointed to exercise the powers of the Crown, together with such other powers as have been statutorily conferred upon them directly.

In theory, there is still only one office of Secretary of State, but several may be invested with the title and powers of the office. By section 5 of and Schedule 1 to the Interpretation Act 1978, 'Secretary of State' means 'one of Her Majesty's Principal Secretaries of State'. Powers and functions entrusted to 'the Secretary of State' can accordingly be exercised by *any* of the principal secretaries of state, of whom there were seventeen in February 2011, each heading a government department and with a seat in the cabinet. Some ministers have traditional titles reflecting their historical functions as servants of the Crown: they include the Lord Chancellor, the Chancellor of the Exchequer, the Lord Privy Seal, the Lord President of the Council, the Chancellor of the Duchy of Lancaster and the Paymaster General. The last four do not run major government departments and their responsibilities vary in different administrations. For example, the Chancellor of the Duchy of Lancaster in the Heath Government (1970–74) had responsibility for the conduct of negotiations for British entry into the European communities. In the Coalition Government formed in May 2010 the Chancellor of the Duchy was Leader of the House of Lords, while the Lord Privy Seal was Leader of the House of Commons, each having responsibility for the management of government business in their respective houses. The paymaster general was the minister for the Cabinet Office with overall responsibility for the work of the office (including Civil Service issues). The Deputy Prime Minister, Nick Clegg (the Leader of the Liberal Democrats), was also invested with the office of Lord President of the Council, and in this dual capacity undertook special responsibility for political and constitutional reform. (His role is given further consideration below.) In some administrations, there is a minister without portfolio, not heading a department but to whom various responsibilities may be assigned. In the Coalition Government the minister without portfolio acts 'as an interface between the Government and the Conservative Party', provides the prime minister 'with strategic thinking on the general direction of Government policy', works with ministerial colleagues on 'social cohesion and big society' and is a member of cabinet and cabinet committees. In the current Johnson Government (from December 2019 onwards), the Lord Privy Seal is also the Leader of the House of Lords. The lord president of the council is also Leader of the House of Commons. The Chancellor of the Duchy of Lancaster was given the responsibility of overseeing the devolution consequences of EU exit and of maintaining the integrity of the union.

The office of Lord Chancellor was greatly reduced in importance with the creation, in May 2007, of the Ministry of Justice. The Secretary of State for Sustice has assumed the title and remaining functions of the Lord Chancellor, and his responsibilities include the constitution (so far as not allocated to the deputy prime minister), democracy and human rights, the courts, law reform, freedom of information, prisons and probation. As Lord Chancellor, he has a particular responsibility for upholding and defending the independence of the judiciary: section 3 of the Constitutional Reform Act 2005. (See, further, Chapter 2.)

The Attorney General and the solicitor general, as law officers of the Crown for England and Wales, the Advocate General for Scotland and the Attorney General and Advocate General for Northern Ireland are (non-cabinet) ministers who act as the government's chief legal advisers and have important responsibilities in relation to the law and its enforcement. The Attorney General, a minister with 'a bewildering range of roles' (Daintith and Page, *The Executive in the Constitution* (1999), p. 232), has a special responsibility to uphold the rule of law and a significant involvement in the criminal justice system, in particular in overseeing the Crown Prosecution Service and the other main prosecuting authorities. In acting as the government's principal legal adviser the Attorney General is required to act independently, in the sense that his legal advice is meant to be impartial. Concern has focused on the tension in his role 'between being a party politician and a member of the Government' – and as such bound by the principle of collective ministerial responsibility – 'and the giving of independent and impartial legal advice' (*The Governance of Britain: A Consultation on the Role of the Attorney General*, Cm 7192/2007, p. 2). This concern was intensified by the circumstances attending the decision to invade Iraq in 2003 when, it appears, there were attempts by ministers to influence the Attorney General's advice to the cabinet on the legality of the projected invasion. In performing his functions relating to legal proceedings, both criminal and civil – for instance, in bringing proceedings for contempt of court, or for the enforcement of public rights, or in making decisions on prosecutions – the Attorney General has a constitutional role as 'guardian of the public interest' (see as to this *Attorney General* v. *Blake* [1998] Ch. 439). Here again there may be tension between this role and the Attorney General's position as a minister and member of the government. While entitled to consult ministerial colleagues as to where the public interest lies, the Attorney General is required by convention to exercise an independent judgment uninfluenced by considerations of party advantage. (See, further, House of Lords Constitution Committee, *Reform of the Office of Attorney General*, 7th Report of 2007–08, HL 93; and Joint Committee on the Draft Constitutional Renewal Bill, *1st Report of 2007–08*, HL 166, HC 551, Chapter 3.)

The simultaneous wearing of these various 'government' and 'independent' hats has proved problematic. In September 1984, allegations were made that the prosecution of a civil servant, Clive Ponting, under section 2 of the Official Secrets Act 1911, had been undertaken on the insistence of the Secretary of State for Defence, supported by the prime minister. Mrs Thatcher denied the allegation in a letter to Dr David Owen MP, saying that the decision to prosecute had been taken by the law officers without consulting any of their ministerial colleagues, and adding:

you must know that the Attorney-General acts in a totally independent and non-political capacity in making decisions on prosecutions. It would be improper for me or my colleagues to interfere in any way with his discretion in the exercise of that function and I confirm that we did not do so in Mr Ponting's case. [*The Times,* 17 September 1984.]

Prime Minister Thatcher's statement was corroborated by the Attorney General himself in Parliament: HC Deb vol. 73, col 180, 12 February 1985.

When the Attorney General brought proceedings for an injunction in the *Crossman Diaries* case (see Chapter 3), he acted on his own judgment (albeit after consulting ministerial colleagues) in his capacity as guardian of the public interest (see Edwards, *The Attorney-General, Politics and the Public Interest* (1984), pp. 337–42). When, a decade later, another Attorney General brought proceedings in Australia for injunctions to prevent the publication of Peter Wright's book, *Spycatcher,* he acted on a different conception of his role. Questioned in the House of Commons about his part in decisions not to bring criminal or civil proceedings in respect of the publication of certain other books about espionage and the security services, the Attorney General (Sir Michael Havers) replied:

When I am wearing my hat as Attorney-General and prosecutor, nobody can influence me and I would not accept any attempt to influence me from anybody. When the Government are acting as Government in civil proceedings I happen, by tradition, to be the nominal plaintiff and that is what has happened here.

Later, with reference to the decision to take proceedings in Australia against *Spycatcher,* he said:

[T]his was a Government decision and, of course, like my fellow Ministers, I accept collective responsibility.

Pressed to confirm that it was 'the Attorney-General's duty to determine the public interest before commencing the injunctive process to ban a book, and not the duty of Ministers collectively', the Attorney General made an evasive reply. (See HC Deb vol. 106, cols 623–4, 1 December 1986.) In contempt proceedings connected with the *Spycatcher* litigation, the Attorney General was said to be acting 'in a quite different capacity independently of the government of the day … as "guardian of the public interest in the due administration of justice"' (Sir John Donaldson MR in *Attorney General* v. *Newspaper Publishing plc* [1988] Ch. 333, 362). Paragraph 6.27 of the *Ministerial Code* (2005) reaffirmed the distinction between civil proceedings 'in which the Law Officers are involved in a representative capacity on behalf of the Government, and action undertaken by them in the general interest, for example, to enforce the law on behalf of the general community'. (This passage has not reappeared in subsequent versions of the code, but the distinction remains valid.)

In 2006, there was a controversial decision by the director of the Serious Fraud Office to drop an investigation into allegations that the firm BAE Systems had bribed officials of the Saudi Arabian Government in order to secure an arms contract. The Attorney General had agreed with the director's decision after consulting other ministers on the public interest considerations (in particular, the risk that the Saudi Government might withhold cooperation in security matters if the investigation continued). Lord Lester of Herne Hill was subsequently to comment that the BAE case 'shows how fragile and inadequate are our present constitutional arrangements for protecting the Rule of Law' (Constitutional Affairs Committee, *5th Report of 2006–07*, HC 306, para 46; and see, further, *R (Corner House Research)* v. *Director of the Serious Fraud Office* [2008] UKHL 60, [2009] 1 AC 756, noted by Spencer [2008] *CLJ* 456 and considered further in Chapters 2 and 10).

Is it realistic to expect the law officers to keep their political and public-interest responsibilities in separate mental compartments? As a Lord of Appeal, Lord Steyn, has remarked extra-judicially, the Attorney General is 'a political figure responsive to public pressure': see (1996) 146 *NLJ* 1770. Should the office of Attorney General be removed from the political arena, as an independent office outside government? How might such an independent officer be held accountable for his or her actions? See the consideration of these matters by the Constitutional Affairs Committee (*5th Report of 2006–07*, HC 306) and the Justice Committee (*4th Report of 2007–08*, HC 698).

After extended review of the Attorney General's role, the then government reasserted, in its *Response to the Justice Committee Report on the Draft Constitutional Renewal Bill*, Cm 7689/2009, p. 2, that:

> The Government's settled view is that the Attorney General should remain the Government's chief legal adviser, a Minister and member of one of the Houses of Parliament, and that the Attorney General should continue as the Minister responsible for superintending the prosecuting authorities.

The government acknowledged that greater clarity was needed as to the Attorney General's role in relation to criminal prosecutions, and to this end a protocol was adopted between the Attorney General and the prosecuting departments to clarify their respective relationships. The protocol (Attorney General's Office, July 2009) confirmed that the Attorney General would not make key prosecution decisions in individual criminal cases unless required to do so by law or exceptionally to safeguard national security.

Although not a cabinet minister, the Attorney General attends cabinet meetings as required and may serve on cabinet committees.

Next in rank below full or senior ministers (most of whom head departments and sit in the cabinet) are ministers of state, who are attached to departments headed by cabinet ministers. Ministers of state are often appointed to take charge (under the departmental minister) of a particular section of a department and are designated accordingly – for example, the minister for Europe in the Foreign and Commonwealth Office. Others have tasks allotted to them by the departmental minister at his or her discretion. Departments also include junior ministers known as parliamentary secretaries (or parliamentary under-secretaries of state if the senior minister is a Secretary of State), some of whom, too, may be appointed to named offices. In the Home Office in May 2020, there were, besides the Secretary of State (Home Secretary), three ministers of state (one of whom was unpaid), a lords minister, and three parliamentary under-secretaries of state. Statutory powers are not conferred on subordinate ministers, who act as delegates of the Secretary of State or other senior minister at the head of the department, in whom powers are legally vested and who remains responsible to Parliament for their exercise. Ministers may be assisted in their parliamentary and political work by members of Parliament appointed by them (with the approval of the prime minister) as parliamentary private secretaries, who are unpaid and do not themselves rank as ministers.

Government whips have posts with titles that do not indicate their parliamentary functions of managing government business, backbench liaison and party discipline: the chief whip in the House of Commons has the title of parliamentary secretary to the Treasury and the deputy chief whip that of treasurer of Her Majesty's household.

A minister must, by convention, be a member of one or other house of Parliament. By statute, there may be no more than ninety-five holders of ministerial office in the House of Commons at any time (House of Commons Disqualification Act 1975, section 2(1)) – a rule designed to prevent executive dominance of the house. (The Ministerial and other Salaries Act 1975 limits the number of ministerial salaries that can be paid, but this restriction may be subverted by the appointment of unpaid ministers.) The number of MPs involved in government (including whips and parliamentary private secretaries) has generally been upwards of 130 in recent years. The principle of collective responsibility (see below) usually assures the government of the support at least of this substantial body of MPs (the 'payroll vote') for its policies and bills. The Public Administration Committee, noting that the payroll vote 'now comprises a fifth (20 per cent) of the voting strength of the whole House' and 'well over a third (39 per cent) of the members of the governing party', has drawn attention to the consequences of this for the independence of Parliament and the effectiveness of its scrutiny of the executive. (See the Committee's *9th Report of 2009–10*, HC 457, paras 22–35.)

Since the financial responsibilities of Parliament are exercised by the House of Commons alone, the Chancellor of the Exchequer, the chief secretary to the Treasury (who also usually has a seat in the cabinet) and the financial secretary are invariably members of the lower house. In the 1964–70 and 1974–79 Labour Governments, the only heads of principal departments who were peers were the Lord Chancellor and (briefly in 1965–66) the colonial secretary. A peer, Lord Carrington, held successively the portfolios of defence, energy and foreign and Commonwealth affairs in the 1970–74 and 1979–83 Conservative administrations. Lord Young of Graffham was a member of Mrs Thatcher's cabinet from 1984 to 1989, successively as Minister without Portfolio, Secretary of State for Employment and Secretary of State for Trade and Industry. The Lord Chancellor was invariably a peer until 2007, but, since the Constitutional Reform Act 2005, it has not been necessary for this office to be held by a peer and in 2007, a member of the House of Commons (Mr Jack Straw) became the first member of that house to take office as Lord Chancellor. In the final months of Gordon Brown's premiership there were, in addition to the Leader of the House of Lords, two secretaries of state heading major departments who were members of that house, Lord Mandelson as Business Secretary and Lord Adonis as Transport Secretary. In the Coalition Government formed in May 2010, there were two cabinet ministers who were peers, Lord Strathclyde as Leader of the House of Lords, and Baroness Warsi, as Minister without Portfolio. In the 2019 Johnson Government, there is only one cabinet minister who is a peer, Baroness Evans of Bowes Park who is the Lord Privy Seal and Leader of the House of Lords. Peers may also hold office as ministers of state or parliamentary secretaries and some will have been appointed as life peers so that they could serve as ministers – in increasing numbers in recent years, raising questions 'about why such appointments are being made and their impact on government and Parliament' (Public Administration Committee, *8th Report of 2009–10*, HC 330, para 14).

A continual increase in the number of ministers (from eighty-one in 1950 to 119 in January 2010) prompted an inquiry by the Public Administration Committee (*9th Report of 2009–10*, HC 457), which drew attention to 'a growing consensus that the ever increasing number of ministers harms the effectiveness of government'.

Ministers generally have a quite short tenure of office. In the eight years from 1983 to 1991, as Richard Rose notes, seven different ministers were in charge of the Department of Trade and Industry (*Too Much Reshuffling of the Cabinet Pack?* (1991), p. 3). The Department of Transport was headed successively by eleven different ministers in the Conservative administrations of 1979–97 and by four different ministers from 2006 to May 2010. In the first decade of the twenty-first century to May 2010, there were seven successive home secretaries. Rose discovered that in the period 1964–91, the average length of time for which a cabinet minister headed a department was two-and -a-half years; in the Labour Government between 1997 and 2010, it was not much over a year. This rapid turnaround has only been exacerbated by successive changes in prime minister and changes in policy direction over Brexit. Few ministers bring to their departments an appropriate specialised knowledge and few remain long enough to acquire it. The National School of Government provides induction seminars for new ministers and specific training courses for ministers (e.g., on working with select committees and on public communications).

It is impossible for a departmental minister to be kept informed in detail about the immense and multifarious activity of a modern government department or to take the management of the department's business into his or her own hands. Overloaded ministers rely greatly on their permanent secretaries and other senior officials in the running of their departments, but a managerially minded minister may take a close interest in the department's organisational structure and decision-making processes. Ministers in the Thatcher administration were encouraged to adopt a managerial role, but it is questionable whether ministers in general have the aptitude, experience or inclination for departmental management. Christopher Foster and Francis Plowden observe (*The State Under Stress* (1996), p. 177) that if efficiency and the control of public expenditure are to be achieved:

> then the civil service is a more hopeful instrument of such changes than politicians can ever be. They are in a better position to retain and restore old notions of good administration and civil service management, at the same time as learning to manage contracts and agencies as efficiently as the best private-sector management, because they have a long-term interest in government.
>
> But the price of achieving such levels of efficiency is that the role of the minister must be limited.

Ministers, these authors say (p. 246), must have 'more time to focus on those things ... for which they are most needed – leadership, policy-making and persuasion'. (See also Foster, *British Government in Crisis* (2005), pp. 205–6.) The lightening of ministers' workloads was one objective of the devolution of operational management to executive agencies within the departments, a reform initiated in 1988 and now an established feature of departmental organisation (see, further, below).

In developing policies and reviewing the work of the department, a minister has the help of subordinate ministers, parliamentary private secretaries, senior officials and possibly one or more special policy advisers brought in from outside government (see, further, below). Ministers heading the departments decide how they can best be run, but since 2005 have been required to establish corporate management boards to provide a collective, strategic leadership of the department and management of its performance. The *Ministerial Code* 2019 provides (para 3.5):

> Secretaries of State should chair their departmental board. Boards should comprise other Ministers, senior officials, a Lead Non-Executive and non-executive board members, (largely drawn from the commercial private sector and appointed by the Secretary of State in

> accordance with Cabinet Office guidelines). The remit of the board should be performance
> and delivery, and to provide the strategic leadership of the department.

(Further details about the purpose, composition and work of these 'enhanced departmental boards' are given in a protocol accessible on the Cabinet Office website.)

Collective ministerial responsibility for the whole of government policy entitles each cabinet minister to claim a share in general policy-making, including policies on important issues emerging from other departments. But ministers immersed in the 'urgent minutiae' of departmental life (Barbara Castle, *The Castle Diaries, 1974–76* (1980), p. 523) seldom have time to inform themselves adequately about extra-departmental matters. When these arise in cabinet or cabinet committee, departmental ministers may simply remain passive, or else take positions urged on them previously by ministerial colleagues, or follow briefs prepared by their own civil servants. Some ministers are more assertive and try to take a full part in government policy-making. Whether they are able to do so will depend on their standing with their colleagues and the prime minister, their membership of the inner cabinet, if there is one, and of relevant cabinet committees, and their ability to limit their involvement in departmental administration by delegating responsibility to subordinate ministers. There is, however, a continuing problem of 'ministerial overload' which diminishes the effectiveness of their role in government. (See Laughrin (2009) 80 *Pol Q* 339. Departmental management boards may doubtless be of some help in this respect: see above.) The Chancellor of the Exchequer is in a special position as, being responsible for public expenditure, he or she is bound to take a close interest in the policies and spending decisions of other ministers. It is a convention that no departmental expenditure can properly be incurred without the approval of the Treasury, and the chancellor, as a former holder of the office has remarked, 'has his finger in pretty well every pie in government' (Nigel Lawson, *The View from No 11* (1993 edn.), p. 273). In the Blair Government (1997–2007), then Chancellor Gordon Brown was able, from his power base in the Treasury, to exert a potent influence in many areas of domestic policy.

By convention, some kinds of decision are taken on the personal responsibility of the minister concerned, without engaging the collective responsibility of ministerial colleagues. This applies, for instance, to decisions of the Home Secretary in extradition cases. (See HL Deb vol. 606, col 185WA, 11 November 1999.)

In principle, all secretaries of state and other cabinet ministers are equal in status, although there is an informal ranking of them by the prime minister. Sometimes, a minister is designated as first Secretary of State, and the prime minister may nominate a deputy prime minister (e.g., Whitelaw, 1979–88; Howe, 1989–90; Heseltine, 1995–97). Mr John Prescott was given the title of Deputy Prime Minister in 1997 and, from 2001 to 2007, held office as Deputy

Prime Minister and First Secretary of State. In the Coalition Government formed in 2010, Mr Nick Clegg took office as Deputy Prime Minister and Lord President of the Council. His responsibilities were specified as follows in the Cabinet Office's *List of Ministerial Responsibilities* (July 2010):

> The Deputy Prime Minister, the Lord President of the Council, is the deputy head of Government with special responsibility for political and constitutional reform:
>
> - Introducing fixed term Parliaments
> - Legislating to hold a referendum on the Alternative Vote system for the House of Commons and to create fewer and more equal sized constituencies
> - Supporting people with disabilities to become MPs
> - Introducing a power for people to recall their MP
> - Developing proposals for a wholly or mainly elected second chamber
> - Speeding up implementation of individual voter registration
> - Considering the 'West Lothian question' [see pp. 316–318 above]
> - Introducing a statutory register of lobbyists
> - Reforming party funding
> - Supporting all postal primaries
>
> The Deputy Prime Minister also has policy responsibility for the Electoral Commission, Boundary Commission and Independent Parliamentary Standards Authority.

In answer to a question in the House of Commons, Mr Clegg outlined his ministerial responsibilities as follows (HC Deb vol. 512, col 148, 22 June 2010):

> As Deputy Prime Minister, I support the Prime Minister in the oversight of the full range of Government policy and initiatives. I have taken particular responsibilities for co-ordinating the Government's domestic policies through my chairmanship of the Cabinet Sub-Committee on home affairs. Within the Government, I am responsible for our ambitious programme of political and constitutional reform, supported in this House by my colleague the Parliamentary Secretary, Cabinet Office . . .

A deputy prime minister may act on behalf of the prime minister during his or her illness or absence, answering in the House of Commons for the whole government, but has no entitlement to be appointed prime minister if that office becomes vacant. (See Brazier [1988] *PL* 176; Hennessy, *The Hidden Wiring* (1996), pp. 14–19.) The current Johnson Government does not include a deputy prime minister. This became a potential issue when the incumbent Prime Minister, Boris Johnson, was unable to work, having contracted Covid-19, leading to his hospitalisation. In those extraordinary circumstances, a range of cabinet ministers, some of whom also fell ill with Covid-19, stood in for the prime minister, particularly to deliver daily briefings on the pandemic.

6.3.1.1 Conduct of Ministers

A rulebook, formerly called *Questions of Procedure for Ministers* and updated from time to time under successive prime ministers, was, from the middle of the twentieth century, issued to ministers on their appointment. It set out guidelines on a variety of questions of cabinet procedure and ministerial conduct and was described, with a dash of hyperbole, as 'the nearest thing we have to a written constitution for British Cabinet government' (Hennessy, *Cabinet* (1986), p. 7). This document was formerly withheld from the public and classified as confidential. The 1992 edition was released into the public domain; the heavens did not fall. Anxieties about the standards of conduct of ministers and other public servants led to the setting up in 1994 of the Nolan Committee on Standards in Public Life. (See Peter Hennessy's racy account of the Nolan Inquiry: *The Hidden Wiring* (1996), ch. 8.) In its *1st Report* (Cm 2850-I/1995) the committee recommended the revision and strengthening of *Questions of Procedure for Ministers*. The amended document, now entitled the *Ministerial Code*, is reissued, with whatever revisions are considered necessary, on the authority of each succeeding prime minister. The *Code* does not have the force of law but ministers are expected to be guided by its principles and 'to behave in a way that upholds the highest standards of propriety' (*Ministerial Code* (2019), para 1.1). The *Code* is to be read (para 1.3):

against the background of the overarching duty on Ministers to comply with the law and to protect the integrity of public life.

Ministers are expected to observe the 'Seven Principles of Public Life' set out on p. 14 of the *1st Report* of the Nolan Committee and in Annex A to the Code, under the headings: selflessness; integrity; objectivity; accountability; openness; honesty; leadership. More specifically, the Code lists ten principles of conduct that ministers are directed to observe: these are set out at p. 218 above.

The *Code* declares that it 'provides guidance to Ministers on how they should act and arrange their affairs' in order to uphold the required standards and that (para 1.6):

Ministers are personally responsible for deciding how to act and conduct themselves in the light of the Code and for justifying their actions and conduct to Parliament and the public.

Then it is added:

Ministers only remain in office for so long as they retain the confidence of the Prime Minister. He is the ultimate judge of the standards of behaviour expected of a Minister and the appropriate consequences of a breach of those standards.

The *Code* is a prime-ministerial document in the sense that successive prime ministers make alterations to it on their own authority, although, in practice, after some consultation with ministerial colleagues and senior officials. Reports of the Committee on Standards in Public Life and the Select Committee on Public Administration have also contributed to the *Code*'s form and content. The *Code* has a hybrid nature, setting out prime-ministerial instructions and practical guidance that may be varied from time to time, but also reaffirming principles of good government and conventions of a binding character (relating for instance to ministerial accountability to Parliament). It exemplifies, as Peter Hennessy has remarked ('Introduction', in Amy Baker, *Prime Ministers and the Rule Book* (2000)):

> the 'coral-reef' nature of much of British constitutional practice – how a cluster of guidelines can grow and harden, first into expectations, then into conventions and ultimately into a code if not quite into a fully-fledged constitutional artefact.

That the *Ministerial Code* should be 'the Prime Minister's property' has been deplored as a 'constitutional anomaly' with disturbing implications for the accountability of prime minister and ministers alike: 'There is an urgent need to find a proper guardian for the code' (Blick, Byrne and Weir, 'Democratic Audit' (2005) 58 *Parl Aff* 408, 415). This is particularly problematic given the extent to which the prime minister's foreword to the code may be used for political purposes, rather than focusing predominantly on the need to uphold ministerial standards. The most recent foreword by Boris Johnson, for example, starts by setting out that:

> The mission of this Government is to deliver Brexit on 31st October for the purpose of uniting and re-energising our whole United Kingdom and making this country the greatest place on earth.

After referring to the standards set out in the code, including 'no breach of collective responsibility' the foreword adds:

> Crucially, there must be no delay – and no misuse of process or procedure by any individual Minister that would seek to stall the collective decisions necessary to deliver Brexit and secure the wider changes needed across our United Kingdom.

The Public Administration Committee joined in the call for an investigatory machinery that would be 'manifestly independent of the Executive' (*7th Report of 2005–06*, HC 1457, paras 21–25). In response, the government agreed to the appointment of an independent adviser on ministers' interests with the duty of investigating alleged breaches of the *Code* when requested by the prime minister to do so. The adviser publishes an annual report that is laid before Parliament. The holder of the post of independent adviser is a personal appointment by the prime minister. It is for the prime minister to decide whether an investigation by the adviser is necessary and what should be the consequences of a finding that the *Code* has been breached. There has been some controversy surrounding when the prime minister fails to refer a minister for investigation by the independent advisor (see the report of the Public Administration Select Committee *The Prime Minister's Adviser on Ministers Interests: Independent or Not?* 2010–2012, HC 1761 and the committee's account of the government's response, 2012–2013, HC 976). Even more worrying is the modification of paragraph 1.4 of the Ministerial Code (discussed in Chapter 3), replacing a duty to refer ministers to the independent advisor, when the prime minister feels this warrants an investigation, with a discretionary power to refer the minister either to the independent advisor or to the Cabinet Office.

Similar codes have been adopted in Scotland and Wales: the code for Wales must be approved by the Welsh National Assembly. Provision for a *Ministerial Code* for Northern Ireland was made by section 28A of the Northern Ireland Act 1998: ministers are required to act in accordance with its provisions.

What might be done to strengthen the effectiveness of the *Ministerial Code*? (Cf. the Public Administration Committee's *9th Special Report of 2007–08*, HC 1056.)

6.3.1.2 Ministerial Solidarity

The convention of collective ministerial responsibility obliges ministers to support and defend the policies and decisions of the government to which they belong; the conventional rule is reaffirmed in para 2.3 of the *Ministerial Code* (2019): 'Decisions reached by the Cabinet or Ministerial Committees are binding on all members of the Government.' In para 2.1, it said:

> The principle of collective responsibility requires that Ministers should be able to express their views frankly in the expectation that they can argue freely in private while maintaining a united front when decisions have been reached. This in turn requires that the privacy of opinions expressed in Cabinet and Ministerial Committees, including in correspondence, should be maintained.

The classic or strict version of the principle requires a minister to resign from office if he or she feels bound to express public dissent from government policies.

The principle of collective solidarity began as a political expedient for countering the authority of the king and managing Parliament; it was fortified by the development of party cohesion in the nineteenth century. Lord Salisbury gave his emphatic endorsement to the principle in 1878:

> **House of Lords, 8 April 1878 (Parl Deb 3rd series vol. 239, cols 833-4)**
>
> **Lord Salisbury:** Now, my Lords, am I not defending a great Constitutional principle, when I say that, for all that passes in a Cabinet, each Member of it who does not resign is absolutely and irretrievably responsible, and that he has no right afterwards to say that he agreed in one case to a compromise, while in another he was persuaded by one of his Colleagues. Consider the inconvenience which will arise if such a great Constitutional law is not respected ... It is, I maintain, only on the principle that absolute responsibility is undertaken by every Member of a Cabinet who, after a decision is arrived at, remains a Member of it, that the joint responsibility of Ministers to Parliament can be upheld, and one of the most essential conditions of Parliamentary responsibility established.

The principle is in the interest of the government, which is able to present a united front against the opposition. In this respect, it seems to be essentially a feature of the party political system, and we find that a similar convention is observed by the opposition, whose frontbench spokesmen are expected to uphold opposition party policies. But it can also be claimed that the convention has a wider 'constitutional' function, in that it makes for coherent and accountable government and the loyalty of ministers to policies that have been approved by the electorate. It is the collective responsibility of ministers that 'welds the separate functions of Government into a single Administration' (Peter Hennessy, *The Hidden Wiring* (1996), p. 102, quoting from an internal government document).

The obligation of ministerial solidarity is most convincingly justified in principle if governmental decisions are reached collectively. One Home Office minister (Mike O'Brien) expressed this in saying (Standing Committee B on the Freedom of Information Bill, 27 January 2000, cols 323–4) that collective responsibility:

> is the bedrock of the Government, of whichever party. It is a safeguard under our constitution that any Minister who makes a decision or speaks on behalf of a Department or the Government as a whole requires the collective consent of other Ministers to make that statement, propound the policy or deliver that decision ... That protection, which is for the citizen as well, must be ensured.

Ministers who have contributed to a decision are properly required to support and defend it. In a modern government, it is, however, impossible for all ministers to take part in all decisions: most questions must necessarily be decided in cabinet or a ministerial committee of the cabinet or within government departments or by interdepartmental discussion. These decisions must be accepted as having been taken on behalf of the government as a whole. Nevertheless, a principle of collective decision-making is embedded in our governmental system. All major departments are represented in the cabinet by the departmental minister, and ministers whose responsibilities are affected will generally be members of the relevant ministerial committee. The flexibility of the conventional arrangements does, however, allow for a less collegiate style of decision-making through informal networks, unacknowledged ad hoc groups and bilateral exchanges between an interventionist prime minister and departmental ministers. In these circumstances, ministerial solidarity may serve merely to strengthen the position of the prime minister or a cabal of senior ministers. A government that practises collective decision-making to the greatest extent that is feasible has the strongest claim on individual ministers to give their loyal support to the decisions reached.

Questions of ministerial solidarity were severely tested in the Westland affair of 1985–6. Political arguments about rescue plans for the Westland helicopter company culminated in 1986 in the resignation of two senior ministers, in circumstances that raised questions about the conventions of ministerial responsibility. For the present, we shall consider the significance of these events in the context of governmental decision-making and the collective responsibility (solidarity) of ministers. (Individual ministerial responsibility is considered in Chapter 9.)

The question at issue was whether Westland plc, a principal supplier of helicopters to the Ministry of Defence, should resolve its financial difficulties through an association with the American company Sikorsky or instead with a consortium of European companies, the British Government participating, in either event, in the reconstruction 'package'. The government's policy was that the choice between Sikorsky and the European consortium was a matter for the Westland Board, the government itself adopting a neutral position. Michael Heseltine, Secretary of State for Defence, came to favour the 'European' solution, and took an active part in fostering a proposal from the European consortium and in publicly urging that the national interest favoured its acceptance. In this, as a parliamentary select committee afterwards observed, he was 'pursuing a policy which was diametrically opposed to the Government's stated policy' (Defence Committee, *4th Report of 1985–86*, HC 519, para 105). The prime minister might have required his resignation on this ground, but did not do so.

Mr Heseltine did, however, resign in January 1986, after a meeting of the cabinet at which it was decided that ministers' statements on the subject of Westland should first be submitted to the Cabinet Office for clearance as being consistent with the government's policy. Mr Heseltine was unable to accept this ruling and afterwards declared that he had resigned because there had been a 'breakdown of constitutional government', in that the prime minister had frustrated collective consideration of the Westland issue, refusing to allow it to be discussed in cabinet and cancelling a ministerial meeting that had been arranged to deal with the matter. (The government's account of these events differed from Mr Heseltine's.) Peter Hennessy remarks on this affair that:

'Each side claimed the other was breaking the rules. Both sides were right' (Minogue and Biddiss (eds.), *Thatcherism: Personality and Politics* (1987), p. 66).

(See also Hennessy, *Cabinet* (1986), pp. 106–11; Marshall, 'Cabinet Government and the Westland Affair' [1986] *PL* 184; Oliver and Austin, 'Political and Constitutional Aspects of the Westland Affair' (1987) 40 *Parl Aff* 20.)

Dissension within government was again dramatically displayed in October 1989, when Chancellor of the Exchequer Nigel Lawson resigned from the office he had held for six years and from the government. Mr Lawson believed that his position had been undermined by differences on questions of economic policy between him and Prime Minister Thatcher, who was disposed to follow the counsel of her economic adviser, Sir Alan Walters, whose opinions (publicly expressed) on some important matters of policy were in opposition to those of the chancellor. In his resignation letter to the prime minister, Mr Lawson declared:

> The successful conduct of economic policy is possible only if there is, and is seen to be, full agreement between the Prime Minister and the Chancellor of the Exchequer. Recent events have confirmed that this essential requirement cannot be satisfied so long as Alan Walters remains your personal economic adviser. I have therefore regretfully concluded that it is in the best interests of the Government for me to resign my office without further ado.

Speaking in the House of Commons on 31 October 1989, Mr Lawson said (HC Deb vol. 159, col 208):

> [F]or our system of Cabinet government to work effectively, the Prime Minister of the day must appoint Ministers whom he or she trusts and then leave them to carry out the policy. When differences of view emerge, as they are bound to do from time to time, they should be resolved privately and, whenever appropriate, collectively.

The strains and fissures in collective, cabinet government in the later days of Mrs Thatcher's premiership were once more to be exposed in the resignation of the Deputy Prime Minister, Sir Geoffrey Howe, in November 1990. Deploring the prime minister's role in the conduct of monetary policy in Europe, he observed in his resignation letter that 'Cabinet government is all about trying to persuade one another from within', adding in his resignation speech that it had become futile 'to pretend that there was a common policy when every step forward risked being subverted by some casual comment or impulsive answer' by the prime minister (HC Deb vol. 180, col 465, 13 November 1990). These resignations contributed to the eventual resignation of Mrs Thatcher herself: see, further, below.

Tony Blair as Prime Minister had a commanding style of leadership and placed a strong emphasis on ministerial unity. A revisionist approach to traditional, 'old Labour' policies and priorities in his first term did not cause serious disaffection at the centre of government or the resignations of senior ministers. The first resignation from the new Labour Government on the ground of policy disagreement was that of Malcolm Chisholm, a Parliamentary Secretary, in 1997 over the reduction of benefits for lone parents. Another junior minister, Peter Kilfoyle, resigned in 2000, disapproving what he saw as the government's disregard of traditional Labour supporters in the regions and their concerns. A more serious reaction was provoked by the military intervention in Iraq in 2003, which led to the resignations of two senior ministers, Robin Cook (President of the Council and Leader of the House of Commons) and Clare Short (Secretary of State for International Development). The former could not support the government's decision to embark on military action without specific authorisation in a United Nations Security Council Resolution. (Two subordinate ministers resigned on the same principle.) Subsequently, Ms Short resigned on the ground of the government's failure to seek a UN mandate authorising the measures necessary for the establishment of a legitimate government in Iraq. She also expressed concerns about the style and organisation of government, in particular a concentration of power in the hands of the prime minister and the downgrading of collective cabinet government. (See Clare Short's resignation statement: HC Deb vol. 505, cols 36–9, 12 May 2003. In her book, *An Honourable Deception?* (2004), p. 71, she remarks that: 'The term collective responsibility is now being used to demand loyalty to decisions on which Cabinet members were not consulted, let alone that were [not] reached collectively.')

There was again a complaint of failure of collective government in the Brown premiership, although in less dramatic circumstances, when Caroline Flint, Minister of State and Minister for Europe in the Foreign and Commonwealth Office, resigned on the stated ground of Mr Brown's 'failure to have an inclusive government', saying that his was 'a two-tier government' and that few were 'allowed into your inner circle' (resignation letter, 5 June 2009).

With respect to cabinet ministers, Christopher Foster has written (*British Government in Crisis* (2005), p. 282):

Solidarity is an important characteristic of a well-functioning Cabinet. While Cabinet ministers must recognise that practicality does not permit all to be involved in every Cabinet decision, all need enough involvement and trust in the system not to think they are being misled.

Whatever its utility, the convention of collective responsibility, if strictly observed, exacts its price. By stifling open dissent, it contributes to secrecy in government: questions of public importance that may be strongly contested between ministers are not aired in a way that enables public opinion to be expressed before decisions are reached – the argument goes on behind the screen of collective responsibility. Also, since the convention extends to all ministers (not only those in the cabinet) and even, if in a weaker form, to parliamentary private secretaries to ministers, some 130 or more MPs on the government side are expected to give unqualified support to government policies as a condition of retaining their positions. In this way, the convention helps to strengthen the government's control over Parliament.

In practice, however, prime ministers often find it impolitic to insist on a strict observance of the obligations of ministerial solidarity. Indeed, on a few occasions the convention has been formally suspended, with a publicly announced 'agreement to differ' on some issue of importance. A famous instance of this occurred in 1932. The National Government, constituted the year before under Ramsay MacDonald to deal with a financial crisis, proposed to introduce tariffs; four cabinet ministers, convinced free-traders, were unable to agree. In the emergency, it was considered important to keep the government together, so a compromise was reached by which the dissenting ministers were allowed to speak and vote against tariffs, while remaining in the government. This arrangement has been regarded with disfavour by most writers on the constitution. Jennings described it as 'an attempt to break down the party system and to substitute government by individuals for government by political principles' (*Cabinet Government* (3rd edn. 1959), p. 281). In 1975, there was again an agreement to differ, on the issue of United Kingdom membership of the European Communities. The Labour Government had decided to submit the question of continued membership (on the terms renegotiated by the government) to a referendum and to recommend the electorate to vote for remaining in the community. Seven cabinet ministers who dissented from the government's recommendation were allowed to oppose it in the referendum campaign.

House of Commons, 23 January 1975 (HC Deb vol. 884, col 1746)

The Prime Minister (Mr Harold Wilson): ... When the outcome of renegotiation is known, the Government will decide upon their own recommendation to the country, whether for continued membership of the Community on the basis of the renegotiated terms, or for withdrawal, and will announce their decision to the House in due course ...

The circumstances of this referendum are unique, and the issue to be decided is one on which strong views have long been held which cross party lines. The Cabinet has, therefore, decided that, if when the time comes there are members of the Government, including members of the Cabinet, who do not feel able to accept and support the Government's recommendation, whatever it may be, they will, once the recommendation has been announced, be free to support and speak in favour of a different conclusion in the referendum campaign.

House of Commons, 7 April 1975 (HC Deb vol. 889, col 351W)

The Prime Minister: In accordance with my statement in the House on 23rd January last, those Ministers who do not agree with the Government's recommendation in favour of continued membership of the European Community are, in the unique circumstances of the referendum, now free to advocate a different view during the referendum campaign in the country.

This freedom does not extend to parliamentary proceedings and official business. Government business in Parliament will continue to be handled by all Ministers in accordance with Government policy. Ministers responsible for European aspects of Government business who themselves differ from the Government's recommendation on membership of the European Community will state the Government's position and will not be drawn into making points against the Government recommendation. Wherever necessary Questions will be transferred to other Ministers. At meetings of the Council of Ministers of the European Community and at other Community meetings, the United Kingdom position in all fields will continue to reflect Government policy.

I have asked all Ministers to make their contributions to the public campaign in terms of issues, to avoid personalising or trivialising the argument, and not to allow themselves to appear in direct confrontation, on the same platform or programme, with another Minister who takes a different view on the Government recommendation.

This arrangement helped to keep the government together. But was it also in the public interest?

In 1977, collective responsibility was again suspended to allow dissenting ministers to vote against the principle of the European Assembly Elections Bill – which provided, in accordance with government policy, for direct elections to the European Parliament – at its second reading. Questioned in the House of Commons about collective responsibility, Prime Minister Callaghan replied (HC Deb vol. 933, col 552, 16 June 1977):

I certainly think that the doctrine should apply, except in cases where I announce that it does not.

This was brusquely said and has been cited as a cynical disregard of constitutional proprieties. But we must ask with Marshall (*Constitutional Conventions: The Rules and Forms of Political Accountability* (1986), p. 8) whether it does 'represent a breach of any constitutional duty to the House of Commons if freedom to speak or vote against cabinet policy [is] willingly conceded by the Cabinet to individual Cabinet Ministers?' The 2010 version of the *Ministerial Code* formally acknowledged that the obligations of collective responsibility may be explicitly set aside (para 2.1: see above). This qualification of the principle of ministerial solidarity was in accordance with provisions of the Conservative/Liberal Democrat Coalition agreement (*The Coalition: Our Programme for Government*, May 2010) which allowed Liberal Democrat ministers openly to oppose, or argue for alternatives to, policies adopted by the government or to abstain in Parliament on implementing measures in relation to a number of issues such as the renewal of Trident, the construction of new nuclear power stations, tax allowances for married couples and higher education funding. The two parties would be permitted to take different sides in the referendum campaign on the alternative vote system. A report by the Institute for Government (*United We Stand? Coalition Government in the UK*, 2010) comments as follows:

> Such developments may have the . . . benefit of helping to foster a more 'grown up' political culture in which the pretence that members of a Cabinet must agree on all matters at all times is dropped, and a degree of public debate among ministers is accepted as a normal part of politics.

In a similar manner, the convention of collective responsibility was suspended by the then Prime Minister, David Cameron, prior to the Brexit referendum on the UK's continued membership of the EU (Hansard HC Deb vol. 604, col 28, 5 January 2016).

> It is the nature of a referendum that it is the people, not the politicians, who decide, and as I indicated before Christmas, there will be a clear Government position, but it will be open to individual Ministers to take a different personal position while remaining part of the Government. Ultimately, it will be for the British people to decide this country's future by voting in or out of a reformed European Union in the referendum.

Formal suspensions of the convention have been rare, but a more commonplace and frequent mitigation of collective responsibility is provided by the 'unattributable ministerial leak'. The current version of the *Ministerial Code* does not include the exception to the principle of collective ministerial responsibility, explaining that the principle applies 'save where it is explicitly set aside'. Moreover, Boris Johnson draws attention to this principle in his foreword, stating that there 'must be . . . no breach of collective responsibility'. This suggests that the current prime minister wishes to reverse the trend of suspending collective responsibility.

Patrick Gordon Walker, *The Cabinet* (rev edn. 1972), pp. 33-4, 35, 38-9

The unattributable leak involves the disclosure of . . . matters that are secret only because of the doctrine of collective responsibility – such as the subject of Cabinet discussion, Cabinet decisions, views assigned to different Ministers and the like. The leak gives information known only to members of the Cabinet; being unattributable, it does not breach the doctrine that Ministers do not attack one another in public.

An element of concealment was inherent in the very concept of collective responsibility. The doctrine that the Cabinet must appear to be united presupposed Cabinet divisions that had not been reconciled. Ministers must in the nature of things have differences but they must outwardly appear to have none. Collective responsibility must therefore to some extent be a mask worn by the Cabinet.

The self-same conditions of mass democracy that gave rise to collective responsibility produced the unattributable leak. The maintenance of secrecy imposed by the doctrine became intolerable. This for two main reasons.

First, Ministers were political creatures living in a political world. As party leaders they accepted the need for the doctrine of collective responsibility: but as political creatures they felt it sometimes necessary to let their political views be unofficially known.

Secondly, the Press began to try and tear away the mask from the face of the Cabinet: their readers became increasingly interested in being informed about 'secrets' that were felt to be of a political and not a security nature . . . From [the 1880s] the unattributable leak became a feature of the Cabinet system. The main motives for leaks by Ministers became the desire to inform – or to mislead – their followers in the Parliamentary party about the stand they had taken in the Cabinet on a particular issue; or the attempt to mobilize party or public opinion behind a view that was being argued in Cabinet . . .

Thus the doctrine of collective responsibility and the unattributable leak grew up side by side as an inevitable feature of the Cabinet in a mass two-party system. In every Cabinet the leak will be deplored and condemned; but it is paradoxically necessary to the preservation of the doctrine of collective responsibility. It is the mechanism by which the doctrine of collective responsibility is reconciled with political reality. The unattributable leak is itself a recognition and acceptance of the doctrine that members of a Cabinet do not disagree in public.

Brian Harrison (*The Transformation of British Politics 1860–1995* (1996), p. 291) remarks that during the Thatcher cabinets 'a competitive leaking to the press was part of the weaponry deployed by "wets" and "dries" in their battle for control over policy'. What Harrison calls 'the art of competitive leaking' continued to be displayed in John Major's Government, which was said to have become 'as leaky as a sieve' (Kenneth Clarke, cited by Peter Hennessy, *The Prime Minister* (2000), p. 445), and did not diminish after Labour took office in 1997.

Leaking is practised by prime ministers as well as by other members of the cabinet. If a necessary palliative of collective responsibility, it makes little contribution to open government: leaked information is notoriously unreliable and at its worst the practice is a technique for misleading the public (see Cockerell, Hennessy and Walker, *Sources Close to the Prime Minister* (1984), ch. 7). A.P. Tant ('"Leaks" and the Nature of British Government' (1995) 66 *Pol Q* 197) regards leaks as a reflection of the pathology of British government, which he sees as being deficient in both responsibility and efficiency. Tant distinguishes the 'deliberate unauthorised' leak and the 'authorised but unacknowledged' leak. The former kind, while 'constitutionally irresponsible', may sometimes be in the national interest: Tant gives the example of information about the inadequacy of Britain's air defences leaked to Winston Churchill in the 1930s. Of the latter kind, Tant writes:

> It is a well-known and accepted part of British political life that from time to time political adversaries use 'authorised but unacknowledged' leaks to discredit or undermine each other's policies. Equally, government uses this strategy to 'fly kites' – in instances where a potentially contentious policy proposal may find its way into the public arena first via a leak. If the public reaction is particularly hostile, government is able to argue that it never had any intention of implementing this particular policy; it was merely part of the discussions surrounding possible options. If, on the other hand, there is a muted response, government knows it is relatively 'safe' to proceed with the policy. Whatever the outcome, it is clear that this tactic in fact compromises the principles of responsible government.

Christopher Foster (above, p. 282) has written: 'A Cabinet that has insufficient understanding of its collective interest not to leak will sooner or later be destroyed.'

It happens from time to time that a minister flouts convention by disagreeing in public with government policy. This may result in his or her dismissal. When a junior naval minister made a speech in 1981 criticising the government's proposed reduction of the surface fleet, he was promptly dismissed by Mrs Thatcher, who said: 'Ministers should fight departmental battles within the Department and not outside' (HC Deb vol. 5, col 151, 19 May 1981). But sometimes the breach results in nothing more than a prime-ministerial rebuke or is simply overlooked. In 1974, after a minister of state had publicly criticised a government decision to complete the delivery of warships to a tyrannical regime in Chile, then Prime Minister Harold Wilson was asked in the House of Commons to say what his policy was with regard to collective responsibility. He replied (HC Deb vol. 873, col 1103, 14 May 1974):

> All members of the Government share a collective responsibility for the policies of Her Majesty's Government. I have recently reminded my right hon and hon Friends in the

administration that, where any conflict of loyalties arises, the principle of the collective responsibility of the Government is absolute and overriding in all circumstances.

Dissenting ministers sometimes choose to resign in emphatic repudiation of government policy, and, in these instances, we seem to see the convention of collective responsibility dramatically confirmed. When Ian Gow, a Minister of State at the Treasury, resigned in protest against the signing of the Anglo-Irish Agreement in November 1985, he said in his resignation letter: 'I cannot support this change of policy; it follows that I cannot remain in your Government.' Instances of resignation in dissent from government policy have been given above, but resignation (like dismissal) is by no means automatic in the event of serious policy disagreement or even an open breach of ministerial solidarity and is often a matter of political calculation; in this respect, it appears that we are dealing with an 'optional convention' (Madgwick, in Herman and Alt (eds.), *Cabinet Studies: A Reader* (1975), p. 98).

Dissent among cabinet ministers is nowadays often revealed to the public in one way or another, and ministerial solidarity is less strictly insisted on than formerly. The dilution of the convention has alarmed some observers. Nevil Johnson discerned a 'retreat into constitutional anarchy' if collective responsibility could at any time be waived by the prime minister, and expressed the sombre belief that 'our constitution has atrophied to a point at which it expresses only one principle, namely that any rule or convention thought to be part of it may be suspended or evaded if the government of the day believes that this is required for the sake of holding together the party in power' (letter to *The Times*, 22 June 1977). But an inflexible insistence on ministerial solidarity is not manifestly for the public good, and its relaxation might contribute to more open and honest government and better informed public debate. Political controversy often takes place *within* rather than *between* the political parties – especially when there is a consensus on particular policies between the party leaderships – and collective responsibility may confine or even effectively suppress this necessary conflict.

Anthony Wedgwood Benn, 'Democracy in the Age of Science' (1979) 50 *Pol Q* 7, 18–19

[T]he constitutional convention of collective Cabinet responsibility which is thought to be central to the working of the British Constitution has considerable implications for secrecy of government. Under this doctrine the myth of Cabinet unity on all matters discussed is fostered. Cabinets are, of course, rarely united in their views. Indeed, were it so there would be no Cabinet discussion at all . . .

Common sense and ordinary personal loyalty must require defeated minorities to accept the majority decision and to explain and defend it. But there is no reason whatsoever why this necessary and sensible principle should be extended to the necessarily false pretence

> that no alternative policies were considered, no real debate took place, and that everyone present was convinced of the merits of the majority view – as distinct from accepting that it was the majority view and that as such it should be supported. The narrow interpretation of collective Cabinet responsibility denies citizens essential knowledge of the processes by which their government reaches its decisions.

A similar view was expressed by Lord Falconer, a former Lord Chancellor, who was reported in *The Times*, 2 June 2009 as saying that collective responsibility 'needed radical overhaul so that dissenting ministers could voice concerns during debate before a final policy decision'. (Such open dissent would, no doubt, be enthusiastically exploited by opposition parties. Does this matter?)

6.3.2 The Prime Minister

The office of prime minister is the creation of convention, and the role and powers of the prime minister still depend mainly on convention and political circumstances. In the course of a reply to a parliamentary question about the extent of his powers, the then Prime Minister Tony Blair said on 15 October 2001:

> The Prime Minister's roles as the head of Her Majesty's Government, her principal adviser and as Chairman of the Cabinet are not . . . defined in legislation. These roles, including the exercise of powers under the royal prerogative, have evolved over many years, drawing on convention and usage, and it is not possible precisely to define them.

Few powers are vested in the prime minister by statute – the office is barely acknowledged in legislation – but like other ministers, although with a preeminent authority, the prime minister may make use of prerogative powers that have devolved on ministers or are exercised by the sovereign only on ministerial advice. A number of public appointments are made directly by the prime minister (e.g., of the interception of communications commissioner, the intelligence services commissioner and surveillance commissioners: see the Regulation of Investigatory Powers Act 2000, sections 57(1) and 59(1) and the Police Act 1997, section 91(1)) and many others are made by the sovereign on prime-ministerial advice: these include government ministers, the cabinet secretary, the Civil Service commissioners and the parliamentary ombudsman. The prime minister's primary role, as Blick and Jones say (*Premiership* (2010), p. 137), is that of public leadership. Other ministers will often be expected to consult the prime minister about the exercise of powers vested in them, especially if public controversy is likely to be caused.

Legislation surrounding the Brexit process has also placed specific requirements on the prime minister, mostly to ensure that the prime minister acts so as to avoid a 'no deal' exit from the European Union. For example, the European Union (Withdrawal) Act 2019, section 1(4), states that 'the Prime Minister must seek an extension' to the Article 50 TEU negotiation period following a motion of the house in favour of an extension to the Article 50 period. The European Union (Withdrawal) (No 2) Act 2019 goes further. It states that the 'Prime Minister must seek to obtain from the European Council an extension of the period under Article 50(3) of the Treaty on European Union' if, by 19 October, there has been neither a resolution of the House of Commons accepting the Withdrawal Agreement, or to agree to leave the EU on 31 October 2019 with no deal. An appendix to the legislation set out the wording of the letter that must be sent to the prime minister in order to request an extension until 31 January 2020. Given the failure to fulfil the requirements of this section, Boris Johnson requested an extension until 31 January 2020. However, he did so reluctantly. He sent an unsigned copy of the appendix to the legislation, accompanied with a signed letter from Britain's ambassador to the EU, explaining that the letter was required due to the request of Parliament to seek an extension, and signed letter from the prime minister making it clear that it remained government policy to leave the EU on 31 October 2019, even if this meant leaving with no deal.

It is now an established convention that the prime minister should be a member of the House of Commons. The last peer to hold the office was Lord Salisbury (from 1895 to 1902); the Earl of Home disclaimed his peerage and sought election to the House of Commons when he became Prime Minister in 1963.

The prime minister customarily holds the titular position of First Lord of the Treasury and since 1968 has held the office of Minister for the Civil Service, with another minister exercising day-to-day responsibility. Exceptionally, the prime minister has taken control of a major department, as when Harold Wilson assumed overall responsibility for the Department of Economic Affairs from 1967 to 1968 (but with a Secretary of State in direct charge of the department). In any event, the prime minister has a general authority to intervene in any sphere of government and often takes a leading role in foreign relations – as did Tony Blair – dealing directly with other heads of government. (The prime minister represents the United Kingdom on the European Council, which gives strategic leadership to the European Union: see Chapter 5.) Mrs Thatcher as Prime Minister took a close and assertive interest in the development of economic policy.

John Mackintosh wrote in 1962 that the description of British government simply as 'Cabinet government' had become misleading, for 'the country is governed by the Prime Minister' (*The British Cabinet* (1st edn. 1962), p. 451; see also the 3rd edn. 1977, ch. 20). The description had been made famous by Sir Ivor Jennings' pioneering study, *Cabinet Government* (1936). Richard Crossman agreed with, and developed, this thesis in a vivid manner in *Inside View* (1972), pp. 62–7. Crossman listed the principal conventional powers wielded by a prime minister which enabled him to exert 'when he is successful, a dominating personal control'. In particular, the prime minister: (1) appointed ministers and could sack any minister at any time; (2) decided the agenda of the cabinet; (3) decided on the organisation and membership of cabinet committees and the issues to be put to them; (4) approved appointments of senior civil servants and certain appointments made by ministers to high public office; (5) had personal control of government publicity. The powers identified by Crossman remain in the prime minister's hands at the present day. The list can be extended, for instance to include powers to change the structure of government departments and to formulate and enforce the *Ministerial Code*. (See also Crossman's 'Introduction', in Walter Bagehot, *The English Constitution* (2nd edn. 1964) and note Geoffrey Marshall's critical comments on Crossman's views [1991] *PL* 1.)

Another former Cabinet minister, Tony Benn, emphasised the 'immense concentration of power in the hands of the Prime Minister' and the need to bring it under greater democratic control (*Arguments for Democracy* (1981), ch. 2). In *The Hidden Wiring* (1996), pp. 86–90, Peter Hennessy lists some fifty functions and powers of the prime minister, with a chilling final item:

> Symbolically enough, the last act a British Prime Minister would take is not a matter for the Cabinet but one for the PM alone. The Polaris or Trident missile would erupt from the Atlantic thanks to a prime ministerial decision made by the Premier under the Royal Prerogative in the name of the Queen.

The argument of prime-ministerial dominance seemed to be confirmed by the premiership of Mrs Thatcher, who became Prime Minister in 1979 with the determination to head a 'conviction government' firmly committed to a range of policies on which she herself held strong views. Initially, she was compelled to conciliate and compromise in a cabinet in which those who shared her political outlook were in a minority, but in 1981, she made changes in her ministerial team so as to bring about 'a major shift in the balance of power within the Cabinet' in her favour (King (ed.), *The British Prime Minister* (2nd edn. 1985), p. 105). Moreover, by displacing some important decision-making to informal, ad hoc groups of ministers convened by her, she diminished the role of cabinet, and she intervened more frequently and assertively than most premiers in the business of departmental ministers and in relation to the appointment of senior civil servants. This is not to say that prime-ministerial powers increased under Mrs Thatcher, but she exerted the available powers to the full, thus demonstrating the dominant authority that can be wielded by a prime minister who has a secure political base, a clearly envisaged set of political objectives, single-mindedly pursued, and a determination to act in a leadership role rather than to foster consensus.

Michael Foley, in *The Rise of the British Presidency* (1993), a wide-ranging study of the premiership (in particular that of Mrs Thatcher), discerned profound and lasting changes in the political system that had transformed the prime minister's position. He concluded (p. 263) that:

> it would be no exaggeration to assert that what this country has witnessed over the last generation has been the growing emergence of a British presidency.

Contrariwise, even Mrs Thatcher failed on occasion to get her way, as in June 1989, when she was obliged to agree to terms of entry to the Exchange Rate Mechanism of the European Monetary System, under threats of resignation from the chancellor and the foreign secretary. Moreover, the resignation of Mrs Thatcher in 1990 demonstrated the limits of prime-ministerial power. She survived, initially, resignations of senior cabinet ministers provoked by her ideologically driven policies and authoritarian style of government (characterised by Hugo Young as a 'marked indifference to the normal protocols of collective responsibility': *One of Us* (1993 edn.), p. 196); however, when her leadership came to be seen as damaging to her party's electoral prospects, the support of her ministerial colleagues ebbed away and a party coup brought about her downfall. (See Alderman and Carter, 'A Very Tory Coup: The Ousting of Mrs Thatcher' (1991) 41 *Parl Aff* 125; Brazier, 'The Downfall of Margaret Thatcher' (1991) 54 *MLR* 471.)

Mrs Thatcher's successor, John Major, was of a conciliatory disposition and, as head of a refractory ministerial team, practised a collegial style of governance, not characterised by strong leadership. With Tony Blair, there was a reversion to a 'command and control' premiership (see Peter Hennessy, *The Prime Minister* (2000), ch. 18), with centralised and informal processes of decision-making tending to displace collective discussion in cabinet and cabinet committees. The dominance of Mr Blair and his preference for doing business in small, informal groups of ministers, officials and policy advisers were evident in the period leading up to and during the Iraq conflict of 2003 (see Hennessy, 'Informality and Circumscription: The Blair Style of Government in War and Peace' (2005) 76 *Pol Q* 3). Collective decision-making was displaced by a style of government wryly described by Hennessy as 'sessions on the sofa in the Prime Minister's study': (2005) 58 *Parl Aff* 6, 10. (See, further, Foster, *British Government in Crisis* (2005), ch. 12; Kavanagh, 'The Blair Premiership', in Seldon (ed.), *Blair's Britain 1997–2007* (2007).) The dominant authority exerted by Blair as Prime Minister may seem to support the 'presidential' thesis of British government, but aspects of his premiership would throw doubt on this conclusion. A striking feature of the Blair premiership was the unrelenting competition between him and the Chancellor of the Exchequer, Gordon Brown, who claimed and was to a great extent accorded a leading role in questions of social and economic policy – so much so that commentators have spoken of a dyarchy or duopoly of Blair and Brown. There was, too, some impairment of Blair's governing authority in the later years of his premiership, in the aftermath of the Iraq war. (See, on these matters, Hennessy (2005) 58 *Parl Aff* 6; Bevir and Rhodes, (2006) 54 *Political Studies* 671; Kavanagh, above.)

While it is difficult to refute the conclusion of the House of Lords Constitution Committee (*4th Report of 2009–10*, HL 30, para 96) that 'There has been a trend towards the Prime Minister playing a more dominant role in the UK's political system', the committee acknowledged that this trend has been uneven. The presidential thesis continues to find support (see, e.g., Allen, *The Last Prime Minister* (2nd edn. 2003); Heffernan and Webb, in Poguntke and Webb (eds.), *The Presidentialization of Politics* (2005)), but a less polarised, more shifting constellation of central powers seems closer to the reality.

James Barber, *The Prime Minister Since 1945* (1991), pp. 130–3

The debate on the Prime Minister's power continues and will continue because no absolute conclusions can be drawn. The available evidence is always partial, open to different interpretations and subject to normative judgements (what we believe 'ought to be'). The bold lines of the debate between the advocates of the presidential and chairmanship approaches have advantages, but such approaches can undervalue the shifting pattern of behaviour and the ups and downs of political life, not just between different Prime Ministers but in the experience of each Prime Minister. Three main factors are involved: first the constitutional and political frameworks in which Prime Ministers operate; second, the circumstances that they face; and third, their personality and personal qualities.

The constitutional and political frameworks, Barber reminds us, 'are built on precedent and convention'. These change only slowly and prime ministers 'have to work within the context created by Cabinet and parliamentary government'. The circumstances that face a prime minister, by the same token, 'are constantly changing and are unpredictable', while the personal qualities 'vary markedly between Prime Ministers':

By putting the three factors together – constitutional and political frameworks, circumstance and personality – the picture that emerges is one of fluctuating powers, whereby at some times a Prime Minister may appear to have a presidential-like position, whereas at others he/she is subject to obvious constraints.

In a similar vein, Martin Smith (in Rhodes and Dunleavy (eds.), *Prime Minister, Cabinet and Core Executive* (1995), p. 110) remarks that:

the power of the Prime Minister and the cabinet is not fixed but varies according to the resources available, the rules of the game, administrative ability, political support, political strategies, relationships within the core executive and external circumstances.

(See, further, Smith, *The Core Executive in Britain* (1999), ch. 4; the same author in Rhodes (ed.), *Transforming British Government*, vol. 1 (2000), ch. 2.)

In an illuminating exploration of the theme of prime-ministerial power, Andrew Blick and George Jones challenge the proposition that the premiership has evolved into a dominant British presidency, entailing the extinction of cabinet government, and propose a new interpretation of the office of prime minister. The analysis by these authors of the 'mist-shrouded institution' of the premiership emphasises its flexibility, the varying styles of different prime ministers and the accrual as well as dispersal ('fusion' and 'fission') of powers, functions and staff into and away from the premiership in the course of its history.

Andrew Blick and George Jones, *Premiership: The Development, Nature and Power of the Office of the British Prime Minister* (2010), pp. 199–200

The underlying role of the British premiership is to provide public leadership. This task is its central role and is more important and relatively more resource-consuming within No.10 than anywhere else in Whitehall. After a transitional period in the eighteenth and nineteenth centuries the Prime Minister, in practice, eclipsed the monarch as the most prominent individual supplier of public leadership in the UK, subject to the emerging convention of collective Cabinet supremacy. The manner and means through which leadership is exercised by the office of Prime Minister have varied substantially; and such mutability is necessary to the effective execution of this task.

The premiership is best seen as a cluster of functions, rights and personnel centring on the person occupying the post of Prime Minister. It emerged casually and gradually from the early eighteenth century. Initially its legitimacy was challenged but during the course of the eighteenth and nineteenth centuries it became more practically entrenched. Codification of the office of Prime Minister has been slow and remains incomplete. The vague formal existence of the institution has always afforded a high degree of discretion to those, both premiers and their aides, responsible for its exercise, subject to various constraints and enticements . . .

The premiership has monopolised certain power resources and is able at times to hoard a preponderant proportion of others. If these resources are held or deployed in the correct combination in the appropriate circumstances, No.10 can unilaterally ensure that government pursues courses of action over certain issues at particular times.

These authors find indications in the Blair premiership of the appearance of a new phase in the historical development of the institution, characterised notably by the establishment of a quasi-prime-ministerial department and seemingly also by a less assured commitment, among those in the central executive, to the principle of collective government. Tendencies in this latest phase, they conclude, 'suggest that Cabinet as a whole has been seriously undermined, although not extinguished'. They do not, however, exclude the possibility of a resurgence of cabinet.

The Minister for the Cabinet Office in the Coalition Government affirmed its determination 'to create proper Cabinet government', which will 'make decisions collectively and not resort to the kind of sofa government that caused so many problems, for example, in the entry to the Iraq war' (HC Deb vol. 511, col 315, 9 June 2010).

It is difficult to comment on the development of the role of prime minister following Tony Blair. The Coalition Government of 2010–2015 was of a different character, with the role of prime minister supplemented by the role of the Deputy Prime Minister, held by Nick Clegg, the Leader of the Liberal Democrats. Moreover, following the Brexit referendum, there has been a series of prime ministers – David Cameron, Theresa May and Boris Johnson. Their role as prime minister was dominated by Brexit, an issue that does not divide on party lines, such that the role of the prime minister during this period adds little to our understanding of the role in general. We may learn little of this potential move from a prime ministerial to a presidential approach until after Brexit, when there is a longer period of one particular prime minister being in office in circumstances when that period of office is not dominated by one major issue that cuts across party lines. Indications of the reaction of Boris Johnson as Prime Minister during the Covid-19 crisis also suggest a move towards a more presidential style of government. This is demonstrated, in particular, through Prime Minister Johnson's use of statements to announce the existence of new rules during lockdown, before these rules had been enacted, including through a text message sent to all UK-registered mobile phones.

(See further on these issues below, pp. 898–900.)

6.3.2.1 The Prime Minister's Office and the Cabinet Office

Cabinet government assumes a collective leadership of ministers, even if one of their number is *primus inter pares*. Indeed, this is the basis of the 'collective responsibility' of ministers to Parliament. Some maintain that the collective leadership of cabinet government, in accommodating the views of different ministers through bargain and compromise, cramps decision-making and results in makeshift policies. For instance, Peter Riddell, citing a former cabinet secretary's discovery of 'the hole in the centre of government', says that the hole 'results from the strength, and vested interests, of individual departments and the increasing load on Prime Ministers that inhibits a strategic view' (*The Times*, 20 April 1998). This has led to arguments for *strengthened* power at the centre, with more resources of information, policy analysis and advice being made available to the prime minister to assist him or her in developing the general strategy of the government.

At the centre of government is the Cabinet Office. Its head (under Cabinet Office ministers) is the cabinet secretary, Britain's most senior civil servant, who is the prime minister's principal official adviser and is also the head of the

Civil Service. The Cabinet Office is responsible for supporting the prime minister in leading the government, the deputy prime minister in a coalition government and also the cabinet as a whole, while the civil servants (including specialist policy advisers) in No 10, the Prime Minister's Office, work exclusively for the prime minister. Peter Madgwick saw the dual role of the Cabinet Office as a 'central ambiguity of British government' (*British Government: The Central Executive Territory* (1991), p. 101), while Peter Hennessy drew attention to an 'ever closer fusion' between the Prime Minister's Office and an expanded Cabinet Office under the Blair Government (*The Prime Minister* (2000), p. 516). The ambiguity has not been resolved and the Constitution Committee was perplexed by different authoritative accounts of the relationship between the two offices, explained as being either 'functionally distinct' or fused, the Prime Minister's Office being a 'subset' or 'business unit' of the Cabinet Office. The committee urged that the nature of the relationship should be clarified (*4th Report of 2009–10*, HL 30, paras 11–26).

Both the Cabinet Office and the Prime Minister's Office have been enlarged and strengthened in recent years. In the Coalition Government, a team of six ministers was located in the Cabinet Office: the deputy prime minister, the minister for the Cabinet Office, a minister of state (providing policy advice to the prime minister), the minister for civil society, the minister for political and constitutional reform, and the minister without portfolio. Units and agencies in the Cabinet Office focus on the development of policies in such matters of concern to government as the constitution, Civil Service reform and government purchasing, while a strategy unit works with No 10 and government departments 'to develop and design policy solutions to the strategic challenges facing the country'. Between 1997 and 2010, the staff of No 10 had doubled in size to almost 200; it is headed by a permanent secretary as a senior official adviser to the prime minister.

The linked Cabinet and Prime Minister's offices provide a powerful motor at the centre of government, but their expanded resources are still by no means comparable with those of a government department, and in arguing for a strengthened support system, some have called for the establishment of a prime minister's department. In contrast, George Jones has argued against such a 'major constitutional change', which would 'shift responsibility from ministers and the cabinet to the Prime Minister' and undermine collective cabinet government: Jones, 'The United Kingdom', in Plowden (ed.), *Advising the Rulers* (1987), pp. 63–4: see too Blick and Jones, *Premiership* (2010), pp. 46, 77, 200–203. The Constitution Committee received contradictory evidence, both favouring and opposing the establishment of a department of the prime minister, or of the prime minister and cabinet, and concluded that the creation of such an office would not 'significantly enhance the effective functioning or accountability of government' (*4th Report of 2009–10*, HL 30, paras 98–110).

The traditional model of collective, 'ministerial' government has undergone a progressive shift to a more directive style of governance. Evolutionary developments at the centre have provided the prime minister with more powerful instruments for the development, coordination and presentation of policy: a prime minister's department in all but name?

6.3.3 The Cabinet

In the mid-nineteenth and early twentieth centuries, the British governmental system was commonly described as one of 'Cabinet government', expressing a principle that the prime minister and senior ministers assembled in cabinet are the supreme governing authority in the state and that it is here that policies are agreed on and the most important decisions are taken. Whether this was ever wholly true may perhaps be doubted: have ministers ever had the knowledge, the inclination – or the time – to become actively involved in subjects beyond their own portfolios? In any case, and as we have seen, this view has not wholly accorded with modern governmental practice.

The prime minister decides on the membership of the cabinet and allocates portfolios, although for an incoming Labour prime minister, there is a constraint in the party rule, which requires cabinet places to be found for the elected members of the Parliamentary Committee (shadow cabinet). Secretaries of state and other heads of principal government departments nowadays always have seats in the cabinet. Since the Second World War, the size of the cabinet has varied between sixteen and twenty-four members. After the election of Conservative Government in 2019, the cabinet of Boris Johnson has twenty-two, as follows:

- Prime minister, first lord of the Treasury and minister for the Civil Service.
- First Secretary of State, Secretary of State for Foreign and Commonwealth Affairs.
- Chancellor of the Exchequer.
- Lord Chancellor, Secretary of State for Justice.
- Secretary of State for the Home Department.
- Chancellor of the Duchy of Lancaster.
- Secretary of State for Defence.
- Secretary of State for Health and Social Care.
- Secretary of State for Business, Energy and Industrial Strategy.
- Secretary of State for International Trade, President of the Board of Trade and Minister for Women and Equalities.
- Secretary of State for Work and Pensions.
- Secretary of State for Education.
- Secretary of State for Environment, Food and Rural Affairs.
- Secretary of State for Housing, Communities and Local Government.
- Secretary of State for Transport.
- Secretary of State for Northern Ireland.
- Secretary of State for Scotland.

- Secretary of State for Wales.
- Leader of the House of Lords, Lord Privy Seal.
- Secretary of State for International Development.
- Secretary of State for Digital, Culture, Media and Sport.
- Minister without portfolio.

Other ministers may be authorised to attend cabinet regularly, or on specific occasions, without being admitted to membership. In the current Boris Johnson cabinet, the following also attend cabinet meetings: the chief secretary to the Treasury; the Leader of the House of Commons and lord president of the council; the parliamentary secretary to the Treasury (chief whip); and the Attorney General.

All members of the cabinet have, in principle, an equal voice, but it is not usual for a vote to be taken. The prime minister normally sums up at the end of a discussion and declares what he or she takes to be the cabinet view.

Patrick Gordon Walker, *The Cabinet* (rev edn. 1972), p. 15

A secret of the smooth adaptability of the British Constitution is that the Cabinet, which is central to the political life of the nation, is unknown to the law and thus extra-constitutional. Many constitutional changes and amendments that in other countries might have to be formally made are in Britain brought about by developments in the form and functions of the Cabinet. All that is necessary is that these developments should be accepted and carried on by successive Governments: often they may scarcely be noticed as constitutional innovations and may not be recognised and analysed until after they have passed into normal practice.

The modern cabinet is the result of the slow growth of constitutional convention and has received only incidental recognition from the law (e.g., in the Ministerial and Other Salaries Act 1975, Schedule 1). No powers are formally vested in it. The cabinet is not, however, correctly described as 'extra-constitutional' simply because it belongs to the conventional part of the constitution rather than to the part governed by law. The fact that firm rules about its composition, functions and procedure are lacking does mean, as Gordon Walker indicates, that changes in its role and operating practice may occur without formality or publicity. This feature has led one commentator to speak of the 'plasticity' of cabinet government (Peter Hennessy, *Cabinet* (1986), p. 4).

Paragraph 2.2 of the *Ministerial Code* (2019) states that the business of cabinet and of ministerial committees of the cabinet consists, in the main, of:

a. questions which significantly engage the collective responsibility of the Government because they raise major issues of policy or because they are of critical importance to the public;

b. questions on which there is an unresolved argument between departments.

The *Code* adds that: 'Matters wholly within the responsibility of a single Minister and which do not significantly engage collective responsibility need not be brought to the Cabinet or to a Ministerial Committee unless the Minister wishes to inform his colleagues or to have their advice ... When there is a difference between departments, it should not be referred to the Cabinet until other means of resolving it have been exhausted.'

For Bagehot, writing in 1867, the cabinet was a body chosen 'to rule the nation' and was 'the most powerful body in the State' (*The English Constitution* (Fontana edn. 1963), pp. 67, 68). Since then power has drained away from the cabinet – to the great departments of state, the prime minister, cabinet committees, coteries of senior ministers, and even to organisations and groups outside government. Richard Crossman expressed the view in 1963 that the cabinet was becoming one of the 'dignified' (rather than 'efficient') elements of the constitution ('Introduction' to Bagehot, above, at p. 54); he repeated his view in his *Diaries of a Cabinet Minister* (3 vols, 1975–77), but his account of the actual working of the cabinet gives a more equivocal impression of cabinet power.

Richard Rose, *Politics in England: Change and Perspective* (5th edn. 1989), pp. 97–8

The Cabinet is the court of last resort for the resolution of differences between ministers, but it takes relatively few decisions. One reason is the pressure of time: the Cabinet meets only once or twice a week [in recent years only once a week], and its agenda is extremely crowded by routine business, such as reports on pending legislation and foreign affairs, and by the need to deal with emergencies. A second reason is practical: most Cabinet ministers will not be informed about most of the work of other departments and have little interest in discussing activities for which they are not personally responsible. A third reason is organizational: it is possible to examine issues in formal or informal Cabinet committees.

The Cabinet is a framework within which many decisions can be taken committing the whole of the Cabinet *outside* the formal setting of a full Cabinet meeting. When a crisis requires prompt action, there may not be time to discuss matters with nonexpert ministers, and the full Cabinet may only be told about a decision when it is a *fait accompli*. During the Falklands War, for example, Mrs Thatcher constituted a small 'War Cabinet' to supervise military operations to which the whole of the Cabinet was committed. Actions that give little prospect of political controversy can be taken within a ministry. Measures low in controversy may be settled by bilateral discussions between two ministries, with the object of producing an agreement that will be formally ratified by Cabinet. Ministers who have not been involved in negotiations prefer to let recommendations pass without question, in the expectation that their bargains will similarly be approved when they appear on the Cabinet agenda.

Graham P. Thomas, *Prime Minister and Cabinet Today* (1998), p. 192

It is impossible to definitely state the role of the Cabinet and what its functions are. A great deal depends on the personalities involved and the political circumstances at any particular time. It is no longer the case (if it ever was) that the Cabinet directs and oversees government policy on a continuous basis. The sheer scale and complexity of governmental responsibilities make this impossible; many crucial decisions, especially those relating to defence, security and key financial and economic issues, are kept away from Cabinet and taken by the Prime Minister and a close circle of colleagues and advisers. The use made by successive Prime Ministers of the Cabinet, the extent to which it has acted in a collegiate manner as opposed to being in a sense a 'rubber stamp' for prime ministerial initiatives, has varied since the war. Thus the Cabinet is best seen as a part of a wider central executive, acting basically as a body to ratify decisions taken elsewhere, receiving reports rather than initiating action. On the other hand, its importance should not be ignored. Although rarely a policy-making body, its consent to major initiatives must usually be obtained and not even the most determined Prime Minister could prevail against the opposition of the majority of his or her colleagues for long.

Martin Smith held it to be a 'constitutional myth of collective responsibility, which sees the cabinet as the central decision-maker in government', whereas in reality 'the majority of decisions, most of the time, are made elsewhere' (*The Core Executive in Britain* (1999), p. 72).

In the 1945–51 Attlee Government, the decision to develop a British atomic bomb was made by the prime minister and an inner group of leading ministers in a cabinet committee, Mr Attlee taking the view that 'the fewer people who were aware of what was happening, the better' (Mackintosh, *The British Cabinet* (3rd edn. 1977), p. 502). The issue was not discussed in cabinet. Similarly, in the 1974–79 Labour Government, the critical decisions on development of the improved Polaris missile (Chevaline) and on support for a NATO programme of new theatre nuclear weapons in Europe were taken not by the cabinet but by small groups of senior ministers. In 1984, a controversial decision by the Conservative Government to ban trade union membership at GCHQ in Cheltenham was taken by a group of ministers without discussion in the cabinet. The decision to allow British bases to be used for the American air attack on Tripoli in April 1986 was taken by the prime minister after consulting three cabinet ministers: other ministers learned of the raid from the radio news. (See Peter Hennessy, *Whitehall* (1989), pp. 317–18; Hugo Young, *One of Us* (1993 edn.), p. 476.) A contentious decision to close thirty-one coal pits in 1992 was taken by the prime minister together with ministers in economic departments without cabinet discussion or approval (*The Times*, 16 October 1992).

Collective decision-making in cabinet suffered a marked decline during the 'Thatcher years' (1979–90) when Mrs Thatcher reduced the number of cabinet meetings, asserted a dominating authority in cabinet (at all events from 1981) and channelled decision-making to cabinet committees and informal meetings with small groups of ministers. Sir Christopher Foster remarks that 'full cabinet discussion of policy became rare' and that cabinet itself 'had become little other than a formal or ritual occasion' ((2004) 67 *MLR* 753, 760). It was on the ground of a failure of collective – or, as he expressed it, 'constitutional' – government that Mr Heseltine, Secretary of State for Defence, justified his resignation from the government during the Westland affair in January 1986. In his resignation statement, he deplored what he saw as a denial of opportunity for full, collective discussion by ministers of the issues of helicopter procurement, European collaboration and the defence industrial base arising from the reconstruction of the Westland helicopter company. (Mr Heseltine's resignation statement was published in *The Times* on 10 January 1986. The Westland affair was considered above, pp. 483–484.) Nigel Lawson gives a more ambivalent assessment of cabinet government under Mrs Thatcher (*The View from No 11* (1993 edn.)). Remarking that 'in general and for good reason, key decisions were taken in smaller groups', he continues (p. 125):

> The Cabinet's customary role was to rubber stamp decisions that had already been taken, to keep all colleagues reasonably informed about what was going on, and to provide a forum for general political discussion if time permitted.

Lawson also refers, however, to Mrs Thatcher's 'increasingly complex attempts to divide and rule' through very small, hand-picked groups (p. 128).

Mr Major has said of his premiership (1990–97) that 'I was very keen to bring Cabinet Government back' (*Evidence to the Public Administration Committee*, HC 821-i of 1999–00, Q8) and the Major years saw a partial revival of traditional decision-making in cabinet and cabinet committees. As Patrick Weller observed, however, the 'party and parliamentary circumstances' of Major's administrations were crucial in this: 'Every prime minister in the last fifty years who relied heavily on cabinet has been in a parlous political situation, either in Parliament or in the polls' ('Cabinet Government: An Elusive Ideal?' (2003) 81 *Pub Adm* 701, 714). In any event it appears that Major became disinclined to bring matters to cabinet for fear of leaks (Hennessy, *The Prime Minister* (2000), p. 444).

Any revival of the cabinet under Major did not survive the premiership of Blair: cabinet and its committees were again overshadowed by informal processes of decision-making, in ad hoc meetings and bilateral discussions between the prime minister and individual ministers – a 'creeping bilateralism', it is said, such as characterised the Thatcher years (Hennessy, *The Blair Revolution in Government?* (2000), p. 13). (See also Hennessy, *The Prime Minister* (2000), pp. 517–23.) Before and during the Iraq war in 2003 the cabinet, in its brief weekly meetings, was not kept fully informed; in particular, the Attorney General's written advice on the question of legal authority for the war was not made available to the cabinet. The prime minister and the foreign and defence secretaries briefed the cabinet orally, but relevant and informative papers written by officials were not discussed in cabinet or cabinet committee. (A subsequent ruling by the Information Tribunal that the minutes of the cabinet meetings should be disclosed was overridden by ministerial veto. See p. 670 below.) In the year before the start of the war, there were frequent informal meetings of the prime minister and a small number of leading ministers, officials and military officers, and during the conflict there was oversight by an informal 'war cabinet' consisting of the prime minister, three secretaries of state and prime-ministerial official advisers. The Defence and Overseas Policy Committee of the cabinet did not meet during the Iraq crisis. (On these matters, see Clare Short's evidence to the House of Commons Foreign Affairs Committee, HC 813 of 2002–03, vol. III, QQ 63–156; Short, *An Honourable Deception?* (2004), pp. 147, 186–7, 247, 254–5; Butler Report, *Review of Intelligence on Weapons of Mass Destruction* (HC 898 of 2003–04), paras 606–11.)

The role of the cabinet in the working of central government is fluid and variable, and if cabinet has suffered a decline it is not yet moribund. G.W. Jones' observation in 1975 that 'for the most politically important issues the Cabinet is the effective decision-making body' (in Thornhill (ed.), *The Modernization of British Government* (1975), p. 31) may need qualification but has not yet been falsified. In *Premiership* (2010), Blick and Jones demonstrate that the role of cabinet (like that of the prime minister) is indeterminate and fluctuating, but that cabinet has not been displaced as a central player in the governmental process.

It may be difficult to refute Martin Burch's conclusion that 'the idea that the Cabinet is in supreme control of decision-making must be judged untenable' ('The Demise of Cabinet Government?', in Robins (ed.), *Political Institutions in Britain* (1987), p. 33), yet although not formally invested with any legal powers, cabinet is still constitutionally 'the supreme decision-making body in government' and 'the ultimate arbiter of government policy' as it is declared to be on the Cabinet Office website. Cabinet remains capable of reasserting itself, most evidently, perhaps, when its members judge that a prime minister is approaching (or has passed) his or her 'use-by' date, as Mrs Thatcher discovered in 1990 and as Mr Blair avoided discovering in the late summer of 2006 only by announcing that he was to resign within a year.

(See further on the cabinet system, Burch and Holliday, *The British Cabinet System* (1996); James, *British Cabinet Government* (2nd edn. 1999), chs. 3, 5 and 6; Thomas, *Prime Minister and Cabinet Today* (1998), ch. 9; Foster, 'Cabinet Government in the Twentieth Century' (2004) 67 *MLR* 753; Bevir and Rhodes (2006) 54 *Political Studies* 671; King, *The British Constitution* (2007), pp. 322–31.)

6.3.3.1 Neither 'Prime Ministerial' nor 'Cabinet' Government: The 'Core Executive' Thesis

There is a continuing ebb and flow in the power relationship of prime minister and cabinet, and it may be better to see contemporary British government as an example of neither prime ministerial nor cabinet government. A number of political scientists have in recent years advanced the thesis that to think in terms of there being a 'core executive' may, instead, be a more accurate and helpful approach to take. (See, e.g., Dunleavy and Rhodes, 'Core Executive Studies in Britain' (1990) 68 *Pub Adm* 3; Rhodes and Dunleavy (eds.), *Prime Minister, Cabinet and Core Executive* (1995); Smith, *The Core Executive in Britain* (1999).) The 'core executive' thesis recognises that power in the centre has grown, without overstating the power of the prime minister. It also avoids discussing these matters as if the 'decline' of the traditional model of cabinet government is something necessarily to be lamented and is even, in some sense, improper or unconstitutional. Walter Bagehot and Ivor Jennings were great constitutionalists. And they were great exponents of cabinet government as a model and as a practice. But we do not necessarily have to follow them in this particular in order to stay loyal to the constitution.

The core executive thesis, in outline, runs as follows: that there is a small number of agencies at the centre of the executive branch of government in the United Kingdom that 'fulfil essential policy setting and general business coordination and oversight functions above the level of departments' (Burch and Holliday, 'The Blair Government and the Core Executive' (2004) 39 *Government and Opposition* 1, 3). These agencies comprise the Prime Minister's Office, the Cabinet Office, the Treasury, the Foreign and Commonwealth Office, the central government law officers and offices managing the governing party's parliamentary and mass support bases (see, further, Burch and Holliday, *The British Cabinet System* (1996)).

The following extracts demonstrate the variety of advantages that proceeding in these terms may bring to the analysis of contemporary British Government.

Patrick Weller, 'Cabinet Government: An Elusive Ideal?' (2003) 81 *Pub Adm* 701, 703–4, 716

We need to avoid the assumption that there is a zero sum game, that if prime ministers are powerful then cabinet has 'lost' influence. Prime ministerial influence and cabinet government are not polar alternatives . . .

We should not be overwhelmed by recent events, by being surprised by the management and practices of recent prime ministers. The argument that prime ministers are powerful and the cabinet has been relegated to become one of the 'dignified' parts of the constitution is scarcely recent, even if it is constantly rediscovered. The explicit theoretical debate began with John Mackintosh [*The British Cabinet* (1962)] who emphasized that 'the country is governed by the Prime Minister who leads, coordinates and maintains a series of ministers'.

The prime ministers on whose experience he drew were those who held office in the 1940s and the 1950s or earlier; Lloyd George and Chamberlain are described as dominant figures who almost did away with cabinet decision making. The thesis thus predates the 1960s and 1970s, yet often these are the very times to which commentators now look as a period when cabinet government flourished . . . Indeed, arguments about dominant prime ministers can be found in the descriptions of the governments of Gladstone and Peel . . .

Cabinet remains a useful forum for maintaining . . . collective support; indeed that still seems the most persuasive reason for the regular meetings of cabinet, whether they are seen as a focus group or a political forum. Indeed these traditional political functions of cabinet – exchanging information, taking the political temperature, geeing up ministers, providing a sense of solidarity, setting the tone, emphasising the current issues and their resolution – can be undertaken almost independently of policy functions. Hence the fact that often when big issues [come] to cabinet, the intent [is] as much to solidify support as [to] determine any direction. Every government seems to still use cabinet for these political purposes, as insurance and to lock in support.

But the pressure and complexity of modern government means that a weekly meeting of busy ministers no longer seems the best way to make timely and sophisticated policy. So prime ministers choose to work with the principal players in and around those regular meetings. The weaknesses of cabinet are . . . well established: too much information, too little time, too many busy people. Modern practices take this pressure into account by segmenting and organizing the decision-making . . .

If that is an accurate diagnosis, then cabinet is simply evolving as it did a century ago.

From 1997, the Labour Government's efforts to counter departmentalism and the fragmentation of the machinery of government emphasised the need for coordinating or 'joining up' the activities of departments and other agencies providing services by establishing a strong and unified strategic centre or core.

Martin Burch and Ian Holliday, 'The Blair Government and the Core Executive' (2004) 39 *Government and Opposition* 1, 8, 12, 20–1

[C]hanges at the core under Labour mark the latest stage in the evolution of Britain's still functioning system of cabinet government . . . [T]he Blair reforms . . . reflect an acceleration of pre-existing trends, with the result that the executive arm of government has been substantially enhanced . . .

[T]he British core is increasingly coordinated and coherent, and increasingly proactive and performance-driven. It also adopts a negotiating, collaborative style designed to maximise its leverage over the rest of Whitehall . . . That it does so reflects a recognition on the part of central actors that highly departmentalized government is not an ideal model for effective administration in an age when policy problems and solutions frequently cut across departmental boundaries and fiefdoms.

Looking at the structures now in place, it is clear that the Centre has more capacity to play a significant policy role. The extent to which that capacity is exploited, and with what success, of course depends on the motivation and skill of key actors, and on the circumstances in which they find themselves at any given moment in time. Furthermore, the notion, sometimes heard, that this amounts to the demise of cabinet government in Britain is something that we seriously question. It is true that the positions of the PM and his aides have been reinforced, but against that needs to be balanced an important and growing role for the Chancellor in domestic policy. There may also be less collective government than under, say, Major or Callaghan. However, each of those premiers was frequently crippled by crisis, and they had little option but to adopt a collective stance. Compared with Thatcher, Blair does not look markedly less collective in approach.

Pulling all this together, what we can say is that collective government still operates fully from time to time, and partially (in smaller groups of ministers) all the time on specific policy issues. In many ways, it simply has to, as the UK has neither a presidential institutional structure nor presidential institutional capacity. Thus, although bouts of prime ministerial dominance may infect particular governments now and then, they cannot be sustained because the system is not in essence presidential and is not designed to support them. The result is that British government exists, at the Centre, in permanent tension between individual (PM) and collective (cabinet) government, veering by time and issue from one tendency to the other. Under Blair, the resources of the PM have been increased, but the balance of the system as a whole has not been totally transformed. Thus, while there has clearly been substantial change, there has not been a revolution. Rather, the changes that have taken place are in keeping with UK traditions and practice.

R.A.W. Rhodes, 'Understanding Governance: Ten Years On' (2007) 28 *Organization Studies* 1243, 1247, 1255

There is a conventional debate about the British executive that focuses on the relative power of the prime minister and cabinet . . . This mainstream analysis assumes the best way to look at the executive is to look at key positions and their incumbents. Instead of such a positional approach, the executive can be defined in functional terms. So, instead of asking which position is important, we can ask which functions define the innermost part or heart of British government? The core functions of the British executive are to pull together and integrate central government policies and to act as final arbiters of conflicts between different elements of the government machine. These functions can be carried out by institutions other than prime minister and cabinet; for example, the Treasury and the Cabinet Office. By defining the core executive in functional terms, the key question becomes: 'Who does what?'

Rhodes adds that 'the power of the British centre is all too often overstated':

> At the heart of this argument about core executive power is the claim that the centre can coordinate effectively. But we know that central coordination is the 'philosopher's stone' of modern government, ever sought, but always beyond reach because it assumes both agreement on goals and a central coordinator.

If the foregoing analysis is correct, it is worth noting at this stage one significant consequence. This is that parliamentary mechanisms and systems of accountability are not based on the notion of the core executive, but continue to be structured around particular government departments (see, further, Chapter 9). There is no House of Commons select committee, for example, on the core executive (although the Public Administration and Constitutional Affairs Committee does examine matters of public administration and government structure in the round). While it does from time to time happen, it continues to be rare for select committees to work together on policy problems that span different government departments (for an example of such cooperation, see the joint inquiry into arms export controls conducted in the 2009–10 Parliament by the Business, Innovation and Skills, Defence, Foreign Affairs and International Development Committees, HC 202 of 2009–10). For further information on these matters, see Chapter 9.

6.3.4 Ministerial Committees of the Cabinet

Much of the work on government policy that was formerly the business of the cabinet is now carried out in cabinet committees (ministerial committees of the cabinet). Such committees have existed since the early nineteenth century, but a fully organised committee system became established as a normal part of cabinet government only after the Second World War. Cabinet committees deal with matters of continuing governmental concern such as economic policy, home and social affairs, energy, defence and foreign policy, and the EU. A new administration may retain much of the previous government's standing committee structure, but the Coalition Government formed in May 2010 established a 'tighter' system of fewer cabinet committees, intended to be 'genuine decision-making bodies' (Minister of State, Cabinet Office, HC Deb vol. 511, col 320, 9 June 2010). Ad hoc committees or subcommittees may be appointed to deal with specific and immediate issues of policy and are wound up when the work entrusted to them has been completed.

The prime minister, acting in a coalition government in consultation with the deputy prime minister, establishes and dissolves cabinet committees, appoints the chairs and members and specifies the terms of reference. Each coalition cabinet committee had a chair from one party and a deputy chair from the other party.

Rodney Brazier, *Ministers of the Crown* (1997), p. 158

From the point of view of the departmental Minister, a Ministerial Committee can reduce a problem to its essentials, and allow disagreeing Ministers to debate the key issues. With luck he will be able to find agreement in the Committee, especially given that other Ministers are acutely aware that they will bring matters to committees from time to time and that if they are helpful to this Minister over his problem, he may reciprocate over theirs. From the point of view of the Cabinet, this method of doing business should save its time: fewer policy matters will be referred to it for discussion (although Committee decisions may be submitted for ratification), and unresolved matters will only be considered to the extent of concentrating on outstanding points of dispute. Given the delegation of ministerial responsibility within departments, it is clearly sensible that junior Ministers should be full members of some Ministerial Committees, and indeed they are – although they are outnumbered by Cabinet Ministers on them.

On the role of cabinet committees, see also Constitution Committee, *4th Report of 2009–10*, HL 30, paras 129–37. Every cabinet committee, said Richard Crossman, 'is a microcosm of the Cabinet' (*Inside View* (1972), p. 56); the committees are empowered, like cabinet itself, to take binding decisions on behalf of the government. These decisions are often of considerable importance. For instance, it was a ministerial committee that made the decision, in 1980, to acquire the Trident nuclear missile system. Cabinet committees, it is stated on the Cabinet Office website, 'reduce the burden on Cabinet by enabling collective decisions to be taken by a smaller group of ministers'. While ministers and departments are to use their judgment in deciding whether an issue requires committee clearance, they are advised that policy or other proposals will need to be considered by a cabinet committee where:

- the proposal takes forward or impacts on a coalition agreement;
- the issue is likely to lead to significant public comment or criticism;
- the subject matter affects more than one department;
- the ministers concerned have failed to resolve a conflict between departments through interdepartmental correspondence and discussions.

The cabinet committee system was formerly not a publicly acknowledged part of the constitution: governments did not announce the establishment or even admit the existence of cabinet committees. Mrs Thatcher let in some light by disclosing the existence (but not the membership or responsibilities) of four principal ministerial standing committees. A greater concession to open government was made in 1992 when Mr Major gave details of the membership and terms of reference of sixteen standing ministerial committees and ten sub-committees; updated lists have been published subsequently. Details of the proceedings of the committees are not made public.

After the 2010 general election, the following cabinet committees – fewer in number than in recent previous administrations – were established by the Coalition Government. In the Boris Johnson cabinet of 2019, the cabinet committees include: an EU Exit Strategy Committee, an EU Exit, Economy and Trade Committee, and an EU Exit Operations Committee, in addition to the more common Domestic Affairs and the Union Committee, a Parliamentary Business and Legislation Committee, and a National Security Council.

The system of ministerial committees is anything but a tidy arrangement and governmental decision-making is diffused not only among these committees but through a constantly changing network of informal groups, interdepartmental meetings and correspondence between ministers. In consequence, cabinet committees have sometimes failed to meet, their business being instead dealt with in unminuted discussions between the prime minister and the departmental ministers concerned. (See Foster, 'Cabinet Government in the Twentieth Century' (2004) 67 *MLR* 753, 760–1, 767–71.) Many matters are, of course, decided wholly within individual government departments.

6.3.5 Government Departments

The central government of the United Kingdom, as a former head of the home Civil Service, Sir William Armstrong, remarked, 'is a federation of departments' (Peter Hennessy, *Whitehall* (1989), p. 380). Departments are the power-houses of government, continually involved in the development and execution of government policies. Statutory powers vested in ministerial heads of departments and prerogative powers delegated to them are alike available to the departments for carrying out their functions.

The prime minister, it is stated in para 4.1 of the *Ministerial Code* (2010), 'is responsible for the overall organisation of the executive and the allocation of functions between Ministers in charge of departments'. In so acting, the prime minister exercises devolved prerogative power and no formalities are ordinarily prescribed: in practice, machinery of government changes, if significant, are announced to Parliament in a written ministerial statement. If statutory functions are to be transferred, this can be done by a transfer of functions order – an order in council made under the Ministers of the Crown Act 1975. The opportunities for parliamentary scrutiny and debate on machinery of government changes are limited and this weakness in accountability has been a matter of concern to the House of Commons Public Administration Committee. (See the committee's several reports, HC 672 of 2006–07, HC 90, 160, 514 of 2007–08 and HC 540 of 2008–09.) The Institute for Government notes that:

> To change the shape of Whitehall – and by extension to alter the trajectory of ministerial careers – at the stroke of a pen is one of the most powerful tools at the disposal of the British Prime Minister.

The institute proposes reforms to improve accountability to Parliament and ensure that organisational changes are 'well-considered, properly planned and implemented in a sustainable way, and . . . positively build the capacity of UK central government' (*Making and Breaking Whitehall Departments* (2010)).

Changes in departmental structure are frequently made, departments being created, dissolved, amalgamated and divided in accordance with the priorities of successive governments. A feature of the 1960s and early 1970s was the bringing together of a number of related governmental functions in new departments, some of them of considerable size and popularly described as 'giant' departments. For instance, a reconstituted Ministry of Defence absorbed the Admiralty, the War Office and the Air Ministry in 1964; a Department of the Environment, set up in 1970, took over the functions of three former ministries (Housing and Local Government, Public Building and Works, and Transport); and the Department of Trade and Industry, also created in 1970, assumed the functions of the Ministry of Technology and the Board of Trade. A result of these and other amalgamations was that all major departments could be represented in the cabinet without increasing its size. It was also hoped that the making and implementation of policies would be better coordinated by grouping related functions together in a single department.

Repeated changes in departmental responsibilities are costly and disruptive of the work of administration, but the reallocation of functions has continued in a quest for greater efficiency or in response to changing priorities. For instance, health and social security, combined in 1968, were again separated in 1988; the Department of Social Security was absorbed in 2001 into a new Department for Work and Pensions. The Department of Trade and Industry dissolved into four departments in 1974 but trade and industry were again merged in 1983, then to be transmuted in 2007 into a Department for Business, Enterprise and Regulatory Reform, only to be absorbed in 2009 by a new Department for Business, Innovation and Skills. A Department of National Heritage was created in 1992, to be reconstituted as the Department of Culture, Media and Sport in 1997. A Department for International Development was created in 1997, giving a greater prominence to policies that previously fell to a wing of the Foreign and Commonwealth Office. Other changes included the creation of a Department for Constitutional Affairs in 2003, then to be incorporated, together with the criminal justice functions of the Home Office, in a new Ministry of Justice in 2007. The decision to create a justice ministry, however commendable, was one of constitutional importance and was not preceded by consultation with the judges or parliamentary debate; the lord chief justice first learned of it from a newspaper report. (See Constitutional Affairs Committee, *The Creation of the Ministry of Justice*, 6th *Report of 2006–07*, HC 466.)

In 2010, the Comptroller and Auditor General reported (*Reorganising Central Government*, HC 452 of 2009–10) that in the four years from 2005 to 2009 there had been over ninety reorganisations of government departments and their associated bodies, at a cost of approximately £200 million a year. Since 1980, twenty-five departments had been created, of which thirteen no longer existed. It was not possible to discover whether the reorganisations had achieved value for money.

There is no legal definition of a government department and there can be disagreement about the bodies that are properly so described: even different official lists do not agree in this matter. (See, e.g., Smith et al., 'Central Government Departments and the Policy Process' (1993) 71 *Pub Adm* 567; Hogwood, 'Whitehall Families: Core Departments and Agency Forms in Britain' (1995) 61 *International Review of Administrative Sciences* 511; see, also, the definition proposed by Rodney Brazier, *Ministers of the Crown* (1997), pp. 32–3.)

Departments are sometimes headed by ministers not in the cabinet (e.g., the Attorney General's Office). There are also *non-ministerial departments* – bodies with departmental status that are headed by officials, for instance, the Charity Commission for England and Wales, the Crown Prosecution Service, HM Revenue and Customs, the Office of Fair Trading, the Serious Fraud Office and the UK Statistics Authority. For each of these, some or other minister has ultimate responsibility.

The functions of most government departments are broadly indicated by their names, but the work of departments changes as issues rise or fall in urgency or salience and as governments come and go or modify their policies, and from time to time responsibility for particular programmes is reallocated between departments. The Home Office, a department of ancient origin, was for a long time charged with a wide and heterogeneous range of functions: it was once said that 'all domestic matters not assigned by law or established custom to some other Minister fall to the Home Secretary, so that he has been described as "a kind of residual legatee"' (Sir Frank Newsam, *The Home Office* (2nd edn. 1955), p. 12). Since 2000, a number of traditional Home Office responsibilities have been transferred to other departments, for example, elections, human rights, data protection, freedom of information, prisons and probation – these being now responsibilities of the Ministry of Justice. The Home Office is still a very large department, responsible for immigration, asylum and nationality, drugs policy, crime, counterterrorism and police.

Responsibilities for law reform, legal services and the administration of justice, formerly divided between a number of departments, were in 2007 brought together in the new Ministry of Justice, whose responsibilities span 'criminal, civil and family justice, democracy, rights and the constitution' (see the ministry's website, www.justice.gov.uk). Decisions taken in the Home Office and the Ministry of Justice often directly affect individuals (e.g., prisoners, asylum-seekers and people facing deportation or extradition) and the law reports reveal frequent instances of legal challenge (by way of judicial review) to decisions taken in these two departments.

The Treasury is a department of wide-ranging influence and power at the centre of government. It is both a finance and an economics department and, since its approval is required for all government expenditure, departments are constrained in adopting policies that cost money by the need for the Treasury's agreement. Departmental estimates of expenditure ('supply estimates') must be approved by the Treasury before being presented to Parliament.

To a great extent we live under a system of 'departmental government'. Most governmental decisions are made in the departments, sometimes in negotiation with outside interest groups. The bulk of legislation is initiated in government departments. The departments act within a general framework of government policy, but have policies and interests of their own. Government being a 'federation of departments' (above) may dissolve into a 'departmentalism' characterised by uncoordinated policy-making, conflicts of interest and inconsistent decisions. In reporting on the Westland affair (above, pp. 483–484), the House of Commons Select Committee on Trade and Industry expressed its 'deepest concern at the lack of co-ordination on matters of major policy formulation between two departments of State' (*2nd Report of 1986–87*, HC 176, para 14). In 1996, the Scott Report (HC 115 of 1995–96) revealed disagreements between the Department of Trade and Industry and the Foreign and Commonwealth Office on exports of defence-related goods.

Policies can often be successfully implemented only through coordinated action by several departments. The Public Administration Committee has noted that, while departments are organised vertically, 'many of the most intractable problems of modern government have a horizontal or inter-connected nature – for example, social exclusion encompasses a range of issues and multiple departmental responsibilities' (*7th Report of 2000–01*, HC 94, para 7). The institutional machinery for achieving the necessary cooperation of departments is to be found in the cabinet, ministerial committees, the Cabinet Office and the Treasury, but these have not always been effective to ensure coherent policy-making and implementation. In 1999, the government White Paper *Modernising Government* (Cm 4310) emphasised the need to challenge departmentalism and engage, in a 'holistic' or 'joined-up' way, with issues that crossed departmental boundaries. The programme of 'joining up' government was developed in the Cabinet Office paper, *Wiring it Up* (2000), and the Institute for Government concluded in its report, *Shaping Up: A Whitehall for the Future* (2010), that there had been 'real improvement' over the previous ten years, but that 'significant barriers' to coordinated policy and delivery between departments still remained.

Centralised control and coordinating mechanisms, while necessary, can, if too prescriptive, have a debilitating effect on departments. In evidence to the Constitution Committee, the Better Government Initiative said (Constitution Committee, *4th Report of 2009–10*, HL 30, *Evidence* p. 171):

> The scale and complexity of modern government is best served if there is clear attribution of responsibilities to departmental ministers … Secretaries of State and their Departments should normally have primary responsibility for initiating, and always for developing policies and legislation in their policy areas. In that and other respects Departments ought to be allowed without micro-management to get on with what is not assigned to the Centre.

A former Cabinet Secretary, Lord Wilson of Dinton, remarks (in Moran, Rein and Goodwin, *The Oxford Handbook of Public Policy* (2006), ch. 7):

> The best answer in an imperfect world is likely to be a creative tension between departments and the centre of government in which neither is ever certain of winning.

Government departments produce annual reports on their performance: these are scrutinised by select committees of the House of Commons and may be debated on the floor of the house.

6.3.6 Arm's Length Bodies

At a remove from the centre of government and the departments we enter a zone of 'delegated governance'.

Matthew Flinders, *Delegated Governance and the British State* (2008), p. 3

Delegation is a central concept in the study of modern governance. The modern state could not function without delegation. The delegation of functions and responsibilities to semi-independent or 'parastatal' actors operating on the boundaries or fringe of the state arguably empowers governments to address a wide range of social issues simultaneously without having to be involved with the minutiae of day-to-day socio-political interactions … In recent years the extent of delegation has increased markedly as numerous governments have attempted to achieve increased levels of efficiency, effectiveness, and responsiveness through the radical restructuring of their administrative systems by introducing various forms of arm's length agencies.

Flinders observes that delegation has transformed the state, such that government 'takes place within a broader context of governance in which governmental actors operate within an increasingly fragmented, complex, and delegated administrative environment'. The traditional Westminster model of British Government, he goes on to say, 'provides a smokescreen behind which lies a highly diffuse and fragmented state system' (pp. 1, 94).

In the White Paper *Putting the Frontline First* (Cm 7753/2009) it is said that arm's length bodies:

> Undertake important functions across the full range of government activities – ranging from funding arts to helping people back into work – and drive performance and results by focusing on delivery.

Existing at arm's length from government, it is said that they 'provide autonomy – and share risks – over personnel, finance and other management matters' (*Reforming Arm's Length Bodies*, HM Treasury, 2010, p. 6).

Arm's length bodies are generally understood to include non-ministerial departments (see above), executive agencies and non-departmental public bodies.

6.3.6.1 Executive Agencies

In 1988, the government launched a programme of organisational reform in the departments, which was based on the idea of 'accountable management', responsibility for 'blocks' of work being delegated to Civil Service managers, who would be given control of resources, with a large measure of operational independence, and would be held accountable for results. The scheme was introduced following a report by the Prime Minister's Efficiency Unit, *Improving Management in Government: The Next Steps* (1988). Its main recommendation, accepted by the government, was explained by the prime minister in the House of Commons (HC Deb vol. 127, col 1149, 18 February 1988) as being that:

> to the greatest extent practicable the executive functions of Government, as distinct from policy advice, should be carried out by units clearly designated within Departments, referred to in the report as 'agencies'. Responsibility for the day-to-day operations of each agency should be delegated to a chief executive. He would be responsible for management within a framework of policy objectives and resources set by the responsible Minister, in consultation with the Treasury.

In the Coalition Government in 2010, there were around fifty-five executive agencies; they included the Central Office of Information, HM Courts Service, the Highways Agency, the National Offender Management Service, Jobcentre Plus, the UK Border Agency and the Identity and Passport Service. Most of the administrative work of central government is now carried out by civil servants in the executive agencies. Similar agencies are attached to the devolved administrations.

The policies, budgets and tasks of the executive agencies are settled by the responsible minister. For each agency, a 'framework document' is drawn up (and published), which specifies, among other matters, the functions, aims and objectives of the organisation, its chief executive's financial freedoms and responsibilities, and its relationship with the minister and departmental officials. The setting of performance targets and monitoring of the extent to which they have been met is a mechanism for improving the efficiency and quality of service of the agencies. Each agency is reviewed, usually at three-yearly intervals; its efficiency and effectiveness – and scope for improvement – are assessed and a decision is taken whether it should continue as an agency, be abolished or privatised, or whether some of its functions should be contracted out to the private sector.

The executive agencies are intended to have a large measure of autonomy in *operational* matters, while *policy* remains the responsibility of the minister and the 'core' department. This distinction has proved problematic. Policy and operations impact on each other and are not easily separated. Moreover, 'Ministers retain the right to look at, question and, if necessary, intervene in the operation of their agencies if public or parliamentary concerns require this' (*Next Steps Report 1997*, Cm 3889/1998, p. v). If ministers withdraw from engagement in agency matters, 'a vacuum of governance will occur' (*Better Government Services: Executive Agencies in the 21st Century*, Report of the Agency Policy Review 2002, para 25). In the early 1990s, ministerial interventions in the Prison Service executive agency were especially frequent, with resulting confusion as to the respective roles of minister and chief executive (for the accountability problems this generated, see Tomkins, *The Constitution after Scott* (1998), pp. 45–9). It has been suggested that executive agency status is not appropriate 'where day-to-day provision of the service is liable to give rise to issues of policy, or at least of political controversy, such that the minister is bound to become engaged in them, and . . . obliged to intervene in the day-to-day performance of the function' (Memorandum by Lord Armstrong, Select Committee on the Public Service, *Special Report*, HL 68 of 1996–97, p. 1).

It is claimed that the executive agency initiative 'has brought a much clearer focus on the executive functions of government by setting clear aims, objectives, and targets and giving chief executives the management authority they need in order to deliver them' (*Government Response to the Public Service Committee*, Cm 4000/1998, para 41). The agency programme is generally considered to have brought about greater efficiency in the delivery of public services. Having said that, it raises important issues of accountability to Parliament, considered in Chapter 9.

Despite the initial growth of next step agencies, the approach of New Labour was a focus on joined up as opposed to devolved government, leading to the reduction in next step agencies. The Coalition Government, which came to power in 2010, pushed this reduction further, having declared a 'bonfire of the quangos'. The number of next step agencies was reduced from around 140 at its peak, to around 40 by 2014, a figure that has remained more or less stable ever since.

The introduction of executive agencies was effected without enabling legislation. Why was this not needed?

(See, further, Davies and Willman, *What Next?* (1991); Greer, *Transforming Central Government: The Next Steps Initiative* (1994); O'Toole and Jordan, *Next Steps: Improving Management in Government?* (1995); Freedland, in Sunkin and Payne (eds.), *The Nature of the Crown* (1999), ch. 5; *Better Government Services: Executive Agencies in the 21st Century*, Report of the Agency Policy Review 2002; Jenkins, *Politicians and Public Services* (2008); *Reforming Arm's Length Bodies* (HM Treasury, 2010); Talbot and Talbot, 'One Step Forward, Two Steps Back? The Rise and Fall of Government's Next Step Agencies', [2019] Civil Service World, 23 September 2019.)

6.3.6.2 Non-Departmental Public Bodies (NDPBs)

On the fringes of central government, there is a large constellation of commissions, boards, committees and other bodies, which, unlike executive agencies, are not located in departments, but which are involved in manifold ways in the processes of government. *Advisory* committees are set up to provide independent and expert advice to ministers and to enlist the cooperation of outside interest groups in government policy-making, while *executive* bodies perform various administrative, regulatory or commercial functions on behalf of government. These NDPBs are sometimes termed 'fringe bodies', and the acronym 'quango' (quasi-autonomous non-governmental organisation) has been coined for them, but they are in fact closely linked with central government and their functions are often of a governmental nature. (We are not dealing in this section with tribunals, NHS bodies or public corporations, such as the BBC.)

An official description of an NDPB runs as follows (*Classification of Public Bodies: Guidance for Departments*, Cabinet Office, 2016, p. 13):

> NDPBs have a role in the process of national government but are not part of a government department. They operate at arm's length from ministers, though a minister will be responsible to Parliament for the NDPBs.

Such bodies have been set up to harness expertise only available outside the Civil Service or to carry out functions which it is thought should be detached from direct ministerial control and should be free from the constraints of Civil Service organisation. For some public functions, NDPBs have the particular advantage that they can exercise their judgment independently of the political preferences of the government of the day. Our main concern in this section is with executive NDPBs, but the advisory bodies also have an important role in support of government. (They include, for example, the Civil Justice Council, the Sentencing Council and the Law Commission.) The following are some of the better-known executive NDPBs:

- Advisory, Conciliation and Arbitration Service (ACAS).
- British Council.
- Criminal Cases Review Commission.
- Criminal Injuries Compensation Authority.
- Environment Agency.
- Health and Safety Executive.
- National Probation Service.
- Parole Board of England and Wales.

Since NDPBs have very diverse functions and have not developed in a coherent fashion, there is a lack of consistency in their legal status, organisation, funding and degree of autonomy. Brian Hogwood ((1995) 48 *Parl Aff* 207, 209) cautions that 'any attempt to define quangos by listing distinguishing characteristics will break down, since some of these characteristics will not apply to some quangos and some will be shared by other types of bodies'. Hogwood's caveat is borne in mind in offering the following list of main features of NDPBs:

1. NDPBs function at arm's length from ministers with substantial operational autonomy, but within limits set by any relevant statute and by government policy.
2. Most executive NDPBs are set up by statute, but some are incorporated under Royal Charter or under the Companies Act. (Advisory bodies may be set up by administrative action.)
3. The members of the managing boards of NDPBs are usually appointed by ministers.
4. NDPBs (unlike executive agencies) are not normally Crown bodies, but there are exceptions (e.g., the Advisory, Conciliation and Arbitration Service and the Health and Safety Executive).
5. Some NDPBs are entirely financed by government, some are partially so financed, while some (especially advisory bodies) may receive no government funding.
6. Executive NDPBs publish their accounts and an annual report.
7. NDPBs employ their own staffs, who are not normally civil servants.

In the 1980s and early 1990s, there was public concern that political considerations were influencing appointments, and that NDPBs were coming to be occupied by party (at that time Conservative) placemen. As a result, the making of appointments to executive NDPBs (and NHS bodies) was one of the matters examined by the Nolan Committee in its Inquiry into Standards in Public Life (see the *Nolan Report* (1995)).

The Nolan Committee recommended the appointment of a new, independent commissioner for public appointments who would monitor, regulate and advise on ministerial appointments to NDPBs and NHS bodies. Provision for the new office was made by order in council and the first commissioner, appointed by the Crown, took office in 1995. The commissioner issued a *Code of Practice for Ministerial Appointments to Public Bodies*, which sets out a number of principles to be observed in making appointments to public bodies, placing emphasis on selection on merit (the 'overriding principle'), independent scrutiny of the appointments process, openness and transparency in appointments and procedures, and the promotion of equality of opportunity and diversity. Scotland and Northern Ireland have their own commissioners for public appointments. This has now been replaced by the *Governance Code*, which came into force on 1 January 2017. This code sets out principles of public appointments that focus on ministerial responsibility for appointments, selflessness, integrity, merit, openness, diversity, assurance and fairness.

The Thatcher Government undertook a critical scrutiny of the work of NDPBs and many were abolished as 'non-essential' or reduced in size and scope. A considerable number, however, survived this culling and new ones continued to be created. The succeeding Labour Government also committed itself 'to keeping the number of NDPBs to a minimum' (HC Deb vol. 310, col 68W, 6 April 1998), and between 1997 and 2009 the total number fell by ninety-one (over 10 per cent), although at 31 March 2009, there were still 766 NDPBs sponsored by the UK Government (*Public Bodies 2009*, p. 6). Efforts to reduce the number of NDPBs have been provoked by concerns, sometimes exaggerated, about issues of cost, accountability and ministerial patronage. The Efficiency in Government Unit in its *Essential Guide to British Quangos* (2005) found a great duplication of effort among NDPBs and presented a list of what it said were 'the 9 most useless quangos' as well as a list of 'the 10 most costly NDPBs'. (See, too, *Reforming Arm's Length Bodies*, HM Treasury, 2010, ch. 2.) Contrariwise, governments have acknowledged the 'enormous contribution' of public bodies 'to providing and delivering public services in the UK' ('Foreword', *The Governance of Public Bodies: A Progress Report*, Cm 3557/1997). No government can do without the expert services that can be secured by these means, and the desirability of keeping some executive functions separate from government departments is generally admitted.

Nevertheless, in 2010, both real and inflated concerns about the role of NDPBs provoked a renewed and more radical commitment by the Coalition Government to reduce their number, with the declared aim of increasing accountability and reducing costs. Prime Minister Cameron instructed ministers to review the public bodies within their areas of responsibility to determine whether each of them could be justified as meeting one of three tests, subsequently formulated as follows by the minister for the Cabinet Office: 'does it perform a technical function, do its activities require political impartiality or does it need to act independently to establish facts?' (HC Deb vol. 516, col 25WS, 14 October 2010). Those found wanting would be abolished and their functions, if still necessary, would be transferred to government departments, the presumption being that bodies spending public money and deliberating on policy should be accountable, through ministers, to Parliament. See now the Public Bodies Bill 2010–11 which, if enacted, will confer extensive powers on ministers to abolish, merge or modify a large number of public bodies, as specified in the schedules to the bill.

The government's handling of this matter was condemned in a strongly worded report of the House of Commons Public Administration Committee (*5th Report of 2010–11*, HC 537), which stated that the government 'did not consult properly on these proposals' (para 29) and that it had failed to apply its tests either consistently or coherently (para 37). There has been a reduction in the number of agencies, with the government website currently listing 408 agencies and other public bodies.

It may be noted that the advantages of the NDPB model still commend themselves to the government: the Coalition's Budget Responsibility and National Audit Bill, introduced into the House of Lords in October 2010, would set up a new executive NDPB, the Office for Budget Responsibility, which was created in 2010, to provide independent analysis of the UK's public finances and to make fiscal and economic forecasts independently of the Treasury.

6.3.6.3 Control and Accountability

The independence that is believed necessary to the proper functioning of non-departmental bodies gives rise to problems of control and accountability. Organisations to which governmental functions and public money are entrusted cannot be left to operate as uncontrolled baronies. Powers of inter-vention – for example, to give binding directions or to call for information – are generally reserved to the minister, who also has the ultimate power of dismissal (or non-renewal of appointments) of board members of NDPBs. Ministers are accountable to Parliament for the exercise of these powers and, more generally, for 'the degree of independence which an NDPB enjoys; for its usefulness as an instrument of government policy; and so ultimately for the overall effectiveness and efficiency with which it carries out its functions' (*Public Bodies: A Guide for Departments* (2006), ch. 2, para 6.1). Ministers are not, however, formally answerable for the day-to-day activities of these bodies.

The Coalition Government has sought to justify its 'bonfire of the quangos' on the grounds both that it will save costs and that it will enhance accountability. In its *5th Report of 2010–11*, HC 537, the Public Administration Committee concluded (at para 137) that the Public Bodies Bill would deliver neither objective: 'the current approach is not going to deliver significant cost savings or result in greater accountability', the committee warned.

The accounts of almost all executive NDPBs are audited on behalf of Parliament by the Comptroller and Auditor General, who may also conduct 'value for money' audits of the economy, efficiency and effectiveness of their operations and report the results to the House of Commons. (See the National Audit Act 1983, sections 6, 7 and 9; *Audit and Accountability of Central Government*, Cm 5456/2002, para 6; HC Deb vol. 379, col 322W, 30 January 2002.) The select committees of the House of Commons that monitor the work of the principal government departments are empowered to examine the 'associated public bodies' of these departments, although the resources of the committees do not allow for a regular and systematic scrutiny of all of them. Executive NDPBs will normally be included in the list of public authorities in Schedule 1 to the Freedom of Information Act 2000 (as that list is amended from time to time by orders made under section 4 of the Act), and the Act's provisions, giving rights of access to information, will accordingly apply to these bodies. Executive NDPBs are set performance targets and their progress in meeting these is reported annually to Parliament. By such means, most of these unelected public bodies have been made subject to a measure of accountability. Since 2008, House of Commons select committees have conducted pre-appointment hearings of ministers' proposed appointments of the chairs or chief executives of a number of NDPBs: the committees' recommendations are not binding on ministers but are taken into account by them before proceeding with an appointment. (See Liaison Committee, *2nd Report of 2009–10*, HC 426, paras 60–72.)

Executive NDPBs may have grant-giving or licensing powers, or provide legal services, enforce standards, levy charges, or conduct or supervise investigations of individuals' complaints. Persons may suffer detriment if powers such as these are improperly exercised. Initially, only very few NDPBs were within the jurisdiction of the parliamentary ombudsman to inquire into allegations of maladministration, but the Parliamentary and Health Service Commissioners Act 1987 extended this jurisdiction to a number of important executive bodies (see Schedule 1). All executive NDPBs (as well as those advisory NDPBs that have direct dealings with members of the public) now fall within the parliamentary ombudsman's jurisdiction unless there are exceptional reasons against this, such as that they are within the jurisdiction of another ombudsman.

A degree of control is also exercised by the courts, in that bodies performing public functions are subject to judicial review. Public bodies created by statute are held by the courts to the limits of their statutory powers under the doctrine of ultra vires: a case of this kind was *Anisminic Ltd* v. *Foreign Compensation Commission* [1969] 2 AC 147, in which the House of Lords struck down a decision of the commission as having been made outside its jurisdiction. A public body is also open to legal challenge on the grounds that it misapplied the rules (even if non-statutory) under which it operates (*R* v. *Criminal Injuries Compensation Board, ex p Schofield* [1971] 1 WLR 926); or failed to act fairly in deciding a question affecting the rights or interests of an individual (*R* v. *Gaming Board, ex p Benaim and Khaida* [1970] 2 QB 417; *R* v. *Parole Board, ex p Wilson* [1992] QB 740); or failed to take account of relevant considerations (*R* v. *Human Fertilisation and*

Embryology Authority, ex p Blood [1999] Fam 151); or acted irrationally (cf. *R v. Radio Authority, ex p Bull* [1998] QB 294); or, if exercising judicial functions, was lacking in the necessary independence from the executive (*R (Brooke) v. Parole Board* [2008] EWCA Civ 29, [2008] 3 All ER 289). Executive NDPBs, in exercising 'functions of a public nature', are public authorities for the purposes of the Human Rights Act (see section 6).

Despite this range of methods of accountability, a report of the Public Administration Select Committee (*Who's Accountable? Relationships Between Government and Arm's-Length Bodies, 5th Report of 2014–15* HC 110) concluded that accountability for arm's-length bodies in the UK was inconsistent with 'overlaps, confusion and clutter'. Moreover:

> The Cabinet Office's public bodies reform programme has been limited to just one form, the non-department public body, and we have been presented with no evidence that it has increased accountability. In the interested of continued accountability, when functions are moved in-house, the same or greater transparency much apply. Clear information enables democratic scrutiny and counters the disillusionment that stems in part from lack of understanding. We have called for a more professional and transparent approach to the management of the hundreds of public bodies which surround central Government . . .
>
> But above all, we have concluded that the Government must focus on relationships and engagement with public bodies . . . The Government has not yet placed enough emphasis on these human factors that contribute to the success of arm's length government.

An Australian Royal Commission on Government Administration has warned (Parliamentary Paper No 185/1976, para 4.4.26) that, taken to extremes, the creation of non-departmental bodies:

> could represent a substantial modification of the constitutional system through the addition of what would amount to a fourth branch of government, separate from the executive branch and largely exempt from the operation of the constitutional conventions which harness the executive to the legislature.

(See, further, Weir and Hall, *Ego Trip: Extra-governmental Organisations in the UK* (1994); Ridley and Wilson (eds.), *The Quango Debate* (1995); Skelcher, *The Appointed State* (1998); Flinders and Smith (eds.), *Quangos, Accountability and Reform* (1999); Flinders, *Delegated Governance and the British State* (2008); Flinders, 'The Politics of Patronage in the United Kingdom' (2009) 22 *Governance* 547; House of Commons Public Administration Committee, *Smaller Government: Shrinking the Quango State, 5th Report of 2010–11*, HC 537; House of Commons Public Administration Select Committee *Who's Accountable? Relationship Between Government and Arm's-Length Bodies, 5th Report of 2014–5*, HC 110.)

6.3.7 The Civil Service

The Civil Service of the state comprises what were formerly distinguished as the home Civil Service and the diplomatic service. (There is a separate Northern Ireland Civil Service.) A concise description of civil servants is that they are servants of the Crown employed in a civil (i.e., non-military) capacity in government departments, but there is no all-purpose legal definition of a civil servant. For many years, the generally accepted definition was that adopted by the Tomlin Royal Commission on the Civil Service in 1931 (Cmd 3909). Civil servants, it said, are:

> servants of the Crown, other than holders of political or judicial offices, who are employed in a civil capacity and whose remuneration is paid wholly and directly out of monies voted by Parliament.

This definition is still serviceable but has been modified in more recent government publications. The *Civil Service Statistics 2004: Sources and Definitions* had the following:

> A civil servant is a servant of the Crown working in a civil capacity who is not: the holder of a political (or judicial) office; the holder of certain other offices in respect of whose tenure of office special provision has been made; a servant of the Crown in a personal capacity paid from the Civil List.

This revised definition takes account of those civil servants who are employed in government departments or executive agencies that are financed by means of trading funds and not from money voted annually by Parliament. (See the Government Trading Funds Act 1973 and the Government Trading Act 1990.) However, members of the judiciary are not civil servants (*Gilham* v. *Ministry of Justice* [2019] UKSC 44).

The Civil Service was formerly managed under the royal prerogative but has been given a statutory framework by the Constitutional Reform and Governance Act 2010. For the purposes of this act, the Civil Service of the State does not include: (a) the Secret Intelligence Service; (b) the security service; (c) GCHQ and (d) the Northern Ireland Civil Service. Apart from the specific exclusions, no general definition of the Civil Service or of a civil servant is provided by the act.

The minister for the Civil Service (an office traditionally held by the prime minister) is empowered by the Act to manage the Civil Service (excluding the diplomatic service) and 'the Secretary of State' (i.e., whichever one of the secretaries of state is entrusted with this responsibility: see above) has the power to manage the diplomatic service (Constitutional Reform and

Governance Act 2010, section 3). These powers include the power to make appointments.

To ensure that civil servants are made aware of their constitutional responsibilities with regard to Parliament, the act provides (section 3(6)):

> In exercising his power to manage the civil service, the Minister for the Civil Service shall have regard to the need to ensure that civil servants who advise Ministers are aware of the constitutional significance of Parliament and of the conventions governing the relationship between Parliament and Her Majesty's Government.

The minister for the Civil Service may delegate a management function to any other servant of the Crown. In practice, the minister for the Cabinet Office is charged with day-to-day responsibility for the Civil Service (other than the diplomatic service), and under ministers the cabinet secretary is the official head of the service.

At common law, civil servants hold office at the pleasure of the Crown and can be dismissed at any time. (See *Dunn* v. *R* [1896] 1 QB 116; *Hales* v. *R* (1918) 34 TLR 589; *Denning* v. *Secretary of State for India* (1920) 37 TLR 138.) This rule has in the past sometimes been explained as resting on an implied term in the contract of employment, but is better regarded as a rule of constitutional law established by the courts on the basis of public policy (and attributed by the majority of their Lordships in *Council of Civil Service Unions* v. *Minister for the Civil Service* [1985] AC 374 to the prerogative). But public policy changes over time, and the modern view of the nature of public employment is expressed in legislation which extends to civil servants rights such as protection against unfair dismissal enjoyed by other employees. (See the Employment Rights Act 1996, section 191.) In practice, civil servants are not notably insecure in their employment, although dismissals for inefficiency or disciplinary offences do occur and some civil servants have lost their jobs when departments have been merged or dissolved or functions have been contracted out to the private sector. An aggrieved civil servant may be able to appeal to the Civil Service Appeal Board, a non-statutory internal tribunal, which can award compensation or recommend reinstatement. Civil servants benefit in general from protection against discrimination as provided by the Equality Act 2010 (see Equality Act 2010, section 50).

6.3.7.1 The Civil Service: Principles and Conduct

Recruitment of civil servants has long been based on the principle of selection on merit in fair and open competition, and this principle is now expressly affirmed in section 10(2) of the Constitutional Reform and Governance Act 2010. In order to insulate recruitment from political influence, responsibility for appointments has been entrusted since 1855 to independent Civil Service commissioners. In recent decades, responsibility for appointment of the great

majority of civil servants was progressively delegated to ministers, but appointment to the most senior positions required approval of the commissioners. The
Constitutional Reform and Governance Act established the Civil Service
Commission as a statutory body. It has the duty of publishing (after consulting
the minister for the Civil Service) a set of recruitment principles, which must
be followed in all Civil Service appointments. The commission monitors
observance of the recruitment principles by the appointing authorities and
the principles may provide that the approval of the commission must be
obtained for appointments in certain circumstances (e.g., to positions of
a certain seniority). The commission investigates complaints that the requirement of selection on merit on the basis of fair and open competition has not
been followed in the making of an appointment.

   A former head of the home Civil Service defined the essential principles of
the service as follows (*The Civil Service: Continuity and Change*, Cm 2627/
1994, para 2.7):

> The particular standards that bind the Civil Service together are integrity, impartiality,
> objectivity, selection and promotion on merit and accountability through Ministers to
> Parliament.

In the 1980s and 1990s, developments such as the establishment of executive
agencies (above), the 'market testing' of departmental activities and the
retrenchment of Civil Service personnel and functions, associated with
a long tenure of government by the same political party, affected traditional
understandings and practices in the Civil Service (see Tomkins, *The
Constitution after Scott* (1998), ch. 2). Officials were more exposed to public
criticism and relationships with ministers came increasingly under strain (see
William Plowden's observations on the 'flawed relationship' in *Ministers and
Mandarins* (1994), pp. 102–9). John Garrett MP spoke of the 'dismemberment'
of government and of a threat to the integrity of the Civil Service in a 'process
of moving from a unified Civil Service of some 30 main departments to a Civil
Service which consists of 30 ministerial headquarters; about 150 executive
agencies and units; hundreds of quangos . . . and thousands of contracts with
private contractors, all of which are trying to make a profit' – all these
enterprises having 'varying standards of service delivery, public accountability
and staff relations' (Treasury and Civil Service Committee, *5th Report of
1993–94*, HC 27, vol. II). There was widespread concern that traditional values
of the Civil Service were being eroded and the government was persuaded in
1996 to introduce, by prerogative order in council, a *Civil Service Code* to give
clearer definition to principles of the Civil Service and the duties of civil
servants and of ministers towards them. Section 5(1) of the Constitutional
Reform and Governance Act 2010 now places a duty on the minister for the
Civil Service to publish a code of conduct for the Civil Service (excluding the

diplomatic service). Any such code must be laid before Parliament (for the information of members). Its provisions form part of the terms and conditions of service of civil servants. There are similar provisions for a code of conduct for the diplomatic service (section 6 of the Act) and separate codes of conduct may be published to cover civil servants serving the Scottish Government or the Welsh Assembly Government (sections 5(2), (3) and 6(6), (7). A similar code applies to the Northern Ireland Civil Service. The Civil Service and diplomatic service codes must require civil servants 'to carry out their duties with integrity, honesty, objectivity and impartiality.

The *Civil Service Code* sets out the values and standards of behaviour that are expected of civil servants and their rights and responsibilities. It defines the values of the Civil Service as follows.

Civil Service Values

The Civil Service is an integral and key part of the government of the United Kingdom. It supports the Government of the day in developing and implementing its policies, and in delivering public services. Civil servants are accountable to ministers, who in turn are accountable to Parliament.

As a civil servant, you are appointed on merit on the basis of fair and open competition and are expected to carry out your role with dedication and a commitment to the Civil Service and its core values: integrity, honesty, objectivity and impartiality. In this code:

- 'integrity' is putting the obligations of public service above your own personal interests
- 'honesty' is being truthful and open
- 'objectivity' is basing your advice and decisions on rigorous analysis of the evidence
- 'impartiality' is acting solely according to the merits of the case and serving equally well Governments of different political persuasions.

These core values support good government and ensure the achievement of the highest possible standards in all that the Civil Service does. This in turn helps the Civil Service to gain and retain the respect of ministers, Parliament, the public and its customers.

This Code sets out the standards of behaviour expected of you and other civil servants. These are based on the core values which are set out in legislation. Individual departments may also have their own separate mission and values statements based on the core values, including the standards of behaviour expected of you when you deal with your colleagues.

In succeeding paragraphs, the *Code* gives details of the standards of behaviour expected of civil servants. It emphasises the *impartiality* of civil servants, while at the same time underlining their obligation of loyalty to the administration in which they serve, reflecting the fundamental and longstanding convention that the Civil Service is non-political and is expected to give loyal service to administrations of every political complexion.

You must:

- serve the Government, whatever its political persuasion, to the best of your ability in a way which maintains political impartiality and is in line with the requirements of this Code, no matter what your own political beliefs are
- act in a way which deserves and retains the confidence of ministers, while at the same time ensuring that you will be able to establish the same relationship with those whom you may be required to serve in some future Government
- comply with any restrictions that have been laid down on your political activities.

You must not:

- act in a way that is determined by party political considerations, or use official resources for party political purposes
- allow your personal political views to determine any advice you give or your actions.

A civil servant who has reason to believe that he or she is being required to act in a way that conflicts with the *Code*, or that another civil servant is acting in such a way, should normally raise the matter with senior officials in the department, but failing a reasonable response may appeal to the Civil Service Commission. After investigating a complaint, the commission may make recommendations to the department about how the matter should be resolved: section 9 of the Constitutional Reform and Governance Act 2010 and the Civil Service Code. A general account of appeals heard by the commission is given in its annual report.

A new government, while it may introduce a number of political advisers of ministers into the departments, normally keeps in office the senior Civil Service personnel who have advised its predecessors. In each department, the permanent secretary, as its official head, having ensured the removal of files and documents of the previous minister from the sight of his or her successor, assumes the role of objective adviser to the new political head of the department.

By section 1(1)(b) of the House of Commons Disqualification Act 1975, civil servants are ineligible for membership of the House of Commons, and under rules first laid down in 1953 (Cmd 8783), they are subject to restrictions on participation in political activities. In 1978, the Armitage Committee recommended relaxations of the rules so as to allow a wider freedom to take part in political activity (Cmnd 7057); the government accepted the recommendations and the rules were liberalised in 1984. The rules now applicable are to be found in section 4.4 of the *Civil Service Management Code*. Civil servants are divided into three groups: the politically free (industrial and non-office grades) who may take part in all political activities; a politically restricted group (primarily members of the senior Civil Service) who are debarred from national political activity but may be given permission to take part in local politics; and an intermediate group, comprising all other staff, who may, with permission, take part in national or local politics. Permission, where required, 'should normally only be refused where civil servants are employed in sensitive areas in which the impartiality of the Civil Service is most at risk' (Annex A to section 4.4 of the Code), for example, civil servants closely engaged in policy assistance to ministers. The ECtHR dismissed a challenge to the restrictions on political activity in *Ahmed* v. *United Kingdom* (1998) 29 EHRR 1.

Should civil servants give total and unqualified loyalty to the government or do they have, in any circumstances, an overriding responsibility to the Crown, to Parliament or to the public?

Civil Service Management Code, para 4.1.1

Civil servants are servants of the Crown and owe a duty of loyal service to the Crown as their employer. Since constitutionally the Crown acts on the advice of Ministers who are answerable for their departments and agencies in Parliament, that duty is, subject to the provisions of the Civil Service Code, owed to the duly constituted Government.

This authoritative statement acknowledges that a civil servant's duty to the government of the day is not unqualified, but is subject to the principles set out in the *Civil Service Code*, which reminds of the duty of civil servants to comply with the law and uphold the administration of justice. Civil servants (other than members of the security and intelligence services) are secured by the Public Interest Disclosure Act 1998 (the 'Whistleblower's Act') against dismissal or other sanctions if they make 'protected disclosures' of malpractices such as a criminal offence, a miscarriage of justice, a risk to health or safety, etc.

6.3.7.2 Civil Servants and Ministers

It does not sufficiently explain the role of civil servants to say that they advise ministers on policy and execute ministers' decisions. In government departments and agencies, very many decisions are necessarily taken by civil servants themselves without reference to ministers, and these decisions will often involve an element of policy-making. Moreover, the senior civil servants who advise ministers can draw on an accumulated departmental experience and expert knowledge of the department's affairs in pressing for acceptance by their minister (perhaps a newcomer to the department, seldom as well versed in its business) of the 'departmental view'.

Peter Kellner and Lord Crowther-Hunt, *The Civil Servants* (1980), p. 187

The concept of the departmental view is difficult to define, or to reconcile with any conventional constitutional theory. Broadly, it consists of the ideas and assumptions that, independently of which party is in office, flow from the knowledge and experience that are generated by civil servants working together. However much civil servants as individuals move around, they add their increment of information to the pool of knowledge about motorway building, or kidney machines, or food subsidies. Such knowledge does not exist in a moral or political vacuum: and so, by an often complex chemistry, a department's knowledge translates into a departmental view. Some of the greatest conflicts between ministers and their Permanent Secretaries occur when the minister's intentions conflict with the departmental view.

There have been ministers in both Conservative and Labour Governments who have, from time to time, asserted that they have been obstructed by civil servants committed to departmental policies contrary to those being pursued by the minister. Among Labour ministers who have made this claim are Tony Benn, Barbara Castle and Richard Crossman (see Theakston, *The Labour Party and Whitehall* (1992), ch. 2). Michael Heseltine, a cabinet minister in the Major Government, said to the Public Service Committee (*Evidence*, HC 265 of 1995–96, Q9):

[A] Minister in charge of a department can give orders, but if he gives orders which are outside the broad conventions, there are endless ways in which his orders will be frustrated. The most obvious is that he will be told that this is not government policy, that he will be told that he has not got authority for what he said, that in some way it is unwise to take a decision on this matter at this stage because other events are about to unfold.

(See, also, Tony Benn, in Sutherland (ed.), *The Rape of the Constitution?* (2000), p. 46.) It is reported that at a cabinet meeting in March 2002 several ministers gave vent to intemperate criticism of the performance and reliability of civil servants in their departments (see Rawnsley, *The End of the Party* (2010), p. 291).

By the same token, it may be said that civil servants have a legitimate constitutional role as a counterweight to politicians and an obligation to 'speak truth unto power'. Sir Brian Cubbon said to the Treasury and Civil Service Committee (*5th Report of 1993–94*, HC 27, vol. III, Appendix 31, para 8):

An apolitical civil service is one of the checks and balances that makes it tolerable to have Ministers who have so much more power than Parliament. Ministers' total dependence for support on apolitical civil servants means that they cannot secretly abuse their power without the knowledge of those who owe them no political allegiance and they cannot take decisions without the discipline of face-to-face discussion with them.

Witnesses appearing before the Public Administration Committee in 2006–7 suggested that 'civil service independence had a political function, in balancing the strong executive power of British governments', and the committee was not persuaded 'that ministers should have the ability to act without any checks on their behaviour, or that the civil service should be considered as wholly the creature of a current administration' (*3rd Report of 2006–07*, HC 122, paras 31–2).

Of course, arguments of this kind do not justify *obstruction* by civil servants of the policies of elected governments. This seems sometimes to have occurred but is not a normal feature of the relations between civil servants and ministers. A Fabian Society study group concluded in 1982 (cited by Theakston, above, at p. 40):

> It is doubtful if the civil service as a whole has a conscious political position of its own to defend. A united government can rapidly secure the support of the civil service in carrying through major and sharp changes of policy, and a strong minister – with the support of the Prime Minister and his colleagues – can impose his will on the government machine.

Government is most effectively conducted by a partnership of ministers and civil servants. In the 1980s and 1990s, this balanced arrangement was disturbed by a tendency for ministers to devalue and dispense with the advice of civil servants and to rely on politically committed outsiders for policy advice. Keith Dowding, writing in 1995 (*The Civil Service* (1995), p. 124), found that 'the power and influence of civil servants over their ministers have diminished during the last decade'. (The dislocation of the relationship is examined in depth by Christopher Foster and Francis Plowden, *The State under Stress* (1996).) This trend continued under Labour administrations from 1997, as ministers relied increasingly for policy support on special advisers, advisory NDPBs, task forces and other sources outside the traditional, permanent Civil Service. This trend continued in the Coalition Government, and the Conservative Governments and minority governments of David Cameron, Theresa May and Boris Johnson, and the 2019 majority government of Boris Johnson. If civil servants exert less influence on ministers than formerly, this may reflect a lack of adaptability of the Civil Service to the demands of modern government. Sir Christopher Foster, a well-informed observer, says of civil servants: 'They were excellent in a world in which changes were evolutionary and marginal, where there were not too many changes at once and none requiring profound reforms'; but, he adds, 'they were not good at organisational or culture change' and 'rarely gave much direct attention to citizens or the consumers of the public services they provided' ('Civil Service Fusion' (2001) 54 *Parl Aff* 425, 439–40). In its inquiry into *Good Government* (*8th Report of 2008–09*, HC 97), the Public Administration Committee received evidence that was, in part, strongly critical of the performance of the Civil Service. The committee concluded that such criticism was overstated, that the calibre and professionalism of civil servants were of a high order, but that the service as a whole was lacking in operational management skills and needed to be 'better geared to the demands of modern government' (paras 25–9).

The Labour Government undertook a Civil Service reform programme with a view to strengthening leadership, planning and performance in the service while preserving its core values such as selection on merit, integrity and impartiality. (See *Civil Service Reform* (Cabinet Office 2009); *The State of the Service* (Institute for Government 2009); *Putting the Frontline First: Smarter Government* (Cm 7753/2009).) But ministers have themselves sometimes undervalued the contribution that civil servants can make to more effective formulation and implementation of policy. Sir Christopher Foster, in a memorandum for the Public Administration Committee (HC 307 of 2004–05, p. 59), observed that:

> the belief that the public sector can be satisfactorily run by politicians issuing instructions, as if private sector managers, is deeply flawed, even if an ample supply of superb private sector managers were on offer. The public sector is essentially different. It requires an effective partnership between Ministers, with their political policy objectives and experience, and experienced civil servants capable of providing the administrative expertise on which effective delivery depends.

He also looked for the 'revival of an earlier tradition by which the Civil Service regularly probed, tested and sometimes challenged new policy proposals, even those in the manifesto, to test their sense and practicality', while acknowledging that 'Ministers must ultimately decide'. Paragraph 5.2 of the *Ministerial Code* (2010) reminds ministers that they 'have a duty to give fair consideration and due weight to informed and impartial advice from civil servants, as well as to other considerations and advice in reaching policy decisions'.

(See, further, Foster, 'The Civil Service Under Stress' (2001) 79 *Pub Adm* 725; Foster, *British Government in Crisis* (2005), chs 2 and 15; Burnham and Pyper, *Britain's Modernised Civil Service* (2008); Richards, *New Labour and the Civil Service* (2008); Greer, 'Whitehall', in Hazell (ed.), *Constitutional Futures Revisited* (2008).)

6.3.7.3 Special Advisers

In recent decades, ministers have looked outside the departments for advice from persons sympathetic to their policies. With prime-ministerial approval, they have appointed temporary advisers to provide them with political advice or the benefit of specialised skills (e.g., in economics). On taking office as Prime Minister in March 1974, Harold Wilson decided to experiment in this way, authorising cabinet ministers to appoint political advisers who would give advice from a perspective different from that of the 'Whitehall mandarin' and help ministers 'to play a constructive part in the collective business of the Government as a whole' (Harold Wilson, *The Governance of Britain* (1976),

Appendix). The practice has continued under subsequent administrations and is now an established feature of British government.

The role of special advisers has been given statutory recognition by the Constitutional Reform and Governance Act 2010, which includes provisions applicable to special advisers appointed by ministers with the approval of the prime minister. Section 7(5) acknowledges their political role in providing that the *Civil Service Code* need not require special advisers 'to carry out their duties with objectivity or impartiality'. The minister for the Civil Service must, however, publish a code of conduct for special advisers, and the code must provide that a special adviser may not authorise public expenditure or exercise any power in relation to the management of the Civil Service or any statutory or prerogative power (section 8(1), (5)). The minister must lay before Parliament any special advisers' code and also an annual report about special advisers in service, giving information about their number and cost (sections 8(8) and 16). Broadly analogous provisions apply to special advisers serving the Scottish Executive or the Welsh Assembly Government.

Ministerial Code (2019), paras 3.2 and 3.3

With the exception of the Prime Minister and the Deputy Prime Minister, Cabinet Ministers may each appoint up to two special advisers (paid or unpaid). The Prime Minister may also authorise the appointment of special advisers for Ministers who regularly attend Cabinet. Where a Minister has additional responsibility additional advisers may be allowed. All appointments, including exceptions to this rule, require the prior written approval of the Prime Minister, and no commitments to make such appointments should be entered into in the absence of such approval. All special advisers will be appointed under terms and conditions set out in the *Model Contract for Special Advisers* and the *Code of Conduct for Special Advisers*.

All special advisers must uphold their responsibility to the Government as a whole, not just to their appointing Minister. The responsibility for the management and conduct of special advisers, including discipline, rests with the Minister who made the appointment. Individual Ministers will be accountable to the Prime Minister, Parliament and the public for their actions and decisions in respect of their special advisers. It is, of course, also open to the Prime Minister to terminate employment by withdrawing his consent to an individual appointment.

As temporary civil servants, special advisers are subject in general to the same rules of conduct as other civil servants but with important exceptions – in particular, special advisors 'are exempt from the general requirement that civil servants should be appointed on merit and behave with impartiality and objectivity or that they need to retain the confidence of future governments of a different political complexion' (*Code of Conduct for Special Advisers*). They are not, however, to take part in public political controversy.

It is intended that special advisers should supplement or counter the conventional wisdom of the departments, follow up the implementation of ministerial decisions and maintain direct links with the party and with outside interest groups. The best special advisers, it has been said, 'combine expert knowledge of a field of policy, political commitment and an understanding of the Whitehall machine' (*Top Jobs in Whitehall*, Report of an RIPA Working Group (1987), p. 56).

The Constitutional Reform and Governance Act 2010 does not place an overall limit on the number of special advisers. At 31 March 2020 (the most recent date for which data is available), there were 102 special advisers in post, including 51 working for the prime minister. In general, it appears that special advisers make a useful contribution in supporting ministers and are able to work in a constructive relationship with established civil servants. Some observers have perceived a threat to the tradition of a politically neutral Civil Service, bringing a collective experience and objective judgment to bear on government policy-making. However, the Committee on Standards in Public Life reported: 'Almost all witnesses made clear their view that special advisers were valuable components of the machinery of Government' (*6th Report*, Cm 4557-I/2000, para 6.26). The Phillis Review (*An Independent Review of Government Communications*, Cabinet Office, 2004) said in its report:

> Members of the duly constituted government have a right to make arrangements with which they are comfortable to help them represent (and protect) themselves in a highly adversarial and increasingly intrusive culture. We believe special advisers to be an integral part of modern government, and their political affiliation is both welcomed by Ministers and an important buttress to the impartiality of the Civil Service. However, we did receive a great deal of evidence on the role that special advisers have and should have in support of government communications.

Special advisers have on occasion in the recent past resorted to the manipulation of news ('spinning') in their efforts to present the government in the most favourable light. They are enjoined by their *Code of Conduct* to 'observe discretion and express comment with moderation, avoiding personal attacks'.

The position of special advisors, and their place in government, became very topical in 2020 over the role of Dominic Cummings, the special advisor to the prime minister. In spite of evidence that Dominic Cummings had breached guidelines regarding the Covid-19 lockdown, and also the first coronavirus regulation, Dominic Cummings continued to receive the support of the prime minister. As such, he was able to keep his position in the face of persistent calls from both the left and right wing media, and from MPs from the Conservative Party as well as opposition parties, for his resignation. One junior minister himself resigned over the lack of accountability of Dominic Cummings. This has raised serious questions as to the power, role and, in particular, accountability of special advisors.

7

The Powers of Government

Contents

No one in the modern state is untouched by the power of government. The editors of a recent volume of essays on executive power write in their introduction that:

> at the opening of the twenty-first century, governments have become the most powerful organs of nation states. They determine the direction, if not always the detail, of domestic policy. They decide how public money should, and should not, be spent. Foreign policy is made almost entirely by governments. And control of military power is likewise the preserve of the executive. Whatever the truth of the claim that, in this era of apparent globalization, states are no longer the only or even the most powerful units of political power, within nation states governments still retain very considerable power. This is not to say that their power can never be checked. Governments may rule, but they do not always rule supreme. In democracies the personnel of the executive is subject to the verdict of the electorate; the policies of the executive may be subject to political or parliamentary accountability; and the legality of executive action may be reviewed by the courts of law.

(Craig and Tomkins (eds.), *The Executive and Public Law: Power and Accountability in Comparative Perspective* (2006), p. 1.)

If anything, Brexit will add to the powers of the UK executive. This is evident in two ways. First, powers that had been transferred to the European Union will be repatriated to the UK. This may require the creation of more agencies in the UK in order to administer these powers previously regulated by the EU. Second, there is a growing trend in legislation implementing Brexit to grant large delegated powers to ministers to implement the Withdrawal Agreement, or to remedy deficiencies in retained EU law caused by Brexit. Moreover, legislation frequently creates new bodies to generate guidelines, codes and regulations as well as overseeing activities post-Brexit. This leads to the situation where there is simultaneously a growth in executive power, but one that is accompanied by the 'carving out' of the state – in other words, governmental powers are being transferred more and more to non-governmental agencies.

Brexit has also illustrated a tension between different understandings of governmental power – which David Howarth refers to as the 'Whitehall' and the 'Westminster' vision of representative government (Howarth, 'Westminster versus Whitehall: Two Incompatible Views of the Constitution', U.K. Const. L. Blog (10 April 2019) (available at https://ukconstitutionallaw.org/)). The 'Whitehall' vision focuses on the powers of the government. It regards the role of the government, as the executive, to implement its electoral mandate. The job of Parliament is to facilitate the enactment of this legislative programme, particularly as the government has a majority of seats in the Commons and so is able to get the votes it needs to ensure its legislation is enacted. Moreover, its ministers should be able to implement these policy requirements with little impediment from Parliament. The 'Westminster' vision focuses more on the powers of Parliament to scrutinise the actions of the government, holding it to account both in terms of its legislative programme and its executive decision-making.

These alternative accounts have come into focus through the Brexit process for two reasons. First, during 2019, the Conservative Governments of both Theresa May and Boris Johnson were minority governments, until the general election in December 2019 returned a majority Conservative Government. This situation means that backbench and opposition MPs have a greater ability to scrutinise the actions of the executive. Second, the main policy objective of Boris Johnson's Government is to implement the Brexit referendum. This can be used to provide an argument for a strengthening of executive power to achieve this policy objective: the government is not just implementing a policy choice found in manifesto, which contains an array of issues that may have persuaded the electorate to vote for that particular political party, but is implementing a specific policy choice that received a majority of votes cast in a referendum on that issue. The government is implementing the will of the people. Does this mean that there should be less scrutiny over the government when it is implementing Brexit?

In this chapter, we are concerned with the power and, more particularly, with the *powers* (plural) of British government. A considerable proportion of the chapter is devoted to exploring the law- and rule-making powers of government. As such, it should be read alongside what is said about delegated legislation in Chapters 2 (pp. 144–148) and 3 (pp. 199–204), and what is said about parliamentary oversight and legislative procedure in Chapter 9. When thinking about these powers, we need to do so in the light of whether we think this gives too much power to the executive and, if so, whether there are sufficient powers of oversight from Parliament or from the courts. These themes will be developed in more detail in later chapters.

7.1 Executive Power

Even in the first half of the nineteenth century the condition of working people in Britain was relieved or exacerbated by Acts of government – by the Corn Laws, Enclosure Acts, Poor Laws, Public Health Acts and Factory Acts. But the increase since that time in the activity of government and its impact on the daily life and work of the community has been immeasurable. Nineteenth-century governments were not called on to regulate a welfare state and did not attempt to manage the economy, foster industrial development or protect the environment. They concerned themselves little if at all with consumer protection, energy conservation, restrictive trade practices, immigration, full employment or equal pay for men and women. They had no need to be troubled with the construction and use of motor vehicles, the location of airports or the disposal of nuclear wastes. All these and many other new activities and concerns have made enormous claims on the resources of government in our time.

Report of the Royal Commission on the Constitution, vol. I (Cmnd 5460/1973)

The subject matter of government

[227]. Throughout most of the nineteenth century government was concerned mainly with law and order, external affairs and defence, the regulation of overseas trade and the raising of revenue; it exercised a narrow range of regulatory functions, but its attitude in domestic affairs was mostly passive and non-interventionist . . . The situation today is quite different; there are now very few areas of public and even personal life with which government can be said to have no concern at all.

[228]. This expansion of government, while a constant feature of modern history, has markedly quickened its pace at certain times. In [the twentieth] century two periods stand out, both associated with the world wars.

[229]. The first period extended from 1908 to 1919. It began with the extensive social reforms which were embodied in the Old Age Pensions Act 1908, the Labour Exchanges Act 1909 and the National Insurance Act 1911. There followed in war-time the imposition of a widening range of administrative and economic controls. After the war those controls were quickly wound up, but many of the new government departments, including those established for Pensions, Labour, Air and Scientific and Industrial Research, remained in being, and

two additional departments, for Transport and Health, were set up. Each of these new departments represented an enlarged area of government intervention.

[230]. The second period of rapid expansion was the decade from 1940. Apart again from the complex apparatus of war-time controls, finally dismantled in the 1950s, there were major developments in the social services and in the economic and environmental fields. Legislation was passed to bring about major changes in the arrangements for education, social security, health, agriculture, and town and country planning, and the Government's direct involvement in industry and the economy was increased through a series of Acts providing for the nationalisation of basic industries. Changes in the character of economic intervention were also implicit in the acceptance by the war-time Government of responsibility for maintaining full employment.

[231]. In these and other ways government responsibilities have ... widened immensely. The range of subjects that may now be raised in Parliament provides some illustration of this. We have examined a recent series of Parliamentary Questions to see how far it would have been appropriate to put them at the beginning of the century. Our analysis covered Questions receiving both oral and written reply in the House of Commons in one week in June 1971. There were 718 Questions in all, and we estimate that between 80 and 90 per cent of them could not have been tabled in 1900 since they related to matters which were not then of government concern.

The system of government in the early twenty-first century remains, even though in the throes of reform, in many respects the same as that with which Britain entered the First World War, after the nineteenth-century Reform Acts had laid the foundations of parliamentary democracy and the Parliament Act 1911 had curbed the powers of the House of Lords. In carrying out their increased commitments, British governments have been able to use the constitutional powers traditionally available to the Crown and have also captured powers from other institutions – from Parliament and from local government – although it might be without any change in the formal location of the power. Governments have often tried to remove restraints on the exercise of their powers and have invented new techniques for putting their policies into effect. But far from being something malign, the growth of governmental power has followed inevitably from the increase in the tasks of government and has been stimulated, at least in part, by the demands of social justice and public welfare.

The Conservative Governments from 1979 to 1997 espoused a political principle or ideology of reducing the role of the state, but if this was accomplished in certain respects (e.g., through policies of privatisation and the 'contracting out' and 'market testing' of services), it was also associated with an accretion of powers to central government. As W.H. Greenleaf observes (*The British Political Tradition*, vol. III, Part II (1987), p. 994), 'a government of explicitly libertarian intent still accepts a very elaborate public agenda indeed'. In the early years of the twenty-first century, we continue to inhabit a Britain of big government, ample public spending and centralised power. This trend continued through the Coalition Government and the more recent

Conservative minority and majority Governments. This can only continue post-Brexit, given that tasks that had been transferred to the EU will now be returned to the UK. Moreover, the response to the Covid-19 pandemic has further increased public spending – through the provision of furlough schemes for those unable to work from home following business closures, and schemes to help the self-employed. Nevertheless, there is a continuing trend to reduce the role of the state by transferring functions to non-governmental organisations.

Governments decide on their objectives and policies in response to innumerable and varied – often overlapping and sometimes contradictory – influences, among which are party policies, interest group pressures, media campaigns, departmental studies, parliamentary opinion, perceptions of public demand, foreign governments and, up to exit day, during the transition period and potentially beyond, the EU. Michael Hill (*The Policy Process* (6th edn. 2013), ch. 5) distinguishes three elements in the process – party-political commitments or programmes; bargaining with influential pressure groups; and the input of civil servants – and emphasises that these elements are 'mixed in varying combinations and often in all stages of the process'. A participatory (or 'deliberative') model of democracy would go further, to include arrangements for greater *public* involvement (through extensive consultation, citizens' juries and discussion in a variety of forums) in the formation of policies.

Robert Leach, in Maurice Mullard (ed.), *Policy-Making in Britain* (1995), pp. 34–5

Policies emerge in a variety of ways. Sometimes they seem to result from a relatively closed process internal to government, from the work of civil servants in major departments of state, perhaps aided by a handful of specialist outside advisers, but with little apparent public debate. Examples might include much of defence policy and some of the more technical aspects of economic policy, such as the decision of Nigel Lawson to maintain the value of sterling in line with that of the German mark from 1985. Such relatively technical policy issues often seem to exclude much of what is usually understood by political activity. Indeed, Lawson's policy of shadowing the mark was so little debated in public that even his own prime minister seemed for a time to be unaware of it. Yet even fairly abstruse technical issues may become caught up in a wider political debate, as indeed subsequently happened with Britain's membership of the Exchange Rate Mechanism.

Public policy may be more commonly perceived as the outcome of an overtly political process involving a highly public debate between political parties. Policy proposals may indeed be derived from party principles or ideologies, or connected with formal commitments in party manifestos. The privatisation programme of the Thatcher and Major governments and the introduction of competition and commercial principles into the operation of public services clearly reflect a particular and contested political philosophy.

The role of organised groups may, however, often be more significant than that of the party in the emergence of specific public policies. The debate between rival interests may take place largely in the corridors of power in Westminster and Whitehall, or it may be fought out in the public arena. It may involve the services of specialist consultants operating behind the scenes, influencing or purporting to influence key decision-makers, or it may involve highly visible public demonstrations. The conflict between rival interests may broadly parallel the party divide, or it may cut across party positions, as in the case of Sunday trading [in 1994] where conflicting pressures upon and within the Conservative Party, involving major retailing, trade union and religious interests, persuaded the Cabinet to allow a free vote.

The role of the wider public in the policy process is more debatable. The electorate is often held to give a 'mandate' to the party that forms the government, and this mandate may be cited to suggest public support for specific policies, particularly those included in the party's election manifesto. However, the notion of a mandate raises considerable theoretical and practical difficulties. Public influence may be more obvious in the negative sense, as a constraint inhibiting certain policies. Thus it was long assumed in the post-war era up until the 1970s that a government that abandoned a commitment to full employment would be decisively rejected by the electorate. More recently there has been a widespread assumption that commitments to increased public spending and taxation would spell disaster at the polls. Such assumptions may not always be correct, but if they are held by ministers, their advisers and other influentials, they are likely to have a significant impact.

Clear evidence of public opposition to specific policies has sometimes led to their reversal – the most notable example being the abolition [in 1992] of the Community Charge (or poll tax) only three years after its introduction as the 'flagship' of government policy. Rather more rarely, public opinion may pressurise a government to act, a possible example being the legislation to control dangerous dogs. Such instances frequently raise questions about the media presentation of particular events and issues. 'Public opinion' is often interpreted, and perhaps essentially moulded, by the press and electronic media, pushing issues such as homelessness or child abuse onto the public policy agenda.

So far, UK public policy has been related essentially to political activities and pressures from within the country. Clearly, however, public policy in the United Kingdom is often constrained by pressures and developments outside. The political system is far from closed. Key policy decisions may be abruptly forced on governments by forces beyond their control. Examples would include the devaluation of the pound sterling in 1967, or the United Kingdom's departure from the Exchange Rate Mechanism in 1992. More routinely, policy is clearly constrained by UK membership of various international associations, most obviously the European Union.

The choice of new policies is invariably constrained by an inheritance of policies and commitments from previous governments that have become 'embedded in public laws and public institutions': a government 'accepts the great bulk of its inheritance of legislation, willingly or *faute de mieux*'. Inherited policies may prove to be politically irreversible or may be sustained by inertia or lack of time to review them. (See Rose and Davies, *Inheritance in Public Policy: Change without Choice in Britain* (1994).) Nevertheless, governments do take office with new policies to implement and will modify or rescind some of their inherited programmes.

Once a policy has been decided, the means must be found to implement it. Implementation of policy is a complex process that depends for its success on a variety of factors, including the availability of the necessary resources of manpower and money, an efficiently designed implementation programme and the cooperation or at least submission of those affected by the policy. Fundamentally, it brings into question the authority and powers of government.

7.2 The Government's Powers

Among the power resources available to government for implementing its policies, Terence Daintith makes a useful distinction between the coercive power or the resource of force, which he terms *imperium*, and the power to employ the government's material resources of wealth or property, which he terms *dominium* ('Legal Analysis of Economic Policy' (1982) 9 JLS 191). The use of coercion by government requires express legal authority, to be found in a body of '*imperium* law', which consists almost entirely of statutes and delegated legislation, but includes some remaining prerogative powers. The use by the government of its *dominium*, if expenditure is involved, must be covered by parliamentary authorisation – the annual Appropriation Act or specific legislation. Daintith includes in '*dominium* law' 'those legal devices of the common law, such as contracts, gifts and other transfers, through which the wealth of government may be deployed' (ibid, p. 215). The government often prefers to rely on *dominium*, which is more flexible in use and may exact a lower political cost than recourse to *imperium*.

When the government requires an addition to its coercive powers, primary legislation by Parliament will normally be necessary, but delegated legislation may suffice if there is existing statutory authority for recourse to it, or, very rarely, power to legislate under the prerogative may be available. Again, if the government needs to make provision for expenditure on a continuing basis, for which annual parliamentary appropriation is considered constitutionally insufficient, it is expected to obtain authorisation in a specific act of Parliament.

Imperium law and *dominium* law invest the government with a host of executive powers by which policies are carried out in detail. Such powers generally include some (often considerable) degree of discretion as to the way in which they are exercised. The exercise of governmental power in modern conditions frequently involves an informal, administrative rule-making, which is a kind of self-regulation by the government. This 'quasi-legislation' does not (indeed cannot) effect alterations in statute or common law, but, as we shall see, it can affect private interests and may have legal consequences. (See, further, below.) In some instances, the government seeks to achieve its objects by the use of guidance – a hybrid technique that sometimes includes an element of legal authority and sometimes depends simply on the government's persuasive power. In *Secretary of State for the Environment, Food and Rural Affairs* v. *Downs* [2009] EWCA Civ 664, [103], Sullivan LJ said:

> Whether a particular provision or provisions should be included in primary or delegated legislation, in a Statutory Code of Practice, or in non-statutory policy guidance, is pre-eminently a matter of political judgment.

All the powers of government are subject to constraints. Some of these are inherent in the specific powers themselves: for example, the power to legislate depends on parliamentary consent, and the exercise of discretionary powers under statute or common law is subject to legal limits supervised by the courts. Other constraints stem from the European context in which British governments must function (Chapter 5). Then there are the countervailing powers possessed to varying degrees by opposition parties, organised groups, local authorities, multinational corporations and international organisations. In an analysis that rests on an idea of 'governance' rather than of 'government', some see the central executive as only one actor in a world of policy communities or 'networks', in which policies emerge through bargaining and agreement at a remove from Parliament and the public. But this analysis seems to underrate the primacy of government and Parliament in the constitutional system. Admittedly, the forces of limitation may be so powerful, especially in combination, as to compel government to make concessions or even to relinquish a policy. Or again the government may be driven to use one form of power instead of another, or to exhort or bargain rather than command. Some goals are in any event beyond the capacity of government to achieve, whatever the outpouring of laws, guidance or admonition.

But this is not to say that government in the UK is feeble and constricted. We have a central executive that is unconfined by a written constitution or a federal structure and unchecked by the balancing arrangements of a thoroughgoing separation of powers. It has established an ascendancy over the House of Commons and can dominate local government. In what the Memorandum of Dissent to the Kilbrandon Report described as 'the largest and most centralised unitary state in Western Europe' (Cmnd 5460-I/1973, para 34), the government has at its disposal great and far-reaching powers for putting its policies into effect.

Although recent events may appear to have limited governmental power, it is important to put these events in context. The 2017 general election result delivered a minority Conservative Government, which entered into a 'confidence and supply' agreement with the DUP. This weakened the power of the government, enabling Westminster to place restrictions over the powers of the executive. In addition, Brexit cuts across party lines. Within each political party – save for the SNP and the Liberal Democrats – there are members who are ideologically in favour of leaving and of remaining in the European Union, in addition to different beliefs as to the specific way in which Brexit should be implemented and as to the future relationship between the EU and the UK. Brexit also has large social, economic, legal and constitutional consequences, meaning that MPs may be more willing to challenge governmental policy than they might otherwise be. While the government may find it harder to implement its policies on Brexit, it may not face the same difficulties on other issues or post-Brexit. We can already see evidence of this change in the first parliamentary session of the majority Conservative Government following the general election in December 2019. Where there may be possible future limits is as regards growing devolution from Westminster to Scotland and Wales. This is moving towards a quasi-federal structure that may, post-Brexit, place further restrictions on the powers of Westminster, particularly given the creation of joint powers and the need for these governments to work together to create common frameworks.

7.2.1 Parliamentary Legislation

For many of its purposes, the government needs to obtain an Act of Parliament. In particular, an Act is necessary for implementing government policies that require changes in the law, the imposition of charges on the public or the assumption of new legal powers. Our present concern is with parliamentary legislation as a resource of government; attention will be given in Chapter 9 to Parliament's scrutinising function in the passage of government bills.

Putting aside the Consolidated Fund and Appropriation Acts (which formally authorise expenditure), the annual Finance Act (for the raising of taxes), the quinquennial Armed Forces Acts and Acts to consolidate the law, public Acts may be passed in order to change existing policy or launch an entirely new policy but also to correct deficiencies in existing legislation or to provide 'running repairs to the machinery that has been established for securing policy objectives but without any intention of altering those objectives' (Burton and Drewry, *Legislation and Public Policy* (1981), distinguishing, at pp. 36–40, between 'policy' and 'administration' bills).

7.2.1.1 Making of Government Bills

Governments adopt a programme of legislation in each session of Parliament to give effect to collectively agreed policies (sometimes prefigured in the governing party's election manifesto). Departments make their bids for legislation to be included in the programme, which is managed by the cabinet's Legislation Committee, balancing departmental interests with those of the government as a whole. The sources of legislative proposals include:

- recommendations of the Law Commission;
- EU obligations: in particular, EU directives that must be transposed into national law (under the current provisions of the Withdrawal Agreement, these will continue during the transition period, ending at the end of the implementation period completion day – currently 31 December 2020);
- an adverse ruling by a UK court, the ECJ (until the end of the implementation period completion day) or the ECtHR;
- unanticipated events requiring an urgent legislative response (for example, the Covid-19 pandemic, giving rise to the Coronavirus Act 2020).

Departments proposing to bring forward bills for adoption are reminded that, 'before seeking a slot in the Government's legislative programme' they 'should consider whether primary legislation is necessary' and departments 'should always consider whether the ends they wish to achieve could be reached by purely administrative means'. (*Guide to Making Legislation* (Cabinet Office, 2017), para 5.3).

A bill proposed for a slot in the programme must be submitted for collective agreement in the Parliamentary Business and Legislation (PBL) Committee and, in respect of its policy, in the relevant cabinet committee. The agreement of Treasury ministers has to be obtained for any public expenditure or tax implications of the bill.

Both in formulating policy and once it has been decided to introduce a bill, the government may embark on a process of consultation with outside interests, and sometimes issues consultation documents (such as preliminary 'Green' or firmer 'White' Papers), which invite public comment. Consultation can help to improve and legitimise a bill and win the support of those whose cooperation is needed if the legislation is to be effective.

In *Making the Law* (1992), the Hansard Society Commission on the Legislative Process reported much dissatisfaction with the extent and manner of consultation and made a number of recommendations for more timely, open and sufficient consultation so that bills could be got into 'a form fit for enactment, without major alteration, before they are presented to Parliament'. Instead, as it found, consultation often continued during a bill's passage through Parliament and consequential government amendments might be introduced at a late stage of the parliamentary process. In 1997 the Modernisation Committee of the House of Commons noted criticisms that there had been little, if any, consultation with the house before bills were formally introduced, and that consultation with bodies outside Parliament with a legitimate concern in the legislation had been 'patchy and spasmodic' (*1st Report of 1997–98*, HC 190). Subsequently, the government issued a *Code of Practice on Consultation* (updated in 2008), which urged departments to consult widely throughout the process of policy development and set out criteria for effective consultation. The House of Lords Constitution Committee reported in 2004 that there had been a positive development since *Making the Law* (above): proposed measures were being regularly put out for consultation and there was wide dissemination of consultation documents to interested parties (*14th Report of 2003–04*, HL 173).

Pre-legislative scrutiny by Parliament as well as consultation with outside bodies are facilitated if bills are published in draft form well before their formal introduction. Five draft bills were published in 1994–5, to be introduced in the following session of Parliament, and this salutary precedent has since been followed in respect of many major bills, for example, the Freedom of Information Bill, the Mental Health Bill, the Corporate Manslaughter Bill, the Climate Change Bill and the Constitutional Renewal Bill (subsequently enacted with revisions as the Constitutional Reform and Governance Act 2010). The Constitution Committee in its *14th Report of 2003–04* (above) recognised that some bills are not suitable for publication in draft but added that 'the occasions when bills are not published in draft should be the exception rather than the rule' (para 31). The government 'remains committed to the publication of bills in draft for pre-legislative scrutiny wherever possible' (Constitution Committee, *21st Report of 2008–09*, HL 160, Appendix 1). (See, further, the *Guide to Making Legislation* (Cabinet Office, 2009), ch. 22; Constitution Committee, *8th Report of 2008–09*, HL 66; below, pp. 546–547, with regard to pre-legislative scrutiny).

Nevertheless, there is no clear evidence of a consistent approach of using Green or White papers, or publishing draft bills. In a recent report, the Constitution Committee of the House of Lords (*The Legislative Process: Preparing Legislation for Parliament, 4th Report 2017–19* HL Paper 27), concluded that:

> pre-legislative scrutiny is seen as an optional extra to the legislative process: it may or may not take place and it does so in relative isolation to the other stages of scrutiny which legislation undergoes. Pre-legislative scrutiny should be considered an integral part of the wider legislative process. This may mean adapting other parts of the process to take account of pre-legislative scrutiny when it occurs. We do not, in this report, prescribe how this might occur, but as one example we recommend that the business managers of the House of Commons and the House of Lords should take into account whether a bill has undergone pre-legislative scrutiny when considering how much parliamentary time to allocate to the bill when it is passing through Parliament.
>
> There is a case for greater resources to be made available for committees undertaking pre-legislative scrutiny, in order to facilitate a detailed legal, policy and financial examination of the proposals in a draft Bill and its associated documents, including impact assessments.

Once a bill has been allocated a slot in the programme and collective agreement has been given to its policy, the sponsoring department gives instructions to parliamentary counsel for drafting the bill for presentation to Parliament. Their essential task 'is to give effect to the government's intentions in a form capable of withstanding Parliamentary and later judicial scrutiny' (Daintith and Page, *The Executive in the Constitution* (1999), p. 250). This work has often to be done under great pressure of time and on the basis of incomplete instructions, with the consequence that Parliament has sometimes received an unfinished and flawed bill in need of extensive amendment. (See, further, Page, 'Their Word is Law: Parliamentary Counsel and Creative Policy Analysis' [2009] *PL* 790.)

Explanatory notes are published together with the bill to inform Parliament and others of the background, structure and content of the bill. An impact assessment is also published if the bill has an impact on business, the environment, charities or the voluntary sector, identifying the interests affected and estimating the likely impact in terms of costs and benefits. For every bill, an equality impact statement must be published, drawing attention to any effects of the bill regarding race, gender or disability. A memorandum must be produced for the Legislation Committee with regard to the bill's compatibility with convention rights, and the explanatory notes must also deal with any human rights aspects of the bill. Finally, the bill is approved by the Parliamentary Business and Legislation Committee for introduction in one or other House of Parliament.

From the government's point of view, Parliament is part of the machinery by which its policies are implemented. The approving and legitimating function of Parliament dominates the perspective not only of the government front-bench but also, in general, that of backbenchers on the government side. The improvement of a bill as an instrument of the government's policy is part of this function and is carried out chiefly on the initiative of the government itself. Opposition members will often cooperate in the work of improvement of an uncontroversial bill, but if they oppose a bill will fight for concessions or – wholly rejecting the policy on which a bill is based – will set to work to defeat, weaken or delay it if they can. In short, government and opposition act, with respect to contested bills, on different conceptions of the parliamentary function. But Parliament as an institution normally acts in accordance with the government's conception of its role, which is to support, perfect and enact the government's bills. For this reason, it is commonly said that parliamentary legislation is in reality a function of government.

When a government bill is introduced in Parliament it has usually already been firmly shaped in a process of departmental and interdepartmental or cabinet discussion and consultation with outside interests. Accommodations will have been reached and bargains struck, even though the bill may still be far from polished or water-tight in its detail. Its passage through Parliament is generally assured, albeit that the government may not be able to resist all amendments.

Thus, the parliamentary process is not wholly conformable to the government's will and there may be a continuing necessity to accommodate the misgivings of backbenchers, the probing of opposition and the unresolved concerns of outside interests. This is evidenced in research, most notably the recent work by Meg Russell and Daniel Gover, which examined in detail the enactment of legislation, through carrying out interviews in addition to tracking legislative amendments.

Russell and Gover, *Legislation at Westminster: Parliamentary Influence in the Making of British Law* (OUP, 2017), pp. 264–5

Our central focus in this chapter is parliament's influence in the legislative process. As set out in Chapter 1 (and detailed in the appendices), we conducted over 120 interviews with people closely involved in the process, in Westminster, Whitehall, and beyond. Quotations from these interviews have informed the analysis throughout the book, with respect to developments on particular bills and the contribution of specific actors. But we also asked all interviewees their opinion on one very central question: 'how influential is parliament on government legislation?'. Respondents were encouraged to interpret this question in their own ways, and it elicited a very wide range of answers. The responses cannot readily be sorted into clear-cut categories, and hence our interpretation here is purely qualitative. Nonetheless for indicative purposes, some of these comments are very illuminating.

Although there were many differences among interviewees, it was notable that those furthest from the lawmaking process tended to be the most sceptical about parliament's power – expressing views closer to those propagated by critical external commentators. For example, one outside group representative stated that he found the 'very question depressing beyond belief', and considered this 'testament to the weakness of parliamentary democracy and the strength of the party system and cabinet government'. Another suggested that 'largely, if it's a government bill, government has the whip hand', while a third described trying to influence bills through parliament as 'a frustrating process'. One Commons backbencher described parliament as 'normally not very influential', while another even suggested that its influence was 'nil, basically'.

This degree of negativity was rare, and there were various more ambivalent or nuanced responses. For example another backbencher replied 'well, not effective enough', while a Conservative peer with long ministerial experience observed that parliamentary influence on bills 'varies a great deal depending on the subject matter'. A Liberal Democrat MP likewise suggested that if seeking change to 'a manifesto commitment, a core policy that goes to the core of the sort of party it is, you ain't going to get very far', whereas on 'a new issue that's come up where people's positions aren't entrenched, you've got more traction'. These are thoughtful and broadly sensible reflections, but of course not supported by the extent of change to manifesto-based policy in the Identity Cards Bill, and particularly in the Health Bill.

If the executive did indeed have the whip hand, we might expect those who have the greatest experience working inside government to be the most dismissive of parliament and its power. It was therefore striking that among our interviewees the most strongly positive responses regarding parliamentary influence came from this group. This was primarily because such people chose to interpret the question in a different way—going beyond immediately visible change. For example when asked 'how influential is parliament on government legislation?' a former cabinet minister responded

'Enormously. It's a widespread illusion that it isn't.' Civil servants who had worked on bill teams very often spoke in similar terms. One described parliament as 'extremely influential', suggesting that it's 'not fully understood, either by the media or by the general public about how much influence parliament has'. Initial responses from other bill team officials included, respectively, 'very influential', 'massively influential', 'immensely', and '100 per cent'.

Further discussion with these government insiders showed that they took a wider view of the role of parliament, beyond simply considering its ability to amend bills during their passage (for further detail of this culture see particularly Chapter 3). A former minister suggested that parliament was 'more influential than many think it is because much of the influence is unseen'. The former cabinet minister already cited elaborated by saying 'just about all legislation is affected by parliament. It's a widespread and completely wrong myth that government goes ahead without parliament.' Likewise another interviewee with long cabinet experience responded to the question as follows:

I think much more than people might think, in that if you just focus on the narrow dialogue between parliament and government at the ... public bill stage of a bill, you ignore the fact that there's [often] been pre-legislative scrutiny, there's been a draft bill, but also ministers do take account of what they know the view of parliament is when they draft the bill. So, actually, it's a sort of progressive influence, and it gets crystallized at the public bill stage, but actually a lot of it happens long before then.

This echoed a comment from one of the bill team officials cited above, that 'it doesn't start and end with the bill itself; it's a constant dialogue with parliament that is influential on what happens'. Another such official went even further, claiming that 'civil servants do – as indeed do ministers – actually default to parliament, as being the basis for everything we do.'

Most bills (about three-quarters of the total number), and, in particular, those of substantial political importance, are introduced in the House of Commons. (Bills whose main purpose is financial cannot begin in the House of Lords.) The first reading of a bill is purely formal: the title is read out and a minister nods his or her assent. The motion for the second reading of the bill is normally debated on the floor of the house, but a few uncontroversial bills are debated in a second reading committee. The second reading debate provides the government with an opportunity to explain the aims and principles of the bill and to outline its main provisions. This is also an opportunity for opposition parties to deliver their challenge to the policy of the bill. If the bill fails to be given a second reading it can go no further, although it is extremely rare for a government bill to be defeated on the motion for second reading. There have been only two instances since 1924: the defeat by one vote of the Reduction of Redundancy Rebates Bill in 1977 and that of the Shops Bill by fourteen votes in 1986.

For the committee stage in the House of Commons, most bills are referred to a public bill committee, with a membership of between sixteen and fifty MPs, reflecting party strengths in the house. Among the members there is, besides the sponsoring minister, a government whip, who has responsibility for ensuring the attendance and support of government backbenchers on the committee. Proceedings in the committee are normally timetabled in accordance with a programme agreed by the house after discussion between the parties. A public bill committee may be given power to send for 'persons, papers and records' and the proceedings may begin with hearings of oral evidence from the minister, officials and other witnesses called by the committee. The committee then considers the bill in detail, clause by clause, and amendments to the bill may be made. From the government's point of view, the committee stage provides it with an opportunity of making improvements to its bill. J.A.G. Griffith observes (*Parliamentary Scrutiny of Government Bills* (1974), p. 38):

> If moved by the Government, the purpose of an amendment is most likely to be to correct a drafting error or to make minor consequential changes, to record agreements made with outside bodies which were uncompleted when the bill was introduced, to introduce new matter, or occasionally to meet a criticism made by a Member either during the second reading debate or at an earlier part of the committee stage, or informally.

A minority government, or one with a slender majority, may have difficulty in managing the proceedings of public bill committees and, like the Labour Government of 1974–9, may be unable to avoid numerous defeats there. If it resorts to taking the committee stage on the floor of the house, this may hold up other items of its legislative programme. (As to the rather loose convention that the committee stage of bills of 'first class constitutional importance' should be taken on the floor of the house, see above, pp. 192–199 and 549–550.)

At the report stage, the bill is considered as a whole and the government has an opportunity to reverse defeats suffered in committee, and also to introduce new amendments embodying promised concessions or the results of its further reflections on the bill. Many government amendments may be tabled and, although it is expected that amendments at this stage will be kept to a minimum, it is often the case that insufficient time is available for scrutiny on report. The third reading allows a final brief debate on the principles of the bill as amended; only minor verbal amendments may be made at this stage.

The subsequent passage of the bill through the House of Lords enables the government to continue the process of refinement of the bill in response to arguments and pressures brought to bear on it. Here, too, amendments may be carried against the government. Lords' amendments must be considered by the Commons, and if the Commons disagrees with any of them, there has to be further consideration of the disputed amendments by the Upper House. The bill may go back and forth between the two houses a number of times until agreement is reached; if the Lords remain adamant, the government can in the last resort, and if time allows, overcome their resistance by using the procedure of the Parliament Acts 1911 and 1949 (below, pp. 772–773).

By introducing some of its less controversial bills in the House of Lords, the government is able to make full use of the resources of both houses in processing its legislation through Parliament. The Parliament Acts do not, however, apply to bills introduced in the House of Lords.

The procedure for the enactment of a public bill is not without its hazards for the government. Even if it has a sufficient majority to overwhelm opposition parties, they may by exploiting the procedures of Parliament cause trouble for the government in its efforts to get a bill enacted intact and on time. The government's own backbenchers cannot always be coerced by the whips and, in recent years, numbers of them have shown a robust willingness to vote in the opposition lobby (see, further, Cowley, *The Rebels: How Blair Mislaid his Majority* (2005); Whitaker (2006) 59 *Parl Aff* 350; Kalitowski (2008) 61 *Parl Aff* 694). Minority governments are especially vulnerable, as was shown in the 1976–7 session when a minority Labour Government failed to secure the passage of seven of its bills. This has also been illustrated during the 2017–19 Conservative Government of Theresa May and the 2019 Government of Boris Johnson, both of which suffered defeats on important legislation relating to Brexit, including seeing Brexit-related legislation lapse as it was not enacted prior to the dissolution of Parliament at the end of the 2017–19 parliamentary session.

But, in ordinary circumstances, the obstacles of the parliamentary process can be overcome. Governments have normally enjoyed the support of mainly loyal majorities in the House of Commons; opposition parties are usually open to bargaining, and if persistently obstructive can be curbed by use of a programme motion (formerly known as the guillotine), which allocates time to specific clauses of a bill or the bill as a whole, or a closure motion which is used to bring debate on legislation to an end. Programme motions are rarely, if ever, defeated. However, on 22 October 2019, the programme motion on the European Union (Withdrawal Agreement) Bill, which would have only allocated three sitting days to its passage through the House of Commons, was defeated by 322 votes to 308 (HC Deb vol. 666, col 922, 22 October 2019). The programme motion having failed, the bill was placed 'in limbo'. It was this defeat that led the then minority Conservative Government to seek a further vote in favour of an early general election and, when that did not receive the requisite number of votes, to propose what became the Early Parliamentary General Election Act 2019, giving rise to the general election on 12 December 2019.

In a full session, the government can generally achieve the passage of something between thirty and sixty bills substantially (sometimes entirely) in the form in which they are wanted. In urgent cases, a public bill can be passed in a few days or even hours. Such speed of enactment, which is not conducive to well-judged law-making, has been a feature of legislation on terrorism. For instance, the Criminal Justice (Terrorism and Conspiracy) Act 1998, enacted in response to a terrorist bombing in Omagh, was read the first time in the House of Commons shortly before 4pm on 2 September 1998 and had passed both houses and been given the royal assent by 1.30am on 4 September. The Anti-Terrorism, Crime and Security Act 2001 (with 129 sections and 8 schedules) was introduced on 12 November 2001 and given the royal assent on 13 December. The Prevention of Terrorism Bill introduced in the House of Commons on 22 February 2005, although strongly contested and passing back and forth between Lords and Commons, received the royal assent on 11 March 2005. More recent instances of such fast-track legislation have included the Criminal Evidence (Witness Anonymity) Bill 2008 and the Northern Ireland Bill 2009. By contrast, the legislative passage of the Terrorism Act 2006 lasted five months and that of the Counterterrorism Act 2008 lasted ten months.

More recently, the Northern Ireland (Executive and Exercise of Functions) Act 2018 was enacted in two days, with just one day in each house. This legislation empowered civil servants, on a temporary basis, to govern Northern Ireland given the failure of the Northern Ireland Assembly to agree on a first minister and deputy first minister and in the face of court decisions challenging the legality of some of the measures enacted by civil servants. Further legislation has been enacted to continue government by civil servants in Northern Ireland. In addition, there are recent examples of non-governmental bills that have been fast-tracked through the House of Commons – the European Union (Withdrawal) Act 2019 (commonly known as the Cooper Bill) and the European Union (Withdrawal) (No 2) Act 2019 (commonly known as the Benn Bill). Both of these pieces of legislation were designed to prevent a 'no-deal' exit from the European Union by requiring the prime minister to ask the European Union for an extension for the Article 50 deadline. In both instances, the extension was requested and granted. Further examples of recent fast-track legislation include the European Union (Withdrawal Agreement) Act 2020, which received a mere three days' scrutiny in the House of Commons, in spite of its complex constitutional implications; the Terrorist Offenders (Restriction of Early Release) Act 2020 (which, argu-ably, breaches the ECHR, given that it retrospectively increases the length of a sentence to be served before being eligible for a parole hearing, when previously these prisoners would have been subject to automatic release) and the Coronavirus Act 2020. The constitutional implications of fast-track legis-lation were considered by the Constitution Committee, *15th Report of 2008–09*, HL 116; see, too, the *Government's Response* in the Committee's *2nd Report of 2009–10*, HL 11.

Governments must govern, and they have a proper interest in getting their bills enacted. Procedural innovations have often been designed to protect this interest rather than to improve the effectiveness of parliamentary scrutiny. There is, indeed, a tension between these aims, and its balanced resolution should be the constant concern of parliamentary reformers. For example, considerations of efficiency might favour the introduction of 'framework' bills restricted to broad principles, the substance to be supplied by subordinate legislation, but such a development could debilitate parliamentary control of the executive. Several bills presented to Parliament by Conservative Governments between 1979 and 1997 did indeed provide it with a very incomplete statement of the whole legislative scheme, extensive rule-making powers being delegated to ministers for filling in the detail. Among statutes of this kind were the Social Security Act 1986, the Education Reform Act 1988, the Legal Aid Act 1988 and the Child Support Act 1991. The practice was seen as 'downgrading the role of Parliament'. (See McAuslan and McEldowney, *Law, Legitimacy and the Constitution* (1985), p. 23.) A lavish delegation of powers of subordinate legislation is still a feature – perhaps an unavoidable feature – of many statutes, such as the Pollution Prevention and Control Act 1999 and the Financial Services and Markets Act 2000. The latter Act includes no fewer than 400 delegated powers. Part 1 of the Civil Contingencies Act 2004 was said by one Cabinet Office minister to be 'heavily reliant on supporting regulations and guidance' (HC Deb vol. 436, col 551 W, 7 July 2005). Two notable 'framework' bills introduced in Parliament in 2010–11 were the Localism Bill (including some 150 order-making powers) and the Public Bodies Bill. The House of Lords Delegated Powers and Regulatory Reform Committee has noted (*7th Report of 2008–09*, HL 83, para 23) that:

> it has been a longstanding feature of social security legislation, since at least the 1970s, that the overall framework is set out in Acts and matters of greater detail are left to subordinate legislation . . .

One of the concerns of this committee is to ascertain whether a bill 'sufficiently particularises the principles on which, and the circumstances in which, secondary legislation may be passed, and so avoids being characterised as a "skeleton bill"': *7th Report of 1999–2000*, HL 36, Appendix 2, para 3.

In spite of these concerns, skeleton bills continue to be enacted and have been, in particular, a feature of legislation required to implement Brexit. One such example is the Healthcare (European Economic Area and Switzerland Arrangements) Act 2019. The Act only has eight sections, section 1 of which states that: 'The Secretary of State may make payments, and arrange for payments to be made, in respect of the cost of healthcare provided in an EEA state or Switzerland', with section 2 empowering the Secretary of State to make regulations to achieve this purpose or to give effect to a healthcare agreement. Both the Delegated Powers and Regulatory Reform Committee and the Constitution Committee of the House of Lords regarded the broad powers in what is now section 2 of the Act as 'inappropriately wide' and inadequately justified. (Delegated Powers and Regulatory Reform Committee, *Thirty Ninth*

Report 2017–19, HL paper 226) para 13 and the House of Lords Constitution Committee *Healthcare (International Arrangements) Bill, 18th Report 2017–19*, HL paper 291) para 8.)

The passage of bills was sometimes facilitated by informal agreement between 'the usual channels' (linking government and opposition) on time-tabling of the bill and in 2000 sessional orders introduced procedures for the regular programming of legislation on an experimental basis. The sessional orders were made permanent in 2004: see now *House of Commons Standing Orders: Public Business* (2019), Nos 83A–83I. By this means, it was hoped, the government would be assured of getting its legislation through in a reasonable time while opposition parties and backbenchers would have a full opportunity to debate and vote on the issues of most concern to them. Programme motions are tabled after cross-party discussions through the usual channels and, in the words of a Leader of the House of Commons, 'the essence of the success of programming lies in the spirit of cooperation between those acting for Government and Opposition on a particular Bill' (HC Deb vol. 425, col 1314, 26 October 2004). An agreed programme avoids the need for the government to resort to imposed and arbitrary guillotines on discussion. But the spirit of cooperation is often lacking: programme motions may be con-tested and agreement may not be reached. Programming may fail to ensure adequate scrutiny of the bill's provisions, with many clauses not being debated.

The system of programming has strengthened the government's control of parliamentary time and this can be countered only if the house is able to take the management of timetabling into its own hands. The ability of Parliament to take control over programming motions is illustrated by the enactment of the European Union (Withdrawal) Act 2019 and the European Union (Withdrawal) (No 2) Act 2019. The first was enacted following a proposed amendment to a motion enacted under Standing Order No. 14. The second was enacted by MPs using Standing Order No. 24 to propose an urgent question. The urgent question proposed a suspension of Standing Order No. 14, proposing instead an alternative programme motion which allocated time for the specific enactment of the European Union (Withdrawal) (No 2) Bill. As discussed above, the Commons voted against the programme motion pro-posed by the government for the European Union (Withdrawal Agreement) Bill 2019.

The parliamentary scrutiny of bills is further considered below, pp. 544–554.

7.2.1.2 Implementation and Effectiveness of Legislation

Acts of Parliament commonly provide that their provisions will come into force on some specified future date (and not immediately following royal assent) or may entrust to a minister the power to make a commencement order bringing the provisions into force (or successive orders for different provisions of the Act). The coming into force of the Act's provisions may accordingly be delayed, for example until administrative arrangements have been put in place for their effective implementation. Events may indeed occur that persuade the minister – or successive ministers – that it is not appropriate to make a commencement order. In *R* v. *Secretary of State for the Home Department, ex p Fire Brigades Union* [1995] 2 AC 513, the House of Lords held that while the minister is under no duty in such cases to bring the provisions of the Act into force, his or her discretion whether or not to do so is not absolute and unfettered; rather, the minister is under a continuing legal duty to consider whether it is appropriate to appoint a commencement date. The act in this case had made provision for a new criminal injuries compensation scheme. The minister was held to have acted unlawfully in deciding to renounce the statutory scheme, instead adopting under the prerogative a different scheme of compensation. To act in this manner, said Lord Browne-Wilkinson, was to 'frustrate the will of Parliament expressed in a statute'.

When a government bill has been passed by Parliament and the Act duly brought into force, it is still not certain that the government will have achieved its objective. The need for parliamentary consent is not the only limitation of the government's power to carry its policies into effect by legislation. Public or group consent is another limiting factor, insofar as the efficacy of an Act may depend on the cooperation or acquiescence of those affected by it. 'Legislation', it has been said, 'is not the end of the policy process, merely a step en route' (Marsh and Rhodes (eds.), *Implementing Thatcherite Policies* (1992), p. 4). The process of implementation of much legislation involves bargaining and compromise, and may be impeded if not thwarted by an adverse or lukewarm response from implementing agencies or from those on whom the Act places new obligations or restrictions. The Industrial Relations Act 1971 failed to accomplish its main purposes when it encountered intense opposition from the trade union movement and only limited and equivocal support among employers (see Moran, *The Politics of Industrial Relations* (1977), ch. 8). The Caravan Sites Act 1968, which required local authorities to provide caravan sites for gypsies residing in or resorting to their areas, was not effective to ensure sufficient accommodation for gypsies: many authorities failed to comply with their obligations and the Secretary of State rarely used the coercive powers available to him under the Act. (Section 80 of the Criminal Justice and Public Order Act 1994 abolished the duty to provide sites and the present policy – currently under review – is to ensure the provision of sites for gypsies and travellers through the planning system and funding local authorities to create sites.) The community charge or poll tax, introduced by the Local Government Finance Act 1988, proved a lamentable and costly failure, being administratively complex, redolent of unfairness and widely unpopular (see Butler, Adonis and Travers, *Failure in British Government: The Politics of the Poll Tax* (1994)). It was abolished in 1992. The Child Support Act 1991 was badly flawed and had unexpected and untoward consequences that successive reviews and amendments to the Act failed to redress. Implementing regulations were found by the Court of Appeal in *Smith* v. *Smith* [2004] EWCA Civ 1318,

[2005] 1 WLR 1318 to be marred by 'sloppy, untidy' drafting that had created a muddle resulting in 'absurdity and injustice'. It was eventually recognised that the system of child support established by the Act could not achieve its objectives and a report by Sir David Henshaw in 2006, concluding that the system should be fundamentally redesigned, was accepted by the government. An 'operational improvement plan' was adopted and a new Child Maintenance and Enforcement Commission was established in 2008, with stronger enforcement powers, to take over responsibility for child support.

Legislation may fail because it is insufficiently prepared, wrongly targeted or excessively complex, and the efficacy of a statute may be blunted if insufficient resources of money, administrative machinery, personnel or publicity are committed to its implementation. Several of these deficiencies marred the Child Support legislation (above), demonstrating, as the Social Security Committee of the House of Commons observed, 'that policy can come close to being frustrated and derailed by over-hasty implementation and poor levels of administrative performance' (*5th Report of 1996–97*, HC 282, para 18). Provisions of the Criminal Justice Act 2003 were said by the Court of Appeal in *R* v. *Bradley* [2005] EWCA Crim 20, [2005] 1 Cr App R 397 to be 'conspicuously unclear in circumstances where clarity could easily have been achieved' and to have been brought into force prematurely, before appropriate training could be given to judges and magistrates. (See, also, as to the Dangerous Dogs Act 1991, Hood et al., 'Assessing the Dangerous Dogs Act: When Does a Regulatory Law Fail?' [2000] *PL* 282.)

(The complex relation between policy and implementation is perceptively discussed by Ham and Hill, *The Policy Process in the Modern Capitalist State* (2nd edn. 1993), ch. 6. Sir Christopher Foster has identified factors contributing to a decline in the quality of legislation in (2000) 53 *Parl Aff* 328, 336–40; see also his *British Government in Crisis* (2005), ch. 4 and pp. 134–5. Foster remarks (p. 53) that 'good, or at least plausible, policy ideas are often reflected in bad legislation'.)

The parliamentary legislative process results in a verbal text which is authoritative but has to be interpreted. The courts, in the exercise of their power of interpretation, aided by recourse to a fund of common law principles, may give to an Act a meaning and effect contrary to what the government had in view in introducing the legislation. A striking instance was the decision of the House of Lords in *Anisminic Ltd* v. *Foreign Compensation Commission* [1969] 2 AC 147. In this case a statutory provision that a determination by the Foreign Compensation Commission should 'not be called in question by any court of law' was held ineffective to prevent a court from setting aside a 'determination' that went beyond the legal powers of the Commission. As J.A.G. Griffith remarks, the decision 'shows how, on occasion, the courts will resist the strongest efforts of the government to exclude them from reviewing executive discretion' (*The Politics of the Judiciary* (5th edn. 1997), p. 106). The strength of this resistance was illustrated further in the recent Supreme Court decision of *R (Privacy International)* v. *Investigative Powers Tribunal* [2019] UKSC 22, [2019] 2 WLR 1219. In this case, a clause not only claimed that determinations and decisions of the Investigative Powers Tribunal (IPT) 'shall not be subject to appeal or be liable to be questioned in any court' but also specifically included decisions as to whether the IPT had jurisdiction within the range of those that could not be questioned by a court – in other words, decisions as to the scope of powers of the IPT. A majority of the Supreme Court concluded that this wording did not exclude judicial review of the court over purported determinations of the IPT as to whether it had the jurisdiction to act; in other words, it did not exclude judicial review for legal errors made by the IPT when determining the scope of its powers.

The decision of the House of Lords in *Pepper (Inspector of Taxes)* v. *Hart* [1993] AC 593 has had the effect of permitting the courts to refer to parliamentary materials as an aid to statutory construction if an Act is ambiguous or obscure or if its literal meaning leads to an absurdity. In particular, a court may have regard to statements made in Parliament by the minister or other promoter of a bill to ascertain 'the intention with which the legislation is placed before Parliament' (per Lord Griffiths). It is the intention of Parliament that is decisive, but if a minister has made a clear and unambiguous statement as to the effect of words in the bill, it is assumed that Parliament 'passed the Bill on the basis that the provision would have the effect stated' (per Lord Browne-Wilkinson). Whether this is a justified assumption is questioned by Baker [1993] *CLJ* 353. Scott Styles observes that the reference by the courts to ministerial statements 'will in practice mean that the courts are directly deferring to the opinions of government ministers' and discerns in this 'a major shift in the British constitution': 'The rule of Parliament: statutory interpretation after *Pepper v Hart*' (1994) 14 *OJLS* 151. For further (and ongoing) argument, see Lord Steyn (2001) 21 *OJLS* 59; Vogenauer (2005) 25 *OJLS* 629; Sales (2006) 26 *OJLS* 585; and Kavanagh (2005) 121 *LQR* 98. Recent cases evidence a 'retreat from *Pepper v Hart*': see *R* v. *Secretary of State for the Environment, Transport and the Regions, ex p Spath Holme Ltd* [2001] 2 AC 349, 391–3, 407–8; *Wilson* v. *First County Trust Ltd* [2003] UKHL 40, [2004] 1 AC 816, [56]–[60], [139]–[140]; *Harding* v. *Wealands* [2006] UKHL 32, [2007] 2 AC 1, [81]; and *Yarl's Wood Immigration Ltd* v. *Bedfordshire Police Authority* [2008] EWHC 2207 (Comm), [155]. See, too, Greenberg (2008) 124 *LQR* 181.

The Hansard Society Commission on the Legislative Process recommended (*Making the Law* (1992), para 393) that the operation of major Acts should be reviewed by parliamentary select committees two or three years after they come into force. This proposal having won support from the House of Lords Constitution Committee (*14th Report of 2003–04*, HL 173) and the Law Commission (*Post-Legislative Scrutiny*, Cm 6945/2006, Law Com 302), the government accepted the case for systematic parliamentary post-legislative scrutiny. In *Post-legislative Scrutiny – The Government's Approach*, Cm 7320/2008, it said that after internal departmental scrutiny of an Act:

> the basis for a new process for post-legislative scrutiny should be for the Commons committees themselves, on the basis of a Memorandum on appropriate Acts submitted by the relevant Government department, and published as a Command paper, to decide whether to conduct further post-legislative scrutiny of the Act in question.

Such reviews would take place between three and five years after royal assent. An instance of post-legislative scrutiny was that of the Licensing Act 2003 carried out by the Culture, Media and Sport Committee of the House of Commons in 2008 (*6th Report of 2008–09*, HC 492). Some legislation provides for post-enactment scrutiny to be conducted by specially appointed reviewers: for example, the operation of the Prevention of Terrorism Act 2005 is reviewed annually by the independent reviewer of terrorism legislation, as provided by section 14 of the Act. Post-legislative review is systematically undertaken by the Scottish Parliament. The Public Audit and Post-Legislative Scrutiny Committee (renamed in 2016) is tasked with carrying out post-legislative scrutiny. Post-legislative scrutiny also regularly takes place in the Welsh Assembly, being undertaken by specific committees as opposed to a specialist committee tasked with post-legislative scrutiny (recent examples include scrutiny of the Higher Education (Wales) Act 2015, The Human Transplantation (Wales) Act 2015 and the Local Government – Active Travel (Wales) Act 2013).

There is more that can be demanded of legislation than that it should effectively implement the government's policy. A requirement of principle was expressed as follows by Sir John Donaldson MR in *Merkur Island Shipping Corpn v. Laughton* [1983] 2 AC 570, 594–5 (with particular reference to the Trade Union and Labour Relations Act 1974, the Trade Union and Labour Relations (Amendment) Act 1976 and the Employment Act 1980):

> At the beginning of this judgment I said that whilst I had reached the conclusion that the law was tolerably clear, the same could not be said of the way in which it was expressed. The efficacy and maintenance of the rule of law, which is the foundation of any parliamentary democracy, has at least two pre-requisites. First, people must understand that it is in their interests, as well as in that of the community as a whole, that they should live their lives in accordance with the rules and all the rules. Second, they must know what those rules are. Both are equally important and it is the second aspect of the rule of law which has caused me concern in the present case . . .
>
> In industrial relations it is of vital importance that the worker on the shop floor, the shop steward, the local union official, the district officer and the equivalent levels in management should know what is and what is not 'offside'. And they must be able to find this out for

themselves by reading plain and simple words of guidance. The judges of this court are all skilled lawyers of very considerable experience, yet it has taken us hours to ascertain what is and what is not 'offside', even with the assistance of highly experienced counsel. This cannot be right.

We have had to look at three Acts of Parliament, none intelligible without the other. We have had to consider section 17 of the Act of 1980, which adopts the 'flow' method of Parliamentary draftsmanship, without the benefit of a flow diagram. We have furthermore been faced with the additional complication that subsection (6) of section 17 contains definitions which distort the natural meaning of the words in the operative subsections ... But I do not criticise the draftsman. His instructions may well have left him no option. My plea is that Parliament, when legislating in respect of circumstances which directly affect the 'man or woman in the street' or the 'man or woman on the shop floor' should give as high a priority to clarity and simplicity of expression as to refinements of policy. Where possible, statutes, or complete parts of statutes, should not be amended but re-enacted in an amended form so that those concerned can read the rules in a single document. When formulating policy, ministers, of whatever political persuasion, should at all times be asking themselves and asking parliamentary counsel: 'Is this concept too refined to be capable of expression in basic English? If so, is there some way in which we can modify the policy so that it can be expressed?' Having to ask such questions would no doubt be frustrating for ministers and the legislature generally, but in my judgment this is part of the price which has to be paid if the rule of law is to be maintained.

(See also the remarks of Lord Diplock in the House of Lords [1983] 2 AC 570, 612 and the example offered by Cowley, *The Rebels: How Blair Mislaid his Majority* (2005), pp. 29–34.)

7.2.2 Delegated Legislation

Putting aside an exceptional and very limited power of legislation under the prerogative (below), the executive is 'constitutionally forbidden to make law except with the express authority of Parliament' (Sedley LJ in *Secretary of State for the Home Department* v. *Pankina* [2010] EWCA Civ 719, [2010] 3 WLR 1526, at [19]: see the judge's exploration of the principle in this case). Many Acts of Parliament do, however, confer power on the administration to legislate for specified purposes. In formal constitutional terms, Parliament as the supreme law-giver delegates a circumscribed portion of legislative competence to a minister of the Crown or other public authority. The reality is that the government, in drawing up a bill for enactment by Parliament, decides how much detailed regulation of the subject matter to include in the bill itself and what powers to keep in its own hands for carrying out the purposes of the bill.

The delegation of legislative power by Parliament to the sovereign or to ad hoc authorities was known in Tudor times and even earlier, but the expansion of governmental activity in the nineteenth and twentieth centuries brought about a great increase in delegated legislation. By the 1930s, the number of departmental regulations issued annually was fifteen or twenty times that of Acts passed by Parliament. This abundant production of law by agencies other than Parliament was viewed by some with an exaggerated alarm as a triumph of bureaucracy over the constitution (e.g., Lord Hewart, *The New Despotism* (1929)). Others, like Harold Laski (*Parliamentary Government in England* (1938), p. 216), recognised that:

> It would be foolish for Parliament to waste its time legislating separately upon applications or extensions of general principles about which it has already legislated. To say, for example, that a poison is a substance declared to be such by the Home Office in consultation with the Pharmaceutical Society is, under proper safeguards, infinitely more sensible than for the Cabinet to ask Parliament for a separate statute on each occasion when it is desirable to restrict the sale of some chemical substance on the ground of its poisonous nature.

The government responded to criticism of the practice of delegated legislation (and the vesting of judicial and quasi-judicial powers in ministers) by setting up the Committee on Ministers' Powers (Donoughmore Committee), which reported in 1932. The committee expressed its general conclusion on the subject of delegated powers in saying (Cmd 4060, pp. 4–5):

> We do not agree with those critics who think that the practice is wholly bad. We see in it definite advantages, provided that the statutory powers are exercised and the statutory functions performed in the right way. But risks of abuse are incidental to it, and we believe that safeguards are required, if the country is to continue to enjoy the advantages of the practice without suffering from its inherent dangers.

The committee added:

> But in truth whether good or bad the development of the practice is inevitable.

It went on to give reasons why the delegation of legislative powers was necessary (pp. 51–2). The reasons were restated, as follows, in 1967.

Select Committee on Procedure, 6th Report of 1966–67, HC 539, Appendix 8: Memorandum by Mr Speaker's Counsel, para 6

The advantages and justifications of delegated legislation may be summarised as follows:

(a) The normal justification is its value in relieving Parliament of the minor details of law making. The province of Parliament is to decide material questions affecting the public interest; and the more procedure and subordinate matters can be withdrawn from their cognizance the greater will be the time afforded for the consideration of more serious questions involved in legislation.

(b) Another advantage is *speed of action*. Action can be taken at once in a crisis without public notice which might prejudice the object of the exercise. For instance an increase in import duties would lose some of its effect if prior notice was given and importers were able to import large quantities of goods at the old lower rate of duty.

(c) Another advantage is in dealing with *technical* subjects. Ministers and Members of Parliament are not experts in the variety of subjects on which legislation is passed eg trade marks, patents, designs, diseases, poison, legal procedure and so on. The details of such technical legislation need the assistance of experts and can be regulated after a Bill passes into an Act by delegated legislation with greater care and minuteness and with better adaptation to local and other special circumstances than they can be in the passage of a Bill through Parliament.

(d) Another is that it enables the Department to deal with *unforeseen circumstances* that may arise during the introduction of large and complicated schemes of reform. It is not possible when drafting legislation on a new subject, to forecast every eventuality and it is very convenient to have power to adjust matters of detail by Statutory Instrument without of course going beyond the general principles laid down in the Bill.

(e) Another is that it provides *flexibility*. Circumstances change and it may be desirable to take power to deal quickly with changing circumstances rather than wait for an amending Bill. [For example, the Electronic Communications Bill provided for delegation of powers 'to ensure flexibility in a field where the technology is changing rapidly in ways which cannot be anticipated at present': Delegated Powers and Deregulation Committee, 5th Report of 1999–2000, HL 30, Memorandum by the DTI, p 5, para 4.]

(f) Finally, there is the question of emergency; and in time of war it is essential to have wide powers of delegated legislation.

The Cabinet Office has outlined the factors to be considered in deciding whether provision should be made in a bill for the delegation of legislative power.

Cabinet Office, *Guide to Making Legislation* (2017), para 16.1

These are some of the factors to consider when deciding whether the bill should confer power to make provision by secondary legislation:

- the matters in question may need adjusting more often than Parliament can be expected to legislate for by primary legislation;
- there may be rules which will be better made after some experience of administering the new Act and which it is not essential to have as soon as it begins to operate;
- the use of delegated powers in a particular area may have a strong precedent and be uncontroversial;
- there may be transitional and technical matters which it would be appropriate to deal with by delegated powers.

On the other hand:

- the matters, though detailed, may be so much of the essence of the bill that Parliament ought to consider them along with the rest of the bill;
- the matters may raise controversial issues running through the bill which it would be better for Parliament to decide once in principle rather than arguing several times over (and taking up scarce Parliamentary time in so doing).

More generally, the guidance notes at paragraph 16 that:

- Any provisions in the bill that delegate legislative powers will be scrutinised closely by Parliament and, in particular, by the House of Lords Delegated Powers and Regulatory Reform Committee. So when preparing instructions to the OPC care needs to be taken to ensure that the proposed powers to make subordinate legislation and the form of Parliamentary scrutiny chosen are justified. The Bill team should also make sure that the Minister is content with what is proposed and alerted to any proposed delegated powers which may prove controversial.
- The role of the House of Lords Delegated Powers and Regulatory Reform Committee (DPRRC) is 'to report whether the provisions of any bill inappropriately delegate legislative power or whether they subject the exercise of legislative power to an inappropriate degree of parliamentary scrutiny'.
- A memorandum to the DPRRC in respect of any powers in the bill to make delegated legislation, by statutory instrument or otherwise, is required by PBL Committee before it will approve a bill for introduction. This is usually drafted by the departmental legal adviser and should be shared in draft with the PBL Secretariat, the Government Whips' Office in the Lords and Parliamentary Counsel for comment before it is submitted to the PBL Committee.

The House of Lords Delegated Powers and Regulatory Reform Committee has also produced 'Guidance for Departments on the Rule and Requirements of the Committee' (July 2014). The guidance states that the memorandum sent to the committee should clearly identify every provision for delegated legislation, the purpose of the power and why the power has been left to delegated legislation. The memorandum should fully explain both why delegation is necessary and why the matter cannot be included in the bill, as well as justifying the full extent of the power and the choice of parliamentary control over such powers, particularly where there is a removal or relaxation of parliamentary control.

The complex activity of a modern industrial society necessitates a far-reaching governmental regulation in the interests of public safety, health and welfare. Much of this regulation is carried out by means of the numerous powers of delegated legislation committed to the government. From the 1950s to the 1990s, the UK issued an annual average of 2,100 statutory instruments, rising to an annual average of 3,200 in the 1990s and 4,200 in the 2000s. The annual average is currently around 3,000 a year (see House of Commons Library, 'Acts and Statutory Instruments: The Volume of UK Legislation 1850 to 2019' Briefing Paper CBP 7438, 17 June 2019). Although delegated legislation is an executive function, it is subject to a measure of parliamentary supervision and to a check of another sort in the processes of consultation with outside interests. (See, further, below.) The Hansard Society Commission on the Legislative Process concluded that, on balance, 'the main advantages of making greater use of delegated legislation outweigh the very real disadvantages', having regard in particular to the desirability of keeping primary legislation 'as clear, simple and short as possible' (*Making the Law* (1992), paras 262–3). The greater flexibility of delegated legislation may, however, dispose a government to proceed in this way even when the subject matter is of an importance that demands the fuller parliamentary scrutiny applied to primary legislation. There have been complaints that issues of policy and principle, instead of being included in the bill and submitted to Parliament, are left to be settled by ministers in delegated legislation. Lord Simon of Glaisdale has spoken in this connection of an aggrandisement of the executive at the expense of Parliament, citing the Child Support Act 1991, which delegated over 100 regulation-making powers to ministers (HL Deb vol. 533, col 747, 11 December 1991). The Procedure Committee concluded in 1996 that there was 'too great a readiness in Parliament to delegate wide legislative powers to Ministers, and no lack of enthusiasm on their part to take such powers' (*4th Report of 1995–96*, HC 152, para 14; see also Procedure Committee, *1st Report of 1999–2000*, HC 48 para 26.). The House of Lords responded to these misgivings in setting up a committee – now named the Delegated Powers and Regulatory Reform Committee – which has, as part of its task, the examination of bills to determine whether their provisions 'inappropriately delegate legislative power' and to report to the house before the bill has reached the committee stage of detailed consideration. The House of Lords Committee does valuable work in checking excessive delegation in government bills.

Of particular recent concern has been the vast range of delegated powers, including Henry VIII clauses, included in the European Union (Withdrawal) Act 2018 and the European Union (Withdrawal Agreement) Act 2020 (discussed in Chapter 4). The breadth of these powers was criticised in numerous reports both from the House of Lords Constitution Committee and the House of Lords Delegated Powers and Regulatory Reform Committee. In particular, both criticised the use of 'appropriate' as a trigger for the use of delegated powers. For example, what is now section 8 of the 2018 Act, states, inter alia, that 'a Minister of the Crown may by regulations make such provision as the Minister considers appropriate to prevent remedy or mitigate any failure of retained EU law to operate effectively'. The clause remained in the bill and became law in spite of the repeated criticism of its breadth and repeated recommendations from both committees that 'appropriate' be replaced with 'necessary'. Section 8 also includes a Henry VIII clause, section 8(5) of which states that the regulations 'may make any provision that could be made by an Act of Parliament'. While both committees recognised that this power may be necessary in order to make technical changes to legislation to ensure its effective operation post-Brexit, nevertheless there were concerns about the potential abuse and breadth of this power, meaning that there was a need for safeguards and scrutiny over the use of these powers. The government did take account of the recommendations of these committees regarding potential improvements to parliamentary scrutiny over the use of these powers, including the requirement for ministers to provide an explanatory memorandum, although the recommendation that ministers explain in these statements why measures were necessary was rejected, these explanatory memorandums are required to explain why the measure in question does no more than is appropriate. The Act also establishes a 'sift committee' in the House of Commons and the House of Lords, whose job it is to determine whether the minister has recommended the right resolution procedure for the enactment of delegated legislation and to make recommendations as to the appropriate resolution procedure. Similar committees are proscribed for the devolved legislatures. (See House of Lords Delegated Powers and Regulatory Reform Committee, *European Union (Withdrawal) Bill 3rd Report 2017–19* HL Paper 22; *European Union (Withdrawal) Bill, 12th Report 2017–19* HL Paper 73; *European Union (Withdrawal) Bill: Government Amendments, 23rd Report 2017–19* HL paper 124; *European Union (Withdrawal) Bill: Further Government Amendments 24th Report 2017–19* HL paper 128; and the House of Lords Constitution Committee *European Union (Withdrawal) Bill: Interim Report 3rd Report 2017–19* HL paper 19; *European Union (Withdrawal) Bill 9th Report 2017–19* HL paper 69.)

If the subject matter of delegation is of a constitutional character or is otherwise of particular importance, the power to legislate may be conferred on the monarch in council. Orders in council are drawn up in the department principally concerned and are formally ratified by the sovereign and a small group of ministers meeting as the Privy Council. Among many enabling acts that make this kind of provision is the Civil Contingencies Act 2004, which invests the government with a wide power to make emergency regulations by order in council for dealing with emergencies threatening the UK.

Orders in council made under statutory authority are to be distinguished from *prerogative* orders in council (see below), which are a type of primary, not delegated, legislation.

Other statutes give powers to ministers of the Crown to legislate by means of instruments variously named as regulations, directives, rules, orders, etc. Law-making powers are also delegated to local authorities and to certain other public bodies (e.g., the Financial Services Authority and the Sea Fish Industry Authority), but our present concern is with powers conferred on ministers of the Crown. These powers are the means to a comprehensive ministerial regulation (within the statutory framework) of many public services and other activities, including the NHS, social security, fair trading, environmental planning, food standards, health and safety at work, road traffic and so on.

An important innovation was the Deregulation and Contracting Out Act 1994, which conferred power on ministers to amend or repeal by ministerial order primary legislation that was considered to impose unnecessary burdens on business. Restrictions on the scope of the power were considered to limit its effectiveness, and strengthened provision was made by the Regulatory Reform Act 2001, authorising ministers to make regulatory reform orders to remove or reduce burdens 'affecting persons in the carrying on of any activity'. Within a few years, the government was persuaded that the powers in the 2001 Act were 'too technical and limited' and that ministers needed enlarged powers to enable them to remove unnecessary bureaucratic restrictions and to bring about 'swift and efficient regulatory reform', to the benefit of business and the public and voluntary sectors. The Legislative and Regulatory Reform Bill that was introduced to achieve these ends would have provided ministers with unprecedented power, subject only to minimal restrictions, to repeal or amend any legislation for any purpose. As we saw in Chapter 2, the bill was widely condemned as constitutionally outrageous and in response to well-mounted challenges from within and outside Parliament, the government agreed to significant concessions, introducing amendments to the bill in the course of its passage so as to limit its scope and introduce safeguards. Consequently, the Legislative and Regulatory Reform Act 2006 provides ministers with wide, but no longer untrammelled, powers to amend Acts of Parliament and secondary legislation.

7.2.2.1 Statutory Instruments

The legislative powers delegated to ministers or to the monarch in council are exercised, for the most part, in the form of statutory instruments, which are defined in the following terms by section 1 of the Statutory Instruments Act 1946:

> 1 (1) Where by this Act or any Act passed after the commencement of this Act [on 1 January 1948] power to make, confirm or approve orders, rules, regulations or other subordinate legislation is conferred on His Majesty in Council or on any Minister of the Crown then, if the power is expressed –
> (a) in the case of a power conferred on His Majesty, to be exercisable by Order in Council;
> (b) in the case of a power conferred on a Minister of the Crown, to be exercisable by statutory instrument,

any document by which that power is exercised shall be known as a 'statutory instrument' and the provisions of this Act shall apply thereto accordingly.

(1A) Where by any Act power to make, confirm or approve orders, rules, regulations or other subordinate legislation is conferred on the Welsh Ministers and the power is expressed to be exercisable by statutory instrument, any document by which that power is exercised shall be known as a 'statutory instrument' and the provisions of this Act shall apply to it accordingly.

(2) Where by any Act passed before the commencement of this Act power to make statutory rules within the meaning of the Rules Publication Act 1893, was conferred on any rule-making authority within the meaning of that Act, any document by which that power is exercised after the commencement of this Act shall, save as is otherwise provided by regulations made under this Act, be known as a 'statutory instrument' and the provisions of this Act shall apply thereto accordingly.

The regulations referred to in section 1(2) are the Statutory Instruments Regulations 1947 (SI 1948/1) as amended.

In broad terms, the effect of the section is as follows. By section 1(1), an instrument made under a post-1947 Act is a statutory instrument either if it is an order in council or if it is made by a minister of the Crown (or by the Welsh ministers) and the empowering Act expressly provides that the power is to be exercised by statutory instrument. Section 1(2) deals with instruments made under pre-1948 Acts. All such instruments made by ministers or by the monarch in council are statutory instruments unless exempted by the Statutory Instruments Regulations: instruments so excepted are those having an executive and not a legislative character. Statutory instruments are subject to the provisions of the Statutory Instruments Act relating to publication and the procedure for laying before Parliament. (See below.) The exercise by the government of powers of delegated legislation may also be subject to conditions specified in the enabling act.

Consultation Merits of Statutory Instruments Committee, *29th Report of 2005–06*, HL 149, para 85

Proper consultation is a crucial part of the process of determining the most effective way of achieving a policy objective and, where legislation is deemed to be necessary, of getting an instrument right before it is laid. It should be remembered that the House cannot amend an instrument: it can only accept or reject it. It is important therefore that, when an instrument comes before Parliament, it should have been exposed to those who will be affected by its provisions and its suitability reviewed in the light of their reactions.

Some enabling acts oblige the minister concerned to consult organised interests or other bodies before making regulations. The particular organisations to be consulted may be specified by the Act or may be left to the judgment of the minister in accordance with some general formula. A typical example of the latter kind occurs in the Medicines Act 1968. The Act empowers health and agriculture ministers to make regulations and orders for certain purposes, and section 129(6) provides:

> Before making any regulations under this Act and before making any order under this Act . . . the Ministers proposing to make the regulations or order shall consult such organisations as appear to them to be representative of interests likely to be substantially affected by the regulations or order.

Does a provision of this kind give the minister an unfettered discretion as to the organisations to be consulted? No: it is a matter for the minister's judgment, but 'subject always to bona fides and reasonableness': see *Agricultural Training Board* v. *Aylesbury Mushrooms Ltd* [1972] 1 WLR 190 (noted by Foulkes (1972) 35 *MLR* 647). Is there any limitation at all on the discretion of a minister who is empowered to make regulations after consultation with 'any organisation appearing to him to be appropriate'? The discretion is not absolute: the minister must fairly and reasonably consider which organisations are appropriate: cf. *R* v. *Post Office, ex p Association of Scientific, Technical and Managerial Staffs* [1981] 1 All ER 139, 141–2.

Some enabling acts combine a general formula with a direction to consult named organisations. Section 14(3) of the Building Act 1984 provides:

> Before making any building regulations . . . the Secretary of State shall consult the Building Regulations Advisory Committee for England and such other bodies as appear to him to be representative of the interests concerned.

In *R* v. *Secretary of State for Social Services, ex p Association of Metropolitan Authorities* [1986] 1 WLR 1, the court was concerned with the 'kind or amount' of consultation that would satisfy a statutory requirement to consult certain organisations before making regulations. Webster J said:

> [T]he essence of consultation is the communication of a genuine invitation to give advice and a genuine receipt of that advice. In my view it must go without saying that to achieve consultation sufficient information must be supplied by the consulting to the consulted party to enable it to tender helpful advice. Sufficient time must be given by the consulting to the consulted party to enable it to do that, and sufficient time must be available for such advice to be considered by the consulting party. Sufficient, in that context, does not mean ample, but at least enough to enable the relevant purpose to be fulfilled. By helpful advice, in this context, I mean sufficiently informed and considered information or advice about aspects of

> the form or substance of the proposals, or their implications for the consulted party, being aspects material to the implementation of the proposal as to which the Secretary of State might not be fully informed or advised and as to which the party consulted might have relevant information or advice to offer.

In determining whether there has been proper consultation, a court will have regard, said Webster J, to the circumstances as they would have appeared to the Secretary of State, acting in good faith at the relevant time. In this case, the judge held that the minister had not given sufficient time to the applicant association to respond adequately to his invitation to them to comment on the proposed regulations. He accordingly granted the association a declaration that the minister had failed to comply with his statutory duty to consult them.

In *R (Moseley)* v. *London Borough of Haringey* [2014] UKSC 56, [2014] 1 WLR 3947, the council was required to consult 'such ... persons as it considers likely to have an interest in the operation of the scheme' when determining how to implement the council tax reduction scheme. The council sent out a questionnaire to residents who were receiving council tax benefits to explain how the new scheme would operate and providing a questionnaire and information booklet. However, the information provided to residents did not make it clear that there were other ways in which the council could have made good on the shortfall in its budget and implemented the council tax reduction scheme other than the specific measures set out by the council in its questionnaire and information booklet. As such, the council had failed to carry out its duty to consult. The council should have made reference to other ways in which it could have made up for the shortfall in its budget, and why Haringey had chosen to do so by its specific version of the council tax reduction scheme.

Even when consultation has not been fulfilled, a further question arises as to the appropriate remedy. In *R* v. *Secretary of State for Social Services, ex p Association of Metropolitan Authorities,* [1986] 1 WLR 1, the judge declined to strike down the regulations which, he said, had 'become part of the public law of the land'. (Is it questionable whether they had so become?) In deciding to exercise his discretion in this way, Webster J noted that there had not been a total failure of consultation: administrative inconvenience would be caused by the revocation of the regulations, and they were in any event being replaced by new, consolidating regulations. He expressed the view that 'it is not necessarily to be regarded as the normal practice, where delegated legislation is held to be ultra vires, to revoke the instrument, but that the inclination would be the other way, in the absence of special circumstances making it desirable to revoke that instrument ... in principle I treat the matter as one of pure discretion'. In *R (C)* v. *Secretary of State for Justice* [2008] EWCA Civ 882, [2009] QB 657, however, the Court of Appeal declined to endorse this dictum of Webster J. Buxton LJ said:

As with any administrative decision, the court has discretion to withhold relief if there are pressing reasons for not disturbing the status quo. It is, however, wrong to think that delegated *legislation* has some specially protected position in that respect. If anything, the imperative that public life should be conducted lawfully suggests that it is more important to correct unlawful legislation, that until quashed is universally binding and used by the public as a guide to conduct, than it is to correct a single decision, that affects only a limited range of people.

Similarly, Keene LJ said that a finding that delegated legislation is ultra vires should normally lead to its being quashed 'and only in unusual circumstances would one expect to find a court exercising its discretion in such a way as to allow such legislation to remain in force'.

In *R* v. *Secretary of State for Health, ex p United States Tobacco International* [1992] QB 353, the company was the sole UK manufacturer of oral snuff. It had been encouraged by the government to manufacture and market its product and had received a government grant to help it in setting up its UK operation. Some three years later, the Secretary of State for Health was advised by the Committee on Carcinogenicity (COC), an independent body of scientific experts, that oral snuff should be banned on health grounds. The Secretary of State then announced that he proposed to make regulations under section 10 of the Consumer Protection Act 1987 banning the marketing of oral snuff. By section 11(5) of the Act he was required, before making the regulations, to consult organisations appearing to him to be representative of interests that would be substantially affected. The Secretary of State invited the company to make representations to him, but then refused its request to be shown the advice and reasons that had been submitted to him by the COC. The company applied for judicial review of the decision to make the regulations, on the ground, inter alia, that the Secretary of State had failed in his statutory duty of consultation. The divisional court held that the Secretary of State had a duty, in consulting, to be fair and to act in accordance with natural justice. What was required to meet the standards of fairness and natural justice would depend on the facts of the particular case, but in the present case, where the company had been 'encouraged to embark upon a substantial commercial operation' in the UK, where the regulations 'impinged almost exclusively' on the company, and since 'the effect of the regulations was likely to be catastrophic' to the company's UK business, a high degree of fairness and candour was required to be shown by the Secretary of State. The court held that in refusing to disclose the COC's advice and reasons the Secretary of State had acted unfairly and unlawfully, and it ordered that the regulations should be quashed. (On judicial review and requirements as to consultation, see, further, Chapter 10.)

As a general rule, ministers are not under a legal duty to consult affected persons or organisations if the enabling act imposes no such requirement: see *Bates* v. *Lord Hailsham* [1972] 1 WLR 1373. The development of public law in more recent times has, however, qualified the generality of this principle and the better view is now that executive rule-making may in particular circumstances be subject to duties of consultation, on grounds of fairness, rationality or an established practice of consultation. In contrast, courts may be disinclined to infer such a duty if Parliament, in delegating power to legislate, has itself provided a control mechanism such as the negative resolution procedure (considered below at p. 573). (See, on this question, *R (C)* v. *Secretary of State for Justice*, above, at [35]–[38].) In any event, it is the regular practice of government departments to consult affected interests before regulations are made. Consultation is often essential if the regulations are to be properly tailored to the objectives sought and if the support is to be won of interests whose cooperation is needed for them to work effectively. The government's *Code of Practice on Consultation* (2008) is intended to provide a framework of standards and advice for departments in their formal, written consultation exercises in order to 'help improve the transparency, responsiveness and accessibility of consultations'. The *Code* recommends a minimum period of twelve weeks for responding to a consultation and encourages the giving of feedback, indicating what responses were received and how they influenced the decisions taken. An impact assessment of the effects of the proposed legislation (including any impact on human rights or race, disability and gender equality) is normally attached to consultation documents.

7.2.2.1.1 Consideration of Relevant Matters

The enabling act may direct the minister to 'have regard to' specified matters in making regulations. For example, section 1(3) of the Industrial Development Act 1982 provides that the Secretary of State, in exercising his powers to make orders specifying areas of Britain as 'development areas' or 'intermediate areas':

> shall have regard to all the circumstances actual and expected, including the state of employment and unemployment, population changes, migration and the objectives of regional policies.

Even in the absence of an express requirement of this kind, there is an implied obligation to have regard to relevant factors, to be gathered from the provisions and objects of the Act, and to disregard irrelevant factors in exercising a statutory power. Moreover, the delegated power must be used for the purposes for which it was conferred by the Act and not for unauthorised purposes. (See *Attorney General for Canada* v. *Hallet & Carey Ltd* [1952] AC 427 and *Customs and Excise Comrs* v. *Cure & Deeley Ltd* [1962] 1 QB 340.) Failure to observe these conditions may result in the invalidity of the regulations.

7.2.2.1.2 Publication

Section 2(1) of the Statutory Instruments Act 1946 provides for the publication of statutory instruments:

> Immediately after the making of any statutory instrument, it shall be sent to the King's printer of Acts of Parliament and numbered in accordance with regulations made under this Act, and except in such cases as may be provided by any Act passed after the commencement of this Act or prescribed by regulations made under this Act, copies thereof shall as soon as possible be printed and sold by or under the authority of the King's printer of Acts of Parliament.

The Statutory Instruments Regulations 1947 (SI 1948/1) exclude certain instruments from the requirement of publication. For example, instruments classified as local by reason of their restricted application (and by analogy with local and personal or private acts), those of which it is certified that their publication would be contrary to the public interest, temporary instruments and bulky schedules to instruments need not be published. Regulations that are not statutory instruments as defined by the 1946 Act escape the Act's requirements for publication. It may be too – the matter is not free from doubt – that sub-delegated legislation, authorised by an instrument itself made under delegated power (or by virtue of the prerogative), is not covered by the 1946 Act. (See Craig, *Administrative Law* (8th edn. 2016).)

The requirement of publication of an instrument after it has been made is generally considered to be directory only and not mandatory, so that failure to publish does not invalidate the instrument: see *R* v. *Sheer Metalcraft Ltd* [1954] 1 QB 586. (For discussion of this question, see Lanham (1974) 37 *MLR* 510, [1983] *PL* 395; Campbell [1982] *PL* 569.) Section 3(2) of the 1946 Act allows a qualified defence to a person charged with an offence against an instrument that has not been published in accordance with the Act.

7.2.2.1.3 Parliamentary Procedure

When a government bill that confers a power of delegated legislation is being prepared, a decision has to be made on the appropriate form of parliamentary control.

For some instruments, no parliamentary control is thought necessary and these are not required even to be laid before Parliament: they include, for example, commencement orders bringing Acts of Parliament into operation and instruments of a purely local nature. This is unexceptionable for routine instruments of these kinds, but in 1996 Sir Richard Scott found it to be a clear 'violation of . . . democratic constitutional principle' that there was no requirement to lay before Parliament orders made by the Secretary of State for Trade under section 1 of the Import, Export and Customs Powers (Defence) Act 1939, although the section conferred on him an extremely wide power to control exports and allowed for the creation of new criminal offences (*Scott Report* (1996), vol. I, para C1.25–6). The matter is now regulated by the Export Control Act 2002, which provides for parliamentary scrutiny of control orders made under it.

Every statutory instrument laid before Parliament is accompanied by an impact assessment (describing its impact on business or on voluntary or public sector bodies) and an explanatory memorandum stating the purpose of the instrument and describing its policy objective.

A few instruments have simply to be laid before Parliament so that members may be informed of them, without any further parliamentary procedure being prescribed. A disturbing instance of recourse to this unexacting procedure was considered by the Supreme Court in *Ahmed and others* v. *HM Treasury* [2010] UKSC 2, [2010] 2 WLR 378, at [5] and [49], but a more typical example is section 2(4) of the Stock Transfer Act 1982, which provides that the power conferred by the act on the Treasury to make orders amending the Act's schedule of 'specified securities':

> shall be exercisable by statutory instrument which shall be laid before Parliament after being made.

To comply with such a provision, copies of the instrument must be delivered to the Votes and Proceedings Office of the House of Commons and to the Office of the Clerk of the Parliaments in the House of Lords. (Instruments of a financial nature are laid before the Commons only.) Section 4(1) of the Statutory Instruments Act 1946 provides that statutory instruments required to be laid before Parliament after being made 'shall be so laid before the instrument comes into operation'. But in urgent cases, an instrument may be brought into operation before being laid, if an explanation of the reasons is sent to the relevant parliamentary authorities. The government gave an undertaking to Parliament on 8 November 1971 that there would normally be an interval of twenty-one days between the laying of an instrument and its coming into operation (HC Deb vol. 825, col 649). This undertaking, or convention, was unintentionally broken when a ministerial order was laid before Parliament on 19 June 2001 and expressed to come into force on the next day. When the mistake was discovered, the order was immediately revoked and a new order in similar terms was laid before Parliament to come into force twenty-one days later. (See HC Deb vol. 371, col 20 W, 2 July 2001.)

Departments have sometimes accidentally neglected to lay an instrument before Parliament as required by the enabling act and have taken corrective action when the failure has come to light. The effect of such a failure on the validity of the instrument has not been definitely determined and may depend on the terms in which the requirement to lay the instrument is expressed in the enabling act. In some cases, the direction to lay may not be mandatory.

Suppose, however, that an Act provides that regulations made under its provisions:

> shall not be made unless a draft of the regulations has been laid before Parliament and approved by a resolution of each House.

What should be the consequence, in this case, of a failure to lay the regulations before they are made? (Cf. *R* v. *Secretary of State for Social Services, ex p Camden London Borough Council* [1987] 1 WLR 819; and see Campbell [1987] *PL* 328.)

Most general statutory instruments have not only to be laid before Parliament but are subject to a further procedure for enabling Parliament to exercise a degree of control. In practice, the choice between the available procedures is made by the department responsible for the enabling bill. A basic distinction can be made between 'affirmative' and 'negative' control procedures, although there are sub-varieties of each class. Under the affirmative procedure, the instrument or a draft of it has to be approved by resolutions of both houses (exceptionally of the Commons only). Under the negative procedure, the instrument becomes law unless it, or a draft of it, is disapproved by a resolution, usually of either house. Examples follow of provision for each kind of procedure.

The Regulation of Investigatory Powers Act 2000. Section 28 of this Act provides for 'directed surveillance' of individuals and section 29 for the use of 'covert human intelligence sources' as methods of investigation by state agencies. Schedule 1 lists the public authorities (police forces, the intelligence services and others) able to conduct such investigations. Under section 30, the Secretary of State has power, exercisable by statutory instrument, to make orders amending Schedule 1. Section 30(7) provides that no such order shall be made that *adds* any public authority to the list in the schedule, 'unless a draft of the order has been laid before Parliament and approved by a resolution of each House'.

The Transport Act 2000. Part 2 (Local Transport) of this Act confers various powers on specified ministers to make regulations and orders, chiefly concerning matters of detailed procedure. Section 160(1) provides that any such power is to be exercised by statutory instrument. Then it is provided by section 160(2): 'A statutory instrument containing regulations or an order made by a Minister of the Crown under this Part . . . shall be subject to annulment in pursuance of a resolution of either House of Parliament.'

To a great extent, departments follow precedent in choosing between the affirmative and negative procedures or in providing only for the laying of an instrument before Parliament for its information, but there are no firm rules or criteria governing the matter. A memorandum by the Civil Service

Department in 1972 (Joint Committee on Delegated Legislation, HC 475 of 1971–72, Appendix 8) concluded that:

> This is an area of legislation where criteria have not been considered desirable. Ministers and Parliament have instead preferred to maintain flexibility as to the choice of Parliamentary procedure, so that the procedure adopted has been determined by reference to the circumstances of each particular case, rather than by the application of a set of rules.

Governments have continued to take the view that it is not practicable to lay down precise criteria in this matter. In practice, the negative procedure is most often chosen: only about one-sixth of instruments subject to parliamentary procedures require an affirmative resolution. The affirmative procedure obliges the government to move for approval of the instrument and allow a debate (which, in the House of Commons, is usually held in a standing committee, so saving the government time on the floor of the house) and is generally reserved for instruments that raise issues of principle or are of some special importance. For example, the affirmative procedure is usually preferred for powers whose exercise will substantially modify Acts of Parliament, powers to impose financial charges and powers to create new offences of a serious nature. Parliament is provided with an explanatory memorandum for each instrument laid before it, giving an explanation of 'what the instrument does and how it does it'.

It is one of the functions of the House of Lords Delegated Powers and Regulatory Reform Committee to report whether bills that provide for delegated legislation 'subject the exercise of legislative power to an inappropriate degree of parliamentary scrutiny'.

An enabling act may exceptionally incorporate a formula allowing the government to apply either the affirmative or the negative procedure in its discretion. Schedule 2, para 2(2) to the European Communities Act 1972 provides:

> Any statutory instrument containing an Order in Council or any order, rules, regulations or scheme made in the exercise of a power so conferred [by this Act], if made without a draft having been approved by resolution of each House of Parliament, shall be subject to annulment in pursuance of a resolution of either House.

More stringent versions of the affirmative procedure are applicable to 'remedial orders' to be made under section 10 of the HRA (see Schedule 2 to the Act) and (on certain conditions) legislative reform orders to be made under section 1 or 2 of the Legislative and Regulatory Reform Act 2006 (see sections 15 and 18): 'super-affirmative' procedures. These procedures are intended to provide the opportunity for a fuller and better-informed consideration of the orders by both houses.

The legislative powers assumed by the government are sometimes very great, and the scrutiny and control applied by Parliament to their exercise is of a weak kind. (Parliamentary control of delegated legislation is more fully considered in Chapter 9; see also consideration of 'Henry VIII' clauses in Chapter 2, above, pp. 146–148.) The exercise of delegated legislative power is open to challenge, in proceedings for judicial review, just as are the executive acts of government. A court may be called on to decide whether the delegated power has been exceeded or used for an improper (unauthorised) purpose, or in some other way misused (see, e.g., *EN (Serbia)* v. *Secretary of State for the Home Department* [2009] EWCA Civ 630, [2010] 3 WLR 182, at [81–3], and see, further, Chapter 10).

Does the delegation of law-making power to the executive offend in any way against the constitutional principle of the separation of powers?

For a thorough account of the making of delegated legislation, see Page, *Governing by Numbers: Delegated Legislation and Everyday Policy-Making* (2001). See also Merits of Statutory Instruments Committee, *29th Report of 2005–06*, HL 149 and *13th Report of 2007–08*, HL 70. Wider aspects of regulation are considered by Ogus, 'Regulation Revisited' [2009] *PL* 332.

7.2.3 Prerogative Legislation

The *Case of Proclamations* (1611) 12 Co Rep 74 established that the Crown has no power, by virtue of the prerogative, to alter the general law. Only in certain limited fields does the Crown retain a prerogative power to legislate, usually by order in council.

The Civil Service was formerly established under the royal prerogative and was regulated by prerogative orders in council, but the Constitutional Reform and Governance Act 2010 put the Civil Service of the state on a statutory footing. (Some parts of the Civil Service, such as the Secret Intelligence Service and the Security Service, remain within the domain of the prerogative: see sections 1(2) and 3(4) of the Act.)

An instance of prerogative legislation was noted by Diplock LJ in *Post Office* v. *Estuary Radio Ltd* [1968] 2 QB 740, 753:

> It still lies within the prerogative power of the Crown to extend its sovereignty and jurisdiction to areas of land or sea over which it has not previously claimed or exercised sovereignty or jurisdiction. For such extension the authority of Parliament is not required. The Queen's Courts, upon being informed by Order in Council or by the appropriate Minister or Law Officer of the Crown's claim to sovereignty or jurisdiction over any place, must give effect to it and are bound by it.

Prerogative must yield to statute, however, and the extent of the UK's territorial sea is now established by the Territorial Sea Act 1987 and orders in council made under the Act.

In the First World War, prerogative orders in council were among the instruments of economic warfare. (See the Reprisals Orders in Council of 1915 and 1917: SR & O 1915, III, p 107; SR & O 1917, pp. 951, 952.) When the Falklands conflict of 1982 necessitated the requisitioning of ships, the government was able to invoke the prerogative of the Crown:

At the Court at Windsor Castle

The 4th day of April 1982
Present,
The Queen's most excellent majesty in council
Whereas it is expedient in view of the situation now existing in relation to the Falkland Islands that Her Majesty should be enabled to exercise in the most effectual manner the powers at law vested in Her for the defence of the realm including Her Majesty's dependent territories:

Now, therefore, Her Majesty is pleased, by and with the advice of Her Privy Council, to order, and it is hereby ordered, as follows:

1. This Order may be cited as the Requisitioning of Ships Order 1982.
2. A Secretary of State or the Minister of Transport . . . or the Lords Commissioners of the Admiralty may requisition for Her Majesty's service any British ship and anything on board such ship wherever the ship may be.
3. [Power to delegate functions under Article 2.]
4. The owner of any ship or thing requisitioned under this Order shall receive such payment for the use thereof during its employment in Her Majesty's service and such compensation for loss or damage to the ship or thing occasioned by such employment as may be provided by any enactment relating to payment or compensation in respect of the exercise of powers conferred by this Order and, in the absence of such an enactment, such payment or compensation as may be agreed between a Secretary of State [or the Minister or the Lords Commissioners] and the owner or, failing such agreement, as may be determined by arbitration.
5. In this Order:

   'Secretary of State' means any of Her Majesty's Secretaries of State;
   'Requisition' in relation to any ship or thing means take possession of the ship or thing or require the ship or thing to be placed at the disposal of the requisitioning authority;
   'British ship' means a ship registered in the United Kingdom or any of the following countries–

   (a) the Isle of Man;
   (b) any of the Channel Islands;
   (c) any colony;
   (d) any country outside Her Majesty's dominions in which Her Majesty has jurisdiction in right of the Government of the United Kingdom.

The government (in its manifestation as the monarch in council) has full power under the prerogative to legislate for a few remaining colonies (those once conquered by or ceded to the Crown): see *R (Bancoult)* v. *Secretary of State for Foreign and Commonwealth Affairs (No 2)* [2008] UKHL 61, [2009] 1 AC 453; to create new courts of common law (see *Re Lord Bishop of Natal* (1864) 3 Moo PCCNS 115); and for a few other limited purposes.

In *Bancoult*, above, a deplorable recourse to the prerogative power to legislate by order in council survived challenge in the House of Lords: see pp. 199–200 above.

7.2.4 Executive Powers

The government possesses a considerable number of executive powers – powers that do not extend to alteration of the law but may affect the rights or obligations of those with respect to whom they are exercised.

Most executive powers of government derive from statute and are vested in the 'Secretary of State', a designated minister or (less often) in government departments. When power is conferred on a departmental minister, it does not necessarily follow that he or she must personally decide whether to exercise the power. In practice, the decision may be taken by a subordinate minister or, very frequently, by officials on the minister's behalf.

Carltona Ltd v. *Commissioners of Works* [1943] 2 All ER 560 (CA)

Under the Defence (General) Regulations 1939 (SR & O 1939 No 927), the commissioners of works were authorised to requisition land if it appeared to them to be necessary to do so in the national interest. The powers of the commissioners were by statute exercisable by the minister of Works and Planning. An official of the Ministry of Works and Planning signed on behalf of the commissioners of works a notice to the owners of a factory stating that possession would be taken of the factory premises. The owners argued unsuccessfully that the requisition was invalid because the minister had not personally directed his mind to the question.

Lord Greene MR: . . . In the administration of government in this country the functions which are given to ministers (and constitutionally properly given to ministers because they are constitutionally responsible) are functions so multifarious that no minister could ever personally attend to them. To take the example of the present case no doubt there have been thousands of requisitions in this country by individual ministries. It cannot be supposed that this regulation meant that, in each case, the minister in person should direct his mind to the matter. The duties imposed upon ministers and the powers given to ministers are normally exercised under the authority of the ministers by responsible officials of the department. Public business could not be carried on if that were not the case. Constitutionally, the decision of such an official is, of course, the decision of the

> minister. The minister is responsible. It is he who must answer before Parliament for anything that his officials have done under his authority, and, if for an important matter he selected an official of such junior standing that he could not be expected competently to perform the work, the minister would have to answer for that in Parliament. The whole system of departmental organisation and administration is based on the view that ministers, being responsible to Parliament, will see that important duties are committed to experienced officials. If they do not do that, Parliament is the place where complaint must be made against them.

See, further, Freedland, 'The Rule against Delegation and the *Carltona* Doctrine in an Agency Context' [1996] *PL* 19; and note the observations on *Carltona* in *Bushell* v. *Secretary of State for the Environment* [1981] AC 75, 95 and *DPP* v. *Haw* [2007] EWHC 1931 (Admin), [2008] 1 WLR 379.

Acts properly done by departmental officials on the minister's behalf are in law considered to be the acts of the minister himself. (See also *Re Golden Chemical Products Ltd* [1976] Ch. 300.) It has been conjectured that certain powers affecting personal liberty, such as the extradition of a fugitive offender, must be exercised by the minister personally. It may be, too, that a minister's discretion to devolve decision-making to officials is not unqualified and would be open to challenge on the ground of irrationality if, say, the designated official were of wholly inappropriate standing or qualification: cf. *R* v. *Secretary of State for the Home Department, ex p Oladehinde* [1991] 1 AC 254, 282, 284, 303; *R* v. *Secretary of State for the Home Department, ex p Doody* [1994] 1 AC 531, 566; *DPP* v. *Haw* (above) at [29].

Exceptionally, statute may require that a power entrusted to a minister of the Crown is to be exercised by the minister personally. There are provisions to this effect, for instance, in section 6(1) of the Intelligence Services Act 1994 and sections 7(1) and 8(6) of the Regulation of Investigatory Powers Act 2000. By convention, certain powers, which perhaps could lawfully be exercised by officials on behalf of ministers, are exercised by ministers in person – for example, the making of deportation orders. (See HC Deb vol. 271, col 514 W, 13 February 1996; HC Deb vol. 365, col 489 W, 26 March 2001. As to the preliminary decision to deport, cf. *Oladehinde* above at 303.)

The executive powers of government are many and of great variety. They include powers to grant licences, authorise certain kinds of business, make appointments to public offices, remove or deport (certain classes of) persons from the UK, approve by-laws of public bodies, make compulsory purchase orders, give directions, require information and award contracts, loans and subsidies. Under various 'default' powers, ministers may take over the functions of other public authorities.

Powers conferred on ministers will involve a greater or lesser degree of discretion as to their exercise. The nature and limits of the discretion must be looked for in the empowering Act, which may qualify the minister's discretion in a number of ways. In particular, it may appear that the minister: (i) may exercise the power only if a certain state of affairs exists, or if he believes it to exist; (ii) must consult or receive representations from certain persons (or even obtain another's consent) before exercising the power; (iii) must have regard to specified factors in deciding whether, or how, to exercise the power; (iv) may exercise the power only for specified purposes. An example is section 7 of the Industrial Development Act 1982, which confers a discretionary power ('the Secretary of State may ...') qualified by a number of conditions that impose duties on the minister, while leaving considerable scope for his subjective judgment. The section reads as follows.

Selective Financial Assistance for Industry in Assisted Areas

7. (1) For the purposes set out in the following provisions of this section the Secretary of State may, with the consent of the Treasury, provide financial assistance where, in his opinion –

    (a) the financial assistance is likely to provide, maintain or safeguard employment in any part of the assisted areas; and

    (b) the undertakings for which the assistance is provided are or will be wholly or mainly in the assisted areas.

(2) The purposes mentioned in subsection (1) above are –

    (a) to promote the development or modernisation of an industry;

    (b) to promote the efficiency of an industry;

    (c) to create, expand or sustain productive capacity in an industry, or in undertakings in an industry;

    (d) to promote the reconstruction, reorganisation or conversion of an industry or of undertakings in an industry;

    (e) to encourage the growth of, or the proper distribution of undertakings in, an industry;

    (f) to encourage arrangements for ensuring that any contraction of an industry proceeds in an orderly way.

(3) Subject to the following provisions of this section, financial assistance under this section may be given on any terms or conditions, and by any description of investment or lending or guarantee, or by making grants, and may, in particular, be –

    (a) investment by acquisition of loan or share capital in any company ...

    (b) investment by the acquisition of any undertaking or of any assets,

    (c) a loan ...

    (d) any form of insurance or guarantee to meet any contingency ...

(4) Financial assistance shall not be given under this section in the way described in subsection (3)(a) above unless the Secretary of State is satisfied that it cannot, or cannot appropriately, be so given in any other way; and the Secretary of State, in giving financial assistance in the way so described, shall not acquire any shares or stock in a company without the consent of that company.

> (5) In this section 'industry', unless the context otherwise requires, includes any description of commercial activity, and references to an industry include references to any section of an industry.
> (6) In this section 'the assisted areas' means the development areas, the intermediate areas and Northern Ireland.

A requirement to 'have regard to' specified factors (which we have already encountered in relation to delegated legislation) appears, for example, in section 11 of the Countryside Act 1968:

> In the exercise of their functions relating to land under any enactment every Minister, government department and public body shall have regard to the desirability of conserving the natural beauty and amenity of the countryside.

This is a rather weak kind of limitation on a minister's power, for it leaves him or her free to have regard, and give greater weight, to other considerations in reaching a decision.

Exceptionally, a statute may specify matters to which a minister exercising a power is *not* to have regard (e.g., the Immigration and Asylum Act 1999, section 97(2)).

Often a minister's power may appear to be virtually unfettered, for example, if the minister is authorised to act 'if it appears to him to be desirable in the public interest' that he should do so, or simply 'if he thinks fit'. More recently, statutory provisions have provided an even more unfettered discretion to the minister, empowering him to act when 'he considers it appropriate'. But even in these cases, the minister must exercise his or her discretion in accordance with the policy or objectives of the Act: see *Attorney General for Canada v. Hallet & Carey Ltd* [1952] AC 427, 450; *Padfield* v. *Minister of Agriculture, Fisheries and Food* [1968] AC 997, *R (on the application of Palestine Solidarity Campaign Ltd)* v. *Secretary of State for Communities and Local Government* [2020] UKSC 16, [2020] 1 WLR 1774.

In using discretionary power, a minister must observe not only statutory constraints but also the principles of administrative law developed by the courts in exercising judicial review. (See Chapter 10.)

7.2.4.1 Prerogative Powers

Some executive powers depend not on statute but on the prerogative. When the government – or the responsible minister – grants a royal pardon (through submission of advice to the sovereign), terminates a prosecution by entering a *nolle prosequi*, concludes a treaty with a foreign government or sends armed forces to quell a disturbance in a British city or a distant colony, it exercises a prerogative of the Crown (those constitutional powers which remain exercisable only by the monarch were considered in Chapter 6: here we are concerned with *ministerial* exercises of prerogative powers).

The principal prerogative powers exercised by ministers were most recently identified in a briefing paper of the House of Commons library.

House of Commons Library, 'The Royal Prerogative' Briefing Paper Number 03861, 17 August 2017, chap. 2

It is difficult to give a comprehensive catalogue of prerogative powers. This is because prerogative covers diverse subjects and there is uncertainty of the law in many instances where an ancient power has not been used in modern times. Constitutional lawyers Bradley, Ewing and Knight summarise the main areas where the prerogative is used today as follows:

- Powers relating to the legislature, e.g. – the summoning and proroguing of parliament; the granting of royal assent to bills; legislating by Order in Council (such as for overseas territories) or by letters patent; creating schemes for conferring benefits upon citizens where Parliament appropriates the necessary finance.
- Powers relating to the judicial system, e.g. – various functions carried out through the Attorney General and the Lord Advocate; pardoning of convicted offenders or remitting or reducing sentences.
- Powers relating to foreign affairs, e.g. – the power to acquire additional territory; the making of treaties (although Parliament has had a veto over treaty-making powers in some circumstances since 201022), the declaration of war and the making of peace; restraining aliens from entering the UK and the issue of passports.
- Powers relating to the armed forces e.g. – the Sovereign is commander in chief of the armed forces of the Crown and the control, organisation and disposition of the armed forces are within the prerogative.
- Appointments and honours, e.g. – appointment of ministers, judges and many other holders of public office; creation of peers and conferring of honours and decorations.
- Immunities and privileges, e.g. – statutes do not bind the Crown unless expressly stated (usually by the formulation "this Act binds the Crown" or similar).
- The prerogative in times of emergency, e.g. – requisitioning of ships or seizure of neutral property in a time of war.
- Miscellaneous prerogatives – various other historic powers relating to such things as royal charters, mining precious metals, coinage, franchises for markets, treasure trove, printing, guardianship of infants. This should not be considered an exhaustive list.

There are three main prerogative powers recognised under the common law which still reside in the jurisdiction of the Sovereign. While these powers are recognised as in the jurisdiction of the Sovereign personally, this does not mean that the Sovereign does not act according to the advice of the Government. In all of these cases, the Government provides advice which would be expected to be followed.

The Appointment of a Prime Minister. The Sovereign appoints the Prime Minister, but must appoint that person who is in the best position to receive the support of the majority in the

House of Commons. The Cabinet Manual is a Government document that sets out the main laws, rules and conventions affecting the conduct and operation of government. It says that in the necessity of discussions on who will form a Government following an election, "The Sovereign would not expect to become involved in any negotiations, although there are responsibilities on those involved in the process to keep the Palace informed."

Prorogation and Summoning of Parliament. The prorogation and summoning of Parliament remains a prerogative power of the Crown, although its dissolution is now a statutory provision under the Fixed-term Parliaments Act 2011. The Deputy Private Secretary to HM The Queen confirmed, in a letter to the Chair of the Political and Constitutional Reform Committee of 16 March 2015, that The Queen would "always act on the advice of the Government of the day" as to setting the first meeting of a Parliament.

Royal Assent to Legislation. In 1708, Queen Anne was the last Sovereign to refuse royal assent to a bill passed by Parliament. Additionally, no monarchs since the sixteenth century have signed Bills themselves and Queen Victoria was the last to give the Royal Assent in person in 1854. De Smith's Judicial Review suggests that the power of Royal Assent may fall outside the court's jurisdiction as being concerned with the processes of Parliament, and therefore may not be able to be challenged by judicial review.

To this list of powers there may be added the distribution (by the prime minister) of functions between government departments, the appointment of official advisers and the management of the government's business in the cabinet and its committees through a variety of ad hoc arrangements.

Foreign relations (including the making of treaties and the declaration of war) are conducted under the prerogative. In 1982, while negotiations were taking place for a settlement of the Falklands conflict, the leader of the opposition urged that 'the House of Commons has the right to make a judgement on this matter before any decision is taken by the government that would enlarge the conflict'. Refusing to accede to this demand, the prime minister said 'it is an inherent jurisdiction of the government to negotiate and to reach decisions. Afterwards, the House of Commons can pass judgment on the government'. (HC Deb vol. 23, cols 597–8, 11 May 1982.) There was no explicit parliamentary authorisation for the subsequent military engagement. Again, the government did not seek parliamentary authority for the commitment of armed forces to military operations in Yugoslavia in 1999 or in Afghanistan in 2001. By the same token, the government sought (and obtained) the approval of the House of Commons before going to war in Iraq in 2003, and this precedent could be seen as establishing a convention that would be binding on future governments. In a powerful report, the House of Lords Constitution Committee recommended in 2006 that Parliament's role in deciding to deploy Britain's armed forces abroad be strengthened and formalised, and that the government should not in the future be able to rely solely on the prerogative as it had in the past: *Waging War, 15th Report of 2005–06*, HL 236. In 2007, following an opposition day debate, the House of Commons resolved that a precedent was 'set by the Government in 2002 and 2003 in seeking and obtaining the approval of the House for its decision in respect of military action against Iraq [and] is of the view that it is inconceivable that any Government would in practice depart from this precedent'. (HC Deb, 15 May 2007, col 579–582). The *Cabinet Manual* describes the convention as follows:

> 5.36 Since the Second World War, the Government has notified the House of Commons of significant military action, either before or after the event, by means of a statement and has in some cases followed this with a debate on a motion for the adjournment of the House.
>
> 5.37 In the two most recent examples of significant military action, in Iraq and Libya, Parliament has been given the opportunity for a substantive debate. Debates took place in Parliament shortly before military action in Iraq began in 2003. In relation to Libya, the Prime Minister made a statement in the House of Commons on 18 March 2011 in advance of military action, which was followed by a government motion for debate on 21 March, expressed in terms that the House 'supports Her Majesty's Government [. . .] in the taking of all necessary measures to protect civilians and civilian-populated areas'.
>
> 5.38 In 2011, the Government acknowledged that a convention had developed in Parliament that before troops were committed the House of Commons should have an opportunity to debate the matter and said that it proposed to observe that convention except when there was an emergency and such action would not be appropriate.

Nevertheless, in spite of the emergence of this convention, concerns have arisen over its scope and possible exceptions to the convention. Most recently, in April 2018, the UK took part in air strikes in Syria following the decision of the prime minister and the cabinet. There was no prior debate. Rather, following political pressure from opposition parties, two debates took place in Parliament after the use of military force. Concerns about this, and other exceptions, modifications or even possible breaches of the convention, prompted a report into the convention by the Public Administration and Constitutional Affairs Committee. The reported noted the difficulty surrounding the scope and application of the convention, in addition to its origins. It recommended that the *Cabinet Manual* be modified both to recognise the existence of the need for parliamentary scrutiny over the deployment of military force which began to emerge in Parliament after the Second World War, in addition to greater clarity as to the possible exceptions to the convention (Public Administration and Constitutional Affairs Committee, 'The Role of Parliament in the UK Constitution: Authorising the Use of Military Force' (20th Report of 2017–19 Session, HC 1891). More specifically, it recommended that:

> 130. Nothing should compromise the ability of governments to use military force when our national or global security is threatened, but a clearer role for the House of Commons is necessary in order to underline the legitimacy of the use of military force, and to give

the public confidence that the Government is being held to account. Expanding the role of the House of Commons, and of its committees, and giving them greater and, in some instances, full access to information would strengthen both the scrutiny and development of policy in relation to foreign affairs and defence. There are precedents in other jurisdictions for committees having access to high-level information of this kind. Making the necessary arrangements so that Members of the House of Commons could be trusted to carry the responsibilities that would come with being given access to high-level and top-secret information will strengthen accountability, legitimacy and public confidence in the decisions taken.

131. The House of Commons must have access to as much of the information as possible so it can carry out effective scrutiny of the Government's use of military force. In the twenty-first century, this means access to all but the most sensitive information at the earliest opportunity. This should include a summary of any relevant legal issues. Committees of the House should if possible be able to scrutinise foreign affairs and defence policy before the point of conflict is reached, so that the opinion of the House is clear and can inform the development of Government policy in advance of the need for military deployment.

132. In situations such as the conflict in Syria in 2013, where there was time to debate UK engagement in the conflict in advance, an appropriate committee, such as the Intelligence and Security Committee, with full access to relevant information, would be able to inform and reassure the House of Commons on the scope of the action proposed by the Government. Such a committee should be composed of Members of the House who both understand the trust and responsibility being placed on them in terms of keeping sensitive information confidential, and in whose advice and judgement the rest of the House can have confidence.

133. The Government should in its response to this report set out what arrangements it feels would be appropriate for committees of the House of Commons to be given access where possible to the most relevant information which have informed the Government's decisions about foreign affairs, military action and intelligence.

134. The House of Commons should consider and approve a substantive motion setting out the core principles of the convention governing the relationship between the Government and Parliament in relation to decisions to take military action. We propose a draft resolution for discussion:

'That this House:–

(1) recognises that Her Majesty's Government exercises Her Majesty's prerogative power to authorise the use of the UK's armed forces on her behalf on the basis that the use of force is legitimate and has the confidence of the House;

(2) recognises that, in order to strengthen the legitimacy of the use of military force and maintain this confidence, a convention has become established that Her Majesty's Government has a duty to inform and consult the House in relation to the deployment of the UK's armed forces in armed conflict, and to consult and seek prior authorisation from the House before engaging in military conflict, except in the following circumstances:

a) where arrangements for prior authorisation could compromise the effectiveness of UK operations and the safety of British servicemen and women;

b) where arrangements for prior authorisation could compromise the UK's sources of secret intelligence;

    c) where arrangements for prior authorisation could undermine the effectiveness or security of the UK's operational partners; or

    d) where a legal basis for action has previously been agreed by Parliament;

  (3) requires, in each instance where UK armed forces have engaged in conflict without the prior authorisation of the House, that the Government shall explain its decisions to the House and be held to account for them, and that to this end a Minister of the Crown shall make an oral Statement to the House, or shall provide oral evidence to a committee of the House, on the engagement at the earliest opportunity;

  (4) requires Her Majesty's Government, in each instance where UK forces have engaged in military conflict, to inform the House of the basis for its policy and decisions by facilitating the provision of all relevant information and intelligence material to such bodies of the House as the House shall determine, under arrangements for confidentiality which the House shall approve.'

The government's response was to recognise the need for the flexibility of the convention, such that there was no real need to place the convention and its restrictions on a more formal setting.

As regards the ratification of treaties, the conventional practice known as the 'Ponsonby Rule' was put on a statutory footing by Part 2 of the Constitutional Reform and Governance Act 2010. Ratification is still an exercise of prerogative power but is subject to the Act's requirements of laying before Parliament and may, as a general rule, be forestalled by a resolution of the House of Commons that the treaty should not be ratified (see sections 20–5).

A strong case can be made for replacing all the rather ill-defined and wide-ranging powers that currently rest on prerogative with a statutory code, bringing clarity and appropriate safeguards to the definition of these powers as a whole, and not only in the context of the deployment of the armed forces (see Tomkins, *Our Republican Constitution* (2005), ch. 4). Several private members' bills have been introduced in Parliament that would, if enacted, have codified aspects of the prerogative, but none were passed into law (see, e.g., the Armed Forces (Parliamentary Approval for Participation in Armed Conflict) Bill 2005, presented by Clare Short MP and the Constitutional Reform (Prerogative Powers and Civil Service etc.) Bill 2006, presented by Lord Lester of Herne Hill). The Labour Government conceded in 2004 that 'it is possible, and sometimes desirable, that [the prerogative] should be replaced by either statute or conventions on parliamentary scrutiny where circumstances make that appropriate' (*Government Response to the Public Administration Committee*, Cm 6187/2004). Measures of this kind already taken have been described above, but the government still insisted that prerogative powers 'can provide flexibility in dealing with specific or exceptional circumstances that are not covered by statutory provisions' (*Review of the Executive Royal Prerogative Powers: Final Report*, Ministry of Justice, 2009, para 109). In its report *Taming the Prerogative* (HC 422 of 2003–04) the Public Administration Committee gave its approval to a draft bill submitted by Professor Rodney Brazier (included in Appendix 1 to the report). The draft bill, in the committee's summary (para 55):

> Would require governments to list the prerogative powers exercised by Ministers within six months of the Act's passing. The list would then be considered by a committee (probably a joint committee of both Houses) and appropriate legislation would be framed to put in place statutory safeguards where these are required.

The draft bill itself included specific provision for controls on the exercise of executive powers relating to the use of the armed forces, the ratification of treaties and the issue and revocation of passports. In the result, the government declined to proceed to comprehensive legislation on the lines proposed in the draft bill (see *Government Response*, Cm 6187/2004).

7.2.4.2 Nature of the Prerogative

It is disputed whether the prerogative covers all executive Acts of the Crown that are not based on statute. Two classic definitions of the prerogative may be compared. Blackstone, in his *Commentaries on the Laws of England* ((8th edn. 1778), Book 1, ch. 7, p. 239), wrote:

> By the word prerogative we usually understand that special pre-eminence, which the king hath, over and above all other persons, and out of the ordinary course of the common law, in right of his regal dignity. It signifies, in its etymology, (from *prae* and *rogo*) something that is required or demanded before, or in preference to, all others. And hence it follows, that it must be in its nature singular and eccentrical; that it can only be applied to those rights and capacities which the king enjoys alone, in contradistinction to others, and not to those which he enjoys in common with any of his subjects: for if once any one prerogative of the crown could be held in common with the subject, it would cease to be prerogative any longer. And therefore Finch [*Law* (1627), p. 85] lays it down as a maxim, that the prerogative is that law in case of the king, which is law in no case of the subject.

This definition of the prerogative limits it to those common law powers that are possessed by the Crown alone. Dicey has a different definition in *The Law of the Constitution* (10th edn. 1959), pp. 424–5:

> The prerogative appears to be both historically and as a matter of actual fact nothing else than the residue of discretionary or arbitrary authority, which at any given time is legally left in the hands of the Crown . . . From the time of the Norman Conquest down to the Revolution of 1688, the Crown possessed in reality many of the attributes of sovereignty. The

prerogative is the name for the remaining portion of the Crown's original authority . . . Every act which the executive government can lawfully do without the authority of the Act of Parliament is done in virtue of this prerogative.

Initial references to 'authority' and 'sovereignty' notwithstanding, the concluding words of this passage express a comprehensive view of the prerogative.

Blackstone's and Dicey's views have both received judicial and academic approval, although, in general, the courts have followed Dicey. It is therefore debatable whether the government is rightly said to exercise the prerogative of the Crown when, for example, it engages an employee or purchases goods or makes grants of money, these being acts that any other person may perform. Perhaps these are simply things that the Crown can do by virtue of its corporate capacity at common law – although, in making payments of money, it must act within the limits of parliamentary authorisation of expenditure. (Cf. Harris (1992) 108 *LQR* 626 and (2010) 126 *LQR* 373; and Cohn (2005) 25 *OJLS* 97.) The power of the Crown, as a corporation sole, to deal with its property or spend money was acknowledged in the judgments of the Law Lords in *R (Hooper)* v. *Secretary of State for Work and Pensions* [2005] UKHL 29, [2005] 1 WLR 1681. See also the discussion in *R (Shrewsbury & Atcham BC)* v. *Secretary of State for Communities and Local Government* [2008] EWCA Civ 148, [2008] 3 All ER 548. It is also questionable whether the prerogative label should be attached to governmental Acts that have no effect on the rights or duties of persons under English law, as when the government publishes official information or issues a passport. But these actions, too, have been held to belong to the prerogative: see *Jenkins* v. *Attorney General* (1971) 115 Sol Jo 674; and *R* v. *Secretary of State for Foreign and Commonwealth Affairs, ex p Everett* [1989] QB 811. Again, the making of a treaty by the Crown has no effect on the domestic law, but the treaty-making power is regarded by the courts as part of the prerogative: see *Blackburn* v. *Attorney General* [1971] 1 WLR 1037 and *Ex p Molyneaux* [1986] 1 WLR 331. (On the whole question, see Sir William Wade, *Constitutional Fundamentals* (rev edn. 1989), pp. 58–64.)

Whichever definition we accept, it is clear that prerogative powers are creatures of the common law, in the sense that the common law defines the scope of prerogative powers. This was illustrated most powerfully in a recent decision of the Supreme Court concerning the prerogative power of prorogation.

R (Miller) v. *Prime Minister; Cherry* v. *Advocate General for Scotland* [2019] UKSC 41, [2020] AC 373

The Prime Minister, Boris Johnson, instructed members of the Privy Council to advise Her Majesty Queen Elizabeth to prorogue Parliament from a date between 9 and 12 September until 14 October. This meant that Parliament would be prorogued for five weeks, an unusually long period when compared with recent prorogations of Parliament intended to enable the prime minister to prepare a new Queen's Speech, where Parliament was normally only prorogued for around four to six days. It also meant Parliament would be prorogued for five of the eight weeks in the run-up to what was then the exit day of the UK from the EU treaties – 31 October 2019. Lady Hale and Lord Reed, the President and Deputy President of the Supreme Court, delivered the unanimous decision of an eleven-bench Supreme Court, which concluded that the advice given by the prime minister was unlawful, meaning, in turn, that the prerogative order in council proroguing Parliament was itself unlawful and null and void.

> [40]. The legal principles of the constitution are not confined to statutory rules, but include constitutional principles developed by the common law … In their application to the exercise of governmental powers, constitutional principles do not apply only to powers conferred by statute, but also extend to prerogative powers …

The Supreme Court recognised two constitutional principles of the common law that placed restrictions on the prerogative power of prorogation: parliamentary sovereignty and parliamentary accountability. The Supreme Court then concluded (in para [50]) that:

> [50]. For the purposes of the present case, therefore, the relevant limit upon the power to prorogue can be expressed in this way: that a decision to prorogue Parliament (or to advise the monarch to prorogue Parliament) will be unlawful if the prorogation has the effect of frustrating or preventing, without reasonable justification, the ability of Parliament to carry out its constitutional functions as a legislature and as the body responsible for the supervision of the executive. In such a situation, the court will intervene if the effect is sufficiently serious to justify such an exceptional course.

The specific use of the prerogative power of prorogation in this instance 'had the effect of frustrating or preventing the constitutional role of Parliament in holding the Government to account' as (at para [56] – [57]):

> [56]. . . . . This was not a normal prorogation in the run-up to a Queen's Speech. It prevented Parliament from carrying out its constitutional role for five out of a possible eight weeks between the end of the summer recess and exit day on the 31st October. Parliament might have decided to go into recess for the party conferences during some of that period but, given the extraordinary situation in which the United Kingdom finds itself, its members might have thought that parliamentary scrutiny of government activity in the run-up to exit day was more important and declined to do so, or at least they might have curtailed

the normal conference season recess because of that. Even if they had agreed to go into recess for the usual three-week period, they would still have been able to perform their function of holding the government to account. Prorogation means that they cannot do that.

[57]. Such an interruption in the process of responsible government might not matter in some circumstances. But the circumstances here were, as already explained, quite exceptional. A fundamental change was due to take place in the Constitution of the United Kingdom on 31st October 2019. Whether or not this is a good thing is not for this or any other court to judge. The people have decided that. But that Parliament, and in particular the House of Commons as the democratically elected representatives of the people, has a right to have a voice in how that change comes about is indisputable. And the House of Commons has already demonstrated, by its motions against leaving without an agreement and by the European Union (Withdrawal) (No 2) Act 2019, that it does not support the Prime Minister on the critical issue for his Government at this time and that it is especially important that he be ready to face the House of Commons.

Moreover,

[61]. It is impossible for us to conclude, on the evidence which has been put before us, that there was any reason – let alone a good reason – to advise Her Majesty to prorogue Parliament for five weeks, from 9th or 12th September until 14th October. We cannot speculate, in the absence of further evidence, upon what such reasons might have been. It follows that the decision was unlawful.

In deciding the case in this manner, the Supreme Court deftly avoided a discussion as to whether the prerogative power of prorogation was non-justiciable – in other words, that it was not an issue that could be decided on by the courts. Although courts can control the manner in which prerogative powers are exercised, they can only do so when the prerogative power in question is justiciable. This limitation is not present for controls over the scope of prerogative powers. The judgment has been welcomed by some as a clear assertion of the court of its ability to ensure that the government acts within the proper sphere of its powers. Moreover, there is evidence of the Supreme Court being sensitive of its need to respect the proper role of the government and Parliament. The Supreme Court recognised that controlling the prerogative power of prorogation was an 'exceptional course' and, as such, it would only interfere when the impact on parliamentary sovereignty and parliamentary accountability was 'sufficiently serious to justify so exceptional a course'. Moreover, there are suggestions in the judgment that the court would have been deferential to any justification provided by the government for its particular use of the prerogative power of prorogation – hence the reference to the fact there was not 'any reason – let alone a good reason' for proroging Parliament for so long.

Nevertheless, a distinction between the scope of a prerogative power, and how it is exercised, can be difficult to maintain, particularly if the scope of a prerogative power is narrowed to such an extent that it can only really be used for one purpose. Is the judgment of the Supreme Court effectively concluding that prorogation can only be used to enable the preparation of the Queen's Speech to being a new parliamentary session? In addition, there are concerns that the Supreme Court is developing constitutional limits that have little, if any, democratic mandate.

7.2.4.3 Prerogative and Statutory Powers

In using either prerogative or other common law powers, the government is free of the constraints of an enabling statute; it may therefore prefer to take this course when it is available rather than obtain statutory authority for its actions. But there is an important limitation on the government's freedom to act in this way. If statutory powers already exist that cover the same ground as a prerogative power, the government is, in general, not free to choose between them, but must act under the statute.

Attorney General v. *De Keyser's Royal Hotel Ltd* [1920] AC 508 (HL)

During the First World War, the government took possession of De Keyser's Royal Hotel in London for the accommodation of staff officers. Afterwards, the owners of the hotel sued the Crown (by the procedure known as petition of right, which has since been superseded) for compensation for the use and occupation of the hotel. The main ground of their claim was that the hotel had been taken under the Defence Act 1842, which provided for compensation. The government's reply was that the hotel had been occupied under the prerogative power to take property for the defence of the realm, which (it was contended) imported no duty to pay compensation.

The House of Lords held that the government could not lawfully act on the prerogative power when there was a statute authorising it to take the property and prescribed the conditions on which that could be done. The taking could be justified only by the statute, and its provisions as to compensation must be observed. The reasoning of their Lordships is indicated by the following passages.

Lord Atkinson: . . . It is quite obvious that it would be useless and meaningless for the Legislature to impose restrictions and limitations upon, and to attach conditions to, the exercise by the Crown of the powers conferred by a statute, if the Crown were free at its pleasure to disregard these provisions, and by virtue of its prerogative do the very thing the statutes empowered it to do. One cannot in the construction of a statute attribute to the Legislature (in the absence of compelling words) an intention so absurd. It was suggested that when a statute is passed empowering the Crown to do a certain thing which it might theretofore have done by virtue of its prerogative, the prerogative is merged in the statute. I confess I do not think the word 'merged' is happily chosen. I should prefer to say that when such a statute, expressing the will and intention of the King and of the three estates of the realm, is passed, it abridges the Royal Prerogative while it is in force to this extent: that the Crown can only do the particular thing under and in accordance with the statutory provisions, and that its prerogative power to do that thing is in abeyance. Whichever mode of expression be used, the result intended to be indicated is, I think, the same – namely, that after the statute has been passed, and while it is in force, the thing it empowers the Crown to do can thenceforth only be done by and under the statute, and subject to all the limitations, restrictions and conditions by it imposed, however unrestricted the Royal Prerogative may theretofore have been.

Lord Moulton, after discussing the legislation culminating in the Defence Act 1842, said:

What effect has this course of legislation upon the Royal Prerogative? I do not think that it can be said to have abrogated that prerogative in any way, but it has given to the Crown statutory powers which render the exercise of that prerogative unnecessary, because the statutory powers that have been conferred upon it are wider and more comprehensive than those of the prerogative itself. But it has done more than this. It has indicated unmistakably that it is the intention of the nation that the powers of the Crown in these respects should be exercised in the equitable manner set forth in the statute, so that the burden shall not fall on the individual, but shall be borne by the community.

This being so, when powers covered by this statute are exercised by the Crown it must be presumed that they are so exercised under the statute, and therefore subject to the equitable provision for compensation which is to be found in it. There can be no excuse for reverting to prerogative powers simpliciter – if indeed they ever did exist in such a form as would cover the proposed acquisition, a matter which is far from clear in such a case as the present – when the Legislature has given to the Crown statutory powers which are wider even than anyone pretends that it possessed under the prerogative, and which cover all that can be necessary for the defence of the nation, and which are moreover accompanied by safeguards to the individual which are in agreement with the demands of justice.

Whether the prerogative power, had it been available to the government in this case, would have permitted the taking of property without compensation, did not fall to be decided. (On this question, see *Burmah Oil Co Ltd* v. *Lord Advocate* [1965] AC 75.) The principle in *De Keyser*, that prerogative must give way to statute, applies only where the statute is in force. (In *R* v. *Secretary of State for the Home Department, ex p Fire Brigades Union* [1995] 2 AC 513 the House of Lords held that the Secretary of State could not rely on the prerogative in introducing a scheme for the compensation of victims of crime when to do so involved renouncing the scheme established by Parliament in the Criminal Justice Act 1988, which he chose not to bring into force by a commencement order.)

Statute and prerogative sometimes co-exist, for Parliament may have provided additional or alternative powers without intending to abridge the prerogative. In some statutes, indeed, we find the prerogative expressly preserved: for example, section 33(5) of the Immigration Act 1971. In other cases, it is a question of construction of the relevant statute whether it has displaced, in whole or in part, a pre-existing prerogative. The inference should not, however, be readily drawn that the government remains free, when Parliament has provided a precisely regulated power, to resort to general (often ill-defined) prerogative powers to achieve its ends.

R v. *Secretary of State for the Home Department, ex p Northumbria Police Authority* [1989] QB 26 (DC and CA)

Section 4(4) of the Police Act 1964 provided that the police authority for a police area 'may … provide and maintain such vehicles, apparatus, clothing and other equipment as may be required for police purposes of the area'. In May 1986, the Home Secretary sent a circular letter to chief officers of police and police authorities, saying that plastic baton rounds and CS gas would be made available to chief officers of police from a central store, for use in situations of serious public disorder. A police force might be supplied with these items, even if the police authority did not agree, if the chief constable's request for them was endorsed by an inspector of constabulary. The Northumbria Police Authority, in an application for judicial review, sought a declaration that the circular was ultra vires, arguing that the Home Secretary had no power to issue plastic baton rounds or CS gas to a chief constable without the consent of the local police authority.

The divisional court held that the only *statutory* power of equipping police forces was that conferred on police authorities by section 4(4) of the Police Act (above), but that the Home Secretary could make use of a *prerogative* power to supply a police force with equipment needed for the maintenance of peace. The Court of Appeal decided, differing in this from the divisional court, that section 41 of the Police Act (authorising the Home Secretary to provide and maintain services for promoting the efficiency of the police) allowed the minister to supply equipment to a police force without the consent of the police authority. Having so decided it was not strictly necessary for the Court of Appeal to consider whether a prerogative power was available to the Home Secretary for this purpose, but the matter had been fully argued and the court gave its attention to this question also.

Did a prerogative power exist that could justify the Home Secretary's action? There was undoubtedly a prerogative of defence of the realm or war prerogative, and the Court of Appeal held that this, or a related prerogative, extended to keeping the peace and maintaining order in peacetime.

> **Nourse LJ**: ... It has not at any stage in our history been practicable to identify all the prerogative powers of the Crown. It is only by a process of piecemeal decision over a period of centuries that particular powers are seen to exist or not to exist, as the case may be. From time to time a need for more exact definition arises.

Nourse LJ saw the war prerogative as being founded on a 'wider prerogative' of protection of the realm and the subjects within it. He continued:

> The wider prerogative must have extended as much to unlawful acts within the realm as to the menaces of a foreign power. There is no historical or other basis for denying to the war prerogative a sister prerogative of keeping the peace within the realm ... [T]he scarcity of references in the books to the prerogative of keeping the peace within the realm does not disprove that it exists. Rather it may point to an unspoken assumption that it does.

Are we to see this case as one in which an existing prerogative power was given 'a more exact definition', or was such a power significantly extended, or a new power created (one not found in the books: cf. *Entick* v. *Carrington*, above, pp. 112–114)?

The Court of Appeal had then to consider the argument that, having regard to *Attorney General* v. *De Keyser's Royal Hotel*, any prerogative power of keeping the peace had been abridged by section 4(4) of the Police Act. This argument was rejected.

> **Croom-Johnson LJ**: ... It is clear that the Crown cannot act under the prerogative if to do so would be incompatible with statute. What was said here is that the Secretary of State's proposal under the circular would be inconsistent with the powers expressly or impliedly conferred on the police authority by section 4 of the Police Act 1964. The Divisional Court rejected that submission for reasons with which I wholly agree; namely that section 4 does not expressly grant a monopoly, and that granted the possibility of an authority which declines to provide equipment required by the chief constable there is every reason not to imply a Parliamentary intent to create one.

> **Purchas LJ**: ... It is well established that the courts will intervene to prevent executive action under prerogative powers in violation of property or other rights of the individual where this is inconsistent with statutory provisions providing for the same executive action. Where the executive action is directed towards the benefit or protection of the individual, it is unlikely that its use will attract the intervention of the courts. In my judgment, before the courts will hold that such executive action is contrary to legislation, express and unequivocal terms must be found in the statute which deprive the individual from receiving the benefit or protection intended by the exercise of prerogative power.

Is this ruling consistent with the principle affirmed in *Attorney General* v. *De Keyser's Royal Hotel Ltd*? (See, further, Bradley [1988] *PL* 298.)

It has been argued by the government that the Civil Contingencies Act 2004, providing a wide range of powers for dealing with emergencies, leaves room for use of the prerogative 'in cases of particular urgency or disruption where the statute may not operate effectively' (*Review of the Executive Royal Prerogative Powers: Final Report*, Ministry of Justice 2009, paras 66–76).

In addition to placing restrictions on the scope of prerogative powers, legislation can place a further limit on prerogative powers in that they cannot be used to frustrate legislation.

R (Miller) v. *Secretary of State for Exiting the European Union* [2017] UKSC 5, [2018] AC 61

Miller and others argued that the government could not use its general prerogative power of entering into treaties in order to notify the European Union of the United Kingdom's intention to withdraw from the European Union. One of the arguments was that, if the government were to do so, it would frustrate, inter alia, the European Communities Act 1972. In delivering the majority judgment of the court, Lord Neuberger explained this restriction on prerogative powers as follows (at para [50]):

> Further, ministers cannot frustrate the purpose of a statute or a statutory provision, for example by emptying it of content or preventing its effectual operation. Thus, ministers could not exercise prerogative powers at the international level to revoke the designation of Laker Airways under an aviation treaty as that would have rendered a licence granted under a statute useless: *Laker Airways Ltd v Department of Trade* [1977] QB 643 – see especially at pp 718–719 and 728 per Roskill LJ and Lawton LJ respectively. And in *Fire Brigades Union* cited above, at pp 551–552, Lord Browne-Wilkinson concluded that ministers could not exercise the prerogative power to set up a scheme of compensation for criminal injuries in such a way as to make a statutory scheme redundant, even though the statute in question was not yet in force. And, as already mentioned in para 35 above, he also stated that it was inappropriate for ministers to base their actions (or to invite the court to make any decision) on the basis of an anticipated repeal of a statutory provision as that would involve ministers (or the court) pre-empting Parliament's decision whether to enact that repeal.

7.2.5 Administrative Rule-Making (Quasi-Legislation)

Public authorities, in particular ministers or government departments acting in the name of ministers, frequently adopt rules without statutory authority which are intended to regulate the way in which they will exercise statutory or other discretionary powers. These are rules of administrative practice, not of law, and rule-making of this kind has been described as administrative quasi-legislation (see Megarry, 'Administrative Quasi-Legislation' (1944) 60 *LQR* 125; and Ganz, *Quasi-Legislation: Recent Developments in Secondary Legislation* (1987)). Such 'quasi-legislative' rules may be described as 'tertiary rules' (distinguishing them from primary or parliamentary legislation and secondary or delegated legislation: cf. Baldwin, *Rules and Government* (1995), pp. 80 et seq.) or simply as 'administrative rules'. They are a type of what is commonly called 'soft law'.

Quasi-legislative rules are a means by which the administration injects specific policies into the exercise of its discretionary powers. The courts have recognised that public authorities are entitled to adopt policies or rules for their own guidance in exercising discretions conferred on them. (See *British Oxygen Co Ltd* v. *Board of Trade* [1971] AC 610.) In *R (Alconbury Developments Ltd)* v. *Secretary of State for the Environment, Transport and the Regions* [2001] UKHL 23, [2003] 2 AC 295, at [143], Lord Clyde said:

> 1 The formulation of policies is a perfectly proper course for the provision of guidance in the exercise of an administrative discretion. Indeed policies are an essential element in securing the coherent and consistent performance of administrative functions. There are advantages both to the public and the administrators in having such policies. Of course there are limits to be observed in the way policies are applied. Blanket decisions which leave no room for particular circumstances may be unreasonable. What is crucial is that the policy must not fetter the exercise of the discretion. The particular circumstances always require to be considered. Provided that the policy is not regarded as binding and the authority still retains a free exercise of discretion the policy may serve the useful purpose of giving a reasonable guidance both to applicants and decision makers.

(See also *Walumba Lumba* v. *Secretary of State for the Home Department* [2011] UKSC 12.)

In *Secretary of State for the Home Department* v. *Pankina* [2010] EWCA Civ 719, [2010] 3 WLR 1526 (pp. 201–202 above), Sedley LJ observed that the formulation of policies by ministers, while formerly not part of 'the technical analysis of state powers ... has come in recent years to be recognised as a significant part of the constitutional framework'.

Administrative policies and rules help to ensure consistent decisions that further the administration's objectives and, applied reasonably, make for public confidence in the integrity and fairness of official conduct. It is therefore unsurprising that much administrative activity is regulated by such self-imposed rules. They may be expressed as broad principles, standards or guidelines, or may prescribe in quite specific detail the terms on which action will be taken. In speaking generally of 'administrative rules', we should keep in mind that they may differ in this way. Let us look at some examples.

7.2.5.1 Naturalisation

The Home Secretary, in deciding on an application for naturalisation as a British citizen, has to be satisfied that the applicant fulfils certain requirements, among them that he or she is 'of good character' (British Nationality Act 1981, section 6(1) and Schedule 1). For the assessment of this element (which has existed in the law since 1844 and is not defined in the Act) a number of rules or criteria have evolved. These are set out in 'Nationality Policy: Naturalisation as a British Citizen by Discretion' Version 4.0 issued by the Home Office on 23 September 2019, which gives guidance to Home Office staff in deciding on applications for naturalisation. Applicants may be refused naturalisation on character grounds in cases, for example, of involvement (or reasonably suspected involvement) in criminal activity; bankruptcy, debt or non-payment of taxes; notorious anti-social behaviour; deception or false statements in pursuing the application; and evasion of immigration control. (These factors, with their limits and exceptions, are set out in 'Nationality: Good Character Requirement' version 1, published for Home Office Staff on 14 January 2019 (available at https://assets.publishing.service.gov.uk/government/uploads/system/uploads/attachment_data/file/770960/good-character-guidance.pdf).

Is a requirement of 'good character' best left to ministerial discretion, subject to self-imposed criteria, or should the attempt be made to formulate precise and objective rules in legislation?

7.2.5.2 Passports

The Home Secretary (or the foreign secretary in respect of overseas applications) has a discretionary power under the prerogative to grant and withdraw passports. The exercise of this discretion is governed not by rules of law but by a set of departmental rules initially adopted by the Foreign and Commonwealth Office. The most recent iteration of these rules is found in a statement by Theresa May, then in her role as Secretary of State for the Home Department, on 25 April 2013, during the Conservative Party/Liberal Democrat Party Coalition Government:

Passports are issued when the Home Secretary is satisfied as to:

i   the identity of an applicant; and
ii the British nationality of applicants, in accordance with relevant nationality legislation; and
iii there being no other reasons (as set out below) for refusing a passport. IPS may make any checks necessary to ensure that the applicant is entitled to a British passport.

A passport application may be refused or an existing passport may be withdrawn. These are the persons who may be refused a British passport or who may have their existing passport withdrawn:

i a minor whose journey was known to be contrary to a court order, to the wishes of a parent or other person or authority in whose favour a residence or care order had been made or who had been awarded custody; or care and control; or

ii a person for whose arrest a warrant had been issued in the United Kingdom, or a person who was wanted by the United Kingdom police on suspicion of a serious crime; or

iii a person who is the subject of:

- a court order, made by a court in the United Kingdom, or any other order made pursuant to a statutory power, which imposes travel restrictions or restrictions on the possession of a valid United Kingdom passport; or
- bail conditions, imposed by a police officer or a court in the United Kingdom, which include travel restrictions or restrictions on the possession of a valid United Kingdom passport; or
- an order issued by the European Union or the United Nations which prevents a person travelling or entering a country other than the country in which they hold citizenship; or
- a declaration made under section 15 of the Mental Capacity Act 2005.

iv A person may be prevented from benefitting from the possession of a passport if the Home Secretary is satisfied that it is in the public interest to do so. This may be the case where:

- a person has been repatriated from abroad at public expense and their debt has not yet been repaid. This is because the passport fee supports the provision of consular services for British citizens overseas; or
- a person whose past, present or proposed activities, actual or suspected, are believed by the Home Secretary to be so undesirable that the grant or continued enjoyment of passport facilities is contrary to the public interest.

There may be circumstances in which the application of legislative powers is not appropriate to the individual applicant but there is a need to restrict the ability of a person to travel abroad.

The application of discretion by the Home Secretary will primarily focus on preventing overseas travel. There may be cases in which the Home Secretary believes that the past, present or proposed activities (actual or suspected) of the applicant or passport holder should prevent their enjoyment of a passport facility whether overseas travel was or was not a critical factor.

Professor Brazier commented (Public Administration Committee, *4th Report of 2003–04*, HC 422, Appendix 1, para 22):

the citizen's possession of a passport should not depend largely on the exercise of Ministerial discretion based on non-statutory rules devised by Ministers themselves – especially given that those rules have never been approved by Parliament. If the executive is to decide whether a citizen can enter and leave his or her own country then that must be on the basis of law approved by the legislature.

It has been judicially confirmed that the Secretary of State can properly apply a set of policies or rules in the exercise of the power to grant or withdraw passports, but the rules must not be applied in an arbitrary or unfair manner: *R* v. *Secretary of State for Foreign and Commonwealth Affairs, ex p Everett* [1989] QB 811. It was the intention of the Labour Government to introduce comprehensive legislation on the procedures for issuing passports (*Review of the Executive Royal Prerogative Powers: Final Report*, Ministry of Justice, 2009, para 38). However, to date, this has not materialised.

Governments frequently adopt non-statutory administrative rules instead of resorting to more formal, legislative procedures, and it is claimed that their use makes for efficient administration.

Robert Baldwin, 'Governing with Rules: The Developing Agenda', in Richardson and Genn (eds.), *Administrative Law and Government Action* (1994), pp. 167–8

[A]dministrative rules are said to routinize the exercise of discretion swiftly and inexpensively; encourage consistency; increase the incorporation of expertise and experience into decisions; enhance publicity and participation; give a flexibility lacking in primary and secondary legislation; allow non-technical language to be employed so as to make the rules accessible; enable rules to be couched in persuasive terms rather than in the form of commands; encourage compromises to be effected between those with different interests; deal with broad policy issues in a manner not possible with more precise primary and secondary rules; and allow rules to be introduced where more formal legislation is inappropriate or of doubtful practical or political feasibility.

As against these claims, Baldwin notes that the making of administrative rules is not subject to parliamentary control or to requirements of accountability such as promulgation and consultation. Questions arise of *transparency* and *accessibility*. (See, further, Baldwin, *Rules and Government* (1995), pp. 80–121.)

Non-statutory administrative rules have not always been published. They may have been kept secret within the administration, or perhaps privately notified to bodies primarily concerned. Even when publicly announced, with or without full details – in published circulars, government White Papers, departmental publications or ministerial statements or answers in Parliament – they have not always been easily accessible. Administrative rules often raise important issues of public concern or have a substantial impact on individual interests. The question whether rules should be published has in general been a matter for the government itself to decide, but a decision adversely affecting individual rights is unlawful if based on unpublished policy: *Walumba Lumba* v. *Secretary of State for the Home Department* [2011] UKSC 12 (esp. at [26]–[39]). In 1971, the government agreed to 'bear in mind' the need for publicity when significant changes affecting the public were made in administrative rules, and in particular undertook that where a rule had been announced in Parliament, subsequent changes of significance would also be announced there. (Parliamentary Commissioner for Administration, *First Report*, Cmnd 4729/1971, para 2.) In the *Code of Practice on Access to Government Information* (2nd edn. 1997, Part I, para 3(ii)), the government undertook to publish, or otherwise make available, such rules, procedures and internal guidance to officials 'as will assist better understanding of departmental action in dealing with the public', subject to certain exceptions on grounds of confidentiality. This appears to have given a stimulus to the publication of administrative rules (e.g., the Immigration Directorate's Instructions to immigration officers, first published in 1998). Rules are often accessible online, on government websites – particularly through www.gov.uk. The Freedom of Information Act 2000 generally assures access to information about administrative rules that have no bearing on security or law enforcement matters.

Exceptionally, non-statutory rules are made subject to a parliamentary procedure. In particular, the immigration rules made by the Home Secretary are not expressly authorised by the Immigration Act 1971, but the Act assumes or acknowledges the fact that the minister may make rules. Section 3(2) provides:

> The Secretary of State shall from time to time (and as soon as may be) lay before Parliament statements of the rules, or of any changes in the rules, laid down by him as to the practice to be followed in the administration of this Act for regulating the entry into and stay in the United Kingdom of persons required by this Act to have leave to enter, including any rules as to the period for which leave is to be given and the conditions to be attached in different circumstances . . .
>
> If a statement laid before either House of Parliament under this subsection is disapproved by a resolution of that House passed within the period of forty days beginning with the date of laying . . ., then the Secretary of State shall as soon as may be make such changes or further changes in the rules as appear to him to be required in the circumstances, so that the statement of those changes be laid before Parliament at latest by the end of the period of forty days beginning with the date of the resolution . . .

If disapproved by Parliament the rules do not cease to apply, but the minister is obliged to make whatever changes in the rules he or she thinks necessary and lay a statement of the revised rules before Parliament.

The immigration rules are a peculiar amalgam of explanations of statutory provisions, information about administrative practice and procedures, and directions to be followed by officials in carrying out their duties. Their hybrid character has troubled the courts, which were at first disposed to regard them as delegated legislation: see *R* v. *Chief Immigration Officer, Heathrow, ex p Salamat Bibi* [1976] 1 WLR 979, 985 (per Roskill LJ). Subsequently, the Court of Appeal in *R* v. *Secretary of State for the Home Department, ex p Hosenball* [1977] 1 WLR 766 took the view that they were not delegated legislation or rules of law in the strict sense but 'rules of practice laid down for the guidance of immigration officers and tribunals who are entrusted with the administration of the Act' (per Lord Denning at 780). In a penetrating analysis of the constitutional status of the immigration rules, Sedley LJ in *Secretary of State for the Home Department* v. *Pankina* [2010] EWCA Civ 719, [2010] 3 WLR 1526 concluded that they have been 'elevated to a status akin to that of law and made the source of justiciable rights'.

Rules of the kind we are considering cannot alter the law or abridge rights conferred by law. But such rules may supplement the law in allowing concessions to which there is no legal entitlement or in laying down the conditions on which discretionary benefits will be granted. A statement of the relevant legal rules will therefore often give an incomplete account of the circumstances in which claims are admitted by the administration. An example can be found in the set of rules adopted by the Inland Revenue in 1971 for the remission of arrears of tax when the arrears resulted from a failure of the department to act on information supplied by the taxpayer. (The rules were published in the Government's reply to a *Report from the Select Committee on the Parliamentary Commissioner for Administration*, Cmnd 4729/1971.) Extra-statutory concessions allowed by the revenue departments were formerly not necessarily publicised, but these as well as other concessions by HM Revenue and Customs are now published in the guide *Extra-Statutory Concessions*, which is updated from time to time. The following passage is taken from the introduction to the guide:

> An Extra-Statutory Concession is a relaxation which gives taxpayers a reduction in tax liability to which they would not be entitled under the strict letter of the law. Most concessions are made to deal with what are, on the whole, minor or transitory anomalies under the legislation and to meet cases of hardship at the margins of the code where a statutory remedy would be difficult to devise or would run to a length out of proportion to the intrinsic importance of the matter.

Some former extra-statutory concessions were incorporated into legislation – most recently by the Enactment of Extra-Statutory Concessions Order 2018.

The government cannot lawfully apply an administrative rule by which benefits of any kind are *withheld* from those who are legally entitled to them. However, government departments do adopt and act on their own interpretations of statutory provisions under which entitlements may arise, and these may be less favourable to claimants than other, perhaps equally tenable, interpretations. Unless and until the government's view is successfully challenged in the courts as being plainly wrong or irrational, it will effectively determine the question of entitlement.

The making and application of non-statutory administrative rules and statements of policy may be open to challenge on the ground that they are not in accordance with law. A court can also intervene if the administration disregards or misconstrues rules of its own making: see *R* v. *Criminal Injuries Compensation Board, ex p Lain* [1967] 2 QB 864; *R* v. *Chief Immigration Officer, Gatwick, ex p Kharrazi* [1980] 1 WLR 1396; and *R (Raissi)* v. *Secretary of State for the Home Department* [2008] EWCA Civ 72, [2008] QB 836, at [107]–[127]. (Note also the reasoning of Lord Goff in *R* v. *Secretary of State for the Home Department, ex p Pierson* [1998] AC 539, 569–70 and compare Lord Browne-Wilkinson's dissenting speech at 576–7.) An administrative rule may be set aside by a court if found to be irrational or to be manifestly unjust, oppressive, or partial and unequal in its operation as between different classes of person: see, e.g., *R* v. *Immigration Appeal Tribunal, ex p Manshoora Begum* [1986] Imm AR 385.

The publication of non-statutory rules may give rise to a 'legitimate expectation' by those affected that the rules will be properly and fairly applied, and the courts may protect this expectation even though it is not a legal right: *Attorney General of Hong Kong* v. *Ng Yuen Shiu* [1983] 2 AC 629; *R* v. *Secretary of State for the Home Department, ex p Khan* [1984] 1 WLR 1337; *Nadarajah* v. *Secretary of State for the Home Department* [2005] EWCA Civ 1363; *R (Bhatt Murphy)* v. *Independent Assessor* [2008] EWCA Civ 755. However, this protection is normally through a provision of procedural mechanisms and it is increasingly rare for the courts to protect a legitimate expectation generated by soft law, particularly when this is combined with no individual representation or detrimental reliance. (Legitimate expectations are further discussed in Chapter 10.)

It is questionable whether the practice of administrative rule-making is under adequate constitutional control (see Baldwin and Houghton, 'Circular Arguments: The Status and Legitimacy of Administrative Rules' [1986] PL 239).

7.2.6 Guidance and Codes of Practice

Guidance is a means by which the government seeks to influence the conduct of public authorities (such as local authorities, health authorities, the police and magistrates), or of private individuals or organisations (such as employers or farmers). Guidance may be used in preference to coercive powers because it is believed that existing, perhaps long-established, practices are better modified through persuasion and cooperation than by a machinery of legal duties and sanctions. Guidance is also preferred when it is thought that the body concerned should have freedom to use its own discretion rather than be subject to governmental regulation in the performance of its tasks. This may be because it possesses an expertise that the government lacks, because it is an elected body answerable primarily to its own electors rather than to the government, or for other reasons of principle or policy.

Guidance ranges from the formal, published and explicit to informal pressures, inducements and advice where 'much is likely to happen behind the scenes, in committees or even in private discussions' (Blondel et al. (1969–70) 5 *Government and Opposition*, 67, 71). Christine Parker and John Braithwaite remark that 'cooperative and persuasive strategies', although not always appropriate, 'are likely to be more effective than coercive law in achieving long-term compliance with norms, and coercive law is most effective when it is in reserve as a last resort' ('Regulation', in Cane and Tushnet (eds.), The *Oxford Handbook of Legal Studies* (2003), pp. 133–4). (See also Karen Yeung's discussion of such 'suasion techniques' and their potentiality for abuse of power: 'Regulating Government Communications' [2006] *CLJ* 53, 71–4, 78–80.)

Some forms of guidance have a statutory basis. A statute may both empower a minister to give guidance to a public body and prescribe the duty of that body with respect to any guidance given. The strongest form of guidance gives rise to a duty to act in accordance with it. This is the case, for example, with the National Data Guardian. Section 1(2) of the Health and Social Care (National Data Guardian) Act 2018 states that the Data Guardian 'may publish guidance about the processing of health and adult social care date in England'. Section 1(3) provides that:

> The following must have regard to such guidance –
>
> (a) a public body exercising functions that relate to the health service, adult social care or adult carer support in England;
> (b) a person (other than a public body) providing –
>   (i) services as part of the health service,
>   (ii) adult social care, or
>   (iii) adult carer support,
>   pursuant to arrangements with a public body falling within paragraph (a).

A less stringent obligation is imposed by some statutes that require those to whom guidance is issued to 'have regard to' or 'take account of' or 'act under' the guidance. The Housing Act 1996 is an example. Section 182(1) provides:

> In the exercise of their functions relating to homelessness and the prevention of homelessness, a local housing authority ... shall have regard to such guidance as may from time to time be given by the Secretary of State.

The Homelessness Code of Guidance having effect under this provision is intended to secure 'fair, consistent and good practice amongst housing authorities', but they are not legally bound to comply with it. (See *De Falco v. Crawley Borough Council* [1980] QB 460, 478, 482; cf. *R v. Police Complaints Board, ex p Madden* [1983] 1 WLR 447.) They are, however, obliged to take account of the *Code* and give fair consideration to its provisions before reaching a decision. A public authority is open to challenge in proceedings for judicial review if it disregards, misconstrues or misapplies guidance that it is required to take into account or departs from it without good and sufficient reason: see *Samuels v. Birmingham City Council* [2019] UKSC 28, [2019] 4 All ER 773. Guidance of this kind will also be unlawful if it contradicts or undermines the provisions of the relevant Act: *R v. Secretary of State for the Environment, ex p Tower Hamlets London Borough Council* [1993] QB 632; *R v. Secretary of State for the Environment, ex p Lancashire County Council* [1994] 4 All ER 165; and *R v. Brent London Borough Council, ex p Awua* [1996] AC 55. See also *R (Bapio Action Ltd) v. Secretary of State for the Home Department* [2008] UKHL 27, [2008] 1 AC 1003.

Another kind of legal effect is sometimes given by statute to forms of guidance or codes of practice. Section 203 of the Trade Union and Labour Relations (Consolidation) Act 1992 authorises the Secretary of State to issue codes of practice containing such practical guidance as he or she thinks fit for the purpose of promoting the improvement of industrial relations or desirable practices in relation to trade union ballots and elections, etc. Section 207(3) provides:

> In any proceedings before a court or employment tribunal or the Central Arbitration Committee any Code of Practice issued . . . by the Secretary of State shall be admissible in evidence, and any provision of the Code which appears to the court, tribunal or Committee to be relevant to any question arising in the proceedings shall be taken into account in determining that question.

It is common for statutes to provide that codes of guidance (especially if they have legal effects of the sorts mentioned above) shall be subject to parliamentary procedures similar to those applied to delegated legislation. For example, draft codes prepared by the secretary of state under the Trade Union and Labour Relations (Consolidation) Act 1992 must be laid before Parliament and may be issued only after approval by both houses (section 204(2)). More commonly, the negative control procedure (see above) is prescribed: for example, by section 4 of the Environment Act 1995 for guidance issued to the Environment Agency. Provision for parliamentary control is, however, sometimes wanting, even where it is plainly appropriate. In *R v. Secretary of State for Social Services, ex p Stitt* (1991) 3 Admin LR 169, the Court of Appeal was perturbed to find that the power of the secretary of state (then under the Social Security Act 1988) to give *binding directions* to social fund officers as to whether particular kinds of need should be met by payments from the fund was exercisable without any parliamentary supervision – even though such directions were equivalent to delegated legislation. Similar concerns arise as to the guidance issued by the Health and Social Care Data Guardian, discussed above.

A great deal of ministerial guidance has no statutory basis and is without any legislative element. It may nevertheless be effective in influencing the conduct of those to whom it is directed, especially when it is based on clear constitutional understandings or if the means of compulsion are available in reserve. The following are examples concerning local authorities.

Local authorities have been the recipients of much guidance from central government. Conscious of their own powers and their democratic base, they have not always responded favourably to government's attempts to influence them in the performance of their functions. But most circulars to local authorities contain guidance of a politically uncontroversial nature which is generally followed. Such guidance will often interpret and expand on primary and secondary legislation. For example, section 70(1) of the Town and Country Planning Act 1990 allows a local planning authority to grant planning permission for a development and attach 'such conditions as they think fit'. This wide power has been circumscribed through a number of judicial decisions (e.g., *Newbury DC* v. *Secretary of State for the Environment* [1981] AC 578). Paragraph 55 of the National Planning Policy Framework sets out a sixfold test that local planning authorities should follow when deciding on any condition to be attached to a planning consent. An updated version of Circular 11/95 seeks to amplify and reclassify the various judicial decisions and help local authorities and decision-makers in the execution of their duties.

Planning policy statements (PPSs) have evolved to have a different function from circulars. PPSs provide decision-makers with the objectives to which planning controls should be put and provide guidance on the means and methods that should be followed. For example, PPS 4, issued by the Department of Communities and Local Government in December 2009, is entitled 'Planning for Sustainable Economic Growth' . PPS 4 sets out the government's overarching objective for planning as the achievement of sustainable economic growth. It gives guidance on what this objective implies for the preparation of development plans and the determining of planning applications. It is in PPS 4 that the policy on restricting new out-of-town retail development is to be found, as well as the methods that local authorities and retailers should employ in determining where a new supermarket should be located. Such guidance is political in nature and changes between different governments and even between different ministers within the same administration. Decision-makers on planning applications are required to take the guidance into account as 'material considerations' and the department (or its inspectors) will be guided by it in the determination of planning appeals and in dealing with called-in planning applications.

When guidance fails to yield results the government may resort to legislation. A 1977 circular asked local education authorities to provide parents with certain information about schools in their areas. The response was disappointing and the guidance was replaced by a statutory obligation: section 8 of the Education Act 1980 required local education authorities to publish their arrangements for admission of pupils to maintained schools and such other information about their policy and arrangements for primary and secondary education as the secretary of state might by regulations require. (See now the School Standards and Framework Act 1998, section 92.)

There are limits to what can be lawfully achieved by guidance. The government may not override a discretionary power that a public body has under statute by giving it guidance, and the public body may not abdicate its discretion by treating the guidance as binding on it: see *R* v. *Police Complaints Board, ex p Madden* [1983] 1 WLR 447. Again, the government's interpretations of the law expressed in advisory circulars have no legal authority. While a departmental interpretation may acquire 'vitality and strength' through being accepted and acted on in practice (see *Coleshill and District Investment Co Ltd* v. *Minister of Housing and Local Government* [1969] 2 All ER 525, 538) and may have some limited persuasive force in the judicial construction of a statutory provision (cf. *Wicks* v. *Firth* [1983] 2 AC 214, 230–1; *R* v. *DPP, ex p Duckenfield* [1999] 2 All ER 873, 895), it is to be disregarded if untenable (e.g., *R* v. *Wandsworth London Borough Council, ex p Beckwith* [1996] 1 WLR 60, 65). A person whose interests are affected by the department's interpretation may seek a declaration from the courts that it is wrong in law.

Royal College of Nursing of the United Kingdom v. *Department of Health and Social Security* [1981] AC 800 (CA and HL)

Section 1 of the Abortion Act 1967 provides that a person is not guilty of an offence of abortion when a pregnancy is terminated 'by a registered medical practitioner' if the treatment is carried out in an NHS hospital (or approved private clinic) after a certificate has been given by two doctors as to the necessity for the abortion (and subject to certain other specified conditions).

The Department of Health and Social Security issued a circular to health authorities and the medical and nursing professions stating its view that it was lawful for a nurse to administer the drug that induced labour and the termination of pregnancy, provided that a registered medical practitioner personally decided on and initiated the process of induction (by inserting a catheter into the woman's body) and remained responsible for the subsequent treatment carried out by the nurse. The circular said:

> [T]he Secretary of State is advised that the termination can properly be said to have been termination by the registered medical practitioner provided it is decided upon by him, initiated by him, and that he remains throughout responsible for its overall conduct and control in the sense that any actions needed to bring it to conclusion are done by

> appropriately skilled staff acting on his specific instructions but not necessarily in his presence.

The Royal College of Nursing, wishing to have the law clarified, brought proceedings for a declaration that the department's advice was wrong in law. Woolf J held that, although a nurse might play a large part in the procedure approved by the circular, it was still treatment by a registered medical practitioner, and accordingly was lawful. The Court of Appeal reversed this decision, holding that in these circumstances the pregnancy was, in fact, terminated by the nurses. Lord Denning MR concluded his judgment by saying (at 806–7):

> If the Department of Health want the nurses to terminate a pregnancy, the Minister should go to Parliament and get the statute altered. He should ask them to amend it by adding the words 'or by a suitably qualified person in accordance with the written instructions of a registered medical practitioner'. I doubt whether Parliament would accept the amendment. It is too controversial. At any rate, that is the way to amend the law: and not by means of a departmental circular.

The House of Lords by a majority allowed an appeal by the department and restored the ruling of Woolf J. The procedure approved by the circular was held to be in conformity with the requirement of the Abortion Act, which was that a registered medical practitioner should accept responsibility for all stages of the treatment. Parts of the treatment could properly be carried out, in accordance with established medical practice, by nursing staff under his instructions.

(See also *Gillick* v. *West Norfolk and Wisbech Area Health Authority* [1986] AC 112; *R* v. *Secretary of State for the Environment, ex p Greenwich London Borough Council* [1989] COD 530; *R* v. *Secretary of State for Health, ex p Pfizer Ltd* [1999] Lloyd's Rep Med 289; *R (Axon)* v. *Secretary of State for Health* [2006] EWHC 37 (Admin), [2006] QB 539; Yeung [2006] *CLJ* 53, 74–83; Beatson, in Forsyth and Hare (eds.), *The Golden Metwand and the Crooked Cord* (1998), pp. 235–43.)

7.2.7 Voluntary Agreement and Self-Regulation

The agreements to be considered here include both legally enforceable contracts (to which the government, like a private individual, may be a party) and agreements not intended to have legal consequences, and perhaps also lacking the element of 'bargain' or consideration necessary for a binding contract, which the government may make with either public bodies or private organisations. 'Voluntary agreement' provides another mechanism for achieving governmental objectives, and one that is in some circumstances preferable from the government's point of view to legislation. Anthony Barker has written (in Hague *et al.* (eds.), *Public Policy and Private Interests* (1975), p. 354):

> In advanced industrial nations, the official and legal systems increasingly interpenetrate with the economic and social systems. So, 'government' is expected to take some kind of 'responsibility' for almost everything that is wanted, or needed, or is thought to have gone wrong.
>
> This has created a vast public demand for 'government responsibility' of some kind in almost every significant walk of the nation's life: protecting the customer, defending the environment and regulating business relationships. Yet even the largest and most interventionist government machine cannot do everything itself. Because it controls the state and can make laws, the government obviously has the means of offering semi-official status to private groups and interests, who are willing and able to enter into a constructive relationship.

If the government wishes to see the adoption of new or improved standards or practices in a trade, industry or profession, it can sometimes achieve this by negotiating a scheme of self-regulation with the appropriate traders', manufacturers' or professional organisation. A code of practice or set of rules agreed to and supervised by the organisation may bring about the desired result, when a legislative scheme would, perhaps, be controversial or difficult to administer.

Codes of practice or similar arrangements have been negotiated by government departments with, among others, the Confederation of British Industry and other business organisations (prompt payment of bills submitted by small firms); the Trades Union Congress (employees' rights to contract out of the political levy); the Society of Motor Manufacturers and Traders (action on vehicle defects affecting safety); the Brewers' Society (tenancies and rents in the licensed trade); the Association of British Insurers (use by insurance companies of genetic information about persons seeking insurance); principal industrial users of hydrofluorocarbons (reduction of hydrofluorocarbon emissions to the atmosphere); the industry biotechnology body SCIMAC (postponement of commercial growing of genetically modified crops pending evaluation); the National Farmers' Union and other organisations (measures to help farmland birds, biodiversity and water quality). A notable instance is the agreement between the government and the Association of British Insurers (revised in 2005) by which the association, in return for specific government commitments to increased expenditure on flood management and on measures to reduce the risk of flooding, acceded to a 'Statement of Principles' designed to ensure the continued availability of flood insurance. (See HC Deb vol. 439, cols 33–5WS, 11 November 2005.) In February 2011, in the so-called Merlin Agreement, the major British banks reached a settlement with the government on lending, pay and bonuses, and support for small businesses (see HC Deb vol. 523, cols 311–13, 9 February 2011).

A well-known instance of this mode of regulation was the agreement of 1977, afterwards renegotiated and renewed from time to time, between the health ministers and the tobacco industry, represented by the Tobacco Manufacturers' Association and the Imported Tobacco Products Advisory Council, on tobacco advertising. The Conference of Medical Royal Colleges, among others, called for legislative controls, but the Secretary of State for Social Services said in the House of Commons on 9 May 1980 (HC Deb vol. 984, col 783):

> [I]t has been the view of successive Governments that they should seek to achieve their health objectives by voluntary agreement ... In other words, this is a field where our tradition of proceeding by persuasion and consent rather than legislation and compulsion has a great deal to commend it. It would be wrong to force sudden abrupt changes on an industry on which tens of thousands of families depend. So long as progress by agreement is possible, it would be wrong to introduce legislation, for instance on advertising, although no Government could rule that out for all time.

In 2002, the Labour Government gave its support to a private member's bill, introduced in the House of Lords, providing for the prohibition of advertising and promotion of tobacco products. The bill was passed by the Lords and was then taken over by the government for its passage through the House of Commons to become the Tobacco Advertising and Promotion Act 2002.

Provision for compensation of the victims of uninsured drivers is made by the terms of an agreement of 1999 between the Secretary of State for the Environment, Transport and the Regions and the Motor Insurers' Bureau (replacing an agreement of 1988; the original agreement was made in 1946). A separate agreement provides for the compensation of victims of untraced drivers. Lord Denning described these agreements as being 'as important as any statute' (*Hardy* v. *Motor Insurers' Bureau* [1964] 2 QB 745, 757).

In some instances, there is a statutory basis for the adoption of voluntary codes of practice: an important example is section 8 of the Enterprise Act 2002, which empowers the Office of Fair Trading, as part of its general function of promoting good practice in activities affecting the interests of consumers, to make arrangements to approve consumer codes produced by suppliers of goods or services. It was said of such codes (then prepared under earlier legislation) that they were 'intended to *supplement* the requirements of the law by obtaining the agreement of trade associations on behalf of their members to raise their standards of trading' (Borrie, 'Laws and Codes for Consumers' [1980] *Jnl of Business Law* 315, 322).

In the regulation of commercial institutions concentrated in the City of London, governments were formerly inclined to favour persuasion rather than compulsion and fostered the establishment of self-regulatory agencies, such as the Panel on Takeovers and Mergers (set up in 1968): see *R* v. *Panel on*

Take-overs and Mergers, ex p Datafin [1987] QB 815, 825. (The Companies Act 2006 has adopted a fundamentally different approach in placing takeover regulation in a statutory framework, empowering the Takeover Panel to make rules for the regulation of takeovers.) The government's former preference for voluntary agreement and self-regulation in dealing with City institutions was shown by events of July 1983. The director general of Fair Trading had referred the rule book of the Stock Exchange to the Restrictive Practices Court for a determination of its compatibility with the public interest. The Secretary of State for Trade and Industry intervened, and reached an agreement with the Council of the Stock Exchange. In return for the termination of the proceedings before the court and the exemption of the Stock Exchange from the restrictive trade practices legislation, the council undertook to make certain changes in its structure and rules. (In particular, minimum scales of commission would be phased out.) The government performed its side of the bargain by securing the passage of the Restrictive Trade Practices (Stock Exchange) Act 1984, which exempted rules and regulations of the Stock Exchange from the Restrictive Trade Practices Act 1976 and formally terminated the proceedings already begun in the Restrictive Practices Court. Arrangements were made for the Bank of England and the government to monitor the implementation by the Stock Exchange of the changes to which it had agreed. (See Graham Zellick's comments on this episode: 'Government Beyond Law' [1985] *PL* 283, 291–3.) The Financial Services Act 1986 established a supervisory system for the investment industry, which was based on rule-making by self-regulatory organisations, but the complexity and failures of financial self-regulation induced the government to introduce legislation to provide for a new, unified system of regulation by a single public body, the Financial Services Authority. Under the Financial Services and Markets Act 2000, the authority exercised the former regulatory responsibilities of three self-regulating organisations, the Bank of England and a number of other bodies such as the Building Societies Commission. The Treasury is at present consulting on a new framework of financial regulation with a leading role assigned to the Bank of England.

When self-regulation fails, recourse to legislation is likely. To give three examples: first, governments were for a long time unwilling to introduce legislation to resolve the difficulties caused to small businesses by delayed payment of debts by large firms and instead attempted to foster prompt payment by means of a code of practice agreed with the Confederation of British Industry and other business organisations. The code having had little effect, the government resorted to legislation in the Late Payment of Commercial Debts (Interest) Act 1998, giving suppliers a right to claim interest on late payment of commercial debt. Second, the private security industry was for many years left to regulate itself through its trade association and inspectorate organisation, but self-regulation was only partially effective and a statutory regime was introduced by the Private Security Industry Act 2001.

Third, the government was in favour of self-regulation by the electronic communications industry but took the precaution of making anticipatory provision for statutory regulation in Part 1 of the Electronic Communications Act 2000. This part of the Act was to lapse at the end of five years from royal assent unless an order should be made to bring it into force, in the event that the industry's self-regulatory scheme had not worked satisfactorily. (No such order was made and Part 1 accordingly lapsed in 2005.)

On grounds of democratic principle governments have refrained from seeking to regulate the conduct of the press, preferring to support self-regulation by the newspaper and magazine industry through the Editors' Code of Practice of the Independent Press Standards Organisation, a body established by the industry itself. The prevention of malpractice in advertising also depends largely on self-regulation. The Advertising Standards Authority, an independent body set up by the advertising industry, monitors observance of advertising codes of practice drawn up by the Committees on Advertising Practice and the Broadcast Committee on Advertising Practice, composed from industry representatives, and adjudicates on complaints of breaches of the codes.

Voluntary agreement, it has been said, can be 'a more cost-effective instrument' for the government than legislation, and its basis in consent may provide a better prospect than the use of law and sanctions for gaining the government's ends (Baggott, 'By Voluntary Agreement: The Politics of Instrument Selection' (1986) 64 *Pub Adm* 51). Agreed codes of practice and similar arrangements can relieve the government of administrative costs and may be more effective in getting the cooperation of the individuals or firms concerned in applying the agreed code according to its spirit, whereas those bound by regulations may be more disposed to look for loopholes in them. Self-administered codes, it is said, are flexible in that they can be continually reviewed by those best informed about their effects and promptly updated as conditions change. There are, however, certain disadvantages and hazards – both for the government and for the public interest – in voluntary agreements as mechanisms for the implementation of policy. In the bargaining that precedes them, the government as well as the private-sector body may have to make concessions, and the government may secure something less than a complete realisation of its objectives. Private bodies are brought into the making of policy as well as its implementation, and the process has often taken place behind closed doors, secluded from democratic control.

(See, generally, Ogus, 'Rethinking Self-Regulation' (1995) 15 *OJLS* 97; Black, 'Constitutionalising Self-Regulation' (1996) 59 *MLR* 24; Moran, 'The Rise of the Regulatory State in Britain' (2001) 54 *Parl Aff* 19; Harlow and Rawlings, *Law and Administration* (3rd edn. 2009), pp. 323–37.)

The government enters into a great many ordinary commercial contracts for the procurement of goods or services. As a massive purchaser from the private sector (latterly estimated to have been as much as £175 billion a year), it has sometimes been able to use its purchasing power to advance its social and economic policies. Governments have in the past applied 'buy British' policies, giving preference to firms considered important to the economy, and formerly imposed a 'fair wages' condition on all government contractors. (This last was based on a House of Commons resolution, which was rescinded in 1983.) But the extent to which these collateral aims could be pursued was always limited, in particular by the Treasury's insistence on 'value for money' in contracting and the need to justify departures from this principle to the Public Accounts Committee of the House of Commons. Membership of the EU brought further constraints. EU directives (implemented in the UK by sets of public contracts regulations) provide for equal opportunities to bid for public contracts without discrimination on grounds of nationality and require competitive tendering for most classes of public contracts and clear statements of award criteria. Preferential treatment for domestic suppliers and products is accordingly prohibited. (For the situation post-implementation period completion day, see 'The Public Procurement (Amendment etc.) (EU Exit) Regulations 2019.) Much defence contracting, however, falls outside the EU rules (see Article 346 of the TFEU), and the Ministry of Defence (the largest single customer of British industry, placing over 50,000 new contracts each year) takes account of wider factors in its purchasing decisions, such as security of supply, support for key technologies, future export potential, sustainable development (minimising environmental impact) and the desirability of sustaining British industrial capabilities. (On the pursuit of social and environmental goals in procurement, see Arrowsmith (1995) 111 *LQR* 234; Davies, *The Public Law of Government Contracts* (2008), ch. 9.)

Government policies for the 'contracting out' of public services have significantly extended the use of the instrument of contract by public authorities. Both Conservative and Labour governments have resorted, on a large scale, to contracts with private-sector companies in making provision for the delivery of public services. Part 2 of the Deregulation and Contracting Out Act 1994 facilitated contracting out by empowering ministers to transfer public functions to the private sector without the need for specific legislation (see Freedland [1995] *PL* 21).

Many contracted-out services are of a routine nature, such as catering, vehicle fleet management and office and building services, but the range of contracted-out operations has increased greatly in recent years. For instance, the recruitment of senior civil servants is commonly contracted out by departments to private-sector recruitment agencies or search consultants (the department remaining responsible for the final selection). Government departments place many contracts for consultancy services, to engage skills (e.g., for IT projects) not available among civil servants. Under public private partnership (PPP) arrangements, private-sector firms have been awarded contracts bringing them into 'partnership' with government on long-term projects such as hospital building, road construction, provision of social housing and the refurbishment of public buildings. The most widely used form of PPP is the private finance initiative used, for example, for funding new schools, hospitals and prisons, under a contract requiring the contractor to design, construct, finance and operate the service in return for regular rental payments. In 'The Politics of Public-Private Partnerships' (2005) 7 *British Journal of Politics and International Relations* 215, Matthew Flinders discusses the 'host of political issues and tensions' raised by arrangements of these kinds. A full account is given by Harlow and Rawlings, *Law and Administration* (3rd edn. 2009), pp. 413–36.

The 'hollowing-out' of the state that is brought about by extensive recourse to such arrangements may contribute to the 'efficient, economical and effective provision of public services' (Foster and Plowden, *The State Under Stress* (1996), p. 118), but as the services are removed from direct ministerial control, private bodies acquire powers that need to be properly regulated and there must be accountability for their use. It is questionable whether this can be effectively achieved through the instrument of contract. Fundamental questions of propriety and accountability are raised in particular by the contracting out of such operations as prison management, prison escort services, immigration removal centres and secure training centres. (Eleven prisons in England and Wales are run by private sector companies.)

(See, further, Vincent-Jones, *The New Public Contracting* (2006); Davies, *The Public Law of Government Contracts* (2008). Harlow and Rawlings, *Law and Administration* (3rd edn. 2009), ch. 8, is an illuminating survey of the pervasiveness of public contracting in the modern British state.)

Part III

Accountability

8

Parties, Groups and the People

Contents

This chapter and the following two are concerned principally with questions relating to accountability and, in particular, to the accountability of government. We have divided our discussion of accountability into three broad areas, although it is important to stress that these areas should be seen as operating with and alongside one another and not in opposition to one another. (However, this is not to say that there are no tensions between the various forms or institutional mechanisms of accountability.) In this chapter, we consider what might rather loosely be called popular accountability and ask 'what role or roles does the British constitution accord to its people?' In Chapter 9, we focus on questions of parliamentary accountability, which, traditionally, has been the most important form of governmental accountability in the British constitutional order. In Chapter 10, we consider the role of the courts in providing, for example, for mechanisms whereby government actions and decisions may be judicially reviewed.

It is important to recognise how all three of these means of accountability can interact with one another – sometimes in a complementary and at other times in a contradictory manner. This has been clearly illustrated throughout the Brexit process. The use of a referendum to determine whether the UK should remain in or leave the European Union provided for a greater role for the people in the UK constitution. The importance of this role was stressed further by the way in which the then Conservative Government was quick to accept the outcome of the referendum, in spite of the fact that the prime minister, a large number of Cabinet ministers and of MPs more generally had campaigned for the UK to remain in the EU. The referendum outcome led to the resignation of the then Prime Minister, David Cameron, and his replacement with Theresa May.

Theresa May's inability to push her Withdrawal Agreement through Parliament resulted in her resignation – demonstrating how Parliament is able to hold the executive to account. Boris Johnson also faced opposition from Parliament, with both backbenchers and opposition MPs using standing orders in a manner that enabled them to prevent a no-deal Brexit. Both of these will be discussed further in Chapter 9. It will be interesting to see if these developments of greater control over the executive by the legislature will continue when Westminster has a Conservative Government with a strong majority, backed by the people in the recent December 2019 general election, as opposed to a minority Conservative Government.

The courts have also played a role. The Supreme Court sat not once but twice in its maximum number of eleven Justices of the Supreme Court. In *R (Miller)* v. *Secretary of State for Exiting the European Union* [2017] UKSC 5, [2018] AC 61, the Supreme Court concluded that the government could not use the prerogative power to trigger Article 50 and begin the process of negotiations to leave the EU. Instead, legislation was required to empower the prime minister to trigger the Article 50 process. In *R (Miller)* v. *Prime Minister; Cherry v Lord Advocate* [2019] UKSC 41, [2020] AC 373, the Supreme Court concluded that there were constitutional limits on the prerogative power of prorogation, the prime minister's advice to Queen Elizabeth to prorogue Parliament breached these constitutional limits and so was unlawful. Both of these cases controlled executive powers. Moreover, the latter demonstrated how members of the Westminster Parliament were able to use the courts to control the executive, as well as exerting their power in Parliament. The control of courts over the executive will be discussed further in Chapter 10.

One question that remains is the extent to which the role of the people in the UK constitution will continue post-Brexit. Will referendums be used more frequently, or will the experience of the Brexit referendum mean that referendums are used less often? Should they only be used 'once in a generation' to determine important constitutional issues, or should it be possible for the people to speak again, having spoken on a similar issue in the recent past? It also remains to be seen how far the growth in controls over the executive through the Brexit process can be explained by the existence of a minority government, the fact that Brexit causes rifts inside and across political parties, and that it is of such constitutional importance that MPs may be more willing to defy party lines. These issues will be explored in more depth in this and the following chapters.

8.1 The People in the Constitution

An ideal conception of a democratic society is one in which the people continuously and actively participate in political affairs. In the real world, societies that fall short of this ideal are nevertheless termed democratic if by their constitutions the people freely elect a government and can at frequent intervals dismiss it and elect another. To this extent, at least, the constitution of the UK is democratic (see pp. 51–59 above). Periodic elections provide for an accountability of the government to the people – in their role as the electorate – who have, in this respect, a place in the constitutional system.

According to a modern theory of democracy fathered by Joseph Schumpeter (*Capitalism, Socialism, and Democracy* (6th edn. 1987)), the intermittent electoral role of the people is as much popular involvement in the practice of government as can take place or is desirable. In this theory, the people choose, from competing elites, the government whose business it is to make policies and laws and provide leadership, and do not themselves attempt to decide on issues or influence policy-making. Democracy, says Schumpeter, 'means only that the people have the opportunity of accepting or refusing the men who are to rule them' (at pp. 284–5). Does this bleak and limited (but, its adherents say, realistic) conception of democracy fit the theory and practice of the British constitution? Do elections provide only a retrospective accountability of government, and not the possibility of choosing between or influencing policies? In our representative democracy, what role and what influence or power are allowed to the people in the government of the country between elections? David Judge has drawn attention to the 'paradox' that 'parliamentary representation serves to include "the people" in decision-making, indirectly and infrequently through the process of elections; yet, simultaneously, it serves to exclude them from direct and continuous participation in the decision-making process' ('Whatever Happened to Parliamentary Democracy in the United Kingdom?' (2004) 57 *Parl Aff* 682, 683).

The official or dominant theory of the British constitution has never located a supreme authority in the people and when a concept of sovereignty was invented it was, as we saw in Chapter 2, attributed not to the people but to the Crown in Parliament. Since the seventeenth century, there have been writers, radical politicians and reformers – from the Levellers to Thomas Paine to the Chartists – who have claimed sovereignty for the people or have declared the people to be the constituent power of the state, by whose consent political authority is exercised. These ideas, in various forms (and various understandings of what was meant by 'the people'), flamed by turns bright and dim outside the pale of the pre-democratic constitution. Even the establishment of democracy in the nineteenth and twentieth centuries did not supplant the official theory with one of popular sovereignty. McKenzie and Silver wrote in 1968 (*Angels in Marble: Working Class Conservatives in Urban England*) of the 'modest role accorded "the people" in British political culture', and continued (p. 251):

> Though modern constitutions typically locate the source of sovereignty in 'the people', in Britain it is the Crown in Parliament that is sovereign. Nor is this a merely technical point. The political culture of democratic Britain assigns to ordinary people the role, not of citizens, but of subjects.

Or as Vernon Bogdanor tersely notes, the British constitution 'knows nothing of the people' (*Power and the People* (1997), p. 15).

Yet Dicey acknowledged that the electorate had come to possess – or at least to share in – the political as opposed to the legal sovereignty in the state (*The Law of the Constitution* (1885), pp. 73–6), and to declare, in his arguments for the referendum, that the time had arrived 'for the formal recognition of a principle which in fact, if not in theory, forms part of our constitutional morality' ((1910) 212 *Quarterly Review* 538, 550). The role of the people in the UK constitution increased following the use of referendums to decide key constitutional issues – as will be discussed further in this chapter. There is also now a system of e-petitions, online petitions asking the government to respond to a particular issue or question. Once a petition obtains 10,000 signatures, it can give rise to a response from the government. An e-petition with 100,000 signatures can prompt a debate on the issue in Westminster Hall. While the use of e-petitions may raise political salience of an issue, there is no guarantee that the government's response will be in favour of the issue raised, or that a debate in Westminster Hall will lead to a future change in the law.

There was also a growing political recognition of the need for a potentially greater role of the people, not just in terms of their role in prompting legislative change, or through sporadic referendums, but also in terms of playing a role in constitutional reform. The experience of Brexit prompted manifesto commitments towards greater constitutional change by most of the major political parties. The Liberal Democrats and the Brexit Party both proposed a move towards a written constitution, with a focus on greater citizen involvement and a change to the voting system. The Liberal Democrats also proposed a written federal constitution. The Labour Party also advocated constitutional change, initiated through a 'UK wide Constitutional Convention, led by citizens' assemblies', this convention to be given a broad mandate for constitutional change (Labour Party Manifesto 2019, p. 81). However, although advocating constitutional change in their manifesto, the Conservative Government would institute this change through a commission on the constitution, democracy and rights, with no specific role of the people in the discussion of these issues by the commission.

As such, it remains that the most realistic programme for creating a role for the people, and popular participation, in the working of the constitution is to focus on 'the unfashionable cause of reviving party politics' as argued by Katwale in Finch and Oppenheim (eds.), *A Future for Politics* (2009), p. 34. Or do political parties merely empower a political class that is detached from the general body of citizens, as maintained by O'Brien in the same volume (pp. 43–4)? (See, too, Fieschi, 'How British Parties Lost Our Favour' (2007) 60 *Parl Aff* 143.) Party membership remains low when expressed in terms of a percentage of the electorate (around 1.7 per cent in 2019) and is not fully representative of the country, with a higher representation of males, from the south, from middle-class backgrounds and of middle age or above. (See House of Commons Library: 'Briefing Paper: Membership of UK Political Parties' August 2019; Bale, Webb and Poletti, *Footsoldiers: Political Party Membership in the 21st Century* (Routledge, 2019) and The 'Party Members Project' at https://esrcpartymembersproject.org/.)

The unresolved role of the people in the constitution lies at the heart of arguments about the electoral system, referendums, the relation between electors and their representatives in Parliament, and the public's 'right to information'. If the people were acknowledged in constitutional theory as the source of political authority, debates on these matters would be conducted in different terms. New ways forward might be opened up, towards greater democracy in the public and semi-public institutions of society.

8.2 Elections

The Electoral Commission, *Election 2005: Turnout* (2005), p. 53

Elections underpin our democracy, ensuring that our representative institutions are both accountable to public opinion and legitimised by it. They provide an opportunity for politicians and political parties to outline their ideas and to defend their performance. Elections can interest, inform and empower people and, by doing so, can help to build political engagement.

Following the coming into force of the Fixed-Term Parliaments Act 2011, the maximum duration of Parliament is five years, with section 1 of the Act fixing polling days to take place every five years. Prior to this Act, section 7 of the Parliament Act 1911 also provided that the maximum duration of Parliament was five years. The 2011 Act, inter alia, transformed the maximum into the standard length of a Parliament. Prior to the 2011 Act, there were examples of Parliaments running for the full five years (in 1992–7 and in 2005–10, for example), but at other times the prime minister would request a dissolution after only four years (such was the preferred practice of both Margaret Thatcher and Tony Blair, for example). Exceptionally, Parliament has lasted only a very short time, as in 1950–1 and 1974.

The Fixed-Term Parliaments Act 2011 provides for two ways in which Parliament may seek an early general election; following a vote of no confidence and a motion for an early parliamentary general election. If a vote of no confidence succeeds, then there is a period of two weeks in which an alternative government can be formed – which becomes a new government following a vote of confidence in that government. Failing this, a general election is called (section 2(3)-(5)). It is theoretically possible for an early general election to be stopped by a vote of confidence in the same government that was voted down in the earlier vote of no confidence, although it is hard to imagine the political circumstances under which this would occur. A motion for an early general election requires a vote by two-thirds of the whole house if it is to succeed in dissolving Parliament (section 2 (1)–(2)). It was believed that this would remove from the prime minister the power to decide when to request a dissolution of Parliament. However, history has demonstrated that this is not the case. Theresa May was able to call an early general election in 2017, in spite of the high hurdle of requiring two-thirds of the votes of the entire house. It is hard to vote against a motion in favour of an early general election without giving the impression that you are afraid that your political party will lose the next general election. Moreover, section 1(7) of the Act preserves the discretion of the prime minister to set the date of the general election following a vote in favour of a motion calling for an early general election. This would seem to preserve the power of the prime minister in reality to continue to determine whether and when to hold an early general election. Nevertheless, Boris Johnson failed to obtain sufficient votes in favour of an early parliamentary general election three times. These exceptions are probably best understood as ones that prove the rule – concerns over the use of a general election to push through a no-deal Brexit in the face of parliamentary disapproval provided a justification for refusing to vote for an early general election without this looking as an admission of defeat before the election even took place.

Recent events have also demonstrated a further way in which an early general election can be called. The Fixed-Term Parliaments Act 2011 can be modified by legislation. This is demonstrated by the Early Parliamentary General Election Act 2019, which provided for the early parliamentary general election that took place on 12 December 2019. The Act was enacted quickly through Parliament – being placed before the House of Commons for its first reading on 29 October 2019 and the Act receiving royal assent on 31 October 2019.

1 Early Parliamentary General Election

(1) An early parliamentary general election is to take place on 12 December 2019 in consequence of the passing of this Act.

(2) That day is to be treated as a polling day appointed under section 2(7) of the Fixed-Term Parliaments Act 2011.

(3) This early parliamentary general election is to be treated as taking place in accordance with section 2 of that Act for the purposes of –
(a) section 96A(9) of the Welfare Reform Act 2012 (benefit cap: review), and
(b) section 23(8) of the Small Business, Enterprise and Employment Act 2015 (duty on Secretary of State to publish reports on economic impact on business activities of regulatory provisions).

(4) For the purposes of regulation 29(4) of the Representation of the People (Scotland) Regulations 2001 (S.I. 2001/497) (which sets out a period for objecting to applications for registration), regulation 8(3) of those Regulations applies as if 2 December 2019 were not a bank holiday.

The 2019 Act does not overturn the provisions of the Fixed-Term Parliaments Act 2011. It is best understood as providing for a specific exception of the 2011 Act, a general election taking place on 12 December 2019 by virtue of this act of Parliament, rather than through a motion for an early general election or a vote of no confidence. Nevertheless, it raises difficult issues as to the relationship between these two Acts of Parliament and the status of constitutional legislation more generally. There are no provisions in the Fixed-Term Parliaments Act 2011 that aim to entrench its provisions. As such, it is, arguably, possible for its terms to be impliedly repealed. However, it is also possible to argue that the Fixed-Term Parliaments Act 2011 is a constitutional statute, therefore it is one that it is not capable of being overturned by implication. Understood in this way, it is perhaps surprising that section 1 (1) of the 2019 Act did not say: 'Notwithstanding the provisions of sections 2(1) to (5) of the Fixed-Term Parliaments Act 2011, an early parliamentary general election is to take place on 12 December 2019 in consequence of the passing on this Act.' Arguably, however, it is not clear that Fixed-Term Parliaments Act 2011 *is* a constitutional statute – given that this issue has not yet arisen before the Supreme Court. Neither is it clear that its provisions could only be expressly repealed. Given the context of the enactment of the 2019 Act in the immediate aftermath of the third failed attempt of Boris Johnson to call an early general election, it would have been clear to MPs voting for the 2019 Act that they were doing so in order to call an election through a means other than the provisions of the Fixed-Term Parliaments Act. In addition, it is arguable that, if the Fixed-Term Parliaments Act 2011 is a constitutional statute, then so, too, is the Early Parliamentary General Elections Act 2019. A conflict between two constitutional statutes would not be resolved in the same manner as a conflict between a constitutional statute and an ordinary statute. The courts would be conscious of the need to prevent Parliament inadvertently undermining the provisions of both Acts, reading the latter constitutional statute as providing a specific exception to the earlier constitutional statutes means of calling an early parliamentary general election, but otherwise leaving the provisions of the 2011 Act untouched. However, one interprets these two legislative provisions, the failure to include a 'notwithstanding' provision in the 2019 Act can also be read as a deliberate political choice, demonstrating a lack of willingness on the part of the government, or Parliament, to concede the existence of constitutional statutes and the need for their provisions to be overturned in a distinct manner.

The Early Parliamentary General Election Act 2019 can be seen as further evidence of the ability of the prime minister to control the timing of a general election, in spite of the provisions of the Fixed-Term Parliaments Act 2011. Although initially failing to call an early general election, the prime minister was able to enact legislation to achieve the same purpose, requiring merely a majority vote to the programme motion to enact the legislation quickly, and to obtain consent to the legislation. However, it is important to recognise three things. First, the Commons could have voted against the programme motion, or could have successfully placed and voted on amendments to the 2019 Act. Second, although the later Act did not require a two-thirds vote, it did require the consent of both the House of Commons and the House of Lords *and* royal assent. The House of Lords could have vetoed the legislation in practice, a delay in and of itself thwarting the aim of the legislation. Although the House of Lords may have felt constrained in doing so, given the clearly expressed desire of the Commons to dissolve Parliament and call an early general election. Third, the prime minister could not unilaterally choose the date of the general election. The date was set by legislation requiring consent of both houses.

The Scottish Parliament, the Welsh and Northern Irish Assemblies, the Greater London Authority (and mayor) and local authorities (and combined authority mayors) are each elected to fixed terms. European parliamentary elections are held every fifth year. As we shall see, a bewildering variety of electoral systems are used for these different elections.

The franchise, which is governed by the Representation of the People Acts 1983 and 1985, as amended, is possessed by all adult British citizens, Commonwealth citizens and citizens of the Republic of Ireland who are not disqualified by law (e.g., as members of the House of Lords), are resident in a constituency and are included in the electoral register for that constituency. The procedures for registration have in the past been defective, with the result that large numbers of eligible electors were omitted from the register and consequently disabled from voting. It has been estimated that approximately 3.5 million people who were entitled to vote were not on the electoral register and that about 91 per cent of the eligible electorate were, in fact, registered to vote (Electoral Commission, *Understanding Electoral Registration* (2005)). The Representation of the People Act 2000 introduced a new system of 'rolling registration' by which the register remains in force indefinitely and is continually updated, electors being able to register at any time of the year instead of by reference to a single annual qualifying date. The Act Also made it easier for homeless persons to register. However, it does not appear that these provisions significantly affected registration rates. The Electoral Registration Act 2006 was designed to improve the process of registration so as to ensure that registers should be as complete and accurate as possible, and the Act placed a duty on electoral registration officers to take all necessary steps to ensure comprehensive registers. A new system of 'individual voter registration' was introduced by the Political Parties and Elections Act 2009. This system has helped to improve voter registration. However, glitches occurred due to the strain of overuse of the system, which meant that the deadline for registration for the Brexit referendum was extended.

British citizens who are resident abroad may qualify for the vote as 'overseas electors' under the Representation of the People Act 1985, as amended, if they were included as being resident in the UK in a parliamentary register of electors within the preceding fifteen years. (As of December 2007, 14,330 British citizens living abroad were registered as overseas voters: see HC Deb vol. 479, col 1965 W, 10 September 2008.)

From 1945 to 1997, the turnout of voters at general elections fluctuated between 71 per cent and 84 per cent of the electorate. In the 2001 election the turnout was 59.4 per cent, the lowest since 1918; in subsequent elections, it has climbed modestly, but remains low in comparison with the period before 1997. Turnout in the 2005 election was 61.4 per cent, with a 65.1 per cent turnout for the 2010 election; 66.1 per cent for the 2015 election; 68.8 per cent for the 2017 election and 67.3 per cent for the 2019 general election.

The votes of the electorate in a general election not only determine the composition of the House of Commons but, directly or indirectly, also decide which of the competing parties will form a government. The 2010 general election was the first in the UK since February 1974 in which no party secured an overall majority of seats in the House of Commons; it resulted in the first Coalition Government that the UK has seen since the Second World War. The 2017 general election produced a minority Conservative Government, supported through a 'confidence and supply' agreement with the Democratic Unionist Party. Views about the best system of election will differ accordingly as emphasis is placed on electoral choice of a government, or on the desirability of a truly representative elected house from which a government, reflecting the balance of parties in the house, will emerge.

8.2.1 Review of Constituency Boundaries

Within the constraints of the existing plurality (or 'first-past-the-post' (FPTP)) electoral system, it is clearly desirable that votes should be, as nearly as possible, of equal value: a vote in Hammersmith should, in principle, be worth as much as a vote in Huntingdon. If this is to be substantially achieved, the boundaries of constituencies should be drawn in such a way that their electorates do not differ too greatly in size. Other factors (such as geographical boundaries) may also have to be taken into account, but it is of the greatest importance that the process should not be influenced by considerations of party advantage.

The Parliamentary Constituencies Act 1986, consolidating previous legislation (and as amended by the Boundary Commissions Act 1992), provided for constituencies to be kept under review by four permanent Boundary Commissions, one each for England, Scotland, Wales and Northern Ireland. The Parliamentary Voting System and Constituencies Act 2011 made significant amendments to this legislation. It provided that the overall size of the House of Commons should be capped at 600 constituencies (the 2010 general election had returned a house of 650 MPs). However, the Electoral Registration and Administration Act 2013 amended this provision, delaying its implementation from 1 June 2015 to 1 June 2020, delaying the inevitable redrawing of almost all parliamentary constituencies. The manifesto of the new majority Conservative Government contains a promise to revisit and redraw constituency boundaries. At the time of writing, the Parliamentary Constituencies Bill 2019–20 was making its progress through Parliament.

At the same time, the rules were changed such that the equal size of constituencies became the *paramount* consideration (previously it had been one of several considerations that the Boundary Commissions were to balance against one another). The government had intended only three concessions to be made to the demands of geography, all in northern Scotland: the constituencies of the Western Isles, of Orkney and Shetland, and of Ross, Skye and Lochaber are to remain, in spite of the fact that each has a much smaller electorate than the norm. The rigidity to this change to the rules led to protests from Wales, from Cornwall and Devon and from the Isle of Wight and elsewhere, where it was felt that more consideration needed to be given to geography, as well as to historical and cultural ties. After extensive and unusually prolonged wrangling in the House of Lords, the rules were softened slightly, such that it may be (at the discretion of the Boundary Commissions) that marginally greater room for manoeuvre remains. Whether the exercise of this discretion will result in an increased resort to the courts, as claims for judicial review are brought, remains to be seen. There may be a strong likelihood of this, as other opportunities for public participation in decision-making by the Boundary Commissions were altered (and arguably reduced) by the 2011 Act. (For an earlier instance of judicial review in the context of constituency boundaries, see R v. *Boundary Commission for England, ex p Foot* [1983] QB 600.)

The latest report of the Boundary Commission of September 2018 proposes sweeping changes to the current constituency boundaries, with only '80 of the existing 533 constituencies in England remaining unchanged' [para 69].

8.2.2 Fairness of the Contest

In a general election, the election is of members of Parliament to represent constituencies. In modern times, however, elections have become less about electing individual members of Parliament and more about electing a government. No member of the electorate actually has a vote on who should, and who should not, be in the government, but the overwhelming majority of the electorate now use their votes as if this is what they are for. As such, the free choice of the electorate may be impaired if the competing parties have unequal opportunities of making their policies known to the people, because of differences in financial resources or access to the media of communication. Electoral law and practice should as far as possible ensure that in these respects none of the parties is at an unfair disadvantage in the election campaign. It is also in the public interest that new political groups or independent candidates are not prevented from entering the contest to challenge the policies of established parties.

Election results are only very rarely challenged in modern Britain. As far as parliamentary elections are concerned, whereas between 1870 and 1914, there were 151 challenges resulting in 69 MPs being unseated, between 1918 and 2005 there were only seven successful challenges, the most recent of these coming in 1924. The mechanism for challenging an election result in a parliamentary constituency is known as an election petition; such petitions are heard by an especially constituted election court (Representation of the People Act 1983, sections 120 and 123). This mechanism was employed in respect of the Oldham East and Saddleworth constituency following the 2010 general election. The election court ruled that the winning candidate (Mr Phil Woolas, for Labour) had engaged in the illegal practice of making false statements in relation to another candidate's personal character or conduct (contrary to section 106 of the Representation of the People Act 1983): see *Watkins v. Woolas* [2010] EWHC 2702 (QB). The decision of the Election Court was upheld on Mr Woolas' unsuccessful claim for judicial review: see *R (Woolas) v. Parliamentary Election Court* [2010] EWHC 3169 (Admin). The result was that the courts certified to the Speaker of the House of Commons that the election of Mr Woolas was void, with the consequence that a by-election had to be held in the constituency. Mr Woolas was barred from seeking re-election for three years. Following the 2015 general election, there was an unsuccessful petition against the election of Alistair Carmichael to the seat of Orkney and Shetland (*Morrison v. Alistair Carmichael MP and Alistair Buchan* [2015] ECIH 71).

8.2.2.1 Election Deposit

Every candidate in a parliamentary election is required to deposit a sum of money with the returning officer, and this sum is forfeited if the candidate fails to poll more than a prescribed percentage of the votes cast in the constituency. The amount of the deposit was fixed at £150 in 1918, and the threshold below which the deposit was forfeited was 12.5 per cent of the votes cast. In 1983, the Home Affairs Committee of the House of Commons considered the requirement of the deposit (*1st Report of 1982–83*, HC 32-I, para 70):

Though it is sometimes argued that there is no reason why any individual who wishes to stand for Parliament should be prevented from doing so by financial considerations, there are valid reasons for imposing some form of constraint. Candidates in parliamentary and European elections automatically acquire a number of advantages and privileges, such as free postage for their election addresses, free use of publicly maintained buildings for public meetings ... and, not least, a great deal of publicity. These privileges are capable of being abused, and it is generally accepted that a deposit of £150 would do little to prevent any number of frivolous or deliberately disruptive candidates from participating in election campaigns and distributing propaganda of a racially inflammatory or otherwise anti-social character.

Although the committee found that there had been little serious abuse of electoral privileges, it was of the opinion that a safeguard was needed (e.g., to discourage candidates who set out to confuse voters by assuming a name similar to that of a well-known candidate) and proposed that the deposit should be increased to £1,000. The Government accepted this recommendation and also decided that the votes threshold should be reduced to 5 per cent of the poll (e.g., 2,500 votes in a poll of 50,000). A bill was introduced in 1984 to give effect to these and other changes in electoral law; in the course of its passage the government reached a compromise with opposition parties to fix the deposit at £500 (see the Representation of the People Act 1983, Schedule 1, rules 9(1) and 53(4), as amended). The Home Affairs Committee returned to the matter in 1998, recommending that the deposit should be raised to £700 and thereafter be index-linked, but this was not acted on and the figure remains at £500.

The requirement of a deposit may discourage some serious independent candidates and creates difficulties for less affluent political parties, deprived at least for the period of the election campaign of what may add up to a substantial sum. For these reasons, it has several times been proposed that the deposit should be abolished and that there should instead be a large increase in the number of supporting signatures required for a nomination – from the present ten to, say, 0.5 per cent of the constituency electorate (250–400 in most constituencies). Governments have declined to adopt this solution, mainly on the ground that candidates who would poll only a handful of votes might yet have little difficulty in obtaining the additional number of signatures to a nomination (*Representation of the People Acts*, Cmnd 9140/ 1984, para 5.4). But the exaction of a substantial deposit may shut out fresh ideas and make it difficult for a new political movement or minority group to take the parliamentary way of advancing its cause. (See, generally, Blackburn, *The Electoral System in Britain* (1995), pp. 222–31.)

8.2.2.2 Election Expenditure and the Funding of Political Parties
The power of money could undermine the fairness of the electoral contest if there were no restriction on expenditure in the campaign. This was

appreciated as early as 1883, when a Corrupt and Illegal Practices Prevention Act established a ceiling for expenditure by each candidate. Ever since then, the legal focus in the UK (unlike in the USA, for example, where the opposite approach is taken) has been to limit *expenditure by* political parties rather than *donations to* political parties.

The limitation of control to *constituency* expenditure continued until the end of the twentieth century, even though the main focus of election contests had shifted decisively to the national campaign. Expenditure by a candidate, a candidate's election agent and by third parties is controlled by sections 73–76ZA of the Representation of the People Act 1983 (as amended, most recently, by the Political Parties and Elections Act 2009, section 21). A candidate's election expenses must, in general, be *paid* by the candidate's election agent and no expense in excess of (at present) £500 may lawfully be *incurred* 'with a view to promoting or procuring the election of a candidate' – whether by presenting the candidate or his or her views to the electors or by disparaging another candidate – except by the candidate, the candidate's election agent or persons authorised by the agent. The Act makes provision for maximum amounts of expenditure that may be incurred by or on behalf of a candidate in any constituency. The precise rules are complex, depending on a fixed amount that is added to in terms of expenditure per elector. In the 2015 general election, following an increase in spending limits, the total limit was around £39,400, depending on the nature of the constituency and its electorate. A much higher maximum applies at by-elections, to which the parties devote a more intensive effort. In recent general elections, the average recorded constituency expenditure per candidate has been well below the permitted maximum for all the parties.

The maximum sum allowed to be spent by a third party in support of or in opposition to a candidate was formerly fixed at £5 by section 75 of the Representation of the People Act 1983, but this draconian limit was challenged in the ECtHR in the case of *Bowman* v. *United Kingdom* (1998) 26 EHRR 1. Shortly before the 1992 general election, Mrs Bowman, Executive Director of the Society for the Protection of the Unborn Child, distributed 25,000 leaflets in Halifax giving details of the voting records and views on abortion of the three main candidates in the Halifax constituency. She was charged with an offence under section 75 in having incurred expense in excess of £5 with a view to promoting or procuring the election of a candidate. Although acquitted on the technical ground that the summons had been issued out of time, she claimed that her prosecution had violated her right to freedom of expression under Article 10 of the ECHR (on which, see further Chapter 11). The European Court held by a majority that the limitation of her expenditure to £5 – in effect, a total barrier to publishing the information – was disproportionate to the legitimate aim (as the court recognised it to be) of securing equality between candidates. It followed that there had been a violation of

Article 10. In consequence of this decision, section 75 was amended so as to raise the limit on expenditure by a third party to £500.

Expenditure on the *national* campaign was until recently not limited by law, even though national leaders and issues had come to dominate election campaigns. In *R v. Tronoh Mines Ltd* [1952] 1 All ER 697, McNair J decided that the prohibition of unauthorised election expenditure (then contained in the Representation of the People Act 1949) did not extend to general propaganda in support of a political party, even if it incidentally assisted particular candidates of that party. The decision led, as David Butler remarks, 'to the innovation of expensive nation-wide advertising' (Committee on Standards in Public Life, *Fifth Report*, vol. 2, Cm 4057-II/1998, p 221). The main parties spend considerable sums in the national campaign on such things as public opinion research, poster campaigns, cinema and press advertising, and broadcasting. (Broadcasting time is provided without charge for party political broadcasts (PPBs), but production can be a costly matter.) The following returns of total campaign expenditure in Great Britain were made by the parties after the 2015 election:

Conservative	£15.59 million
Labour	£12.09 million
Liberal Democrat	£3.53 million

This marks a reduction in expenditure from the Conservative Party (from £16.68 million in 2010) and from the Liberal Democrats (from £4.79 million in 2010). In contrast, there was a marked increase in expenditure by the Labour Party (from £8.01 million in 2010). This brought the spending of the two major political parties closer to one another than the marked contrast in expenditure in the 2010 general election, although expenditure was not as equal as in the 2005 general election, where these two parties each spent very similar amounts (£17.85 million for the Conservatives; £17.94 million by Labour). Total party political expenditure in 2005 was just over £41 million, whereas in 2010 the total figure was just over £31 million. In 2015, it was just over £37 million. The difference is almost entirely explained by the far lower sum that the Labour Party spent in 2010. It is hard to draw comparisons with the 2017 and 2019 general election spending. Both of these elections were early general elections, making them of a different character, particularly the 2019 general election.

In 1998, the majority of the Committee on Standards in Public Life concluded that limits should be imposed on national campaign expenditure by political parties and other campaigning individuals and organisations (*Fifth Report*, vol. 1, Cm 4057-I/1998, para 10.31). The government in response brought forward proposals for national expenditure limits that were enacted in the Political Parties, Elections and Referendums Act 2000. The Act imposes limits on registered political parties' campaign expenditure for parliamentary general elections, normally applicable to the period of 365 days ending with the date of the election. The maximum amount a party may spend depends on the number of constituencies it is contesting, an allowance of £30,000 being made for each constituency contested. Accordingly, a party contesting all the constituencies in the UK in the 2010 general election was able to spend up to £19.5 million on the national campaign. The Act also sets limits on expenditure by third parties intended to promote or oppose the election of a political party or its candidates. (Similar controls are applied to expenditure by political parties and by third parties in elections to the European Parliament and the devolved legislatures in Scotland, Wales and Northern Ireland.)

Hayden Phillips, conducting a *Review of the Funding of Political Parties*, reported in 2007 that 'the attempt to curb campaign expenditure in the Political Parties, Elections and Referendums Act 2000 has not worked as intended' (see his report, *Strengthening Democracy: Fair and Sustainable Funding of Political Parties*). The 2000 Act, he claimed, 'has proved inadequate to the challenge'. Its approach, built around a particular understanding of 'campaign expenditure', was simultaneously 'inadequate and excessively complicated', the current regulations being 'complex, difficult to understand and burdensome to implement'. What seems to be needed is a holistic approach that combines regulation of expenditure with regulation of party-political funding more generally: that is, a single regime that governs not only expenditure but also income, donations and loans. Further, what is needed is a regime that combines regulation of local and national expenditure, and also combines regulation of expenditure during elections with regulation of expenditure between elections. To achieve this will require cross-party agreement. To date, this has been sorely lacking, and we continue with the patchwork complexity that has been the unwelcome (and wholly unnecessary) hallmark of this area of our law for far too long. (Consequently, the Phillips Review led to only modest change: see the White Paper, *Party Finance and Expenditure in the United Kingdom* (Cm 7329, 2008) and the Political Parties and Elections Act 2009; for commentary, see Fisher (2009) 62 *Parl Aff* 298 and (2010) 63 *Parl Aff* 778.)

Party government depends on strong and well-organised political parties, capable of carrying out the study and research necessary for the formulation of realistic policies, and able to present them effectively to the public. These things cannot be done without adequate financial resources. The two main parties derive their income in part from individual contributions and local fundraising efforts, and in part from corporate contributions. The Conservative Party benefits from company donations and the Labour Party from trade union subventions; both parties have also been helped by substantial donations from wealthy business magnates. Reported donations received by the main parties were as follows for the period July to September 2019:

Conservative	£5,775,445
Labour	£5,476,086
Liberal Democrat	£3,298,001

There has been growing concern in recent decades about the sufficiency of resources for a vigorous party system and a similar concern about donations from individuals attempting to buy political influence or to secure decisions from a government favourable to their commercial interests.

The Houghton Committee recommended in 1976 that a system of state aid for political parties should be introduced to maintain the level of activity and efficiency required if the parties were to fulfil effectively their role in the working of democracy. (See the *Report of the Committee on Financial Aid to Political Parties*, Cmnd 6601/1976.) A few years later the Hansard Society's Commission on the Financing of Political Parties proposed a scheme by which the parties would be able to claim state aid related to their popular support, measured by individual contributions of money to the parties (*Paying for Politics* (1981)).

In 1997, the prime minister asked the Committee on Standards in Public Life 'to review issues in relation to the funding of political parties and recommend any changes in present arrangements'. In its *Fifth Report* (Cm 4057-I/1998) the committee rehearsed the arguments for and against state aid for political parties and found them to be finely balanced. It was not persuaded that the state should provide funding for political parties' general activities, but recognised that the parties had been obliged 'to concentrate their resources on campaigning and routine administration at the expense of long-term policy development'. To help the parties to put more effort into the development of policies, the committee proposed that a modest policy development fund (initially of about £2 million per annum) should be established 'to enable the parties represented in the House of Commons to fulfil better what is, after all, one of their most vital functions'. The committee also proposed that donations to political parties of £5,000 or more should be publicly disclosed and that foreign donations should not be permitted.

The government brought forward legislation to implement the main recommendations of the committee and provision was made by the Political Parties, Elections and Referendums Act 2000 for the registration of political parties as the basis for the control of donations (and of election expenditure, as we have seen). A party proposing to field candidates in elections must be registered with the Electoral Commission. (There is a separate registration scheme for Northern Ireland.) A registered political party is required to report to the Electoral Commission donations of above £7,500 to the central organisation or above £1,500 at the local level. The commission maintains a public register of reported donations. It is unlawful for a party to receive 'foreign' donations, from individuals not registered to vote in the UK or companies that are not incorporated in the EU or do not carry on business in the UK. Anonymous donations are not permitted. The Act does not provide for full state funding of political parties.

We saw above the judgment of Hayden Phillips that the Act has not worked as it was intended to do in curbing expenditure by political parties. The all-party House of Commons Constitutional Affairs Committee was similarly of the view that the 2000 Act had enjoyed only limited success in the arena of party funding. Reporting in late 2006, the committee concluded that 'the current system of party financing in the UK is unstable' and that not address-ing the issue 'could lead to increased dependency on large donations ... and the subsequent further erosion of public confidence due to the increasing appearance of money buying power and influence' (*Party Funding*, 1st Report of 2006–07, HC 163, para 48).

There has been an increasing realisation that over-reliance by the parties on wealthy benefactors is harmful to the political process, in that donors may hope for favourable treatment (for instance, concessions in the development of policy or the awarding of contracts) from the recipient party when in govern-ment. Allegations in 2006 that peerages were 'bought' with cash donations (in some instances disguised as 'loans') caused a lengthy furore. The Metropolitan Police undertook an inquiry into possible offences under the Honours (Prevention of Abuses) Act 1925. No prosecutions were brought, but the affair led to a change in the law such that loans (as well as donations) to political parties must now be reported to the Electoral Commission (see the Electoral Administration Act 2006).

(For full accounts of the various ways in which money influences democ-racy, parties and elections in Britain, see Ewing, *The Cost of Democracy: Party Funding in Modern British Politics* (2007); and Rowbottom, *Democracy Distorted: Wealth, Influence and Democratic Politics* (2010).)

8.2.2.3 The Media

The fairness of the electoral contest is put into question by partisanship in the media of communication. Most newspapers display a political bias, sometimes combined with an attempt at objectivity. There has been an unsurprising tendency for a capitalist press that is concentrated in the hands of a few owners, most of whom have other commercial interests, to uphold established view-points and propagate a conservative political consensus. (See Hollingsworth, *The Press and Political Dissent* (1986).) For much of the twentieth century, the national press gave preponderant support to the Conservative Party. It has been argued that the tabloid press influenced voting behaviour in the 1992 election and 'almost certainly made the difference between a Conservative victory and a hung Parliament' (Thomas, 'Labour, the Tabloids, and the 1992 General Election' (1998) 12 *Contemporary British History* 80). The balance was redressed in the 1997 election, 'a landmark in the political history of Britain's press [and] the first campaign in which Labour secured the support of most national daily newspapers' (Butler and Kavanagh, *The British General Election of 1997* (1997), p. 156). These authors commented that 'it would be naïve to regard the 1997 election as instituting a long-term "realignment" of Britain's newspapers' (p. 184). Nevertheless, the shift was consolidated in the 2001 general election, with increased newspaper support for Labour. By the time of the 2010 election, the Conservatives had won back the support of most newspapers, and a number of papers that had traditionally supported Labour advocated editorially that electors should vote for the Liberal Democrats.

Even in the age of the internet, the independence and diversity of the press remains essential if the public are to be able to acquire the information needed for the exercise of political choice in a mature democracy. The authors of the *Minority Report* of the Royal Commission on the Press (Cmnd 6810/1977), convinced of a 'manifest political imbalance in Britain's national press', argued for governmental measures that would achieve greater diversity in the press without prejudice to its freedom. By way of contrast, the majority were not in favour of public measures to correct political partisanship in the press, such as the establishment of a public launch fund to help new newspapers. They expressed their 'firm belief . . . that the press should be left free to be partisan', restrained only by the law and a strengthened Press Council (since replaced by another self-regulatory body, the Press Complaints Commission).

Although the ownership of media (newspapers and commercial broadcasting) is subject to the restraints of general competition law, governments have recognised the need for special limitations of media ownership to ensure that 'a significant number of different media voices' can be heard. The Department of Culture, Media and Sport, in para 1.7 of a *Consultation on Media Ownership Rules* (2001), set out the case for a plurality of media sources:

Plurality ensures that no individual or corporation has excessive power in an industry which is central to the democratic process.

A plurality of owners should secure a plurality of sources of news and editorial opinion, which is vital given the position that newspapers and current affairs occupy at the heart of public debate. A healthy democracy depends on a culture of dissent and argument, which would inevitably be diminished if there were only a limited number of providers of news.

At the limit, even though a single source might produce impartial, high-quality content, they would be able to dictate exactly what constituted 'news' itself, and their inclusion or omission of stories could slant the whole news agenda in a particular direction.

Plurality maintains our cultural vitality. Different media companies produce different styles of programming and publishing, which each have a different look and feel to them. A plurality of approaches adds to the breadth and richness of our cultural experience.

More recently, governments have adopted a 'deregulatory' standpoint, favouring a relaxation of specific controls on media ownership, while insisting that rules are to remain in place when necessary as 'safeguards of democratic debate'. The Communications Act 2003 established a new regulatory body, the Office of Communications (OFCOM), which is invested with general competition powers (exercising a jurisdiction concurrent with that of the Competition and Markets Authority). The Act made changes to the newspaper merger regime. The Secretary of State, advised by OFCOM, is empowered to intervene, with a view to enforcement action, in newspaper mergers on public interest grounds, including the need for a sufficient plurality of views in newspapers. Similarly, the Secretary of State may intervene in cross-media mergers on public interest grounds, including the need for a sufficient plurality of persons with control of media enterprises. OFCOM is required to review media ownership rules at least every three years and may recommend further reforms to the Secretary of State. (See, generally, House of Lords Communications Committee, *The Ownership of the News*, 1st Report of 2007–08, HL 122, and the Government response, Cm 7486/2008.)

Political broadcasts were first transmitted by the BBC in 1924 and ITV began to do so in 1956. Subsequently, the holders of licences to provide television and radio services under the Broadcasting Act 1990 were required by the terms of the licences to include party political broadcasts (PPBs) in the licensed service, in accordance with rules made by the regulatory authorities. In a *Review of Party Political Broadcasting* of 2003, the Electoral Commission said that PPBs offered political parties 'their only opportunity to present an unmediated broadcast message directly to the electorate' and emphasised their effectiveness as direct campaigning tools available to the parties. New arrangements for PPBs were made by the Communications Act 2003. OFCOM must include in the licences for commercial public service broadcasters (Channel 3, Channel 4 and Channel 5 and national radio services) requirements to broadcast PPBs in accordance with rules made by OFCOM, having regard to the views of the Electoral Commission. The BBC and (in Wales) Sianel Pedwar Cymru determine their own policies for the allocation of PPBs, but must have regard to any views expressed by the Electoral Commission. Consistency in allocation of PPBs is sought through a broadcasters' liaison group, which aims to reach consensus on allocation policy, taking into account the views of political parties. Allocations for a forthcoming general election are made to parties (registered with the Electoral Commission) on the basis of the number of candidates being fielded and previous electoral support.

Extensive radio and television coverage of general elections occurs in news programmes, reports from party press conferences, interviews of party leaders, etc. Broadcast programmes relating to the election are exempt from the prohibition of unauthorised expenditure imposed by section 75(1) of the Representation of the People Act 1983 (see above). But section 93(1) formerly provided that a candidate might not take part in a broadcast about his or her constituency for the purpose of promoting his or her election unless every other candidate in the constituency consented. This meant that a candidate could (in effect) veto any broadcast in which another candidate in his or her constituency was to take part. This provision was repealed by section 144 of the Political Parties, Elections and Referendums Act 2000: instead, it is provided that each broadcasting authority is to adopt a code of practice with respect to the participation of candidates in broadcast items about a constituency. In drawing up the code, a broadcasting authority must have regard to any views expressed by the Electoral Commission.

The 2010 general election was the first in which leadership debates were broadcast between the leaders of the three main political parties. Three such debates were held, broadcast respectively by Sky, ITV and the BBC. The detailed rules concerning the conduct of the debates were agreed between the broadcasters and the political parties. The SNP petitioned the Court of Session for judicial review of the legality of the exclusion of the SNP's leader from these debates. The challenge was unsuccessful, not least because separate arrangements were in place ensuring full and impartial coverage of the election in Scotland: see *Scottish National Party, Petitioners* [2010] CSOH 56.

Difficulties have surrounded the subsequent organisation of these debates, which are regulated by agreement between the broadcasters and the political parties. In 2015, four separate debates were held. A live question and answer session was broadcast on Channel 4 and Sky News featuring the then leaders of the Conservative Party (David Cameron) and the Labour Party (Ed Miliband). Both were interviewed separately and faced questions from the audience, but they did not take part in a head-to-head debate. Second, ITV held a debate with seven party leaders, David Cameron, Ed Miliband, Nick Clegg (Liberal Democrats), Nigel Farage (UKIP), Nicola Sturgeon (SNP), Natalie Bennett (Green Party) and Leanne Wood (Plaid Cymru). Third, a debate between opposition party leaders was held on the BBC, featuring the leaders of Labour, the SNP, UKIP, Plaid Cymru and the Green Party. Fourth, the BBC broadcast a *Question Time* special programme with David Cameron, Ed Miliband and Nick Clegg.

Due to the timing of the snap general election in 2017, there was little time to organise a leaders' debate and Theresa May, then Prime Minister and leader of the Conservative Party, quickly ruled out her appearance. A leaders' debate was, however, held on ITV between the seven major parties, which both Jeremy Corbyn, then leader of the Labour Party, and Theresa May declined to attend. Channel 4 and Sky News jointly broadcast a programme in which Theresa May and Jeremy Corbyn were interviewed separately and received questions from the audience. The BBC hosted the final leaders' debate with the main party leaders. Jeremy Corbyn did attend this debate. The Conservative Party sent Amber Rudd, then Home Secretary, as opposed to Theresa May.

Leadership debates were again held in 2019. ITV hosted a debate between Jeremy Corbyn (Labour) and Boris Johnson (Conservative). The BBC held a *Question Time* leadership special, with leaders of the Conservative, Labour, SNP (Nicola Sturgeon) and Liberal Democrat (Jo Swinson) parties. The BBC also hosted a live debate between the leaders of the seven main political parties:

Conservative, Labour, Liberal Democrat, SNP, Green, UKIP and Plaid Cymru; a live head-to-head debate between Jeremy Corbyn and Boris Johnson; and a special edition of *Question Time* aimed at the under 30s. Channel 4 held a debate that focused on the environment, which was attended by all party leaders except the prime minister (an ice sculpture was placed on the empty podium created by Boris Johnson's non-attendance). The proposed debate on Sky News between Boris Johnson, Jeremy Corbyn and Jo Swinson was cancelled.

There have been calls for these debates to be regularised, perhaps through a statutory framework and an independent commission to oversee their regulation. However, these calls were rejected by the House of Lords Select Committee on Communications (*Broadcast General Election Debates 2nd Report 2014* HL 171). The Hansard Society repeated calls for the debates to be formalised in 2018 (Hansard Society, *Audit of Political Engagement 15: The 2018 Report*). Following an e-petition and a Westminster Hall debate, a private members' bill was presented to the Commons – the General Election (Leaders' Debate) Bill 2019, which failed to make progress through Parliament. Given the importance of ensuring impartiality, and the importance of the role played by the broadcast and social media in election campaigns, it is to be hoped that the leaders' debates will be regularised in the future, particularly given the difficulties of ensuring fairness and the lack of judicial review over decisions of the broadcasters to refuse to allow leaders of particular political parties to attend debates.

Section 320 of the Communications Act 2003 requires the providers of television and radio services (other than the BBC – see below) to preserve 'due impartiality' in matters of political or industrial controversy or relating to current public policy. OFCOM is required by section 319 of the Act to draw up and keep under review a broadcasting code that is to include provision for ensuring, inter alia, compliance with the impartiality requirements of section 320 and that news is reported with due accuracy. OFCOM investigates breaches of the code and in serious cases may impose sanctions on the broadcaster. The BBC is not subject to a statutory duty of impartiality, but the Framework Agreement between the Secretary of State for Culture, Media and Sport and the BBC (Cm 6872/2006) imposes an obligation on the BBC to 'do all it can to ensure that controversial subjects are treated with due accuracy and impartiality' in the output of news or in dealing with matters of public policy or of political or industrial controversy. (For this purpose, 'a series of programmes may be considered as a whole'.) The BBC Trust (the sovereign body in the BBC) must draw up and keep under review a code of guidance as to the rules to be observed by the BBC in performance of this obligation, and must do all it can to ensure that the code is complied with.

The duty of impartiality is important, for it would be rash to deny the possibility of an influence of television, in particular, on political attitudes and the outcome of elections. The formal requirement of impartiality leaves a great deal to the judgment of the broadcasting authorities; the independence of these bodies, in particular their immunity from covert governmental pressure, is something that calls for constant vigilance.

Apart from PPBs, political advertising is prohibited in the broadcast media (but not in the print media) in the UK. This ban was unsuccessfully challenged by Animal Defenders International (ADI), a group that campaigns against cruelty to animals. An advertisement prepared by ADI had failed to clear the Broadcast Advertising Clearance Centre on the basis that its transmission would breach the prohibition on political advertising. In upholding the statutory ban (in section 321 of the Communications Act 2003), the House of Lords attached considerable importance to the fact that, in legislating on the matter, Parliament had paid particularly close attention to the relevant case law of the ECtHR and had sought carefully to weigh considerations of free speech against the other public interests in play: see *R (Animal Defenders International)* v. *Secretary of State for Culture, Media and Sport* [2008] UKHL 15, [2008] 1 AC 1312. This decision was upheld by a majority judgment of the Grand Chamber of the European Court of Human Rights (*Animal Defenders International Ltd* v. *United Kingdom* [2013] ECHR 48876/08.

The domestic courts will not intervene in the exercise of judgment by the broadcasting authorities, unless their decision is so unreasonable as to be perverse or they have acted in breach of their legal obligations. As well as *Scottish National Party, Petitioners* and *Animal Defenders International* (above), see, to similar effect, *Attorney General (ex rel McWhirter)* v. *Independent Broadcasting Authority* [1973] QB 629; *Wilson* v. *Independent Broadcasting Authority* 1979 SC 351; *Wilson* v. *Independent Broadcasting Authority (No 2)* 1988 SLT 276; *R* v. *BBC and ITC, ex p Referendum Party* [1997] COD 459; and *R (Prolife Alliance)* v. *BBC* [2003] UKHL 23, [2004] 1 AC 185.

A modest but useful reform of electoral law was brought about by the Registration of Political Parties Act 1998 in protecting parties registered under the act from misuse of their names by persons seeking to mislead the electorate. In *Sanders* v. *Chichester* [1995] 03 LS Gaz R 37, an election court of the Queen's Bench Division had held that a candidate in the 1994 European parliamentary election was not prohibited from describing himself as a 'literal democrat'. (On other occasions, candidates had declared themselves to be standing for the 'conservatory party' or the 'new labour party'.) A revised scheme of registration was introduced by Part II of the Political Parties, Elections and Referendums Act 2000, obliging every party that wishes to put up candidates at an election to be registered with the Electoral Commission. A party is not permitted to register under a name that is the same as that of a registered party or is likely to lead voters to confuse it with a registered party. Further provision to prevent the registration of party names designed to mislead voters is made by the Electoral Administration Act 2006. (Registration is also the basis for the restrictions on campaign expenditure by political parties and for controls on accounting systems and funding of parties.)

8.2.3 The Electoral System

The electoral system in use affects both the 'value' of a vote in terms of its efficacy to secure the election of a preferred representative to Parliament, and also the likelihood that the government elected into power will reflect the interests or policy preferences of the electorate. The system adopted in the UK for elections to the House of Commons is that known variously as the 'first-past-the-post' (FPTP), 'plurality' or 'relative majority' system. Some other Commonwealth countries (e.g., Canada and India) and the USA also make use of this system, but in most democratic countries, in Europe and elsewhere, different systems are preferred. A nationwide referendum was held in May 2011 on whether this electoral system should be replaced with a version of the 'alternative vote' (AV) system; in the result, a large majority voted to stick with FPTP. (See Threlfall, 'The Purpose of Electoral Reform for Westminster' (2010) 81 *Pol Q* 522.)

8.2.3.1 FPTP

In the FPTP system, voting takes place in single-member constituencies and the candidate with the most votes is elected. It is not the object of this system to produce an elected house that will be a 'mirror of the nation' in the sense that it accurately represents the different parties, interests or viewpoints in society. For many years, the system has supported the alternation in government of two main parties, usually assuring to one or other of them an absolute majority in the House of Commons. The tendency of FPTP to disfavour small parties (unless their support is regionally concentrated) and to give a disproportionate benefit in seats won to the party with the largest share of the popular vote has tended to work in favour of single-party government. Parties have been able to come forward with policies for government, rather than for bargaining, and general elections have acquired virtually the character of referendums in which the people have decided which party should form the government. Richard Rose wrote in 1974 (*The Problem of Party Government*, p. 115):

> The argument for the existing procedure is simply stated: the British electoral system is intended to manufacture majority government. It does this by giving disproportionately more seats to the most successful party. The element of distortion in the ratio of votes to seats is usually considered a small price to pay for the greater advantage of fixing responsibility for government upon a single party with a majority in the House of Commons. A purely proportional allocation of seats in accordance with votes would result in neither the Conservative nor Labour party gaining a majority in the Commons. The

weakest rather than the strongest of the three parties, the Liberals, could decide who governs.

For much of the twentieth century, FPTP worked reasonably well, at least in the period from 1931 to 1970 when an overwhelming majority of voters gave their support to the two main parties. In the ten general elections held in that period the two major parties together won an average of 90.74 per cent of the vote (their joint share never falling below 85 per cent). In all but one of those elections, the party that formed the government – including the National Governments of 1931 and 1935 dominated by the Conservatives – had won more votes than any other party: the exception was the 1951 election, which was won by the Conservatives in spite of Labour's having a 0.8 per cent larger share of the total vote. Every government in that period had an absolute majority of seats in the House of Commons. Thus, the system was manufacturing majority government, and since the great majority of those voting (the turnout of voters then averaging 76.71 per cent) gave their votes to one or other of the two main parties, it seems a reasonable inference that those parties stood for a range of viewpoints that were widely held in the community.

The FPTP system may, then, be credited, no doubt in combination with other factors, with the continuation until the 1970s of stable, single-party government enjoying broad popular support. Contrariwise, critics of the system observed that parties were not fairly represented in Parliament in proportion to votes cast for them, and that the Liberal Party, with substantial but dispersed support among voters, was invariably excluded from a share in government. A party could achieve power having won less than 50 per cent of the total vote, and, indeed, this had become the norm.

In the two general elections of 1974, the distorting effects of FPTP on parliamentary representation became more apparent. In each of these elections, the Liberals, with over 18 per cent of the total vote, won only 2 per cent of the seats, and it was observed that more than ten times as many votes were needed to elect a Liberal MP as to elect a Labour or Conservative MP. Mirroring the 1951 result, the February 1974 election was won by the Labour Party with a smaller share of the total vote than that of the Conservatives, and Labour took office as the first government since the Second World War not to have an absolute majority in the House of Commons.

Until 2010, general elections again produced majority government, but they also demonstrated the disproportionality that may result from the FPTP system. Consider, for example, the results of the 1992, 1997 and 2005 elections (source: Kavanagh and Butler, *The British General Election of 2005* (2005).) The result in 2010 gave rise to a Coalition Government, led by the Conservative Party and supported by the Liberal Democrats. In 2015, there was what appeared to be a return to normal, with the general election giving rise to a Conservative majority, albeit a smaller majority than in earlier elections. This was caused, in particular, by the fall in support for the Liberal Democrats. The 2015 election also cast doubt on the traditional classification of the UK as a 'two-party' system, demonstrating a considerable rise in support for the Scottish Nationalist Party in Scotland. The 2017 election produced a minority Conservative Government, supported by a confidence and supply agreement with the DUP. The most recent election, which took place on 12 December 2019, saw a return to a strong Conservative majority Government.

The 1992 General Election

Electorate: 43,249,721
   Votes cast: 33,612,693 (77.7 per cent turnout)

Party	Votes	% of total vote	Seats won
Conservative	14,092,891	41.9	336
Labour	11,559,735	34.4	271
Liberal Democrat	5,999,384	17.8	20
Welsh and Scottish Nationalist	783,991	2.3	7
Others (Northern Ireland and minor parties)	1,176,692	3.5	17

The 1997 General Election

Electorate: 43,757,478
   Votes cast: 31,286,597 (71.5 per cent turnout)

Party	Votes	% of total vote	Seats won
Conservative	9,602,857	30.7	165
Labour	13,516,632	43.2	418
Liberal Democrat	5,242,894	16.8	46
Welsh and Scottish Nationalist	782,570	2.5	10
Others (Northern Ireland and minor parties)	2,141,644	6.8	20

The 2005 General Election

Electorate: 44,261,545
   Votes cast: 27,123,652 (61.3 per cent turnout)

Party	Votes	% of total vote	Seats won
Conservative	8,772,473	32.3	197
Labour	9,547,944	35.2	356
Liberal Democrat	5,981,847	22.1	62
Welsh and Scottish Nationalist	587,105	2.2	9
Others (Northern Ireland and minor parties)	2,234,256	8.2	22

The 2010 General Election

Electorate: 45,600,000
Votes cast: 29,691,380 (65.1 per cent turnout)

Party	Votes	% of total vote	Seats won
Conservative	10,700,000	36.1	306
Labour	8,600,000	29.0	258
Liberal Democrat	6,800,000	23.0	57
Welsh and Scottish Nationalist	657,000	2.3	9
Others (Northern Ireland and minor parties)	1,031,000	3.6	20

The 2015 General Election

Electorate: 46,354,197
Votes cast: 30,697,525 (66.2 per cent turnout)

Party	Votes	% of total vote	Seats won
Conservative	11,334,726	36.9	331
Labour	9,347,324	30.4	232
Liberal Democrat	2,415,882	7.9	8
Scottish Nationalist Party	1,454,436	4.7	56
Welsh Nationalist	181,604	0.6	3
UK Independence Party	3,881,099	12.6	1
Green Party	1,156,149	3.8	1
Others (Northern Ireland and minor parties)	5,963,543	19.1	22

The 2017 General Election

Electorate: 46,843,896
Votes cast: 32,181,757 (68.7 per cent turnout)

Party	Votes	% of total vote	Seats won
Conservative	13,636,684	42.4	318
Labour	12,877,918	40	262
Liberal Democrat	2,371,861	7.4	12
Scottish Nationalist Party	977,568	3	35
Welsh Nationalist	164,466	0.5	4
UK Independence Party	594,068	1.8	0
Green Party	525,665	1.6	1
Others (Northern Ireland and minor parties)	1,197,993	3.3	18

The 2019 General Election

Electorate: 47,587,254
  Votes cast: 30,697,525 (67.3 per cent turnout)

Party	Votes	% of total vote	Seats won
Conservative	13,966,451	43.6	365
Labour	10,295,907	32.2	203
Liberal Democrat	3,696,423	11.5	11
Scottish Nationalist Party	1,242,380	3.9	48
Welsh Nationalist	153,265	0.5	4
Green Party	865,697	2.7	1
Others (Northern Ireland and minor parties)	4,173,825	5.6	18

The Conservative Government elected in 1992, with 42 per cent of the total vote, enjoyed an absolute majority in the House of Commons, yet, on a principle of strict proportionality, the Conservatives would have been entitled to no more than 274 seats (out of 651) – not enough for the formation of a majority government. Similarly, the Conservative Government elected in 2019 had a strong majority in the House of Commons, but would have been entitled to 283 (out of 650) if the seats were distributed on a proportionate basis. In 1997, 2001 and 2005, the Labour Party achieved absolute majorities respectively of 179 (63 per cent of the seats) with 43 per cent of the vote; 166 (again 63 per cent of the seats) with 41 per cent of the vote; and 66 (55 per cent of the seats) with 35 per cent of the vote. Mrs Thatcher's Conservative Party likewise enjoyed three-figure majorities in the House of Commons with about 40 per cent of the votes cast in the general elections of 1983 and 1987.

The Liberal Democrats have been strikingly penalised by the dispersion of their support over the country. In 1992, with 18 per cent of the vote, they won only 3 per cent of the seats. They did somewhat better in subsequent general elections by concentrating their effort on winnable seats, and in 2005 their 22 per cent of the vote gave them sixty-two seats (9.6 per cent of the seats). However, their fall in popularity following the Coalition Government led to a drastic reduction in vote share and seats. The most striking impact of the FPTP voting system is demonstrated in the differences between the outcome of the 2017 and 2019 general election. Although the Liberal Democrats increased their share of the vote from 7.4 per cent in 2017 to 11.5 per cent in 2019, this led to a reduction in seats from twelve to eleven.

These results show that FPTP may discriminate severely against third parties, which naturally regard their under-representation in the House of Commons as unfair. It is also objected against this system that a party can be put in power with much less than a majority of votes and may govern without having to accommodate its policies to the interests of a majority of voters represented by the other parties in Parliament (the argument of 'elective dictatorship'). Other questionable features of the FPTP system were demonstrated in the general elections of 1997, 2001 and 2005, in each of which most MPs were elected with the support of a minority of the voters in their constituencies. General elections have commonly distorted the regional representation of parties, yielding a substantial under-representation of Labour voters in southern shires and of Conservative voters in northern cities. In 1997, the Conservatives failed to win any seats in Scotland with 17.5 per cent of the vote or in Wales with 19.6 per cent. An increase in their Welsh vote to 21 per cent in 2001 still brought them no seats there but almost exactly the same share of the Welsh vote in 2005 gave them three seats.

Among other matters, the 2010 election, which resulted in no one party having an overall majority of seats in the House of Commons, shows that even between the two biggest parties results can appear odd under the FPTP system. Compare, for example, the 258 seats that Labour won in 2010 with 29 per cent of the vote with the 165 seats that the Conservatives had won in 1997 with nearly 31 per cent of the vote. Likewise, compare the 306 Conservative seats in 2010 (with 36.1 per cent of the vote) with the 356 Labour seats in 2005 (with 35.2 per cent of the vote): in the one case, 35 per cent of the vote was enough for a comfortable overall majority, whereas, in the other, 36 per cent of the vote yielded 'only' 47 per cent of the seats, twenty seats short of an overall majority. There can also be disparities when we compare the results of the same party over time. In 2017, for example, the Conservative Party formed a minority government with 318 seats and 42.4 per cent of the vote. In 2019, the Conservative Party won a large majority with 365 seats and 43.6 per cent of the vote. This difference arose from an increase of 329,767 more votes between 2017 and 2019.

As the disproportionality of the FPTP system became increasingly evident, many advocated its replacement by one or other system of proportional representation (PR). It was argued that FPTP was undemocratic in failing to reflect the preferences of voters and, in effect, disenfranchising the numerous classes of voters who, in casting their votes for candidates other than the winner in a constituency, make no contribution to the national election result. (See Blackburn, *The Electoral System in Britain* (1995), pp. 362–4.) PR would be likely to bring about coalition governments and a more consensual style of politics, parties of the left or right having to temper their policies and reach accommodations with parties of the centre. It is said that a new politics of this kind would accord with a broad consensus that exists in society at large and is artificially polarised by a two-party system. (See, e.g., Finer (ed.), *Adversary Politics and Electoral Reform* (1975), pp. 30–1; V Bogdanor, *The People and the Party System* (1981), p. 205; Wright, 'British Decline: Political or Economic?' (1987) 40 *Parl Aff* 41.) However, given the manifesto commitment of the current Conservative Government to keep FPTP, there is unlikely to be any change to the voting system any time soon.

It must not be supposed that the FPTP or plurality system is universally disfavoured. The rationale for plurality elections, as Sanford Lakoff explains (*Democracy: History, Theory, Practice* (1996), p. 178):

is that voters should be encouraged to form and support large amalgamated parties so as to reduce the prospect that minority parties can exercise vetoes over majorities and to improve the chance that elected governments will not be composed of coalitions not chosen by the voters but arranged among the parties.

Coalition governments resulting from PR are not necessarily more representative of the views and interests of the electorate than a single-party government elected by a minority of votes. As J.A. Chandler remarks, 'it is by no means evident that a coalition will fully represent the interests of all those who voted for one of the members of that coalition' ('The Plurality Vote: A Reappraisal' (1982) 30 *Political Studies* 87, 88; see his development of this argument at pp. 88–91). Chandler argues further that the FPTP system is more likely than PR to produce governments that are responsive to public opinion throughout their tenure of office (p. 92):

Within a plurality system a relatively small loss of votes will result in a disproportionately large loss of seats for the largest parliamentary parties and will be likely to threaten their ability to form part of a government. Any party operating under such conditions must take great care not to alienate many of their supporters at the time of the last election unless they can be replaced by new converts to their cause. In comparison a party operating under a system of PR could afford to alienate a much larger number of voters before suffering a correspondingly large loss of seats and a threat to its chances of holding or obtaining power.

The objection that FPTP encourages 'adversary politics' is countered by those who say that PR induces a 'coalition politics' that disregards real divisions of interest in society and suppresses the productive confrontation of ideas. It is also said that PR would reduce the power of voters to dismiss governments. As Tony Benn has remarked: 'In countries that have proportional representation the electorate can only stir the mixture of political parties forming the governing coalition, but can rarely get rid of the whole bunch and replace them with others' (*Industry, Technology and Democracy*, IWC Pamphlet No 60 (1978), p. 7). Karl Popper, too, has decried the effect of PR on the 'decisive issue' of getting rid of a government by voting it out of office, and sees coalition government as leading to a 'decay of responsibility' ('The Open Society and its Enemies Revisited', *The Economist*, 23 April 1988, p. 25). In a similar vein, the following passage focuses on the role of elections in a democracy.

Michael Pinto-Duschinsky, 'Send the Rascals Packing' (1999) 36 *Representation* 117, 118

Elections and representation in the legislature are not ends in themselves. They produce democracy only if they provide the means by which the populace can hope to exercise direct

> and effective control over the government. Not all elections are 'democratic'. In order to qualify as such, they need to affect the composition of a government. In short, democratic elections are not principally about membership of the legislature. The key condition of people power is that the voters should have a direct effect on the selection and – even more important – on the expulsion of Prime Ministers and cabinets.

In PR systems, it has been noted, 'small parties often have excessive power in creating or dissolving coalitions and/or in making decisions within the legislature or coalition': consequently 'fairness in translating votes to seats may lead to unfairness in translating seats to power' (Blau, 'Fairness and Electoral Reform' (2004) 6 *British Journal of Politics and International Relations* 165, 173).

G. Bingham Powell, Jr, *Elections as Instruments of Democracy* (2000), p. 26

[T]he majoritarian [e.g. the present Westminster] and proportional approaches to democracy envision rather different roles for elections in connecting the preferences of citizens and the formation of policy-making coalitions. The majoritarian vision sees elections as enabling citizens directly to choose between alternative governments (incumbent or prospective or both), with the winner taking office and making the policies after the election. The proportional vision sees elections as choosing representatives who can bargain for their voters' interests in postelection policy making. Although all national elections aggregate the desires of thousands of voters into a much smaller number of representative policy-makers, the majoritarian view favors much greater aggregation, while the proportional view emphasizes the importance of equitable reflection of all points of view into the legislature.

A powerful defence of plurality voting in a two-party system is presented by Brian Harrison, *The Transformation of British Politics 1860–1995* (1996), pp. 212–17 and by Kelly (2008) 79 *Pol Q* 260; but compare the exposure of its deficiencies by Stuart Weir and David Beetham, *Political Power and Democratic Control in Britain* (1999), ch. 3.

8.2.3.2 The Alternative Vote

A system that does not necessarily ensure PR but allows more voters to influence the result than does FPTP is the AV system (used for elections to the Australian House of Representatives). This system requires the winning candidate to have received more than half of the votes cast. Voters in single-member constituencies list the candidates in order of preference: if no candidate gets an overall majority of first-preference votes, the candidate with fewest first-preference votes is eliminated and his or her supporters' second-preference votes are redistributed among the remaining candidates.

A candidate who then achieves over 50 per cent of the votes is elected; otherwise, the process is repeated until one candidate obtains an overall majority. The system may be seen as fairer than FPTP, in that a candidate must secure an absolute majority of votes to win the seat and it allows a wider choice to voters, with fewer 'wasted' votes. This is the system that would have replaced FPTP for British parliamentary elections had there been a 'yes' vote in the 2011 referendum.

Before the 1997 general election, a joint consultative committee of the Labour Party and the Liberal Democrats agreed that a commission on voting systems should be appointed early in the new Parliament to recommend an appropriate proportional alternative to FPTP. The choice between the recommended option and FPTP was then to be submitted to a referendum.

An Independent Commission on the Voting System under the chairmanship of Lord Jenkins of Hillhead was appointed by the Prime Minister, Tony Blair, in December 1997. The Report of the Jenkins Commission was published eleven months later (Cm 4090-I/1998). The commission examined the merits and deficiencies of FPTP and, although not required by their terms of reference to come to a view as to whether FPTP should be retained or replaced, were evidently sceptical about the advantages claimed for it. The commission went on to consider what alternative system to recommend. They were impressed by the case for the 'single transferable vote' (see below), especially in its maximisation of voter choice, but were dissuaded from recommending it on the grounds that it was inherently complex, was confusingly different from the systems to be used for the European elections, the Scottish Parliament, the Welsh Assembly and the London Assembly, and was difficult to reconcile with the maintenance of a link between MPs and geographical constituencies. Consequently, the commission decided to recommend a mixed system. While rejecting the AV system on its own as not achieving greater proportionality than FPTP and capable of producing substantially unfair results, the commission concluded that these demerits could be overcome in an additional member system which it described as 'AV with top-up members' (also known as 'AV-plus'). This system, they said, while resembling the German mixed system:

stems essentially from the British constituency tradition and proceeds by limited modification to render it less haphazard, less unfair to minority parties, and less nationally divisive in the sense of avoiding large areas of electoral desert for each of the two major parties.

The recommendations of the Jenkins Commission were never implemented. The nearest that the Labour Governments of 1997–2010 came to introducing electoral reform for British parliamentary elections was in 2010, when a proposal to hold a referendum on whether FPTP should be replaced with

AV was included in the Constitutional Reform and Governance Bill of 2009–10. However, the proposal was dropped from the legislation before it was passed and there is nothing about electoral reform in the Constitutional Reform and Governance Act 2010. As we have seen, it was under the Coalition Government, and not under Labour, that the 2011 referendum on AV was held.

8.2.3.3 Some Varieties of PR

The single transferable vote (STV) version of PR has many advocates in the UK. Although not used on the continent of Europe or in many countries elsewhere, it applies in Ireland and for elections to the Upper House of the Australian Parliament (the Senate). STV was in use in Northern Ireland from 1920 to 1929 and was reintroduced in 1973 for local government elections in the province and for elections to the Northern Ireland Assembly. The assembly reconstituted in 1998 following the Belfast Agreement is elected by STV in six-member constituencies (see the Northern Ireland (Elections) Act 1998 and the Northern Ireland Act 1998, sections 33–4). STV is also used for the election of Northern Ireland's representatives in the European Parliament and it was introduced for local government elections in Scotland as from 2007.

STV is based on large, multi-member constituencies. If this system were to be introduced in the UK, it is likely that most constituencies would have three, four, five or six members, with the five-member constituency of about 300,000 voters as the norm. The voter indicates an order of preference among the candidates named on the ballot paper. The following is a concise explanation of this system (taken from the Plant Report, *Democracy, Representation and Elections* (1991), p. 8):

> The system and methods of calculation involved are complex; but put simply, voters have to list candidates in order of preference, and candidates have to reach a quota in order to be elected. If a candidate passes this quota, any votes for that candidate in 'excess' of the quota are redistributed according to second preferences. If no candidate reaches the quota, the lowest placed candidate drops out and his/her second preferences are transferred. This process continues down the order until the required number of candidates has been elected – bringing in third, fourth and possibly even fifth preferences, if necessary. The more seats per constituency, the more proportional the overall result is likely to be.

Various methods may be used for transferring surplus votes in accordance with voters' preferences. (For a full account of the system, see, e.g., Bogdanor, *What is Proportional Representation?* (1984), ch. 5; Farrell, *Electoral Systems* (2001), ch. 6.)

STV achieves a high level of proportionality between the votes cast for each party and the parliamentary seats that each party receives. STV also increases the power of the voter, in that he or she can express a preference between candidates who are members of the same party: in this respect, a general election also functions as a *primary* election of those who will be a party's representatives in the legislature. The voter can also choose to vote across party lines, giving his or her preferences to candidates, of whatever party, who support a particular cause that he or she favours. The adoption of the system could result in the election of more women and members of ethnic minorities to Parliament.

Some of the merits claimed for STV are speculative in a UK context. The Hansard Society Commission on Electoral Reform in its 1976 report noted that the system has never been used in a country with a population as large as that of Britain. The report also said (para 106) that it was uncertain to what extent voters would be able to discriminate between candidates of the same party by reference to their political standpoints: 'The selection of candidates will still be made by the political parties, and certainly in Ireland there is no conscious attempt to produce a slate of candidates across the political spectrum within a party.' STV could have a 'localising' effect on politics and the behaviour of MPs, who would be at risk of displacement by candidates of their own parties and liable to be unseated as a result of second preferences recorded by voters of other parties. The effect might be to weaken the role of parties in the political system.

An alternative form of PR, widely used in Western Europe and elsewhere, is the list system, which is designed to achieve a representation of *political parties* in proportion to votes cast rather than – as with STV – a fair representation of the decisions of *voters*, irrespective of their support for parties. There are several kinds of list system. In some varieties, each party presents regional or local lists of its candidates, placed in an order of the party's preference, to electors in multi-member constituencies. Votes are cast for parties and seats are distributed between the parties in proportion to their shares of the votes, a party's seats being allotted to its candidates in the listed order. This 'closed-list' system gives an influential role to the party leadership, which draws up the lists, the voter having no power to modify the party's rank order of candidates. In the more flexible 'open-list' system the voter may express a preference between candidates on the party list so that the party's order of preference can be varied. There are several different procedures for allocating seats to the parties in proportion to the votes cast for them.

Pure list systems have not been much favoured by those campaigning for PR in the UK. A closed-regional list system was, however, the government's chosen method to replace FPTP for elections in Great Britain to the European Parliament and was brought into effect by the European Parliamentary Elections Act 1999. (See now the consolidating European Parliamentary Elections Act 2002, as amended.)

The additional member system (AMS) is a mixed system that combines one or other version of the list system with a majoritarian system (such as AV) or with FPTP. Each voter has two votes, one to be cast for a constituency candidate and the other for a party list. The disproportionality resulting from the election of the constituency members is corrected by the allocation of additional members from the party lists. AMS has been adopted for elections to the Scottish Parliament, the Welsh Assembly and the London Assembly (see Chapter 4).

8.3 The People and Government

Do the people exercise any influence or control over government *between* general elections? Are governments 'responsive' to the views and demands of the people?

It seems clear enough that governments are not indifferent to public opinion and pay some regard to it in their decision-making. A government is, in a sense, engaged in a continuous election campaign and is influenced, throughout its term of office, by its assessments of electoral consequences. The 'rule of anticipated reactions' (Carl Friedrich, *Constitutional Government and Politics* (1937), pp. 16–18) may lead a government to refrain from actions that it is thought would provoke widespread unpopularity, evasion or non-cooperation among the public. As Jock Bruce-Gardyne and Nigel Lawson say (*The Power Game* (1976), p. 184):

> All governments are continuously influenced by *anticipated* public opinion. The act of deference, however, occurs within the secrecy of the Cabinet room, so the people never learn of the triumphs they have won. The people complain that their opinions are ignored, while ministers are frustrated by the constraints of (real or imagined) popular sentiment.

Of course, the government may be wrong in its assessment of public opinion. On many specific issues, the public will be sharply divided in its opinions, while, on others, it will be generally indifferent, and again a widely held opinion may fail to be publicly expressed, or what is represented as public opinion may be only that of an articulate minority. But this is not to say that public opinion, however crudely expressed or interpreted, has no impact on government.

Lines of communication lead from the constituencies to the government through the party organisation and MPs' postbags, but a more reliable source of information about public opinion on particular issues is nowadays provided by opinion surveys. Although by no means an exact science, the technique of opinion polling has been refined in recent decades, and political parties commission opinion surveys and make use of polls in planning the tactics of election campaigns. Governments carry out research into public reactions to existing and proposed new policies, employing consultants, setting up citizens' panels, task forces and 'focus groups' or publishing Green Papers. The Home Secretary said on 3 July 1998 (HC Deb vol. 315, col 287WA): 'In line with the practice of successive administrations, the Department routinely consults the public, interested parties and client groups by way of consultation papers and research projects on a wide range of policies and proposed legislation.' Advisory bodies on which outside interests are represented provide further channels of communication.

Ordinary citizens can participate in governmental decision-making in limited ways, using the opportunities provided by land-use planning procedures, or taking part in campaigns against unwanted local development or controversial national legislation (such as the Shops Bill 1986, defeated after 'some of the most extensive and effective lobbying of MPs ever seen in Britain': Peter Riddell, *Financial Times*, 16 April 1986, p. 17). It is, however, mainly through political parties and organised interests or pressure groups (see below) that the citizen can participate in government. Exponents of a 'participatory democracy' envisage a greater role for the individual citizen in workplace and local community politics, as well as in political parties, and a resulting heightened public awareness of national political issues. The democratic principle, as Anthony Arblaster observes, 'could beneficially be applied far more widely in modern societies than it presently is' (*Democracy* (1987), p. 105).

8.3.1 Referendums

It is rare for a general election to be fought on a single main issue, and the result of an election indicates, at most, an undifferentiated approval of a whole range of policies. Only a referendum makes it possible for the electorate to give a clear judgment on a single issue of immediate relevance.

Our constitution embodies the principle of representative, not direct, democracy, and the referendum has not in the past been a normal feature of the system, although various statutes provided for local referendums on the promotion of private bills, the Sunday opening of cinemas, the establishment of public libraries and the 'local option' for the licensing of public houses. The Local Government Act 2000 requires the holding of binding local referendums on the adoption of certain forms of executive governance, including a directly elected mayor (see Chapter 4).

National referendums have in the past been urged for such contentious issues as Irish home rule (Dicey was among those who argued for a referendum on home rule at the turn of the last century) and food taxes, on which Stanley Baldwin proposed a referendum in 1930. In 1911, the Conservative opposition made an unsuccessful attempt to amend the Parliament Bill so as to provide for referendums on bills of constitutional importance (e.g., those affecting the Crown or the franchise or the powers of either House of Parliament). It was not until 1972 that Parliament approved the use of a referendum other than for a local government matter. The Northern Ireland (Border Poll) Act 1972 provided for a referendum in which the electors of Northern Ireland were to vote on the question whether the province should remain part of the UK or be joined with the Republic of Ireland.

The first nationwide referendum was held in 1975. The UK joined the European Communities in 1972 without the terms of entry being submitted to the people for approval. In its manifesto for the February 1974 general election, the Labour Party undertook that it would renegotiate the terms of membership and that if the negotiations were successful, 'the people should have the right to decide the issue through a General Election or a Consultative Referendum'. In March 1975, the renegotiations were concluded and the government announced that it would recommend the British people to vote in favour of staying in the community: 'The Government will accept their verdict' (*Report on Renegotiation*, Cmnd 6003, para 153).

Legislation was necessary to provide for the first nationwide referendum to be held in the UK. In the referendum held in accordance with the Referendum Act 1975, the electorate voted on 5 June 1975 on the question: 'Do you think that the United Kingdom should stay in the European Community (the Common Market)?' (This formulation of the question seemed to some observers to 'tilt the balance in favour of the status quo': see Kellas, in Banting and Simeon (eds.), *The Politics of Constitutional Change in Industrial Nations* (1985), p. 151.) Of those voting, 67.2 per cent (in a turnout of 65 per cent of the electorate) voted to stay in the community.

Although referendums are a relatively recent addition to the UK constitution, it is at least arguable that a practice – some would even argue a constitutional convention – exists of the need for referendums in two related areas: the European Union and devolution.

8.3.1.1 The European Union

As discussed above, the first national referendum was used to confirm the UK's membership of the EU. Prior to the Brexit referendum in 2016, there was both a series of calls for referendums on matters relating to Europe and the imposition of referendum requirements regarding some modifications of the nature of the UK's relationship with the European Union. Developments in the EU stimulated demands for a referendum in the 1990s. A backbench MP, fearful of the implications of the Maastricht Treaty, introduced a Referendum Bill in February 1992 to require a national referendum as a precondition for the ratification of treaties that would have the effect of diminishing the powers of Parliament: 'no such profound constitutional change should take place without reference to the people' (Mr Richard Shepherd, HC Deb vol. 204, col 581, 21 February 1992; the bill made no headway). Amendments were moved by backbenchers to the European Communities (Amendment) Bill 1993 in both houses to provide for a referendum on ratification of the Maastricht Treaty: although lost, they were supported by dissidents in all three main parties. Subsequently, there were demands (and another doomed referendum bill) for a referendum on developments in the EU towards monetary union and a single currency, and a Referendum Party was launched in 1994 with the single object of securing a referendum on 'the future structure of Europe'. The European Union Act 2011 imposed referendum requirements in order to ratify any proposed amendment to the EU Treaties, as well as with regard to the other possible transfers of power from the UK to the EU. These provisions were overturned on exit day by the European Union (Withdrawal) Act 2018.

No mention of the impact of referendums on the UK constitution is complete without mention of the Brexit referendum – the referendum on the UK's continued membership of the EU. Following increasing tensions in his own party concerning divisions over Europe, in addition to the growth in support of the UK Independence Party, which called for the UK's exit from the EU, the Conservative Party manifesto promised the holding of an 'in-out' referendum on the UK's continued membership of the European Union. Following the election of a Conservative Government in 2015, the European Union Referendum Act 2015 was duly enacted, providing for the Brexit referendum. On 23 June 2016, 51.9 per cent of those participating voted to leave the EU and 48.1 per cent voted to remain. The 2015 Act had not provided for a legal obligation on the part of the UK Government to implement the outcome of the referendum. Nevertheless, the government announced that it would adhere to the outcome of the referendum and initiate the process for the UK's withdrawal from the EU Treaties set out in Article 50 TEU. This was in spite of the fact that the Prime Minister, David Cameron, and a large number of the government and MPs had campaigned to remain in the European Union.

8.3.1.2 Devolution and Independence

The Labour Government elected in 1997 said that it would proceed with legislation to establish a Scottish Parliament and a Welsh Assembly only with the support of the relevant electorates. Provision for referendums in the two countries was made by the Referendums (Scotland and Wales) Act 1997. In the Scottish referendum, voters were to be asked to choose between the two propositions: 'I agree that there should be a Scottish Parliament' and 'I do not agree that there should be a Scottish Parliament'. A second ballot paper offered a further choice between alternatives: 'I agree that a Scottish Parliament should have tax-varying powers' and 'I do not agree that a Scottish Parliament should have tax-varying powers'. In the Welsh referendum, there was only one pair of alternatives, voters being asked whether they agreed or disagreed 'that there should be a Welsh Assembly'. In the subsequent referendums, in Scotland on 11 September 1997 and in Wales a week later, the affirmative proposition was carried in each case. (See Chapter 4 and see, further, Munro [1997] *PL* 579.) A further referendum was held in March 2011 in Wales on whether the National Assembly for Wales should assume further legislative powers. Legislative authority for the holding of this referendum was provided by sections 103–4 of the Government of Wales Act 2006 (see also the National

Assembly for Wales Referendum (Assembly Act Provisions) (Referendum Question, Date of Referendum, etc.) Order 2010). The Scotland Act 2016 and the Wales Act 2017, which amended the Scotland Act 1998 and the Government of Wales Act 2006 respectively, provided that the Scottish Parliament and the Welsh Assembly are 'not to be abolished except on the basis of a decision' of the people of Scotland or Wales 'voting in a referendum'. (See section 63A Scotland Act 1998 and section A1 Governance of Wales Act 2006.)

A referendum was held in Northern Ireland, in accordance with the Northern Ireland Negotiations (Referendum) Order 1998 (SI 1998/1126), after the multi-party political agreement concluded in Belfast on Good Friday 1998. Voters in Northern Ireland were asked: 'Do you support the agreement reached at the multi-party talks on Northern Ireland as set out in Command Paper 3883?' Of the 81 per cent of electors who voted on 22 May 1998, 71 per cent supported the agreement. (See, further, Chapter 4.) Section 1 of the Northern Ireland Act 1998 also makes it clear that Northern Ireland is to remain part of the United Kingdom and 'shall not cease to be so without the consent of a majority of the people of Northern Ireland voting in a poll'. Were the people of Northern Ireland to vote in favour of leaving the UK and joining Ireland, the Act places the UK Government under a legal obligation to agree proposals between the UK and Ireland to achieve this objective and to lay these proposals before the Westminster Parliament.

In 2014, Scotland held a referendum on Scottish independence. Given the lack of legal certainty surrounding whether Scotland held the power to enact legislation to hold a referendum, the Scottish Government sought, and was granted, an order from the UK Government under section 30 of the Scotland Act 1998 empowering the Scottish Government to hold an independence referendum. By 53.3 per cent to 47.7 per cent, Scotland voted to remain a part of the United Kingdom. Following the UK's exit from the European Union, there have been calls for a second independence referendum in Scotland. In 2017, the Scottish First Minister, Nicola Sturgeon, succeeded in obtaining a vote from the Scottish Parliament to approve a request for the UK Government to make a second section 30 order, transferring to Scotland the power to hold a second independence referendum. Theresa May, then UK Prime Minister, made it clear that she would not be willing to make such an order until after the Brexit negotiations had been concluded. Following the recent general election in 2019, which saw an increase in support for the SNP in Scotland, there have been further calls for a second independence referendum, and votes in the Scottish Parliament in favour of seeking a second independence referendum. However, proposed talks between the Scottish and the UK governments were put on hold by the Scottish government in the light of the Covid-19 pandemic.

Referendums and proposals for referendums have also been forthcoming on other issues. Proposals for the establishment of a Greater London Authority with an elected assembly and mayor were submitted in 1998 to an electorate consisting of local government electors in London boroughs and City of London wards. In accordance with the Greater London Authority (Referendum) Act 1998 a single question was presented to the voters: 'Are you in favour of the Government's proposals for a Greater London Authority, made up of an elected mayor and a separately elected assembly?' In a turnout of 34 per cent, a majority of 72 per cent voted 'Yes'. The ability to create an elected mayor, following a local referendum, was established in the Local Government Act 2000. Since 2007, elected mayors have also been able to be created via appointment.

In May 2011, voters decided not to replace the FPTP electoral system used for parliamentary elections with the AV system.

Before any referendum is held, questions of principle and procedure have to be settled – for example, whether the referendum is to be binding on the government or only advisory, how the referendum question is to be worded, and whether a majority of votes in favour of a proposal is to be sufficient or is to be effective, say, only if it constitutes a specified percentage of the electorate. The Political Parties, Elections and Referendums Act 2000 made general provision for such matters. The Act governs the conduct of referendums in the UK, with the object of ensuring that each side in a referendum campaign should have a fair opportunity of presenting its case to the electorate. The Act provides for a system of controls administered by the Electoral Commission. Individuals, political parties or other organisations taking part in a referendum campaign must register with the commission. As 'permitted participants', they are subject to expenditure controls, which, in respect of registered political parties, are based on the percentage of the vote secured by the party at the previous general election. Special arrangements apply to 'umbrella organisations' designated by the Electoral Commission as representing those campaigning on each side of the question. The government, local authorities and other publicly funded bodies are prohibited from publishing promotional material in relation to a referendum in the twenty-eight days before the poll. The Secretary of State must consult the Electoral Commission before making orders regulating the conduct of referendums. The formulation of the question to be put to the voters is determined by the legislation providing for a referendum. The Electoral Commission considers the proposed wording as specified in the bill or draft statutory instrument and declares its view of the intelligibility of the question (see section 104 of the Act). It takes considerations of fairness into account – for instance, that the words and phrases used in the question should not be intentionally 'leading' and should not have positive or negative connotations. The commission is required to publish reports on the administration of referendums. The first occasion for these arrangements to be tested in a *nationwide* context came only in 2011 with the AV referendum. In 2009–10, the House of Lords Constitution Committee conducted an inquiry into the use of *Referendums in the United Kingdom* (see the Committee's 12th Report of 2009–10, HL 99). The committee surveyed the arguments for and against the use of referendums in the context of a parliamentary democracy such as the UK. These may be summarised as follows. *Arguments for*: that referendums enhance the democratic process, that they can settle an issue, that they can be a protective device (that is, a safeguard against controversial decisions), that they can enhance citizen engagement and that they can promote voter education. *Arguments against*: that referendums are used merely as a tactical device (or as a political tool), that they are dominated by elite groups, that they fail to deal with complex issues, that there is little voter desire for them and that they are expensive to run. The committee concluded that, in spite of the 'significant drawbacks' to their use, 'they are most appropriately used in relation to fundamental constitutional issues' (para 94). The committee's view was that it was impossible to provide a 'precise definition', but indicated that the following would fall within the scope of being a fundamental constitutional issue: abolition of the monarchy; departure from the EU; secession of any nation from the UK; abolition of either House of Parliament; reform of the electoral system for the House of Commons; the adoption of a written constitution; and changing the UK's currency (para 94).

Is it true to say that 'the arguments against the referendum are also arguments against democracy' (Bogdanor, *The People and the Party System* (1981), p. 93)? Or, by the same token, are referendums incompatible with the principle of representative parliamentary democracy and with the authority of an elected Parliament? (Compare the views expressed in the Lords' debate on an abortive Parliamentary referendum bill on 31 January 2001: HL Deb vol. 621, cols 763 et seq.) This often depends on the nature of the referendum. While there is clear evidence that the Scottish independence referendum helped to further deliberative democracy, the same cannot be said for the recent Brexit referendum. At all events it can no longer be said that the referendum is something alien to the British constitution. Neither is it the case that there is a clear practice establishing when referendums should be used, or whether referendums should only be politically advisory or should always produce a legal obligation on the government to respond to the referendum outcome. The UK constitution needs still to resolve the tension that referendums create between direct and representative democracy and between the will of the people and the will of Parliament. While the outcome of the 2019 general election may have resolved this issue as regards Brexit, the bigger issue as to the nature of the UK constitution remains to be resolved.

(See, further, Tierney, *Constitutional Referendums: The Theory and Practice of Republican Deliberation* (Oxford University Press, 2012); McHarg, Mulle, Page and Walker (eds.), *The Scottish Independence Referendum: Constitutional and Political Implications* (OUP, 2016); Qvortrup, *The Referendum and other Essays on Constitutional Politics* (Hart, 2018).)

8.4 Political Parties and Pressure Groups

The system of parliamentary government in the UK is one of party government. Yet Jean Blondel noted in 1963 (*Voters, Parties and Leaders*, p. 87) that political parties in Britain were 'private associations to which the law does not give more rights and duties than to other private organisations'. The law of the constitution did not, until recently, regulate political parties and indeed barely acknowledged their existence. But the working of the constitution depends on parties, which are 'the chief motivating force of our main governmental institutions'. (Memorandum of Dissent to the Kilbrandon Report, Cmnd 5460-I/1973, para 311. The authors of the memorandum considered that any scheme for constitutional reform must concern itself with the political parties.)

Report of the Committee on Financial Aid to Political Parties (Cmnd 6601/1976), para 9.1

Effective political parties are the crux of democratic government. Without them democracy withers and decays. Their role is all pervasive. They provide the men and women, and the policies for all levels of government – from the parish council to the European Parliament. The parties in opposition have the responsibility of scrutinising and checking all the actions of the Executive. Parties are the people's watchdog, the guardian of our liberties. At election times it is they who run the campaigns and whose job it is to give the voters a clear-cut choice between different men and different measures. At all times they are the vital link between the government and the governed. Their function is to maximise the participation of the people in decision-making at all levels of government. In short they are the mainspring of all the processes of democracy. If parties fail, whether from lack of resources or vision, democracy itself will fail.

Parties are important in a study of the constitution because they engage individuals in the political process, bring about the election of MPs (and also members of the devolved legislatures and UK members of the European Parliament), provide governments and opposition to governments, and are engines (although not the only ones) for the creation of public policy.

Parties are the motor of our system of government, yet membership of the main parties has fallen steeply in recent decades, and fewer than 2 per cent of the electorate are now members of a political party. As Hayden Phillips reported in 2007 (*Strengthening Democracy: Fair and Sustainable Funding of Political Parties*), 'fifty years ago one in 11 of the electorate belonged to a political party; today that ratio is down to one in 88'. Is this decline a threat to the working of democracy in our country? (See, further, Parvin and McHugh, 'Defending Representative Democracy: Parties and the Future of Political Engagement in Britain' (2005) 58 *Parl Aff* 632.)

Since independent members are rarely elected to the House of Commons (none were elected in 1983, 1987 or 1992, one in 1997 and 2001, and two in 2005), the selection of candidates by the political parties is a crucial factor in determining the membership of the house. This was clearly demonstrated in the recent 2019 general elections, where none of the MPs who had had the whip removed from the Conservative Party for voting against the government on Brexit were successful in being re-elected when standing as an independent candidate. Selection in a safe seat is virtually equivalent to election, and many of those selected will serve for long periods in Parliament. Among them will be future holders of ministerial office and prime ministers. The selection procedures used by the parties are therefore a matter affecting the public interest. The parties' rules for the selection of candidates differ, but, in each case, selection is a function of the local party organisation, subject to a degree of central control.

Political parties are all engaged to some degree in formulating policies. Parties that aim to take office, whether alone or as part of a coalition, will devise a comprehensive range of policies for government. Some minor parties have more limited objectives that they hope to achieve through pressure and bargaining. The parties have their own procedures and conventions for the making of policy. These procedures vary as to the extent to which policy-making is a matter for the party leadership, for the party conference or for other party bodies such as specially created policy forums.

A stimulus to the development of party policies is provided by non-party organisations (or 'think tanks') of the right, left or centre. These include on the right: the Institute of Economic Affairs, Civitas, the Centre for Policy Studies and the Adam Smith Institute; on the left: the Fabian Society and the Institute for Public Policy Research (the latter founded 'to provide an alternative to the free market think tanks'). CentreForum, founded (as the Centre for Reform) in 1998, is close to the Liberal Democrats. There are other organisations that campaign or stimulate discussion on constitutional reform, among them the Constitution Unit, the Institute for Government, Democratic Audit and DEMOS.

(See, generally, Bogdanor, 'The Constitution and the Party System in the Twentieth Century' (2004) 57 *Parl Aff* 717; McHugh and Needham (eds.), 'The Future of Parties' (2005) 58 *Parl Aff* 499 (Special Issue).)

Pressure groups are bodies of people organised to exert influence or pressure on government without themselves seeking, through the electoral process, to assume governmental responsibility. In general, they are clearly distinguishable from political parties, which hope to enter government, or at least to establish for themselves a strong base in Parliament by fielding candidates in elections. The distinction becomes blurred when single-issue parties, such as the Legalise Cannabis Alliance, are formed to contest elections.

It was aptly said by Bill Jones (in Jones et al., *Politics UK* (5th edn. 2004), p. 235) that: 'The ability to form organisations independent of the state is one of the hallmarks and, indeed, preconditions of a democratic society.' Pressure groups have grown in number and following in the UK while the membership of political parties has declined. Dennis Kavanagh, *British Politics: Continuities and Change* (4th edn. 2000), p. 178, commented as follows:

> More than half the adult population are subscribing members of at least one organization (such as a trade union) and many belong to a number of groups. (The Royal Society for the Protection of Birds has more members than all of the British political parties put together!)

Individuals may find that their views on specific issues are more likely to have an impact via pressure-group activity than through membership of a political party, or that their particular interests are better defended by a group set up with the protection of those interests as its object. R.T. McKenzie (in Kimber and Richardson (eds.), *Pressure Groups in Britain* (1974), p. 280) was in no doubt:

> that pressure groups, taken together, are a far more important channel of communication than parties for the transmission of political ideas from the mass of the citizenry to their rulers.

Pressure groups are like political parties in expressing the demands of sections of the public, but, unlike most parties, they campaign for a specific interest or cause rather than for a wide range of policies. It is usual to distinguish two kinds of pressure group. 'Interest' or 'sectional' groups represent people with social, occupational or economic interests in common, and their main purpose is to protect and further those interests. Among them are professional bodies, producers' groups such as trade unions, industrial and commercial associations, the National Farmers Union and the two 'peak' organisations, the Confederation of British Industry and the Trades Union Congress. The main concern of many sectional organisations is to provide services to their members, and some also control entry to a trade or profession and seek to maintain standards of competence: it may be only occasionally that they resort to lobbying and the tactics of pressure. But some sectional groups are engaged in a continuous dialogue with government, and many try to maintain a constant moderating influence on the government departments whose policies may affect their interests.

The other kind of pressure group is the 'promotional' or 'cause' group, which is an organisation of persons for the promotion of a cause which its members support. Cause groups are also of great number and variety. Some examples are: Amnesty International; the Campaign for Freedom of Information; the Child Poverty Action Group; the Campaign to Protect Rural England; Friends of the Earth; Greenpeace; the Howard League for Penal Reform; the Joint Council for the Welfare of Immigrants; Liberty (the

National Council for Civil Liberties); the National Society for the Prevention of Cruelty to Children; and Shelter. Many of the cause groups put much of their effort into giving assistance to people in need, but all seek by publishing information, mounting public campaigns or exerting direct pressure on government to achieve legal reforms or the expenditure of public money or other favourable official response to the cause advocated. Some cause groups have only a brief life, campaigning on transitory issues such as a road-building scheme or the closure of a hospital, but others continue for many years, as, indeed, do the needs or injustices that give rise to them.

Pressure groups sometimes work through or in alliance with a political party, hoping in this way to influence the policies of an existing or future government. The League Against Cruel Sports, for example, has concentrated its efforts on the Labour Party and was at the forefront of the campaign that led to the enactment of the Protection of Wild Mammals (Scotland) Act 2002 and the Hunting Act 2004. In contrast, Mediawatch-UK (formerly the National Viewers' and Listeners' Association) and the Country Land and Business Association have had more influence in the Conservative Party.

Ernest Bevin remarked that the Labour Party had grown out of the bowels of the trade union movement, and the trade unions have been closely linked with the Labour Party throughout its history. More recently, the bond has loosened, but it has not been severed. The unions affiliated to the party provide a substantial part of its income, have 50 per cent of the votes in the party conference and elect several members of the party's national executive committee. The leader and deputy leader of the Labour Party are chosen by an electoral college voting in three sections – members of the Commons and European Parliamentary Labour Parties; individual members of the party; and members of affiliated trade unions and other affiliated organisations – each section having one-third of the votes.

Sectional groups do not enjoy a similar organic relationship with the other political parties, but business interest groups, while not affiliated to the Conservative Party, have traditionally been informally linked with it and have been able to influence party policy in economic and industrial matters. The Institute of Directors, for instance, has had close links with the Conservative leadership and was considered to have made a significant contribution to the Thatcher Government's measures to limit trade union power and immunities.

Government legislation often bears the stamp of successful pressure by outside interests and is sometimes virtually the product of negotiation with affected groups. (As to pre-legislative consultation, see Chapter 7.) Some policies are not so much influenced by *pressure* as produced in a joint effort by a government department and one or more groups with which it shares a common interest. For example, a continuous dialogue takes place between the Department for Environment, Food and Rural Affairs and the National Farmers Union on questions of agricultural policy. (Retiring presidents of the

National Farmers' Union have an excellent prospect of being awarded knighthoods.) The close relationships between departments and pressure groups have led observers to speak of a 'colonisation' of government by groups, or of 'policy communities' composed of government departments and insider groups.

Pressure groups also look for support in Parliament and have done so increasingly in recent decades (see Norton (1997) 50 *Parl Aff* 357, 360). Besides lobbying MPs and briefing them with information and arguments, pressure groups instigate parliamentary questions, draft suggested amendments to bills and give evidence to select committees. (A great part of the evidence received by select committees is provided by pressure groups.) Opposition frontbenchers, lacking the resources of the Civil Service, often depend on groups to provide them with the expertise and information needed for the effective scrutiny of government bills. Many MPs act as parliamentary advisers or consultants to companies, trade unions or other outside bodies such as the Countryside Alliance or the Caravan Club. Pressure groups often have links with all-party groups in the House of Commons through which they seek to further their interests or causes – for instance, the all-party groups on disability, food and health, nuclear energy, refugees and the retail industry. All-party groups engage the active interest of MPs in a great variety of policy questions, drawing on the experience and specialised knowledge of the outside groups. Contrariwise, funding or other support received by all-party groups from outside interests may compromise their objectivity: the House of Commons has adopted rules requiring all-party groups to notify the Parliamentary Commissioner for Standards of financial and other material benefits (e.g., secretarial services) received by them.

Public campaigns and parliamentary pressure organised by groups have induced governments to legislate and have succeeded in putting on the statute book such measures as the Television Act 1954 (providing for commercial television) and the Vaccine Damage Payments Act 1979. Groups have often made a significant contribution to the content of government legislation, as was seen, for instance, in the role of the disability organisations in helping to shape the Disability Discrimination Act 1995. Interest groups were acknowledged by the government to be 'active participants in the policy-making process' that led to the enactment of the Food Standards Act 1999: the government 'placed a very strong emphasis on consulting affected interests throughout all stages' (Grant, *Pressure Groups and British Politics* (2000), pp. 70–6). The Campaign for Freedom of Information can take much of the credit for the enactment of the Freedom of Information Act 2000 (considered below). Pressure groups have also played an important part in the enactment of private members' legislation, such as the Abortion Act 1967, the Unsolicited Goods and Services Act 1971, the Protection of Children Act 1978, the Environment and Safety Information Act 1988, the Copyright (Visually Impaired Persons) Act 2002 and the Autism Act 2009. By the same token, sometimes pressure groups have campaigned successfully against governmental initiatives, such as the proposed imposition of VAT on books and newspapers in 1985 and the Shops Bill in 1986.

Interest and cause groups are an important part of the machinery by which government is controlled in the modern democratic state. They are a means by which citizens can express their demands on government between elections and they help to make government responsive to bodies of opinion and interests that it might otherwise disregard. Therefore, they contribute to a more *participatory* democracy and to better informed government. An ideal may, indeed, be constructed of a representative democracy in which the periodic assertion of the full power of the people in general elections is supplemented by a continuous interchange between government and a multiplicity of groups which aggregate and articulate the demands of individuals. In this way, the power to influence government is diffused and government itself, encompassed by assertive and competing groups, proceeds by bargaining instead of coercion.

This *pluralist* vision of society does not, however, correspond with reality. For one thing, not all interests have a representative organisation, and organised groups are markedly unequal in resources and influence. Those which express the values and objectives of 'the establishment' may be readily embraced by government, while the claims of the deprived and vulnerable go unheard. Then again, the processes of bargaining with interest groups are for the most part unstructured and secret; groups may advance their sectional interests by 'whispering into important ears rather than proclaiming their arguments in public debate' (Frank Bealey, *Democracy in the Contemporary State* (1988), p. 174). Concerns as to how this may be most appropriately regulated were usefully examined by the House of Commons Public Administration Committee in its report on *Lobbying: Access and Influence in Whitehall* (1st Report of 2008–09, HC 36). In the absence of statutory regulation of covert political lobbying, organisations representing professional lobbyists have set up an independent body, the UK Public Affairs Council, which is to create a register of lobbyists and monitor the observance of a set of guiding principles and a code of conduct for the industry.

Sanford Lakoff (*Democracy: History, Theory, Practice* (1996), p. 295) observes in this connection:

> So long as the interest groups are not so dominant as to dictate outcomes, and so long as they are pluralized enough to exercise countervailing power against each other, the public interest is well served by lobbying. Where the public interest is inarticulate and undefined, or where particular lobbies are effective in gaining control over the direction of public policy, abuses occur.

In urging their own narrow, sectional interests, interest groups may disregard and obscure the wider issues of policy involved. Wyn Grant remarks (in

'Pressure Politics: A Politics of Collective Consumption?' (2005) 58 *Parl Aff* 366, 367–8) that 'NIMBY' ('not in my back yard') protesters:

> often deploy broader environmental or health arguments, but this should not conceal their main purpose which is to protect their own particular interests. They rarely argue, for example, that air traffic in general should be restrained, only that planes should not fly over their house. They do not usually offer constructive alternatives: the phone mast should be removed, but they rarely suggest where it might go.

Government may be assailed by the contrary demands of opposed pressure groups and, as Wyn Grant shows, a government faced with such conflicting claims may itself be divided, different departments responding according to their own policy preoccupations.

Not all groups are truly representative of those on whose behalf they claim to act; some, as Wyn Grant observes, may be run by 'a self-perpetuating oligarchy' whose supporters have little opportunity to influence the policies or strategies adopted by the leadership ('Pressure Politics' (2001) 54 *Parl Aff* 337, 345).

It became apparent in the early 1990s that some outside bodies were bypassing the normal channels of communication with government departments in seeking particular favours from MPs or ministers, sometimes employing consultants claiming to provide a privileged access to government and sometimes endeavouring to purchase information or influence for cash (e.g., payments to MPs for asking parliamentary questions). Following the first report of the Committee on Standards in Public Life (Cm 2850/1995), which censured these abuses, the House of Commons admonished members not to pursue initiatives in Parliament in return for remuneration or favours from outside bodies, strengthened the rules on disclosure of financial interests and approved a code of conduct for MPs (subsequently revised: see now HC 735 of 2008–09).

The code prohibits paid advocacy by MPs on behalf of any outside body, and agreements and remuneration for parliamentary services must be disclosed. The house also established an independent parliamentary commissioner for standards who monitors the operation of the code, maintains the register of members' interests, advises on questions of conduct of MPs and investigates allegations of misconduct. The commissioner is supported by the Committee on Standards and Privileges, which considers any complaints against MPs referred to it by the commissioner for further investigation. The machinery for maintaining standards has been strengthened and clarified in the light of experience and in response to reports of the Committee on Standards in Public Life (in particular its *Eighth Report*, Cm 5663/2002).

Some pressure groups have adopted a 'test case strategy', assisting individuals to bring cases in courts or tribunals with the object of establishing precedents that will result in changes in administrative practice favourable to the interests of a whole class of persons. The Child Poverty Action Group (CPAG) is one group to have pursued this strategy. Pressure groups may also be given leave to intervene in proceedings to which they are not parties, so as to present arguments to the court on aspects of the public interest that are affected by the litigation. It is a marked feature of appeal court litigation in the UK that such 'public interest interventions' have occurred more frequently in recent years. Liberty and JUSTICE have been particularly notable as intervening parties in litigation in cases concerned with civil liberties, for example (see the valuable survey of the issues in JUSTICE, *To Assist the Court: Third Party Interventions in the UK* (2009)). Trades unions have also played a part – for instance, recently in *R (UNISON)* v. *Lord Chancellor* [2017] UKSC 51, [2017] 3 WLR 409, where UNISON successfully challenged the lord chancellor's decision to raise tribunal fees and to reduce the threshold below which tribunal fees could be remitted.

In *Re E (A Child)* [2008] UKHL 66, [2009] 1 AC 536, the House of Lords was critical of the way in which the Northern Ireland Human Rights Commission (a statutory body) had intervened in the proceedings.

> **Lord Hoffmann:** ... In recent years the House has frequently been assisted by the submissions of statutory bodies and non-governmental organisations on questions of general public importance. Leave is given to such bodies to intervene and make submissions, usually in writing but sometimes orally from the bar, in the expectation that their fund of knowledge or particular point of view will enable them to provide the House with a more rounded picture than it would otherwise obtain. The House is grateful to such bodies for their help.
>
> An intervention is however of no assistance if it merely repeats points which the appellant or respondent has already made. An intervener will have had sight of their printed cases and, if it has nothing to add, should not add anything. It is not the role of an intervener to be an additional counsel for one of the parties. This is particularly important in the case of an oral intervention. I am bound to say that in this appeal the oral submissions on behalf of the NIHRC only repeated in rather more emphatic terms the points which had already been quite adequately argued by counsel for the appellant. In future, I hope that interveners will avoid unnecessarily taking up the time of the House in this way.

The Conservative Government was also critical of the way in which pressure groups and others were bringing legal actions, viewed by some as an intention to 'play politics' in the courts and to cause unnecessary delay to legitimate government projects. This led to the enactment of Part 4 of the Criminal Justice and Courts Act 2015, which made it more difficult for pressure groups to bring legal challenges directly or to intervene in legal challenges. This Act requires courts not to grant standing, or to refuse to make an award or grant relief, if it appears to the court to be 'highly likely that the outcome for the applicant would not have been substantially different if the conduct complained of had not occurred' (Senior Courts Act 1981 section 31 (2B) and section 31 (3D) as amended). This may make it extremely difficult for pressure groups to bring direct actions, as although the action challenged may have an impact on individuals, it may not have an impact on the pressure group itself. This does not prevent pressure groups from supporting actions brought by those whose interests are harmed by governmental action. However, the 2015 Act provides a disincentive for doing so. It is harder to obtain protective cost orders, meaning that pressure groups may face larger costs if they bring judicial challenges. Moreover, the court may order intervenors to pay costs and may not require other parties to cover the costs of intervenors unless there are 'exceptional circumstances that make it appropriate to do so' (Criminal Justice and Courts Act 2015, section 88). In its recent manifesto, the Conservative Government stated that it would establish a constitution, democracy and rights commission, including a statement that the Conservative Party 'will ensure that judicial review is available to protect the rights of the individuals against an overbearing state, while ensuring that it is not abused to conduct politics by another means or to create needless delays' (Conservative Party Manifesto 2019, p. 48). This looks remarkably like the arguments used to implement the 2015 reforms, which suggests that, in the future, it may be even more difficult for pressure groups to bring legal challenges or to intervene in judicial review proceedings.

Some groups have adopted tactics of 'direct action' to press their demands, their protests sometimes involving breaches of the law. Lord Hoffmann referred in *R v. Jones* [2006] UKHL 16, [2007] 1 AC 136, at [89], to the 'long and honourable history' of civil disobedience on conscientious grounds, and continued:

> People who break the law to affirm their belief in the injustice of a law or government actions are sometimes vindicated by history. The suffragettes are an example which comes immediately to mind. It is the mark of a civilised community that it can accommodate protests and demonstrations of this kind. But there are conventions which are generally accepted by the law-breakers on one side and the law-enforcers on the other. The protesters behave with a sense of proportion and do not cause excessive damage or inconvenience. And they vouch the sincerity of their beliefs by accepting the penalties imposed by the law. The police and prosecutors, on the other hand, behave with restraint and the magistrates impose sentences which take the conscientious motives of the protesters into account. The conditional discharges ordered by the magistrates in the cases which came before them exemplifies their sensitivity to these conventions.

(Note Lord Hoffmann's qualification of these remarks in paras [90]–[94].)

All in all we may say with Sanford Lakoff (above, p. 170) that pressure groups, together with other institutions of civil society, 'act as a buffer against the expansion of the state's power and sphere of action'. More positively, they can provide experience, expertise and a measure of popular participation in the making and implementation of public policy. We may also note, as does Brian Harrison (*The Transformation of British Politics 1860–1995* (1996), p. 178) that 'without the enterprise, the impatience, the energy, and the dedication cause groups evoke, democracies would lose much of their vitality, and might not survive at all.'

(See, further, Harden and Lewis, *The Noble Lie* (1986), ch. 6; Hirst, *Representative Democracy and its Limits* (1990); Harlow and Rawlings, *Pressure Through Law* (1992); Grant, *Pressure Groups and British Politics* (2000); Coxall, *Pressure Groups in British Politics* (2001); Jordan and Maloney, *Democracy and Interest Groups: Enhancing Participation?* (2007); Grant, 'The Changing Pattern of Group Politics in Britain' (2008) 3 *British Politics* 204.)

8.5 Open Government

If the principle of responsible government is to be maintained, there must be sufficient public access to information about governmental activities and decisions. Openness in government is necessary if Parliament, groups and the public are to be able to contribute to the making of policy, and if the actions of government are to be properly scrutinised and evaluated, and the decision-makers held accountable.

R v. *Shayler* [2002] UKHL 11, [2003] 1 AC 247

Lord Bingham: . . . Modern democratic government means government of the people by the people for the people. But there can be no government by the people if they are ignorant of the issues to be resolved, the arguments for and against different solutions and the facts underlying those arguments. The business of government is not an activity about which only those professionally engaged are entitled to receive information and express opinions. It is, or should be, a participatory process. But there can be no assurance that government is carried out for the people unless the facts are made known, the issues publicly ventilated. Sometimes, inevitably, those involved in the conduct of government, as in any other walk of life, are guilty of error, incompetence, misbehaviour, dereliction of duty, even dishonesty and malpractice. Those concerned may very strongly wish that the facts relating to such matters are not made public. Publicity may reflect discredit on them or their predecessors. It may embarrass the authorities. It may impede the process of administration. Experience however shows, in this country and elsewhere, that publicity is a powerful disinfectant. Where abuses are exposed, they can be remedied. Even where abuses have already been remedied, the public may be entitled to know that they occurred.

Without openness and a 'right to know', ministerial responsibility to Parliament is enfeebled, opposition to governments disarmed and democracy undermined. The effective use of parliamentary questions, the work of select committees and political campaigning by opposition parties or pressure groups all depend on the availability of information. Secrecy, by way of contrast, begets arbitrariness and misgovernment. In the words of Lord Jenkins of Putney, it is wrong to deprive the electorate of information about the processes of government, 'for where they are bad they remain bad and get worse in the dark' (HL Deb vol. 483, col 175, 17 December 1986). 'The first task of the opposition in Parliament', say J.A.G. Griffith and Michael Ryle, 'is to minimise secrecy in government' (*Parliament* (2nd edn. 2003), p. 477).

British governments have traditionally maintained a high degree of secrecy about their operations. The political culture has not in the past included any idea of 'participatory democracy' that could have supported claims by individuals or groups to be provided with information about government. The assumption discerned by Nevil Johnson in a note issued by the head of the Civil Service in 1985 that 'in some sense all information gained in the course of duty is the private property of the Government of the day and, therefore, to be disclosed only if its disclosure is regarded as desirable and duly authorised' (Memorandum to the Treasury and Civil Service Committee, *7th Report of 1985–86*, HC 92-II, p. 172) seemed to reflect a persisting ethos of British governments. Governmental secrecy was for many years fortified by the draconian section 2 of the Official Secrets Act 1911. The all-embracing section 2 was repealed by the Official Secrets Act 1989 but this Act, although limited to specified categories of information, is still wide-ranging in its application of criminal sanctions to unauthorised disclosures of official information and it admits no defence of the public interest in proceedings for contravention of its provisions: see *R* v. *Shayler* (above) and see further Chapter 11. Civil servants remain in any event subject to disciplinary proceedings for disclosures of information in breach of internal Civil Service rules and instructions.

Some of the principal conventions of the constitution – in particular those of collective and individual ministerial responsibility – have contributed to the maintenance of governmental secrecy by enforcing an internal governmental discipline in the control of information. The courts admit no right in common law to obtain information about the processes of government. In *R* v. *Secretary of State for Defence, ex p Sancto* (1992) 5 Admin LR 673, the court was of the opinion that a minister's refusal to disclose to the parents of a soldier the report of a board of inquiry into his accidental death was, in the particular circumstances, 'outrageous', but could give no remedy because there was no public 'right to know' and no legal duty to disclose the report. A party to litigation may be able to obtain an order for the production of official information needed to prove his or her case – but only if the court is not persuaded that the public interest precludes disclosure of the information. Indeed, some judges formerly took the view that a valid ground of objection to the disclosure of information in legal proceedings was 'to protect from inspection by possible critics the inner working of government while forming important governmental policy' (Lord Wilberforce in *Burmah Oil Co Ltd* v. *Bank of England* [1980] AC 1090, 1112). While an argument of this kind would not usually prevail today against the right to a fair trial assured by the HRA, it remains a struggle to persuade courts that they should rule in favour of openness in the face of government claims that secrecy is necessary: see, for an acute example, *R (Binyam Mohamed)* v. *Secretary of State for Foreign and Commonwealth Affairs* [2010] EWCA Civ 65, [2010] 3 WLR 554, discussed in Chapter 2.

British governments have in the past held it to be entirely a matter for their discretion whether and to what extent official information should be made available to the public or to interested organisations. It has been a perennial concern that governments are unduly restrictive in withholding information from the public (and from Parliament) and that secrecy is sometimes maintained not for reasons of the public interest, but to protect the government from criticism or embarrassment.

In 1968, the Fulton Committee on the Civil Service observed that the administrative process was 'surrounded by too much secrecy' and that 'the public interest would be better served if there were a greater amount of openness' (Cmnd 3638, para 278). The government in its response drew attention to measures already taken to disclose more information (*Information and the Public Interest*, Cmnd 4089/1969). Among these was the practice, begun in 1967, of issuing 'Green Papers' setting out policy proposals and inviting public comment and discussion before decisions were taken. In 1976, the Prime Minister, Mr Callaghan, announced in Parliament that in future more background information on major policies would be published. This undertaking was followed by the 'Croham Directive', an instruction to official heads of departments circulated by Sir Douglas Allen (afterwards Lord Croham), Head of the Home Civil Service. In terms of the directive, departments were to publish 'as much as possible of the factual and analytical material used as the background to major policy studies'. While initiatives such as these increased the flow of information to some extent, they had only a modest effect in opening the processes of government to public scrutiny.

If the government controls access to information, it may use its power – and indeed has done so – to 'manage' the release of news and information in its political interest by selective 'leaking', non-attributable briefings to lobby journalists, the manipulation of statistics (e.g., on hospital waiting lists or levels of crime) and similar expedients (see Daintith [2002] *PL* 13). The question of misuse or 'spinning' of information so as to delude the public was highlighted in 2002–3 when it was alleged that the Blair Government had made unfounded assertions about Iraq's possession of weapons of mass destruction in order to justify the decision to go to war. On this sorry episode and the wider issues raised, see the Intelligence and Security Committee, *Iraqi Weapons of Mass Destruction: Intelligence and Assessments* (Cm 5972/2003) and *Government Response* (Cm 6118/2004); Foreign Affairs Committee, *9th Report of 2002–03*, HC 813 and *Government Responses* (Cm 6062/2003 and 6123/2004); Runciman (ed.), *Hutton and Butler: Lifting the Lid on the Workings of Power* (2004); and Yeung, 'Regulating Government Communications' [2006] *CLJ* 53.

8.5.1 Freedom of Information

Access to information is now provided through the Freedom of Information Act 2000. Its enactment replaced the *Code of Practice on Access to Government Information*, which was introduced by a Conservative Government and came into effect in 1994. The code was not legally enforceable, but compliance was supervised by the parliamentary ombudsman. A complaint that information had been improperly withheld could be taken (through an MP) to the parliamentary ombudsman who might, at his or her discretion, investigate the complaint and recommend (but not order) that information should be made available. The *Code of Practice* was not sufficiently publicised and public recourse to its provisions was at a low level. Nonetheless, it scored a number of successes in terms of open government. The Labour Government published a White Paper, *Your Right to Know* (Cm 3818) and a draft freedom of information bill. The latter met with widespread criticism. It was seen by the organisation Liberty as 'deeply flawed', by the Campaign for Freedom of Information as weaker than the *Code of Practice* it was to replace, and was generally regarded as falling well short of the principles of openness affirmed in the government's White Paper. In response to the criticisms some changes were made to the bill, but disappointment remained that the government had not modified its basic structure and scheme. In the face of continuing criticism in both houses some significant improvements were made to the bill.

The Freedom of Information Act 2000 is comprehensive in its application to 'public authorities', including government departments, the National Assembly for Wales, the Northern Ireland Assembly, NHS bodies, publicly owned companies, local authorities, educational establishments, NDPBs, the armed forces and the police (see Schedule 1). Further bodies and offices may be included by orders made by the Secretary of State (sections 4 and 5): these may include private bodies that have functions of a public nature or provide services under contract with a public authority. In all, some 115,000 bodies are covered by the act, far more than had been subject to the *Code of Practice on Access*. The security and intelligence services are excluded from the Act's provisions. (Separate legislation governs the position in Scotland: see the Freedom of Information (Scotland) Act 2002.)

The 2000 Act, which came fully into force only in 2005, allows any person, whether or not a citizen of the UK or resident in this country, to request the disclosure of information from a public authority to which the Act applies. The authority is then, in general, obliged to inform the applicant whether it holds information of the description requested (the duty to 'confirm or deny') and, if the information is held, to communicate it to the applicant promptly and in any event within twenty working days. (Information known to officials but *unrecorded* is not covered by the Act.) As far as is reasonably practicable, the information is to be provided by the means requested – by supplying a copy of written information, allowing inspection of a record or providing a summary of the information held. An authority will not be obliged to comply with a request if the cost of doing so exceeds the 'appropriate limit' fixed by regulations. If the cost is estimated to be above the limit, the authority may refuse the request or require payment of the whole or part of the cost.

All freedom of information laws exempt some categories of information from disclosure. The 1997 White Paper *Your Right to Know* (Cm 3818) proposed that requests for disclosure should in each case be assessed by reference to a test of harm: in general, disclosure would be denied only if it would cause 'substantial' harm to one of a limited number of protected interests. The Act takes a different approach, dispensing with a general test of this kind. It provides for twenty-three exemptions from the obligations of disclosure. Most of these are 'class' exemptions, applicable without the need to satisfy a test of harm or prejudice. Information relating to national security is exempted on this basis (a minister's certificate providing conclusive evidence that the exemption is required for safeguarding national security). There is also, for instance, a class exemption for information held by an authority for the purposes of criminal investigations or certain other investigations or proceedings conducted by the authority. Another broad class exemption covers information relating to the formulation or development of government policy, communications between ministers, advice by law officers and the operations of any ministerial private office. Some of these classes are of wide scope and, none being subject to a harm test, may allow public authorities to withhold much information of a factual nature not manifestly requiring to be kept secret in the public interest. Personal information and information supplied in confidence are also protected on a class basis, as is information intended for future publication (it may be at some undetermined date).

Besides the class exemptions there is a set of exemptions – such as those relating to defence, international relations, the economy, commercial interests and law enforcement – which apply if disclosure of the information would be likely, by reason of its contents, to prejudice the interest in question. A requirement of (the probability of) 'prejudice' seems to be a weaker test than that of 'substantial harm' proposed in *Your Right to Know*. What has been criticised as a 'catch-all' provision allows the withholding of information if in 'the reasonable opinion of a qualified person' (e.g., a minister of the Crown) it would be likely to prejudice the maintenance of the convention of collective responsibility of ministers, inhibit the free and frank provision of advice or exchange of views, or otherwise prejudice the effective conduct of public affairs.

Some of the exemptions are expressed as being *absolute*, so that the duty to disclose (or to confirm or deny that the information exists) can have no application: these include, for instance, the exemptions for court records relating to particular proceedings, information provided in confidence and information supplied by or relating to the security and intelligence services. Most of the exemptions are not absolute and in these cases the public authority must disclose the information unless 'in all the circumstances of the case, the public interest in maintaining the exemption outweighs the public interest in disclosing the information'. (See section 2.) This applies, for instance, to the exemption for information relating to the formulation or development of government policy, and, in this case, it is further provided (section 35(4)) that 'regard shall be had to the particular public interest in the disclosure of factual information which has been used, or is intended to be used, to provide an informed background to decision-taking'. The effect is that material such as internal reports, the evaluation of policy options and interdepartmental communications in the course of formulating policy are protected from disclosure, subject to the balancing test, while factual and background information used in the policy-making process is not only subject to balancing but (in the words of a government minister) is given 'a strong steer towards disclosure' (Lord Falconer of Thoroton, HL Deb vol. 612, col 827, 20 April 2000).

The expression 'public interest' in section 2 is not defined. How is it to be understood? Is it in the public interest that the government or public authority should not be exposed to embarrassment or mistrust or ill-informed criticism? The Information Commissioner's Office (on which see below) publishes guidance on this and many other matters of how the freedom of information legislation is to be understood, but its guidance note on the meaning of the 'public interest' test raises the question posed here without offering a definitive answer. In practice, much will depend on the specific exemption that is relied on.

If a public authority refuses to disclose the information requested, it must give reasons for doing so. An applicant who complains of a refusal to disclose information (or to confirm or deny its existence) must first seek internal review by the public authority concerned in accordance with its complaints procedure. If not satisfied with the result, the complainant may bring the matter before the information commissioner.

The Act confers supervisory and enforcement powers on the independent information commissioner (see www.ico.gov.uk). The commissioner has responsibility for the administration of the Act; he or she is to promote good practice by public authorities and their observance of the statutory requirements, and gives guidance to individuals and organisations about their rights and obligations under the law. His or her office employs more than 280 people and in 2008 received 2,600 freedom of information complaints, as well as 26,000 data protection complaints. A complainant against a refusal to disclose information (or to confirm or deny) may apply to the information commissioner for a decision as to whether the public authority has complied with the requirements of the Act. Unless the commissioner makes no decision on the application (giving reasons for not doing so), he or she notifies the complainant and the public authority of the decision reached in a formal 'decision notice'. If the commissioner has found that the authority is in breach of its obligation to make disclosure – whether in having wrongly concluded that the information sought was exempt from disclosure, or that (in the case of a 'contents' exemption) disclosure would cause prejudice, or that (in the case of any non-absolute exemption) the public interest in disclosing the information was outweighed by the public interest in maintaining the exemption – the commissioner can overrule the authority's decision and specify in the decision notice the steps it must take to comply with the Act. Either the complainant or the public authority may appeal to the First-Tier Tribunal (Information Rights) against a decision notice, and either party may further appeal to the Upper Tribunal and from there to the Court of Appeal. (The tribunal also hears appeals against notices issued under the Data Protection Act 1998 and the Environmental Information Regulations 2004.) Several cases have now reached the courts, but the judgments in these cases tend to focus on points of detail (albeit sometimes important detail) rather than broad points of principle: see, for example, *Common Services Agency v. Scottish Information Commissioner* [2008] UKHL 47, [2008] 1 WLR 1550; *BBC v. Sugar* [2009] UKHL 9, [2009] 1 WLR 430; *BBC v. Sugar (No 2)* [2010] EWCA Civ 715, [2010] 1 WLR 2278; *HM Treasury v. Information Commissioner* [2009] EWHC 1811 (Admin), [2010] 2 WLR 931; *Evans v. Information Commissioner* [2015] UKHL 382 (AAC); *Innes v. Information Commissioner* [2014] EWCA Civ 1086, [2015] 1 WLR 210; *Department for Work and Pensions v. Information Commissioner* [2016] EWCA Civ 758, [2017] 1 WLR 1; *Department of Health v. Information Commissioner* [2017] EWCA Civ 374, [2017] 1 WLR 3330 and *Stunt v. Associated Newspapers Ltd (Information Commissioner Intervening)* [2018] EWCA Civ 1780, [2018] 1 WLR 6060.

Some decisions of the information commissioner can be overridden by executive order under section 53 of the Act. This 'executive override' applies to a decision of the commissioner that a public authority must disclose information on the ground that the public interest in disclosure prevails over the public interest in maintaining the exemption. A Cabinet minister or the Attorney General may *in this case only* give the commissioner a certificate that 'he has on reasonable grounds formed the opinion' that the authority was not in breach of its obligation to make disclosure. Reasons for the opinion must be given. A copy of the certificate must be laid before each House of Parliament. The issue of an overriding certificate is in principle open to judicial review. Such a certificate was used for the first time in 2009 to prevent the disclosure of Cabinet minutes pertaining to discussion in 2003 of the Attorney General's advice as to the legality of the Iraq war (for the ruling of the Information Tribunal, see *Cabinet Office v. Information Commissioner*, EA/2008/0024 and EA/2008/0029, 27 January 2009; for the

Secretary of State's ministerial override, see HC Deb vol. 488, cols 153–68, 24 February 2009). A considerable body of previously secret information was subsequently published by the Iraq Inquiry (see www.iraqinquiry.org.uk); for analysis, see the excellent Weller, *Iraq and the Use of Force in International Law* (2010), ch. 6–7 (the key passages as regards how limited Cabinet discussion was of the legality of the Iraq war are at pp. 229 and 250).

An override certificate was also used to prevent the disclosure of memos written by Prince Charles to various government departments. The issue of this certificate was challenged in *R (Evans)* v. *Attorney General* [2015] UKSC 21, [2015] 2 WLR 813. The Supreme Court, in a majority decision, concluded that the Attorney General was not entitled to issue a certificate. The majority agreed that section 53 could not empower the Attorney General to issue a certificate merely because he disagreed with the conclusion of the tribunal. Lord Neuberger's judgment provided a strong criticism of the very purpose of section 53. Its provisions potentially breached two aspects of the rule of law: the basic principle that a court decision is binding between the parties, including the executive, and that decisions of the executive are capable of being reviewed by the court. To empower the Attorney General to issue a certificate to overrule the decision of the Upper Tribunal, merely because the Attorney General disagreed with its outcome, would undermine both of these principles. As such, 'reasonable grounds' had to be read down by the court, so as to prevent its provisions from undermining the rule of law. For Lord Neuberger, this meant interpreting 'reasonable grounds' so as to include legal or factual errors, or where there had been a change of circumstances since the judicial decision. Lord Mance provided a different reading to section 53, concluding that the courts would review the 'reasonable grounds' provided by the Attorney General by a more stringent standard of review than *Wednesbury* unreasonableness. Insufficient justification of these reasonable grounds had been provided in this case. The dissent, most notably that of Lord Wilson, disagreed with both interpretations of section 53. The judgment demonstrates that, at least as regards the implementation of section 53 of the Act, courts will closely scrutinise the justification provided for issuing a certificate to overturn the decision of the Upper Tribunal.

The commissioner may investigate a public authority's compliance with the Act on his or her own initiative and issue an 'enforcement notice' if the authority is found to be in breach of its obligations. The authority may appeal to the tribunal against such a notice and it is subject to the executive override on the question of public interest (as above).

As well as providing a right to information for individual applicants, the Act requires public authorities to adopt and publish schemes for the publication of information as a matter of course. A publication scheme must specify the classes of information that the authority intends to publish, the manner of publication and whether fees are payable. In adopting (or reviewing) a scheme, an authority is to have particular regard to the public interest in allowing public access to information that it holds as well as the public interest in the publication of reasons for decisions made by it.

Despite its limitations, the Freedom of Information Act has provided a valuable reinforcement of governmental accountability and a worthwhile extension of the rights of the individual. The Select Committee on Constitutional Affairs said in its *7th Report of 2005–06* (HC 991, para 13):

> It is clear to us that the implementation of the FOI Act has already brought about significant and new releases of information and that this information is being used in a constructive and positive way by a range of different individuals and organisations. We have seen many examples of the benefits resulting from this legislation and are impressed with the efforts made by public authorities to meet the demands of the Act. This is a significant success.

Perhaps the most notorious example to date of the use of the freedom of information legislation is in the context of the MPs' allowances scandal of 2009, in which the 2000 Act was used by journalists in pursuit of details as to how MPs had used (and abused) their complex systems of allowances and expenses (see Chapter 1). The argument that the Act did not apply to MPs for reasons pertaining to parliamentary privilege was roundly dismissed by the Divisional Court: see *Corporate Officer of the House of Commons* v. *Information Commissioner* [2008] EWHC 1084 (Admin), [2009] 3 All ER 403; for commentary, see Leyland [2009] *PL* 675. (The Supreme Court subsequently ruled that parliamentary privilege was likewise no bar to parliamentarians being prosecuted for the offence of false accounting, contrary to section 17 of the Theft Act 1968: see *R* v. *Chaytor and others* [2010] UKSC 52.)

In an echo of British governments' traditional preference for secrecy over openness, Tony Blair in his memoirs (*A Journey* (2010), pp. 516–17) cited the Freedom of Information Act as one of the great errors of his time in office. The terms in which he expressed himself are striking:

> Freedom of information. Three harmless words. I look at those words as I write them, and feel like shaking my head till it drops off my shoulders. You idiot. You naïve, foolish, irresponsible nincompoop. There is really no description of stupidity, no matter how vivid, that is adequate. I quake at the imbecility of it.
>
> Once I appreciated the full enormity of the blunder, I used to say – more than a little unfairly – to any civil servant who would listen: Where was Sir Humphrey when I needed him? We had legislated in the first throes of power. How could you, knowing what you know, have allowed us to do such a thing so utterly undermining of sensible government?
>
> Some people might find this shocking. Oh, he wants secret government; he wants to hide the foul misdeeds of the politicians and keep from 'the people' their right to know what is being done in their name.

> The truth is that the FOI Act isn't used, for the most part, by 'the people'. It's used by journalists . . .
>
> But another and much more important reason why it is a dangerous Act is that governments, like any other organisations, need to be able to debate, discuss and decide issues with a reasonable level of confidentiality. This is not mildly important. It is of the essence. Without the confidentiality, people are inhibited and the consideration of options is limited in a way that isn't conducive to good decision-making. In every system that goes down this path, what happens is that people watch what they put in writing and talk without committing to paper. It's a thoroughly bad way of analysing complex issues.

There are two main problems with this position. First, the exemptions in the Act more than adequately cater for the limitations to freedom of information that Mr Blair is eager to reinforce. Second, it was a serious criticism of his own government that decision-making was too often undertaken informally, without adequate minute-taking and in small clusters of advisers rather than in open cabinet discussion: see, e.g., the Butler Report of 2004: *Review of Intelligence on Weapons of Mass Destruction* (HC 898 of 2003–04, para 611).

Mr Blair's views about freedom of information can be contrasted with those of his immediate successor. Gordon Brown said in a speech in October 2007, four months after becoming Prime Minister, that: 'Although FOI can be inconvenient, at times frustrating and indeed embarrassing for governments, freedom of information is the right course, because government belongs to the people, not the politicians. Wherever possible, that should be the guiding principle behind the implementation of our Freedom of Information Act.' (Quoted by the information commissioner in evidence to the House of Commons Justice Committee, *3rd Report of 2008–09*, HC 146, Ev 16.)

(On freedom of information, see Birkinshaw and Varney, *Government and Information Rights: The Law Relating to Access, Disclosure and their Regulation* (5th edn. 2019); Wadham, Harris and Matcalfe, *Blackstone's Guide to the Freedom of Information Act* (5th edn. 2013); Worthy, 'The Future of Freedom of Information in the UK' (2008) 79 *Pol Q* 100; Little and Stopforth, 'The Legislative Origins of the MP's Expenses Scandal' (2013) 76 MLR 83; Coppel, *Information Rights* (4th edn. 2014).)

9

Parliament and the Responsibility
of Government

Contents

9.1 Introduction: Responsible Government

Our constitutional system is one of 'responsible government'. The idea of political (or constitutional) responsibility is wide enough to include a number of values (no fewer than twelve are identified by Gilbert, 'The Framework of Administrative Responsibility' (1959) 21 *Journal of Politics* 373), but in the present context two are of particular importance. The first is indicated by A.H. Birch, *Representative and Responsible Government* (1964), pp. 17–18, in saying that 'the term "responsible" is commonly used to describe a system of government in which the administration is responsive to public demands and movements of public opinion.' The responsibility of government in this sense implies that it is responsive to (takes heed of, defers to) demands, pressure or influence exerted by the public, or on its behalf by institutions or organisations that have an acknowledged place in the constitutional system. We may take the correlative of 'responsiveness' to be 'control', so that a responsive government is one that submits to control by the public or by representative bodies. 'Control' is a central concept of constitutional thought and practice, and it needs some elucidation.

A dictionary definition of control gives as synonyms 'command', 'restraint' and 'a check', and it is evident that the word may be used in strong or weak senses. Even mere influence can be thought of as a relative power, or control in a weak sense, so that control extends in a series from a power of direction at one extreme to inducement or influence at the other. It is helpful for our purposes to retain the full range of meaning. If control were to be restricted to the power of directing the actions of subordinates, the usefulness of this term in describing the working of the constitution would be very limited, and in practice it is not so restricted. The weaker forms of control are of great importance in our system of government. Carl Friedrich has written that, apart from power, 'influence is probably the most important basic concept of political science' (*Constitutional Government and Politics* (1937), pp. 16–17). Control in whatever degree is exercised a priori before the relevant action or decision is taken. (For a useful analysis of the nature and forms of control, see Dunsire, 'Control over Government' (1984) 26 *Malaya Law Review* 79.)

The second concept embodied in the idea of political responsibility is that of accountability (or 'responsibility' in a narrow sense: see pp. 59–62 above). Accountability implies obligations: in the first place, an obligation to *give account* – to answer, disclose, explain or justify – which may be called 'explanatory accountability'. Next to it is 'amendatory' or 'remedial' accountability, the obligation to *account for* action or inaction – to 'answer for' whatever has been revealed of error or misgovernment, and correct or make due reparation for it. It is this sense of accountability that is meant in phrases such as 'held accountable for', with its connotations of blame and penalty. Amendatory accountability is evidently retrospective or a posteriori. (See Mulgan, '"Accountability": An Ever-Expanding Concept?' (2000) 78 *Pub Adm* 555.)

Like control, accountability (of either kind) may be strong or weak. There may be a strict legal liability to account, or an obligation founded on established convention, or a merely voluntary – and perhaps limited – acceptance of the demands of accountability. Accountability complements control. A fully responsible government is responsive, submitting to constitutional controls, and is subject to accountability in both the explanatory and the amendatory forms. In an ideal system, the machinery of control prescribes or indicates limits, guidelines or policies for government; explanatory accountability provides a flow of information before, during and after the exercise of control; and amendatory accountability enables blame to be attached to government for failure of policy or abuse of power, and redress or amendment to be exacted.

As we consider the various institutions and structures through which political control and accountability are made effective against the government, we need to be aware that these organisations are themselves possessors of power and may have their own interests and objectives. As M.J.C. Vile observes (*Constitutionalism and the Separation of Powers* (1967), p. 333):

> There have grown up new and powerful means of controlling government, but like the earlier mechanisms of control they are not neutral instruments, but organisations which must themselves be subject to control. Indeed, there can *never* be a 'neutral' control system, for we must never lose sight of the fact that these 'controls' are not pieces of machinery in the mechanical sense. The mechanical analogy is a dangerous one. They are all, without exception, patterns of behaviour, they are all procedures operated by human beings, and they can never be neutral.

We should also be aware that control and accountability function as restraints on government and make demands on public resources. These must be accepted in a system of responsible government and indeed such restraints can contribute to the rationality (prudence, consistency and competence) of government. But there is a balance to be struck between their claims and the need for governmental effectiveness, because, after all, as L.J. Sharpe tells us (in J.A.G. Griffith (ed.), *From Policy to Administration* (1976), p. 132):

> government in a democracy must possess the capacity to govern; that is to say, it must have that functional effectiveness that makes a reality [of] the choice between alternative policies that democracy claims to offer the electorate.

In the description of the British constitutional system as one of responsible government, what is primarily meant is that the government is responsible to Parliament and, more precisely, to the House of Commons. In other words, ours is a system of parliamentary government in which the government's authority depends on its having the confidence of the elected house. (As we saw in Chapter 4, this model also applies, albeit with a number of variations, to the devolved institutions in Scotland, Wales and Northern Ireland.) The aspect of responsibility that is emphasised in this description is the liability of the government to be dismissed by a vote of the Commons (subject to an appeal to the electorate). Dorothy Pickles has written (*Democracy* (1970), p. 148): 'The essential requirement in a parliamentary democracy is that Parliament shall retain the power to dismiss Governments.' In practice, such dismissals have been a rarity in Britain. Governments were defeated on votes of confidence only three times in the twentieth century – in 1924 (twice) and 1979 – and on no occasion since, but the requirement that the government must retain the confidence of the House of Commons is still a fundamental principle of the constitution. In the last resort, it is sustained by the government's dependence on the House of Commons for 'supply' (finance) and the passing of legislation.

In practice, the power of Parliament to dismiss the government is a contingent power, which can be asserted only in circumstances of minority government or breakdown of party solidarity, or if, in a coalition government, the coalition partners should separate or fail to sustain parliamentary support for their joint venture. In normal circumstances, as John Mackintosh says, 'the House of Commons is enmeshed with and supports the government of the day' (Mackintosh (ed.), *People and Parliament* (1978), p. 210). It is, indeed, a paradoxical feature of the modern constitution that for the control and account-ability of government we rely mainly on an elected house in which a majority see it as their principal function to maintain the government in power. But the ultimate, collective responsibility of the government to Parliament is not without meaning. The need to retain the confidence of the house imposes restraints. It compels governments to explain, justify, bargain and concede.

John Stuart Mill, *Considerations on Representative Government* (1861), p. 104

Instead of the function of governing, for which it is radically unfit, the proper office of a representative assembly is to watch and control the government: to throw the light of publicity on its acts; to compel a full exposition and justification of all of them which any one considers questionable; to censure them if found condemnable, and, if the men who compose the government abuse their trust, or fulfil it in a manner which conflicts with the deliberate sense of the nation, to expel them from office, and either expressly or virtually appoint their successors.

It was not true when Mill was writing, but over the course of the twentieth century it became the case that, ordinarily, a government with an absolute majority in the House of Commons can rely on party cohesion and discipline to assure it of the confidence of the house. Defeats in the House of Commons, even on important issues, are not considered to require a government to resign, unless the house has been expressly invited to treat the issue as one of confidence in the government. (The classic statement of parliamentary government in the era of John Stuart Mill remains Bagehot, *The English Constitution* (1867).)

In the Parliament of March–September 1974, a minority Labour Government faced a House of Commons in which supporters of opposition parties outnumbered Labour MPs by over thirty. The prime minister explained the government's position to the house.

House of Commons, HC Deb vol. 870, cols 70–1, 12 March 1974

The Prime Minister (Mr Harold Wilson): ... The Government intend to treat with suitable respect, but not with exaggerated respect, the results of any snap vote or any snap Division ...

> In case of a Government defeat, either in such circumstances or in a more clear expression of opinion, the Government will consider their position and make a definitive statement after due consideration. But the Government will not be forced to go to the country except in a situation in which every hon. Member in the House was voting knowing the full consequences of his vote.
>
> I am saying that if there were to be anything put to the House which could have those consequences, every hon. Member would have it explained to him in the House by the Government before he voted.

(A similar statement was made by Ramsay MacDonald as head of a minority government in 1924: see Jennings, *Cabinet Government* (3rd edn. 1959), p. 494.)

A prime minister may announce that an issue will be treated as one of confidence with the object of overcoming dissidence in the ranks of his or her parliamentary party by the threat that the government's continuance in power would be put at risk. Mr Major as Prime Minister resorted to this expedient on several occasions in relation to policy on the EU, as in November 1992 on a motion to proceed with the European Communities (Amendment) Bill and again in the following year in moving 'that this House has confidence in the policy of Her Majesty's Government on the adoption of the Protocol on Social Policy' (HC Deb vol. 229, col 625, 23 July 1993: see also col 627). Rebels on the Conservative backbenches were once more coerced during the passage of the European Communities (Finance) Bill, the prime minister saying that the passage of the bill 'in all its essentials is inescapably a matter of confidence' (HC Deb vol. 250, col 30, 16 November 1994).

Defeats in the House of Commons do not ordinarily put the government in jeopardy. The 1974 Labour Government suffered seventeen defeats in the House of Commons in that year alone. In the 1974–79 Parliament, the Labour Government – again without an overall majority from 1976 – suffered *forty-two defeats* before being obliged to appeal to the electorate. (See Norton, *Dissension in the House of Commons 1974–1979* (1980), p. 441.)

Philip Norton, 'The House of Commons and the Constitution: The Challenges of the 1970s' (1981) 34 *Parl Aff* 253, 254–5, 266–7

As a result of the political developments of the nineteenth century, the House of Commons became the dominant element of the triumvirate of the Queen-in-Parliament, but these very developments (the introduction of near-universal male suffrage and the resulting party government) served to move the House from an important position in the decision-making process to a somewhat ambivalent one related to, yet not part of, the main decision-making machinery. The outputs of the Queen-in-Parliament continued to be legally omnipotent as a result of the judicially self-imposed if not universally revered doctrine of 'parliamentary sovereignty', but those outputs were the results of decisions taken elsewhere. To adapt the

House of Commons to the changed political circumstances, and especially to the new relationship between it and the government, its functions were variously redefined. These functions find no delineation in one formal, binding document. There does appear, though, to be some general if at times tenuous agreement on the main functions of the post-1867 House [following the extension of voting rights by the Representation of the People Act 1867]: To provide, by convention, the personnel of government (a function shared with the Lords); to constitute a 'representative' assembly, members being returned to defend and pursue the interest of their constituents and de facto of wider interests (which may be categorised as the specific and general functions of representation); in pursuance of the representative function, to legitimise the actions and the legislative measures advanced by Her Majesty's government, and prior to giving legitimisation to subject the government and its measures to a process of scrutiny and influence. The House fulfils a number of other functions, including a minor shared legislative role, but the foregoing constitute the most important.

In fulfilling the function of scrutiny and influence, MPs found themselves faced with a serious limitation. To be effective, scrutiny rested primarily on the existence of the House's sanction of defeating the government in the division lobbies – its ability to deny legitimisation to a measure or part of it – but the MPs in the government party proved unwilling to utilise this power. Much of this refusal was for political reasons: members of the governing party wanted to support the government and normally approved of its measures. On those occasions when they were inclined to vote with the opposition, they were restrained from doing so by what they perceived to be a constitutional convention: that a government defeat in the division lobbies would necessitate the government either resigning or requesting a dissolution. As Arthur Balfour commented in 1905, it appeared to be assumed in various parts of the House 'that the accepted constitutional principle is that, when a government suffers defeat, either in supply or on any other subject, the proper course for His Majesty's responsible advisers is either to ask His Majesty to relieve them of their office or to ask His Majesty to dissolve parliament'. This view remained current until at least the 1970s . . . A consequence was cohesion in the division lobbies. Sustenance of the government in office was equated with sustaining the government in every division. The greater the degree of cohesion (or at least the fewer the defeats), the more this appeared to be borne out in practice. The result was an apparent paradox. On the one hand, the power of the House to ensure effective scrutiny and influence of government, to determine the boundaries in which it could operate, was based upon its power to defeat the government, to deny assent to its measures. On the other hand, given the assumption that a defeat would bring the government down, a majority of the House was not prepared to use it. Hence the ease with which government measures went through and the criticisms levelled at the Commons for failing to fulfil effectively the tasks expected of it. The events of the 1970s served to resolve this paradox.

The belief that a defeat in the division lobbies necessitated the government's resignation or an election was based on no authoritative source nor upon any continuous basis of practice. In that sense, the belief could be described as constituting a constitutional 'myth'. Nevertheless, so long as members continued in this belief, it influenced their behaviour. It took the defeats of the 1970s to make members realise that defeats could be imposed upon the government without there necessarily being any wider constitutional implications. The constitutional reality, as it had been since 1841, was that a government was required by convention to resign (or dissolve) in the event only of losing a vote of confidence; in the event of losing a division on an item central to its policy, it had the discretion as to whether to resign (or request a dissolution) or seek a vote of confidence from the House; in the event of defeat on any other matter, it had to consider only whether to accept the defeat or seek its reversal at a later stage. This distinction was given clear recognition by Stanley Baldwin in the House of Commons in April 1936. The response of the governments of the 1970s to the defeats suffered was in line with precedent. The popular view that there was a deviation from previous practice is incorrect. What changed was not the basis of the government's response but the number of defeats. Whereas previous defeats had been few and far between, and did not impact themselves upon members' consciousness, the defeats of the 1970s were too numerous to be ignored. Members began to realise the implications of their own actions and to realise that they could effect changes in the measures of government without necessarily threatening its life. This was to generate a change in attitude and to resolve the paradox of the House depending upon a power it was not willing to use. Members proved willing to overcome the constraints of party to employ the power that resided with them. Government could no longer rely upon the loyalty of its own backbenchers to see all its measures through in the form desired. (Nor upon the electorate and the electoral system to provide it with an overall majority.) In consequence, members restored to themselves the means by which they could achieve more effectively their function of scrutiny and influence.

The revived independence of backbench MPs and their willingness to vote against their own government did not evaporate after 1979, but the substantial overall majorities enjoyed by Conservative Governments from 1979 to 1992 reduced the incidence of government defeats in the House of Commons. After the 1992 election, John Major's Government had a less secure and diminishing majority, and was more vulnerable to backbench rebellion. (Mutinousness among 'Eurosceptic' Conservative backbenchers led to the withdrawal of the whip from eight of their number in November 1994 for five months.) The Labour Government that came to power in 1997 with a majority of 179 and was returned to office in 2001 with a majority of 167 and again in 2005 with a reduced but still seemingly safe majority of sixty-six was not immune from back-bench rebellion and, on occasion, defeat in the house, as will be seen later. (See, further, Norton (ed.), *Parliament in the 1980s* (1985), ch. 2; Cowley, *The Rebels: How Blair Mislaid his Majority* (2005).)

Influence and scrutiny – or 'controlling' and 'calling to account' – are functions of Parliament that depend largely on the acceptance by ministers of the Crown of their collective and individual responsibility to Parliament. The responsibility of ministers is the mainspring of the working relationship between Parliament and government. As Michael Rush remarks, it 'underpins all debates, all parliamentary questions, all committee activity – the means by which Parliament seeks to exercise its scrutiny' (Pyper and Robins (eds.), *Governing the UK in the 1990s* (1995), p. 109).

Ministerial responsibility to Parliament is besides a link in a chain of accountability of the government to the people, for, as Mark Bovens says: 'In some sense, the people's representatives render account to the voters at election time' ('Analysing and Assessing Accountability: A Conceptual Framework' (2007) 13 *European LJ* 447, 455).

9.2 Individual Ministerial Responsibility

'One of the fundamentals of our system of Government', wrote Lord Morrison (*Government and Parliament* (3rd edn. 1964), p. 332), 'is that some Minister of the Crown is responsible to Parliament, and through Parliament to the public, for every act of the Executive.' According to this convention, every minister is responsible to Parliament for his or her own official conduct, and a minister who heads a department also has ultimate responsibility for everything done by that department. This is known as the convention of individual ministerial responsibility. (For the collective responsibility of ministers, see Chapter 6.)

A convention in these terms is necessary, first, to enable Parliament to make good the 'explanatory accountability' of government: for every branch of the government's business, there must be an identifiable minister who has an obligation to answer and explain to Parliament. This obligation is owed primarily to the house of which the minister is a member, in the great majority of cases the House of Commons. If the minister is a peer, he or she answers to the House of Lords and is not directly answerable to the Commons; junior ministers in the Commons will answer in that house for a department headed by a peer, and the peer may be invited to give evidence to select committees of the Commons. The lack of accountability to the Commons of senior ministers in the Lords was considered by the Procedure Committee in its *3rd Report of 2009–10*, HC 496, but the matter has yet to be resolved.

The performance by Parliament of its functions of controlling the executive and holding it accountable for errors and malpractice depends on getting from ministers the relevant facts and explanations. This is underlined in para K8.2 of the Scott Report on arms to Iraq (HC 115 of 1995–96):

> The obligation of Ministers to give information about the activities of their departments and to give information and explanations for the actions and omissions of their civil servants, lies at the heart of Ministerial accountability.

The Scott Report revealed, however, that the government had failed lamentably in its observance of this obligation in pursuing its policies on defence sales to Iran and Iraq between 1984 and 1990. Sir Richard Scott found that there had been 'a consistent undervaluing by Government of the public interest that full information should be made available to Parliament' (para D1.165) and observed that 'the withholding of information by an accountable Minister should never be based on reasons of convenience or for the avoidance of political embarrassment, but should always require special and carefully considered justification' (para K8.5).

The *Ministerial Code* (2019) enjoins ministers to be 'as open as possible with Parliament and the public, refusing to provide information only when disclosure would not be in the public interest' and declares it to be 'of paramount importance that Ministers give accurate and truthful information to Parliament, correcting any inadvertent error at the earliest opportunity'. (See, further, above, pp. 217–219.) These statements of principle first appeared in the 1997 edition of the *Ministerial Code* in response to an important initiative taken by both Houses of Parliament in that year, following a recommendation of the Public Service Committee of the House of Commons (*2nd Report of 1995–96*, HC 313, the committee's recommendation itself coming as a direct consequence of the findings of the Scott Report (above)). Each house passed a resolution on ministerial accountability to Parliament in terms that were subsequently incorporated into the *Ministerial Code*. (See HC Deb vol. 292, cols 1046–7, 19 March 1997 and HL Deb vol. 579, cols 1055–62, 20 March 1997.) These resolutions translated the formerly unwritten convention of ministerial responsibility into a clear parliamentary rule, which was no longer unilaterally alterable by government. (See Tomkins, *The Constitution After Scott* (1998), p. 62; although cf. Woodhouse, 'Ministerial Responsibility: Something Old, Something New' [1997] *PL* 262.)

In addition, the convention of individual ministerial responsibility is traditionally supposed to fix the blame on the minister heading a department for every failure of departmental policy or administration, whether it is the minister him- or herself who was at fault, or a civil servant, or if the failure resulted from a defect of departmental organisation. The minister must, in this orthodox version, submit to the judgment of Parliament and, if the failure is a serious one, should resign from office without waiting for a vote of censure.

Crichel Down

The traditional view of ministerial responsibility seemed to be vindicated by the resignation in 1954 of the Minister of Agriculture, Sir Thomas Dugdale, following the notorious episode of Crichel Down. In 1938, some land in Dorset had been acquired by the Air Ministry from its owners for use as a bombing range. (Powers of compulsory acquisition were available, but it had not proved necessary to resort to them.) After the war, the land was no longer needed for the purpose for which it had been acquired, and it was transferred to the Ministry of Agriculture and by them to the Commission for Crown Lands, which let it to a tenant of its choice. A request by one of the former owners to buy back his land was refused, and neighbouring landowners who had been given to understand that they would be able to bid for tenancies of the land were denied the opportunity to do so. These events led to an official inquiry that came to the conclusion (since criticised for its partiality: see Nicolson, *The Mystery of Crichel Down* (1986)) that civil servants in the Ministry of Agriculture had acted in a high-handed and deceitful manner: *Report of the Public Inquiry into the Disposal of Land at Crichel Down* (Cmd 9176/1954). As a consequence of this report and of widespread criticism, in Parliament and outside, of the conduct of his department, the minister resigned. He said in the House (HC Deb vol. 530, col 1186, 20 July 1954):

> I, as Minister, must accept full responsibility to Parliament for any mistakes and inefficiency of officials in my Department, just as, when my officials bring off any successes on my behalf, I take full credit for them.

But this seemingly unequivocal demonstration of individual ministerial responsibility in its traditional sense was, in fact, blurred by some of the attendant circumstances. First, civil servants concerned in the case had been named and criticised in the report of the inquiry: it was not only the minister who had to take the blame. Second, the minister himself (and two junior ministers) had taken a personal part in the transactions relating to Crichel Down, and he was to admit to the house that his decisions had been taken with knowledge of the main facts of the case. (See Nicolson, above, pp. 54–5, 61, 76–7, 90–1.) In reality, it seems that, its iconic status as the leading example of a minister falling on his sword because of mistakes made by others and where he himself had done nothing wrong notwithstanding, Sir Thomas Dugdale's resignation actually owed more to the fact that his policies had fallen out of favour with both the cabinet and the Conservative backbenchers, who had begun to lose confidence in him (see Tomkins, *The Constitution after Scott* (1998), p. 56). In the Crichel Down debate on 20 July 1954, the Home Secretary attempted to clarify the convention.

House of Commons, HC Deb vol. 530, cols 1285–7, 20 July 1954

The Home Secretary (Sir David Maxwell Fyfe): . . . There has been criticism that the principle operates so as to oblige Ministers to extend total protection to their officials and to endorse their acts, and to cause the position that civil servants cannot be called to account and are effectively responsible to no one. That is a position which I believe is quite wrong, and I think it is the cardinal error that has crept into the appreciation of this situation. It is quite untrue that well-justified public criticism of the actions of civil servants cannot be made on a suitable occasion. The position of the civil servant is that he is wholly and directly responsible to his Minister. It is worth stating again that he holds his office 'at pleasure' and can be dismissed at any time by the Minister; and that power is none the less real because it is seldom used . . .

I would like to put the different categories where different considerations apply. I am in agreement with the right hon. Gentleman who has just spoken, that in the case where there is an explicit order by a Minister, the Minister must protect the civil servant who has carried out his order. Equally, where the civil servant acts properly in accordance with the policy laid down by the Minister, the Minister must protect and defend him.

I come to the third category, which is different . . . Where an official makes a mistake or causes some delay, but not on an important issue of policy and not where a claim to individual rights is seriously involved, the Minister acknowledges the mistake and he accepts the responsibility, although he is not personally involved. He states that he will take corrective action in the Department. I agree with the right hon. Gentleman that he would not, in those circumstances, expose the official to public criticism . . .

But when one comes to the fourth category, where action has been taken by a civil servant of which the Minister disapproves and has no prior knowledge, and the conduct of the official is reprehensible, then there is no obligation on the part of the Minister to endorse what he believes to be wrong, or to defend what are clearly shown to be errors of his officers. The Minister is not bound to defend action of which he did not know, or of which he disapproves. But, of course, he remains constitutionally responsible to Parliament for the fact that something has gone wrong, and he alone can tell Parliament what has occurred and render an account of his stewardship.

(See, further, the discussion of the Crichel Down affair by Jacob, *The Republican Crown* (1996), pp. 168–74.)

9.2.1 A Convention of Resignation?

The traditional view that a minister is bound to resign in atonement for departmental misconduct does not take account of the great increase in the work of government departments in modern times, which has made it impossible for ministers to supervise directly or even know about the bulk of their departments' everyday business, including decisions taken by officials in the minister's name. It has also been shown that the traditional view, with its emphasis on the sanction of ministerial resignation, does not accord with the facts of political life. Professor S.E. Finer looked for ministerial resignations in the period 1855–1955 that had been 'forced by overt criticism from the House of Commons' and so might be attributed to the convention of ministerial responsibility. He found that there had been only twenty such resignations in the century, 'a tiny number', as he wrote, 'compared with the known instances of mismanagement and blunderings'. The following passage gives his conclusions.

S.E. Finer, 'The Individual Responsibility of Ministers' (1956) 34 *Pub Adm* 377, 393–4

The convention implies a form of punishment for a delinquent Minister. That punishment is no longer an act of attainder, or an impeachment, but simply loss of office.

If each, or even very many charges of incompetence were habitually followed by the punishment, the remedy would be a very real one: its deterrent effect would be extremely great. In fact, that sequence is not only exceedingly rare, but arbitrary and unpredictable. Most charges never reach the stage of individualisation at all: they are stifled under the blanket of party solidarity. Only when there is a minority Government, or in the infrequent cases where the Minister seriously alienates his own back benchers, does the issue of the individual culpability of the Minister even arise. Even there it is subject to hazards: the punishment may be avoided if the Prime Minister, whether on his own or on the Minister's initiative, makes a timely re-shuffle. Even when some charges get through the now finely woven net, and are laid at the door of a Minister, much depends on his nicety, and much on the character of the Prime Minister. Brazen tenacity of office can still win a reprieve. And, in the last resort – though this happens infrequently – the resignation of the Minister may be made purely formal by reappointment to another post soon afterwards.

We may put the matter in this way: whether a Minister is forced to resign depends on three factors, on himself, his Prime Minister and his party . . . For a resignation to occur all three factors have to be just so: the Minister compliant, the Prime Minister firm, the party clamorous. This conjuncture is rare, and is in fact fortuitous. Above all, it is indiscriminate – which Ministers escape and which do not is decided neither by the circumstances of the offence nor its gravity. A Wyndham and a Chamberlain go for a peccadillo, a Kitchener will remain despite major blunders.

A remedy ought to be certain. A punishment, to be deterrent, ought to be certain. But whether the Minister should resign is simply the (necessarily) haphazard consequence of a fortuitous concomitance of personal, party and political temper.

Is there then a 'convention' of resignation at all?

A convention, in Dicey's sense, is a rule which is not enforced by the Courts. The important word is 'rule'. 'Rule' does not mean merely an observed uniformity in the past; the notion includes the expectation that the uniformity will continue in the future. It is not simply a description; it is a prescription. It has a compulsive force.

Now in its first sense, that the Minister alone *speaks* for his Civil Servants to the House and to his Civil Servants for the House, the convention of ministerial responsibility has both the proleptic and the compulsive features of a 'rule'. But in the sense in which we have been considering it, that the Minister *may be punished, through loss of office* for all the misdeeds and neglects of his Civil Servants which he cannot prove to have been outside all possibility of his cognisance and control, the proposition does not seem to be a rule at all.

What is the compulsive element in such a 'rule'? All it says (on examination) is that if the Minister is yielding, his Prime Minister unbending and his party out for blood – no matter how serious or trivial the reason – the Minister will find himself without Parliamentary support. This is a statement of fact, not a code. What is more, as a statement of fact it comes very close to being a truism: that a Minister entrusted by his Prime Minister with certain duties must needs resign if he loses the support of his majority. The only compulsive element in the proposition is that if and when a Minister loses his majority he ought to get out rather than be kicked out.

> Moreover, even as a simple generalisation, an observed uniformity, the 'convention' is, surely, highly misleading? It takes the wrong cases: it generalises from the exceptions and neglects the common run. There are four categories of delinquent Ministers: the fortunate, the less fortunate, the unfortunate, and the plain unlucky. After sinning, the first go to other Ministries; the second to Another Place [i.e. to the House of Lords]; the third just go. Of the fourth there are but twenty examples in a century: indeed, if one omits Neville Chamberlain (an anomaly) and the 'personal' cases . . ., there are but sixteen. Not for these sixteen the honourable exchange of offices, or the silent and not dishonourable exit. Their lot is public penance in the white sheet of a resignation speech or letter . . . It is on some sixteen or at most nineteen penitents and one anomaly that the generalisation has been based.

The resignation of Sir Thomas Dugdale in the Crichel Down affair (above) was in accordance with Finer's thesis: the minister had lost the confidence of MPs of his own party, and the cabinet did not find it expedient to outface its backbench supporters.

Between 1955 and 1982 there were only two resignations of senior ministers (Profumo and Jellicoe) that can be put down to an acknowledgment by the ministers concerned of their responsibility to Parliament (the resignation of Maudling in 1972 would not seem to fall into this category) and, in each case, the resignation was connected with the minister's own conduct, not the actions of his department. In 1982, the unexpected Argentine invasion of the Falkland Islands and public and parliamentary criticism of the role of the Foreign and Commonwealth Office was followed by the resignations of the Foreign Secretary (Lord Carrington), the Lord Privy Seal (Mr Humphrey Atkins), who had been the spokesman for the Foreign Office in the House of Commons, and a minister of state who had conducted the negotiations with Argentina on the Falkland Islands question. In resigning, the ministers accepted responsibility to Parliament for a failure of policy, afterwards attributed in part to defects in the machinery of government, misjudgments by ministers and officials of Argentine intentions and faulty decisions by ministers. (See *Falkland Islands Review*, Cmnd 8787/1983.)

It has been remarked that the resignation of Lord Carrington and his colleagues 'continues to shine like a beacon of honour in an era when most ministers in trouble appear to hang on to their office as if it were a personal freehold rather than a Crown possession' (Hennessy, *The Prime Minister* (2000), p. 415). The invasion of the Falklands had caused a loss of confidence among parliamentarians – not least those of the government party – and the public in the organisation and leadership of the Foreign Office, and the ministers concerned rightly concluded that their resignations were required for a restoration of that confidence. But the circumstances were unusual, and most administrative failures are of a more limited kind which do not bring into question the whole departmental organisation or the leadership of ministers. It is not likely that a minister's head will be demanded or proffered in such cases. But if the error is serious and has grave consequences, critical attention may be focused on the minister. His or her response will depend on the factors of personality, party and politics indicated by Professor Finer (above).

The Maze Break-Out

In September 1983, there was a mass break-out of republican prisoners from the Maze Prison in Belfast, an event described in a leading article in *The Times* (8 February 1984) as 'a fearful blow to the authority of the state in Northern Ireland'. It was serious enough to raise the question of the responsibility of ministers. Those concerned were the Secretary of State in charge of the Northern Ireland Office, Mr James Prior, and the Under-Secretary of State responsible for the prison service, Mr Nicholas Scott, who had been in office for only three months at the time of the break-out. His predecessor, Lord Gowrie, had moved to the Privy Council Office as Minister for the Arts.

A report by Sir James Hennessy on security arrangements at the Maze Prison (HC 203 of 1983–84) found that there had been deficiencies in the management and physical security of the prison, and that faulty procedures and laxity and negligence of staff had facilitated the escape. For this state of affairs, the report held the prison governor to be primarily responsible; there was also some criticism of the prison department of the Northern Ireland Office for its oversight of security at the prison. The government accepted the report and its recommendations. The prison governor resigned, but no ministers did so. For reasons that may be surmised, the prime minister was not disposed to press for Mr Prior's resignation; neither did the Labour opposition wish to see him replaced at the Northern Ireland Office by any other Tory minister.

Shifts in the understanding of ministerial responsibility prompted the Treasury and Civil Service Committee to remark: 'If Crichel Down is dead and Ministers are not accountable to Parliament for some actions of their officials, then who is?' (*7th Report of 1985–86*, HC 92.)

Resignations of ministers as a result of sexual escapades, imprudent remarks, questionable financial transactions, acceptance of payment for asking parliamentary questions and other instances of personal default or misjudgment occurred with unwonted frequency in the 1980s and 1990s. Not all such resignations can be seen as arising from the minister's responsibility to Parliament and will often have been precipitated by public opinion, a press campaign or the concerns of ministerial colleagues and government backbenchers for the political fortunes of the party (or by a combination of these factors). Such was the case in the resignation in 2001 of Peter Mandelson, Secretary of State for Northern Ireland, whose position had become untenable following allegations that he had been less than candid and had misled ministerial colleagues and the public about his involvement in a passport application by a businessman with whom he was associated. (The former minister was afterwards acquitted of any improper conduct in an independent inquiry by Sir Anthony Hammond: *Review of the Circumstances Surrounding an Application for Naturalisation by Mr S P Hinduja in 1998*, HC 287 of 2000–01.)

The Blair Government's second term of office (2001–5) yielded a crop of senior ministerial resignations. First, there was the resignation of Stephen Byers as Secretary of State for Transport, Local Government and the Regions in 2002 after extensive criticism, from opposition MPs and in the media, of certain of his decisions said to show inept judgment and of his deficient management of his department. In resigning, Mr Byers acknowledged errors of judgment and said that he had become 'a distraction from what the government is achieving'. Later in that year, Estelle Morris resigned as Secretary of State for Education and Skills, following criticism of her handling of problems connected with checks on the background of teachers and procedures for the determination of 'A' level grades, as well as the failure to meet literacy and numeracy targets set by her predecessor. In resigning, she admitted to weaknesses in her strategic management of her department and in her dealings with the media.

Neither of these resignations can be attributed to errors or maladministration by departmental officials. Both ministers resigned on the ground of deficiencies, admitted by them, in their official conduct as ministers and in the running of their departments, not for misconduct in their personal lives. Each resignation followed sustained criticism of the minister from opposition MPs and in the media. Diana Woodhouse concludes ('UK Ministerial Responsibility in 2002: The Tale of Two Resignations' (2004) 82 *Pub Adm* 1, 6): 'Whatever the reasons for the resignations of Morris and Byers, they provide additional precedents for a resigning convention within the departmental context.' She sees these resignations as vindicating a 'role responsibility' of ministers – a minister's obligation to provide effective leadership and supervision of his or her department and to account to Parliament for the proper performance of this role, with resignation as the ultimate sanction for failure.

Woodhouse also draws attention to the significant part played by media criticism in these resignations, asking whether 'there has been a shift in the location of accountability, away from politicians, and particularly Parliament, to the media.'

A third resignation was that of David Blunkett as Home Secretary in December 2004 after his private office had intervened with the Immigration and Nationality Directorate regarding an application by his lover's nanny for indefinite leave to remain in the UK. Mr Blunkett at first publicly denied any intervention by his office but when presented with contradictory evidence he resigned, saying that he would not hide behind or blame his officials and took responsibility for what had occurred. Nicholas Bamforth has commented that as Blunkett's initial (inadvertently false) denial was made to the media and not to Parliament, his resignation evidences a broadening of ministerial responsibility to Parliament so as to embrace ministerial statements made outside the house ('Political Accountability in Play' [2005] *PL* 229). Mr Blunkett re-entered the cabinet as Secretary of State for Work and Pensions after the general election of May 2005, but his renewed tenure of office was short-lived. In October 2005 it came to light that, after leaving his previous office, he had failed to inform the Advisory Committee on Business Appointments about paid posts taken up by him, as required of ex-ministers by the *Ministerial Code*. Mr Blunkett acknowledged his mistake and resigned. Here we see the convention of ministerial responsibility extending to a minister's former actions when not in office, although the obligation in which he had defaulted arose from his tenure of his previous office, in which he had become bound by the provisions of the *Code*.

The toll of resignations continued in Gordon Brown's premiership with a cluster of five resignations in the single month of June 2009 (Blears, Hoon, Hutton, Purnell and Smith), but these were attributable less to ministerial responsibility to Parliament than to a collapse of ministerial confidence in the twilight of the Brown Government (together with, in some cases, the taint of improper expenses claims).

By the same token, we find ministers continuing, in cases of departmental failure, blunders or misconduct, to invoke the distinctions formulated in the Crichel Down and Maze Prison cases, disclaiming any obligation to resign for errors of subordinates. On the occasion of another prison escape – of IRA prisoners from Brixton in 1991 – Home Secretary Kenneth Baker declined to resign for what he described as 'operational failures' by officers of the prison department. Even for action in which he had himself taken a part and for which he was held to have been guilty, in his official capacity as Secretary of State for the Home Department, of contempt of court (see *M* v. *Home Office*, above, pp. 129–134), the same Mr Baker did not contemplate resignation.

After further escapes from prison an inquiry into prison security (Learmont Report, Cm 3020/1995) found serious management failures and inefficiency in the Prison Service (an executive agency of the Home Office): the Director-General of the Service (Mr Lewis) was dismissed as bearing 'operational' responsibility while the Home Secretary, Michael Howard, survived. (See Barker, 'Political Responsibility for UK Prison Security: Ministers Escape Again' (1998) 76 *Pub Adm* 1; Polidano, 'The Bureaucrat who Fell under a Bus: Ministerial Responsibility, Executive Agencies and the Derek Lewis Affair in Britain' (1999) 12 *Governance* 201.) The tally of non-resignations was added to when criticism of ministers in the Scott Report on arms to Iraq (HC 115 of 1995–96) was brazened out, the government taking refuge in Sir Richard Scott's finding that, although ministers had misled Parliament, they had done so without 'duplicitous intention' (see Tomkins, *The Constitution after Scott* (1998), ch. 1).

The case of Charles Clarke, Home Secretary from 2004 to 2006, raises points of interest. It was disclosed in April 2006 that about 1,000 foreign criminals, who should have been considered for deportation or removal, had completed their prison sentences and been released without any consideration by the Immigration and Nationality Directorate of the Home Office of deportation or removal action. For this failure in the Home Office, Mr Clarke offered his resignation to the prime minister who declined to accept it, and he remained in office. In a statement in the House of Commons (HC Deb vol. 445, col 573, 26 April 2006), Mr Clarke apologised for what had occurred, saying that he took responsibility for what he acknowledged to be a systemic failure in the department and promising to take action to put things right. Some days later, the prime minister, in carrying out a cabinet 'reshuffle', decided to remove Mr Clarke from office as Home Secretary. Dissatisfied with this decision, Mr Clarke declined other cabinet posts that were offered to him and resigned from the government. Mr Clarke was an able minister who was well placed to correct deficiencies in the Home Office, but the fiasco of the foreign criminals left at large had caused considerable embarrassment to the government. What does this episode reveal about the working of the doctrine of ministerial responsibility? (In 2007, responsibility for prisons was transferred from the Home Office to the Ministry of Justice.)

While not able to supervise in detail all that is done by a department, the departmental minister nevertheless has a responsibility for ensuring that the department is efficiently organised and has effective systems for delivering its services, appropriate rules of conduct for its staff and controls in place for preventing error or malpractice. There should be a limit to the ability of ministers to escape responsibility by attributing blame to their officials.

The *Ministerial Code*

It is impossible to deny the impact of the *Ministerial Code* on ministerial resignations, particularly in the light of the parliamentary expenses scandal. Through providing a code of conduct, it provides a stronger means of exerting political pressure, particularly through the media in addition to that provided by criticism of the opposition. During the Coalition Government of 2010–15, David Laws, in 2010, and Maria Miller in 2014 resigned over expenses issues. Liam Fox resigned on 14 October 2011 due to a breach of the *Ministerial Code*.

Perhaps the clearest impact of the *Ministerial Code* can be found in the resignations of Priti Patel and Amber Rudd, both of which occurred during the May Governments. Priti Patel was forced to resign as Secretary of State for International Development on 8 November 2017. Priti Patel had met with Israeli political organisations and politicians during a holiday to Israel and had not informed the government of these meetings, in breach of the *Ministerial Code*. There was severe criticism in the media of Ms Patel's conduct. In her resignation letter, Ms Patel stated that her actions 'fell below the high standards that are expected of a Secretary of State' and although they 'were meant with the best of intentions' they 'fell below the standards of transparency and openness'.

Amber Rudd's resignation demonstrates how breaches of the *Ministerial Code* can lead to the indirect resignation of a minister over a failed policy issue. Amber Rudd's resignation was entwined with the Windrush immigration scandal. The scandal arose due to the adoption of the 'hostile environment' policy towards immigrants. This was applied to many from Caribbean countries who had been invited to emigrate to the UK to help cover the post-war labour shortage. The first arrivals travelled on the ship MV *Empire Windrush*, which arrived in the UK in 1948. At the time of their arrival in the UK, most were British subjects or from Commonwealth nations and therefore enjoyed the same rights as UK nationals. However, under the 'hostile environment' policies, many were not able to provide documentation to prove their entitlement to reside in the UK. This was made more problematic as the Home Office had destroyed records of the landing cards issued on arrival to the Windrush migrants. As such, many were denied access to the NHS, to social services, and some were threatened with deportation. The policy was put in place before Amber Rudd became Home Secretary – indeed it was implemented by Theresa May, who was then Home Secretary and who was the Prime Minister at the time the Windrush scandal came to light. Amber Rudd was asked to appear before the Home Affairs Select Committee. At the committee, she was asked whether the Home Office had targets for immigration. She denied the existence of targets. However, targets had been in place at the time. Amber Rudd resigned as she had inadvertently misled the Select Committee, thereby breaching the *Ministerial Code*. Had this not taken place, it is not clear that Amber Rudd would have resigned in the face of the Windrush scandal alone. As such, her resignation illustrates the impact of the *Ministerial Code* in holding ministers to account.

It could be argued that Amber Rudd was right not to resign over the Windrush scandal. Although it came to light during her time as Home Secretary, it was implemented before she held that office. As such, it is arguably not her responsibility. However, Amber Rudd is also not guilty of having deliberately misled the Select Committee. She did not knowingly lie, rather she failed to keep herself fully informed of the situation. In her resignation letter, she pointed out that 'Since appearing before the select committee, I have reviewed the advice I was given on this issue and became aware of information provided to my office which makes mention of targets. I should have been aware of this, and I take full responsibility for the fact that I was not.'

Ministerial resignations continued to occur over scandals over personal conduct during the Coalition Government, and both May administrations. The Coalition Government saw the resignation of Mark Harper, who employed someone without permission to work in the UK while holding a ministerial role with responsibility to oversee controls over illegal workers and of Andrew Mitchell, who resigned over accusations that he had referred to police officers as 'fucking plebs' – although it later transpired that this was not the case. The most scandalous resignation was that of Chris Huhne in 2012. Chris Huhne's car had been issued a speeding ticket while he had been driving. However, he had asked his wife, Vicky Pryce, to claim that she had been driving the car so that she would receive the penalty points on her licence. He then lied about this when questioned. He was later prosecuted and jailed.

The May Governments of 2016–17 and 2017–2019 saw a handful of resignations for inappropriate behaviour – Damian Green, who lied about having pornographic images on his work computer, as well as the resignations of Michael Fallon and Christopher Pincher. There were sixty ministerial resignations in total during these two May administrations. Most of these were over Brexit, where ministers resigned as they were unable to back Theresa May's withdrawal deal, or the continued threat to leave the EU with no deal. Brexit also caused the resignation of two prime ministers – David Cameron who had campaigned in favour of the UK remaining in the EU and Theresa May, who failed to secure support for her Withdrawal Agreement and failed to ensure the UK left the EU on 29 March 2019 as she had promised. Rather than being seen as a resurgence of support for individual ministerial responsibility, this rise in resignations is best understood as illustrating the divisive nature of Brexit both within and across party lines.

If resignations in deference to ministerial responsibility are rare – it would perhaps reflect badly on the quality of British Government if they were frequent – the power of the House of Commons to censure and dismiss individual ministers hardly exists except on the plane of theory. Motions of censure can always be defeated by a majority government. They are, in any event, likely to be treated as putting in issue the house's confidence in the government as a whole, and therefore its survival. (See, e.g., HC Deb vol. 951, col 1129, 14 June 1978.) A minister threatened with a motion of censure who believed that he or she had lost the support of party and colleagues would be unlikely to await the formal vote. Nevertheless, the power remains in reserve and awareness of it underlies much that is said and done in Parliament; it is one of the conditioning elements in the behaviour of MPs and ministers. This idea was expressed in elevated terms by an MP and former minister in the course of committee proceedings on a government bill.

House of Commons Standing Committee F (British Nationality Bill) vol. V of 1980–81, cols 1916–17, 12 May 1981

Mr J. Enoch Powell: Where an Act of Parliament gives discretion to a Minister, it gives him that discretion as a person responsible in all his actions to Parliament. The discretion of a Minister under this Bill or any similar Act is not arbitrary in the sense that it is an irresponsible discretion. He exercises all such discretions in the light of his answerability to Parliament, and any such cases and any such decision can be raised, and theoretically could be made the subject of a vote of censure upon the Minister, in either House of Parliament . . .

> We ... take it for granted that if in the opinion of Parliament, as the supreme protection of the body of citizens and of every citizen individually, that discretion is exercised unjustly, improperly or unwisely in any way, Parliament is capable of bringing that Minister to account, and willing to do so.

The ultimate sanction of ministerial resignation continues to have constitutional validity. As Peter Barberis says, 'the bottom line of sacrifice must, in principle, remain visible and generally understood in order to give guts to the other dimensions of accountability' (*The Civil Service in an Era of Change* (1997), p. 141). The House of Commons Public Service Committee (*2nd Report of 1995–96*, HC 313) also stood firm on this point:

> [T]he attempt to ensure Ministers are accountable by seeking their resignation may be an informal and highly political affair. It cannot be reduced to firm rules and conventions. Nevertheless ... it remains an essential component of the control of government. It is, in effect, the final stage in a process of accountability.

Yet there are, as Barberis notes (above), other dimensions of accountability, and the principle of ministerial responsibility is not exhausted by its potentiality for inducing resignations. It supports and gives focus to all the available instruments for the scrutiny of the executive, such as parliamentary questions, debates and select committee inquiries. Even if, as in the usual case, a minister is able to disclaim personal responsibility for departmental errors or failures, he or she is still expected to 'accept responsibility' in the sense of having to give an account to Parliament of the circumstances, take into consideration views expressed in the house and inform it of disciplinary or remedial action taken.

'Where things go wrong, the Minister is responsible for putting them right and for telling Parliament how he has done so' (Mr Roger Freeman, Chancellor of the Duchy of Lancaster, Public Service Committee, *1st Special Report of 1996–97*, HC 67, Annex A, para 11). In July 1998, the Legg Inquiry into the 'Sandline affair' (breaches of an embargo on the supply of arms to Sierra Leone) revealed failures of communication in the Foreign Office and errors of judgment by officials such that (as *The Economist* commented on 1 August 1998) 'one part of the Foreign Office knew about the breach of an arms embargo that another part of the Foreign Office had gone to some trouble to impose'. (See *Report of the Sierra Leone Arms Investigation*, HC 1016 of 1997–98.) The Foreign Secretary (Robin Cook), in making a statement in the House of Commons on the Legg Report, drew attention to its finding that 'most of the trouble originated from systemic and cultural factors' in the Foreign Office. Acknowledging his responsibility for the department, he announced 'a programme of 60 different measures to improve the management of the Foreign Office' (HC Deb vol. 317, cols 19 et seq., 27 July 1998).

Again in 2006, after a series of management failures in the Home Office, it was declared by the Home Secretary (John Reid) to be 'not fit for purpose' and he made a number of changes to improve its organisation and performance (see HC Deb vol. 449, cols 323–5, 19 July 2006), as did the prime minister when, the following year, aspects of its work were transferred to the Ministry of Justice, as noted above.

9.2.2 Responsibility of Civil Servants

In constitutional theory, the responsibility of civil servants is absorbed by the responsibility of ministers to Parliament, with its corollary of the anonymity and exclusively internal responsibility of officials to their departmental minister. In replying to a report of the Expenditure Committee on the Civil Service, the government declared (Cmnd 7117/1978, para 3):

> their belief that the interests of the country will continue to be best served by a non-political, permanent Civil Service working under the close policy supervision of the Government of the day. They distinguish between the responsibility of the Civil Service to the Government and the responsibility of the Government to Parliament. Ministers alone are responsible to Parliament for policy, and any extension of the accountability of civil servants must recognise the overriding responsibility of the Departmental Minister for the work and efficiency of his department. The Government do not therefore favour developments which would detract from the principle that the advice tendered to Ministers by civil servants should be confidential and objective . . .

The traditional view of the constitutional position of civil servants was restated in 1985, in a note by Sir Robert Armstrong, Head of the Home Civil Service, issued after consultation with the permanent secretaries of government departments. The note, as revised in 1996, declared:

> The Civil Service as such has no constitutional personality or responsibility separate from the duly constituted Government of the day. It is there to provide the Government of the day with advice on the formulation of the policies of the Government, to assist in carrying out the decisions of the Government, and to manage and deliver the services for which the Government is responsible . . . In the determination of policy the civil servant has no constitutional responsibility or role distinct from that of the Minister.

Professor Vernon Bogdanor said of the Armstrong Code that it 'failed . . . to take account of the fact that the role of the civil servant was changing with the establishment of agencies (above, pp. 515–524) and other developments requiring officials to be far more involved in policy initiatives than traditional doctrines would allow' (Memorandum to the Select Committee on the Public

Service: *Special Report of 1996–97*, HL 68, p 36, para 10). Although the Armstrong Memorandum has been superseded by the *Civil Service Code* (above, pp. 527–528), it has been declared by the Cabinet Office to be still 'a valuable statement of constitutional principles' (Public Service Committee, *2nd Report of 1995–96*, HC 313-I, p. xiii, note 13). Governments have continued to insist that civil servants owe their loyalty to the duly constituted government and are accountable to the minister in charge of their department and not to Parliament. 'The way in which our constitution works', said Sir Robin Butler to the Public Administration Committee in 1997, 'is that the Minister accounts to Parliament and the civil servants account to the Minister' (Minutes of Evidence, HC 285 of 1997–98, Q70). This principle is reaffirmed in section 4.1.1 of the *Civil Service Management Code*:

> Civil servants are servants of the Crown and owe a duty of loyal service to the Crown as their employer. Since constitutionally the Crown acts on the advice of Ministers who are answerable for their departments and agencies in Parliament, that duty is, subject to the provisions of the Civil Service Code owed to the duly constituted Government.

The provisions of the Constitutional Reform and Governance Act 2010 (which placed the Civil Service on a statutory footing for the first time) do not affect any substantive changes to these arrangements.

The absence of direct constitutional responsibility of civil servants to Parliament is not total and has been qualified by recent changes in the machinery of government. A direct personal responsibility of officials to Parliament has for many years been formally acknowledged in one instance: the accounting officer of a department, who is usually the permanent secretary, is responsible for the departmental accounts and answers personally to the Public Accounts Committee of the House of Commons for the regularity and propriety of departmental expenditure and the observance of proper economy. This responsibility qualifies the accounting officer's duty to the minister. If the accounting officer believes that any projected departmental expenditure would be irregular or improper, it is his or her duty to make a formal objection to it. The minister may override the objection by giving the officer a written instruction, but the matter is then reported to the Comptroller and Auditor General and is made known to the Public Accounts Committee. A similar procedure applies if the accounting officer is concerned that proposed action may not achieve value for money. (See the *Ministerial Code* (2019), paras 5.3–5.5.) In 1991, a departmental accounting officer submitted a memorandum of dissent to the minister for overseas development, objecting that expenditure on the Pergau hydro-electric scheme in Malaysia would not be a prudent and economic use of aid funds. He was overruled by the minister. Afterwards, the accounting officer appeared before the Public Accounts Committee to give a full account of the circumstances: Public Accounts Committee, *17th Report of*

1993–94, HC 155. (For the subsequent judicial review of the minister's decision, see below, p. 794) The most recent report of the chair of the Committee of Public Accounts noted that there had not been a marked increase in the use of ministerial direction letters over expenditure, in spite of the statement made by Elizabeth Truss, the Chief Secretary to the Treasury, encouraging the use of these directions in order to ensure urgent expenditure to ensure readiness for Brexit (House of Commons, Committee of Public Accounts, *Fourth Annual Report of the Chair of the Committee of Public Accounts 3rd Special Report 2017–19*, HC 2370).

Senior civil servants are frequently called on to appear before other parliamentary select committees, in particular the 'departmentally related' committees, and may be questioned about the work of their respective departments. Their evidence is constrained by ministerial responsibility and is subject to limits established by the government, as we shall see, but the *Ministerial Code* (2019) says that ministers should 'require civil servants who give evidence before Parliamentary Committees on their behalf and under their direction to be as helpful as possible in providing accurate, truthful and full information' to the committees. A considerable amount of information about the detail of departmental administration is provided to the committees by officials. 'In practice', as Peter Barberis observes, 'civil servants do answer to Parliament, most visibly through select committees', and he adds that the load of explanatory accountability 'is now borne by civil servants as well as by ministers' (*The Civil Service in an Era of Change* (1997), p. 144). Government, however, withholds formal recognition from this development: 'The Government's commitment to a permanent, non-political civil service means that there can be no question of apportioning between the Minister and his civil servants part or parallel shares in a single line of accountability to Parliament' (Public Service Committee, *1st Special Report of 1996–97* (Government Response), HC 67).

A direct responsibility of civil servants has from time to time been exacted by committees or tribunals of inquiry that have identified civil servants as being to blame for administrative failures. The Scott Report on arms to Iraq (HC 115 of 1995–6) made numerous criticisms of individual civil servants for errors of judgment, neglect of duty, want of frankness and other 'thoroughly reprehensible' conduct. (Disciplinary action was subsequently taken against two officials in the Foreign and Commonwealth Office: Public Service Committee, *Minutes of Evidence*, HC 285 of 1997–98, Appendix 2.) In 1999, the Foreign Affairs Committee in its report on the 'Sandline affair' (above, p. 693: *2nd Report of 1998–99*, HC 116) concluded that certain named officials had 'failed in their duty' in not keeping ministers informed of events – a judgment not accepted by the government (see its Response to the Committee, Cm 4325/1999). Subsequently, the inquiry into the Conservative Government's handling of the BSE epidemic found that there had been 'institutional and political failure up to the highest levels', naming and criticising both senior civil servants and ministers (*Report of the BSE Inquiry*, HC 887 of 1999–2000). The conduct of officials came under scrutiny in both the Hutton and Butler Reports in 2004 consequent on the invasion of Iraq (HC 247 and HC 898 of 2003–04). No individual official was found to have been seriously culpable: in particular, the misleading dossier of September 2002 on Iraqi weapons of mass destruction, drawn up by the Joint Intelligence Committee under the chairmanship of John Scarlett, was said by Butler to be the result of collective failures, such that Scarlett should not be expected to resign as head of the Secret Intelligence Service.

The establishment of executive agencies in government departments (see above, p. 526) has given Civil Service managers or 'chief executives' of the agencies an enhanced responsibility and independence in carrying out their tasks. The Treasury and Civil Service Committee perceived the implications of this development for democratic control and accountability, saying in its *8th Report of 1987–88* (HC 494, paras 46–7):

> The traditional system of accountability does not seem to us to be entirely consistent with the increased delegation of responsibility to individual civil servants . . . [T]hose who are to make the decisions should be publicly answerable for them . . . We certainly do not advocate abandoning the principle of ministerial accountability, but modifying it so that the Chief Executive who has actually taken the decisions can explain them, in the first instance. In the last resort the Minister will bear the responsibility if things go badly wrong and Parliament will expect him or her to put things right, but the process of Parliamentary accountability should allow issues to be settled at lower levels, wherever possible.

The government agreed to the committee's recommendation that chief executives of agencies should be appointed as accounting officers, with direct, personal responsibility to the Public Accounts Committee for the use of public money (see above) and that they should appear and give evidence before other parliamentary select committees (albeit 'on behalf of ministers') on the day-to-day operational matters delegated to them (*Civil Service Management Reform: The Next Steps*, Cm 524/1988, p. 9).

Executive agencies operate under published framework documents describing their organisation and responsibilities, and they publish annual reports and accounts as well as three-year business plans, which set out their objectives, related to three-year funding agreements with their departments. Chief executives are set publicly announced performance targets and are responsible to ministers for achieving them and generally for the management of the agencies. Ministers remain responsible for the broad issues of policy relating to agencies, the targets set for them and the resources provided. Correspondence from MPs and written parliamentary questions that bear on the functions delegated to agencies are referred by ministers to the chief executives for reply. (Their replies to referred parliamentary questions are published in the *Official*

Report (Hansard).) An MP who is dissatisfied with a chief executive's response can raise the matter with the minister, who remains ultimately accountable.

These extensive delegations to agency chief executives have intensified debate about the location of responsibility to Parliament. Governments remain firm in their insistence on the traditional doctrine and have refused to accept arguments that chief executives should be personally and directly accountable to Parliament for the matters assigned to them. (See *Taking Forward Continuity and Change*, Cm 2748/1995; and *Government Response to House of Lords Select Committee on the Public Service*, Cm 4000/1998.) Perhaps Lord Mackay of Ardbrecknish, a minister of state, was not mindful of the government's official standpoint in saying to the Public Service Committee of the House of Lords: 'We [ministers] are accountable to Parliament. And the Chief Executives themselves, perhaps at a non-policy level, at the administration level, are also accountable to Parliament' (Public Service Committee, *Special Report of 1996–97*, HL 68, Ev, Q 885). Official doctrine and reality seem to diverge in the evolving relations of ministers and their agencies to Parliament.

The division of responsibilities between ministers and their agencies is expressed in official pronouncements in terms that responsibility for *policy* is owed by the minister to Parliament, while *operational* responsibility is delegated to the chief executive and is owed to the minister. But the distinction between 'policy' and 'operations' is problematic and becomes blurred in practice, since ministers have authority to intervene in operational matters and have sometimes done so frequently and in detail. The formula does nothing to illuminate the shadowy contours of ministerial responsibility. Christopher Foster remarks that the diffusion of power in government, of which executive agencies are an instance, 'has diffused responsibility and made it harder to apportion blame fairly' (*British Government in Crisis* (2005), p. 153).

The Public Administration Committee, in its *3rd Report of 2006–07*, HC 122, concluded that there was 'no consensus about the respective responsibilities of ministers and civil servants' and received evidence of an 'accountability gap' in which 'politicians and civil servants can hide behind each other, so that no one is really held to account'. In its response, the government adhered to the orthodox view of the accountability of ministers and civil servants (Public Administration Committee, *10th Special Report of 2007–08*, HC 1057, Appendix):

> There is a clear democratic line of accountability which runs from the electorate through MPs to the Government of the day. The Government – whatever its political complexion – is supported by the Civil Service in developing and implementing its policies. Civil servants are accountable to Ministers, who in turn are accountable to Parliament. It is this line of accountability which makes clear that ultimately Ministers are accountable to the electorate.

The actions of civil servants may be the subject of investigation by the parliamentary commissioner for administration (ombudsman) (see, further, below). The ombudsman's inquiries into maladministration by government departments may lead to findings that particular civil servants have been at fault, but those concerned are not usually named in the resulting report to Parliament.

(See, generally, Woodhouse, *Ministers and Parliament: Accountability in Theory and Practice* (1994); Giddings (ed.), *Parliamentary Accountability: A Study of Parliament and Executive Agencies* (1995); Tomkins, *The Constitution After Scott* (1998); Barberis, 'The New Public Management and the New Accountability' (1998) 76 *Pub Adm* 451; Riddell, *Parliament under Blair* (2000), ch. 4; Hogwood, Judge and McVicar, 'Agencies and Accountability', in Rhodes (ed.), *Transforming British Government* (2000); Elder and Page, 'Accountability and Control in Next Steps Agencies', in Rhodes, ibid.; Hansard Society Commission, *The Challenge for Parliament: Making Government Accountable* (2001); Woodhouse, 'Ministerial Responsibility', in Bogdanor (ed.), *The British Constitution in the Twentieth Century* (2003); Baldwin and Forman, 'Ministers and Parliament: Responsibility and Accountability', in Baldwin, (ed.), *Parliament in the 21st Century* (2005).)

9.3 The Power of Parliament

We are not now concerned with the 'sovereignty' of Parliament, or that supreme law-making power that belongs not to Parliament alone but to the monarch in Parliament, and which, in reality, is mainly at the disposal of the government. Our present interest is in the power of Parliament, in particular the House of Commons, to perform its functions of controlling and scrutinising the executive – these terms being taken in a wide sense: 'controlling' to include influencing or restraining, and 'scrutinising' (or calling to account) to include extracting information, criticising and procuring reparation or redress. In carrying out these tasks, Parliament relies less on its formal powers (e.g., to enforce the production of papers or punish for contempt) than on the conventional responsibility owed to it by ministers, and the practices and procedures that have crystallised about this convention.

> ### Joint Committee on Conventions, *First Report: Conventions of the UK Parliament,* HL 265-I, HC 1212-I of 2005–06, para 3
>
> This is a free country, and the Westminster Parliament is one of the things which make it so. Parliament is a complex mechanism, but at its heart is a simple balance: the balance between enabling the Government to do things, and holding them to account – asking questions, proposing alternatives, forcing them to reveal information and justify their actions.

Bernard Crick, *The Reform of Parliament* (rev. 2nd edn. 1970), pp. 79–81

Politics, not law, must explain the concept and practice of Parliamentary control of the Executive. In modern conditions any such control can only be something that does not threaten the day-to-day political control of Parliament by the Executive. The hope for any worth-while function of control by Parliament would be grim indeed if it depended on the ultimate deterrent of the vote: the undoubted Constitutional right of Parliament to vote against the Queen's Ministers and the Convention by which they would then resign. But control, on both sides, is indeed political. Governments respond to proceedings in Parliament if the publicity given to them is likely to affect public confidence in the Government, or even if the weakness with which the Government puts up its case, even in purely Parliamentary terms, begins to affect the morale of its own supporters (though it takes a very long succession of bleak days for the Government in the House before the country begins to be affected).

The only meanings of Parliamentary control worth considering, and worth the House spending much of its time on, are those which do *not* threaten the Parliamentary defeat of a government, but which help to keep it responsive to the underlying currents and the more important drifts of public opinion. All others are purely antiquarian shufflings. It is wholly legitimate for any modern government to do what it needs to guard against Parliamentary defeat; but it is not legitimate for it to hinder Parliament, particularly the Opposition, from reaching the public ear as effectively as it can. Governments must govern in the expectation that they can serve out their statutory period of office, that they can plan – if they choose – at least that far ahead, but that everything they do may be exposed to the light of day and that everything they say may be challenged in circumstances designed to make criticism as authoritative, informed and as public as possible.

Thus the phrase 'Parliamentary control', and talk about the 'decline of Parliamentary control', should not mislead anyone into asking for a situation in which governments can have their legislation changed or defeated, or their life terminated (except in the most desperate emergency when normal politics will in any case break down, as in Chamberlain's 'defeat' in 1940). Control means *influence*, not direct power; *advice*, not command; *criticism,* not obstruction; *scrutiny*, not initiation; and *publicity*, not secrecy. Here is a very realistic sense of Parliamentary control which *does* affect any government. The Government will make decisions, whether by existing powers or by bringing in new legislation, in the knowledge that these decisions, sooner or later, will find their way to debate on the Floor of one of the Houses of Parliament. The type of scrutiny they will get will obviously affect, in purely political terms, the type of actions undertaken. And the civil service will administer with the knowledge that it too may be called upon to justify perhaps even the most minute actions . . .

Governments deserve praise in so far as they expose themselves, willingly and helpfully, to influence, advice, criticism, scrutiny, and publicity; and they deserve blame in so far as they try to hide from unpleasant discussions and to keep their reasons and actions secret. Parliaments deserve praise or blame as to whether or not they can develop institutions whose control is powerful in terms of general elections and not of governmental instability. This 'praise' and 'blame' is not moralistic: it is prudential . . . So Parliamentary control is not

> the stop switch, it is the tuning, the tone and the amplifier of a system of communication which tells governments what the electorate want (rightly or wrongly) and what they will stand for (rightly or wrongly); and tells the electorate what is possible within the resources available (however much opinions will vary on what is possible) and – on occasion – what is expected of them.

Ours is a system of *party* government in which political parties present themselves and their programmes to the electorate, with the object of winning a parliamentary majority and forming a government committed to the implementation of party policies. This is facilitated through the first-past-the-post electoral system, which tends to produce governments with large working majorities. In this system, it is an essential function of Parliament (albeit not its *overriding* function) to sustain the government. Parliament is quite different in this respect from the United States Congress, which is established, on the principle of the separation of powers, as a separate branch of government with independent powers enabling it to oversee and check the executive branch. Ronald Butt has written (*The Times*, 18 May 1978, p. 18):

> The essence of effective parliamentary control over government is not simply that the House of Commons should stop a government from doing things. It is that the Commons should positively support and sustain the government of the day – and preferably from the position in which a clear majority of MPs has been elected by the people to do just that.

In practice, it is the majority party in the House of Commons that, in speech and vote, performs the function of sustaining the government. This underlines the fact that when we speak of Parliament or the House of Commons doing things, it is often only a part of the house that is meant. Besides being an institution, Parliament is a place in which different political forces, in competition or in combination, pursue a variety of objectives.

So, when we consider Parliament's functions of controlling and scrutinising the executive, we have to distinguish between the House of Commons as an institution and the forces within it. Generally, when the house seems to assert itself as a body against the executive we find only that intra-party disagreement on a specific issue of policy has resulted in temporary defections or an ad hoc combination of members. A particular combination of circumstances was provided in 2019 that led to a series of large governmental defeats: a minority government; a key policy issue (Brexit) that caused division within as well as across political parties; this policy issue had large social, political and constitutional ramifications meaning that MPs may have been more willing to risk losing the party whip; key personalities forming alliances across political parties and the growing role of the SNP. The select committees that seem to speak for Parliament in a dialogue with government are only groups of party members who have temporarily vacated their embattled positions to find common ground in scrutinising parts of the administration. Parliament, as Ian Gilmour says (*The Body Politic* (2nd edn. 1971), p. 246), is 'rather a place than a body of persons' – a place in which backbenchers and opposition parties (sometimes in strange alliances) can be seen to do the work that, as by a metaphor, is described as the work of Parliament.

This is not to deny Parliament its institutional character, which it possesses in law, as an inheritance of history, and in the convictions of some, at least, of its members who have a sense of being parliamentarians as well as party men or women. It is important to maintain the idea of a shared duty to 'watch and control' the executive, of whatever party.

9.3.1 Opposition

In the words of the Houghton Report on *Financial Aid to Political Parties* (Cmnd 6601/1976, para 9.1): 'The parties in opposition have the responsibility of scrutinising and checking all the actions of the Executive.' Brian Harrison remarks more trenchantly that 'the British two-party adversarial system is designed ... to subject government to a continuous barrage of criticism' (*The Transformation of British Politics 1860–1995* (1996), p. 422).

The legitimacy of opposition parties is confirmed by law, convention and the political culture of the UK. The opposition is recognised as having rights and is part of the constitutional system – as much part of it as is the government.

> **Ivor Jennings, *Cabinet Government* (3rd edn. 1959), pp. 15–16**
>
> Democratic government ... demands not only a parliamentary majority but also a parliamentary minority. The minority attacks the Government because it denies the principles of its policy. The Opposition will, almost certainly, be defeated in the House of Commons because it is a minority. Its appeals are to the electorate. It will, at the next election, ask the people to condemn the government, and, as a consequence, to give a majority to the Opposition. Because the Government is criticised it has to meet criticism. Because it must in course of time defend itself in the constituencies it must persuade public opinion to move with it. The Opposition is at once the alternative to the Government and a focus for the discontent of the people. Its function is almost as important as that of the Government. If there be no Opposition there is no democracy. 'Her Majesty's Opposition' is no idle phrase. Her Majesty needs an Opposition as well as a Government.

When this passage was written, the 'two-party system' – in which a single-party majority government faced an opposition dominated by the other major party – appeared to be firmly established. A system of adversary politics offered the electorate a clear-cut choice between party programmes. Since the 1950s, the two major parties have seen a decline in their combined share of the total vote at general elections, and in 1976–9, the smaller parties were able to bargain for concessions from a minority Labour Government. Although majority government was subsequently restored, the challenge to the two-party system did not fade away; a reconstituted third force, the Liberal Democrats, repudiate the model of adversary politics and have campaigned for a new political system based on proportional representation. They entered into the Coalition Government in 2010 while remaining committed to electoral reform. As we saw in the previous chapter, the Jenkins Commission on the Voting System recommended a 'broadly proportional' system, which would have a tendency to result in coalition governments. The Scottish Government was a coalition (between the Labour Party and the Liberal Democrats) after it came to power in 1999 until 2007, when the Scottish National Party formed a minority government, this situation being repeated in the 2011 and 2016 general election. In the Scottish Parliament, three parties, Labour, the Conservatives and the Liberal Democrats, with a handful of others, then formed the opposition. Since 1999, Wales has seen both minority administrations (Labour) and coalitions (of Labour and the Liberal Democrats), with substantial representation in the Welsh Assembly of Plaid Cymru and the Conservatives. Following the 2016 election, and subsequent changes, the Welsh Assembly is led by a Labour Government supported by the sole Liberal Democrat member of the Welsh Assembly. In Northern Ireland since 2007 (after a restoration of devolved government), the executive has been dominated by two parties (the Democratic Unionist Party and Sinn Fein), with substantial representation in the Assembly of the Ulster Unionist Party and the Social Democratic and Labour Party. In each of the devolved governments, multiparty politics prevails. Even at Westminster, and even under the current electoral system, we may yet see the emergence of a genuinely multi-party politics. While this appeared to be emerging due to the rise of the Liberal Democrats, culminating in the Coalition Government of 2010 to 2015, the subsequent fall in seats for the Liberal Democrats appeared to mark a return to two-party politics. However, the rise of SNP members in Westminster marks a new challenge to this perception of Westminster.

Having said that, a majority coalition government may confront opposition parties in much the same dominating way as does a majority single-party government.

At the present time, the constitution accords a special status to the official opposition which, as Nevil Johnson has written, is to be seen as an institution, having been 'institutionalised for the modern electorate as the standing possibility of an alternative government to replace the one in power' ('Opposition in the British Political System' (1997) 32 *Government and Opposition* 487). Since 1937, there has been statutory provision for the payment of a salary to the leader of the opposition. By section 1(1)(b) of and Schedule 2 to the Ministerial and other Salaries Act 1975, salaries are now paid to the leader of the opposition, the chief opposition whip and not more than two assistant opposition whips in the Commons, and to the leader of the opposition and the chief opposition whip in the Lords. The leader of the opposition is defined by section 2(1) of the Act as follows:

> In this Act 'Leader of the Opposition' means, in relation to either House of Parliament, that Member of that House who is for the time being the Leader in that House of the party in opposition to Her Majesty's Government having the greatest numerical strength in the House of Commons.

Thus, it is by reference to party strengths in the Commons that the leaders of the opposition in both houses are designated. Any doubt as to the identity of the leader of the opposition in either house is settled conclusively by the decision of the Speaker of that house (section 2(2), (3)).

The status and privileges of the official opposition and its leader in the House of Commons are supported by rules, conventions and practices of the house. The leader of the opposition is normally consulted by the prime minister in the event of a national emergency. He or she and other members of the opposition frontbench (those who are privy councillors) may be informed of confidential matters of state 'on Privy Council terms'. It is customary for opposition members to chair a proportion of the select committees of the House and in particular to take the chair of the Public Accounts Committee and of the Joint Committee on Statutory Instruments.

Conventions known as the Douglas-Home Rules (which had their genesis in 1964 in the last year of the Douglas-Home premiership) allow confidential pre-election contacts between senior civil servants and leaders of opposition parties on machinery of government questions in preparation for a possible change of government. (See House of Commons Library Standard Note SN/PC/03318, 22 May 2014, available on the UK Parliament website.)

A number of 'opposition days' are set aside in the House of Commons for debates on subjects chosen by opposition parties. Standing Order No. 14(2) provides:

> Twenty days shall be allotted in each session for proceedings on opposition business, seventeen of which shall be at the disposal of the Leader of the Opposition and three of which shall be at the disposal of the leader of the second largest opposition party; and matters selected on those days shall have precedence over government business.

Smaller parties are, from time to time, allowed an opposition day by agreement with one of the two principal opposition parties. Apart from the formal allocation of opposition days, the address in reply to the Queen's Speech at the beginning of a session allows for debate on opposition amendments, and time is always made available for official opposition motions of censure.

Discussions continually take place between government and opposition 'through the usual channels' on the arrangement of parliamentary business.

Robert Blackburn and Andrew Kennon (eds.), *Griffith and Ryle on Parliament: Functions, Practice and Procedures* (2nd edn. 2003), pp. 409–11

Supplementing the necessary measure of agreement between the parties on how business shall be conducted, day-to-day contact is needed. The programme for the next week is announced by the Leader of the House each Thursday, but is discussed with opposition spokesmen before its announcement. Amongst other matters on which agreement is normally come to, after discussion between government and opposition, are the length of debate on a motion, and whether a bill is to be debated in committee on the floor of the House or in standing committee. A particularly important area of agreement relates to the timetabling of bills as they progress through the House, especially in standing committee when, more often than not, the two sides agree on the number of sittings that will be needed ... [On timetabling. see above, pp. 544–554.]

Important and sometimes controversial discussions take place through the usual channels on how many chairs of select committees shall be held by the opposition and, particularly, which chairs. Agreement through the usual channels will also be come to on how long the respective last speakers (the 'winders-up') in an important debate will need. The whips will consult front-bench Members, and also those on the back benches with a special interest in the proceedings, and the Speaker will be informed accordingly.

All this does not mean that what takes place on the floor of the House or in committee is ritualised and wholly predictable. The plans may be interrupted and set aside by some unexpected event in the House or in the world outside. Back-benchers on either side of the House may rebel against the arrangements agreed by their leaders and quite frequently do. Chief whips on both sides of the House have a common interest in limiting such back-bench unrest and may work together to this end.

The principal actors in the discussions that take place between the two sides in the House are the Leader of the House and the shadow Leader, and the government chief whip and the opposition chief whip. These are 'the usual channels'. The government chief whip, together with the Leader of the House, is responsible for seeing that the government's timetable runs smoothly at all levels: sessionally, weekly and daily. It requires good judgment and careful execution to ensure that government bills make their way through the Commons and the Lords to emerge as Acts of Parliament in accordance with the government's timetable ...

On a day-to-day basis, there has to be a considerable flow of information between the parties through the medium of the whips' offices. The nature of parliamentary business is such that only seldom is anything to be gained by one side keeping its intentions secret from the other side. It is in the interests of neither side to surprise the other ...

Occasionally co-operation between the parliamentary parties breaks down and the 'usual channels' are closed for a time ... Such occasions are short-lived, however. Business is delayed, pairing ceases, votes are called on trivial matters and everyone's personal convenience suffers. For different reasons, therefore, it suits both sides to come to agreements and there is sufficient strength on both sides for genuine compromises to be reached.

Matters that are settled through the usual channels to the mutual satisfaction of government and opposition may be unwelcome to independently minded backbenchers: Mr Tony Benn once caustically described the usual channels as 'the most polluted waterways in the world' (HC Deb vol. 207, col 6, 27 April 1992).

On the opposition frontbench in the House of Commons there is a 'shadow cabinet', which directs the strategy of the opposition and organises its tactical response to forthcoming government business in the house. (There will also be one or more shadow cabinet members in the House of Lords, one of them the leader of the opposition in the Lords.) Members of the shadow cabinet hold 'portfolios' corresponding to those of ministers of the Crown. Both the Conservative shadow cabinet (or Consultative Committee) and the Labour shadow cabinets are appointed by the party leader.

The frontbench team speaks for the official opposition and its members are expected to observe a convention of collective responsibility and refrain from public dissent from party policies. Compliance with this convention may be enforced by the leader of the opposition, as happened when Mr Enoch Powell was dismissed from the Conservative shadow cabinet in 1968 after a speech on immigration which was considered by Mr Heath to be damaging to the Conservative position on race relations. In 1982, the Labour opposition leader dismissed three frontbench spokesmen for voting contrary to a shadow cabinet injunction in a debate on the Falklands crisis. (See, further, Brazier, *Ministers of the Crown* (1997), pp. 52–4.) More recently, members of the shadow cabinet resigned over policy divergence with Jeremy Corbyn and over Brexit.

The opposition is under certain disadvantages in delivering its challenge to the government in the House of Commons. The government controls the parliamentary timetable and commands, in the guillotine (now programme motions), a powerful weapon of last resort for restricting debate. The opposition, however, has its own weapons. A minister of the Crown once conceded that 'delaying tactics of a strenuous nature' are a legitimate weapon of opposition (Mr Iain Macleod, HC Deb vol. 655, col 432, 7 March 1962) and it is one that can be used to considerable effect. If the opposition considers itself unfairly treated, it may withhold cooperation from the government in the conduct of parliamentary business, shutting off 'the usual channels'. It was no idle threat when, the government having decided to guillotine a strongly contested social security bill, an opposition spokesman said in the House on 6 May 1980 (HC Deb vol. 984, col 114):

> [T]he Opposition will not counsel Labour Members to co-operate in the normal running of business in the House. The Government have a large majority but it will not be possible on many days for them to do what they want when they want to do it.

In 1993–4, the Labour opposition, affronted by the drastic guillotining of two social security bills, withheld cooperation with the government for four months. As a last resort, opposition may be carried to the point of deliberate obstruction: filibustering, contrived points of order, repeated interventions in speeches and other time-wasting devices can be used by an opposition that considers its rights to have been violated. (See, e.g., HC Deb vol. 990, cols 522–50, 6 August 1980). But the confrontation between the parties is seldom taken to these lengths, and in general the government remains in effective control of the proceedings of the house. One striking series of exceptions, which saw the Commons taking over the business of the house from the government, occurred during 2019, both in the governments of Theresa May (from 2017–19) and of Boris Johnson (2019), discussed below.

The opposition is unable to match the government in information and resources. An attempt to redress the balance was made on 20 March 1975 when the House of Commons resolved (HC Deb vol. 888, cols 1933–4) that provision should be made 'for financial assistance to any Opposition party in this House to assist that party in carrying out its Parliamentary business'. In accordance with a formula then laid down, and revised in subsequent resolutions, opposition parties have been able to claim payments towards expenditure on their parliamentary work, the amounts being related to a party's numerical strength in the house and its electoral support. The money may be used, for example, for the employment of research assistants to frontbenchers and for expenses of the party leader's and whips' offices. (An additional sum is made available for the travelling expenses of opposition spokespersons.) The original scheme was proposed by the then Leader of the House, Mr Edward Short, and the finance provided became known as 'Short money'. A scheme known as 'Cranborne money' (from Viscount Cranborne, then Leader of the House of Lords) was introduced in 1996 to provide funding for the first and second opposition parties in the House of Lords, modified in 2010 so as to remove the eligibility of the second opposition party (HL Deb vol. 719, cols 1429–35, 24 June 2010).

The Short and Cranborne money schemes were considered by the Committee on Standards in Public Life (*Fifth Report*, Cm 4057-I/1998), which declared its belief that:

> the Short money scheme is founded on the sound principle that, in a parliamentary democracy, the party in government should be held to account and kept in check by a vigorous and well-prepared opposition.

The committee proposed that the levels of Short and Cranborne funding should be reviewed by the political parties in the respective Houses of Parliament with a view to increasing them and that a portion of Short money should be earmarked for funding the office of the leader of the opposition in the House of Commons. The government having approved these recommendations, resolutions of both houses provided for substantial increases respectively in Short and Cranborne money, the former including a sum specifically identified for the office of the leader of the opposition (HC Deb vol. 332, cols 427 et seq., 26 May 1999). The House of Lords resolution also provides for financial assistance for the parliamentary work of cross-bench peers (HL Deb vol. 638, cols 817 et seq., 30 July 2002). The scheme was amended by a Commons resolution in 2016 (HC Deb vol. 607, col 1714, 23 May 2016). The money is available to all opposition parties in the House of Commons that have secured two seats, or one seat and more than 150,000 votes at the last general election. It is intended to fund the opposition parties in carrying out their parliamentary business, to fund travel and associated expenditure and to fund the running costs of the leader of the opposition. (See House of Commons Members Estimate Committee *Consolidated List of Provisions of the Resolutions of the House Relating to Expenditure Charged to the Estimate for House of Commons: Members as at 16 July 2018 First Report 2017–19*, HC 1442.) A party in government does not qualify for financial assistance under the Short and Cranborne schemes. The Liberal Democrats, which had previously received Short and Cranborne money as a party in opposition, were deprived of their allocations on entering the Coalition Government in May 2010. (See, further, Chapter 8 as to the funding of non-parliamentary activities of political parties.)

The opposition performs a dual role: it both opposes the government, functioning as 'an orchestration of all discontents' (Bernard Crick, *New Statesman*, 18 June 1960, p. 883), and presents itself to the electorate as an alternative government. It is the latter role that is said to make for 'Responsible Opposition', meaning an opposition that accepts the basic political structure and obeys the rules of the parliamentary game. Acceptance of parliamentary democracy is not, however, incompatible with radical policies for institutional change.

A 'responsible' opposition, aspiring to power, will criticise the government and expose its weaknesses. It will use whatever strength it has to exact concessions from the government. Continuous scrutiny by opposition parties in a public arena compels governments to defend, to explain and sometimes to moderate their policies.

Ronald Butt, *The Power of Parliament* (2nd edn. 1969), pp. 317–18

Just as a Government must anticipate the reactions of its backbenchers and prepare to meet them, so it must do the same in relation to the Opposition. Of course, an Opposition attack is much less menacing than a widespread tide of rebellion within the governing party. Nevertheless, although a Cabinet, to satisfy a particular demand inside its own party, may be prepared to brave the Opposition storm, in many other cases it will modify its policies in the light of what it expects the Opposition case to be. If it suspects that the Opposition will have an attractive case, it will do its best, within broad limits, to make that case less attractive – or to steal and adapt the Opposition's clothes. In this broad sense, therefore, the voice of Opposition contributes to the policy-making of Government in any given Parliament and is not simply a factor in deciding what the composition of the *next* Parliament should be. For example, although Conservative Party opinion prompted the production of the Commonwealth Immigrants Act which became law in 1962, an assessment of Opposition feeling was an important factor in preventing the Government from going further. As it was, the Bill was fought bitterly by the Labour Opposition. This was a generally popular measure but had the Government taken it so far as to have appeared to ordinary people to be unreasonable … then many more people might have been swung against it and the Opposition would have been presented with a very much stronger case. To see this point, one has only to try to envisage what shape the measure might have taken had the Labour Opposition not expressed such uncompromising hostility, *in advance*. Indeed, leaving aside the question of the Opposition's part in determining the issues and outcome of any next election, one has only to try to imagine the silence of the Opposition during any Parliament to comprehend what difference it would make to the current conduct of politics.

Apart from the real if indirect effect it has on the evolution of Government policy, the Opposition can also, by a carefully fought and reasoned campaign, get the details of legislation amended. Many, perhaps most, crucial amendments to Bills are in the name of the Minister concerned, yet they may well have arisen from the activity of the Opposition. Thus the capital gains provisions of the 1964 Labour Government were heavily amended by the Chancellor. Yet the detailed pressure for amendment and the exposure of weak elements in the Government's original proposal came from the Conservative Opposition. The Government's acceptance of some of them cannot be explained in terms of its small majority but rather reflected the Chancellor's understanding that he had to meet a powerful Opposition case.

In British politics, everything depends on the convention that the power of the majority should not be used to steamroller into silence the protests of the minority. If numbers were all that counted, a Government majority could any day silence the minority Opposition, and it is owing less to the formal rules of Parliament than to an acceptance of the spirit of common procedures that it does not do so.

It is a principal virtue of ministerial responsibility that it provides a justification and opportunities for opposition parties to 'harry and embarrass ministers': see Kam, 'Not Just Parliamentary "Cowboys and Indians": Ministerial Responsibility and Bureaucratic Drift' (2000) 13 *Governance* 365.

The two-party system acknowledges only a modest role for minor parties in the proceedings of Parliament. The Conservative and Labour Parties, which have for many years dominated politics in the UK, have been able to frustrate the development of a multiparty system by their incorporation of a wide spectrum of political viewpoints, each of these parties being in some way a coalition; and their dominance has been sustained by the FPTP electoral system. Nevertheless, the third party, the Liberal Democrats, have increased their share of the vote and have urged their claim to greater recognition and weight in the business of the House of Commons.

Nevil Johnson, 'Opposition in the British Political System' (1997) 32 *Government and Opposition* 487, 508–10

The British political system clearly belongs to the still relatively small group of mature democratic regimes. All such regimes necessarily acknowledge opposition, both as an entailment of their basic political values and as an expression of the social pluralism which sustains democratic government. But in such societies opposition can be and is embodied in different political habits and procedures. Both formal institutions and the patterns of parties may diffuse opposition so that it finds expression more in the multiplicity of points of opposition within a society and its political system than in the presence of a single focal point for opposition. But in some liberal democracies opposition is highly focused and institutionalised, and of these Britain is the pre-eminent example.

Perhaps the British view of opposition retains its fascination precisely because it is unusual in its clarity of definition as the institutionalisation of an alternative government and, therefore, as a necessary component of a system of democratic government worthy of that name. It is still seen as the means of enabling the electorate to change its government and to punish those office-holders in whom it has lost faith. The failings of the principle are the encouragement it offers to the over-simplification of the issues arising in political life, the exaggeration of adversarial relationships in the public sphere, and a certain kind of brutal disregard for those parties which are not players in the big league. And after all there can only be two in any big league. The virtues of this approach are to be found in the protection it offers against the domination of public life by in-bred and often introverted party oligarchies. It does in a certain sense open the doors to the people and there is underlying it a coherent normative theory of popular government and democratic control. Despite the fact that it has not actually been widely exported and when it has, has often failed, there are still grounds for believing that 'loyal Opposition' remains one of the great political inventions of the British.

Previous editions remarked that the Liberal Democrat breakthrough into government in 2010 and the prospect of continuing electoral volatility could herald a new kind of politics, affecting the makeup of both governments and oppositions. However, this was not to be, at least in terms of the role of the Liberal Democrats. The 2015 general election saw a significant fall in support for the Liberal Democrats, falling from 23 per cent to 7.9 per cent of votes cast, with a corresponding fall in MPs from fifty-seven to eight. This share of the vote stayed more or less the same in the 2017 general election, however, the number of seats rose from eight to twelve. In 2019, the Liberal Democrats saw a significant rise in the percentage of votes cast – rising to 11.5 per cent. However, they lost one seat – that of their then leader Jo Swinson, who subsequently stepped down as leader of the party. However, the fall in support for the Liberal Democrats was supplemented by a rise in support for the SNP, which obtained fifty-six seats in the 2015 general election, with a 4.7 per cent share of votes cast. This fell to thirty-five seats in 2017, and forty-eight seats in 2019. The SNP played a crucial role in siding against the government with regard to Brexit, as will be discussed below. While this may have signalled a move towards more deliberative politics, which provides a greater role for the opposition, the large majority of the Conservative Party in the 2019 general election would suggest that this increase in the power of the opposition parties will dwindle in the current Parliament.

9.3.2 Backbenchers

Backbenchers on both sides of the House of Commons have a role in the checking of government. Although they generally give their primary loyalty to their party, they have also other interests and loyalties, and will often speak in the house for their constituencies, or on behalf of outside groups with which they are associated, or to argue the cases of individuals who complain of unfair treatment by government departments. This pleading of special interests, or checking of the detail of administration, is rather a function of backbenchers than of organised parties. The procedure and practice of the house provide for it in a number of ways.

Backbench members can raise issues of concern to them or their constituents in a daily half-hour adjournment debate and other adjournment debates in the chamber of the house, and also in the 'parallel chamber' in Westminster Hall. The Westminster Hall sittings, providing an additional forum for the scrutiny and accountability of government in politically non-contentious matters, have substantially increased the amount of time available for backbench members' debates. Standing Order No. 24 (emergency debates) provides an opportunity for backbenchers (as well as opposition frontbench MPs) to raise urgent issues on the floor of the house, even though a subsequent debate is only rarely allowed (for one example of a strategic use of Standing Order No. 24, see below). Backbenchers make frequent use of question time in the house (see below) and write to ministers (many thousands of letters each year) about the grievances of constituents. Even if much of this backbench activity has no obvious impact on the government, an administration that did not have to submit to it could afford to be less careful and more high-handed.

Important reforms have been brought about by private members' bills – for example, the liberalisation of the laws on abortion, homosexual behaviour and divorce, the abolition of capital punishment, the ending of theatre censorship and, more recently, the Public Interest Disclosure Act 1998 (giving protection to 'whistleblowers' who disclose malpractices of their employers), the Female Genital Mutilation Act 2003, the Autism Act 2009 and the Green Energy (Definition and Promotion) Act 2009. Recent successful private members' bills include the Assaults on Emergency Workers (Offences) Act 2018, the Preventing and Combating Violence Against Women and Domestic Violence (Ratification of Convention) Act 2017 and the House of Lords (Expulsion and Suspension) Act 2015.

Standing orders give precedence to private members' bills on thirteen Fridays in each session, and there is a further (rather remote) chance for a private member's bill to reach the statute book by way of the '10-minute rule' procedure (SO No. 23), by which a backbencher may move for leave to bring in a bill, allowing a brief speech to be made in favour of the proposed bill. This procedure was recently used successfully to enact the Guardianship (Missing Persons) Act 2017, introduced by Kevin Hollinrake MP, although its provisions have still not been implemented through the requisite secondary legislation.

Although a private member's bill has no prospect of being enacted in the teeth of government opposition, if the bill has support on both sides of the house, the government may stay its hand, help the bill on its way or promise to introduce a bill of its own. For example, the strength of the support for bills on Crown immunity in NHS hospitals and on official secrecy introduced by a backbencher, Mr Richard Shepherd, helped to persuade the government to bring forward legislation of its own (the National Health Service (Amendment) Act 1986 and the Official Secrets Act 1989). Again, the government was induced by backbench pressure and a series of private members' bills to introduce its own bill which became the Disability Discrimination Act 1995. Usually, no more than two or three private members' bills are enacted in any year and reforms could be introduced to facilitate their passage into law (see House of Commons Reform Committee, *1st Report of 2008–09*, HC 1117; and Brazier and Fox, 'Enhancing the Backbench MP's Role as a Legislator' (2010) 63 *Parl Aff* 201).

The most remarkable recent examples of private members' bills are the bills introduced by Cooper and Letwin, which became the European Union (Withdrawal) Act 2018 and by Benn and Burt, which became the European Union (Withdrawal) (No 2) Act 2018. They are remarkable as they were enacted neither through the means of the ballot for private members' bills nor the ten-minute rule. Moreover, both were enacted to prevent key government policies and had constitutional consequences, requiring the prime minister to seek an extension to the Article 50 Brexit negotiations. This occurred through the combined actions of backbench and opposition MPs, and will be discussed further below.

A government is more concerned to retain the loyalty and support of its own backbenchers than to placate the opposition. If disaffection should break out among its backbenchers, the government's management of the house becomes difficult, the signs of disunity affect its reputation in the country and it may suffer defeats in the house in circumstances of maximum publicity, as occurred most notably in 2019, where the government was defeated three times on a series of 'meaningful votes' to endorse Theresa May's Withdrawal Agreement.

In recent decades, government backbenchers have shown an increased willingness to use their votes independently – even on occasion to inflict defeats on the government, knowing that such defeats do not normally put the government's survival in question. Between 1970 and 1979, both Conservative and Labour Governments suffered numerous defeats, on the floor of the house and in standing committees, as a result of backbench defection. Between 1979 and 1992, Conservative Governments with comfortable majorities were less vulnerable to defeat, but nevertheless saw new immigration rules voted down by the house in 1982 and the loss of the Shops Bill in 1986, suffered defeats in committee and repeatedly had their majorities reduced by backbench revolts. After 1992, Conservative backbenchers showed a revived independence and joined with opposition MPs to inflict significant defeats on the Major Government, notably in votes on the Maastricht Treaty in July 1993, on VAT on domestic fuel in December 1994 and on European fisheries policy in December 1995.

The Labour Governments elected with commanding Commons majorities in 1997 and 2001 and a reduced but still substantial majority in 2005 were confronted by increasingly assertive Labour backbenchers. In Mr Blair's first term, the government experienced significant backbench rebellions in votes on such matters as a reduction in lone-parent benefit (1997), restrictions on eligibility for incapacity benefit (1999), the partial privatisation of National Air Traffic Services (2000) and the Freedom of Information Bill (2000). In the Parliament elected in 2001, substantial backbench rebellions were provoked by provisions in a number of government bills, among them the Anti-Terrorism, Crime and Security Bill (2001), the Education Bill (2002), the Nationality, Immigration and Asylum Bill (2002), the Criminal Justice Bill (2003) and the Health and Social Care (Community Health and Standards) Bill (2003). In January 2004, seventy-two Labour MPs voted against the government at the second reading of the Higher Education Bill (providing for top-up fees) and a succession of revolts marked the passage of the Asylum and Immigration (Treatment of Claimants etc.) Bill (2004). On the question of Iraq, large cohorts of Labour backbenchers, resisting pressure from both ministers and the whips, voted against the government on successive occasions, notably on 26 February and (on a motion authorising military action) 18 March 2003. The latter, as Philip Norton remarks, was, at the time, 'the largest parliamentary party rebellion of any Prime Minister on a question of high policy' ('Governing Alone' (2003) 56 *Parl Aff* 543, 550). In the 2005–6 session, the government suffered notable rebellions by its backbenchers in votes on the Identity Cards Bill and the Education and Inspections Bill, and was twice *defeated* in votes on the Terrorism Bill and twice again on the Racial and Religious Hatred Bill. In March 2007, a revolt by a large number of Labour backbenchers against the proposed renewal of the Trident nuclear weapons system was overcome only with the support of opposition MPs.

In the early months of the Coalition Government, revolts were so frequent as to become the norm, although the numbers of dissenting MPs were modest. The Coalition Government was defeated seven times in the House of Commons, most notably as regards the motion in response to the use of chemical weapons in Syria and the request to deploy British troops in 2013 (HC Deb vol. 566, cols 1547–1556). Cameron's majority government from 2015–16 was defeated only three times, and May's majority government from 2015–16 was defeated only once.

The situation was radically different during May's minority government, which was defeated on thirty-three divisions, with some of these arising from opposition day motions, where May instructed her party to abstain. The biggest rebellions occurred over Brexit, the first being the rebellion which gave rise to the enactment of the meaningful vote, found in section 13 of the European Union (Withdrawal) Act 2018. This provision placed legal requirements on the ratification of the Withdrawal Agreement, including a vote in the House of Commons in favour of the Withdrawal Agreement and a series of votes should a Withdrawal Agreement fail to be agreed on by a series of fixed dates in the run up to the first Article 50 deadline of 29 March 2019. May also suffered the largest defeat on a government motion in a time of universal suffrage, losing the first meaning vote on her Withdrawal Agreement by 202 votes in favour to 432 against (January 2019). Theresa May would go on to suffer three further defeats on the Withdrawal Agreement (12 and 29 March 2019). It was these defeats in particular, leading to the failure to achieve the government's promise to deliver Brexit, that led to May's resignation as leader of the Conservative Party in June 2019. The May government also saw a defeat on an opposition motion holding the government as a whole in contempt of the house for failing to comply with a motion of the house to publish the full legal advice of the Attorney General on the EU Withdrawal Agreement and the Framework for the Future Relationship. (18 December 2018). Similar problems arose for the Johnson Government of 2019, which, despite lasting less than six months, was defeated twelve times. Johnson's Government failed to win a division until 15 October 2019, a full six weeks after its first sitting.

As will be discussed in more detail below, this unprecedented series of defeats can be explained due to the unusual combination of Brexit and a minority government. It is also the case that these defeats were not purely due to backbench rebellion. Backbench rebellion over Brexit continued, despite Boris Johnson making it clear that the party whip would be removed and MPs voting against the government and in favour of what became the European Union (Withdrawal) (No 2) Act 2019 would be expelled from the party. Boris Johnson expelled twenty-one Conservative MPs from the party, including Kenneth Clarke, Dominic Grieve, Philip Hammond, David Gauke, Sir Nicholas Soames, Sir Oliver Letwin, Justine Greening, Rory Stewart and Sam Gyimah. However, it is important to note that each of those expelled from the party who then stood for election (either as an independent or as a member of another political party) failed to win a seat in the December 2019 general election. This would suggest a return to the normal rate of fewer backbench rebellions under the current Conservative majority Government.

Current research also suggests that, in addition to group backbench rebellion to seek modifications to legislation, particularly towards the end of the second or third term of a majority government, individual backbench MPs may be more likely to rebel when to do so draws the attention of constituents to their views. (See, further, Cowley, *Revolts and Rebellions: Parliamentary Voting under Blair* (2002); Cowley and Stuart, 'Parliament: More Bleak House than Great Expectations' (2004) 57 *Parl Aff* 301 and 'Parliament: Hunting for Votes' (2005) 58 *Parl Aff* 258; Whitaker, 'Backbench Influence on Government Legislation?' (2006) 59 *Parl Aff* 350; Slapin, Kirkland, Lazzaro, Leslie and O'Grady, 'Ideology, Grandstanding, and Strategic Party Disloyalty to the British Government' (2018) 112 *American Political Science Review*, 15.)

Even though the majority of government bills pass through the House of Commons unscathed, the influence of government backbenchers is not to be measured solely in government defeats. A less obvious but continuous and powerful restraint (or spur) operates on government through the *anticipated reactions* of its backbenchers. A recent study by Meg Russell and Dan Gover points out five main ways in which legislation can be influenced by backbenchers, who may: influence the content of legislation before it is introduced; pursue changes through proposing amendments to government legislation; through voicing private concerns and obtaining changes in exchange for support on pivotal votes; in addition to restricting the government who are constrained by anticipated reactions of backbench MPs and through the mere power they exert when they support the government. This influence continued through the Coalition Government of 2010 to 2015.

Meg Russell and Daniel Gover, *Legislating at Westminster: Parliamentary Actors and Influence in the Making of British Law* (OUP, 2017), pp. 144–5

Government backbench influence should therefore be conceived not only in terms of what changed on the bills, but also what didn't. On many issues the government was simply supported by its backbenchers. In some cases this was because the policy issues were uncontroversial, with little attempt by the opposition or others to 'politicize' them (as illustrated in Chapter 4). But on other occasions opposition parliamentarians sought to press the government, and made little progress because backbench opinion was solid. This applied for example to Labour's protests about the coalition's Savings Accounts and Health in Pregnancy Grant Bill, and its attempts to complete the pilot study on ID cards, or to negotiate refunds for those who had already purchased the cards. In all three cases ministers could hence proceed unimpeded. In contrast, in the case of John McDonnell's proposed amendments to Labour's Employment Bill, it was the opposition that applied counteractive pressure, alongside more mainstream backbenchers.

During coalition the distinction between the two partners made the possibility of dividing the government more obvious and ... sometimes specifically sought to do so with its amendments. Maintaining the support, or at least acquiescence, of Liberal Democrat backbenchers was crucial to securing the government's programme. On occasion these members expressed their displeasure by abstaining in divisions, rather than actively rebelling. Hence on the Welfare Reform Bill a Labour peer said of the Liberal Democrats that 'all I asked was not to vote with us but to simply come in and listen to the debate' (since government backbenchers often just arrive at the sound of the division bell and pass through whichever lobby their whips advise). Abstentions (as well as rebellious votes) contributed to several defeats on the bill in the Lords. But in no case were these sufficient to deny the government its majority in the Commons. This period illustrates clearly the fine line that ministers must sometimes walk in order to maintain their parliamentary majority, and the latent power of government backbenchers.

Cross-party combinations of backbenchers can be formidable. It was such a combination (the 'unholy alliance' led by Mr Foot and Mr Powell) that in 1969 defeated a scheme for the reform of the House of Lords which was supported by both the government and the official opposition. At a remove from the battleground of party politics, all-party subject groups of members (such as the all-party disability group), often linked with outside interests, can on occasion exert a significant influence on government policy. (See, further, Judge, *Backbench Specialisation in the House of Commons* (1981), pp. 141–4; James, *British Government* (1997), pp. 170–94; Whitaker, 'Backbench Influence on Government Legislation?' (2006) 59 *Parl Aff* 350.)

A significant reform was achieved in June 2010 when the recommendation of the Wright Committee (*First Report, Select Committee on Reform of the House of Commons*, HC 1117 of 2009–10) that a backbench business committee should be established was adopted by the House of Commons, which had induced the government to relinquish, in Commons proceedings relating to non-government, backbench business, 'their iron grip on the procedures and agenda of the House' (Leader of the House, HC Deb vol. 511, col 779, 15 June 2010). This new select committee of eight members, elected by a secret ballot of MPs, is empowered 'to determine the backbench business to be taken in the House and in Westminster Hall' on the thirty-five days at its disposal in each session of Parliament (see HC Standing Order No. 152 J), business of a kind previously arranged by the government's managers in the Whips' Office. In the words of Graham Allen MP: 'The committee is about taking the chunk of business that all of us accept is the province, property and interest of Back-Benchers, pulling it together and taking a Back-Bench view on how best to use it. Rather than the Leader of the House deciding that we should have a general debate next week on something or other, there would be a process by which all of us, collectively, could decide what that debate should be about' (HC Deb vol. 511, col 819, 15 June 2010). The House of Commons Procedure Committee, which carried out a review of the committee after its first year, recommended that the committee continue (*Review of Backbench Committee 2nd Report of 2012–13*, HC 168, 22 November 2012).

A threat to the independence of backbenchers is presented by the provisions of the Parliamentary Voting Systems and Constituencies Act 2011, which fixes the number of parliamentary constituencies in the UK at 600, reducing the membership of the House of Commons from 650. With no reduction proposed in the number of ministers and parliamentary private secretaries, the effect of the change may be to increase the proportion of MPs on the 'payroll vote', altering the balance of power between the executive and Parliament and diminishing the ability of backbenchers to hold ministers to account. The Parliamentary Constituencies Bill 2019–20 does propose modifications to the way in which constituency boundaries will be drawn. However, clause 5 of the Bill, if enacted, repeals the legislative requirement to reduce the number of MPs from 650 to 600.

9.3.3 The House of Commons

There are occasions, although not very frequent, when members on both sides of the House of Commons combine to assert the power of the house against what they see as an encroachment by the executive on its rights or privileges. On these rare but instructive occasions, we see the house acting as a body to claim its constitutional authority over the executive. One such instance occurred in 1980.

Following the seizure of American hostages in Iran on 4 November 1979, the UK Government introduced in the House of Commons on 8 May 1980 the Iran (Temporary Powers) Bill, providing for economic sanctions against Iran. The minister in charge of the bill assured the house that the bill and orders to be made under it would apply only to future contracts, and would not affect the implementation of those already made by British exporters. The bill was duly passed by both houses and received the royal assent on 15 May 1980.

On 18 May, it was agreed at a meeting of the foreign ministers of the member states of the European Community that sanctions should be jointly applied against Iran and should extend to all contracts entered into after 4 November 1979. Since the Iran (Temporary Powers) Act 1980 did not apply to contracts already made, the government proposed to rely on earlier legislation, the Import, Export and Customs Powers (Defence) Act 1939, under which orders could be made prohibiting the export of goods to Iran under contracts entered into at any time after 4 November 1979. When this decision was announced in the House of Commons by the Lord Privy Seal (speaking for the Foreign Office), he was strongly criticised, from both sides of the house, by members who considered that the house had been misled. After the announcement an opposition MP sought and obtained leave from the Speaker to move the adjournment of the house 'for the purpose of discussing a specific and important matter that should have urgent consideration' and, the required support of not fewer than forty members having been given, an emergency debate was set down for the next day. On 20 May 1980, the Lord Privy Seal made the following statement to the House (HC Deb vol. 985, cols 254–5):

> After my statement yesterday about decisions taken on the implementation of sanctions against Iran by Foreign Ministers of the European Community meeting informally in Naples over the weekend, the House made its view very clear that the inclusion of retrospection, however limited, was unacceptable.
>
> The Government have therefore decided that sanctions will not be retrospective. No orders will be laid before the House which ban the supply of goods under arrangements made before the date on which those orders were laid. Last night we informed our European Community partners and the Government of the United States that, in view of the opposition of this House to retrospection, we would no longer be prepared to proceed to apply any element of retrospection among the decisions that we agreed to at the meeting in Naples.

Governmental accountability is from time to time exacted on the floor of the House of Commons when issues are debated which transcend party loyalties. Such was the Debate on 29 April 2009, when the government was defeated in an Opposition day motion calling on it to extend the limited settlement rights in the UK conceded to Gurkhas and their families: HC Deb vol. 491, cols 890–931, 988–999. The clearest example of the combined power of members of the house against the government is illustrated through the many ways in which the house defeated the government on issues relating to Brexit in 2019.

9.3.4 Brexit and the Minority Governments of 2019

As discussed above, 2019 saw the enactment of two private members' bills outside the normal channels, in addition to a series of governmental defeats – including the largest government defeat since universal suffrage. Difficulties arose due to a conflict between the Commons and the government's plan to leave the European Union on 29 March 2019, the end of the two-year negotiation period established by Article 50 TEU. Both backbench MPs and members of the opposition were unhappy with the Withdrawal Agreement obtained by the then Prime Minister, Theresa May. The house was able to exert its power due to a combination of circumstances: the minority governments of Theresa May and later Boris Johnson in 2019; the intra- in addition to interparty divisions on Brexit; the use of the courts and a creative use of standing orders (and some would argue creative interpretation of standing orders by the then Speaker, John Bercow). That the government was able to remain in power despite these defeats was due to the provisions of the Fixed-Term Parliaments Act 2011, and an unwillingness on the part of the opposition to hold a general election when to do so may defeat the purpose of delaying Brexit.

The first catalyst was section 13 of the European Union (Withdrawal) Act 2018, which was itself a product of a successful House of Lords amendment, supported by backbenchers in the Commons, which gave rise to a government concession. The section provided, inter alia, that the Withdrawal Agreement could not be ratified without a vote of the House of Commons in favour of the Withdrawal Agreement and the Framework for the Future Relationship, and a motion in the House of Lords to take note of the vote in the Commons. The programme motion for debate on the Withdrawal Agreement was put before the Commons on 4 December 2018. This motion was successfully amended following an amendment proposed by Dominic Grieve, such that any motion proposed by the government under the provisions of section 13 would not be neutral motions according to Standing Order No. 24B. This was to become important later on, allowing for further possibilities for the House of Commons to challenge the government's policy on Brexit in 2019, which arose following the government's abandonment of its programme motion.

Following a series of further debates, the first meaningful vote took place on 15 January 2019, giving rise to the largest governmental defeat since the establishment of universal suffrage. Following this defeat, Theresa May invited the opposition to table a motion of no confidence in the government, under the provisions of the Fixed-Term Parliaments Act 2011, a vote that the government won by 325 to 306 votes. The Commons went on to reject the Withdrawal Agreement on two further occasions, on the 12 and 29 March 2019. In addition to these votes, the Commons voted on a motion in neutral terms on 29 January, in favour of rejecting a no-deal exit from the European Union and for renegotiating the Northern Ireland backstop; voted against the government's statement on Europe on 14 February, and voted on 27 February in favour of the government seeking an extension to the Article 50 negotiation period (in contradiction of governmental policy), should the Commons fail to vote in favour of the Withdrawal Agreement on 12 March. Following a further vote against leaving with no deal, and a vote in favour of asking the EU for a further extension, the prime minister asked the European Union to extend the Article 50 negotiation period.

This, in and of itself, demonstrates the strength of the power of the Commons when united against a weak government on a key, yet divisive, issue. Section 13 also provided for a series of indicative votes, where the Commons voted on various options in response to the UK's exit from the European Union. However, these votes also show the difficulties that can arise when the Commons seeks to work together. Although there was a majority in the Commons that the UK should not leave the EU with no deal, there was no consensus as to the precise path the UK should take in its further negotiations with the EU on the Withdrawal Agreement. While the Commons may be better equipped to prevent governmental action, it is harder placed to direct action itself.

Nevertheless, 2019 also saw the House of Commons work together to provide clear direction to prevent leaving the EU with no deal and to require the government to seek an extension to the Article 50 process, with the enactment of two private members' bills which had cross-party support. As mentioned above, these private members' bills were enacted in a novel manner, neither through the ballot nor through the ten-minute rule. Rather, the first bill was able to pass due to a business motion proposed by Sir Oliver Letwin MP (Conservative) on 3 April 2019, which required the house to debate all three readings of the European Union (Withdrawal) (No 5) Bill 2019, proposed by Yvette Cooper MP (Labour) and himself on that date. Having succeeded in obtaining a majority in the Commons, the bill was then debated on that date, before being debated in the House of Lords, which proposed amendments to the bill that were accepted on 8 April 2019. The bill became the European Union (Withdrawal) Act 2019, which required the prime minister to propose a motion in the house seeking approval for an extension of the Article 50 negotiation period until a date of the prime minister's choosing.

The second private members' bill was enacted in September, following the announcement of the prime minister of his intention to prorogue Parliament from between 9 and 12 September until 14 October. The Commons returned from its summer recess on 3 September. On that date, Sir Oliver Letwin MP applied for an emergency debate under Standing Order No. 24, which proposed that the provisions of Standing Order No. 14, which prioritises governmental business, should not apply on 4 September, instead enabling all three stages of the European Union (Withdrawal) (No 6) Bill, proposed by, inter alia, Hilary Benn MP (Labour) and Alistair Burt MP (Conservative), to be passed through the House on that day. The use of Standing Order No. 24 in this novel manner was permitted by the Speaker, in spite of its previously being thought that Standing Order No. 24 could only be used for neutral motions. The Speaker disagreed with this interpretation of Standing Order No. 24B, enabling the motion to be tabled. Having obtained a majority in favour of the motion, the European Union (Withdrawal) (No 6) Bill 2019 passed through all three stages of Parliament in one day. The House of Lords also, after a long debate, agreed to modify the usual process of a bill through the house in order to expedite the bill's progress through the Lords. The bill received royal assent on 9 September; just prior to the prorogation of Parliament. The bill became the European Union (Withdrawal) (No 2) Act 2019, whose provisions required the prime minister to seek a further extension to the Article 50 period until 31 January 2020, unless the Commons voted either in favour of the Withdrawal Agreement, or to leave the EU with no deal, by 19 October 2019. An appendix to the Act set out the wording of the letter that the prime minister should send to the European Council. In spite of Parliament's sitting on a Saturday, neither vote was achieved and the prime minister, reluctantly, sent the letter requesting an extension as per the wording of the appendix, although this was not signed by the prime minister. It was accompanied by a signed letter from the prime minister explaining that this was not the policy of the government, which still wished to leave the EU on 31 October 2019, and a further letter from the British ambassador to the EU explaining that the letter had been sent to the European Council as per legislative instruction.

Both of these bills required an extraordinary combination of circumstances: a minority government; a key policy issue against a tight deadline that was outside the autonomous control of the government or Parliament; a creative use of standing orders; approval of this use by the Speaker; cross-party support in order to ensure sufficient votes to proposed business orders and support emergency debates; and sufficient votes in the Commons and the Lords in favour of legislation that was against the wishes of the government. They demonstrate the potential power of the Commons in these circumstances. However, although these events set a precedent, and could provide a further control over governmental action more generally, it is difficult to see how these events could repeat themselves in the near future. The backbenchers who rebelled were expelled from the Conservative party and either did not stand for election in December 2019, or failed to obtain a seat in Parliament. There is also now a large Conservative majority. Given the large risks involved, action of the house to curb the government is only likely to succeed in extreme circumstances. In 2019 this involved not only Brexit, but the unlawful prorogation of Parliament by Boris Johnson and the enactment of legislation to hold an early parliamentary general election. Only time will tell whether, these precedents having been set, they will be used again when the house feels it is necessary to challenge actions of the government.

9.4 Control and Scrutiny

We are reminded in a briefing paper of the Hansard Society (*House of Commons Reform* (2009)) that it is the constitutional obligation of MPs, individually and collectively, 'to scrutinise the executive, holding the government of the day to account on behalf of the public'. The effectiveness of parliamentary control and scrutiny of government depends much less on the formal powers of Parliament than on the recognition by governments of the authority of Parliament and their voluntary submission to the constraints of parliamentary government. In the view of some parliamentarians, successive governments have failed in these respects in their constitutional duty to Parliament. These discontents were expressed by Alan Beith (a Liberal Democrat) in the following motion in the House of Commons (HC Deb vol. 316, col 932, 21 July 1998):

> That this House, reiterating the importance of a strong parliamentary democracy in Britain, deplores the fact that successive governments have increasingly diluted the role of Parliament by making announcements to the media before making them to this House; by undermining the legitimate revising role of the House of Lords; by giving access to lobbyists at a time when the representations of elected Members are dealt with in an increasingly dilatory fashion; by inhibiting the rights of backbenchers to make criticisms of their own side; by encouraging planted supplementary questions which fail to hold the Executive to account; and by responding to questions and arguments with meaningless soundbites and partisan rhetoric instead of constructive answers.

Grounds for some of these strictures may appear later in this chapter. For the present, we may note that in the debate on Mr Beith's motion particular concern was expressed about governments' breaches of the principle, declared in the *Ministerial Code* (1997) (reaffirmed in subsequent editions, including 2019), that 'when Parliament is in session, the most important announcements of Government policy should be made, in the first instance, in Parliament.' The Speaker from time to time rebuked ministers for lapses in the observance of this convention (see, e.g., HC Deb vol. 306, col 565, 12 February 1998) but they continued to occur. In response to criticism in a report of the Public Administration Committee of the House of Commons, the government undertook to strengthen the provision of the *Code* on this point: see now the more precise requirements set out in paras 9.1–9.7 of the *Ministerial Code* (2019).

A more optimistic view than that expressed in Mr Beith's motion (above) has been taken by some observers, among them Philip Norton who discerned 'an improvement in the capacity of Parliament to subject government to scrutiny and to influence what government does' (in Pyper and Robins (eds.), *Governing the UK in the 1990s* (1995), p. 100). The same author placed emphasis on parliamentary procedure as a factor constraining government: all governments must operate *through* Parliament and its procedures (such as those relating to the passage of bills) present obstacles to arbitrary or unconsidered action by government. (See Norton, 'Playing by the Rules: The Constraining Hand of Parliamentary Procedure' (2001) 7 *Jnl Legislative Studies* 13.)

By way of contrast, developments in the organisation and working of central government (e.g., the creation of executive agencies, the accrual of power to the Prime Minister's Office and the Cabinet Office, the more prominent role of special advisers to ministers and the contracting out of governmental functions) present new challenges to parliamentary scrutiny. In the judgment of the Hansard Society Commission on Parliamentary Scrutiny (*The Challenge for Parliament: Making Government Accountable* (2001), p. 6), Parliament's:

> response to developments has been inadequate. It has failed to adapt sufficiently and remains, in many ways, the last unreformed part of the constitution. As a result Parliament is not effectively performing its core tasks of scrutinising and holding Government to account.

The Power Report (*Power to the People* (2006)) was persuaded of the inability of Parliament to control an executive which had acquired greatly enhanced power, concluding that 'the Executive in Britain is now more powerful in relation to Parliament than it has probably been since the time of Walpole ['the first Prime Minister' d. 1745]'. However, as Seaward and Silk remark (in Bogdanor (ed.), *The British Constitution in the Twentieth Century* (2003), p. 186), 'it is easy to overstress the growth in executive powers, and just as striking, over the course of the century, has been the survival of a belief in the importance of scrutiny and accountability, and the development of devices to assist that process.'

(See, generally, Tomkins, 'What Is Parliament For?', in Bamforth and Leyland (eds.), *Public Law in a Multi-layered Constitution* (2003), ch. 3; Giddings (ed.), *The Future of Parliament* (2005); Brazier et al., *New Politics, New Parliament?* (2005); Finch and Oppenheim (eds.), *A Future for Politics* (2009); Hansard Society, *The Reform Challenge* (2010); Wright, 'What Are MPs For? (2010) 81 *Pol Q* 298.)

9.4.1 Policy and Administration

9.4.1.1 Debates

The main contest between the parties takes place in debates on the floor of the house. Battle is joined on such general issues as unemployment, immigration or the government's expenditure plans, or debate may focus on specific governmental decisions such as the closure of a hospital, the deportation of a non-British resident or the sale of arms to a foreign government.

Each session begins with a debate on the address in reply to the Queen's Speech, continuing over some five or six days, which allows for challenges by the opposition to the government's legislative programme. Debates are held in every session on certain matters, such as budget proposals, foreign affairs, reports of the Public Accounts Committee and developments in the EU. Debates on policy and administration initiated by the government, opposition parties and backbenchers continue throughout the session, interspersed with debates on legislation and other business of the house. Debates on particular subjects may be arranged through 'the usual channels' or – on the days allotted for backbench business in the house – determined by the Backbench Business Committee (above). As an exercise in 'control', debates are most effective when governmental proposals are presented to the house, possibly in a Green Paper, before they have become firm, as a test of parliamentary and public opinion.

Since what is said in a debate on the floor of the house rarely affects the result of the vote at its end or induces the government to reverse a decision already taken, it is apparent that debates are not a strong instrument of control. But they are an essential part of the continuous parliamentary scrutiny of government, compelling it to explain and defend its policies and decisions.

Philip Norton, *The Commons in Perspective* (1981), p. 119

[G]eneral debates are . . . not without some uses in helping to ensure a measure of scrutiny and influence, however limited. A debate prevents a Government from remaining mute. Ministers have to explain and justify the Government's position. They may want to reveal as little as possible, but the Government cannot afford to hold back too much for fear of letting the Opposition appear to have the better argument. The involvement of Opposition spokesmen and backbenchers ensures that any perceived cracks in the Government's position will be exploited. If it has failed to carry its own side privately, the Government may suffer the embarrassment of the publicly expressed dissent of some of its own supporters, dissent which provides good copy for the press. On some occasions, Ministers may even be influenced by comments made in debate. They will not necessarily approach an issue with closed minds, and will normally not wish to be totally unreceptive to the comments of the Opposition (whose co-operation they need for the efficient despatch of business) or of their own Members (whose support they need in the lobbies, and among whom morale needs to be maintained); a Minister who creates a good impression by listening attentively to views expressed by Members may enhance his own prospects of advancement . . . A Minister faced by a baying Opposition and silence behind him may be unnerved and realise that he is not carrying Members on either side with him, and in consequence may moderate or even, in extreme cases, reverse his position.

(See also Adonis, *Parliament Today* (2nd edn. 1993), pp. 142–8; and, for a sceptical view, Weir and Beetham, *Political Power and Democratic Control in Britain* (1999), pp. 382–4.)

Adjournment debates initiated by backbenchers on local or narrow issues of administration may take place in an almost empty house and attract no publicity, but a minister is obliged to attend and answer what is not always a skilfully presented case. If the minister is not often persuaded to change his or her mind, the debate may serve at least to bring into the open the way in which a decision was reached. The Backbench Business Committee considers applications for debates on sitting Tuesdays at 2:30pm. These debates take place on days allotted to the backbenches by the government, or can also take place in Westminster Hall. Westminster Hall is also used for debates raised through e-petitions.

Foster and Plowden have noted – and deplored – a recent decline in the significance and value of debates in the House of Commons, which these authors find to be no longer central to the parliamentary process or, as they formerly were, 'a stringent check on ministerial misbehaviour'. A factor in this trend has been, they say, 'the catastrophic decline in the attention the media give to parliamentary debates, precipitous since 1992' (*The State under Stress* (1996), pp. 203–4), and they call for a revival of 'the great tradition of parliamentary debate' on important issues (at p. 238). 'The main arena of British political debate', says Peter Riddell, 'is now the broadcasting studio rather than the chamber of the House of Commons' (*Parliament under Blair* (2000), p. 160). Our media culture is not, on the whole, of the reflective, analytical kind that might focus attention on Parliament and help to revitalise debate in the house. Despite consistent criticism of debate – particularly in the light of debates on Brexit – very little has changed. Reforms would appear to require a change in culture and not merely a modification of parliamentary rules.

9.4.1.2 Questions

The House of Commons Procedure Committee declared in its *3rd Report of 2001–02* (HC 622, para 1):

> The right of Members of the House of Commons to ask questions of Ministers, to seek information or to press for action, is an essential part of the process by which Parliament exercises its authority and holds the Government to account.

Any MP (other than a minister or, by convention, the leader of the opposition) may ask questions of ministers by giving notice to the Table Office. If an oral answer in the house is required, the question is marked with an asterisk; other questions are given a written answer. Since 2007, question time in the house has been divided into two, so that in addition to tabled questions, time is set aside for open, 'topical' questions on any subject within the minister's responsibilities.

Questions to ministers 'should relate to the public affairs with which they are officially connected, to proceedings pending in Parliament, or to matters of administration for which they are responsible' Erskine May, *Parliamentary Practice*, (25th edn., 2019) para 22.9. The requirement that a question must relate to matters with which they are connected or for which they are responsible to Parliament will generally exclude questions about matters within the competence of the devolved institutions in Scotland, Wales and Northern Ireland. Likewise out of order are questions about the activities of local authorities, the European Commission, privatised industries, NDPBs and the police. For instance, when the Home Secretary was asked a series of questions with reference to a demonstration by Tamils in Parliament Square about the number of people arrested or charged, the cost of policing the demonstration and the number of police officers involved, a Home Office minister replied on behalf of the Secretary of State: 'The Home Office does not hold this information. These are operational matters for the Commissioner of the Metropolitan Police' (HC Deb vol. 492, cols 270–1 W, 6 May 2009). Ministers can, however, be asked about the exercise of any powers they may have in respect of such bodies – for instance, powers of appointment, or to give directions, issue guidance, approve expenditure or call for reports.

Questions relating to the day-to-day operations of an executive agency are referred by the minister to the agency chief executive for reply by letter, which is placed in the library of the house, but a member who is dissatisfied with the reply given may raise the matter again with the minister. (Ministers also sometimes deal in this way with questions about NDPBs.)

A minister is not compellable to answer any question, and there are many matters on which ministers customarily refuse to give answers. Among these are confidential exchanges with foreign governments, matters affecting national security, surveillance and telephone interception operations, proceedings in cabinet and ministerial committees, internal discussion and advice, matters that are sub judice, commercial confidences and confidential information about individual persons and companies. Information requested may be refused on the grounds that it is not available or could only be obtained at disproportionate cost. Departments apply a general rule that a cost exceeding a certain sum justifies refusal to give a written answer. All these are matters of ministerial practice, not of parliamentary convention.

Although ministers cannot be compelled to answer questions fully or, indeed, at all, they are required by the house in terms of its resolution of 19 March 1997 (above, p. 574), as reaffirmed in para 1.3d of the *Ministerial Code* (2019), to be:

> as open as possible with Parliament and the public, refusing to provide information only when disclosure would not be in the public interest which should be decided in accordance with the relevant statutes and the Freedom of Information Act 2000.

The government agreed in 1996 that if ministers refused to provide a full answer to a parliamentary question, otherwise than on the ground of disproportionate cost, they should give reasons that related to the exemptions allowed then by the Code of Practice on Access to Government Information. (The undertaking was not always faithfully observed.) The Code of Practice has since been superseded by the Freedom of Information Act 2000. The government's *Guidance to Officials on Drafting Answers to Parliamentary Questions* now states:

> If you conclude that material information must be withheld and the PQ cannot be fully answered as a result, draft an answer which makes this clear and explains the reasons, such as disproportionate cost or the information not being available, or explains in terms similar

> to those in the Freedom of Information Act (without resorting to explicit reference to the Act itself or to section numbers) the reason for the refusal. For example, 'The release of this information would prejudice commercial interests'. Take care to avoid draft answers which are literally true but likely to give rise to misleading inferences.

A member who is refused an answer may raise the matter in an adjournment debate or ask the question again (but only after an interval of three months, unless circumstances have changed). Another recourse for a member who is refused an answer or is dissatisfied with the answer given is to write to the department concerned with a request for the information. This brings the matter within the scope of the Freedom of Information Act and may entitle the member to obtain the information in accordance with the provisions of that Act.

Draft answers to questions are prepared for ministers by officials. The government's *Guidance to Officials on Drafting Answers to Parliamentary Questions* reminds officials that 'It is of paramount importance that Ministers give accurate and truthful information to Parliament' and should be 'as open as possible with Parliament and the public, refusing to provide information only when disclosure would not be in the public interest'. It continues:

> It is a civil servant's responsibility to Ministers to help them fulfil those obligations. It is the Minister's right and responsibility to decide how to do so. Ministers want to explain and present Government policy and actions in a positive light. Ministers will rightly expect a draft answer that does full justice to the Government's position.

Officials are admonished not to 'omit information sought merely because disclosure could lead to political embarrassment or administrative inconvenience'.

The Procedure Committee of the House of Commons monitors the performance of government departments in answering questions and in reporting its conclusions annually to Parliament may draw attention to failures in openness and accuracy in answers given. (see Hough [2003] *PL* 211). The committee produced a report in 2013, (Monitoring Written Parliamentary Questions, 7th Report of Session 2012–13), which concluded that:

> Written Parliamentary questions are a vital tool for the accountability of Government. The effectiveness of this form of accountability depends on Members receiving answers which are both timely and which respond adequately and appropriately to the question which has been asked. As the committee charged with considering the practice and procedure of the House in the conduct of public business, we have a central role in ensuring the

continued accountability of Government to this House. The task which we have taken on as the recipients of complaints about inadequate and late answers, and in assessing the performance of departments in the timeliness of answering PQs, is an important addition to our role in ensuring accountability. We will continue to discharge it rigorously and in full acknowledgement that good scrutiny contributes to good government. We look forward to making further reports to the House on the discharge of this aspect of our responsibilities.

In its most recent report, on the 2016–17 session, the committee noted with approval that nine out of ten written questions received an answer within five sitting days, as well as noting an upward trend in questions. The committee also proposed to undertake an evaluation of the quality of answers provided in the 2018 session onwards. (*Written Parliamentary Questions: Progress Report for Session 2016–17, Monitoring in the 2017 Parliament and Electronic Tabling Second Report 2017–19*, HC 661).

Written answers are given to 'unstarred' questions and also to questions put down for oral answer that are not reached in the time allotted on the floor of the house. (Over 50,000 questions were tabled for written answer in the year after the 2017 Queen's Speech, and over 39,000 questions were tabled in the 2016–17 session of Parliament.) A considerable amount of information is elicited from the government in written answers. A member may put down any number of unstarred questions (whereas a member may not have more than two oral questions tabled on any one day) and can coordinate his or her questions to different departments so that a picture is built up of the government's whole operations in the area in question.

Questions for oral answer are taken for about an hour on Mondays, Tuesdays, Wednesdays and Thursdays. Ministers answer in accordance with a rota that is customarily arranged after consultation through the usual channels, more time being set aside for the major (or most controversial) departments. In addition, 'cross-cutting' questions, covering the responsibilities of a number of departments, can be asked in the 'parallel chamber' of Westminster Hall. On any day, the speaker may give permission, in a case of urgency or an important unexpected event, for an urgent question, which has not been tabled, to be answered on the same day by the responsible minister. (The former Speaker, John Bercow, demonstrated a greater readiness to allow urgent questions. It remains to be seen whether this will continue with the appointment of the new Speaker, Lindsay Hoyle.) The prime minister answers questions for thirty minutes on Wednesdays.

A member who receives an oral answer can go on to ask a supplementary question, of which no prior notice need have been given, and other members may put supplementaries if they catch the Speaker's eye. The leader of the opposition has the right to question the prime minister through supplementaries, and regularly engages in gladiatorial combat with the prime minister on Wednesdays.

Among questions to the prime minister, who accepts a responsibility to answer for the whole range of governmental activities, are 'open questions', which are designed not to reveal the subject matter of the supplementary question that will follow. This allows the MP to raise a supplementary that is topical on the day when the question comes up for answer and also provides an element of surprise. The inscrutable character of open questions ensures that they will not be transferred to other, more directly responsible, ministers, which might happen if the real purport of the question were apparent on its face.

House of Commons, HC Deb vol. 666, col 958–9, 23 October 2019

Dr Rupa Huq (Ealing Central and Acton) (Labour) asked the Prime Minister if he would list his official engagements for Wednesday 23 October.

The Prime Minister (Boris Johnson): The whole House will be shocked by the appalling news that 39 bodies have been discovered in a lorry container in Essex. This is an unimaginable and truly heartbreaking tragedy, and I know that the thoughts and prayers of all Members are with those who lost their lives and their loved ones. I am receiving regular updates. The Home Office will work closely with Essex police to establish exactly what happened, and my right hon. Friend the Home Secretary will make an oral statement immediately after this Question Time.

This morning, I had meeting with ministerial colleagues and others. In addition to my duties in this House, I shall have further such meetings later today.

Dr Huq: I completely associate myself with the Prime Minister's remarks about the tragedy in Essex – I do not normally do that, but on this occasion I am completely with him.

It is good to see the Prime Minister at Prime Minister's Question Time. Until today, I think he had only ever done one – in 100 days. We all know that he has a long list of shortcomings, so could he – *[Interruption.]* Will he do something about one that he does have some control over and get rid of Dominic Cummings?

It will be evident that the purpose of this supplementary question was not to obtain information. While supplementaries may have the object of challenging government policies, some are 'planted' by the government side to elicit a politically favourable response. In any event, it may be questioned whether the kind of point-scoring duel typically arising from open questions contributes anything to the accountability of government.

In the 2016–17 parliamentary session, 4,422 questions were tabled for oral answer by ministers, of which 3,362 were answered in the house. There were 34,711 questions tabled for written answer (*Sessional Returns 2016–17*).

Questions put by backbenchers on the government side may reflect their constituency and other interests or their unease about aspects of government policy, and in this way they play their part in the scrutiny of ministers. Government backbenchers may also table questions with the object of balancing hostile questions asked by opposition members. On one occasion, it came to light that civil servants had assisted ministers in the preparation of a 'bank' of favourable questions to be supplied to sympathetic backbenchers. A select committee that considered this incident advised (*Report from the Select Committee on Parliamentary Questions*, HC 393 of 1971–72, para 36):

> it is not the role of the Government machine to seek to redress the party balance of Questions on the Order Paper, and civil servants should not in future be asked to prepare Questions which have this object.

The government agreed to lay down a new rule in accordance with this recommendation (HC Deb vol. 847, cols 462–3 W, 6 December 1972).

Select Committee on Procedure, *3rd Report of 1990–91*, HC 178

In evidence to the committee, the principal clerk of the Table Office outlined the purposes of parliamentary questions, whether oral or written:

> (a) a vehicle for individual backbenchers to raise the individual grievance of their constituencies;
> (b) an opportunity for the House as a whole to probe the detailed actions of the Executive;
> (c) a means of illuminating differences of policy on major issues between the various political parties, or of judging the parliamentary skills of individual Members on both sides of the House;
> (d) a combination of these or any other purposes, for example a way of enabling the Government to disseminate information about particular policy decisions. [Standing orders now make provision for written ministerial statements and policy announcements are expected to be made in this way rather than in answer to ministerially inspired questions.]

The committee said in its report that there should be added to these 'the obtaining of information by the House from the Government and its subsequent publication'. The report continued (para 27):

> [T]he relative prominence assumed by the different purposes of parliamentary questions has tended to vary from one era to another. This is especially true of oral questions, which, certainly so far as the main Departments are concerned, have taken on a markedly more partisan aspect over recent decades, especially perhaps since the late 1960s. The notion that an oral question is designed as a genuine enquiry to obtain factual information belongs – sadly, some might say – to a growing extent in the past. Increasingly, in recent Parliaments, questions have become vehicles for supplementaries aimed at establishing a specific political point as part of the ideological clash between the parties. Indeed, it is often

> claimed that very few Members now table an oral question unless they already know the
> likely answer.

The committee noted other strands of question time that had been emphasised in evidence to it, 'notably the raising of constituency matters and the pursuit of campaigns on issues that either cut across party lines or which do not have a strong ideological content'. In any event, the committee did not believe that parliamentary accountability was 'incompatible with the increased use of Question Time for the exposure of policy differences between the parties'.

(See, further, Procedure Committee, *Parliamentary Questions*, HC 622 of 2001–02 and *Government Response* (Cm 5628/2002); Hough, 'Ministerial Responses to Parliamentary Questions: Some Recent Concerns' [2003] *PL* 211; Giddings and Irwin, 'Objects and Questions', in Giddings (ed.), *The Future of Parliament* (2005); Procedure Committee of the House of Commons, *Monitoring Written Parliamentary Questions 7th Report 2012–13* HC1095).

9.4.1.3 Select Committees

Besides ad hoc committees set up from time to time for particular investigations, the House of Commons has some thirty select committees that are appointed each session in accordance with standing orders. They include the Committee on Standards and Privileges, whose predecessor, the Committee of Privileges, dates from the seventeenth century, the Committee of Public Accounts, first set up in 1861, and such more recent creations as the Environmental Audit Committee and the Select Committees on Public Administration and Constitutional Affairs and Regulatory Reform. Select committees may also be formed in response to specific requirements – for example, the Select Committee on Exiting the European Union. Not all of these committees are concerned with the control or scrutiny of the executive, but this is the essential function of the select committees established in 1979 'to examine the expenditure, administration and policy' of the principal government departments and the public bodies associated with them.

Governments have not always regarded the establishment of select committees that can question their policies and investigate the details of administration with enthusiasm. The 'departmentally related' select committees set up in 1979 owe their existence to backbench pressure and the persistence of a reform-minded Minister and Leader of the House, Mr St John-Stevas, just as an earlier, more limited experiment with specialist committees is associated with Mr Richard Crossman, Leader of the House from 1966 to 1968. The committees established in the 1966–70 Parliament – on agriculture, science and technology, education and science, race relations and immigration, Scottish affairs, and overseas aid – did some useful work but were at first regarded with scepticism by many MPs and with suspicion by the government, which tried to influence the selection of members and the choice of subjects to be investigated. The Committee on Agriculture, which showed a particular independence of spirit, was soon wound up. It became evident that too great an assertiveness by the committees would result in counter-measures by the government – a reminder that the traditions of British parliamentary government do not easily accommodate rival institutions that will 'balance' the power of the executive.

Nevertheless, it was increasingly realised by backbenchers that in select committees they could take part in a concerted and informed scrutiny of the administration that was more effective than their sporadic efforts on the floor of the house. The system developed in a rather piecemeal way until in 1978 the Procedure Committee recommended a new structure of committees that 'would cover the activities of all departments of the United Kingdom Government, and of all nationalised industries and other quasi-autonomous governmental organisations' (*1st Report of 1977–78*, HC 588, para 5.22). The new departmentally related committees were established on a firm footing in the standing orders of the house in 1979. In the 2017–19 parliament there were nineteen of these committees, each of them 'shadowing' one or more government departments and their associated bodies: business, energy and industrial strategy; culture, media and sport; defence; digital, education, environment; food and rural affairs; exiting the European Union; foreign affairs; health and social care; home affairs; housing, communities and local government; international development; international trade; justice; Northern Ireland affairs; Scottish affairs; transport; Treasury; Welsh affairs; work and pensions.

If it is to keep the work of a department and its satellite public bodies under effective review, a committee may need to appoint a sub-committee to carry out simultaneous inquiries. A committee may meet concurrently with any other committee of *either* house and committees may make available to each other evidence taken by them in the course of their inquiries. From 1999, four Commons committees – those for defence, foreign affairs, international development and trade and industry – worked together in scrutinising the government's policy on strategic export controls: in acknowledging the work of this 'quadripartite committee', a Foreign Office minister paid it the compliment of having 'given the government so much trouble' in its 'detailed and expert analysis' (HC Deb vol. 359, col 32WH, 14 December 2000; see, further, Yihdego (2008) 61 *Parl Aff* 662). The four committees – now defence; foreign affairs; international development; and international trade – continue this scrutiny and are known collectively as the Committees on Arms Export Controls.

The standard number of members of a 'departmental' (departmentally related) committee is eleven, although the Northern Ireland Committee has a maximum membership of thirteen. In the 2017–19 session, the Exiting the European Union Committee had a membership of twenty one. Since 1979, members have been appointed on the nomination of an all-party Committee of

Selection, which would have regard to the balance of parties in the house. In practice, however, government and opposition whips exercised a covert and decisive influence, as has been seen from time to time when backbenchers of independent spirit have been deprived of their places on select committees. When two Labour MPs were excluded from, respectively, the Foreign Affairs Committee and the Transport, Local Government and the Regions Committee, seemingly for the vigour with which they had performed their function of critical scrutiny, the House of Commons delivered a rare cross-party rebuke to the government in voting to restore the two members to their places on the committees. (See HC Deb vol. 372, cols 35 et seq., 16 July 2001; vol. 372, cols 508 et seq., 19 July 2001.)

A House of Commons committee declared it to be 'wrong in principle that party managers should exercise effective control of select committee membership' (Liaison Committee, *1st Report of 1999–2000*, HC 300, para 13). The government initially disfavoured any change in the system of nomination (see the government's *Response*, Cm 4737/2000) but a new Leader of the House (Mr Robin Cook) proved more flexible and the matter was considered afresh by the Modernisation Committee, chaired by the Leader of the house. In its *1st Report of 2001–02*, HC 224, that committee proposed that nominations to all select committees should be placed 'in the hands of an independent authoritative body', a new Committee of Nomination, which would 'command the confidence of the House on both sides'. When the matter came before the house for decision, MPs were not persuaded of the case for such a committee, which, it was objected, would assume powers belonging properly to the parties in Parliament and the house as a whole. The influence of the whips may perhaps be discerned in this outcome. (See HC Deb vol. 385, cols 648 et seq., 13 May 2002.)

Reform-minded MPs continued to campaign for a new system of election to select committees, and a House of Commons Reform Committee (*Rebuilding the House*, HC 1117 of 2008–09) insisted that 'It should be for the House and not for the Executive to choose which of its Members should scrutinise the Executive.' It recommended that the chairs of departmental select committees – and also of some comparable select committees such as the Public Administration Committee and the Committee of Public Accounts – should be elected by the whole house and further that the members of those committees should be elected by secret ballot of members of each political party in the house, in accordance with an agreed division of seats between the parties on each committee. (A majority of the members of each committee belong to the party or parties in government.) The proposed reform was implemented, as regards the committee chairs, by new Standing Order No. 122B. Chairs are allocated to the parties in proportion to their representation in the house and their election by the house now takes place by secret ballot. (The Committee of Public Accounts is always to be chaired by a member of the official opposition.) The Reform Committee's recommendation that members of select committees should be elected by parties in a secret ballot was endorsed in a resolution of the House on 4 March 2010 (HC Deb vol. 506, col 1095).

The departmental select committees are the preserve of backbenchers: front-bench spokespersons for government and opposition are not appointed to them. Committee chairs serve on a Liaison Committee, which coordinates the work of select committees and makes representations on their behalf (on staffing, powers, etc.) to the house. The Liaison Committee's report, *Shifting the Balance* (HC 300 of 1999–2000), assessed the effectiveness of the departmental and other scrutinising committees, and proposed reforms for strengthening them in their task of holding the executive to account. Few of the recommendations were implemented and the committee expressed disappointment with the government's response (*Shifting the Balance: Unfinished Business*, HC 321-I of 2000–01). The project was resumed by the Modernisation Committee under its reform-minded chairman and Leader of the House, Mr Robin Cook. Its *1st Report of 2001–02* (above) made twenty-two recommendations for enabling select committees to perform their task of scrutiny more effectively. The proposed reforms included additional staff and resources for committees, an alternative parliamentary career structure devoted to scrutiny, with salaries for committee chairs, and a clear definition of committees' common objectives. These proposals were approved by the House of Commons on 14 May 2002 (HC Deb vol. 385, cols 648 et seq.). Following this resolution, the Commons Liaison Committee defined the 'core tasks' of select committees with a role in holding the government to account: these committees, it is said, 'now provide the central scrutiny agenda for the accountability of ministers and their departments to Parliament' (*Annual Report of the Liaison Committee for 2004*, HC 419 of 2004–05). These core tasks were refreshed in 2012, which included a recommendation that select committees should report their performance against these objectives at the end of each session (*Select Committee Effectiveness, Resources and Powers*, 2nd Report of Session 2012–13, HC 697 of 2012–13). The primary purpose of select committees is 'to examine the expenditure, administration and policy of the principal government departments … and associated public bodies' (House of Commons Liaison Committee *The Effectiveness and Influence of the Select Committee System*, Fourth Report 2017–19, HC 186, p. 17).

The core tasks, endorsed by the House in 2013, are set out as follows, in guidance to each committee.

Overall aim: To hold Ministers and Departments to account for their policy and decision-making and to support the House in its control of the supply of public money and scrutiny of legislation

Strategy: Examine the strategy of the department, how it has identified its key objectives and priorities and whether it has the means to achieve them, in terms of plans, resources, skills, capabilities and management information

Policy: Examine policy proposals by the department, and areas of emerging policy, or where existing policy is deficient, and make proposals

Expenditure and Performance: Examine the expenditure plans, outturn and performance of the department and its arm's length bodies, and the relationships between spending and delivery of outcomes

Draft Bills: Conduct scrutiny of draft bills within the committee's responsibilities

Bills and Delegated Legislation: Assist the House in its consideration of bills and statutory instruments, including draft orders under the Public Bodies Act

Post-Legislative Scrutiny: Examine the implementation of legislation and scrutinise the department's post-legislative assessments

European Scrutiny: Scrutinise policy developments at the European level and EU legislative proposals

Appointments: Scrutinise major appointments made by the department and to hold pre-appointment hearings where appropriate

Support for the House: Produce timely reports to inform debate in the House, including Westminster Hall, or debating committees, and to examine petitions tabled

Public Engagement: Assist the House of Commons in better engaging with the public by ensuring that the work of the committee is accessible to the public

In its most recent report, the Liaison Committee recommended a modification to these tasks, both to reduce the number of tasks and to include a section setting out how committees should deliver these tasks. It also recommended a modification to Standing Order No. 152 in order to clarify that select committees can investigate the actions of bodies associated to ministries (*The Effectiveness and Influence of the Select Committee System, Fourth Report 2017–19*, HC 186, ch. 2).

Each of the departmental committees has power 'to send for persons, papers and records'. This formal power is rarely exercised, the committees preferring to proceed by invitation rather than command, but some initial refusals to appear or provide evidence have led to the service of formal orders by the serjeant-at-arms. The committees cannot themselves enforce their orders, but a refusal to comply could be reported to the house, which might treat the refusal as a contempt. Members of neither house can be compelled to attend by the select committee, although by convention ministers do attend and, for the most part, this is adhered to. MPs and ministers may be ordered to attend select committees or produce documents only by the house itself. (See Leopold [1992] *PL* 541; Blackburn and Kennon, *Griffith and Ryle on Parliament* (2nd edn. 2003), paras 11–095–11–101.)

The Leader of the House of Commons gave the following assurance on behalf of the government on 25 June 1979 (HC Deb vol. 969, col 45):

> There need be no fear that departmental Ministers will refuse to attend Committees to answer questions about their Departments or that they will not make every effort to ensure that the fullest possible information is made available to them.
>
> I give the House the pledge on the part of the Government that every Minister from the most senior Cabinet Minister to the most junior Under-Secretary will do all in his or her power to co-operate with the new system of Committees and to make it a success.

These undertakings have been renewed subsequently and *in general* have been honoured by ministers – although *former* ministers have refused to give evidence to committees (Baroness Thatcher in 1994 in the Foreign Affairs Committee's inquiry into the Pergau Dam affair) or have attended reluctantly after initial refusal (Mrs Edwina Currie in 1989 in the Agriculture Committee's inquiry into salmonella in eggs). In 2002, the Transport, Local Government and the Regions Committee expressed its dissatisfaction that no Treasury minister or official had consented to appear before it to answer questions about rail franchising or funding proposals for London Underground, although the Treasury had been closely involved in decisions taken. The Treasury, it said, 'is ever more powerful and influential but is unwilling to be fully accountable' to the scrutinising committees (Liaison Committee, *1st Report of 2001–02*, HC 590, Appendix R, para 8; see also Transport, Local Government and the Regions Committee, *1st Special Report of 2001–02*, HC 771). In 2009, the JCHR, in examining allegations of UK complicity in torture, complained that ministers had refused to give oral evidence to the committee and had provided only partial answers to requests for information. The committee concluded that ministers had been determined to avoid parliamentary scrutiny and accountability on these matters (*23rd Report of 2008–09*, HL 152, HC 230; see also the government's *Reply*, Cm 7714/2009). Successive prime ministers consistently refused to appear before select committees until, in April 2002, Mr Blair announced that he would, in future, submit to questioning by the Liaison Committee at least once every six months, and this practice has been followed by his successors. (It is a noteworthy feature of our unwritten constitution that the terms on which ministers answer to Parliament can sometimes be a matter for unilateral decision by the prime minister.)

Other ministers, as well as civil servants and special advisers, appear frequently before the departmental committees, are questioned at length and in detail, and are usually helpful to the committees in their inquiries. Committees may summon named civil servants to appear before them and the government acknowledges a presumption that a request for attendance of a particular official will be agreed to, but this is subject to the right of ministers 'to decide which official or officials should represent them' (*Departmental Evidence and Response to Select Committees*, below, paras 43–4). Moreover, 'Civil servants who give evidence to Select Committees do so on behalf of their Ministers and under their directions' (para 40) and so may be instructed not to answer particular questions or disclose certain information. In 1984 the government declined to allow the director of GCHQ and a trade union official employed there to give evidence to the Select Committee on Employment, which was inquiring into a ban on trade union membership at GCHQ (see Employment Committee, *1st Report of 1983–84*, HC 238). In the course of its inquiry into the Westland affair (above, pp. 483–484) in 1986, the Defence Committee wished to question five officials about their conduct in the affair, but ministers refused to allow them to attend. The committee criticised this refusal as an evasion of accountability to Parliament and was supported in this by the Treasury and Civil Service Committee: see Defence Committee, *4th Report of 1985–86*, HC 519; and Treasury and Civil Service Committee, *7th Report of 1985–86*, HC 92. The government said in its reply that it did not believe 'that a Select Committee is a suitable instrument for inquiring into or passing judgement upon the actions or conduct of an individual civil servant' (*Westland plc* (Cmnd 9916/1986), para 44). Guidelines subsequently issued to civil servants insist that questions by select committees about the conduct of individual officials (raising the possibility of criticism or blame) should not be answered by civil servants: it is the responsibility of the minister to make any necessary inquiry and then to inform the committee of what happened and of any corrective action taken. (See *Departmental Evidence and Response to Select Committees*, below, paras 73–8.) In the Trade and Industry Committee's Arms Exports to Iraq inquiry, the government refused to assist the committee in facilitating the giving of evidence by two retired officials, on the grounds that they would not have access to departmental papers and could not give evidence on behalf of ministers (*2nd Report of 1991–92*, HC 86; see, further, Weir and Beetham, *Political Power and Democratic Control in Britain* (1999), pp. 412–13; and Erskine May, *Parliamentary Practice* (22nd edn. 1997), pp. 760–1).

Some categories of information are withheld from select committees. The criteria to be applied by officials are set out in the so-called 'Osmotherly Rules' (formerly entitled a *Memorandum of Guidance for Officials Appearing before Select Committees*) of which the 1980 edition was issued by an official of that name. The guidance has since been revised from time to time and has become less restrictive in recent editions. It is now entitled 'Giving Evidence to Select Committees: Guidance for Civil Servants' https://assets.publishing.service.gov.uk/government/uploads/system/uploads/attachment_data/file/364600/Osmotherly_Rules_October_2014.pdf). It states (para 53) as its 'central principle' that officials should be as forthcoming and helpful as possible to select committees, and that any withholding of information 'should be decided in accordance with the law and care should be taken to ensure that no information is withheld which would not be exempted if a parallel request were made under the FOI [Freedom of Information] Act'. Information is not to be disclosed, for instance, if it relates to national security or would be likely to cause harm to defence, international relations or the economy, or if it concerns the private affairs of individuals or was supplied to the government in confidence. As regards the discussion of government policy, the guidance states (para 33):

> Officials should as far as possible confine their evidence to questions of fact and explanation relating to government policies and actions. They should be ready to explain what those policies are; the justification and objectives of those policies as the Government sees them; the extent to which those objectives have been met; and also to explain how administrative factors may have affected both the choice of policy measures and the manner of their implementation. Any comment by officials on government policies and actions should always be consistent with the principle of civil service political impartiality. Officials should as far as possible avoid being drawn into discussion of the merits of alternative policies, including their advice to Ministers. If official witnesses are pressed by the Committee to go beyond these limits, they should make clear to the Committee that they are unable to answer the questions as the line of questioning is for the relevant Minister and that they are not authorised by their Minister to go any further. Select Committees should respect this position and it is then for the Committee to decide whether to request the Minister to provide the evidence.

In a memorandum provided to the Liaison Committee by the clerks to the committee in 2004 it is said:

> At least since the 1970s, there has been a continuing struggle between committees and successive Governments to establish a modus operandi on attendance by civil servants. The Government's position is set out in the so called Osmotherly rules. These have, however, never been approved by the House, which asserts that it is not for Ministers unilaterally to abridge or fetter its powers to call evidence. On the other hand, political reality implies that these powers cannot be enforced against the wishes of a Government with a majority in the House. The resulting agreement to disagree, on this point, together with undertakings by Government, most notably set out in the Resolution of 19 March 1997 [above, p 574], have created informal conventions which normally enable committees to carry out their work without major hindrance. However, periodically there are refusals of cooperation over particular Government witnesses.

Various instances of difficulty experienced by committees in securing information or the attendance of witnesses have been recounted by the Liaison Committee (see, e.g., *Shifting the Balance: Unfinished Business*, HC 321 of 2000–01, paras 118–26). However, in its most recent report, the committee reported that, although there had been some continuing struggles, there had been no irresolvable disputes over civil servants giving evidence since this issue was last discussed in 2014 (House of Commons Liaison Committee *The Effectiveness and Influence of the Select Committee System Fourth Report*

2017–19, HC 186, p. 70). When the government refused in 1998 to provide the Foreign Affairs Committee with copies of telegrams received at the Foreign Office relating to breaches of an embargo on the supply of arms to Sierra Leone, the committee asked that the matter be debated in the house: Foreign Affairs Committee, *1st Special Report of 1997–98*, HC 760 and *2nd Special Report of 1997–98*, HC 852. The issue between the government and the committee was not yet resolved when it was raised for debate on an opposition motion. The motion was defeated, the government having affirmed its readiness to provide the committee with a summary of the telegrams on a confidential basis: HC Deb vol. 315, cols 865 et seq., 7 July 1998. In 2003, the Foreign Affairs Committee, in its report on *The Decision to Go to War in Iraq*, was 'strongly of the view that we were entitled to a greater degree of co-operation from the Government on access to witnesses and to intelligence material'. It regarded the government's 'refusal to grant us access to evidence essential to our inquiries as a failure of accountability to Parliament' (*9th Report of 2002–03*, HC 813; see also the committee's *2nd Report of 2005–06*, HC 522).

The relative weakness of select committees (despite their formal power to send for persons, papers and records) in the face of a refusal to produce documents has been contrasted with the experience of the (non-statutory) Hutton Inquiry into the Circumstances Surrounding the Death of David Kelly CMG (HC 247 of 2003–04), which was able to secure production of all the documents that it required, some of which had been denied to the Foreign Affairs Committee. (See the Memorandum to the Liaison Committee by the clerks to the committee, cited above; Foreign Affairs Committee, *1st Special Report of 2003–04*, HC 440, paras 9–12; *Annual Report of the Liaison Committee for 2003*, HC 446 of 2003–04, paras 87–91.) In its *Annual Report for 2004*, HC 419 of 2004–05, the Liaison Committee was encouraged by the new assurance, now found in para 40 of 'Giving Evidence to Select Committees: Guidance for Civil Servants' that 'the presumption is that requests for information from Select Committees will be agreed to'. This has heralded a greater readiness to cooperate with the committees. Recent reports of the Liaison Committee have confirmed that, in general, the committees have been able to maintain positive working relationships with the departments: see, *The Effectiveness and Influence of the Committee System Fourth Report 2017–19*, HC 1860.

However, difficulties have arisen where private individuals have refused to appear before committees to give evidence. This has become an issue as committees have begun to take on the role of scrutinizing the performance of private individuals who exercise power in society, in addition to carrying out inquiries on matters of public interest falling in the sphere of the department that the committee shadows. In 2016, the house resolved to admonish two employees of News International for contempt after they had deliberately misled the Culture, Media and Sport Committee about their knowledge of phone-hacking. In 2018, the house ordered Mr Dominic Cummings to attend a meeting of the Digital, Culture, Media and Sport Committee after he had refused to comply with an order of the committee to attend a meeting. Mr Cummings still failed to attend, leading to the house referring this matter to the Committee of Privileges as a potential contempt of Parliament. (See House of Commons, Digital, Culture, Media and Sport Committee *Failure of a Witness to Answer an Order of the Committee: Conduct of Mr Dominic Cummings, 3rd Special Report 2017–19* HC 1115). The committee recommended that Mr Cummings be admonished by the house for his behaviour (House of Commons Committee of Privileges *Conduct of Mr Dominic Cummings First Report 2017–19*, HC 1490). The report of the Liaison Committee on this issue recognizes the minimal impact of this form of punishment on private individuals (House of Commons Liaison Committee *The Effectiveness and Influence of the Select Committee System Fourth Report 2017–19*, HC 186, para 184).

> The key question for the House is whether the admonishment of those who have defied a committee or lied to it has made it less or more likely that future witnesses will consider that the risks attached to defiance or deliberate deceit are high enough to deter them from that course. For those with a lack of a sense of public obligation and perhaps without a reputation or a share price to defend or protect they may not be. And, from this perspective, the stakes for defying an order to produce papers are similarly low.

However, the committee did not reach a conclusion on whether Westminster should follow the lead of the Scottish Parliament and the Welsh Parliament, establishing a statutory obligation to attend committee meetings. It did conclude, however, that 'the option of doing nothing is unacceptable' (para 186). While there may be concerns about involving courts, nevertheless this has worked successfully in other parliamentary systems. Moreover, the reasons for refusing to attend to give evidence could be evaluated in a court without transgressing parliamentary privilege. This may also reassure individuals – including Mr Cummings who wished to give evidence before committees 'under oath' and wished the MPs at the committee to also be 'under oath'. This may also be required given the ability of those who refuse to give evidence to place their side of the story on blogs and through other forms of social media, where it may not be possible to hear the other side. Nevertheless, given recent events, it is unlikely that any progress on this issue will be made in the near future.

High hopes have been expressed for what the departmental committees might achieve, as when a Leader of the House said that they were intended to 'redress the balance of power' between Parliament and the executive (HC Deb vol. 969, col 36, 25 June 1979). As such, the committees have an important role in the scrutiny of the executive. Ministers and civil servants are questioned in depth in a way that is impossible on the floor of the house, and are obliged to explain and justify their actions. Departmental activities are investigated, in many hours of questioning, by members who have acquired some proficiency in the subject and can call on the assistance of expert advisers. Not only the departments themselves but others involved with or affected by their policies – local authorities, political parties, pressure groups, industrialists, trade unions – may be called to give evidence. The committees have prised many facts and explanations from the departments that could not have been extracted in any other way, and their published reports (300 or more in a parliamentary session) constitute a considerable body of information about the processes of government.

The Treasury Committee assumed a new role for itself in 1998 after the establishment (by the Bank of England Act 1998) of a Monetary Policy Committee of the Bank of England with responsibility for setting interest rates. The Treasury Committee decided to hold regular non-statutory 'confirmation hearings' on appointments of members of the Monetary Policy Committee to satisfy itself and Parliament that those appointed were of 'demonstrable professional competence and personal independence of the government'. It has held to the view that it should be given power by statute to confirm nominations to the Monetary Policy Committee (e.g., *9th Report of 2000–01*, HC 42). In 2003, the Public Administration Committee argued that there were 'solid reasons for Parliament to take a more assertive approach to public appointments' and recommended that select committees should have the right to hold meetings with proposed appointees to key positions and be empowered to require competition for a post to be reopened if they were of the opinion that the person proposed was unsuitable (*4th Report of 2002–03*, HC 165). The government initially rejected this recommendation. Scrutiny of major appointments has long been one of the 'core tasks' of the select committees and it has been common practice for them to hold evidence sessions with incumbents of major posts soon *after* appointment.

A more constructive approach was taken by the government in its *Governance of Britain* Green Paper (Cm 7170/2007, paras 76–9) in proposing that government nominees for certain key positions – in particular, those with a role in protecting the public interest or holding the executive to account – should be subject to (non-binding) appointment hearings by the relevant select committee. The proposal was welcomed by select committees and the government listed fifty posts (including, for example, the chair of the Judicial Appointments Commission, the information commissioner and the parliamentary ombudsman) that it considered suitable for pre-appointment hearings: some additional posts were agreed between the Liaison Committee and the government in May 2008. In March 2018, the Liaison Committee asked the Public Administration and Constitutional Affairs Committee to look into pre-appointment hearings. Following their recommendations, the Liaison Committee published revised guidelines, incorporating two recommended changes: the requirement for candidates to fill out a written questionnaire and this being used to determine whether an oral hearing is needed; and, where the committee has concerns, to inform ministers of their concerns in private and to seek further information before agreeing their report. The Public Administration and Constitutional Affairs Committee also concluded that it was for Parliament to determine which appointments should be subject to pre-appointment hearings. However, in its response to the report, the government disagreed, concluding that ministers were responsible for these appointments to Parliament and so should determine when pre-appointment hearings are needed. The Liaison Committee, in its most recent report, agreed that it should be for Parliament and not the government to decide when pre-appointment hearings are needed, with the list provided by the Cabinet Office being regarded as merely providing guidance. (See Public Administration and Constitutional Affairs Committee, *Pre-Appointment Hearings: Promoting Best Practice 10th Report 2017–19*, HC 909; Liaison Committee, *Review of Pre-Appointment Hearings*, 19 June 2019. See, further, Hazell, Hursit, Mehta and Waller, 'Improving Parliamentary Scrutiny of Public Appointments' Constitution Unit, July 2017.)

Another of the core tasks of select committees is the scrutiny of draft bills, in this way making a useful contribution to the quality of legislation. It can be difficult to assess the contribution of select committees to the legislative process. Legislative amendments made due to recommendations in a select committee report may also be adopted due to support for the changes from other sources – for instance pressure groups – or because of the anticipated reaction of backbench MPs. However, research suggests that select committees can be influential in modifying governmental policies, albeit that this is more likely to be the case for minor as opposed to major policy changes (see Benton and Russell, 'Assessing the Impact of Parliamentary Oversight Committees: The Select Committees in the British House of Commons' (2013) 66 *Parliamentary Affairs* 772).

Understandably, select committees have played an important role scrutinis-ing Brexit legislation. Sixty-six inquiries and fifty-six of the 267 committee reports for the 2017–19 parliamentary session concerned issues relating to Brexit. Again, research suggests that the extent to which committee reports influence the government depends on the nature of the policy change recom-mended in the report, with the government more willing to accede to sug-gested minor as opposed to large policy changes. (See, further, Lynch and Whitaker, 'Select Committees and Brexit: Parliamentary Influence in a Divisive Policy Area' (2019) 72 *Parliamentary Affairs* 923.)

Some draft bills are submitted for scrutiny to a joint committee of both houses: the draft Parliamentary Buildings (Restoration and Renewal) Bill and the draft Domestic Abuse Bill are recent examples from the 2017–19 parlia-mentary session. The government's response to the report of the joint committee on the draft Parliamentary Buildings (Restoration and Renewal) Bill demonstrated a willingness to respond to and agree to some of the recommendations proposed by the committee.

Between the departments and the committees that shadow them there is a continual dialogue, the departments replying to the committees' reports (normally within two months) and their replies sometimes stimulating further inquiry. It has been found possible in the committees 'for people of widely disparate views to work together exclusively as parliamentarians' (Mr Edward du Cann MP, in evidence to the Select Committee on Procedure (Finance), HC 365-vi of 1981–82, Q 459). The committees do not usually vote on party lines and generally strive for consensus, which adds weight to reports that are often sharply critical of government policy or its administration. This has continued even throughout scrutiny over Brexit, the exception being the Select Committee on Exiting the European Union, which has provided a number of divisions in its reports.

It is sometimes difficult to assess the impact of the committees on governmental decision-making, especially where a committee's work relates more to an overall policy theme rather than to a specific set of proposals. That said, even if a committee's report has no observable result, it may bring new evidence and argument into the debate within government or may contribute to the climate of opinion in which departments must operate.

There has also been some effect on the house as a whole. Select committee reports may be specifically debated in the house: three estimates days are set aside for such debates in each session, but the main forum for debating select committee reports is the parallel chamber in Westminster Hall. In addition, many reports are relevant to the subject matter of other debates. For example, the report of the Foreign Affairs Committee on the 'patriation' of the Canadian constitution (see Chapter 3) provided much material for the debates in Parliament. The Treasury Committee's annual report on the budget is brought to the attention of MPs in debates on the Finance Bill. Members of the committees are also better equipped to play their part on the floor of the house, in the striving for accountability that takes place there.

The select committees are Parliament's best method for enforcing the accountability of government, and in this they have had some success, although their achievement has been partial and uneven. Recent changes in the working methods and objectives of the departmental committees, particularly through the election of most committee chairs, have made possible a more systematic and effective scrutiny of the executive. A change of culture is also required. Governments are ambivalent in their attitude to select committees: as Peter Riddell remarks, 'Too often, select committees have been seen by ministers and civil servants as a problem to be tackled, and if possible neutralised, than as a potentially important factor in policy making and implementation, and legislation' (*Parliament under Blair* (2000), p. 214). The committees themselves cannot be wholly detached from the contest of the parties in Parliament, which are engaged there in a perpetual election campaign. Members of the committees are supportive of their party, may be hopeful of office, yet are called on to assert themselves as parliamentarians in confronting and restraining the executive. In this, they sometimes falter, although it is perhaps remarkable that they are often able to transcend party differences in exposing the errors and deficiencies of government policy and administration.

Not everyone would welcome an extension of the bipartisan role of select committees, seen by some as contributing to a sterile 'government by consensus'. Tony Benn, for instance, believed that the select committees 'have become effectively a network of coalitions, knitting government and opposition backbenchers together through a common desire to reach unanimous conclusions' (in Sutherland (ed.), *The Rape of the Constitution?* (2000), p. 48). Surely this judgment underrates the achievement of the committees in holding the government to account?

The Security and Secret Intelligences Services are not overseen by any of the parliamentary select committees. An Intelligence and Security Committee, established under the Intelligence Services Act 1994, reinforced by the Justice and Securities Act 2013, examines and oversees the expenditure, administration and policy of the Security Service, the Secret Intelligence Service and GCHQ. The committee consists of nine members of the Lords and Commons who are appointed by the House of Parliament from which the member is drawn, following consultation with the prime minister and the leader of the opposition. Its annual reports are laid before Parliament, although the 'ISC must exclude any matter from any report to Parliament if the Prime Minister, after consultation with the ISC, considers that the matter would be prejudicial to the continued discharge of the functions of the Security Service, the Secret Intelligence Service, the Government Communications Headquarters' or any other individual carrying out activities related to the intelligence services. A former Director of Public Prosecutions, Lord Macdonald, has written that the committee can be seen by the public to be a fake and that it 'fails to deliver the scrutiny that's so critical to public support' (*The Times*, 17 November 2010).

On the strengths and weaknesses of the select committees of the House of Commons, see, further, Woodhouse, *Ministers and Parliament* (1994), ch. 10; Giddings, 'Select Committees and Parliamentary Scrutiny' (1994) 47 *Parl Aff* 669; Weir and Beetham, *Political Power and Democratic Control in Britain* (1999); Riddell, *Parliament under Blair* (2000); Maer and Sandford, *Select Committees Under Scrutiny* (2004); Natzler and Hutton, 'Select Committees: Scrutiny *a la Carte*?', in Giddings (ed.), *The Future of Parliament* (2005); Norton, 'Parliament: The Best of Times, The Worst of Times', in Jowell and O'Cinneide, *The Changing Constitution* (9th edn., 2019). The work of the Commons' select committees is reviewed annually by the Liaison

Committee. See also its recent comprehensive report 'The Effectiveness and Influence of the Select Committee System' 4th Report of the 2017–19 session, HC 1860.

9.4.1.4 Parliamentary Ombudsman

The office of parliamentary commissioner for administration (or 'parliamentary and health service ombudsman', the name by which the officer is commonly known) was established by the Parliamentary Commissioner Act 1967 for the investigation of complaints by members of the public of injustice resulting from 'maladministration' by government departments. The role also includes that of the health service commissioner, whose powers are set out in the Health Service Commissioners Act 1993. The model for the new office was the Scandinavian ombudsman, but unlike the officers of this title in Sweden, Denmark, Norway and Finland, the British parliamentary ombudsman was to be harnessed to the legislature and to function as an extension of parliamentary scrutiny and control. The office was intended, as the government said in 1965, to provide members of Parliament with 'a better instrument which they can use to protect the citizen' (*The Parliamentary Commissioner for Administration*, Cmnd 2767/1965, para 4).

The parliamentary ombudsman is an independent officer, appointed by the Crown – in practice, on the motion of the prime minister with the agreement of the leaders of the main opposition parties and of the chairman of the House of Commons Select Committee on Public Administration – and answerable to the House of Commons. Appointment to the office of parliamentary ombudsman is now subject to a pre-appointment hearing by the Public Administration Committee. The Law Commission would go further and is consulting on its preliminary proposal that it should be for Parliament to nominate to the monarch its preferred candidate for the post of parliamentary ombudsman (*Public Services Ombudsmen*, Consultation Paper No 196 (2010), paras 3.32–3.35). The ombudsman is appointed for a non-renewable term of no more than seven years and may be dismissed only on a joint address by both Houses of Parliament.

The ombudsman (Rob Behrens CBE in 2020) can at present undertake an investigation only at the request of an MP, to whom he reports the result. He makes an annual report to Parliament and other reports as he thinks fit and he is supported by the Select Committee on Public Administration and Constitutional Affairs, which itself reports to the house on the work of the ombudsman and takes up with the departments any cases in which there has been an inadequate response to the ombudsman's findings.

The linkage with Parliament has been a controversial feature of the institution, for the 'MP filter' has operated in an arbitrary way – some MPs rarely or never refer complaints to the ombudsman while others do so frequently – and is a hindrance to the ordinary citizen in need of a clear and simple remedy for grievances against the administration. Direct access to the ombudsman or equivalent officer by members of the public is allowed in almost every other country that has this institution, and there is direct access to the health service ombudsman and the local government ombudsman. A survey carried out for the Cabinet Office, *Review of the Public Sector Ombudsmen in England* (Collcutt Report) (2000), was emphatic in recommending the abolition of the MP filter and was supported in this by the Select Committee on Public Administration. The government at that time accepted this recommendation (HC Deb vol. 372, col 464 W, 20 July 2001). In 2016, the government produced the draft Public Service Ombudsman Bill, which proposed the removal of the MP filter. In its most recent report on the work of the ombudsman, the Public Administration and Constitutional Affairs Committee was critical of the lack of momentum behind the draft bill and, again, urged the need for the ability of the ombudsman to initiate his own investigations, in addition to responding to complaints made directly to the ombudsman (*PHSO Annual Scrutiny 2017/18: Towards a Modern and Effective Ombudsman Service 16th Report 2017–19*, HC 1855).

A previous ombudsman, while recognising that the MP filter does symbolise the close constitutional relationship between the ombudsman and Parliament, has found that the filter can discourage individuals from coming forward with complaints and has suggested that 'the anachronistic barrier to citizen access it now represents outweighs its symbolic value' (Abraham (2008) 61 *Parl Aff* 535, 543). She supported the provisional proposal of the Law Commission for a 'dual track approach', which would retain the option of reference to the ombudsman by an MP while allowing the alternative of direct access by a complainant to the ombudsman (*Administrative Redress: Public Bodies and the Citizen*, Law Com No 322, HC 6 of 2010–11, paras 5.34–5.43; Law Com Consultation Paper No 196 (2010), paras 4.97–4.106). Some complainants, unaware of the present restriction, apply directly to the ombudsman, who has adopted a practice that mitigates the effect of the present rule. If the complaint seems to be 'clearly investigable', the ombudsman sends it with the complainant's consent to his or her constituency MP, inviting the member to refer it to the ombudsman for investigation. The current ombudsman also referred to the filter as 'an unnecessary restriction' and called on the government to proceed with the draft legislation, drawing attention to the Council of Europe's Venice Principles for the protection and promotion of ombudsman institutions that could be used to further guide the legislation (*The Ombudsman's Casework Report 2019* HC 63, p. 11).

The ombudsman can investigate the complaint of a member of the public 'who claims to have sustained injustice in consequence of maladministration' by a scheduled government department or authority (Parliamentary Commissioner Act 1967, section 5(1) and Schedule 2), but he is not authorised to question the *merits* of a decision taken, without maladministration, in the exercise of discretion (section 12(3)). The ombudsman has stated the four basic requirements a complaint must satisfy if it is to be accepted for investigation (*Annual Report* (1983), HC 322 of 1983–84, para 17) as follows:

(1) the department or authority concerned must be one within my jurisdiction; (2) there must be some evidence from which it may reasonably be inferred that there has been *administrative* fault; (3) I have to be satisfied that there is an apparent link between the alleged maladministration and the personal injustice which the aggrieved person claims to have suffered; and (4) I also need to be satisfied that there is some prospect of my intervention, if I find the complaint justified, leading to a worthwhile remedy for the aggrieved person or some benefit to the public at large.

These are still, in essentials, the requirements for acceptance of a complaint for investigation – although it should be added that the complainant must first have pursued any internal complaints process of the public body concerned.

'Maladministration' is not defined in the Act, but its intended scope appears from the 'Crossman catalogue' of procedural improprieties instanced by Mr Richard Crossman in the second reading debate on the Parliamentary Commissioner Bill in the House of Commons: 'bias, neglect, inattention, delay, incompetence, inaptitude, perversity, turpitude, arbitrariness and so on' (HC Deb vol. 734, col 51, 18 October 1966). The ombudsman has provided an expanded list of examples, going beyond the Crossman catalogue, though not intended to be a comprehensive definition of maladministration (*Annual Report* (1993), HC 290 of 1993–94, para 7):

rudeness (though that is a matter of degree);
unwillingness to treat the complainant as a person with rights;
refusal to answer reasonable questions;
neglecting to inform a complainant on request of his or her rights or entitlements;
knowingly giving advice which is misleading or inadequate;
ignoring valid advice or overruling considerations which would produce an uncomfortable
    result for the overruler;
offering no redress or manifestly disproportionate redress;
showing bias whether because of colour, sex, or any other grounds;
omission to notify those who thereby lose a right of appeal;
refusal to inform adequately of the right of appeal;
faulty procedures;
failure by management to monitor compliance with adequate procedures;
cavalier disregard of guidance which is intended to be followed in the interest of equitable
    treatment of those who use a service;
partiality; and failure to mitigate the effects of rigid adherence to the letter of the law where
    that produces manifestly inequitable treatment.

Maladministration has 'nothing to do with the nature, quality or reasonableness of the decision itself', per Lord Donaldson MR in *R v. Local Commissioner for Administration, ex p Eastleigh Borough Council* [1988] QB 855, 863. It has been said that 'maladministration comes in many different guises' and that while it may overlap with unlawful conduct, they are not synonymous: Henry LJ in *R v. Local Commissioner for Administration, ex p Liverpool City Council* [2001] 1 All ER 462, at [17]. The ombudsman cannot investigate if the complaint is simply that a department's decision affecting the complainant was wrong, if there is no suggestion that the complainant's case was mishandled in some way, for example, by disregarding relevant facts, drawing unjustified conclusions, mislaying information, giving inaccurate or misleading advice – 'and so on'. Injustice – also undefined – may be experienced as hardship, or financial loss, or the forfeiture of some benefit, or simply as distress, anxiety or inconvenience, or 'the sense of outrage aroused by unfair or incompetent administration' (Sedley J in *R v. Parliamentary Commissioner for Administration, ex p Balchin* [1996] EWHC Admin 152, at [15]–[16]).

The investigatory jurisdiction of the parliamentary ombudsman extends to most kinds of administrative action by some 350 government departments and agencies and other public bodies. There are some notable exclusions, such as public service personnel matters, contractual or other commercial transactions and decisions from which there is a right of appeal to a tribunal or a remedy in a court of law (see, further, section 5 of and Schedule 3 to the 1967 Act). Contracted-out functions performed on behalf of listed departments remain subject to the ombudsman's jurisdiction. (See the Deregulation and Contracting Out Act 1994, section 72.)

The ombudsman has wide powers for carrying out his investigations and may adopt whatever investigative procedure he considers appropriate in the circumstances of the case. He has the same powers as the High Court to compel witnesses to attend for examination and may require any minister or civil servant to provide relevant information or documents. (However, material relating to the proceedings of the cabinet and its committees may be withheld from him.) The ombudsman is subject to the ordinary supervisory jurisdiction of the courts and his findings may be set aside if he should exceed his statutory powers, act unlawfully or fail to consider a relevant factor (see, e.g., *R v. Parliamentary Commissioner for Administration, ex p Dyer* [1994] 1 WLR 621 and comment by Marsh [1994] *PL* 347; and *R v. Parliamentary Commissioner for Administration, ex p Balchin (No 2)* [1999] EWHC Admin 484, (1999) 2 LGLR 87 and comment by Giddings [2000] *PL* 201).

If the ombudsman finds injustice caused by maladministration, he may recommend to the department concerned whatever action he thinks should be taken by way of redress, but has no power of enforcement. Departments normally comply with the ombudsman's recommendations, although compliance has occasionally been grudging and exceptionally has been refused. Redress may take the form of an *ex gratia* payment, so as to restore the complainant to the position in which he or she would have been had the maladministration not occurred, or an apology, or the reversal of the decision of which complaint was made. A department may also revise its procedures, standing instructions or staff training with a view to avoiding similar failures in the future. If it appears to the ombudsman that an injustice will not be remedied, he may make a special report on the case to Parliament (section 10(3) of the 1967 Act).

9.4.1.4.1 The Channel Tunnel Rail Link: Exceptional Hardship

In February 1995, for only the second time in the history of the office, the ombudsman laid a special report before each House of Parliament (under section 10(3) of the Parliamentary Commissioner Act 1967) stating his view that injustice had been caused to persons in consequence of maladministration and had not been remedied (HC 193 of 1994–5). Complaints had been forwarded by MPs to the ombudsman from householders who had been unable to sell their properties as a result of the blight caused by the prolonged delay in settling the route of the Channel Tunnel Rail Link. Existing compensation schemes did not cover a number of persons who, as the ombudsman found, had suffered 'exceptional or extreme hardship' as a result of the delay. He concluded that the Department of Transport, in failing to consider *ex gratia* redress for householders who had been affected in this extreme degree, had been guilty of maladministration resulting in injustice. The department did not agree and made no offer of redress.

The Select Committee on the Parliamentary Commissioner acted on the ombudsman's special report in taking evidence from the ombudsman and the department and, in line with the principle that maladministration included 'a failure to mitigate the effects of rigid adherence to the letter of the law where that produces manifestly inequitable treatment', agreed with the ombudsman that maladministration causing injustice had occurred. The committee recommended that the department should reconsider the payment of compensation to those who had suffered exceptional hardship. While continuing to deny that maladministration had occurred, the department agreed to reconsider the question of redress 'out of respect for the PCA Select Committee and the office of the Parliamentary Commissioner'. The department subsequently formulated a scheme for identifying and compensating those who had suffered exceptional hardship (see James and Longley [1996] *PL* 38).

In the 2005–6 parliamentary session, the ombudsman twice reported to Parliament under section 10(3) of the Parliamentary Commissioner Act 1967 that injustice had been caused by maladministration and that the government did not intend to remedy it.

9.4.1.4.2 A Debt of Honour

In *A Debt of Honour* (HC 324 of 2005–06) the ombudsman dealt with a complaint about the administration by the Ministry of Defence of a scheme for making ex gratia payments to (among others) British civilians who had been interned and ill-treated by the Japanese during the Second World War. The complainant had been denied compensation on the ground that the scheme, as varied after its introduction, was limited to British claimants born in the UK or with a parent or grandparent who had been born there. The ombudsman found that there had been maladministration in the manner in which the scheme was brought into effect (with the criteria for eligibility left unclear) and also by reason of inconsistency in its operation. Maladministration on the first ground was admitted by the government, which made due apology and modest financial recompense, but the finding of inconsistency was initially rejected. The ombudsman's section 10(3) report was considered by the Public Administration Committee, which concluded that there was 'ample evidence to support the Ombudsman's finding of maladministration'; at the same time the ministry's further investigations led it to acknowledge that there had indeed been inconsistencies in the operation of the scheme and that errors had been made. In the event, the minister agreed to make changes to the eligibility criteria and to ensure that the new criteria would be properly introduced and applied.

9.4.1.4.3 Trusting in the Pensions Promise; Equitable Life

Between 2004 and 2006, the ombudsman investigated the actions of several government bodies that had led to the referral by MPs of over 200 complaints to her office. These related to certain final salary occupational pension schemes that had been wound up with insufficient assets to pay the promised benefits, so that scheme members suffered substantial financial losses. In *Trusting in the Pensions Promise* (HC 984 of 2005–06) the ombudsman's principal finding was that the government had, in promoting the schemes, provided inaccurate, incomplete, unclear and inconsistent information which had misled participants as to the risks involved. She concluded that this constituted maladministration and that, as a result, the complainants had suffered injustice in financial losses sustained as well as in their 'sense of outrage, and considerable distress, anxiety and uncertainty'. She recommended that the government should consider appropriate arrangements for the restoration of benefits to those who had suffered loss. The government rejected the ombudsman's findings of maladministration and her principal recommendations, whereupon she laid her report before Parliament under section 10(3) of the 1967 Act. The Public Administration Committee supported the Ombudsman's conclusions (*6th Report of 2005–06*, HC 1081), saying:

> In future, we hope that the Government will engage with the Ombudsman positively, and start from the presumption that it is her job to determine whether or not maladministration has occurred, not its own.

Several individuals who had suffered loss in consequence of the winding-up of company pension schemes brought proceedings for judicial review of the government's decision, taken on its behalf by the Secretary of State for Work and Pensions, to reject the ombudsman's findings. In *R (Bradley)* v. *Secretary of State for Work and Pensions* [2008] EWCA Civ 36, [2009] QB 114, the Court of Appeal rejected the claimants' argument that the findings of the ombudsman were binding on the secretary of state, but held that, in declining to accept a finding of maladministration, the minister must have cogent reasons for his decision – that is to say, must not act irrationally. In the event, the court held that the secretary of state had acted irrationally in rejecting the ombudsman's principal finding of maladministration and that his decision must accordingly be quashed. This case usefully clarified the test to be applied in judicial review of the rejection of a finding by the ombudsman of maladministration (see Varuhas (2009) 72 *MLR* 102).

It was not the end of the pensions scandal. Policyholders who had suffered loss from the near-collapse of the insurer Equitable Life complained to the ombudsman that Equitable's inability to meet its obligations was the result of a failure, over a period of years, of the responsible government departments and agencies in their duty of prudential regulation of the insurer. The ombudsman's special report, *Equitable Life: A Decade of Regulatory Failure* (HC 815 of 2007–08), ran to five volumes and was the outcome of an extremely complex investigation over four years. Concluding, inter alia, that regulation had been carried out in a 'passive, reactive and complacent manner' and that the regulators' actions were 'largely ineffective and often inappropriate', the ombudsman made ten findings of maladministration and found that injustice to individuals had resulted in six of these cases. She recommended that, in addition to an apology from the public bodies concerned, a scheme for compensation should be established and funded by the government. In 2009, the then government accepted only in part the ombudsman's findings of maladministration and injustice, apologised for its failings, but declined to establish the recommended compensation scheme, proposing instead a limited scheme for ex gratia payments to individuals who had suffered a disproportionate impact: *The Prudential Regulation of the Equitable Life Assurance Society*, Cm 7538/2009. The government's response provoked much critical reaction, including a further report from the ombudsman (*Injustice Unremedied*, HC 435 of 2008–09), laid before Parliament under section 10(3) of the Parliamentary Commissioner Act 1967 – the fifth special 'unremedied injustice' report by the ombudsman since the creation of the office in 1967 – and a report from the Public Administration Committee (*Justice Denied?* HC 219 of 2008–09). In proceedings for judicial review of the government's response, the Administrative Court in *R (Equitable Members Action Group)* v. *HM Treasury* [2009] EWHC 2495 (Admin), applying the principles established in *Bradley* (above), upheld some grounds of challenge while rejecting others. The government's limited scheme for ex gratia compensation was held not to be irrational (see, further, Elliott [2010] *CLJ* 1), although the government made some adjustments to its proposed scheme as a consequence of the administrative court's rulings on maladministration and injustice.

The Conservative-Liberal Democrat *Coalition Agreement* of May 2010 included an undertaking to implement the ombudsman's recommendation of an independent scheme 'to make fair and transparent payments to Equitable Life policyholders'. The Coalition Government accepted all ten findings of maladministration made by the ombudsman and established an independent commission to design a compensation scheme. Legislation was enacted to authorise the Treasury to fund payments to persons adversely affected by government maladministration in the regulation of Equitable Life: see the Equitable Life (Payments) Act 2010. The amount to be allocated by the government towards the payment scheme (£1.5 billion) was announced in the House of Commons on 20 October 2010 (HC Deb vol. 516, col 960). (The Equitable Members Action Group contests the fairness of the government's compensation proposals and further litigation is in prospect.)

Thousands of complaints are received by the parliamentary ombudsman each year. In 2018–19, the office handled 29,841 complaints, some of those being received in the previous year when the office had relocated from London to Manchester and had not been able to handle as many complaints. Of those, 24,183 were either not yet ready for the office or should not be taken forward, and 5,658 were decided. Complaints can be declined as a result of being outside the ombudsman's jurisdiction or because the complaint was not first addressed to the body complained about, or if on initial consideration there is no evidence of maladministration or no worthwhile outcome appears likely. Many complaints are resolved 'through intervention' of the ombudsman or his staff, the public body being invited to provide an appropriate remedy, otherwise a full investigation is undertaken. (In 2018–19, 444 complaints were resolved through intervention, alongside 3,597 assessment decisions, with 746 investigations that were upheld or partly upheld and 871 investigations that were not upheld: PCSO *Annual Report and Accounts* 2018–19.)

As well as securing redress for victims of maladministration, the ombudsman has a wider 'public benefit' role in seeking to enhance standards of service to the public by bringing about improvements in departmental procedures and decision-making, and encouraging good practice in dealing with complaints. The ombudsman's reports may recommend improvements and in 2007 she published a set of *Principles of Good Administration*, a blueprint, as she has said, for humanising the bureaucracy of the state and a template for shaping administrative practice to fit the needs of citizens (Abraham, 'Good Administration: Why We Need it More than Ever' (2009) 80 *Pol Q* 25). A consolidated publication includes the *Principles of Good Administration* together with *Principles of Good Complaint Handling* and *Principles for Remedy*. (The current version is available at www.ombudsman .org.uk/about-us/our-principles/ombudsmans-introduction-principles.) For its part, the government has issued a guidance document for civil servants, *The Ombudsman in Your Files* (rev edn. 1997, available at https://assets .publishing.service.gov.uk/government/uploads/system/uploads/attachment_ data/file/61193/guide-handling-of-ombudsman-cases.pdf), which seeks to encourage good practice and an avoidance of conduct that may lead to complaints.

The jurisdiction of the parliamentary ombudsman embraces maladministration by scheduled public bodies in relation to England and, in respect of reserved matters, also in relation to Wales, Scotland and Northern Ireland. Separate ombudsman schemes are established in Scotland, Wales and Northern Ireland. (See the Scottish Public Services Ombudsman Act 2002, the Public Services Ombudsman (Wales) Act 2005 and the Public Services Ombudsman Act (Northern Ireland) 2016.) These schemes are not qualified by a parliamentary or assembly 'filter' and complaints may be taken directly to the ombudsman. Health complaints in England are investigated by the health service ombudsman for England in the final stage of the health service complaints system. This office is at present concurrently held by Rob Behrens as Parliamentary and Health Service Ombudsman.

Difficulties were formerly experienced by an individual whose complaint involved more than one sector of public administration, central or local. The ombudsman noted that constraints in existing legislation 'prevented the Ombudsman from providing a seamless, accessible and responsive service'. (See *Reform of Public Sector Ombudsmen Services in England* (2005), para 28.) In her *Annual Report for 2005–06*, HC 1363, she emphasised 'the need to reform the legislative framework governing working arrangements between Ombudsmen to allow them to publish joint reports and share information'. Cooperation between the parliamentary ombudsman, the health service ombudsman for England and the local government ombudsmen for England was enabled by the Regulatory Reform (Collaboration etc. Between Ombudsmen) Order 2007 (SI 2007/1889). The ombudsmen may undertake joint investigations in cases relevant to more than one of their jurisdictions and may issue joint reports.

The Law Commission has considered the exclusion by section 5 of the 1967 Act of the ombudsman's jurisdiction where the complainant has a remedy by way of recourse to a court or tribunal (except where it is unreasonable to expect the complainant to resort to the legal remedy). It has provisionally proposed that the statutory bar should be reformed, allowing the ombudsman to open an investigation even if the complainant has access to a court or tribunal, while having jurisdiction to decline to investigate in the light of this factor: in effect, a presumption in favour of investigation. (See Law Commission Consultation Paper No 196 (2010), paras 4.25–4.47.) Further proposals for reform of the system of public sector ombudsmen were made by the Law Commission in *Administrative Redress: Public Bodies and the Citizen* (2010), Law Com No 322, Part 5 and Consultation Paper No 196 (above). (See, too, the following articles:

Abraham (2008) 61 *Parl Aff* 206, 370, 535, 681 and (2009) 80 *Pol Q* 25; O'Brien [2009] *PL* 466; Kirkham, Thompson and Buck (2009) 62 *Parl Aff* 600.)

In 2019, the ombudsman published *The Ombudsman's Casework Report 2019* (HC 63), which is designed to be the first of a series of annual reports highlighting the casework of the PHSO. This report highlights the work of the ombudsman, providing an account of complaints that can serve as a means of facilitating good practice. The report also highlights the diverse nature of the complaints investigated by the PHSO, ranging from failure of the Child Support Agency to secure the payment of child support arrears, to poor recordkeeping, failures to take enforcement actions, delayed diagnoses and a failure to react to signs of sepsis, the prescription of the wrong medication and the failure of probation providers (available at www.ombudsman.org.uk/sites/default/files/Ombudsman_Casework_Report_2019.pdf).

9.4.2 Legislation

Legislation as a governmental function was considered in Chapter 7; what follows should be read in the light of the material considered there.

9.4.2.1 Primary Legislation

The passage of government bills through Parliament is a process in part collaborative and in part adversarial, the mixture depending on the extent to which the bill arouses party controversy. The parliamentary process not only provides the formal legitimation of government legislation but allows for the delivery of an attack on the principle of the bill – mainly at second reading – and for argument on the detail of its provisions – mainly at the committee stage. Ministers are obliged to explain and defend the bill, which is given a public and critical scrutiny. Most government bills presented to Parliament have been put into reasonably firm shape by the responsible department, often in consultation with outside interests (see Chapter 7), and, when this is the case, debates and scrutiny in Parliament may have only a modest effect on the outcome of the legislation. However, where it appears that the government is acting in undue haste, or where its proposals are ill-thought through, parliamentary debate may secure a greater degree of amendment.

J.A.G. Griffith, 'Standing Committees in the House of Commons', in S.A. Walkland and Michael Ryle (eds.), *The Commons Today* (rev. edn. 1981), pp. 121–2, 130–1

Amendments may have one or more of a great variety of purposes. Whether moved by the Opposition or by a government backbencher, an amendment may be intended to cause political mischief, to embarrass the Government, to discover what are the Government's real intentions and whether (in particular) they include one or more specific possibilities, to placate interests outside Parliament who are angered by the bill, to make positive improvements in the bill the better to effect its purposes, to set out alternative proposals, to initiate a debate on some general principle of great or small importance, to ascertain from the Government the meaning of a clause or sub-section or to obtain assurances on how they will be operated, to correct grammatical errors or to improve the draftsmanship of the bill. If moved by the Government, the purpose of an amendment is most likely to be to correct a drafting error or to make minor consequential changes, to record agreements made with outside bodies which were uncompleted when the bill was introduced, to introduce new matter, or occasionally to meet a criticism made by a Member either during the second reading debate or at an earlier part of the committee stage, or informally.

Not all of these purposes, if fulfilled, are likely to make the bill 'more generally acceptable'. Apart from the trivialities of minor errors, the occasions of an amendment falling within that phrase are when an opposition amendment is accepted by the Government or when a government amendment goes some way to meet an objection. This of course, may, at the same time, make the bill less acceptable to some of the government supporters. This is not to say that committee debates seldom, if ever, result in the improvement of a bill. It is to say, however, that very many amendments are not put forward with that purpose, and of those that are, not all have that effect.

More importantly, much of what takes place during committee on a controversial bill is an extension and an application of the general critical function of the House and there is little or no intention or expectation of changing the bill. The purpose of many Opposition amendments is not to make the bill more generally acceptable but to make the Government less generally acceptable . . .

If the value of the proceedings in standing committee on government bills is judged by the extent to which Members, other than Ministers, successfully move amendments, then the value is small. It has been as rare for ministerial amendments to be rejected as for other Members' amendments to be successfully moved against government opposition. Party discipline is largely maintained in standing committee. Not surprisingly when the latter rarity occurs it is often on bills concerned with matters of the highest social controversy like race relations or immigration policy. For it is on such matters that the Whip is most likely to be defied.

On the other hand, minor reforms are quite often successfully achieved by persuading the Minister to 'look again' when the matter is before the committee and not infrequently he may propose some compromise on report.

But more important than the making of amendments is the scrutiny to which Ministers and their policies are subjected. Committee rooms are not large and do not have that sense of space and support which can be felt on the floor of the House (though that also can no doubt be at times a very lonely place). For hour after hour and for week after week a Minister may be required to defend his bill against attack from others who may be only slightly less knowledgeable than himself. His departmental brief may be full and his grasp of the subject considerable but even so he needs to be constantly on the alert and any defects he or his policy reveals will be very quickly exploited by his political opponents.

The effectiveness of standing committee (now 'public bill committee') proceedings depends largely on the ability of MPs to inform themselves adequately about the background, objectives and machinery of the bill. Outside interests affected by a bill will often supply MPs on the committee with facts, arguments and draft amendments. Modest adjustments to the bill may be won or conceded. Committees rarely manifest such potency as when, in 1985, the combined resistance of government and opposition backbenchers in the committee proceedings caused the government to abandon its Civil Aviation Bill.

The Procedure Committee recommended that committees on bills should normally be authorised to hold 'a limited number of sittings in select committee form, calling witnesses and receiving written submissions' about the factual and technical background to the bill, before proceeding to the usual examination of clauses and debating of amendments (*1st Report of 1977–78*, HC 588). An experiment on these lines was approved by the House of Commons in 1980 and as the result standing orders provided that a bill might be committed, on the motion of any member, to a 'special standing committee' with power to send for persons, papers and records and receive oral evidence at not more than three morning sittings. At these hearings the committee could examine ministers, civil servants, outside experts and pressure group representatives, before going on to the detailed consideration of the bill's clauses. A special standing committee on the Criminal Attempts Bill in the 1980–1 session heard evidence on the bill from a High Court judge, a member of the Law Commission (which had produced an initial draft of the bill) and two academic lawyers. A number of improvements to the bill resulted from these hearings. Subsequently, the procedure was seldom used, but in 1999 the Immigration and Asylum Bill was committed to a special standing committee that received oral and written evidence from civil rights groups, refugee organisations and church groups. The Adoption and Children Bill was also committed to a special standing committee in October 2001.

The Modernisation Committee recommended in 2006 that special standing committees should be the norm for government bills originating in the Commons (*1st Report of 2005–06*, HC 1097). In response to this report, changes were made to the House of Commons' standing orders in 2006 to provide that government bills that commenced in the Commons and were subject to programming (timetabling) would normally be referred to a committee – renamed a 'public bill committee' – which would have power to receive written and oral evidence. Provision to this effect is to be found in Standing Order No. 84A and it is now standard practice for government bills starting in the Commons that are programmed (the great majority) to be sent to a public bill committee, which may receive written submissions and take oral evidence from ministers, officials and other witnesses before proceeding to the detailed scrutiny of the clauses of the bill. In an assessment of the introduction of public bill committees, Jessica Levy (*Strengthening Parliament's Powers of Scrutiny?*, The Constitution Unit, 2009) has written:

> As a result of the introduction of evidence-gathering legislative committees, the Commons committee stage has become more informed, more transparent and characterised by improved debate. Oral evidence sessions in particular have provided interested organisations and individuals outside parliament with an additional forum in which to express their views and offer expert advice and opinions on elements of proposed government legislation.

There is evidence that the ability of public bill committees to take evidence has been a positive development on the whole. However, there remain issues when the timetabling of a bill is restricted, minimizing the opportunity for evidence to be obtained and analysed. Moreover, even when evidence is available, debate in the house often focuses more on issues of principle and policy than it does on evidence. In short, the extent to which these developments enhance legislative scrutiny may well depend on the subject matter of the bill – some may lend themselves more readily to evidence-based scrutiny – and the role of outside pressure groups. (See, further, Brazier, Kalitowski and Rosenblatt with Korris, *Law in the Making*, Hansard Society, 2008, pp. 221–4; Fox and Korris, *Making Better Law*, Hansard Society, 2010, pp. 141–5; Thompson, 'More of the Same or a Period of Change? The Impact of Bill Committees in the Twenty-First Century House of Commons' (2013) 66 *Parliamentary Affairs* 459; Thompson, 'Evidence Taking under the Microscope: How Has Oral Evidence Affected the Scrutiny of Legislation in House of Commons Committees?' (2014) 9 *British Politics* 385; Thompson, 'Debunking the Myths of Bill Committees in the House of Commons' [2016] 36 *Politics* 36; Russell and Gover, *Legislation at Westminster: Parliamentary Actors and influence in the making of British Law* (2017).)

The Lords meet as a whole house at the committee stage, either in the chamber as a committee of the whole house or in the grand committee in a committee room. The proceedings are the same in each case and are broadly similar to those in the Commons, but in the grand committee, no voting takes place and decisions must be unanimous. It is possible, but rare, for a bill to be considered in a special public bill committee, taking oral and written evidence. A special public bill committee was used for the Sentencing (Pre-consolidation Amendments) Bill in 2019, for example. Very occasionally a public bill is referred, after a second reading in the House of Lords, to a select committee of that house for examination of the policy and contents of the bill. This procedure was followed in 2004 in regard to the Constitutional Reform Bill, which had not been published in draft or given pre-legislative scrutiny. Some significant amendments to the bill resulted from the deliberations of this committee.

Pre-legislative scrutiny by Parliament of government proposals for legislation has been briefly considered above (pp. 546–547). The benefits of pre-legislative scrutiny were enumerated by the House of Commons Modernisation Committee (*1st Report of 1997–98*, HC 190, para 20):

> There is almost universal agreement that pre-legislative scrutiny is right in principle, subject to the circumstances and nature of the legislation. It provides an opportunity for the House as a whole, for individual backbenchers, and for the Opposition to have a real input into the form of the actual legislation which subsequently emerges, not least because Ministers are likely to be far more receptive to suggestions for change before the Bill is actually published. It opens Parliament up to those outside affected by legislation. At the same time such pre-legislative scrutiny can be of real benefit to the Government. It could, and indeed should, lead to less time being needed at later stages of the legislative process … Above all, it should lead to better legislation and less likelihood of subsequent amending legislation.

The Modernisation Committee's proposals were acted on in the submission of a number of draft government bills to pre-legislative scrutiny, either by the appropriate departmental committee or by a specially constituted select committee or a joint committee of both houses. In the recent 2017–19 session, ten draft bills were laid before Parliament. Most of these bills were scrutinized by the appropriate select committee. The Draft Domestic Abuse Bill and the Draft Parliamentary Buildings (Restoration and Renewal) Bill were both considered in an especially composed joint committee.

Pre-legislative scrutiny is, however, as the Modernisation Committee has noted, 'in the gift of the Government' (*1st Report of 2005–06*, HC 1097, para 56) and many bills have escaped this salutary process. There was no draft bill of the hugely constitutionally important European Union (Withdrawal Agreement) Act 2020, whose provisions were changed from the first bill laid before Parliament in the 2017–19 session to the second bill laid before Parliament in the 2019–21 session, and which was enacted through the House of Commons in just three days. The House of Lords Constitution Committee recommended in 2004 that 'the decision as to which draft bills should be subject to pre-legislative scrutiny should be negotiated between the Government and the Liaison Committee of the House of Commons' (*14th Report of 2003–04*, HL 173), but the government in its reply took the view that the current process (involving the 'usual channels' and consultation with the Liaison Committee) was satisfactory. The deputy Leader of the House of Commons undertook on 25 October 2010 that 'our normal practice will be to introduce important bills in draft' and promised a considerable increase in the number of government bills to be given pre-legislative scrutiny (HC Deb vol. 517, col 21).

In 2017–19, the Constitution Committee of the House of Lords published a series of reports on the legislative process. In its report, *The Legislative Process: Preparing Legislation for Parliament 4th Report 2017–19*, HL Paper 27, the committee recommended that draft bills should be published more frequently, as well as being subject to more frequent pre-legislative scrutiny. In its response to this report, the government noted that the Parliamentary Business and Legislation Cabinet Committee 'always encourages departments to publish draft legislation' for pre-legislative scrutiny (available at www.parliament.uk/documents/lords-com mittees/constitution/Legislative-process-inquiry/20180126_Leader-to-Baroness-Taylor-of-Bolton_The%20LegislativeProcessPreparingLegislationforParliament. pdf). However, no further commitment was forthcoming.

As McKay and Johnson have noted (*Parliament and Congress: Representation and Scrutiny in the Twenty-First Century* (2010), p. 463): 'There is a general consensus that legislation which follows this route is better in quality than that which does not.' (See, further, Power, *Parliamentary Scrutiny of Draft Legislation 1997–1999* (2000); Brazier, *Parliament, Politics and Law Making* (2004), ch. 4; Kennon, 'Pre-Legislative Scrutiny of Draft Bills' [2004] *PL* 490; Smookler, 'Making a Difference? The Effectiveness of Pre-Legislative Scrutiny' (2006) 59 *Parl Aff* 522; Fox and Korris, *Making Better Law*, Hansard Society, 2010, pp. 46–8, 137–41; Russell and Gover, *Legislation at Westminster: Parliamentary Actors and Influence in the Making of British Law* (2017), ch. 3.)

In its efforts to get to grips with legislation during its passage, Parliament is hindered by a number of deficiencies of the legislative process: inadequate preparation of bills, the overwhelming torrent and complexity of legislation, late introduction of government amendments, reluctance of governments to give ground or seem to weaken in response to the – often partisan – challenges to its bills, and unwillingness of the government's own backbenchers to withhold support for the government's measures. These are among the factors that have contributed to a frequent production of insufficiently scrutinised and flawed legislation. This is not to say that there have not been useful reforms in parliamentary scrutiny such as we have indicated above, and it would be wrong to conclude that Parliament has been supine or ineffective in performing its scrutinising role. Brazier, Kalitowski and Rosenblatt with Korris (*Law in the Making* (Hansard Society, 2008)) have shown that 'Parliament, as a whole and through its constituent parts, does make a difference to legislation, sometimes in major ways, and more frequently through many minor but significant changes.' In a more recent report, the Hansard Society (Fox and Korris, *Making Better Law*, 2010), has called for a renewed programme of reform:

> While the consideration of bills is largely dominated by partisan battle, the key relationship in the legislative process is between Parliament and the executive. To enhance the scrutiny of bills, and thus improve the quality of legislation, Parliament needs to take greater control

of the legislative process, stand up to government more often, and make better use of the existing tools and procedures available to it.

However, it is equally important not to underestimate the many ways in which a range of political actors can exercise indirect influence over the content of legislation. In the conclusion of their extensive study, *Legislation at Westminster: Parliamentary Actors and Influence in the Making of British Law* (2017), Russell and Gover conclude that (at p. 282):

parliament's influence on government legislation is extensive, and is exerted in various different ways throughout the policy process. Ideas for policies in bills are frequently urged upon government by parliamentarians (often working in conjunction with pressure groups). Mechanisms such as debates, private members' bills, and EDMs – generally presented as weak, and as quite distinct from the legislative process – play an important part in setting the policy agenda. So do select committees. During the policy formulation stage, and indeed later, after bills have been introduced, parliamentarians publicly test the arguments, and continue using these mechanisms to influence the detail. In formulating major bills, ministers will always be careful to consult inside their own parliamentary party; and at the drafting stage, the ability to get a bill through parliament is paramount to government planning. If all of this fails, and objections are raised which can potentially garner majority support in parliament, bills often go on to be amended. This usually occurs in an outwardly consensual way, via government concessionary amendments.

(See, further, Fox and Korris, *Making Better Law* (2010); House of Lords Constitution Committee, *Parliament and the Legislative Process*, 14th Report of 2003–04, HL 173, *The Legislative Process: Preparing Legislation for Parliament*, 4th report of 2017–19 HL 27, *The Legislative Process: The Passage of Bills Through Parliament*, 24th Report of 2017–19 HL 393.)

9.4.2.2 Delegated Legislation

Delegated or secondary legislation (considered as a function of government in Chapter 7) is produced by the executive in great quantity. Many statutes empower the executive to make far-reaching rules or orders in order to give effect in detail to the provisions of what may often be described as a 'framework' act, which commonly authorises ministers (in so-called Henry VIII clauses) to adapt, amend or repeal primary legislation. A recent instance was the Sanctions and Anti-Money Laundering Bill 2017–9, of which the Delegated Powers and Regulatory Reform Committee of the House of Lords said (*7th Report of Session 2017–19* HL Paper 38, paras 16–17):

> We accept that, in the light of the UK's withdrawal from the European Union, it is reasonable for Government to establish a comprehensive mechanism that will allow them to ensure that the UK is able to comply with its international obligations with respect to sanctions, particularly those obligations which arise under the UN Charter. We also accept that it is appropriate for this mechanism to operate through the exercise of delegated powers, because of the need to react quickly in response to global events and to ensure timely compliance with the UK's international obligations; and that these powers need to be drawn widely because of the variety of circumstances in which they may need to be applied.
>
>   However, we are also mindful of the fact that clause 1, when read together with the other provisions of Part 1, confers exceptionally wide powers which are capable of being applied to a very wide range of persons, with a very wide discretion being given to Ministers to determine the persons against whom sanctions measures may be applied. The sanctions measures are inherently intrusive with the potential to have a significant impact on the rights of individuals.

Similar criticisms have been made of both Acts designed to implement Brexit – the European Union (Withdrawal) Act 2018 and the European Union (Withdrawal Agreement) Act 2020.

Parliamentary control of delegated legislation is severely restricted. A bill that is published in draft for pre-legislative scrutiny may give Parliament and its committees an incomplete picture, for it is not accompanied by drafts of statutory instruments to be made under powers delegated by its provisions. Statutory instruments can normally only be approved or disapproved as a whole, without amendment. In the House of Commons, a 'prayer' or motion to annul a negative instrument is unlikely to be debated on the floor of the house and may fail to be debated at all within the forty-day period fixed by section 5 of the Statutory Instruments Act 1946. Debates on affirmative instruments on the floor of the house are generally subject to a time limit of ninety minutes. In practice, an instrument is more likely to be debated in a delegated legislation committee, to which a negative instrument may be referred on the motion of a minister of the Crown. (Affirmative instruments are automatically so referred unless a minister tables a motion to the contrary.) Debate in the committee takes place on a neutral motion – that the committee 'has considered' the instrument – which does not allow for any recommendation to be made to the house: the committee can only express its disapproval of an instrument by voting that it has not considered it. The effective vote on the instrument is taken subsequently on the floor of the house: indeed, once a negative instrument has been debated in the committee, there is usually no vote on the prayer for annulment. Although the official opposition can generally secure a debate on an instrument to which it is strongly opposed, a very large proportion of prayers on negative instruments are not debated at all, and the procedures do not provide for an adequate parliamentary consideration of the general run of statutory instruments. The Procedure Committee has described the parliamentary procedures for debating and deciding on statutory instruments as 'palpably unsatisfactory' (*4th Report of 1995–96*, HC 152) and as being 'urgently in need of reform' (*1st Report of 1999–2000*, HC 48). Director of the Hansard Society, Dr Ruth Fox, was of like mind in saying that 'scrutiny of statutory instruments remains wholly inadequate' and has urged that the affirmative resolution procedure 'should allow for amendment rather than just adoption or rejection' (*The Reform Challenge* (2010), p. 10). A court, in considering the interpretation and effect of an item of delegated legislation, may take account of the inadequacies of the negative procedure as an instrument of parliamentary control: see *R* v. *Secretary of State for the Environment, Transport and the Regions, ex p Spath Holme Ltd* [2001] 2 AC 349 (CA) at [68], (HL) at 382–3; *R (Public Law Project)* v. *Lord Chancellor* [2015] UKSC 39, [2017] 2 All ER 423, [27]-[28].

In 2003, the House of Lords established a Select Committee on the Merits of Statutory Instruments, now the Secondary Legislation Scrutiny Committee, to consider statutory instruments laid before each house and decide whether the special attention of the Lords should be drawn to an instrument on any of the following grounds:

(a) that it is politically or legally important or gives rise to issues of public policy likely to be of interest to the House;

(b) that it may be inappropriate in view of changed circumstances since the enactment of the parent Act;

(c) that it may inappropriately implement European Union legislation;

(d) that it may imperfectly achieve its policy objectives.

The working methods of this committee were most recently described in *Accessing the Scrutiny Work of the Committee and Information Relating to Secondary Legislation, 45th Report 2017–19* HL Paper 312. It is particularly concerned to identify negative instruments of special interest on any of the specified grounds. Following the enactment of the European Union (Withdrawal) Act 2018, the committee has also performed the sifting function over measures enacted under the 2018 Act to remedy deficiencies in retained EU law following the UK's exit from the European Union. From 2018–19, the committee split into two sub-committees to better enable it to deal with this function. There is as yet no equivalent House of Commons' committee that could enable a better informed and more focused scrutiny of statutory instruments in that house.

A technical examination of statutory instruments laid before Parliament, and other instruments of a general and not local character, is carried out by the Joint Committee on Statutory Instruments, composed of members of both houses. (Instruments laid only before the House of Commons are considered by the Commons members of the committee sitting without the peers.) The committee determines whether the special attention of each house should be drawn to any instrument on grounds not impinging on its merits or policy – for example, if its drafting appears to be defective, or if it is excluded by the enabling act from challenge in the courts, or if there is doubt whether it is intra vires, or if it 'appears to make some unusual or unexpected use of the powers conferred by the statute under which it is made'. (See Standing Order No. 151.) Before reporting to the house, the committee must give the department concerned an opportunity to provide an explanation.

When a significant technical defect is discovered by the joint committee, the department concerned is usually willing to amend the instrument. If it declines to do so, members may attempt to use such opportunities as are provided by the affirmative or negative procedure to oppose the instrument in the house. If no parliamentary procedure is prescribed by the enabling act, other occasions may be found for raising the question on the floor of the house. But an 'adverse report by the Committee has no effect on the manner in which an instrument is considered, and there is no procedure to prevent a substantive decision [by the House of Commons] before the Committee has completed its consideration' (Procedure Committee, *1st Report of 1977–78*, HC 588, para 3.8). Both the Procedure Committee and the Joint Committee on Statutory Instruments have urged the adoption of a standing order precluding any decision by the house on a statutory instrument before it has been considered by the joint committee. (See Procedure Committee, *1st Report of 1999–2000*, HC 48.) Provision to this effect is already made in standing orders of the House of Lords.

The Regulatory Reform Committee of the House of Commons scrutinises and reports on draft orders laid before the house under the Legislative and Regulatory Reform Act 2006. (See, as to this Act, pp. 565, 574 above.) A wider scrutiny of statutory delegations of legislative power is carried out by the Delegated Powers and Regulatory Reform Committee of the House of Lords (see, further, p. 562 above).

(See, generally, Hayhurst and Wallington, 'The Parliamentary Scrutiny of Delegated Legislation' [1988] PL 547; *Report of the Hansard Society Commission on the Legislative Process* (1992), paras 364–87; Brazier (ed.), *Parliament, Politics and Law Making* (2004), ch. 5; Salmon, 'Scrutiny of Delegated Legislation in the House of Lords' (2005) *The Table* 46; Fox and Korris, *Making Better Law* (2010), pp. 43–5, 161–5; Select Committee on the Constitution, *The Legislative Process: The Delegation of Powers*, 16th Report 2017–19 HL Paper 225.)

9.4.3 Finance

'The real power to have in Parliament is control over money' (Mr Edward du Cann MP, in Englefield (ed.), *Commons Select Committees: Catalysts for Progress?* (1984), p. 38). Parliament exercises a formal financial control over the government in that its authority has to be obtained for taxation and the expenditure of public money. In practice, the financial control and account-ability of government depend on a variety of parliamentary procedures of which some have been relatively effective and others decidedly weak. Public finance and expenditure, the process of 'getting and spending', was until recently neglected by parliamentary reformers. But the raising and expenditure of public money involves choices between different policy goals and can profoundly affect the prosperity of the country and the distribution of wealth in society.

Taxation may be proposed only by ministers on behalf of the Crown and has to be authorised by Parliament (see above, p. 66). Much of it is provided for in permanent legislation, but rates of income, corporation and other taxes are fixed for the year, and new taxes may be introduced, in an annual finance bill, which follows the presentation of the budget and the approval of budget ('ways and means') resolutions in the House of Commons. The house accordingly has opportunities to debate proposals for taxation when fiscal legislation and budget resolutions are before it. The government is, admittedly, unlikely to agree to significant alterations to the budget and, as the Treasury and Civil Service Committee noted, 'Although the tablets of stone on which the Finance Bill is written can in theory be amended during its consideration, in practice the Government's reputation is at stake and so major substantive amendments are rare' (*6th Report of 1981–82*, HC 137, para 2.1). Yet it has been remarked that the Commons debates on the finance bill 'are often some of the best argued and most effective of any held in the House' (Blackburn and Kennon, *Griffith and Ryle on Parliament* (2nd edn. 2003), para 6–188), and the hazards of politics may, exceptionally, compel the government to give way, as in December 1994 when it retreated from the imposition of additional VAT on domestic fuel. Contrariwise, the Treasury Select Committee has expressed dissatisfaction with procedure on the finance bill, 'which lets badly drafted and insufficiently tested tax legislation onto the statute book every year' (*3rd Report of 2000–01*, HC 73, para 54).

In 1997 the Labour Government announced measures for wider consult-ation on budget proposals, in particular through publication of a 'Pre-Budget Report' (*Financial Statement and Budget Report*, HC 85 of 1997–98, para 1.30). The Pre-Budget Report appeared in the autumn and set out the government's provisional proposals for the budget, allowing several months for consultation with outside bodies and consideration by the Treasury Committee of the House of Commons. The 2010–15 Coalition Government replaced the pre-budget report with the autumn statement, a practice that continued until 2017. In 2017, the budget was moved from spring to the autumn, accompanied by a spring statement. In 2019, there was no autumn budget due to the general election, this taking place, instead, in March 2020. The Treasury Committee reports each year on the budget and the spring statement, having examined Treasury officials and the Chancellor of the Exchequer on the tax proposals.

Another source of government revenue, borrowing, largely escapes parliamentary scrutiny, although it has been of great importance in the management of the economy. The Select Committee on Procedure (Finance) recommended that the House of Commons should be given formal power to approve the government's annual borrowing requirement (*1st Report of 1982–83*, HC 24), but the government did not accept this.

The fundamental principle relating to *expenditure* by the government is stated in the introductory sections to the government's annual supply estimates as follows:

> Under long-established constitutional practice it is for the Crown (the Government) to demand money, the House of Commons to grant it and the House of Lords to assent to the grant.

Money is 'granted' (i.e., expenditure is authorised) by Parliament only on the 'demand' of the Crown. This exclusive financial initiative of the Crown has been an important element in the establishment of the government's ascendancy over Parliament. The rule, as Gordon Reid says (*The Politics of Financial Control* (1966), p. 44), provides governments with 'a powerful controlling technique' and 'protects parties in government from the political embarrassment of having to vote against a wide range of alternative proposals, initiated in other parts of the House, and designed to appeal to the electorate'. Parliament may not increase the items of expenditure submitted to it by the government or vote for the expenditure of money on objects of its own choice.

Nevertheless, the formal requirement that expenditure must be authorised by Parliament opens up the possibility of an exercise of some control or influence by the House of Commons over the government's spending policies. The importance of this was underlined by David Howarth MP (as he then was) in reminding us (citing Aaron Wildavsky) that 'policy is expenditure and expenditure is policy' because 'a policy that does not have resources attached to it is generally just hot air, and any spending decision is, in reality, a decision about what to spend money on, as opposed to spending money on something else, and therefore is a policy decision' (HC Deb vol. 498, col 958, 4 November 2009).

The bulk of government expenditure is approved annually by Parliament in voting 'supply'. Estimates of departmental expenditure are laid before the Commons by the Treasury and, once approved by resolution of the house, are confirmed by legislation: an appropriation Act is passed for the year in question, giving authority for the money to be issued from the Consolidated Fund. Expenditure that does not require the annual approval of Parliament consists of certain payments charged directly by statute on the Consolidated Fund – for example, salaries and pensions of judges and the Speaker of the House of Commons, payments to the EU (at least until the end of implementation period completion day) and payments to the National Loans Fund to service the national debt. Some departmental activities are financed through trading funds, which fall outside the parliamentary supply process.

The detailed scrutiny by the House of Commons of the proposed supply expenditure of government departments was abandoned long ago, and the government's estimates presented to the house came to be passed 'on the nod'. In 1880, the house voted to reduce an estimate by £80, the cost of providing food for the pheasants in Richmond Park (Einzig, *The Control of the Purse* (1959), p. 271), but a century later, a vote of £500 million would be approved without debate. Supply days had come to be used for debating questions of policy or administration chosen by the opposition rather than for the detailed examination of departmental estimates. (These are now 'opposition days', which are unconnected with the supply procedure.) Since 1982, three days have been allotted in each session for debates on the estimates, the subjects for debate being chosen on the recommendation of the Liaison Committee. Five days, spread over 2018 and 2019, were spent debating the estimates of the 2017–19 session. These debates, too, are usually on matters of general policy, focusing on reports from the departmental select committees, and voting on estimates has become a formality. At the end of the twentieth century, the Procedure Committee of the House of Commons concluded that the power of the house over expenditure had become 'if not a constitutional myth, very close to one' (*6th Report of 1998–99*, HC 295, para 4).

However, there have been substantial improvements in the comprehensiveness and quality of the financial information provided to Parliament. Several of the departmental committees have responded by taking a greater interest in the material provided, examining departmental estimates or the departments' annual reports that describe their activities and performance over the previous year and set out their future spending plans. This is one of the 'core tasks' of the committees (see above, pp. 734–735), although their coverage of government expenditure is not complete or systematic.

In 1997, the government announced that public expenditure planning, instead of looking only to the year ahead, would in future be based on forward spending reviews, led by the Treasury, departments being set 'firm plans and fixed budgets for three years at a time'. In the spending review process, government departments engage in discussions with the Treasury on the spending budgets to be allocated to them for the years ahead, differences being referred to the Public Expenditure Committee of senior ministers (commonly and unhistorically known as the 'Star Chamber') for resolution. The spending review of October 2010 fixed the spending budgets for the four years (rather than three as formerly) from 2011–12 to 2014–15. In 2015, the then chancellor delivered a combined autumn statement and spending review. The next spending review, for 2020–21 took place in 2019. A multi-year review was planned for 2020, but this was delayed from March to July in the light of the Covid-19 pandemic. Spending reviews are examined by the Treasury Committee and debated in the House of Commons.

A reform that took full effect from 2001–2 was the change to a system of resource-based supply and accounting, in place of the traditional, exclusively cash-based system. Parliament approves expenditure expressed in terms of costs to be incurred, as well as the cash actually to be spent, in the year ahead. Resource estimates and accounts (replacing the former cash-based appropriation accounts) provide Parliament with more comprehensive financial information, yielding benefits in improved departmental decision-making and parliamentary control.

However, the system of authorisation and monitoring of government expenditure was still flawed, being too complicated and affected by a mismatch between documents presented to Parliament and the systems of control used within government, since Treasury budgets, Estimates and resource accounts measured and reported expenditure in different ways. Following cross-party discussions over several years, the government presented a set of proposals in the White Paper *Alignment (Clear Line of Sight) Project*, Cm 7567/2009, in order to achieve 'better alignment between budgets, Estimates and accounts and simplifying and streamlining Government's financial reporting documents, thereby improving Parliament's ability to scrutinise planned and actual expenditure' (para 1.3). The Liaison Committee, as well as other committees of the House of Commons, welcomed the proposals, which would 'enable the House to track spending plans clearly as they are translated from plans for future years into precise figures requiring legislative authority for each year, and into actual spending recorded in the accounts' (*2nd Report of 2008–09*, HC 804). The government's alignment proposals were approved by the House of Commons on 5 July 2010 (HC Deb vol. 513, cols 85–108). Finance is the area in which above all others the Commons possesses legal and constitutional superiority over the Lords: see further on this point below.

However, despite these improvements, there continue to be criticisms of the level of scrutiny over financial matters. In 2011, the Leigh-Pugh Report recommended the establishment of a budget committee, supported by a parliamentary budget officer (Sir Edward Leigh and Dr John Pugh *Options to Improve Parliamentary Scrutiny of Government Expenditure*). Since then, there have been two reports of the Procedure Committee, both making recommendations for more effective scrutiny, and the second report strongly supporting the establishment of a budget committee in the Commons (Procedure Committee, *Authorising Government Expenditure: Steps to More Effective Scrutiny*, 5th Report 2016–17 HC 190 and *Should There Be a Commons Budget Committee? Tenth Report 2017–19* HC 1482). In its latter report, the committee concluded (at p. 35) that:

In many respects the House's scrutiny of Estimates does not live up to expectations:

- Formal scrutiny of annual Estimates is limited, and the resulting legislation passes both Houses almost by default.
- The House has limited opportunities for proper examination of the sums the Government has asked it to appropriate.
- The departmental select committee system does not provide the systematic quality assurance and scrutiny of Estimates which the Government claims is undertaken once its spending plans are presented to Parliament.

This disadvantages Members in their understanding of how public money is being used, and their capacity to make recommendations to Government about how it might be better spent.

It remains to be seen whether the house will agree to act on these recommendations and create a budget committee.

(See, further, Daintith and Page, *The Executive in the Constitution* (1999), chs 4–6; White and Hollingsworth, *Audit, Accountability and Government* (1999); McEldowney and Lee, 'Parliament and Public Money', in Giddings (ed.), *The Future of Parliament, Change or Decay* (2005); Brazier and Ram, *The Fiscal Maze: Parliament, Government and Public Money* (2006); McEldowney, 'Public Expenditure and the Control of Public Finance', in Jowell and Oliver (eds.), *The Changing Constitution* (8th edn. 2015); McKay and Johnson, *Parliament and Congress* (2010), pp. 225–6, 254–67, 299–301.)

9.4.3.1 Public Accounts Committee

Parliament also needs to check that expenditure by the government has been for the purposes authorised and that value for money has been obtained. Since 1861 this ex post facto scrutiny has been carried out on behalf of the House of Commons by its Public Accounts Committee, of which the chairman is always, by convention, a member of the opposition. The work of the committee is closely linked with that of the independent National Audit Office (NAO) headed by the Comptroller and Auditor General, which examines and reports to Parliament on the annual accounts of government departments, executive agencies and a wide range of other public bodies, drawing attention to any losses, extravagance or impropriety that have been discovered. Besides this financial audit, the NAO conducts special investigations during the year into the 'economy, efficiency and effectiveness' with which government departments and other public bodies have used their resources, presenting the results to Parliament in a succession of 'value for money' (VFM) reports (around sixty a year). Facts recounted in the VFM reports must be agreed with the department or public body concerned. Recent reports have covered such matters as 'Challenges in using data across government'; 'Serious and organized crime'; 'NHS waiting times for elective and cancer treatment'; 'Windrush generation and the Home Office' and

'Renewing the EastEnders set'. The VFM reports are considered by the Public Accounts Committee, which questions departmental accounting officers and other senior officials on the matters to which the office has drawn attention, and itself reports to Parliament on the results of its inquiries. The government's reply to the report is published in a Treasury minute. The committee's reports to Parliament have, over the years, revealed many instances of waste and failure of financial control, and the committee is said to have 'contributed significantly to the maintenance of high standards in the handling of public money by the Civil Service' (Procedure Committee, *1st Report of 1977–78*, HC 588, para 8.3).

The importance of the Public Accounts Committee's work appears from its report on the Chevaline project (*9th Report of 1981–82*, HC 269). The Ministry of Defence embarked on this programme for the improvement of the Polaris missile system in the late 1960s, and the first cost estimate for the project was £175 million. The Secretary of State for Defence informed the House of Commons of the project in January 1980 and announced that the estimated cost had risen to £1,000 million. The committee decided to investigate Chevaline and in due course reported to Parliament its finding of significant weaknesses in the department's management and control of the project, with serious underestimates of costs and timescales. The committee also drew attention to more general grounds for disquiet (para 15):

> In the case of Chevaline a major project costing £1,000 million continued for over ten years without Parliament being in our view properly informed of its existence and escalating costs. Expenditure each year was included in the normal way in the Defence Estimates and Appropriation Accounts; our criticism is that the costs were not disclosed, and that there was no requirement that they should be disclosed. Incidental and oblique references to a Polaris enhancement programme made in Parliament or to Parliamentary committees in our view do not provide sufficient information for Parliament to discharge its responsibility to scrutinise major expenditure proposals and to exercise proper financial control over supply.

The government in reply agreed to provide the Public Accounts Committee with financial information about major defence projects in future (*Treasury Minute*, Cmnd 8759/1982). The committee has since carried out annual examinations of major defence projects and these regularly reveal poor project management, mounting delays and inflated costs. Inquiries in 2005 and 2009 into the purchase of Chinook Mk3 helicopters found that this procurement had been flawed by a catalogue of errors from the start and was one of the worst examples of equipment procurement the committee had ever seen: *8th Report of 2004–05*, HC 386 and *8th Report of 2008–09*, HC 247.

The Public Accounts Committee works on non-party lines and its reports, which are in practice unanimous, are debated each year in the House of

Commons. The great majority of the committee's recommendations are accepted by the government.

It is important that the Comptroller and Auditor General should be independent of government. The office was formerly thought to be too closely associated with the Treasury; the government agreed to a change in the status of the office only under considerable backbench pressure and after a private member's bill to reform the system of state audit had won widespread support from MPs. The National Audit Act 1983 established the Comptroller and Auditor General as an officer of the House of Commons who is appointed by the Crown on an address from the house, moved by the prime minister with the agreement of the chairman of the Public Accounts Committee. On the appointment of a new Comptroller and Auditor General in 2009 there was, for the first time, a pre-appointment hearing by the Public Accounts Committee. The Comptroller may be dismissed only on resolutions of both houses.

After a review of the governance arrangements for the National Audit Office in 2008, it was decided to reconstitute the office as a corporate body to be managed by a board with a majority of non-executive members, including the chair, and with the Comptroller and Auditor General as chief executive. Following the enactment of the Budget Responsibility and National Audit Act 2011, the Comptroller is appointed by the monarch on an address of the House of Commons for a non-renewable ten-year term. The chair of the NAO is appointed by the same process, for a once renewable term of three years. The NAO is to support and advise the Comptroller and monitor the performance of his or her functions.

9.5 The House of Lords

In considering the control and accountability of government, we have concentrated on the role of the House of Commons. We have, however, already noted some of the ways in which the House of Lords takes part in the supervision of the executive – for example, through the work of its select committees on the EU and on the Merits of Statutory Instruments, and its participation with the House of Commons in the Joint Committee on Statutory Instruments. We have also noted the establishment of the Lords' Delegated Powers and Regulatory Reform Committee and that peers join with MPs in the JCHR, which considers a range of matters relating to human rights in the UK (see further Chapter 11). We have also seen that draft bills may be referred to joint committees of the two houses for pre-legislative scrutiny.

The House of Lords has no departmentally related committees like those of the Commons, but since 1979 there has been a Lords' Select Committee on Science and Technology which enquires into government policy and other matters of public concern affecting science and technology. It has reported on such subjects as renewable energy, science teaching in schools, radioactive waste management and the science and technology of healthy living in an aging society. The committee work of the house has since expanded with the establishment of new sessional (permanent) committees on communications (the media and the creative industries), economic affairs, food, poverty, health and the environment and the constitution. The terms of reference of the Constitution Committee are:

> to examine the constitutional implications of all public bills coming before the House; and to keep under review the operation of the constitution.

In recent times, the Constitution Committee has been critical of a range of bills, notably so with regard to a number of those concerned with constitutional reform. See, for example, its reports on the following bills: the Constitutional Reform and Governance Bill (*11th Report of 2009–10*, HL 98); the Parliamentary Voting Systems and Constituencies Bill (*7th Report of 2010–11*, HL 58); the Fixed-Term Parliaments Bill (*8th Report of 2010–11*, HL 69); the Public Bodies Bill (*6th Report of 2010–11*, HL 51); and the European Union (Withdrawal) Bill (*3rd Report 2017–19*, HL Paper 19, *9th Report 2017–19*, HL Paper 69). A glance at the Lords' second reading debates on bills such as these will show that the reports of the Constitution Committee are extensively cited and relied on by peers from all sides of the house.

In addition to its legislative scrutiny work, the Constitution Committee also conducts policy inquiries into various aspects of constitutional affairs. Among its most notable such reports are the following: *Waging War: Parliament's Role and Responsibility* (*15th Report of 2005–06*, HL 236); *Surveillance: Citizens and the State* (*2nd Report of 2008–09*, HL 18); *Fast-track Legislation: Constitutional Implications and Safeguards* (*15th Report of 2008–09*, HL 116); *The Cabinet Office and the Centre of Government* (*4th Report of 2009–10*, HL 30); *Referendums in the United Kingdom* (*12th Report of 2009–10*, HL 99); *The Process of Constitutional Change* (*15th Report 2010–12*, HL Paper 177); *Scottish Independence: Constitutional Implications of the Referendum* (*8th Report 2013–14*, HL Paper 188); *The Union and Devolution* (*10th Report 2015–16*, HL Paper 149); *English Votes for English Laws* (*6th Report 2016–17*, HL Paper 61); *Parliamentary Scrutiny of Treaties* (*20th Report 2017–19* HL Paper 345) and a series of reports on the legislative process (*4th Report 2017–19*, HL Paper 27; *16th Report 2017–19*, HL Paper 279 and *24th Report 2017–19*, HL Paper 393).

The house also sets up ad hoc committees from time to time, inquiring for instance into proposals for a bill of rights, human cloning and stem cell research, HIV and AIDS in the UK and intergenerational fairness. One such committee conducted a thorough inquiry into the law of murder, making an important contribution to the debate on the subject of the mandatory life sentence for this crime: *Report from the Select Committee on Murder and Life Imprisonment*, HL 78 of 1988–99. Rodney Brazier remarks that 'the expertise at the disposal of Lords select committees gives them considerable authority' (*Ministers of the Crown* (1997), p. 259).

A bill normally has to be passed in identical terms by both houses before being given the royal assent, and disagreement between the houses is commonly resolved through the process known as 'ping-pong' as the bill travels back and forth between the two houses. The powers of the House of Lords in relation to primary legislation are, however, substantially restricted by the Parliament Acts 1911 and 1949. A money bill passed by the House of Commons, if sent up to the House of Lords at least one month before the end of the session, may be presented for the royal assent if it has not been passed by the Lords without amendment within one month. For this purpose a 'money bill' is a public bill dealing *only* with such matters as central government taxation, supply, appropriation and government loans, and must have been certified as such by the Speaker of the House of Commons. (The annual finance bill is not necessarily a money bill as it may deal with other matters besides taxation. Issues relating to the Speaker's certification were debated in the House of Lords on 29 November 2010: HL Deb vol. 722, cols 1269–82; see further House of Lords Constitution Committee, *Money Bills and Commons Financial Privilege, 10th Report of 2010–11*, HL 97.) Any other public bill – except a bill to extend the maximum duration of Parliament beyond five years – may be presented for the royal assent if it has been passed by the Commons in two successive sessions and the Lords have rejected it in each of those sessions, provided that a year has elapsed between the second reading of the bill in the House of Commons in the first session and its third reading in that house in the second session. So far seven bills have been passed without the consent of the Lords under the procedure of the Parliament Acts: the Government of Ireland Act 1914, the Welsh Church Act 1914, the Parliament Act 1949, the War Crimes Act 1991, the European Parliamentary Elections Act 1999, the Sexual Offences (Amendment) Act 2000 and the Hunting Act 2004. The power to overcome the resistance of the Lords by this means is one of last resort, and most differences between the houses (or between the government and peers contesting its legislation) are resolved by compromise or concession.

The question whether the prohibition on the use of the Parliament Acts for the passage of a bill to extend the life of a Parliament beyond five years (see above) could itself be deleted by an Act passed by the machinery of those Acts was a matter on which differing views were expressed by the Law Lords in *R (Jackson)* v. *Attorney General* [2005] UKHL 56, [2006] 1 AC 262: yes, said Lord Bingham [32]: no, said Lords Nicholls [57]–[59], Steyn [79], Hope [118], [122], Carswell [175] and Baroness Hale [164]; probably no, said Lords Rodger [139] and Brown [194].

When the Labour Government that came to power in 1945 embarked on a radical programme of nationalisation which was threatened by the existence of a Conservative majority in the House of Lords, the leader of the Conservative peers, Lord Salisbury, urged self-restraint and reached an agreement with Lord Addison, Leader of the House, to the effect that the Upper House should not reject a 'manifesto' bill considered to have been approved by the electorate. In 1967, another leader of the Conservative opposition in the Lords reaffirmed the 'Salisbury (or Salisbury-Addison) doctrine' with respect to manifesto bills: it should be assumed that any such bill had been approved by the electorate and, while the Lords might properly amend it in order that the Commons might reconsider a matter, they should not insist on the amendment if the Commons remained firm. The House of Lords Constitution Committee concluded that, technically, the Salisbury-Addison did not apply to a coalition government (*Constitutional Implications of Coalition Government, 5th Report 2013–14*, HL Paper 130). Nevertheless, the behaviour of the House of Lords during that period reinforced the application of the convention. Questions also arose as to whether the convention should apply during a minority government. A report of the Constitution Committee revealed mixed perceptions as to the scope and application of the convention, it being regarded, for example, as not applying to Liberal Democrat peers (*The Salisbury-Addison Convention, 5th Report 2017–19*, HL Paper 28).

Nevertheless, there is a consensus that restraint should also be exercised with regard to non-manifesto bills passed by the Commons. This applies both to coalition and minority governments. However, in certain circumstances the Upper House would be justified in using its delaying power, rejecting the bill or insisting on an amendment.

House of Lords, HL Deb vol. 280, cols 419–20, 16 February 1967

Lord Carrington: . . . [T]his House, the unelected Chamber, should not, except in the last resort and in quite exceptional circumstances, override the opinion of the House of Commons which has been elected by the people of this country. If we did not adopt such a course it would be impossible for any Labour Government to govern, since obviously much of the legislation which is introduced is bitterly opposed by those of us in the Conservative Party. It would really not be possible for a two-Chamber system of Government to operate, nor would it be a justifiable position for the unelected Chamber to control the timing of the Government's legislative programme by using its delaying powers . . .

There could arise a matter of great constitutional and national importance, on which there was known to be a deep division of opinion in the country or perhaps on which the people's opinion was not known. In a case of this kind, it seems to me that the House of Lords has a right, and perhaps a duty, to use its powers, not to make a decision, but to afford the people of this country and Members of the House of Commons a period for reflection and time for views to be expressed.

(The convention was explored in more detail in Chapter 3.)

The terms on which a reformed second chamber should engage with the House of Commons would need to be renegotiated in order to settle the rules, conventions or practices governing the relationship (see further below).

Even as constrained by law and practice, the House of Lords was able to cause considerable difficulty to the 1974–9 Labour Government, which had at best only a very slender overall majority in the Commons and did not always command the voting strength to remove Lords' amendments. The Upper House set aside its customary restraint and caused the government's supporters in the Commons to suffer a diet of three-line whips and late nights in the chamber. The government was compelled to accede to major Lords' amendments to some of its bills. A Trade Union and Labour Relations (Amendment) Bill introduced in the 1975–6 session was passed only after its reintroduction in the succeeding session and under the threat of invoking the Parliament Acts to overcome the Lords' opposition. The passage of this legislation was prolonged by some four months.

The renewed assertiveness of the Lords continued under subsequent Conservative governments, and opposition parties made well-organised and effective use of the Upper House in delivering their challenge to the government. Cross-bench and dissenting Conservative peers not infrequently joined them so as to inflict defeat on the Conservative government in its traditional bastion. A notable instance of this sort occurred in 1984, when the Local Government (Interim Provisions) Bill, which provided for the cancellation of forthcoming elections in Greater London and the metropolitan counties and the establishment of nominated bodies in place of the elected councils, suffered a wrecking amendment in the House of Lords that obliged the government to keep the elected authorities in being until their abolition took effect under the Local Government Act 1985. In the 1984–5 session, the Lords undermined the Government's Education (Corporal Punishment) Bill by amending it to provide for the abolition of corporal punishment in state schools, in place of provision for parental choice. The government abandoned the bill and introduced legislation in terms of the Lords' amendment in the following session (the Education (No 2) Act 1986, section 47; see now the Education Act 1996, section 548, as amended).

Conservative governments proved more vulnerable to defeat in the Lords than in the Commons. Between 1979 and 1990, 148 defeats were inflicted on government bills in the Lords, and in the majority of cases the Lords' amendments were accepted by the government or the bill was otherwise modified to placate opposition in the Upper House. The Lords were no less assertive in the 1990s, when defeats or the threat of them in the Lords obliged the government to make concessions on a number of bills, among them the Education (Schools) Bill in 1992, the Railways Bill in 1993, the Police and Magistrates' Courts Bill in 1994, the Pensions Bill in 1995, the Police Bill and the Crime (Sentences) Bill in 1997. In other instances, the government stood firm, using its Commons majority to overcome radical Lords' amendments – for example, regarding the Criminal Justice and Public Order Bill in 1994.

The willingness of the House of Lords to assert its independence and vote against the legislation of a Conservative government should not be exaggerated. Although the Conservatives did not always have an overall majority of the 'effective House' (all peers except those with leave of absence or without writs of summons), there was generally a loyal Conservative majority among the regularly voting peers. A study confirming this also found that cross-bench peers 'overwhelmingly support the Conservatives' (Adonis, 'The House of Lords in the 1980s' (1988) 41 *Parl Aff* 380, 382). When a strong attack, supported by a number of cross-bench and a few Conservative peers, was mounted on the Local Government Finance Bill (introducing the community charge or 'poll tax') in 1988 strenuous efforts by the government chief whip assured the defeat of an amendment relating the charge to ability to pay, in a huge turnout of over 500 peers, including many who had rarely attended the house before.

It was to be expected that the Labour Government elected in May 1997 would face a combative House of Lords. This proved to be so, the Lords inflicting thirty-six defeats on government bills in the 1997–8 parliamentary session. The Teaching and Higher Education Bill proceeded back and forth between Lords and Commons, in contention on the subject of student tuition fees in Scotland, until – as the matter came before the House of Lords for the seventh time – the government made a concession that was accepted by the peers. (The Parliament Acts could not have been used in this instance as the bill had begun in the House of Lords.) In 1998, the House of Lords gave a striking demonstration of its capacity for the discomfiture of government in repeatedly rejecting the government's 'closed list' system of proportional representation in the European Parliamentary Elections Bill, compelling the government to resort to the Parliament Acts to secure the bill's passage.

Even as the process of reform of the House of Lords got underway in the course of the 1997–2001 Parliament, the Upper House continued to exert to the full the powers available to it. The Parliament Acts were again invoked by the Labour Government to overcome the Lords' resistance and ensure the enactment of the Sexual Offences (Amendment) Act 2000, providing for an equal age of consent for homosexuals and heterosexuals. The government's attempt in the Local Government Bill 2000 to bring about the repeal of the notorious section 28 of the Local Government Act 1988 (prohibiting local authorities from 'promoting' homosexuality) was frustrated by the Lords. The bill having begun in the Upper House, the Parliament Acts were inapplicable and the government relinquished the repealing clause in order to save the bill. Challenges from the House of Lords to a number of other government bills were overcome when Lords' amendments were reversed by the Commons, or peers were placated by concessions, but the government was unable to rescue its Criminal Justice (Mode of Trial) (No 2) Bill (restriction of jury trial) or its

Tobacco Advertising Bill. Following the 2001 general election, the (partially reformed) Upper House reasserted its power. In the 2001–5 Parliament, government defeats in the Lords were of an unprecedented frequency and wrested significant concessions from the government during the passage of, among others, the Anti-Terrorism, Crime and Security Bill in 2001, the Police Reform Bill in 2002, the Criminal Justice Bill in 2003 and the Constitutional Reform Bill in 2005. The Hunting Bill received the royal assent in 2004 only by recourse to the Parliament Acts.

In the first session of the new Parliament elected in May 2005, further defeats in the Lords compelled the government to compromise on provisions in the Racial and Religious Hatred Bill and the Terrorism Bill in 2005, and the Identity Cards Bill in 2006. (See, further, Russell and Sciara, *The House of Lords in 2005: A More Representative and Assertive Chamber?* (2006).) Subsequently, the Lords induced further significant retreats or concessions from the Labour Government. The Fraud (Trials without a Jury) Bill was killed off in 2007 when the Lords voted to delay further debate on the bill for six months. There was a notable defeat in 2008 of the provision for forty-two days' pre-charge detention in the Counter-Terrorism Bill. In proceedings in the Lords on the Coroners and Justice Bill in 2009, the government accepted 254 amendments and lost 6 votes, obliging the government to remove provision for non-jury inquests from the bill. Their Lordships' ability and willingness to subject government bills to detailed, prolonged and oftentimes critical scrutiny has survived into the coalition era. Numerous government measures have met with sustained opposition in the Upper House, not least the Parliamentary Voting Systems and Constituencies Act 2011 and the Public Bodies Bill 2010–11.

Neither did this series of governmental defeats cease during the 2010–15 coalition government, during the Conservative majority Government of 2015–17, or the series of Conservative minority Governments from 2017–2019. The government was defeated forty-eight times in 2010–2012; twenty-six times in 2012–13; fourteen times in 2013–14; eleven times in 2014–15; sixty times in 2015–16; thirty-eight times in 2016–17 and sixty-two times in 2017–19. This pattern demonstrates, unsurprisingly, that the House of Lords is more able to defeat minority governments. The House of Lords was particularly active over the scrutiny of legislation to secure Brexit, with a series of defeats on the Trade Bill, the Healthcare (International Arrangements) Bill, and particularly the European Union (Withdrawal) Bill. The influential section 13 – the so-called 'meaningful vote'– was initiated by an amendment in the House of Lords; although the subsequent government amendment, and the final version of this section, differed in content from that originally proposed in the House of Lords.

This recital of government defeats and consequent revisions of policy exacted by the Lords may be seen as supporting the case for a confident Upper House with the ability to frustrate ill-considered or flawed legislation.

Contrariwise, the unrestrained activity of the House of Lords in dealing with government bills in opposition to the will of the Commons has raised questions about the legitimacy of a house with a largely nominated and still in part hereditary membership.

It is aptly said by Paul Carmichael and Brice Dickson (*The House of Lords* (1999), p. 17) that: 'Although the Lords' delaying power is constitutionally important ... there is little doubt that in the routine work of Parliament the major legislative function of the House of Lords is in the examination and revision of government legislation passed by the Commons or introduced in the Upper House before being passed to the Commons for consideration.' The scale of this work was evident in the 2007–8 session, when the Lords made 2,036 amendments to government bills brought up from the Commons. The great majority of Lords' amendments to government bills are the government's own amendments, incorporating second thoughts or concessions arising from the proceedings in the Commons or the continuing efforts of outside interests. Some other amendments are accepted by the government in recognition of their utility or from a willingness to compromise. In these respects, the House of Lords performs an essential revising function. Amendments to which the government remains opposed are generally removed when the bill is sent back to the House of Commons, and the lords, unless taking a strong stand on what they regard as a matter of principle, usually defer to the democratic character of the elected house and do not insist on amendments with which the Commons disagrees.

The House of Lords carries out a necessary scrutiny and improvement of bills that have left the Commons after an incomplete examination, in particular under the constraints of timetabling or when amendments are introduced at a late stage. An important instance was the Equality Bill in 2009, now the Equality Act 2010, for which there was inadequate time in the final (report and third reading) stages in the Commons to debate the large number of amendments and new clauses that had been tabled by the government and by members on both sides of the house, and it was left to the Lords to undertake the necessary scrutiny work. As David Lipsey has noted, 'Many bills are only scrutinised in their entirety because the Lords does so' ((2009) 80 *Pol Q* 400, 401). The House of Lords also has a useful role in facilitating the legislative programmes of government, through the introduction of less controversial government bills in that house. But as a check and restraint on government, the House of Lords has not enjoyed the legitimacy of a representative chamber, and the anomalous composition of the unreformed house imported an element of imbalance into the constitution. The challenge for reformers, however, is how to bring democracy to the Upper House without compromising on the quality or expertise of its work.

The lords have equal powers with the Commons with regard to statutory instruments, other than financial instruments laid before the Commons only, and therefore have a power of veto over most affirmative and negative instruments. This power has seldom been used, but in 1968 the Conservative majority in the House of Lords voted to reject an affirmative instrument, the Southern Rhodesia (United Nations Sanctions) Order. The result of this unprecedented vote was that inter-party talks then taking place on the reform of the House of Lords were suspended. Having made their protest, the lords approved a substantially similar order soon afterwards. The house has generally refrained from voting against statutory instruments, but on 20 October 1994 it agreed to a motion affirming 'its unfettered freedom to vote on any subordinate legislation submitted for its consideration' (HL Deb vol. 558, cols 356 et seq.). Peers supporting the motion acknowledged that the lords should vote against an instrument only as a last resort.

The lords asserted themselves in February 2000 when two items of delegated legislation relating to Greater London Authority elections were laid before Parliament. Again in March 2007, the lords declined to approve a draft instrument relating to the licensing of casinos. (See the detailed discussion of the lords' role in regard to statutory instruments in the report of the Joint Committee on Conventions, HL 265, HC 1212 of 2005–06, paras 190–234.) In 2015, the House of Lords was asked to approve the Tax Credits (Income Thresholds and Determination of Rates) (Amendments) Regulations 2015. The House of Lords rejected a fatal amendment to these regulations, but voted in favour of two amendments that suspended the consideration of the regulations by the House of Lords until either the government published its response to the analysis of these regulations by the Institute of Fiscal Studies, or provided a scheme for a renewable, three-year transition period. The government reacted strongly to this defeat, claiming that the House of Lords had breached convention, by effectively undermining the primacy of the House of Commons on an issue of spending and taxation, in addition to there not being exceptional circumstances to justify the House of Lords defeating delegated legislation. The government then announced a review of the powers of the House of Lords – the Strathclyde Review (*Strathclyde Review: Secondary legislation and the primacy of the House of Commons* Cm 9177, December 2015). The review recommended that a new procedure should be created, such that defeats of the House of Lords over delegated legislation could be overruled by the House of Commons. The review also advocated that these new provisions should be placed on a statutory basis. The Commons Public Administration and the Constitutional Affairs Committee and the Lords Constitution Committee and Delegated Powers and Regulatory Reform Committee rejected these suggestions. (*The Strathclyde Review: Statutory Instruments and the Power of the House of Lords*, 8th Report 2015–16, HC 752, *Delegated Legislation and Parliament: A Response to the Strathclyde Review*, 9th Report 2015–16, HL Paper 116 and *Special Report: Response to the Strathclyde Review*, 25th Report 2015–16, HL Paper 119). All recognized that the House of Lords could and should have the power to vote against delegated legislation.

9.5.1 Reform

The need for the reform of the House of Lords has been generally acknowledged and it was a Conservative Deputy Leader of the House who remarked in 1967 that the hereditary element in the composition of the house was 'not really a rational basis on which to run a second chamber in a democracy' (see Morgan, *The House of Lords and the Labour Government 1964–1970* (1975), p. 172). A carefully worked-out scheme of reform was incorporated in the Parliament (No 2) Bill 1968, but a campaign of filibustering by backbenchers on both sides of the House of Commons and the press of more urgent matters caused the Labour Government to drop the bill. (Its scheme of a two-tier house of voting and non-voting peers is described in the White Paper *House of Lords Reform*, Cmnd 3799/1968.) A Labour Party policy review of 1989 proposed an elected second chamber whose members would 'particularly reflect the interests and aspirations of the regions and nations of Britain' and which would have an extended power to delay, for the whole life of a Parliament, legislation affecting fundamental rights (*Meet the Challenge, Make the Change* (1989), pp. 55–6). Labour Party policy in the 1990s became more reticent as to the composition of a reformed second chamber, but was committed to the removal of the hereditary element. The Labour Party and the Liberal Democrats reached agreement on a two-stage programme of reform, which was reflected in the Labour manifesto for the 1997 general election.

The manifesto promised that as an initial, self-contained reform, 'the right of hereditary peers to sit and vote in the House of Lords will be ended by statute'. This was to be 'the first stage in a process of reform to make the House of Lords more democratic and representative'. In January 1999, the government announced the appointment of a royal commission, with Lord Wakeham as chairman, with terms of reference requiring it 'to consider and make recommendations on the role and functions of a second chamber; and to make recommendations on the method or combination of methods of composition required to constitute a second chamber fit for that role and for those functions'. At the same time, a House of Lords Bill was introduced in the House of Commons, providing for the removal of the right of hereditary peers (then some 750 in number) to sit and vote in the Upper House. In order to facilitate the passage of the bill through the House of Lords, the government agreed to an amendment (the 'Weatherill amendment') to allow ninety-two hereditary peers to remain in the house until the second stage of reform was implemented. Of this number, ninety would be elected from the existing hereditary peers in accordance with arrangements in new standing orders (also providing for by-elections to maintain the number at ninety) while two other hereditary peers holding great offices of state (the Earl Marshal and the Lord Great Chamberlain) would remain as members of the House ex officio. The bill duly received the royal assent as the House of Lords Act 1999.

Pending further reform the House of Lords was to continue as a house of predominantly appointed peers, together with twenty-six Church of England bishops and the Law Lords. (The latter were to migrate to the new Supreme Court in 2009.) The prime minister, who formally recommends those to be appointed by the monarch as life peers under the Life Peerages Act 1958, announced that he would forego his right of veto over nominations of peers by opposition leaders and that his power to nominate cross-bench (non-party) peers would be transferred to an independent appointments commission. No one party would be in a position to dominate the transitional house. The non-statutory Appointments Commission was established in May 2000: it has seven members, one nominated by each of the three main political parties and four (including the chair) who are non-partisan. Persons recommended by the commission must have 'independence, integrity and a commitment to the highest standards of public life'. By March 2010, fifty-five individuals had been recommended by the commission to the prime minister for appointment by the monarch to non-party-political peerages. In 2019, there were 661 life peers eligible to vote in the House of Lords. The prime minister continues to nominate directly to the monarch distinguished public servants on their retirement for appointment to non-party-political peerages (no more than ten in any one Parliament). The Appointments Commission also has the role of scrutinising all nominations for peerages, in particular those made by the political parties (other than peerages to be conferred on persons who are to serve in the Upper House as ministers). It reports to the prime minister any concerns it may have about the propriety of nominations, but does not have a veto.

The report of the Wakeham Royal Commission (*A House for the Future*, Cm 4534/2000) made 132 recommendations. It proposed relatively modest changes in the legislative and scrutinising functions of the lords, which were intended to enhance their role in the legislative process and enable them more effectively to hold the executive to account, but without significantly enlarging their powers or disturbing the existing balance between the two houses. The principal recommendations of the Wakeham Commission related to the composition of the Upper House, which was to consist of about 550 members. The Law Lords would remain and there would be thirty-one representatives of the different religious faiths. For the rest, the house would be composed of a majority of appointed members and a minority of elected regional members (65, 87 or 195 according to the several options proposed). All appointments would be the responsibility of a new, statutory Appointments Commission, which would be required to maintain a political balance reflecting each party's share of the votes in the most recent general election, and also to ensure that at least 20 per cent of the total membership of the house should be cross-bench (independent) members. Under this arrangement, no single party would have an overall majority in the House. (On the Wakeham Report, see Shell [2000] *PL* 193; Oliver [2000] *PL* 553; Russell and Cornes (2001) 64 *MLR* 82.)

The government's initial response to the Wakeham Report was positive. The government's proposals for the second stage of reform were published in a White Paper, *Completing the Reform* (Cm 5291/2001), and were seen to deviate from the Royal Commission Report in some important respects. While adhering to the Wakeham principle of a largely appointed Upper House with a minority (20 per cent in the White Paper) of regionally elected members and entrusting the appointment of cross-bench members to a statutory Appointments Commission, the White Paper would leave nomination of the political members in the hands of the political parties.

The White Paper followed Wakeham in leaving the powers and functions of the House of Lords substantially unchanged, but for a new power to delay a statutory instrument for up to three months, in place of the existing veto power over delegated legislation.

If the Wakeham Report had been widely regarded as over-cautious, if realistic, and as including some well-devised and sensible proposals, the White Paper met with a generally hostile response, not least among Labour backbenchers, was deprecated by Lord Wakeham himself and was criticised as a timid and executive-minded approach to the unfinished business of reform. There was particular dissatisfaction with the proposal that a majority of members should be nominees of the political parties and much support for the view that a substantial majority of members should be democratically elected. (See HL Deb vol. 630, cols 561 et seq., 9 January 2002; HC Deb vol. 377, cols 702 et seq., 10 January 2002.) More than 300 MPs signed an early day motion calling for a wholly or substantially elected second chamber, and the Public Administration Committee was unanimous in recommending that 60 per cent of the members should be elected in a chamber of no more than 350 members in total (5th *Report of 2001–02*, HC 494-I). The government, conceding that consensus on the composition of a reformed second chamber had not been achieved, agreed in May 2002 to the establishment of a joint committee of both houses (its membership to be settled through 'the usual channels') to explore afresh the options for reform and to bring forward alternative proposals to be voted on by each house. The joint committee (of twelve MPs and twelve peers) presented seven options: a wholly appointed house, a wholly elected house and a house of 20, 40, 50, 60 or 80 per cent elected members. In February 2003, the House of Lords voted by a substantial majority in favour of a wholly appointed house, but there was no majority support for any of the proposed options in the Commons (which voted decisively against a wholly appointed house and also against an additional option of abolition of the House of Lords – the 80 per cent elected option was defeated by only three votes).

Following this impasse, the reform project stalled. An attempt to revive it was made in 2007 with the publication of a White Paper (*House of Lords*

Reform, Cm 7027/2007), in which the government put forward for discussion the model of a hybrid house of 540 members, half of them to be elected and at least 20 per cent to be non-party-political appointments. In debates on the White Paper, the Commons gave preference to a fully elected second chamber, whereas the lords supported a wholly appointed house. This lack of consensus between the houses as to the composition of a reformed second chamber was followed by a resumption of cross-party talks with a view to a comprehensive reform package to include the size and composition of the house, electoral systems and the balance of powers. The talks proceeded on the basis that a wholly or mainly elected chamber was supported by the Commons and the three major political parties – or, at all events, their leaderships.

The outcome of the consultations was the publication of yet another White Paper, *An Elected Second Chamber: Further Reform of the House of Lords* (Cm 7438/2008), 'intended to generate discussion and inform debate', whereupon final proposals for reform would be included in a general election manifesto. However, the Labour Government's efforts to complete the reform of the House of Lords were extinguished in the general election of May 2010. The Coalition Government stepped into the breach in that year, when the deputy prime minister took the chair of a cross-party committee to negotiate the terms of a draft Lords reform bill. The draft bill, published in May 2011 (Cm 8077), proposed an 80 per cent elected house, using the single transferable vote system of election. It was submitted to a joint committee, which approved the recommendation for the 80 per cent elected and 20 per cent nominated composition of the House of Lords. The House of Lords Reform Bill was introduced in the Commons in 2012, where emphasis was placed both on the need to ensure the democratic accountability of the house, as well as to stem the tide of the rising membership of the House of Lords. However, the government withdrew the bill after its second reading, following a large Conservative rebellion, and it became clear that there would be insufficient support in the Commons for the bill. Shortly after the withdrawal of the bill, Lord Steel proposed the House of Lords Reform Bill, which became the House of Lords Reform Act 2014. Although this Act does not tackle the perceived democratic deficit of the House of Lords, it provides a modest solution to the size of the second chamber, providing a means for members to resign, in addition to providing that those peers who do not attend the House of Lords at all during a session of the house that lasts six months or more ceases to be a peer from the following session, subject to narrow exceptions. Members also lose their membership of the house if convicted of a serious offence.

There have been no subsequent measures to reform the second chamber, although calls for its reform persist. Despite this, research demonstrates that the second chamber continues to play an important role in the Westminster Parliament, often strengthening the ability of backbench and opposition MPs to hold the executive to account for its actions and playing an important role in the scrutiny of legislation.

(On the work of the House of Lords and reform proposals, see Shell, *The House of Lords* (2007); Russell and Sciara, 'The Policy Impact of Defeats in the House of Lords' (2008) 10 *British Jnl of Politics* 571; Russell, 'A Stronger Second Chamber?' (2010) 58 *Pol Stud* 866; Lord Bingham, 'The House of Lords: Its Future?' [2010] *PL* 261; Russell, *The Contemporary House of Lords: Westminster Bicameralism Revived* (OUP, 2013); Ballinger, *The House of Lords 1911–2011: A Century of Non-Reform* (Hart, 2014); Norton, *Reform of the House of Lords* (Manchester University Press, 2017.)

10

The Courts: Judicial Review and Liability

Contents

10.1 Nature and Foundations of Judicial Review

The decision of a minister, local authority or other public officer or body may be challenged in court by recourse to the machinery of judicial review. Judicial review is to be distinguished from appeal, which is sometimes available as a means of contesting an administrative decision. Judicial review is the exercise of an ancient and inherent supervisory jurisdiction of the court, by which excess or abuse of public power may be restrained or remedied. Its origins lie in the common law. Contrariwise, appeal to a court against an administrative Act is possible only where provision for it is made by statute.

A clear explanation of the distinction between review and appeal can be seen in the recent Supreme Court decision of *Michalak v. General Medical Council and others* [2017] UKSC 71, [2017] 1 WLR 4193. Dr Michalak had been dismissed from her job at an NHS Trust hospital. She brought a claim for unfair dismissal before an employment tribunal. Before the employment tribunal had reached its decision, the NHS Hospital Trust referred Dr Michalak to the General Medical Council (GMC) regarding her fitness to continue as a medical practitioner. Although the trust later withdrew its referral, the GMC had, by that stage, begun investigations into the complaint. Dr Michalak argued before the employment tribunal that the NHS Hospital Trust and the GMC had discriminated against her, on grounds of gender, race and disability. The trust argued that the employment tribunal did not have the ability to hear the appeal. This was because of section 120(7) of the Equality Act 2010, which prevents employment tribunals from hearing cases that may be 'subject to an appeal or proceedings in the nature of an appeal' that was available to the applicant 'by virtue of an enactment'. The trust argued that, as Dr Michalak could bring proceedings for judicial review, these proceedings were 'in the nature of an appeal'. Therefore, Dr Michalak could not bring her case for unfair dismissal before the employment tribunal.

The Supreme Court disagreed (*Michalak* v. *General Medical Council and others* [2017] UKSC 71, [2017] 1 WLR 4193, [20]). Judicial review is not the same as an appeal. According to Lord Kerr:

> In its conventional connotation, an 'appeal' ... is a procedure which entails a review of an original decision in all its aspects. Thus, an appeal body may examine the basis on which the original decision was made, assess the merits of the conclusions of the body or court from which the appeal was taken and, if it disagrees with those conclusions, substitute its own. Judicial review, by contrast, is *par excellence*, a proceeding in which the legality of or the procedure by which a decision was reached is challenged.

Moreover, Dr Michalak's action for judicial review was not available to her by 'virtue of an enactment' because 'judicial review originated as a common law procedure and not by virtue of any enactment'. [31]. While appeals are provided for by statute, judicial review is a creature of the common law.

The distinctive features of judicial review were considered by the House of Lords in *Chief Constable of the North Wales Police* v. *Evans* [1982] 1 WLR 1155. The Law Lords noted that judicial review is concerned not with the merits or demerits of the decision reached by an administrative authority – with whether that decision was right or wrong – but with the process by which the decision was reached. Lord Hailsham LC said:

> [I]t is important to remember in every case that the purpose of the remedies [in judicial review] is to ensure that the individual is given fair treatment by the authority to which he has been subjected and that it is no part of that purpose to substitute the opinion of the judiciary or of individual judges for that of the authority constituted by law to decide the matters in question. The function of the court is to see that lawful authority is not abused by unfair treatment and not to attempt itself the task entrusted to that authority by the law. There are passages in the judgment of Lord Denning MR (and perhaps in the other judgments of the Court of Appeal) in the instant case . . . which might be read as giving the courts carte blanche to review the decision of the authority on the basis of what the courts themselves consider fair and reasonable on the merits. I am not sure whether the Master of the Rolls really intended his remarks to be construed in such a way as to permit the court to examine, as for instance in the present case, the reasoning of the subordinate authority with a view to substituting its own opinion. If so, I do not think this is a correct statement of principle. The purpose of judicial review is to ensure that the individual receives fair treatment, and not to ensure that the authority, after according fair treatment, reaches on a matter which it is authorised by law to decide for itself a conclusion which is correct in the eyes of the court.

In *R* v. *Cambridge Health Authority, ex p B* [1995] 1 WLR 898, 905, Sir Thomas Bingham MR said that a court exercising judicial review has 'one function only, which is to rule upon the lawfulness of decisions'. In *R (St Helens BC)* v. *Manchester PCT* [2008] EWCA Civ 931, May LJ said the following (at [13]):

> Judicial review is a flexible but not entirely unfenced jurisdiction. This stems from certain intrinsic features. The court's relevant function is to review decisions of statutory and other public authorities to see that they are lawful, rational and reached by a fair and due process. The public authority is normally the primary decision-maker with a duty to apprehend the facts underlying the decision by a fair procedure which takes properly into account all relevant facts and circumstances. If the public authority does this, the court will not normally examine the merits of the factual determination. Accordingly, a court hearing a judicial review application normally receives evidence in writing only and does not set about determining questions of disputed fact. The court will therefore not normally entertain oral evidence nor cross-examination of witnesses on their written evidence.

The jurisdiction and powers of an appellate court or tribunal depend on the particular provision made in the relevant statute, but, in broad terms, we may say that appeal is concerned with merits, while judicial review is concerned with legality and process. Again, whereas an appellate court is usually empowered to substitute its own decision for that of the body appealed from, a court exercising review cannot normally do this: it is restricted to granting one or more of certain specific remedies – for instance, an order setting aside the decision of the administrative body. The courts, as Jaffey and Henderson observe, 'have by historic warrant and general consent a valuable and indispensable role in the administrative process'. Their task, say these authors, 'is to contain administrative activity within the bounds of delegated power: to apply to administrative action the test of "legality"' ((1956) 72 *LQR* 345, 346).

This is all very well as a matter of constitutional theory but, as we shall see, the line between 'appeal on the merits' and 'review of legality' is not always so clear in practice. It may also be that, as judicial review has developed and expanded, the line has blurred further. We will return to this matter later in the chapter.

The justification for judicial review has been looked for in the principle that powers granted to a public body must not be exceeded. This is the ultra vires principle: the act of a public authority that falls outside the limits of its jurisdiction or powers is unlawful and will be prevented or, after the event, set aside by the reviewing court. Where power is conferred by statute, it will be for the court to determine what limits Parliament has imposed on the use of the power and whether those limits have been exceeded. However, difficulties arise with this justification both when the court relies on limits other than those expressly set out in legislation, and when the court controls prerogative powers. Two justifications have been found: that the court is relying the implied intentions of Parliament, or that the court is drawing on common law principles to set the limits of the power of administrative bodies.

Daymond v. *South West Water Authority* [1976] AC 609 (HL)

Section 30 of the Water Act 1973 authorised water authorities 'to fix, and to demand, take and recover such charges for the services performed, facilities provided or rights made available by them . . . as they think fit'. The South West Water Authority imposed a charge for sewerage services on a householder, Daymond, whose house was not connected to a public sewer. Daymond contested the validity of the charge:

> **Viscount Dilhorne:** . . . Section 30 must have been intended to entitle water authorities to demand, take and recover their charges from some persons and classes of persons. Is it to be inferred that it was the intention of Parliament that they should be at liberty to charge anyone they thought fit in Great Britain? That has only to be stated to be rejected for it is, to my mind, inconceivable that Parliament should have intended to entrust such an extensive power of taxation to a non-elected body. Is it then to be inferred that it was intended to give them only power to charge those living in their area and those who came into it and made use of their services, facilities and rights? I think that such a limitation must be implied.
>
> If that is to be inferred, is it also to be inferred that they are completely at liberty to charge such of those persons as they think fit? . . .
>
> The natural inference to be drawn from a provision which only says that a statutory body can demand, take and recover such charges for the services it performs, the facilities it

> provides and the rights it makes available, as it thinks fit, is, in my opinion, that it can charge
> only those who avail themselves of its services, facilities and rights.

There was no other provision in the Act indicating that any different interpretation was to be placed on section 30. The House of Lords decided (by
a majority) that the charge imposed on Daymond was not permitted by the
statute.

What a statute permits, or does not permit, may be spelled out clearly and
unmistakably in the language used: what is intra vires and what ultra vires is
immediately apparent. Often, however, the statutory language is equivocal
and has to be interpreted (as in *Daymond*, above). In this task, the court
may be assisted by *presumptions* – for instance, the presumption that
Parliament would not have intended to authorise interference with fundamental rights unless its intention to do so appears 'by irresistible inference
from the statute read as a whole' (Lord Reid in *Westminster Bank
v. Minister of Housing and Local Government* [1971] AC 508, 529).
Presumptions of this kind derive from the common law, which is to say
that the courts have developed them, and so we see that judicially created
principles may be applied by the courts in deciding what a statute permits to
be done. It has been questioned whether, in this case, the courts are really
giving effect to the unexpressed but presumed intention of Parliament or
are rather simply requiring statutory powers to be exercised in conformity
with principles that the courts see it as their responsibility to uphold, and
that have their source in a judicial conception of the rule of law. If this is so,
it would seem that the judges are not acting – or at all events are not acting
exclusively – on a principle of ultra vires. Rather, they are enforcing the rule
of law, taken to mean not only that precisely limited statutory powers must
not be exceeded, but that powers must not be used – we should say abused –
in ways or for purposes that run counter to the principles of justice and fair
dealing evolved by the courts in the long experience of judging and developing the common law.

In recent years, the ultra vires theory of the basis of judicial review has
been strongly challenged by those who find the source and justification of
review in the common law. In their view, the principles applied by the
courts are not derived from an implied – and altogether fictional – intention
of Parliament, but rest on the historic function and character of courts 'as
guardians and pronouncers of values anchored in society and culture'
(Cotterrell, in Richardson and Genn (eds.), *Administrative Law and
Government Action* (1994), p. 17) – values that the courts have 'discovered'
in, or transplanted into, the common law. Paul Craig and Nicholas
Bamforth, 'Constitutional Analysis, Constitutional Principle and Judicial
Review' [2001] *PL* 763 say (at p. 767) that proponents of the common law
model (they are among them):

> argue that the principles of judicial review are in reality developed by the courts. They are the creation of the common law. The legislature will rarely provide any indication as to the content and limits of what constitutes judicial review. When legislation is passed the courts will impose the controls which constitute judicial review which they believe are normatively justified on the grounds of justice, the rule of law, etc. . . . The courts will decide on the appropriate procedural and substantive principles of judicial review which should apply to statutory and non-statutory bodies alike. Agency action which infringes these principles will be unlawful. A finding of legislative intent is not necessary for the creation or general application of these principles.

By the same token, the courts have generally continued to explain the review jurisdiction in terms of ultra vires, as providing a basis for their far-reaching power of control that is overtly respectful of parliamentary sovereignty. (See, e.g., *R v. Lord President of the Privy Council, ex p Page* [1993] AC 682, 701; *Boddington v. British Transport Police* [1999] 2 AC 143, 164, 171.) Some academic commentators, too, remain wedded to ultra vires as the comprehensive, unifying principle of the judicial review of statutory powers and have mounted a spirited defence of this principle. For them it is no mere fiction to say that Parliament, in granting manifold powers to ministers, local authorities, NDPBs and other agencies, does so on an unexpressed condition that the powers must be used rationally, fairly and for the purposes for which they are given. Even though a large measure of discretion is allowed in exercising the power – the statute using some such expression as 'the minister may, if he thinks fit ...' – it is argued that Parliament cannot be indifferent as to whether the power is diverted to collateral ends that are not compatible with the statutory purpose, or is used in an arbitrary manner that disregards the rights or legitimate expectations of individuals, or defies reason. If the courts devise principles to forestall abuses such as these, are they not acting to reinforce the will of Parliament?

(The ultra vires controversy has attracted a considerable literature. Significant contributions to the debate can be found in Forsyth (ed.), *Judicial Review and the Constitution* (2000). See, further, Elliott, *The Constitutional Foundations of Judicial Review* (2001); Craig and Bamforth [2001] *PL* 763; Barber (2001) 21 *OJLS* 369; Halpin (2001) 64 *MLR* 500; Allan [2002] *CLJ* 87; Leslie (2010) 30 *LS* 301.)

Although the focus is often on judicial review as a means of protecting the individual and providing remedies for wrongs done, we should not lose sight of a broader aim of review. Lord Woolf regards judicial review as 'primarily concerned with enforcing public duties on behalf of the public as a whole and as only concerned with vindicating the interests of the individual as part of the process of ensuring that public bodies do not act unlawfully and do perform their public duties' (*Protection of the Public: A New Challenge* (1990), pp. 33–4). If review is to have a deeper effect in improving the quality of administration and the official treatment of members of the public, it must generate clear principles that can provide guidance to administrators, who in their turn must accept a responsibility to act on the guidance so given. In these respects, it must be said that the achievement of judicial review has been modest. Although it has developed greatly in recent decades as a means of redress for wrongs, the principles of review are still somewhat lacking in clarity and precision, while the reaction of the administration to this burgeoning jurisdiction has been mixed, by turns unaware, acquiescent, sceptical or hostile, and less often conscientiously receptive. There are some indications, however, that a more positive administrative response may be emerging. (See, further, Rawlings, 'Judicial Review and the "Control of Government"' (1986) 64 *Pub Adm* 135; Richardson and Sunkin, 'Judicial Review: Questions of Impact' [1996] *PL* 79; Barker, 'The Impact of Judicial Review: Perspectives from Whitehall and the Courts' [1996] *PL* 612; Halliday, 'The Influence of Judicial Review on Bureaucratic Decision-Making' [2000] *PL* 110; Sunkin and Pick, 'The Changing Impact of Judicial Review' [2001] *PL* 736; Hertogh and Halliday (eds.), *Judicial Review and Bureaucratic Impact* (2004). On the tensions – damaging or creative? – that may arise between the judiciary and the executive, see Loveland, 'The War Against the Judges' (1997) 68 *Pol Q* 162; and Woolf, 'Judicial Review: The Tensions Between the Executive and the Judiciary' (1998) 114 *LQR* 579.)

Judicial review is a procedure that is known to both English and Scots law. While the principal *grounds* on which judicial review may be sought are largely the same in the two jurisdictions, there are several differences of *procedure*. The questions 'against whom may judicial review be sought?' and 'who may seek judicial review?', for example, are answered differently in English and Scots law (see, further, below). In both English and Scots law, judicial review has its own procedure, which is different in a variety of respects from ordinary private law procedure. This has been true in English law since 1977 and in Scots law since 1985. In England, the procedure is known as the claim for judicial review. It is governed by Part 54 of the Civil Procedure Rules. In Scotland, the procedure is known as the petition for judicial review. It is governed by Rule 58 of the Rules of the Court of Session. The procedures are designed to allow for a relatively speedy process. Unmeritorious claims or petitions can be dispensed with quickly. The procedure is not principally designed to allow courts to resolve substantial disagreements of fact. In most judicial review cases, there will be no disagreement between the parties as to the facts: the issue will be whether the government minister or other public authority has acted (or is proposing to act) lawfully or not. For this reason, most evidence in judicial review cases will be written rather than oral and there will not be extensive cross-examination. In both English and Scots law, judicial review procedure is exclusive: if a litigant wishes to argue that an authority subject to judicial review has acted unlawfully, the judicial review procedure is normally the only procedure available to them. (The leading authority on this point in English law is *O'Reilly* v. *Mackman* [1983] 2 AC 237; in Scots law, the issue of exclusivity is clear from the terms of Rule 58.)

The remedies available in judicial review allow the courts to quash an unlawful decision, to order that a duty be performed, to prohibit an unlawful decision from being taken or to make a declaration (in Scots law, a declarator) – an authoritative ruling on a question of law in contention between the parties. In English law, the first three of these remedies were formerly known as *certiorari*, *mandamus* and prohibition. They are now known as quashing, mandatory and prohibiting orders. In Scots law, they are known as reduction, implement and suspension. It is important to note that damages, while theoretically available, are granted in judicial review cases only rarely. This is because of the nature of the argument in judicial review. As we have seen, the argument in judicial review focuses less on whether the claimant (or petitioner) should be compensated and more on whether the public authority under review has acted lawfully or not. Damages and compensatory remedies are, however, beginning to grow in importance in public law, not least (as we saw in Chapter 5) under the influence of EU and European human rights law. We consider their availability against the Crown and other public authorities when we examine questions of liability later in this chapter.

Judicial review procedure and remedies are considered in greater depth in the literature on administrative law: see, among others, Blair, *Scots Administrative Law: Cases and Materials* (1999), chs 10–11; Craig, *Administrative Law* (8th edn. 2016), chs 24–7; Endicott, *Administrative Law* (3rd edn. 2018), chs 10–11; Harlow and Rawlings, *Law and Administration* (3rd edn. 2009), ch. 15.

Also in the literature on administrative law can be found consideration of other institutions of administrative justice, such as tribunals. While they hear and decide hundreds of thousands of cases every year and while they make a distinctive and important contribution to administrative justice and to several areas of our substantive law (notably immigration law and the law of social security), tribunal decisions may be regarded as a source of constitutional law only very rarely (an instance being some decisions on freedom of information, on which, see pp. 672–673). For these reasons, tribunals are not considered in detail in this book. Their governing statute, which effected the most significant reorganisation of tribunals in half a century, is the Tribunals, Courts and Enforcement Act 2007.

10.2 Grounds of Review

In *Council of Civil Service Unions* v. *Minister for the Civil Service* (the *GCHQ* case) [1985] AC 374, 410, Lord Diplock said:

> Judicial review has I think developed to a stage today when … one can conveniently classify under three heads the grounds upon which administrative action is subject to control by judicial review. The first ground I would call 'illegality', the second 'irrationality' and the third 'procedural impropriety'.

In identifying these categories, Lord Diplock had no intention of setting a limit to the expansion of judicial review, for he added: 'That is not to say that further development on a case by case basis may not in course of time add further grounds.' We shall consider the grounds of review under Lord Diplock's three heads, albeit that in our consideration of irrationality, we shall also consider questions of proportionality. For reasons that we shall explore, these now need, at least in some cases, to be read together. It is important to recognise that the various heads of review are not entirely distinct. As Lord Irvine LC remarked in *Boddington* v. *British Transport Police* [1999] 2 AC 143, 152:

> Categorisation of types of challenge assists in an orderly exposition of the principles underlying our developing public law. But these are not watertight compartments because the various grounds for judicial review run together. The exercise of a power for an improper purpose may involve taking irrelevant considerations into account, or ignoring relevant considerations; and either may lead to an irrational result. The failure to grant a person affected by a decision a hearing, in breach of principles of procedural fairness, may result in a failure to take into account relevant considerations.

The grounds of review, with one relatively minor exception concerning ultra vires (see below), are largely the same in English law and in Scots law. The Court of Session was quick to accept that Lord Diplock's formulation of the grounds of review in the *GCHQ* case also applied in Scots law: see *City of Edinburgh DC* v. *Secretary of State for Scotland* 1985 SC 261.

10.2.1 Illegality

If a public authority acts in bad faith, deliberately exceeding the limits of its power, it is guilty of illegality. Such conduct is rare, and when a public authority acts illegally, it is generally as a consequence of an error of law, be it in misinterpreting a statute or disregarding common law principles that govern the exercise of public power. At one time, it was held that only certain errors of law would affect the validity of a decision, namely those that related to the scope of the decision-maker's powers (jurisdictional error) or that appeared on the face of the record of the decision taken, but in English law, these limitations have been overcome and it is now clear that any relevant error of law (affecting the decision reached) can result in the decision being quashed by the court. (See *Anisminic* v. *Foreign Compensation Commission* [1969] 2 AC 147. This is not the case in Scots law, where the distinction between ultra vires and intra vires errors of law continues to be important: see, e.g., *Watt* v. *Lord Advocate* 1977 SLT 130, 1979 SLT 137.) Lord Griffiths summarised the English law position as follows (in *R* v. *Lord President of the Privy Council, ex p Page* [1993] AC 682, 693):

> If [administrative bodies] apply the law incorrectly they have not performed their duty correctly and judicial review is available to correct their error of law so that they may make their decision upon a proper understanding of the law.

Administrative action may be shown to be invalid on the simple ground that the public authority has stepped outside limits clearly fixed by a statute conferring the power: here we may surely still say that the authority has acted ultra vires. Such action is properly described as illegal. For an important example, see *Ahmed and others* v. *HM Treasury* [2010] UKSC 2, [2010] 2 WLR 378, considered above, pp. 200–201. When reading legislation, courts often apply the principle of legality, reading down broad delegations of power such that general words do not grant power to the executive to act contrary to fundamental common law rights (*R (UNISON)* v. *Lord Chancellor* [2017] UKSC 51, [2017] 3 WLR 409 and *R (Evans)* v. *Attorney General* [2015] UKSC 21, [2015] AC 1787).

In addition, an exercise of power – or a failure to exercise it – falls within the scope of illegality if such conduct runs counter to the policy and objects of the empowering Act or defeats the purpose for which the power was given. We may distinguish several ways in which this kind of default, or illegality, may occur.

(1) *Extraneous or improper purposes.* A power-conferring statute will doubtless be found to give a discretion to the public officer or body concerned. Any such discretion may be exercised only for the purposes – to be discovered by construing the Act as a whole – for which it was given and not for extraneous purposes of the decision-maker.

In *R* v. *Secretary of State for Foreign Affairs, ex p World Development Movement* [1995] 1 WLR 386, we see a striking instance of a minister's decision being held unlawful because it was not within the statutory purpose. The Overseas Development and Co-operation Act 1980 authorised the minister to provide financial assistance 'for the purpose of promoting the development or maintaining the economy' of a country outside the UK. It was held by the Divisional Court that this provision did not empower the minister 'to disburse money for unsound development purposes': in this instance, the contemplated development (the Pergau Dam in Malaysia) was 'so economically unsound that there is no economic argument in favour of the case'. The minister had taken into account the 'wider perspective' of the UK's political and commercial relations with Malaysia in approving the project, but the decision to give financial aid to so uneconomical a scheme was not permitted by the Act. Following the court's decision, funds set aside for the Pergau Dam were reallocated for emergency aid in Bosnia, Rwanda and other parts of the world. See the analysis of this case by Harden, White and Hollingsworth [1996] *PL* 661.

This kind of abuse of power was also seen in *Porter* v. *Magill* [2001] UKHL 67, [2002] 2 AC 357. Under section 32 of the Housing Act 1985, local authorities had power to dispose of land in furtherance of lawful public purposes. Westminster City Council adopted a policy of increasing the sales of residential properties in the city and in particular to sell 250 properties a year in eight marginal electoral wards. The aim of this policy was not the achievement of proper housing objectives; rather, it was contemplated that purchasers would, as owner-occupiers, be likely to vote Conservative and that the composition of the electorates in the eight marginal wards would be altered so as to improve the prospects of the Conservative Party in the 1990 council elections. The House of Lords held that the council's adoption and implementation of this policy was a deliberate misuse of the statutory power for an unauthorised and improper purpose and was unlawful.

It may often be difficult – if not impossible – to find clear evidence that power was being used by the administration for an improper purpose. This can be seen in the latest instalment in the series of actions for judicial review concerning the Chagos Islands – *R (Bancoult) (No 3)* v. *Secretary of State for Foreign and Commonwealth Affairs* [2018] UKSC 3, [2018] 1 WLR 973. Mr Bancoult challenged the decision of the Secretary of State for Foreign and Commonwealth affairs to create a marine protected area around the Chagos Islands. The marine protected area would include a ban on residence on the islands, in addition to a ban on commercial fishing. Mr Bancoult and others who had been removed from these islands, argued that the marine protected area had been granted for an improper purpose – namely, to ensure that he and other former residents of the Chagos Islands were unable to return to the islands. Bancoult was only able to find evidence to support this claim through WikiLeaks, which put into the public domain a diplomatic cable that allegedly supported the granting of the marine protected area for an improper purpose. The evidence obtained through WikiLeaks was originally not disclosed to the court. After this disclosure on appeal, the Court of Appeal and the Supreme Court held that it did not provide sufficient evidence to support the argument that the creation of the marine protected area had been motivated by an improper purpose. The evidence related to information from American officials who did not, ultimately, take the decision. Moreover, although the decision to create a marine protected area had been made by the minister against the advice of officials, there was no evidence to support that he had been motivated by the improper purpose of ensuring the Chagos Islanders were unable to return.

In spite of these difficulties, there are examples of cases where courts have struck down administrative decisions that were motivated by an improper purpose. In *R* v. *Ealing London Borough Council, ex p Times Newspapers Ltd* (1986) 85 LGR 316 (DC), for example, Ealing London Borough Council was, by virtue of the Public Libraries and Museums Act 1964, a library authority. As such, it was empowered to provide a public library service and was under a duty to provide a comprehensive and efficient service for all persons in the borough (section 7).

Times Newspapers Ltd and other newspaper groups were engaged in a bitter industrial dispute with dismissed print workers and their trade unions. In response to representations from the unions and as a way of supporting their cause, Ealing Council, acting in concert with other library authorities, banned from public libraries in the borough all copies of newspapers and periodicals published by the newspaper groups concerned in the dispute. A resident in the borough applied for judicial review of the decision. The Divisional Court held that it was ultra vires and void as an abuse of the council's power.

> **Watkins LJ:** . . . I am of the opinion that the ban imposed by the borough councils was for an ulterior object. It was inspired by political views which moved the borough councils to interfere in an industrial dispute and for that purpose to use their powers under the Act of 1964. Parliament, I am sure, did not contemplate such action as that to be within the power it conferred when it enacted section 7.

(2) *Frustration of the statutory purpose.* Statutes empower administrative bodies to act to achieve specific purposes. It is for the court to determine the purpose of the Act. If the court determines that executive powers are being used to frustrate the purpose of this Act, then the court can strike down the action of the executive. The key case in this area is *Padfield*.

Padfield v. *Minister of Agriculture, Fisheries and Food* [1968] AC 997 (HL)

A milk marketing scheme for England and Wales had been established under the Agricultural Marketing Act 1958. Under the scheme, producers had to sell their milk to a milk marketing board, which itself fixed the prices to be paid, on a regional basis. The Act provided machinery for dealing with complaints made by producers to the minister about the operation of the scheme. A complaint would be referred, 'if the Minister in any case so directs', to a committee of investigation, which would consider the complaint and make a report to the minister. If the committee reported that anything done under the scheme was contrary to the interest of the complainants and was not in the public interest, the minister was empowered (although not obliged) to make an order amending the scheme. Producers in the southeastern region complained to the minister that the prices being paid to them by the board were too low and asked that their complaint should be referred to the committee of investigation. The minister refused to refer the complaint and the producers applied to the court for an order commanding him to refer it.

Plainly, the minister was not under a duty to refer every complaint to the committee of investigation and he argued that the Act gave him an unfettered discretion ('if the Minister . . . so directs') whether or not to refer. The House of Lords rejected this. Although the discretion was expressed in unqualified terms, it must be exercised (per Lord Reid) 'to promote the policy and objects of the Act'. The minister had given his reasons for refusing to refer the complaint and their Lordships went on to examine these. The minister had said, in the first place, that the complaint raised wide issues, affecting the interests of other regions and the price structure as a whole. Second, if the committee were to uphold the complaint, the minister was concerned that he would be expected to give effect to its recommendations: the implication here, as their Lordships saw it, was that a report by the committee might generate pressure on the minister to take corrective action, against his judgment, and put him in a politically embarrassing position.

The House of Lords held (Lord Morris dissenting) that the considerations on which the minister had taken his decision left altogether out of account the merits of the complaint and showed that he had misdirected himself in law. That the complaint raised wide issues and affected other regions was not a good ground for refusing to refer it to the committee of investigation; on the contrary, these were matters that the committee was well qualified to investigate. As to the possibility of political embarrassment, that was manifestly a bad reason and, as Lord Upjohn remarked, was 'alone sufficient to vitiate the Minister's decision which ... can never validly turn on purely political considerations'. Consequently, the minister was directed to reconsider the complaint according to law.

The result of this decision was that the minister duly reconsidered the complaint and referred it to the committee of investigation. The committee reported in favour of the complainants: it was then for the minister to decide whether there were 'other public interests which outweigh the public interest that justice should be done to the complainers' (per Lord Reid in *Padfield*). The minister concluded that it would not be in the public interest to give effect to the committee's report.

This outcome shows the limits of judicial review, which does not allow a court to substitute its own judgment of what is good policy for that of the minister. Yet even the final decision of the minister in this case would have been reviewable if he had again acted under a misapprehension as to what was legally required of him in exercising his statutory discretion.

In this case, the statute did not oblige the minister to give reasons for a refusal to refer a complaint to the committee. He chose to give reasons and they were found to be bad in law. Suppose that he had given no reasons. The Law Lords were in no doubt that even so a court could intervene if the circumstances indicated that the minister had acted contrary to the policy and objects of the statute. This point was elaborated as follows by Lord Keith in *R v. Secretary of State for Trade and Industry, ex p Lonrho plc* [1989] 1 WLR 525, 539–40:

> The absence of reasons for a decision where there is no duty to give them cannot of itself provide any support for the suggested irrationality of the decision. The only significance of the absence of reasons is that if all other known facts and circumstances appear to point

> overwhelmingly in favour of a different decision, the decision-maker, who has given no reasons, cannot complain if the court draws the inference that he had no rational reason for his decision.

More recently, in *R (Rights of Women)* v. *Lord Chancellor and Secretary of State for Justice* [2016] EWCA Civ 91, [2016] 3 All ER 473. The Legal Aid, Sentencing and Punishment of Offenders Act 2012 (LASPO) empowers the Lord Chancellor to enact regulations determining those eligible for legal aid. The Lord Chancellor enacted regulations that allowed for legal aid for victims of domestic abuse, but only when victims were able to provide evidence for their claim that was under twenty-four months old. The court construed LASPO as requiring that legal aid be granted to those in need, albeit against a backdrop of withdrawing civil legal services from some categories of case for cost-saving purposes. The court received evidence of when victims of domestic violence would be unable, for good reasons, to bring claims until more than twenty-four months after evidence could be obtained to support their claim – for instance, where it took time for women to find a place of safety for themselves and their children before being able to bring a claim of domestic violence. The 'formidable catalogue of areas of domestic violence not reached by a statute whose purpose is to reach such cases' demonstrated that there was no 'rational connection' between the twenty-four-month period and the purpose of LASPO ([44]-[45]).

Statutes commonly specify the purposes for which a power is conferred and so expressly indicate the limits of the discretion allowed. In other cases, restrictions on an exercise of statutory power may be inferred from the general purposes of the Act or from fundamental principles which, it is presumed, Parliament will have intended to uphold. It is for the court to determine the purpose of legislation. Even when courts focus on the specific wording of legislation to determine its purpose, this can give rise to divergent opinions on whether administrative actions were taken for an improper purpose.

R (Palestine Solidarity Campaign Ltd) v. *Secretary of State for Housing, Communities and Local Government* [2020] UKSC 16, [2020] 1 WLR 1774

The case concerned the local government pension scheme. The Public Service Pensions Act 2013 required local authorities to maintain a separate pension fund for their employees. These funds were to be administered according to regulations, enacted according to the provisions of the 2013 Act. This included a requirement for local authorities to formulate an investment strategy for the money in those pension schemes, according to guidelines issued by the Secretary of State. One of these guidelines stated that pension policies could not be used to pursue boycotts, divestment or sanctions against foreign nationals or UK defence industries, unless formal sanctions or embargoes had been put in place by the UK government. Also, local authorities could not devise investment strategies that were contrary to UK foreign or defence policy. The question arose as to whether these guidelines had been made for an improper purpose.

The majority concluded that the guidance *had* been issued for an improper purpose. Section 3(1) of the 2013 Act had empowered the minister to enact such provisions as he 'considers appropriate'. However, Lord Wilson, on behalf of the majority, concluded that 'the power cannot be as broad as that' as 'no statutory discretion is unfettered' (at [23]). Lord Wilson then looked at section 3 in more detail, and the Schedules linked to the 2013 Act, to determine the limits on this broad discretionary power. He noted that the legislation and regulations that empowered the Secretary of State to issue guidelines referred to issues of administration, management, or policy that focused on how local authorities should administer investments in pension schemes. By issuing guidelines requiring local authorities to uphold UK foreign policies, the Secretary of State had issues guidelines for an improper purpose – directing in which bodies local authorities could invest their money as opposed to directing how to administer the pension scheme. This conclusion was reinforced by the assessment by the majority that the pension scheme was private money, designed to provide pensions for employees, as opposed to public money.

Lady Arden and Lord Sales disagreed. They argued that the guidelines were limited to providing information to local authorities who were taking investment decisions that were not purely based on financial considerations – in other words, maximising the return on the pension fund. In those situations, the state does have a legitimate interest in how local authorities invest their funds and it was not an improper purpose to require these local authorities not to breach governmental policies. The minority read the 2013 Act more broadly and did not think that the wording of specific provisions in the Act had limited the power of the Secretary of State to issuing guidelines purely about how pension schemes were to be managed.

This case provides the most recent account of the application of the principles in *Padfield*. As the case clearly illustrates, the difference between the majority and the minority did not concern the scope of *Padfield*, but its application to a particular statute. For Lord Wilson:

[20]. The *Padfield* case [1968] AC 997, cited in para 1 above, arose out of the statutory requirement in England and Wales that producers of milk should sell it only to the Milk Marketing Board. Producers in the south east of England complained to the minister about the price paid to them by the board. Statute provided that, "if the Minister ... so directs", a committee had to consider their complaint. The minister declined to direct the committee to do so. The House of Lords upheld the claim of the producers that he had acted unlawfully in declining to give the direction. Of the four judges in the majority, one (Lord Hodson) applied long-recognised principles of judicial review. But Lord Reid, supported by Lord Pearce at p 1053 and Lord Upjohn at p 1060, reached his decision by reference to a different principle which he explained as follows at p 1030:

"Parliament must have conferred the discretion with the intention that it should be used to promote the policy and objects of the Act [which] must be determined by construing the Act as a whole . . . if the Minister . . . so uses his discretion as to thwart or run counter to the policy and objects of the Act, then our law would be very defective if persons aggrieved were not entitled to the protection of the court."

[21]. In *R v Secretary of State for the Environment, Transport and the Regions, Ex p Spath Holme Ltd*[2001] 2 AC 349 the House of Lords applied the principle identified in the *Padfield* case, albeit in reaching a conclusion that the Secretary of State's order was not unlawful. His order, under challenge by a landlord, capped otherwise justifiable increases in the rent which had been registered as payable under regulated tenancies. The order was made pursuant to a power conferred in wide terms by section 31 of the Landlord and Tenant Act 1985. The landlord argued that Parliament's object in granting the power was that it should be used only in order to counter inflation but the appellate committee held that it had wider objects which extended to the purpose behind the capping order. Lord Bingham of Cornhill said at p 381:

'no statute confers an unfettered discretion on any minister. Such a discretion must be exercised so as to promote and not to defeat or frustrate the object of the legislation in question . . . The object is to ascertain the statutory purpose or object which the draftsman had in mind when conferring on ministers the powers set out in section 31.'

Lord Nicholls of Birkenhead said at p 396:

'The present appeal raises a point of statutory interpretation: what is the ambit of the power conferred on the minister by section 31(1) . . . ? No statutory power is of unlimited scope . . . Powers are conferred by Parliament for a purpose, and they may be lawfully exercised only in furtherance of that purpose . . . The purpose for which a power is conferred, and hence its ambit, may be stated expressly in the statute. Or it may be implicit. Then the purpose has to be inferred from the language used, read in its statutory context and having regard to any aid to interpretation which assists in the particular case. In either event . . . the exercise is one of statutory interpretation.'

[22]. In *R (Ben Hoare Bell Solicitors) v Lord Chancellor* [2015] 1 WLR 4175, the Divisional Court of the Queen's Bench Division upheld a challenge by solicitors to the lawfulness of a regulation which withheld remuneration under the Civil Legal Aid scheme for work done on behalf of applicants for judicial review unless their applications eventually met with a specified result. The court chose to divide the challenge into two sections. It rejected the first, which it entitled '"Strict" ultra vires', and upheld the second, which it entitled 'The *Padfield* statutory purpose ground'. With respect, it is not obvious that such was a helpful division of an inquiry into whether the impugned provision exceeded the scope of the statutory power under which it was claimed to have been made. For those who continue to insist on Latin, an inquiry by reference to the principle in the *Padfield* case is an inquiry into whether the provision is ultra vires: *de Smith's Judicial Review*, 8th ed (2018), para 5-018.

Lady Arden and Lord Sales, in dissent, set out the principle of *Padfield* as follows:

[63]. This is an important principle of statutory construction, which for present purposes is encapsulated in the following passage from the speech of Lord Reid in *Padfield* [1968] AC 997, 1030:

'Parliament must have conferred the discretion with the intention that it should be used to promote the policy and objects of the Act; the policy and objects of the Act must be determined by construing the Act as a whole and construction is always a matter of law for the court. In a matter of this kind it is not possible to draw a hard and fast line, but if the Minister, by reason of his having misconstrued the Act or for any other reason, so, uses his discretion as to thwart or run counter to the policy and objects of the Act, then our law would be very defective if persons aggrieved were not entitled to the protection of the court. So it is necessary first to construe the Act.'

[64]. We would make a number of observations. First, it is not the practice of Parliament to insert 'purpose' clauses into legislation, and indeed the policies or objects of particular legislation may be quite complex. They may be deduced from the context, including the constitutional position. The relevant constitutional background which sets the context in which the 2013 Act falls to be construed includes the constitutional responsibility of central government for the conduct of the UK's international affairs, for promoting the country's economy and for seeking to preserve internal good order and harmonious relations between different parts of society.

[65]. In *R v Secretary of State for the Environment, Transport and the Regions, Ex p Spath Holme Ltd* [2001] 2 AC 349 ('*Spath Holme*'), the House of Lords gave important guidance regarding the operation of the *Padfield* principle. Lord Bingham of Cornhill, referring to observations by Lord Simon of Glaisdale and Lord Diplock in *Maunsell v Olins* [1975] AC 373, 393, emphasised at [2001] 2 AC 349, 385ᴇ–ɢ and 391ᴀ–ʙ that a statute may well have more than one statutory objective. As Lord Simon (speaking for himself and Lord Diplock) said in *Maunsell v Olins*, in the passage relied on by Lord Bingham:

'For a court of construction to constrain statutory language which has a primary natural meaning appropriate in its context so as to give it an artificial meaning which is appropriate only to remedy the mischief which is conceived to have occasioned the statutory provision is to proceed unsupported by principle, inconsonant with authority and oblivious of the actual practice of parliamentary draftsmen. Once a mischief has been drawn to the attention of the draftsman he will consider whether any concomitant mischiefs should be dealt with as a necessary corollary.'

[66]. The Bill leading to the 2013 Act laid down a common framework for pension provision within the public service so that the framework could be adapted to each sector as circumstances required. So, it was clear that the detail had to be filled in by secondary legislation and it is not surprising to find that the powers to make secondary legislation were given in broad terms. One of the purposes of the legislation, as one might expect, was to establish sound governance arrangements for the new schemes.

[67]. The second point is that it is not good enough if the minister misconstrues the legislation in good faith. This is because the courts are the authoritative organ for the interpretation of a statutory power. We do not have any equivalent of the *Chevron* doctrine in the United States (*Chevron v Natural Resources Defence Council* (1984) 467 US 837),

where it was held that where a statute directed to a government agency was ambiguous, the court will follow any permissible reading adopted by the agency.

[68]. Thirdly, as Lord Nicholls explained in *Spath Holme*[2001] 2 AC 349, 396ᴅ–ɢ, the *Padfield* principle depends upon the proper interpretation of the relevant statutory provision; and 'an appropriate starting point is that language is to be taken to bear its ordinary meaning in the general context of the statute' (p 397ʙ). 'The overriding aim of the court must always be to give effect to the intention of Parliament as expressed in the words used': *Spath Holme*, p 388ᴅ, per Lord Bingham. Here, the language of section 3(1), according to its ordinary meaning, especially when it is read in context and alongside section 3(2) of and Schedule 3 to the 2013 Act, is apt to confer a very wide discretion upon the Secretary of State (as the responsible authority) to promulgate regulations which 'make such provision in relation to a [public service pension scheme]' as the Secretary of State 'considers appropriate'. We do not think that the limitation for which the claimants contend can be read into section 3(1). Again, we agree with Sir Stephen Richards, who said (para 21):

> 'I find it . . . helpful to put the question in terms of whether the legislation permits wider considerations of public interest to be taken into account when formulating guidance to administering authorities as to their investment strategy; and . . . given the framework nature of the statute and the broad discretion it gives to the Secretary of State as to the making of regulations and the giving of guidance, I can see no reason why it should not be so read.'

Divergence arose here concerning whether to interpret legislative provisions as providing a restriction on the guidance the Secretary of State could produce, or whether to focus more broadly on the general purpose of the legislation. It can be difficult to determine, therefore, the precise purpose of legislation that the administration is not meant to contravene. Moreover, as the judgment of Lady Arden and Lord Sales makes clear, Parliament rarely provides an account of the purpose of legislation. This can lead to problems: what considerations led courts to the conclusion that Parliament had not intended to authorise such action as was taken by the council in the *Ealing* case or the Lord Chancellor in the *Rights of Women* case? In considering whether power has been used for an improper purpose, we may need to invoke common law principles rather than speculate about Parliament's intention. T.R.S. Allan regards the decision in the *Ealing* case as an application of a principle of equality – 'the right to be free from unfair or hostile discrimination at the hands of the state' – which, he claims, is fundamental to the rule of law: *Law, Liberty, and Justice* (1993), pp. 170–1. Other cases that may perhaps be explained in this way include *Wheeler v. Leicester City Council* [1985] AC 1054 and *R v. Lewisham London Borough Council, ex p Shell UK Ltd* [1988] 1 All ER 938. (See Allan, above, p. 790; for a more sceptical interpretation of *Wheeler v. Leicester City Council*, see Tomkins, *Public Law* (2003), pp. 179–80. However, there are dangers in developing such rights-base approaches to judicial review – see Varuhas 'The

Reformation of English Administrative Law? "Rights", Rhetoric and Reality'
(2013) 72 *Cambridge Law Journal* 369 for a criticism of this general approach
to administrative law.)

The reasoning in these cases – as in *Padfield* itself – was closely bound up
with the statute that conferred decision-making power in the first place. But
what if there is no such statute? What if the public authority is purporting to
exercise a prerogative, rather than a statutory power, for example? *R* v.
Secretary of State for the Home Department, ex p Fire Brigades Union [1995]
2 AC 513 shows that *Padfield* illegality may also apply in this context. If
a minister purports to exercise a prerogative power improperly, he or she
may be acting illegally, just as he or she would be were he or she to exercise
a statutory power improperly. In *ex p Fire Brigades Union*, a majority of the
House of Lords held that the Home Secretary had acted unlawfully in seeking
to use his prerogative powers to effect a change in the system of criminal
injuries compensation, which had been approved by Parliament. In the *Fire
Brigades Union* case, the use of the prerogative power frustrated a specific
power of the minister to specify the day on which a statutory compensation
scheme, set out in legislation, to come into force. In *R (Miller)* v. *Secretary of
State for Exiting the European Union* [2017] UKSC 5, the Supreme Court
concluded, inter alia, that prerogative powers could not be used to frustrate
legislation by rendering legislation as a whole devoid of purpose. The majority
of the Supreme Court concluded that the purpose of the European
Communities Act 1972 would be frustrated were the prime minister to use
her prerogative power to trigger Article 50, notifying the European Union of
the UK's intention to leave the European Union. Moreover, in *R (Miller)*
v. *Prime Minister; Cherry* v. *Advocate General for Scotland* [2019] UKSC 41,
[2020] AC 373, counsel for Miller and Cherry argued that the prime minister
had advised the monarch to prorogue Parliament for an improper purpose.
The Supreme Court decided the case in a different manner, and the English
high court had concluded that the prerogative power of prorogation was non-
justiciable, meaning that the head of review of improper purpose could not
apply. This leaves open the possibility of a challenge that a justiciable prerogative power has been exercised for an improper purpose.

(3) *Irrelevant considerations*. It is further necessary, if the exercise of discretionary power is to satisfy the requirement of legality, that the deciding
authority should take account of all considerations that are relevant to its
decision and disregard irrelevant considerations: arbitrary action in violation
of these constraints is held to be illegal. A statute may itself specify considerations to be taken into account. However, the factors that are or are not
relevant to the exercise of a power will often be a matter of construction or
inference. As Lord Bridge observed in *R* v. *Tower Hamlets London Borough
Council, ex p Chetnik Developments Ltd* [1988] AC 858, 873, 'if the purpose
which the discretion is intended to serve is clear, the discretion can only be
validly exercised for reasons relevant to the achievement of that purpose.'

It is not always clear in advance what the courts will deem to be a relevant or irrelevant consideration. This is amply illustrated in the following case.

R (Corner House Research) v. *Director of the Serious Fraud Office* [2008] UKHL 60, [2009] 1 AC 756

The director of the Serious Fraud Office (SFO) decided to abandon a criminal investigation into British Aerospace (BAE) in connection with alleged bribery relating to a lucrative arms contract signed between the UK and Saudi Arabia, for which BAE was the main contractor. It was alleged, and the Divisional Court accepted, that the director of the SFO had acted unlawfully in deciding to halt the investigation as, in doing so, he had surrendered to a threat apparently made by the Saudi Arabia Government to the effect that were the investigation not halted, the Saudis would cease all intelligence cooperation with the UK. This, it was further alleged, would be so gravely contrary to the national security interests of the UK that it would risk placing British lives in jeopardy. Had such a threat been made by a party within the domestic jurisdiction of the courts, that party would be liable for prosecution for attempting to pervert the course of justice.

The Divisional Court ruled ([2008] EWHC 714 (Admin), [2008] 4 All ER 927) that the director's decision was unlawful not because he had no power to take into account relevant considerations of national security but because, in this case, he had not so much taken them into account as surrendered to them. The potentially grave consequences that *might* have followed *had* the Saudis carried out their threat notwithstanding, the court noted that there was in fact no 'specific, immediate threat' to national security or public safety. The court further noted that steps could and should have been taken to resist the threat. That not all such steps were taken in this case was critical to the court's judgment, which was founded on the proposition that 'submission to a threat is lawful only when it is demonstrated to a court that there was no alternative course open to the decision-maker' (see *R* v. *Coventry City Council, ex p Phoenix Aviation* [1995] 3 All ER 37).

The judgment of the Divisional Court in *Corner House* was expressed in unusually robust terms, with numerous references to high constitutional principle and the importance of the rule of law. It is clear that the court considered that it had itself been affronted by the Saudis' threat, as that threat had been directed not only at the UK's political, diplomatic and security interests, but also at the independence and integrity of its legal system. However, all of this notwithstanding, the judgment of the Divisional Court was swiftly overturned by a unanimous House of Lords. Their Lordships ruled that the Divisional Court had asked itself the wrong question. The issue was not whether the director had done everything possible to avoid having to accede to what their Lordships described as an 'ugly' and 'extremely distasteful' threat; rather the question was 'whether, in deciding that the public interest in pursuing an important investigation into alleged bribery was outweighed by the public interest in protecting the lives of British citizens, the Director made a decision outside the lawful bounds of the discretion entrusted to him by Parliament' (Lord Bingham, at [38]). The director of the SFO had not *wanted* to abandon the investigation. Indeed, he had strongly resisted political pressure to abandon it for as long as he could. But, in the end, he did abandon it, and he did so after it had been explained to him that the threat of withdrawal of Saudi intelligence cooperation was real and that the consequences entailed an equally real risk to British lives. Lady Hale stated (at [52]–[53]) that 'the only question is whether it was lawful for [the director] to take this into account' and ruled that 'put like that, it is difficult to reach any other conclusion than that it was indeed lawful for him to take it into account.'

This last sentence reveals how the Divisional Court and the House of Lords reached such different conclusions in the case: all depends on how the question is framed. For the House of Lords, the *only* question was whether the director was entitled to take national security and public safety considerations into account. While the Divisional Court accepted that he could do so, for that court this was not the only question. There was an additional issue: namely whether the director should also take into account the reason *why* national security and public safety considerations had come into play. Here, the *only* reason why they had done so was because of the threat made by the Saudi authorities – a threat that, to repeat, would have been unlawful had it been made by someone subject to the domestic jurisdiction of the courts. The House of Lords thought this issue to be irrelevant. Their Lordships seemed entirely unconcerned that an ostensibly independent prosecutor felt himself required to abandon a criminal investigation because (and only because) a third party made an ugly and distasteful threat to the UK Government. Neither was there any attempt made to examine the strength, the veracity or the reasonableness of the claims made about security and safety. The director had taken these claims at face value, and so did the Law Lords.

The decision of the House of Lords in *Corner House* has been widely criticised: see, for example, Jowell (2008) 13 *JR* 273. Lord Steyn made his views clear when he said that for 'our country, through its judicial branch' to have succumbed to a threat from Saudi Arabia was 'a deeply depressing event' (see [2009] *PL* 228, 234).

A rather different sort of case in which, again, there was disagreement among the judges as to whether a consideration was relevant or irrelevant is *R (Sainsbury's)* v. *Wolverhampton City Council* [2010] UKSC 20, [2010] 2 WLR 1173. The case concerned a dispute between the two supermarket rivals, Sainsbury's and Tesco, both of which wanted to build a supermarket on a particular site. Each owned part of the site, but one would have to sell its share to the other for the site to be developed in the way that either desired. Neither would agree to sell to the other. The local authority decided to use its statutory powers of compulsory purchase to settle the issue in Tesco's favour. In so deciding, it took into account the fact that Tesco had undertaken to assist the local authority with the regeneration of another site elsewhere in the city (Tesco was of the view that this regeneration would be uneconomical but agreed nonetheless to assist if it and not Sainsbury's was permitted to build the supermarket; the local authority was of the view that it was strongly in the local public interest for this second site to be regenerated). The Supreme Court was split 4:3 on the question of whether the local authority was permitted to take into account the regeneration of the second site when considering the future of the first site. The majority held that this was an immaterial consideration (under section 70 of the Town and Country Planning Act 1990) and that the local authority's decision was therefore unlawful. The majority founded its approach on the view that powers of compulsory purchase, strikingly invasive of rights to private property as they may be, should be narrowly construed. The minority, by contrast, placed greater emphasis on the responsibility of a local authority to act in the public interest, taking into account the whole of its area, and accorded weight to the council's opinion that the regeneration of the second site was sorely needed.

Four further observations may be made on relevant and irrelevant considerations. First, a consideration is legally relevant only if it is something that the decision-maker is obliged (on a right understanding of any applicable statute) to take into account and is not merely a factor that may properly be taken into account (*CREEDNZ Inc* v. *Governor-General* [1981] 1 NZLR 172, 183, approved on this point by the House of Lords in *Re Findlay* [1985] AC 318, 333). Second, the weight to be attached to the relevant considerations is a matter for the judgment of the decision-maker – subject to *Wednesbury* unreasonableness (on which see below): *Tesco Stores Ltd* v. *Secretary of State for the Environment* [1995] 1 WLR 759, 764, 780; see, further, Herling, 'Weight in Discretionary Decision-Making' (1999) 19 *OJLS* 583. Third, irrelevant considerations and improper purposes overlap and may often be more or less alternative ways of characterising the same unlawful action. It has been remarked that 'When a decision-maker pursues a purpose outside of the four corners of his powers, he mostly does so by taking an "irrelevant consideration" into account' (S de Smith, Lord Woolf and J Jowell, *Judicial Review of Administrative Action* (1995), para 6–063). Fourth, there can be overlap between relevant and irrelevant considerations and rationality. These points are illustrated in the following case.

R (DSD) v. *Parole Board of England and Wales* [2018] EWHC 694 (Admin), [2018] 3 All ER 417

The Parole Board had been asked to decide whether to release John Warboys – who now wished to be known as John Radford – following his conviction for a series of serious sexual offences – including one rape – between 2006 and 2008 involving twelve victims. The Parole Board decided to release Mr Radford. The decision was subject to strong public criticism. Radford was known as the 'black cab rapist' and it was believed that he had committed serious sexual offences against far more women than the twelve victims that had given rise to his conviction. Although these had been mentioned in the dossier before the Parole Board, the Parole Board had not requested further evidence of these other possible offences. Neither had they been taken into account when the Parole Board decided to release Radford. DSD and another (NBV) brought an action for judicial review to overturn the decision of the Parole Board. NBV had been one of Mr Radford's victims who had given evidence at his trial. DSD and NBV had also brought successful litigation against Radford and the Metropolitan Police. One of their arguments was that the Parole Board had failed to take account of a relevant consideration when deciding to release Radford – they had failed to take account of evidence of Radford's wider offending beyond the crimes for which he was convicted. When reaching decisions, the Parole Board determines the extent to which a convicted offender poses a risk to the public, such that continued detention is necessary for the protection of the public. Counsel for DSD argued that evidence of wider offending was a relevant consideration for the determination of the risk to public safety.

The High Court disagreed. First, the legislation had not provided a clear account of the considerations that the Parole Board had to take into account when determining whether the continued detention of a prisoner was necessary for the protection of the public. Second, it was not clear that the need to take account of wider convictions could be inferred from the legislation. In particular, it was not clear that evidence of wider convictions was always necessary. Moreover, evidence of wider convictions may not always be available and may not always be relevant to the future risk posed by a particular prisoner.

The High Court also concluded that the decision to release Radford was not irrational. Nevertheless, it concluded that, on the particular circumstances of the case, it was irrational for the Parole Board to have reached its conclusion without carrying out further investigation as to Radford's wider convictions. This was because in Radford's case, further investigation of the wider convictions would have assisted the Parole Board in determining whether his expressions of remorse for his crimes were genuine, particularly given that Radford had only recently changed his mind and accepted his conviction, expressing remorse, having previously denied his crimes. Consequently, the original decision of the Parole Board was quashed. The Parole Board investigated the wider convictions more thoroughly and, as a result of their investigations, overturned their earlier decision and refused to grant parole to Radford.

Of particular note is the comment of the court concerning the definition of relevant considerations in paragraph 141 of the judgment:

> The distinction between relevant considerations, properly so called, and matters which may be so obviously material in any particular case that they cannot be ignored, is not merely one

of legal classification; it has important consequences. If a consideration arises as a matter of necessary implication because it is compelled by the wording of the statute itself, the decision-maker must take it into account, and any failure to do so is, without more, justiciable in judicial review proceedings. If, on the other hand, the logic of the statute does not compel that conclusion or, in the language of Laws LJ, there is no implied lexicon of the matters to be treated as relevant, then it is for the decision-maker and not for the court to make the primary judgment as to what should be considered in the circumstances of any given case. The court exercises a secondary judgment, framed in broad *Wednesbury* terms, if a matter is so obviously material that it would be irrational to ignore it.

The court determines which considerations are relevant and, if a public body fails to take account of a consideration that the court deems relevant, or takes account of a consideration that the court deems irrelevant, then the court essentially corrects the decision of the public body. The public body is then free to decide again, ensuring it takes account of the considerations deemed relevant by the court. *DSD* illustrates caution on the part of the court, restricting its definition of relevant considerations to those 'so obviously material in any particular case', especially when this is a 'necessary implication' of the statute empowering the public body. The court is also concerned to ensure that it is the public body that determines the particular weight to be given to these relevant considerations. However, *DSD* also gives rise to problems. How can a consideration not be relevant, while at the same time it is irrational for the public body not to carry out a further investigation and gather evidence relating to this particular consideration? The High Court attempts to square this circle by distinguishing between the consideration, and the requirement to obtain evidence. While it was not irrational to conclude that Radford could be released, or unlawful to have reached this decision without taking account of his wider convictions, it was nevertheless irrational to fail to find evidence of these wider convictions. However, it is hard to see why this is the case: why is it irrational to fail to seek further evidence of wider convictions if this evidence is not a relevant consideration? Second, it could be argued that this conclusion turns on the difference between the general and the specific. It is not generally required for parole boards to take account of wider convictions, meaning that this is not a relevant consideration. Nevertheless, it is irrational not to find further evidence of wider convictions on the specific facts of Radford's case. While this may be a logical distinction, it may be hard to apply this in practice and may lead to further confusion as to whether factors that should influence a public body when exercising its decision-making powers are best described as relevant considerations, giving rise to a challenge for illegality, or are really concerned with the rationality of the decision.

(4) *Unlawful delegation.* A public body on which power is conferred by statute may not divest itself of the power by delegating it to some other body, unless such delegation is expressly or impliedly authorised by the statute (see,

e.g., *H Lavender & Son Ltd* v. *Minister of Housing and Local Government* [1970] 1 WLR 1231). The non-delegation rule is qualified in an important – and controversial – way by section 69 of the Deregulation and Contracting Out Act 1994, which authorises ministers to delegate any of a wide range of statutory functions vested in themselves to persons outside government (see Freedland [1995] *PL* 21). The rule against delegation is to be contrasted with the *Carltona* principle (above, pp. 577–578) by which decision-making may be *devolved* to subordinate officers within the organisation of the authority entrusted with the power.

(5) *Fettering of discretion.* When a statute grants a discretionary power to a public authority, it is to be inferred that the authority must not do anything to constrain or fetter its discretion so that it is prevented from exercising the discretion in the manner, and with respect to all the matters, contemplated by the statute. An authority must not, for instance, make a contract or adopt a policy that nullifies or abridges its discretion, thus defeating the purpose for which the discretion was given.

That said, it is lawful (and common practice) for an authority to adopt a policy regarding the exercise of a discretionary power and, indeed, it may be helpful to persons affected and make for consistency if this is done. There may also be situations in which a public authority is required to adopt a policy, as in *R (Purdy)* v. *Director of Public Prosecutions* [2009] UKHL 45, [2010] 1 AC 345, where the director of public prosecutions was required to adopt a policy concerning when he would pursue a conviction for assisted suicide in order to protect the Article 8 ECHR rights of those wishing to ask others to help them to end their lives. Any such policy must, however, be in conformity with the objects of the statute and must not be applied in an inflexible way and without consideration of individual circumstances. (See *British Oxygen Co Ltd* v. *Board of Trade* [1971] AC 610; and *Re Findlay* [1985] AC 318.) Once a policy has been produced and published, the public body must follow this policy and cannot, instead, apply an unpublished contradictory policy (*R (Lumba)* v. *Secretary of State for the Home Department* [2011] UKSC 12, [2012] AC 245). The court will ensure that a published policy is applied to those falling within the scope of this policy, unless there are good reasons to not do so (*Mandalia* v. *Secretary of State for the Home Department* [2015] UKSC 59, [2015] 1 WLR 4546).

10.2.2 Irrationality

It is often said that an administrative decision may be vitiated by 'unreasonableness'. Sometimes this word is used loosely 'as a general description of the things that must not be done' (per Lord Greene MR in the *Wednesbury* case), including action that is more properly described as illegal. Unreasonableness is, however, a distinct ground for challenging a decision, but then it bears a stricter, technical sense. In *Associated Provincial Picture Houses Ltd v. Wednesbury Corpn* [1948] 1 KB 223, 230, Lord Greene MR said:

> It is true to say that, if a decision on a competent matter is so unreasonable that no reasonable authority could ever have come to it, then the courts can interfere. That, I think, is quite right; but to prove a case of that kind would require something overwhelming . . . [I]t must be proved to be unreasonable in the sense that the court considers it to be a decision that no reasonable body could have come to. It is not what the court considers unreasonable, a different thing altogether.

Lord Greene gave the example, suggested in an earlier case, of a red-haired teacher, dismissed because she had red hair; in other words, 'something so absurd that no sensible person could ever dream that it lay within the powers of the authority'. However, there are problems even with this extreme example. Is it really the case that to dismiss a red-haired teacher is irrational, or is it rather that hair colour is not a relevant consideration when determining teaching ability? This problem has led some to conclude that *Wednesbury* unreasonableness adds nothing. It may be more accurate to conclude that the scope of *Wednesbury* depends on whether courts adopt a broad or a narrow definition of 'relevant considerations', as discussed in *DSD* above.

The courts have repeatedly emphasised that only a high degree of unreasonableness, commonly labelled 'irrationality', allows a court to intervene. Lord Diplock in *Council of Civil Service Unions* v. *Minister for the Civil Service* [1985] AC 374, 410 said that:

> what can now be succinctly referred to as '*Wednesbury unreasonableness*' . . . applies to a decision which is so outrageous in its defiance of logic or of accepted moral standards that no sensible person who had applied his mind to the question to be decided could have arrived at it.

Evidently the justification for judicial intervention on this ground is meant to be an exacting one. In *R* v. *Secretary of State for the Home Department, ex p Brind* [1991] 1 AC 696, 757–8, Lord Ackner said:

> This standard of unreasonableness, often referred to as 'the irrationality test', has been criticised as being too high. But it has to be expressed in terms that confine the jurisdiction exercised by the judiciary to a supervisory, as opposed to an appellate, jurisdiction. Where Parliament has given to a minister or other person or body a discretion, the court's jurisdiction is limited, in the absence of a statutory right of appeal, to the supervision of the exercise of that discretionary power, so as to ensure that it has been exercised lawfully. It would be a wrongful usurpation of power by the judiciary to substitute its, the judicial

view, on the merits and on that basis to quash the decision. If no reasonable minister properly directing himself would have reached the impugned decision, the minister has exceeded his powers and thus acted unlawfully and the court in the exercise of its supervisory role will quash that decision. Such a decision is correctly, though unattractively, described as a 'perverse' decision. To seek the court's intervention on the basis that the correct or objectively reasonable decision is other than the decision which the minister has made is to invite the court to adjudicate as if Parliament had provided a right of appeal against the decision – that is, to invite an abuse of power by the judiciary.

This exacting standard is particularly evident in cases where courts are asked to evaluate policy choices of the executive, particularly concerning socioeconomic or financial issues. In *R (JK)(Burundi)* v. *Secretary of State for the Home Department* [2017] EWCA Civ 433, [2017] 1 WLR 4567, the court was asked to review the decision of the Secretary of State to reduce the weekly amount payable to asylum seekers, specifically the amount payable as support for the dependent children of asylum seekers. The amount had been reduced by 30 per cent, from £52.96 to £36.95. The applicants argued that in reaching this conclusion, the Secretary of State had failed to put the interests of the child first, had failed to comply with the requirements of an EU regulation concerning support for asylum seekers (the RCD), and had exercised his discretion irrationally. The Court of Appeal concluded that the Secretary of State had not acted unlawfully. In doing so, it noted the difficulties that arise when courts are asked to investigate the determination of social assistance, seeing this as a case 'exemplifying the importance of judicial reserve or restraint and calling for a proper appreciation of the different provinces of the executive and the judiciary' (at [86]). In the words of Gross LJ at [87]:

Provided, however, that the Secretary of State has complied with the RCD minimum standard and assessed essential living needs rationally and reasonably, then the value judgment of what does and does not comprise an essential living need is for her and not for the court. Within the boundary thus demarcated, the inclusion or exclusion of any particular item belongs within the Secretary of State's sphere rather than that of the court. Policy choices for such areas, concerning resource allocation and implications for the public purse, fall properly to the Secretary of State for decision. In this way, while the court retains the power and the duty to adjudicate upon threshold questions, the 'judicialisation' of public administration, very much including the provision of welfare services, can beneficially be avoided; so too, the realities of public sector finances can be taken into account.

Wednesbury unreasonableness or irrationality is a mechanism of judicial control that is not appropriately applied to every kind of administrative decision. As Lord Phillips MR observed in *R (Asif Javed)* v. *Secretary of State for the Home Department* [2002] QB 129, at [49]: 'The extent to which the exercise of a statutory power is in practice open to judicial review on the ground of irrationality will depend critically on the nature and purpose of the enabling legislation.' In *R* v. *Ministry of Defence, ex p Smith* [1996] QB 517, 554, Sir Thomas Bingham MR warned of the caution demanded in applying the irrationality test to decisions of a 'policy-laden' nature:

> The greater the policy content of a decision, and the more remote the subject matter of a decision from ordinary judicial experience, the more hesitant the court must necessarily be in holding a decision to be irrational.

The House of Lords had earlier accepted this restriction of review for irrationality in *Nottinghamshire County Council* v. *Secretary of State for the Environment* [1986] AC 240 and *R* v. *Secretary of State for the Environment, ex p Hammersmith London Borough Council* [1991] 1 AC 521. Both cases concerned decisions of the Secretary of State in matters of local government finance, and in each of them the decision had been presented to the House of Commons for approval, as required by the enabling act, and had been approved by affirmative resolution of that house. In each case, a challenge to the decision on the ground of irrationality was dismissed. Lord Bridge in the *Hammersmith* case expressed the principle of both cases in saying (at p. 597):

> The formulation and the implementation of national economic policy are matters depending essentially on political judgement. The decisions which shape them are for politicians to take and it is in the political forum of the House of Commons that they are properly to be debated and approved or disapproved on their merits. If the decisions have been taken in good faith within the four corners of the Act, the merits of the policy underlying the decisions are not susceptible to review by the courts and the courts would be exceeding their proper function if they presumed to condemn the policy as unreasonable.

It must be emphasised that other grounds of challenge remain open in such cases. The legality of a decision is a matter for the courts, and approval by resolution of one or both houses cannot legitimise a decision that is vitiated by illegality.

'Perverse', 'irrational', 'absurd': so high a degree of folly appears to be demanded by the *Wednesbury* principle that one might doubt that any public authority would ever succeed in attaining it. Nevertheless, examples can be provided where this exacting standard is met. In *R (Rogers)* v. *Swindon NHS Primary Care Trust* [2006] EWCA Cil 392, [2006] 1 WLR 2649 (CA), the claimant was a patient with primary breast cancer. She had been prescribed the drug Herceptin by her oncologist, which was licensed for the treatment of late-stage breast cancer but not (at the material time) for the earlier stage from which she suffered. She came within the eligible group of patients for whom the drug was likely to be effective and to increase her life expectancy, and she applied to the primary care trust (PCT) for her treatment to be funded by the NHS. It was the PCT's general policy to fund drug treatment not approved by the National Institute for Clinical Excellence (NICE) only where a patient had a special healthcare problem that presented an exceptional need for treatment having regard to the funds available. In the case of Herceptin, however, the PCT decided to fund treatment in exceptional circumstances without regard to cost. The claimant was denied funding because she was not considered to be an exceptional case. At first instance, her claim for judicial review of that decision was dismissed on the ground that the PCT's policy in relation to Herceptin was not irrational.

However, the Court of Appeal allowed the appeal, holding that in deciding whether the PCT's policy was irrational, the question to be considered was whether there were any relevant exceptional circumstances that could justify the trust refusing treatment to one patient in the eligible group but granting it to another. Once financial considerations had been ruled out, as they had been here, and once it had been decided not to rely on NICE without exception, the personal characteristics of a particular patient other than those based on healthcare were irrelevant, the Court of Appeal ruled, and the only relevant consideration was the clinical need of the patient. The PCT's policy of funding Herceptin in exceptional circumstances for patients in the eligible group, without regard to financial considerations, was irrational since no persuasive ground could be identified in clinical terms for treating one patient who fulfilled the clinical requirements for treatment differently from others in the group. Accordingly, the only reasonable approach was to fund patients who were properly prescribed the drug by their doctor.

As the Court of Appeal made plain, had the PCT decided on grounds of cost that Herceptin was not available on the NHS to patients in the earlier stage of breast cancer, it would have been far more difficult, if not impossible, for a court to have ruled that the decision was irrational: on this matter, see R v. *Cambridge Health Authority, ex PB* [1995] 1 WLR 898 (for commentary, see Syrett [2006] *PL* 664 and, generally, King, 'The Justiciability of Resource Allocation' (2007) 70 *MLR* 197).

If the standard of review under *Wednesbury* unreasonableness is lowered in certain policy-making contexts, it is intensified in other circumstances. As Laws LJ has remarked, the *Wednesbury* principle 'constitutes a sliding scale of review, more or less intrusive according to the nature and gravity of what is at stake' (*R v. Secretary of State for Education and Employment, ex p Begbie* [2000] 1 WLR 1115, 1130). A more exacting standard of rational decision-making has been applied by the courts when 'fundamental' or 'constitutional' rights are said to have been in question: see, for example, *Bugdaycay v. Secretary of State for the Home Department* [1987] AC 514, 531; and *R v. Ministry of Defence, ex p Smith* [1996] QB 517, 554. The latter case is particularly important. It concerned the administrative discharge of four members of Her Majesty's Armed Services on the sole basis that they were homosexual. No allegations of sexual misconduct were made against them. Although the court did not conclude that their dismissals had been irrational in the circumstances, nevertheless, they recognised that a higher standard of scrutiny was required when determining whether a decision which restricted human rights was reasonable or not. The Court of Appeal confirmed that, when human rights are involved, '[t]he more substantial the interference with human rights, the more the court will require by way of justification before it is satisfied that the decision is reasonable.'

However, even this intensified test of irrationality was subsequently found by the ECtHR not to be sufficient to meet the demands of the European Convention. Article 13 of the convention provides that 'Everyone whose rights and freedoms as set forth in this Convention are violated shall have an effective remedy before a national authority.' Having lost in the Court of Appeal, the claimants in *ex p Smith* took their case to the ECtHR. In *Smith and Grady v. United Kingdom* (1999) 29 EHRR 493 the European Court declared (at [138]) that:

> the threshold at which the High Court and the Court of Appeal could find the Ministry of Defence policy irrational was placed so high that it effectively excluded any consideration by the domestic courts of the question of whether the interference with the applicants' rights answered a pressing social need or was proportionate to the national security and public order aims pursued, principles which lie at the heart of the Court's analysis of complaints under Article 8 [right to respect for private and family life] of the Convention.

For this reason, the ECtHR held that the judgment of the Court of Appeal in *ex p Smith* violated the claimants' rights under Article 13 of the Convention: even an intensified test of *Wednesbury* unreasonableness is not an 'effective remedy' in these circumstances, the court held.

Since the coming into force of the HRA, the House of Lords has held that, in cases concerning convention rights, standards of proportionality should be used instead of notions of *Wednesbury* unreasonableness. Nevertheless the formulation of *Wednesbury* to provide for a more stringent scrutiny of decisions that harm fundamental or constitutional rights still has relevance as regards decisions that restrict fundamental common law rights that are not convention rights, either because they are not protected by the list of convention rights found in Schedule 1 to the Human Rights Act 1998, or because there is no clear decision of the European Court of Human Rights confirming that the convention would apply to the applicant's situation. There is also obiter dicta to suggest that the UK courts may be prepared to apply a test of proportionality as regards the breach of fundamental common law rights that protect human rights. (See, in particular, *R (Youssef) v. Secretary of State for Foreign and Commonwealth Affairs* [2016] UKSC 3, [2016] AC 1457.)

There are other accounts of *Wednesbury* – that a decision is *Wednesbury* unreasonable if it is 'beyond the range of responses open to a reasonable decision-maker' (*R* v. *Ministry of Defence, ex p Smith* [1996] QB 517, 554), and we arrive at the 'simple test' of 'whether the decision in question was one which a reasonable authority could reach' (Lord Cooke of Thorndon in *R* v. *Chief Constable of Sussex, ex p International Trader's Ferry Ltd* [1999] 2 AC 418, 452). The applicable standard is elucidated by Lord Woolf in *R* v. *North and East Devon Health Authority, ex p Coughlan* [2001] QB 213, para 65, as follows:

> Rationality, as it has developed in modern public law, has two faces: one is the barely known decision which simply defies comprehension; the other is a decision which can be seen to have proceeded by flawed logic (though this can often be equally well allocated to the intrusion of an irrelevant factor).

We can also find evidence of cases where *Wednesbury* appears to have been applied in a very exacting manner, although this may often be in cases where different members of the judiciary express contradictory views.

Keyu v. Secretary of State for Foreign and Commonwealth Affairs [2015] UKSC 69, [2016] AC 1355

The case concerned the tragic events that took place on 11 and 12 December 1948, where members of a Scots Guards patrol shot and killed twenty-four unarmed civilians in the village of Batang Kali, in Selangor. At that time, Selangor was part of the British Protected State in the Federation of Malaya, and is now part of Malaysia. The claimants had asked the Secretary of State to hold an inquiry into the shootings, exercising a discretionary power under section 1 of the Inquiries Act 2005, arguing that the killings were unjustified murder thus requiring an inquiry. When the Secretary of State refused, the claimants challenged this decision, focusing on their rights under Article 2 ECHR, a potential requirement for an investigation under the provisions of customary international law and, more importantly for the purposes of this chapter, arguing that the decision of the Secretary of State was irrational according to the *Wednesbury* standard of rationality. The case is more well-known for its contribution to the argument as to whether proportionality should be adopted as a general standard of review in English administrative law (see below). However, it also illustrates tension in the approach to *Wednesbury* itself, illustrated in particular in the contrast between the approach of Lord Neuberger and Lady Hale.

The Secretary of State had provided a range of reasons for why an inquiry should not be held. These included the difficulty of establishing the truth of events that had taken place so long ago; problems for witnesses, many of whom would now have died and others who would be in their 80s and who may have difficulty recalling events that took place sixty years ago; the different legal backdrops of when the events occurred and today; the difficulty and costs of obtaining evidence; that understanding whether these events that took place so long ago were motivated by race may have little impact on race relations in the present day; and that inadequacies of earlier inquiries were not sufficient to justify a further inquiry. Lord Neuberger agreed with the Court of Appeal's assessment that 'the Secretaries of State considered everything which they were required to consider; did not have regard to any irrelevant considerations; and reached rationality decides which were open to them.' ([128]), adding that the secretaries of state 'clearly considered the request for an inquiry seriously and rejected it for reasons which are individually defensible and relevant, and which cumulatively render it impossible to characterise their conclusion as unreasonable, let alone irrational' ([129]). Lord Neuberger also accepted that it was not unreasonable for the Secretary of State to have reached this decision without quantifying the precise likely costs of an inquiry.

Lady Hale, however, reached the opposite conclusion. In doing so, she listed nine factors that she believed a rational decision-maker would have to take into account.

> [309]. Any rational decision-maker would take into account, at the very least, the following salient points about the background history:
>
> (1) The enormity of what is alleged to have taken place. If the guardsmen did indeed kill innocent and unarmed villagers in cold blood, then even by the different standards of the time, this was a grave atrocity which deserves to be acknowledged and condemned.
> (2) The inadequacy of the initial investigation. There were many people present at the scene who could have been asked for their accounts. It was totally unacceptable to assume that the guardsman and their police escorts were telling the truth but that the survivors and civilian eye-witnesses would not do so.
> (3) The weight which should be accorded to the confessions made in 1970. Although originally given to a newspaper, four were repeated under caution to the police. They were enough to cast serious doubt in the official account and to prompt a serious police inquiry.
> (4) The premature termination of that inquiry, which was obviously being conscientiously conducted by DCS Williams, and his view that this was a political decision, unsurprising given that it happened very shortly after the change of government in 1970.
> (5) The evidence obtained from the Royal Malaysian Police inquiry in the 1990s. Although some of the relatives and survivors had previously given their accounts to others, this evidence had only recently come to light.
> (6) The petering out of that inquiry, in the face, it would appear, of an unhelpful attitude of the British authorities when the Malaysian Police wished to pursue their inquiries here.
> (7) The thorough analysis of all of the available evidence in *Slaughter and Deception at Batang Kali*. The authors did not have a particular point of view, being determined to

> undermine the official account, but they collected together a great deal of information and analysed it in great detail.
>
> (8) The evidence from the archaeologist, Professor Black, as to what exhuming and examining the bodies of the deceased could show and how it would help in determining the facts.
>
> (9) The persistence and strength of injustice felt by the survivors and families of the men who were killed, which has led them twice to petition the Queen and to launch these proceedings.

That is quite a list! It was not clear at all that this range of factors would be required to be taken into account by the Secretary of State according to section 1(1) of the Inquiries Act 2005, which states that 'A Minister may cause an inquiry to be held under this Act in relation to a case where it appears to him that – (a) particular events have caused, or are capable of causing, public concern, or (b) that there is public concern that particular events may have occurred'. The list is longer than the account of the range of factors the Secretary of State listed as having taken into account. It, in turn, provides a potentially stronger constraint on the powers of the Secretary of State.

This is reinforced by further statements in Lady Hale's judgment, where she sets out what she regards as the advantages and disadvantages that a rational decision-maker would have to take into account when determining whether to hold a public inquiry into the killings. The advantages included the real possibility of reaching the truth, the importance of the British authorities finally seeking to make good and the huge importance of setting the record straight. These had to be weighed against the disadvantages of finding the facts given the passage of time, the lower impact of the findings of the inquiry on current practices given the changes that had taken place since the events occurred and the not inconsiderable costs of holding an inquiry. For Lady Hale (at [312]),

> The reasons given by the Secretaries of State focused on what might now be learned of contemporary relevance, either to the organisation and training of the army or to promoting race relations, from conducting an inquiry. They did not seriously consider the most cost-effective form which such an inquiry might take. They did not seriously consider the 'bigger picture': the public interest in properly inquiring into an event of this magnitude; the private interests of the relatives and survivors in knowing the truth and seeing the reputations of their deceased relatives and survivors vindicated; the importance of setting the record straight – as counsel put it, balancing the prospect of the truth against the value of the truth.

This would appear to suggest that Lady Hale is concerned that the Secretary of State failed to take account of relevant considerations. However, the real concern in her judgment is that the Secretary of State gave too much weight to the lack of relevance of the inquiry to the improvement of current conduct or improving current race relations and to the potential cost of an inquiry; while giving too little weight to the value of establishing the truth. This is evident in her conclusion that 'if the Divisional Court had not set the bar to establishing the truth so high, it might well have concluded that the value of establishing the truth, which would serve all the beneficial purposes which it identified, was overwhelming' and, as such, 'the *Wednesbury* test does have some meaning in a case such as this' ([313]).

Given this potential flexibility in meaning, it is not surprising that the argument of *Wednesbury* unreasonableness is often urged; although it does not always succeed. (See, generally, Lord Irvine, 'Judges and Decision-Makers: The Theory and Practice of *Wednesbury* Review' [1996] *PL* 59; Laws, '*Wednesbury*', in Forsyth and Hare (eds.), *The Golden Metwand and the Crooked Cord* (1998); Hickman, *Public Law after the Human Rights Act* (2010), ch. 7.)

10.2.3 Proportionality

In 1980, the Committee of Ministers of the Council of Europe adopted a recommendation to member states (No R(80)2) 'concerning the exercise of discretionary powers by administrative authorities'. One of the principles that it recommended should be followed in the exercise of discretionary power was that the administrative authority:

> maintains a proper balance between any adverse effects which its decision may have on the rights, liberties or interests of persons and the purpose which it pursues.

This is the principle of 'proportionality', which has become central in the jurisprudence both of the CJEU and of the ECtHR. Respect for the principle of proportionality requires that an authority exercising a power that necessarily has a disadvantageous effect on private rights or interests, if able to choose between alternative measures, should adopt the least onerous and should not impose a sanction, restriction or penalty that is disproportionate in severity or extent to the aim pursued. The principle of proportionality is used in English law in specific circumstances: when applying EU law (or retained EU law post-implementation period completion day); when applying convention rights under the provisions of the Human Rights Act 1998; as a standard of review when applying the doctrine of substantive legitimate expectations (see, e.g., *R (Nadarajah)* v. *Secretary of State for the Home Department* [2005] EWCA Civ 1363, and *Paponette* v. *AG of Trinidad and Tobago* [2010] UKPC 32, [2012] 1 AC 1); and in certain applications of fundamental common law rights, particularly when applying the principle of legality (see, e.g., *R* v. *Secretary of State for the Home Department ex p Leech* [1994] QB 198; *R* v. *Secretary of State for the Home Department, ex p Daly* [2001] UKHL 26, [2001] 2 AC 532; *R (UNISON)* v. *Lord Chancellor* [2017] UKSC 51, [2017] 3 WLR 409). However, there have been recent calls for proportionality to be adopted as a general standard of review in English law, with these debates being played out in the Supreme Court. Although proportionality has not yet been adopted as a general standard of review, there have been moves in this direction, in addition to criticisms of such a move.

Prior to exit day, and during the implementation period, UK courts are required to apply EU law in a manner that has regard to the principle of proportionality, this being a general principle of European Union law. Post-implementation period completion day, section 6(3) of the European Union (Withdrawal) Act 2018 requires UK courts to continue to interpret retained EU law 'in accordance with any retained principles of EU law', which would include the principle of proportionality. However, the Supreme Court – and if the powers under the European Union (Withdrawal Agreement) Act 2020 are used, potentially other courts – may depart from decisions of the CJEU when interpreting retained EU law. As such, this provides the possibility that proportionality may not be used, or may be applied differently, as regards retained EU law. Proportionality has played a particular role when determining whether UK laws restrict the four fundamental freedoms in EU law – that is, the free movement of goods, services, capital and people (see, e.g., *R* v. *Chief Constable of Sussex, ex p International Trader's Ferry Ltd* [1999] 2 AC 418). When applying EU law in this manner, the proportionality test is applied more or less stringently, the test being modified on occasion such that actions are only unlawful when they are manifestly disproportionate (see, e.g., *R (Sinclair Collis)* v. *Secretary of State for Health* [2011] EWCA Civ 437, [2012] QB 394). Post-implementation period completion day, the four freedoms should no longer play a role in UK law, although it remains to be seen whether standards of proportionality will apply to possible derogations from the common frameworks that will regulate the UK market post-implementation period completion day.

The main impact of the principle of proportionality has been as regards its application to the Human Rights Act 1998. The ECtHR uses the notion of proportionality in a particular way. This may be explained with reference to *Smith and Grady* v. *United Kingdom* (1999) 29 EHRR 493 (see above). Smith and Grady argued that the investigations into their personal lives that led to their administrative discharge from the armed services infringed their rights under Article 8 ECHR. Article 8 is in the following terms:

1. Everyone has the right to respect for his private and family life, his home and his correspondence.
2. There shall be no interference by a public authority with the exercise of this right except such as is in accordance with the law and is necessary in a democratic society in the

> interests of national security, public safety or the economic well-being of the country, for the prevention of disorder or crime, for the protection of health or morals, or for the protection of the rights and freedoms of others.

It will be seen that the structure of Article 8 is as follows. Paragraph 1 contains the rights protected (i.e., the right to respect for private and family life, home and correspondence). Paragraph 2 contains the requirements that must be met for state or public interference with these rights to be justified. Three requirements must be met: (a) the interference must be 'in accordance with the law'; (b) the interference must be 'necessary in a democratic society'; and (c) the interference must be for a certain prescribed aim, such as national security, public safety, etc. In terms of its structure, Article 8 is typical of the convention: Articles 9–11 (concerning the rights to freedom of thought, expression and assembly) are structured identically (see, further, Chapter 11). It is with regard to the second of these requirements that proportionality comes into play: the ECtHR interprets the test of necessity in a democratic society as, in essence, a test of proportionality. The court asks if there is a 'pressing social need' justifying the interference. On the facts of *Smith and Grady*, the court ruled that there was not and that Article 8 was violated as a result. As we saw above, the court then went on to rule that, because the test of irrationality employed by the Court of Appeal did not enable that court to examine whether the interference with Article 8 rights was *necessary* (only whether it was *reasonable*), judicial review on grounds of irrationality failed to provide an 'effective remedy' within the meaning of Article 13.

The decisive move to allow arguments of proportionality to be made in domestic courts in cases concerning convention rights came in *R (Daly)* v. *Secretary of State for the Home Department* [2001] UKHL 26, [2001] 2 AC 532. It should be noted that this development was arguably not strictly required by the HRA. This is for two reasons: first, Article 13 is not one of the convention rights that is domestically incorporated under that Act and, second, proportionality is a ground of review that, as we have seen, was developed by the *Court* of Human Rights in its *case law*. The *text* of the convention itself does not use the term. The convention itself talks of necessity in a democratic society, but the court has chosen to interpret that notion through the lens of proportionality. The HRA does not incorporate the case law of the ECtHR into domestic law. It incorporates only the text of the convention rights themselves. What the HRA says about the case law of the ECtHR is that domestic courts 'must take [it] into account' (section 2(1)). While such case law must be *taken into account*, it does not necessarily have to be *followed*, at least not according to a strict reading of section 2. (Under the *Ullah* principle, however, the House of Lords has ruled that a clear and constant line of authority from the Strasbourg court ought generally to be followed by the UK courts: *R (Ullah)* v. *Special Adjudicator* [2004] UKHL 26,

[2004] 2 AC 323. The *Ullah* principle is a matter of some controversy and is discussed in Chapter 11.) By way of contrast, the UK courts are required to ensure that public authorities do not act contrary to convention rights (Human Rights Act 1998, section 6) and that, so far as it is possible to do so, legislation is read and given effect to in a manner that is compatible with convention rights (Human Rights Act 1998, section 3). To fulfil these obligations, courts have to determine the content of convention rights. An assessment of proportionality is often necessary to achieve this task.

In *Daly* v. *Secretary of State for the Home Department* [2011] UKHL 26, [2001] AC 2 AC 532 (HL), the House of Lords ruled that domestic courts should follow the ECtHR in adopting proportionality as a ground of review in cases concerning convention rights. The test of review to be adopted in such cases was set out in the opinion of Lord Steyn, with which all their Lordships hearing the appeal agreed.

> **Lord Steyn:** ... The contours of the principle of proportionality are familiar. In *de Freitas v Permanent Secretary of Ministry of Agriculture, Fisheries, Lands and Housing* [1999] 1 AC 69 the Privy Council adopted a three-stage test. Lord Clyde observed, at p 80, that in determining whether a limitation (by an act, rule or decision) is arbitrary or excessive the court should ask itself:
>
> > 'whether: (i) the legislative objective is sufficiently important to justify limiting a fundamental right; (ii) the measures designed to meet the legislative objective are rationally connected to it; and (iii) the means used to impair the right or freedom are no more than is necessary to accomplish the objective.'
>
> Clearly, these criteria are more precise and more sophisticated than the traditional grounds of review. What is the difference for the disposal of concrete cases? Academic public lawyers have in remarkably similar terms elucidated the difference between the traditional grounds of review and the proportionality approach: see Jowell, 'Beyond the rule of law: towards constitutional judicial review' [2000] *PL* 671 [his Lordship cited further academic authorities to similar effect]. The starting point is that there is an overlap between the traditional grounds of review and the approach of proportionality. Most cases would be decided in the same way whichever approach is adopted. But the intensity of review is somewhat greater under the proportionality approach. Making due allowance for important structural differences between various convention rights, which I do not propose to discuss, a few generalisations are perhaps permissible. I would mention three concrete differences without suggesting that my statement is exhaustive. First, the doctrine of proportionality may require the reviewing court to assess the balance which the decision maker has struck, not merely whether it is within the range of rational or reasonable decisions. Secondly, the proportionality test may go further than the traditional grounds of review inasmuch as it may require attention to be directed to the relative weight accorded to interests and considerations. Thirdly, even the heightened scrutiny test developed in *R v Ministry of Defence, ex p Smith* [1996] QB 517, 554 is not necessarily appropriate to the protection of

human rights. It will be recalled that in *Smith* the Court of Appeal reluctantly felt compelled to reject a limitation on homosexuals in the army. The challenge based on article 8 of the Convention for the Protection of Human Rights and Fundamental Freedoms (the right to respect for private and family life) foundered on the threshold required even by the anxious scrutiny test. The ECtHR came to the opposite conclusion: *Smith and Grady v United Kingdom* (1999) 29 EHRR 493 . . . [T]he intensity of the review, in similar cases, is guaranteed by the twin requirements that the limitation of the right was necessary in a democratic society, in the sense of meeting a pressing social need, and the question whether the interference was really proportionate to the legitimate aim being pursued.

The differences in approach between the traditional grounds of review and the proportionality approach may therefore sometimes yield different results. It is therefore important that cases involving Convention rights must be analysed in the correct way. This does not mean that there has been a shift to merits review. On the contrary, as Professor Jowell [2000] *PL* 671, 681 has pointed out the respective roles of judges and administrators are fundamentally distinct and will remain so.

The UK courts have now adopted a four-stage approach to proportionality. The clearest account of this test is found in *R (Quila)* v. *Secretary of State for the Home Department* [2011] UKSC 45, which concerned the modification of immigration rules. Visas had been granted for spouses moving to the UK in order to marry a UK national, where both parties to the marriage were over the age of eighteen. This was changed so as to require both parties to be over the age of twenty-one, with the aim of reducing forced marriages between UK nationals and those wishing to obtain the right to reside in the UK. The applicants argued that this was a disproportionate restriction on their right to marry. Lord Wilson provided a clear account of the four-stage test as follows, at [45]:

The amendment had a legitimate aim: it was 'for the protection of the rights and freedoms of others', namely those who might otherwise be forced into marriage. It was 'in accordance with the law'. But was it 'necessary in a democratic society'? It is within this question that an assessment of the amendment's proportionality must be undertaken. In *Huang v Secretary of State for the Home Department, Kashmiri v Secretary of State for the Home Dept* [2007] UKHL 11, [2007] 4 All ER 15, [2007] 2 AC 167, Lord Bingham suggested, at [19], that in such context four question generally arise, namely:

(a) is the legislative objective sufficiently important to justify limiting a fundamental right?
(b) are the measures which have been designed to meet it rationally connected to it?
(c) are they no more than are necessary to accomplish it?
(d) do they strike a fair balance between the rights of the individual and the interests of the community?

This four-stage process has become firmly established in English cases applying the Human Rights Act 1998. (See *Bank Mellat* v. *HM Treasury (2)* [2013] UKSC 39, [2014] AC 700; *R (Nicklinson)* v. *Ministry of Justice* [2014] UKSC 38, [2015] AC 657; *R (Tigere)* v. *Secretary of State for Business, Innovation and Skills* [2015] UKSC 57, [2015] 1 WLR 3820; *R (Steinfeld)* v. *Secretary of State for International Development* [2018] UKSC 32.)

Smith and Grady v. *United Kingdom* suggests that there are two apparent differences between the *Wednesbury* rationality test and proportionality applied under the Human Rights Act. First, when applying proportionality, courts are the primary decision-makers. Second, proportionality is a more exacting form of review than rationality, meaning that it is easier for an applicant to demonstrate that a decision is disproportionate than it is to demonstrate that the decision is irrational.

It is clear that it is the job of the court to determine the content of a convention right, in order to assess whether a public authority acted contrary to this right or whether legislation can be read and given effect in a manner compatible with the convention right. This can illustrated by *R (SB)* v. *Denbigh High School* [2006] UKHL 15, [2007] 1 AC 100 and *Belfast City Council* v. *Miss Behavin'* [2007] UKHL 19, [2007] 1 WLR 1420. In *Denbigh High School*, the claimant, who was a pupil at the school, had been sent home for wearing to school a type of Islamic dress (the *jilbab*) that was not permitted under the school's rules on uniform. The *shalwar kameez* was permitted but the more restrictive *jilbab* was not. The pupil sought judicial review of the school's decision to send her home, arguing that it violated her right (under Article 9 of the ECHR) to freedom of thought, conscience and religion. The Court of Appeal held for the pupil, ruling that the school's decision was disproportionate because the school had not had specific regard in its decision-making to the fact that the matter engaged the pupil's convention rights. In order to satisfy the demands of proportionality, the Court of Appeal ruled, the decision-maker (here the school) was required itself to ensure that its decision was proportionate. The House of Lords unanimously overturned the Court of Appeal's ruling, as well as its reasoning, insisting that proportionality is a question of law for the court to rule on, rather than a matter which decision-makers in public administration are themselves required, in terms, to consider. According to Lord Bingham, the Court of Appeal's approach would have introduced 'a new formalism' and would have been 'a recipe for judicialisation on an unprecedented scale' ([31]). Upholding the school's decision, Lord Bingham stated at [33]–[34] that:

> the school did not reject the [claimant's] request out of hand: it took advice, and was told that its existing policy conformed with the requirements of mainstream Muslim opinion.

> The school was in my opinion fully justified in acting as it did. It had taken immense pains to devise a uniform policy which respected Muslim beliefs but did so in an inclusive, unthreatening and uncompetitive way . . .

Miss Behavin' is in similar terms. Here, the local authority rejected an application to license a sex shop in a particular location in Belfast. The claimants argued that the decision was unlawful on grounds of proportionality, as the local authority had failed to consider their right to freedom of expression under Article 10 of the ECHR. The House of Lords had no difficulty in applying the rule in *Denbigh High School* and held for the local authority. Proportionality requires more of the court than the older test of irrationality. As Lady Hale expressed it in *Miss Behavin'* (at [31]):

> The role of the court in human rights adjudication is quite different from the role of the court in an ordinary judicial review of administrative action. In human rights adjudication, the court is concerned with whether the human rights of the claimant have in fact been infringed, not with whether the administrative decision-maker properly took them into account.

It is not that the court reviews the reasonableness of the decision of the administrative decision-maker; it is that the court comes to a judgment of its own. It is outcomes, not decision-making processes, that are determinative. And the question for the court is not whether the decision-maker's preferred outcome was within the range of reasonable responses (the enhanced *Wednesbury/ex p Smith* question) but whether it was compatible with convention rights. To answer this question the court has to come to a decision of its own. (See also *R (Lord Carlile of Berriew)* v. *Secretary of State for the Home Department* [2014] UKSC 60, [2015] AC 945.)

Thus, it is clear that, in interpreting convention rights and working out their implications and limits, the courts have a new constitutional role to perform in the difficult enterprise of reconciling the interests of society with the rights and freedoms of the individual. A court may have to undertake this task albeit that the legislature, or the executive, has chosen to strike the balance in a particular way between the rights of the individual and the interests of society.

What is less clear, however, is whether proportionality really does provide a more stringent form of review in all cases. The ECtHR allows a 'margin of appreciation', a certain freedom of action, to state authorities, recognising that they have a greater awareness of local circumstances than an international court does, which may justify a restriction of convention rights. In *Hatton* v. *United Kingdom* (2003) 37 EHRR 28, at [97], the European Court reiterated 'the fundamentally subsidiary role of the Convention':

> The national authorities have direct democratic legitimation and are, as the Court has held on many occasions, in principle better placed than an international court to evaluate local needs and conditions. In matters of general policy, on which opinions within a democratic society may reasonably differ widely, the role of the domestic policy maker should be given special weight.

The doctrine of the margin of appreciation is not applicable in the domestic context, but our courts concede to the legislature and executive 'a discretionary area of judgment within which policy choices may legitimately be made' (Lord Steyn in *R* v. *A (No 2)* [2001] UKHL 25, [2002] 1 AC 45, at [36]). 'In some circumstances', said Lord Hope in *R* v. *DPP, ex p Kebilene* [2000] 2 AC 326, 381:

> it will be appropriate for the courts to recognise that there is an area of judgment within which the judiciary will defer, on democratic grounds, to the considered opinion of the elected body or person whose act or decision is said to be incompatible with the Convention.

One way in which this can occur is when the test for proportionality is itself modified, in line with case law from the ECtHR. One such example occurs when the issue before the court concerns general measures of economic policy, or of social strategy, where measures require an analysis of questions of economic or social judgment. In *R (Carmichael and Rourke)* v. *Secretary of State for Work and Pensions* [2016] UKSC 58, the Supreme Court was asked to determine whether the controversial 'bedroom tax' contravened convention rights. The 'bedroom tax' imposed a cap on housing benefit. Housing benefit is calculated according to the maximum rent (social sector) for a particular dwelling. However, this was reduced when the dwelling had more bedrooms than would be needed by those occupying the house, this calculation depending on assessments of those who could be expected to share a room – for instance, those living together as man and wife, children of the same sex or children of a different sex under the age of ten. Additional bedrooms were allowed for those requiring overnight care. Carmichael and Rourke argued that the rules discriminated against those with disabilities. In determining whether convention rights had been breached, the Supreme Court confirmed that the appropriate test was to assess whether the provisions of the 'bedroom tax' were 'manifestly without reasonable foundation'. Lord Toulson, giving the judgment of the court, confirmed that the 'manifestly without reasonable foundation' test was required by the ECtHR as this concerned 'choices about welfare systems involving policy decisions on economic and social matters which are pre-eminently matters for national authorities'. Nevertheless, the Supreme Court examined the regulations relating to the 'bedroom tax' carefully to determine whether they were without reasonable foundation. The court concluded that it was 'manifestly without reasonable foundation' for the rules not to include the need for an extra bedroom when a married couple were unable to share the same room because of the disability of one party to the marriage, given that the rules would allow for an extra room where children were unable to share a room because of the disabilities of one of the children. It was also manifestly without reasonable foundation to allow for an extra room for an overnight carer needed for an adult, but not to do the same when an extra room was needed for an overnight carer for a child.

In addition to applying a less rigorous test of proportionality in line with case law of the ECtHR, there are also examples of where UK courts apply proportionality less stringently through applying a concept of 'deference' to the decisions made by an elected legislature or a democratic government. This aspect of 'deference' can also be understood as providing a greater area of discretionary judgment to the executive.

In *Bank Mellat* v. *HM Treasury* (No 2), [2014] UKSC 39, [2014] AC 700, the bank argued that a measure adopted under Schedule 7 to the Counter-Terrorism Act 2008 prohibiting all persons operating in the financial sector from entering into transactions with Bank Mellat, on the grounds that it was a major Iranian commercial bank and that the Treasury believed that Iran was developing nuclear weapons, breached the bank's convention rights. In this case, Lord Sumption observed (at [21]) that

> The measures have been opened up to judicial scrutiny by the express terms of the Act because they may engage the rights of designated persons or others under the European Convention on Human Rights. Even so, any assessment of the rationality and proportionality ... of a Schedule 7 direction must recognise that the nature of the issue requires the Treasury to be allowed a large margin of judgment. It is difficult to think of a public interest as important as nuclear non-proliferation. The potential consequences of nuclear proliferation are quite serious enough to justify a precautionary approach. In addition, the question whether some measure is apt to limit the risk posed for the national interest by nuclear proliferation in a foreign country, depends on an experienced judgment of the international implications of a wide range of information, some of which may be secret. This is pre-eminently a matter for the executive. For my part, I wholly endorse the view of Lord Reed JSC that 'the making of government and legislative policy cannot be turned into a judicial process'.

Nevertheless, the Supreme Court did conclude that the measure was disproportionate. The Schedule 7 measure only applied to Bank Mellat. No measures had been taken against other Iranian commercial banks, in spite of there being no clear distinction between Bank Mellat and these banks and the fact that the risk related to international banks more generally and was not specifically related to the activities of Bank Mellat. As such, the measures were disproportionate.

This restraint on judicial intervention is commonly expressed as a requirement to show 'deference' to the decision-maker, but in *R (Prolife Alliance)* v. *BBC* [2003] UKHL 23, [2004] 1 AC 185, at [75], Lord Hoffmann remarked that the question is rather one of deciding, as a matter of law, 'which branch of government has in any particular instance the decision-making power and what the legal limits of that power are'. Accordingly, he continued (at [76]), 'when a court decides that a decision is within the proper competence of the legislature or executive, it is not showing deference. It is deciding the law.' A similar analysis was applied by Lord Bingham in *A* v. *Secretary of State for the Home Department* [2005] 2 AC 68, at [29] (see further on this case Chapter 11). (Compare the approach of Lord Steyn in 'Deference: A Tangled Story' [2005] *PL* 346.)

In *Huang* v. *Secretary of State for the Home Department* [2007] UKHL 11, [2007] 2 AC 167, the House of Lords was invited to set out a general theory of deference, but their Lordships were unanimous in declining the invitation. Such an approach has been eschewed in favour of the more context-specific, case-by-case method familiar to the common law. (Compare *International Transport Roth* v. *Secretary of State for the Home Department* [2003] QB 728, where Laws LJ had attempted to distil a number of the relevant principles.) Bearing in mind that what follows is in general terms and that there may always be exceptions, we may expect greater judicial deference to other decision-makers where the court acknowledges the greater expertise of the decision-maker or where it acknowledges that it lacks expertise, as in some cases concerning national security (e.g., *R (Binyam Mohamed)* v. *Secretary of State for Foreign and Commonwealth Affairs* [2010] EWCA Civ 65, [2010] 3 WLR 554); or where the court acknowledges the appropriateness of the decision being made by a body that is democratically elected or democratically accountable (e.g., *R (Alconbury)* v. *Secretary of State for the Environment* [2001] UKHL 23, [2003] 2 AC 295; *R (Countryside Alliance)* v. *Attorney General* [2007] UKHL 52, [2008] 1 AC 719; *R (Animal Defenders International)* v. *Secretary of State for Culture, Media and Sport* [2008] UKHL 15, [2008] 1 AC 1312; but compare *Re G (Adoption: Unmarried Couple)* [2008] UKHL 38, [2009] 1 AC 173, in which a markedly less deferential approach was taken: see Herring (2009) 125 *LQR* 1).

(The controversies surrounding deference have spawned a voluminous literature, of which the following is representative: Allan [2006] *CLJ* 671; King (2008) 28 *OJLS* 1; Young (2009) 72 *MLR* 554; Kavanagh, *Constitutional Review under the UK Human Rights Act* (2009), chs 7–9; Hickman, *Public Law after the Human Rights Act* (2010), ch. 5; Allan (2010) 60 *UTLJ* 41.)

The greater the 'deference', or the greater the discretionary area of judgment accorded to the decision-maker, the less likely it is that the new proportionality test will yield results that would not have been obtained under the older standards of *Wednesbury* unreasonableness. In this respect, as Thomas Poole has suggested, proportionality is somewhat reminiscent of irrationality in its flexibility, such that it can be 'applied almost infinitely forcefully or infinitely cautiously, producing an area of discretionary judgement that can be massively broad or incredibly narrow – and anything else in between' ('The Reformation of English Administrative Law' [2009] *CLJ* 142, 146).

Both the distinct nature of the test for proportionality, and the variable intensity of review with which both the test of proportionality and *Wednesbury* unreasonableness can be applied, have influenced the call for English law to adopt proportionality as a general standard of review. Contrariwise, our courts were initially wary of accepting the principle of proportionality as a distinct ground of review in domestic cases. While there were a few cases that followed a line of reasoning analogous to proportionality (see, e.g., *R v. Barnsley Metropolitan Borough Council, ex p Hook* [1976] 1 WLR 1052) and while arguments of proportionality were increasingly raised and addressed in the courts, outside the context of EU law, the courts were deeply reluctant to add proportionality to the grounds of judicial review. The reasons for this were outlined by Lord Donaldson MR in the Court of Appeal and by Lord Ackner in the House of Lords in *R v. Secretary of State for the Home Department, ex p Brind* [1991] 1 AC 696 (note, however, that others of their Lordships in *Brind* spoke in terms more favourable to the adoption of proportionality as a ground of judicial review, albeit that none of their Lordships considered that *Brind* was the appropriate case to introduce such a reform). Lord Donaldson reminded us (at 722) that:

> it must never be forgotten that [judicial review] is a *supervisory* and not an *appellate* jurisdiction ... Acceptance of 'proportionality' as a separate ground for seeking judicial review ... could easily and speedily lead to courts forgetting the supervisory nature of their jurisdiction and substituting their view of what was appropriate for that of the authority whose duty it was to reach that decision.

Lord Ackner agreed. He suggested that the use of a proportionality test would inevitably require the court to make 'an inquiry into and a decision upon the merits' of the matter and would, as such, amount to a 'wrongful usurpation of power' (at 762).

It is still the case that proportionality is not a general test of review in administrative law. This was confirmed by both the Court of Appeal in England and the Inner House of the Court of Session in Scotland: see *R (Association of British Civilian Internees: Far East Region) v. Secretary of State for Defence* [2003] QB 1397; *Somerville v. Scottish Ministers* [2006] CSIH 52, 2007 SC 140; *Browne v. Parole Board of England and Wales* [2018] EWCA Civ 2024. Nevertheless, a series of cases in the UK Supreme Court provide evidence of a possible move to adopt proportionality as a general test, although, in the words of Lord Neuberger in *Keyu v. Secretary of State for*

Foreign and Commonwealth Affairs [2015] UKSC 69, [2016] AC 1355, at [132]-[133]:

> It would not be appropriate for a five-Justice panel of this court to accept, or indeed to reject, this argument which potentially has implications which are profound in constitutional terms and very wide in applicable scope. Accordingly, if a proportionality challenge to the refusal to hold an inquiry would succeed, then it would be necessary to have this appeal (or at any rate this aspect of this appeal) re-argued before a panel of nine Justices . . . The move from rationality to proportionality, as urged by the appellants, would appear to have potentially profound and far-reaching consequences, because it would involve the court considering the merits of the decision at issue: in particular it would require the courts to consider the balance which the decision-maker has struck between competing interests (often a public interest against a private interest) and the weight to be accorded to each such interest . . .

The first clear judicial statements suggesting a potential move to the adoption of proportionality as a general test of review in English law are found in the judgment of Lord Mance in *Kennedy* v. *Charity Commission* [2014] UKSC 20, [2015] AC 455, [54]:

> As Professor Paul Craig has shown (see e.g. 'The Nature of Reasonableness Review' (2013) 66 CLP 131), both reasonableness review and proportionality involve considerations of weight and balance, with the intensity of the scrutiny and the weight to be given to any primary decision-maker's view depending on the context. The advantage of the terminology of proportionality is that it introduces an element of structure into the exercise, by directing attention to factors such as suitability or appropriateness, necessity and the balance or imbalance of benefits and disadvantages. There seems no reason why such factors should not be relevant in judicial review even outside the scope of convention and EU law. Whatever the context, the court deploying them must be aware that they overlap potentially and that the intensity with which they are applied is heavily dependent on the context.

Lord Mance is making three points relevant to the issue as to whether proportionality should be adopted as a general standard of review. First, he argues that both *Wednesbury* unreasonableness and proportionality require 'considerations of weight and balance' either to determine that a decision is irrational or disproportionate. Second, he is rejecting the claim that both *Wednesbury* unreasonableness and proportionality are monolithic tests. In other words, it is not the case that *Wednesbury* or proportionality have only one clear application, such that *Wednesbury* rationality is always a less stringent form of review than the more stringent form of review found in the proportionality test. Each test applies more or less stringently according to the context of the particular decision to which the test has been applied. This has been illustrated in the case law discussed above, with regard to the application of both irrationality and proportionality. As such, it may well be the case that the same outcome is achieved, regardless of whether the courts apply a test of rationality or proportionality. Third, Lord Mance provides a distinct advantage of a test of proportionality – it provides a more structured approach to judicial review through the application of the four stage test discussed above. These factors can be just as relevant to cases outside of convention rights and EU law as other cases.

These arguments can be found in a series of recent Supreme Court cases: *Bank Mellat v. HM Treasury (2)* [2013] UKSC 38, [2014] AC 700; *Pham v. Secretary of State for the Home Department* [2015] UKSC 19, [2015] 1 WLR 1591; *Keyu v. Secretary of State for Foreign and Commonwealth Affairs* [2015] UKSC 69, [2016] AC 1355; *R (Youssef) v. Secretary of State for Foreign and Commonwealth Affairs* [2016] UKSC 3, [2016] AC 1457. There is also a clear line of argument running through these cases that proportionality may be more suited to cases involving rights than cases that involve other areas of judicial review. Proportionality lends itself more to fundamental rights cases both in terms of the applicability of the four-stage structure, and in terms of these cases providing a reason for a more stringent form of judicial review – albeit that other aspects of fundamental rights cases may call for less stringency, rights cases that also involve issues of national security, for example. Nevertheless, it is still the case that proportionality is not a general test of review, although it is at least arguable that it can now be applied in cases involving fundamental rights, as can be seen by this account from Lord Carnwath, providing the judgment of the court, in *R (Youssef) v. Secretary of State for Foreign and Commonwealth Affairs* at [55]-[57]:

[55]. In *R (Keyu) v Secretary of State for Foreign and Commonwealth Affairs* [2015] 3 WLR 1665 (decided since the hearing in this appeal) this court had occasion to consider arguments, in the light of *Kennedy* and *Pham*, that this court should authorise a general move from the traditional judicial review tests to one of proportionality. Lord Neuberger of Abbotsbury PSC (with the agreement of Lord Hughes JSC) thought that the implications could be wide ranging and 'profound in constitutional terms', and for that reason would require consideration by an enlarged court. There was no dissent from that view in the other judgments. This is a subject which continues to attract intense academic debate: see, for example, the illuminating collection of essays in *The Scope and Intensity of Substantive Review: Traversing Taggart's Rainbow*, ed Wilberg and Elliott, 2015. It is to be hoped that an opportunity can be found in the near future for an authoritative review in this court of the judicial and academic learning on the issue, including relevant comparative material from other common law jurisdictions. Such a review might aim for rather more structured guidance for the lower courts than such imprecise concepts as 'anxious scrutiny' and 'sliding scales'.

[56]. Even in advance of such a comprehensive review of the tests to be applied to administrative decisions generally, there is a measure of support for the use of

proportionality as a test in relation to interference with 'fundamental' rights: *Keyu*, paras 280–282, per Lord Kerr of Tonaghmore JSC, para 304, per Baroness Hale of Richmond DPSC. Lord Kerr referred to the judgment of Lord Reed JSC in *Pham* (paras 113, 118–119) where he found support in the authorities for the proposition that:

> 'where Parliament authorises significant interferences with important legal rights, the courts may interpret the legislation as requiring that any such interference should be no greater than is objectively established to be necessary to achieve the legitimate aim of the interference: in substance, a requirement of proportionality.' (Para 119.)

See also my own judgment in the same case (para 60), and those of Lord Mance JSC (paras 95–98) and Lord Sumption JSC (paras 105–109), discussing the merits of a more flexible approach in judging executive interference with important individual rights, in that case the right to British citizenship.

[57]. On the other hand, in many cases, perhaps most, application of a proportionality test is unlikely to lead to a different result from traditional grounds of judicial review. This is particularly true of cases involving issues of national security. In *Bank Mellat v HM Treasury (No 2)* [2014] AC 700 (which concerned another security council regime, relating to nuclear weapons), there was not only majority and minority agreement as to the steps involved in an assessment of 'proportionality' (demanded in that case by the relevant statute), but also, within that context, general recognition that on issues of national security a large margin of judgment was accorded to the Executive: paras 20–21 per Lord Sumption JSC, para 98 per Lord Reed JSC. The difference turned on contrasting views as to the allegedly discriminatory nature of the restrictions in that case.

Whether it is satisfactory for the two tests of irrationality and proportionality to continue side by side, the one applying when there is no issue of convention rights arising and the other when there is such an issue, is open to debate. For a forceful defence of the status quo, see Taggart, 'Proportionality, Deference, Wednesbury' [2008] *NZLR* 423; for a critique of this position, see Hunt, 'Against Bifurcation', in Dyzenhaus, Hunt and Huscroft (eds.), *A Simple Common Lawyer: Essays in Honour of Michael Taggart* (2009), ch. 6. For equally strong arguments in the opposite direction, see Craig, 'The Nature of Reasonableness Review' (2013) 66 CLP 131 and Williams, 'Structuring Substantive Review' (2017) Public Law 99. See also the collection of essays in Wilberg and Elliott (eds.), *The Scope and Intensity of Substantive Review: Traversing Taggart's Rainbow* (Hart, 2015) for a comprehensive account of the different arguments.

10.2.4 Procedural Impropriety and Unfairness

The grounds of review considered thus far relate to the substance of public or governmental decisions. The final ground of judicial review concerns fair procedures. In the *GCHQ* case, Lord Diplock referred to this ground of review as 'procedural impropriety'. 'Breach of the rules of natural justice' is an older expression covering much the same ground. There are two established rules of natural justice: the 'rule against bias' and the 'duty to hear the other side', alternatively and more straightforwardly known as the 'duty to act fairly'. We shall consider each in turn.

10.2.4.1 Bias

If the decision-maker has a pecuniary interest in the matter to be decided, he or she is automatically disqualified from making the decision. This was settled in the classic case of *Dimes* v. *Grand Junction Canal Proprietors* (1852) 3 HLC 759 and applies even if no allegation of the decision-maker actually being biased can be made. That other direct interests, in addition to pecuniary interests, may likewise lead to automatic disqualification for bias was demonstrated by the decision of the House of Lords in *R* v. *Bow Street Stipendiary Magistrate, ex p Pinochet (No 2)* [2000] 1 AC 119. The case concerned the relationship of Lord Hoffmann to a party (Amnesty International Charity Ltd) related to another (Amnesty International) that had intervened in litigation before him who had advocated for a particular outcome. Even though no allegation of actual bias was made against his Lordship, the House of Lords held that the decision of which he had been part could not stand.

In addition to cases of automatic disqualification, a decision-maker may be disqualified from making a decision where the 'fair-minded and informed observer, having considered the facts, would conclude that there was a real possibility' of bias (*Porter* v. *Magill* [2001] UKHL 67, [2002] 2 AC 357, at [103] (Lord Hope)). This is known as apparent bias. The *Porter* v. *Magill* 'fair-minded and informed observer' test has been applied in numerous subsequent cases, a notable instance being *Helow* v. *Secretary of State for the Home Department* [2008] UKHL 62, 2009 SC (HL) 1. Like *Pinochet*, the allegation here concerned the bias of a senior judge but, unlike that case, here the issue was one of apparent bias rather than automatic disqualification. Helow was a Palestinian whose family were supporters of the Palestinian Liberation Organisation (PLO). She sought asylum in the UK but her application was refused. She then sought judicial review of this decision. Her case was heard in the Court of Session. The judge, Lady Cosgrove, dismissed Helow's petition for judicial review. Lady Cosgrove is Jewish and is a member of the International Association of Jewish Lawyers and Jurists (IAJLJ). The IAJLJ's quarterly publication had carried a number of articles that were, in Lord Hope's words, 'markedly antipathetic' to the PLO. The House of Lords was unanimous in ruling that Lady Cosgrove's membership of the IAJLJ did not constitute apparent bias in the circumstances of this case. Lord Hope stated (at [5]) that 'had there been anything to indicate that Lady Cosgrove had by word or deed associated herself with these views so as to indicate that they were her views, too, I would have had no difficulty in concluding that the test of apparent bias set out in *Porter v Magill* ... was satisfied.' But there was no evidence of anything of this sort and, despite the fact that Lady Cosgrove had been a 'high-profile member of the Scottish branch' of the IAJLJ (as Lord Walker described it at [27]), their Lordships were clear that the test for apparent bias had not been made out and that the judge's decision to dismiss Helow's petition for judicial review should stand. (For criticism of the 'informed observer' test for bias, see Olowofoyeku [2009] *CLJ* 388.)

The rule against bias may cause difficulties in administrative or governmental circumstances where the decision-maker has been elected to the position whereby it may make a decision on the basis of a manifesto or campaign commitment to resolve certain issues in a particular way. Take, for example, a planning authority, composed of democratically elected councillors who have been elected on a manifesto commitment to support – or to block – certain sorts of development. To what extent may such electoral commitments constitute bias? This problem was addressed in *R* v. *Secretary of State for the Environment, ex p Kirkstall Valley Campaign* [1996] 3 All ER 304. The judgment makes clear that the normal test for bias (as now articulated by Lord Hope in *Porter* v. *Magill*, although at the time the *Kirkstall Valley* case was decided the test was slightly different) should be applied in the normal way in such a context: 'In the case of an elected body the law recognises that members will take up office with publicly stated views on a variety of policy issues', said Sedley J. In such cases, he continued, 'the court will be concerned to distinguish ... legitimate prior stances or experience from illegitimate ones.' The judge ruled that, on the facts, the claimants had failed to demonstrate bias. This approach was approved and applied by the Court of Appeal in *R (Lewis)* v. *Redcar and Cleveland Borough Council* [2008] EWCA Civ 746, [2009] 1 WLR 83, in which Pill LJ stated as follows (at [62]):

> There is no doubt that councillors who have a personal interest, as defined in the authorities, must not participate in council decisions. No question of personal interest arises in this case. The committee which granted planning permission consisted of elected members who would be entitled, and indeed expected, to have and to have expressed views on planning issues. When taking a decision councillors must have regard to material considerations, and only to material considerations, and to give fair consideration to points raised, whether in an officer's report to them or in representations made to them at a meeting of the planning committee. Sufficient attention to the contents of the proposal which on occasions will involve consideration of detail must be given. They are not, however, required to cast aside views on planning policy they will have formed when seeking election or when acting as councillors. The test is a very different one from that to be applied to those in a judicial or quasi-judicial position.

These matters have been affected by the regime of convention rights introduced into our law by the HRA. Article 6(1) of the Convention, which is domestically incorporated under the Act, provides that 'In the determination of his civil rights and obligations ... everyone is entitled to a fair and public hearing ... by an independent and impartial tribunal.' There are many circumstances in which our governmental system provides for decisions to be made by ministers or administrators rather than by an 'independent and impartial tribunal'. Under the planning system, for example, the final decision on the most complex and controversial planning applications – on matters such as whether Heathrow Airport should have a new terminal or runway, or whether there should be a new high-speed rail link between London and the Channel Tunnel – will be made by the Secretary of State. The one thing that the Secretary of State clearly is not is an independent and impartial tribunal. In *R (Alconbury)* v. *Secretary of State for the Environment* [2001] UKHL 23, [2003] 2 AC 295, the House of Lords held that this aspect of Britain's planning system did not violate Article 6. The simplest solution would have been for their Lordships to rule that Article 6 is not engaged in these circumstances: that a decision on a planning application is not the determination of a 'civil right' for the purposes of Article 6 (after all, developers submitting planning applications can hardly be said to be 'on trial', and the right contained in Article 6 is described in the convention as the right to a fair trial). However, this elegant solution was effectively unavailable to the House of Lords because of the case law of the ECtHR, which has vastly expanded the scope of Article 6 so as to include within it decisions such as those at stake in the planning process (for critical analysis, see Gearty (2001) 64 *MLR* 129). While the House of Lords is not technically bound by this case law, their Lordships knew that had the claimants lost in the House of Lords on this ground, they would surely have mounted a successful appeal to the European Court in Strasbourg. Accordingly, the House of Lords ruled that Article 6 was not violated because, first, the decision-making of the Secretary of State was subject to judicial review and, second, the Secretary of State's decision-making in this context was closely related to sensitive questions of national environmental and social policy, in respect of which the Secretary of State should be accountable primarily to Parliament rather than to the courts (see, e.g., Lord Slynn at [48], Lord Nolan at [60], Lord Hoffmann at [68] and Lord Clyde at [139]–[144]).

What, however, if the decision-maker is making a straightforwardly administrative decision, rather than one that impacts on sensitive policy concerns? Does the decision-maker then need to be 'independent and impartial'? This issue arose in *Runa Begum* v. *Tower Hamlets London Borough Council* [2003] UKHL 5, [2003] 2 AC 430, in which the House of Lords chose not to distinguish *Alconbury* but to follow it. Mrs Begum was homeless. The local authority offered her a secure tenancy of a two-bedroom flat. Mrs Begum did not want to live in the area in which the flat was located. She requested a review, as she was legally entitled to do. As provided in the relevant statutory regulations, the reviewing officer was someone who was not involved in the original decision to allocate the flat and was senior to the officers who had been so involved. The reviewing officer rejected Mrs Begum's reasons for refusing the flat as unreasonable. Mrs Begum argued that the review violated her rights under Article 6, in that the reviewing officer was not 'independent and impartial'. The House of Lords unanimously held that Article 6 was not violated. Two reasons were furnished in the opinions of their Lordships: first, that the reviewing officer was subject to judicial supervision (via a statutory appeal on a point of law – the equivalent for present purposes of judicial review) and, second, that, as Lord Hoffmann expressed it (at [43]), 'regard must be had to democratic accountability, efficient administration and the sovereignty of Parliament'. The courts, he said (at [59]), should be 'slow to conclude that Parliament has produced an administrative scheme which does not comply with Convention rights'.

What their Lordships were seeking to avoid in this case was the prospect of convention rights being used to undermine the UK's well-established system of administrative justice in the welfare state. Benefits such as housing are administered under complex statutory schemes by local authorities. While the administration of such schemes is, of course, subject to statutory appeals and to judicial review, it has always been Parliament's intention and it has always been deemed to be in the interests of good administration for these schemes to be administered by professionals employed by local authorities (or, in the case of other aspects of social security, by government departments) and not by independent and impartial figures. As in *Alconbury*, the most elegant way of ruling that these schemes do not violate Article 6 would have been for their Lordships to rule that Article 6 is simply not engaged, but, as we have seen, that would be to risk running counter to the (deeply controversial) case law of the ECtHR on this issue. The result is that their Lordships felt that they had little option but to accept that Article 6 is engaged, albeit that they then had to find a way of holding that it was not violated. The solution in *Alconbury* relied on notions of democratic accountability for contested policy questions (hence Lord Hoffmann's reference to 'democratic accountability' above). From a constitutional point of view, that seems fair enough. But in *Begum*, a different solution was required – the reviewing officer can hardly be said to have been engaged in decision-making on delicate matters of policy and, in any event, she was not democratically accountable: she was an officer of the local authority, not a minister or a councillor – hence Lord Hoffmann's additional references (above) to 'efficient administration and the sovereignty of Parliament'. Now, it is hardly the scheme of the HRA that fundamental constitutional rights should be enjoyed only if and in so far as they do not impede efficient administration or the sovereignty of Parliament, but Lord Hoffmann was backed into a corner in ruling in these terms because any alternative result would either (as Lord Bingham expressed it at [5]) bring about 'the emasculation (by over judicialisation) of administrative welfare schemes' or would be destined to be overturned by the ECtHR.

The inelegance of the reasoning in these cases – and particularly of *Begum* – has continued to disturb our courts (and, we stress, it is the reasoning rather than the outcome which is disliked: Lord Bingham's point about emasculation by over-judicialisation is powerfully made and is surely correct). A different approach was therefore taken by the Supreme Court in *Ali* v. *Birmingham City Council* [2010] UKSC 8, [2010] 2 AC 39. In this case, the Supreme Court took the approach that at least some sorts of administrative decisions as to welfare and benefits should be held not to engage Article 6 in the first place. In the leading judgment, Lord Hope attempted to draw a distinction between 'the class of social security and welfare benefits that are of the kind ... whose substance the domestic law defines precisely' and 'those benefits which are, in their essence, dependent upon the exercise of judgment by the relevant authority' (at [43]). Whereas the former may be regarded as 'civil rights' within the meaning of Article 6(1), the latter, the court ruled, should not be so regarded: 'cases where the award of services or benefits in kind is not an individual right of which the applicant can consider himself the holder, but is dependent upon a series of evaluative judgments by the provider as to whether the statutory criteria are satisfied and the need for it ought to be met, do not engage Article 6(1)' (Lord Hope at [49]).

Elegant as this solution appeared, it did not meet with approval from the ECtHR. In *Ali* v. *United Kingdom* [2015] ECHR 40378/10, (2015) 63 EHRR 968, the fourth chamber of the court rejected this distinction, concluding that the determination of whether Ali should be allocated a house was a determination of a civil right triggering the application of Article 6(1) ECHR. In reaching this conclusion, the court described the determination of a civil right as follows, at para 53:

> a dispute over a 'right' which can be said, at least on arguable grounds, to be recognised under domestic law, irrespective of whether it is protected under the Convention. The dispute must be genuine and serious; it may relate to the actual existence of a right in the first place as well as to its scope and the manner of its exercise; and finally, the result of the proceedings must be directly decisive for the right in question, mere tenuous connections or remote consequences not being sufficient to bring article 6(1) into play.

The government had adopted the argument of the Supreme Court, stating that the determination of a housing right was not sufficiently identifiable. While an individual may have a right to be housed, that individual did not have a right to be housed in a particular house. It also required a double value judgment by governmental authorities: first to determine whether Ali had a right to housing and, second, to determine a suitable house to be provided for Ali to satisfy her right to housing. These arguments were insufficient to convince the ECtHR, although it did conclude that, in Ali's case, there was sufficient scrutiny of the decision of the housing officer by the homelessness review officer and the courts. This was because of the specific nature of Ali's claim. The housing officer had sent Mrs Ali a letter, offering her a particular property and explaining that, should Mrs Ali reject this property without good reason, then the housing authority would consider that it had discharged their duty to house her. Mrs Ali claimed that she had not received the letter. Instead, she had phoned the housing officer, had been given the address of the property, but then refused the property after visiting. The housing officer then wrote to Mrs Ali explaining that the council had fulfilled their housing duty. Mrs Ali complained, raising the lack of the receipt of the letter as one of her grounds of complaint. When hearing her appeal, the homelessness review officer had been able to reinvestigate the facts surrounding Mrs Ali's refusal to accept a house. Moreover, the case did not involve an element of injustice or unfairness. Even had Mrs Ali received the letter, she would still have refused the property; her grounds for refusing did not relate to the letter. There were also procedural safeguards in place as the homelessness review officer could not take part in the initial decision regarding the housing of Mrs Ali, and Mrs Ali was allowed to make representations to the homelessness review officer. Moreover, the decision could be reviewed by the court, which, although it could not fully reinvestigate the facts, could determine if the housing officer and the homelessness review officer had taken account of all of the relevant considerations and had not made a material error of relevant facts. As such, there was sufficient due inquiry into the facts by an independent tribunal when the scheme of decision-making was taken as a whole.

Nevertheless, the ruling in *Ali* v. *United Kingdom* has given rise to no change in domestic law. In *Poshteh* v. *Kensington Royal London Borough Council* [2017] UKSC 36, [2017] AC 624, the Supreme Court refused to follow the chamber decision of the ECtHR, concluded that housing decisions were not the determination of a civil right and thus did not require to be taken by an independent and impartial tribunal. Mrs Poshteh was a refugee from Iran who had been granted indefinite leave to remain the UK. Prior to her arrival in the UK, she had been subject to imprisonment and torture in Iran. As she was a homeless individual, Kensington LBC had a duty to find accommodation for her. However, Mrs Poshteh refused the permanent accommodation she had been offered. In particular, she stated that the small round window and other small window in the accommodation reminded her of where she had been held prisoner in Iran. The Supreme Court concluded that *Ali* v. *Birmingham City Council* had been designed to provide the definitive answer in domestic law as to whether the provision of housing was the determination of a civil right for the purposes of Article 6 ECHR. Moreover, the ECtHR had failed to give sufficient weight to the concerns of the judicialisation of the welfare process expressed in *Ali* v. *Birmingham City Council*. The decision in *Ali* v. *United Kingdom* also was not based on a clear and consistent line of case law, having decided a new issue, and had given too much weight to a statement found in an statement of Hale LJ – as she then was – that no longer reflected either the view of Lady Hale or of the Supreme Court more generally. As such, the Supreme

Court declined to change UK law until the issue of housing rights was determined by the Grand Chamber of the ECtHR.

Clearly, this issue is not yet resolved. While it may have made no difference in *Ali*, where the ECtHR concluded that there had been sufficient review of the decision of the housing officer by an independent and impartial tribunal, this may not be true in all cases. In *Poshteh*, for example, the Supreme Court examined whether the decision of the housing officer had made an error of law, failing to give sufficient weight to the impact of the house offered to Mrs Poshteh on her mental health. There was no analysis of the facts here – for instance, questioning witnesses to assess the strength of Mrs Poshteh's reaction on seeing the house, or through evaluating her medical records. Rather, the court focused on the difficult situation of the housing officer, trying to pay attention to Mrs Poshteh's situation when balancing her needs against other deserving applicants with a very small supply of available housing. Would the ECtHR regard this as a sufficiently detailed assessment of the facts for the purposes of correcting the original decision being made by a housing officer who is not independent from the council required to house Mrs Posheth? Moreover, by removing these evaluations from the scope of Article 6, housing officers will be better able to perform their job of allocating housing as fairly as possible, without the fear of potential legal actions. It remains to be seen whether these factors will influence the Grand Chamber of the ECtHR.

10.2.4.2 Duty to Act Fairly

A public authority is manifestly guilty of procedural impropriety if, in exercising a statutory power, it fails to comply with procedural safeguards – for instance, a duty to consult those affected – incorporated in the Act. Power-conferring statutes do not, however, always expressly provide safeguards against unfair treatment of the individual, and the common law may then 'supply the omission of the legislature' (Byles J in *Cooper* v. *Wandsworth Board of Works* (1863) 14 CBNS 180, 194) and impose standards of procedural fairness on the decision-maker. 'However widely the power is expressed in the statute, it does not authorise that power to be exercised otherwise than in accordance with fair procedures': Lord Browne-Wilkinson in *R* v. *Secretary of State for the Home Department, ex p Pierson* [1998] AC 539, 574.

The duty to act fairly requires decision-makers to give to persons affected a fair opportunity to make representations, and to take those representations into account, before reaching a decision. The duty was for a time considered to arise only if the decision to be taken was of a judicial or 'quasi-judicial' character and was to have no application to purely executive action not involving a 'duty to act judicially', but this limitation was eradicated by the House of Lords in *Ridge* v. *Baldwin* [1964] AC 40. Liberated by this decision, the courts have extended the requirements of the duty to act fairly to a wide range of administrative decision-making.

As it has with regard to bias and the requirements of impartiality, since the coming into force of the HRA, Article 6 of the ECHR has likewise had an impact on the duty to act fairly. A particularly notable and important case is *Wright*.

R (Wright) v. Secretary of State for Health [2009] UKHL 3, [2009] 1 AC 739

This case was concerned with the provisional listing of care workers on a list of persons unsuitable for working with vulnerable adults (the 'POVA' list) under the Care Standards Act 2000 (the relevant provisions of which are no longer in force, having been replaced by the Safeguarding Vulnerable Groups Act 2006). A tribunal hearing was available before full listing, but not before provisional listing, yet the consequences of being listed on POVA even provisionally could be devastating. People commonly remained provisionally listed for between five and nine months – all of this without being afforded a hearing. The House of Lords unanimously held that these arrangements were in violation of Article 6(1) and issued a declaration of incompatibility accordingly.

Lady Hale: . . . First, are we here concerned with a civil right at all? This is uncontroversial. As Lord Hoffmann explained in *Runa Begum v Tower Hamlets London Borough Council* [2003] 2 AC 430, the scope of the concept of civil rights has been greatly expanded from the sorts of dispute which the original framers of the Convention had in mind. But since 1981 it has been held to include the right to practise one's profession *(Le Compte, Van Leuven and De Meyere v Belgium (1981) 4 EHRR 1; Bakker v Austria* (2003) 39 EHRR 548). The right to remain in the employment one currently holds must be a civil right, as too must the right to engage in a wide variety of jobs in the care sector even if one does not currently have one.

More controversial is the second question. Does provisional listing amount to a 'determination' of a civil right, given that the listed person will eventually have the opportunity of taking the case before the Care Standards Tribunal? No one disputes that the tribunal provides a full merits hearing which is article 6 compliant in every way. But it is a general principle, frequently reiterated by the European Court of Human Rights, that 'article 6 does not apply to proceedings relating to interim orders or other provisional measures adopted prior to the proceedings on the merits, as such measures cannot, as a general rule, be regarded as involving the determination of civil rights and obligations' . . .

There are exceptions to that general rule. Some interim measures have such a clear and decisive impact upon the exercise of a civil right that article 6(1) does apply . . . It is one thing temporarily to freeze a person's assets, so that he cannot divest himself of them before an issue is tried; it is another thing to deprive someone of their employment by operation of law. If article 6 applies to the suspension of a doctor from medical practice (as in *Le Compte*), it must apply to the permanent separation of a person from her current employment.

This, too, the Secretary of State accepts. But there are cases in which provisional listing may not have quite such a drastic effect. The scheme allows for a temporary suspension or transfer to a non-care position. However, it is unlikely that an employer will take this option.

They will have to employ another person to do the work which the listed person was employed to do. The reality is that that particular job will be lost to the listed person for good. Of course, some listed people will no longer be employed in care positions and so will not lose their existing jobs. Much was made on behalf of the Secretary of State of the wide range of jobs, even within the care sector, which remained open to a listed person, including any job in an independent or NHS hospital. But, once again, the reality is that a listed person is most unlikely to be able to obtain such a job or to keep it if she does disclose that she has been listed. The main answer to this point, however, is that the scheme cannot assume that article 6(1) will never apply to provisional listing. There will undoubtedly be some cases, perhaps the majority, where it does apply. While the Strasbourg court has the luxury of looking back at the particular circumstances of a concrete case, and deciding whether there has been a breach of article 6 in that case, our national law has to devise a scheme which will be generally applicable before the particular impact of the decision is known . . .

The difficult question is how the requirements of article 6 apply in cases such as this. It is a well-known principle that decisions which determine civil rights and obligations may be made by the administrative authorities, provided that there is then access to an independent and impartial tribunal which exercises 'full jurisdiction' . . . What amounts to 'full jurisdiction' varies according to the nature of the decision being made. It does not always require access to a court or tribunal even for the determination of disputed issues of fact. Much depends upon the subject matter of the decision and the quality of the initial decision-making process. If there is a 'classic exercise of administrative discretion', even though determinative of civil rights and obligations, and there are a number of safeguards to ensure that the procedure is in fact both fair and impartial, then judicial review may be adequate to supply the necessary access to a court, even if there is no jurisdiction to examine the factual merits of the case. The planning system is a classic example (*Alconbury*); so too, it has been held, is the allocation of 'suitable' housing to the homeless (*Runa Begum*) . . .

[In the Court of Appeal] Dyson LJ considered that there were two reasons why the failure to afford the care worker an opportunity to make representations before provisional listing could not be cured by the possibility of being taken off the list . . . by judicial review, or by the later access to the tribunal. The first was that denial of the right to make representations was 'not a mere formal or technical breach. It is a denial of one of the fundamental elements of the right to a fair determination of a person's civil rights, namely, the right to be heard' . . . Secondly, the detrimental effect of provisional listing was often irreversible and incurable. Hence he concluded that there should be a right to make representations before provisional listing, unless it was outweighed by the immediate need to protect vulnerable adults from harm.

My Lords, the scheme appears premised on the assumption that permanently to ban a person from a wide variety of care positions does require a full merits hearing before an independent and impartial tribunal. That premise is, in my view, correct. The issue is what should be done on the way to that decision. How is a proper balance to be struck between the need to protect the vulnerable adults, who may be at risk from a care worker who has been referred to the Secretary of State, and the need to protect the care worker from suffering irreversible damage to her civil rights, as a result of allegations which later turn out to be unfounded, even frivolous or malicious, or at the very least blown up out of all proportion?

No one can be in any doubt of the need for some scheme such as this to protect children and vulnerable adults from being harmed by the people who regularly come into contact with them in the course of work. The most practicable way of providing such a scheme may well be to have a list of banned individuals which is maintained administratively and where the initial decisions are made by officials. [The High Court] was told that there are about 900,000 care workers within the scope of the scheme. Referrals run at the rate of 200 a month. There were then about 2,000 provisional listings and about 500 confirmed listings but only 37 cases had gone to the tribunal. If the process is working as it should, many people will accept that they should indeed be on the list.

However, in my view, Dyson LJ was entirely correct in his conclusion that the scheme as enacted in the Care Standards Act 2000 does not comply with article 6(1), for the reasons he gave. The process does not begin fairly, by offering the care worker an opportunity to answer the allegations made against her, before imposing upon her possibly irreparable damage to her employment or prospects of employment.

The content of the right to a fair hearing has also been influenced by Article 5 (4) ECHR, which provides for procedural protections for those who are deprived of their liberty. However, it is important to recognise that the common law protections still continue to play a clear role, with courts referring to the requirements of natural justice to determine the content of a right to a fair hearing, leading to a conclusion that these protections, in turn, ensure that Articles 6 or 5 ECHR have not been breached.

R (Osborn) v. Parole Board [2013] UKSC 61, [2014] AC 1115

Osborn had been released on licence from his prison sentence. However, while on release, he broke the conditions of his licence. His case was heard by the Parole Board, which revoked his licence. The Parole Board considered his appeal on paper, with written representations. Osborn argued that Article 5(4) ECHR and the common law right to a fair hearing required that the Parole Board grant him an oral hearing. The Supreme Court declined to conclude that an oral hearing should be granted for all Parole Board hearings concerning breach of licence conditions, or when determining whether a prisoner serving a life sentence should be released, once the prisoner had served the mandatory component of their life sentence. Lord Reed, giving the judgment of the court, summarised their conclusions as follows, at [2]:

(i) In order to comply with common law standards of procedural fairness, the board should hold an oral hearing before determining an application for release, or for a transfer to open conditions, whenever fairness to the prisoner requires such a hearing in the light of the facts of the case and the importance of what is at stake. By doing so the board will also fulfil its duty under section 6(1) of the Human Rights Act 1998 to act compatibly with article 5.4 of the European Convention for the Protection of Human Rights and Fundamental Freedoms, in circumstances where that article is engaged.

It is impossible to define exhaustively the circumstances in which an oral hearing will be necessary, but such circumstances will often include the following. (a) Where facts which appear to the board to be important are in dispute, or where a significant explanation or mitigation is advanced which needs to he heard orally in order fairly to determine its credibility. The board should guard against any tendency to underestimate the importance of issues of fact which may be disputed or open to explanation or mitigation. (b) Where the board cannot otherwise properly or fairly make an independent assessment of risk, or of the means by which it should be managed and addressed. That is likely to be the position in cases where such an assessment may depend on the view formed by the board (including its members with expertise in psychology or psychiatry) of characteristics of the prisoner which can best be judged by seeing or questioning him in person, or where a psychological assessment produced by the Ministry of Justice is disputed on tenable grounds, or where the board may be materially assisted by hearing evidence, for example from a psychologist or psychiatrist. Cases concerning prisoners who have spent many years in custody are likely to fall into the first of these categories. (c) Where it is maintained on tenable grounds that a face-to-face encounter with the board, or the questioning of those who have dealt with the prisoner, is necessary in order to enable him or his representatives to put their case effectively or to test the views of those who have dealt with him. (d) Where, in the light of the representations made by or on behalf of the prisoner, it would be unfair for a 'paper' decision made by a single member panel of the board to become final without allowing an oral hearing: for example, if the representations raise issues which place in serious question anything in the paper decision which may in practice have a significant impact on the prisoner's future management in prison or on future reviews.

(ii) In order to act fairly, the board should consider whether its independent assessment of risk, and of the means by which it should be managed and addressed, may benefit from the closer examination which an oral hearing can provide.

(iii) The board should also bear in mind that the purpose of holding an oral hearing is not only to assist in its decision-making, but also to reflect the prisoner's legitimate interest in being able to participate in a decision with important implications for him, where he has something useful to contribute . . . .

(viii) The board should guard against any temptation to refuse oral hearings as a means of saving time, trouble and expense . . .

(xi) In applying this guidance, it will be prudent for the board to allow an oral hearing if it is in doubt whether to do so or not.

(xii) The common law duty to act fairly, as it applies in this context, is influenced by the requirements of article 5.4 as interpreted by the European Court of Human Rights. Compliance with the common law duty should result in compliance also with the requirements of article 5.4 in relation to procedural fairness.

Osborn also illustrates how the requirements of natural justice vary according to the subject matter. In *R* v. *Secretary of State for the Home Department, ex p Doody* [1994] 1 AC 531, 560, Lord Mustill addressed the question of what fairness required of a decision-maker:

> My Lords, I think it unnecessary to refer by name or to quote from, any of the often-cited authorities in which the courts have explained what is essentially an intuitive judgement. They are far too well known. From them, I derive that (1) where an Act of Parliament confers an administrative power there is a presumption that it will be exercised in a manner which is fair in all the circumstances. (2) The standards of fairness are not immutable. They may change with the passage of time, both in the general and in their application to decisions of a particular type. (3) The principles of fairness are not to be applied by rote identically in every situation. What fairness demands is dependent on the context of the decision, and this is to be taken into account in all its aspects. (4) An essential feature of the context is the statute which creates the discretion, as regards both its language and the shape of the legal and administrative system within which the decision is taken. (5) Fairness will very often require that a person who may be adversely affected by the decision will have an opportunity to make representations on his own behalf either before the decision is taken with a view to producing a favourable result; or after it is taken, with a view to procuring its modification; or both. (6) Since the person affected usually cannot make worthwhile representations without knowing what factors may weigh against his interests fairness will very often require that he is informed of the gist of the case which he has to answer.

Fairness is not to be ossified as a set of rigid rules that must be followed as a matter of course. It may or may not, for example, require an oral hearing, or a right to be legally represented, or a right to cross-examine witnesses, or the giving of reasons for a decision. On these variables, see, respectively, *Lloyd* v. *McMahon* [1987] 1 AC 625, *R (Smith)* v. *Parole Board* [2005] UKHL 1, [2004] 1 WLR 923, *R (Osborn)* v. *Parole Board* [2013] UKSC 61, [2014] AC 1115 (oral hearing); *R* v. *Board of Visitors of HM Prison the Maze, ex p Hone* [1988] AC 379, *R (AT)* v. *University of Leicester* [2014] EWHC 4593 (Admin) (legal representation); *Bushell* v. *Secretary of State for the Environment* [1981] AC 75 (cross-examination). A court will consider the whole process by which a decision is reached and, rather than focusing on particular details, will decide whether the individual concerned has, in the end, been fairly treated.

There are some classes of case in which the duty to act fairly is given a particularly narrow construction by the courts so as to impose only a minimal restraint on the public authority. For example, in a number of cases the courts have taken the view that the ordinary standards of fairness must give way to the judgment of a minister in matters of national security, for instance, when a person is deported from the UK on this ground (see, e.g., *R* v. *Secretary of State for the Home Department, ex p Hosenball* [1977] 1 WLR 766 and *R* v. *Secretary of State for the Home Department, ex p Cheblak* [1991] 1

WLR 890). Ordinary understandings of due process as regards civil procedure in the courts may likewise be diluted, sometimes alarmingly so, on the basis of claims as to the interests of national security (see, e.g., *A* v. *United Kingdom* (2009) 49 EHRR 29 and *Secretary of State for the Home Department* v. *AF* [2009] UKHL 28, [2009] 3 WLR 74). (Case law concerning national security is considered in more detail in Chapter 11.) Protecting confidentiality may, likewise, reduce the extent of the law's safeguarding of procedural fairness: *R* v. *Gaming Board, ex p Benaim and Khaida* [1970] 2 QB 417.

Two aspects of the duty to act fairly seem to have grown in importance in recent years: the duty to give reasons and the significance attached to public consultation. There is still no general duty to give reasons imposed on administrative bodies by the common law. Nevertheless, there is a growing range of exceptions where the courts will conclude that the requirements of procedural fairness include a duty to give reasons. In *R* v. *Civil Service Appeal Board, ex p Cunningham* [1991] 4 All ER 310 (CA), Mr Cunningham had been dismissed from the Prison Service following an alleged assault on a prisoner. He appealed against this dismissal to the Civil Service Appeal Board, which concluded that Mr Cunningham had, indeed, been unfairly dismissed. Nevertheless, the Home Office refused to reinstate him. The board did not provide him with reasons. Mr Cunningham brought an action for judicial review, arguing that the failure to give reasons breached the provisions of natural justice. The Court of Appeal concluded that Mr Cunningham should have been given reasons. In reaching this conclusion, the court drew on three features: the 'character of the decision-making body'; the framework, including statutory, under which the decision-making body operates; and whether the decision-making body was determining rights, such that natural justice required the individual whose rights had been affected to be given reasons. These were applied in *R* v. *Secretary of State for the Home Department, ex parte Doody* [1994] 1 AC 531.

The extent to which the common law was willing to find a duty to give reasons, particularly when this was required by the nature of the interest or right of the applicant harmed by a particular decision, led commentators to conclude that the exceptions had eclipsed the rule (see Paul Craig, 'The Common Law, Reasons and Administrative Justice' (1994) 53 *Cambridge Law Journal* 282 and Mark Elliott, 'Has the Common Law Duty to Give Reasons Come of Age Yet?' (2011) *Public Law* 56). Two Court of Appeal cases concerning planning decisions have broadened the duty to give reasons even further, focusing not on how reasons are required for those individuals affected by administrative decisions, but also on how the giving of reasons serves the public more generally, and may be more likely to be required with regard to decisions that concern a 'protected public interest'. In *R (Campaign to Protect Rural England)* v. *Dover District Council* [2016] EWCA Civ 936, planning permission had been granted for a housing development in Kent, including on part of the Kent Downs, an area of outstanding natural beauty.

Central government policy required local authorities to refuse to grant planning permission for building in these areas, unless there were exceptional circumstances. The Campaign to Protect Rural England (CPRE) challenged the granting of planning permission, arguing that the district council had a duty to give reasons for its decision. The Court of Appeal upheld their claim, concluding that 'A local planning authority which is going to authorise a development which will inflict substantial harm on an Area of Outstanding Natural Beauty must surely give substantial reasons for doing so' [21]. This appeared to suggest that any decision affecting a protected public interest – such as areas of outstanding natural beauty – would trigger a general duty to give reasons. The duty to give reasons also arose from European Union law. In *Oakley* v. *South Cambridgeshire District Council* [2017] EWCA Civ 71, [2017] 1 WLR 3765, Cambridge City Football Club had asked for permission to develop a new football stadium on green belt land. Permission was originally refused by the planning officer, due to special protection of the green belt and the decision being contrary to the local authority's local development plan. This decision was reversed by the planning committee of the district council, which granted planning permission. Local residents challenged this decision, arguing, inter alia, that the council should have provided reasons. Although the Court of Appeal also drew on the importance of a protected public interest – in this case, the green belt – the court appeared to grant a duty to give reasons on narrower grounds. The council had overturned the decision of the planning officer that had been in line with the council's own local development plans.

R (CPRE Kent) v. *Dover District Council* [2017] UKSC 79, [2018] 1 WLR 108

The Supreme Court confirmed the decision of the Court of Appeal, relying on the duty in EU law. The court also discussed the common law duty to give reasons, appearing to favour the narrower interpretation of the duty found in *Oakley*. The statements of Lord Carnwath, giving the judgment of the court, are instructive:

> [51]. Public authorities are under no general common law duty to give reasons for their decisions; but it is well established that fairness may in some circumstances require it, even in a statutory context in which no express duty is imposed (see *R v Secretary of State for the Home Department, ex parte Doody* [1994] 1 AC 531; *R v Higher Education Funding Council, ex parte Institute of Dental Surgery* [1994] 1 WLR 242, 263A-D; *De Smith's Judicial Review* 7th ed (2013) para 7-009). *Doody* concerned the power of the Home Secretary (under the Criminal Justice Act 1967 section 61(1)), in relation to a prisoner under a mandatory life sentence for murder, to fix the minimum period before consideration by the Parole Board for licence, taking account of the 'penal' element as recommended by the trial judge. It was held that such a decision was subject to judicial review, and that the prisoner was entitled to be informed of the judge's recommendation and of the reasons for the Home Secretary's decision:

'To mount an effective attack on the decision, given no more material than the facts of the offence and the length of the panel element, the prisoner has virtually no means of ascertaining whether this is an instance where the decision-making process has gone astray. I think it important that there should be an effective means of detecting the kind of error which entitle the court to intervene, and in practice I regard it as necessary for this purpose that the reasoning of the Home Secretary should be disclosed. If there is any difference between the penal element recommended by the judges and actually imposed by the Home Secretary, this reasoning is bound to include, either explicitly or implicitly, a reason why the Home Secretary has taken a different view' p 565, per Lord Mustill.

It is to be noted that a principal justification for imposing the duty was seen as the need to reveal any such error as would entitle the court to intervene, and so make effective the right to challenge the decision by judicial review.

[52]. Similarly, in the planning context, the Court of Appeal has held that a local planning authority generally is under no common law duty to give reasons for the grant of planning permission (*R v Aylesbury Vale District Council, Ex p Chaplin* (1997) 76 P & CR 207, 211–212, per Pill LJ). Although this general principle was reaffirmed recently in *R (Oakley) v South Cambridgeshire District Council* [2017] 1 WLR 3765, the court held that a duty did arise in the particular circumstances of that case: where the development would have a 'significant and lasting impact on the local community', and involved a substantial departure from Green Belt and development plan policies, and where the committee had disagreed with its officers' recommendations. Of the last point, Elias LJ (giving the leading judgment, with which Patten LJ agreed) said, at para 61:

'The significance of that fact is not simply that it will often leave the reasoning obscure. In addition, the fact that the committee is disagreeing with a careful and clear recommendation from a highly experienced officer on a matter of such potential significance to very many people suggests that some explanation is required ... the dictates of good administration and the need for transparency are particularly strong here, and they reinforce the justification for imposing the common law duty.'

His conclusion was reinforced by reference to the United Kingdom's obligations under the Aarhus Convention: para 62; see to similar effect my own comments on the relevance of the Convention, in *Walton v Scottish Ministers* [2013] PTSR 51, para 100. Sales LJ agreed with the result, but expressed concern that the imposition of such duties 'might deter otherwise public-spirited volunteers' from council duties, and might also introduce 'an unwelcome element of delay into the planning system': para 76.

[53]. Mr Cameron QC (for the Council) submitted that this decision should be 'treated with care', against the background of the Government's decision in 2013 to abrogate the statutory duty to give reasons for grant of permission, planning law being a creature of statute: see *Hopkins Homes Ltd v Secretary of State for Communities and Local Government* [2017] 1 WLR 1865, para 20. The factors identified by Elias LJ could arise in many cases, and lead to the common law duty becoming a general rule. He asked us to prefer the view of Lang J (*R (Hawksworth Securities plc) v Peterborough City Council* [2016] EWHC 1870 (Admin) at [81]) that a common law duty to give reasons would arise only 'exceptionally' and that 'generally, the requirements of fairness will be met by public access

to the material available to the decision-maker'. The present case, he submitted, was not exceptional in that sense, either in principle or on its own facts.

[54]. In my view *Oakley* was rightly decided, and consistent with the general law as established by the House of Lords in *Doody*. Although planning law is a creature of statute, the proper interpretation of the statute is underpinned by general principles, properly referred to as derived from the common law. *Doody* itself involved such an application of the common law principle of 'fairness' in a statutory context, in which the giving of reasons was seen as essential to allow effective supervision by the courts. Fairness provided the link between the common law duty to give reasons for an administrative decision, and the right of the individual affected to bring proceedings to challenge the legality of that decision.

[55]. *Doody* concerned fairness as between the state and an individual citizen. The same principle is relevant also to planning decisions, the legality of which may be of legitimate interest to a much wider range of parties, private and public: see *Walton v Scottish Ministers* [2013] PTSR 51, paras 152–153 per Lord Hope of Craighead DPSC. Here a further common law principle is in play. Lord Bridge saw the statutory duty to give reasons as the analogue of the common law principle that 'justice should not only be done, but also be seen to be done' (see para 25 above). That principle of open justice or transparency extends as much to statutory inquiries and procedures as it does to the courts: see *Kennedy v Information Comr (Secretary of State for Justice intervening)* [2015] AC 455, para 47 per Lord Mance JSC, para 127 per Lord Toulson JSC. As applied to the environment it also underpins the Aarhus Convention, and the relevant parts of the EA Directive. In this respect the common law, and European law and practice, march together (compare *Kennedy* para 46 per Lord Mance JSC).

In the application of the principle to planning decisions, I see no reason to distinguish between a ministerial inquiry, and the less formal, but equally public, decision-making process of a local planning authority such as in this case.

[56]. The existence of a common law duty to disclose the reasons for a decision, supplementing the statutory rules, is not inconsistent with the abrogation in 2013 of the specific duty imposed by the former rules to give reasons for the grant of permission. As the explanatory memorandum made clear, that was not intended to detract from the general principle of transparency (which was affirmed), but was a practical acknowledgement of the different ways in which that objective could normally be attained without adding unnecessarily to the administrative burden. In circumstances where the objective is not achieved by other means, there should be no objection to the common law filling the gap.

[57]. Thus in *Oakley* the Court of Appeal were entitled in my view to hold that, in the special circumstances of that case, openness and fairness to objectors required the members' reasons to be stated. Such circumstances were found in the widespread public controversy surrounding the proposal, and the departure from development plan and Green Belt policies; combined with the members' disagreement with the officers' recommendation, which made it impossible to infer the reasons from their report or other material available to the public. The same combination is found in the present case, and, in my view, would if necessary have justified the imposition of a common law duty to provide reasons for the decision.

There is still no general common law duty to give reasons. And it is clear from the assessment of the Supreme Court that the common law duty to provide reasons in *CPRE Kent* arose not just from the fact that the decision affected a protected public interest, but also because the council had reversed the original decision of the planning officer, which had been in line with the protection of this public interest and the local planning policies applied in this area. However, this still expands the duty to give reasons through focusing on the need to ensure reasons are provided to the public more generally when protected public interests are at play, rather than merely focusing on when individuals require reasons for decisions that affect their particular interests. Moreover, the reference to needs for greater public transparency may, in future, give rise to the development of a general duty to provide reasons, with specific exceptions.

With regard to consultation rights, the government has promulgated a code of practice on consultation (currently available at https://assets.publishing .service .gov.uk/government/uploads/system/uploads/attachment_data/file/100807/ file47158.pdf), as well as consultation principles (currently available at https:// assets.publishing.service.gov.uk/government/uploads/system/uploads/attach ment_data/file/691383/Consultation_Principles__1_.pdf). While the courts have not gone so far as to require a general duty of consultation, in spite of the statements of Cranston J that 'the common law duty of consultation is well-established' (*R (Crompton)* v. *Wiltshire Primary Care Trust* [2009] EWHC 1824 (Admin), at [104]), duties of consultation can arise from a legitimate expectation, *R* v. *Liverpool City Council, ex p Liverpool Taxi Fleet Operators' Association* [1972] 2 QB 299 (CA) and *R (Greenpeace)* v. *Secretary of State for Trade and Industry* [2007] EWHC 311 (Admin), [2007] Env LR 29, it also being part of the common law duty to act fairly. European Union law has also imposed duties of consultation, particularly with regard to environmental law. The courts have simultaneously been developing the common law to augment enforceable rights to effective consultation.

R (Moseley) v. *Haringey London Borough Council* [2014] UKSC 56, [2014] 1 WLR 3947

All councils were required to move from a system of council tax benefit schemes to council tax reduction schemes. While council tax benefits had been set centrally, council tax reduction schemes were to be set by local councils. The legislation governing this change required that councils had to 'consult such other persons as it considers are likely to have an interest in the operation of the scheme' before establishing its scheme. Haringey London Borough Council approved recommendations to reduce council tax relief for all claimants except pensioners. While pensioners could still claim up to 100 per cent council tax relief, others would need to pay between 18 per cent and 21 per cent of their council tax, from which they had been previously exempt. In order to fulfil its consultation obligations, the council had published a consultation document online and delivered hard copies of the documents to residents in receipt of council tax benefits. The document provided information on the council's scheme, but did not explain that the council could have found other ways to make up the shortfall that would occur with the move from council tax benefits to the council tax reduction scheme. Following the consultation process, the council adopted its proposed scheme. Moseley and others challenged the decision, arguing that the consultation process had not been carried out in the proper manner.

The Supreme Court agreed. In reaching its conclusion, Lord Wilson endorsed the 'Sedley criteria' set out by Sedley, as legal counsel, in *R v. Brent London Borough Council, ex p Gunning* (1985) 84 LGR 168, and later approved by the Court of Appeal in *ex p Baker* [1995] 1 All ER 75 and *R v. North and East Devon Health Authority, ex p Coughlan* [2001] QB 213: 'First that consultation must be at a time when proposals are still at a formative stage. Second, that the proposer must give sufficient reasons for any proposal to permit of intelligent consideration and response. Third ... that adequate time must be given for consideration and response and, finally, fourth, that the product of consultation must be conscientiously taken into account in finalising any statutory proposals.' By merely providing information on the council's proposed scheme, without making it clear that there could be other, alternative schemes and setting out these possible alternatives, the council had failed to fulfil its statutory duty of consultation. In reaching this conclusion, Lord Wilson, at [24], drew on the common law conceptions of fairness, as well as information as to the specific statute setting out the council's duty to consult:

> Fairness is a protean concept, not susceptible of much generalized enlargement. But its requirements in this context must be linked to the purposes of consultation. In *R (Osborn) v Parole Board* [2014] AC 1115, this court addressed the common law duty of procedural fairness in the determination of a person's legal rights. Nevertheless the first two of the purposes of procedural fairness in that somewhat different context, identified by Lord Reed JSC in paras 67 and 68 of his judgment, equally underlie the requirement that a consultation should be fair. First, the requirement 'is liable to result in better decisions, by ensuring that the decision-maker receives all relevant information and that it is properly tested': para 67. Second, it avoids 'the sense of injustice which the person who is the subject of the decision will otherwise feel': para 68. Such are two valuable practical consequences of fair consultation. But underlying it is also a third purpose, reflective of the democratic principle at the heart of our society. This third purpose is particularly relevant in a case like the present, in which the question was not: 'Yes or no, should we close this particular care home, this particular school etc.?' It was: 'Required, as we are, to make a taxation-related scheme for application to all the inhabitants of our borough, should we make one in the terms which we here propose?'

Lord Reed, however, reached the same conclusion as to the content of this particular duty to consult through reflecting on the content of legislation, rather than the common law. Nevertheless, Lord Wilson's statements, combined with the approach of the Supreme Court to the duty to give reasons in *CPRE Kent*, suggest a move towards regarding the content of procedural fairness not just in terms of its better ability to reach correct outcomes, or to uphold the dignity of the individual, but also to facilitate the protection of public interests and the facilitation of democracy. It remains to be seen how far this trend will influence the future development of the right to procedural fairness.

10.2.4.2.1 Legitimate Expectations

The rules of natural justice clearly apply when a decision affects the legal rights or interests of a party. In addition, since *Schmidt* v. *Secretary of State for Home Affairs* [1969] 2 Ch. 149, it has also been the case that the duty to act fairly will apply when a party has a 'legitimate expectation' that this will be so. In *Schmidt*, Lord Denning MR ruled (at 170) that:

> an administrative body may, in a proper case, be bound to give a person who is affected by their decision an opportunity of making representations. It all depends on whether he has some right or interest, or, I would add, some legitimate expectation, of which it would not be fair to deprive him without hearing what he has to say.

Even if a decision will affect no existing right or legally recognised interest, the decision-maker may be bound to consult or allow a hearing to a party who has a 'legitimate expectation' that that will be done. In *R* v. *Board of Inland Revenue, ex p MFK Underwriting Agents* [1990] 1 WLR 1545, 1569–70, Bingham LJ ruled as follows:

> If a public authority so conducts itself as to create a legitimate expectation that a certain course will be followed it would often be unfair if the authority were permitted to follow a different course to the detriment of one who entertained the expectation, particularly if he acted on it.

Conduct giving rise to a legitimate expectation may be an agreement or undertaking, a regular practice (such as one of regular consultation of affected parties) or an announcement of procedures to be followed. A 'clear and unambiguous representation' is generally required, although what will constitute such a representation is not always as straightforward as it might be. See, for example, *R (Wheeler)* v. *Office of the Prime Minister* [2008] EWHC 1409 (Admin), where it was held that ministerial statements undertaking that there would be a referendum in the UK before the EU's Constitutional Treaty could be ratified did not generate a legitimate expectation that a referendum would be held before the Lisbon Treaty could be ratified. (See, further, Watson (2010) 30 *LS* 633.)

In the cases considered so far, what the party expected was to be consulted. (Another example of this is the *GCHQ* case itself: *Council of Civil Service Unions* v. *Minister for the Civil Service* [1985] AC 374.) This may be termed a procedural expectation: what the party expected was that a particular procedure would be followed. But what if a party legitimately expected not that a particular procedure would be followed but that a certain decision would not be made at all? What if a party expected a substantive outcome? In spite of original reluctance (see, in particular, the Court of Appeal in *R* v. *Secretary of State for the Home Department, ex p Hargreaves* [1997] 1 WLR 906), it is now the case that courts will uphold substantive legitimate expectations, albeit it in limited circumstances. The key case is *R* v. *North and East Devon Health Authority, ex p Coughlan* [2001] QB 213 (CA). Miss Coughlan was a severely ill and disabled woman in long-term care in Mardon House, a purpose-built care home managed by the health authority. She and other patients had been moved from an NHS hospital to Mardon House in 1993, having agreed to this on an assurance by the health authority that Mardon House would be their home for life. In 1998, the authority decided to close Mardon House and transfer responsibility for the care of the patients to a local authority social services department. It was accepted that this decision could not be impugned on grounds of irrationality.

Miss Coughlan brought proceedings for judicial review of the health authority's decision to close Mardon House. Her case that the decision was flawed rested on a number of grounds, one of which was that the 'home for life' promise made to her had given rise to a legitimate expectation and that to frustrate it would be an abuse of power. *Coughlan* illustrates that the courts will give substantive protection to a legitimate expectation even where the authority has not acted *Wednesbury* unreasonably. However, it also illustrates that the courts will do this only in certain, limited, circumstances. Lord Woolf set out the law as follows:

Lord Woolf: . . . There are at least three possible outcomes. (a) The court may decide that the public authority is only required to bear in mind its previous policy or other representation, giving it the weight it thinks right, but no more, before deciding whether to change course . . . (b) On the other hand the court may decide that the promise or practice induces a legitimate expectation of, for example, being consulted before a particular decision is taken . . . (c) Where the court considers that a lawful promise or practice has induced a legitimate expectation of a *benefit which is substantive*, not simply procedural, authority now establishes that here too the court will in a proper case decide whether to frustrate the expectation is so unfair that to take a new and different course will amount to an abuse of power.

This account raises more questions than it answers. How do we determine whether a lawful promise or practice gives rise to a substantive legitimate expectation, or whether the public authority is only required to bear in mind its previous policy or representation? Do the courts only grant a procedural legitimate expectation when public authorities make specific representations as to procedures, or may they arise in other circumstances? These questions are not easy to answer and the law still remains a little unclear.

As set out in *Coughlan*, a promise would be more likely to have binding effect if made 'to a category of individuals who have the same interest' than if 'made generally or to a diverse class, when the interests of those to whom the promise is made may differ or, indeed, may be in conflict'. Accordingly:

> most cases of an enforceable expectation of a substantive benefit . . . are likely in the nature of things to be cases where the expectation is confined to one person or a few people, giving the promise or representation the character of a contract.

In *Coughlan*, the promise was limited to a few individuals and what was promised was of great importance to Miss Coughlan. Whether the decision could nevertheless be justified by an overriding public interest was to be determined not by the health authority but by the court, which was not persuaded that any such overriding consideration had been established. In particular, the only consequences for the authority of upholding this promise would be financial. The court concluded that the decision to close Mardon House constituted unfairness amounting to an abuse of power. In addition, the court agreed with the judge in the court below that the decision was a breach of Miss Coughlan's right to respect for her home under Article 8 of the ECHR (not yet, at that time, given domestic legal effect by the HRA). (For comment on this case, see Craig and Schønberg [2000] *PL* 684; and Roberts (2001) 64 *MLR* 112.)

The circumstances that were held to justify this result in *Coughlan* were the extraordinary importance of what had been promised, the fact that the promise was limited to a small number of individuals and the fact that there would be no consequences other than financial for the authority in holding them to their promise. Absent these circumstances, and the courts will generally hold that public authorities should be able to change their minds and to adapt policy, even in the face of earlier assurances to the contrary, as long as in doing so they are acting reasonably in the *Wednesbury* sense. See *R (Bhatt Murphy)* v. *Independent Assessor* and *R (Niazi)* v. *Secretary of State for the Home Department* [2008] EWCA Civ 755, which show that it will be in rare circumstances, if at all, that a policy that was later changed could, by itself, give rise to a substantive legitimate expectation. In these circumstances, it is more likely that an individual will receive what is referred to in *Niazi* as a 'secondary procedural legitimate expectation – that is, a requirement to make representations as to why the old policy should continue to apply to the applicant, or possibly requirements or consultation or pipeline measures. Moreover, these procedural protections are more likely to apply when the applicant can point to a series of interactions between the applicant and the public body in the specific application of this policy (see *R (Luton)* v. *Secretary of State for Education* [2011] 217 (Admin)).

The law of legitimate expectations is still under development. Judges and legal academics alike seem prone to offer repeated attempts to classify and categorise the various circumstances in which legitimate expectations may arise and the various consequences that may follow for claimants once they have shown that they are in possession of a legitimate expectation. While the case law on legitimate expectations now includes a number of House of Lords, Privy Council and Supreme Court authorities (see *R (BAPIO)* v. *Secretary of State for the Home Department* [2008] UKHL 27, [2008] 1 AC 1003, *R (Bancoult)* v. *Secretary of State for Foreign and Commonwealth Affairs* [2008] UKHL 61, [2009] 1 AC 453, *Paponette* v. *A-G* [2010] UKPC 32, [2012] 1 AC 1, *Mandalia* v. *Secretary of State for the Home Department* [2015] UKSC 59, [2015] 1 WLR 4546, *R (Gallaher)* v. *Competition and Markets Authority* [2018] UKSC 25, [2019] AC 96, *Re Finucane's Application for Judicial Review (Northern Ireland)* [2019] UKSC 7, [2019] 3 All 191), there is still no definitive ruling from the Supreme Court on the proper scope of legitimate expectations in our public law, with most of the important judgments stemming from the Court of Appeal.

Nevertheless, there are a few further clarifications that have been made by the case law. First, the doctrine of legitimate expectations no longer applies in situations where the applicant is not aware of the policy or promise on which the legitimate expectation is based. In these circumstances, as confirmed in *Mandalia* v. *Secretary of State for the Home Department* [2015] UKSC 59, [2015] 1 WLR 4546, the applicant relies on a 'principle no doubt related to the doctrine of legitimate expectation, but free-standing' [29] stemming from *R (Nadarajah)* v. *Secretary of State for the Home Department* [2005] EWCA Civ 1363.

However, care must be taken over the extent to which 'fairness' or 'consistency' has become a new general principle of the law. In *R (Gallaher)* v. *Competition and Markets Authority* [2018] UKSC 25, [2019] AC 96, Lord Sumption, in agreement with Lord Carnwath's leading judgment, concluded that:

> [50] ... In public law, as in most other areas of law, it is important not unnecessarily to multiply categories. It tend to undermine the coherence of the law by generating a mass of disparate special rules distinct from those applying in public law generally or those which apply to neighbouring categories. To say that a decision-maker must treat persons equally unless there is a reason for treating them differently begs the question what counts as a valid reason for treating them differently. Consistency of treatment is, as Lord Hoffmann

> observed in *Matedeen v Pointu* [1999] 1 AC 98, ay para 9 "a general axiom of rational behaviour" … Absent a legitimate expectation of a different result arising from the decision-maker's statement or conduct, a decision which is rationally based on relevant considerations is mostly unlikely to be unfair in any legally cognisable sense. In the present case nothing than the OFT said or did could have given rise to any other expectation than that it would act rationally.

This statement is difficult to reconcile with *Mandalia*, which was not referred to in *Gallaher*. The difference appears to turn on whether there is a promise or policy and the awareness of the applicant of that policy. Where a promise or policy exists and the applicant is aware of this, then the courts apply the doctrine of legitimate expectation. When the promise or policy exists, but the applicant is not aware of its existence (e.g., it is an internal policy that is not communicated to the applicant), then the principle of consistency applies. When there is no general policy or no specific representation – as in *Gallaher*, where the applicants wished that a promise made to one party, but not to Gallaher, should also be applied to Gallaher – the applicant can only rely on rationality grounds of judicial review.

Second, *Re Finucane's Application for Judicial Review (Northern Ireland)* [2019] UKSC 7, [2019] 3 All 191 makes it clear that detrimental reliance on a specific policy or promise is not needed in order to establish a legitimate expectation. However, detrimental reliance may be taken into account when determining whether there are good grounds for a public body to go back on its promise.

Third, a consistent line of authority appears to be emerging that a test of proportionality is used to determine whether going back on a legitimate expectation would amount to an abuse of power. This stems from the statement of Laws LJ in *Nadarajah* v. *Secretary of State for the Home Department* [2005] EWCA Civ 1363 (at [68]):

> Where a public authority has issued a promise or adopted a practice which represents how it proposes to act in a given area, the law will require the promise or practice to be honoured unless there is good reason not to do so. What is the principle behind this proposition? It is not far to seek. It is said to be grounded in fairness, and no doubt in general terms that is so. I would prefer to express it rather more broadly as a requirement of good administration, by which public bodies ought to deal straightforwardly and consistently with the public. In my judgment this is a legal standard which, although not found in terms in the European Convention on Human Rights, takes its place alongside such rights as fair trial, and no punishment without law. That being so there is every reason to articulate the limits of this requirement – to describe what may count as good reason to depart from it – as we have come to articulate the limits of other constitutional principles overtly found in the European Convention. Accordingly a public body's promise or practice as to future conduct may only be

denied, and thus the standard I have expressed may only be departed from, in circumstances where to do so is the public body's legal duty, or is otherwise, to use a now familiar vocabulary, a proportionate response (of which the court is the judge, or the last judge) having regard to a legitimate aim pursued by the public body in the public interest. The principle that good administration requires public authorities to be held to their promises would be undermined if the law did not insist that any failure or refusal to comply is objectively justified as a proportionate measure in the circumstances.

The test of proportionality is also used in *Paponette* v. *A-G* [2010] UKPC 32.

In spite of these clarifications, there is still considerable debate as to the foundation and the scope of substantive legitimate expectations. The most recent Supreme Court case in *Finucane* did little to clarify the law and arguably added to the confusion (Elliott, 'Legitimate Expectation: Reliance, Process and Substance' [2019] CLJ 260). Whether the doctrine of legitimate expectation is rooted in 'fairness', in the notion of 'good administration' or (as Sedley LJ and others would prefer) in 'abuse of power' is open to debate (see Knight [2009] *PL* 15).

The question that lies at the heart of the ongoing debate about the proper scope of this area of law is: to what extent should the courts insist that public authorities act consistently with what they have said in the past? How, in other words, should the line be drawn between, on the one hand, affording to public authorities the freedom to develop policy in what they perceive to be the public interest and, on the other hand, affording to individuals some degree of legal protection in the event that a change in policy results in unfairness? These are not easy questions and it seems inevitable that at some point the Supreme Court will have to consider in more detail whether the answers given in *Coughlan* are the most appropriate ones.

10.3 Scope and Limits of Judicial Review

10.3.1 Scope of Judicial Review

Judicial review is available only against certain persons or bodies. English law and Scots law differ markedly from one another in how they delimit the scope of judicial review. In English law, judicial review is available only against persons or bodies performing public functions. Scots law has set itself against a public/private distinction in this regard. In Scots law, a decision will be judicially reviewable if it can be said that there is a 'tripartite relationship' between (1) the source of the decision-making power, (2) the decision-maker and (3) the person or persons affected by the decision (see *West* v. *Secretary of State for Scotland* 1992 SC 385). Judicially reviewable bodies in English law clearly include ministers and their departments, local authorities and NDPBs. In addition, the English courts, led by the Court of Appeal's decision in *R* v.

Panel on Take-overs and Mergers, ex p Datafin plc [1987] QB 815, have extended the judicial review jurisdiction to certain 'self-regulating' organisations constituted in the private sector but with some form of 'governmental' function. Although not set up by the government or themselves entrusted with statutory powers, bodies such as these carry out their regulatory functions in each case as an integral part of a system of governmental control supported by statutory powers and sanctions. That said, however, not all 'regulatory' bodies are subject to judicial review under this approach: English courts have declined to review the exercise of regulatory responsibilities by the chief rabbi, the managers of an independent school, the Football Association, the Jockey Club and the Insurance Ombudsman Bureau, the functions performed by these bodies being based on agreement, voluntary submission or not having a sufficiently 'governmental' character. (For a recent example, see *R (Holmcroft Properties Ltd) v. KPMG LLP* [2018] EWCA Civ 2093, where the functions of an independent reviewer for customer redress arrangements were not amendable to judicial review as appertaining predominantly to the determination of private law rights; and see, further, Campbell, 'The Nature of Power as Public in English Judicial Review' [2009] *CLJ* 90. In many of these cases, Scots law would include these bodies within the scope of judicial review. A golf club, for example, was held by the Court of Session to be judicially reviewable, whereas this outcome would be unlikely in English law: see *Crocket* v. *Tantallon Golf Club* 2005 SLT 663 and cf. *R* v. *Disciplinary Committee of the Jockey Club, ex p Aga Khan* [1993] 1 WLR 909.)

The matter is complicated by the fact that, in both English and Scots law, not every Act of a potentially judicially reviewable body falls within the judicial review jurisdiction, for these bodies may take action on the plain of private law, for instance, in engaging employees or making commercial contracts. The ordinary remedies of private law must then be pursued. (See, e.g., *R* v. *BBC, ex p Lavelle* [1983] 1 WLR 23 and *Blair* v. *Lochaber District Council* 1995 SLT 407.) Judicial review is a remedy of last resort: if an alternative remedy is available, it must be pursued before turning to judicial review.

Following the reorganisation of tribunals provided for by the Tribunals, Courts and Enforcement Act 2007, the question arose as to the extent to which judicial review would lie in respect of tribunal decisions. Despite earlier divergence between the English and Scots courts, the Supreme Court in *R (Cart)* v. *Upper Tribunal* [2011] UKSC 28, [2012] AC 663 and *Eba* v. *Advocate General for Scotland* [2011] UKSC 29, [2012] 1 AC 710 adopted the same criteria in both English and Scots law. These cases confirmed that the High Court will only hear an appeal from the Upper Tribunal on a matter of law when the case raises an important point of principle or practice, or where there are other compelling reasons for the high court to hear the claim (see J Bell, 'Rethinking the Story of *Cart v Upper Tribunal* and its Implications for Administrative law' (2019) 39 *OJLS* 74.

10.3.2 Standing

Only those who have sufficient standing in law – *locus standi* – may bring proceedings for judicial review (Senior Courts Act 1981, section 31). Historically, this is a matter that is dealt with differently in English and Scots law, with the English law of standing being considerably more generous than Scots law. In Scots law, a petitioner had to have both 'title' and 'interest'. 'Title' meant that the petitioner must be a party 'to some legal relation which gives him some right which the person against whom he raises the action either infringes or denies' (*D & J Nicol* v. *Trustees of the Harbour of Dundee* 1915 SC (HL) 7). 'Interest' had been interpreted relatively narrowly and, in particular, had been interpreted against special interest groups seeking what might be termed 'representative standing': see, e.g., *Scottish Old People's Welfare Council, Petitioners* 1987 SLT 179 and also *Rape Crisis Centre* v. *Secretary of State for the Home Department* 2000 SC 527.

This narrow approach to standing was criticised by Lord Hope (see [2001] *PL* 294). In *AXA General Insurance* v. *The Lord Advocate* [2011] UKSC 46, Lord Hope, at para [62], stated that 'the time has come to recognise that the private law rule that title and interest has to be shown has no place in applications to the court's supervisory jurisdiction that lie in the field of public law'. In *Walton* v. *First Minister* [2012] UKSC 44, the Supreme Court was required to determine whether Mr Walton was a 'person aggrieved' under the Roads (Scotland) Act 1984. After concluding that Mr Walton satisfied this test, Lord Reed also considered standing under the common law. He concluded, at para [90] that the Supreme Court in *AXA General Insurance* had 'clarified the approach which should be adopted to the question of standing to bring an application to the supervisory jurisdiction. In doing so it intended to put an end to the unduly restrictive approach which had too often obstructed the proper administration of justice: an approach which presupposed that the only function of the court's supervisory jurisdiction was to redress individual grievances, and ignore the constitutional function of maintaining the rule of law.' This has now been placed on a statutory footing by section 89 of Courts Reform (Scotland) Act 2014, which inserts section 27B(2)(a) into the Court of Session Act 1988, mirroring the English test of 'sufficient interest'.

The sufficiency of the claimant's interest is not considered in isolation: account is taken of the nature of the duty imposed on the public authority and the subject matter of the claim. In *IRC* v. *National Federation of Self-Employed and Small Businesses* (the *Fleet Street Casuals* case) [1982] AC 617, 630, Lord Wilberforce said:

> There may be simple cases in which it can be seen at the earliest stage that the person applying for judicial review has no interest at all, or no sufficient interest to support the application: then it would be quite correct at the threshold to refuse him leave to apply. The right to do so is an important safeguard against the courts being flooded and public bodies

harassed by irresponsible applications. But in other cases this will not be so. In these it will be necessary to consider the powers or the duties in law of those against whom the relief is asked, the position of the applicant in relation to those powers or duties, and to the breach of those said to have been committed. In other words, the question of sufficient interest cannot, in such cases, be considered in the abstract, or as an isolated point: it must be taken together with the legal and factual context. The rule requires sufficient interest *in the matter to which the application relates.*

If the claimant is not a mere busybody and appears to have an arguable case, the court will generally grant permission to proceed with the claim for judicial review without a full examination of the claimant's standing, leaving this to be resolved when the substance of the case unfolds at the subsequent hearing of the claim.

The interest of the claimant in the matter 'need not be any recognisable legal interest and need not involve any assertion of any infringement of the rights of the [claimant]' (Hobhouse LJ in *Crédit Suisse* v. *Allerdale Borough Council* [1997] QB 306, 356). Lord Fraser said in the *Fleet Street Casuals* case (above) that the claimant must have a 'reasonable concern' with the matter to which the claim relates. The case itself establishes that a taxpayer will not normally have such a reasonable concern or sufficient interest in the dealings of the Inland Revenue with other taxpayers. By the same token, in *R* v. *Her Majesty's Treasury, ex p Smedley* [1985] QB 657, where the question in issue was the legality of certain payments to be made by the Treasury to the European Community, the Court of Appeal was of the opinion that since this question was a serious and urgent one, the claimant did have standing to raise it, 'if only in his capacity as a taxpayer'. In *R* v. *Secretary of State for Foreign Affairs, ex p Rees-Mogg* [1994] QB 552 there was (surprisingly, perhaps?) no dispute as to the claimant's standing to challenge the government's proposed ratification of the TEU, and the Divisional Court considered the claim on its merits, although the claimant was only a citizen with 'a sincere concern for constitutional issues'. The similar approach was taken in *R (Wheeler)* v. *Office of the Prime Minister* [2008] EWHC 1409 (Admin) where, again, no objection to the claimant's standing seems to have been raised, the claimant unsuccessfully arguing that a referendum should have been held before the UK ratified the Lisbon Treaty.

The courts may be disposed to take a liberal view of standing to enable matters of public importance to be raised (see *R* v. *Felixstowe Justices, ex p Leigh* [1987] QB 582 and *R* v. *Secretary of State for Employment, ex p Equal Opportunities Commission* [1995] 1 AC 1), and an 'increasingly liberal approach' to standing was noted by the Divisional Court in *R* v. *Secretary of State for Foreign Affairs, ex p World Development Movement Ltd* [1995] 1 WLR 386 in holding that the claimants, a non-partisan pressure group which campaigned to increase the amount and quality of British aid to developing countries, had a sufficient interest to challenge the minister's decision to provide financial support for the construction of the Pergau Dam in Malaysia from the aid budget although, as Dawn Oliver has noted, the decision 'did not adversely affect the interests of any individuals' (*Common Values and the Public-Private Divide* (1999), p. 32). Other pressure groups such as the Child Poverty Action Group, Greenpeace, the Joint Council for the Welfare of Immigrants and Help the Aged have also succeeded in establishing their standing to bring proceedings for judicial review in 'public interest challenges' on behalf of their clients or as promoters of public causes. While standing was denied to the pressure group in *R v. Secretary of State for the Environment, ex p Rose Theatre Trust Co* [1990] 1 QB 504, the case is out of line with the developing trend of the case law and in any event had the distinguishing feature that the group in question had been formed ad hoc, for the specific purpose of saving the Rose Theatre. More recently, in *R (DSD) v. Parole Board of England and Wales* [2018] EWHC 694 (Admin) (discussed above) a decision of the Parole Board was challenged by the Lord Mayor of London, as well as one of the victims of the crimes for which John Radford (formerly Warboys) had been convicted and a victim of the crimes of which he was suspected. Standing was denied to the lord mayor of London, as, although the lord mayor had responsibilities for crime and justice, including support for the victims of crime, these did not include oversight of the workings of the Parole Board. The lord mayor also had other means through which he could comment on these issues – for instance, through the media. Standing was granted, however, to the victims, in part because the Secretary of State had decided not to challenge this decision and the victims were therefore the best placed litigants to ensure the upholding of the rule of law. (For a critical assessment of the broadening of standing see Harlow, 'Public Law and Popular Justice' (2002) 65 *MLR* 1.)

It should be noted that if a legal challenge relates to the violation of a 'convention right' under the HRA, a claimant must show that he or she is a 'victim' of the alleged violation (section 7(1)). This is a more stringent obligation than satisfying the 'sufficient interest' test in judicial review.

10.3.3 Ouster Clauses

Statutes have sometimes provided expressly for the exclusion of judicial review. Such 'ouster' or 'privative' clauses are strictly construed by the courts in order to preserve, to the fullest possible extent, the right of the citizen to challenge the legality of action affecting his or her interests. A particularly strong judicial counterstroke was delivered in *Anisminic Ltd v. Foreign Compensation Commission* [1969] 2 AC 147, in which the House of Lords was confronted by a statutory provision that the 'determination' by the commission of any application made to it under the Act 'shall not be called in question in any court of law'. It was held that an error of law made by the commission in rejecting an application had the result that its purported determination was a nullity and that the court was not prevented from granting a declaration to that effect, for 'determination' must be construed to mean a determination that the commission, directing itself correctly in law, had power to make and not a purported determination which lay outside its powers. This construction of the statutory ouster provision drained it of practical effect.

Ouster provisions will ordinarily be ineffective to exclude judicial review not only when the decision under challenge results from an error of law (as in *Anisminic*), but further when the decision is a nullity by reason of 'any other error which would justify the intervention of the court on judicial review including a breach of the requirements of fairness' (Lord Woolf MR in *R v. Secretary of State for the Home Department, ex p Fayed* [1998] 1 WLR 763, 771).

The ouster clause in *Anisminic* failed because it could not exclude judicial review over 'purported' determinations. Later case law clarified that 'purported' determinations were determinations that included jurisdictional errors – that is, errors as to whether an inferior court or tribunal had the power to make a particular determination. All legal errors would be deemed to be jurisdictional. As such, any ouster clause could not remove judicial review for legal errors. The most recent Supreme Court case on ouster clauses is *Privacy International*.

R (Privacy International) v. *Investigatory Powers Tribunal* [2019] UKSC 22, [2019] 2 WLR 1219

This case concerned legislation that appeared to be designed to successfully remove judicial review from determinations of the Investigatory Powers Tribunal (IPT). The ouster clause stated that 'determinations, awards, orders and other decisions of the tribunal (including decisions as to whether they have jurisdiction) shall not be subject to appeal or be liable to be questioned in any court' (Regulation of Investigatory Powers Act 2000, section 67(8)). In both the High Court and the Court of Appeal, the words 'including decisions as to whether they have jurisdiction' were interpreted as having successfully removed judicial review over decisions of the IPT. In *Anisminic*, the court relied on a presumption that Parliament would not want to remove the supervisory jurisdiction of the court over decisions of inferior courts or tribunals. However, the statutory provision made it clear that Parliament had expressly stated that courts could not review decisions of the IPT, even when the mistake made by the IPT was one as to whether it had the power to act. The Supreme Court, however, concluded that the clause was not sufficient to remove judicial review of the court over determinations of the IPT.

While there is a majority in favour of the failure of the ouster clause to remove judicial review, there is a difference between the reasoning of the four justices of the Supreme Court, resulting in turn in a difference in the extent to which Parliament can exclude judicial review. Lord Carnwath, with whom

Lady Hale and Lord Kerr agreed, focused on the distinction between 'determinations' and 'purported' determinations in *Anisminic*. He concluded that the specific exclusion of decisions as to whether the IPT had jurisdiction only referred to real and not purported decisions as to whether the tribunal had jurisdiction. Therefore, the ouster clause did not remove the power of the high court to conduct judicial review over purported determinations of jurisdiction – those determinations that were incorrect where the IPT had mistakenly thought it had the power to act when it did not. In reaching this conclusion, Lord Carnwath relied on *R (Cart)* v. *Upper Tribunal* [2011] UKSC 28, [2012] AC 663, where the Supreme Court had adopted a principled and pragmatic approach to determining its power to review decisions of the Upper Tribunal. It is for the court to determine a proportionate and principled review over the decisions of inferior courts and tribunals. In doing so, it will apply a general presumption of interpretation that Parliament would not wish to remove judicial review – this applying equally to judicial review over inferior courts and tribunals as it does to judicial review over administrative bodies.

Lord Lloyd-Jones also concluded that the ouster clause would not succeed. But he did so for different reasons. The case law from *Anisminic* through to *R* v. *Hull University Visitor, ex parte Page* [1993] AC 682 had made it clear not only that all legal errors were classified as jurisdictional errors, but also that the interpretative presumption had changed. It was no longer the case that courts would presume that Parliament did not wish to remove the power of the court to review decisions of tribunals where they had made jurisdictional errors, but rather tha courts would presume that Parliament did not wish to remove the power of the court to check for legal errors made by inferior courts and tribunals. As such, the wording of section 67(8) was not sufficiently clear to remove judicial review. In other words, while it may be true that all errors of law are classified as jurisdictional errors, it is not the case that all jurisdictional errors are legal errors. As the statutory provision did not specifically remove judicial review over legal errors, the ouster clause did not remove judicial review for legal errors made by the IPT. In reaching this conclusion, Lord Lloyd-Jones did not apply the general presumption against ouster clauses as applied to administrative bodies – this general presumption did not apply to decisions of inferior courts and tribunals.

The minority – Lord Sumption, with whom Lord Kerr agreed and Lord Wilson who delivered his own judgment – disagreed. Lord Wilson provided the strongest dissent. He went so far as to state that he 'deprecates' the reasoning in *Anisminic* (at [219]). Nevertheless, he did not go so far as to suggest it should be overturned. For Lord Wilson, it would have been clear to Parliament from the case law that ouster clauses like the one in *Anisminic* could not remove judicial review of jurisdictional errors made by inferior courts and tribunals. Parliament had expressly stated that judicial review for jurisdictional errors had been excluded. As such, it was clear that Parliament wished to oust judicial review over determinations of the IPT. Lord Sumption's

judgment was more subtle. He focused on the wording of the legislation that
granted power to the IPT, as well as its function and composition. The
statutory provisions provided the IPT with a broad range of decision-making
powers where it was clearly performing a judicial function. The legislation
made it clear that the IPT was to make substantive determinations in its area of
jurisdiction that were not subject to judicial review by the court. However,
Lord Sumption also recognised that courts presume that Parliament would not
wish to remove the power of higher courts to check the actions of lower courts
and tribunals. Specifically, while the legislation had given the IPT the power to
make a broad range of judicial determinations, it had not specifically removed
the power of the court to check that the IPT had not made a procedural error
when determining the scope of its jurisdiction. In reaching this conclusion,
Lord Sumption, relied on the judgment of Lord Mance in *Lee* v. *Ashers Baking
Co Ltd* [2018] UKSC 49, [2018] 3 WLR 1227.

If this were not confusing enough, six of the seven justices of the Supreme
Court also considered a further issue – which was technically obiter dicta for
the three justices of the Supreme Court in the majority – as to whether, and if
so how, it would be possible for Parliament to oust judicial review from
decisions of the Supreme Court. Lord Lloyd-Jones did not provide an answer
to this broader question, as it was not necessary for him to do so in order to
reach a decision. Lord Carnwath, however, stated (at para [144]) that:

> ... although it is not necessary to decide the point, I see a strong case for holding that,
> consistently with the rule of law, binding effect cannot be given to a clause which purports
> wholly to exclude the supervisory jurisdiction of the High Court to review a decision of an
> inferior court or tribunal, whether for excess or abuse of jurisdiction, or error of law. In all
> cases, regardless of the words used, it should remain ultimately a matter for the court to
> determine the extent to which such a clause should be upheld, having regard to its purpose
> and statutory context, and the nature and importance of the legal issue in question; and to
> determine the level of scrutiny required by the rule of law.

In other words, Lord Carnwath proposed a more 'flexible approach' to ouster
clauses (at para [131]). It is the role of the court to determine the scope of
judicial review of the courts, based on their understanding of the rule of law.
Rather than focusing on 'such elusive concepts as jurisdiction (wide or narrow), ultra vires, or nullity' the courts should focus on 'a natural application of
the constitutional principle of the rule of law (as affirmed by section 1 of the
[Constitutional Reform Act] 2005), and as an essential counterpoint to the
power of Parliament to make law. The constitutional roles both of Parliament
as the maker of the law, and of the High Court, and ultimately of the appellate
courts, as the guardians and interpreters of that law, are thus respected' (at
para [132]).

Lord Sumption disagreed. Rather than its being the role of the court to determine the scope of judicial review, Lord Sumption's focus is on the intention of Parliament as set out in the express wording of legislation. Lord Sumption rejected Lord Carnwath's approach as it gave priority to the rule of law over the sovereignty of Parliament. However, he was willing to accept a less radical interpretation of the relationship between these two constitutional principles – that 'judicial review is necessary to sustain parliamentary authority. This is because Parliament can express its will only by written texts, to which effect can be given only if there is a supreme interpretative and enforcing authority. That authority by its nature resides in courts of law' (at para [208]). Furthermore, he stated (at para [210])

> . . . If Parliament on the true construction of an enactment has created a tribunal of legally limited jurisdiction, then it must have intended that those limits should have effect in law. The only way in which a proposition can have effect in law, is for it to be recognised and applied by the courts. Parliament's intention that there should be legal limits to the tribunal's jurisdiction is not therefore consistent with the courts lacking the capacity to enforce the limits. Ms Rose, correctly to my mind, described this as giving effect to the sovereignty of Parliament, not limiting it. In order to escape this conceptual difficulty, Parliament would have to create a tribunal of unlimited jurisdiction or one with unlimited discretionary power to determine is own jurisdiction. A sufficiently clear and all-embracing ouster clause might demonstrate that Parliament had indeed intended to do that. But it would be a strange thing for Parliament to intend, and although conceptually possible, it has never been done.

These contradictory statements illustrate a deeper tension running through judicial review – how far is it the role of courts to determine the content of the principles of judicial review, particularly when faced with the interpretation of statutory provisions? Lord Carnwath's dictum suggests that it is for the courts and the courts alone to determine these principles according to the rule of law. If this requires courts to contradict the express wording of Parliament then this is necessary to hold Parliament in check given its law-making power. For Lord Sumption, courts should not focus on determining broad principles of the rule of law, but specific and more precise legal principles. Moreover, they should use legislation more proactively to determine the scope of judicial review. To do otherwise is to undermine parliamentary sovereignty. To add to the confusion, Lord Wilson appears to give partial support to Lord Carnwath – although he would have limited this to the impossibility of Parliament legislating to remove judicial review over inferior courts and tribunals with limited jurisdiction for jurisdictional errors (at [236]).

Where does this leave the ability of Parliament to oust judicial review? If we accept the dictum of Lord Carnwath and his reasoning, then it would require very specific and broad wording. One such possible example is the government's (mainly unsuccessful) attempt to introduce an extraordinarily wide-ranging ouster clause in the Asylum and Immigration (Treatment of Claimants etc.) Act 2004. This clause is specifically referred to in the judgment of Lord Carnwath. It attracted stringent criticism (see above, pp. 106–107 and see, further, Woolf (2004) 63 *CLJ* 317 and Rawlings (2005) 68 *MLR* 378). We may be left with the conclusion that, while it may be theoretically possible to oust judicial review over the decisions of a specific inferior court or tribunal, it may be politically impossible to obtain a majority in Parliament to do so. (See Elliott and Young (2019) 78 *CLJ* 490).

10.3.4 Judicial Review of Prerogative Powers

It was formerly held that while the courts could determine the existence and extent of any prerogative, and whether its use had been restricted by statute (above, pp. 590–594), they might not question or review the grounds on which, in a particular case, a prerogative power had been exercised. Judges in a number of cases disclaimed competence to review prerogative acts, as when Lord Denning MR said in *Blackburn* v. *Attorney General* [1971] 1 WLR 1037, 1040 that ministers in negotiating and signing a treaty 'exercise the prerogative of the Crown. Their action in so doing cannot be challenged or questioned in these courts'. Contrariwise, there were indications in the case law that judicial review was not wholly excluded, as when Lord Devlin, in *Chandler* v. *DPP* [1964] AC 763, 810, equated prerogative with other discretionary powers, saying that the courts could intervene to correct 'excess or abuse'. In *R* v. *Criminal Injuries Compensation Board, ex p Lain* [1967] 2 QB 864, a case subsequently marked as a turning point, it was held by the Divisional Court that the actions of a public body set up by the government – under the prerogative, as the court saw it – to make awards of compensation to victims of criminal offences could be the subject of judicial review. It remained for the House of Lords to put the law on a new basis in the *GCHQ* case.

Council of Civil Service Unions v. *Minister for the Civil Service (the 'GCHQ' Case)* [1985] AC 374 (HL)

In 1983, the prime minister (as minister for the Civil Service) issued an instruction that the conditions of service of civil servants employed at GCHQ, a military and signals intelligence centre, should be revised so as to exclude the right of trade union membership. The instruction was given under Article 4 of the Civil Service Order in Council 1982, an order made by virtue of what was assumed by the court to be a prerogative power, that of regulating the conduct of the Civil Service. The minister's action was taken without prior consultation with trade unions representing staff at GCHQ.

The unions applied for judicial review, seeking a declaration that the instruction was invalid. They argued that the prerogative power to vary the terms and conditions of employment of civil servants was subject to review by the courts, and further that the GCHQ staff had a legitimate expectation, arising from a well-established practice of consultation before their conditions of service were altered, that the minister would not make such an alteration without first consulting the staff or their trade union representatives.

Glidewell J accepted these arguments and granted a declaration that the instruction was invalid. The Court of Appeal set aside the declaration and the unions appealed to the House of Lords. There it was argued for the minister that the instruction was not open to review because the power to issue it had its source in the prerogative. This argument was rejected by all of their Lordships. Lords Fraser and Brightman were persuaded to this conclusion because the power exercised in this case had been *delegated* to the minister by the prerogative order in council and it must be an implied condition of any such delegation that the power should be exercised fairly – a matter appropriate for review. The majority, however, were of the opinion that even a *direct* exercise of prerogative power was in principle reviewable.

> **Lord Scarman:** . . . I believe that the law relating to judicial review has now reached the stage where it can be said with confidence that, if the subject matter in respect of which prerogative power is exercised is justiciable, that is to say if it is a matter upon which the court can adjudicate, the exercise of the power is subject to review in accordance with the principles developed in respect of the review of the exercise of statutory power. Without usurping the role of legal historian, for which I claim no special qualification, I would observe that the royal prerogative has always been regarded as part of the common law, and that Sir Edward Coke had no doubt that it was subject to the common law: *Prohibitions del Roy* (1607) 12 Co Rep 63 and the *Proclamations' Case* (1611) 12 Co Rep 74. In the latter case he declared, at p 76, that 'the King hath no prerogative, but that which the law of the land allows him'. It is, of course, beyond doubt that in Coke's time and thereafter judicial review of the exercise of prerogative power was limited to inquiring into whether a particular power existed and, if it did, into its extent: *Attorney General v De Keyser's Royal Hotel Ltd* [1920] AC 508. But this limitation has now gone, overwhelmed by the developing modern law of judicial review. . . . Just as ancient restrictions in the law relating to the prerogative writs and orders have not prevented the courts from extending the requirement of natural justice, namely the duty to act fairly, so that it is required of a purely administrative act, so also has the modern law . . . extended the range of judicial review in respect of the exercise of prerogative power. Today, therefore, the controlling factor in determining whether the exercise of prerogative power is subject to judicial review is not its source but its subject matter.
>
> **Lord Diplock:** . . . It was the prerogative that was relied on as the source of the power of the Minister for the Civil Service in reaching her decision of 22 December 1983 that membership of national trade unions should in future be barred to all members of the home civil service employed at GCHQ.
>
> My Lords, I intend no discourtesy to counsel when I say that, intellectual interest apart, in answering the question of law raised in this appeal, I have derived little practical assistance

from learned and esoteric analyses of the precise legal nature, boundaries and historical origin of 'the prerogative', or of what powers exercisable by executive officers acting on behalf of central government that are not shared by private citizens qualify for inclusion under this particular label. It does not, for instance, seem to me to matter whether today the right of the executive government that happens to be in power to dismiss without notice any member of the home civil service upon which perforce it must rely for the administration of its policies, and the correlative disability of the executive government that is in power to agree with a civil servant that his service should be on terms that did not make him subject to instant dismissal, should be ascribed to 'the prerogative' or merely to a consequence of the survival, for entirely different reasons, of a rule of constitutional law whose origin is to be found in the theory that those by whom the administration of the realm is carried on do so as personal servants of the monarch who can dismiss them at will, because the King can do no wrong.

Nevertheless, whatever label may be attached to them there have unquestionably survived into the present day a residue of miscellaneous fields of law in which the executive government retains decision-making powers that are not dependent upon any statutory authority but nevertheless have consequences on the private rights or legitimate expectations of other persons which would render the decision subject to judicial review if the power of the decision-maker to make them were statutory in origin. From matters so relatively minor as the grant of pardons to condemned criminals, of honours to the good and great, of corporate personality to deserving bodies of persons, and of bounty from moneys made available to the executive government by Parliament, they extend to matters so vital to the survival and welfare of the nation as the conduct of relations with foreign states and – what lies at the heart of the present case – the defence of the realm against potential enemies. . . .

My Lords, I see no reason why simply because a decision-making power is derived from a common law and not a statutory source, it should *for that reason only* be immune from judicial review.

Qualifications of the availability of review that are indicated in the above passages are that the exercise of the prerogative power must relate to a subject matter that is 'justiciable' (Lord Scarman) and must affect the 'private rights or legitimate expectations of other persons' (Lord Diplock). Lord Roskill was in agreement with Lords Scarman and Diplock in being unable to see 'any logical reason why the fact that the source of the power is the prerogative and not statute should today deprive the citizen of that right of challenge to the manner of its exercise which he would possess were the source of the power statutory'. He made some additional remarks on the subject of the 'justiciability' of the power.

Lord Roskill: . . . But I do not think that the right of challenge can be unqualified. It must, I think, depend upon the subject matter of the prerogative power which is exercised. Many

> examples were given during the argument of prerogative powers which as at present advised I do not think could properly be made the subject of judicial review. Prerogative powers such as those relating to the making of treaties, the defence of the realm, the prerogative of mercy, the grant of honours, the dissolution of Parliament and the appointment of ministers as well as others are not, I think, susceptible to judicial review because their nature and subject matter are such as not to be amenable to the judicial process. The courts are not the place wherein to determine whether a treaty should be concluded or the armed forces disposed in a particular manner or Parliament dissolved on one date rather than another.

The prerogative power exercised in this case was not of a kind to fall within Lord Roskill's 'excluded categories' and their Lordships were in agreement that the minister's action was in principle open to review. They were also agreed that in the circumstances the GCHQ staff had, prima facie, a legitimate expectation that they would be consulted, as on all previous occasions, about the change to be made to their conditions of service.

However, it was held that the appellants' legitimate expectation and the duty of fairness arising from it were overridden by the requirements of national security. The government claimed that it was on the ground of national security that the decision had been made to change the conditions of service at GCHQ. Their Lordships accepted the government's claims and, for this reason, held against the unions. It has been persuasively argued that in coming to this conclusion 'the Law Lords were too easily satisfied by some very exiguous evidence': Drewry (1985) 38 *Parl Aff* 371, 380. (See, further, on the *GCHQ* case and on other case law concerning national security Chapter 11.)

(There has been extensive commentary on this case and the conclusions of the Law Lords have attracted criticism on a variety of grounds: particular attention should be given to the rulings on justiciability and national security. (See, e.g., Drewry (1985) 38 *Parl Aff* 371; Ewing [1985] *CLJ* 1; Griffith [1985] *PL* 564; Lee [1985] *PL* 186; Morris [1985] *PL* 177; Wade (1985) 101 *LQR* 153; Walker [1987] *PL* 62.)

The barrier of justiciability erected in the *GCHQ* case has not foreclosed a continuing if cautious advance in judicial review of the exercise of prerogative powers. In *R* v. *Secretary of State for Foreign and Commonwealth Affairs, ex p Everett* [1989] QB 811 it was held by the Court of Appeal that the discretionary power to issue a passport, considered by the court to belong to the prerogative, was open to review. It was a matter 'affecting the rights of individuals and their freedom of travel' (per Taylor LJ) and raised issues no less justiciable than those commonly arising in the courts in immigration cases. In *R* v. *Secretary of State for the Home Department, ex p Bentley* [1994] QB 349, the question was whether the exercise of the prerogative of mercy might in some circumstances be reviewable, the fact that it had been included in Lord Roskill's catalogue of non-justiciable prerogative powers in the *GCHQ* case notwithstanding. The Divisional Court concluded that, within limits to be determined from case to case, judicial review of this prerogative was possible (see, to similar effect, *Lewis* v. *Attorney General of Jamaica* [2001] 2 AC 50).

In *R (Bancoult)* v. *Secretary of State for Foreign and Commonwealth Affairs* [2008] UKHL 61, [2009] 1 AC 453, the House of Lords accepted that legislation made under the prerogative should be subject to judicial review 'on ordinary principles of legality, rationality and procedural impropriety in the same way as any other executive action' (Lord Hoffmann, at [35], and Lord Rodger, at [105]). Mark Elliott and Amanda Perreau-Saussine state that, as such, *Bancoult* was 'the first English decision to establish clearly that the prerogative itself – as distinct from secondary powers derived from exercises of the prerogative – exists in the shadow of the rule of law' ('Pyrrhic Public Law: *Bancoult* and the Sources, Status and Content of Common Law Limitations on Prerogative Power' [2009] *PL* 697, 716; on the substance of the dispute in *Bancoult* and on its grave injustice, see pp. 199–200, above).

The two most recent important cases on the control of prerogative powers did not concern judicial review over the way in which prerogative powers are exercised, but over the scope of prerogative powers and the extent to which they may be frustrated by legislation.

R (Miller) v. *Secretary of State for Exiting the European Union* [2017] UKSC 5, [2018] AC 61

Gina Miller and others brought an action for judicial review challenging the decision of the government to use its prerogative power to inform the European Council of the UK's decision to exit the European Union. The majority of the Supreme Court concluded that the UK Government did not have a prerogative power to trigger the Article 50 TEU process required to leave the European Union. Although the minority disagreed with this conclusion, their disagreement is best understood not as a disagreement as to the relevant legal principles to be applied, but as to how they were applied to the European Communities Act 1972. The limits on the scope of prerogative powers are set out by Lord Neuberger (at para [50]-[51]) as follows:

[50] ... it is a fundamental principle of the UK constitution that, unless primary legislation permits it, the Royal Prerogative does not enable ministers to change statute law or common law. As Lord Hoffmann observed in *R (Bancoult) v Secretary of State for Foreign and Commonwealth Affairs (No 2)* [2009] AC 453 at para 44 'since the 17th century the prerogative has not empowered the Crown to change English common or statute law'. This is, of course, just as true in relation to Scottish, Welsh or Northern Irish law. Exercise of ministers' prerogative powers must therefore be consistent both with the common law as laid down by the courts and with statutes as enacted by Parliament.

> [51]. Further, ministers cannot frustrate the purpose of a statute or statutory provision, for example by emptying it of content of preventing its effectual operation. Thus, ministers could not exercise prerogative powers at the international level to revoke the designation of Laker Airways under an aviation Treaty as that would have rendered a licence granted under a statute useless: *Laker Airways Ltd v Department of Trade* [1977] QB 643 – see especially at pp 718-719 and p 728 per Roskill and Lawton LJJ respectively. And in Fire Brigades Union cited above, at pp 551-552, Lord Browne-Wilkinson concluded that ministers could not exercise the prerogative power to set up a scheme of compensation for criminal injuries in such a way as to make a statutory scheme redundant, even though the statute in question was not yet in force.

The majority concluded that to use the prerogative power to withdraw from the European Union would modify domestic law, as it would remove European Union law rights which had been incorporated into domestic law through the European Communities Act 1972. It would also frustrate the purposes of the 1972 Act by rendering it devoid of purpose. The purpose of the Act was to ensure the UK's membership of the EU. This would be frustrated were the UK to exit the union. Lord Neuberger also stated (at para [81]) that it would be 'inconsistent with long-standing and fundamental principle for such a far-reaching change to the UK constitutional arrangements to be brought about by ministerial decision or ministerial action alone'.

The minority disagreed. Withdrawing from the European Union would not modify domestic law. This is because of the dualist nature of the UK. International law is not automatically incorporated into UK law. Rather, it requires legislation to incorporate its provisions into domestic law. Withdrawal from the EU would not modify domestic law but would, instead, remove a source of international law – EU law is not domestic law. Neither would withdrawal from the EU frustrate the purposes of the European Communities Act 1972. The purpose of the Act was to incorporate EU law 'from time to time created or arising by or under the Treaties' into domestic law (European Communities Act 1972, section 2(1)). To withdraw from the EU would not frustrate the purposes of the Act. The Act would still be able to incorporate EU law into domestic law. However, by withdrawing from the EU, the law arising by or under the treaties at the time of withdrawal would be, effectively, no law at all. This did not render the mechanism for incorporating these obligations – be what they may – into domestic law.

The *Miller* decision has generated much critical commentary. (See Craig, 'Miller, Structural Constitutional Review and the Limits of Prerogative Power' [2017] *Public Law* 48; Mark Elliott, 'The Supreme Court's Judgment in *Miller*: In search of Constitutional Principle' (2017) 76 *CLJ* 257; Young, 'R *(Miller) v Secretary of State for Exiting the European Union: Thriller or Vanilla?*' (2017)

42 *European Law Review* 280; Phillipson, 'EU Law as an Agent of National Constitutional Change: *Miller v Secretary of State for Exiting the European Union* (2017) 36 *YEL* 46, as well as special editions of *Public Law* and the *Modern Law Review*.) In terms of its control over prerogative powers, however, the controversy arises not from the legal principles it relies on, but on their specific application and their consequences. It is important not to let one's view of the desirability, or otherwise, of the UK's exit from the EU cloud ones assessment of the case.

What is more important is how it illustrates further tensions between how courts approach judicial review cases. How far is it the role of the court to act as guardian of the constitution, preventing the executive from abusing its powers, even perhaps when this means overriding clearly expressed statutory provisions? Should courts, instead, focus merely on providing an interpretation of legislation as expressed by Parliament? These tensions are even more prevalent in the second *Miller* decision.

R (Miller) v. *Prime Minister; Cherry* v. *Advocate General for Scotland* [2019] UKSC 41, [2020] AC 373

The case concerned the prime minister's advice to the monarch to prorogue Parliament from a date between the 9 and 12 September until 14 October 2019. It will be recalled that the Supreme Court, in a unanimous decision of eleven justices, concluded that the decision was unlawful. The Supreme Court reached this conclusion by using the common law constitutional principles of parliamentary sovereignty and parliamentary accountability to place limits on the extent of the prerogative power of prorogation. In particular:

> [50]. For the purposes of the present case, therefore, the relevant limit upon the power to prorogue can be expressed in this way: that a decision to prorogue Parliament (or to advise the monarch to prorogue Parliament) will be unlawful if the prorogation has the effect of frustrating or preventing, without reasonable justification, the ability of Parliament to carry out its constitutional functions as a legislature and as the body responsible for the supervision of the executive. In such a situation, the court will intervene if the effect is sufficiently serious to justify such an exceptional course.

The prorogation for such a long period of time, in the run-up to Brexit, where Parliament had already granted a role to the legislature as regards the UK's exit from the EU, and the Commons had enacted private members' bills to direct governmental policy, amounted to a sufficiently serious restriction on parliamentary sovereignty and parliamentary accountability so as to justify the intervention of the court. As the government had failed to provide a justification, the decision to advise the prime minister to prorogue Parliament was quashed.

(The judgment has split opinion in the academic community – Craig, 'The Supreme Court, Prorogation and Constitutional Principle' [2020] *PL* 248; Loughlin, 'A Note on Craig on *Miller; Cherry*' [2020] *PL* 278; Craig, 'Response to Loughlin's note on *Miller; Cherry*' [2020] *PL* 282; Thiel, 'Unconstitutional Prorogation of Parliament' [2020] *PL* 529; Young, '*R (Miller) v Prime Minister; Cherry v Advocate General for Scotland*: Re-inventing the Constitution, or Re-imagining Constitutional Scholarship?' (forthcoming).)

10.4 Conclusion: The Advance of Judicial Review

Recent decades have witnessed a significant expansion of recourse to judicial review, of the readiness of the courts to intervene in administrative decision-making and in the development of the principles of review. In the following passage, Martin Loughlin reflects on the tension between the idea of administration and the idea of law, describing the main perspectives on the nature and resolution of that tension:

Martin Loughlin, 'The Underside of the Law: Judicial Review and the Prison Disciplinary System' (1993) 46 *CLP* 23, 25–6

The traditional – and predominant – view of administrative law which has emerged in this country might be labelled the Whig view. [Reference is made here to, inter alios, Dicey, Lord Hewart, *The New Despotism* (1929) and Sir William Wade, *Administrative Law* (6th edn. 1988; see now 10th. edn 2009).] It is a view which not only focuses on the centrality of courts in administrative law but which also views courts as the guardians of liberty. This Whig view is rooted in a profound distrust of all executive power and it tends to equate progress – the onward march of liberty – with the growth in the number of administrative decisions which are subjected to review by the courts. Courts are special primarily because they are the repositories of certain customary values. What underpins this Whig view, then, is the belief in the common law as 'the golden metwand' which maintains a balance between the individual and the state. Within this image, law is not to be seen as a theoretical science founded on reason but is based on 'artificial reason' which is rooted in experience. The common law – our customary inheritance – embodies immutable ideas of right and justice which the judiciary, in oracular fashion, are called upon to proclaim.

Throughout this century, this traditional view has been subjected to challenge. The pace of social change, the great extension of the sphere of influence of the executive, and the changing character of law all serve to undermine the view that the judiciary, through their access to the accumulated wisdom of the common law, possess a unique appreciation of how the business of government ought to be conducted. The challengers to the Whig view may, rather crudely, be placed into two broad camps: the de-mythologisers and the modernisers – the radicals and the reformers. The radical challenge seeks to undermine the Whig view largely by exposing the sham and hypocrisy of legal rhetoric; in effect, they seek to strip the mask of justice from the face of power. Law, in this radical view, is essentially an expression of power relations in society: 'laws are merely statements of a power relationship and nothing more' (Griffith ['The Political Constitution' (1979) 42 *MLR*1], p 18). In a reversal of the Whig view, the de-mythologisers see the courts, not as the guardians of liberty, but as the bastions of privilege. The values of the common law are the values of an old order which, with the emergence of democracy, must change. Our courts, being absorbed in the culture of the common law, do not provide a solution to the quest for administrative justice but, far from it, must be viewed as part of the problem. [Reference is made here to, inter alios, Griffith, *The Politics of the Judiciary* (4th edn. 1991; see now 5th edn. 1997).]

Aspects of the radical critique can also be identified in the analysis of the reformers. The reformers recognise that the foundations of a modern legal order cannot be rooted simply in the acceptance of the authority of the judiciary as carriers of traditional wisdom. The pace of social, economic and technological change has been such as to devalue much of that customary wisdom. The reformist solution, however, is to seek to modernise the common law tradition; to reinterpret that tradition in the language of rights. Rights rather than remedies, principles not precedents are what is required. The modernisers reject the radical claim; they believe that reason – not power – lies at the heart of law. Law is based on principle not policy. Above all, the reform or modernising movement is a rationalising movement; it seeks to expose the skeleton of rights enmeshed within the corpus of the common law. [Reference is made here to, inter alios, Dworkin, *Law's Empire* (1986) and Allan: see his *Law, Liberty, and Justice* (1993) and *Constitutional Justice* (2001).]

The growth of judicial activism and the deeper penetration of review since the 1960s may be attributed to a continual accrual of broad statutory powers to the executive, together with an increasingly powerful judicial perception of the limitations of ministerial responsibility to Parliament. In *R* v. *Secretary of State for the Home Department, ex p Fire Brigades Union* [1995] 2 AC 513, 567, Lord Mustill drew attention to the latter of these factors:

In recent years . . . the employment in practice of . . . specifically Parliamentary remedies has on occasion been perceived as falling short, and sometimes well short, of what was needed to bring the performance of the executive into line with the law, and with the minimum standards of fairness implicit in every Parliamentary delegation of a decision-making function. To avoid a vacuum in which the citizen would be left without protection against a misuse of executive powers the courts have had no option but to occupy the dead ground in a manner, and in areas of public life, which could not have been foreseen 30 years ago.

(For a defence of the continuing importance and effectiveness of ministerial responsibility to Parliament, see Tomkins, *Public Law* (2003), ch. 5.)

The awakening from 'the long sleep of public law' (Lord Justice Sedley, *Freedom, Law and Justice* (1999), p. 11) and the increasingly interventionist temper of the judges in matters of public administration have attracted a variety of responses. The question raised is a fundamental one of the role of the judges in the constitution and their relation to Parliament and the executive. It is beyond argument that there were several leading public law judges in the 1990s who considered that the judicial role in constitutional and administrative law in the UK was too weak and too small, and that it should be significantly augmented: see, for example, Sedley, 'The Sound of Silence: Constitutional Law Without a Constitution' (1994) 110 *LQR* 270; Woolf, *'Droit Public* – English Style' [1995] *PL* 57; Laws, 'Law and Democracy' [1995] *PL* 72; Steyn, 'The Weakest and Least Dangerous Department of Government' [1997] *PL* 84.

The effect of their remarkable efforts over recent years, combined with breakthrough legislative interventions such as, most obviously, the HRA, has transformed the judicial contribution to our public law in a process that, one suspects, remains ongoing (among the best accounts of this is Hickman, *Public Law after the Human Rights Act* (2010)). But, while many of the leading cases discussed in this chapter point avowedly to an enhanced judicial role (from *Padfield* to *Daly* to *Privacy International* via *GCHQ*, *Coughlan* and *Miller* and *Miller; Cherry*), restraint has also been a continuing theme of the courts' case law, as witnessed in decisions as diverse as *Alconbury*, *Denbigh High School* and *R (Wheeler)* v. *Office of the Prime Minister*, for example. While many of the key cases raise acute questions of political accountability, political judgment and political propriety, as well as questions of legality (*Corner House* and *Bancoult*, for instance), we can hardly be said to be governed by judges yet. Indeed, a notable refrain in the case law is that the courts will often try to strengthen rather than to undermine Parliament's roles in law-making and in scrutinising the executive: the decision of the Supreme Court in *Ahmed* v. *HM Treasury* and the powerful opinions of Lords Bingham and Mance in *Bancoult* being examples. Lord Sumptions's Reith lectures (www .bbc.co.uk/programmes/m00057m8), as well as the work of the Judicial Power Project (https://judicialpowerproject.org.uk/) provide a stringent critique of a perceived transfer of power from the legislature to the courts (see also Sumption, *Trials of the State: Law and the Decline of Politics* (2020)).

However, it would be wrong to conclude that courts are not sensitive to the need to be wary of performing a political as opposed to a legal function. While we can point to cases that mark a more activist stance, with *Privacy International* marking a new high point, these cases often include strong dissents. Moreover, decisions are highly contextually sensitive. Courts tend to intervene more greatly in order to protect access to courts or fundamental common law rights. They are sensitive to the limits of their power, modifying standards of review, even in the field of human rights, in order to preserve the division between politics and law.

10.5 Liability of the Crown

We move now from matters of judicial *review* to matters of *liability*. As we saw above, the principal purpose of judicial review is not to allow claimants to sue public authorities for damages: rather, it is to allow the courts to review the legality of the exercise of public powers. While judicial review is now the most significant court procedure in public law, it is not the only one. From time to time litigants will wish not merely to seek a review of the legality of government actions and decisions, but will desire remedies in private law – remedies which will often include damages. Where a litigant claims that the government or another public authority has acted in breach of contract or has acted negligently, for example, it will not be judicial review procedure that the litigant needs to employ. Rather, the litigant will wish to sue, arguing that the government or public authority is liable in the law of contract or tort.

Questions of liability in public law are divided into two: first, we consider the special position of the Crown. This will generally be relevant when a litigant wishes to proceed against a department or minister of central government. In the next section, we will examine the principles of liability against other public authorities – especially local authorities. As we shall see, there has been substantial and significant case law in recent years on the liability of public authorities in negligence.

There is one further complicating feature that needs to be borne in mind when considering proceedings against, and the liability of, the Crown: this is one of the areas of public law that is most different as between English and Scots law. English law was traditionally more protective of the Crown than was Scots law. However, two factors have conspired to dilute the differences at the expense, unfortunately, of the integrity and former advantages that were enjoyed by litigants in Scots law. The first is that, in a variety of cases, Scots law has been reinterpreted to bring it into line with English law, meaning that litigants wishing to proceed against the Crown in Scots law have found fresh hurdles placed in their way (see, e.g., *Macgregor* v. *Lord Advocate* 1921 SC 847 (relying on English authorities to hold that the Crown could not be sued in tort, despite Scots authorities to the contrary) and *Lord Advocate* v. *Dumbarton District Council* 1988 SLT 546 (IH), [1990] 2 AC 580 (HL), with the House of Lords overruling the Inner House of the Court of Session on the extent of the Crown's immunity from statute). The second is that, when the English law of Crown proceedings was reformed by the Crown Proceedings Act 1947, the legislation, some of which applied to Scotland as well as to England, was written in such a way as to ignore the differences that had existed between English and Scots law in this area, making the Scots law position both more complex and more protective of the Crown than it had formerly been. The Crown Proceedings Act 1947 was designed to make it easier to proceed against the Crown, yet its effect in Scotland was in a number of respects precisely the opposite – in particular as regards the (non-) availability of interdict (i.e., injunction) against the Crown (see *McDonald* v. *Secretary of State for Scotland* 1994 SC 234). Only in 2005 did the House of Lords move to remedy this problem (see *Davidson* v. *Scottish Ministers* [2005] UKHL 74, 2006 SC (HL) 41; see, in greater detail, Tomkins, 'The Crown in Scots law', in McHarg and Mullen (eds.), *Public Law in Scotland* (2006), ch. 13).

As far as English law is concerned, until 1947 the citizen was under many disabilities, both procedural and substantive, as a litigant against the Crown. The procedural disabilities were associated with the archaic mode of proceeding by petition of right. A claim by petition of right required the leave of the Crown, granted by the sovereign on the advice of the Attorney General, and the Crown benefited from an array of procedural privileges. The most serious defect in the substantive law was the Crown's immunity from liability in tort ('the King can do no wrong'), and it was the need to remedy this defect that led to the enactment of the Crown Proceedings Act 1947. The Act effected a broader reform of the law, abolishing (with limited exceptions) the procedure of petition of right (section 13), removing most of the disabilities of the private litigant and approximating Crown proceedings to ordinary civil proceedings between citizens. Despite these far-reaching reforms of the law and procedure, some rules remain that are peculiar to Crown liability, while actions by and against the Crown retain certain distinctive features. (The petition of right procedure was unknown in Scots law – see the Crown Suits (Scotland) Act 1857 – and Scots law, unlike English law, did not traditionally consider that 'the King can do no wrong'.)

Under the Crown Proceedings Act 1947 the court may, in general, make any such order against the Crown as it has power to make 'in proceedings between subjects' (section 21(1)) and in particular may award a sum of money (whether a debt due or damages). Although there can be no order for execution of judgment against the Crown, the court will issue a certificate of any order made by it and the appropriate government department is required to pay to the claimant the sum certified as being payable (section 25).

Section 21(1) of the Crown Proceedings Act preserves the immunity which the Crown enjoyed at English common law from injunctions and orders of specific performance, but provides that in lieu of such orders the court may grant a declaratory order (declaration). However, the crucial difference between the two remedies is that, unlike injunctions, there is no such thing as an interim declaration. Section 21 extends to Scotland. But in Scotland, until 1947, the Crown did not enjoy an immunity from interdict – this is one of the respects in which the 1947 Act failed to adequately take the differences between English and Scots law into account. Section 21(1) applies only to 'civil proceedings'. This phrase has now been interpreted in both English and Scots law as excluding judicial review proceedings. thus, section 21(1) notwithstanding, injunctions are available against the Crown in judicial review (see *M* v. *Home Office* [1994] 1 AC 377 and *Davidson* v. *Scottish Ministers* [2005] UKHL 74, 2006 SC (HL) 41).

Section 21(2) of the Act provides that the court shall not grant any injunction or other order against an *officer* of the Crown (including a minister and any Crown servant) if the effect would be 'to give any relief against the Crown which could not have been obtained in proceedings against the Crown'. This provision was for a time understood to disallow the grant of an injunction against a minister in any case in which he or she had acted in an official capacity (see *Merricks* v. *Heathcoat-Amory* [1955] Ch. 567 and *R* v. *Secretary of State for Transport, ex p Factortame Ltd* [1990] 2 AC 85, 146–8). Fortunately, this view was repudiated by the House of Lords in *M* v. *Home Office* (above). Scots law was brought into line with *M* v. *Home Office* in *Davidson* v. *Scottish Ministers* (above).

The restrictions on remedies imposed by section 21 must give way in appropriate cases to EU law, which requires that effective protection should be given to EU rights. This was made clear by the ECJ in its ruling in Case C-213/89 *R* v. *Secretary of State for Transport, ex p Factortame Ltd (No 2)* [1991] 1 AC 603, 644, in which it was held that:

> a national court which, in a case before it concerning Community law, considers that the sole obstacle which precludes it from granting interim relief is a rule of national law must set aside that rule.

It is not clear how far this will be preserved post-implementation period completion day. The European Union (Withdrawal) Act 2018 will preserve the principle of effective legal protection as concerns the interpretation of retained EU law. However, under the provisions of section 5, this will only require legislative provisions enacted prior to exit day to give way to retained EU law.

10.5.1 Contractual Liability

Section 1 of the Crown Proceedings Act 1947 provides:

> Where any person has a claim against the Crown after the commencement of this Act, and, if this Act had not been passed, the claim might have been enforced, subject to the grant of His Majesty's fiat, by petition of right, ... then, subject to the provisions of this Act, the claim may be enforced as of right, and without the fiat of His Majesty, by proceedings taken against the Crown for that purpose in accordance with the provisions of this Act.

The government is different from private contracting parties by reason of its responsibilities for the public interest – a difference that is expressed in certain rules affecting its capacity to bind itself by contract. In particular, the government – like other public authorities – may not contract in such a way as to fetter the exercise of its public powers or the discharge of its public duties. This rule most commonly applies to discretionary powers conferred by statute and was crisply expressed in relation to the Crown by Woolf J in *R* v. *IRC, ex p Preston* [1983] 2 All ER 300, 306:

> the Crown cannot put itself in a position where it is prevented from performing its public duty . . . If it seeks to make an agreement which has that consequence, that agreement is of no effect.

(This proposition was upheld in the House of Lords: [1985] AC 835, 862.) Contrariwise, the making of a contract, so far from being an unlawful fettering of discretionary powers, is normally a legitimate exercise of discretion: it is only if a contract is incompatible with the purposes for which a power was given that it offends against the rule.

The rule against fettering of discretion is not limited, in its application to the Crown, to statutory discretionary powers. The Crown has an ultimate responsibility for the public welfare, which may demand the exercise of its prerogative or common law powers, even though such necessary action runs counter to specific contractual undertakings previously given. How is this conflict of public and private interests to be resolved?

Rederiaktiebolaget Amphitrite v. *The King* [1921] 3 KB 500 (Rowlatt J)

During the First World War, the British Government was operating a 'ship for ship' policy, by which neutral ships were not allowed to leave British ports unless replaced by other ships of the same tonnage. The suppliants in a petition of right were a Swedish steamship company that had sought and been given an express assurance that if their ship, the *Amphitrite*, brought a cargo of approved goods to a British port, it would be allowed to leave, the 'ship for ship' policy notwithstanding. The *Amphitrite* discharged its cargo of approved goods at Hull but, in spite of the undertaking given, was detained. The company, having sold the ship to avoid further loss, claimed damages from the Crown for breach of contract. Rowlatt J gave judgment for the Crown.

> **Rowlatt J:** . . . I have not to consider whether there was anything of which complaint might be made outside a Court, whether that is to say what the Government did was morally wrong or arbitrary; that would be altogether outside my province. All I have got to say is whether there was an enforceable contract, and I am of opinion that there was not. No doubt the Government can bind itself through its officers by a commercial contract, and if it does so it must perform it like anybody else or pay damages for the breach. But this was not a commercial contract; it was an arrangement whereby the Government purported to give an assurance as to what its executive action would be in the future in relation to a particular ship in the event of her coming to this country with a particular kind of cargo. And that is, to my mind, not a contract for the breach of which damages can be sued for in a Court of law. It

> was merely an expression of intention to act in a particular way in a certain event. My main reason for so thinking is that it is not competent for the Government to fetter its future executive action, which must necessarily be determined by the needs of the community when the question arises. It cannot by contract hamper its freedom of action in matters which concern the welfare of the State.

The broad rule of 'executive necessity' affirmed by Rowlatt J in this case has caused disquiet. Denning J in *Robertson v. Minister of Pensions* [1949] 1 KB 227 sought to limit its application, saying that the 'defence of executive necessity' would avail the Crown only 'where there is an implied term to that effect or that is the true meaning of the contract'. Certainly the rule does not give the government carte blanche to renounce its contracts. It is generally accepted – as by Rowlatt J himself in the above passage – that it does not apply to ordinary commercial contracts such as are made by the government in great number. The undertaking given by the government in the *Amphitrite* case was of a very unusual kind, and, in the conditions of war, a court would naturally have been unwilling to restrict the government in making decisions that might be dictated by unexpected emergencies. The rule is probably to be understood as meaning that the Crown is not bound by a contractual undertaking that proves to be incompatible with the necessary exercise of its powers in a matter of compelling public interest. Even so limited, the rule is open to question. Is the Crown not sufficiently protected by its immunity from orders of specific performance?

A rare instance of the application of the *Amphitrite* principle was *Crown Lands Commissioners v. Page* [1960] 2 QB 274, in which the Court of Appeal held that a lease by the Crown must be treated as impliedly subject to the 'proper exercise in the future of the Crown's executive authority'; therefore, no covenant of quiet enjoyment could be implied in favour of the tenant that would limit the Crown's future exercise of its discretionary powers.

In practice, the government seldom needs to invoke the rule of executive necessity, for a standard condition of government contracts, known as the 'break clause', which is generally included in government contracts of substantial value, allows the government to terminate the contract at any time in its discretion. The break clause is not open to the reproach of unfairness, which attends the rule of executive necessity, or at least not to the same extent, for the clause includes provision for compensation of the contractor in respect of work already done and for wasted expenditure.

10.5.2 Tortious Liability

Petition of right was not available in English law against the Crown for claims in tort, this immunity being derived from the maxim 'the King can do no wrong', which was understood as excluding not only the personal liability of the sovereign but the vicarious liability of the Crown for the torts of its servants (on the extension of this immunity to Scotland, see *Macgregor* v. *Lord Advocate* 1921 SC 847). An action could be brought against a Crown servant who had personally committed the tort and the Crown would then normally – if the tort were committed in the course of employment – undertake the defence of the case and make an ex gratia payment of any damages awarded. If it was not possible to identify a particular Crown servant who was responsible for the tort, the Crown might cooperate by nominating an official against whom the action might be brought, but this device became unworkable when the courts refused to admit the personal liability of Crown servants who had themselves committed no tort. (See *Adams* v. *Naylor* [1946] AC 543 and *Royster* v. *Cavey* [1947] KB 204.)

Parliament might have reformed the law by simply enacting in general terms that the Crown should henceforth be liable in tort. This was not done. Instead, section 2(1) of the Crown Proceedings Act 1947 provides that the Crown shall be liable in tort to the same extent as if it were 'a private person of full age and capacity', under three heads:

(a) in respect of torts committed by its servants or agents;
(b) in respect of any breach of those duties which a person owes to his servants or agents at common law by reason of being their employer; and
(c) in respect of any breach of the duties attaching at common law to the ownership, occupation, possession or control of property.

Section 2(2) adds one further ground, in providing that the Crown may be liable for breach of statutory duty, provided that the duty 'is binding also upon persons other than the Crown and its officers'.

Although these four categories cover almost the whole ground of tortious liability, there are some few instances of liability that fall outside them, so that a residue of Crown immunity appears to survive. This can be illustrated by reference to *Collins* v. *Hertfordshire County Council* [1947] KB 598, in which the managers of a hospital were held liable for the death of a patient that occurred because the hospital operated a negligent system for the provision of dangerous drugs. The duty resting on the hospital – to maintain a safe system – was not one that would fall within any of the categories of liability in the Crown Proceedings Act if the defendant in such a case should be the Crown. Doubtless in some cases of this kind, the Crown, while not itself in breach of any duty, would be vicariously liable for the negligent act of a servant under section 2(1)(a), but it might not always be possible to establish that any particular Crown servant had committed a tort.

Proceedings under any of the four heads may be brought only if the liability arises in respect of Her Majesty's Government in the United Kingdom;

a certificate issued by a Secretary of State that any alleged liability does not so arise is declared to be conclusive (section 40(2)(b), (3)). An action was defeated by such a certificate in *Trawnik* v. *Lennox* [1985] 1 WLR 532, a case that arose from actions of the British military authorities in Germany.

Section 2(1)(a), above, provides for the vicarious liability of the Crown for torts of its 'servants or agents'. Whether any person is to be considered a servant of the Crown for the purpose of vicarious liability is a matter primarily for the common law, but section 2(6) provides that the Crown is not to be liable for the act of any 'officer' of the Crown (defined in section 38(2) as including 'any servant of His Majesty' and, accordingly, a minister of the Crown) unless the officer was directly or indirectly appointed by the Crown and paid wholly out of moneys provided by Parliament or certain other central government funds. The main effect of this provision is to exclude the vicarious liability of the Crown for torts committed by the police (who are paid in part out of local tax).

The question of the Crown's vicarious liability will arise most often in relation to the tort of negligence, making it necessary to decide whether the Crown's servant or agent owed a duty of care to the claimant. Such a duty may be owed by officers performing public functions, as in *Home Office* v. *Dorset Yacht Co Ltd* [1970] AC 1004, and, in principle, a duty may attach to those giving official information or advice (cf. *Hedley Byrne & Co* v. *Heller & Partners* [1964] AC 465). But the question of the existence of a duty of care is decided by the courts in the light of public policy, which will often be found to argue against the imposition of liability for negligence in the exercise of public powers. In particular, the courts show a marked reluctance to import a duty of care into discretionary decision-making by ministers or officials, and 'the more that general policy factors have to be taken into account in making the decision the less suitable is the case for adjudication by the courts' (per Browne-Wilkinson V-C in *Lonrho plc* v. *Tebbit* [1991] 4 All ER 973, 984). (See, further on these matters, below.)

(The domestic law on these matters may be contrasted with principles of state liability under EU law: see above, pp. 368–371.)

10.5.3 Liability in Restitution

The leading case on the Crown's liability in restitution is the *Woolwich* case.

Woolwich Equitable Building Society v. *Inland Revenue Commissioners* [1993] AC 70 (HL)

The Inland Revenue Commissioners (the Revenue) had claimed payment of certain sums of money by way of tax from the building society (Woolwich). Woolwich, while disputing its liability to the tax, had paid the sums claimed. In proceedings for judicial review, Woolwich then successfully challenged the validity of the regulations on which the claims for tax had been based, so establishing that the claims had been unlawful. The Revenue thereon repaid the capital sums, but without interest.

Woolwich brought proceedings against the Revenue for interest on the sums repaid. It was argued for the Revenue that no interest was payable, on the ground that, even though Woolwich had not been liable to pay the tax, the repayment of the capital was not legally due and had been made voluntarily. It was admitted that if Woolwich had a valid claim for repayment of the capital on the principles of restitution, interest would be recoverable. No immunity from liability in restitution could be or was asserted by the Crown, and the House of Lords was concerned with the application of the common law principles of restitution to the circumstance of payment in response to an unlawful demand of taxation from the Crown.

Lord Goff: ... I now turn to the submission of Woolwich that your Lordships' House should, despite the authorities to which I have referred, reformulate the law so as to establish that the subject who makes a payment in response to an unlawful demand of tax acquires forthwith a prima facie right in restitution to the repayment of the money. This is the real point which lies at the heart of the present appeal ...

The justice underlying Woolwich's submission is, I consider, plain to see. Take the present case. The revenue has made an unlawful demand for tax. The taxpayer is convinced that the demand is unlawful, and has to decide what to do. It is faced with the revenue, armed with the coercive power of the state, including what is in practice a power to charge interest which is penal in its effect. In addition, being a reputable society which alone among building societies is challenging the lawfulness of the demand, it understandably fears damage to its reputation if it does not pay. So it decides to pay first, asserting that it will challenge the lawfulness of the demand in litigation. Now, Woolwich having won that litigation, the revenue asserts that it was never under any obligation to repay the money, and that it in fact repaid it only as a matter of grace. There being no applicable statute to regulate the position, the revenue has to maintain this position at common law.

Stated in this stark form, the revenue's position appears to me, as a matter of common justice, to be unsustainable; and the injustice is rendered worse by the fact that it involves, as Nolan J pointed out [1989] 1 WLR 137, 140, the revenue having the benefit of a massive interest-free loan as the fruit of its unlawful action. I turn then from the particular to the general. Take any tax or duty paid by the citizen pursuant to an unlawful demand. Common justice seems to require that tax to be repaid, unless special circumstances or some principle of policy require otherwise; prima facie, the taxpayer should be entitled to repayment as of right.

Lord Goff went on to consider possible objections to 'the simple call of justice' and found them unpersuasive. On the contrary, he found a number of reasons that reinforced the justice of Woolwich's case and concluded:

> I would therefore hold that money paid by a citizen to a public authority in the form of taxes or other levies paid pursuant to an ultra vires demand by the authority is prima facie recoverable by the citizen as of right. As at present advised, I incline to the opinion that this principle should extend to embrace cases in which the tax or other levy has been wrongly exacted by the public authority not because the demand was ultra vires but for other reasons, for example because the authority has misconstrued a relevant statute or regulation. It is not however necessary to decide the point in the present case, and in any event cases of this kind are generally the subject of statutory regimes which legislate for the circumstances in which money so paid either must or may be repaid.

Lords Browne-Wilkinson and Slynn agreed that money paid to the Revenue pursuant to an ultra vires demand was recoverable. Lords Keith and Jauncey delivered dissenting speeches. In this case, as the Law Commission observed, the House of Lords 'overturned the traditional common law rule on overpaid levies, which allowed recovery only on grounds recognised by the private law, and substituted a new public law rule providing that such levies are prima facie recoverable' (Law Com 227, para 1.8; see, further, Beatson (1993) 109 *LQR* 401; and see also *Deutsche Morgan Grenfell* v. *Inland Revenue Commissioners* [2006] UKHL 49, [2007] 1 AC 558).

10.6 Liability of Public Authorities

Public authorities not enjoying the 'shield of the Crown' – not being government departments or Crown servants – have never been immune from liability in tort and may sue or be sued in ordinary civil proceedings.

10.6.1 Contractual Liability

In principle, an incorporated public body has capacity to make contracts for any purpose that falls within its competence as defined by the relevant statute (putting aside bodies incorporated under the prerogative). In the case of local authorities, a general power to make contracts derives from section 111(1) of the Local Government Act 1972, authorising an authority in England or Wales to 'do any thing ... which is calculated to facilitate, or is conducive or incidental to, the discharge of any of their functions'. A similar provision exists in respect of local authorities in Scotland. Power to enter into 'public–private partnership' agreements (engaging private resources for local authority purposes) is given by the Local Government (Contracts) Act 1997, and various other statutes confer powers on local authorities to make specific classes of contract. An authority is not permitted to contract otherwise than for such authorised purposes: a contract made for an ultra vires purpose is null and void, as was the loan guarantee contract entered into by the local authority in *Crédit Suisse* v. *Allerdale Borough*

Council [1997] QB 306. (In certain circumstances, the other party to such an ultra vires contract is protected by the provisions of the Local Government (Contracts) Act 1997.)

Section 135 of the Local Government Act 1972 provides that a local authority *may* make standing orders to regulate the making of contracts and *must* make such orders with respect to contracts for the supply of goods or materials or the execution of works. Standing orders relating to contracts for goods, materials or works must provide for competition for such contracts and must regulate the procedure for inviting tenders. Standing orders are internal rules to be complied with by those acting for the authority, but section 135(4) provides that a contractor shall not be bound to inquire whether standing orders have been observed and that non-compliance 'shall not invalidate any contract entered into by or on behalf of the authority'.

The pursuit of collateral policies in local authority purchasing is restricted by section 17 of the Local Government Act 1988, which specifies a number of 'non-commercial matters' that must be excluded from the contracting process. In their contracting procedures, local authorities, like central government bodies, are bound to observe the requirements of the European Community directives on procurement and the regulations implementing these in the UK. The common law also imposes restrictions, for example, in the rule against fettering of discretion (*Ayr Harbour Trustees* v. *Oswald* (1883) 8 App Cas 623; cf. *R* v. *Lewisham London Borough Council, ex p Shell UK Ltd* [1988] 1 All ER 938).

10.6.2 Tortious Liability

The tortious (or, in Scotland, the delictual) liability of public authorities has in recent years been the subject of a large number of high-profile appeals to the Supreme Court. This is a difficult area of law, on which EU law and, even more so, European human rights law has exerted considerable influence. It is an area of law that has become contested and controversial. The Law Commission considered it in detail over a four-year period, producing significant proposals for change in 2008. The proposals were not well received, however, and in its final report on the matter it made no substantive recommendations for reform (see, further on all this, below). (The basic principles of this area of law are broadly the same in English and in Scots law: see, e.g., *Mitchell* v. *Glasgow City Council* [2009] UKHL 11, [2009] 1 AC 874.)

The starting point in considering the tortious liability of public authorities (other than the Crown) is double-edged: on the one hand, there is no general cloak of immunity for public authorities but, on the other hand, there is no general right to damages for harm caused by an ultra vires act of a public authority.

One area of difficulty in considering the liability in tort of public authorities is the relationship in determining the limits of such liability between public law concepts (ultra vires, irrationality, etc.) and private law concepts (duty of care, breach of duty, etc.). Formerly, it appeared that a negligence action could succeed against a public authority only if the authority had acted *Wednesbury* unreasonably (see, e.g., *Home Office* v. *Dorset Yacht Co Ltd* [1970] AC 1004, per Lord Diplock). More recently, the courts appear to have relaxed this rule (see, especially, *Barrett* v. *Enfield London Borough Council* [2001] 2 AC 550, considered below). However, public law concepts have not been rendered wholly irrelevant when considering questions of liability in tort and, in particular, in negligence. Where the decision of the public authority is characterised as being 'non-justiciable', for example, the authority will not be liable in negligence. Matters of justiciability will be determined with reference to public law concepts. The recent Supreme Court cases of *Michael* v. *Chief Constable of South Wales Police* [2015] UKSC 2, [2015] 2 WLR 343, *Robinson* v. *Chief Constable of West Yorkshire Police* [2018] UKSC 4, [2018] AC 736 and *Poole Borough Council* v. *GN* [2019] UKSC 25 mark a change in the reasoning process of the courts. These cases contain clear statements that the same principles apply when bringing a claim against a public authority and a private individual. Moreover, they appear to mark a move away from the use of broad arguments from public policy towards an application of specific types of tortious claim, focusing more on a distinction between acts or omissions.

Where it is argued that a public authority is liable in negligence (or, indeed, in other torts) the detail of the statutory scheme under which the authority was acting will be central to the determination of liability. A critical question used to be whether the authority was exercising a statutory duty or a statutory power. Following *Robinson* (above), the focus of the court is more on whether the harm caused by a public authority was due to an act or an omission; rephrased by Lord Reed in *Poole Borough Council* v. *GN* as a difference between 'causing harm (making things worse) and failing to confer a benefit (not making things better)' (at para [28]). Different lines of authority apply to the distinction between statutory duties and powers. The leading cases with regard to statutory duties are *X* v. *Bedfordshire County Council* [1995] 2 AC 633 and *Barrett* v. *Enfield London Borough Council* [2001] 2 AC 550 (but see also *Phelps* v. *Hillingdon London Borough Council* [2001] 2 AC 619, which is particularly important on vicarious liability). The leading authorities with regard to statutory powers are *Stovin* v. *Wise* [1996] AC 923 and *Gorringe* v. *Calderdale Metropolitan Borough Council* [2004] 1 WLR 1057. These last two cases made it clear that it continues to be the case that litigants are very unlikely to be able to show that a public authority has acted negligently in the exercise of a statutory power unless they can show that the authority has acted *Wednesbury* unreasonably. These cases now have to be read in light of the distinction between causing a harm and not making things better. Liability in tort law normally does not apply in those instances in which A, whether a public body or a private individual, failed to make things better for

B. However, the statutory background imposing duties or powers on a public authority may provide evidence that a duty of care can nevertheless arise.

Robinson v. *Chief Constable of West Yorkshire Police* [2018] UKSC 4, [2018] AC 736

Mrs Robinson was a 'relatively frail woman' aged 76, walking on a town centre shopping street. At the same time, the police were attempting to arrest a suspected drug dealer. Concerned that the drug dealer may escape arrest, while eager to ensure that the drug dealer was caught expeditiously to prevent him from getting rid of any illegal drugs he may have been carrying, two police officers moved in to arrest the drug dealer, with two others ready to move in from the other side. A struggle ensued. As a result of the struggle, the two police officers and the suspected drug dealer knocked Mrs Robinson to the ground, falling on top of her, injuring her in the process. Mrs Robinson sought damages from the police for personal injury.

Applying established case law, it would appear that Mrs Robinson would have little chance of success. Any case for the tort of negligence requires the establishment of a duty of care, a breach in this duty of care, and a link between this breach of a duty and the harm caused. The leading case on establishing a duty of care, *Caparo* v. *Dickman* [1990] 2 AC 605, established a three-point test: reasonable foreseeability; proximity and whether it was fair, just and reasonable to impose a duty of care on the specific facts. *Hill* v. *Chief Constable of West Yorkshire* [1989] AC 53 had concluded, on public policy grounds, that there was no general duty of care owed by the police to the public concerning how they carried out their investigations. As such, applying the 'fair, just and reasonable' test to the facts, it would appear that the police did not owe a duty of care to Mrs Robinson, unless there was a specific exception that could apply in her case.

The Supreme Court disagreed. Lord Reed drew on the decision of the Supreme Court in *Michael* v. *Chief Constable of South Wales* (above), concluding (at para [21]) that 'the proposition that there is a *Caparo* test which applies to all claims in the modern law of negligence, and that in consequence the court will only impose a duty of care where it considers it fair, just and reasonable to do so on the particular facts is mistaken'. Instead, the court should 'adopt an approach based, in the manner characteristic of the common law, on precedent, and on the development of the law incrementally and by analogy with established authorities'. Lord Reed then proceeded to give an account of the approach to the tortious liability of public authorities as follows:

> [32]. At common law, public authorities are generally subject to the same liabilities in tort as private individuals and bodies: see, for example, *Entick v Carrington* (1765) 2 Wils KB 275 and *Mersey Docks and Harbour Board v Gibbs* (1866) LR 1 HL 93. Dicey famously stated that 'every official, from the Prime Minister down to a constable or a collector of taxes, is under

the same responsibility for every act done without legal justification as any other citizen': *The Law of the Constitution* 3rd ed (1889), p 181. An important exception at common law was the Crown, but that exception was addressed by the Crown Proceedings Act 1947, section 2.

[33]. Accordingly, if conduct would be tortious if committed by a private person or body, it is generally equally tortious if committed by a public authority: see, for example, *Dorset Yacht Co Ltd v Home Office* [1970] AC 1004, as explained in *Gorringe's* case [2004] 1 WLR 1057, para 39. That general principle is subject to the possibility that the common law or statute may provide otherwise, for example by authorising the conduct in question: *Geddis v Proprietors of Bann Reservoir* (1878) 3 App Cas 430. It follows that public authorities are generally under a duty of care to avoid causing actionable harm in situations where a duty of care would arise under ordinary principles of the law of negligence, unless the law provides otherwise.

[34]. On the other hand, public authorities, like private individuals and bodies, are generally under no duty of care to prevent the occurrence of harm: as Lord Toulson JSC stated in *Michael's* case [2015] AC 1732, para 97, 'the common law does not generally impose liability for pure omissions'. This 'omissions principle' has been helpfully summarised by Tofaris and Steel, 'Negligence Liability for Omissions and the Police' [2016] CLJ 128:

> 'In the tort of negligence, a person A is not under a duty to take care to prevent harm occurring to person B through a source of danger not created by A unless (i) A has assumed a responsibility to protect B from that danger, (ii) A has done something which prevents another from protecting B from that danger, (iii) A has a special level of control over that source of danger, or (iv) A's status creates an obligation to protect B from that danger.'

[35]. As that summary makes clear, there are certain circumstances in which public authorities, like private individuals and bodies, can come under a duty of care to prevent the occurrence of harm: see, for example, *Barrett v Enfield London Borough Council* [2001] 2 AC 550 and *Phelps v Hillingdon London Borough Council* [2001] 2 AC 619, as explained in *Gorringe's* case [2004] 1 WLR 1057, paras 39–40. In the absence of such circumstances, however, public authorities generally owe no duty of care towards individuals to concur a benefit upon them by protecting them from harm, any more than would a private individual or body: see, for example, *Smith v Littlewoods Organisation Ltd* [1987] AC 241, concerning a private body, applied in *Mitchell v Glasgow City Council* [2009] AC 874, concerning a public authority.

[36]. That is so, notwithstanding that a public authority may have statutory powers or duties enabling or requiring it to prevent the harm in question. A well-known illustration of that principle is the decision of the House of Lords in *East Suffolk Rivers Catchment Board v Kent* [1941] AC 74. The position is different if, on its true construction, the statutory power or duty is intended to give rise to a duty to individual members of the public which is enforceable by means of a private right of action. If, however, the statute does not create a private right of action, then 'it would be, to say the least, unusual if the mere existence of

the statutory duty [or, a fortiori, a statutory power] could generate a common law duty of care': *Gorringe's case* [2004] 1 WLR 1057, para 23.

[37]. A further point, closely related to the last, is that public authorities, like private individuals and bodies, generally owe no duty of care towards individuals to prevent them from being harmed by the conduct of a third party: see, for example, *Smith v Littlewoods Organisation Ltd* [1987] AC 241 and *Mitchell v Glasgow City Council* [2009] AC874. In *Michael's* case [2015] AC1732, para 97 Lord Toulson JSC explained the point in this way:

> 'It is one thing to require a person who embarks on action which may harm others to exercise care. It is another matter to hold a person liable in damages for failing to prevent harm caused by someone else.'

There are however circumstances where such a duty may be owed, as Tofaris and Steele indicated in the passage quoted above. They include circumstances where the public authority has created a danger of harm which would not otherwise have existed, or has assumed a responsibility for an individual's safety on which the individual has relied. The first type of situation is illustrated by the *Dorset Yacht* case, and in relation to the police by the case of *Attorney General of the British Virgin Islands v Hartwell* [2004] 1 WLR 1273, discussed below. The second type of situation is illustrated, in relation to the police, by the case of *An Informer v A Chief Constable* [2013] QB 579, as explained in *Michael's* case [2015] AC1732, para 69.

Lord Reed then turned to the cases concerning the liability of the police in particular, concluding (at para 55]) that

> *Hill's* case is not, therefore, authority for the proposition that the police enjoy a general immunity from suit in respect of anything done by them in the course of investigating or preventing crime. On the contrary, the liability of the police for negligence or other tortious conduct resulting in personal injury, where liability would arise under ordinary principles of the law of tort, was expressly confirmed. Lord Keith spoke of an 'immunity', meaning the absence of a duty of care, only in relation to the protection of the public from harm through the performance by the police of their function of investigating crime.

When applied to Mrs Robinson, the court concluded that the police did owe her a duty of care. The police had harmed Mrs Robinson when carrying out an action, as opposed to failing to prevent harm occurring to Mrs Robinson.

Lord Reed's shift in focus was motivated by concerns to remove policy considerations from the courts when established rules of tort law were capable of deciding the case before the court. Lord Hughes, however, was less willing to rule out the use of policy considerations when determining the scope of liability of public authorities. He was concerned, in particular, of the impact that imposing liability on the police may have on their ability to carry out their duties. For Lord Hughes, it was these policy reasons, and not the distinction between acts and omissions, that played the main role in ascertaining whether the police owed a duty of care to Mrs Robinson.

Robinson does not change the law. Rather, it provides clarification of the case law. In *Poole Borough Council* v. *GN* (above), Lord Reed summarised the impact of *Robinson* as follows (at paras [64] and [65]):

> [64]. *Robinson* did not lay down any new principle of law, but three matters in particular were clarified. First, the decision explained, as *Michael* had previously done, that *Caparo* did not impose a universal tripartite test for the existence of a duty of care, but recommended an incremental approach to novel situations, based on the use of established categories of liability as guides, by analogy, to the existence and scope of a duty of care in cases which fall outside them. The question whether the imposition of a duty of care would be fair, just and reasonable forms part of the assessment of whether such an incremental step ought to be taken. It follows that, in the ordinary run of cases, courts should apply established principles of law, rather than basing their decisions on their assessment of the requirements of public policy. Secondly, the decision re-affirmed the significance of the distinction between harming the claimant and failing to protect the claimant from harm (including harm caused by third parties), which was also emphasised in *Mitchell* and *Michael*. Thirdly, the decision confirmed, following *Michael* and numerous older authorities, that public authorities are generally subject to the same general principles of the law of negligence as private individuals and bodies, except to the extent that legislation requires a departure from those principles. That is the basic premise of the consequent framework for determining the existence or non-existence of a duty of care on the part of a public authority.
>
> [65]. It follows (1) that public authorities may owe a duty of care in circumstances where the principles applicable to private individuals would impose such a duty, unless such a duty would be inconsistent with, and is therefore excluded by, the legislation from which their powers or duties are derived; (2) that public authorities do not owe a duty of care at common law merely because they have statutory powers or duties, even if, by exercising their statutory functions, they could prevent a person from suffering harm; and (3) that public authorities can come under a common law duty to protect from harm in circumstances where the principles applicable to private individuals or bodies would impose such a duty, as for example where the authority has created the source of danger or has assumed a responsibility to protect the claimant from harm, unless the imposition of such a duty would be inconsistent with the relevant legislation.

Older case law now needs to be read in the light of these three recent Supreme Court cases. We turn first to the case law concerning negligence and statutory duties. In *X* v. *Bedfordshire County Council* (above), several claimants argued that their local authorities had acted negligently, inter alia, in not investigating serious allegations of parental abuse and neglect, and in failing to commence appropriate measures of child protection. The local authorities applied to have

the claims struck out. The House of Lords ruled in favour of the local authorities. In *X* v. *Bedfordshire County Council*, the House of Lords focused on the
existence of a duty of care, holding that it would not be 'fair, just and reasonable' to impose a duty of care on local authorities in respect of their responsibilities under child protection legislation. A variety of overlapping reasons was
offered in support of this conclusion: (1) a duty of care was a blunt instrument
that would cut across the whole statutory scheme; (2) the statutory scheme was
interdisciplinary, involving multiparty, collective decision-making (potentially
including parents, teachers, social workers, educational psychologists, the
police and others), giving rise to a problem of who, in particular, should owe
any duty of care; (3) imposing liability would lead to problems of apportion-
ment of responsibility; (4) alternative remedies were available, such as complaints to the local government ombudsmen; (5) imposing a duty of care would
risk encouraging defensive administration (whereby decision-makers make
decisions principally in order to escape liability, rather than making decisions
that are necessarily in the best interests of the parties); and (6) a finding of
liability would impose a burden on scarce public resources, both financial and
human.

Barrett v. *Enfield London Borough Council* (above) was a negligence case
about a child who was already in local authority care. Relying on decisions such
as *X* v. *Bedfordshire County Council* the local authority applied to have Mr
Barrett's claim struck out. The House of Lords ruled that the claim should not
be struck out. *X* v. *Bedfordshire County Council* was distinguished. Their
Lordships ruled that the public policy considerations on which the court had
relied in *X* in deciding that it would not be fair, just and reasonable to impose
a duty of care in the circumstances of that case 'did not have the same force in
respect of decisions taken once the child was in care'. Their Lordships ruled
that *Barrett* should be allowed to proceed to full trial. The key issue at that trial,
their Lordships thought, would be whether the local authority had breached its
duty of care to Mr Barrett.

Following *Poole Borough Council* v. *GN* (above, at para [74]), 'the decision in
X (Minors) v Bedfordshire can no longer be regarded as good law in so far as it
ruled out on grounds of public policy the possibility that a duty of care might
be owed by local authorities or their staff towards children with whom they
came into contact in the performance of their functions under the 1989 Act, or
in so far as liability for inflicting harm on a child was considered, in the
Newham case, to depend on 'an assumption of responsibility'. The differences
between *X* and *Barrett* can now be explained through an analysis of whether
the claim for liability is as regards an act or an omission by the public authority
and, if for an omission, whether there was an assumption of responsibility for
this omission. In *X*, the social workers advising the council in child abuse cases
had not assumed any responsibility towards the children or their parents. They
were not providing advice to the claimants. Neither was it reasonably foreseeable that the claimants would rely on information provided in the reports to

the council. In *Barrett*, however, the local authority assumed responsibility for a child once the child had been placed in their care. Similarly, In *Phelps* v. *Hillingdon* (above), a duty of care existed as it was reasonably foreseeable that the parents of a child would rely on the advice of an educational psychologist providing information to the council concerning the educational needs of the child.

Similarly, *Stovin* v. *Wise* (above) and *Gorringe* (above) are also to be read as cases concerning omissions. *Poole Borough Council* v. *GN* now provides the leading authority on cases concerning the extent to which local authorities owe a duty of care with regard to care packages provided to children. *GN* concerned a severely disabled child. This child, his younger brother and his mother, were housed in council housing in Poole. Unfortunately, they were housed next to a family who persistently targeted the family, subjecting them to harassment and abuse. This behaviour was such that the younger child ran away from home, leaving a suicide note. Eventually, after five years of abuse and harassment, the family were moved. They brought an action in damages for the physical and psychological harm suffered as a result of the abusive behaviour of their neighbours.

GN followed the approach of *Michael* v. *Chief Constable of South Wales Police* (above), which had, in turn, relied on *Stovin v Wise* and *Gorringe*, concluding that there was only a narrow set of circumstances in which an individual could be liable for the harm caused by a third party. Applied to the facts of *GN*, it would require the family who abused GN to be under the control of Poole Borough Council, or where Poole Borough Council had assumed responsibility to protect GN and his family. Although Poole Borough Council had investigated the incidents of abuse and had monitored GN's position, it was not providing advice to GN and his family 'on which they could be expected to rely' [81]. The council had not taken GN or his family into care. Also, GN and his family had not entrusted their safety to the council, neither could it be said that the council had assumed responsibility for the safety of the family. Therefore, although it was no longer the case that public policy reasons would automatically mean that there was no duty of care owed by the council to GN, on the application of these specific principles, no duty of care was owed.

It remains to be seen how far this focus on existing principles of tort law, rather than an approach based on an assessment of policy reasons for when it would be fair, just and reasonable to impose a duty of care, and a specific focus on acts and omissions and assumptions of responsibility, will change the law. It is likely that the more recent cases discussed above would have been decided the same way even if broader policy arguments had been taken into consideration (see, e.g., the explanation of Lord Hughes in *Robinson*). Nevertheless, it marks a move away from the courts balancing policy issues towards a focus on established case law. It can only be hoped that this will bring more clarity to the law. However, the criticism of the distinction between acts and omissions suggests that full clarification may not yet have been reached.

A public authority may have the defence to an action in tort that the act done was authorised by statute. For instance, an authority is not liable in tort for a nuisance resulting from its performance, without negligence, of a statutory duty. If, however, a nuisance is caused by the authority in exercising a public power, it will ordinarily be liable if the power could have been exercised without causing the nuisance. (See, e.g., *Marcic* v. *Thames Water Utilities Ltd* [2003] UKHL 66, [2004] 2 AC 42.)

Damages for a tort committed by a public authority or officer are assessed on ordinary principles, but exemplary damages may be awarded if the authority was guilty of 'oppressive, arbitrary or unconstitutional action' in performing public functions. (*Rookes* v. *Barnard* [1964] AC 1129, 1225–6. See also *Holden* v. *Chief Constable of Lancashire* [1987] QB 380; *Kuddus* v. *Chief Constable of Leicestershire* [2001] UKHL 29, [2002] 2 AC 122.)

In addition to negligence, there is a separate tort of breach of statutory duty. Even though ministers and other public authorities are under a large number and range of statutory duties, it is rare for an action for breach of statutory duty to succeed (apart from in some cases concerning industrial accidents). The courts will generally not allow an action for breach of statutory duty to proceed unless two conditions are met: first, that Parliament evinced an intention that the statutory duty in question should be actionable in this way and, secondly, that the duty was intended to confer a benefit only on a particular group and not on the public at large (see *O'Rourke* v. *Camden London Borough Council* [1998] AC 188; *Phelps* v. *Hillingdon London Borough Council* [2001] 2 AC 619).

A further tort – misfeasance in public office – provides a remedy for abuse of power by a public officer. The elements of the tort, as identified by the House of Lords in *Three Rivers District Council* v. *Bank of England (No 3)* [2003] 2 AC 1, are that a public officer caused injury or loss to the claimant by an unlawful act, either ('targeted malice') with the intention of causing such injury or ('untargeted malice') knowing that the act was unlawful and that it would probably injure the claimant, or being reckless, in deliberate disregard of a serious risk that injury to the claimant would result from the conduct known to be unlawful. (See also *Watkins* v. *Home Office* [2006] UKHL 17, [2006] 2 AC 395.)

10.6.2.1 Conclusion: Reform?

The liability in tort of public authorities is an area of our law that has attracted trenchant criticism for more than twenty years. It remains to be seen whether the trio of recent decisions in the Supreme Court will stem this tide of criticism.

For a short period, House of Lords case law was in favour of developing the law of negligence in a principled fashion, the high point being *Anns* v. *Merton London Borough Council* [1978] AC 728. But *Anns* was overruled in *Murphy* v. *Brentwood District Council* [1991] 1 AC 398, leading to the incremental development of the law, where it was decided on a case-by-case basis whether it is 'fair, just and reasonable' to impose a duty of care, etc. In the words of the Law Commission, this has resulted in a body of law that is both 'uncertain and unprincipled' (*Administrative Redress: Public Bodies and the Citizen*, Law Com 322, 2010, para 1.18). *Michael, Robinson* and *GN* mark a move away from the consideration of broad policy considerations, focusing instead on established case law determining duties of care for acts and omissions, and the assumption of responsibility for third parties. However, this was not fully endorsed by all of the justices of the Supreme Court in *Robinson*.

The JUSTICE–All Souls report on *Administrative Justice* (1988) recommended that a remedy for wrongful administrative action should be introduced by legislation, 'which might take some such form as the following' (para 11.83):

> Subject to such exceptions and immunities as may be specifically provided, compensation in accordance with the provisions of this Act shall be recoverable by any person who sustains loss as a result of either:
>
> (a) any act, decision, determination, instrument or order of a public body which materially affects him and which is for any reason wrongful or contrary to law; or
> (b) unreasonable or excessive delay on the part of any public body in taking any action, reaching any decision or determination, making any order or carrying out any duty.

It is added that 'wrongful' and 'public body' would need to be carefully defined. (Among those who expressed reservations as to this proposal was Lord Woolf, in *Protection of the Public: A New Challenge* (1990), pp. 57–8.) To date, no such remedy has been enacted into law.

In 2008, the Law Commission published a consultation paper, *Administrative Redress: Public Bodies and the Citizen* (CP 187), in which it was proposed that a return be made to what the Law Commission considered to be a more principled and less incrementalist approach. The starting point was that 'as a matter of justice, claimants should be entitled to obtain redress for loss caused by clearly substandard administrative action' (*Administrative Redress: Public Bodies and the Citizen*, Law Com 322, 2010, para 1.13). To this end, the Law Commission proposed a package of reforms. First, it suggested that damages ought to be more widely available in judicial review, especially where a public authority is shown to have been at 'serious fault'. Second, it suggested that the ordinary principles of the private law of negligence should apply to public authorities when they are exercising powers which they share with individuals. Only when they are engaged in what the Law Commission called 'truly public' activities should special rules apply and, even then, damages should be available where the claimant could prove 'serious fault' on the part of a public body. These proposals, which the Law Commission conceded it had been unable fully to cost, were not well received, not least by the government, who strongly resisted them (and for academic criticism, see, e.g., Cornford [2009] *PL* 70). Very shortly after the close of the consultation period the House of Lords handed down its ruling in *Van*

Colle/Smith, in which, as we saw, such appetite for reform as their Lordships displayed was found only in the partially dissenting opinion of Lord Bingham. In the light of all this, the Law Commission gave up, recognising in its final report (*Administrative Redress: Public Bodies and the Citizen*, Law Com 322, 2010) that 'it is impractical to attempt to pursue the reform of state liability any further at this time' (para 1.6). The Law Commission did not accept many of the criticisms levelled at its 2008 proposals, and the 2010 report seeks to defend them and to rebut some of the criticism.

On the considerable impact of EU law on questions of liability against the state and against public authorities, see Chapter 5 (above, pp. 368–371).

(See, generally on this area of law, Fairgrieve, *State Liability in Tort: A Comparative Law Study* (2003); Harlow, *State Liability: Tort Law and Beyond* (2004); Oliphant (ed.), *The Liability of Public Authorities in Comparative Perspective* (2016), in addition to the work of the Law Commission cited above.)

Part IV
Liberty

Liberty and the Constitution

Contents

When we think about civil liberties, we normally do so in terms of our rights to freedom of expression and freedom of assembly. This is unsurprising, as these areas are crucial to the maintenance of democracy. Without freedom of expression – both for MPs and for individuals – it is difficult for individuals to communicate their views to political institutions and even more difficult for them to hold governmental officials to account for their actions. The right to peaceful protest empowers those who may otherwise have no access to the media – social or otherwise – or to lobbying groups to communicate their message. They are also both rights that can require balancing with other rights. Freedom of expression protects speech that can harm others; but we need to ensure that in doing so it does not place too great a restriction on the right to privacy, or the right not to be discriminated against on the grounds of your race, gender, religion, sexual orientation or disability. While we protect a right to peaceful protest, these protests may need to be balanced with the rights of others to use the highway. When we think of other liberties in the context of the United Kingdom – for instance, the right to liberty and security of the person found in Article 5 ECHR – we normally do so to point out the extent to which these have been restricted in order to protect national security.

All these issues will be addressed in depth in this chapter. However, it is impossible to discuss civil liberties without referring to the measures adopted by the UK in response to the Covid-19 pandemic in 2020. As healthcare is a devolved issue, England, Scotland, Wales and Northern Ireland each enacted its own delegated legislation to implement 'lockdown' measures to delay the spread of Covid-19. These measures required the widespread closing of businesses, subject to exceptions for essential services such as food retailers, newsagents, pharmacies, petrol stations, launderettes and dry cleaners, post offices, funeral directors, and those providing health and dental care services and veterinary services. It also placed restrictions on movement. Under the first stage of lockdown measures, people were not allowed to leave their place of residence unless for a 'reasonable excuse' – to obtain basic necessities; to take exercise; to seek medical assistance; to provide care or assistance for the vulnerable; to donate blood; to travel to work (where it is not reasonably possible to work from home); to attend a funeral; to fulfil a legal obligation; to access critical public services; to move house where reasonably necessary; for children to continue to visit parents who are not part of their household as per existing contact arrangements; and to avoid injury or illness or to escape the risk of harm. The regulations also prohibited public gatherings of two people of more, subject to specific exceptions. In addition to placing these restrictions on movement, the regulations created new criminal offences and empowered the police to take such action as was necessary to enforce these restrictions, including dispersing gatherings, and extended the powers of arrest in England and Wales to empower police officers to arrest an individual if the police officer reasonably believes this is necessary to maintain public health or public order.

While these measures appear draconian out of context, they are understandable in the context of such a serious threat to the health of the nation that, at the time of writing, had already caused more than 40,000 deaths in the UK and over 400,000 deaths worldwide, in spite of these measures being put in place. Only history will tell whether the measures were a proportionate and effective means of tackling such a pandemic. As will be seen in the following, ensuring an effective protection of civil liberties often requires a delicate balance of competing rights. While the situations below do not require a delicate balance between civil liberties and the right to life, they nevertheless frequently present situations in which it is reasonable to disagree whether the correct balances were made. The response to the Covid-19 pandemic also illustrates three themes that run through any assessment of the protection of civil liberties: the need for certainty and clarity; the importance of analysing how rules are enforced in practice; and the need for adequate legal and political checks over any proposed restriction on civil liberties.

The response to the Covid-19 pandemic demonstrates the difficulties that can arise when regulations are insufficiently clear. More problematically, it illustrates deeper rule of law issues that can arise where guidelines or widely publicised advice appears to contradict the legally binding regulations. For example, advice was provided that it was a reasonable excuse to leave your house for exercise only once a day. Yet, at the time this advice was given, only the Welsh Regulations restricted leaving the house for exercise to once a day. There was no similar restriction in the English, Scottish or Northern Irish Regulations. Moreover, there was widespread dissemination of the advice to ensure that, when you are outside, you exercise 'social distancing' by remaining two metres apart from others. However, there was no specific provision in any of the regulations requiring this. It was also widely believed that the only reasonable excuses for leaving home under the first stage of lockdown regulations was to buy food, to exercise, or to travel to work, in spite of the regulations in force at that time providing a longer list of 'reasonable excuses'. More fundamentally, the rule of law is undermined when 'advice' is presented as a legally binding rule when this is not the case. On 23 March 2020, for example, Prime Minister Boris Johnson announced on television that he was giving 'the British people a very simple instruction – you must stay home' adding that 'if you do not follow the rules, the police will have powers to enforce them, including through fines and dispersing gatherings.' Most listening to this message would have had the impression that the rules mentioned by the prime minister were already in force. This would have been potentially reinforced by the text message sent by the government to all UK mobile phones on 24 March: 'New rules in force now: you must stay at home.' Not only was this text message misleading – it was not the case that everyone must stay at home given the existence of reasonable excuses for leaving the home, – but also, more fundamentally, the rules referred to had not yet been enacted. The various regulations enforcing these measures across the UK did not come into force until 26 March. While it is understandable that the government needed to react quickly in response to the pandemic, this is no excuse for intimating that the police had the power to enforce rules that had not been enacted and prior to the police being provided with specific powers of enforcement.

Second, throughout the first stage of the lockdown, concerns arose as to the way in which the police had been enforcing their powers, from the imposition of roadblocks, the use of drones to spy on those exercising in the Peak District National Park, to statements that the police would be checking shopping baskets to ensure that supermarket customers really were purchasing only essential items of food. However, it was not clear that the regulations authorised the use of roadblocks or drones. Neither was it the case that the regulations limited the 'reasonable excuse' to leave the house to buy food to the purchase of essential food items – however that may be determined. These difficulties resulted in the production of a series of guidelines as to how the provisions would be enforced.

Third, and perhaps most fundamentally of all, it is important to ensure that there are sufficient legal and political checks over any measures restricting civil liberties. Again, it is at least arguable that these checks were lacking, or were, at best, minimal. The Coronavirus Act 2020 completed its passage through the House of Commons in one day. The Health Protection (Coronavirus, Restrictions) (England) Regulations 2020 were made on 26 March at 1pm and laid before Parliament on the same day at 2:30pm, having come into force already at 1pm. Moreover, at the time they were laid before Parliament, Parliament was in recess, making it impossible for scrutiny of its provisions. In addition, it was enacted (some would argue controversially) under the Public Health (Control of Diseases) Act 1984. This did not require the prior declaration of an emergency, or even the need for the existence of an emergency (with the potential of both political and legal control) prior to the enactment of regulations. Moreover, in contrast to measures enacted under the Civil Contingencies Act 2004, which lapse after a period of seven days unless each House of Parliament enacts a resolution approving of these measures, measures enacted under the Public Health (Control of Diseases) Act 1984 lapse only after twenty-eight days if they are not approved by the House of Commons. In addition, unlike in the 2004 Act, there is no requirement that the measures enacted are proportionate or necessary. Although each of the regulations lapses after six months, requires the minister to revisit whether they are still needed every three weeks and also requires that the minister lift the regulations when that minister deems this necessary, there is no requirement for parliamentary approval, with scrutiny only occurring through questions or debates. Moreover, the Westminster Parliament was still in recess when the regulations were first renewed. It is to be hoped that proper parliamentary debate, in addition to future court controls, will ensue to ensure that measures remain in place when needed, and are lifted in a sensible and proportionate manner when they are no longer required.

This chapter will continue with an overview of the relevant sources of law in the UK, before analysing the convention rights incorporated into UK law through the Human Rights Act 1998, looking at the impact of the convention on anti-terrorism and national security as a case study. It will then examine two case studies – freedom of expression and freedom of assembly. These case studies illustrate the themes mentioned above, in addition to the need to recognise the continuing role of the common law even after the enactment of the Human Rights Act 1998.

11.1 Sources of Protection

11.1.1 Common Law

The common law's traditional approach to the protection of rights, exempli-fied in such leading cases as *Entick v Carrington* (1765) 19 St Tr 1029 (on which, see p. 112), centres upon the notion of 'residual liberty'. According to this approach, we are free to do anything that is not legally prohibited. As Sir Robert Megarry V-C expressed it in *Malone v Metropolitan Police Commissioner* [1979] Ch. 344, 'everything is permitted except what is expressly forbidden' (see above, pp. 114–116). Even liberty in its most basic sense of freedom from physical restraint is seen as having this residual character: the writ of habeas corpus, for protecting the individual from unlawful restriction of his or her liberty, may be unavailing if the restriction can be justified in terms of statutory provision such as Schedule 2, paragraph 16 to the Immigration Act 1971 (as amended), sections 2, 3 or 4 of the Mental Health Act 1983 (as amended by the Mental Health Act 2007), section 41 of the Terrorism Act 2000 or section 2 of the Terrorism Prevention and Investigative Measures Act 2011.

This approach may be contrasted with a constitutional order in which liberty is protected by force of a *positive* list of rights – a list of statements to the effect that no matter what the state or the government claims to be able to do, there are some matters that are protected, such that the state or the government may not interfere with them at all (or, at least, such that the state or the government may interfere with them only on strictly limited conditions). This is the approach that is now taken in UK law under the authority of the Human Rights Act. However, even before the passage of this Act, certain cases had begun to explore the possibility that, inherent in the common law, there may be individual, fundamental or constitutional rights that may be relied on to delimit lawful state or governmental action. An early instance was *Hubbard v Pitt* [1976] QB 142, in which Lord Denning, in a dissenting judgment, would have vindicated 'the right to demonstrate and the right to protest on matters of public concern'. In *Secretary of State for Defence v Guardian Newspapers Ltd* [1985] AC 339, 361, Lord Scarman said with reference not to the common law but to a statutory provision (section 10 of the Contempt of Court Act 1981, which gives to publishers of newspapers and others a qualified immunity from compulsion to disclose their sources of information) that:

> [Counsel for the *Guardian*] described the section as introducing into the law 'a constitutional right'. There being no written constitution, his words will sound strange to some. But they may more accurately prophesy the direction in which English law has to move under the compulsions to which it is now subject than many are yet prepared to accept.

(See, further, below, on the Contempt of Court Act 1981.)

Since the mid-1990s judicial references to 'constitutional rights' and to 'constitutional statutes' have multiplied. 'In the present state of its maturity', said Laws LJ in *Thoburn v Sunderland City Council* [2003] QB 151, at [62], 'the common law has come to recognise that there exist rights which should properly be classified as constitutional or fundamental'. In a widely cited judgment, for example, Steyn LJ ruled in *R v Secretary of State for the Home Department, ex p Leech* [1994] QB 198, 210, that 'the principle of our law that every citizen has a right of unimpeded access to the court ... must rank as a constitutional right'. And in *R v Ministry of Defence, ex p Smith* [1996] QB 517, the Court of Appeal accepted that judicial scrutiny of administrative discretion under the doctrine of irrationality (or *Wednesbury* unreasonableness: see Chapter 10) should be intensified in what was described as 'the human rights context'. The *principal* use to which the notion of common law 'constitutional rights' has been put is, as in the *Leech* case, that of statutory interpretation. The position was summarised (as we saw in Chapter 2) in Lord Hoffmann's important dictum in *R v Secretary of State for the Home Department, ex p Simms* [2000] 2 AC 115 (HL) (emphasis added):

> Parliamentary sovereignty means that Parliament can, if it chooses, legislate contrary to fundamental principles of human rights. The Human Rights Act 1998 will not detract from this power. The constraints upon its exercise by Parliament are ultimately political, not legal. But the principle of legality means that Parliament must squarely confront what it is doing and accept the political cost. *Fundamental rights cannot be overridden by general or ambiguous words.* This is because there is too great a risk that the full implications of their unqualified meaning may have passed unnoticed in the democratic process. *In the absence of express language or necessary implication to the contrary, the courts therefore presume that even the most general words were intended to be subject to the basic rights of the individual.* In this way the courts of the United Kingdom, though acknowledging the sovereignty of Parliament, apply principles of constitutionality little different from those which exist in countries where the power of the legislature is expressly limited by a constitutional document.

That there are limits to the extent to which the common law will recognise rights as being 'constitutional' in character was laid down in *Watkins v Home Office* [2006] UKHL 17, [2006] 2 AC 395, in which the House of Lords reversed a judgment of the Court of Appeal which had held that, in the words of Lord Bingham, 'if there is a right which may be identified as a constitutional right, then there may be a cause of action in misfeasance in a public office for infringement of that right without proof of damage'. The House of Lords reinstated the rule – which can be traced back for more than 300 years – that the tort of misfeasance in a public office requires special damage. Lord Rodger stated (at [58]-[64]) that:

> the Court of Appeal's decision is noteworthy for the novel use which it makes of the concept of a 'constitutional right' ... For such an innovation to be workable, it would have to be possible to identify fairly readily what were to count as 'constitutional rights' for this purpose ... There is, however, no magic in the term 'constitutional right' ... It is in the sphere of interpretation of statutes that the expression 'constitutional right' has tended to be used, more or less interchangeably with other expressions [his Lordship cited *ex p Leech* (above) and related case law]. The term 'constitutional right' works well enough, alongside equivalent terms, in the field of statutory interpretation. But, even if it were otherwise suitable, it is not sufficiently precise to define a class of rights whose abuse should give rise to a right of action in tort without proof of damage ... In using the language of 'constitutional rights', the judges were, more or less explicitly, looking for a means of incorporation [of the ECHR] *avant la lettre*, of having the common law supply the benefits of incorporation without incorporation. Now that the Human Rights Act is in place, such heroic efforts are unnecessary.

Similar concerns as to the identification of fundamental rights of the common law can be found in more recent decisions of the Supreme Court, concerning both the content and the source of fundamental common law rights.

Moohan v. *Lord Advocate* [2014] UKSC 67, [2015] AC 901

The petitioners were prisoners in Scotland who wished to challenge the ban on prisoner voting, such that they could vote in the Scottish independence referendum. Having concluded that the right to vote in Article 3 of the First Protocol only applied to the election of a national or European legislature, and did not apply to referendums, the court then turned to examine whether the right to vote was a fundamental common law right. While Lord Hodge recognized the right to vote as a 'basic or constitutional right', nevertheless, (at [34]), he did:

> not think that the common law has been developed so as to recognise a right of universal and equal suffrage from which any derogation must be provided for by law and must be proportionate. It is important to bear in mind, as the Lord Ordinary in para 70 of his opinion, the historical development of the right to vote. Parliaments were initially summoned and the franchise created by the King's writ. In the fifteenth century parliamentary legislation in both Scotland and England and Wales sought to regulate the franchise. In Scotland the Election of Commissioners Act 1681 established the county franchise which survived until 1832. Since then the franchise has been extended by statute. It has thus been our constitutional history that for centuries the right to vote has been derived from statute. The UK Parliament through its legislation has controlled and controls the modalities of the expression of democracy. It is not appropriate for the courts to develop the common law in order to supplement or override the statutory rules which determine our democratic franchise. In *In re McKerr* [2004] 1 WLR 807, para 30, Lord Nicholls of Birkenhead stated:

'The courts have always been slow to develop the common law by entering, or re-entering, a field regulated by legislation. Rightly so, because otherwise there would inevitably be the prospect of the common law shaping powers and duties and provisions inconsistent with those prescribed by Parliament. *R v Lyons* [2003] 1 AC 976 is a recent instance where the House rejected a submission having this effect.'

His concerns were echoed by Baroness Hale, who asserted that: 'It would be wonderful if the common law had recognised a right of universal suffrage. But, as Lord Hodge JSC has pointed out, it has never done so . . . It makes no more sense to say that sentenced prisoners have a common law right to vote than it makes to say that women have a common law right to vote, which is clearly absurd' (at [56]).

Lord Kerr, however, was not so convinced, particularly by the claim that common law rights cannot exist in tandem with statutory provisions. Although he accepted that, to the extent that legislation specifically contradicted a right then reliance on common law could not succeed, he was nevertheless of the opinion that 'the common law can certainly evolve alongside statutory development' (at [86]), although, having reached his conclusion that the right to vote in a referendum did fall within the scope of Article 3 of the First Protocol, his statements on this matter are purely obiter.

Lord Kerr built on these statements in a later case in the Supreme Court.

El Gizouli v. *Secretary of State for the Home Department* [2020] UKSC 10, [2020] 2 WLR 857

It was alleged that El Gizouli's son was a member of the Islamic State of Iraq and had been one of a party of men who had carried out twenty-seven beheadings. He was being held by the USA, which had requested mutual legal assistance from the UK that would assist in his prosecution. The UK had a longstanding policy of not providing mutual legal assistance where this could be used in evidence for the prosecution of crimes carrying the death penalty without an assurance that the US authorities would not seek to impose the death penalty. However, after a series of exchanges with the US authorities, the UK eventually provided this assistance without the accompanying assurance. El Gizouli argued that this disclosure was both contrary to the Data Protection Act 2018 and the common law. The Supreme Court upheld the claim under the provisions of the Act. The majority of the Supreme Court also concluded that there was no fundamental right of the common law that would prevent the government acting in a manner that could facilitate the imposition of the death penalty, thereby undermining the right to life. Any such development of the right to life would be more than a merely incremental development of the common law and, therefore, beyond the powers of the court. Nevertheless, Lord Kerr, who provided the leading judgment in the case, concluded that there was a fundamental common law right against the facilitation of the death penalty.

Lord Kerr asserted (at [105]) that:

> The common law will not develop in an area where Parliament has legislated definitively. But that is not the case here. The HRA does not prevent the common law from upholding rights or obligations that are outside the scope or jurisdiction of the ECHR. Moreover, nothing can be inferred from the fact that Parliament has not legislated to prohibit the provision of assistance without death penalty assurances.

He then drew on evidence from a range of sources – the European Convention of Human Rights; European Union law; Privy Council case law discussing cases where the imposition of the death penalty was delayed; the Bill of Rights which prevents 'cruel and unusual punishment'; British contemporary values supporting the abolition of the death penalty; and the illogicality that results in a legal system that prevents deportation of individuals for crimes where the death penalty could be imposed without assurances that it will not be imposed while allowing for evidence to be provided as regards crimes for which the death penalty could be imposed without such assurances. He then concluded (at [142]):

> Drawing all these factors together, I believe that the time has arrived where a common law principle should be recognised whereby it is deemed unlawful to facilitate the trial of any individual in a foreign country where, to do so, would put that person in peril of being executed. This is not a conclusion of the considerable and controversial variety suggested by the respondent. It is a natural and inevitable extension of the prohibition (in the common law as well as under the HRA) of extradition or deportation without death penalty assurances. If it appears to be an incremental step, that is only because this is the first time the matter has come before the courts for consideration, largely because the two previous occasions since 2001 on which – according to the respondent – MLA was provided without a death penalty assurance, that was done without public knowledge and so without the possibility of judicial scrutiny.

These cases amply illustrate the tensions that arise when determining the content of a fundamental common law right: should the courts only rely on longstanding principles of the common law, or should they also rely on: international law provisions; UK legislation implementing aspects of a fundamental common law right; prevailing legal and political culture; and background philosophical positions concerning rights? There is also considerable confusion as to when a fundamental common law principle is sufficiently clear as to become a fundamental common law right, such that provisions of legislation should be read down and any specific authority to restrict the right can only be so far as is necessary to achieve a legitimate objective.

These difficulties make it hard to provide a definitive account of the rights protected by the common law. Other constitutional rights and liberties to have been recognised by judicial decisions are the right to life, 'the most fundamental of all human rights' (*R* v. *Lord Saville of Newdigate, ex p A* [2000] 1 WLR 1855); the right to freedom of expression (*Derbyshire County Council* v. *Times Newspapers* [1993] AC 534, on which see, further, below); the right to refuse to answer police questions (*Rice* v. *Connolly* [1966] 2 QB 414); and the right of a person in custody to consult a solicitor – 'one of the most important and fundamental rights of a citizen' (Hodgson J in *R* v. *Samuel* [1988] QB 615, 630) and a common law right as well as being protected by section 58(1) of the Police and Criminal Evidence Act 1984 (*R* v. *Chief Constable of South Wales, ex p Merrick* [1994] 1 WLR 663; on the rather different position in Scotland, see *Cadder* v. *HM Advocate* [2010] UKSC 43, 2010 SLT 1125) and the right of access to justice (*R (UNISON)* v. *Lord Advocate* [2017] UKSC 51, [2017] 3 WLR 409). To these, we may add the privilege against self-incrimination, 'deep rooted in English law' (Lord Griffiths in *Lam Chi-ming* v. *R* [1991] 2 AC 212, 222), although 'statutory interference with the right is almost as old as the right itself' (Lord Mustill in *R* v. *Director of Serious Fraud Office, ex p Smith* [1993] AC 1, 40; and see the Criminal Justice and Public Order Act 1994, sections 34–9; and also *Saunders* v. *United Kingdom* (1996) 23 EHRR 313). We have already met with 'the two fundamental rights accorded … by the rules of natural justice or fairness': the right to a hearing and to absence of personal bias in decisions affecting an individual's legal rights (*O'Reilly* v. *Mackman* [1983] 2 AC 237, 279): see Chapter 10.

A v. *Secretary of State for the Home Department (No 2)* [2005] UKHL 71, [2006] 2 AC 221 represents something of both the strengths and the limitations of the common law's protection of liberty. In a resounding judgment, a panel of seven Law Lords unanimously ruled that, in Lord Bingham's words (at [52]): 'The principles of the common law … compel the exclusion of third party torture evidence as unreliable, unfair, offensive to ordinary standards of humanity and decency and incompatible with the principles which should animate a tribunal seeking to administer justice.' Their Lordships were not, however, prepared to rule that the Secretary of State, the security services or the police would be acting unlawfully if they acted on information derived from torture in another country – if, for example, an individual was arrested and detained in the UK as a result of information extracted by torture in another jurisdiction, that would not necessarily be unlawful. The value of their Lordships' principal ruling, on the exclusion of third-party torture evidence, was substantially undermined by the standard of proof a majority of the Law Lords thought appropriate. The majority (Lords Hope, Rodger, Carswell and Brown) ruled that such evidence should be excluded only if it is established, on a balance of probabilities, that it was obtained by torture. The judges in the minority were scathing about this aspect of the ruling: Lord Bingham described it (at [59]) as 'a test which, in the real world, can never be satisfied' and Lord Nicholls stated that (at [80]) it will, in practice, 'largely nullify the principle . . . that courts will not admit evidence procured by torture'. His Lordship went on to say, bluntly, that 'That would be to pay lip-service to the principle' and that 'That is not good enough'. The judges in the minority (Lords Bingham, Nicholls and Hoffmann) would have preferred a standard of proof whereby once a party to proceedings had plausibly shown that evidence may have been procured by torture, such evidence should not be admitted unless and until the court or tribunal had inquired into the matter and had positively satisfied itself that it had not been so obtained.

As the *A* case suggests, we must not exaggerate the achievement of the courts in the defence of constitutional rights. Judicial vindication of individual rights has not been consistently evident, for example, in cases concerning immigrants or refugees (see, e.g., *R* v. *Secretary of State for the Home Department, ex p Swati* [1986] 1 WLR 477; *Rajput* v. *Immigration Appeal Tribunal* [1989] Imm AR 350; and *R* v. *Secretary of State for the Home Department, ex p Abdi* [1996] 1 WLR 298) and has very frequently faltered when countered by pleas of 'national security' (see below). Judicial decisions have sometimes drastically curtailed or diluted the rights of the individual against the state: see, for instance, *Duncan* v. *Jones* [1936] 1 KB 218 (below, p. 982, concerning freedom of expression and police powers) and *Liversidge* v. *Anderson* [1942] AC 206 (below, pp. 936–937, concerning personal freedom and executive discretion). Judges, as Griffith remarks, 'are concerned to preserve and to protect the existing order', and he cautions us against looking to them as 'the strong, natural defenders of liberty' (*The Politics of the Judiciary* (5th edn. 1997), p. 342). Griffith continues:

> In the societies of our world today judges do not stand out as protectors of liberty, of the rights of man, of the unprivileged, nor have they insisted that holders of great economic power, private or public, should use it with moderation. Their view of the public interest, when it has gone beyond the interest of governments, has not been wide enough to embrace the interests of political, ethnic, social or other minorities. Only occasionally has the power of the supreme judiciary been exercised in the positive assertion of fundamental values. In both democratic and totalitarian societies, the judiciary has naturally served the prevailing political and economic forces.

If we take this view of the judiciary as being closely identified with the governing elite in society, and as disposed to support established interests, we will not have confidence in the courts as resolute protectors of individual rights. Yet Griffith acknowledges that the judges have played a part in sustaining liberty and the rule of law (pp. 337–9), while warning that we must not expect too much of them. Other writers are more optimistic in looking to the common law, shaped by the judges, for the elaboration and defence of constitutional rights. (See, e.g., Allan, *Law, Liberty, and Justice* (1993), ch. 6; and Sir

John Laws, 'Is the High Court the Guardian of Fundamental Constitutional Rights?' [1993] *PL* 59.)

11.1.2 Statute

The single most important statute concerning liberty in Britain is now the Human Rights Act, which we consider in detail in section 2 of this chapter. It should not be thought, however, that the HRA is the only statute relevant to the topic of liberty. The extension of the franchise is a matter governed by statute: Acts for this purpose were passed in 1832, 1867, 1884, 1918 and 1928: see now the Representation of the People Act 1983, as amended, in addition the Scottish Elections (Franchise and Representation) Act 2020 and the Senedd and Elections (Wales) Act 2020, which extend the franchise to sixteen and seventeen year olds for the Scottish Parliament and the Welsh Senedd respectively. Rights to freedom of information and to data protection are likewise governed by statute (see, e.g., the Data Protection Act 2018, the Freedom of Information Act 2000 and the Freedom of Information (Scotland) Act 2002). A range of important statutes prohibit various forms of discrimination. Parliament first legislated in the field of race relations in the mid-1960s (see the Race Relations Acts of 1965 and 1968) and in the field of sex discrimination in the early 1970s (see the Equal Pay Act 1970 and the Sex Discrimination Act 1975). See now the Equality Act 2010, an enactment as important to the protection and advancement of equality as the HRA is to liberty. More recent legislation has been enacted to protect LGBTQI rights – for example, the Gender Recognition Act 2004 and the Marriage (Same Sex Couples) Act 2013.

In addition, specific provisions in numerous other Acts have conferred or confirmed important rights: for instance, section 28 of the Police and Criminal Evidence Act 1984 provides that an arrest is not lawful unless the person arrested is informed that he or she is under arrest and of the ground for the arrest. (A similar requirement previously existed at common law: *Christie v. Leachinsky* [1947] AC 573.)

While statute is a source of protection of liberty in numerous instances, it may also be a threat to liberty. The Police and Criminal Evidence Act 1984 extended the powers of the police as regards stop and search, arrest, detention and search and seizure. The Public Order Act 1986, as amended by the Crime and Courts Act 2013, extended the powers of the police to regulate protest (see, further, below, pp. 999–1011). The Official Secrets Act 1989 made inroads into the extent to which the right to freedom of expression could be enjoyed (see, further, below, p. 1028). The Criminal Justice and Public Order Act 1994, the Anti-Social Behaviour, Crime and Policing Act 2014, the Investigatory Powers Act 2016, the Civil Contingencies Act 2004 and the Crime and Courts Act 2013, as well as numerous other statutes, have all had a substantial impact on various civil liberties and human rights. On top of all of this is the considerable range of counterterrorism legislation that has been passed in recent years (on which, see below).

The Coalition Government that took office in May 2010 promised to introduce legislation that would repeal a range of statutory incursions into our liberties. The Identity Documents Act 2010 abolished the scheme of ID cards and the National Identity Register, which had been promoted by the previous government. It also enacted the Protection of Freedoms Act 2012.

11.1.3 Statutory Interpretation

The common law provides no defensive shield for fundamental rights against the unequivocal provision of statute (compare sections 3 and 4 of the HRA, considered in Chapter 2 (above, pp. 87–93)). Indeed, the courts have given effect to the proscriptions of statute even when these were not expressly stated but appeared more or less unambiguously from the scheme and purpose of the Act (see, e.g., *Re London United Investments plc* [1992] Ch. 578: privilege against self-incrimination held to have been impliedly displaced by statute). By the same token, the judges have held it to be consistent with a proper respect for statute to apply certain presumptions of parliamentary intent in the interpretation of statutes when the statutory language is unclear or ambiguous, or leaves the matter in question undetermined. These presumptions give effect to a principle that rights and liberties recognised by the common law (as the judges have developed it) are not to be overridden as a by-product of statutory language that is not clearly directed to bringing about that result. Parliament, it is supposed, must have intended to leave such rights and liberties intact unless a contrary intention is clearly expressed or is a *necessary* (not merely a 'possible' or 'reasonable') implication of the terms of the statute. Likewise, as Purchas LJ observed in *Hill* v. *Chief Constable of South Yorkshire* [1990] 1 WLR 946, 952, a statute that gives rights to interfere with the liberty of the citizen 'ought to be construed strictly against those purporting to exercise those rights'. See now on this matter the dictum of Lord Hoffmann in *ex p Simms* (above) and of Lord Reed in R (*UNISON*) v. *Lord Chancellor* (at pp. 100–101).

This judicial tendency was formerly most evident in that 'particular vigilance' in which lawyers were trained in the field of the protection of property rights (Lord Radcliffe in *Burmah Oil Co Ltd* v. *Lord Advocate* [1965] AC 75, 118): see, for example, *Central Control Board* v. *Cannon Brewery Co Ltd* [1919] AC 744, 752. But the courts have also been able to protect, against indirect or accidental displacement by statute, such rights as personal liberty, freedom of movement, access to the courts, the right to communicate confidentially with a legal adviser under legal professional privilege and the right not to be punished for an act which was not an offence at the time it was done. (See *DPP* v. *Bhagwan* [1972] AC 60 (the right of a British subject to enter the UK); *Waddington* v. *Miah* [1974] 1 WLR 683 (non-liability to retrospective penalty);

R v. *Hallstrom, ex p W* [1986] QB 1090 (liberty of the subject); and *R (Morgan Grenfell & Co Ltd* v. *Special Commissioner of Income Tax* [2002] UKHL 21, [2003] 1 AC 563 (legal professional privilege)).)

However, here, as elsewhere, the judicial record has not been consistent, for the courts have on occasion strained the language of statute in favour of the power-wielding authority so as to restrict the individual's zone of freedom. The following case is an example (and see, too, *R (Haw)* v. *Secretary of State for the Home Department* [2006] EWCA Civ 532, [2006] QB 780).

R v. *Z* [2005] UKHL 35, [2005] 2 AC 645

Section 3 of the Terrorism Act 2000 provides that 'an organisation is pro-scribed if (a) it is listed in Schedule 2 [to the Act] or (b) it operates under the same name as an organisation listed in that Schedule'. The consequences of proscription could hardly be more serious: section 11 of the Act makes it a criminal offence, punishable by up to ten years' imprisonment, to belong or even to profess to belong to a proscribed organisation. A number of defendants were charged with being members of the Real Irish Republican Army ('Real IRA'), contrary to section 11. They argued in their defence that the Real IRA was not proscribed, as it was not listed in Schedule 2 to the Terrorism Act, whereas the 'Irish Republican Army' (IRA) *was* proscribed, as was the 'Continuity Army Council'; the Real IRA, however, was not. The trial judge accepted the defence and acquitted the defendants on that ground. The Attorney General for Northern Ireland referred the matter to the Court of Appeal of Northern Ireland, which ruled, contrary to the trial judge, that a person does commit an offence under section 11 if he or she belongs, or professes to belong, to the Real IRA. On appeal to the House of Lords, their Lordships unanimously agreed with the Court of Appeal. The House of Lords noted that the Real IRA was distinguished from other organisations in other contexts: the Northern Ireland (Sentences) Act 1998 provides for the acceler-ated release of certain prisoners convicted of terrorist offences, but not if the prisoners are supporters of a specified organisation. Four such organisations have been specified by the Secretary of State: the Continuity IRA, the Real IRA, the Irish National Liberation Army and the Loyalist Volunteer Force. In this context, care has been taken to distinguish the IRA from both the Continuity IRA and the Real IRA, as they have been recognised as different for these purposes from the IRA itself. Nonetheless, the House ruled that in the context of the Terrorism Act 2000 the inclusion on the list of proscribed organisations of the IRA was to be read as including the Real IRA. Counsel for the defendants conceded that the Real IRA is a terrorist organisation deserving of proscription but he insisted that the task of the courts is to interpret the provision that Parliament has actually enacted and not (in the words of Lord Bingham at [16]) 'to give effect to an inferred intention of Parliament not fairly to be derived from the language of the statute'. Lord Carswell defended the decision of the House of Lords by referring (at [49]) to the 'mischief' rule of interpretation: namely, that the courts will have regard not only to the language of the statute but also to the mischief that the statute was intended to remedy. Parliament had intended that the Real IRA be proscribed, even if it had not stated so expressly, and the Act should be interpreted accordingly. Is such a method of interpretation appropriate in the criminal context or, indeed, when fundamental rights such as the right to liberty and to security of the person are at stake?

The scope of the criminal law will clearly have a direct impact on the extent of freedom: behaviour that is criminalised is behaviour that we are not at liberty to engage in. Where criminal offences are badly drafted in statute, or where they seem over-inclusive, or where they may involve reverse burdens of proof, the courts have in recent years sought to interpret the offences in the light of the requirements of human rights law, with a view to clarifying exactly what must be proved by the prosecution for a conviction to be secured. Examples include *R v. Keogh* [2007] EWCA Crim 528, [2007] 1 WLR 1500 (concerning certain offences under the Official Secrets Act 1989) and *R v. G* [2009] UKHL 13, [2010] 1 AC 43 (concerning certain offences under the Terrorism Act 2000). Nevertheless, legislation still continues to be interpreted in a manner that broadens criminal activity – in *R v. Choudary* [2016] EWCA Crim 61, [2018] 1 WLR 695, for example, section 12 of the Terrorism Act 2000, which criminalises the 'support' of terrorist offences, the court held that 'support' was not limited to practical or tangible help and extended to include encouragement, emotional support, mental help, or writing or speaking in favour of an activity.

(On statutory interpretation and the protection of liberty, see, further, Sales 'Legislative Intention, Interpretation, and the Principle of Legality' (2019) 40 Statute Law Review 53, and Allan, 'Principle, Practice, and Precedent: Vindicating Justice, According to Law' [2018] CLJ 269.)

11.1.4 Delegated Legislation

The courts do not owe to the subordinate legislation of governmental bodies the deference shown to Acts of Parliament. A power of legislation delegated by Parliament to the executive is taken as not extending to the violation of fundamental rights unless Parliament has clearly provided otherwise. A court may accordingly hold subordinate legislation invalid if, without such parliamentary authorisation, its provisions infringe a fundamental or 'constitutional' right: *Ahmed v. HM Treasury* [2010] UKSC 2, [2010] 2 WLR 378 is an important recent example. *R (Bancoult) v. Secretary of State for Foreign and Commonwealth Affairs (No 2)* [2008] UKHL 61, [2009] 1 AC 453, by contrast, is a significant example going the other way, where the legality of an order in council was upheld despite its grave impact on fundamental rights. Both *Ahmed* and *Bancoult* were considered in Chapter 3 (pp. 200–201).

11.2 Liberty and the HRA

The general scheme of the HRA was outlined in Chapter 5 (pp. 351–353). In addition, the impact of the Act on the sovereignty of Parliament was considered in Chapter 2 (pp. 86–93) and its impact on domestic judicial review law was examined in Chapter 10 (pp. 819–828). What we are concerned with in this section, which should be read in the light of what was said in these previous chapters, is the Act's impact on the protection of liberty under the British constitution. It may be said that the enactment of the HRA confirmed a transformation, which, as we have seen, was already beginning to take place in the common law, from individual liberties to positive rights. As Sedley LJ observed in *Redmond-Bate* v. *DPP* [2000] HRLR 249, 257, the Act has brought about (or has reinforced) a 'constitutional shift' away from the conception of rights as mere residual liberties:

> A liberty, as AP Herbert repeatedly pointed out, is only as real as the laws and bylaws which negate or limit it. A right, by contrast, can be asserted in the face of such restrictions and must be respected, subject to lawful and proper reservations, by the courts.

11.2.1 The Convention Rights

Before we go any further, we need to set out the terms of the convention rights that are incorporated into domestic law under section 1 of the HRA. These are set out in Schedule 1 to the Act, as follows:

Human Rights Act 1998, Schedule 1

Article 2: Right to Life
1. Everyone's right to life shall be protected by law. No one shall be deprived of his life intentionally save in the execution of a sentence of a court following his conviction of a crime for which this penalty is provided by law.
2. Deprivation of life shall not be regarded as inflicted in contravention of this Article when it results from the use of force which is no more than absolutely necessary:

  (a) in defence of any person from unlawful violence;
  (b) in order to effect a lawful arrest or to prevent the escape of a person lawfully detained;
  (c) in action lawfully taken for the purpose of quelling a riot or insurrection.

Article 3: Prohibition of Torture
No one shall be subjected to torture or to inhuman or degrading treatment or punishment.

Article 4: Prohibition of Slavery and Forced Labour
1. No one shall be held in slavery or servitude.
2. No one shall be required to perform forced or compulsory labour.
3. For the purpose of this Article the term 'forced or compulsory labour' shall not include:
    (a) any work required to be done in the ordinary course of detention imposed according to the provisions of Article 5 of this Convention or during conditional release from such detention;
    (b) any service of a military character or, in case of conscientious objectors in countries where they are recognised, service exacted instead of compulsory military service;
    (c) any service exacted in case of an emergency or calamity threatening the life or well-being of the community;
    (d) any work or service which forms part of normal civic obligations.

Article 5: Right to Liberty and Security
1. Everyone has the right to liberty and security of person. No one shall be deprived of his liberty save in the following cases and in accordance with a procedure prescribed by law:
    (a) the lawful detention of a person after conviction by a competent court;
    (b) the lawful arrest or detention of a person for non-compliance with the lawful order of a court or in order to secure the fulfilment of any obligation prescribed by law;
    (c) the lawful arrest or detention of a person effected for the purpose of bringing him before the competent legal authority on reasonable suspicion of having committed an offence or when it is reasonably considered necessary to prevent his committing an offence or fleeing after having done so;
    (d) the detention of a minor by lawful order for the purpose of educational supervision or his lawful detention for the purpose of bringing him before the competent legal authority;
    (e) the lawful detention of persons for the prevention of the spreading of infectious diseases, of persons of unsound mind, alcoholics or drug addicts or vagrants;
    (f) the lawful arrest or detention of a person to prevent his effecting an unauthorised entry into the country or of a person against whom action is being taken with a view to deportation or extradition.
2. Everyone who is arrested shall be informed promptly, in a language which he understands, of the reasons for his arrest and of any charge against him.
3. Everyone arrested or detained in accordance with the provisions of paragraph 1(c) of this Article shall be brought promptly before a judge or other officer authorised by law to exercise judicial power and shall be entitled to trial within a reasonable time or to release pending trial. Release may be conditioned by guarantees to appear for trial.
4. Everyone who is deprived of his liberty by arrest or detention shall be entitled to take proceedings by which the lawfulness of his detention shall be decided speedily by a court and his release ordered if the detention is not lawful.
5. Everyone who has been the victim of arrest or detention in contravention of the provisions of this Article shall have an enforceable right to compensation.

Article 6: Right to a Fair Trial

1. In the determination of his civil rights and obligations or of any criminal charge against him, everyone is entitled to a fair and public hearing within a reasonable time by an independent and impartial tribunal established by law. Judgment shall be pronounced publicly but the press and public may be excluded from all or part of the trial in the interests of morals, public order or national security in a democratic society, where the interests of juveniles or the protection of the private life of the parties so require, or to the extent strictly necessary in the opinion of the court in special circumstances where publicity would prejudice the interests of justice.

2. Everyone charged with a criminal offence shall be presumed innocent until proved guilty according to law.

3. Everyone charged with a criminal offence has the following minimum rights:

   (a) to be informed promptly, in a language which he understands and in detail, of the nature and cause of the accusation against him;

   (b) to have adequate time and facilities for the preparation of his defence;

   (c) to defend himself in person or through legal assistance of his own choosing or, if he has not sufficient means to pay for legal assistance, to be given it free when the interests of justice so require;

   (d) to examine or have examined witnesses against him and to obtain the attendance and examination of witnesses on his behalf under the same conditions as witnesses against him;

   (e) to have the free assistance of an interpreter if he cannot understand or speak the language used in court.

Article 7: No Punishment without Law

1. No one shall be held guilty of any criminal offence on account of any act or omission which did not constitute a criminal offence under national or international law at the time when it was committed. Nor shall a heavier penalty be imposed than the one that was applicable at the time the criminal offence was committed.

2. This Article shall not prejudice the trial and punishment of any person for any act or omission which, at the time when it was committed, was criminal according to the general principles of law recognised by civilised nations.

Article 8: Right to Respect for Private and Family Life

1. Everyone has the right to respect for his private and family life, his home and his correspondence.

2. There shall be no interference by a public authority with the exercise of this right except such as is in accordance with the law and is necessary in a democratic society in the interests of national security, public safety or the economic well-being of the country, for the prevention of disorder or crime, for the protection of health or morals, or for the protection of the rights and freedoms of others.

Article 9: Freedom of Thought, Conscience and Religion

1. Everyone has the right to freedom of thought, conscience and religion; this right includes freedom to change his religion or belief, and freedom, either alone or in community with others and in public or private, to manifest his religion or belief, in worship, teaching, practice and observance.

2. Freedom to manifest one's religion or beliefs shall be subject only to such limitations as are prescribed by law and are necessary in a democratic society in the interests of public safety, for the protection of public order, health or morals, or for the protection of the rights and freedoms of others.

Article 10: Freedom of Expression

1. Everyone has the right to freedom of expression. This right shall include freedom to hold opinions and to receive and impart information and ideas without interference by public authority and regardless of frontiers. This Article shall not prevent States from requiring the licensing of broadcasting, television or cinema enterprises.

2. The exercise of these freedoms, since it carries with it duties and responsibilities, may be subject to such formalities, conditions, restrictions or penalties as are prescribed by law and are necessary in a democratic society, in the interests of national security, territorial integrity or public safety, for the prevention of disorder or crime, for the protection of health or morals, for the protection of the reputation or rights of others, for preventing the disclosure of information received in confidence, or for maintaining the authority and impartiality of the judiciary.

Article 11: Freedom of Assembly and Association

1. Everyone has the right to freedom of peaceful assembly and to freedom of association with others, including the right to form and to join trade unions for the protection of his interests.

2. No restrictions shall be placed on the exercise of these rights other than such as are prescribed by law and are necessary in a democratic society in the interests of national security or public safety, for the prevention of disorder or crime, for the protection of health or morals or for the protection of the rights and freedoms of others. This Article shall not prevent the imposition of lawful restrictions on the exercise of these rights by members of the armed forces, of the police or of the administration of the state.

Article 12: Right to Marry and Found a Family

Men and women of marriageable age have the right to marry and to found a family, according to the national laws governing the exercise of this right.

Article 14: Prohibition on Discrimination

The enjoyment of the rights and freedoms set forth in this Convention shall be secured without discrimination on any ground such as sex, race, colour, language, religion, political or other opinion, national or social origin, association with a national minority, property, birth or other status.

Article 1 of the First Protocol: Protection of Property
Every natural or legal person is entitled to the peaceful enjoyment of his possessions. No one shall be deprived of his possessions except in the public interest and subject to the conditions provided for by law and by the general principles of international law.

The preceding provisions shall not, however, in any way impair the right of a State to enforce such laws as it deems necessary to control the use of property in accordance with the general interest or to secure the payment of taxes or other contributions or penalties.

Article 2 of the First Protocol: Right to Education
No person shall be denied the right to education. In the exercise of any functions which it assumes in relation to education and to teaching, the State shall respect the right of parents to ensure such education and teaching in conformity with their own religious and philosophical convictions.

Article 3 of the First Protocol: Right to Free Elections
The High Contracting Parties undertake to hold free elections at reasonable intervals by secret ballot, under conditions which will ensure the free expression of the opinion of the people in the choice of the legislature.

Article 1 of the Thirteenth Protocol: Abolition of the Death Penalty
The death penalty shall be abolished. No one shall be condemned to such penalty or executed.

11.2.1.1 Absolute and Qualified Rights
The convention rights set out in Schedule 1 to the HRA replicate the corresponding articles of the European Convention in their full extent, including the exceptions and qualifications that are expressed in a number of those articles. Some of the convention rights may be described as absolute, in the sense that they may not in any circumstances be overridden or abridged by the authorities of the state. Among these rights are Article 2, the right to life; Article 3, the right not to be subjected to torture or to inhuman or degrading treatment or punishment; Article 4(1), the right not to be held in slavery or servitude; Article 5(1), the right to liberty and security of person; and Article 7, the right not to be convicted or punished under retroactive criminal law. That said, however, account must always be taken of the terms in which the right is formulated in the article that confers it and, in particular, of any specified

limits of the right, in order to discover its dimensions or scope. For instance, Article 5(1) allows the detention of persons – in accordance with procedures prescribed by law – on six specified grounds. Note also the terms of Articles 2(2) and 7(2). Yet, within their defined limits, such rights may be protected absolutely from restriction.

Article 6, the right to a fair trial, encompasses a number of ancillary rights such as the right to a public hearing and the presumption of innocence in criminal proceedings. While the fundamental right to a fair trial is absolute, the several constituent rights in Article 6 are not and may have to be balanced against wider interests of the community. (See *Brown* v. *Stott* [2003] 1 AC 681, 704, 708, 719, 728, and *O'Halloran and Francis* v. *United Kingdom* [2007] ECHR 15809/02.)

Even if a convention right is expressed in unqualified terms, there is a role for the courts in determining its scope. In respect of Article 3, for instance, it will be for the court to determine whether ill-treatment of an individual attributable to a public authority is of such severity as to be 'inhuman or degrading' (see, e.g., *R (Q)* v. *Secretary of State for the Home Department* [2003] EWCA Civ 364, [2004] QB 36 and see, further, below).

Where *positive* obligations arise by implication from convention articles (on which see below), these are not absolute: they are to be 'interpreted in a way which does not impose an impossible or disproportionate burden on the authorities': *R (Pretty)* v. *Director of Public Prosecutions* [2001] UKHL 61, [2002] 1 AC 800.

Some convention rights are not absolute but, rather, 'qualified', in that they may be restricted by the state on specified grounds. Particular notice should be taken of the qualifications expressed in the second paragraphs of Articles 8–11. These paragraphs allow the exercise of the respective rights and freedoms to be restricted by authorities of the state if three conditions are met: namely, if the restriction is prescribed by law; if it is 'necessary in a democratic society'; and if it serves a certain, prescribed aim or objective, as listed in the respective article. (On the meaning of the phrase 'necessary in a democratic society' and on its connection to notions of proportionality, see Chapter 10.) Each of the paragraphs in question admits, as grounds for restriction of the respective rights, the interest of public safety and the need to protect health or morals or the rights and freedoms of other persons. National security and the prevention of disorder or crime appear among additional grounds of limitation in Articles 8, 10 and 11 (but not in Article 9), while other grounds are specific to a single article: for instance, Article 11(2) allows the exercise of the right to freedom of assembly and association by members of the armed forces, the police or public servants to be restricted by law.

The structure of Articles 8–11 reflects the aim of the convention to strike a just balance between the general interests of a democratic society and the fundamental rights of the individual, but with a particular emphasis on the latter. (See the *Belgian Linguistic Case (No 2)* (1968) 1 EHRR 252; and *Klass*

v. *Germany* (1978) 2 EHRR 214, 237.) Permitted restrictions of convention rights are to be narrowly interpreted (*Sunday Times* v. *United Kingdom* (1979) 2 EHRR 245, para 65). In *Sporrong* v. *Sweden* (1982) 5 EHRR 35, para 69, the European Court said that the search for a fair balance between the demands of the general interest of the community and the individual's fundamental rights 'is inherent in the whole of the Convention'. Accordingly, the above requirements are applicable not only in respect of Articles 8–11 but whenever a restriction of a convention right is sought to be justified.

11.2.1.2 Positive and Negative Obligations

The HRA makes it unlawful for a public authority in the UK to act in a way that is incompatible with a convention right; 'act', for this purpose, includes a failure to act (HRA, section 6(1), (6)). This plainly means that a public authority is under a (negative) obligation not to infringe the right itself, but it may also be bound by a positive duty to take appropriate action to ensure that the convention right is protected from violation, whether by the authority's own agents or by others. Article 14, for instance, provides explicitly that the right not to suffer discrimination (in the enjoyment of convention rights) is to be 'secured'. More generally, the authorities may be obliged to provide 'a regulatory framework of adjudicatory and enforcement machinery in order to protect the rights of the individual' (Butler-Sloss P in *Venables* v. *News Group Newspapers Ltd* [2001] Fam 430, at [25]). Domestic courts, following decisions of the ECtHR, have identified a positive duty arising from Article 2 (the right to life), expressed in *Osman* v. *United Kingdom* (1998) 29 EHRR 245, para 115, as a duty 'not only to refrain from the intentional and unlawful taking of life, but also to take appropriate steps to safeguard the lives of those within [the state's] jurisdiction'. This duty may oblige the authorities to put in place measures to counter threatened criminal acts that put life at risk: see, for instance, *Venables* v. *News Group Newspapers Ltd*, above; *R (A)* v. *Lord Saville of Newdigate* [2001] EWCA Civ 2048, [2002] 1 WLR 1249; and *Re Officer L* [2007] UKHL 36, [2007] 1 WLR 2135. But compare *Van Colle* v. *Chief Constable of Hertfordshire* [2008] UKHL 50, [2009] 1 AC 225, *Mitchell* v. *Glasgow City Council* [2009] UKHL 11, [2009] 1 AC 874 and *Michael* v. *Chief Constable of South Wales Police* [2015] UKSC 2, [2015] 2 WLR 343, considered in Chapter 10. (see Tofaris and Steel, 'Negligence Liability for Omissions and the Police' [2016] 75 CLJ 128.)

Article 2 may also give rise to a 'procedural obligation' to conduct an effective investigation in a case in which death has resulted from neglect, negligence or the use of force in which agents of the state are alleged to have been involved: see, for example, *R (Amin)* v. *Secretary of State for the Home Department* [2003] UKHL 51, [2004] 1 AC 653; *R (Middleton)* v. *West Somerset Coroner* [2004] UKHL 10, [2004] 2 AC 182; *Savage* v. *South Essex Partnership NHS Trust* [2008] UKHL 74, [2009] 1 AC 681. This can even apply to events that took place before the Human Rights Act 1998 came into force if there was a genuine connection between the death and the coming into force of the Act

(*Re Finucane's application for judicial review (Northern Ireland)* [2019] UKSC 7, [2019] 3 All ER 191). In *Gentle* v. *Prime Minister* [2008] UKHL 20, [2008] 1 AC 1356, the House of Lords ruled that the Article 2 procedural obligation did not extend so far as to confer on the mothers of two British soldiers killed in Iraq a right to require the government to establish an independent public inquiry into the circumstances surrounding the invasion of Iraq in 2003. A similar obligation – that is, a duty to investigate – may be founded on Article 3 (the prohibition on torture, degrading and inhuman treatment): see *R (Ali Zaki Mousa)* v. *Secretary of State for Defence* [2011] EWCA 1334. See also the Baha Mousa Inquiry (https://webarchive.nationalarchives.gov.uk /20120215203921/http://www.bahamousainquiry.org/report/index.htm).

The extent to which Article 3 imposes positive obligations of a *substantive* nature was explored by the House of Lords in the following case.

R (Limbuela) v. Secretary of State for the Home Department [2005] UKHL 66, [2006] 1 AC 396

Section 95 of the Immigration and Asylum Act 1999 provides that the Secretary of State may arrange for the provision of a range of support services for asylum-seekers 'who appear to the Secretary of State to be destitute or to be likely to become destitute' within a certain period of time. Section 55 of the Nationality, Immigration and Asylum Act 2002 provides, by way of exception, that the Secretary of State may refuse support services to asylum-seekers whose claims for asylum were not made as soon as reasonably practicable after the person's arrival in the UK. (In practice, this provision has restricted benefits and support services to those asylum-seekers who claimed asylum only at the port of entry: a claim made at any point after the person had passed the point of immigration control was likely to be regarded as having been made too late, unless there were special circumstances: see the opinion of Lord Hope at [39].) Section 55(5) (a) of the 2002 Act provides that: 'This section shall not prevent the exercise of a power by the Secretary of State to the extent necessary for the purpose of avoiding a breach of a person's Convention rights.' This provision needs to be read together with section 6(1) of the HRA, which provides that: 'It is unlawful for a public authority to act in a way which is incompatible with a Convention right.'

Mr Limbuela, an Angolan national, maintained that he arrived in the UK at an unknown airport accompanied by an agent and that on the same day he claimed asylum at the Asylum Screening Unit at Croydon. He was provided with emergency accommodation but it was subsequently decided that he had not claimed asylum as soon as reasonably practicable and he was evicted from his accommodation. He spent two nights sleeping rough, during which time he had no money and no access to food or to washing facilities. After being advised to contact a solicitor, he obtained interim relief and permission to seek judicial review. He argued that his treatment violated his rights under Article 3 (in that he was subjected to inhuman or degrading treatment). The leading speech in a unanimous House of Lords was delivered by Lord Hope:

Lord Hope: ... [A]rticle 3 may be described in general terms as imposing a primarily negative obligation on states to refrain from inflicting serious harm on persons within their jurisdiction. The prohibition is in one sense negative in its effect, as it requires the state – or, in the domestic context, the public authority – to refrain from treatment of the kind it describes. But it may also require the state or the public authority to do something to prevent its deliberate acts which would otherwise be lawful from amounting to ill-treatment of the kind struck at by the article ...

But the European Court has all along recognised that ill-treatment must attain a minimum level of severity if it is to fall within the scope of the expression 'inhuman or degrading treatment or punishment': *Ireland v United Kingdom* (1978) 2 EHRR 25, 80, para 167; *A v United Kingdom* (1998) 27 EHRR 611, 629, para 20; *V v United Kingdom* (1999) 30 EHRR 121, para 71. In *Pretty v United Kingdom* 35 EHRR 1, 33, para 52, the court said:

> 'As regards the types of "treatment" which fall within the scope of article 3 of the Convention, the court's case law refers to "ill-treatment" that attains a minimum level of severity and involves actual bodily injury or intense physical or mental suffering. Where treatment humiliates or debases an individual showing a lack of respect for, or diminishing, his or her human dignity or arouses feelings of fear, anguish or inferiority capable of breaking an individual's moral and physical resistance, it may be characterised as degrading and also fall within the prohibition of article 3. The suffering which flows from naturally occurring illness, physical or mental, may be covered by article 3, where it is, or risks being, exacerbated by treatment, whether flowing from conditions of detention, expulsion or other measures, for which the authorities can be held responsible.'

It has also said that the assessment of this minimum is relative, as it depends on all the circumstances of the case such as the nature and context of the treatment or punishment that is in issue. The fact is that it is impossible by a simple definition to embrace all human conditions that will engage article 3 ...

The first question that needs to be addressed is whether the case engages the express prohibition in article 3. It seems to me that there can only be one answer to this question if the case is one where the Secretary of State has withdrawn support from an asylum-seeker under section 55(1) of the 2002 Act. The decision to withdraw support from someone who would otherwise qualify for support under section 95 of the 1999 Act because he is or is likely to become, within the meaning of that section, destitute is an intentionally inflicted act for which the Secretary of State is directly responsible. He is directly responsible also for all the consequences that flow from it, bearing in mind the nature of the regime which removes from asylum-seekers the ability to fend for themselves by earning money while they remain in that category. They cannot seek employment for at least 12 months, and resort to self-employment too is prohibited. As the Court of Appeal said in *R (Q) v Secretary of State for the Home Department* [2004] QB 36, 69, para 57, the imposition by the legislature of a regime which prohibits asylum-seekers from working and further prohibits the grant to them, when they are destitute, of support amounts to positive action directed against asylum-seekers and not to mere inaction. This constitutes 'treatment' within the meaning of the article ...

It is possible to derive from the cases which are before us some idea of the various factors that will come into play in this assessment: whether the asylum-seeker is male or female, for example, or is elderly or in poor health, the extent to which he or she has explored all avenues of assistance that might be expected to be available and the length of time that has been spent and is likely to be spent without the required means of support. The exposure to the elements that results from rough-sleeping, the risks to health and safety that it gives rise to, the effects of lack of access to toilet and washing facilities and the humiliation and sense of despair that attaches to those who suffer from deprivations of that kind are all relevant . . .

It was submitted for the Secretary of State that rough sleeping of itself could not take a case over the threshold. This submission was based on the decision in *O'Rourke v United Kingdom*, (Application No 39022/97) (unreported) 26 June 2001. In that case the applicant's complaint that his eviction from local authority accommodation in consequence of which he was forced to sleep rough on the streets was a breach of article 3 was held to be inadmissible. The court said that it did not consider that the applicant's suffering following his eviction attained the requisite level to engage article 3, and that even if it had done so the applicant, who was unwilling to accept temporary accommodation and had refused two specific offers of permanent accommodation in the meantime, was largely responsible for the deterioration in his health following his eviction. As Jacob LJ said in the Court of Appeal [2004] QB 1440, 1491, para 145, however, the situation in that case is miles away from that which confronts section 55 asylum-seekers who are not only forced to sleep rough but are not allowed to work to earn money and have no access to financial support by the state. The rough sleeping which they are forced to endure cannot be detached from the degradation and humiliation that results from the circumstances that give rise to it.

As for the final question, the wording of section 55(5)(a) shows that its purpose is to prevent a breach from taking place, not to wait until there is a breach and then address its consequences. A difference of view has been expressed as to whether the responsibility of the state is simply to wait and see what will happen until the threshold is crossed or whether it must take preventative action before that stage is reached. In *R (Q) v Secretary of State for the Home Department* [2004] QB 36 the court said that the fact that there was a real risk that the asylum-seeker would be reduced to the necessary state of degradation did not of itself engage article 3, as section 55(1) required the Secretary of State to decline to provide support unless and until it was clear that charitable support had not been provided and the individual was incapable of fending for himself: p 70, para 63. But it would be necessary for the Secretary of State to provide benefit where the asylum-seeker was so patently vulnerable that to refuse support carried a high risk of an almost immediate breach of article 3: p 71, para 68. In *R (Zardasht) v Secretary of State for the Home Department* [2004] EWHC 91 (Admin) Newman J asked himself whether the evidence showed that the threshold of severity had been reached. In *R (T) v Secretary of State for the Home Department* 7 CCLR 53 the test which was applied both by Maurice Kay J in the Administrative Court and by the Court of Appeal was whether T's condition had reached or was verging on the degree of severity described in *Pretty v United Kingdom* 35 EHRR 1.

> The best guide to the test that is to be applied is, as I have said, to be found in the use of the word 'avoiding' in section 55(5)(a). It may be, of course, that the degree of severity which amounts to a breach of article 3 has already been reached by the time the condition of the asylum-seeker has been drawn to his attention. But it is not necessary for the condition to have reached that stage before the power in section 55(5)(a) is capable of being exercised. It is not just a question of 'wait and see'. The power has been given to enable the Secretary of State to avoid the breach. A state of destitution that qualifies the asylum-seeker for support under section 95 of the 1999 Act will not be enough. But as soon as the asylum-seeker makes it clear that there is an imminent prospect that a breach of the article will occur because the conditions which he or she is having to endure are on the verge of reaching the necessary degree of severity the Secretary of State has the power under section 55(5)(a), and the duty under section 6(1) of the Human Rights Act 1998, to act to avoid it.

Professor Sandra Fredman has written of this case that it shows how in a human rights framework positive duties play a 'pivotal role'. 'The House of Lords in *Limbuela*', she adds, 'has articulated a basic value of our unwritten constitution, namely that the state is responsible for preventing destitution which arises as a consequence of the statutory regime' (see Fredman, 'Human Rights Transformed: Positive Duties and Positive Rights' [2006] *PL* 498, 519–20; see, further, Fredman, *Human Rights Transformed: Positive Rights and Positive Duties* (2008)).

That there are limits, however, to the extent to which the courts will rule that convention rights impose positive obligations on the state is illustrated by *E v. Chief Constable of the Royal Ulster Constabulary* [2008] UKHL 66, [2009] 1 AC 536 and by the tragic case of *N v. Secretary of State for the Home Department* [2005] UKHL 31, [2005] 2 AC 296. N, born in Uganda, sought asylum in the UK. Her claim was refused and the Secretary of State proposed to deport her. She suffered from advanced HIV/AIDS. With medical treatment, her condition had stabilised such that, if the treatment continued, she could live for decades. However, without continuing treatment (principally medication), her prognosis was 'appalling': as Lord Nicholls reported it (at [3]), 'she will suffer ill-health, discomfort, pain and death within a year or two.' As Lord Nicholls went on to say (at [4]): 'The cruel reality is that if [N] returns to Uganda her ability to obtain the necessary medication is problematic. So if she returns to Uganda and cannot obtain the medical assistance she needs to keep her illness under control, her condition will be similar to having a life-support machine switched off.' She argued that, in these circumstances, deporting her to Uganda would be incompatible with her rights under Article 3. The House of Lords unanimously rejected this argument. Lord Nicholls ruled (at [15]-[17]) that 'Article 3 does not require contracting states to undertake the obligation of providing aliens indefinitely with medical treatment lacking in their home countries ... Article 3 cannot be interpreted as requiring contracting states to admit and treat AIDS sufferers from all over the world for the rest of their lives.' Were this an exceptional case, he suggested, 'the pressing humanitarian considerations of her case would prevail' (at [9]) but, alas, it was far from exceptional, the prevalence of AIDS worldwide, and particularly in southern Africa, being 'a present-day human tragedy on an immense scale' (at [9]). (The ECtHR subsequently endorsed the judgment of the House of Lords in this case: *N v. United Kingdom* (2008) 47 EHRR 39.)

11.2.1.3 Scope of Protection

As we have seen, section 6(1) of the HRA provides that 'It is unlawful for a public authority to act in a way which is incompatible with a Convention right'. Section 6(1) does not apply (section 6(2)(a)) if the public authority was compelled to act as it did as a result of primary legislation or (section 6(2)(b)) if it acted so as to give effect to such legislation, *its incompatibility with convention rights notwithstanding*. In this way, section 6(2) is 'intended to preserve the sovereignty of Parliament', as the Law Lords stated in *R v. Secretary of State for Work and Pensions, ex p Hooper* [2005] UKHL 29, [2005] 1 WLR 1681 (at [51], [70], [80], [92], [105]). As we saw in Chapter 2, incompatible primary legislation does not cease to be valid (sections 3(2) (c) and 4(6)).

The Act does not define a public authority or provide a list of persons or bodies that have this status. Rather, it is left to the courts to determine whether any particular person or body qualifies as a public authority. It is plain that, for instance, ministers, government departments, local authorities, the director of public prosecutions, the security services, and police, prison and immigration officers and such like are public authorities for the purposes of the Act, and governmental bodies of these kinds have been characterised by writers and the courts as 'standard' or 'core' public authorities. In *Aston Cantlow Parochial Church Council v. Wallbank* [2003] UKHL 37, [2004] 1 AC 546, Lord Nicholls said that behind the 'instinctive classification' of such organisations 'as bodies whose nature is governmental lie factors such as the possession of special powers, democratic accountability, public funding in whole or in part, an obligation to act only in the public interest, and a statutory constitution' (at [7], acknowledging the valuable article by Dawn Oliver, 'The Frontiers of the State: Public Authorities and Public Functions under the Human Rights Act' [2000] *PL* 476). A body of this class, added Lord Nicholls, 'is required to act compatibly with Convention rights in everything it does'. Such a body is not itself capable of having convention rights or of being the 'victim' of the breach of such a right.

Besides the core public authorities, other bodies are brought within the reach of section 6(1) by section 6(3):

> In this section 'public authority' includes:
>
> (a) a court or tribunal, and
> (b) any person certain of whose functions are functions of a public nature, but does not include either House of Parliament or a person exercising functions in connection with proceedings in Parliament.

Then it is provided in section 6(5):

> In relation to a particular act, a person is not a public authority by virtue only of subsection 3(b) if the nature of the act is private.

Section 6(3)(b) and (5) was elucidated, in the course of proceedings on the Human Rights Bill, with the example of Railtrack (since dissolved), which had statutory public powers and functioned as a safety regulatory authority, but might also carry out private transactions, for instance, in the acquisition or development of property (HL Deb vol. 583, col 796, 24 November 1997). Some of the functions of such 'hybrid' or 'functional' public authorities are of a public nature, but they may also engage in private activity and to that extent will fall outside section 6(1). Being non-governmental organisations they may, however, themselves enjoy convention rights (see Article 34 of the ECHR and section 7(1), (7) of the HRA).

The question whether a body is a hybrid public authority in that certain of its functions are 'of a public nature' (section 6(3)(b)) is one of fact and degree (*Aston Cantlow Parochial Church Council* v. *Wallbank*, above). 'Factors to be taken into account', said Lord Nicholls (at [12]), 'include the extent to which in carrying out the relevant function the body is publicly funded, or is exercising statutory powers, or is taking the place of central government or local authorities, or is providing a public service.'

Whether a body is a hybrid public authority has proved to be a particularly difficult issue in the context of the provision of residential accommodation. Where an individual falls within the scope of section 21 of the National Assistance Act 1948 – one of the pillars of the welfare state – a local authority becomes liable to make arrangements for their residential accommodation (typically in a care home or a nursing home). Frequently, a local authority will contract out the actual provision of such accommodation. In *YL* v. *Birmingham City Council* [2007] UKHL 27, [2008] 1 AC 95, the House of Lords ruled by the narrowest of margins that, in such circumstances, the company or body providing the accommodation is not a hybrid public authority within the meaning of section 6(3)(b). If the local authority had itself provided the accommodation, it would have been bound by the HRA to ensure that its decisions respected the convention rights of the residents. But this fact did not mean, in the view of the majority, that an otherwise private company or body, to whom this function was contracted out, should be likewise bound. On the facts of *YL*, the majority ruled, while the residents retained convention rights enforceable against the local authority, their legal remedies against the provider of the accommodation lay in the private law of contract. Lords Scott, Mance and Neuberger constituted the majority; Lord Bingham and Lady Hale dissented. The decision was widely criticised (see, e.g., Elliott [2007] *CLJ* 485; and Williams [2008] *EHRLR* 524) and, at least as far as residential accommodation is concerned, the result in *YL* has been overturned by legislation: section 145 of the Health and Social Care Act 2008 (and see, further, *R (Weaver)* v. *London and Quadrant Housing Trust* [2009] EWCA Civ 587, [2010] 1 WLR 363). However, other than in this context, it may be argued that the restrictive approach favoured by the majority in *YL* may continue to apply.

Even before the decision of the House of Lords in *YL*, the restrictive approach taken in the case law had been strongly criticised by legal commentators: see Craig (2002) 118 *LQR* 551; Sunkin [2004] *PL* 643; for an alternative view, see Oliver [2004] *PL* 329. Parliament's Joint Committee on Human Rights has also voiced powerful criticisms of the courts' case law on this matter: see its *9th Report of 2006–07*, HL 77, HC 410.

While neither house of the UK Parliament is a public authority for the purposes of section 6 of the HRA (see section 6(3)), the Scottish Parliament and the Scottish ministers have no power to act incompatibly with the convention rights (Scotland Act 1998, sections 29(2)(d) and 57(2)). The devolved institutions in Wales and Northern Ireland are likewise core public authorities.

Section 7 of the HRA provides the avenues of redress for persons who claim that their convention rights have been infringed by a public authority:

> 7(1) A person who claims that a public authority has acted (or proposes to act) in a way which is made unlawful by section 6(1) may:
> (a) bring proceedings against the authority under this Act in the appropriate court or tribunal, or
> (b) rely on the Convention right or rights concerned in any legal proceedings, but only if he is (or would be) a victim of the unlawful act.

The concept of a 'victim' is adopted from the ECHR (Article 34) and its jurisprudence: a person is a victim of an unlawful act for the purposes of section 7 only if he or she would have standing to bring proceedings in the ECtHR as a victim of an alleged violation of the convention (section 7(7)). While a non-governmental organisation or a group or association of individuals may qualify as a victim, this will be so only if its own rights have been infringed by the unlawful act and it is not acting in the interests of its members or others who may be affected – unless persons whose rights have been infringed have specifically authorised it to act as their representative.

A victim need not have suffered actual detriment: a person who is a 'potential' victim as being at particular risk of a violation of his or her convention right may have standing. For instance, a pupil at a school that practised corporal punishment could be a victim of inhuman treatment contrary to Article 3 of the Convention even though he or she had not as yet been punished in this way. (See *Campbell and Cosans* v. *United Kingdom* (1982) 4 EHRR 293.)

In reliance on section 7, the victim of an alleged violation of a convention right may, according to the circumstances, bring civil proceedings, or a claim for judicial review, or raise the question of violation by way of defence to civil or criminal proceedings brought by a public authority. It is provided by section 8 that a court or tribunal which finds the act of a public authority to be unlawful under section 6(1) may grant whatever relief or remedy within its powers that it considers 'just and appropriate', and, in particular, may award damages if satisfied that that is necessary, in all the circumstances of the case (including any other relief or remedy granted), 'to afford just satisfaction' to the victim. In deciding on damages, the court must take into account the principles applied by the ECtHR in awarding compensation. The principles to be applied in the award of damages under section 8 are considered by Lord Millett in *Cullen* v. *Chief Constable of the Royal Ulster Constabulary* [2003] UKHL 39, [2003] 1 WLR 1763, at [75]-[84] and, in relation to a violation of Article 6 (the right to a fair trial), by Lord Bingham in *R (Greenfield)* v. *Secretary of State for the Home Department* [2005] UKHL 14, [2005] 1 WLR 673, at [7]-[19]. See, further, Law Commission No 266, *Damages under the Human Rights Act 1998* (Cm 4853/2000); Law Commission, *Remedies Against Public Bodies: A Scoping Report*, Clayton [2005] *PL* 429; Varuhas, 'A Tort-Based Approach to Damages under the Human Rights Act 1998' (2009) 72 MLR 750.

It is expressly provided that courts and tribunals are public authorities for the purposes of the HRA (section 6(3)(a)). Accordingly a court cannot lawfully give a judgment or make any order which is incompatible with convention rights. It might seem to follow that the courts must, in any legal proceedings, protect the convention rights of an individual party to the proceedings from infringement, whether by the action of a public authority or by that of a private person. In this respect, the convention rights would have a *horizontal* effectiveness in proceedings between private persons as well as being *vertically* effective against public authorities. The argument for horizontal effect also finds some support in the interpretative obligation, placed on the courts by section 3 of the Act, which is applicable to all legislation, even in cases involving private persons only (as in *Ghaidan* v. *Godin-Mendoza* [2004] UKHL 30, [2004] 2 AC 557: see Chapter 2). (For a period, the question of horizontality was strongly contested: see Wade [1998] *EHRLR* 520; Hunt

[1998] *PL* 423; Buxton, (2000) 116 *LQR* 48; Wade (2000) 116 *LQR* 217; Bamforth (2001) 117 *LQR* 34.)

In *Venables* v. *News Group Newspapers Ltd* [2001] Fam 430, Butler-Sloss P expressed the view (at [25]-[27], [111]), that while the courts have a positive obligation to protect the convention rights of the individual and must apply the convention principles to existing causes of action in private law cases, that obligation 'does not ... encompass the creation of a free-standing cause of action based directly upon the articles of the Convention'. While this view is compelling, the courts have given effect to convention rights in disputes between individuals by 'absorbing' such rights into causes of action that already exist. In particular, the action for breach of confidence has been developed by the courts so as to give greater effect to the convention right to personal privacy (Article 8) than was formerly the case in our domestic law. The leading authority is *Campbell* v. *Mirror Group Newspapers* [2004] UKHL 22, [2004] 2 AC 457, which has been considered and applied in numerous instances since, the following being prominent examples: *Douglas* v. *Hello!* [2005] EWCA Civ 595, [2006] QB 125; *Murray* v. *Express Newspapers* [2008] EWCA Civ 446, [2009] Ch. 481. As may be imagined, elements of the media have been vocal in their disapproval of this extension of privacy rights, arguing that their rights to freedom of expression have been accorded insufficient weight: see, further, below, pp. 927–928.

11.2.1.4 Strasbourg Case Law and the UK Courts: The *Ullah* Principle

Section 2 of the HRA provides that our courts (and tribunals) 'must take into account' relevant decisions of the ECtHR when determining an issue in relation to a convention right. There is no statutory obligation on our courts to *follow* the ECtHR's case law: the obligation is to take it into account. However, in *R (Ullah)* v. *Special Adjudicator* [2004] UKHL 26, [2004] 2 AC 323, the House of Lords ruled (at [20], per Lord Bingham) that domestic courts 'should, in the absence of some special circumstances, follow any clear and constant jurisprudence of the Strasbourg court ... The duty of national courts is to keep pace with the Strasbourg jurisprudence as it evolves over time: no more, but certainly no less.' Two reasons were offered in support of this considerable tightening of the provision in section 2: first, the ECtHR has the unique authority to expound the correct interpretation of the convention and, second, section 6(3) of the HRA (as we have just seen) includes domestic courts within the notion of 'public authorities'.

The *Ullah* principle has been cited with approval in numerous cases since – for example, *R (Animal Defenders International)* v. *Secretary of State for Culture, Media and Sport* [2008] UKHL 15, [2008] 1 AC 1312 – and has been followed in key cases even when, in doing so, the House of Lords has been required to depart from its earlier case law. The most notable example of this came in *Secretary of State for the Home Department* v. *AF* [2009] UKHL 28, [2010] 2 AC 269. *AF* is the leading case on the fairness of legal proceedings involving the use of a 'special advocate'. A special advocate is a lawyer appointed from a list maintained by the Attorney General in cases in which the government asserts that information cannot be disclosed in the ordinary way to a party in legal proceedings because of the sensitivity (for reasons of national security) of the material in issue. In such circumstances a security-cleared special advocate will be appointed to 'represent' the individual, although the relationship between the special advocate and the individual is very different from the usual relationship between a lawyer and his or her client. The sensitive (or 'closed') material will be served only on the special advocate, and once it has been served there can generally be no further communication between the special advocate and the individual concerned. Special advocates and 'closed material proceedings' are now used in a wide variety of legal proceedings in cases concerned with national security, including cases concerned with asset-freezing and associated financial restrictions (*Bank Mellat* v. *HM Treasury* [2010] EWCA Civ 483, [2010] 3 WLR 1090), employment law (*Tariq* v. *Home Office* [2010] EWCA Civ 462, [2010] ICR 1034), the Parole Board (*Roberts* v. *Parole Board* [2005] UKHL 45, [2005] 2 AC 738) and Terrorism Prevention and Investigation Measures (TPIMs), which replaced control orders (the subject of *AF*, for example; see, further on control orders, below, pp. 947–949). They were, controversially, expanded to include any civil law proceedings under the provisions of the Justice and Security Act 2013 where national security issues were engaged. However, they cannot be used in relation to a 'criminal cause or matter' and this includes the judicial review of a decision not to prosecute for misconduct in a public office as regards potential complicity in the rendition of terrorist suspects (*R (Belhaj)* v. *Director of Public Prosecutions* (1) [2018] UKSC 33, [2018] 3 WLR 435).

In *Secretary of State for the Home Department* v. *MB* [2007] UKHL 46, [2008] AC 440, the House of Lords had ruled that, in the context of control orders, the use of special advocates and closed material procedure was compatible with the right to a fair trial in Article 6 of the ECHR unless, looking at the process as a whole, the procedure involved significant injustice to the individual concerned. (This was the majority's view: Lord Hoffmann dissented, ruling that the use of closed material would always be fair as long as a special advocate were appointed.) The test set down by the majority in *MB* was so vague that it proved impossible for the lower courts to apply consistently and the matter returned to the House of Lords for a fresh ruling: this is *AF*. One week before oral argument in *AF*, the ECtHR decided *A* v. *United Kingdom* (2009) 49 EHRR 29. One of the issues for the ECtHR in that case was whether hearings before the Special Immigration Appeals Commission concerning an individual's certification as a 'suspected international terrorist' were fair under Article 5(4) of the ECHR. Such hearings included the use of closed material and special advocates.

In *AF*, a panel of nine Law Lords unanimously ruled that there were no material differences as far as fairness of procedure is concerned between this regime and that of control orders. Lord Phillips ruled that *A* v. *United Kingdom* 'establishes that the [individual] must be given sufficient information about the allegations against him to enable him to give effective instructions in relation to those allegations. Provided that this requirement is satisfied there can be a fair trial notwithstanding that the [individual] is not provided with the detail or the sources of the evidence forming the basis of the allegations' (*AF*, at [59]). The national security context can reduce the information given to the individual but *A* v. *United Kingdom* makes it clear that 'non-disclosure cannot go so far as to deny a party knowledge of the essence of the case against him, at least where he is at risk of consequences as severe as those normally imposed under a control order' (at [65]). While some of their Lordships welcomed this (most notably Lord Scott, with Lord Hope in support) at least one other strongly lamented it (Lord Hoffmann). All were agreed that they were effectively bound by *A* v. *United Kingdom* – a clear, recent and unanimous verdict of the Grand Chamber, after all. Lord Carswell stated (at [108]) that: 'Whatever latitude [the] formulation [in section 2 of the HRA] may permit, the authority of a considered statement of the Grand Chamber is such that our courts have no option but to accept and apply it.'

It is clear that there are important differences between *MB* and *AF*. The latter decision requires significantly more by way of disclosure in some cases. In a series of decisions following their Lordships' ruling in *AF*, the Home Secretary felt compelled to discharge a number of individuals from control orders because, in his view, it would be unsafe to disclose in open court some of the material on which the government was relying as justification for the control order. Tension was initially resolved through the introduction of 'gisting'. When the government relies on secret evidence, it must ensure that the individual is given the 'gist' of the case against him. The gist should be sufficient to ensure that the individual is able to instruct the special advocate to act on his behalf. Despite this resolution, issues still remain as to whether the UK courts were ensuring that gisting did indeed satisfy the requirements of Article 6 ECHR, particularly given that the information required was on a sliding scale, more being required for decisions concerning detention and less required for other legal decisions. In *Home Office* v. *Tariq* [2011] UKSC 35, [2012] 1 AC 452, the Supreme Court concluded that less information was required in an employment law decision, where Tariq had argued that he had unfairly had his security clearance removed, and been suspended from his work as an immigration officer, after a family member had been arrested with regard to a suspected terrorist investigation. The 'sliding scale' of gisting was eventually approved by the Strasbourg court: *Tariq* v. *United Kingdom* (Application nos 4658/11 and 3960/12).

A quite different attitude towards Strasbourg authority was shown by the Supreme Court in *R* v. *Horncastle* [2009] UKSC 14, [2010] 2 WLR 47 (decided by a panel of seven justices). In *Al-Khawaja* v. *United Kingdom* (2009) 49 EHRR 1, a chamber of the ECtHR ruled that Article 6 is breached where a statement by a person who had not himself or herself been called as a witness is admitted as evidence in a criminal trial. In this ruling, the chamber relied on the long-established Strasbourg rule that proceeding in this way will violate Article 6 where the statement admitted is the 'sole or decisive' evidence against the defendant (see *Doorson* v. *Netherlands* (1996) 22 EHRR 330). The UK requested that the chamber's decision in *Al-Khawaja* be referred to the Grand Chamber. The Supreme Court was referred to *AF* (above), where, in Lord Phillips' words in *Horncastle*, the House of Lords had considered itself 'bound to apply a clear statement of principle by the Grand Chamber in respect of the precise issue that was before' it. Horncastle's counsel invited the Supreme Court to adopt this approach, but the court declined to do so. Lord Phillips stated (at [11]) that:

> The requirement [in section 2 of the HRA] to 'take into account' the Strasbourg jurisprudence will normally result in this court applying principles that are clearly established by the Strasbourg court. There will, however, be rare occasions where this court has concerns as to whether a decision of the Strasbourg court sufficiently appreciates or accommodates particular aspects of our domestic process. In such circumstances it is open to this court to decline to follow the Strasbourg decision, giving reasons for adopting this course.

This is what the Supreme Court did in this case, giving seventy pages of reasoned analysis as to why, in its view, the common law as supplemented with various statutory provisions (especially the Criminal Justice Act 2003 and the Criminal Evidence (Witness Anonymity) Act 2008) achieved a better balance between the interests of the accused and any countervailing public interest than would a blanket reliance on the Strasbourg 'sole and decisive' test. Much of the Supreme Court's seventy pages was clearly directed at the Grand Chamber. In its decision in *Al-Khawaja* v. *United Kingdom* [2011] ECHR 26766/05, the Grand Chamber took account of the concerns expressed by the Supreme Court. It recognized that Article 6 was breached when a conviction is based 'solely or to a decisive degree on depositions that have been made by a person whom the accused has had no opportunity to examine or have examined', while also recognizing that special circumstances may mean that Article 6 is not breached. In particular, the Grand Chamber recognized the conviction may be possible if a witness would not appear in person due to fear of intimidation, or where there were counterbalancing factors that would ensure that the rights of defence found under Article 6 ECHR would be protected.

In a similar manner, the Court of Appeal refused to follow the decision of the Grand Chamber in *Vinter* v. *UK* [2013] ECHR 6606/09 concerning the compatibility of the UK's life sentence regime with Article 3 ECHR. Although life sentences are not, per se, contrary to Article 3, any life sentence must include the possibility of release, with a possibility of review to determine whether those serving a life sentence should be released. The Grand Chamber concluded that there was insufficient clarity as to the prospect of review and release. In *Attorney Generals Reference (No 60 of 2103), R v. McLoughlin; R v. Newell* [2014] EWCA Crim 188, [2014] 3 All ER 73, the Court of Appeal reached the opposite conclusion. The court concluded that the Lifer Manual, which regulated the conditions of those serving life sentences, was sufficiently clear and did provide the requisite real hope and possibility of release to comply with Article 3 ECHR. This was particularly true as the Manual, although setting out a policy, was not able to fetter the decision of the Secretary of State and any decision of the Secretary of State would be subject to judicial review requiring the Secretary of State, inter alia, to act in a manner compatible with convention rights when applying this policy. The issue returned to the European Court of Human Rights in *Hutchinson* v. *UK* [2015] ECHR 57592/08, where the court took account of the issues raised by the Court of Appeal in response to *Vinter* and concluded that UK law did comply with convention rights.

Recognising this, the Supreme Court has now offered a fresh articulation of the *Ullah* principle, in which it appears in a more qualified form, as follows:

Manchester City Council v Pinnock [2010] UKSC 45, [2010] 2 WLR 1441 (at [48]; emphasis added)

This court is not bound to follow every decision of the European Court [of Human Rights]. Not only would it be impractical to do so: it would sometimes be inappropriate, as it would destroy the ability of the court to engage in the constructive dialogue with the European court which is of value to the development of Convention law: see, eg, *R v Horncastle*. Of course, we should usually follow a clear and constant line of decisions by the European court: *Ullah*. But we are not actually bound to do so or (in theory, at least) to follow a decision of the Grand Chamber ... Section 2 of the 1998 Act requires our courts to 'take into account' European court decisions, not necessarily to follow them. Where, however, there is a clear and constant line of decisions *whose effect is not inconsistent with some fundamental substantive or procedural aspect of our law, and whose reasoning does not appear to overlook or misunderstand some argument or point of principle,* we consider that it would be wrong for this court not to follow that line.

In *Moohan* v. *Lord Advocate*, Lord Wilson provided a timeline of the weakening of the *Ullah* principle [104], prior to summarizing the current law as follows (at [105]) which explains both that the ECHR should not be considered as a ceiling, as well as not a floor of human rights protections:

The effect of the above is that protracted consideration over the last six years has led this court substantially to modify the *Ullah* principle. The present case does not require further consideration of the current status of Lord Bingham's opinion that our courts must 'certainly

> [do] no less' than to keep pace with the jurisprudence of the ECtHR. For present purposes the relevant part of his opinion was we must do 'no more', or, as Lord Brown at one time considered, 'certainly [do] no more', than to keep pace with it. At any rate where there is no directly relevant decision of the ECtHR with which it would be possible (even if appropriate) to keep pace, we can and must do more. We must determine for ourselves the existence or otherwise of an alleged convention right. And, in doing so, we must take account of all indirectly relevant decisions of the ECtHR and, in particular, of such principles underlying them as might, whether as currently expressed or as subject to the natural development apt to a living instrument, inform our determination.

(See, further, Lord Hoffmann, 'The Universality of Human Rights' (2009) 125 *LQR* 416; Baroness Hale, '*Argentoratum Locutum*: Is Strasbourg or the Supreme Court Supreme?' (2012) 12 HRLR 65; Lord Irvine of Lairg, 'A British Interpretation of Convention Rights' [2012] PL 237; Sales, 'Strasbourg Jurisprudence and the Human Rights Act: A Response to Lord Irvine' [2012] PL 253; Fenwick and Masterman, 'The Conservative Project to "Break the Link" Between British Courts and Strasbourg": Rhetoric or Reality?' (2017) MLR 1111.)

11.2.1.5 The Future of the HRA

At the 2010 general election, all three of the main political parties in the UK were pledged to repeal the HRA and to replace it with a British Bill of Rights. The Liberal Democrats have long wanted to see a bill of rights as part of a written constitution for the UK. The Labour and Conservative parties shared a concern that the courts had gone too far in protecting individuals' rights under the HRA and had afforded too little weight to individuals' responsibilities and to the broader public interest. Among the contexts in which this concern was most keenly felt in government was that of counter-terrorism, where decisions such as *AF* (above) were regarded as getting the balance wrong between rights on the one hand and national security on the other. In 2009–10 the Conservative Party's appetite for reform of the HRA seemed considerably greater than did that of the Labour Party, and the Conservative critique of the Act was more sharply focused than was Labour's. As the Constitution Unit stated in February 2010, 'there can be no doubt of the Conservative commitment to repeal the Human Rights Act' (Constitution Unit, *The Conservative Agenda for Constitutional Reform* (2010), p. 63). David Cameron pledged to repeal the HRA in a series of speeches delivered as leader of the opposition in 2006–09, as did his shadow justice secretaries. The Conservatives were concerned not only about the balance struck between rights and responsibilities (in terrorism cases, but also in asylum cases and elsewhere) but also about the extent to which the HRA required British courts to enforce norms of European law, a variant of Conservative Party 'Euroscepticism' informing the argument. Much of the Conservatives' ire seems to have been directed at section 2, as interpreted in *Ullah*. Another element of the Conservatives' position was that traditional English (British?) liberties such as the right to trial by jury should be more visibly protected in a British Bill of Rights.

Human rights lawyers, by contrast, are keen to preserve the HRA and are concerned that any attempt to repeal it and to replace it with a British Bill of Rights would dilute rather than strengthen the protection that our law affords to fundamental rights.

An independent commission on a UK Bill of Rights was established by the Coalition Government in March 2011. The commission failed to reach a consensus, with views ranging from those wishing to withdraw from, or renegotiate, the UK's membership of the ECHR to those who opposed a British Bill of Rights precisely because its enactment might be used as a means of weakening rights protections by the potential withdrawal from the ECHR. There have been consistent pledges by the Conservative Party to amend the Human Rights Act 1998. In the manifesto for the 2015 general election, the Conservative Party pledged to 'scrap the Human Rights Act', again suggesting that it should be replaced with a British Bill of Rights. In addition to the earlier concerns as to terrorism and asylum cases, there were concerns as to the application of convention rights to the military, particularly when carrying out military activities abroad, as well as the 'living tree' approach to interpretation adopted by the European Court of Human Rights. In the 2017 general election, the Conservative Party manifesto placed the reform of the Human Rights Act on hold until after Brexit had been completed. In 2019, the issue of the Human Rights Act resurfaced. The manifesto included a pledge – which was included in the Queen's Speech of December 2019 – to establish a constitution, democracy and rights commission. The task of this commission is to examine 'broader aspects of our Constitution' post-Brexit – including the protection of human rights. There was a promise to 'update the Human Rights Act' to 'ensure there is a proper balance between the rights of individuals, our vital national security and effective government' (p. 48). At the time of writing, no commission had been appointed.

11.2.2 Convention Rights and National Security: A Case Study

Probably the greatest single challenge that the new regime of convention rights has had to face thus far is that posed by the threat of terrorism and national and international security. The terrorist outrages of 11 September 2001, universally referred to as '9/11', in the USA and the wars and the accumulation of 'emergency powers' that have followed have generated a substantial volume of both legislation and case law in numerous jurisdictions, the UK included. The British Government's principal response to 9/11 was to introduce the legislation that (very quickly) became the Anti-Terrorism, Crime and Security Act 2001. Bearing in mind that the UK already possessed one of the most comprehensive counterterrorism statutes in Europe (the Terrorism Act 2000, weighing in at 131 sections and 16 schedules – a total of 155 pages), the 2001 Act, with its 129 sections and 8 schedules (coming to 118 pages) was a significant addition, to say the least. But it is not only a question of quantity. The range of powers contained in the 2001 Act is extraordinary: it includes provisions on terrorist property and freezing orders, on disclosure of information, on racial hatred and religiously aggravated offences, on weapons of mass destruction, on the security of pathogens and toxins, on security in the nuclear and aviation industries, on police powers of fingerprinting, personal search and seizure, on the retention of communications data and on bribery and corruption, as well as other matters. Of these, the provisions with regard to the disclosure and retention of information were particularly controversial (see Tomkins [2002] *PL* 205, 209).

Most controversial of all the powers contained in the 2001 Act were the powers in Part 4 of the Act regarding the indefinite detention without trial of persons suspected to be international terrorists – a form, for all the government's protestations to the contrary, of internment. Certain aspects of these Part 4 powers were found by the House of Lords to be unlawful (see *A v. Secretary of State for the Home Department* [2004] UKHL 56, [2005] 2 AC 68, considered in detail below) and they were subsequently abolished and replaced with new powers to impose 'control orders': see the Prevention of Terrorism Act 2005 (see below). However, remaining aspects of the Anti-Terrorism, Crime and Security Act 2001 remain in force.

In 2006, Parliament added the Terrorism Act 2006 to its vast range of counterterrorism measures. Among other matters, this Act created new criminal offences of encouraging or glorifying terrorism (section 1) and extended the maximum period for which persons arrested on suspicion of terrorist offences may be detained from seven to twenty-eight days (section 23).

Laws such as these pose a great variety of challenges for the protection of convention rights. Since the time of Thomas Hobbes, if not before, all governments have regarded their first responsibility to be to secure, as best they can, peace and order within the jurisdiction (see Hobbes, *Leviathan* (1651), ch. 17). If a government were to fail adequately to secure the realm against internal or external threats to national security, it would be unlikely to remain in office for long. In the face of what we are led to believe about the nature and range of current threats, such onerous responsibilities should be taken neither lightly nor for granted. The problem, however, is that it is principally the government that leads us to believe that the threats are severe, as it is the government that has ownership of the country's secret intelligence assessments. Suspicions are bound to arise that the government is at least sometimes tempted to exaggerate the nature or the level of the threat so as to obtain greater powers for itself or so that it can argue that greater resources need to be devoted to seeking to counter the threat. The 'fiasco' (as Lord Hoffmann described it in *A v. Home Secretary* (above, at [94])) over non-existent Iraqi weapons of mass destruction in the months leading up to the invasion of March 2003 did nothing to alleviate such suspicions. (See, further, the *Review of Intelligence on Weapons of Mass Destruction* (chaired by Lord Butler), HC 898 of 2003–04.)

The undoubted importance of security notwithstanding, however, measures taken in its name clearly engage a number of convention rights: the prohibition on torture (Article 3), the right to liberty (Article 5), the right to a fair trial (Article 6), the right to privacy (Article 8), freedom of expression (Article 10) and freedom of assembly (Article 11), among others, are all affected by the measures contained in Britain's counterterrorism legislation.

11.2.2.1 National Security Before the HRA

Part of the reason why this poses such a challenge to the regime of convention rights is because courts in the UK have traditionally been notoriously weak in upholding civil liberties in the face of government claims to national security. This is a story that spans almost a century of case law, going all the way back to the First World War. An overview of six leading cases follows, by way of background to the case law that has developed, since 9/11, under the HRA.

R v. Halliday, ex p Zadig [1917] AC 260

Section 1 of the Defence of the Realm Act 1914 conferred on the government the power 'during the continuance of the present war to issue regulations for securing the public safety and the defence of the realm'. Regulation 14B of the Defence of the Realm (Consolidation) Regulations, made under the authority of section 1 of the 1914 Act, provided that 'where . . . it appears to the Secretary of State that for securing the public safety or the defence of the realm it is expedient in view of the hostile origin or associations of any person that he shall be subjected to such obligations and restrictions as are hereafter mentioned, the Secretary of State may by order require that person . . . to be interned in such place as may be specified'. The Secretary of State ordered the internment of Mr Arthur Zadig, apparently on the sole ground that Zadig had been born in Germany (he had lived in Britain for more than twenty years and had become naturalised in 1905). Zadig was charged with no criminal offence. He challenged the legality of his internment and of Regulation 14B on which it was based. Altogether thirteen judges heard Zadig's case: five in the Divisional Court, three in the Court of Appeal and five in the House of Lords. Of these, twelve held for the government that both Zadig's internment and Regulation 14B were lawful. The one dissentient was Lord Shaw in the House of Lords, whose opinion stands as one of the true (and rare) landmarks of the judicial protection of liberty in Britain in the face of claims to national security. In response to Zadig's various and detailed legal arguments the House of Lords was dismissive in the extreme. Lord Finlay LC ruled, for example, that 'It appears to me to be a sufficient answer' to his arguments 'that it may be necessary in a time of great public danger to entrust great powers to His Majesty in Council' (at 268). His internment was described as 'not punitive but precautionary' (at 269) and as 'expedient' in the 'interests of the nation' (at

270). Dissenting, Lord Shaw described Zadig's internment as 'a violent exercise of arbitrary power' (at 277). Noting that the Act of 1914 said nothing about persons of hostile origins and nothing about internment, his Llordship ruled that Regulation 14B could not be justified with reference to the Defence of the Realm Act and was ultra vires. (For commentary on the case, see Foxton, 'R v. Halliday, ex p Zadig in Retrospect' (2003) 119 *LQR* 435; Ewing and Gearty, *The Struggle for Civil Liberties: Political Freedom and the Rule of Law in Britain 1914–1945* (2000), ch. 2.)

Liversidge v. Anderson [1942] AC 206

In many ways, this case is the Second World War equivalent of *ex p Zadig*. Like *Zadig*, it is concerned with internment and again like *Zadig*, *Liversidge* v. *Anderson* saw a strongly worded lone dissent – this time from Lord Atkin (who was, as Atkin J, one of the twelve judges who ruled in the government's favour in *ex p Zadig*). In the years that have passed since the Second World War, it is Lord Atkin's dissent that has been championed. But this is unfair: of the two, it is Lord Shaw's dissent in *ex p Zadig* that ought to be held up as the leading example of judicial liberalism in the face of government claims to national security (a point made strongly both by Foxton and by Ewing and Gearty, above). That said, the point made by Lord Atkin that the majority of their Lordships had shown themselves to be 'more executive minded than the executive' (at 244) is deservedly often repeated in commentaries on the case law considered here. There are a number of differences between *Zadig* and *Liversidge* v. *Anderson*. In the latter case, the relevant statute, section 1 of the Emergency Powers (Defence) Act 1939, expressly provided that regulations made by the Crown under that section could include regulations 'for the detention of persons whose detention appears to the Secretary of State to be expedient in the interests of the ... defence of the realm' (section 1(2)). The relevant regulation was Regulation 18B of the Defence (General) Regulations 1939, which provided that: 'If the Secretary of State has reasonable cause to believe any person to be of hostile origin or associations ... he may make an order against that person directing that he be detained.' Liversidge was detained on an order signed by Sir John Anderson, the Home Secretary. He sought a declaration that his detention was unlawful and damages for false imprisonment. Argument in the House of Lords focused on the words 'If the Secretary of State has reasonable cause to believe' in Regulation 18B. The majority of their Lordships ruled that the courts could not inquire whether in fact the Secretary of State had reasonable grounds for his belief that it was expedient to order a person's detention. Viscount Maugham proclaimed that: 'To my mind this is so clearly a matter for executive discretion and nothing else that I cannot myself believe that those responsible for the [regulation] could have contemplated for a moment the possibility of the action of the Secretary of State being subject to the discussion, criticism and control of a judge in a court of law' (at 220). In the exercise of this power, the Secretary of State was 'answerable to Parliament', not to the courts (at 222). Lord Atkin complained that the view of the majority had altered the meaning of the words in Regulation 18B from 'If the Secretary of State has reasonable cause to believe' to 'If the Secretary of State *thinks* he has reasonable cause to believe' (at 245). He ruled that this was not what the regulation meant and, applying this ruling to the facts of *Liversidge*, he held that the Secretary of State did not have reasonable cause to believe that it was expedient to detain him. (In the companion case of *Greene* v. *Secretary of State for Home Affairs* [1942] AC 284, decided by the House of Lords on the same day as *Liversidge* v. *Anderson*, Lord Atkin ruled that, on the facts of that case, the Secretary of State did have reasonable cause to believe that Greene's detention was expedient within the terms of Regulation 18B; for a detailed analysis, see Simpson, *In the Highest Degree Odious: Detention without Trial in Wartime Britain* (1992); and see, further, Ewing and Gearty, The *Struggle for Civil Liberties: Political Freedom and the Rule of Law in Britain 1914–1945* (2000), ch. 8.)

R v. *Secretary of State for Home Affairs, ex p Hosenball* [1977] 1 WLR 766

Mr Hosenball was an American citizen who had been lawfully resident in Britain and Ireland for all his adult life. He was a journalist who worked on *Time Out* and the *London Evening Standard*. In 1976, the Home Secretary informed him that he was to be deported to the USA for the reason that he had 'obtained for publication information harmful to the security of the United Kingdom'. Hosenball asked for further particulars of what was alleged against him but was not provided with any. He was given a hearing before a special panel of three 'advisors'. At the hearing, the advisors had sight of evidence from the security service that Hosenball and his lawyers were not permitted to examine. Neither was the advisors' report to the Home Secretary disclosed to Hosenball. After receiving the report, the Home Secretary renewed the deportation order. The Divisional Court and the Court of Appeal unanimously rejected Hosenball's application for judicial review. Lord Denning MR ruled as follows (at 778): 'if this were a case in which the ordinary rules of natural justice were to be observed, some criticism could be directed upon it . . . But this is no ordinary case. It is a case in which national security is involved: and our history shows that, when the state itself is endangered, our cherished freedoms may have to take second place. Even natural justice itself may suffer a set-back. Time after time Parliament has so enacted and the courts have loyally followed.' After citing *ex p Zadig* and *Liversidge* v. *Anderson*, Lord Denning went on to note that although these were wartime authorities, 'times of peace hold their dangers too'. He concluded as follows (at 782–3): 'Great as is the public interest in the freedom of the individual and the doing of justice to him, nevertheless in the last resort it must take second place to the security of the country itself . . . There is a conflict here between the interests of national security on the one hand and the freedom of the individual on the other. The balance between these two is not for a court of law. It is for the Home

Secretary . . . He is answerable to Parliament for the way [he balances the two] and not to the courts here.' Since the 1970s, Mr Hosenball has continued to enjoy an illustrious and prize-winning career as an investigative journalist, most recently for Reuters. (The advisory panel was replaced in 1997 by the Special Immigration Appeals Commission (SIAC), following the ruling of the ECtHR in *Chahal* v. *United Kingdom* (1996) 23 EHRR 413 that the advisory panel system violated Article 5(4) of the Convention; see, further, on SIAC below.)

Council of Civil Service Unions v. *Minister for the Civil Service* (the 'GCHQ' case) [1985] AC 374

We encountered this important case in the previous chapter, where it was examined for what it states about the grounds of judicial review in domestic law. Here we are concerned with what the case has to say about national security. As will be recalled, the case concerned Mrs Thatcher's decision as Prime Minister and Minister for the Civil Service that the several thousand people working at GCHQ should not be permitted to form or to join trade unions. The Council of Civil Service Unions argued that the decision was procedurally unfair, in that Mrs Thatcher had not consulted them in advance as she was legally required to do. The fact that the unions were successful in this argument notwithstanding, they lost the case, for the reason that Mrs Thatcher claimed in the Court of Appeal and the House of Lords that her decision was taken in the interests of national security. (This argument was not made at earlier stages of the litigation.) Lord Fraser ruled that: 'The question is one of evidence. The decision on whether the requirements of national security outweigh the duty of fairness in any particular case is for the government and not for the courts; the government alone has access to the necessary information, and in any event the judicial process is unsuitable for reaching decisions on national security' (at 402). Lord Diplock expressed the point more pithily: 'national security,' he said, 'is *par excellence* a non-justiciable question' (at 412).

R v. *Secretary of State for the Home Department, ex p Cheblak* [1991] 1 WLR 890

Cheblak, like *Hosenball* (above), concerned the Home Secretary's powers to deport persons from the UK whose deportation is, in his view, 'conducive to the public good for reasons of national security' (Immigration Act 1971, section 3(5)). Abbas Cheblak was a writer and scholar who campaigned for human rights in the Arab world and for a peaceful solution to the Israeli/Palestinian conflict. He had lived in Britain for sixteen years. Like Hosenball, Cheblak sought judicial review of the Home Secretary's decision to deport him. Like Hosenball, Cheblak was unsuccessful in the Divisional Court and the Court of Appeal. The Court of Appeal ruled that national security was a matter 'exclusively' for the government. In the absence of evidence of bad faith or that the Home Secretary had exceeded the limitations on his authority imposed by statute, the courts will accept that the Home Secretary had good reason to make a deportation order on national security grounds without requiring him to produce evidence to substantiate those grounds. In the light of this ruling, it is remarkable that Lord Donaldson MR should have gone out of his way to state in the course of his judgment that: 'Judges are exhorted by commentators to be "robust" . . . I agree that judges should indeed be "robust" and I hope that we are' (at 906). He then went on to say that 'although they give rise to tensions at the interface, "national security" and "civil liberties" are on the same side. In accepting, as we must, that to some extent the needs of national security must displace civil liberties, albeit to the least possible extent, it is not irrelevant to remember that the maintenance of national security underpins and is the foundation of all our civil liberties' (at 906–7). A decade later, the investigative journalist Nick Cohen returned to the *Cheblak* case. This is what he reported:

Nick Cohen, 'Return of the H-Block', *Observer*, 18 November 2001

In 1991, during the Gulf War . . . 50 Palestinians [were] interned because of their 'links to terrorism', and 35 Iraqi 'soldiers', captured in Britain and held as prisoners of war in a camp on the Salisbury Plain . . .

I was a reporter on the *Independent* at the time, who generally believed that the representatives of the state were honest and competent . . . [A]long with most others who watched the arrests I promised I was never going to make that mistake again. The Gulf War was one of those clarifying moments when the artifice of authority became transparent.

The internees were innocent. Not just in the legal sense of not being guilty beyond reasonable doubt, but irrefutably innocent. The Iraqi 'soldiers' weren't a fifth column. They were engineering and physics students whose scholarships came from the Iraqi military. Their arrest wasn't the great espionage coup the press had hailed. Iraqi assets in Britain had been frozen at the start of hostilities. Before he returned to Baghdad, the Iraqi ambassador sent the Bank of England the students' names and addresses. He asked that their grants be paid until the fighting was over. They were locked-up instead, and many showed their loyalty to Saddam by asking for political asylum . . .

The interned Palestinians included those rare moderates the Foreign Office dedicates so much time to finding in the Middle East. Abbas Cheblak was an advocate of Arab-Israeli rapprochement who had written a sympathetic study of the Jews of Iraq and criticised the invasion of Kuwait. The Home Office may have got a clue that MI5 had blundered when it heard that the campaign to free him was being organised by the editor of the *Jewish Quarterly*.

The behaviour of the state confirmed that the arrests were a PR operation designed to gull a mulish press and public into thinking all was well. The 'terrorists' homes weren't searched. Interrogations were perfunctory or non-existent. Although the internees weren't told why they were in jail, MI6 leaked that MI5 was arresting people on the basis of information in files which were 20 years out of date. The case against Ali el-Saleh, a computer salesman from Bedford, seemed to be that his wife's sister had married a man whose uncle was Abu Nidal. El-Saleh and Cheblak spoke with embarrassing sadness of how they had lost their

> homes in Palestine and had hoped to make a new life for themselves and their children as free and grateful British citizens.
>
> At the end of the war, the Home Office released all the detainees. It might still have deported them if there was a hint of a suspicion that they were terrorists. Ministers quietly allowed anyone who wanted to remain in Britain to do so. There was no disciplinary action against the MI5 officers involved. The judiciary, which hadn't squeaked while the principles of English law were assaulted and battered, was briefly criticised, but the complaints died away. The scandal was all but forgotten as the childish need to believe in benign authority reasserted itself.

Secretary of State for the Home Department v. *Rehman* [2001] UKHL 47, [2003] 1 AC 153

This is the final of our six pre-HRA national security cases. It is another deportation case. Rehman appealed the Secretary of State's decision to deport him to SIAC, which, as was mentioned above, replaced the previous system of advisory panels in 1997. SIAC upheld Rehman's appeal on the basis that as a number of the Secretary of State's claims against him could not be substantiated on the facts, it could not be said that he had offended against national security. For SIAC, being a threat to national security could constitute grounds for deportation only if it could be shown that the deportee had engaged in, promoted or encouraged 'violent activity that is targeted at the UK, its system of government or its people'. The Secretary of State appealed, arguing that this was too narrow a definition of national security. In his view, the UK's national security could be threatened by action targeted at an altogether different jurisdiction, even if no British subjects were directly involved. Both the Court of Appeal and the House of Lords unanimously agreed with the Secretary of State. The House of Lords further ruled that determining what measures are required to be taken in the interests of national security is a 'matter of judgment and policy' for the Secretary of State (Lord Hoffmann, at [50]). Judicial oversight of executive decision-making in this area is narrowly confined to three matters: first, 'the factual basis for the executive's opinion . . . must be established by evidence'; second, SIAC would be able to reject the Secretary of State's opinion on the ground that it was *Wednesbury* unreasonable; and, third, if deportation would entail a substantial risk that the deportee would be subject in the country to which he is deported to treatment contrary to Article 3 of the ECHR, the court may, on the authority of *Chahal v United Kingdom* (1996) 23 EHRR 413, order the deportation to be stopped (Lord Hoffmann, at [54]; see further on this aspect of the ECtHR's ruling in *Chahal*, below). The House of Lords conceded that 'it cannot be proved to a high degree of probability that [Rehman] has carried out any individual act which would justify the conclusion that he is a danger' (Lord Hutton, at [65]). Nonetheless, their Lordships ruled that SIAC was wrong to allow Rehman's appeal for the reasons it had given and the case was remitted to SIAC for redetermination. Their Lordships' opinions in *Rehman* were handed down on 11 October 2001, one month exactly after 9/11. Lord Hoffmann added the following 'postscript' to his opinion in the case (at [62]):

> I wrote this speech some three months before the recent events in New York and Washington. They are a reminder that in matters of national security the cost of failure can be high. This seems to me to underline the need for the judicial arm of government to respect the decisions of ministers of the Crown on the question of whether support for terrorist activities in a foreign country constitutes a threat to national security. It is not only that the executive has access to special information and expertise in these matters. It is also that such decisions, with serious potential results for the community, require a legitimacy which can be conferred only by entrusting them to persons responsible to the community through the democratic process. If the people are to accept the consequences of such decisions, they must be made by persons whom the people have elected and whom they can remove.

11.2.2.2 National Security after the HRA

We can now examine the extent to which the HRA and the case law decided under it have had an impact on matters touching on national security. The most immediately striking case is the decision of the House of Lords in *A v. Secretary of State for the Home Department* [2004] UKHL 56, [2005] 2 AC 68, to which we shall turn first. However, as we shall see in the next section, this is far from the only case we need to examine: confining our attention to this case alone, important though it is, would leave a seriously misleading impression.

A v. Secretary of State for the Home Department [2004] UKHL 56, [2005] 2 AC 68

A panel of nine Law Lords heard this case. By a majority of 8:1 they ruled, overturning a unanimous Court of Appeal (see [2004] QB 335), that the indefinite detention without trial of suspected international terrorists, as provided for by Part 4 of the Anti-Terrorism, Crime and Security Act 2001, was unlawful as being both a disproportionate interference with the right to liberty under Article 5 of the ECHR and a discriminatory measure in breach of Article 14 of the ECHR. In the course of their opinions, several of their Lordships voiced concerns about governmental claims regarding national security that are quite different from the sorts of approach taken in the case law considered in the previous section. Lord Rodger stated, for example, at [177] that 'national security can be used as a pretext for repressive measures that are really taken for other reasons', while Baroness Hale stated at [226] that 'Unwarranted declarations of emergency are a familiar tool of tyranny.' Even Lord Walker, who dissented and who would have upheld the legality of the measures, conceded at [193] that 'a portentous but non-specific appeal to the interests of national security can be used as a cloak for arbitrary and oppressive action on the part of government' and that 'national security can be the last refuge of the tyrant.'

When it introduced the Anti-Terrorism, Crime and Security Bill into Parliament, the government knew that the provisions concerning indefinite detention without trial would be in breach of Article 5. As a result, the government 'derogated' from Article 5 for the purposes of these provisions. Derogation from the convention is governed by Article 15 of the ECHR, which provides as follows:

1. In time of war or other public emergency threatening the life of the nation any High Contracting Party may take measures derogating from its obligations under this Convention to the extent strictly required by the exigencies of the situation, provided that such measures are not inconsistent with its other obligations under international law.
2. No derogation from Article 2, except in respect of deaths resulting from lawful acts of war, of from Articles 3, 4 (paragraph 1) and 7 shall be made under this provision . . .

Section 1(2) of the HRA provides that the convention rights (as defined in section 1(1)) 'are to have effect for the purposes of this Act subject to any designated derogation'. Such a designated derogation, in respect of Article 5 of the ECHR and the provisions concerning indefinite detention without trial, was made by the Secretary of State: see the Human Rights Act 1998 (Designated Derogation) Order 2001 (SI 3644/2001).

The regime under Part 4 of the Act did not represent what the government claimed it would ideally like to be able to do to suspected international terrorists. Ideally, the government claimed, suspected international terrorists would be deported. However, this option is not always available as a result of the ruling of the ECtHR in *Chahal v United Kingdom* (1996) 23 EHRR 413. In that case, the European Court held that it would be a breach of Article 3 of the Convention for a high contracting party to deport a person where 'substantial grounds have been shown for believing that the person in question, if expelled, would face a real risk of being subjected to treatment contrary to Article 3 in the receiving country' (at [74]). Article 3 is non-derogable: as we have just seen, the terms of Article 15(2) make it impossible for a high contracting party to derogate from Article 3. This is the problem that the regime of indefinite detention without trial was meant to be the solution to. (The ruling in *Chahal* was reaffirmed by a unanimous Grand Chamber of the ECtHR in *Saadi* v. *Italy* (2009) 49 EHRR 30.)

This explains why Part 4 applied only to those persons who were subject to immigration control. Nationals cannot be deported in any event.

For the House of Lords to rule (as the majority did) that the scheme of indefinite detention without trial was in breach of Article 5, their Lordships first had to deal with the legality of the derogation. If the derogation from Article 5 was lawful, the Act's interference with the right to liberty could not be unlawful. It is this aspect of their Lordships' ruling that most closely touches on issues of national security, as we shall see. There is one preliminary point, however, that must be addressed first. What is the test that the courts should employ to determine whether a purported derogation is lawful? Article 15, while referred to in the HRA, is *not* one of the convention rights incorporated into domestic law by section 1 of the HRA. Like Article 13, Article 15 was deliberately excluded. This suggests that, when considering the legality of a purported derogation, domestic courts should do no more (and no less) than apply the ordinary principles of judicial review: legality, rationality, procedural propriety and, in the context of convention rights (as here, Articles 5 and 14 both being incorporated under the HRA), proportionality (see Chapter 10). Yet this is not the approach their Lordships took. Most of the Law Lords appear simply to have assumed that the criteria in Article 15 should be applied in assessing the legality of the derogation. Only Lord Scott directly addressed this issue (at [151]). While he confessed (at [152]) to having 'doubts' and 'difficulty' in understanding how the domestic courts could, in effect, enforce Article 15 when it had not been incorporated into domestic law, he set such doubts aside and considered the case on this footing on the basis that the Attorney General, arguing the government's case, had 'expressly accepted' that this was how the case should proceed. It seems to have been a curiously generous concession on the government's part.

It will be seen that there are two main tests contained in Article 15(1), both of which must be satisfied for a derogation to be lawful. The first is that the derogation must be made in 'time of war or other public emergency threatening the life of the nation'; the second is that the measures taken must be 'strictly required by the exigencies of the situation'. In *A*, eight of the Law Lords (i.e., all bar one, Lord Hoffmann) accepted that the derogation was made in time of public emergency threatening the life of the nation. Of these eight, all but one (Lord Walker) held that the derogating measures were not strictly necessary and were therefore unlawful. We deal with each of these points in turn.

Public Emergency Threatening the Life of the Nation. Lord Bingham ruled, 'not without misgiving (fortified by reading the opinion of … Lord Hoffmann)' (at [26]), for the Secretary of State on this point for two main reasons: first, because under the case law of the ECtHR states are given a very wide margin of appreciation in determining whether there is such a public emergency and, second, because 'great weight should be given to the judgment of the Home Secretary, his colleagues and Parliament on this question' (at [29]). Lord Bingham expressly relied on Lord Hoffmann's opinion in *Rehman* (above) in support of this position. Lord Hope stated that, while he was 'content . . . to accept that the questions whether there is an emergency and whether it threatens the life of the nation are pre-eminently for the executive and Parliament' and that while the 'judgment that has to be formed on these issues lies outside the expertise of the courts . . . it is nevertheless open to the judiciary to examine the nature of the situation that has been identified by government as constituting the emergency' (at [116]). On such an examination there was, in Lord Hope's view, 'ample evidence . . . to show that the government were fully justified in taking the view . . . that there was an emergency threatening the life of the nation' (at [118]). Lord Scott was more guarded: he stated that 'For my part, I do not doubt that there is a terrorist threat to this country . . . But I do have very great doubt whether the "public emergency" is one that justifies the description of "threatening the life of the nation". Nonetheless, I would, for my part, be prepared to allow the Secretary of State the benefit of the doubt on this point and accept that the threshold criterion of Article 15 is satisfied' (at [154]). Baroness Hale ruled in the following terms, at [226]:

> The courts' power to rule on the validity of the derogation is [one] of the safeguards enacted by Parliament in this carefully constructed package. It would be meaningless if we could only rubber-stamp what the Home Secretary and Parliament have done. But any sensible court, like any sensible person, recognises the limits of its expertise. Assessing the strength of a general threat to the life of the nation is, or should be, within the expertise of the Government and its advisers. They may, as recent events have shown, not always get it right. But courts too do not always get things right. It would be very surprising if the courts were better able to make that sort of judgment than the Government. Protecting the life of the nation is one of the first tasks of a Government in a world of nation states. That does not mean that the courts could never intervene. Unwarranted declarations of emergency are a familiar tool of tyranny. If a Government were to declare a public emergency where patently there was no such thing, it would be the duty of the court to say so. But we are here considering the immediate aftermath of the unforgettable events of 11 September 2001. The attacks launched on the United States on that date were clearly intended to threaten the life of that nation. SIAC were satisfied that the . . . material before them justified the conclusion that there was also a public emergency threatening the life of this nation. I, for one, would not feel qualified or even inclined to disagree.

Lord Hoffmann was the only one of their Lordships to come to a different view on this point. We quoted from his opinion on the matter in Chapter 1, above (p. 17).

We may ask the following question: how did Lord Hoffmann know that the threat faced by the UK, while serious, did not threaten the life of the nation? We may ask a similar question of Lord Hope (see above): how did Lord Hope know that the life of the nation *was* threatened? After all, none of their Lordships saw the 'closed material', presumably containing intelligence assessments and the like, which had been examined by SIAC. The question is the more pressing because the majority of their Lordships did not actually need to answer it at all. Given that a majority held that the measures taken (in terms of indefinite detention without trial) were, in any event, not strictly required, why could not the House of Lords do as the JCHR had done in its various parliamentary reports on the 2001 Act and leave the question open as to whether the UK faced a public emergency threatening the life of the nation? The House of Lords could have quashed the derogation order and made a declaration of incompatibility in respect of the relevant provisions of the Act without having to decide this question at all.

Strictly Required. It is to the 'strictly required' point that we can now turn. On this matter, their Lordships were considerably more persuasive than, with respect, they were with regard to the previous issue. There were two flaws with the government's scheme, both of which undermined its claim that detention without trial was 'strictly required' within the meaning of Article 15(1). The first was that while the government conceded that the threat from international terrorism was not limited to non-nationals, the power to detain without trial was so limited (see, e.g., Lord Bingham, at [32]). If measures short of indefinite detention without trial were sufficient for British citizens suspected of involvement in or support for international terrorism, then so too were they sufficient for non-nationals. The second was that all those detained under the scheme were 'free to leave' the UK if they chose to do so – indeed, as we have seen, the government claimed that it wanted the detainees to leave and would have deported them if it had been legal to do so. A number of those detained did indeed leave the UK for other countries. One left for France, where he was subsequently released. Yet, if the detainees were such a threat to the UK that their indefinite incarceration was required, why allow them to leave for and be released in other countries, where they would be relatively free to plot their treachery? These twin irrationalities within the scheme fatally undermined it. As Baroness Hale expressed it, at [228], [231]:

> There is every reason to think that there are British nationals living here who are international terrorists within the meaning of the Act; who cannot be shown to be such in a court of law; and who cannot be deported to another country because they have every right to be here. Yet the Government does not think that it is necessary to lock them up. Indeed, it has publicly stated that locking up nationals is a Draconian step which could not at present be justified. But it has provided us with no real explanation of why it is necessary to lock up one group of people sharing exactly the same characteristics as another group which it does not think necessary to lock up . . . The conclusion has to be that it is not necessary to lock up the nationals. Other ways must have been found to contain the threat which they present. And if it is not necessary to lock up the nationals it cannot be necessary to lock up the foreigners. It is not strictly required by the exigencies of the situation.

Discrimination. The final aspect of their Lordships' ruling in *A* concerned discrimination. We saw above why the government presented the measures in Part 4 as 'immigration measures' that could apply only to persons subject to immigration control (i.e., to non-nationals). While the Court of Appeal accepted this analysis, the majority of the House of Lords did not. For the majority of their Lordships, the appropriate comparator with the detainees was not those with no right of abode who are not suspected international terrorists but those with a right of abode who are suspected international terrorists (see, e.g., Lord Bingham, at [53]–[54], and Lord Nicholls, at [76]). Seen in this light, the measures in Part 4 were discriminatory and were, accordingly, held to be in breach of Article 14 of the ECHR as well as being in breach of Article 5.

(For immediate reaction to the *A* case, see the four case notes on the decision at (2005) 68 *MLR* 654 by Hickman, Tierney, Dyzenhaus and Hiebert; see also Lord Lester [2005] *PL* 249; Tomkins [2005] *PL* 259; Feldman [2005] *CLJ* 271. While there are criticisms of aspects of the decision in a number of these pieces, the decision was subjected to sustained critique in two later pieces: Finnis (2007) 123 *LQR* 417; and Campbell [2009] *PL* 501.)

11.2.2.3 Analysis and Subsequent Events

Professor Feldman ([2005] *CLJ* 271, 273) described the decision of the House of Lords in *A* as 'perhaps the most powerful judicial defence of liberty since *Leach* v. *Money* (1765) 3 Burr 1692 and *Somersett* v. *Stewart* (1772) 20 St Tr 1' and claimed that it 'will long remain a benchmark in public law'. In the light of the case law, from *Zadig* to *Rehman*, surveyed above, the decision in *A* is indeed remarkable. Four factors, however, ought to qualify our assessment of its importance and impact. The first is that there was nothing in their Lordships' opinions that had not already been argued for, extremely power-fully, by a series of committees reviewing the operation of the 2001 Act. The parliamentary Joint Committee on Human Rights and a group of privy counsellors appointed under section 122 of the Act to review it had already concluded that Part 4 of the Act was not 'a sustainable way of addressing the problem of terrorist suspects in the United Kingdom', that 'it should be replaced' with a new scheme that applied equally to nationals and non-nationals alike and that did not require a derogation from Article 5 of the ECHR (*Report of the Privy Counsellor Review Committee*, HC 100 of 2003–4, p. 5). Moreover, it was not only in respect of the Part 4 powers of indefinite detention without trial that these reviewing committees were deeply critical of the 2001 Act. The *Report of the Privy Counsellor Review Committee* was, in this sense, not only an equally powerful but also a more complete defence of liberty than anything the Law Lords were able to provide.

Second, while the ruling on the '*strictly required*' point was certainly ground-breaking, the ruling on the '*public emergency threatening the life of the nation*' point somewhat undercut other aspects of the decision. David Dyzenhaus expresses the argument well when he says that such 'victory for the rule of law' as the case secured was not only qualified but 'unstable' (Dyzenhaus, 'Deference, Security and Human Rights', in Goold and Lazarus (eds.), *Security and Human Rights* (2007), p. 128). Thomas Poole puts it yet more starkly, detecting 'a trace of schizophrenia' in the approaches taken by their Lordships to deference and to the intensity of judicial review (Poole, 'Courts and Conditions of Uncertainty in "Times of Crisis"' [2008] *PL* [2008 234, 239].

Third, we should bear in mind 'what happened next'. The provisions of the 2001 Act concerning indefinite detention without trial were replaced with new provisions under the Prevention of Terrorism Act 2005. Under section 2(1) of the 2005 Act, the Secretary of State was able to impose a 'control order' on any individual (whether a British national or not):

> if he (a) has reasonable grounds for suspecting that the individual is or has been involved in terrorism-related activity; and (b) considers that it is necessary, for purposes connected with protecting members of the public from a risk of terrorism, to make a control order imposing obligations on that individual.

Control orders included a considerable range of restrictions on an individual, including, most controversially, the imposition of restrictions on movement that would see individuals being placed under curfew, effectively confined to their home for long periods of each day, in addition to a restriction of movement outside the home. Control orders were challenged in numerous cases. Many of these concerned the fairness of legal proceedings in control orders cases, which relied on 'closed material' that was not disclosed to the controlled person but only to a security-cleared 'special advocate' (see above). The most significant substantive challenge to control orders came in *Secretary of State for the Home Department* v. *JJ* [2007] UKHL 45, [2008] 1 AC 385. Here the House of Lords ruled by a 3:2 majority that particular control orders had been improperly made, but their Lordships were unanimous in upholding the legality of the control order regime. The case focused on the length of the curfew that could be imposed under a control order. Too long a curfew, the majority held, and the control order would be a 'deprivation of liberty' (in breach of Article 5) rather than a mere 'restriction of freedom of movement'. Lords Hoffmann and Carswell dissented on this point: in their view, the concept of deprivation of liberty should be confined to actual imprisonment; and control orders, while restrictive in numerous ways, were not akin to actual imprisonment. The longest curfew imposed in the control orders considered in *JJ* was eighteen hours (that is, the controlled person was under a curfew for eighteen out of every twenty-four hours). This was regarded by the majority as too long to be compatible with Article 5. Lord Brown (one of the judges in the majority) suggested that sixteen hours might be the cut-off.

In the face of subsequent parliamentary pressure, emanating principally from the JCHR, to reform the regime of control orders, the government was able to resist, proclaiming that 'as a result of the House of Lords' judgments …, the control orders legislation is fully compliant with the European Convention on Human Rights' (JCHR, *20th Report of 2007–08*, HL 108, HC 554, para 68). The JCHR responded angrily, remarking that their Lordships had been unhelpful and, indeed, misguided. Lord Brown's suggestion that a sixteen-hour curfew would not generally breach Article 5 of the ECHR was strongly criticised, not least because (as the politicians on the JCHR would have foreseen even if Lord Brown did not) it led directly to the government *increasing* the length of the curfews imposed in a number of other control orders from twelve to sixteen hours! The JCHR argued that the Prevention of Terrorism Act 2005 should be amended to make it clear that a control order could impose no curfew of more than twelve hours. This was one of many JCHR recommendations on control orders that the government swept aside on the basis that the Law Lords had not required such an amendment. It was not just the length of the curfew that the JCHR was concerned about: it was the way in which the House of Lords singled this issue out as being of prime importance. In the JCHR's view, the court should have had regard not only to the length of the curfew but also to 'the nature, effects and manner of implementation' of the totality of the restrictions imposed by the control order (see JCHR, *20th Report of 2007–08*, HL 108, HC 554, paras 82–9). (See, further, *Secretary of State for the Home Department* v. *AP* [2010] UKSC 24, [2010] 3 WLR 51.)

Control orders proved to be exceptionally controversial. The Coalition Government set about reviewing a number of aspects of the counterterrorism laws and policies that they had inherited from their predecessors in office. In January 2011, the Home Secretary published the results of this review and announced that control orders would be replaced by a new scheme of 'terrorism prevention and investigation measures' (TPIMs). These were introduced in the Terrorism Prevention and Investigation Measures Act 2011, which repealed the control order by repealing the Prevention of Terrorism Act 2005. TPIMs were designed to be less restrictive of civil liberties. TPIMs replaced the controversial lengthy curfews with a more flexible requirement of overnight residence. The restrictions of movement were replaced with measures designed to impose specific exclusions over tightly drawn areas rather than broader restrictions on movement – for example, to prevent visiting certain mosques or community centres rather than preventing individuals from travelling beyond certain distances from a home. TPIMs also allowed electronic tagging, and restrictions on communications. The new legislation also removed the ability to relocate a terrorist suspect away from their family and their community. TPIMs also had greater court oversight, being subject to quasi-automatic review in the High Court, albeit that this was often through closed material proceedings, and were limited in time to a maximum of two years. However, unlike the control orders legislation which required annual renewal, the 2011 Act only requires an annual review from the independent reviewer of terrorism legislation. Renewal of the 2011 Act is only required every five years.

In its post-legislative scrutiny report, prior to the need to renew the 2011 Act in 2016, the Joint Committee on Human Rights was critical of some of its provisions. In particular, the committee was concerned about the lack of parliamentary engagement with the annual review reports of the independent reviewer of terrorism legislation. In addition, the committee remained concerned that, just as with the control order regime, TPIMs were being used more as preventive rather than an investigative measure; repeating concerns over the breadth of the power granted to impose a TPIM where the Home Secretary 'reasonably considers it necessary for purposes connected with protecting the public from a risk of terrorism' (Terrorism Prevention and Investigation Measures Act 2011, section 3). As is clear from its concluding remarks, it was difficult to see how TPIMs were needed, yet, at the same time, the lack of clear public knowledge and information made it hard for any institution to reach a conclusive answer on this issue (*Post-Legislative Scrutiny: Terrorism Prevention and Investigation Measures Act 2011, 10th Report 2013–14*, HL Paper 113, HC 1014) p. 28:

> At the conclusion of our review we are left with the distinct impression that, in practice, TPIMs may be withering on the vine as a counter-terrorism tool of practical utility. No new TPIM has been imposed since October 2012. Soon there will only be one TPIM in force. It remains to be seen whether any new TPIMs will be imposed in the foreseeable future . . . We do not feel that we are sufficiently informed about the threat picture, however, to be able to conclude with confidence that the power to impose some form of civil restriction orders such as TPIMs is no longer required, or to recommend that the Secretary of State should exercise the power the Act gives her to repeal it if it is no longer necessary.

Nevertheless, in the face of growing perceived threats to the UK from foreign-terrorist fighters, not only were TPIMs renewed, but also further measures were adopted in legislation to protect national security. This threatens evidence through acts of terrorism in Europe, particularly the *Charlie Hebdo* attack in Paris. First, the UK enacted the Counter-Terrorism and Security Act 2015, which was semi-fast-tracked through Parliament, partly to implement UN Security resolutions, although these were rarely discussed in parliamentary debate. The Act empowered the police to retain passports and travel documents, and to impose temporary exclusion orders (TEOs) to prevent those with a right to reside in the UK, whom the Home Secretary reasonably suspects have been involved in a terrorist organisation abroad, from returning to the UK. TEOs may only be imposed after the court has given permission, or with subsequent court authorisation in cases of urgency. The 2015 Act also amended the TPIM regime. In particular, it changed the standard that needed to be met for the Home Secretary to impose a TPIM, substituting 'reasonably believes' for 'is satisfied, on the balance of probabilities'. It remains the case, however, that TPIMs are rarely imposed. In February 2020, in response to a written question, it was revealed that there had been four TPIMs in place from 1 December 2018 to 20 February 2019; four from 1 March 2019 to 31 May 2019, three from 1 June to 31 August 2019 and five from 1 September to 20 November 2019. (See Blackbourn and Walker, 'Interdiction and Indoctrination: The Counter-Terrorism and Security Act 2015' (2016) 79 MLR 840.)

In 2019, the UK Parliament enacted the Counter-Terrorism and Border Security Act 2019. In addition to placing further restrictions on freedom of expression (discussed below), the legislation creates a new offence of entering into or remaining in 'designated areas', with the Secretary of State being empowered to designate areas in order to protect the public from a risk of terrorism. It also introduced a power to stop, question, search and detain individuals at ports in order to determine whether they are, or have been, involved in hostile activity.

It is hard to deny that the legislation imposes large restrictions on civil liberties, often purely on a belief or suspicion of their involvement in terrorism, the focus being on prevention as opposed to investigation. However, it is also hard to deny evidence of an escalation in terrorism since the previous edition of this book, which took account of the terrorist incidents in 9/11 and 7/7. From 2010 to 2017, there had been a series of individual terrorism-motivated acts of violence, most notably the murder of soldier Stephen Rigby in 2013 and the murder of Jo Cox, MP, in 2016. The former was motivated by Islamic extremism and the latter by white supremacism. The following year, 2017, however, saw an escalation in acts of terrorism, both in number and in scale. March 2017 witnessed the Westminster attack, with four killed and almost fifty injured by Khalid Mahsood, believed to be motivated by Islamic extremism, who drove a car into pedestrians on Westminster Bridge, before running into the grounds of the Palace of Westminster and fatally stabbing a police officer. The Manchester Arena bombing occurred in May 2017, when an Islamist suicide bomber killed twenty-two and injured 139 people, many of whom were children and teenagers, leaving an Ariana Grande concert. In June 2017, the London Bridge attack killed eight and injured at least forty-eight people when three Islamists drove a van into pedestrians on London Bridge. Later in the same month, a British man drove a van into Muslim worshippers outside Finsbury Park Mosque. In September, there was an attack on the Parsons Green tube station, where a bomb caused injuries, but no fatalities. There were further incidents in 2018 and 2019, culminating in 2019 with the London Bridge stabbing. The last motivated the enactment of emergency terrorism legislation – the Terrorist Offenders (Restriction of Early Release) Act 2020. The legislation was designed to respond specifically to the London Bridge attack, given that this had been carried out by an individual who had been automatically released after serving one-third of his sentence, as per the legal regime in place at the time. The 2020 Act creates different rules for prisoners convicted of terrorist offences, replacing automatic release with a Parole Board hearing to determine whether release should be granted, this taking place after a prisoner has served half as opposed to one-third of their sentence. Both of these elements were given retrospective effect – that is, they would apply to prisoners currently serving their sentence. The retrospective effect of the lengthening of the time served before a parole hearing was criticised as breaching civil liberties by the Constitution Committee of the House of Lords (*Terrorist Offenders (Restriction of Early Release) Bill, 3rd Report 2019–21*, HL Paper 23).

The final factor we should bear in mind when assessing the impact of the House of Lords' decision in *A* is the extent to which the more robust – or more critical – attitude the majority of their Lordships displayed towards the relationship between personal freedom and national security has – or has not – been sustained in subsequent case law. Subsequent decisions suggest that, rather than becoming the 'benchmark' that Professor Feldman had predicted, the *A* case is already beginning to look more like a one-off. Consider the following examples.

In *R (Gillan)* v. *Metropolitan Police Commissioner* [2006] UKHL 12, [2006] 2 AC 307, the House of Lords ruled that what had been described in a lower court as the 'extraordinary' and 'sweeping' stop and search powers contained in the Terrorism Act 2000 (sections 44–7) may lawfully be used in the context of the police stopping apparently peaceful protesters from approaching an international arms fair to protest against Britain's involvement in the arms trade. The appellants' argument that the powers should be read as being available only where there were reasonable grounds for considering that their use was necessary and suitable for the prevention of terrorism was dismissed. The ECtHR subsequently ruled (in *Gillan* v. *United Kingdom* (2010) 50 EHRR 45) that the use of these powers in the applicants' cases constituted an unlawful interference with their Article 8 rights. The contrast between the House of Lords and the ECtHR in *Gillan* is stark. The Home Secretary stated of these powers that they 'represented an unacceptable intrusion on an individual's human rights and must be repealed' (HC Deb vol. 522, col 307, 26 January 2011). The powers were repealed and replaced with more tightly defined powers (see the Protection of Freedoms Act 2012, sections 59 to 61). The Act also required the Secretary of State to produce a code of practice as to how the powers should be used. As with control orders, it is notable that it took a change of government rather than a ruling of a UK court to bring about a change in the law.

In *R (Al Jedda)* v. *Secretary of State for Defence* [2007] UKHL 58, [2008] 1 AC 332, the House of Lords ruled that UN Security Council Resolutions authorised British military detention in Iraq and severely restricted the relevance of Article 5 to that detention. Once again, the decision stands in a stark contrast to the significantly more robust approach to UN Security Council resolutions adopted by the ECJ in Joined Cases C-402/05 P and C-415/05 P *Kadi v Council* [2008] ECR I-6351, considered in Chapter 5: see above, pp. 376–380.

In *RB (Algeria)* v. *Secretary of State for the Home Department* [2009] UKHL 10, [2010] 2 AC 110, the House of Lords ruled, among other matters, that the Home Secretary may lawfully deport Abu Qatada to Jordan, where he has been convicted in his absence of terrorist offences; these convictions, it is claimed, having been secured on the basis of evidence obtained by torture. The European Court of Human Rights reached the opposite conclusion – that it was not lawful to deport Abu Qatada, given the likelihood that his trial in Jordan would give rise to a flagrant denial of justice, such as to amount to a nullification of the right to a fair trial found in Article 6. This was satisfied given the real risk that evidence obtained by torture would be used in this trial.

To this rather depressing list may be added further House of Lords decisions, discussed elsewhere in this book, such as *R (Corner House)* v. *Director of the Serious Fraud Office* [2008] UKHL 60, [2009] 1 AC 756 (above, pp. 804–805) and *R (Bancoult)* v. *Secretary of State for Foreign and Commonwealth Affairs* [2008] UKHL 61, [2009] 1 AC 453 (above, pp. 200–201). Rather more promising, from a civil liberties point of view, were the decisions of the Supreme Court in *Ahmed* v. *HM Treasury* [2010] UKSC 2, [2010] 2 WLR 378 (above, p. 200) and *Belhaj* v. *Straw; Rahmatullah* v. *Ministry of Defence* [2017] UKSC 3, [2017] AC 964).

These decisions do not exactly return us to the twentieth-century depths of *Zadig, Liversidge, Hosenball* and *Cheblak* but, equally, they hardly make for an inspiring, robust or sustained defence of liberty. Even in the era of the HRA, our highest court seems to find it remarkably difficult to escape the legacy of ambivalence and compromise that so marked its contributions to this field in earlier times. (In this regard, it is interesting to compare the record of lower courts that, on one view, may offer more in terms of protection of civil liberties: see Tomkins (2010) 126 *LQR* 543.) Some commentators have provocatively asserted that the cases summarised here demonstrate the 'futility' of the HRA (see Ewing and Tham [2008] *PL* 829). Others have sought vigorously to dispute this, praising the courts for doing the best that can reasonably be expected in difficult circumstances (e.g., Kavanagh [2009] *PL* 287). It may be that a better view would be to see the judicial record as being decidedly mixed. We should write off neither the courts nor the HRA as futile, but neither is there much to celebrate. Indeed, there is plenty about which we should be gravely concerned. Just because we now have an HRA in the UK is evidently no reason to be complacent about the state of our national security and counterterrorism law.

(There is considerable literature on all this. Representative of it are the following: Arden (2005) 121 *LQR* 604; Dyzenhaus, *The Constitution of Law: Legality in a Time of Emergency* (2006); Feldman [2006] *PL* 364; Goold and Lazarus (eds.), *Security and Human Rights* (2007); Ewing, *Bonfire of the Liberties* (2010); Poole [2008] *PL* 234; Bates (2009) 29 *LS* 99; Kavanagh (2010) 73 *MLR* 836; Walker [2010] *PL* 4; Fenwick (2010) 63 *CLP* 153; Tomkins (2011) 64 *CLP* 215; Tomkins,

'Parliament, Human Rights and Counter-Terrorism', in Campbell, Ewing and Tomkins (eds.) *The Legal Protection of Human Rights: Sceptical Essays* (OUP, 2011); Davis and de Londras (eds.), *Critical Debates on Counter-Terrorism Judicial Review* (CUP. 2014).)

11.3 Freedom of Expression

The final two sections of this chapter are case studies of liberty and constitutional law in Britain. Our case studies consider both common law and statute. Neither focuses exclusively on protection under the HRA: rather, one of the themes of the case studies is that protection under that Act needs to be understood in the context of what the law already offered. We recognise that numerous such case studies could have been selected. Police powers of arrest and detention, or the scope of the protection afforded to privacy, are examples. The two we have selected are freedom of expression and freedom of assembly. Neither is dealt with comprehensively – for reasons of space, we have had to be selective in our choice of materials. Within the broad area of freedom of expression we have been particularly selective, focusing only on what might be called freedom of political expression. Other important areas of free speech law (such as obscenity, defamation, film and theatre censorship and broadcasting regulation) are not considered in any detail.

(On other areas of law concerning personal liberty, see Fenwick, *Civil Rights: New Labour, Freedom and the Human Rights Act* (2000); Whitty, Murphy and Livingstone, *Civil Liberties Law: The Human Rights Act Era* (2001). On other areas of freedom of expression, see Feldman, *Civil Liberties and Human Rights in England and Wales* (2nd edn. 2002), chs 13–17; Barendt, *Freedom of Speech* (2nd edn. 2005); Bailey, Harris and Jones, *Civil Liberties: Cases and Materials* (6th edn. 2009), chs 9–12; Fenwick and Edwards, *Fenwick on Civil Liberties and Human Rights* (5th edn. 2016); Amos, *Human Rights Law* (2nd edn. 2014).)

11.3.1 Freedom of Expression and Democracy

Freedom of speech, or expression, has two aspects: it is both a liberty of the individual to impart information and the freedom (or perhaps more naturally the 'right') of others to receive it. This twofold freedom can be supported, by a variety of arguments, as being essential to 'self-realisation, social life, politics, economic activity, art, and knowledge' (Richard Abel, *Speech and Respect* (1994), pp. 28–9; see, further, Barendt, *Freedom of Speech*, above). A principal justification of freedom of expression is its contribution to the buttressing of democracy, and we shall consider it mainly from this perspective. It is believed that democracy is most secure, responsive and efficient – most likely to realise the high hopes placed in it – if there is a free exchange of information and opinions and freedom to criticise those who exercise governing power. This is a necessary freedom if the accountability of government is to be assured. Additionally, freedom of expression, in fostering ideas, argument and understanding, counters officially sanctioned nostrums and versions of the facts, and enables citizens – and voters – to make informed choices. Accordingly, freedom of the press and other media of communication is rightly regarded as a bulwark of democracy.

Judges have recognised this, Lord Bingham, for instance, saying in *McCartan Turkington Breen v. Times Newspapers Ltd* [2001] 2 AC 277, 290–1, that 'the proper functioning of a modern participatory democracy requires that the media be free, active, professional and inquiring. For this reason the courts, here and elsewhere, have recognised the cardinal importance of press freedom.' For Lord Steyn in *R v. Secretary of State for the Home Department, ex p Simms* [2000] 2 AC 115, 126:

> freedom of speech is the lifeblood of democracy. The free flow of information and ideas informs political debate. It is a safety valve: people are more ready to accept decisions that go against them if they can in principle seek to influence them. It acts as a brake on the abuse of power by public officials. It facilitates the exposure of errors in the governance and administration of justice of the country.

In *R (Animal Defenders International) v. Secretary of State for Culture, Media and Sport* [2008] UKHL 15, [2008] 1 AC 1312, Lord Bingham returned to the theme, observing as follows (at [27]–[28]):

> Freedom of thought and expression is an essential condition of an intellectually healthy society. The free communication of information, opinions and argument about the laws which a state should enact and the policies its government at all levels should pursue is an essential condition of truly democratic government. These are the values which Article 10 [of the ECHR] exists to protect, and their importance gives it a central role in the Convention regime, protecting free speech in general and free political speech in particular.
>
> The fundamental rationale of the democratic process is that if competing views, opinions and policies are publicly debated and exposed to public scrutiny the good will over time drive out the bad and the true prevail over the false. It must be assumed that, given time, the public will make a sound choice when, in the course of the democratic process, it has the right to choose. But it is highly desirable that the playing field of debate should be so far as practicable level. This is achieved where, in public discussion, differing views are expressed, contradicted, answered and debated.

The importance of freedom of expression in a democracy was directly in issue in the following case.

Derbyshire County Council v. Times Newspapers Ltd [1993] AC 534 (HL)
Articles published in the *Sunday Times* alleged that Derbyshire County Council had entered into improper financial transactions to the prejudice

of its pension fund. The council brought an action against the publishers claiming damages for libel. The defendants applied to have the action struck out as disclosing no cause of action, thus raising as a preliminary point of law the question whether a local authority could sue for libel in respect of words reflecting on the conduct of its governmental and administrative functions. The authorities established that both trading and non-trading corporations could sue for libel calculated to injure their business or governing reputations; was a local authority, itself a body corporate, in a different position?

Morland J was not persuaded that it was and declined to strike out the council's action, but the Court of Appeal reversed his decision, holding that a local authority could not sue for libel. The council appealed to the House of Lords, which unanimously dismissed the appeal, Lord Keith giving the only speech:

> Lord Keith: ... There are ... features of a local authority which may be regarded as distinguishing it from other types of corporation, whether trading or non-trading. The most important of these features is that it is a governmental body. Further, it is a democratically elected body, the electoral process nowadays being conducted almost exclusively on party political lines. It is of the highest public importance that a democratically elected governmental body, or indeed any governmental body, should be open to uninhibited public criticism. The threat of a civil action for defamation must inevitably have an inhibiting effect on freedom of speech. In *City of Chicago v Tribune* Co (1923) 139 NE 86 the Supreme Court of Illinois held that the city could not maintain an action of damages for libel. Thompson CJ said, at p 90:
>
> > 'The fundamental right of freedom of speech is involved in this litigation, and not merely the right of liberty of the press. If this action can be maintained against a newspaper it can be maintained against every private citizen who ventures to criticise the ministers who are temporarily conducting the affairs of his government. Where any person by speech or writing seeks to persuade others to violate existing law or to overthrow by force or other unlawful means the existing government, he may be punished ... but all other utterances or publications against the government must be considered absolutely privileged. While in the early history of the struggle for freedom of speech the restrictions were enforced by criminal prosecutions, it is clear that a civil action is as great, if not a greater, restriction than a criminal prosecution. If the right to criticise the government is a privilege which, with the exceptions above enumerated, cannot be restricted, then all civil as well as criminal actions are forbidden. A despotic or corrupt government can more easily stifle opposition by a series of civil actions than by criminal prosecutions.'
>
> After giving a number of reasons for this, he said, at p 90:
>
> > 'It follows, therefore, that every citizen has a right to criticise an inefficient or corrupt government without fear of civil as well as criminal prosecution. This absolute privilege is founded on the principle that it is advantageous for the public interest that the citizen

should not be in any way fettered in his statements, and where the public service or due administration of justice is involved he shall have the right to speak his mind freely.'

These propositions were endorsed by the Supreme Court of the United States in *New York Times Co v Sullivan* (1964) 376 US 254, 277. While these decisions were related most directly to the provisions of the American Constitution concerned with securing freedom of speech, the public interest considerations which underlaid them are no less valid in this country. What has been described as 'the chilling effect' induced by the threat of civil actions for libel is very important. Quite often the facts which would justify a defamatory publication are known to be true, but admissible evidence capable of proving those facts is not available. This may prevent the publication of matters which it is very desirable to make public. In *Hector v AG of Antigua and Barbuda* [1990] 2 AC 312 the Judicial Committee of the Privy Council held that a statutory provision which made the printing or distribution of any false statement likely to undermine public confidence in the conduct of public affairs a criminal offence contravened the provisions of the constitution protecting freedom of speech. Lord Bridge of Harwich said, at p 318:

> 'In a free democratic society it is almost too obvious to need stating that those who hold office in government and who are responsible for public administration must always be open to criticism. Any attempt to stifle or fetter such criticism amounts to political censorship of the most insidious and objectionable kind. At the same time it is no less obvious that the very purpose of criticism levelled at those who have the conduct of public affairs by their political opponents is to undermine public confidence in their stewardship and to persuade the electorate that the opponents would make a better job of it than those presently holding office. In the light of these considerations their Lordships cannot help viewing a statutory provision which criminalises statements likely to undermine public confidence in the conduct of public affairs with the utmost suspicion.'

It is of some significance to observe that a number of departments of central government in the United Kingdom are statutorily created corporations, including the Secretaries of State for Defence, Education and Science, Energy, Environment and Social Services. If a local authority can sue for libel there would appear to be no reason in logic for holding that any of these departments (apart from two which are made corporations only for the purpose of holding land) was not also entitled to sue. But as is shown by the decision in *Attorney-General v Guardian Newspapers Ltd (No 2)* [1990] 1 AC 109, a case concerned with confidentiality [on which, see below], there are rights available to private citizens which institutions of central government are not in a position to exercise unless they can show that it is in the public interest to do so. The same applies, in my opinion, to local authorities. In both cases I regard it as right for this House to lay down that not only is there no public interest favouring the right of organs of government, whether central or local, to sue for libel, but that it is contrary to the public interest that they should have it. It is contrary to the public interest because to admit such actions would place an undesirable fetter on freedom of speech.

The conclusion must be, in my opinion, that under the common law of England a local authority does not have the right to maintain an action of damages for defamation.

Lord Keith did, however, note the possibility that individual councillors or officers of a local authority might sue for libel if publication of defamatory matter about the authority reflected on them personally. This qualification provoked the response that 'a suit launched by an individual is not demonstrably less chilling than an action by a council' (Loveland (1994) 14 *LS* 206, 217). As Christopher Forsyth remarks (in Beatson and Cripps (eds.), *Freedom of Expression and Freedom of Information* (2000), p. 88): '[I]f free and vigorous criticism of public authorities is a necessary part of a democratic society how can free and vigorous criticism of the individuals in charge of those public authorities be avoided?'

These issues arose in *Reynolds* v. *Times Newspapers Ltd* [2001] 2 AC 127 in proceedings for libel brought by a politician and former taoiseach (prime minister) of Ireland, arising out of allegations published in the *Sunday Times* that he had misled and lied to the Dáil (the Irish equivalent of Parliament) and cabinet colleagues. It was contended for the newspaper that the defence of qualified privilege (forfeited only on proof of malice) should be available in a case such as this arising out of political discussion and reflecting on the reputation of Mr Reynolds as taoiseach and as an elected member of the Dáil in the exercise of his public responsibilities. It was argued that the common law should be developed so as to admit a new category of qualified privilege covering the publication of 'political information', which would give due recognition to the investigative role of the media in a democratic society. The House of Lords declined to develop the law in this way. A generic category of qualified privilege, protecting the publication of political information whatever the circumstances (in the absence of proof of malice) would not, said Lord Nicholls in the leading speech, give adequate protection to reputation and would be unsound in principle in distinguishing political discussion from discussion of other matters of serious public concern. The elasticity of the established common law approach was to be preferred, by which the court should 'have regard to all the circumstances when deciding whether the publication of particular material was privileged because of its value to the public' – or, more simply, 'whether the public was entitled to know the particular information'. Lord Nicholls listed, by way of illustration, ten specific matters to be taken into account by the court (at 205), adding that the court 'should be slow to conclude that a publication was not in the public interest and, therefore, the public had no right to know, especially when the information is in the field of political discussion'.

In *Jameel* v. *Wall Street Journal Europe* [2006] UKHL 44, [2007] 1 AC 359, at [28], Lord Bingham stated that the decision in *Reynolds* 'carried the law forward in a way which gave much greater weight than the earlier law had done to the value of informed public debate of significant public issues'. Nevertheless, there were concerns that the defence failed to provide clarity to the law, or to facilitate public debate. Lord Nicholls's ten criteria in *Reynolds* aimed to ensure that protection was given to journalism that adhered to principles of responsible journalism. Even with the simplification in *Jameel*, with its focus on looking, first, at whether the publication was in the public interest and, second, at whether it was reasonable and fair, failed to overcome the potential chilling effect. It was also not clear how far the defence could apply to publications by those who were not journalists, who may not know of or adhere to standards of responsible journalism. In addition, it was hard to determine the application of the defence of actual malice. Section 4 of the Defamation Act 2013 overturned the *Reynolds* defence, replacing it with a new defence of publication on a matter of public interest. The defendant needs to show, first, that the statement complained of concerned a matter of public interest and, second, that she reasonably believed that publishing the statement was in the public interest. While this new statutory provision has made it clearer that the defence of publication on a matter of public interest can also apply to citizen-journalists, bloggers etc., the courts have continued to rely on the standards of responsible journalism set out in *Reynolds* to determine whether the defendant's belief that publishing the statement was in the public interest was reasonable (see *Economou v. de Freitas* [2018] EWCA Civ 2591). It remains to be seen whether this section will further responsible journalism ensuring that MPs and others are held accountable for their actions.

11.3.2 The *Spycatcher* Cases

A constraint on freedom of expression may result from the equitable doctrine of breach of confidence, which has been fashioned and refined by the courts over many years. We saw in Chapter 3 that, in *Attorney General* v. *Jonathan Cape Ltd* [1976] QB 752, this doctrine was carried over from the sector of domestic and commercial relationships so as to provide a legal sanction for cabinet confidentiality, although one that proved inapplicable to the particular facts of that case. The doctrine was again relied on by an Attorney General in the *Spycatcher* cases in attempts to prevent publication by newspapers of matters that it was believed should be kept secret in the public interest.

Peter Wright, a former member of the Security Service MI5, gave an account of his experiences in the service in his book, *Spycatcher*, which was to be published in Australia. The book described the organisation and operations of the security service and contained allegations of serious misconduct by members of the service, including a 1974 plot to instigate rumours intended to undermine the Wilson Government. The Attorney General, acting for the British Government, brought proceedings in the Australian courts for an injunction to prevent the publication of the book. The *Guardian* and the *Observer* then published articles about the Australian proceedings which disclosed allegations made in *Spycatcher*, and subsequently the *Sunday Times* began the publication of a series of extracts from the book. The Attorney General took proceedings in the English courts for injunctions against these newspapers, as well as for interlocutory (interim) relief. (There were also certain collateral proceedings for contempt of court: see *Attorney General v. Newspaper Publishing plc* [1988] Ch. 333; *Attorney General v. Times Newspapers Ltd* [1992] 1 AC 191.) Meanwhile, *Spycatcher* was published in the USA – the British Government had been advised of the impossibility of obtaining a judicial restraint on its publication there – and copies became readily available in the UK.

The ground on which the Attorney General sought relief from the courts, both in Australia and in Britain, was that the information to be published had been acquired by Mr Wright in confidence as an officer of MI5 and that he, or anyone who obtained the information knowing of the circumstances, was under a duty of confidentiality that would be breached by publication of the information.

Interlocutory injunctions were granted against the newspapers and were upheld by a majority of the House of Lords in *Attorney General v. Guardian Newspapers Ltd* [1987] 1 WLR 1248. The Law Lords recognised that the case concerned 'the public right to freedom of expression in the press' and that this public interest and the public interest in the protection of the secrecy of the Security Service would have to be 'weighed against each other and a balance struck between them' (Lord Brandon at 1291). The majority were, however, persuaded of the necessity to restrain publication of the material until a final decision was reached on the Attorney General's application for permanent injunctions. They believed that, although the essential information contained in *Spycatcher* had already become known to some, wider dissemination would do further harm and the need to prevent this must take precedence over the right of the public to be provided with information, at all events until the full trial of the case. The dissenting lords, by way of contrast, thought it wrong to maintain a fetter on the disclosure of information that had become publicly available, and they placed greater emphasis on freedom of speech and the 'legitimate business' of the press of 'collecting, disseminating and commenting upon news which they regard as of interest to their reading public' (Lord Oliver at 1315). The following passage, containing a stinging rebuke, is taken from the dissenting speech of Lord Bridge:

> I can see nothing whatever, either in law or on the merits, to be said for the maintenance of a total ban on discussion in the press of this country of matters of undoubted public interest and concern which the rest of the world now knows all about and can discuss freely. Still less can I approve your Lordships' decision to throw in for good measure a restriction on reporting court proceedings in Australia which the Attorney-General had never even asked for. Freedom of speech is always the first casualty under a totalitarian regime. Such a regime cannot afford to allow the free circulation of information and ideas among its citizens. Censorship is the indispensable tool to regulate what the public may and what they may not know. The present attempt to insulate the public in this country from information which is freely available elsewhere is a significant step down that very dangerous road.

When the case came to full trial in *Attorney General* v. *Guardian Newspapers Ltd (No 2)* [1990] 1 AC 109, the Attorney General's claim for permanent injunctions against the newspapers was refused, and this decision was upheld by the House of Lords. The Law Lords were satisfied that further publication would do no more damage to the public interest than had already been done, since the matter was no longer secret and was in the public domain. Detriment to the public interest was an essential condition of the grant of an injunction, at least if the intended publication was to be made not by the Crown servant himself or his agent but by a third party (such as the newspapers in this case).

Besides insisting on the requirement of detriment, the Law Lords in *Guardian Newspapers Ltd (No 2)* allowed for the possibility of a limited defence of revelation of 'iniquity' as a just cause for breaching confidence. Scott J, in the High Court, had found this defence to be made out, holding that allegations such as that of a plot to 'destabilise' the Wilson Government were not to be suppressed: 'the ability of the press freely to report allegations of scandals in government is one of the bulwarks of our democratic society.' However, the House of Lords held that general publication of mere allegations of this sort, which were not shown to be well-founded, was not justified on the 'iniquity' ground.

While, in the result, the House of Lords gave a clear ruling that the suppression of disclosures of official information on the basis of confidentiality must be supported by proof of harm to the public interest, it was only the prior publication of the information contained in *Spycatcher* that was found to have removed any such harm in this case. In principle, any demonstrated harm resulting from breach of confidentiality should be balanced against the public interest in freedom of expression. Lord Griffiths, for instance, said (at 273) that any detriment 'must be examined and weighed against the other countervailing public interest of freedom of speech and the right of the people in a democracy to be informed by a free press'; and Lord Goff declared (at 283) that 'in a free society there is a continuing public interest that the workings of government should be open to scrutiny and criticism', which can be defeated only by 'some other public interest which requires that publication should be restrained'. These are sterling principles, but everything depends on how such a balancing operation is performed, what is regarded as detrimental to the public interest and what weight is given to freedom of expression.

Their Lordships, it should be noted, were of the opinion that if Peter Wright had been within the jurisdiction of the English courts, an injunction to prevent him from publishing *Spycatcher* in this country might properly have been granted. As a former officer of MI5, he owed a lifelong obligation of confidence to the Crown. The prior publication of the book overseas would not avail him when he had himself brought that about, for he should not be allowed to benefit from his own wrongdoing.

The interim injunctions granted in the first *Spycatcher* case in 1987 (above) resulted in a hearing by the ECtHR of complaints by the newspapers concerned that their rights under Article 10 of the European Convention had been violated: *Observer and Guardian* v. *United Kingdom* (1991) 14 EHRR 153. The Court held that the continuation of the interim injunctions after *Spycatcher* had been published in the USA and the confidentiality of the contents destroyed were not necessary in a democratic society and were a violation of Article 10. (See Leigh, 'Spycatcher in Strasbourg' [1992] *PL* 200.)

(For comment on the *Spycatcher* cases, see, e.g., Williams [1989] *CLJ* 1; Barendt [1989] *PL* 204; Birks (1989) 105 *LQR* 501; Burnet and Thomas (1989) 16 *Jnl of Law and Soc* 210; Michael (1989) 52 *MLR* 389; Leigh [1992] *PL* 200. See also *Lord Advocate* v. *Scotsman Publications Ltd* [1990] 1 AC 812.)

11.3.3 Freedom of Expression as a Common Law 'Constitutional Right'

Even before the HRA came into force, freedom of expression had won recognition in a number of common law cases as a 'constitutional right'. It was so characterised by Browne-Wilkinson LJ in a dissenting judgment in the Court of Appeal in *Wheeler* v. *Leicester City Council* [1985] AC 1054, 1065. For Salmon LJ in *R* v. *Metropolitan Police Commissioner, ex p Blackburn (No 2)* [1968] 2 QB 150, 155, freedom of speech was 'one of the pillars of individual liberty . . . which our courts have always unfailingly upheld' and for Laws J in *R* v. *Advertising Standards Authority Ltd, ex p Vernons Organisation Ltd* [1992] 1 WLR 1289, 1293, it was 'a sinew of the common law'. The courts repeatedly affirmed that Article 10 of the ECHR mirrored the common law – including in *Attorney General* v. *Guardian Newspapers Ltd (No 2)* [1990] 1 AC 109, 283 and *Derbyshire County Council* v. *Times Newspapers Ltd* [1993] AC 534, 551.

Yet in the first cases in which the ECtHR found that the UK had violated the terms of Article 10 (the provision in the convention that protects the right to freedom of expression), it was a decision of the domestic courts rather than a piece of legislation that was found to be in breach. *Sunday Times* v. *United Kingdom* (1979) 2 EHRR 245 concerned an injunction that the House of Lords had granted to the Attorney General, which stopped the *Sunday Times* from publishing a story about the drug Thalidomide. The House of Lords had granted the injunction on the basis that it would be in contempt of court (on which see, further, below) for a newspaper to publish an article where there was a *possibility* that publication would prejudice legal proceedings (see *Attorney General* v. *Times Newspapers* [1974] AC 273). The ECtHR ruled that this (common law) test gave insufficient weight to the newspaper's freedom of expression. (This common law test has now been replaced by section 2(2) of the Contempt of Court Act 1981, which provides that such injunctions may be granted only where there is *substantial* risk of *serious* prejudice to legal proceedings.) In *Observer and Guardian* v. *United Kingdom* (1991) 14 EHRR 153, as we saw in the previous section, the two newspapers successfully argued before the ECtHR that the ruling of the House of Lords in *Attorney General* v. *Guardian Newspapers* [1987] 1 WLR 1248 was in breach of Article 10.

In this light, not all judicial dicta about the compatibility of the common law with values of freedom of expression are to be taken at face value. As Lord Bingham stated in *R (Laporte)* v. *Chief Constable of Gloucestershire* [2006] UKHL 55, [2007] 2 AC 105 (at [34]), 'The approach of the . . . common law to freedom of expression and assembly was hesitant and negative.' That said, however, there are undoubtedly some cases where common law protection of freedom of expression has been high. The following is an example.

R v. *Secretary of State for the Home Department, ex p Simms* [2000] 2 AC 115 (HL)

Two prisoners serving life sentences for murder protested their innocence and wished to have oral interviews with journalists who were willing to investigate the safety of their convictions. They hoped that by this means their cases would be reopened and their convictions referred to the Court of Appeal by the Criminal Cases Review Commission. Acting in accordance with a policy adopted by the Home Secretary, the prison authorities refused to allow the interviews to take place unless the journalists signed written undertakings not to publish any part of the interviews. The journalists having refused to do so, permission for the interviews was denied. The prisoners sought judicial review of the lawfulness of the minister's policy. Their claim was based on the right to freedom of expression as supporting their object of challenging the safety of their convictions.

It was argued for the Home Secretary that the ban on interviews was authorised by provisions of the prison rules, made under power conferred by the Prison Act 1952. As we saw above (p. 902), a statute is not to be interpreted as allowing the infringement of what the courts hold to be a fundamental right unless it expressly or by necessary implication authorises this to be done. In the present case, a similar approach was taken to the interpretation of subordinate legislation and it was held that the Home Secretary's policy was not authorised by the prison rules.

> Lord Hoffmann: . . . What this case decides is that the principle of legality applies to subordinate legislation as much as to Acts of Parliament. Prison regulations expressed in general language are also presumed to be subject to fundamental human rights. The presumption enables them to be valid. But, it also means that properly construed, they do not authorise a blanket restriction which would curtail not merely the prisoner's right of free expression, but its use in a way which could provide him with access to justice.

It was further held that even if the provisions of the prison rules could properly have been construed as permitting a blanket ban, those provisions would have been 'exorbitant in width' in undermining the prisoners' fundamental rights: so construed, the provisions would have been ultra vires and invalid.

11.3.4 Freedom of Expression and Statute

A number of statutes expressly protect particular forms of expression. Parliamentary speech is protected under Article 9 of the Bill of Rights 1689. The Public Interest Disclosure Act 1998 provides limited protection for 'whistleblowers'. Contrariwise, several statutes impose restrictions on freedom of expression: the Obscene Publications Act 1959, the Public Order Act 1986 (as amended) and the Official Secrets Act 1989 are all examples. Under section 3 of the HRA, of course, courts are now required to read and give effect to such legislation in a way which is compatible with convention rights, 'so far as it is possible to do so'. The courts must therefore strive to interpret a statute (whenever enacted) in such a way that it does not constitute or permit a restriction of freedom of expression which is not justified in terms of Article 10(2) of the European Convention. If this is not possible, the court may make a declaration of incompatibility (section 4). In consequence of these provisions, the courts may be called on to reconsider their previous interpretations of statutory provisions and to review the balance between freedom of expression and other interests that is effected by particular statutes.

A statute of particular importance in the context of freedom of expression is the Contempt of Court Act 1981. Section 2 of the Contempt of Court Act, although it makes no express reference to freedom of expression, implicitly recognises its value by placing limits on the rule of strict liability for contempt, which applies to publications tending to interfere with the course of justice in particular legal proceedings. Section 2(2) provides:

> The strict liability rule applies only to a publication which creates a substantial risk that the course of justice in the proceedings in question will be seriously impeded or prejudiced.

This sub-section, as we saw above, was enacted in response to the judgment of the ECtHR in *Sunday Times* v. *United Kingdom* (1979) 2 EHRR 245. It is for the courts to determine whether the test of substantial risk of serious prejudice is met in any particular case. This is an exercise in evaluation rather than in balancing, but the Act's recognition of the value of freedom of expression is downgraded if the words 'substantial' and 'seriously' are not given their full weight. Indeed, the courts may appear to have devalued the requirement that the risk be 'substantial' in holding this to mean only that there must be more than a remote or minimal risk of serious prejudice (*Attorney General* v. *English* [1983] 1 AC 116; *Attorney General* v. *News Group Newspapers Ltd* [1987] QB 1, 15), but it has been remarked that the cases in which section 2(2) has been applied show that its provisions 'limit the scope of the old, common-law, strict liability rule ... in a more than cosmetic way' (Feldman, *Civil Liberties and Human Rights in England and Wales* (2nd edn. 2002), p. 984).

Section 5 of the Contempt of Court Act, which comes into play if the risk specified in section 2(2) is found to exist, provides as follows:

> A publication made as or as part of a discussion in good faith of public affairs or other matters of general public interest is not to be treated as a contempt of court under the strict liability rule if the risk of impediment or prejudice to particular legal proceedings is merely incidental to the discussion.

The policy reflected in this section is that the risk of prejudice to a trial must be accepted if it is an incidental by-product of a discussion in good faith of matters of public concern. Here again it is left to the courts to resolve the conflict between 'fair trial and free press', in deciding whether, in a particular case, the criteria in section 5 ('good faith', 'general public interest', 'merely incidental') are satisfied. (See *Attorney General* v. *English*, above, and *Attorney General* v. *Guardian Newspapers Ltd* [1992] 1 WLR 874; and note that it is for the prosecution to prove that the risk of prejudice to the proceedings resulting from a discussion in good faith of matters of general public interest was *not* merely incidental to the discussion.) Section 5 may be seen, in its qualification of the strict liability rule, as giving effect to the proportionality principle.

The Contempt of Court Act gives further recognition to the claims of freedom of expression – in particular, of the investigatory role of the media – in granting a conditional protection to the confidentiality of sources of information. Section 10 of the Act provides as follows:

> No court may require a person to disclose, nor is any person guilty of contempt of court for refusing to disclose, the source of information contained in a publication for which he is responsible, unless it be established to the satisfaction of the court that disclosure is necessary in the interests of justice or national security or for the prevention of disorder or crime.

The purpose of this section was explained by Lord Diplock in *Secretary of State for Defence* v. *Guardian Newspapers Ltd* [1985] AC 339, 348–9:

> Section 10 ... recognises the existence of a prima facie right of ordinary members of the public to be informed of any matter that anyone thinks it appropriate to communicate to them as such ... Provided that it is addressed to the public at large or to any section of it every publication of information falls within the section and is entitled to the protection granted by it unless the publication falls within one of the express exceptions introduced by the word unless.
> The nature of the protection is the removal of compulsion to disclose in judicial proceedings the identity or nature of the source of any information contained in the

> publication, even though the disclosure would be relevant to the determination by the court of an issue in those particular proceedings.

The need for the protection, Lord Diplock went on to say, was that 'unless informers could be confident that their identity would not be revealed sources of information would dry up.' For this reason, the protection of journalistic sources is regarded by the ECtHR as 'one of the basic conditions for press freedom' (*Goodwin* v. *United Kingdom* (1996) 22 EHRR 123, 143).

X Ltd v. *Morgan Grampian (Publishers) Ltd* [1991] 1 AC 1 (HL)

A company, X Ltd, had prepared a business plan to be used in seeking loan capital. An unknown person purloined a copy of the plan and that person or another (the 'source') provided confidential and damaging information taken from it to Mr Goodwin, a journalist, who used it in writing an article about the company for a journal, *The Engineer*. The company applied for an order requiring Mr Goodwin to disclose to it the notes that he had made of his conversations with the source. This would enable the company to identify the source, take proceedings to recover the stolen document and prevent further dissemination of the damaging information. Mr Goodwin invoked section 10 of the Contempt of Court Act 1981. Hoffmann J ordered the defendant to disclose the notes to the company and this order was upheld by the Court of Appeal and by the House of Lords.

> Lord Bridge: ... [W]henever disclosure is sought, as here, of a document which will disclose the identity of a source within the ambit of section 10, the statutory restriction operates unless the party seeking disclosure can satisfy the court that 'disclosure is necessary' in the interests of one of the four matters of public concern that are listed in the section. I think it is indisputable that where a judge asks himself the question: 'Can I be satisfied that disclosure of the source of *this* information is necessary to serve *this* interest?', he has to engage in a balancing exercise. He starts with the assumptions, first, that the protection of sources is itself a matter of high public importance, secondly, that nothing less than necessity will suffice to override it, thirdly, that the necessity can only arise out of concern for another matter of high public importance, being one of the four interests listed in the section.

The House of Lords was in no doubt that it was 'in the interests of justice' that the company should be able to take remedial action against the source. In weighing this public interest against the public interest in the protection of sources, and concluding that discovery of the source was 'necessary' in the interests of justice, their Lordships were moved by the facts that the source had been a party to a gross breach of confidence, that severe damage would be done to the company's business if further dissemination of the confidential material could not be prevented, and that the publication of the information served no legitimate purpose.

Following the dismissal of his appeal to the House of Lords, Mr Goodwin was fined for contempt of court in his earlier refusal to comply with Hoffmann J's order to disclose his source.

On a complaint by Mr Goodwin that the order to disclose his source had violated his right of freedom of expression under Article 10 of the European Convention, the ECtHR considered, in *Goodwin* v. *United Kingdom* (1996) 22 EHRR 123, whether the undoubted interference with his right was justified under Article 10(2) as having the legitimate aim of protecting the rights of X Ltd (identified in these proceedings as Tetra Ltd). The court answered this question in the negative, on the ground that Tetra's interests in unmasking a disloyal employee, preventing further disclosure and obtaining compensation were not sufficient to outweigh 'the vital public interest in the protection of the applicant journalist's source'. Since the disclosure order was disproportionate to the legitimate aim pursued, it could not be regarded as necessary in a democratic society for the protection of the company's rights.

It has been observed that the tests applied in this case by the ECtHR and the House of Lords 'were substantially the same'. It is said that the two courts reached different conclusions *on the facts*, essentially in their assessment of the damage likely to follow from any further disclosure of the confidential information by the source. (See *Camelot Group plc* v. *Centaur Communications Ltd* [1999] QB 124.) Accordingly, it was not considered that any amendment of section 10 of the Contempt of Court Act was necessary as a consequence of the ruling of the European Court in *Goodwin*. (See, further, *Ashworth Hospital Authority* v. *MGN Ltd* [2002] UKHL 29, [2002] 1 WLR 2033; Costigan, 'Protection of Journalists' Sources' [2007] *PL* 464.)

11.3.5 Freedom of Expression and the HRA

To date, the HRA has not had an enormous impact on freedom of expression, either positively or negatively. An early case was *R* v. *Shayler* [2002] UKHL 11, [2003] 1 AC 247. This case was a challenge to the compatibility with Article 10 of the ECHR of certain provisions of the Official Secrets Act 1989. At the time of its enactment critics saw the Act as one of the Thatcher Government's most obnoxious assaults on freedom of political expression. Section 1 of the 1989 Act makes it an offence for a member or former member of the security and intelligence services without lawful authority to disclose any information relating to security or intelligence that came into that person's possession by virtue of his or her employment in the services. No damage to Britain's national security need actually (or even potentially) be caused by the disclosure and it is no defence to a charge under section 1 that the disclosure was in the public interest (on the ground that, for example, it revealed corruption in the services). In *Shayler*, the House of Lords ruled that, the breathtaking scope of this section notwithstanding, it did not breach the protection of freedom of expression afforded by Article 10. Had the Act's ban on the disclosure of such information been absolute, Lord Bingham suggested (at [36]), Article 10 would have been breached. But, as it was, the Act allowed members and former members of the services to disclose any concerns they may have as to the lawfulness of the service's activities to the Attorney General, to the director of public prosecutions or to the Metropolitan Police commissioner, and to disclose concerns about misbehaviour, irregularity, maladministration or incompetence in the services to the home, foreign or Northern Ireland secretaries, to the prime minister, to the cabinet secretary or to the Joint Intelligence Committee. Their Lordships ruled that such avenues were sufficient, given what Lord Bingham described (at [25]) as 'the need for a security or intelligence service to be secure'. Perhaps the decidedly muted support for freedom of expression that one sees in this case had something to do with the unpromising facts. *Shayler*, a former MI5 officer, had disclosed a series of classified documents relating to the security service to the *Mail on Sunday* newspaper without first having gone through any of the channels for voicing grievances permitted to him under the act. He then fled the country for three years before returning to face his charges. In the event, he was jailed for six months, of which term he served only seven weeks before being released. (See, further, on the scope of offences under the Official Secrets Act *R* v. *Keogh* [2007] EWCA Crim 528, [2007] 1 WLR 1500.)

R (Rusbridger) v. *Attorney General* [2003] UKHL 38, [2004] 1 AC 357 concerned the compatibility with Article 10 of the Treason Felony Act 1848. Section 3 of that Act makes it a criminal offence, among other matters, to 'compass, imagine, invent, devise or intend to deprive or depose our Most Gracious Lady the Queen ... from the style, honour, or royal name of the imperial Crown of the United Kingdom'. This provision had as a prime target editors of newspapers advocating republicanism in Britain. Rusbridger, editor of the *Guardian* newspaper, published a series of articles there in which it was argued that Britain should become a republic. The Attorney General brought no proceedings under the Act of 1848 in respect of the articles. Rusbridger sought a statement from the Attorney General that the 1848 Act would be disapplied in respect of all published advocacy of the abolition of the monarchy other than by criminal violence. When the Attorney General declined to give such a statement, Rusbridger sought judicial review, seeking either a declaration that section 3 of the 1848 Act does not apply in the context of peaceful advocacy of the abolition of the monarchy or, in the alternative, a declaration that section 3 of the 1848 Act is incompatible with Article 10 of the ECHR. The administrative court held that there was no decision by the Attorney General that was susceptible to challenge by way of judicial review. On appeal, the House of Lords agreed, refusing to grant either of the declarations sought by the newspaper. However, several of their Lordships passed comment on section 3 of the 1848 Act. Lord Steyn, for example, stated (at [28]) that: 'The part of section 3 of the 1848 Act which appears to criminalise the advocacy of republicanism is a relic of a bygone age and does not fit the fabric of our modern legal system. The idea that section 3 could survive scrutiny under the Human Rights Act is unreal.' Lord Scott stated (at [40]) that: 'It is as plain as a pike staff . . . that no one who advocates the peaceful abolition of the monarchy and its replacement by a republican form of government is at any risk of prosecution'.

Among the most significant free speech cases thus far in the HRA era is the *Prolife* case, to which we now turn.

R (Prolife Alliance) v. British Broadcasting Corporation [2003] UKHL 23, [2004] 1 AC 185

Television broadcasters must ensure, so far as they can, that their programmes contain nothing likely to be offensive to public feeling. This 'offensive material restriction' is a statutory obligation placed on the independent broadcasters by section 6(1)(a) of the Broadcasting Act 1990. The BBC is subject to a comparable, non-statutory obligation under its agreement with the Secretary of State. Prolife Alliance is a political party that campaigns for 'absolute respect for innocent human life from fertilisation until natural death'. Among its main policies is the prohibition of abortion. In May 2001, Prolife Alliance fielded enough candidates for the June 2001 general election to entitle it to make a party election broadcast in Wales. Early in May 2001, Prolife submitted a tape of its proposed broadcast to the BBC, ITV, Channel 4 and Channel 5. The major part of the proposed programme was devoted to explaining the processes involved in different forms of abortion, with pro-longed and graphic images of the product of suction abortion: aborted foetuses in a mangled and mutilated state, tiny limbs, a separated head, and the like. Representatives of each broadcaster refused to screen these pictures as part of the proposed broadcast. The broadcasters did not raise an objection regarding the proposed soundtrack. As Lord Nicholls put it (at [3]), 'Prolife Alliance was not prevented from saying whatever it wished about abortion.' The objection related solely to the pictures. Prolife submitted two further versions of the proposed broadcast to the broadcasters. In the two revised versions, the images of the foetuses were progressively more blurred. Neither was acceptable. On 2 June, a fourth version was submitted and approved. This version replaced the offending pictures with a blank screen bearing the word 'censored'. The blank screen was accompanied by a sound track describing the images shown on the banned pictures. This version was broadcast in Wales on the evening of the same day, five days before the general election.

Prolife sought judicial review of the broadcasters' decisions. The Court of Appeal held in favour of Prolife, holding that the broadcasters' decisions had failed to have sufficient regard to the issues of freedom of political expression that were at stake. By a 4:1 majority (Lord Scott dissenting) the House of Lords upheld the broadcasters' appeal. Lord Nicholls was one of the majority:

Lord Nicholls: . . . Freedom of political speech is a freedom of the very highest importance in any country which lays claim to being a democracy. Restrictions on this freedom need to be examined rigorously by all concerned, not least the courts . . .

In this country access to television by political parties remains very limited. Independent broadcasters are subject to a statutory prohibition against screening advertisements inserted by bodies whose objects are of a political nature. The BBC is prohibited from accepting payment in return for broadcasting. Party political broadcasts and party election broadcasts, transmitted free, are an exception. These 'party broadcasts' are the only occasions when political parties have access to television for programmes they themselves produce. In today's conditions, therefore, when television is such a powerful and intrusive medium of communication, party broadcasts are of considerable importance to political parties and to the democratic process.

The foundation of Prolife Alliance's case is article 10 of the European Convention on Human Rights. Article 10 does not entitle Prolife Alliance or anyone else to make free television broadcasts. Article 10 confers no such right. But that by no means exhausts the application of article 10 in this context. In this context the principle underlying article 10 requires that access to an important public medium of communication should not be refused on discriminatory, arbitrary or unreasonable grounds. Nor should access be granted subject to discriminatory, arbitrary or unreasonable conditions. A restriction on the content of a programme, produced by a political party to promote its stated aims, must be justified. Otherwise it will not be acceptable. This is especially so where, as here, the restriction operates by way of prior restraint. On its face prior restraint is seriously inimical to freedom of political communication.

That is the starting point in this case. In proceeding from there it is important to distinguish between two different questions. Once this distinction is kept in mind the outcome of this case is straightforward. The first question is whether the content of party broadcasts should be subject to the same restriction on offensive material as other programmes. The second question is whether, assuming they should, the broadcasters applied the right standard in the present case.

It is only the second of these two questions which is in issue before your Lordships. I express no view on whether, in the context of a party broadcast, a challenge to the lawfulness of the statutory offensive material restriction would succeed. For present purposes what matters is that before your Lordships' House Prolife Alliance accepted, no doubt for good reasons, that the offensive material restriction is not in itself an infringement of Prolife Alliance's Convention right under article 10. The appeal proceeded on this footing. The only issue before the House is the second, narrower question. The question is this: should the court, in the exercise of its supervisory role, interfere with the broadcasters' decisions that the offensive material restriction precluded them from transmitting the programme proposed by Prolife Alliance?

On this Prolife Alliance's claim can be summarised as follows. A central part of its campaign is that if people only knew what abortion actually involves, and could see the reality for themselves, they would think again about the desirability of abortion. The disturbing nature of the pictures of mangled foetuses is a fundamental part of Prolife

Alliance's message. Conveying the message without the visual images significantly diminishes the impact of the message. A producer of a party broadcast can be expected to exercise self-control over offensiveness, lest the broadcast alienate viewers whose interest and support the party is seeking. Here, it was common ground that the pictures in the proposed programme were not fictitious or reconstructed or 'sensationalised'. Nor was the use of these images 'gratuitous', in the sense of being unnecessary. The pictures were of real cases. In deciding that, even so, the pictures should not be transmitted the broadcasters must have misdirected themselves. They must have attached insufficient importance to the context that this was a party election broadcast. Any risk of distress could have been safeguarded by transmitting the programme after 10.00pm with a suitably explicit warning at the beginning of the programme.

In my view, even on the basis of the most searching scrutiny, Prolife Alliance has not made out a case for interfering with the broadcasters' decisions. Clearly the context in which material is transmitted can play a major part in deciding whether transmission will breach the offensive material restriction. From time to time harrowing scenes are screened as part of news programmes or documentaries or other suitable programmes . . . But, even in such broadcasts, the extent to which distressing scenes may be shown must be strictly limited, so long as the broadcasters remain subject to their existing obligation not to transmit offensive material. Parliament has imposed this restriction on broadcasters and has chosen to apply this restriction as much to party broadcasts as to other programmes. The broadcasters' duty is to do their best to comply with this restriction, loose and imprecise though it may be and involving though it does a significantly subjective element of assessment.

The present case concerns a broadcast on behalf of a party opposed to abortion. Such a programme can be expected to be illustrated, to a strictly limited extent, by disturbing pictures of an abortion. But the Prolife Alliance tapes went much further. In its decision letter dated 17 May 2001 the BBC noted that some images of aborted foetuses could be acceptable depending on the context: 'What is unacceptable is the cumulative effect of several minutes primarily devoted to such images.' None of the broadcasters regarded the case as at the margin. Each regarded this as a 'clear case in which it would plainly be a breach of our obligations to transmit this broadcast'. In reaching their decisions the broadcasters stated they had 'taken into account the importance of the images to the political campaign of the Prolife Alliance'. In my view the broadcasters' application of the statutory criteria cannot be faulted. There is nothing, either in their reasoning or in their overall decisions, to suggest they applied an inappropriate standard when assessing whether transmission of the pictures in question would be likely to be offensive to public feeling.

I respectfully consider that in reaching the contrary conclusion the Court of Appeal fell into error in not observing the distinction between the two questions mentioned above, one of which was before the court and the other of which was not. Laws LJ said (at [22]) the 'real issue' the court had to decide was 'whether those considerations of taste and offensiveness, which moved the broadcasters, constituted a legal justification for the act of censorship involved in banning the claimant's proposed PEB'. The court's constitutional duty, he said (at [37]), amounted to a duty 'to decide for itself whether this censorship was justified'. The letter of 17 May 2001 gave 'no recognition of the critical truth, the legal principle, that considerations of taste and decency cannot prevail over free speech by a political party at election time save wholly exceptionally': [44] . . .

The flaw in this broad approach is that it amounts to rewriting, in the context of party broadcasts, the content of the offensive material restriction imposed by Parliament on broadcasters. It means that an avowed challenge to the broadcasters' decisions became a challenge to the appropriateness of imposing the offensive material restriction on party broadcasts. As already stated, this was not an issue in these proceedings. Had it been, and had a declaration of incompatibility been sought, the appropriate Government minister would need to have been given notice and, no doubt, joined as a party to the proceedings. Then the wide-ranging review of the authorities undertaken by the Court of Appeal would have been called for.

As it was, the Court of Appeal in effect carried out its own balancing exercise between the requirements of freedom of political speech and the protection of the public from being unduly distressed in their own homes. That was not a legitimate exercise for the courts in this case. Parliament has decided where the balance shall be held. The latter interest prevails over the former to the extent that the offensive material ban applies without distinction to all television programmes, including party broadcasts. In the absence of a successful claim that the offensive material restriction is not compatible with the Convention rights of Prolife Alliance, it is not for the courts to find that broadcasters acted unlawfully when they did no more than give effect to the statutory and other obligations binding on them. Even in such a case the effect of section 6(2) of the 1998 Act would have to be considered. I would allow this appeal. The broadcasters' decisions to refuse to transmit the original version, and the first and second revised versions, of Prolife Alliance's proposed broadcast were lawful.

This approach may be contrasted with that of Lord Scott (dissenting):

Lord Scott: . . . The short issue in the case is whether the broadcasters, the BBC and the ITV companies, acted lawfully in declining to transmit the television programme submitted to them by the Prolife Alliance as the Alliance's desired party election broadcast for the purposes of the 2001 general election.

It is accepted that the broadcasters' refusal to transmit the Prolife Alliance's programme engages article 10 of the European Convention on Human Rights . . .

The right to impart information and ideas does not necessarily entitle those who desire to do so to be supplied with the means or facilities necessary to enable the information to be conveyed to the desired audience. A person who has written a book or a play cannot insist on having it published by a publisher, or placed on someone else's bookstall, or, if a play, staged in someone else's theatre. But radio and television broadcasting are different. Licences are required. And licences are granted on conditions that impose restrictions as to the contents of programmes that can be broadcast. So article 10 is engaged.

It follows that, in the present case, the Prolife Alliance is entitled to say that the criteria applied to its desired party election programme by the broadcasters in deciding whether or not to accept the programme should be no more severe than are 'necessary in a democratic society, in the interests of national security, territorial integrity or public safety, for the prevention of disorder or crime, for the protection of health or morals, for the protection of the reputation or rights of others, for preventing the disclosure of information received in confidence, or for maintaining the authority and impartiality of the judiciary' (Article 10(2)).

I have set out in full the article 10(2) heads under which restrictions on article 10 rights can be justified notwithstanding the obvious inapplicability of most of the heads to the reasons why the Alliance's proposed programme was rejected. I have done so because it seems to me helpful to notice their comprehensive character. The application of restrictions allegedly in the public interest but not justifiable under any of these heads would, in my opinion, constitute a breach of article 10 rights . . .

It was not contended by counsel for the Alliance that a restriction barring the televising of a programme likely to be offensive to public feeling was, per se, incompatible with article 10. Nor should it have been. The reference in article 10(2) to the 'rights of others' need not be limited to strictly legal rights the breach of which might sound in damages and is well capable of extending to a recognition of the sense of outrage that might be felt by ordinary members of the public who in the privacy of their homes had switched on the television set and been confronted by gratuitously offensive material.

Nor, as my noble and learned friend, Lord Nicholls of Birkenhead, has pointed out, was it contended before your Lordships that the content of party election broadcasts should be subject to any textually different restrictions from those applicable to other programmes. The requirement that broadcasts should not offend good taste and decency or be offensive to public feeling is not necessarily an article 10 breach in relation to party election broadcasts any more than it is in relation to programmes generally. The issue, therefore, on the present appeal is a narrow one. It is whether the rejection by the broadcasters of this particular programme, the purpose of which was to promote the cause of the Alliance at the forthcoming general election, was a lawful application by the broadcasters of the conditions by which they were bound. To put the point another way, was their rejection of the Alliance's desired programme necessary in a democratic society for the protection of the right of home-owners that offensive material should not be transmitted into their homes?

The issue is one that is fact-sensitive. The relevant facts seem to me to be these. (1) The Prolife Alliance is against abortion. (2) Its candidates at general elections stand on a single issue, namely, that the abortion law should be reformed so as either to bar abortions altogether or, at least, to impose much stricter controls than at present pertain. This is a lawful issue and one of public importance. (3) The Alliance's desired programme was factually accurate. Laws LJ (at [13]), described what was shown in the programme thus: 'The pictures are real footage of real cases. They are not a reconstruction, nor in any way fictitious. Nor are they in any way sensationalised.' There was no dissent from this description. (4) Laws LJ went on to describe what was shown in the programme as 'certainly disturbing to any person of ordinary sensibilities'. This, too, was not disputed. (5) It was accepted that, if the programme was to be transmitted, it would have to be transmitted in the late evening, and be preceded by an appropriate warning. (6) Television is of major importance as a medium for political advertising. That this is so has throughout been recognised on all sides.

The decision to refuse to broadcast the programme was communicated to the Alliance by a letter of 17 May 2001 from the BBC. The letter said that the BBC, and the ITV broadcasters, had concluded that 'it would be wrong to broadcast these images which would be offensive to very large numbers of viewers'. Was this a conclusion to which a reasonable decision maker, paying due regard to the Alliance's right to impart information about abortions to the electorate subject only to what was necessary in a democratic society to protect the rights of others, could have come?

In my opinion, it was not. The restrictions on the broadcasting of material offending against good taste and decency and of material offensive to public feeling were drafted so as to be capable of application to all programmes, whether light entertainment, serious drama, historical or other documentaries, news reports, party political programmes, or whatever. But material that might be required to be rejected in one type of programme might be unexceptionable in another. The judgment of the decision maker would need to take into account the type of programme of which the material formed part as well as the audience at which the programme was directed. This was a party election broadcast directed at the electorate. He, or she, would need to apply the prescribed standard having regard to these factors and to the need that the application be compatible with the guarantees of freedom of expression contained in article 10.

The conclusion to which the broadcasters came could not, in my opinion, have been reached without a significant and fatal undervaluing of two connected features of the case: first, that the programme was to constitute a party election broadcast; second, that the only relevant criterion for a justifiable rejection on offensiveness grounds was that the rejection be necessary for the protection of the right of home-owners not to be subjected to offensive material in their own homes.

The importance of the general election context of the Alliance's proposed programme cannot be overstated. We are fortunate enough to live in what is often described as, and I believe to be, a mature democracy. In a mature democracy political parties are entitled, and expected, to place their policies before the public so that the public can express its opinion on them at the polls. The constitutional importance of this entitlement and expectation is enhanced at election time.

If, as here, a political party's desired election broadcast is factually accurate, not sensationalised, and is relevant to a lawful policy on which its candidates are standing for election, I find it difficult to understand on what possible basis it could properly be rejected as being 'offensive to public feeling'. Voters in a mature democracy may strongly disagree with a policy being promoted by a televised party political broadcast but ought not to be offended by the fact that the policy is being promoted nor, if the promotion is factually accurate and not sensationalised, by the content of the programme. Indeed, in my opinion, the public in a mature democracy are not entitled to be offended by the broadcasting of such a programme. A refusal to transmit such a programme based upon the belief that the programme would be 'offensive to very large numbers of viewers' (the letter of 17 May 2001) would not, in my opinion, be capable of being described as 'necessary in a democratic society ... for the protection of ... rights of others'. Such a refusal would, on the contrary, be positively inimical to the values of a democratic society, to which values it must be assumed that the public adhere.

(See, further on this case, Barendt [2003] *PL* 580; Macdonald [2003] *EHRLR* 651; Rowbottom (2003) 119 *LQR* 553; and see further on the HRA and freedom of expression *R (Animal Defenders International)* v. *Secretary of State for Culture, Media and Sport* [2008] UKHL 15, [2008] 1 AC 1312 (noted by Sackman (2009) 72 *MLR* 475), considered above, p. 954. See also Blom-Cooper [2008] *PL* 260.)

11.3.6 Conflict of Rights

Different convention rights protected by the HRA may come into conflict. In particular, freedom of expression (Article 10) may conflict with the right to respect for private and family life (Article 8). Each of these rights may be restricted by law so far as necessary in a democratic society, inter alia, for the protection of the rights of others (Articles 8(2) and 10(2)). In case of conflict, it is accordingly necessary for the court to balance one right against the other with reference to the particular circumstances, giving to each right its due value and having regard to the principle of proportionality.

Concern was expressed during the passage of the Human Rights Bill that freedom of the press might be curtailed by judicial decisions giving undue weight to respect for privacy. The press were especially apprehensive of the threat of prior restraint of publication by the granting of interlocutory injunctions by the courts, freezing press comment in matters still to be tried. The government responded with an amendment (now section 12 of the HRA) designed to safeguard press freedom (but not restricted to cases affecting newspapers).

Section 12 applies if a court is considering, in civil proceedings, whether to grant any relief which might affect the exercise of the convention right to freedom of expression. The section is not limited to cases in which one of the parties is a public authority. It is provided in particular (section 12(3)) that interlocutory injunctions – only in exceptional circumstances to be granted without notice, the respondent not being present or represented – are not to be granted unless the court is satisfied that the applicant is likely to succeed on the merits at the trial. Such injunctions will accordingly not be granted simply to preserve the existing position of the parties pending the full trial. Further, in deciding whether to give any relief, the court 'must have particular regard to the importance of the convention right to freedom of expression' (section 12(4)). While this provision demonstrates the importance attached to freedom of expression and the media, it does not 'require the court to treat freedom of speech as paramount' (Sir Andrew Morritt V-C in *Imutran Ltd* v. *Uncaged Campaigns Ltd* [2001] 2 All ER 385, at [18]); it is a 'powerful card' but 'not in every case the ace of trumps' (Brooke LJ in *Douglas* v. *Hello! Ltd* [2001] QB 967, at [49]). In proceedings relating to journalistic, literary or artistic material, the court must also have particular regard to the fact or imminent likelihood of the material being in any event available to the public, the extent to which publication would be in the public interest, and any relevant privacy code.

Concerns over the balance of freedom of expression and privacy came to the forefront following the phone-hacking scandal, where *News of the World* journalists were convicted of hacking into telephone conversations in order to source information for stories. Concerns that this was not a 'one-off' incident led to the establishment of a public inquiry – the Leveson Inquiry. Part 1 of the Inquiry investigated the 'culture, practices and ethics of the press' and Part 2 of the Inquiry would have investigated 'the extent of unlawful or improper conduct' within the media. Although Part 1 of the inquiry was delivered, the current Conservative Government dropped Part 2 of the Inquiry. The inquiry led to the disbandment of the Press Complaints Commission, pushing instead for self-regulation through a series of 'approved' regulators, which would be approved by the Press Recognition Panel. There are currently two press regulators – IPSO and IMPRESS. Although IMPRESS is an approved regulator, which complies with the recommendations of the Leveson Inquiry, IPSO is not an approved regulator. Section 40 of the Crime and Courts Act 2013 was designed to provide a financial incentive for newspapers to sign up to an approved regulator – those publishers who had not signed up would have to pay the legal costs for both sides. This section has not been brought into force and the Conservative Party promised to repeal this in their 2019 mani-festo. The 2013 Act also protects those who have signed up from exemplary damages. The outcome of the Leveson Inquiry was widely rejected by the press, who believed this to place too great a restriction of press freedom. This led some newspapers – including *the Guardian* and *the Financial Times* – to refuse to join either of the press regulators, setting up instead their own independent arbiters.

In 2009–10, controversy erupted in Parliament and in the media about the use of so-called 'super-injunctions'. The story is told in the following extract, taken from the report of the House of Commons Culture, Media and Sport Committee, *Press Standards, Privacy and Libel* (*2nd Report of 2009–10*, HC 362):

> On 12 October 2009, one of the members of our Committee, Paul Farrelly MP, tabled a number of Parliamentary questions, one of which concerned an injunction obtained by Trafigura, a company trading in oil, base metals and other items, preventing the publication of a report on the alleged dumping of toxic waste in the Ivory Coast. Trafigura's solicitors, Carter-Ruck, on learning of Mr Farrelly's question, informed the *Guardian* that it would be a breach of the injunction if the newspaper reported the question, but agreed to seek instructions from Trafigura on a variation of the order. The *Guardian* promptly published,

initially online and then on the front page of its 13 October 2009 issue, the fact that it was unable to report a tabled Parliamentary question. The internal report Trafigura wanted to suppress was already widely available on the internet.

The injunction which both Carter-Ruck and *Guardian* lawyers believed prevented the reporting of Parliamentary proceedings was a so-called 'super-injunction'. This is a court order which requires that, when an injunction is in place, its very existence may not be disclosed or published. The order in the *Trafigura* case was granted on 11 September 2009 by a vacation duty judge, Mr Justice Maddison, at a private hearing of which the *Guardian* had just a few hours' notice. It also applied to other 'persons unknown' and anyone who became aware of its existence. The injunction was drafted by Carter-Ruck and in this case a third level of secrecy was granted in that Trafigura and subsidiary's identities as claimants were replaced by the random initials 'RJW' and 'SJW'. The case never went to a full hearing, because the tabling of Parliamentary questions is protected by parliamentary privilege and due to the publicity which followed, not least on the internet, Trafigura and Carter-Ruck withdrew the injunction. The *Guardian* estimated, however, that it would have cost at least £300,000 to go to a hearing, at a time it was making redundancies.

It appears that the injunction and secondary court order were not specifically drafted with the aim of preventing the reporting of parliamentary discussion, and as a result confusion has arisen over whether the injuncted matter could, indeed, be reported when it was referred to in Parliament.

The Lord Chief Justice, Lord Judge, took the unusual step of issuing a press release, stating: 'I am speaking entirely personally but I should need some very powerful persuasion indeed – and that, I suppose, is close to saying I simply cannot envisage – that it would be constitutionally possible, or proper, for a court to make an order which might prevent or hinder or limit discussion of any topic in Parliament. Or that any judge would intentionally formulate an injunction which would purport to have that effect.'

We warmly welcome his comments.

Section 3 of the Parliamentary Papers Act 1840 provides that 'any extract from or abstract of' a 'report, paper, votes, or proceedings' of Parliament is immune from civil and criminal liability if published in good faith and 'without malice'. The right of the press to report matters in Parliament is also codified in statute in Schedule 1 to the Defamation Act 1996 . . . This clearly covers written questions such as that concerning *Trafigura*. In a debate on libel in Westminster Hall on 21 October 2009, Bridget Prentice, the Parliamentary Under-Secretary of State for Justice, confirmed that section 3 of the 1840 Act remained in force, and therefore that the *Guardian* was free to report the text of the question.

However, the Minister's assurances were subsequently challenged in a submission to us from Carter-Ruck. While the firm accepted that Article 9 of the Bill of Rights provides that no court order could restrain debate in Parliament, it remained adamant that reporting of the question by the *Guardian*, which is subject to common law and statute rather than the Bill of Rights, was restrained under the injunction . . .

The free and fair reporting of proceedings in Parliament is a cornerstone of a democracy. In the UK, publication of fair extracts of reports of proceedings in Parliament made without malice are protected by the Parliamentary Papers Act 1840. They cannot be fettered by a court order. However, the confusion over this issue has caused us the very gravest concern that this freedom is being undermined. We therefore repeat previous recommendations from the Committee on Parliamentary Privilege that the Ministry of Justice replace the Parliamentary Papers Act 1840 with a clear and comprehensible modern statute.

These events involving Trafigura occurred after the conclusion of our oral evidence sessions. In a debate in Westminster Hall on 21 October 2009, Bridget Prentice MP, the Parliamentary Under-Secretary of State for Justice, said that the Ministry of Justice was examining the use of super-injunctions outside the areas of fraud and child protection with the judiciary and lawyers from major newspapers. Notwithstanding the controversy already, Carter-Ruck had also sought to persuade the Speaker of the House of Commons that this debate should not proceed as the case was *sub judice* under the House's own rules. The Speaker, however, exercised his absolute discretion and allowed the debate. We welcome the Speaker's determination to defend freedom of speech in Parliament, as well as the comments by the Lord Chief Justice on the Trafigura affair, and strongly urge that a way is found to limit the use of super-injunctions as far as is possible and to make clear that they are not intended to fetter the fundamental rights of the press to report the proceedings of Parliament . . .

Super-injunctions raise acute concerns about matters of civil procedure, open justice and freedom of expression, as well as other matters. Andrew Geddis has perceptively written that disquiet about the super-injunction in the Trafigura case 'forms a subset of broader concerns about the way in which UK law trenches upon freedom of expression. Such concerns encompass the development of the breach of confidence action into a virtual tort of invasion of privacy, as well as perceived plaintiff-friendly defamation rules that have spurred the growth of "libel tourism". From the perspective of newspaper and other media companies, these cumulative legal impediments are hampering their ability to report fully on matters of public interest.' ('What We Cannot Talk About We Must Pass Over in Silence' [2010] *PL* 443, 450–1. See also Adrian Zuckerman's powerfully argued editorial comment at (2010) 29 *CJQ* 131; see, further, Eady (2010) 29 *CJQ* 411; *Terry (Previously 'LNS')* v. *Persons Unknown* [2010] EWHC 119 (QB), [2010] EMLR 16 .) In May 2011, a committee on super-injunctions (chaired by the Master of the Rolls) published a full report analysing the issues in depth (the report is available via www.judiciary.gov.uk).

11.4 Freedom of Assembly

'The freedom to demonstrate one's views in public – within the law – is fundamental to a democracy' (*Review of the Public Order Act 1936*, Cmnd 7891/1980, para 36). Freedom of assembly bears a close relation to freedom of speech, for in the constitutional context our concern is with assemblies held to further a political campaign or to mount a public protest: such assemblies have the purpose of communication, by argument, pressure or persuasion.

Frederick Schauer, *Free Speech: A Philosophical Enquiry* (1982), pp. 201–2

Much speech takes place in settings in which the only issues as to regulation are those that relate to the content of the communication. Whether we should regulate matter appearing in books, newspapers, and Hyde Park Corner orations, for example, is determined by what is said, and our estimation of the dangers that might flow from the particular communicative content of the speech.

Traditionally, these concerns with content have constituted the only important free speech questions. But as speech has moved into new settings, new considerations not related to content have appeared. When people communicate by picketing, through the use of demonstrations or in parades, interests not related to the content of the communication are implicated. Parades interfere with the flow of traffic, demonstrations may prevent people from going where they wish to go, and picketing may interfere with the operation of a business or office. All of these are legitimate concerns. Yet these settings for communication are becoming increasingly prevalent in contemporary society. Reconciling the free speech interests with the acknowledged importance of traffic- and crowd-control has as a result become an increasingly important problem for free speech theory.

It is tempting to say that this type of communication is less important. Communication by parades, demonstrations and picketing is more emotional than intellectual, and more fully argued statements of the positions involved are available in books, newspapers, magazines and other less obstructive communicative formats. If we cut off 'speech in the streets', there remain readily available alternative forums, and there is little danger that some ideas will remain unsaid. Indeed, restricting speech of this type may well support some of the values protected by a system of freedom of speech, by forcing communication into channels more conducive to rational argument and deliberation, thereby increasing the overall level of civility in public discourse.

Acceptance of such a position, however, requires that we ignore an important phenomenon in contemporary communication. When people first started talking and writing about freedom of speech and freedom of the press, there existed only a few forums for communication. There was no radio or television or cinema, few newspapers, few periodicals, and comparatively few political tracts published for private distribution. It was not at all unreasonable to assume that a mildly expressed and closely reasoned political or social or theological argument would in fact be read or heard by most people having any interest in such matters. But now, with radio, television and film, with almost innumerable newspapers, magazines, books and pamphlets, and with so many people speaking out on so many different subjects, there is perhaps 'too much' speech, in the sense that it is impossible to read or hear even a minute percentage of what is being expressed. There is a din of speech, and our limited capacity to read or to hear has resulted in effective censorship by the proliferation of opinion rather than by the restriction of opinion. We learn no more from a thousand people all speaking at the same time than we learn from total silence.

Under such circumstances it is frequently necessary, literally or figuratively, to shout to be heard. One method of gaining a listener's attention is by the use of offensive words or pictures. Another, more relevant here, is through the use of placards, large groups of people, loud noises and all the other attention-getting devices that are part of parades, picketing and demonstrations. To restrict these methods of communication is to restrict the effectiveness of speech, and also to restrict the extent to which new or controversial ideas may be brought to the attention of potential listeners.

Moreover, important free speech values are served by emotive utterances. This is most apparent under the catharsis argument [discussed by the author in chap. 6 of his book]. But it is equally important under the argument from democracy. As a voter I am interested not only in what others feel about a certain issue, but also in how many people share that view, and in how strongly that opinion is held. As a public official I am equally concerned (or should be) with gauging the extent and the strength of public opinion. In addition, freedom of speech serves a legitimizing function, in holding that people should be bound by official policy if they have had, through speech, the opportunity to participate (even if unsuccessfully) in the process of formulating official policy. In terms of this function, parades, picketing and demonstrations are a way of attempting to influence official policy and are thus a part of the total process.

I am not arguing that parades, demonstrations and picketing should always be protected. Nor am I arguing that there are not good reasons for restricting speech when it takes these forms. What I am arguing is that there are good reasons for recognizing this type of speech as being important, and that there seem to be no good reasons for relegating these forms of communication to some inferior status in the free speech hierarchy. The question is not one of balancing a less legitimate form of speech against legitimate governmental interests in peace and order, but rather is one of balancing an important and legitimate form of communication against important and legitimate governmental interests. When so formulated the problem is a difficult one, but one that is fortunately slightly more susceptible to rational resolution than some other free speech problems.

(See, also, Eric Barendt's discussion of the value of freedom of assembly, in Beatson and Cripps, *Freedom of Expression and Freedom of Information* (2000), pp. 165–9, suggesting that freedom of assembly is also important for other values than freedom of speech, such as in enabling unrepresented groups in society to participate in political activity.)

11.4.1 Common Law: The Classic Authorities

'It can hardly be said', remarked Dicey (*The Law of the Constitution* (1885), p. 271), 'that our constitution knows of such a thing as any specific right of public meeting.' By the same token, he went on to say, if persons holding a meeting did not break the law they could not, as a general rule, be required by the authorities to disperse. This is the traditional view of constitutional 'rights' as merely residual liberties. The potential strength of this approach was famously illustrated in the following case.

Beatty v. *Gillbanks* (1882) 9 QBD 308 (DC)

The Salvation Army was in the habit of marching in procession through the streets of Weston-super-Mare. The objectives were peaceable but the Army was accompanied by vociferous supporters and opposed by a militant organ-isation, the Skeleton Army, which on several occasions violently resisted passage, causing outbreaks of disorder on the streets. Local magistrates pub-lished a notice ordering all persons 'to abstain from assembling to the disturb-ance of the public peace', but, on the following Sunday, the Salvationists set out as usual, and as usual were followed by a large and noisy crowd. The police met the procession and told Beatty, one of the leaders, that they must obey the magistrates' notice and disperse. Beatty refused and, the march continuing, he and other leaders were arrested. None of them had committed acts of violence, but on being brought before justices of the peace they were found to have unlawfully and tumultuously assembled and were bound over (required to find sureties to keep the peace) for twelve months. They appealed by way of case stated to the Divisional Court, which gave judgment for the appellants:.

Field J: I am of opinion that this order cannot be supported. The matter arises in this way. The appellants have, with others, formed themselves into an association for religious exercises among themselves, and for a religious revival, if I may use that word, which they desire to further among certain classes of the community. No one imputes to this association any other object, and so far from wishing to carry that out with violence, their opinions seem to be opposed to such a course, and, at all events in the present case, they made no opposition to the authorities. That being their lawful object, they assembled as they had done before and marched in procession through the streets of Weston-super-Mare. No one can say that such an assembly is in itself an unlawful one. The appellants complain that in consequence of this assembly they have been found guilty of a crime of which there is no reasonable evidence that they have been guilty. The charge against them is, that they unlawfully and tumultuously assembled, with others, to the disturbance of the public peace and against the peace of the Queen. Before they can be convicted it must be shewn that this offence has been committed. There is no doubt that they and with them others assembled together in great numbers, but such an assembly to be unlawful must be tumultuous and against the peace. As far as these appellants are concerned there was nothing in their conduct when they were assembled together which was either tumultuous or against the peace. But it is said, that the conduct pursued by them on this occasion was such, as on several previous occasions, had produced riots and disturbance of the peace and terror to the inhabitants, and that the appellants knowing when they assembled together that such consequences would again arise are liable to this charge.

Now I entirely concede that every one must be taken to intend the natural consequences of his own acts, and it is clear to me that if this disturbance of the peace was the natural consequence of acts of the appellants they would be liable, and the justices would have been right in binding them over. But the evidence set forth in the case does not support this contention; on the contrary, it shews that the disturbances were caused by other people antagonistic to the appellants, and that no acts of violence were committed by them.

In Hawkins' Pleas of the Crown, s 9, it is said, 'An unlawful assembly according to the common opinion is a disturbance of the peace by persons barely assembling together with the intention to do a thing which if it were executed would make them rioters, but neither actually executing it nor making a motion toward the execution of it.' On this definition, standing alone, it is clear that the appellants were guilty of no offence, for it cannot be contended that they had any intention to commit any riotous act. The paragraph, however, continues thus, 'But this seems to be much too narrow a definition. For any meeting whatever of great numbers of people, with such circumstances of terror as cannot but endanger the public peace and raise fears and jealousies among the king's subjects, seems properly to be called an unlawful assembly, as where great numbers, complaining of a common grievance, meet together, armed in a warlike manner, in order to consult together concerning the most proper means for the recovery of their interests; for no man can foresee what may be the event of such an assembly.' Examples are then given, but in each the circumstances of terror exist in the assembly itself, either in its object or mode of carrying it out, and there is the widest difference between such cases and the present. What has happened here is that an unlawful organisation has assumed to itself the right to prevent the appellants and others from lawfully assembling together, and the finding of the justices amounts to this, that a man may be convicted for doing a lawful act if he knows that his doing it may cause another to do an unlawful act. There is no authority for such a proposition, and the question of the justices whether the facts stated in the case constituted the offence charged in the information must therefore be answered in the negative.

Cave J concurred.

Even if the reasoning of Field J on the question of the causation of the disorder was somewhat superficial (see Bevan [1979] *PL* 163, 178; Supperstone, *Brownlie's Law of Public Order and National Security* (2nd edn. 1981), pp. 126–7), the case stands as a beacon in upholding the legality of peaceful public assembly and the principle that a gathering does not become unlawful because other persons are so inflamed by it as to commit acts of violence. The dictum of O'Brien J in *R* v. *Londonderry Justices* (1891) 28 LR Ir 440, 450, is consistent with this principle:

If danger arises from the exercise of lawful rights resulting in a breach of the peace, the remedy is the presence of sufficient force to prevent that result, not the legal condemnation of those who exercise those rights.

Although only rarely since applied by the courts (and more often distin-guished, as in *O'Kelly* v. *Harvey* (1883) 10 LR Ir 285 and *Wise* v. *Dunning* [1902] 1 KB 167), the principle of *Beatty* v. *Gillbanks* has never been over-thrown, has continued to inform public discussion (as in Lord Scarman's *Report on The Red Lion Square Disorders of 15 June 1974*, Cmnd 5919/1975, paras 69–70) and has, in general, guided public authorities in the use of their discretionary powers – for example, to ban the holding of processions (now under section 13 of the Public Order Act 1986): see Gearty, in McCrudden and Chambers (eds.), *Individual Rights and the Law in Britain* (1994), p. 55.

Beatty v. Gillbanks, it has been remarked, 'is essentially concerned with prior control, in the form of formal restraining orders imposed by courts or administrators or by the police, rather than with the duty or power of police officers responding instantly to actual threats to the public peace' (Williams, in Doob and Greenspan (eds.), *Perspectives in Criminal Law* (1985), p. 116). Persons taking part in peaceful public processions or meetings have had to submit to directions given by police on the spot in exercising their preventive powers to preserve the peace. This qualification (or is it more than a 'qualification'?) of the *Beatty* v. *Gillbanks* principle was firmly embedded in the law by the decision in *Duncan* v. *Jones* (below) and the two precedents have endured in uneasy misalliance since that time.

Duncan v. *Jones* [1936] 1 KB 218 (DC)

Mrs Duncan was about to address a meeting in the street opposite the entrance to an unemployed training centre. After a meeting addressed by her in the same place fourteen months previously, a disturbance had taken place inside the centre. On this occasion, police officers, reasonably believing – it was afterwards found – that a breach of the peace might again occur, told Mrs Duncan that the meeting must not be held in that place but may instead be held in another street nearby. When she insisted on addressing those present, she was arrested and subsequently convicted by magistrates of the statutory offence of obstructing a constable in the execution of his duty. Mrs Duncan appealed to the Divisional Court.

> Lord Hewart CJ: There have been moments during the argument in this case when it appeared to be suggested that the Court had to do with a grave case involving what is called the right of public meeting. I say 'called,' because English law does not recognise any special right of public meeting for political or other purposes. The right of assembly, as Professor Dicey puts it, is nothing more than a view taken by the Court of the individual liberty of the subject. If I thought that the present case raised a question which has been held in suspense by more than one writer on constitutional law – namely, whether an assembly can properly be held to be unlawful merely because the holding of it is expected to give rise to a breach of the peace on the part of persons opposed to those who are holding the meeting – I should wish to hear much more argument before I expressed an opinion. This case, however, does not even touch that important question.

Lord Hewart then gave brief attention to 'the somewhat unsatisfactory case' of *Beatty* v. *Gillbanks*, noting that the circumstances and the charge in that case were different from the matter before him and that Field J had there conceded that everyone must be taken to intend the natural consequences of his or her own acts. He continued:

The case stated which we have before us indicates clearly a causal connection between the meeting of [the previous year] and the disturbance which occurred after it . . . In my view, the deputy-chairman was entitled to come to the conclusion to which he came on the facts which he found and to hold that the conviction of the appellant for wilfully obstructing the respondent when in the execution of his duty was right. This appeal should, therefore, be dismissed.

Humphreys J: I agree. I regard this as a plain case. It has nothing to do with the law of unlawful assembly. No charge of that sort was even suggested against the appellant. The sole question raised by the case is whether the respondent, who was admittedly obstructed, was so obstructed when in the execution of his duty.

It does not require authority to emphasize the statement that it is the duty of a police officer to prevent apprehended breaches of the peace. Here it is found as a fact that the respondent reasonably apprehended a breach of the peace. It then, as is rightly expressed in the case, became his duty to prevent anything which in his view would cause that breach of the peace. While he was taking steps so to do he was wilfully obstructed by the appellant. I can conceive no clearer case within the statutes than that.

Singleton J agreed that the appeal should be dismissed.

See, on this case, Wade (1936–39) 6 *CLJ* 175, 179, who wrote that 'the net has closed entirely upon those who from lack of resources, or for other reasons, desire to hold meetings in public places'; Daintith [1966] *PL* 248, who observes that it brought about a 'substantial expansion of police powers'; Ewing and Gearty, *The Struggle for Civil Liberties: Political Freedom and the Rule of Law in Britain 1914–1945* (2000), who describe the case as being 'as noteworthy today for the vacuity of its reasoning as for its long-term deleterious effect on civil liberties' (at p. 265). The courts have repeatedly endorsed the reasoning of *Duncan v. Jones* and have readily upheld the actions of the police in preventing or dispersing demonstrations and in arresting those who persist for breach of the peace: see *Piddington v. Bates* [1961] 1 WLR 162; *Kavanagh v. Hiscock* [1974] QB 600; *Moss v. McLachlan* [1985] IRLR 76. The courts have, it is true, insisted that the police must anticipate 'a real, not a remote, possibility' of a breach of the peace before taking preventive action, but have been reluctant to question the judgment of police officers on the spot as to the necessity for intervention (see, further on this point, below). In *R v. Chief Constable of Sussex, ex p International Trader's Ferry Ltd* [1999] 2 AC 418, 435, Lord Slynn reaffirmed the principle reflected in *Duncan v. Jones* and its progeny in saying: 'I do not accept that *Beatty v. Gillbanks* lays down that the police can never restrain a lawful activity if that is the only way to prevent violence and a breach of the peace.'

The decision in the following case may be thought to invite a reconsideration of *Duncan v. Jones*.

Redmond-Bate v. *Director of Public Prosecutions* [2000] HRLR 249 (DC)

The appellant, Alison Redmond-Bate, and two other women were preaching to passers-by from the steps of Wakefield Cathedral. A crowd of over

100 people gathered and some of them were showing hostility towards the preachers. A constable arrived and, fearing a breach of the peace, asked the women to stop preaching; when they refused, he arrested them for breach of the peace. The appellant was subsequently charged with obstructing the constable in the execution of his duty. She was convicted and, her appeal to the Crown Court having been dismissed, appealed by case stated to the Divisional Court.

The essential question for the court was whether the constable had been acting in the execution of his duty when he asked the women to stop speaking. A constable is not empowered to take preventive action in such circumstances unless he has reasonable grounds to fear that a breach of the peace, in the form of violent conduct, will occur. Even if this requirement is satisfied, there is a further matter to be considered by the constable – and by a court in deciding whether the constable was justified in the action he took. Sedley LJ's judgment (in which Collins J concurred) was mainly directed to this further question:

> **Sedley LJ:** . . . [A] judgment as to the imminence of a breach of the peace does not conclude the constable's task. The next and critical question for the constable, and in turn for the court, is where the threat is coming from, because it is there that the preventive action must be directed. Classic authority illustrates the point. In *Beatty* v. *Gillbanks* (1882) 9 QBD 308 this court (Field, J and Cave, J) held that a lawful Salvation Army march which attracted disorderly opposition and was therefore the occasion of a breach of the peace could not found a case of unlawful assembly against the leaders of the Salvation Army. Field, J, accepting that a person is liable for the natural consequences of what he does, held nevertheless that the natural consequences of the lawful activity of the Salvation Army did not include the unlawful activities of others, even if the accused knew that others would react unlawfully. By way of contrast, in *Wise* v. *Dunning* [1902] 1 KB 167 a Protestant preacher in Liverpool was held by this Court (Lord Alverstone, CJ, Darling and Channell, JJ) to be liable to be bound over to keep the peace upon proof that he habitually accompanied his public speeches with behaviour calculated to insult Roman Catholics. The distinction between the two cases is clear enough: the reactions of opponents would in either case be unlawful, but while in the first case they were the voluntary acts of people who could not properly be regarded as objects of provocation, in the second the conduct was calculated to provoke violent and disorderly reaction.

In regard to *Duncan* v. *Jones*, Sedley LJ said that the court had there 'cast its reasoning somewhat wider than – as it seems to me – is consonant with modern authority'. He was able to distinguish that case from the present one on the basis that the justices in *Duncan* v. *Jones* had found that the appellant, Mrs Duncan, had herself been the source of the threat to public order. Sedley LJ went on to consider the ruling of the Crown Court in the present case:

The Crown Court correctly directed itself that violence is not a natural consequence of what a person does unless it clearly interferes with the rights of others so as to make a violent reaction not wholly unreasonable.

Contrariwise, as to the ruling of the Crown Court that 'lawful conduct can, if persisted in, lead to conviction for wilful obstruction of a police officer', Sedley LJ said:

This proposition has, in my judgment, no basis in law. A police officer has no right to call upon a citizen to desist from lawful conduct. It is only if otherwise lawful conduct gives rise to a reasonable apprehension that it will, by interfering with the rights or liberties of others, provoke violence which, though unlawful, would not be entirely unreasonable that a constable is empowered to take steps to prevent it.

With regard to the present case Sedley LJ went on to say:

The question for [the constable] was whether there was a threat of violence and if so, from whom it was coming. If there was no real threat, no question of intervention for breach of the peace arose. If the appellant and her companions were (like the street preacher in *Wise v. Dunning*) being so provocative that someone in the crowd, without behaving wholly unreasonably, might be moved to violence he was entitled to ask them to stop and to arrest them if they would not. If the threat of disorder or violence was coming from passers-by who were taking the opportunity to react so as to cause trouble (like the Skeleton Army in *Beatty v. Gillbanks*), then it was they and not the preachers who should be asked to desist and arrested if they would not.

On the facts of the case, Sedley LJ could see no lawful basis for the arrest of the appellant or for her conviction. As to a concession by the prosecution that blame would not attach for a breach of the peace to a speaker 'so long as what she said was inoffensive', the judge responded:

This will not do. Free speech includes not only the inoffensive but the irritating, the contentious, the eccentric, the heretical, the unwelcome and the provocative provided it does not tend to provoke violence. Freedom only to speak inoffensively is not worth having.

The conclusion of the court was that the situation perceived by the constable 'did not justify him in apprehending a breach of the peace, much less a breach of the peace for which the three women would be responsible'. The appeal was accordingly allowed.

The principle vindicated in this case was reaffirmed by the Court of Appeal in *Bibby* v. *Chief Constable of Essex* (2000) 164 JP 297. See the comment on these cases by Smith [2000] *CLJ* 425.

11.4.2 Common Law Preventive Powers and Breach of the Peace

Unlike in Scots law, in English law, breach of the peace is not *itself* a criminal offence (for the offence in Scots law, see, e.g., *Smith* v. *Donnelly* 2001 SLT 1007). In *R (Laporte)* v. *Chief Constable of Gloucestershire* [2006] UKHL 55, [2007] 2 AC 105, Lord Brown stated (at [111]) that a breach of the peace, while not itself a criminal offence in English law, 'necessarily involves' the commission of a criminal offence; see, further on this case, below. Under English law, a magistrate may 'bind over' an individual to keep the peace, meaning that the individual may forfeit a sum of money if he or she subsequently breaches the peace (Magistrates' Courts Act 1980, section 115). Refusal to be bound over to keep the peace is an offence in English law, punishable by up to six months' imprisonment. (These principles date back to at least the fourteenth century: see the Justices of the Peace Act 1361; for commentary, see Feldman [1988] *CLJ* 101.) Under the common law, the police possess a preventive power of arrest in anticipation of a breach of the peace. The anticipated breach of the peace must be 'imminent' (see below). This is not only a power: it is, in some circumstances, a duty. Moreover, it is a duty that is shared by the police and by citizens alike. In *Albert* v. *Lavin* [1982] AC 546 Lord Diplock stated (at 565) that:

> every citizen in whose presence a breach of the peace is being, or reasonably appears to be about to be, committed has the right to take reasonable steps to make the person who is breaking or threatening to break the peace refrain from doing so; and those reasonable steps in appropriate cases will include detaining him against his will. At common law this is not only the right of every citizen, it is also his duty, although, except in the case of a citizen who is a constable, it is a duty of imperfect obligation.

The police also possess a power, vehemently contested by civil liberties commentators, to enter private premises to prevent an anticipated breach of the peace (see the controversial decision in *Thomas* v. *Sawkins* [1935] 2 KB 249; see, further, *McLeod* v. *Metropolitan Police Commissioner* [1994] 4 All ER 553; *McLeod* v. *United Kingdom* (1999) 27 EHRR 493; for commentary on *Thomas* v. *Sawkins*, see Ewing and Gearty, *The Struggle for Civil Liberties: Political Freedom and the Rule of Law in Britain* 1914–1945 (2000), pp. 289–95).

'Breach of the peace' is a concept that has been variously defined. In *R* v. *Chief Constable of Devon and Cornwall Police, ex p CEGB* [1982] QB 458, 471, Lord Denning MR went so far as to proclaim that: 'There is a breach of the peace whenever a person who is lawfully carrying out his work is unlawfully and physically prevented by another from doing it . . . If anyone unlawfully and physically obstructs the worker, by lying down or chaining himself to a rig or the like, he is guilty of a breach of the peace.' (Other members of the Court of Appeal offered narrower definitions in this case.) Given the range of intrusive and coercive powers accorded to the police in anticipation of breach of the peace, were such a broad definition to stand, the exercise of such police powers would clearly fall foul of convention rights. In *Percy* v. *DPP* [1995] 1 WLR 1382, the court made it clear that there could be no breach of the peace without violence or the threat of violence. That said, however, the violence does not have to be perpetrated by the person arrested: it is sufficient if violence from another party is a natural consequence of his or her action. The ECtHR has ruled that, given (and subject to) this clarification, arrests for breach of the peace do not (without some further problem) breach Article 5(1) of the ECHR: see *Steel* v. *United Kingdom* (1998) 28 EHRR 603. But cf. *Hashman* v. *United Kingdom* (2000) 30 EHRR 241, where the Court held that a binding over order to be 'of good behaviour' was in breach of Article 10, and *McLeod* v. *United Kingdom* (above), where the court held that a particular use of the *Thomas* v. *Sawkins* power to enter private premises in anticipation of a breach of the peace was not justified and was in breach of Article 8. (For commentary on these cases, see Fenwick and Phillipson, 'Direct Action, Convention Values and the Human Rights Act' (2001) 21 *LS* 535, 553–7.)

In *Moss* v. *McLachlan* [1985] IRLR 76, the Divisional Court confirmed that preventive action may be taken only if the officers 'honestly and reasonably form the opinion that there is a real risk of a breach of the peace in the sense that it is in close proximity both in place and time', but the court's application of this principle to the facts of the case caused controversy. The case arose from the miners' strike of 1984–5. Disorder had occurred at collieries in Nottinghamshire and police were stationed at a road junction in the county to prevent striking miners from taking part in mass pickets at any of four nearby collieries. It was held that the police had acted lawfully in stopping a group of about sixty miners from proceeding in cars to join a mass picket at one or other of the collieries (the nearest being one-and-a-half to two miles away), since there was a substantial risk that an outbreak of violence would result. The likelihood of a breach of the peace, said the court, was 'imminent, immediate and not remote'. Four miners who had refused police orders to turn back were held to be rightly convicted of obstructing the police in the execution of their duty, although it was not shown that any of them had done anything from which an intention to commit acts of violence could be inferred. (For criticism of the decision, see, e.g., Newbold [1985] *PL* 30.)

These issues arose again in the following case.

R (Laporte) v. *Chief Constable of Gloucestershire* [2006] UKHL 55, [2007] 2 AC 105
Ms Laporte was travelling on a coach from London to Gloucestershire in order to take part in a protest against the Iraq war at a US Air Force base at

Fairford, which is in that county. Several coachloads of protesters were making the same journey. The police had received intelligence that a number of the passengers intended to breach the peace and that not all of the protesters would act peacefully. A few miles from Fairford, at a place called Lechlade, the police stopped the coaches, then boarded and searched them. It was apparently impossible for the police to identify with certainty which of the passengers intended to protest violently and which peacefully. All the passengers were ordered to return to London and were escorted throughout the two-and-a-half-hour journey by the police. The coaches were not allowed to stop and no passenger was permitted to disembark until the coaches reached London.

On an application for judicial review, the claimant argued that the police had acted unlawfully (1) in preventing her from travelling to the demonstration at Fairford and (2) in returning her to London in the manner described above. The Divisional Court and the Court of Appeal held against the claimant on the first point (both courts expressly relying on *Moss* v. *McLachlan*, above) and for the claimant on the second point. The House of Lords unanimously allowed the claimant's appeal (and unanimously dismissed the chief constable's cross-appeal). As Lord Brown expressed it (at [115]), the problem with the judgments of the lower courts was, in the view of the Law Lords, that, on the approach adopted there, 'the police are under a duty to take reasonable steps to prevent a breach of the peace *from becoming* imminent (rather than *which is* imminent)'.

While their Lordships declined to overrule the decision in *Moss* v. *McLachlan*, they distinguished it on the facts. Lord Brown (at [118]) said of the case that it had gone 'to the furthermost limits of any acceptable view of imminence, and then only on the basis that those prevented from attending the demonstration were indeed manifestly intent on violence'. Lord Carswell summarised the legal issues in *Laporte* in the following stark manner, at [92]:

> the appellant . . . was prevented from taking part in a lawful demonstration at the Fairford air base. In a country which prides itself on the degree of liberty available to all citizens the law must take this curtailment of her freedom of action seriously.

The significance of their Lordships' ruling in *Laporte* is further revealed in the following passages from the opinion of Lord Bingham.

> **Lord Bingham:** . . . Reduced to essentials, the argument of Mr Emmerson QC for the claimant rested on four propositions:
>
> (1) Subject to Articles 10(2) and 11(2) of the European Convention, the claimant had a right to attend the lawful assembly at RAF Fairford in order to express her strong opposition to the war against Iraq.

(2) The conduct of the Chief Constable ... in stopping the coach on which the claimant was travelling at Lechlade and not allowing it to continue its intended journey to Fairford, was an interference by a public authority with the claimant's exercise of her rights under Articles 10 and 11.

(3) The burden of justifying an interference with the exercise of a Convention right such as those protected by Articles 10 and 11 lies on the public authority which has interfered with such exercise, in this case the Chief Constable.

(4) The interference by the Chief Constable in this case was for a legitimate purpose but

(a) was not prescribed by law, because not warranted under domestic law, and (b) was not necessary in a democratic society, because it was (i) premature and (ii) indiscriminate and was accordingly disproportionate.

Mr Freeland QC, for the Chief Constable, did not contest the correctness of propositions (1), (2) and (3), and it was common ground that the Chief Constable acted in the interests of national security, for the prevention of disorder or crime or for the protection of the rights of others, these being legitimate purposes under Articles 10(2) and 11(2). The remainder of what I have called proposition (4) was, however, strongly contested between the parties.

Mr Emmerson argued that the Chief Constable's interference was not prescribed by law because not warranted by domestic legal authority. According to that authority there is a power and duty resting on constable and private citizen alike to prevent a breach of the peace which reasonably appears to be about to be committed. That is the test laid down in *Albert v Lavin* [1982] AC 546 [above] ... It refers to an event which is imminent, on the point of happening. The test is the same whether the intervention is by arrest or ... by action short of arrest. There is nothing in domestic authority to support the proposition that action short of arrest may be taken when a breach of the peace is not so imminent as would be necessary to justify an arrest. Here, Mr Lambert [the senior police officer at the scene] did not think a breach of the peace was so imminent as to justify an arrest. He recorded that judgment at 10.45am. There is no evidence to suggest that his judgment ever altered. It was, in any event, plainly correct ... The conduct of Mr Lambert was not governed by some general test of reasonableness but by the *Albert v Lavin* test of whether it reasonably appeared that a breach of the peace was about to be committed. By that standard Mr Lambert's conduct, however well-intentioned, was unlawful in domestic law ...

I am persuaded ... that the Chief Constable's interference with the claimant's right to demonstrate at a lawful assembly at RAF Fairford was not prescribed by law ...

I would add ... that if (on which I express no opinion) the public interest requires that the power of the police to control demonstrations of this kind should be extended, any such extension should in my opinion be effected by legislative enactment and not judicial decision. As the Strasbourg authorities ... make clear, Article 10 and 11 rights are fundamental rights, to be protected as such. Any prior restraint on their exercise must be scrutinised with particular care. The Convention test of necessity does not require that a restriction be indispensable, but nor is it enough that it be useful, reasonable or desirable: *Handyside v United Kingdom* (1976) 1 EHRR 737, para 48; *Silver v United Kingdom* (1983) 5 EHRR 347, para 97. Assessment of whether a new restriction meets the exacting Convention test of necessity calls in the first instance for the wide consultation and inquiry and democratic consideration which should characterise the legislative process, not the more narrowly focused process of judicial decision. This is not a field in which judicial development of the law is at all appropriate.

In contending that the police action at Lechlade failed the Convention test of proportionality because it was premature and indiscriminate, Mr Emmerson relied on many of the matters already referred to. The action was premature because there was no hint of disorder at Lechlade and no reason to apprehend an immediate outburst of disorder by the claimant and her fellow passengers when they left their coaches at the designated dropoff points in Fairford and gathered in the designated assembly area before processing to the base. Because the action was premature it was necessarily indiscriminate because the police could not at that stage identify those (if any) of the passengers who appeared to be about to commit a breach of the peace. By taking action when no breach of the peace was in the offing, the police were obliged to take action against the sheep as well as the goats.

Mr Freeland resisted this contention also. He relied on Mr Lambert's belief, held by the courts below to be reasonable, that there would be disorder once the coaches reached Fairford. Given the intelligence known to the police . . ., the items found on the coaches and the unwillingness of the passengers to acknowledge ownership of these items or (in many cases) give their names, Mr Lambert was entitled to find that the 120 passengers had a collective intent to cause a breach of the peace. These considerations justified him in acting when and as he did.

I would acknowledge the danger of hindsight, and I would accept that the judgment of the officer on the spot, in the exigency of the moment, deserves respect. But making all allowances, I cannot accept the Chief Constable's argument. It was entirely reasonable to suppose that some of those on board the coaches might wish to cause damage and injury to the base at RAF Fairford, and to enter the base with a view to causing further damage and injury. It was not reasonable to suppose that even these passengers simply wanted a violent confrontation with the police, which they could have had in the lay-by. Nor was it reasonable to anticipate an outburst of disorder on arrival of these passengers in the assembly area or during the procession to the base, during which time the police would be in close attendance and well able to identify and arrest those who showed a violent propensity or breached the conditions to which the assembly and procession were subject. The focus of any disorder was expected to be in the bell-mouth area outside the base, and the police could arrest trouble-makers then and there . . . There was no reason (other than her refusal to give her name, which however irritating to the police was entirely lawful) to view the claimant as other than a committed, peaceful demonstrator. It was wholly disproportionate to restrict her exercise of her rights under Articles 10 and 11 because she was in the company of others some of whom might, at some time in the future, breach the peace.

This decision may be contrasted with that in *Austin*.

Austin v. Metropolitan Police Commissioner [2009] UKHL 5, [2009] 1 AC 564
Austin concerned the policing in London of the May Day protests of 2001, when the police kept about 3,000 assorted anti-globalisation and anti-capitalist

protesters confined at Oxford Circus for seven hours (from about 2.30pm until about 9.30pm). The House of Lords held that, in the circumstances, this action did not engage Article 5 of the ECHR.

The application of article 5(1) to measures of crowd control is an issue which does not appear so far to have been brought to the attention of the court in Strasbourg. So there is no direct guidance as to whether article 5(1) is engaged where the police impose restrictions on movement for the sole purpose of protecting people from injury or avoiding serious damage to property. The need for measures of crowd control to be adopted in the public interest is not new, however. It is frequently necessary, for example, for such measures to be imposed at football matches to ensure that rival fans do not confront each other in situations that may lead to violence. Restrictions on movement may also be imposed by the police on motorists in the interests of road safety after an accident on a motorway, or to prevent local residents from coming too close to a fire or a terrorist incident. It is not without interest that it has not so far been suggested that restrictions of that kind will breach article 5(1) so long as they are proportionate and not arbitrary.

The restrictions that were imposed by the police cordon in this case may be thought, . . . to have been greater in degree and intensity. But Lord Pannick QC for the respondent submitted that one could not sensibly ignore the purpose of the restriction or the circumstances . . . Ms Williams QC for the appellant, on the other hand, said that the purpose for which the measure was employed was irrelevant. The fact that it was a necessary response and was proportionate was a precondition for establishing the measure's legality for the purpose of . . . article 5(1). But it went no further than that. There was no balance to be struck when consideration was being given to the initial question whether article 5(1) applied to the measures adopted by the police. . .

I would hold . . . that there is room, even in the case of fundamental rights as to whose application no restriction or limitation is permitted by the Convention, for a pragmatic approach to be taken which takes full account of all the circumstances. No reference is made in article 5 to the interests of public safety or the protection of public order as one of the cases in which a person may be deprived of his liberty. This is in sharp contrast to article 10(2), which expressly qualifies the right to freedom of expression in these respects. But the importance that must be attached in the context of article 5 to measures taken in the interests of public safety is indicated by article 2 of the Convention, as the lives of persons affected by mob violence may be at risk if measures of crowd control cannot be adopted by the police. This is a situation where a search for a fair balance is necessary if these competing fundamental rights are to be reconciled with each other. The ambit that is given to article 5 as to measures of crowd control must, of course, take account of the rights of the individual as well as the interests of the community. So any steps that are taken must be resorted to in good faith and must be proportionate to the situation which has made the measures necessary. This is essential to preserve the fundamental principle that anything that is done which affects a person's right to liberty must not be arbitrary. If these requirements are met however it will be proper to conclude that measures of crowd control that are undertaken in the interests of the community will not infringe the article 5 rights of individual members of the crowd whose freedom of movement is restricted by them.

If measures of this kind are to avoid being prohibited by the Convention . . . it must be by recognising that they are not within the ambit of article 5(1) at all. In my opinion measures of crowd control will fall outside the area of its application, so long as they are not arbitrary. This means that they must be resorted to in good faith, that they must be proportionate and that they are enforced for no longer than is reasonably necessary . . . I would hold, in agreement with the Court of Appeal, that the restriction on the appellant's liberty that resulted from her being confined within the cordon by the police on this occasion met these criteria.

The decision of the House of Lords in *Austin* was sharply criticised by Helen Fenwick in 'Marginalising Human Rights: Breach of the Peace, "Kettling" and Public Protest [2009] *PL* 737, in David Mead, *The New Law of Peaceful Protest* (2010), ch. 7 and by David Feldman [2009] *CLJ* 243. In spite of these powerful criticisms, Austin did not succeed in her case before the European Court of Human Rights (*Austin* v. *United Kingdom* [2012] ECHR 36962/09). The European Court of Human Rights placed emphasis on the need to examine potential breaches of Article 5 ECHR in their context and to ensure that sufficient discretion was given to the police to regulate protests on the ground. This, in turn, gave rise to a larger margin of appreciation to be granted to member states when determining whether kettling amounted to a breach of Article 5:

56. As the Court has previously stated, the police must be afforded a degree of discretion in taking operational decisions. Such decisions are almost always complicated and the police, who have access to information and intelligence not available to the general public, will usually be in the best position to make them (see *P.F. and E.F.* v. *The United Kingdom*, cited above, para 41). Moreover, even by 2001, advances in communications technology had made it possible to mobilise protesters rapidly and covertly on a hitherto unknown scale. Police forces in the Contracting States face new challenges, perhaps unforeseen when the Convention was drafted, and have developed new policing techniques to deal with them, including containment or 'kettling'. Article 5 cannot be interpreted in such a way as to make it impracticable for the police to fulfil their duties of maintaining order and protecting the public, provided that they comply with the underlying principle of Article 5, which is to protect the individual from arbitrariness (see *Saadi* v. *UK* [2008] ECHR 13229/03, paras 67-74) . . .

60. Article 5 enshrines a fundamental human right, namely the protection of the individual against arbitrary interference by the State with his or her right to liberty. Subparagraphs (a)-(f) of art 5(1) contain an exhaustive list of permissible grounds on which persons may be deprived of their liberty and no deprivation of liberty will be compatible with art 5(1) unless it falls within one of those grounds (see, amongst many

other authorities, *Al-Jedda v UK* [2011] ECHR 27021/08, para 99, 7 July 2011). It cannot be excluded that the use of containment and crowd control techniques could, in particular circumstances, give rise to an unjustified deprivation of liberty in breach of art 5(1). In each case, art 5(1) must be interpreted in a manner which takes into account the specific context in which the techniques are deployed, as well as the responsibilities of the police to fulfil their duties of maintaining order and protecting the public, as they are required to do under both national and Convention law.

61. The question whether there has been a deprivation of liberty is, therefore, based on the particular facts of the case. In this connection, the Court observes that within the scheme of the Convention it is intended to be subsidiary to the national systems safeguarding human rights (see *A. and Others v. the United Kingdom*, cited above, § 154). Subsidiarity is at the very basis of the Convention, stemming as it does from a joint reading of Articles 1 and 19. The Court must be cautious in taking on the role of a first-instance tribunal of fact, where this is not rendered unavoidable by the circumstances of a particular case. As a general rule, where domestic proceedings have taken place, it is not the Court's task to substitute its own assessment of the facts for that of the domestic courts and it is for the latter to establish the facts on the basis of the evidence before them. Though the Court is not bound by the findings of domestic courts and remains free to make its own appreciation in the light of all the material before it, in normal circumstances it requires cogent elements to lead it to depart from the findings of fact reached by the domestic courts (see Giuliani and Gaggio, cited above, § 180). Nonetheless, since pursuant to Articles 19 and 32 of the Convention it is the Court's role definitively to interpret and apply the Convention, while it must have reference to the domestic court's findings of fact, it is not constrained by their legal conclusions as to whether or not there has been a deprivation of liberty within the meaning of Article 5 § 1 (see, for example, Storck, cited above, § 72)

62. Tugendhat J's judgment at first instance followed a three week trial, during which he considered a substantial body of evidence about the events at Oxford Circus on May Day 2001, including oral testimony and documentary, video and photographic evidence (see para 16 above). He found, *inter alia,* that the information available in advance to the police indicated that the demonstration would attract a 'hard core' of 500 to 1,000 violent demonstrators and that there was a real risk of serious injury, even death, and damage to property if the crowds were not effectively controlled. The police were expecting a crowd to form at Oxford Circus at around 4 p.m. and they were taken by surprise when over 1,500 people gathered there two hours earlier. In the light of the intelligence they had received and the behaviour of crowds at earlier demonstrations on similar themes, the police decided that, if they were to prevent violence and the risk of injury to persons and damage to property, an absolute cordon had to be imposed at 2 p.m. From 2.20 p.m., when a full cordon was in place, no-one in the crowd was free to leave the area without permission. There was space within the cordon for people to walk about and there was no crushing, but conditions were uncomfortable, with no shelter, food, water or toilet facilities. Throughout the afternoon and evening attempts were made by the police to commence collective release, but the violent and

uncooperative behaviour of a significant minority both within the cordon and in the surrounding area outside led the police repeatedly to suspend dispersal. In consequence, full dispersal could not be completed until 9.30 p.m. However, the police permitted approximately 400 individuals who could clearly be identified as not being involved in the demonstration or who were seriously affected by being confined, to leave (see paras 17–25 above). These findings were not disputed by the parties to the present proceedings and the Court sees no ground to depart from them. The first, second and third applicants were confined within the police cordon for approximately second hours and the fourth applicant for five and a half hours.

63. The Court must analyse the applicants' concrete situation with reference to the criteria set out in *Engel* and the subsequent case-law (see para 57 above). Although there were differences between the applicants, in that the first applicant was present in Oxford Circus as a demonstrator whereas the other applicants were passers-by, the Court does not consider that this difference is relevant to the question whether there was a deprivation of liberty.

64. In accordance with the *Engel* criteria, the Court considers that the coercive nature of the containment within the cordon; its duration; and its effect on the applicants, in terms of physical discomfort and inability to leave Oxford Circus, point towards a deprivation of liberty.

65. However, the Court must also take into account the 'type' and 'manner of implementation' of the measure in question. As indicated above, the context in which the measure was imposed is significant.

66. It is important to note, therefore, that the measure was imposed to isolate and contain a large crowd, in volatile and dangerous conditions. As the Government pointed out (see paragraph 42 above), the police decided to make use of a measure of containment to control the crowd rather than having resort to more robust methods, which might have given rise to a greater risk of injury to people within the crowd. The trial judge concluded that, given the situation in Oxford Circus, the police had had no alternative but to impose an absolute cordon if they were to avert a real risk of serious injury or damage (see paragraph 26 above). The Court finds no reason to depart from the judge's conclusion that in the circumstances the imposition of an absolute cordon was the least intrusive and most effective means to be applied. Indeed, the applicants did not contend that, when the cordon was first imposed, those within it were immediately deprived of their liberty (see paragraph 48 above).

67. Moreover, again on the basis of the facts found by the trial judge, the Court is unable to identify a moment when the measure changed from what was, at most, a restriction on freedom of movement, to a deprivation of liberty. It is striking that, some five minutes after the absolute cordon was imposed, the police were planning to commence a controlled release towards the north. Thirty minutes later, a second attempt by the police to begin release was begun but suspended, because of the violent behaviour of those within and outside the cordon. Between about 3 p.m. and 6 p.m. the police kept the situation under review, but the arrival of a new group of protesters and the dangerous conditions within the crowds led them to consider that it would not be safe

to attempt to release those within the cordon. Controlled release was recommended at 5.55 p.m., but stopped at 6.15 p.m.; resumed at 7 p.m. and suspended at 7.20 p.m.; begun again at 7.30 p.m., again abandoned; then carried out continuously, by groups of ten, until the entire crowd had been released at 9.45 p.m. (see para 24 above). Thus, the trial judge found the same conditions which required the police to contain the crowd at 2 p.m. persisted until about 8 p.m., when the collective release was finally able to proceed without interruption (see para 24 above). In these circumstances, where the police kept the situation constantly under close review, but where substantially the same dangerous conditions which necessitated the imposition of the cordon at 2 p.m. continued to exist throughout the afternoon and early evening, the Court does not consider that those within the cordon can be said to have been deprived of their liberty within the meaning of art 5(1). Since there was no deprivation of liberty, it is unnecessary for the Court to examine whether the measure in question was justified in accordance with subparagraphs (b) or (c) of art 5(1).

68. The Court emphasises that the above conclusion, that there was no deprivation of liberty, is based on the specific and exceptional facts of this case. Furthermore, this application did not include any complaint under arts 10 or 11 of the Convention and the Court notes the first instance judge's finding that there had been no interference with the art 10 and 11 rights of freedom of expression and assembly of those contained within the cordon (see para 32 above). It must be underlined that measures of crowd control should not be used by the national authorities directly or indirectly to stifle or discourage protest, given the fundamental importance of freedom of expression and assembly in all democratic societies. Had it not remained necessary for the police to impose and maintain the cordon in order to prevent serious injury or damage, the 'type' of the measure would have been different, and its coercive and restrictive nature might have been sufficient to bring it within Article 5.

The decision in *Austin* does not mean that kettling will always be a lawful police tactic: this was confirmed in *R (Moos and McClure)* v. *Metropolitan Police Cmr* [2011] EWHC 957 (Admin) (see esp. at [56]). Also of note are the JCHR's views as to how containment may be operated in such a way as to ensure compatibility with convention rights: see JCHR, *Demonstrating Respect for Rights: Follow-up*, 22nd Report of 2008–09, HL 141, HC 522, paras 28–9 (and see also JCHR, *Demonstrating Respect for Rights*, 7th Report of 2008–09, HL 47, HC 320. See also Oreb, 'Case Comment: The Legality of "Kettling" after *Austin*' (2013) 76 Modern Law Review 735).

Kettling continues to be used as a means of controlling large demonstrations, with the decision of the European Court of Human Rights having been seen as giving the 'greenlight' to its use for controlling public protests, in spite of the fact that this may impose severe restrictions on those who are merely protesting peacefully, and others who happen to be caught within the police cordon despite having played no role in the protest. However, it is not the only means through which to control protests. A more recent case demonstrates the ability of the police to arrest individuals due to the suspicion that their activities will give rise to an imminent breach of the peace, then holding these individuals in a police station before releasing them without charge. Again, the focus on the need to give sufficient discretion to the police to carry out their activities, and the broad margin of appreciation granted by Article 5 ECHR, suggests that it may be relatively easy for the police to prevent individuals from carrying out peaceful activities that may be suspected of having the potential to disrupt the police.

R (Hicks) v. *Commissioner of Police for the Metropolis* [2017] UKSC 9, [2017] 2 WLR 824

The case concerned police operations surrounding the wedding of the Duke and Duchess of Cambridge in April 2011. Large crowds were expected. However, while most would wish to peacefully enjoy the occasion, the police had received intelligence that other anti-monarchy protestors would also use the event to cause disruption and breach the peace. Hicks was on his way to the 'Not the Royal Wedding' street party when he was stopped and searched and then arrested. Others also wishing to attend the same street party were arrested at Charing Cross Station. Other applicants in the case were dressed as zombies and had been planning to attend the Zombie Picnic, when they were arrested in a coffee shop. All were then detailed at nearby police stations across London, until they were then released without charge after the wedding celebrations were over. The Supreme Court concluded that this did not breach Article 5 ECHR:

> [29]. The fundamental principle underlying article 5 is the need to protect the individual from arbitrary detention, and an essential part of that protection is timely judicial control, but at the same time article 5 must not be interpreted in such a way as would make it impracticable for the police to perform their duty to maintain public order and protect the lives and property of others. These twin requirements are not contradictory but complementary . . . In balancing these twin considerations it is necessary to keep a grasp of reality and the practical implications. Indeed, this is central to the principle of proportionality, which is not only embedded in article 5 but is part of the common law relating to arrest for breach of the peace.
>
> . . .
>
> [31]. In this case there was nothing arbitrary about the decisions to arrest, detain and release the appellants. They were taken in good faith and were proportionate to the situation. If the police cannot lawfully arrest and detain a person for a relatively short time (too short for it to be practical to take the person before a court) in circumstances where this is reasonably considered to be necessary for the purpose of preventing imminent violence, the practical consequence would be to hamper severely their ability to carry out the difficult task of maintaining public order and safety at mass public events. This would run counter to the fundamental principles previously identified.

The Court concluded that there was no breach of Article 5, given that the European Court of Human Rights had recognised that it was not contrary to Article 5 to arrest individuals when this is reasonably considered necessary to prevent an individual from committing an offence. However, in doing so, the Supreme Court was adhering to the minority and not the majority judgment of the European Court of Human Rights in *Ostendorf v. Germany* [2013] ECHR 197. The majority of the court concluded that detention would only be permitted for the prevention of crime when this was pre-trial detention. Individuals could be detained for the purposes of being brought to trail; not for the purposes of preventing crime, where individuals were held pending a determination of the legality of their preventative detention. Nevertheless, in *Eiseman Renyard v. United Kingdom* (2019) Application No 57884/17, the European Court of Human Rights upheld the decision of the Supreme Court in *Hicks*. They concluded that the arrests were not arbitrary as an objective observer would have been satisfied that the individuals who were arrested and detained would in all likelihood be involved in a breach of the peace and the applicants had been released as soon as this imminent risk of a breach of the peace had passed. Also, the detention had only been for a few hours. The uncertain scope of these powers, in addition to their ability to justify detention until protests are completed, may place a large restriction on the right to protest in practice.

11.4.3 Freedom of Assembly as a 'Constitutional Right'

In the traditional understanding of a citizen's rights as being, in general, merely residual liberties, our law formerly took the position that there was no right of assembly but only a liberty for people to assemble within whatever limits and prohibitions the law might impose. As Lord Hewart said in *Duncan* v. *Jones* (above), 'English law does not recognise any special right of public meeting for political or other purposes'. In more recent times, however, the courts came to recognise freedom of assembly as having positive value as a constitutional right. In *Hubbard* v. *Pitt* [1976] QB 142, Lord Denning, in a dissenting judgment, vindicated the right to demonstrate. The defendants in this case had picketed the premises of a firm of estate agents in protest against the firm's alleged anti-social practices directed against tenants in the area. The firm having sued for an injunction and damages for the tort of nuisance, the majority of the Court of Appeal held in interlocutory proceedings that there was a serious issue of private nuisance to be tried, and upheld an interim injunction granted (on different grounds) by the court below. Lord Denning, who would have discharged the injunction, said (at 178):

> Here we have to consider the right to demonstrate and the right to protest on matters of public concern. These are rights which it is in the public interest that individuals should

possess; and, indeed, that they should exercise without impediment so long as no wrongful act is done. It is often the only means by which grievances can be brought to the knowledge of those in authority – at any rate with such impact as to gain a remedy. Our history is full of warnings against suppression of these rights. Most notable was the demonstration at St Peter's Fields, Manchester, in 1819 in support of universal suffrage. The magistrates sought to stop it. At least 12 were killed and hundreds injured. Afterwards the Court of Common Council of London affirmed 'the undoubted right of Englishmen to assemble together for the purpose of deliberating upon public grievances'. Such is the right of assembly. So also is the right to meet together, to go in procession, to demonstrate and to protest on matters of public concern. As long as all is done peaceably and in good order, without threats or incitement to violence or obstruction to traffic, it is not prohibited.

It was time, Lord Denning went on to say, for the courts to recognise the right to demonstrate and to protest. In *Hirst* v. *Chief Constable of West Yorkshire* (1986) 85 Cr App R 143, the defendants, who had been demonstrating outside a furrier's shop against the use of animal fur, were charged with an offence contrary to section 137 of the Highways Act 1980. An offence is committed under this section if a person 'without lawful authority or excuse, in any way wilfully obstructs the free passage along a highway'. The defendants were convicted by justices, but the Divisional Court allowed their appeal, for the justices had not asked themselves whether the conduct of the defendants was in all the circumstances a reasonable use of the highway, such as would have constituted a 'lawful excuse' in terms of the section. The place, the duration and the purpose of the gathering should have been considered. If this were done, said Otton LJ after quoting Lord Denning's dictum (above), the 'balance would be properly struck and … the "freedom of protest on issues of public concern" would be given the recognition it deserves'. The decision in this case was approved by Lords Irvine LC and Hutton in *DPP* v. *Jones* [1999] 2 AC 240 (on which see below).

Article 11 of the ECHR, a convention right under the HRA, protects the right to assemble peacefully, whether in a stationary gathering or in a procession. The ECtHR has held that an assembly may be peaceful and qualify for protection even though it may annoy or cause offence and counterdemonstrators threaten to disrupt it with violence: public authorities are required to take all reasonable and appropriate measures to protect the peaceful demonstrators from disruption by their violent opponents. See *Plattform Ärzte für das Leben* v. *Austria* (1988) 13 EHRR 204. (Compare *Redmond-Bate* v. *DPP*, above, and see *R* v. *Chief Constable of Sussex, ex p International Trader's Ferry Ltd* [1999] 2 AC 418, in which the House of Lords held that the duty of the police to protect lawful activities is *not* absolute and may be qualified by the resources available to them and the demands of other policing requirements.) Restrictions may properly be imposed by law on the right of assembly on the grounds specified in Article 11(2), notably for the prevention of disorder or for the protection of the rights and freedoms of others. In deciding whether any restriction was justified in terms of Article 11(2), the courts must be satisfied that there was a pressing social need for the restriction and that it was proportionate to the legitimate aim pursued. The courts must closely scrutinise legislative provisions that appear to restrict freedom of assembly and must interpret and give effect to such provisions, so far as it is possible to do so, in a way which is compatible with the convention right: section 3(1) of the HRA. Accordingly, legislation should not be read as authorising public authorities – whether the Home Secretary, a local authority or the police – to act incompatibly with the right to freedom of assembly, unless such an interpretation is unavoidable.

11.4.4 Statutory Restrictions on Freedom of Assembly

Public processions and assemblies are subject to the controls for which provision is made in sections 11–14 of the Public Order Act 1986, as amended by the Serious Organised Crime and Police Act 2005. They are summarised in the following memorandum.

> **The National Heritage Committee, *4th Report of 1992–93*, HC 294-III, Appendix 3: Memorandum Submitted by the Home Office**
>
> **Public Order Act 1986**
>
> **Police Powers to Control Assemblies and Processions**
>
> 1. The purpose of the legislation is to give the police adequate powers to prevent and control disorder and to ensure that demonstrations are held without causing undue inconvenience to the rights of others.
> 2. Under sections 12 and 14 of the Public Order Act the police may place conditions (for example, as to numbers, route, location) on those organising and taking part in public assemblies of 20 or more people and public processions if the police reasonably believe that the assembly or procession is likely to result in: serious public disorder; or serious damage to property; or serious disruption to the life of the community; or if its purpose is to coerce.
> 3. A 'public place' within the meaning of the 1986 Act means any highway or any place to which at the material time the public has access, on payment or otherwise, as of right or by virtue of express or implied permission.
> 4. It is an offence for an organiser of a public procession or public assembly or a person taking part in such a procession or assembly knowingly to fail to comply with a condition imposed by the police, but it is a defence to prove that the failure arose from circumstances beyond his control. A constable may arrest without warrant anyone he reasonably suspects is committing such an offence, which is punishable by up to three months' imprisonment or a level 4 fine.

Advance Notice of Processions

5. Under section 11 organisers of public processions are normally required to give 6 days' notice to the police of the date, time and proposed route, and the name and address of the proposed organiser. This requirement does not apply where the procession is one commonly or customarily held in the area or is a funeral procession. There is no such requirement for public assemblies.

Bans on Processions

6. Under section 13 the police can apply to the local authority (but in London direct to the Home Secretary) for a ban on public processions (but not static assemblies) [see, further on this point, below] if serious public disorder cannot be avoided by the imposition of conditions. Before a banning order is made the Home Secretary's consent is required.

It should be noted that the police may impose conditions on processions and assemblies where it is reasonably believed that they may result in 'serious disruption to the life of the community'. These powers may be exercised even if there is no threat of violence or a breach of the peace. Decisions to impose conditions or to ban processions under these statutory provisions are in principle open to judicial review, an important example being *R (Kay)* v. *Metropolitan Police Commissioner* [2008] UKHL 69, [2008] 1 WLR 2723, where it was held that the monthly 'Critical Mass Cycle Ride' in London was a procession 'commonly or customarily' held, even though the cyclists took a different route each month. The police had notified the cyclists that they needed to give six days' notice of the route they proposed to take each month, but the House of Lords ruled that this was not required on a proper construction of section 11 of the Public Order Act 1986. More recently, in *R (Jones)* v. *Metropolitan Police Commissioner* [2019] EWHC 2957 (Admin), the High Court had to determine the meaning of 'assembly' when determining the powers conferred by section 14 of the Public Order Act for a senior police officer present to impose conditions on the location, duration and number of participants of an assembly. The issue arose during the policing of the 'Extinction Rebellion Autumn Uprising' in October 2019. Members would meet to protest in one area, before disbursing and meeting in a series of other locations and times across London. The question arose as to whether this series of meetings was one assembly, or a series of assemblies. The court concluded that each assembly was distinct. As such, conditions imposed by a senior police officer present at the assembly did not travel from that assembly to future assemblies. Rather, if the police wished to impose conditions on future assemblies, it would require the actions of the chief officer of the police and not just the senior police officer present.

A decision to restrict or ban will not necessarily be found to be incompatible with the convention right of freedom of assembly. A general ban on processions in London for a period of two months, imposed under the 1936 Act, was held by the European Commission of Human Rights to be justified in terms of Article 11(2) as being necessary for the prevention of disorder, even though processions with peaceful objectives were caught by the ban: *Christians against Racism and Fascism* v. *United Kingdom* (1980) 21 DR 138. The necessity for any such ban would, however, have to be assessed by the courts with reference to the particular circumstances and with due regard to the principle that it should not be a disproportionate response to the threat of disorder.

The Criminal Justice and Public Order Act 1994 introduced new restrictions, which are applicable in specified circumstances to persons who trespass on land. Section 68 created an offence of aggravated trespass, committed by trespassers whose actions are intended to intimidate, obstruct or disrupt any lawful activity on the land. This provision was principally aimed at hunt saboteurs and those who disrupt events such as the Grand National. The generality of the provision may, however, present a threat to non-violent protesters against, for example, road schemes or the destruction of trees or intensive livestock rearing. Section 70, introducing a new section 14A into the Public Order Act 1986, extended the banning power – previously limited to public processions – to trespassory assemblies (of twenty or more persons) which may result in 'serious disruption to the life of the community' or in significant damage to land or buildings of historical, architectural, archaeological or scientific importance. A chief officer of police, reasonably believing that such disruption or damage may occur, may apply to the district council for an order prohibiting, for a specified period, the holding of *all* trespassory assemblies in the district or part of it, and the council may then make such an order (with or without modifications) if the Secretary of State gives consent. (In London, the Metropolitan Police commissioner may himself make a similar order with the consent of the Secretary of State.) This provision was targeted at the sort of mass trespass that had taken place at Stonehenge, but again a much wider range of activities may fall within the broad terms of the section.

Enacted as a response to particular public order and policing difficulties that it was thought could not be overcome by using the existing law, these provisions of the Criminal Justice and Public Order Act confer far-reaching discretionary powers on the police and effect a further encroachment on freedom to protest. Consider what Peter Thornton, Chairman of the Civil Liberties Trust, wrote with reference to the Act (*The Times*, 8 March 1994):

Public protest is designed to inform, persuade and cajole. It may be a nuisance, it may be intended to be. It is often noisy and inconvenient. But it should not be banned or curbed; nor should peaceful protestors be put at risk of prosecution.

When a meeting or procession is held, for greatest effect, in the streets, the limits of lawful conduct by those attending are narrow and uncertain. Lord Scarman said in his *Report on the Red Lion Square Disorders of 15 June 1974* (Cmnd 5919/1975), p. 38, that here too the right to demonstrate 'of course exists, subject only to limits required by the need for good order and the passage of traffic'. But the restrictions are potentially far-reaching. Those attending a meeting on the highway are at risk of committing the offence of wilful obstruction of the highway, contrary to section 137 of the Highways Act 1980. They may also be guilty of public nuisance: see the restrictive judgment of Forbes J in *Hubbard* v. *Pitt* [1976] QB 142. A right to assemble on the highway was given a qualified recognition in the following case.

Director of Public Prosecutions v. *Jones* [1999] 2 AC 240 (HL)

The defendants were among a group of protesters, more than twenty in number, who had gathered on the grass verge of a public highway adjacent to the perimeter fence of Stonehenge. The local council had made an order under section 14A of the Public Order Act 1986 prohibiting trespassory assemblies in an area that included Stonehenge and the place in which the demonstration took place. The protesters were peaceful and, although the grass verge was part of the public highway, it was found as a fact that they had not caused an obstruction. The defendants were charged with taking part in a trespassory assembly prohibited under section 14A and were convicted. Their conviction was upheld by the Divisional Court and they appealed to the House of Lords.

The defendants were plainly guilty of the offence if their conduct in gathering on the highway constituted a trespass. The appeal raised the question of the extent of the public's right to use the public highway: the Divisional Court had ruled that a non-obstructive, peaceful assembly, such as had taken place on this occasion, exceeded the public's right and so must necessarily be trespassory. One interpretation of earlier case law was that the highway might be used by the public only 'to pass and repass' and at most to do anything *incidental or ancillary* to the right of passage (e.g., stopping to consult a street map or to have a rest). This was the view preferred by the minority (Lords Slynn and Hope) in the House of Lords. Standing or sitting on the highway in order to demonstrate had nothing to do with use of the highway for passing and repassing and accordingly must be a trespass. The majority (Lords Irvine LC, Clyde and Hutton) derived a wider principle from earlier decisions: any reasonable and usual mode of using the highway is lawful, provided that it is consistent with the general public's right of passage. (What is reasonable or usual 'may develop and change from one period of history to another', observed Lord Clyde.) This conclusion was expressed as follows by Lord Irvine LC:

> I conclude ... the law to be that the public highway is a public place which the public may enjoy for any reasonable purpose, provided the activity in question does

not amount to a public or private nuisance and does not obstruct the highway by unreasonably impeding the primary right of the public to pass and repass; within these qualifications there is a public right of peaceful assembly on the highway.

It was held by the majority that an assembly on the highway was not necessarily unlawful; that the ruling of the Divisional Court to the contrary was wrong; and that the assembly in this case had not exceeded the limits of lawful public use of the highway. The defendants' appeal was accordingly allowed.

It was a somewhat unusual feature of this case that the assembly was held on a part of the highway – the grass verge – not normally used for public passage. Had the protesters assembled on the part of the highway along which people passed, the result might have been different. The requirement that a gathering on the highway must be non-obstructive leaves little room for a public right to assemble there.

DPP v. *Jones* was decided before the HRA had come into force. The matter should now be approached from the standpoint of the right of assembly assured by Article 11 of the European Convention. The decision of the House of Lords is doubtless consistent with the result that would be required by an application of Article 11 to the same facts, but the convention right may be more strongly fortified (by the strict limits placed by Article 11(2) on restrictions of the right) than the qualified right admitted by the House of Lords. (See, further, Fenwick and Phillipson, 'Public Protest, the Human Rights Act and Judicial Responses to Political Expression' [2000] *PL* 627.)

Appleby v. *United Kingdom* (2003) 37 EHRR 38 concerned a peaceful protest not on the highway but in a privately owned public space – a shopping mall that, since its construction, formed the centre of a particular town. Protesters wanted to collect signatures for a petition arguing that the only remaining public playing field near the town centre should not be built on, as the local council was apparently planning. The manager of the shopping mall refused to allow the protesters to collect signatures in the mall. The ECtHR held that this ban constituted an infringement of neither Article 10 nor of Article 11. Three reasons were furnished: first, the property rights of the shopping mall owner needed to be borne in mind; second, Articles 10 and 11 do not bestow any freedom of forum for the exercise of their rights; and, third, the restriction on the protesters' ability to communicate their views was limited to the entrance areas and passageways of the mall – they were not prevented from obtaining permission from the individual businesses within the mall, or from distributing leaflets and collecting signatures outside the mall. (For an excellent analysis, see Rowbottom, 'Property and Participation: A Right of Access for Expressive Activities' [2005] *EHRLR* 186.)

Hall and Others v. *Mayor of London* [2010] EWCA Civ 817

Parliament Square Gardens (PSG) comprises the central area of Parliament Square, around which are the Houses of Parliament, Westminster Abbey, the

Supreme Court and the end of Whitehall (commencing with the Treasury and leading to Downing Street and the Cabinet Office). In May 2010, several groups arrived at PSG and set up a camp there, which they named 'Democracy Village'. This was a gathering of diverse groups, campaigning on issues such as the war in Afghanistan, climate change, civil liberties and land reform. (In addition, Mr Brian Haw had been camping lawfully on the pavement next to one side of PSG from 2001 until 2011 (*Mayor of London* v. *Haw* [2011] EWHC 585 (QB); he was not part of Democracy Village.) By virtue of section 384 of the Greater London Authority Act 1999, PSG is vested in the Crown and is under the 'care, control, management and regulation' of the Greater London Authority (GLA). The GLA sought to evict the Democracy Village campers from PSG. The judge made the requisite order for possession. The Court of Appeal was subsequently required to consider whether this order for possession had been made compatibly with Articles 10 and 11 of the ECHR. The Court of Appeal ruled that it had been:

> Lord Neuberger MR: . . . As I have already said, there can be no doubt that the defendants should have the right to express the views which they wish to express; similarly, there is no doubt that they should enjoy the right to assemble together. Such rights are, of course, specifically protected by, respectively, articles 10 and 11 of the Convention. However, as articles 10(2) and 11(2) of the Convention emphasise, these rights, vitally important though they are, must be subject to some constraints, and those constraints include 'restrictions' provided they are, *inter alia*, 'prescribed by law and necessary in a democratic society in the interests of . . . public safety, for the prevention of disorder or crime, . . . for the protection of the [under article 10, "reputation or"] rights ["and", under article 11, "freedoms"] of others'.
>
> The right to express views publicly, particularly on the important issues about which the defendants feel so strongly, and the right of the defendants to assemble for the purpose of expressing and discussing those views, extends to the manner in which the defendants wish to express their views and to the location where they wish to express and exchange their views. If it were otherwise, these fundamental human rights would be at risk of emasculation. Accordingly, the defendants' desire to express their views in Parliament Square, the open space opposite the main entrance to the Houses of Parliament, and to do so in the form of the Democracy Village, on the basis of relatively long term occupation with tents and placards, are all, in my opinion, within the scope of articles 10 and 11.
>
> Having said that, the greater the extent of the right claimed under article 10(1) or article 11(1), the greater the potential for the exercise of the claimed right interfering with the rights of others, and, consequently, the greater the risk of the claim having to be curtailed or rejected by virtue of article 10(2) or article 11(2). . .
>
> In this case, the Mayor considered and refused an application (or, strictly, a letter which he treated as an application) for the establishment and continuance of the Democracy Village on PSG, and he refused it for reasons given in a fairly detailed letter dated 20 May 2010. That letter included the observation that

'[T]he effect of the Democracy Village is to prevent the public from exercising their rights over a very significant part of PSG for a prolonged and indefinite period [and] one impact of the Democracy Village has been to exclude others from exercising their right to protest there. The extent and duration of the impact of the Democracy Village on the lawful, reasonable and ordinary activities on PSG is the primary reason for refusing consent.'

The letter also said that 'The Mayor is seriously concerned about the substantial damage which is being caused by the Democracy Village to PSG', and that 'the cost of reparation to return the Square to its former condition is substantial'. The letter went on to state that

'Permissions for other peaceful protests and rallies on Parliament Square Garden are normally limited to a maximum of 3 hours, in order to allow for proper management, to ensure that the day-to-day business of the city is not impeded, and to allow the maximum number of groups or individuals to use the space to exercise their democratic right to peaceful protest. As this period will be extended in appropriate cases, the Mayor is not prepared to permit camping by significant numbers for a prolonged period.'

The Democracy Village defendants are plainly trespassers on PSG: rightly, that is no longer in contention, although it was debated before the Judge. . .

[W]hen freedom of assembly, and, even more, when freedom of expression, are in play, then, save possibly in very unusual and clear circumstances, article 11, and article 10, should be capable of being invoked to enable the merits of the particular case to be considered. Thus, in *R (Laporte) v Chief Constable of Gloucestershire Constabulary* [2007] 2 AC 105, paragraphs 36 and 37 Lord Bingham made it clear that state authorities have a positive duty to take steps to ensure that lawful public demonstrations can take place, and that any prior restraint on freedom of speech requires 'the most careful scrutiny'.

Given, therefore, that articles 10 and 11 are in play, it seems to me that the decision on the balancing, or proportionality, issue is ultimately one for the court, not the Mayor – see *R (SB) v Governors of Denbigh High School* [2006] UKHL 15; [2007] 1 AC 100 . . . Further, when carrying out that balancing exercise, the court must consider the facts, and, particularly when it comes to article 10 (and article 11), focus very sharply and critically on the reasons put forward for curtailing anyone's desire to express their beliefs – above all their political beliefs – in public.

The Judge concluded . . . that there was 'a pressing social need not to permit an indefinite camped protest on PSG for the protection of the rights and freedoms of others to access all of PSG and to demonstrate with authorisation but also importantly for the protection of health – the camp has no running water or toilet facilities – and the prevention of crime – there is evidence of criminal damage to the flower beds and of graffiti'. He went on to say that he was 'satisfied the GLA and the Mayor are being prevented from exercising their necessary powers of control management and care of PSG and the use of PSG by tourists and visitors, by local workers, by those who want to take advantage of its world renowned setting and by others who want to protest lawfully, is being prevented.'

In my view, insofar as those conclusions amounted to findings of fact, they were, to put it at its lowest, findings which were open to the Judge on the evidence before him. Once those findings were made, there are no grounds for attacking the conclusion reached by the Judge in the following paragraph, namely that '[w]hile the removal of the defendants ... would interfere with their article 10 and article 11 rights, that is a wholly proportionate response and so no defendant has a convention defence ... to the claim for possession.'

It is important to bear in mind that this was not a case where there is any suggestion that the defendants should not be allowed to express their opinions or to assemble together. The claim against them only relates to their activities on PSG. It is not even a case where they have been absolutely prohibited from expressing themselves and assembling where, or in the manner, in which they choose. They have been allowed to express their views and assemble together at the location of their choice, PSG, for over two months on an effectively exclusive basis. It is not even as if they will necessarily be excluded from mounting an orthodox demonstration at PSG in the future. Plainly, these points are not necessarily determinative of their case, but, when it comes to balancing their rights against the rights of others, they are obviously significant factors.

The importance of Parliament Square as a location for demonstrations and the importance of the right to demonstrate each cut both ways in this case. It is important that the Democracy Village members are able to express their views through their encampment on PSG, just opposite the Houses of Parliament. However ... it is equally important to all the other people who wish to demonstrate on PSG that the Democracy Village is removed, in the light of the Judge's finding, in line with the Mayor's view, and (it should be added) the preponderance of the evidence, that the presence of the Democracy Village impedes the ability of others to demonstrate there. Additionally, there are the rights of those who simply want to walk or wander in PSG, not perhaps Convention rights, but nonetheless important rights connected with freedom and self-expression. The fact that Democracy Village have been effectively in exclusive occupation of PSG for over two months is also relevant, especially as there is no sign of the camp being struck, as the defendants have, it may be said, had some seventy days to make their point.

Was Tony Benn justified, in giving evidence in this case in the High Court, in describing the proceedings for eviction as 'an attack on the democratic process'?

Protests in PSG are now regulated by the provisions of the Police Reform and Social Responsibility Act 2011, as amended by the Anti-Social Behaviour, Crime and Policing Act 2011, which extended the control over PSG to the footpaths immediately adjoining PSG and the highways and gardens next to Westminster. These provisions prohibit the use of amplified noise equipment, the erection or use of tents or other structures to facilitate sleeping and the use or intended use of sleeping equipment in these areas. The police and other authorised individuals are empowered to stop activities, ask people to leave the area and, if these instructions are not followed, to confiscate equipment. Under the Parliament Square Byelaws, the Greater London Authority can grant permission to protest on PSG. It is unlawful to protest there without prior permission.

R (Barda) v. *Mayor of London on Behalf of the Greater Authority* [2015] EWHC 3584

In October 2014, Occupy Democracy established a camp in Parliament Square Gardens. There were concerns over the way in which the police exercised their powers, with reports that they were removing backpacks and pizza boxes as 'sleeping equipment'. In response to the first protest, the Greater London Authority (GLA) put up fences around PSG, which continued to be used in response to a series of demonstrations in the following months. The High Court concluded that the erection of fences around PSG for much of the first few months of protest did interfere with the right to protest found in Article 11, given the significance of Parliament as the focus of the demonstration meaning that the place of the protest in sight of the Houses of Parliament was part of the protest. Nevertheless, the fences were a proportionate restriction on the right to protest, particularly given that most of the protests had still been able to take place near to the fenced off area of PSG. The following elements were relevant to the balancing exercise carried out by the court. First, Article 11 was not breached merely by the requirement to ask for prior permission before holding a demonstration. However (at [107]):

> Those organising demonstrations, "as actors in the democratic process", should respect the rules governing conduct of demonstrations by complying with the regulations in force. A failure to do so demonstrates a disregard of the rights and freedoms of others and of the need to manage those competing rights sensibly if they are to be enjoyed to the greatest extent possible. Of course the Convention imposes obligations on contracting states not individuals, but if the individual does not play his part a greater latitude must be allowed to the state in the way it responds. Mr Barda says he objects as a matter of principle to seeking permission to demonstrate; his objection is wholly misplaced. The Convention principles on which he seeks to rely do not operate in a vacuum.

Second, the court weighed the response to the protests by the GLA, taking account of previous protests by the same group and the way in which the GLA only escalated to stronger fencing when their original, less-intrusive methods failed to prevent the use of PSG (at [115-121]):

> Until they learned of it from social media, the GLA knew nothing of Occupy's plans in respect of PSG. Occupy had not sought permission for the demonstration because they disagreed with the need for permission as a matter of principle. In fact, they did not engage with GLA at all. But once GLA learned of them, they could hardly be expected to do nothing in response. On any view, the planned demonstration would present something of a challenge and would require some form of response from those who had responsibility for the management of the square. Contingency planning, in those circumstances, was entirely justified.

It was discovered that the plan was for a nine-day 'occupation' of PSG in October by the group, or a variant of the group, who had previously 'occupied' St Paul's churchyard. The Occupy movement was known to be non-violent but their presence in St Paul's had caused very substantial difficulties and had interfered with the rights of others to use the churchyard. It was now PSG which was to be the site of a static demonstration. The October occupation was to be followed by further monthly demonstrations until the General Election in May 2015.

Showing what, in my judgment, was commendable restraint and good sense, the GLA's initial response was not fences and barricades to protect the Square from occupation, but low level rope and posts. Given the terms of the Byelaws, the effect of the PRSRA, the fact that Occupy had not sought permission for this demonstration, had not informed the GLA directly, had a history of establishing long-term encampments in public or private places, were seeking to encourage large numbers of people to attend the event, were prevented by statute from bringing sleeping equipment onto the site, had provided nothing to indicate that they had made arrangements themselves to marshal demonstrators or to provide them with basic facilities for a prolonged stay, putting up posts, ropes and signs to discourage trespassing on the gardens by those without permission to use them was, in my judgment, plainly proportionate.

In fact, the posts and rope did not prevent the Occupy Democracy event proceeding in the gardens. The demonstrations continued and Ms Demetriou [counsel for Occupy Democracy], quite properly, does not suggest that this 'interference' was unlawful. It plainly was not. But that is significant not only for the period when posts and rope were deployed in mid-October; it is also significant for the rest of the period because it demonstrates that GLA were seeking to calibrate their response to reflect the evidence available to them about the nature of the challenge the Occupy Democracy demonstration posed.

On 21 October fencing was erected around PSG. That followed a period of some days during which Occupy protesters moved over the rope barrier and onto the grassed area. Sleeping equipment was moved onto the grass and material which could be used in breach of the PRSRA [Police Reform and Social Responsibility Act 2011] was seized. There were a number of arrests. It was plain the rope barriers were not being respected and increasing numbers of demonstrators were likely to ignore the Byelaws and the PRSRA and take over parts of PSG, at least for a period of some days. For the reasons set out above, it does not seem to me that, faced with those developments, GLA were confined to the reactive measures provided for by the PRSRA. Fencing off part of the Square was a reasonable and proportionate response.

That level of fencing did not prove entirely effective; there were yet further incidents on PSG between 22 and 26 October 2014 and the Heras fencing around PSG was pushed over. As the briefing for the November demonstration makes clear, GLA continued to fear that tents would be pitched on PSG.

The Occupy Democracy website for December indicated that the demonstrator's plan remained 'Monthly Occupations until General Election'; in other words the threat of an occupation remained very real. In my judgment, GLA were entitled to take measures to prevent the occupation of the Square, in order to protect the Square itself, to protect the

> rights of others to use the Square and to prevent the flouting of the Byelaws and the PRSRA. A failure to maintain a measure of management and control over PSG in these circumstances would inevitably affect adversely the ability of others to exercise their rights in the Square. When the threat of occupation diminished, the fencing was removed.
>
> At no time were Occupy Democracy's protests prevented altogether. Throughout the period, it remained possible for them to mount their protest, albeit in less space and comfort than they would have wished. Their programme of events continued regardless of the limitations imposed on them.

It has to be recognised that the right to protest does not only hinder the rights of others to enjoy PSG. MPs need to be able to walk to the Houses of Parliament free from harassment, abuse, intimidation, and insult in order to facilitate the democratic process. In a recent report, the Constitution Committee of the House of Lords recognised the rights of protestors outside Parliament need to be balanced against the effective functioning of Parliament. They recommended forming a joint group convened by the Metropolitan Police and including, inter alia, the Leader of the House, the Crown Prosecution Service, and the Equality and Human Rights Commission to find a solution to ensure a balance between peaceful protest and the need to ensure MPs were not intimidated and prevented from performing their proper democratic function (*Democracy, Freedom of Expression and Freedom of Association: Threats to MPs, First Report 2019–20*, HC 37, HL Paper 5).

The need to balance freedom of assembly and public order has arisen in an acute form in Northern Ireland. Traditional parades held in the 'marching season', although often taking place peacefully, have sometimes been, or have been perceived as being, triumphalist and intimidatory, and, on some occasions, have resulted in serious public disorder. The Public Processions (Northern Ireland) Act 1998 made a fresh attempt to deal with the problem, with an emphasis on fostering local agreement on contested parades. The Act established an independent body, the Parades Commission for Northern Ireland, which has a duty 'to promote and facilitate mediation as a means of resolving disputes concerning public processions' (section 2(1)(b)). The commission issues a code of conduct applicable to public processions and to meetings of protesters against them, and has power to impose conditions on persons organising or taking part in a procession, having regard not only to considerations of public order but to 'any impact which the procession may have on relationships within the community'. As a last resort, processions and protest meetings can be prohibited by the Secretary of State (sections 11 and 11A). (See, generally, www.paradescommission.org; see, also, *Re E* [2008] UKHL 66, [2009] 1 AC 536; *DB* v. *Chief Constable of Police Service (Northern Ireland)* [2017] UKSC 7, [2017] 3 LRC 252.)

The Public Order Act 1986 contains a series of offences criminalising various actions and forms of behaviour that may catch protesters. The more serious offences of riot, violent disorder, affray and fear or provocation of violence (sections 1–4) are relatively unobjectionable, but it is the more minor offences that may be said to blur the line between the criminal and the merely irritating. Demonstrators whose conduct inclines simply to the boisterous may fall foul of section 5 of the Public Order Act 1986, which makes it an offence to use threatening or abusive ('insulting' was removed in 2014 by the Crime and Courts Act 2013, section 22) words or behaviour, or disorderly behaviour that is likely to cause (but that may not necessarily actually cause) harassment, alarm or distress to another who is within sight or hearing. The government itself remarked of this offence when first proposing it that it was 'not easy to define the offence in a manner which conforms with the normally precise definitions of the criminal law' (*Review of Public Order Law*, Cmnd 9510/1985, para 3.26; see, further, Geddis, 'Free Speech Martyrs or Unreasonable Threats to Social Peace?' [2004] *PL* 853). Smith, *Offences Against Public Order* (1987), p. 117, says of this provision:

> Because of the potential breadth of the language in which the section is drafted, it affords scope for injudicious policing; considerable common sense and restraint on the part of the police will be called for in the application of the section.

Anti-social behaviour legislation has also been used to police protests. Section 35 of the Anti-Social Behaviour, Crime and Policing Act 2014 gives the police the power to order the dispersal of groups of persons in cases where members of the public have been 'harassed, alarmed or distressed' or where there has been an 'occurrence in the locality of crime or disorder' and the exclusion or dispersal of these individuals is necessary to remove or reduce the likelihood of those in the area being harassed, alarmed or distressed, or to prevent disturbance or crime. This power is available only where a senior officer has given an 'authorisation' under section 34 of the Act for a specific locality and for no more than forty-eight hours. A senior officer of at least the rank of inspector may only grant this authorisation 'if satisfied on reasonable grounds that the use of these powers in the locality during that period may be necessary for the purpose of removing or reducing the likelihood' of members of the public in that area being 'harassed, alarmed or distressed' or to prevent the 'occurrence in the locality of crime and disorder'. The senior officer must have 'particular regard' to Articles 10 and 11 when determining whether to make an order. (Note that Scotland has its own legislation in this area: see the Antisocial Behaviour etc. (Scotland) Act 2004.)

In addition to the Public Order Act and the anti-social behaviour legislation, a considerable range of criminal legislation has been added to the statute book since 1997 in an attempt, in particular, to respond to the intimidatory and sometimes violent tactics employed by militant animal rights protesters. Note in particular the Protection from Harassment Act 1997 and provisions of the

Criminal Justice and Police Act 2001 (section 42) and of the Serious Organised Crime and Police Act 2005 (see especially sections 125–7 and 145 of the 2005 Act), and the Counter-Terrorism and Security Act 2015. On the Protection from Harassment Act 1997, see *University of Oxford* v. *Broughton* [2006] EWCA Civ 1305, concerning the long-running protests against the construction of a research laboratory in Oxford.

(See, further, Fenwick and Phillipson, 'Public Protest, the Human Rights Act and Judicial Responses to Political Expression' [2000] *PL* 627 and 'Direct Action, Convention Values and the Human Rights Act' (2001) 21 *LS* 535; Bailey, Harris and Jones, *Civil Liberties: Cases, Materials and Commentary* (6th edn. 2009), ch. 5; Fenwick, 'Marginalising Human Rights: Breach of the Peace, "Kettling" and Public Protest' [2009] *PL* 737; Mead, *The New Law of Peaceful Protest* (2010); Ewing, *Bonfire of the Liberties* (2010), ch. 4.)

Index